Financial Accounting

Third Edition

Financial Accounting:

An Introduction to Concepts, Methods, and Uses

Third Edition

Sidney Davidson, Ph.D., CPA
University of Chicago

Clyde P. Stickney, D.B.A., CPA
Dartmouth College

Roman L. Weil, Ph.D., CPA, CMA
University of Chicago

The Dryden Press
Chicago · New York · Philadelphia
San Francisco · Montreal · Toronto
London · Sydney · Tokyo · Mexico City
Rio de Janeiro · Madrid

Acquisitions Editor: Feeny Lipscomb
Developmental Editor: Elizabeth Widdicombe
Project Editor: Brian Link Weber
Design Director: Alan Wendt
Production Manager: Peter Coveney

Text and cover design by Harry Voigt
Copy editing by Ruth Henoch
Indexing by Cherie Worman

Address orders to:
383 Madison Avenue
New York, New York 10017

Address editorial correspondence to:
One Salt Creek Lane
Hinsdale, Illinois 60521

Library of Congress Catalog Card Number:
ISBN: 0-03-059871
Printed in the United States of America
4 5 6   016   10 9 8 7 6

CBS College Publishing
The Dryden Press
Holt, Rinehart and Winston
Saunders College Publishing

For our wives, with thanks.

Whatever be the detail with which you cram your students, the chance of their meeting in after-life exactly that detail is almost infinitesimal; and if they do meet it, they will probably have forgotten what you taught them about it. The really useful training yields a comprehension of a few general principles with a thorough grounding in the way they apply to a variety of concrete details. In subsequent practice the students will have forgotten your particular details; but they will remember by an unconscious common sense how to apply principles to immediate circumstances.

Alfred North Whitehead
The Aims of Education and Other Essays

Preface

The third edition of this book has the same principal objectives as the previous editions. We view the introductory course in financial accounting as having the following purposes:

- To help the student develop a sufficient understanding of the basic concepts underlying financial statements so that the concepts can be applied to new and different situations.
- To train the student in accounting terminology and methods so that financial statements currently published in corporate annual reports can be interpreted, analyzed, and evaluated.

Most introductory financial accounting textbooks share these, or similar, objectives. The critical differences between textbooks relate to the relative emphases on concepts, methods, and uses.

1 **Concepts** We emphasize the rationale for, and implications of, important accounting concepts. The ability to "conceptualize" material covered is an important part of the learning process. Without such conceptualization, students will have difficulty focusing on relevant issues in new and different situations. Accordingly, we have identified the important accounting concepts early in each chapter. Following these are several numerical examples illustrating their application. Numerous short problems are included at the end of each chapter to check the students' ability to apply the concepts to still different problem situations.

2 **Methods** We attempt to place sufficient emphasis on accounting procedures so that students can interpret, analyze, and evaluate published financial statements,

but not so much emphasis on the procedures that they get bogged down in detail. The determination of just how much accounting procedure is "enough" is a problem faced by all writers of accounting textbooks. Most feel, as we do, that the most effective way to learn accounting concepts is to work numerous problems and exercises. However, when too much emphasis is placed on accounting procedures, there is a tendency for students to be lulled into the security of thinking they understand accounting concepts when they actually do not. The mixture of concepts and procedures in this book is one with which we have experimented extensively and that we have found effective in classroom use.

Our experience is that students do not understand the accounting implications of an event until they can construct the journal entry for that event. Throughout this book, we show journal entries in describing the nature of accounting events. Moreover, most chapters contain questions that require the analysis of transactions with debits and credits. Do not conclude, however, by a glance at this text, that it is primarily procedural. We are more concerned that our students learn concepts; the procedures are required for learning the concepts. Furthermore, we believe that this is the most effective way to train both professional accountants and those who wish merely to be informed users of financial statements.

3 **Uses** We attempt to bridge the gap between the preparation of financial statements and the uses to which the statements might be put. We give extensive consideration to the effects of alternative accounting principles on the measurement of earnings and financial position and to the types of interpretations that should and should not be made. A complete set of financial statements and related notes is presented in Appendix A at the back of the book. Discussion of these financial statements is integrated into each chapter as appropriate. We have also included numerous user-oriented cases at the ends of most chapters.

Changes in This Edition

The major changes in the third edition are as follows:

1 A self-study problem and suggested solution have been added at the end of each chapter to assist students in understanding the concepts and procedures covered in the chapter. Some chapters have several such problems and solutions.

2 Chapter 1 includes an expanded discussion of the objectives of financial reporting and their role in the standard-setting process.

3 The material in Chapters 3 and 4 of the Second Edition has been substantially reordered in this edition. Chapter 3 now contains the general concepts of accrual accounting and the accounting procedures followed under accrual accounting when revenue is recognized at the time of sale. Chapter 4 now contains the concepts and procedures of accrual accounting for manufacturing firms, as well as a discussion of revenue recognition at times other than the time of sale. Instructors wishing to cover only the usual case of revenue recognition at time of sale will find all of the necessary concepts and procedures in Chapter 3. Instructors wishing

to explore revenue recognition in greater depth will find the material in Chapter 4.

4 The discussion of the procedures for preparing the statement of changes in financial position in Chapter 5 starts with a cash definition of funds and then illustrates its preparation using a working capital definition of funds. Regardless of which definition the instructor may prefer to emphasize, we have found that exposure to a cash definition first is most effective for student learning.

5 The discussion of accounting for marketable securities under the lower-of-cost-or-market method in Chapter 7 now includes the accounting for marketable securities classified both as Current Assets and as Investments.

6 The material on liabilities has now been split into two chapters (Chapters 10 and 11). Chapter 10 includes a discussion of the concept of an accounting liability and the accounting procedures for current liabilities, mortgages, notes, and bonds. Chapter 11 now includes the accounting for interest imputation, leases, pensions, and deferred income taxes.

7 Chapter 13, completely revised, covers accounting for intercorporate investments. The discussion follows a logical flow from minority passive investments to minority active investments to majority active investments. The illustration of consolidation procedures has been simplified by having the investment account stated as equity in the subsidiary and by basing the illustration on pre-closing trial balance data. The latter permits the integration of consolidation procedures for the balance sheet and income statement. Complexities in consolidation are presented in an appendix. The material on purchase and pooling of interests has been placed in a problem at the end of the chapter.

8 Chapter 14 is now a new chapter on accounting for changing prices that incorporate the important concepts of FASB *Statement No. 33.*

9 Appendix A presents a complete set of financial statements and notes for General Products Company in accordance with the provisions of SEC *Accounting Series Releases 279, 280,* and *281.* The financial statements have been simplified, relative to those in the Second Edition.

Organization

This book is divided into four major parts as outlined below:

One   Overview of Financial Statements . . . . .Chapter 1
Two   Accounting Concepts and Methods . . . . .Chapters 2–6
Three Measuring and Reporting Assets and Equities . . . . .Chapters 7–14
Four   Synthesis . . . . .Chapter 15

The four parts may be viewed as four tiers, or steps, for coverage of the material. Part One (Chapter 1) presents a general overview of the principal financial statements and the nature of accounting. Part Two (Chapters 2 through 6) discusses the basic accounting model used to generate the principal financial statements. Part Three (Chapters 7 through 14) considers the specific accounting principles or methods used in preparing the financial statements. Finally, Part Four (Chapter 15) serves as a synthesis for the entire book. This organization reflects our view that learning can take place most effectively when the student starts with a broad picture, then breaks up that broad picture into smaller pieces until the desired depth is achieved, and finally synthesizes so that the relationship between the parts and the whole can be kept in perspective.

Chapter 1 presents a brief description of the purpose and concepts underlying the three principal financial statements: the balance sheet, the income statement, and the statement of changes in financial position. The economic, social, and political environment within which these statements are generated is also considered. Particular attention is given to the process by which "generally accepted accounting principles" are set and the role of financial reporting objectives in that process.

Many students feel deluged with the multitude of new terms and concepts after reading Chapter 1. Most of these same students admit later, however, that the broad overview was useful in piecing material together as they later explored individual topics in greater depth.

Chapters 2 through 5 present the basic accounting model that generates the three principal financial statements. In each case, we begin with a description of the important concepts underlying each statement. The accounting procedures employed to generate the statements are then described and illustrated. One of the unique features of the book is the integration in Chapter 3 of the accounting entries for transactions during a period with the related adjusting entries at the end of the period. We have found that when these two types of entries are discussed in separate chapters, students lose sight of the fact that both kinds of entries are required to measure net income and financial position.

Another unique aspect of the text is the early coverage, in Chapter 5, of the statement of changes in financial position. We have two purposes in placing it here. First, this placement elevates the statement to its rightful place among the three principal financial statements. Students can thereby integrate the concepts of profitability and liquidity more effectively and begin to understand that one does not necessarily accompany the other. When the funds statement is covered at the end of the course (in many cases, when time is running out), there is a tendency for the student to think it is less important. Our second purpose for placing this chapter early in the book is that it serves to cement understanding of the basic accounting model in Chapters 2 through 4: Preparing the statement of changes in financial position requires the student to work "backwards" from the balance sheet and income statement to reconstruct the transactions that took place.

Chapter 6 introduces the topic of financial statement analysis. We place it here to serve as a partial synthesis of the first five chapters. Students at this point ask how information in the statements might be used. This chapter presents an opportunity to answer some of these questions, even if at only an elementary level. Effective financial statement analysis requires an understanding of the specific accounting methods discussed in Part Three. Chapter 6 therefore serves as a springboard for what is to come.

Chapters 7 through 14 discuss the various "generally accepted accounting principles" employed in generating financial statements. In each chapter, we not only describe and illustrate the application of the various accounting methods but also consider their effect on the financial statements. This approach reflects our view that students should be able to interpret and analyze published financial statements and to understand the effect of alternative accounting methods on such assessments. We have placed some of the more complicated topics in chapter-end appendixes to provide flexibility in coverage. Some instructors may not wish to use this more advanced material.

The students who have used the previous editions of this book have found that Chapter 15, which synthesizes much of the material in the first fourteen chapters, is in many ways the most useful in the book. Explicit consideration is given to the combined effects of alternative accounting methods on the financial statements and the significance of alternative accounting methods on financial statement analysis. The self-study problem and problems **16** and **17** at the end of Chapter 15 are major review problems for the whole book.

A comprehensive Glossary of financial accounting is included at the end of the book. This glossary serves as a useful reference tool for accounting and other business terms and provides additional descriptions of a few topics considered only briefly in the text, such as *accounting changes.*

Related Materials Accompanying the Text

The following materials have been prepared for use with the text:

Instructor's Manual The instructor's manual, in addition to including responses to all questions and solutions to all exercises and problems, presents suggested course outlines for courses of varying lengths, a list of chapter objectives, helpful teaching hints, detailed lecture and discussion outlines including the numbers of particularly germane problems, and sample examination questions and problems. The instructor's manual also includes a list of check figures for various problems in the text. These check figures can be photocopied and distributed to students if the instructor so desires.

Study Guide A study guide has been prepared by LeBrone C. Harris, James E. Moon, and William L. Stephens. This study guide includes a listing of highlights from each chapter and is then followed by numerous short true/false, matching, and multiple-choice questions, with answers.

Transparencies A set of transparencies is available for many of the exhibits in the text and the problems at the ends of the chapters.

Acknowledgments

We gratefully acknowledge the helpful criticisms and suggestions of our colleagues and others who reviewed the manuscript at various stages: James A. Largay III, Katherine Schipper, Leonard E. Morrissey, and Shyam Sunder.

Our work on this revision was further aided by reviews from:

Thomas G. Black, San Jose State University
Ellen Cox, Duke University
Wagih G. Dafashy, College of William and Mary
John Eber, Illinois Benedictine College
Paul Guttmann, San Jose State University
Ronald Jaffe, Claremont Men's College
Lawrence Kalbers, Wittenberg University
Robyn Lawrence, University of Oregon
L. R. Paquette, Duke University
Dan Yavner, University of Minnesota
Barbara Zorkowski, Bellevue Community College

Some of our former students helped us to improve the clarity of the Questions and Problems and to debug the solutions. We thank them for their help; Carl Texter was especially productive.

Thomas Horton and Daughters, Inc., has graciously given us permission to reproduce material from *Accounting: The Language of Business,* published by them. The Prima, Secunda, and Tertia problems in Chapter 3 were adapted from ones prepared by George H. Sorter. These problems involve working backwards from one financial statement to another, and we have found them useful in cementing understanding.

We thank the following people for their hard work in helping us to prepare the manuscript for this book: Melanie Brennan, Barbara Haskell, Sandra Myers, Raymonde Rousselot, Suzanne Sweet and K. Xenophon-Rybowiak. Cherie Worman prepared the index.

Finally, we thank Peter Coveney, Feeny Lipscomb, Brian Weber and Liz Widdicombe of The Dryden Press for their assistance and patience in the preparation of this book.

S.D.
C.P.S.
R.L.W.

Contents

Financial Accounting

Third Edition

Part One

Overview of Financial Statements

Chapter 1 *Overview of Financial Statements and Reporting Process*

A major function of accounting is providing information useful for making decisions. For example, a corporate treasurer might use a statement of estimated cash receipts and disbursements in deciding if short-term borrowing is necessary. A production manager might use a report on the productivity of various employees in deciding how a special order is to be routed through a factory. A sales manager might use a report on the cost of producing and selling different product lines in recommending the prices that should be charged and the products that should be emphasized by the sales staff. The preparation of reports for use by persons within a firm is referred to as *managerial accounting*. Users of information within a firm are generally free to specify the types of information they need for their decisions; managerial accounting reports are prepared to conform to these needs.

In contrast, *financial accounting* is concerned with the preparation of reports for use by persons outside, or external to, a firm. For example, a bank may desire information on the cash-generating ability of a firm in deciding whether or not to grant a bank loan. A potential investor may desire information on a firm's profitability before deciding to purchase shares of its common stock.

The format and content of financial accounting reports tend to be more standardized than is the case in managerial accounting. Considering the large number of uses and users of financial accounting reports, there is a need for some degree of uniformity in reporting among firms. The most common reports for external users are the financial statements included in annual reports to shareholders and potential investors. These financial statements are prepared in accordance with "generally accepted accounting principles." Such "principles" have evolved over time or have been made "acceptable" by decree from an official rule-making body. The Financial Accounting

2

Standards Board, an independent body in the private sector, and the Securities and Exchange Commission, an agency of the federal government, are the principal rule-making bodies in the United States. Much of this text is devoted to a discussion of the underlying assumptions, rationale, and implications of specific generally accepted accounting principles. Because this text is an introduction to financial accounting, we do not specifically consider managerial accounting reports.

This chapter provides an overview of the principal financial reports, or statements, issued by firms to external users and presents a brief description of the financial reporting process. We first consider the general objectives of financial reporting. We then examine the purpose and content of each of the principal financial statements included in the annual report to shareholders. Finally, we discuss the nature of generally accepted accounting principles and the process through which they are developed. Because this chapter merely introduces material to be covered in greater depth in later chapters, more questions are raised than are answered. We feel, however, that it is helpful to have an overview of financial reporting before embarking on a study of the concepts and procedures employed in preparing various accounting reports.

Objectives of Financial Reporting

Financial accounting reports provide information to investors, creditors, and others who commit financial resources to a firm. The Financial Accounting Standards Board has established a broad set of financial reporting objectives to guide the financial reporting process. These objectives are summarized below.

1. Financial reporting should provide information that is useful to present and potential investors and creditors and other users in making rational investment, credit and similar decisions. The information should be comprehensible to those who have a reasonable understanding of business and economic activities and are willing to study the information with reasonable diligence.

2. Financial reporting should provide information to help present and potential investors and creditors and other users in assessing the amounts, timing, and uncertainty of prospective cash receipts from dividends or interest and from the proceeds from the sale, redemption, or maturity of securities or loans. The prospects for those cash receipts are affected by an enterprise's ability to generate enough cash to meet its obligations when due and its other cash operating needs, to reinvest in operations and to pay cash dividends and may also be affected by perceptions of investors and creditors generally about that ability, which affect market prices of the enterprise's securities.

3. Financial reporting should provide information about the economic resources of an enterprise, the claims on those resources (obligations of the enterprise to transfer resources to other entities and owners' equity), and the effects of transactions, events and claims on those resources.

4. Financial reporting should provide information about an enterprise's financial performance during a period. . . . The primary focus of financial reporting is information about an enterprise's performance provided by measures of earnings and its components.

3

5. Financial reporting should provide information about how an enterprise obtains and spends cash, about its borrowing and repayment of borrowing, about its capital transactions, including cash dividends and other distributions of enterprise resources to owners, and about other factors that may affect an enterprise's liquidity and solvency.

6. Financial reporting should provide information about how management of an enterprise has discharged its stewardship responsibility to owners (stockholders) for the use of enterprise resources entrusted to it. Management of an enterprise is periodically accountable to the owners not only for the custody and safekeeping of enterprise resources but also for their efficient and profitable use and for protecting them to the extent possible from unfavorable economic impacts of factors in the economy such as inflation or deflation and technological and social changes.

7. Financial reporting should include explanations and interpretations to help users understand financial information provided.[1]

The emphasis of financial reporting is on helping present and potential investors and creditors assess the amount and timing of future cash flows (expected return) to them from business enterprises and the uncertainty (risk) of those returns. This general reporting objective is accomplished through a set of financial statements that provide information about (1) an enterprise's economic resources and claims on those resources, (2) an enterprise's financial performance during a period, and (3) an enterprise's sources and uses of cash. The three principal financial statements included in annual reports, discussed in the next section, provide these three types of information. Financial reports should also include explanatory and interpretative comments to help users in understanding the financial information provided. This last objective is accomplished with supporting schedules and notes attached to the three principal financial statements.

Principal Financial Statements

The annual report to shareholders typically includes a letter from the company's president summarizing activities of the past year and assessing the company's prospects for the coming year. Also frequently included are pictures of the firm's products and employees and similar promotional material. The section of the annual report containing the financial statements comprises the following:

1 Statement of financial position.
2 Statement of net income.
3 Statement of changes in financial position.
4 Various supporting statements or schedules.
5 Notes to the financial statements.
6 Opinion of the independent certified public accountant.

---

[1] Financial Accounting Standards Board, *Statement of Financial Accounting Concepts No. 1,* "Objectives of Financial Reporting by Business Enterprises," 1978.

Statement of Financial Position

The statement of financial position, or balance sheet, provides information about the economic resources of a firm and the claims on those resources by creditors and owners as of a specific moment in time. Exhibit 1.1 presents a comparative statement of financial position of the Jonathan Electronics Corporation, as of December 31, 1981 and 1982. As its title suggests, this statement attempts to present an overall view of Jonathan Electronics Corporation's financial position as of the ends of 1981 and 1982. Several aspects of this statement should be noted.

Exhibit 1.1
Jonathan Electronics Corporation
Comparative Statement of
Financial Position
December 31, 1981 and 1982

	December 31	
ASSETS		
Current Assets:[a]	**1981**	**1982**
Cash	$ 75,000	$ 125,000
Accounts Receivable from Customers	75,000	200,000
Merchandise Inventory (at acquisition cost)	150,000	225,000
Total Current Assets	$ 300,000	$ 550,000
Noncurrent Assets (at acquisition cost):[a]		
Land	$ 200,000	$ 200,000
Equipment (net of accumulated depreciation)	700,000	900,000
Buildings (net of accumulated depreciation)	800,000	750,000
Total Noncurrent Assets	$1,700,000	$1,850,000
Total Assets	$2,000,000	$2,400,000
LIABILITIES AND SHAREHOLDERS' EQUITY		
Current Liabilities:[a]		
Accounts Payable to Suppliers	$ 125,000	$ 160,000
Salaries Payable to Employees	25,000	40,000
Income Taxes Payable to Federal Government	50,000	100,000
Total Current Liabilities	$ 200,000	$ 300,000
Noncurrent Liabilities:[a]		
Bonds Payable to Lenders (due 1998)	600,000	700,000
Total Liabilities	$ 800,000	$1,000,000
Shareholders' Equity:		
Common Stock	$ 500,000	$ 550,000
Retained Earnings	700,000	850,000
Total Shareholders' Equity	$1,200,000	$1,400,000
Total Liabilities and Shareholders' Equity	$2,000,000	$2,400,000

[a]The current and noncurrent classification of assets and liabilities is discussed later in this chapter.

Statement at a Moment in Time The statement of financial position presents a snapshot of the firm's financial position as of a given date. (In Exhibit 1.1, one column reports the financial position as of December 31, 1981, and the other, as of December 31, 1982.) The statement presents amounts or levels or *stocks* of various items. (Note here that we are not referring to shares of stock.) *Stocks* are to be contrasted with *flows*. A stock is a measure of the amount of an item at a particular time, whereas a flow is a measure of the increase or decrease in an item over a period of time. For example, to say that Jonathan Electronics Corporation had cash in the amount of $75,000 on December 31, 1981, and $125,000 on December 31, 1982, is to say something about the firm's stock of cash on these particular dates. A parallel statement about flows is to say that the firm's cash receipts and disbursements during the period were such that the cash balance increased, or changed, by $50,000.

Concepts of Assets and Equities The statement of financial position presents a listing of the firm's *assets, liabilities,* and *owners' equity.* When the corporate form of organization is used, ownership is evidenced by shares of stock, and the owners' equity is frequently referred to as *stockholders' equity* or *shareholders' equity.*

Assets are economic resources. An asset is an item that has the ability or potential to provide future services or benefits to a firm. For example, cash can be used to purchase merchandise inventory or equipment. Merchandise inventory can be sold to customers for an amount the firm hopes will be larger than was paid for it. Equipment can be used in transporting the merchandise inventory to customers.

Liabilities are creditors' claims on the resources of a firm. Jonathan Electronics Corporation acquired merchandise inventory from its suppliers but has not yet paid for a portion of the purchases. As a result, these creditors have a claim on the assets of the company. Labor services have been provided by employees for which payment has not been made as of December 31 of each year. These employees likewise have a claim on the assets of the firm. Creditors' claims, or liabilities, result from benefits previously received by a firm, and typically have a specified amount and date at which they become due.

Shareholders' equity is the owners' claim on the assets of a firm. Unlike creditors, the owners have a residual interest. That is, owners have a claim on all assets in excess of those required to meet creditors' claims. The shareholders' equity generally comprises two parts: contributed capital and retained earnings. Contributed capital reflects the assets invested by shareholders in exchange for an ownership interest. Retained earnings represent the earnings, or profits, realized by a firm since its formation in excess of dividends distributed to shareholders. In other words, retained earnings are earnings reinvested by management for the benefit of the shareholders. Management directs the use of a firm's assets so that over time more assets are received than are given up in obtaining them. This increase in assets, after any claims by creditors, belongs to the firm's owners. Most firms reinvest a large percentage of their earnings for growth and expansion rather than distributing all earnings as dividends.

Liabilities plus shareholders' equity are referred to as *total equities,* or simply *equities.*

6

Equality of Assets and Equities As the statement of financial position for Jonathan Electronics Corporation indicates, there is an equality between (1) assets and (2) liabilities plus shareholders' equity. That is,

$$\text{Assets} = \text{Liabilities} + \text{Shareholders' Equity}.$$

The significance of this equality can be grasped by considering the nature of each of the three components. Assets are resources of the firm. Liabilities and shareholders' equity are the claims on these resources. Thus:

$$\text{Resources} = \text{Claims on Resources}.$$

In the statement of financial position, we view the resources from two viewpoints: a listing of the assets under the control of the firm and a listing of the parties external to the firm who have a claim on these assets. Because of the equality of total assets and total equities, the statement of financial position is often called a *balance sheet*.

Balance Sheet Classification The assets and liabilities are classified in the balance sheet as being either *current* or *noncurrent*.

Current assets include cash and other assets that are expected to be turned into cash, or sold, or consumed within approximately 1 year from the date of the balance sheet. Cash, temporary investments in securities, accounts receivable from customers, and merchandise inventories are the most common current assets. Current liabilities include liabilities that are expected to be paid within 1 year. Accounts payable to suppliers, salaries payable to employees, and taxes payable to governmental agencies are examples of current liabilities. Noncurrent assets typically are held and used for several years; they provide a firm with longer-term productive capacity. Noncurrent liabilities plus shareholders' equity are a firm's longer-term sources of capital. The usefulness of the classification of assets and equities as current or noncurrent is discussed when we consider the third principal statement, the statement of changes in financial position.

Valuation The dollar amount shown for each asset and liability listed in the statement of financial position of Jonathan Electronics Corporation is based on one of two valuation bases: (1) cash, or current cash-equivalent, valuation, or (2) acquisition, or historical, cost valuation.

Cash is stated at the amount of cash on hand or in the bank. Accounts receivable are shown at the amount of cash expected to be collected from customers. Liabilities are generally shown at the amount of cash required to discharge debts. These assets and liabilities are sometimes referred to as *monetary items* because they are valued on a cash, or current cash-equivalent, basis.

The remaining assets are shown at either unadjusted or adjusted acquisition cost. For example, merchandise inventory and land are shown at the amount of cash or other resources that the firm originally sacrificed to acquire those assets. Equipment and buildings are likewise shown at acquisition cost, but this amount is adjusted downward to reflect the portion of the assets' services that has been used since acquisition. A large proportion of Jonathan Electronics Corporation's assets are shown at either unadjusted or adjusted acquisition cost. It is unlikely that these amounts are equal to the amounts the company could realize if the assets were sold or the amounts the company would have to pay currently to replace them.

Common stock is stated at the amount originally invested by owners when the firm's stock was first sold. Retained earnings is the sum of all prior years' earnings in excess of dividends.

Assets and Equities Not Shown After you study the balance sheet of Jonathan Electronics Corporation, you may think of several resources of the firm noteworthy by their absence. Consider, for example, the value of a well-trained labor force, dynamic managerial leadership, superior technological abilities, and the good reputation of the company. Because of difficulties in valuing such resources, they do not appear as assets on most firms' balance sheets. Potential liabilities, such as some pending lawsuits against a firm, also do not appear.

We have introduced several asset and liability valuation and inclusion issues here to point out possible deficiencies in the balance sheet as an indicator of a firm's financial position at any moment in time. Later chapters consider these issues more fully.

Statement of Net Income

The statement of net income provides information for assessing a firm's financial performance during a period of time. Exhibit 1.2 presents a statement of net income of Jonathan Electronics Corporation for the year 1982. This statement indicates the *net income, earnings,* or *profits,* of the company for a period of time. Note several aspects of this second principal financial statement.

Statement Reports Activities over Time The income statement presents the results of earnings activity over time and therefore reports *flows.* In contrast, the balance sheet presents a statement of the firm's assets and equities at a specific point in time and reports *stocks.*

Concepts of Net Income, Revenue, and Expense The terms *net income, earnings,* and *profits* are synonyms used interchangeably in corporate annual reports and throughout this text. Generating earnings is a primary activity of most business firms, and the income statement is intended to provide a measure of how successful a firm was in achieving this goal for a given time span. *Net income* is the difference between revenues and expenses for a period.

Revenues are a measure of the inflows of assets (or reductions in liabilities) from selling goods and providing services to customers. During 1982, Jonathan Electronics

Exhibit 1.2
Jonathan Electronics Corporation
Statement of Net Income
for the Year 1982

Revenues:	
Sale of Merchandise	$2,250,000
Sale of Engineering Services	140,000
Interest on Customers' Uncollected Accounts	10,000
Total Revenues	$2,400,000
Less Expenses:	
Cost of Merchandise Sold	$ 900,000
Salaries Expense	400,000
Depreciation Expense	200,000
Selling and Administrative Expenses	350,000
Interest Expense	50,000
Income Tax Expense	200,000
Total Expenses	$2,100,000
Net Income	$ 300,000

Corporation sold merchandise and provided engineering and financing services. From its customers, Jonathan Electronics Corporation received assets, either cash or promises to pay cash in the near future. These promises to pay are called Accounts Receivable from Customers. Thus, revenues were generated and assets increased.

Expenses are a measure of the outflows of assets (or increases in liabilities) used up in generating revenues. The cost of merchandise sold (an expense) is measured by the acquisition cost of merchandise that was sold to customers. Salaries expense is the amount of cash payments or liability to make future cash payments to employees for services received in helping generate revenues during the period. Depreciation expense is a measure of the services of equipment and buildings used during 1982. For each expense there is either a reduction in an asset or an increase in a liability.

A firm strives to generate an excess of net asset inflows from revenues over net asset outflows from expenses required in generating the revenues. When expenses for a period exceed revenues, a firm incurs a *net loss*. The net income measure may be used as an indicator of a firm's accomplishments (revenues) relative to the efforts required (expenses) in pursuing its activities.

Relationship to Balance Sheet The income statement links with the balance sheets at the beginning and the end of the period. Recall that retained earnings represents the sum of all prior earnings of a firm in excess of dividends. The amount of net income for the period helps explain the change in retained earnings between the beginning and end of the period. During 1982, Jonathan Electronics Corporation had net income of $300,000. Assume that dividends declared and paid were

$150,000. The change in retained earnings during 1982 can therefore be explained as follows:

Retained Earnings, December 31, 1981 (stock)	$700,000
Add Net Income for the Year 1982 (flow)	300,000
Subtract Dividends Declared and Paid (flow)	(150,000)
Retained Earnings, December 31, 1982 (stock)	$850,000

This linkage by the income statement of the beginning and ending balance sheets is called *articulation.*

Net income for the period also articulates with changes in the other components of the balance sheet. If we subtract the amount for each balance sheet component at the beginning of the period from the corresponding amount at the end of the period, we get the *change* in each component during the period, as follows:

$$\begin{matrix} \text{Change in} \\ \text{Assets} \end{matrix} = \begin{matrix} \text{Change in} \\ \text{Liabilities} \end{matrix} + \begin{matrix} \text{Change in} \\ \text{Contributed} \\ \text{Capital} \end{matrix} + \begin{matrix} \text{Change in} \\ \text{Retained} \\ \text{Earnings.} \end{matrix}$$

In explaining the change in retained earnings for 1982 of Jonathan Electronics Corporation, we saw that the change in retained earnings is equal to net income minus dividends. Thus:

$$\begin{matrix} \text{Change in} \\ \text{Assets} \end{matrix} = \begin{matrix} \text{Change in} \\ \text{Liabilities} \end{matrix} + \begin{matrix} \text{Change in} \\ \text{Contributed} \\ \text{Capital} \end{matrix} + \begin{matrix} \text{Net} \\ \text{Income} \end{matrix} - \text{Dividends.}$$

For Jonathan Electronics Corporation, these relationships for 1982 are as follows:

$$\$400,000 = \$200,000 \quad + \$50,000 \quad + \$300,000 - \$150,000.$$

Assets increased by $400,000. This increase can be related to an increase in liabilities of $200,000, an increase in contributed capital of $50,000, and the generation of net income of $300,000, offset by the payment of $150,000 in dividends. The significance of the relationships between the balance sheet and income statement is treated in later chapters.

Measurement of Revenues and Expenses As with assets and equities on the balance sheet, the measurement of revenues and expenses is based on either (1) cash, or cash-equivalent, values or (2) acquisition costs. The amount reported as revenue from the sale of merchandise or services is measured by the expected amount of cash to be received from customers. Salary, selling and administrative, interest, and income tax expenses are measured by the amount of cash the firm was required to pay for the services received. Cost of merchandise sold is measured by the acquisition cost of inventory that was sold, and depreciation expense is measured in terms of the

10

acquisition cost of the services of the equipment and buildings that were used during the year.

Holding Gains and Losses Excluded The balance sheet shows assets such as inventory, land, equipment, and buildings at acquisition cost. The income statement thus excludes any holding gains caused by increases in the economic value of those assets. For example, land was acquired for $200,000 several years ago. Suppose that this land had a current appraised value of $500,000 at the end of 1982. This increase in value is not normally recognized as revenue on the income statement until the land is sold. The economist views increases in the market value of a firm's assets as part of its income. The accountant generally recognizes increases in the value of assets only at the time assets are sold. Thus, we see one important difference between the economist's and accountant's definitions of income.

Statement of Changes in Financial Position

The statement of changes in financial position reports the principal sources and uses of funds flowing through a firm during a period of time. Exhibit 1.3 presents a statement of changes in financial position for Jonathan Electronics Corporation for 1982, with "funds" defined as cash. Operations led to a net increase in cash of $400,000. (Recall that not all revenues result in an immediate increase in cash and not all expenses result in an immediate decrease in cash.) Cash was also received when bonds and common stock were issued. Cash was used to pay dividends and to acquire buildings and equipment. Of what significance is a statement explaining or analyzing the change in cash during a period of time? This might be best understood with an example.

Exhibit 1.3
Jonathan Electronics Corporation
Statement of Changes in
Financial Position
for the Year 1982

Sources of Cash:		
Operations	$400,000[a]	
Proceeds from Issue of Bonds	100,000	
Proceeds from Issue of Common Stock	50,000	
Total Sources of Cash		$550,000
Uses of Cash:		
Dividends Declared and Paid	$150,000	
Equipment and Building Acquired	350,000	
Total Uses of Cash		(500,000)
Net Increase in Cash for 1982		$ 50,000

[a]The computation of cash generated by operations and its relationship to net income reported in the income statement are treated in Chapter 5.

Example Diversified Technologies Corporation began business in 1978. In its first 4 years of operations, it had net income of $100,000, $300,000, $800,000, and $1,500,000, respectively. The company has retained all of its earnings for growth and expansion. Early in 1982, the company learned that it was running out of cash despite the retention of earnings. A careful study of the problem revealed that, although the company was operating profitably, it was expanding inventories, buildings, and equipment so fast that funds were not being generated quickly enough to keep pace with its recent growth.

This example illustrates a common phenomenon for business firms. Cash is not generated in sufficient amounts or at the proper times to finance all ongoing or growing operations. If the firm is to continue operating successfully, it must generate more funds than it spends. In some cases the firm can borrow from long-term investors to replenish its cash but future operations must generate funds to repay these loans. The statement of changes in financial position provides information about the principal financing (increases and decreases in debt and capital stock) and investing (purchases and sales of assets) activities of a firm. Because this information helps explain the change in various items on the balance sheet between the beginning and end of a period, the descriptive title, statement of changes in financial position, is used. Some refer to the statement as a "sources and uses of funds statement."

The definition of "funds" could be cash only, or cash plus accounts receivable, or some other definition. Most published statements of changes in financial position use a broader definition of funds than cash only. Funds are defined as cash plus those assets expected to be turned into cash within approximately 1 year, referred to as *current assets,* less those obligations expected to require the payment of cash within approximately 1 year, referred to as *current liabilities.* The excess of current assets over current liabilities, is called *working capital.* It represents a pool of cash or near-cash resources that may help finance ongoing or growing operations. Selecting an appropriate definition of funds for preparing the statement of changes in financial position is discussed in Chapter 5. Several additional aspects of this statement should be noted.

Statement Reports Activities over Time The statement of changes in financial position indicates the increases and decreases in funds during a period and, like the income statement, reports flows.

Relationship to Balance Sheet and Income Statement The statement of changes in financial position helps explain the change in funds between the beginning and end of the period. In this way, the statement articulates or links with the balance sheet. If funds are defined as cash, the statement of changes in financial position analyzes the change in cash reported in comparative balance sheets. If funds are defined as working capital, the statement analyzes the change in current assets minus current liabilities between the beginning and end of the period. The statement of changes in financial position also articulates with the income statement in that operations are a primary source of funds for most firms.

Figure 1.1 summarizes the relationships among the three principal financial statements.

12

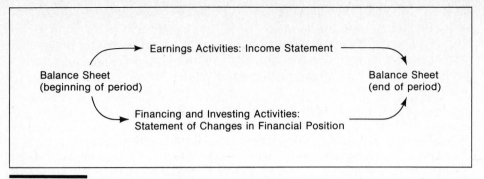

Figure 1.1
Relationships among Principal Financial Statements

Supporting Statements or Schedules

The statements of financial position, net income, and changes in financial position shown in the annual report are usually highly condensed for easy comprehension by the average reader. Some readers are interested in details omitted from these condensed versions. The annual report, therefore, typically includes schedules that provide more detail for some of the items reported in the three main statements. For example, separate schedules must be provided to explain the change in contributed capital and retained earnings, and may be provided to explain changes in other items in the balance sheet.

Notes to the Financial Statements

Every set of published financial statements is supplemented by explanatory notes. These notes are an integral part of the statements. As later chapters make clear, a firm must select the accounting methods followed in preparing its financial statements from a set of generally accepted methods. The notes indicate the actual accounting methods used by the firm. The notes also disclose additional information that elaborates on items presented in the three principal statements. To understand fully a firm's balance sheet, income statement, and statement of changes in financial position requires a careful reading of the notes. We do not present notes to the financial statements for the Jonathan Electronics Corporation because they would not mean much at this stage. Do not conclude, however, that the notes are unimportant merely because they have been omitted from the statements presented in this chapter. See Appendix A, Exhibit A.4, at the back of the book, for examples of notes to the financial statements.

Auditor's Opinion

An important section of the annual report to the shareholders is the opinion of the independent Certified Public Accountant on the financial statements, supporting schedules, and notes. The accountant's opinion is frequently described as the *Ac-*

countant's Report, or sometimes merely as the *Opinion* or *Certificate.* It is often called the report of the *Auditor* or *Certified Public Accountant.*

The auditor's opinion generally follows a standard format, with some variations to meet specific circumstances. An auditor's opinion on the financial statements of Jonathan Electronics Corporation on pages 5, 9, and 11 might be as follows:

> We have examined the comparative balance sheets of Jonathan Electronics Corporation as of December 31, 1981 and 1982, and the related statements of net income and changes in financial position for the year 1982. Our examination was made in accordance with generally accepted auditing standards, and accordingly included such tests of the accounting records and such other auditing procedures as we considered necessary in the circumstances.
>
> In our opinion, the aforementioned financial statements present fairly the financial position of Jonathan Electronics Corporation at December 31, 1981 and 1982, and the results of its operations and changes in financial position for the year 1982 in conformity with generally accepted accounting principles applied on a basis consistent with that of the preceding year.

The opinion usually contains two paragraphs—a *scope* paragraph and an *opinion* paragraph. The scope paragraph indicates the financial presentations covered by the opinion and affirms that auditing standards and practices generally accepted by the accounting profession have been adhered to unless otherwise noted and described. Exceptions to the statement that the auditor's "examination was made in accordance with generally accepted auditing standards" are seldom seen in published annual reports. There are occasional references to the auditor's having relied on financial statements examined by other auditors, particularly for subsidiaries or for data from prior periods.

The opinion expressed by the auditor in the second paragraph is the heart of the accountant's report. The opinion may be *unqualified* or *qualified.* The great majority of opinions are unqualified; that is, there are no exceptions or qualifications to the auditor's opinion that the statements "present fairly the financial position . . . and the results of operations and the changes in financial position . . . in conformity with generally accepted accounting principles applied on a consistent basis."

Qualifications to the opinion result primarily from material uncertainties regarding realization or valuation of assets, outstanding litigation or tax liabilities, or accounting inconsistencies between periods caused by changes in the application of accounting principles. An opinion qualified as to fair presentation is usually noted by the phrase *subject to;* an opinion qualified as to consistency in application of accounting principles is usually noted by *except for,* with an indication of the auditor's approval of the change.

A qualification so material that the auditor feels an opinion cannot be expressed as to the fairness of the financial statements as a whole must result in either a *disclaimer of opinion* or an *adverse opinion.* Adverse opinions and disclaimers of opinion are rare in published reports.

A member of the American Institute of Certified Public Accountants (AICPA), the professional organization of practicing CPAs, is expected to adhere to the pronouncements of the body designated by the AICPA as the official source of generally accepted accounting principles.[2] As will be discussed later in this chapter, the official authoritative body from 1938 to 1959 was the Committee on Accounting Procedure and from 1959 to 1973 was the Accounting Principles Board. Since 1973, the Financial Accounting Standards Board has been given the authority for specifying generally accepted accounting principles. A Certified Public Accountant normally may not attest that statements are in conformity with generally accepted accounting principles when the statements contain material departures from rulings of those bodies. If, however, the CPA can demonstrate that, because of unusual circumstances, departures are required so that the statements are not misleading, then the CPA may attest to statements with material departures from generally accepted accounting principles. The grounds for justifying departures are so stringent, however, that such departures are seldom seen in published financial statements.

Nature and Development of Accounting Principles

Frequent references are made throughout this book to "generally accepted accounting principles." These "principles" are the accounting methods and procedures used by firms in preparing their financial statements. In this section, we consider the nature of these principles and the process through which they are developed.

Nature of Principles in Accounting

Principles in accounting differ from those in fields such as physics and mathematics. In physics and other natural sciences, the criterion for evaluating a principle is the degree to which the predictions indicated by the principle or theory correspond with physically observed phenomena. In mathematics, a principle (or theorem) is judged on its internal consistency with the structure of definitions and underlying axioms. In accounting, principles are judged on their general acceptability by preparers and users of accounting reports. Unlike those in the physical sciences, principles in accounting do not naturally exist awaiting discovery. Unlike mathematics, there is no structure of definitions and concepts in accounting that can be used unambiguously in developing accounting principles. For example, one generally accepted accounting principle is that land is to be stated at its acquisition cost as long as it is held by a firm. Changes in the market value of the land are not reflected in the financial statements until the land is sold. This accounting principle cannot be "proven" to be correct. It has simply been judged to be the generally acceptable method of accounting for land. Recently, however, experience with inflation has led many accountants and financial statement users to question the relevance of historical-cost valuations. In response to this concern, the Financial Accounting Standards Board requires large firms to disclose certain supplemental information on the impact of inflation on certain financial statement items.

---

[2]American Institute of Certified Public Accountants, *Code of Professional Ethics*, 1973, Rule 203.

Development of Principles in Accounting

The discussion above, concerning the nature of accounting principles, suggests that their development is essentially a political process. Various persons or groups have power, or authority, in the decision process that yields generally accepted accounting principles. Some of the more important participants are described below.

Congress In the Securities Act of 1933, the Congress accepted the ultimate legal authority to prescribe the methods of accounting used in preparing financial statements for shareholders of publicly held corporations. Congress has delegated its authority to the Securities and Exchange Commission (SEC), an agency of the federal government. Whereas the SEC has legal authority to prescribe accounting principles, since 1938 it has delegated most of the responsibility for developing accounting principles to the accounting profession.[3] In most cases, the SEC serves as an advisor or consultant on proposed accounting procedures. In a few instances, the SEC has effectively exerted its legal authority by disagreeing with positions taken within the accounting profession.

In recent years, the pronouncements of the SEC have been concerned primarily with format and disclosure in the financial statements. The SEC requires that certain financial statement information be included in the annual report to shareholders. The financial statements for General Products Company in Appendix A are presented in the required format. The annual report to shareholders, along with certain supplementary information, must then be included in the annual report submitted to the SEC (known as the *10-K report*).[4] Among the publications of the SEC are the following:

> *Regulation S-X.* A document pertaining to the form and content of financial statements required to be filed with the SEC.
>
> *Accounting Series Releases.* A series of opinions on accounting principles that, together with *Regulation S-X,* are the primary statements on the form and content of financial statements filed with the Commission.
>
> *Staff Accounting Bulletins.* A series of reports prepared by the SEC staff that discuss certain reporting issues in greater depth than provided in *Regulation S-X* or the *Accounting Series Releases.*

Accounting Profession The accounting profession is composed of practicing accountants, financial managers, controllers, academicians, and others. Each of these groups has its own professional organization or association (American Institute of Certified Public Accountants, National Association of Accountants, Financial Executives Institute, American Accounting Association). The professional organizations

---

[3] Securities and Exchange Commission, *Accounting Series Release No. 4,* 1938. The SEC reaffirmed its delegation of responsibility by recognizing the Financial Accounting Standards Board in *Accounting Series Release No. 150,* 1973.

[4] Securities and Exchange Commission, *Accounting Series Releases No. 279, 280,* and *281,* 1980.

sometimes express positions, or opinions, on proposed accounting principles. Most of the specification of accounting principles has been carried out, however, by officially appointed committees or boards within the accounting profession. Between 1938 and 1959, the Committee on Accounting Procedure of the American Institute of Certified Public Accountants issued Bulletins on various topics. Between 1959 and 1973, the Accounting Principles Board (APB) of the American Institute of Certified Public Accountants issued Opinions. These Bulletins and Opinions were considered to constitute generally accepted accounting principles. The APB was composed of individuals from within the accounting profession, with heavy representation from public accounting firms.

Since 1973, the Financial Accounting Standards Board (FASB) has been the principal agency outside of the federal government responsible for developing accounting principles. The FASB differs from the APB in two important respects. First, the FASB includes substantial representation from several groups of statement preparers and users in addition to members from the public accounting profession. Second, the members of the FASB are employed on a full-time basis and have severed all relations with their previous firms or universities. This severance of relations increases the independence of Board members, and reduces chances for undue influence by their previous employers. The FASB issues Statements on Financial Accounting Standards which have the authority of being considered generally accepted accounting principles.

Standard Setting under the FASB The process of setting accounting principles under the FASB has two noteworthy attributes. First, the FASB follows a rather complex due-process procedure in its deliberations. The process generally followed is summarized as follows:

1 A reporting issue is identified and placed on the Board's agenda.
2 The technical staff of the FASB, in consultation with a group of knowledgeable persons in the accounting and business community (formed in a "task force"), prepares a *Discussion Memorandum* (DM) on the reporting issue. The DM is intended to be an impartial discussion of the principal questions to be considered by the Board.
3 The DM is "exposed" to the public for a period of at least 60 days.
4 A public hearing on the contents of the DM is held. Individuals and organizations have an opportunity at this point to comment on the questions raised and to indicate support for particular positions.
5 The FASB, after considering the oral and written comments received, prepares an Exposure Draft of a Proposed Financial Accounting Standard. The Exposure Draft takes a definitive position on the major issues under consideration.
6 The Exposure Draft is "exposed" to the public for a period of at least 30 days.
7 A second public hearing is frequently held. The comments this time are directed at the content of the Proposed Standard.
8 After additional consideration of the comments received, the Board either (a) adopts the Proposed Standard as an official Statement of Financial Account-

ing Standard, (b) revises the Proposed Standard before making it official, in some cases allowing additional opportunities for public comment (in effect, returning to Step 6), (c) delays issuance of an official Standard but keeps the issue on its active agenda, or (d) decides not to issue an official Standard and takes the issue off of its agenda.

The Board's due-process procedure recognizes that the standard-setting process is a political one and that all constituents must be given an opportunity to speak before the final decision. It also recognizes that accounting standards are judged according to their acceptability to several groups. By involving the various preparer and user groups in the deliberation process, the FASB hopes that these groups will be able to make more informed recommendations and be more tolerant of viewpoints that differ from their own.

A second attribute of the FASB's standard-setting process is its effort to relate specific accounting Standards to more general-purpose financial statement objectives (presented earlier in the chapter). This approach results from criticisms directed at the FASB's predecessors for following a question-by-question approach. Unless the Board's pronouncements are integrated with some underlying set of objectives or purposes of financial statements, the possibility exists that the pronouncements will become internally inconsistent. It is too early to assess whether the FASB will be any more successful in relating its pronouncements to a set of objectives for financial statements than were its predecessors.

Whereas Congress and the SEC have the legal authority to prescribe accounting principles and the FASB has responsibility for doing so, several professional accounting organizations have influence on the decision process.

The *American Institute of Certified Public Accountants* (AICPA) is the national organization of certified public accountants. Its publications and committees are influential in the development of accounting principles and practices. It actively promulgates standards of ethics and reviews conduct within the profession. Among its publications are the following:

Journal of Accountancy. A monthly periodical containing articles, pronouncements, announcements, and practical sections of direct interest to the practicing members of the profession.

Accountants' Index. A series published each quarter (with annual summaries) in which the literature pertaining to the field for the period covered is indexed in detail. The index service is also obtainable through an on-line computer system.

Accounting Trends and Techniques. An annual publication presenting a survey of the accounting aspects of financial reports of some 600 industrial and commercial corporations. It presents statistical tabulations on specific practices, terminology, and disclosures together with illustrations taken from individual annual reports.

In addition to the national organization, there are state societies of certified public accountants that contribute to maintaining high levels of professional performance and to developing procedures and practices.

The American Accounting Association is primarily an organization for accountants in academic work, but it is open to all who are interested in accounting. It participates in the development of generally accepted accounting principles and practice, and it promotes the academic phases of accounting theory, research, and instruction. Among its influential publications are the following:

> *The Accounting Review.* A quarterly periodical containing articles and sections covering a broad span of subjects related to accounting practice, research, and instruction for purposes of both external and internal reporting.

> *Studies in Accounting Research.* A series of research studies on specific theoretical and current topics carried out by members of the American Accounting Association. Among the topics of recent studies have been the theory of accounting measurement, the allocation problem in financial accounting, and alternative income theories.

The *National Association of Accountants* is a national society generally open to all engaged in activities closely associated with managerial accounting. Among its publications are the following:

> *Management Accounting.* A monthly periodical.

> *Research Series.* A series of monographs on subjects of internal and external accounting.

> *Accounting Practice Reports.* A series of summaries of surveys on current practice in a limited area of accounting.

The *Financial Executives Institute* is an organization of financial executives of large businesses, such as chief accountants, controllers, treasurers, and financial vice-presidents. Among its publications are *Financial Executive,* a monthly periodical, and a number of studies on problems confronting accounting and financial management.

Income tax legislation and administration have had a substantial impact on adequate accounting and reporting. Although the income tax requirements in themselves do not establish principles and practices for general external reporting, their influence on the choice of acceptable procedures is substantial. At the federal level, in addition to the *Internal Revenue Code* passed by the Congress, there are the *Regulations* and *Rulings* of the Internal Revenue Service, and the opinions of various courts.

Financial Statement Users The FASB seeks representation from those doing security analysis and thus some representation from user interests. Professional organizations of financial statement users, such as the Financial Analysts Federation and the Investment Bankers Association, frequently comment on proposed accounting principles to the FASB and SEC. Any individual user of financial statements can, of course, comment on existing or proposed accounting principles to the FASB, SEC, or a member of Congress.

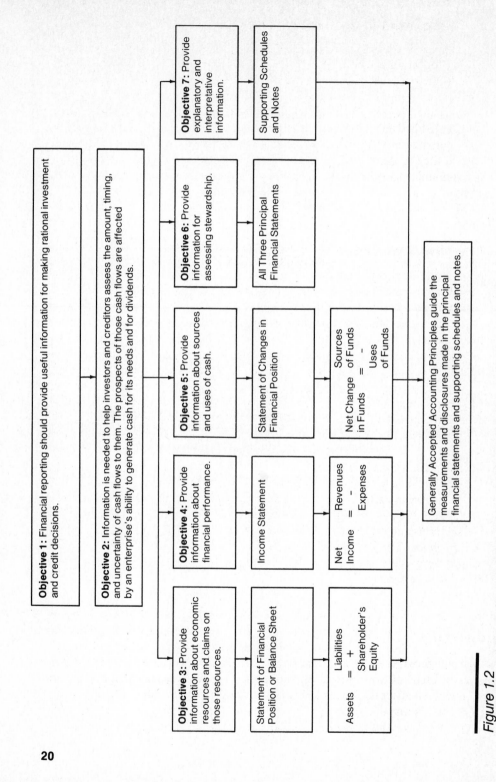

Figure 1.2
Summary of Reporting Process and Principal Financial Statements

Future Development of Accounting Principles

Unless Congress or the SEC unexpectedly decides to exert its legal authority, we see little reason for the future development of accounting principles to differ materially from that in the past. The process will continue to be a political one, with opposing viewpoints attempting to exert influence on the decision process. Positions taken or opinions rendered by participants in this process must be not only carefully developed but also effectively marketed if the positions are to become generally acceptable to the persons involved in preparing and using financial statements. To provide guidance to the standard-setting process, the FASB should continually strive to relate its pronouncements on particular topics to general-purpose financial reporting objectives.

Accounting Terminology

A firm's Annual Report to Shareholders reaches a large group of readers. The members of this group vary in their understanding of business and accounting. If accounting is to fulfill its potential contribution, it should address this broad group of users. Thus, there is a need for a terminology based as much as possible on that of the general citizenry.

Accounting terminology generally follows common usage. Occasionally, however, commonly used words are given restricted technical meanings. For example, the word "reserve" in common usage may indicate that a pool of assets is earmarked or set aside, but in accounting terminology its meaning is altogether different. The term "surplus" may mean "too much" in commonly used terminology, but this is not its meaning when used in accounting. We attempt to prevent the possible confusion that can arise out of these and other similar altered usages of common terminology. Students of accounting can therefore use their vocabulary as developed for general communication. You will find it necessary to learn a rather limited vocabulary of new technical terms and to become aware of technical meanings assigned to a few common words such as *allowance, cost, credit, expense,* and *revenue.* A glossary of accounting terms and other terms with special meanings in accounting appears at the back of this book. The first question at the end of each chapter lists the important accounting terms used in that chapter. Use the glossary to aid in reviewing the meaning of those terms.

Summary

This chapter provides an overview of the objectives of financial reporting, the purpose and content of the three principal financial statements, and the nature and development of generally accepted accounting principles. Figure 1.2 summarizes this material. Perhaps more questions have been raised than answered. We feel, however, that it is helpful to have an overview of the field of financial accounting before embarking on a study of the concepts and procedures employed in preparing various accounting reports.

Chapters 2–5 discuss and illustrate the concepts and procedures underlying the balance sheet, income statement, and statement of changes in financial position. Chapter 6 considers techniques for analyzing and interpreting financial statements. Chapters 7–14 explore more fully the principles of accounting for individual assets and equities, and Chapter 15 provides a synthesis of generally accepted accounting principles.

Now we turn to the study of financial accounting. We recognize that most readers of this book will not choose careers in the field of accounting. Accordingly, emphasis is placed not only on the compilation of the accounting data and preparation of reports, but also on the uses of accounting data for those who will receive it in the form of various reports. Regardless of the reader's interest in accounting, we have found that the most effective means of comprehending the concepts and procedures discussed in this book is careful study of the numerical examples presented in the chapters and diligent working of several problems at the end of each chapter. A comprehensive self-study problem, along with a suggested solution, is presented at the end of each chapter. Frequent reference should also be made to the detailed set of financial statements and notes presented in Appendix A at the back of the book for General Products Company. By the time you have completed your study of the material in this book, you should be able to understand all the items included in these financial statements. These suggestions should be kept in mind as you proceed with your study of accounting.

Problem for Self-Study

The accounting records of Digital Electronics Corporation reveal the following:

Balance Sheet Items:	Dec. 31, 1981	Dec. 31, 1982
Accounts Payable to Suppliers	$250,000	$295,000
Accounts Receivable from Customers	240,000	320,000
Bonds Payable	100,000	120,000
Buildings (net of accumulated depreciation)	150,000	140,000
Cash	30,000	50,000
Common Stock	100,000	100,000
Equipment (net of accumulated depreciation)	140,000	220,000
Income Taxes Payable	40,000	70,000
Land	60,000	70,000
Merchandise Inventory	380,000	400,000
Retained Earnings	500,000	600,000
Salaries Payable	10,000	15,000

Income Statement Items for 1982:

Cost of Merchandise Sold	$ 620,000
Depreciation Expense	40,000
Income Tax Expense	100,000
Insurance Expense	3,000
Interest Expense	10,000
Property Tax Expense	2,000
Rental Revenue (rental of part of building)	30,000
Salary Expense	135,000
Sales Revenue	1,000,000

Dividend Information for 1982:

Dividends Declared and Paid	$ 20,000

a Prepare a comparative balance sheet for Digital Electronics Corporation as of December 31, 1981 and 1982. Classify the balance sheet items into the following categories: current assets, noncurrent assets, current liabilities, noncurrent liabilities, or shareholders' equity.

b Prepare an income statement for Digital Electronics Corporation for the year 1982. Separate income statement items into revenues and expenses.

c Prepare a schedule explaining or accounting for the changes in retained earnings between the beginning and end of 1982.

Suggested Solution

Exhibit 1.4 presents a comparative balance sheet, Exhibit 1.5 presents an income statement, and Exhibit 1.6 analyzes the change in retained earnings for Digital Electronics Corporation for 1982.

Exhibit 1.4
Digital Electronics Corporation
Comparative Balance Sheet
December 31, 1981 and 1982

ASSETS	December 31	
Current Assets:	**1981**	**1982**
Cash	$ 30,000	$ 50,000
Accounts Receivable from Customers	240,000	320,000
Merchandise Inventory	380,000	400,000
Total Current Assets	$ 650,000	$ 770,000
Noncurrent Assets:		
Land	$ 60,000	$ 70,000
Equipment (net of accumulated depreciation)	140,000	220,000
Buildings (net of accumulated depreciation)	150,000	140,000
Total Noncurrent Assets	$ 350,000	$ 430,000
Total Assets	$1,000,000	$1,200,000

Exhibit 1.4 (continued)

LIABILITIES AND SHAREHOLDERS' EQUITY

Current Liabilities:

Accounts Payable to Suppliers	$ 250,000	$ 295,000
Salaries Payable	10,000	15,000
Income Taxes Payable	40,000	70,000
Total Current Liabilities	$ 300,000	$ 380,000

Noncurrent Liabilities:

Bonds Payable	100,000	120,000
Total Liabilities	$ 400,000	$ 500,000

Shareholders' Equity:

Common Stock	$ 100,000	$ 100,000
Retained Earnings	500,000	600,000
Total Shareholders' Equity	$ 600,000	$ 700,000
Total Liabilities and Shareholders' Equity	$1,000,000	$1,200,000

Exhibit 1.5
Digital Electronics Corporation
Income Statement
for the Year 1982

Revenues:

Sales Revenue	$1,000,000	
Rental Revenue	30,000	
Total Revenues		$1,030,000

Expenses:

Cost of Merchandise Sold	$ 620,000	
Salary Expense	135,000	
Property Tax Expense	2,000	
Insurance Expense	3,000	
Depreciation Expense	40,000	
Interest Expense	10,000	
Income Tax Expense	100,000	
Total Expenses		910,000
Net Income		$ 120,000

Exhibit 1.6
Digital Electronics Corporation
Analysis of Change in
Retained Earnings
for the Year 1982

Retained Earnings, January 1, 1982	$500,000
Plus Net Income	120,000
Less Dividends Declared and Paid	(20,000)
Retained Earnings, December 31, 1982	$600,000

Questions and Problems

1 Review the meaning of the following concepts or terms discussed in this chapter.
   a Financial accounting.
   b Managerial accounting.
   c Generally accepted accounting principles.
   d Financial reporting objectives.
   e Balance sheet.
   f Assets.
   g Liabilities.
   h Shareholders' equity.
   i Total equities.
   j Contributed capital.
   k Retained earnings.
   l Acquisition cost.
   m Current cash-equivalent value.
   n Net income, earnings, profits.
   o Net loss.
   p Revenue.
   q Expense.
   r Dividends.
   s Statement of changes in financial position.
   t Funds as cash.
   u Funds as working capital.
   v Stocks versus flows.
   w Articulate.
   x Unqualified, qualified, and adverse auditor's opinions.
   y FASB.
   z SEC.

2 Distinguish between financial accounting and managerial accounting. Suggest several ways in which the managers of a firm might use information presented in the three principal externally directed financial statements discussed in this chapter.

3 Suggest reasons why the format and content of financial accounting reports tend to be more standardized than is the case for managerial accounting reports.

4 What purpose is served by having a broad set of financial reporting objectives, such as those issued by the FASB?

5 One of the more controversial issues in accounting is whether assets, such as land, should be stated on the balance sheet at the amount a firm originally paid to acquire them (acquisition cost) or the amount a firm would have to pay currently to replace them (current replacement cost). Discuss which valuation basis for land is most consistent with the FASB's set of financial reporting objectives.

6 Generally accepted accounting principles are the methods of accounting used by publicly held firms in preparing their financial statements. A principle in physics, such as the law of gravity, serves as a basis for developing theories and explaining the relationships among physical objects. In what ways are generally accepted accounting principles similar to and different from principles in physics?

7 How would the principal financial statements of a not-for-profit hospital, library, or university differ from those presented in the chapter?

8 Prepare a balance sheet of your personal assets, liabilities, and owner's equity. How does the presentation of owner's equity on your balance sheet differ from that in Exhibit 1.1?

9 Suggest procedures you could follow in determining the amounts at which the following resources might be stated on a balance sheet if they were to be recognized as assets:
   a Well-known trademark or other product symbol.
   b Well-trained employee labor force.

10 "Asset valuation and income measurement are closely related." Explain.

11 Suggest reasons why the definition of "funds" in a statement of changes in financial position presented to a bank for a 6-month bank loan might differ from the definition of funds in a statement presented to shareholders and potential investors.

12 Does the unqualified or clean opinion of a certified public accountant indicate that the financial statements are free of errors and misrepresentations? Explain.

13 The text states that the standard-setting process is essentially political in nature. Yet, the FASB is striving to relate its pronouncements to a broad set of financial reporting objectives. Do you see any inconsistency between these two approaches to standard setting?

14 Distinguish between a Discussion Memorandum, an Exposure Draft of a Proposed Financial Accounting Standard, and a Financial Accounting Standard.

15 Various items are classified on the balance sheet or income statement in one of the following ways:

CA—Current assets
NA—Noncurrent assets
CL—Current liabilities
NL—Noncurrent liabilities

CC—Contributed capital
RE—Retained earnings
NI—Income statement item (revenue or expense)
X—Item would generally not appear on a balance sheet or income statement

Using the letters above, indicate the classification of each of the following items:

a Factory.
b Interest revenue.
c Common stock issued by a corporation.
d Goodwill developed by a firm (see Glossary).
e Automobiles used by sales staff.
f Cash on hand.
g Unsettled damage suit against a firm.
h Commissions earned by sales staff.
i Supplies inventory.
j Note payable, due in 3 months.
k Increase in market value of land held.
l Dividends.
m Employee payroll taxes payable.
n Note Payable, due in 6 years.

16 Determine the missing balance sheet amounts in each of the four independent cases below.

	a	b	c	d
Noncurrent Assets	$400,000	$500,000	$340,000	?
Shareholders' Equity	?	250,000	290,000	$140,000
Total Assets	?	?	500,000	?
Current Liabilities	500,000	150,000	?a	?b
Current Assets	600,000	?	?a	?b
Noncurrent Liabilities	100,000	?	?	160,000
Total Liabilities and Shareholders' Equity	?	700,000	?	550,000

aWorking capital = current assets − current liabilities = $70,000.
bWorking capital = current assets − current liabilities = $80,000.

17 The comparative balance sheets of the Sweet Corporation as of December 31, 1981, and December 31, 1982, are presented below:

Sweet Corporation
Comparative Balance Sheets
December 31, 1981 and 1982

	December 31 1981	1982
Total Assets	$500,000	$800,000
Liabilities	$100,000	$160,000
Common Stock	250,000	290,000
Retained Earnings	150,000	350,000
Total Liabilities and Shareholders' Equity	$500,000	$800,000

Dividends declared and paid during 1982 were $80,000.

a Compute net income for the year ending December 31, 1982, by analyzing the change in retained earnings.

b Compute net income for the year ending December 31, 1982, by analyzing the changes in assets, liabilities, and contributed capital during the year.

18 Determine the missing amount affecting retained earnings for the year 1982 in each of the independent cases below.

	a	b	c	d	e
Retained Earnings, December 31, 1981	$80,000	?	$458,000	$120,000	$240,000
Net Income	30,000	$260,000	260,000	?	(60,000)*
Dividends Declared and Paid	10,000	145,000	?	35,000	?
Retained Earnings December 31, 1982	?	766,000	598,000	110,000	180,000

*Net loss.

19 B. Stephens, L. Harris, and G. Winkle, recent business school graduates, set up a management consulting practice on December 31, 1981, by issuing common stock for $950,000. The accounting records of the S, H, & W Corporation as of December 31, 1982, reveal the following:

Balance Sheet Items:

Cash	$ 240,000
Accounts Receivable from Clients	230,000
Supplies Inventory	20,000
Office Equipment (net of depreciation)	260,000
Office Building (net of depreciation)	360,000
Accounts Payable to Suppliers	8,000
Payroll Taxes Payable	40,000
Income Taxes Payable	30,000
Common Stock	950,000

Income Statement Items:

Revenue from Consulting Services	$1,100,000
Rental Revenue (from renting part of building)	150,000
Salaries Expense	890,000
Property Taxes and Insurance Expense	80,000
Supplies Expense	10,000
Depreciation Expense	30,000
Income Tax Expense	80,000

Dividend Information:

Dividends Declared and Paid	$ 78,000

a Prepare an income statement for S, H, & W Corporation for the year ending December 31, 1982. Refer to Exhibit 1.2 for help in designing the format of the statement.

b Prepare a comparative balance sheet for S, H, & W Corporation on December 31, 1981, and December 31, 1982. Refer to Exhibit 1.1 for help in designing the format of the statement.

c Prepare an analysis of the change in retained earnings during 1982.

20 The accounting records of Laser Sales Corporation reveal the following:

	December 31	
Balance Sheet Items:	**1981**	**1982**
Accounts Payable	$1,247,000	$1,513,000
Accounts Receivable	740,000	820,000
Bank Loan Payable (due April 10, 1983)	—	15,000
Bonds Payable (due 1996)	80,000	100,000
Building (net of accumulated depreciation)	460,000	440,000
Cash	270,000	315,000
Common Stock	1,190,000	1,240,000
Equipment (net of accumulated depreciation)	825,000	1,023,000
Income Taxes Payable	25,000	30,000
Land	40,000	50,000
Merchandise Inventory	550,000	610,000
Note Receivable (due June 15, 1983)	—	20,000
Note Receivable (due December 31, 1990)	100,000	100,000
Retained Earnings	430,000	470,000
Salaries Payable	28,000	32,000
Supplies Inventory	15,000	22,000

Income Statement Items for 1982:

Cost of Merchandise Sold	$2,611,000
Depreciation Expense	45,000
Income Tax Expense	55,000
Insurance Expense	8,000
Interest Expense	16,000
Interest Revenue	15,000
Payroll Tax Expense	80,000
Salary Expense	640,000
Sales Revenue	3,500,000

28

Dividend Information:

Dividends Declared and Paid during 1982 . . . . $ 20,000

a Prepare a comparative balance sheet for Laser Sales Corporation as of December 31, 1981 and 1982. Classify the balance sheet items into one of the following categories: current assets, noncurrent assets, current liabilities, noncurrent liabilities, or shareholders' equity.

b Prepare an income statement for Laser Sales Corporation for the year 1982. Separate income items into revenues and expenses.

c Prepare a schedule explaining, or accounting for, the change in retained earnings between the beginning and end of 1982.

21 The purpose of this problem is to illustrate the relationships between the three principal financial statements. Exhibit 1.7 presents a comparative balance sheet for Articulation Corporation as of December 31, 1981 and 1982. Exhibit 1.8 presents an income statement

---

Exhibit 1.7
Articulation Corporation
Comparative Balance Sheets
December 31, 1981 and 1982

	December 31	
ASSETS		
Current Assets:	**1981**	**1982**
Cash	$ 80	$180
Accounts Receivable from Customers	300	340
Merchandise Inventory	150	160
Total Current Assets	$530	$680
Noncurrent Assets:		
Land	$ 40	$ 55
Buildings and Equipment (net of accumulated depreciation)	130	165
Total Noncurrent Assets	$170	$220
Total Assets	$700	$900
LIABILITIES AND SHAREHOLDERS' EQUITY		
Current Liabilities:		
Accounts Payable	$310	$350
Income Taxes Payable	40	60
Total Current Liabilities	$350	$410
Noncurrent Liabilities:		
Bonds Payable	20	25
Total Liabilities	$370	$435
Shareholders' Equity:		
Common Stock	$200	$245
Retained Earnings	130	220
Total Shareholders' Equity	$330	$465
Total Liabilities and Shareholders' Equity	$700	$900

Exhibit 1.8
**Articulation Corporation
Income Statement
for the Year 1982**

Sales Revenue		$1,000
Expenses:		
Cost of Merchandise Sold	$600	
Salary Expense	100	
Depreciation Expense	50	
Interest Expense	20	
Income Tax Expense	120	
Total Expenses		890
Net Income		$ 110

Exhibit 1.9
**Articulation Corporation
Statement of Changes in
Financial Position
for the Year 1982**

Sources of Cash:		
Operations:		
Revenues Increasing Cash	$960	
Expenses Decreasing Cash	790	
Total from Operations	$170	
Issue of Bonds	5	
Issue of Common Stock	45	
Total Sources		$220
Uses of Cash:		
Dividends Declared and Paid	$ 20	
Land Acquired	15	
Buildings and Equipment Acquired	85	
Total Uses		120
Net Change in Cash		$100

and Exhibit 1.9 presents a statement of changes in financial position (funds defined as cash) for Articulation Corporation for the year 1982.

Using amounts from these three financial statements, demonstrate that the following relationships are correct:

a Retained earnings at the beginning of 1982 plus net income for 1982 minus dividends declared and paid for 1982 equal retained earnings at the end of 1982.

b Change in total assets equals change in total liabilities plus change in contributed capital plus net income minus dividends.

c Accounts receivable at the beginning of 1982 plus sales (all on account) to customers less cash collections from customers (see statement of changes in financial position) equal accounts receivable at the end of 1982.

d Buildings and equipment at the beginning of 1982 plus acquisitions of buildings and equipment minus dispositions of buildings and equipment minus depreciation for 1982 equal buildings and equipment at the end of 1982.

e Bonds payable at the beginning of 1982 plus new bonds issued during 1982 minus outstanding bonds redeemed during 1982 equal bonds payable at the end of 1982.

f Common stock at the beginning of 1982 plus common stock issued during 1982 minus outstanding common stock redeemed during 1982 equal common stock at the end of 1982.

22 Refer to the financial statements and notes for General Products Company presented in Appendix A at the back of the book. After studying carefully these financial statements, respond to the following questions.

a With respect to the consolidated balance sheet:

(1) Justify the inclusion of "marketable securities," "inventories," and "property, plant, and equipment—net" as assets.

(2) Identify the valuation methods used in determining the amounts for the various assets shown on General Products Company's balance sheet. (Note: You must refer to some of General Products Company's notes to respond to this question.)

(3) What justification can you see for excluding General Products Company's investment in a well-trained labor force or its good reputation with customers from its balance sheet?

(4) Liabilities and shareholders' equities represent sources of or claims on the assets of a firm. In what sense are "accounts payable," "taxes accrued," and "retained earnings" sources of or claims on the assets of General Products Company?

(5) The "net worth" of a firm has been described as the excess of a firm's assets over its liabilities. Assume that you have agreed to purchase all of the common stock of General Products Company for its net worth as of December 31, 1982. Is $8,200 million, the total shareholders' equity, a reasonable price to pay? Why or why not?

b With respect to the consolidated income statement:

(6) Net income is defined as the excess of revenues over expenses. Using only numerical amounts, rearrange the items in General Products Company 's income statement for 1982 into the following equation:

$$\text{Net Income} = \text{Revenues} - \text{Expenses.}$$

(7) Revenues are a measure of the inflows of assets (or reductions in liabilities) from selling goods and services to customers. Justify the inclusion of "sales" as revenues.

(8) Expenses are a measure of the outflows of assets (or increases in liabilities) used up in generating revenues. Justify the inclusion of "cost of goods sold," "depreciation," and "income taxes" as expenses.

(9) Assuming that "minority interest," and "total shareholders' equity" represent "contributed capital," demonstrate that the following equation is valid for 1982:

$$\frac{\text{Change in}}{\text{Assets}} = \frac{\text{Change in}}{\text{Liabilities}} + \frac{\text{Change in}}{\text{Contributed Capital}} + \text{Net Income} - \text{Dividends.}$$

(10) Net income has been described as a measure of the increase in wealth of a firm for a particular period of time. Do you agree?

c With respect to the consolidated statement of changes in financial position:

(11) What definition of "funds" is used by General Products Company?

(12) The factors causing a change in funds can be classified as follows:

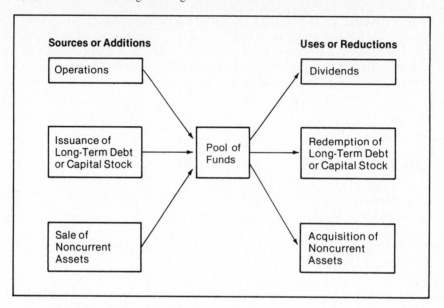

Classify each of the sources and applications of funds for General Products Company for 1982 into one of these six categories.

d Assume that you are a credit officer for a bank contemplating a loan of $500 million to General Products Company as of February 1, 1983. The loan is to be repaid with interest on July 31, 1983. What information from General Products Company's financial statements would you find useful in making this decision?

e Assume that you are an independently wealthy investor contemplating the purchase of $500 million of General Products Company's common stock. What information from General Products Company's financial statements would you find useful in making this decision?

23 The ABC Company started the year in fine shape. The firm made widgets—just what the customer wanted. It made them for $.75 each and sold them for $1.00. The ABC Company kept an inventory equal to shipments of the past 30 days, paid its bills promptly, and collected cash from customers within 30 days after the sale. The sales manager predicted a steady increase of 500 widgets each month beginning in February. It looked like a great year, and it began that way:

January 1 : Cash, $875; receivables, $1,000; inventory, $750.

January : In January, 1,000 widgets costing $750 were sold on account for $1,000. Receivables outstanding at the beginning of the month were collected. Production totaled 1,000 units at a total cost of $750. Net income for the month was $250. The books at the end of January showed:

February 1: Cash, $1,125; receivables, $1,000; inventory $750.

February : This month's sales jumped, as predicted, to 1,500 units. With a corresponding step-up in production to maintain the 30-day inventory, ABC Company made 2,000 units at a cost of $1,500. All receivables from January sales were collected. Net income so far, $625. Now the books looked like this:

March 1 : Cash, $625; receivables, $1,500; inventory, $1,125.

March : March sales were even better: 2,000 units. Collections: On time. Production, to adhere to the inventory policy: 2,500 units. Operating results for the month, net income of $500. Net income to date: $1,125. The books:

April 1 : Cash, $250; receivables, $2,000; inventory, $1,500.

April : In April, sales jumped another 500 units to 2,500, and the manager of ABC Company patted the sales manager on the back. Customers were paying right on time. Production was pushed to 3,000 units, and the month's business netted $625 for a net income to date of $1,750. The manager of ABC Company took off for Miami before the accountant's report was issued. Suddenly a phone call came from the treasurer: "Come home! We need money!"

May 1 : Cash, $000; receivables, $2,500; inventory, $1,875.

a Prepare an analysis that explains what happened to ABC Company. (Hint: Compute the amount of cash receipts and cash disbursements for each month during the period January 1 to May 1.)

b How can a firm show increasing net income but a decreasing amount of cash?

c What insights are provided by the problem about the need for all three financial statements: balance sheet, income statement, and statement of changes in financial position?

Part Two   Accounting Concepts and Methods

Chapter 2   *Measuring Financial Position—Valuation Principles and Accounting Procedures*

Chapter 1 introduced the balance sheet, one of the three principal financial statements. You will recall that the balance sheet presents a snapshot of the resources of a firm (assets) and claims on those resources (liabilities and owners' equity) as of a specific moment in time. The balance sheet derives its name from the fact that it shows the following balance, or equality:

$$\text{Assets} = \text{Liabilities} + \text{Owners' Equity.}$$

That is, a firm's resources are in balance with, or equal to, the claims on those resources by creditors and owners. In the balance sheet, we view resources from two angles: a listing of the specific forms in which they are held (for example, cash, inventory, equipment); and a listing of the persons or interests that have a claim on them (for example, suppliers, employees, governments, shareholders). Our introduction to the balance sheet in Chapter 1 left several important questions unanswered:

1 What limits are set in defining the business entity for which the balance sheet is prepared?
2 Which resources of a firm are recognized as assets?
3 What valuations are placed on these assets?
4 How are assets classified, or grouped, within the balance sheet?
5 Which claims against a firm's assets are recognized as liabilities?
6 What valuations are placed on these liabilities?
7 How are liabilities classified within the balance sheet?
8 What valuation is placed on the owners' equity in a firm, and how is the owners' equity disclosed?

In seeking answers to these questions, we must explore briefly several accounting concepts and conventions that underlie the balance sheet. This discussion not only provides a background for understanding the statement as it is currently prepared, but also permits an assessment of alternative methods of measuring financial position. After this brief introduction to accounting theory, we describe and then illustrate the accounting procedures used in recording transactions and events for presentation in a balance sheet.

Underlying Concepts and Conventions

Accounting Entity

Business activities are carried on through various units, or entities. The identification of the business entity is the starting point in designing an accounting system that will provide data for financial statements. Most problems of identifying the business entity are caused by differences between the definition of the entity used in accounting, or the *accounting entity,* and the definition of the entity prescribed by law, or the *legal entity.* In accounting, we attempt to emphasize substance over form; that is, we focus on the unit, or entity, engaged in business activity even though it may not be recognized as a separate legal entity.

Example 1 Joan Webster operates a hardware store in her neighborhood as a sole proprietorship. According to the laws of most states, Webster's business assets and personal assets are mingled. That is, suppliers of merchandise to the hardware store can obtain payment for their claims from some or all of her personal assets if business assets are insufficient. Even so, the accounting entity is the hardware store alone, because this is the organizational unit carrying on the business activity.

Example 2 Bill White and Roger Green own and manage an apartment complex, called the Leisure Living Apartments, as a partnership. Under the laws of most states, their personal assets as well as the business assets are subject to the claims of creditors. Even so, the accounting entity is the apartment complex alone, because this is the organizational unit carrying on the business activity.

Example 3 The Wilson Corporation operates through its subsidiaries in 23 states. Each subsidiary is organized as a separate legal corporation under the laws of the state in which it is located. The accounting entity is a combination (or consolidation) of Wilson Corporation and all of its 23 subsidiary corporations, because these legally separate units operate as a single business entity. For purposes of internal performance evaluation by management, however, Wilson Corporation might treat each subsidiary as a separate reporting entity. Thus, we see that the scope of the accounting entity can be related to the purpose to be served by the financial statements.

The accounting entity for which a set of financial statements has been prepared can be determined from the heading of each statement. For the three examples above, the headings might read: Webster's Hardware Store, Leisure Living Apartments, and Wilson Corporation and Consolidated Subsidiaries.

Asset Recognition

Assets are resources that have the potential for providing a firm with future economic benefits. That benefit is the ability to generate future cash inflows or to reduce future cash outflows. The resources that are recognized as assets are those (1) for which the firm has acquired rights to their future use as a result of a past transaction or exchange and (2) for which the value of the future benefits can be measured, or quantified, with a reasonable degree of precision.[1]

Example 1 Miller Corporation sold merchandise and received a note from the customer who agreed to pay $2,000 within 4 months. This note receivable is an asset of Miller Corporation, because a right has been established to receive a definite amount of cash in the future as a result of the previous sale of merchandise.

Example 2 Miller Corporation acquired manufacturing equipment costing $40,000 and agreed to pay the seller over 3 years. After the final payment, legal title to the equipment will be transferred to Miller Corporation. Even though Miller Corporation does not possess legal title, the equipment is Miller's asset because it has obtained the rights and responsibilities of ownership and can sustain those rights as long as the payments are made on schedule.

Example 3 Miller Corporation plans to acquire a fleet of new trucks next year to replace those wearing out. These new trucks are not now assets, because no exchange has taken place between Miller Corporation and a supplier and, therefore, no right to the future use of the trucks has been established.

Example 4 Miller Corporation has developed a good reputation with its employees, customers, and citizens of the community. This good reputation is expected to provide benefits to the firm in its future business activities. A good reputation, however, is generally *not* recognized as an asset. Although Miller Corporation has made various expenditures in the past to develop the reputation, the future benefits are considered to be too difficult to quantify with a sufficient degree of precision to warrant recognition as an asset.

Most of the difficulties in deciding which items to recognize as assets are related to unexecuted or partially executed contracts. In Example 3, suppose that Miller Corporation entered into a contract with a local truck dealer to acquire the trucks next year at a cash price of $60,000. Miller Corporation has acquired rights to future benefits, but the contract has not been executed. Unexecuted contracts of this nature

---

[1] Financial Accounting Standards Board, *Statement of Financial Accounting Concepts No. 3,* "Elements of Financial Statements of Business Enterprises," 1980, par. 19. See Glossary for the Board's specific definition of an asset.

are generally not recognized as assets in accounting. Miller Corporation will recognize an asset for the trucks when they are received next year.

To take the illustration one step further, assume that Miller Corporation advances the truck dealer $15,000 of the purchase price upon signing the contract. Miller Corporation has acquired rights to future benefits and has exchanged cash. Current accounting practice treats the $15,000 as an advance on the purchase of equipment and reports it as an asset under a title such as Advances to Suppliers. The trucks would not be shown as assets at this time, however, because Miller Corporation is not yet deemed to have received sufficient future rights to justify their inclusion in the balance sheet. Similar asset-recognition questions arise when a firm leases buildings and equipment for its own use under long-term leases or manufactures custom-design products for particular customers. These issues are discussed more fully in later chapters.

Asset Valuation Bases

An amount must be assigned to each asset in the balance sheet. Several methods of computing this amount might be used.

Acquisition or Historical Cost The acquisition, or historical, cost of an asset is the amount of cash payment (or cash-equivalent value of other forms of payment) made in acquiring the asset. This amount can generally be found by referring to contracts, invoices, and canceled checks. Because a firm is not compelled to acquire a given asset, it must expect the future benefits from that asset to be at least as large as its acquisition cost. Historical cost then is a lower limit on the amount that a firm considered the future benefits of the asset to be worth at the time of acquisition.

Current Replacement Cost Each asset might be shown on the balance sheet at the current cost of replacing it. Current replacement cost is often referred to as an *entry value,* because it represents the amount required currently to acquire, or "enter" into, the rights to receive future benefits from the asset.

For assets purchased frequently, such as merchandise inventory, current replacement cost can often be calculated by consulting suppliers' catalogs or price lists. The replacement cost of assets purchased less frequently, such as land, buildings, and equipment, is more difficult to ascertain. A major obstacle to implementing current replacement cost is the absence of well-organized secondhand markets for many used assets. Ascertaining current replacement cost in these cases requires finding the cost of a similar new asset and then adjusting that amount downward somehow for the services of the asset already used. There may be difficulties, however, in finding a similar asset. With technological improvements and other quality changes, equipment purchased currently will likely be quite different from that acquired 10 years previously but that is still being used. Thus, there may be no similar equipment on the market for which replacement cost can be found. Alternatively, the current replacement cost of an asset capable of rendering equivalent services might be substituted when the replacement cost of the specific asset is not readily available.

This approach, however, is also subject to a high degree of subjectivity in the identification of assets with equivalent service potential.

Current Net Realizable Value Net realizable value is the net amount of cash (selling price less selling costs) that the firm would receive currently if it sold each asset separately. This amount is often referred to as an *exit value,* because it reflects the amount obtainable if the firm currently disposed of the asset, or "exited" ownership. In measuring net realizable value, one generally assumes that the asset is sold in an orderly fashion, rather than through a forced sale at some "distress" price.

Measuring net realizable value entails difficulties similar to those in measuring current replacement cost. There may be no well-organized secondhand market for used equipment, particularly when the equipment is specially designed for a single firm's needs. In this case, the current selling price of the asset (value in exchange) may be substantially less than the value of the future benefits to the firm from using the asset (value in use).

Present Value of Future Net Cash Flows Another possible valuation basis is the present value of future net cash flows. An asset is a resource that provides a future benefit. This future benefit is the ability of an asset either to generate future net cash receipts or to reduce future cash expenditures. For example, accounts receivable from customers will lead directly to future cash receipts. Merchandise inventory can be sold for cash or promises to pay cash. Equipment can be used to manufacture products that can then be sold for cash. A building that is owned reduces future cash outflows for rental payments. Because these cash flows represent the future services, or benefits, of assets, they might be used in the valuation of assets. Because cash can be invested to yield interest revenue over time, today's value of a stream of future cash flows, called the *present value,* is worth less than the sum of the cash amounts to be received or saved over time. The balance sheet is to be prepared as of a current date. If future cash flows are to be used to measure an asset's value, then the future net cash flows must be "discounted" to find their present value as of the date of the balance sheet. Chapters 10, 11, and Appendix B discuss the discounting methodology, but the following example presents the general approach.

Example Miller Corporation sold merchandise to a reliable customer, General Models Company, who promised to pay $10,000 one year from the date of sale. General Models Company signed a "promissory note" to that effect and gave the note to Miller Corporation. Miller Corporation judges that if it invests $9,100 today, it could earn about 10 percent on the investment in a year. At the end of 1 year, it would therefore receive about $10,000. Hence, the *present value* of $10,000 to be received 1 year from today is not $10,000, but is about $9,100. (Miller Corporation is indifferent between receiving approximately $9,100 today and $10,000 one year from today.) The asset represented by General Models Company's promissory note has a present value of $9,100. If the note was stated on the balance sheet as of the date of sale at the present value of the future cash flows, it might be shown at approximately $9,100.

Using discounted cash flows in the valuation of individual assets requires solving several problems. One is the difficulty caused by the uncertainty of the amounts of future cash flows. The amounts to be received can depend on whether or not competitors introduce new products, the rate of inflation, and many other factors. A second problem is allocating the cash receipts from selling a single item of merchandise inventory to all of the assets involved in its production and distribution (for example, equipment, buildings, sales staff's automobiles). A third problem is selecting the appropriate rate to be used in discounting the future cash flows back to the present. Is the interest rate at which the firm could borrow the appropriate one? Or is the rate at which the firm could invest excess cash the one that should be used? Or is the appropriate rate the firm's cost of capital (a concept introduced in managerial accounting and finance courses)? In the example above, the appropriate rate is General Models' borrowing rate, not Miller's earnings rate on investments.

Selecting the Appropriate Valuation Basis

In selecting a valuation basis, we choose the one that is most appropriate for the financial report being prepared.

Example 1 Miller Corporation is preparing its income tax return for the current year. The Internal Revenue Code and Regulations specify that acquisition or adjusted acquisition cost valuation must be used in most instances.

Example 2 A fire recently destroyed the manufacturing plant, equipment, and inventory of Miller Corporation. The firm's fire insurance policy provides coverage in an amount equal to the cost of replacing the assets that were destroyed. Current replacement cost at the time of the fire is appropriate for supporting the insurance claim.

Example 3 Miller Corporation plans to dispose of one of its manufacturing divisions because it has been operating unprofitably. In deciding on the lowest price to accept for the division, the firm considers the net realizable value of each asset.

Example 4 Brown Corporation is considering the purchase of Miller Corporation. In deciding on the highest price to be paid, Brown Corporation would be interested in the present value of the future net cash flows to be realized from owning Miller Corporation.

Generally Accepted Accounting Asset Valuation Bases

The asset valuation basis appropriate for financial statements issued to shareholders and other investors is perhaps less obvious. The financial statements currently prepared by publicly held firms are based on one of two valuation bases: one for monetary assets and one for nonmonetary assets.

41

Monetary assets, such as cash and accounts receivable, are generally shown on the balance sheet at their net present value—their current cash, or cash-equivalent, value. Cash is stated at the amount of cash on hand or in the bank. Accounts receivable from customers are stated at the amount of cash expected to be collected in the future. If the period of time until a receivable is to be collected spans more than 1 year, then the expected future cash receipt is discounted to a present value. Most accounts receivable, however, are collected within 1 to 3 months. The amount of future cash flows is approximately equal to the present value of these flows, and the discounting process is ignored.

Nonmonetary assets, such as merchandise inventory, land, buildings, and equipment, are stated at acquisition cost, in some cases adjusted downward for depreciation reflecting the services of the assets that have been consumed.

The acquisition cost of an asset may include more than its invoice price. Cost includes all expenditures made or obligations incurred in order to put the asset into usable condition. Transportation cost, costs of installation, handling charges, and any other necessary and reasonable costs incurred in connection with the asset up to the time it is put into service should be considered as part of the total cost assigned to the asset. For example, the cost of an item of equipment might be calculated as follows:

Invoice Price of Equipment	$12,000
Less: 2 Percent Discount for Prompt Cash Payment	240
Net Invoice Price	$11,760
Transportation Cost	326
Installation Costs	735
Total Cost of Equipment	$12,821

The acquisition cost of this equipment to be recorded in the accounting records is $12,821.

Instead of disbursing cash or incurring a liability, other forms of consideration (for example, common stock, merchandise inventory, land) may be given in acquiring an asset. In these cases, acquisition cost is measured by the market value of the consideration given or the market value of the asset received, depending on which market value is more reliably measured.

Foundations for Acquisition Cost Accounting's use of acquisition-cost valuations for nonmonetary assets rests on three important concepts or conventions. First, a firm is assumed to be a *going concern.* That is, it is assumed that the firm will remain in operation long enough for all of its current plans to be carried out. Any increases in the market value of assets held will be realized in the normal course of business when the firm receives higher prices for its products. Current values of the individual assets are therefore assumed to be largely unimportant. Second, acquisition-cost valuations are considered to be more objective than those obtained from using the other valuation methods. *Objectivity* in accounting refers to the ability of several independent measurers to come to the same conclusion about the valuation of an asset. It is relatively easy to obtain consensus on what constitutes the acquisition cost of an asset. Differences among measurers can arise in ascertaining an asset's current replacement cost, current net realizable value, or present value of future cash flows. A reasonable degree of consensus is necessary if financial statements are to be subject to audits by independent accountants. Third, acquisition cost generally provides more conservative valuations of assets (and measures of earnings) relative to the other valuation methods. Many accountants feel that the possibility of misleading financial statement users will be minimized when assets are stated at lower rather than higher amounts. Thus, *conservatism* has evolved as a convention to justify acquisition-cost valuations.

The preceding description of generally accepted valuation bases does not justify them. Which basis—the acquisition cost, current replacement cost, current net realizable value, or present value of future cash flows of a firm's assets—is most relevant to investors' decisions is an empirical question for which a definitive answer has not yet been provided. As Chapter 14 discusses, most publicly-held firms are required to provide supplementary information on the current cost of their inventories, property, plant, and equipment. The required disclosure of such information is, to some extent, a response to the recognized deficiencies of historical cost valuations during periods of inflation.

Asset Classification

The classification of assets within the balance sheet varies widely in published annual reports. The principal asset categories are described below.

Current Assets The term *current assets* designates "cash and other assets or resources commonly identified as those which are reasonably expected to be realized in cash or sold or consumed during the normal operating cycle of the business."[2] The operating cycle refers to the period of time that elapses for a given firm during which cash is converted into salable goods and services, goods and services are sold to customers, and customers pay for their purchases with cash. Included in current assets are cash, marketable securities held for the short-term, accounts and notes receivable net of allowance for uncollectible accounts, inventories of merchandise, raw materials, supplies, work in process, and finished goods and prepaid operating costs (for example, prepaid insurance, and prepaid rent). Prepaid costs, or prepayments, are current assets to the extent that if they were not paid in advance, then current assets would be required within the next operating cycle to acquire those services.

Investments A second section of the balance sheet, labeled "Investments," includes long-term investments in securities of other firms. For example, a firm might purchase shares of common stock of a supplier to help assure continued availability of raw materials. Or shares of common stock of a firm in another area of business activity might be acquired to permit the acquiring firm to diversify its operations.

---

[2]Committee on Accounting Research, *Accounting Research Bulletin No. 43*, 1953, Chapter 3.A.

When one corporation (the parent) owns more than 50 percent of the voting stock in another corporation (the subsidiary), a single set of "consolidated" financial statements is usually prepared. That is, the specific assets, liabilities, revenues, and expenses of the subsidiary are merged, or consolidated, with those of the parent corporation. The securities shown in the Investments section of the balance sheet are therefore investments in firms whose assets and liabilities have *not* been consolidated with the parent or investor firm. Consolidated financial statements are discussed in Chapter 13.

The holders of a firm's long-term bonds may require that cash be set aside periodically so that sufficient funds will be available to retire, or redeem, the bonds at maturity. The funds are typically given to a trustee, such as a bank or insurance company, which invests the funds received. Funds set aside for this purpose are shown in a Sinking Fund account and classified under Investments on the balance sheet.

Property, Plant, and Equipment Property, plant, and equipment (sometimes called *plant assets* or *fixed assets*) designates the tangible, long-lived assets used in a firm's operations over a period of years and generally not acquired for resale. This category includes land, buildings, machinery, automobiles, furniture, fixtures, computers, and other equipment. The amount shown on the balance sheet for each of these items (except land) is acquisition cost less accumulated depreciation since the asset was acquired. Frequently, only the net balance, or book value, is disclosed on the balance sheet. Land is presented at acquisition cost.

Intangible Assets Intangible assets include such items as patents, trademarks, franchises, and goodwill. The expenditures made by the firm in developing intangible assets are usually not recognized as assets, because of the difficulty of ascertaining the existence and amount of future benefits. Only when intangible assets are acquired from other entities are they recognized as assets.

Liability Recognition

A liability represents a firm's obligation to make payment of cash, goods, or services in a reasonably definite amount at a reasonably definite future time for benefits or services received currently or in the past.[3]

Example 1 Miller Corporation purchased merchandise inventory and agreed to pay the supplier $8,000 within 30 days. This obligation is a liability, because Miller Corporation has received the goods and must pay a definite amount at a reasonably definite future time.

---

[3] Financial Accounting Standards Board, *op. cit.,* par. 28. See Glossary for the Board's specific definition of a liability.

Example 2 Miller Corporation borrowed $4 million by issuing long-term bonds. Annual interest payments of 10 percent must be made on December 31 of each year, and the $4 million principal must be repaid in 20 years. This obligation is a liability, because Miller Corporation has received the cash and must repay the debt in a definite amount at a definite future time.

Example 3 Miller Corporation provides a 3-year warranty on its products. The obligation to maintain the products under warranty plans creates a liability. The selling price for its products implicitly includes a charge for future warranty services. As customers pay the selling price, Miller Corporation receives a benefit (that is, the cash received). Past experience provides a basis for estimating the proportion of customers who will seek services under the warranty agreement and the expected cost of providing warranty services. Thus, the amount of obligation can be estimated with a reasonable degree of accuracy, and it is shown as a liability.

Example 4 Miller Corporation has signed an agreement with its employees' labor union, promising to increase wages 6 percent and to provide for medical and life insurance. This agreement does not immediately create a liability, because services have not yet been received from employees that would require any payments for wages and insurance. As labor services are received, a liability will arise.

The most troublesome questions of liability recognition relate to unexecuted contracts. The labor union agreement in Example 4 above is an unexecuted contract. Other examples include leases, pension agreements, and purchase-order commitments. Whether or not unexecuted contracts should be recognized as liabilities has been and continues to be controversial.

Liability Valuation

Most liabilities are monetary, requiring payments of specific amounts of cash. Those due within 1 year or less are stated at the amount of cash expected to be paid to discharge the obligation. If the payment dates extend more than 1 year into the future (for example, as in the case of the bonds in Example 2 above), the liability is stated at the present value of the future cash outflows.

A liability that requires delivering goods or rendering services, rather than paying cash, is nonmonetary. For example, magazine publishers typically collect cash for subscriptions, promising delivery of magazines over many months. Cash is received currently, whereas the obligation under the subscription is discharged by delivering magazines in the future. Theaters and football teams receive cash for season tickets and in return incur an obligation to admit the ticket holder to future performances. Landlords receive cash in advance and are obligated to let the tenant use the property. Such nonmonetary obligations are included among liabilities. They are stated, however, at the amount of cash received rather than at the expected cost of publishing the magazines or of providing the theatrical or sporting entertainment. The title frequently used for liabilities of this type is Advances from Customers.

Liability Classification

Liabilities in the balance sheet are typically classified in one of the following categories.

Current Liabilities The term *current liabilities* "is used principally to designate obligations whose liquidation is reasonably expected to require the use of existing resources properly classified as current assets, or the creation of other current liabilities."[4] Included in this category are liabilities to merchandise suppliers, employees, and governmental units. Notes and bonds payable are also included to the extent that they will require the use of current assets within a relatively short period of time, typically during the next 12 months.

Long-Term Debt Obligations having due dates, or maturities, more than 1 year after the balance sheet date are generally classified as long-term debt. Included are bonds, mortgages, and similar debts, as well as some obligations under long-term leases.

Other Long-Term Liabilities Obligations not properly considered as current liabilities or long-term debt are classified as *other long-term liabilities,* or *indeterminate-term liabilities.* Included are such items as deferred income taxes and some deferred compensation obligations.

Owners' Equity Valuation and Disclosure

The owners' equity in a firm is a residual interest.[5] That is, the owners have a claim on all assets not required to meet the claims of creditors.[6] The valuation of the assets and liabilities included in the balance sheet therefore determines the valuation of total owners' equity.

The remaining question concerns the manner of disclosing this total owners' equity. Accounting draws a distinction between contributed capital and earnings retained by a firm. The balance sheet for a corporation generally separates the amounts contributed directly by shareholders for an interest in the firm (that is, capital stock) from the subsequent earnings realized by the firm in excess of dividends declared (that is, retained earnings).

In addition, the amount received from shareholders is usually further disaggregated into the *par* or *stated value* of the shares and *amounts contributed in excess of par value or stated value.* The par or stated value of a share of stock is a somewhat arbitrary amount assigned to comply with corporation laws of each state and will rarely equal the market price of the shares at the time they are issued. As a result, the

---

[4]Committee on Accounting Procedure, *Accounting Research Bulletin No. 43,* 1953, Chapter 3.A.

[5]Although owners' equity is equal to assets minus liabilities, accounting provides an independent method for computing the amount. This method is presented in this and the next two chapters.

[6]Financial Accounting Standards Board, *op. cit.* par. 43. See the glossary at the back of the book for the Board's specific definition of owners' equity.

46

distinction between par or stated value and amounts contributed in excess of par or stated value is of questionable informational value, but is typically shown nonetheless. (These fine points of accounting for owners' equity are discussed in Chapter 12.)

Example 1 Stephens Corporation was formed on January 1, 1982. It issued 15,000 shares of $10-par value common stock for $10 cash per share. During 1982, Stephens Corporation had net income of $30,000 and paid dividends of $10,000 to shareholders. The shareholders' equity section of the balance sheet of Stephens Corporation on December 31, 1982, is as follows:

Common Stock (par value of $10 per share, 15,000 shares issued and outstanding) . . .	$150,000
Retained Earnings	20,000
Total Shareholders' Equity	$170,000

Example 2 Instead of issuing $10 par value common stock as in Example 1, assume that Stephens Corporation issued 15,000 shares of $1 par value common stock for $10 cash per share. (The market price of a share of common stock depends on the economic value of the firm and not on the par value of the shares.) The shareholders' equity section of the balance sheet of Stephens Corporation on December 31, 1982, is as follows:

Common Stock (par value of $1 per share, 15,000 shares issued and outstanding)	$ 15,000
Capital Contributed in Excess of Par Value	135,000
Retained Earnings	20,000
Total Shareholders' Equity	$170,000

The balance sheets of firms that are organized as sole proprietorships or partnerships, rather than as corporations, do not distinguish between contributed capital and earnings retained in the business. The designation of par or stated value is also not used, because these forms of organization do not issue capital stock.

Example 3 Joan Webster operates a hardware store as a sole proprietorship. She contributed $20,000 on January 1, 1982, and used the cash to rent a building, acquire display equipment, and purchase merchandise inventory. During 1982, she had net income of $15,000 and withdrew $10,000 cash for personal use. The owner's equity section of the balance sheet of Webster's Hardware Store on December 31, 1982, is as follows:

Joan Webster, Capital	$25,000[a]
Total Owner's Equity	$25,000

[a]$20,000 + $15,000 − $10,000 = $25,000.

47

Example 4 Bill White and Roger Green own and manage an apartment complex as a partnership. Each partner contributed $50,000 cash to form the partnership on January 1, 1982. During 1982, net income from the apartment complex was $40,000, which the partners shared equally. Bill White withdrew $10,000 and Roger Green withdrew $5,000 from the partnership. The owners' equity section of the balance sheet on December 31, 1982, for the apartment complex is as follows:

Bill White, Capital	$ 60,000[a]
Roger Green, Capital	65,000[b]
Total Owner's Equity.	$125,000

[a]$50,000 + (.50 \times $40,000) - $10,000 = $60,000.
[b]$50,000 + (.50 \times $40,000) - $ 5,000 = $65,000.

Accounting Procedures for Preparing the Balance Sheet

Now that we have explored the concepts and conventions underlying the balance sheet, we are ready to consider the manner in which these concepts and conventions are applied in preparing the statement. Our objective is to develop a sufficient understanding of the accounting process that generates the balance sheet so that the resulting statement can be interpreted and analyzed.

Dual Effects of Transactions on the Balance Sheet Equation

The equality between total assets and total equities (liabilities plus owners' equity) in the balance sheet equation is maintained by reporting the effects of *each* transaction in a way that maintains the equation. Any single transaction will have one of the following four effects or some combination of these effects:

1 It increases both an asset and an equity.
2 It decreases both an asset and an equity.
3 It increases one asset and decreases another asset.
4 It increases one equity and decreases another equity.

To illustrate the dual effects of various transactions on the balance sheet equation, consider the following selected transactions for Miller Corporation during January 1982.

1 On January 1, 1982, 10,000 shares of $10-par value common stock are issued for $100,000 cash.
2 Equipment costing $60,000 is purchased for cash on January 5, 1982.
3 Merchandise inventory costing $15,000 is purchased from a supplier on account on January 15, 1982.
4 The supplier in (3) is paid $8,000 of the amount due on January 21, 1982.
5 The supplier in (3) accepts 700 shares of common stock at par value in settlement of the $7,000 amount owed.

48

6 A fire insurance premium of $600 for coverage between February 1, 1982, and January 31, 1983, is paid in cash on January 31, 1982.

7 Cash of $3,000 is received from a customer on January 31, 1982, for merchandise to be delivered during February, 1982.

Exhibit 2.1 illustrates the dual effects of these transactions on the balance sheet equation. Note that after each transaction assets equal liabilities plus shareholders' equity.

Exhibit 2.1
Illustration of Dual Effects of Transactions on Balance Sheet Equation

Transaction	Assets	=	Liabilities	+	Share-holders' Equity
(1) On January 1, 1982, 10,000 shares of $10 par value common stock are issued for $100,000 cash. (Increase in both an asset and an equity.)	+ $100,000		$ 0	+	$100,000
Subtotal	$100,000	=	$ 0	+	$100,000
(2) Equipment costing $60,000 is purchased for cash on January 5, 1982. (Increase in one asset and decrease in another asset.)	− 60,000 + 60,000				
Subtotal	$100,000	=	$ 0	+	$100,000
(3) Merchandise inventory costing $15,000 is purchased from a supplier on account on January 15, 1982. (Increase in both an asset and an equity.)	+ 15,000		+ 15,000		
Subtotal	$115,000	=	$15,000	+	$100,000
(4) The supplier in (3) is paid $8,000 of the amount due on January 21, 1982. (Decrease in both an asset and an equity.)	− 8,000		− 8,000		
Subtotal	$107,000	=	$ 7,000	+	$100,000
(5) The supplier in (3) accepts 700 shares of common stock at par value in settlement of the $7,000 amount owed. (Increase in one equity and decrease in another equity.)			− 7,000	+	7,000
Subtotal	$107,000	=	$ 0	+	$107,000
(6) A fire insurance premium of $600 for coverage between February 1, 1982, and January 31, 1983, is paid in cash on January 31, 1982. (Increase in one asset and decrease in another asset.)	+ 600 − 600				
Subtotal	$107,000	=	$ 0	+	$107,000
(7) Cash of $3,000 is received from a customer on January 31, 1982, for merchandise to be delivered during February, 1982. (Increase in both an asset and an equity.)	+ 3,000		+ 3,000		
Total—January 31, 1982	$110,000	=	$ 3,000	+	$107,000

The dual effects reported for each transaction may be viewed as an outflow and an inflow. For example, common stock is issued to shareholders and cash is received from them. A cash expenditure is made and equipment is received. A promise to make a future cash payment is given to a supplier and merchandise inventory is received.

Purpose and Use of Accounts

It would be possible to prepare a balance sheet for Miller Corporation as of January 31, 1982, using information from the preceding analysis. Total assets are $110,000. We would need to retrace the effects of each transaction on total assets to determine what portion of the $110,000 represents cash, merchandise inventory, and equipment. Likewise, the effects of each transaction on total liabilities and shareholders' equity would have to be retraced to ascertain which liability and shareholders' equity amounts comprise the $110,000 total. Even with just a few transactions during the accounting period, this approach to preparing a balance sheet would be cumbersome. Considering the thousands of transactions during the accounting period for most firms, some more practical approach to accumulating amounts for the balance sheet is necessary. To accumulate the changes that take place in each balance sheet item, the accounting system uses a device known as an *account*.

Requirement for an Account Because a balance sheet item that changes can only increase or decrease, all an account need do is to provide for accumulating the increases and decreases that have taken place during the period for a single balance sheet item. The balance carried forward from the previous statement is added to the total increases; the total decreases are deducted, and the result is the amount of the new balance for the current balance sheet.

Form of an Account The account may take many possible forms, and several are commonly used in accounting practice.

Perhaps the most useful form of the account for textbooks, problems, and examinations is the *T-account*. This form of the account is not used in actual practice, except perhaps for memorandums or preliminary analyses. However, it satisfies the requirement of an account and it is easy to use. As the name indicates, the T-account is shaped like the letter T and consists of a horizontal line bisected by a vertical line. The name or title of the account is written on the horizontal line. One side of the space formed by the vertical line is used to record increases in the item and the other side to record the decreases. Spaces for dates and other information can, of course, be provided.

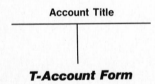

T-Account Form

The form that the account takes in actual records depends on the type of accounting system being used. In manual systems the account may take the form of a single "ledger" sheet with columns for recording increases and decreases; in punched-card systems the account may take the form of a group of cards; in computer systems it may be a group of similarly coded items on a disk. Whatever its form, an account contains the opening balance as well as the increases and decreases in the balance that result from the transactions of the period.

Placement of Increases and Decreases in the Account Given the two-sided account, we must choose which side will be used to record increases and which, decreases. By long-standing custom, the following rules are used:

1 Increases in assets are entered on the left side and decreases in assets on the right side.
2 Increases in liabilities are entered on the right side and decreases in liabilities on the left side.
3 Increases in owners' equity are entered on the right side and decreases in owners' equity on the left side.

This custom has an element of logic. A common form of balance sheet shows assets on the left and liabilities and owners' equity on the right. Following this example, asset balances should appear on the left side of accounts; equity balances should appear on the right. But asset balances will appear on the left only if asset increases are recorded on the left side of the account. Similarly, right-hand equity balances can be produced only by recording equity increases on the right. When each transaction is properly analyzed into its dual effects on the accounting equation, and when the above three rules for recording the transaction are followed, then every transaction results in equal amounts in entries on the left- and right-hand sides of various accounts.

Debit and Credit Two terms may now be added to our vocabulary, *debit* (Dr.) and *credit* (Cr.). These terms have an interesting history, but today they should be thought of merely as convenient abbreviations. *Debit* is an abbreviation for "record an entry on the left side of an account" when used as a verb and is an abbreviation for "an entry on the left side of an account" when used as a noun or adjective. *Credit* is an abbreviation for "record an entry on the right side of an account" when used as a verb and is an abbreviation for "an entry on the right side of an account" when used as a noun or adjective. These terms have no other meaning in accounting. More helpful abbreviations than *debit* and *credit* certainly seem possible, but these terms have become part of the accounting language through centuries of use and are not likely to be displaced. Often, however, the word *charge* is used instead of *debit,* both as a noun and as a verb. In terms of balance sheet categories, a debit or charge indicates (1) an increase in an asset, (2) a decrease in a liability, or (3) a decrease in an owners' equity item. A credit indicates (1) a decrease in an asset, (2) an increase in a liability, or (3) an increase in an owners' equity item.

Any previous associations or meanings of the terms debit and credit should be disregarded in accounting. In popular parlance, to credit people with something means to give them favorable recognition for some achievement, and to debit them means to charge something unfavorable against them. These terms have, however, no such implications in accounting. The best approach is simply to accept the terms *debit* and *credit* as technical terms meaning *left* and *right*.

In order to maintain the equality of the balance sheet equation, the amounts debited to various accounts for each transaction must equal the amounts credited to various accounts. Likewise, the sum of balances in accounts with debit balances at the end of each period must equal the sum of balances in accounts with credit balances.

Summary of Account Terminology and Procedure The conventional use of the account form and the terms debit and credit can be summarized graphically with the use of the T-account form, as follows:

Any Asset Account	
Beginning Balance Increases + Dr.	Decreases − Cr.
Ending Balance	

Any Liability Account	
Decreases − Dr.	Beginning Balance Increases + Cr.
	Ending Balance

Any Owners' Equity Account	
Decreases − Dr.	Beginning Balance Increases + Cr.
	Ending Balance

Reflecting the Dual Effects of Transactions in the Accounts

We are now ready to illustrate the manner in which the dual effects of transactions are reflected in the accounts. We begin by creating three separate T-accounts, one for assets, one for liabilities, and one for shareholders' equity. The dual effects of the transactions of Miller Corporation for January 1982, described earlier in the chapter, are entered in the T-accounts as shown in Exhibit 2.2.

Exhibit 2.2
Summary T-Accounts Showing the
Transactions of Miller Corporation

	Assets		=	Liabilities		+	Shareholders' Equity	
	Increases (Dr.)	Decreases (Cr.)		Decreases (Dr.)	Increases (Cr.)		Decreases (Dr.)	Increases (Cr.)
(1) Issue of Common Stock for Cash	100,000							100,000
(2) Purchase of Equipment for Cash	60,000	60,000						
(3) Purchase of Merchandise on Account	15,000				15,000			
(4) Payment of Cash to Supplier in (3)		8,000		8,000				
(5) Issuance of Common Stock to Supplier in (3)				7,000				7,000
(6) Payment of Insurance Premium in Advance . .	600	600						
(7) Cash Received from Customer in Advance	3,000				3,000			
Balance	110,000				3,000			107,000

You will note that the amount entered on the left side of, or debited to, the accounts for each transaction is equal to the amount entered on the right side of, or credited to, the accounts. Recording equal amounts of debits and credits for each transaction ensures that the balance sheet equation will always be in balance. At the end of January 1982, the assets account has a debit balance of $110,000. The sum of the balances in the liabilities and shareholders' equity accounts is a credit balance of $110,000.

A balance sheet could be prepared for Miller Corporation from the information in the T-accounts. As was the case in the earlier illustration, however, it would be necessary to retrace the entries in the accounts during the period to ascertain which individual assets, liabilities, and shareholders' equity items make up the total assets of $110,000 and the total equities of $110,000.

So that the amount of each asset, liability, and shareholders' equity item can be computed directly, a separate account is used for each balance sheet item, rather than for the three broad categories alone. The recording procedure is the same, except that we must now consider which specific asset or equity account is debited and credited.

The transactions of Miller Corporation for January 1982 are recorded in Exhibit 2.3, using separate T-accounts for each balance sheet item. The number in parentheses refers to the seven transactions we have been considering for Miller Corporation.

53

Exhibit 2.3
**Individual T-Accounts Showing
the Transactions of
Miller Corporation**

Cash (Asset)			
Increases (Dr.)	Decreases (Cr.)		
(1) 100,000	60,000 (2)		
(7) 3,000	8,000 (4)		
	600 (6)		
Balance 34,400			

Accounts Payable (Liability)	
Decreases (Dr.)	Increases (Cr.)
(4) 8,000	15,000 (3)
(5) 7,000	
	0 Balance

Merchandise Inventory (Asset)	
Increases (Dr.)	Decreases (Cr.)
(3) 15,000	
Balance 15,000	

Advance from Customer (Liability)	
Decreases (Dr.)	Increases (Cr.)
	3,000 (7)
	3,000 Balance

Prepaid Insurance (Asset)	
Increases (Dr.)	Decreases (Cr.)
(6) 600	
Balance 600	

Common Stock (Shareholders' Equity)	
Decreases (Dr.)	Increases (Cr.)
	100,000 (1)
	7,000 (5)
	107,000 Balance

Equipment (Asset)	
Increases (Dr.)	Decreases (Cr.)
(2) 60,000	
Balance 60,000	

We can see that the total assets of Miller Corporation of $110,000 as of January 31, 1982, comprise $34,400 in cash, $15,000 in merchandise inventory, $600 of prepaid insurance, and $60,000 in equipment. Total equities of $110,000 comprise $3,000 of advances from customers and $107,000 of common stock.

The balance sheet can be prepared using the amounts shown as balances in the T-accounts. The balance sheet of Miller Corporation after the seven transactions of January 1982 is shown in Exhibit 2.4.

Exhibit 2.4
Miller Corporation
Balance Sheet
January 31, 1982

ASSETS
Current Assets:

Cash		$ 34,400
Merchandise Inventory		15,000
Prepaid Insurance		600
Total Current Assets		$ 50,000

Property, Plant, and Equipment:

Equipment		60,000
Total Assets		$110,000

LIABILITIES AND SHAREHOLDERS' EQUITY
Current Liabilities:

Advance from Customer		$ 3,000

Shareholders' Equity:

Common Stock		107,000
Total Liabilities and Shareholders' Equity		$110,000

An Overview of the Accounting Process

The double-entry recording framework is used in processing the results of various transactions and events through the accounts so that financial statements can be prepared periodically. The accounting system designed around this recording framework generally involves the following operations:

1 Entering the results of each transaction in the *general journal* in the form of a *journal entry,* a process called *journalizing.*
2 Posting the journal entries from the general journal to the accounts in the *general ledger.*
3 Preparing a *trial balance* of the accounts in the general ledger.
4 Making *adjusting* and *correcting* journal entries to accounts listed in the trial balance and posting them to the appropriate general ledger accounts.
5 Preparing financial statements from a trial balance after adjusting and correcting entries.

Each of these operations is described further and illustrated using the transactions of Miller Corporation during January 1982.

Journalizing

Each transaction is initially recorded in the general journal in the form of a *journal entry.* The standard journal entry format is as follows:

Date Account Debited	Amount Debited
Account Credited.	Amount Credited
Explanation of transaction or event being journalized.	

The *general journal* is merely a book or other device containing a listing of journal entries. The general journal is often referred to as the "book of original entry," because transactions initially enter the accounting system through it.

The journal entries for the seven transactions of Miller Corporation during January 1982 are presented below.

(1) Jan. 1, 1982	Cash	100,000	
	Common Stock		100,000
	10,000 shares of $10-par value common stock are issued for cash.		
(2) Jan. 5, 1982	Equipment.	60,000	
	Cash		60,000
	Equipment costing $60,000 is purchased for cash.		
(3) Jan. 15, 1982	Merchandise Inventory	15,000	
	Accounts Payable		15,000
	Merchandise inventory costing $15,000 is purchased on account.		
(4) Jan. 21, 1982	Accounts Payable	8,000	
	Cash		8,000
	Liabilities of $8,000 are paid with cash.		
(5) Jan. 21, 1982	Accounts Payable	7,000	
	Common Stock		7,000
	700 shares of $10-par value common stock are issued in settlement of an account payable of $7,000.		
(6) Jan. 31, 1982	Prepaid Insurance	600	
	Cash		600
	One-year fire insurance premium of $600 is paid in advance.		
(7) Jan. 31, 1982	Cash	3,000	
	Advance from Customer		3,000
	Advance of $3,000 is received from customer for merchandise to be delivered in February 1982.		

Journal entries are useful for indicating the effects of various transactions on a firm's financial statements and in preparing solutions to the problems at the end of each chapter. You will not completely understand an accounting event until you can analyze the event into its required debits and credits and can prepare the journal entry. Consequently, journal entries are used as tools of analysis throughout this text.

56

Posting

At periodic intervals (for example, weekly or monthly), the transactions journalized in the general journal are entered, or posted, to the individual accounts in the general ledger. In manual systems, the *general ledger* is a book with a separate page for each account. In computerized systems, the general ledger takes the form of an access number in a computer's memory bank. The T-account described earlier serves as a useful surrogate for a general ledger account. The journal entries from the general journal of Miller Corporation would be posted to the general ledger accounts in the manner shown previously in Exhibit 2.3.

As with journal entries, T-accounts are useful tools in preparing solutions to accounting problems and are used throughout this text.

Trial Balance Preparation

A trial balance is a listing of each of the accounts in the general ledger with its balance as of a particular date. The trial balance of Miller Corporation on January 31, 1982, is presented in Exhibit 2.5.

Exhibit 2.5
Miller Corporation
Unadjusted Trial Balance
January 31, 1982

Account	Amounts in Accounts with Debit Balances	Amounts in Accounts with Credit Balances
Cash	$ 34,400	
Merchandise Inventory	15,000	
Prepaid Insurance	600	
Equipment	60,000	
Advance from Customer		$ 3,000
Common Stock		107,000
Totals	$110,000	$110,000

An equality between the sum of debit and the sum of credit account balances serves as a check on the arithmetic accuracy of the manner in which the double-entry recording procedure has been carried out during the period. If the trial balance is out of balance, it is necessary to retrace the steps followed in processing the accounting data to locate the source of the error.

Trial Balance Adjustment and Correction

Any errors detected in the processing of accounting data must be corrected. Such corrections are generally few in number. A more important type of adjustment is often necessary to account for unrecorded events that help to measure financial position at the end of the period and net income for the period. This type of adjustment is considered more fully in Chapters 3 and 4. Most corrections and adjustments are made by preparing a journal entry, entering it in the general journal, and then posting it to the general ledger accounts.

Financial Statement Preparation

The balance sheet and income statement can be prepared from the trial balance after adjustments and corrections. Because correcting or adjusting entries are not required for Miller Corporation, the balance sheet presented in Exhibit 2.4 is correct as presented. In subsequent chapters, we consider the accounting procedures for preparing the income statement and the statement of changes in financial position.

The accounting process might be summarized as shown in Figure 2.1. The results of various transactions and events are processed through the accounting system in a flow beginning with the journalizing operation and ending with the financial statements.

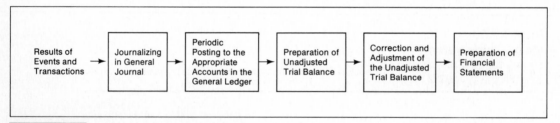

Figure 2.1
Summary of the Accounting Process

The audit of the financial statements by the independent accountant typically flows in the opposite direction. The auditor begins with the financial statements prepared by management and then traces various items back through the accounts to the source documents (for example, sales invoices, canceled checks) that support the entries made in the general journal. Thus, it is possible to move back and forth among source documents, journal entries, general ledger postings, and the financial statements.

Balance Sheet Account Titles

The following list shows balance sheet account titles that are commonly used. The descriptions should help in your understanding the nature of various assets, liabilities, and owners' equities as well as in selecting appropriate terms for solving problems. Alternative account titles can be easily devised. The list does not show all the account titles used in this book or appearing in the financial statements of publicly-held firms.

Assets

Cash on Hand Coins and currency, and such items as bank checks and money orders. The latter items are merely claims against individuals or institutions, but by custom are called "cash."

Cash in Bank Strictly speaking, merely a claim against the bank for the amount deposited. Cash in bank consists of demand deposits, against which checks can be drawn, and time deposits, usually savings accounts and certificates of deposit. In published statements, the two items of Cash on Hand and Cash in Bank usually are combined under the title *Cash.*

Marketable Securities Government bonds, or stocks and bonds of corporations, which the firm plans to hold for a relatively short period of time. The word *marketable* implies that they can be bought and sold readily through a security exchange such as the New York Stock Exchange.

Accounts Receivable Amounts due from customers of a business from the sale of goods or services. The collection of cash occurs some time after the sale. These accounts are also known as "charge accounts" or "open accounts." The general term Accounts Receivable is used in financial statements to describe the figure representing the total amount receivable from all customers but, of course, the firm keeps a separate record for each customer.

Notes Receivable Amounts due from customers or from others to whom loans have been made or credit extended, when the claim has been put into writing in the form of a promissory note.

Interest Receivable Interest on assets such as promissory notes or bonds that has accrued, or come into existence, through the passing of time but that has not been collected as of the date of the balance sheet.

Merchandise Inventory Goods on hand that have been purchased for resale, such as canned goods on the shelves of a grocery store or suits on the racks of a clothing store.

Finished Goods Inventory Completed but unsold manufactured products.

Work-in-Process Inventory Partially completed manufactured products.

Raw Materials Inventory Unused materials from which manufactured products are to be made.

Supplies Inventory Lubricants, cleaning rags, abrasives, and other incidental materials used in manufacturing operations. Stationery, computer disks, pens, and other office supplies. Bags, twine, boxes, and other store supplies. Gasoline, oil, spare parts, and other delivery supplies. Alternative titles, such as *Factory Supplies, Office Supplies, Store Supplies,* and *Delivery Supplies,* could be used.

Prepaid Insurance Insurance premiums paid for future coverage.

Prepaid Rent Rent paid in advance for future use of land, buildings, or equipment.

Advances to Suppliers The general name used to indicate payments made in advance for goods to be received at a later date. If no cash is paid by a firm when it places an order, then no asset is recognized.

Investment in Securities The cost of shares of stock in other companies, where the firm's purpose is to hold the shares for relatively long periods of time.

Land Land occupied by buildings or used in operations.

Buildings Factory buildings, store buildings, garages, warehouses, and so forth.

Equipment Lathes, ovens, tools, boilers, computers, motors, bins, cranes, conveyors, automobiles, and so forth.

Furniture and Fixtures Desks, tables, chairs, counters, showcases, scales, and other such store and office equipment.

Accumulated Depreciation This account shows the cumulative amount of the cost of long-term assets (such as buildings and equipment) that has been allocated to prior periods in measuring net income or to the costs of production. The amount in this account is subtracted from the acquisition cost of the long-term asset to which it relates in ascertaining the *net book value* of the asset to be shown in the balance sheet.

Leasehold The right to use property owned by someone else.

Organization Costs Amounts paid for legal and incorporation fees, for printing the certificates for shares of stock, and for accounting and any other costs incurred in organizing the business so it can begin to function. This asset is seen most commonly on the balance sheets of corporations.

Patents A right granted for up to 17 years by the federal government to exclude others from manufacturing, using, or selling a certain process or device. Under current generally accepted accounting principles, research and development costs must be treated as an expense in the year incurred rather than being recognized as an asset with future benefits.[7] (This treatment seems to us to be at odds with good accounting theory.) As a result, a firm that develops a patent will not normally show it as an asset. On the other hand, a firm that purchases a patent from another firm or from an individual will recognize the patent as an asset. This inconsistent treatment of internally developed and externally purchased patents is discussed more fully in Chapter 9.

Goodwill An amount paid by one firm in acquiring another business enterprise that is greater than the sum of the values assignable to individual, identifiable assets. A good reputation and other desirable attributes are generally not recognized as assets by the firm that creates or develops them. However, when one firm acquires another firm, these desirable attributes are indirectly recognized as assets, because they are a factor in the measurement of goodwill.

Liabilities

Accounts Payable Amounts owed for goods or services acquired under an informal credit agreement. These accounts are usually payable within 1 or 2 months. The same items appear as Accounts Receivable on the creditor's books.

Notes Payable The face amount of promissory notes given in connection with loans from the bank or the purchase of goods or services. The same items appear as Notes Receivable on the creditor's books.

Payroll Taxes Payable Amounts withheld from wages and salaries of employees for federal and state payroll taxes that have not yet been remitted to tax authorities as well as the employer's share of such taxes.

Withheld Income Taxes Amounts withheld from wages and salaries of employees for income taxes that have not yet been remitted to the taxing authority. This is a tentative income tax on the earnings of employees, and the employer acts merely as a tax-collecting agent for the federal and state governments. A few cities also levy income taxes, which the employer must withhold from wages.

Interest Payable Interest on obligations that has accrued or accumulated with the passage of time but that has not been paid as of the date of the balance sheet. The liability for interest is customarily shown separately from the face amount of the obligation.

Income Taxes Payable The estimated liability for income taxes, accumulated and unpaid, based on the taxable income of the business from the beginning of the taxable year to the date of the balance sheet. Because sole proprietorships and part-

---

[7] Financial Accounting Standards Board, *Statement of Financial Accounting Standards No. 2,* "Accounting for Research and Development Costs," 1974.

nerships do not pay federal income taxes directly, this term will appear only on the books of a corporation or other taxable entity.

Advances from Customers The general name used to indicate payments received in advance for goods to be delivered or services to be furnished to customers in the future; a nonmonetary liability. If no cash is received when a customer places an order, then no liability is shown.

Rent Received in Advance Another example of a nonmonetary liability. The business owns a building that it rents to a tenant. The tenant has prepaid the rental charge for several months in advance. The amount applicable to future months cannot be considered a component of income until the rent is earned as service is rendered with the passage of time. Meanwhile the advance payment results in a liability payable in services (that is, in the use of the building). On the records of the tenant the same amount would appear as an asset, Prepaid Rent.

Mortgage Payable Long-term promissory notes that have been given greater protection by the pledge of specific pieces of property as security for their payment. If the loan or interest is not paid according to the agreement, the property can be sold for the benefit of the creditor.

Bonds Payable Amounts borrowed by the business for a relatively long period of time under a formal written contract or indenture. The loan is usually obtained from a number of lenders, each of whom receives one or more bond certificates as written evidence of his or her share of the loan.

Debenture Bonds The most common type of bond, except in the railroad and public utility industries. This type of bond carries no specific security or collateral; instead it is issued on the basis of the general credit of the business. If other bonds have a prior claim on the assets of the business, then the debenture is called *subordinated*.

Convertible Bonds A bond that the holder can *convert* into or "trade in" for shares of common stock. The number of shares to be received when the bond is converted into stock, the dates when conversion can occur, and other details are specified in the bond indenture.

Capitalized Lease Obligations The present value of future commitments for cash payments to be made in return for the right to use property owned by someone else.

Deferred Income Taxes Certain income tax payments are delayed beyond the current accounting period. This item, which appears on the balance sheet of most U.S. corporations, is discussed in Chapter 11.

Owners' Equity

Common Stock Amounts received for the par or stated value of a firm's principal class of voting stock.

Preferred Stock Amounts received for the par value of a class of a firm's stock that has some preference relative to the common stock. This preference is usually with respect to dividends and to assets in the event the corporation is liquidated. Sometimes preferred stock is convertible into common stock.

Capital Contributed in Excess of Par or Stated Value Amounts received from the issuance of common or preferred stock in excess of such shares' par value or stated value. This account is also referred to as *Additional Paid-in Capital* or sometimes as *Premium on Preferred* (or *Common*) *Stock.*

Retained Earnings An account reflecting the increase in net assets since the business was organized as a result of generating earnings in excess of dividend declarations. When dividends are declared, net assets are decreased, and retained earnings are reduced by an equal amount.

Treasury Shares This account shows the cost of shares of stock originally issued but subsequently reacquired by the corporation. Treasury shares are not entitled to dividends and are not considered to be "outstanding" shares. The cost of treasury shares is almost always shown on the balance sheet as a deduction from the total of the other shareholders' equity accounts. Accounting for treasury shares is discussed in Chapter 12.

A balance sheet that includes many of the accounts described in this section is presented in Appendix A, Exhibit A.2, for General Products Company.

Summary

The balance sheet, or statement of financial position, comprises three major classes of items—assets, liabilities, and owners' equity.

Resources are recognized as assets when a firm has acquired rights to their future use as a result of a past transaction or exchange and when the value of the future benefits can be measured with a reasonable degree of precision. Monetary assets are, in general, stated at their current cash, or cash-equivalent, values. Nonmonetary assets are stated at acquisition cost, in some cases adjusted downward for the cost of services that have been consumed.

Liabilities represent obligations of a firm to make payments of a reasonably definite amount at a reasonably definite future time for benefits already received. Owners' equity is the difference between total assets and total liabilities and, for corporations, is typically segregated into contributed capital and retained earnings.

The equality of total assets and total equities (liabilities plus owners' equity) is maintained by recording the effects of each transaction in a dual manner in the accounts. The double-entry recording framework is summarized as follows:

Asset Accounts		=	Liability Accounts		+	Owners' Equity Accounts	
Increases (Debits)	Decreases (Credits)		Decreases (Debits)	Increases (Credits)		Decreases (Debits)	Increases (Credits)

The dual effects of each transaction are initially recorded in journal-entry form in the general journal. These journal entries are then posted to the appropriate asset, liability, and owners' equity accounts in the general ledger. A trial balance of the ending balances in the general ledger accounts is prepared periodically as a check on the mathematical accuracy of the double-entry recording procedure. Any necessary adjustments or corrections of the account balances in the trial balance are then made in the general journal and posted to the accounts in the general ledger. The financial statements are prepared from the adjusted and corrected trial balance. The procedures for preparing the income statement are discussed in Chapters 3 and 4. The statement of changes in financial position is considered in Chapter 5.

Problem for Self-Study

The Electronics Appliance Corporation was organized on September 1, 1982. The following transactions occurred during the month of September.

(1) The firm issues 4,000 shares of $10-par value common stock for $12 cash per share on September 1.

(2) The firm's attorney is given 600 shares of $10-par value common stock on September 2 in payment for legal services rendered in the organization of the corporation. The bill for the services is $7,200.

(3) A factory building is leased for the 3 years beginning October 1, 1982. Monthly rental payments are $5,000. Two months' rent is paid in advance on September 5.

(4) Raw materials are purchased on account for $6,100 on September 12.

(5) A check for $900 is received on September 15 from a customer as a deposit on a special order for equipment that Electronics plans to manufacture. The contract price is $4,800.

(6) Office equipment with a list price of $950 is acquired on September 20. After deducting a discount of $25 for prompt payment, a check is issued in full payment.

(7) The company hires three employees to begin work October 1. A cash advance of $200 is given to one of the employees on September 28.

(8) Factory equipment costing $27,500 is purchased on September 30. A check for $5,000 is issued, and a long-term mortgage liability is assumed for the balance.

(9) The labor costs of installing the new equipment in (8) are $450 and are paid in cash on September 30.

a Prepare journal entries for each of the nine transactions.
b Set up T-accounts and enter each of the nine transactions.

64

c Prepare a balance sheet for Electronics Appliance Corporation as of September 30, 1982.

Suggested Solution

The journal entries for the nine transactions are as follows:

(1) Sept. 1, 1982	Cash		48,000	
	Common Stock			40,000
	Additional Paid-in Capital			8,000
	Issuance of 4,000 shares of $10-par value common stock for $12 cash per share.			
(2) Sept. 2, 1982	Organization Costs		7,200	
	Common Stock			6,000
	Additional Paid-in Capital			1,200
	Issuance of 600 shares of $10-par value common stock in settlement of $7,200 attorney's bill connected with organization of the corporation.			
(3) Sept. 5, 1982	Prepaid Rent		10,000	
	Cash			10,000
	Prepayment of rent for October and November on factory building.			
(4) Sept. 12, 1982	Raw Material Inventory		6,100	
	Accounts Payable			6,100
	Raw materials costing $6,100 are purchased on account.			
(5) Sept. 15, 1982	Cash		900	
	Advances from Customers			900
	An advance of $900 is received from a customer as a deposit on equipment to be manufactured in the future.			
(6) Sept. 20, 1982	Equipment		925	
	Cash			925
	Equipment with a list price of $950 is acquired, after a discount, for $925.			
(7) Sept. 28, 1982	Advance to Employee		200	
	Cash			200
	A cash advance of $200 is given to an employee beginning work on October 1.			
(8) Sept. 30, 1982	Equipment		27,500	
	Cash			5,000
	Mortgage Payable			22,500
	Acquisition of equipment for $5,000 cash and assumption of a $22,500 mortgage for the balance of the purchase price.			
(9) Sept. 30, 1982	Equipment		450	
	Cash			450
	Installation cost on equipment acquired in (8) of $450 is paid in cash.			

Exhibit 2.6 presents T-accounts for Electronics Appliance Corporation and shows the recording of the nine entries in the accounts. The letters A, L, and OE are added after the account titles to indicate the balance sheet category of the accounts. Exhibit 2.7 presents a balance sheet as of September 30, 1982.

Exhibit 2.6
**T-Accounts and Transactions during September 1982
for Electronics Appliance Corporation**

Cash (A)		Advances to Employees (A)	Raw Materials Inventory (A)	Prepaid Rent (A)
(1) 48,000	10,000 (3)	(7) 200	(4) 6,100	(3) 10,000
(5) 900	925 (6)			
	200 (7)			
	5,000 (8)			
	450 (9)			
32,325		200	6,100	10,000

Equipment (A)		Organization Costs (A)	Accounts Payable (L)	Advances from Customers (L)
(6) 925		(2) 7,200	6,100 (4)	900 (5)
(8) 27,500				
(9) 450			6,100	900
28,875		7,200		

Mortgage Payable (L)	Common Stock (OE)	Additional Paid-in Capital (OE)
22,500 (8)	40,000 (1)	8,000 (1)
	6,000 (2)	1,200 (2)
22,500	46,000	9,200

Questions and Problems

1 Review the meaning of the following concepts or terms discussed in this chapter.
   a Accounting entity.
   b Legal entity.
   c Sole proprietorship.
   d Partnership.
   e Corporation.
   f Acquisition cost.
   g Current replacement cost.
   h Current net realizable value.
   i Present (discounted) value of future cash flows.
   j Monetary assets.
   k Nonmonetary assets.
   l Going concern.
   m Objectivity.
   n Conservatism.
   o Plant, or fixed, assets.
   p Intangible assets.
   q Par value.
   r Stated value.
   s Debit.
   t Charge.
   u Credit.
   v Journal entry.
   w General journal.
   x General ledger.
   y T-account.
   z Trial balance.

Exhibit 2.7
Electronics Appliance Corporation
Balance Sheet
September 30, 1982

ASSETS
Current Assets:

Cash	$32,325	
Advances to Employees	200	
Raw Materials Inventory	6,100	
Prepaid Rent	10,000	
Total Current Assets		$48,625

Property, Plant, and Equipment:

Equipment		28,875

Intangibles:

Organization Costs		7,200
Total Assets		$84,700

LIABILITIES AND SHAREHOLDERS' EQUITY
Current Liabilities:

Accounts Payable	$ 6,100	
Advances from Customers	900	
Total Current Liabilities		$ 7,000

Long-term Debt:

Mortgage Payable		22,500
Total Liabilities		$29,500

Shareholders' Equity:

Common Stock, $10-Par Value	$46,000	
Additional Paid-in Capital	9,200	
Total Shareholders' Equity		55,200
Total Liabilities and Shareholders' Equity		$84,700

2 How can you determine from a balance sheet whether the enterprise is a corporation, partnership, or sole proprietorship?

3 Conservatism is generally regarded as a convention in accounting. Indicate who might be hurt by conservatively stated accounting reports.

4 Indicate whether or not each of the following items would be recognized as an asset by a firm according to generally accepted accounting principles.
   a A patent on a new invention purchased from its creator.
   b A firm's chief scientist, who has twice won the Nobel prize.
   c The right to use a building during the coming year. The rent for the period has already been paid.
   d An automobile acquired with the issue of a note payable. Because the note has not been paid, legal title to the automobile has not yet passed to the firm.

67

e A degree in engineering from a reputable university, awarded to the firm's chief executive.

f A contract signed by a customer to purchase $1,000 worth of goods next year.

g A favorable reputation.

5 Indicate whether or not each of the following immediately gives rise to an asset under generally accepted accounting principles. If an asset is recognized, state the account title and amount.

a A check for $300 has been sent to an insurance company for property insurance. The period of coverage begins next month (consider from the standpoint of the firm making the cash expenditure).

b A check for $3,000 is issued as a deposit on specially-designed equipment. The equipment is to have a total purchase price of $20,000 and will be completed and delivered next year (consider from the standpoint of the firm making the cash expenditure).

c Shares of common stock of General Electric Company are acquired with temporarily excess cash for $12,000.

d Merchandise inventory with a list price of $800 is acquired, with payment made in time to secure a 3-percent discount for prompt payment. Cash discounts are treated as a reduction in the acquisition cost of the inventory.

e A well-known scientist has been hired to manage the firm's research and development activity. Employment begins next month. One-twelfth of the annual salary of $90,000 is payable at the end of each month worked.

f Bonds with a face value of $200,000 are purchased for $206,000. The bonds mature in 20 years. Interest is payable by the issuer at the rate of 10 percent annually.

g An order for $700 worth of merchandise is received from a customer.

h Notice has been received from a manufacturer that raw materials billed at $2,000, with payment due in 30 days, have been shipped by freight. The buyer obtains title to the goods as soon as they are shipped by the seller.

6 Indicate whether or not each of the following events immediately gives rise to the recognition of an asset under generally accepted accounting principles. If an asset is recognized, state an account title and amount.

a Raw materials with an invoice price of $4,800 are purchased on account from Greer Wholesalers.

b Defective raw material purchased in part **a** for $400 is returned to Greer Wholesalers and full credit is received.

c The bill of Greer Wholesalers (see parts **a** and **b**) is paid promptly. A discount of 2 percent offered by the seller for prompt payment is taken. Cash discounts are treated as a reduction in the acquisition cost of the raw materials.

d A machine is purchased for $25,000 cash.

e The cost of transporting the new machine in part **d** to the plant site is paid in cash, $450.

f Material and labor costs incurred in installing the machine in part **d** total $300 and are paid in cash.

7 In each of the following transactions, give the title(s) and amount(s) of the asset(s) that would appear on the balance sheet.

a A firm purchases an automobile with a list price of $8,000. The dealer allows a discount of $850 from the list price for payment in cash. Dealer preparation charges on the automobile amount to an extra $200. The dealer collects a 4-percent sales tax on the price paid for the automobile and preparation charges. In addition, the dealer collects a

68

$75 fee to be remitted to the state for this year's license plates and $300 for a 1-year insurance policy provided by the dealer's insurance agency. The firm pays a body shop $75 for painting the firm's name on the automobile.

b A firm acquires land that has been appraised at $2 million by a certified real estate appraiser. The firm pays for the land by giving up shares in the Xerox Corporation at a time when equivalent shares traded on the New York Stock Exchange have a market value of $2,100,000.

c A firm acquires land that has been appraised at $2 million by a certified real estate appraiser. The firm pays for the land by giving up shares in Small Timers, Inc., whose shares are traded only on the Pacific Stock Exchange. The last transaction in shares of Small Timers, Inc., occurred 4 days prior to this asset swap. Using the prices of the most recent trades, the shares of stock of Small Timers, Inc. given in exchange for the land have a market value of $2,100,000.

8 A group of investors owns an office building, which is rented unfurnished to tenants. The building was purchased 5 years previously from a construction company and, at that time, was expected to have a useful life of 40 years. Indicate the procedures you might follow in determining the amount at which the building would be stated under each of the following valuation methods.

a Acquisition cost.

b Adjusted acquisition cost.

c Current replacement cost.

d Current net realizable value.

e Present value of future cash flows.

9 Indicate whether or not each of the following items is recognized as a liability according to generally accepted accounting principles.

a An obligation to provide magazines next year to subscribers who have paid one year's subscription fees in advance (consider from the standpoint of the magazine publisher).

b The reputation for poor quality control on products manufactured.

c An obligation to provide warranty services for three years after customers purchase the firm's products.

d The outstanding common stock of a corporation.

e Unpaid property taxes for the preceding year.

f The amount payable by a firm for a television advertisement that has appeared but for which payment is not due for 30 days.

g A tenant's obligation to maintain a rented warehouse in good repair.

h The firm's president has an incompetent son who is employed in the business.

10 Indicate whether or not each of the following events immediately gives rise to the recognition of a liability under generally accepted accounting principles. If a liability is recognized, state the account title and amount.

a A company hires its president under a 5-year contract beginning next month. The contract calls for $300,000 compensation per year.

b An insurance company receives $2,000 for 6 months' insurance coverage in advance (consider from the standpoint of the insurance company).

c A manufacturer agrees to produce a specially-designed piece of equipment for $3 million. A down payment of $300,000 is received upon signing the contract, and the remainder is due when the equipment is completed. Consider from the standpoint of the manufacturer.

d Additional common stock with a par value of $75,000 is issued for $80,000.

e Employees earned wages totaling $6,000 during the last pay period for which they have not been paid. The employer is also liable for payroll taxes of 8 percent of the wages earned.

f A firm signs a contract agreeing to sell $6,000 of merchandise to a particular customer.

11 Indicate whether or not each of the following events immediately gives rise to the recognition of a liability under generally accepted accounting principles. If a liability is recognized, indicate the account title and amount.

a A $600 check is received from a tenant for 3 months' rent in advance (consider from the standpoint of the lessor, or owner, of the building).

b Utility services received during the past month of $240 have not been paid.

c A $10,000 loan has been received from the bank, with the firm signing a note agreeing to repay the loan with interest at 8 percent in 6 months.

d A firm has signed an agreement with its employees' labor union agreeing to increase the firm's contribution to the union pension fund by $20,000 per month, beginning next month.

e Income taxes on last year's earnings totaling $15,000 have not been paid.

f A firm has signed an employment contract with its controller for a 3-year period beginning next month at a contract price of $200,000 per year.

12 Some of the assets of one firm correspond to the liabilities of another firm. For example, an account receivable on the seller's balance sheet would be an account payable on the buyer's balance sheet. For each of the following items, indicate whether it is an asset or a liability and give the corresponding account title on the balance sheet of the other party to the transaction.

a Advances by Customers.

b Bonds Payable.

c Interest Receivable.

d Prepaid Insurance.

e Rental Fees Received in Advance.

13 The assets of a business total $700,000, and liabilities total $550,000. Present the owners' equity section of the balance sheet under the following assumptions:

a The business is a sole proprietorship owned by William Gleason.

b The business is a partnership. William Gleason has a 35-percent interest, John Morgan has a 40-percent interest, and David Johnson has a 25-percent interest.

c The business is a corporation. Outstanding common stock was originally issued for $80,000, of which $50,000 represented par value. The remainder of the owners' equity represents accumulated, undistributed earnings.

14 Information may be classified with respect to a balance sheet in one of the following ways:

(1) Asset.

(2) Liability.

(3) Owners' equity.

(4) Item would not appear on the balance sheet as conventionally prepared.

Using the numbers above, indicate the appropriate classification of each of the following items:

a Salaries payable.

b Retained earnings.

c Notes receivable.
d Unfilled customers' orders.
e Land.
f Interest payable.
g Work-in-process inventory.
h Mortgage payable.
i Organization costs.
j Advances by customers.
k Advances to employees.
l Patents.
m Good credit standing.
n Common stock.

15 Information may be classified with respect to a balance sheet in one of the following ways:
(1) Asset.
(2) Liability.
(3) Owners' equity.
(4) Item would not appear on the balance sheet as conventionally prepared.

Using the numbers above, indicate the appropriate classification of each of the following items:
a Preferred stock.
b Furniture and fixtures.
c Potential liability under lawsuit (case has not yet gone to trial).
d Prepaid rent.
e Capital contributed in excess of par value.
f Cash on hand.
g Goodwill.
h Estimated liability under warranty contract.
i Raw materials inventory.
j Rental fees received in advance.
k Bonds payable.
l Unexpired insurance.

16 Presented below are journal entries for a series of transactions. Describe the likely transaction that gave rise to each journal entry.

a	Equipment	10,000	
	Cash		2,000
	Note Payable		8,000
b	Cash	6,000	
	Accounts Receivable		4,000
	Advances from Customers		2,000
c	Accounts Payable	2,500	
	Merchandise Inventory		2,500
d	Bonds Payable	100,000	
	Common Stock		40,000
	Additional Paid-in Capital		60,000
e	Cash	800	
	Subscription Fees Received in Advance		800
f	Prepaid Rent	2,000	
	Cash		2,000

71

17 Present journal entries for each of the following transactions of Mailor Corporation during April 1982, its first month of operations.

(1) April 2, 1982: 250,000 shares of $5-par value common stock are issued for $8 cash per share.

(2) April 3, 1982: A building costing $800,000 is acquired. A down payment of $200,000 is made in cash and a 10-percent note maturing on April 3, 1985 is signed for the balance.

(3) April 8, 1982: A machine costing $15,000 is acquired for cash.

(4) April 15, 1982: Merchandise inventory costing $120,000 is acquired on account from various suppliers.

(5) April 18, 1982: A check for $400 is issued for insurance coverage for the period beginning May 1, 1982.

(6) April 20, 1982: A check for $800 is received from a customer for merchandise to be delivered on May 5, 1982.

(7) April 26, 1982: Invoices totaling $80,000 from the purchases on April 15 are paid, after deducting a 2-percent discount for prompt payment. Cash discounts are treated as a reduction in the acquisition cost of inventory.

(8) April 30, 1982: The remaining invoices from the purchases on April 15 are paid after the discount period has lapsed.

18 Present journal entries for each of the following transactions of Area Corporation. You may omit dates and explanations for the journal entries.

(1) 20,000 shares of $10-par value common stock are issued at par value for cash.

(2) Land and building costing $90,000 are acquired with the payment of $25,000 cash and the assumption of a 20-year, 8-percent mortgage for the balance. The land is to be stated at $30,000 and the building at $60,000.

(3) A used lathe is purchased for $4,620 cash.

(4) Raw materials costing $3,600 are acquired on account.

(5) Defective raw materials purchased in **(4)** and costing $650 are returned to the supplier. The account has not yet been paid.

(6) The supplier in **(4)** is paid the amount due, less a 2-percent discount for prompt payment. Cash discounts are treated as a reduction in the acquisition cost of raw materials.

(7) A fire insurance policy providing $100,000 coverage beginning next month is obtained. The 1-year premium of $625 is paid in cash.

(8) A check for $2,000 is issued to Roger White to reimburse him for costs incurred in organizing and promoting the corporation.

(9) A check for $600 is issued for 3 months' rent in advance for office space.

(10) A patent on a machine process is purchased for $35,000 cash.

(11) Office equipment is purchased for $950. A down payment of $250 is made, with the balance payable in 30 days.

(12) $275 is paid to Express Transfer Company for delivering the equipment purchased in **(3)**.

19 Express the following transactions of the Winkle Grocery Store, a sole proprietorship, in journal-entry form. You may omit explanations for the journal entries.

(1) John Winkle contributes $50,000 cash to help set up the grocery store.

(2) A 60-day, 8-percent note is signed in return for a $10,000 loan from the bank.

(3) A building is rented, with the annual rental of $6,000 paid in advance.

(4) Display equipment costing $16,000 is acquired. A check is issued.

(5) Merchandise inventory costing $35,000 is acquired. A check for $8,000 is issued, with the remainder payable in 30 days.

(6) A contract is signed with a nearby restaurant under which the restaurant agrees to purchase $6,000 of groceries each week. A check is received for the first 2 weeks' orders in advance.

20 Express the following independent transactions in journal-entry form. If an entry is not required, indicate the reason. You may omit explanations for the journal entries.

(1) Bonds of the Sommers Company with a face value of $60,000 and annual interest at the rate of 8 percent are purchased for $58,500 cash.

(2) A check for $2,600 is received by a fire insurance company for premiums on policy coverage over the next 2 years.

(3) A corporation issues 20,000 shares of $12-par value common stock in exchange for land, building, and equipment. The land is to be stated at $30,000, the building at $180,000, and the equipment at $75,000.

(4) A contract is signed by a manufacturing firm agreeing to purchase 100 dozen machine tool parts over the next 2 years at a price of $60 per dozen.

(5) 5,000 shares of $1-par value preferred stock are issued to an attorney for legal services rendered in organization of the corporation. The bill for the services is $9,500.

(6) A coupon book, redeemable in future movie viewings, is issued for $60 cash by a movie theatre.

(7) A firm has been notified that it is being sued for $30,000 damages by a customer who incurred losses as a result of purchasing defective merchandise.

(8) Merchandise inventory costing $2,000, purchased on account, is found to be defective and returned to the supplier for full credit.

21 Indicate the effects of the transactions below on the balance sheet equation using the following format:

Transaction Number	Assets	=	Liabilities	+	Owner's Equity
(1)	+$50,000		0		+$50,000
Subtotal	$50,000	=	0	+	$50,000

(1) 5,000 shares of $10-par value common stock are issued at par for cash.

(2) Equipment costing $12,000 is acquired. A down payment of $4,000 is made, with the remainder payable in six months with interest at 9 percent.

(3) Raw materials costing $6,000 are acquired on account.

(4) Installation cost of $800 on the equipment in **(2)** is paid in cash.

(5) The property insurance premium of $420 for the year, beginning on the first day, of next month is paid.

(6) Raw materials acquired in **(3)** for $700 are found to be defective and returned to the supplier for full credit. The account had not yet been paid.

(7) Invoices from the purchases in **(3)** totaling $4,000 are paid after deducting a 1-percent discount for prompt payment. Cash discounts are treated as a reduction in the acquisition cost of raw materials.

(8) 100 shares of $10-par value common stock are issued to the firm's attorney for services in organizing the corporation. The attorney's bill was $1,000.

(9) Customers advanced the firm $250 for merchandise to be delivered next month.

22 Set up T-accounts for the following accounts. Indicate whether each account is an asset, liability, or owners' equity item, and enter the transactions described below:

Cash	Accounts Payable
Merchandise Inventory	Note Payable
Prepaid Insurance	Mortgage Payable
Building	Common Stock—Par Value
Equipment	Additional Paid-in Capital

(1) 30,000 shares of $5-par value stock are issued for $8 cash per share.

(2) A building costing $300,000 is acquired. A cash payment of $60,000 is made, and a long-term mortgage is assumed for the balance of the purchase price.

(3) Equipment costing $5,000 and merchandise inventory costing $7,000 are acquired on account.

(4) A 3-year fire insurance policy is taken out and the $900 premium is paid in advance.

(5) A 90-day, 6-percent note is issued to the bank for a $10,000 loan.

(6) Payments of $8,000 are made to the suppliers in **(3)**.

23 The Patterson Manufacturing Corporation is organized on January 1, 1982. During January 1982, the following transactions occur:

(1) The corporation issues 15,000 shares of $10-par value common stock for $210,000 in cash.

(2) The corporation issues 28,000 shares of common stock in exchange for land, building, and equipment. The land is to be stated at $80,000, the building at $220,000, and the equipment at $92,000.

(3) The corporation issues 2,000 shares of common stock to an attorney in payment of legal services rendered in obtaining the corporate charter.

(4) Raw materials costing $75,000 are acquired on account from various suppliers.

(5) Manufacturing equipment with a list price of $6,000 is acquired. After deducting a $600 discount, the net amount is paid in cash. Cash discounts are treated as a reduction in the acquisition cost of equipment.

(6) Freight charges of $350 for delivery of the equipment in **(5)** are paid in cash.

(7) Raw materials costing $800 are found to be defective and returned to the supplier for full credit. The raw materials had been purchased on account [see **(4)**], and no payment had been made as of the time that the goods were returned.

(8) A contract is signed for the rental of a fleet of automobiles beginning February 1, 1982. The rental for February of $1,400 is paid in advance.

(9) Invoices for $60,000 of raw materials purchased in **(4)** are paid, after deducting a discount of 3 percent for prompt payment. Cash discounts are treated as a reduction in the acquisition cost of raw materials.

(10) Fire and liability insurance coverage is obtained from Southwest Insurance Company. The 2-year policy, beginning February 1, 1982, carries a $400 premium, which has not yet been paid.

(11) A contract is signed with a customer for $20,000 of merchandise that Patterson plans to manufacture. The customer advanced $4,500 toward the contract price.

(12) A warehouse costing $60,000 is acquired. A down payment of $7,000 is made, and a long-term mortgage is assumed for the balance.

(13) Raw materials inventory with an original list price of $1,500 is found to be defective and returned to the supplier. This inventory has already been paid for in **(9)**. The returned raw materials are the only items purchased from this particular supplier during January 1982.

(14) The firm purchased 6,000 shares of $10-par value common stock of the General Cereal Corporation for $95,000. This investment is made as a short-term investment of excess cash. The shares of General Cereal Corporation are traded on the New York Stock Exchange.

The following assumptions will help you resolve certain accounting uncertainties: (i) Transactions **(2)** and **(3)** occurred on the same day as transaction **(1)**. (ii) The invoices paid in **(9)** are the only purchases for which discounts were made available to the purchaser.

a Enter these transactions in T-accounts. Indicate whether each account is an asset, liability, or owners' equity item. Cross-reference each entry to the appropriate transaction number.

b Prepare a balance sheet as of January 31, 1982.

24 The Scott Products Corporation is organized on October 1, 1982. During October the following transactions occur:

(1) The corporation issues 20,000 shares of $5-par value common stock for $7 per share in cash.

(2) The corporation issues 200 shares of $100-par value preferred stock at par value for cash.

(3) The corporation gives $40,000 in cash and 5,000 shares of common stock in exchange for land and building. The land is to be stated at $5,000 and the building at $70,000.

(4) Equipment costing $26,000 is acquired. Cash of $3,000 is paid and an 8-percent note, due in one year, is given for the balance.

(5) Transportation costs on the equipment in **(4)** of $800 are paid in cash.

(6) Installation costs on the equipment in **(4)** of $1,100 are paid in cash.

(7) Merchandise inventory costing $45,000 is acquired on account.

(8) License fees for the year beginning November 1, 1982 of $800 are paid in advance.

(9) Merchandise costing $1,300 from the acquisition in **(7)** is found to be defective and returned to the supplier for full credit. The account had not been paid.

(10) A patent is purchased from its creator for $15,000.

(11) The corporation signed an agreement to manufacture a specially-designed machine for a customer for $60,000, to be delivered in January 1983. At the time of signing, the customer advanced $6,000 of the contract price.

(12) Invoices totaling $30,000 from the purchases in **(7)** are paid, after deducting a 2-percent discount for prompt payment. Cash discounts are treated as a reduction in the acquisition cost of inventory.

a Enter the transactions in T-accounts. Indicate whether each account is an asset, liability, or owners' equity item. Cross-reference each entry to the appropriate transaction number.

b Prepare a balance sheet for Scott Products Corporation as of October 31, 1982.

25 The following transactions occur during March 1982 for Dryden's Book Store, a sole proprietorship, in preparation for its opening for business on April 1, 1982.

(1) H. R. Dryden contributes $6,000 in cash, 100 shares of Western Corporation common stock, and an inventory of books to be sold. The stock of Western Corporation is quoted on the New York Stock Exchange at $15 per share on the day it is contributed, and will be sold when additional cash is needed. The books are to be stated at $2,750.

(2) Two months' rent on a store building is paid in advance in cash. The bookstore will occupy the building on April 1. The monthly rental is $400.

(3) Store fixtures are purchased for $4,000, of which $800 is paid in cash. A note, to be paid in 10 equal monthly installments beginning May 1, is signed for the balance.

(4) Books with an invoice price of $2,600 are purchased on account.

(5) A 1-year insurance policy on the store's contents beginning April 1, 1982, is purchased. The premium of $160 is paid by check.

(6) A check for $320 is issued to the Darwin Equipment Co. for a cash register and other operating equipment.

(7) Merchandise costing $1,800 is ordered from a publisher. Delivery is scheduled for April 15.

(8) The merchandise purchased in **(4)** is paid for by check. Payment is made in time to obtain a 2-percent cash discount for prompt payment. These are the only purchases for which discounts are available. Cash discounts are treated as a reduction in the acquisition cost of merchandise.

(9) An operating license for the year beginning April 1, 1982, is obtained from the city. The fee of $250 is paid by check.

a Enter these transactions in T-accounts. Indicate whether each account is an asset, liability, or owners' equity item. Cross-reference each entry to the appropriate transaction number.

b Prepare a balance sheet for this sole proprietorship as of March 31, 1982.

26 Priscilla Mullins and Miles Standish form a partnership to operate a laundry and cleaning business to be known as Pilgrim's One Day Laundry and Cleaners. The following transactions occur in late June 1982, prior to the grand opening on July 1, 1982.

(1) Standish contributes $400 cash and cleaning equipment that is to be stated at $5,600.

(2) Mullins contributes $3,000 cash and a delivery truck to be stated at $2,500.

(3) The July rent for the business premises of $400 is paid in advance.

(4) Cleaning supplies are purchased on account from the Wonder Chemical Company for $2,500.

(5) Insurance coverage on the equipment and truck for a 1-year period beginning July 1, 1982, is purchased for $425 cash.

(6) The firm borrows $2,000 from the First National Bank. A 90-day, 8-percent note is signed, with principal and interest payable at maturity.

(7) The Wonder Chemical Company account is paid in full after deducting a 2-percent discount for prompt payment. Cash discounts are treated as a reduction in the acquisition cost of supplies.

(8) A cash register is purchased for $700. A down payment of $100 is made, and a note is signed for the remainder, payable in 10 equal installments beginning August 1.

a Enter these transactions in T-accounts. Indicate whether each account is an asset, liability, or owners' equity item. Cross-reference each entry to the appropriate transaction number.

b Prepare a balance sheet for the partnership as of June 30, 1982.

27 Most of the financial records of the Rowland Novelty Company were removed by an employee who, apparently, took all the cash on hand from the store on October 31. From supplementary records, the following information is obtained:

(1) According to the bank, cash in bank was $5,730.

(2) Amounts payable to creditors were $4,720.

76

(3) Rowland's initial contribution to the business was $15,000, and the total interest in the business at the time of the theft was $17,500.

(4) Cost of merchandise on hand was $11,380.

(5) A 1-year fire insurance policy was purchased on September 1 for $900.

(6) Furniture and fixtures are rented from the Anderson Office Supply Company for $200 per month. The rental for October has not been paid.

(7) A note for $1,200 was given by a customer. Interest due at October 31 was $45.

(8) Payments due from other customers amounted to $1,915.

(9) Rowland purchased a license from the city for $300 on July 1. The license allows retail operations for 1 year.

a Determine the probable cash shortage.

b Prepare a well-organized balance sheet presenting the financial position immediately preceding the theft.

28 Comment on any unusual features of the following balance sheet of the Western Sales Corporation shown in Exhibit 2.8.

Exhibit 2.8
Western Sales Corporation
Balance Sheet
for the Year Ended
December 31, 1982

ASSETS

Current Assets:

Cash and Certificates of Deposit	$ 86,500	
Accounts Receivable—Net	193,600	
Merchandise Inventory	322,900	$ 603,000
Investments (substantially at cost):		
Investment in U.S. Treasury Notes	$ 60,000	
Investment in Eastern Sales Corp.	196,500	256,500
Fixed Assets (at cost):		
Land	$225,000	
Buildings and Equipment—Net	842,600	1,067,600
Intangibles and Deferred Charges:		
Prepaid Insurance	$ 1,200	
Prepaid Rent	1,500	
Goodwill	2	2,702
Total Assets		$1,929,802

Exhibit 2.8 (continued)
LIABILITIES AND SHAREHOLDERS' EQUITY
Current Liabilities:

Accounts Payable	$225,300	
Accrued Expenses	10,900	
Income Taxes Payable	89,200	$ 325,400
Long-Term Liabilities:		
Bonds Payable	$500,000	
Pensions Payable	40,600	
Contingent Liability	100,000	640,600
Shareholders' Equity:		
Common Stock—$10-par value, 50,000 shares issued and outstanding	$625,000	
Earned Surplus	338,802	963,802
Total Liabilities and Shareholders' Equity		$1,929,802

29 Financial analysts typically use information from all three of the principal financial statements discussed in Chapter 1 (that is, balance sheet, income statement, and statement of changes in financial position) in making their analyses and interpretations. It is possible, however, to make some general observations about changes in the structure of a firm's assets and equities by studying comparative balance sheets only. These general observations are then examined further by studying the income statement and statement of changes in financial position.

Refer to the comparative balance sheet and related notes of General Products Company in Appendix A at the back of the book. Using this financial statement only, describe the most significant changes that occurred in the structure of General Products Company's assets and equities between 1981 and 1982 (Hint: You may want to begin your analysis by expressing various balance sheet components as a percentage of other components. For example, current assets represent 53.4 percent of total assets on December 31, 1982.)

Chapter 3 *Income Statement—Measurement Principles and Accounting Procedures*

A second principal financial statement is the income statement. This statement provides a measure of the earnings performance of a firm for some particular period of time. As we discussed in Chapter 1 and illustrated for the Jonathan Electronics Corporation in Exhibit 1.2, *net income,* or *earnings,* is equal to revenues minus expenses.

Revenues measure the inflow of net assets (assets less liabilities) from selling goods and providing services. *Expenses* measure the outflow of net assets that are used up, or consumed, in the process of generating revenues. As a measure of earnings performance, revenues reflect the services rendered by the firm, and expenses indicate the efforts required or expended.

This chapter considers the measurement principles and accounting procedures that underlie the income statement. We begin by discussing the concept of an accounting period, the span of time over which earnings performance is measured. Next we describe and illustrate two common approaches to measuring earnings performance: the cash basis and the accrual basis. Finally, the accounting procedures used in applying the accrual basis of accounting are illustrated for a merchandising firm. Chapter 4 explores more fully the application of the accrual basis of accounting for manufacturing, construction, and other types of businesses.

The Accounting Period Convention

The income statement reports earnings performance over a specified period of time. Years ago, the length of this period varied substantially among firms. Income statements were prepared at the completion of some activity, such as after the round-trip voyage of a ship between England and the colonies or at the completion of a construction project.

The earnings activities of most modern firms are not so easily separated into distinguishable projects. Instead, the income-generating activity is carried on continually. For example, a plant is acquired and used in manufacturing products for a period of 40 years or more. Delivery equipment is purchased and used in transporting merchandise to customers for 4, 5, or more years. If the preparation of the income statement were postponed until all earnings activities were completed, the report might never be prepared and, in any case, would be too late to help a reader appraise earnings performance. An accounting period of uniform length is used to facilitate timely comparisons and analyses among firms.

An accounting period of *1 year* underlies the principal financial statements distributed to shareholders and potential investors. Most firms prepare their annual reports using the calendar year as the accounting period. A growing number of firms, however, use a *natural business year.* The use of a natural business year is an attempt to measure performance at a time when most earnings activities have been substantially concluded. The ending date of a natural business year varies from one firm to another. For example, Sears once used a natural business year ending on January 31, which comes after completion of the Christmas shopping season and before the start of the Easter season. American Motors uses a year ending September 30, the end of its model year. A. C. Nielsen (producers of television ratings and other surveys) uses a year ending August 31, just prior to the beginning of the new television season.

Accounting Methods for Measuring Performance

Some earnings activities are both started and completed within a given accounting period. For example, merchandise might be purchased from a supplier, sold to a customer on account, and the account collected in cash, all within a particular accounting period. Few difficulties are encountered in measuring performance in these cases. The difference between the cash received from customers and the cash disbursed to acquire, sell, and deliver the merchandise represents earnings from this series of transactions.

Many earnings activities, however, are started in one accounting period and completed in another. Buildings and equipment are acquired in one period but used over a period of several years. Merchandise is sometimes purchased in one accounting period, sold during the next period, while cash is collected from customers during a third period. A significant problem in measuring performance for a specific accounting period is measuring the amount of revenues and expenses from earnings activities that are in process as of the beginning of the period or are incomplete as of the end of the period. Two approaches to measuring earnings performance are (1) the cash basis of accounting, and (2) the accrual basis of accounting.

Cash Basis of Accounting

Under the *cash basis of accounting,* revenues from selling goods and providing services are recognized in the period when cash is received from customers. Expenses are typically reported in the period in which expenditures are made for merchandise, salaries, insurance, taxes, and similar items. To illustrate the measurement of performance under the cash basis of accounting, consider the following example.

Donald and Joanne Allens open a hardware store on January 1, 1982. They contribute $20,000 in cash and borrow $12,000 from a local bank. The loan is repayable on June 30, 1982, with interest charged at the rate of 12 percent per year. A store building is rented on January 1, and 2 months' rent of $4,000 is paid in advance. The premium of $2,400 for property and liability insurance coverage for the year ending December 31, 1982, is paid on January 1. During January, merchandise costing $40,000 is acquired, of which $26,000 is purchased for cash and $14,000 is purchased on account. Sales to customers during January total $50,000, of which $34,000 is sold for cash and $16,000 is sold on account. The acquisition cost of the merchandise sold during January is $32,000, and various employees are paid $5,000 in salaries.

Exhibit 3.1 presents a performance report for Allens' Hardware Store for the month of January 1982 using the cash basis. Cash receipts from sales of merchandise of $34,000 represent the portion of the total sales of $50,000 made during January which was collected in cash. Whereas merchandise costing $40,000 was acquired during January, only $26,000 cash was disbursed to suppliers, and only this amount is subtracted in measuring performance under the cash basis. Cash expenditures during January for salaries, rent, and insurance are also subtracted in measuring performance, without regard to whether or not the services acquired were fully consumed by the end of the month. Cash expenditures made for merchandise and services exceeded cash receipts from customers during January by $3,400.[1]

As a basis for measuring performance for a particular accounting period (for example, January 1982 for Allens' Hardware Store), the cash basis of accounting is subject to two related criticisms. First, the cost of the efforts required in generating revenues is not adequately matched with those revenues. Performance of one period therefore gets mingled with the performance of preceding and succeeding periods. The store rental payment of $4,000 provides rental services for both January and February, but under the cash basis, the full amount is subtracted in measuring performance during January. Likewise, the annual insurance premium provides coverage for the full year, whereas under the cash basis of accounting, none of this insurance cost will be subtracted in measuring performance during the months of February through December.

The longer the period over which future benefits are received, the more serious is this criticism of the cash basis of accounting. Consider, for example, the investments of a capital-intensive firm in buildings and equipment that might be used for 10, 20,

---

[1] Note that, under the cash method, cash received from owners and through borrowing is not included in the performance report. Only those cash receipts and disbursements from the firm's operating and investing activities are included.

or more years. The length of time between the purchase of these assets and the collection of cash for goods produced and sold can span many years.

A second, and probably less serious, criticism of the cash basis of accounting is that it postpones unnecessarily the time when revenue is recognized. In most cases, the sale (delivery) of goods or rendering of services is the critical event in generating revenue. Collecting cash is relatively routine, or at least highly predictable. In these cases, recognizing revenue at the time of cash collection may result in reporting the effects of earnings activities one or more periods after the critical revenue-generating activity has occurred. For example, sales to customers during January by Allens' Hardware Store totaled $50,000. Under the cash basis of accounting, $16,000 of this amount will not be recognized until February or later, when the cash is collected. If the credit standings of customers have been checked prior to making sales on account, it is highly probable that cash will be collected, and there is little reason to postpone recognition of the revenue.

The cash basis of accounting is used principally by lawyers, accountants, and other professional people. These professionals have relatively small investments in multiperiod assets, such as buildings and equipment, and usually collect cash from their clients soon after services are rendered. Most such firms actually use a *modified cash basis of accounting,* under which the costs of buildings, equipment, and similar items are treated as assets when purchased. A portion of the acquisition cost is then recognized as an expense when services of these assets are consumed. Except for the treatment of these long-lived assets, revenues are recognized at the time cash is received and expenses are reported when cash disbursements are made.

Most individuals use the cash basis of accounting for the purpose of computing personal income and personal income taxes. Where inventories are an important factor in generating revenues, such as for a merchandising or manufacturing firm, the Internal Revenue Code prohibits a firm from using the cash basis of accounting in its income tax returns.

Exhibit 3.1
Allens' Hardware Store
Performance Measurement on a
Cash Basis
for the Month of January 1982

Cash Receipts from Sales of Merchandise		$34,000
Less Cash Expenditures for Merchandise and Services:		
Merchandise	$26,000	
Salaries	5,000	
Rental	4,000	
Insurance	2,400	
Total Cash Expenditures		37,400
Excess of Cash Expenditures over Cash Receipts		($ 3,400)

Accrual Basis of Accounting

Under the *accrual basis of accounting*, revenue is recognized when some critical event or transaction occurs that is related to the earnings process. In most cases, this critical event is the sale (delivery) of goods or the rendering of services. The nature and significance of this critical event are discussed more fully in Chapter 4. Under the accrual basis of accounting, costs incurred are reported as expenses in the period when the revenues which they helped produce are recognized. Thus, an attempt is made to *match* expenses with associated revenues. When particular types of costs incurred cannot be closely identified with specific revenue streams, they are treated as expenses of the period in which services of an asset are consumed or future benefits of an asset disappear.

Exhibit 3.2 presents an income statement for Allens' Hardware Store for January 1982 using the accrual basis of accounting. The entire $50,000 of sales during January is recognized as revenue even though cash in that amount has not yet been received. Because of the high probability that outstanding accounts receivable will be collected, the critical revenue-generating event is the sale of the goods rather than the collection of cash from customers. The acquisition cost of the merchandise sold during January is $32,000. Recognizing this amount as cost-of-goods-sold expense leads to an appropriate matching of sales revenue and merchandise expense in the income statement. Of the advance rental payment of $4,000, only $2,000 applies to the cost of services consumed during January. The remaining rental of $2,000 applies to the month of February. Likewise, only $200 of the $2,400 insurance premium represents coverage used up during January. The remaining $2,200 of the insurance premium provides coverage for February through December and will be recognized as an expense during those months. The interest expense of $120 represents 1 month's interest on the $12,000 bank loan at an annual rate of 12 percent ($= \$12,000 \times .12 \times 1/12$). Although the interest will not be paid until the loan

---

Exhibit 3.2
Allens' Hardware Store
Income Statement
for the Month of January 1982
(Accrual Basis of Accounting)

Sales Revenue		$50,000
Less Expenses:		
Cost of Goods Sold	$32,000	
Salaries Expense	5,000	
Rent Expense	2,000	
Insurance Expense	200	
Interest Expense	120	
Total Expenses		39,320
Net Income		$10,680

becomes due on June 30, 1982, the firm benefited from having the funds available for its use during January; an appropriate portion of the total interest cost on the loan should therefore be recognized as a January expense. The salaries, rental, insurance, and interest expenses, unlike the cost of merchandise sold, cannot be associated directly with revenues recognized during the period. These costs are therefore reported as expenses of January to the extent that services were consumed during the month.

The accrual basis of accounting provides a better measure of earnings performance for Allens' Hardware Store for the month of January than does the cash basis for two reasons:

1 Revenues are measured in a more meaningful way.
2 Expenses are associated more closely with reported revenues.

Likewise, the accrual basis will provide a superior measure of performance for future periods, because activities of those periods will be charged with their share of the costs of rental, insurance, and other services to be consumed. Thus, the accrual basis focuses on the *use* of assets in operations rather than on their financing (that is, the receipt and expenditure of cash).

Most business firms, particularly those involved in merchandising and manufacturing activities, use the accrual basis of accounting. The next section examines in greater depth the measurement principles of accrual accounting.

Measurement Principles of Accrual Accounting

In recognizing revenues and expenses under the accrual basis of accounting, we are concerned with when revenues and expenses are recognized (timing questions) and how much is recognized or reported (measurement questions).

Timing of Revenue Recognition

The earnings process for the acquisition and sale of merchandise might be depicted as shown in Figure 3.1. Revenue could conceivably be recognized at the time of

Figure 3.1
Earnings Process for the Acquisition and Sale of Merchandise

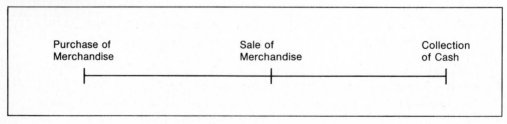

84

purchase, sale, or cash collection, at some point(s) between these events, or even continuously. To answer the timing question, we must have a set of criteria for revenue recognition.

Criteria for Revenue Recognition The criteria currently required to be met before revenue is recognized under the accrual basis of accounting are as follows:

1 All, or a substantial portion, of the services to be provided have been performed.
2 Cash, a receivable, or some other asset susceptible to reasonably precise measurement has been received.

For the vast majority of firms involved in selling goods and services, revenue is recognized at the time of sale (delivery). This method of recognizing revenues is called the *completed-sale,* or in some contexts the *completed-contract,* method of revenue recognition. The goods have been transferred to the buyer or the services have been performed. Future services, such as for warranties, are likely to be insignificant, or if significant, can be estimated with reasonable precision. An exchange between an independent buyer and seller has occurred which provides an objective measure of the amount of revenue. If the sale is made on account, past experience and an assessment of customers' credit standings provide a basis for predicting the amount of cash that will be collected. The sale of the goods or services is therefore the critical revenue-generating event. Under the accrual basis of accounting, revenue is typically recognized at the time of sale.

Measurement of Revenue

The amount of revenue recognized is generally measured by the cash or cash-equivalent value of other assets received from customers. As a starting point, this amount is the agreed-upon price between buyer and seller at the time of sale. Some adjustments to this amount may be necessary, however, if revenue is recognized in a period prior to the collection of cash.

Uncollectible Accounts If some portion of the sales for a period is not expected to be collected, the amount of revenue recognized for that period must be adjusted for estimated uncollectible accounts arising from those sales. Logic suggests that this adjustment of revenue should occur in the period when revenue is recognized and not in a later period when specific customers' accounts are found to be uncollectible. If the adjustment is postponed, reported income of subsequent periods will be affected by earlier decisions to extend credit to customers. Thus, the performance of the firm for both the period of sale and the period when the account is judged uncollectible would be measured inaccurately. These problems are considered further in Chapter 7.

Example Champion's Department Store had sales to customers during 1982 as follows: cash sales, $400,000; sales on account, $600,000. Based on past experience, Champion's estimates that 2 percent of all sales on account will not be collected. The amount of revenue recognized by Champion's for 1982 under the accrual method is determined as follows:

Cash Sales	$ 400,000
Credit Sales	600,000
Total Sales—Gross	$1,000,000
Estimated Uncollectibles (2% × $600,000)	(12,000)
Total Sales—Net	$ 988,000

Sales Discounts and Allowances Customers may take advantage of discounts for prompt payment, or allowances may be granted for unsatisfactory merchandise. In these cases, the amount of cash eventually to be received can be expected to be less than the stated selling price. Appropriate reductions should therefore be made at the time of sale in measuring the amount of revenue to be recognized.

Delayed Payments If the period between the sale of the goods or services and the time of cash collection extends over several years and there is no provision for explicit interest payments, it is likely that the selling price includes an interest charge for the right to delay payment. Under the accrual basis of accounting, this interest element should be recognized as interest revenue during the periods between sale and collection when the loan is outstanding. To recognize all potential revenue entirely in the period of sale would be to recognize too soon the return for services rendered over time in lending money. Thus, when cash collection is to be delayed, the measure of revenue for the current period should be the selling price reduced to account for interest during future periods. Only the *present value* at the time of sale of the amount to be received should be recognized as revenue during the period of sale. For most accounts receivable, the period between sale and collection spans only 2 to 3 months. The interest element is likely to be relatively insignificant in these cases. As a result, in accounting practice no reduction for interest on delayed payments is made for receivables to be collected within 1 year or less. This procedure is a practical expedient rather than a strict following of the underlying accounting theory.

Timing of Expense Recognition

Assets provide future benefits to the firm. *Expenses* are a measurement of the assets consumed in generating revenue. Assets are *unexpired costs* and expenses are *expired costs* or "gone assets." Our attention focuses on *when* the asset expiration takes place. The critical question is "When have asset benefits expired—leaving the balance sheet—and become expenses—entering the income statement as reductions in owners' equity?" Thus:

Balance Sheet   **Income Statement**

Assets or Unexpired Costs ⟶ Expenses or Expired Costs

Expense Recognition Criteria The criteria used in accrual accounting are:

1 Asset expirations directly associated with particular types of revenue are expenses in the period in which the revenues are recognized. This treatment is called the *matching convention,* because cost expirations are matched with revenues.
2 Asset expirations not associated with revenues are expenses of the period in which services are consumed in operations.

Product Costs The cost of goods or merchandise sold is perhaps the easiest expense to associate with revenue. At the time of sale, the asset physically changes hands. Revenue is recognized, and the cost of the merchandise transferred is treated as an expense.

A *merchandising firm* purchases inventory and later sells it without changing its physical form. The inventory is shown as an asset stated at acquisition cost on the balance sheet. Later, when the inventory is sold, the same amount of acquisition cost is shown as an expense (cost of goods sold) on the income statement.

A *manufacturing firm,* on the other hand, incurs various costs in changing the physical form of the goods it produces. These costs are typically of three types: (1) direct material, (2) direct labor, and (3) manufacturing overhead (sometimes called indirect manufacturing costs). Direct material and direct labor costs can be associated directly with particular products manufactured. Manufacturing overhead includes a mixture of costs that provide a firm with a capacity to produce. Examples of manufacturing overhead costs are expenditures for utilities, property taxes, and insurance on the factory, as well as depreciation on manufacturing plant and equipment. The services of each of these items are used up, or consumed, during the period while the firm is creating new assets—the inventory of goods being worked upon or held for sale. Benefits from direct material, direct labor, and manufacturing overhead are, in a sense, transferred to, or become embodied in, the asset represented by units of inventory. Because the inventory items are assets until sales are made to customers, the various direct material, direct labor, and manufacturing overhead costs incurred in producing the goods are included in the manufacturing inventory under the titles Work-in-Process Inventory and Finished Goods Inventory. Such costs, which are assets transformed from one form to another, are called *product costs.* Product costs are assets; they become expenses only when the goods in which they are embodied are sold.

Selling Costs In most cases, the costs incurred in selling, or marketing, a firm's products relate to the units sold during the period. For example, salaries and commissions of the sales staff, sales literature used, and most advertising costs are incurred in generating revenue currently. Because these selling costs are associated with the revenues of the period, they are reported as expenses in the period when the services provided by these costs are used. It can be argued that some selling costs, such as advertising and other sales promotion, provide future-period benefits for a firm and should continue to be treated as assets. However, distinguishing what portion of the cost relates to the current period to be recognized as an expense and what portion relates to future periods to be treated as an asset can be extremely difficult. Therefore, accountants typically treat selling and other marketing activity costs as expenses of the period when the services are used. These selling costs are treated as *period expenses* rather than as assets, even though they may enhance the future marketability of a firm's products.

Administrative Costs The costs incurred in administering, or directing, the activities of the firm cannot be closely associated with units produced and sold and are, therefore, like selling costs, treated as period expenses. Examples include the president's salary, accounting and data-processing costs, and the costs of conducting various supportive activities, such as legal services and corporate planning.

Measurement of Expenses

Expenses represent assets consumed during the period. The amount of an expense is therefore the cost of the expired asset. Thus, the basis for expense measurement is the same as for asset valuation. Because assets are primarily stated at acquisition cost on the balance sheet, expenses are measured by the acquisition cost of the assets that were either sold or used during the period.

Summary

Under the accrual basis of accounting, revenue is typically recognized at the time of sale and stated at the amount of cash expected to be collected from customers. Costs that can be directly associated with particular revenues become expenses in the period when revenues are recognized. The cost of acquiring or manufacturing inventory items is treated in this manner. Costs that cannot be closely associated with particular revenue streams become expenses of the period when goods or services are consumed in operations. Most selling and administrative costs are treated in this manner.

The accounting procedures for preparing the income statement are considered next.

Overview of Accounting Procedures

Relationship between Balance Sheet and Income Statement

Net income, or earnings, for a period is a measure of the excess of revenues (net asset inflows) over expenses (net asset outflows) from selling goods and providing services. Dividends are a measure of the net assets distributed to shareholders. The Retained Earnings account on the balance sheet measures the cumulative excess of earnings over dividends since the firm began operations. The following disaggregation of the balance sheet equation helps to show the relation of revenues, expenses, and dividends to the components of the balance sheet.

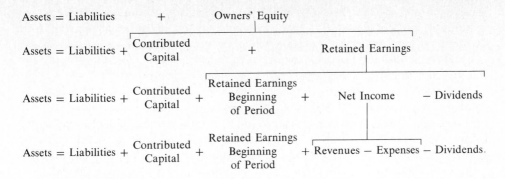

Purpose and Use of Individual
Revenue and Expense Accounts

Revenue and expense amounts could be recorded directly in the Retained Earnings account. For example, the sale of merchandise on account results in an increase in assets (accounts receivable) and retained earnings (sales revenue) and a decrease in assets (merchandise inventory) and retained earnings (cost of merchandise sold). Measuring the *amount* of net income would be relatively simple if revenues and expenses were recorded directly in the Retained Earnings account. Net income would be computed from the following equation:

$$\text{Net Income} = \frac{\text{Retained Earnings}}{\text{End of Period}} - \frac{\text{Retained Earnings}}{\text{Beginning of Period}} + \text{Dividends.}$$

In preparing an income statement, however, we are interested in the components of net income: the sources of revenue and the types of expenses. To help in preparing the income statement, individual revenue and expense accounts are maintained during the accounting period. These accounts begin the accounting period with a zero balance. During the period, revenues and expenses are recorded in the accounts as they arise. At the end of the period, the balance in each revenue and expense account represents the cumulative revenues and expenses *for the period.* These amounts are reported in the income statement, which shows the net income of the period.

Because revenues and expenses are basically components of retained earnings, the balance in each revenue and expense account is transferred at the end of the period to the Retained Earnings account. Each revenue and expense account will then have a zero balance after the transfer. Retained earnings will be increased by the amount of net income (or decreased by the net loss) for the period.

The end result of maintaining separate revenue and expense accounts during the period and transferring their balances to the Retained Earnings account at the end of the period is the same as if revenues and expenses were initially recorded directly in the Retained Earnings account. Using separate revenue and expense accounts facilitates preparation of the income statement in which specific types of revenues and expenses are disclosed. Once this purpose has been served, the need for separate revenue and expense accounts *for a given accounting period* has ended. Having been reduced to a zero balance at the end of the accounting period, these accounts begin the following accounting period with a zero balance and are therefore ready for entry of the revenue and expense amounts of the following period.

The process of transferring the balances in revenue and expense accounts to retained earnings is referred to as the *closing process,* because each revenue and expense account is closed, or reduced to a zero balance. Revenue and expense accounts accumulate amounts for only a single accounting period, and are therefore called *temporary accounts.* On the other hand, the accounts on the balance sheet reflect the cumulative changes in each account from the time the firm was first organized, and are not closed each period. The balances in these accounts at the end of one period are carried over as the beginning balances of the following period. Balance sheet accounts are called *permanent accounts.*

Debit and Credit Procedures for Revenues, Expenses, and Dividends

Because revenues, expenses, and dividends are components of retained earnings, the recording procedures for these items are the same as for any other transaction affecting owners' equity accounts.

Owners' Equity

Decreases (Debit)	Increases (Credit)
	Issues of Capital Stock
Expenses	Revenues
Dividends	

The transaction giving rise to revenue results in an increase in net assets (increase in assets or decrease in liabilities) and an increase in owners' equity. The usual journal entry to record a revenue transaction is therefore:

Asset (A) Increase or Liability (L) Decrease	Amount
Revenue (OE)	Amount
Typical entry to recognize revenue.	

The transaction giving rise to expense results in a decrease in net assets (decrease in assets or increase in liabilities) and a decrease in owners' equity. The usual journal entry to record an expense is therefore:

Expense (OE)	Amount
Asset (A) Decrease or Liability (L) Increase	Amount
Typical entry to record expense.	

Dividends result in a decrease in net assets and a decrease in owners' equity. As we discuss in Chapter 12, dividends may be paid either in cash or in other assets. Although the accounting procedures for dividends are similar regardless of the form of the distribution, we assume that cash is used unless information is provided to the contrary. The usual entry to record the declaration of a dividend by the board of directors of a corporation is:

Retained Earnings (OE)	Amount
Dividends Payable (L)	Amount
Typical entry to record dividend declaration.	

An alternative method of recording the dividend is to debit an account, Dividends Declared. At the end of the accounting period, the balance in the Dividends Declared account is closed to the Retained Earnings account, thereby reducing the balance of Retained Earnings. The end result under both procedures is a debit to Retained Earnings and a credit to Dividends Payable for the amount of dividends declared during the period.

When the dividend is paid, the journal entry is:

Dividends Payable (L)	Amount
Cash (A)	Amount
Typical entry to record dividend payment.	

A conceptual error sometimes made is that of treating dividends as an expense on the income statement. *Dividends are not expenses.* They are not costs incurred in *generating* revenues. Rather, they represent *distributions* of assets arising from current and prior years' operations to the owners of the firm. Because the account, Dividends Declared, is closed in a manner similar to an expense account at the end of the accounting period, the second method of recording the dividend leads some students to regard dividends as expenses. We therefore prefer that dividends declared be debited directly to the Retained Earnings account.

Before illustrating the recording procedures for revenues and expenses, it may be helpful to review briefly the steps in the accounting process.

Review of the Accounting Process

The steps in the accounting process, discussed in Chapter 2, are summarized as follows:

Journalizing Each transaction or series of transactions during the period is recorded in journal-entry form in the general journal (or in a special journal that supplements the general journal).

Posting At periodic intervals, the entries in the general journal are posted to the accounts in the general ledger.

91

Trial Balance At the end of the accounting period, the balance in each general ledger account is calculated and a trial balance is prepared. A trial balance is a listing of all accounts in the general ledger. If the recording process has been carried out properly, the total amount in accounts having debit balances must equal the total amount in accounts having credit balances.

Adjusting Entries During the period, some accounting events may be only partially recorded, not recorded at all, or recorded incorrectly. Before the financial statements can be prepared at the end of the period, the omissions must be accounted for and the errors corrected. The entries to do this are known as *adjusting* entries. These entries are made so that revenues and expenses are reported in the correct accounts and amounts and so that balance sheet accounts show appropriate amounts of assets and equities at the end of the period.

Closing Entries The revenue and expense accounts, as well as the Dividend Declared account, if used, are closed at the end of the accounting period by transferring the balance in each account to Retained Earnings.

Statement Preparation The balance sheet, income statement, statement of changes in financial position, and any desired supporting schedules (for example, an analysis of changes in the Cash, Buildings and Equipment, or Retained Earnings accounts) are then prepared.

Illustration of the Accounting Process for a Merchandising Firm

Stephen's Shoe Store, Inc., has been in business since 1979. A trial balance taken from its general ledger accounts on January 1, 1982, the first day of an accounting period, is shown in Exhibit 3.3. To facilitate understanding, in this illustration the asset accounts are designated (A); the liability accounts (L), and the owners' equity (including revenue and expense) accounts (OE). Trial balances do not usually contain such designations.

Note that the revenue and expense accounts are not included in this trial balance; they have zero balances at the beginning of an accounting period. Two of the accounts in the trial balance, Allowance for Uncollectible Accounts and Accumulated Depreciation, have not previously been considered. These accounts are presented on the balance sheet as deductions from Accounts Receivable and from Building and Equipment, respectively. (See Exhibit 3.9 for balance sheet presentation of these accounts.) Because of this manner of disclosure, they are referred to as *contra accounts*. A contra account accumulates amounts that are subtracted from the amount in another account. The nature and use of these contra accounts are discussed later in this illustration. An asset contra account is designated XA in the trial balance.

Exhibit 3.3
Stephen's Shoe Store, Inc.
Trial Balance
January 1, 1982

	Accounts with Debit Balances	Accounts with Credit Balances
Cash (A)	$ 30,000	
Accounts Receivable (A)	70,000	
Allowance for Uncollectible Accounts (XA)		$ 7,000
Merchandise Inventory (A)	175,000	
Land (A)	100,000	
Building and Equipment (A)	525,000	
Accumulated Depreciation (XA)		85,000
Accounts Payable (L)		135,000
Bonds Payable (L)		100,000
Common Stock (OE)		250,000
Additional Paid-in Capital (OE)		200,000
Retained Earnings (OE)		123,000
Total	$900,000	$900,000

Journalizing

The transactions of Stephen's Shoe Store during 1982 and the appropriate journal entries at the time of the transactions follow.

1 Merchandise costing $355,000 is purchased on account.

(1) Merchandise Inventory (A)	355,000	
Accounts Payable (L)		355,000

2 Sales during the year are $625,000, of which $225,000 are for cash and the remainder are on account.

(2) Cash (A)	225,000	
Accounts Receivable (A)	400,000	
Sales Revenue (OE)		625,000

3 The cost of merchandise sold during 1982 is $390,000.

(3) Cost of Goods Sold (OE)	390,000	
Merchandise Inventory (A)		390,000

4 Salaries of $110,000 are paid in cash during the year.

(4) Salaries Expense (OE)	110,000	
Cash (A)		110,000

5 Customers' accounts of $325,000 are collected.

(5) Cash (A)	325,000	
Accounts Receivable (A)		325,000

6 Payments of $270,000 are made to merchandise suppliers for purchases on account.

(6) Accounts Payable (L)	270,000	
Cash (A)		270,000

7 A premium of $1,500 is paid on January 1, 1982, for a 3-year property and liability insurance policy.

(7) Prepaid Insurance (A)	1,500	
Cash (A)		1,500

The debit in this entry, made on January 1, 1982, is to an asset account, because the insurance provides 3 years of coverage beginning on that date. The entry to reduce the Prepaid Insurance account and to record the insurance expense for 1982 is one of the adjusting entries, illustrated later, made at the end of the accounting period.

8 Warehouse space not needed in the company's operations is rented out for 1 year beginning December 1, 1982. The annual rental of $600 is received at that time.

(8) Cash (A)	600	
Rental Fees Received in Advance (L)		600

9 Annual interest at 8 percent on the long-term bonds outstanding is paid on December 31, 1982; $.08 \times \$100,000 = \$8,000$.

(9) Interest Expense (OE)	8,000	
Cash (A)		8,000

10 A 90-day note was received from a customer on November 1, 1982. The note replaced the customer's open account receivable balance of $10,000 arising from an earlier sale. The note bears interest of 9 percent per year.

94

| (10) Notes Receivable (A) . . . . | 10,000 | |
| Accounts Receivable (A) . . . . | | 10,000 |

11 The board of directors declared a cash dividend of $15,000 on December 28, 1982. The dividend is to be paid on January 20, 1983.

| (11) Retained Earnings (OE) . . . . | 15,000 | |
| Dividends Payable (L) . . . . | | 15,000 |

Posting

The entries in the general journal are posted to the appropriate general ledger accounts. In this illustration, the posting operation takes place on December 31, 1982. The T-accounts in Exhibit 3.4 show the opening balances from the trial balance in Exhibit 3.3 and the effects of transactions (1) through (11).

Trial Balance Preparation

The trial balance prepared at the end of the accounting period before adjusting and closing entries is called an *unadjusted trial balance.* The unadjusted trial balance of Stephen's Shoe Store as of December 31, 1982, is shown in Exhibit 3.5. The amounts in the unadjusted trial balance are taken directly from the ending balances in the T-accounts shown in Exhibit 3.4.

Adjusting and Correcting Entries

The entries in the general journal made during the year result primarily from transactions between the firm and outsiders (for example, suppliers, employees, customers, and governmental units). Other events continually occur, however, for which no specific transaction signals the requirement for a journal entry, but which must be considered in measuring net income for the period and financial position at the end of the period. For example, building and equipment are continually used in the process of generating revenue. Because the services of these assets are consumed during the period, a portion of their acquisition cost must be recorded as an expense. Similarly, insurance coverage expires continually throughout the year. Because the services of the asset are gradually consumed, a portion of the asset, Prepaid Insurance, must be recorded as an expense.

Other kinds of events occur that affect the revenues and expenses of the period but for which a cash transaction with an outsider will not occur until a subsequent period. For example, salaries and wages are earned by administrative employees during the last several days of the current accounting period, but they will not be paid until the following accounting period. Such salaries and wages, although payable in the next period, are expenses of the current period when the labor services are

95

Exhibit 3.4
Stephen's Shoe Store, Inc.
T-Accounts Showing Beginning Balances,
Transactions During 1982, and Ending
Balance before Adjusting Entries

Cash (A)

Bal. 1/1	30,000	110,000	(4)
(2)	225,000	270,000	(6)
(5)	325,000	1,500	(7)
		8,000	(9)
(8)	600		
Bal. 12/31	191,100		

Notes Receivable (A)

Bal. 1/1	0		
(10)	10,000		
Bal. 12/31	10,000		

Land (A)

Bal. 1/1	100,000	
Bal. 12/31	100,000	

Accounts Payable (L)

(6)	270,000	135,000	Bal. 1/1
		355,000	(1)
		220,000	Bal. 12/31

Accounts Receivable (A)

Bal. 1/1	70,000	325,000	(5)
(2)	400,000	10,000	(10)
Bal 12/31	135,000		

Merchandise Inventory (A)

Bal. 1/1	175,000	390,000	(3)
(1)	355,000		
Bal. 12/31	140,000		

Building and Equipment (A)

Bal. 1/1	525,000	
Bal. 12/31	525,000	

Dividends Payable (L)

		0	Bal. 1/1
		15,000	(11)
		15,000	Bal. 12/31

Allowance for Uncollectible Accounts (XA)

	7,000	Bal. 1/1
	7,000	Bal. 12/31

Prepaid Insurance (A)

Bal. 1/1	0	1,500	(7)
Bal. 12/31	1,500		

Accumulated Depreciation (XA)

	85,000	Bal. 1/1
	85,000	Bal. 12/31

Rental Fees Received in Advance (L)

		0	Bal. 1/1
		600	(8)
		600	Bal. 12/31

96

Bonds Payable (L)

	100,000 Bal. 1/1
	100,000 Bal. 12/31

Additional Paid-in Capital (OE)

	200,000 Bal. 1/1
	200,000 Bal. 12/31

Common Stock (OE)

	250,000 Bal. 1/1
	250,000 Bal. 12/31

Retained Earnings (OE)

(11) 15,000	123,000 Bal. 1/1
	108,000 Bal. 12/31

Sales Revenue (OE)

	0 Bal. 1/1
	625,000 (2)
	625,000 Bal. 12/31

Interest Expense (OE)

Bal. 1/1 0	
(9) 8,000	
Bal. 12/31 8,000	

Salaries Expense (OE)

Bal. 1/1 0	
(4) 110,000	
Bal. 12/31 110,000	

Cost of Goods Sold (OE)

Bal. 1/1 0	
(3) 390,000	
Bal. 12/31 390,000	

97

Exhibit 3.5
Stephen's Shoe Store, Inc.
Unadjusted Trial Balance
December 31, 1982

	Accounts with Debit Balances	Accounts with Credit Balances
Cash (A)	$ 191,100	
Accounts Receivable (A)	135,000	
Allowance for Uncollectible Accounts (XA)		$ 7,000
Notes Receivable (A)	10,000	
Merchandise Inventory (A)	140,000	
Prepaid Insurance (A)	1,500	
Land (A)	100,000	
Building and Equipment (A)	525,000	
Accumulated Depreciation (XA)		85,000
Accounts Payable (L)		220,000
Dividends Payable (L)		15,000
Rental Fees Received in Advance (L)		600
Bonds Payable (L)		100,000
Common Stock (OE)		250,000
Additional Paid-in Capital (OE)		200,000
Retained Earnings (OE)		108,000
Sales Revenue (OE)		625,000
Cost of Goods Sold (OE)	390,000	
Salaries Expense (OE)	110,000	
Interest Expense (OE)	8,000	
Totals	$1,610,600	$1,610,600

consumed. Similarly, interest accrues on a firm's notes receivable or payable. Interest will be collected or paid in a subsequent period, but a portion of the interest should be recognized as revenue or expense in the current period.

Adjusting entries are prepared at the end of the accounting period. These entries alter the balances in the general ledger accounts in order to recognize all revenues and expenses for the proper reporting of net income and financial position. Several examples of adjusting entries are illustrated for Stephen's Shoe Store in the following sections.

Recognition of Accrued Revenues and Receivables Revenue is earned as services are rendered. For example, rent is earned as a tenant uses the property. Interest, a "rent" for the use of money, is earned as time passes on a loan. It is usually not convenient, however, to record these amounts as they accrue day by day. At the end of the accounting period, there may be some situations in which revenue has been earned but for which no entry has been made, either because cash has not been received or the time has not arrived for a formal invoice to be sent to the customer. A claim has come into existence that, although it may not be due immediately, should appear on the balance sheet as an asset and be reflected in the revenues of the period. The purpose of the adjusting entry for interest eventually receivable by the lender is to recognize on the balance sheet the right to receive cash in an amount equal to the interest already earned and to recognize the same amount as revenue on the income statement for the period.

Stephen's Shoe Store received a 90-day note from a customer on November 1, 1982. At year-end, the note is included as an asset on the trial balance. Interest earned during November and December, however, is not reflected in the unadjusted trial balance. The note earns interest at the rate of 9 percent per year. By convention in business practice, interest rates stated on loans are almost always stated as annual interest rates. Also, by convention, a year equal to 12 months of 30 days each, or 360 days, is usually assumed to simplify the calculation of interest earned. Interest of $150 is earned by Stephen's Shoe Store, Inc., during November and December. This amount is equal to the $10,000 principal times the 9-percent annual interest rate times the elapsed 60 days divided by 360 days ($150 = $10,000 \times .09 \times 60/360$). The adjusting entry to recognize the asset, Interest Receivable, and the interest earned, is:

(12) Interest Receivable (A)	150	
Interest Revenue (OE)		150

Recognition of Accrued Expenses and Payables As various services are received, their cost should be reflected in the financial statements, whether or not payment has been made or an invoice received. Here, also, it is frequently not convenient to record these amounts day by day. It is likely that some adjustment of expenses and liabilities will be necessary at the end of the accounting period.

Salaries and wages earned during the last several days of the accounting period, which will not be paid until the following accounting period, illustrate this type of adjustment. According to payroll records, employees of Stephen's Shoe Store earned salaries of $6,000 during the last several days of 1982 that were not recorded at year-end. The adjusting entry is:

(13) Salaries Expense (OE)	6,000	
Salaries Payable (L)		6,000

Other examples of this type of adjusting entry include costs incurred for utilities, taxes, and interest.

Allocation of Prepaid Operating Costs Another type of adjustment arises because assets are acquired for use in the operations of the firm but are not completely used during the accounting period in which they are acquired. For example, Stephen's Shoe Store paid $1,500 on January 1, 1982, for a 3-year insurance policy.

During 1982, one-third of the coverage expired, so $500 of the premium should be reflected as insurance expense. The balance sheet on December 31, 1982, should show $1,000 of prepaid insurance among the assets, because this portion of the premium is a future benefit—the asset of insurance coverage to be received over the next 2 years.

The nature of the adjusting entry to record an asset expiration as an expense depends on the recording of the original payment. If the payment resulted in a debit to an asset account, the adjusting entry must reduce the asset and increase the expense for the services used up during the accounting period. Stephen's Shoe Store had recorded in entry (7), as discussed on page 94, the payment of the insurance premium on January 1, 1982, as follows:

(7) Prepaid Insurance (A)	1,500	
Cash (A)		1,500

The adjusting entry is, therefore:

(14) Insurance Expense (OE)	500	
Prepaid Insurance (A)		500

Insurance expense for 1982 is $500, and prepaid insurance in the amount of $1,000 is shown as an asset on the balance sheet on December 31, 1982.

Instead of debiting an asset account at the time the premium is paid, some firms debit an expense account. For example, Stephen's Shoe Store might have recorded the original premium payment as follows:

(7a) Insurance Expense (OE)	1,500	
Cash (A)		1,500

Because many operating costs become expenses in the period in which the expenditure is made (for example, monthly rent), this second procedure for recording expenditures during the year sometimes reduces the number of adjusting entries that must be made at year-end. In the situation with the insurance policy, however, not all of the $1,500 premium paid is an expense of 1982. If the original journal entry had been (7a), the adjusting entry would then be:

(14a) Prepaid Insurance (A)	1,000	
Insurance Expense (OE)		1,000

After the original entry in (7a) and the adjusting entry in (14a), insurance expense for 1982 is reflected in the accounts at $500, and prepaid insurance at $1,000. The *end result* of these two approaches to recording the original payment of the premium is the same. The *adjusting entries,* however, are quite different.

100

Recognition of Depreciation When assets such as buildings, machinery, furniture, and trucks are purchased, their acquisition cost is debited to appropriate asset accounts. Although these assets may provide services for a number of years, eventually their future benefits will expire. Therefore, the portion of an asset's cost that will expire is spread systematically over its estimated useful life. The charge made to the current operations for the portion of the cost of such assets consumed during the current period is called *depreciation.* Depreciation involves nothing new in principle; it is identical with the procedure for prepaid operating costs presented previously. For example, the cost of a building is a prepayment for a series of future services, and depreciation allocates the cost of the services to the periods in which services are received and used.

Various accounting methods are used in allocating the acquisition cost of long-lived assets to the periods of benefit. One widely used method is the *straight-line method.* Under this procedure, an equal portion of the acquisition cost less estimated salvage value is allocated to each period of the asset's estimated useful life. The depreciation charge for each period is computed as follows:

$$\frac{\text{Acquisition Cost} - \text{Estimated Salvage Value}}{\text{Estimated Useful Life in Periods}} = \frac{\text{Depreciation Charge for}}{\text{Each Period.}}$$

Internal records indicate that the Building and Equipment account of Stephen's Shoe Store comprises a store building with an acquisition cost of $400,000 and a group of items of equipment with an acquisition cost of $125,000. At the time the building was acquired, it had an estimated 40-year useful life and a zero salvage value. Depreciation expense for each year of the building's life is calculated to be

$$\frac{\$400,000 - \$0}{40 \text{ years}} = \$10,000 \text{ per year.}$$

At the time the equipment was acquired, it had an estimated useful life of 6 years and an estimated salvage value of $5,000. Annual depreciation is, therefore,

$$\frac{\$125,000 - \$5,000}{6 \text{ years}} = \$20,000 \text{ per year.}$$

The adjusting entry to record depreciation of $30,000 (= $10,000 + $20,000) for 1982 is:

(15) Depreciation Expense (OE)	30,000	
Accumulated Depreciation (XA)		30,000

101

The credit in entry (15) could have been made directly to the Building and Equipment account, because the credit records the portion of the asset's cost which has expired, or become an expense, during 1982. The same end result is achieved by crediting the Accumulated Depreciation account, a contra-asset account, and then deducting the balance in this account from the acquisition cost of the assets in the Building and Equipment account on the balance sheet. Using the contra account enables the financial statements to show both the acquisition cost of the assets in use and the portion of that amount that has previously been recognized as an expense. Showing both acquisition cost and accumulated depreciation amounts separately provides a rough indication of the relative age of the firm's long-lived assets.

Note that the Depreciation Expense account includes only depreciation for the current accounting period, while the Accumulated Depreciation account includes the cumulative depreciation charges on the present assets since acquisition. The Accumulated Depreciation account is sometimes referred to as Allowance for Depreciation.

Valuation of Accounts Receivable When sales are made to customers on account, it is usually expected that some of the accounts will not be collected. Earlier in this chapter, we indicated that the primary objective in accounting for uncollectible accounts is to ensure that sales revenue of the period reflects only the amount of cash expected to be collected. That is, adjustments for anticipated uncollectible accounts should be charged against sales revenue *in the period of the sale*. The principal accounting problem here arises from the fact that individual accounts may not be judged uncollectible until some time after the period of sale. An estimate of the probable amount of uncollectible accounts must therefore be made in the period of sale.

Based on past experience, Stephen's Shoe Store estimates that 2 percent of sales on account during the year will ultimately become uncollectible. Sales on account during 1982 were $400,000. The adjusting entry to provide for estimated uncollectible accounts of $8,000 ($= .02 \times \$400,000$) is:

(16) Sales Contra, Estimated Uncollectibles (OE)	8,000	
Allowance for Uncollectible Accounts (XA)		8,000

The debit entry is to an income statement account. Because revenue should be stated at the amount expected to be collected in cash, the amount in this account is preferably deducted from sales revenue on the income statement as a contra account. Many firms, however, debit an expense account, such as Bad Debt Expense or Uncollectible Accounts Expense, which is included in the expense section rather than the revenue section of the income statement. The effect on net income is the same in either case.

The credit entry to recognize estimated uncollectible accounts is made to a balance sheet account that is shown as a contra to Accounts Receivable. The net amount, accounts receivable less estimated uncollectibles, indicates the amount of cash expected to be collected from customers. Using the contra account permits the

102

disclosure of the total receivables outstanding, as well as the estimated amount that will be collected.

At periodic intervals, individual customers' accounts are reviewed to assess their collectibility. Accounts deemed to be uncollectible are eliminated or "written off." Stephen's Shoe Store ascertained on December 31, 1982, that specific customers' accounts totaling $7,500 would never be collected. The adjusting entry to write off these individual accounts is:

(17) Allowance for Uncollectible Accounts (XA)	7,500	
Accounts Receivable (A)		7,500

Note that net income is not affected by the write-off of the specific customers' accounts. Net income is affected in the period of sale when a provision is made for uncollectible accounts [for example, entry (16) and similar entries made in prior years]. When the $7,500 of specific customers' accounts is written off at the end of 1982, there is no effect on net income. Also note that the amount, accounts receivable less estimated uncollectibles, on the balance sheet is not affected by the write-off, because both the asset and contra asset are reduced by an equal amount. We consider further the accounting treatment of uncollectible accounts in Chapter 7.

Valuation of Liabilities When cash is received from customers before merchandise is sold or services are rendered, the cash receipt creates a liability. For example, Stephen's Shoe Store received $600 on December 1, 1982, as 1 year's rent on warehouse space. When the cash was received, the liability account, Rental Fees Received in Advance, was credited. One month's rent has been earned as of December 31, 1982. The adjusting entry is:

(18) Rental Fees Received in Advance (L)	50	
Rent Revenue (OE)		50

The remaining $550 of the advance rental is yet to be earned and is carried on the December 31, 1982, balance sheet as a liability.

Correction of Errors Various errors and omissions may be discovered at the end of the accounting period as the process of checking, reviewing, and auditing is carried out. For example, the sales for 1 month during the year might have been recorded as $38,700 instead of $37,800. Or the sale to a specific customer might not have been recorded. Entries must be made at the end of the accounting period to correct for these errors. There were no such errors in the accounts of Stephen's Shoe Store.

Trial Balance After Adjusting Entries The adjusting entries are posted or entered in the general ledger in the same manner as entries made during the year. A trial

Exhibit 3.6
Stephen's Shoe Store, Inc.
Trial Balance Before and After Adjusting Entries[a]
December 31, 1982

Accounts	Unadjusted Trial Balance		Adjusting Entries		Adjusted Trial Balance	
	Debit	Credit	Debit	Credit	Debit	Credit
Cash (A)	$ 191,100				$ 191,100	
Accounts Receivable (A)	135,000			$ 7,500 (17)	127,500	
Allowance for Uncollectible Accounts (XA)		$ 7,000	$ 7,500 (17)	8,000 (16)		$ 7,500
Notes Receivable (A)	10,000				10,000	
Interest Receivable (A)			150 (12)		150	
Merchandise Inventory (A)	140,000				140,000	
Prepaid Insurance (A)	1,500			500 (14)	1,000	
Land (A)	100,000				100,000	
Building and Equipment (A)	525,000				525,000	
Accumulated Depreciation (XA)		85,000		30,000 (15)		115,000
Accounts Payable (L)		220,000				220,000
Salaries Payable (L)				6,000 (13)		6,000
Dividends Payable (L)		15,000				15,000
Rental Fees Received in Advance (L)		600	50 (18)			550
Bonds Payable (L)		100,000				100,000
Common Stock (OE)		250,000				250,000
Additional Paid-in Capital (OE)		200,000				200,000
Retained Earnings (OE)		108,000				108,000
Sales Revenue (OE)		625,000				625,000
Interest Revenue (OE)				150 (12)		150
Rent Revenue (OE)				50 (18)		50
Cost of Goods Sold (OE)	390,000				390,000	
Salaries Expense (OE)	110,000		6,000 (13)		116,000	
Interest Expense (OE)	8,000				8,000	
Insurance Expense (OE)			500 (14)		500	
Depreciation Expense (OE)			30,000 (15)		30,000	
Sales Contra, Estimated Uncollectibles (OE)			8,000 (16)		8,000	
Totals	$1,610,600	$1,610,600	$52,200	$52,200	$1,647,250	$1,647,250

[a]This convenient tabular form is often called a *work sheet*. Most work sheets are more elaborate than this one, but their purpose is the same—to display data in a form for easy computations and financial statement preparation. The typical work sheet would not show just two final columns called Adjusted Trial Balance, but would show four columns: Income Statement Debit and Credit, and Balance Sheet Debit and Credit. The horizontal sum of the amounts in an income account is shown in the appropriate debit or credit income statement column of the work sheet. The horizontal sum of the amounts in a balance sheet account is shown in the appropriate debit or credit balance sheet column of the work sheet. See Glossary at *work sheet* for an example.

balance of the general ledger accounts after adjusting entries are made could be prepared. Such a trial balance is called an *adjusted trial balance* and is useful in preparing the financial statements. Exhibit 3.6 presents the trial balance data before and after adjusting entries for Stephen's Shoe Store. The exhibit indicates the effect of the adjustment process on the various accounts. The number in parentheses identifies the debit and credit components of each adjusting entry.

Closing of Temporary Accounts

The purpose of the closing process is to transfer the balances in the temporary revenue and expense accounts (and the Dividends Declared account, if used) to Retained Earnings. Temporary accounts with debit balances are closed by crediting each such account in an amount equal to its balance at the end of the period and debiting Retained Earnings. The usual closing entry for temporary accounts with debit balances is:

Retained Earnings (OE)	X	
Accounts with Debit Balances (OE) (specific account titles)		X

Temporary accounts with credit balances are closed by debiting the temporary account and crediting Retained Earnings. The usual closing entry for temporary accounts with credit balances is:

Accounts with Credit Balances (OE) (specific account titles)	X	
Retained Earnings (OE)		X

After closing entries, the balances in all temporary accounts are zero. The former debit (credit) balances in temporary accounts become debits (credits) in the Retained Earnings account.

Each temporary revenue and expense account could be closed by a separate entry. Some recording time is saved, however, by closing all revenue and expense accounts in a single entry as follows:

(19) Sales Revenue (OE)	625,000	
Interest Revenue (OE)	150	
Rent Revenue (OE)	50	
Cost of Goods Sold (OE)		390,000
Salaries Expense (OE)		116,000
Interest Expense (OE)		8,000
Insurance Expense (OE)		500
Depreciation Expense (OE)		30,000
Sales Contra, Estimated Uncollectibles (OE)		8,000
Retained Earnings (OE)		72,700

The amount credited to Retained Earnings is the difference between the amounts debited to revenue accounts and the amounts credited to expense and sales adjustments accounts. This amount is the net income for the period.[2]

An alternative closing procedure uses a temporary "Income Summary" account. Individual revenue and expense accounts are first closed to the Income Summary account. The income statement is prepared using information on the individual revenues and expenses in the Income Summary account. The balance in the Income Summary account, representing net income for the period, is then closed to Retained Earnings.

For example, the entry to close the Sales Revenue account under this alternative procedure is:

(19a) Sales Revenue (OE)	625,000	
Income Summary (OE)		625,000

The entry to close the Cost of Goods Sold account is:

(19b) Income Summary (OE)	390,000	
Cost of Goods Sold (OE)		390,000

Similar closing entries are made for the other revenue and expense accounts. The Income Summary account will have a credit balance of $72,700 after all revenue and expense accounts have been closed. The balance in the Income Summary account is then transferred to Retained Earnings:

(19c) Income Summary (OE)	72,700	
Retained Earnings (OE)		72,700

The end result of both closing procedures is the same. Revenue and expense accounts, as well as the Income Summary account if one is used, have zero balances after closing entries, and the Retained Earnings account is increased by the net income for the period of $72,700. Exhibit 3.7 shows the Income Summary account for Stephen's Shoe Store after all revenue and expense accounts have been closed at the end of the period.

---

[2] The amount credited to Retained Earnings in the closing entry is called a *plug*. When making some journal entries in accounting, often all debits are known, as are all but one of the credits (or vice versa). Because double-entry recording procedure requires equal debits and credits, the unknown quantity can be found by subtracting the sum of the known credits from the sum of all debits (or vice versa). This process is known as *plugging*.

Exhibit 3.7
**Illustration of Income Summary
Account for Stephen's Shoe
Store, Inc.**

Income Summary Account (OE)				Retained Earnings (OE)		
Cost of Goods Sold	390,000	625,000 Sales Revenue			123,000 Beginning Balance	
Salaries Expense	116,000	150 Interest Revenue				
Interest Expense	8,000	50 Rent Revenue	Dividends 15,000		72,700 Net Income	
Insurance Expense	500	625,200				
Depreciation Expense	30,000				180,700 Ending Balance	
Sales Contra, Estimated Uncollectibles	8,000					
To Close Income Summary Account	72,700					
	625,200					

Financial Statement Preparation

The income statement, balance sheet, and any desired supporting schedules can be prepared from information in the adjusted trial balance. The income statement of Stephen's Shoe Store for 1982 is presented in Exhibit 3.8. The comparative balance sheets for December 31, 1981 and 1982, are presented in Exhibit 3.9. An analysis of changes in retained earnings is presented in Exhibit 3.10.

Exhibit 3.8
**Stephen's Shoe Store, Inc.
Income Statement
for the Year Ending
December 31, 1982**

Revenues:

Sales Revenue	$625,000		
Less Sales Contra, Estimated Uncollectibles	8,000		
Net Sales Revenue		$617,000	
Interest Revenue		150	
Rent Revenue		50	
Total Revenues			$617,200

Less Expenses:

Cost of Goods Sold	$390,000	
Salaries Expense	116,000	
Interest Expense	8,000	
Insurance Expense	500	
Depreciation Expense	30,000	
Total Expenses		544,500
Net Income		$ 72,700

Exhibit 3.9
Stephen's Shoe Store, Inc.
Comparative Balance Sheet
December 31, 1981 and 1982

ASSETS

		December 31, 1981		December 31, 1982
Current Assets				
Cash		$ 30,000		$191,000
Accounts Receivable	$ 70,000		$127,500	
Less Allowance for				
Uncollectible Accounts	7,000		7,500	
Accounts Receivable—net		63,000		120,000
Notes Receivable		—		10,000
Interest Receivable		—		150
Merchandise Inventory		175,000		140,000
Prepaid Insurance		—		1,000
Total Current Assets		$268,000		$462,250
Property, Plant, and Equipment				
Land		$100,000		$100,000
Building and Equipment—at				
acquisition cost	$525,000		$525,000	
Less: Accumulated Depreciation	85,000		115,000	
Building and Equipment—net		440,000		410,000
Total Property, Plant, and				
Equipment		$540,000		$510,000
Total Assets		$808,000		$972,250

LIABILITIES AND SHAREHOLDERS' EQUITY

	December 31, 1981	December 31, 1982
Current Liabilities		
Accounts Payable	$135,000	$220,000
Salaries Payable	—	6,000
Dividends Payable	—	15,000
Rental Fees Received in Advance	—	550
Total Current Liabilities	$135,000	$241,550
Long-Term Debt		
Bonds Payable	100,000	100,000
Total Liabilities	$235,000	$341,550
Shareholders' Equity:		
Common Stock—at par value	$250,000	$250,000
Additional Paid-in Capital	200,000	200,000
Retained Earnings	123,000	180,700
Total Shareholders' Equity	$573,000	$630,700
Total Liabilities and Shareholders' Equity	$808,000	$972,250

Exhibit 3.10
Stephen's Shoe Store, Inc.
Analysis of Changes in
Retained Earnings
for the Year Ending
December 31, 1982

Retained Earnings, December 31, 1981		$123,000
Net Income	$72,700	
Less Dividends	15,000	
Increase in Retained Earnings		57,700
Retained Earnings, December 31, 1982		$180,700

Summary

Measurements of net income *for the period* and of financial position *at the end of the period* are closely related. Revenues result from selling goods or rendering services to customers and lead to increases in assets or decreases in liabilities. Expenses indicate that services have been used in generating revenue and result in decreases in assets or increases in liabilities. Because revenues represent provisional increases in owners' equity, revenue transactions are recorded by crediting (increasing) an owners' equity account for the specific type of revenue and by debiting either an asset or liability account. Expenses represent provisional decreases in owners' equity and are recorded by debiting (decreasing) an owners' equity account for the specific type of expense and crediting either an asset or a liability account. After the revenue and expense accounts have accumulated the revenues earned and expenses recognized during the period, the balances in these temporary accounts are transferred, or closed, to the Retained Earnings account at the end of the period.

Some events will not be recorded as part of the regular day-to-day recording process during the period because no explicit transaction between the firm and some external party (such as a customer, creditor, or governmental unit) has taken place to signal the requirement for a journal entry. Such events require an adjusting entry at the end of the period so that periodic income and financial position can be properly reported on an accrual basis.

Problem 1 for Self-Study

Harris Equipment Corporation was organized on January 2, 1982, with the issuance of 10,000 shares of $10-par value common stock for $15 cash per share. The following transactions occurred during 1982:

(1) January 2, 1982: A building costing $80,000 and equipment costing $40,000 were acquired. Cash in the amount of $60,000 was given and a 10-percent mortgage assumed for the balance of the purchase price. Interest is payable on January 2 of each year, beginning one year after the purchase.

109

(2) January 2, 1982: A 2-year fire insurance policy was taken out on the building and equipment. The insurance premium of $1,200 for the 2-year period was paid in advance (debit an asset account).

(3) During 1982: Merchandise acquired on account totaled $320,000. Payments to these suppliers during 1982 totaled $270,000.

(4) During 1982: Sales of merchandise totaled $510,000, of which $80,000 was for cash and $430,000 was on account. Collections from credit customers during 1982 totaled $360,000.

(5) During 1982: Salaries paid to employees totaled $80,000.

(6) During 1982: Utility bills totaling $1,300 were paid.

(7) November 1, 1982: A customer advanced $600 toward the purchase price of merchandise to be delivered during January 1983.

(8) November 1, 1982: A customer gave a $1,000, 9-percent, 90-day note in settlement of an open account receivable.

(9) December 1, 1982: A portion of the building was rented out for a 3-month period. The rent for the period of $900 was received in advance (credit a revenue account).

Give the journal entries to record these nine transactions during 1982. Omit explanations for the journal entries.

Suggested Solution

(1) Jan. 2, 1982	Building	80,000	
	Equipment	40,000	
	Cash		60,000
	Mortgage Payable		60,000
(2) Jan. 2, 1982	Prepaid Insurance	1,200	
	Cash		1,200
(3) During 1982	Merchandise Inventory	320,000	
	Accounts Payable		320,000
During 1982	Accounts Payable	270,000	
	Cash		270,000
(4) During 1982	Cash	80,000	
	Accounts Receivable	430,000	
	Sales Revenue		510,000
During 1982	Cash	360,000	
	Accounts Receivable		360,000
(5) During 1982	Salary Expense	80,000	
	Cash		80,000
(6) During 1982	Utilities Expense	1,300	
	Cash		1,300
(7) Nov. 1, 1982	Cash	600	
	Advances from Customers		600

110

(8) Nov. 1, 1982	Note Receivable	1,000	
	Accounts Receivable		1,000
(9) Dec. 1, 1982	Cash	900	
	Rent Revenue		900

Problem 2 for Self-Study

Refer to the data for Harris Equipment Corporation in the preceding self-study problem. Give the adjusting entries on December 31, 1982, to reflect the following items. You may omit explanations to the journal entries.

(10) The building acquired on January 2, 1982, has a 20-year estimated life and zero salvage value. The equipment has a 7-year estimated life and $5,000 salvage value. The straight-line depreciation method is used.

(11) After a physical inventory is taken at the end of the year, the cost of merchandise sold during 1982 is determined to be $180,000.

(12) Interest expense on the mortgage liability for 1982 is recognized.

(13) The company estimates that 2 percent of all sales on account will not be collected.

(14) Specific customers' accounts totaling $1,200 are written off as uncollectible.

(15) Salaries earned by employees during the last three days of December total $800 and will be paid on January 4, 1983.

(16) Interest revenue is recognized on the note receivable [see transaction **(8)** in the preceding self-study problem].

(17) An adjusting entry is made to record the proper amount of rent revenue for 1982 [see transaction **(9)** in the preceding self-study problem].

(18) Dividends of $25,000 are declared. The dividend will be paid on January 15, 1983 (debit Retained Earnings).

Suggested Solution

(10) Depreciation Expense	9,000	
Accumulated Depreciation		9,000
($80,000 − $0)/20 = $4,000; ($40,000 − $5,000)/7 = $5,000.		
(11) Cost of Goods Sold	180,000	
Merchandise Inventory		180,000
(12) Interest Expense	6,000	
Interest Payable		6,000
$60,000 × .10 = $6,000.		
(13) Sales Contra, Estimated Uncollectibles	8,600	
Allowance for Uncollectible Accounts		8,600
.02 × $430,000 = $8,600.		

111

(14) Allowance for Uncollectible Accounts	1,200	
Accounts Receivable		1,200
(15) Salary Expense	800	
Salaries Payable		800
(16) Interest Receivable	15	
Interest Revenue		15
$\$1,000 \times .09 \times 60/360.$		
(17) Rent Revenue	600	
Rental Fees Received in Advance		600
(18) Retained Earnings	25,000	
Dividends Payable		25,000

Questions and Problems

1 Review the meaning of the following concepts or terms discussed in this chapter.

a Revenue.
b Expense.
c Net income or net loss.
d Accounting period.
e Natural business year or fiscal period.
f Cash basis of accounting.
g Accrual basis of accounting.
h Unexpired costs.
i Expired costs.
j Matching convention.
k Product cost.
l Period expense.
m Expense versus dividend.
n Temporary and permanent accounts.
o General journal entries.
p Adjusting entries.
q Closing entries.
r Unadjusted trial balance.
s Adjusted trial balance.
t Contra account.

2 What factors would a firm likely consider in its decision to use the calendar year versus a fiscal year as its accounting period?

3 Which of the following types of businesses are likely to have a natural business year?
a A ski resort in Vermont.
b A professional basketball team.
c A grocery store.

4 Distinguish between a revenue and a cash receipt. Under what conditions will they be the same?

5 Distinguish between an expense and a cash expenditure. Under what conditions will they be the same?

6 "Accrual accounting focuses on the use, rather than the financing, of assets." Explain.

7 "Depreciation on equipment may be a product cost or a period expense depending on the type of equipment." Explain.

8 "Revenue and expense accounts are useful accounting devices but they could be dispensed with." What is an alternative to using them?

9 Why are revenue and expense accounts closed at the end of each accounting period?

112

10 Before the books have been closed for an accounting period, what types of accounts will have nonzero balances? After the books have been closed, what types of accounts will have nonzero balances?

11 If each transaction occurring during an accounting period has been properly recorded, why is there a need for adjusting entries at the end of the period?

12 What is the purpose of using contra accounts? What is the alternative to using them?

13 Conservatism is generally regarded as a convention in accounting. Indicate who might be hurt by conservatively stated accounting reports.

14 Under the accrual basis of accounting, cash receipts and disbursements may precede, coincide with, or follow the period in which revenues and expenses are recognized. Give an example of each of the following:
  a A cash receipt that precedes the period in which revenue is recognized.
  b A cash receipt that coincides with the period in which revenue is recognized.
  c A cash receipt that follows the period in which revenue is recognized.
  d A cash disbursement that precedes the period in which expense is recognized.
  e A cash disbursement that coincides with the period in which expense is recognized.
  f A cash disbursement that follows the period in which expense is recognized.

15 Assume that the accrual basis of accounting is used and that revenue is recognized at the time the goods are sold or services are rendered. How much revenue is recognized during the month of May in each of the following transactions?
  a Collection of cash from customers during May for merchandise sold and delivered in April, $8,200.
  b Sales of merchandise during May for cash, $9,600.
  c Sales of merchandise during May to customers to be collected in June, $2,400.
  d A store building is rented to a toy shop for $800 a month, effective May 1. A check for $1,600 for 2 months' rent is received on May 1.
  e Data in part **d**, except that collection is received from the tenant in June.

16 Indicate the amount of revenue recognized, if any, from each of the following related events, assuming that the accrual basis of accounting is used.
  a Purchase orders are received from regular customers for $8,400 of merchandise. A 2-percent discount is allowed, and generally taken, for prompt payment.
  b The customers' orders are filled and shipped by way of the company's trucking division.
  c Invoices totaling $8,400 are sent to the customers.
  d The merchandise is received by customers in the correct quantities and according to specifications.
  e Checks in the amount of $8,232 ($= .98 \times \$8,400$) are received from customers in payment of the merchandise.
  f On reinspection, several days later, merchandise with a gross invoice price of $600 is found to be defective by customers and returned for appropriate credit.

17 Indicate which of the following transactions or events immediately gives rise to the recognition of revenue under the accrual basis of accounting.
  a The receipt of an order from a customer for merchandise.
  b The shipment of goods that have been paid for in advance.

113

c The issue of additional shares of common stock.

d The completion of a batch of men's suits by a clothing factory.

e The sale of tickets by a major league baseball team for a game in two weeks.

f Same as part **e**, except that sale was made by Ticketron, a ticket broker.

g The deduction of a medical insurance premium from an employee's paycheck (from the standpoint of the employer).

h Transaction **g**, from the standpoint of the insurance company when the premium is received.

i The interest earned on a savings account between interest dates.

j A collection of cash from accounts receivable debtors.

k The rendering of accounting services to a customer on account.

18 Give the amount of expense recognized, if any, from each of the following related events, assuming that the accrual basis of accounting is used.

a The purchasing department notifies the stockroom that the supply of $\frac{1}{2}$-inch plywood has reached the minimum point and should be reordered.

b A purchase order is sent to Central Lumber Company for $10,000 of the material.

c An acknowledgment of the order is received. It indicates that delivery will be made in 15 days but that the price has been raised to $10,200.

d The shipment of plywood arrives and is checked by the receiving department. The correct quantity has been delivered.

e The purchase invoice arrives. The amount of $10,200 is subject to a 2-percent discount if paid within 10 days. Cash discounts are treated as a reduction in the acquisition cost of inventory.

f On reinspection, plywood with a gross invoice price of $200 is found to be defective and returned to the supplier.

g The balance of the amount due the Central Lumber Company is paid in time to obtain the discount.

h The plywood is sold to customers for $12,000.

19 Assume that the accrual basis of accounting is used and that revenue is recognized at the time goods are sold or services are rendered. Indicate the amount of expense recognized during March, if any, from each of the following transactions or events.

a An insurance premium of $1,800 is paid on March 1 for one year's coverage beginning on that date.

b On April 3, a utilities bill totaling $460 for services during March is received.

c $700 worth of supplies was purchased on account during March. $500 of these purchases on account was paid in March and the remainder was paid in April. On March 1, supplies were on hand that cost $300. At March 31, supplies that cost $350 were still on hand.

d Data of **c**, except that $200 of supplies was on hand at March 1.

e Property taxes of $4,800 on an office building for the year were paid in January.

f An advance of $250 on the April salary is paid to an employee on March 29.

20 In the business world, many transactions are routine and repetitive. Because accounting records business transactions, many accounting entries are also routine and repetitive. Knowing one-half of an entry in the double-entry recording system often permits a reasoned guess about the other half. The items below give the account name for one-half of an entry. Indicate your best guess as to the name of the account of the *routine* other half of

114

the entry. Also indicate whether the other account is increased or decreased by the transaction.

a Debit: Cost of Goods Sold.

b Debit: Accounts Receivable.

c Credit: Accounts Receivable.

d Debit: Accounts Payable.

e Credit: Accounts Payable.

f Credit: Accumulated Depreciation.

g Debit: Retained Earnings.

h Credit: Prepaid Insurance.

i Debit: Property Taxes Payable.

j Debit: Merchandise Inventory.

21 J. Thompson opened a hardware store on January 1, 1982. Thompson invested $10,000 and borrowed $8,000 from the local bank. The loan is repayable on June 30, 1982, with interest at the rate of 9 percent per year.

Thompson rented a building on January 1, and paid 2 months' rent in advance in the amount of $2,000. Property and liability insurance coverage for the year ending December 31, 1982, was paid on January 1 in the amount of $1,200.

Thompson purchased $28,000 of merchandise inventory on account on January 2 and paid $10,000 of this amount on January 25. The cost of merchandise on hand on January 31 was $15,000.

During January, cash sales to customers totaled $20,000 and sales on account totaled $9,000. Of the sales on account, $2,000 had been collected as of January 31.

Other costs incurred and paid in cash during January were as follows: utilities, $400; salaries, $650; taxes, $350.

a Prepare an income statement for January, assuming that Thompson uses the accrual basis of accounting with revenue recognized at the time goods are sold (delivered).

b Prepare an income statement for January, assuming that Thompson uses the cash basis of accounting.

c Which basis of accounting do you feel provides a better indication of the operating performance of the hardware store during January? Why?

22 Management Consultants, Inc., opened a consulting business on July 1, 1982. Roy Bean and Sarah Bower each contributed $7,000 cash for shares of the firm's common stock. The corporation borrowed $8,000 from a local bank on August 1, 1982. The loan is repayable on July 31, 1983, with interest at the rate of 9 percent per year.

Office space was rented on August 1, with 2 months' rent paid in advance. The remaining monthly rental fees of $900 per month were made on the first of each month, beginning October 1. Office equipment with a 4-year life was purchased for cash on August 1 for $4,800.

Consulting services rendered for clients between August 1 and December 31, 1982, were billed at $15,000. Of this amount, $9,000 was collected by year-end.

Other costs incurred and paid in cash by the end of the year were as follows: utilities, $450; salary of secretary, $7,500; supplies, $450. Unpaid bills at year-end are as follows: utilities, $80; salary of secretary, $900; supplies, $70. All supplies acquired were used.

a Prepare an income statement for the 5 months ended December 31, 1982, assuming that the corporation uses the accrual basis of accounting, with revenue recognized at the time services are rendered.

b Prepare an income statement for the 5 months ended December 31, 1982, assuming that the corporation uses the cash basis of accounting.

c Which basis of accounting do you feel provides a better indication of operating performance of the consulting firm for the period? Why?

115

23 Feltham Company acquired used machine tools costing $75,000 from various sources. These machine tools were then sold to Mock Corporation. Delivery costs paid by Feltham Company totaled $4,500. Mock Corporation had agreed to pay $100,000 cash for these tools. Finding itself short of cash, however, Mock Corporation offered $110,000 of its par-value bonds to Feltham Company. These bonds promised 8 percent interest per year. At the time the offer was made, the bonds could have been sold in public bond markets for $98,000.

Feltham Company accepted the offer and held the bonds for 3 years. During the 3 years, it received interest payments of $8,800 per year, or $26,400 total. At the end of the third year, Feltham Company sold the bonds for $95,000.

a What profit or loss did Feltham Company recognize on the sale of machine tools to Mock Corporation?

b What profit or loss would Feltham Company have recognized on the sale of machine tools if it had sold the bonds for $98,000 immediately upon receiving them?

c What profit or loss would Feltham Company have recognized on the sale of machine tools if it had held the bonds to maturity, receiving $8,800 each year for another 5 years and $110,000 at the time the bonds matured?

24 The particular time when various events and transactions are recorded in the accounts is often a matter of clerical efficiency. For each of the items below, describe the likely entry during each month and the adjusting entry at the end of each month, assuming that financial statements are prepared monthly.

a The rental on buildings and equipment of $600 is paid in advance at the beginning of each month.

b Property taxes for the calendar year of $3,600 are paid on July 1.

c Selling and office supplies, $375, are purchased once each month but used each day in small amounts.

d A firm rents out excess office space at the rate of $500 a month, payable in advance for each calendar quarter of the year.

25 Give the journal entry that should be made upon the receipt of each of the following invoices by the South Appliance Company, assuming that no previous entry has been made.

(1) From Western Electric Supply Company, $385, for repair parts purchased.

(2) From Touch & Rose, certified public accountants, $800, for services in filing income tax returns.

(3) From the General Electric Company, $12,365, for refrigerators purchased.

(4) From the White Stationery Company, $250, for office supplies purchased.

(5) From the Showy Sign Company, $540, for a neon sign acquired.

(6) From Schutheis and Schutheis, attorneys, $1,000, for legal services in changing from the corporate to the partnership form of organization.

(7) From the Bell Telephone Company, $65, for telephone service for next month.

(8) From the Madison Avenue Garage, $43, for gasoline and oil used by the delivery truck.

(9) From the Municipal Electric Department, $105, for electricity used for lighting last month.

26 The General Supply Company received a $10,000, 3-month, 9-percent promissory note, dated December 1, 1982, from Widen Stores to apply on its open accounts receivable.

a Present journal entries for the General Supply Company from December 1, 1982,

116

through collection at maturity. The books are closed quarterly. Include the closing entry.

b Present journal entries for Widen Stores from December 1, 1982, through payment at maturity. The books are closed quarterly. Include the closing entry.

27 Selected transactions of the Burlson Company are described below. Present dated journal entries for these transactions and adjusting entries at the end of each month from January 15, 1982, through July 1, 1982. Assume that only the notes indicated were outstanding during this period. The accounting period is 1 month.

(1) The company issued a $6,000, 2-month, 10-percent promissory note on January 15, 1982, in lieu of payment on an account due that date to the Grey Wholesale Company.

(2) The note in **(1)** and interest were paid at maturity.

(3) The company issued a $2,000, 3-month, 9-percent promissory note to the Grey Wholesale Company on the date of purchase of merchandise, April 1, 1982.

(4) The note in **(3)** and interest were paid at maturity.

28 On January 1, 1982, the Office Supplies Inventory account of the Harris Company had a balance of $4,200. During the ensuing quarter, supplies were acquired on account in the amount of $9,000. On March 31, 1982, the inventory was taken and calculated to amount to $2,500.

Present journal entries to record the above acquisition and adjustments at the end of March in accordance with each of the following sets of instructions, which might be established in an accounting systems manual:

a An expense account is to be debited at the time supplies are acquired.

b An asset account is to be debited at the time supplies are acquired.

29 The sales, all on account, of the Devine Company in 1982, its first year of operation, were $900,000. Collections totaled $750,000. At December 31, 1982, it was estimated that $1\frac{1}{2}$ percent of sales on account during the year would likely be uncollectible. On that date, specific accounts in the amount of $2,500 were written off.

Present journal entries for the transactions and adjustments of 1982 related to sales and customers' accounts.

30 The Florida Realty Company rents office space to Maddox Consultants at the rate of $600 per month. Collections have been made for rental through April 30, 1982. The following transactions occurred on the date indicated:

(1) May 1, 1982: Collection, $600.

(2) June 1, 1982: Collection, $1,200.

(3) August 1, 1982: Collection, $1,800.

Present journal entries for the above transactions and for adjusting and closing entries from May 1 to August 31, inclusive, as they relate to both companies, assuming that each company closes its books monthly.

31 Present journal entries for each of the following separate sets of data:

a On January 15, 1982, a $6,000, 2-month, 12-percent note was received by the company. Present adjusting entries at the end of each month and the entry for collection at maturity.

b The company uses one Merchandise Inventory account to record the beginning inventory and purchases during the period. The balance in this account on December 31,

117

1982, was $580,000. The inventory of merchandise on hand at that time was $60,000. Present the adjusting entry.

c The company rents out part of its building for office space at the rate of $900 a month, payable in advance for each calendar quarter of the year. The quarterly rental was received on February 1, 1982. Present collection and adjusting entries for the quarter. Assume that the books are closed monthly.

d The company leases branch office space at $3,000 a month. Payment is made by the company on the first of each 6-month period. Payment of $18,000 was made on July 1, 1982. Present payment and adjusting entries through August 31, 1982. Assume that the books are closed monthly.

e The balance of the Prepaid Insurance account on October 1, 1982, was $400. On December 1, 1982, the company renewed its only insurance policy for another 2 years, beginning on that date, by payment of $3,000. Present journal entries for renewal and adjusting entries through December 31, 1982. Assume that the books are closed quarterly.

f The Office Supplies on Hand account had a balance of $400 on December 31, 1982. Purchases of supplies in the amount of $580 were recorded in the Office Supplies Expense account during the month. The physical inventory of office supplies on December 31, 1982, was $340. Present any necessary adjusting entry at December 31, 1982.

g An office building was constructed at a cost of $560,000. It was estimated that it would have a useful life of 50 years from the date of occupancy, October 31, 1982, and a residual value of $80,000. Present the adjusting entry for the depreciation of the building in 1982. Assume that the books are closed annually at December 31.

h Experience indicates that 1 percent of the accounts arising from sales on account will not be collected. Sales on account during 1982 were $400,000. A list of uncollectible accounts totaling $800 as of December 31, 1982, was compiled. Present journal entries for the annual provision for uncollectible accounts and the write-off of specific customers' accounts as of December 31, 1982. The books are closed annually.

32 Give the journal entry to record each of the transactions below as well as any necessary adjusting entries on December 31, 1982, assuming that the accounting period is the calendar year and the books are closed on December 31.

a Morrissey's Department Store had sales of $600,000 during 1982. Of this total, $350,000 were for cash and $250,000 were on account. Accounts totaling $220,000 were collected. Past experience indicates that 2 percent of sales on account will probably become uncollectible. Specific accounts totaling $3,500 were found to be uncollectible during the year.

b Harrison's Supply Company received a 90-day note from a customer on December 1, 1982. The note in the face amount of $3,000 replaced an open account receivable of the same amount. The note is due with interest at 9 percent per year on March 1, 1983.

c Thompson's Wholesale Company purchased a 2-year insurance policy on September 1, 1982, paying the 2-year premium of $9,600 in advance.

d William's Products Company acquired a machine on July 1, 1982, for $20,000 cash. The machine is expected to have a $4,000 salvage value and a 4-year life.

e Greer Electronics Company acquired an automobile on September 1, 1981, for $5,000 cash. The automobile is expected to have $1,400 salvage value and a 4-year life.

f Devine Company rented out excess office space for the 3-month period beginning December 15, 1982. The first month's rent of $6,400 was received on this date.

g Prentice Products Corporation began business on November 1, 1982. It acquired office supplies costing $5,000 on account. Of this amount, $4,000 was paid by year-end. A physical inventory indicates that office supplies costing $2,400 were on hand on December 31, 1982.

33 a Machine A costs $10,000, has accumulated depreciation of $4,000 as of year-end, and is being depreciated on a straight-line basis over 10 years with an estimated salvage value of zero. How old is machine A as of year-end?

b Machine B has accumulated depreciation (straight-line basis) of $6,000 at year-end. The depreciation charge for the year is $2,000. The estimated salvage value of the machine at the end of its useful life is zero. How old is machine B as of year-end?

34 In recording the adjusting entries of the Hammond Sales Company, Inc., at the end of 1982, the following adjustments were omitted:

(1) Depreciation on the delivery truck of $3,000.

(2) Insurance expired on the delivery truck of $600.

(3) Interest accrued on notes payable of $150.

(4) Interest accrued on notes receivable of $330.

Indicate the effect (exclusive of income tax implications) of these omissions on the following items in the financial statements prepared on December 31, 1982.

a Current assets.

b Noncurrent assets.

c Current liabilities.

d Selling expenses.

e Net income.

f Retained earnings.

35 A corporation known as the Kirby Collection Agency is organized by Betty Kirby and Charles Stevens on January 1, 1982. The business of the firm is to collect overdue accounts receivable of various clients on a commission basis. The following transactions occurred during January:

(1) Kirby contributes office supplies worth $3,000 and cash of $12,000. She is issued stock certificates for 500 shares with a par value of $30 a share.

(2) Stevens contributes $3,000 in cash and office equipment valued at $9,000. He is issued stock certificates for 400 shares.

(3) The Kirby agency collects $400 on an account that was turned over to it by the Jiggly Market. The commission earned is 50 percent of the amount collected.

(4) The stenographer's salary during the month, $600, is paid.

(5) A bill is received from Lyband and Linn, certified public accountants, for $400 to cover the cost of installing a computer system.

(6) The amount due the Jiggly Market [see **(3)**] is paid.

(7) An office is leased for the year beginning February 1, 1982, and the rent for 2 months is paid in advance. A check is drawn for $900.

(8) An automobile is purchased on January 30 for $4,500; $2,500 is paid by check, and an installment contract, payable to the Scotch Automobile Sales Company, is signed for the balance.

a Open T-accounts and record the transactions during January.

b Prepare an adjusted, preclosing trial balance as of January 31, 1982. Indicate, by **"R"** or **"E,"** accounts that are revenue or expense accounts.

119

36 The balance sheet accounts of Hanover Camera Repair Shop at July 1, 1982, are as follows:

Cash	$1,920	
Repair Parts Inventory	600	
Office Supplies Inventory	80	
Equipment	2,200	
Accumulated Depreciation		$ 300
Accounts Payable		2,500
B. Greer, Capital		2,000
	$4,800	$4,800

A summary of the transactions for July is as follows:

(1) Performed repair services, for which $900 in cash was received immediately.

(2) Performed additional repair work, $200, and sent bills to customers for this amount.

(3) Paid creditors, $400.

(4) Took out insurance on equipment on July 1, and issued a check to cover 1 year's premium of $96.

(5) Paid $60 for a series of advertisements that appeared in the local newspaper during July.

(6) Issued a check for $130 for rent of shop space for July.

(7) Paid telephone bill for the month, $35.

(8) Collected $100 of the amount charged to customers in item **(2)**.

(9) The insurance expired during July is calculated at $8.

(10) Cost of repair parts used during the month, $180.

(11) Cost of office supplies used during July, $40.

(12) Depreciation of equipment for the month is $30.

a Open T-accounts and insert the July 1 balances. Record the transactions for the month in the T-accounts, opening additional T-accounts for individual revenue and expense accounts as needed.

b Prepare an adjusted, preclosing trial balance at July 31, 1982.

c Enter closing entries in the T-accounts using an Income Summary account.

d Prepare an income statement for the month of July and a balance sheet as of July 31, 1982.

37 The trial balance of Jones Shoe Repair Shop at February 28, 1982, is shown below. The books have not been closed since December 31, 1981.

Cash	$ 5,920	
Accounts Receivable	15,200	
Supplies Inventory	4,800	
Prepaid Insurance	1,040	
Equipment	65,000	
Accumulated Depreciation		$ 10,600
Accounts Payable		6,980
W. R. Jones, Capital		62,360
Sales		46,060

Salaries and Wages Expense	26,600	
Cost of Outside Work	2,040	
Advertising Expense	900	
Rent Expense	1,200	
Power, Gas, and Water Expense	880	
Supplies Used	—	
Depreciation Expense	—	
Miscellaneous Expense	2,420	
	$126,000	$126,000

A summary of the transactions for the month of March 1982 is as follows:

(1) Sales: for cash, $26,000; on account, $17,600.

(2) Collections on account, $22,000.

(3) Purchases of outside work (repair work done by another shoe repair shop for Jones), $1,600, on account.

(4) Purchases of supplies, on account, $2,800.

(5) Payments on account, $6,000.

(6) March rent paid, $1,200.

(7) Supplies used (for the quarter), $4,960.

(8) Depreciation (for the quarter), $3,820.

(9) March salaries and wages of $13,290 are paid.

(10) Bills received but not recorded or paid by the end of the month: advertising, $300; power, gas, and water, $620.

(11) Insurance expired (for the quarter), $300.

a Open T-accounts and enter the trial balance amounts.

b Record the transactions for the month of March in the T-accounts, opening additional T-accounts as needed. Cross-number the entries.

c Enter closing entries in the T-accounts using an Income Summary account.

d Prepare an adjusted, preclosing trial balance at March 31, 1982, an income statement for the 3 months ending March 31, 1982, and a balance sheet as of March 31, 1982.

38 The trial balance of Cunningham's Hardware Store on September 30, 1982, is as follows:

Cash	$ 88,400	
Accounts Receivable	54,500	
Merchandise Inventory	136,300	
Prepaid Insurance	800	
Equipment	420,000	
Allowance for Uncollectible Accounts		$ 6,500
Accumulated Depreciation		166,000
Accounts Payable		68,200
Note Payable		10,000
Salaries Payable		2,500
Capital Stock		300,000
Retained Earnings		146,800
Total	$700,000	$700,000

Transactions during October and additional information are as follows:

(1) Sales, all on account, total $170,000.

(2) Merchandise inventory purchased on account from various suppliers is $92,600.

(3) Rent for the month of October of $23,500 is paid.

(4) Salaries paid to employees during October are $41,200.

(5) Accounts receivable of $68,300 are collected.

(6) Accounts payable of $77,900 are paid.

(7) Miscellaneous expenses of $6,400 are paid in cash.

(8) The premium on a 1-year insurance policy was paid on June 1, 1982.

(9) Equipment is depreciated over a 10-year life. Estimated salvage value of the equipment is considered to be negligible.

(10) Employee salaries earned during the last two days of October but not paid are $3,200.

(11) Based on past experience, the firm estimates that 1 percent of all sales on account will become uncollectible.

(12) Specific customers' accounts of $2,700 are determined to be uncollectible.

(13) The note payable is a 90-day, 12-percent note issued on September 30, 1982.

(14) Merchandise inventory on hand on October 31, 1982, totals $155,900.

a Prepare general journal entries to reflect the transactions and other events during October. Indicate whether each entry records a transaction during the month **(T)** or is an adjusting entry at the end of the month **(A)**.

b Set up T-accounts and enter the opening balances in the accounts on September 30, 1982. Record the entries from part **a** in the T-accounts, creating additional accounts as required.

c Prepare an adjusted, preclosing trial balance as of October 31, 1982.

d Prepare an income statement for the month of October.

e Enter the appropriate closing entries at the end of October in the T-accounts, assuming that the books are closed each month. Use an Income Summary account.

f Prepare a balance sheet as of October 31, 1982.

39 The following unadjusted trial balance is taken from the books of the Kathleen Clothing Company at July 31, 1982. The company closes its books monthly.

Accounts Payable		$ 12,952
Accounts Receivable	$ 18,257	
Accumulated Depreciation		8,240
Advances by Customers		540
Allowance for Uncollectible Accounts		1,200
Capital Stock		40,000
Cash	9,000	
Equipment	2,640	
Depreciation Expense	—	—
Dividends Payable	—	—
Furniture and Fixtures	12,000	
Income Tax Expense		—
Income Tax Payable		3,500
Insurance Expense	—	—
Leasehold	10,800	
Merchandise Cost of Goods Sold	—	—

122

Merchandise Inventory	49,500	
Miscellaneous Expense	188	
Prepaid Insurance	450	
Rent Expense	—	—
Retained Earnings		13,068
Salaries and Commissions Expense	2,020	
Salaries and Commissions Payable		500
Sales		25,000
Sales Contra, Estimated Uncollectibles	—	—
Supplies Inventory	145	
	$105,000	$105,000

Additional data:

(1) Depreciation on equipment is to be calculated at 10 percent of cost per year (assume zero salvage value).

(2) Depreciation on furniture and fixtures is to be calculated at 20 percent of cost per year (assume zero salvage value).

(3) The leasehold represents long-term rent paid in advance by Kathleen. The monthly rental charge is $600.

(4) One invoice of $420 for the purchase of merchandise from the Peoria Company on account was recorded during the month as $240. The account has not yet been paid.

(5) Commissions unpaid at July 31, 1982, are $340. All salaries have been paid. The balance in the Salaries and Commissions Payable account represents the amount of commissions unpaid at July 1.

(6) Merchandise with a sales price of $350 was recently delivered to a customer, and charged to Accounts Receivable, although the customer had paid $350 in advance.

(7) The estimated uncollectible account rate is 1 percent of the charge sales of the month. Charge sales were 70 percent of the sales of the month.

(8) An analysis of outstanding customers' accounts indicates that two accounts totaling $210 should be written off as uncollectible.

(9) The balance in the Prepaid Insurance account relates to a 3-year policy that went into effect on January 1, 1982.

(10) A dividend of $3,000 was declared on July 31, 1982.

(11) The inventory of merchandise on July 31, 1982, was $33,600.

Present adjusting journal entries at July 31, 1982. Use only the accounts listed in the trial balance.

40 The adjusted trial balance of Life Photographers, Inc., at June 30, 1982, is as follows:

Exhibit 3.11
Life Photographers, Inc. Adjusted Trial Balance
June 30, 1982

Accounts Payable		$ 3,636
Accounts Receivable	$ 3,900	
Accumulated Depreciation		2,000
Advertising Expense	1,500	
Cameras and Equipment	15,500	

Exhibit 3.11 *(Continued)*

Cash	2,994	
Common Stock		10,000
Depreciation Expense—Cameras and Equipment	180	
Depreciation Expense—Furniture and Fixtures	105	
Electricity Expense	300	
Equipment Repairs Expense	180	
Furniture and Fixtures	9,600	
Insurance Expense	330	
Photographic Supplies Expense	1,950	
Photographic Supplies on Hand	3,390	
Prepaid Insurance	270	
Rent Expense	1,425	
Retained Earnings		14,138
Revenue—Commercial Photography		18,090
Revenue—Printing Service		4,680
Salaries Expense	10,800	
Telephone Expense	120	
	$52,544	$52,544

a Present the journal entries to close the revenue and expense accounts directly to Retained Earnings as of June 30, 1982.

b Set up in T-account form the revenue, expense, and retained earnings accounts. Insert the trial balance amounts and record the closing entries from part **a**.

41 (Problems 41 through 43 are adapted from problems by George H. Sorter.) The following data relate to the Prima Company:

(1) Postclosing trial balance at December 31, 1982:

DEBITS

Cash	$ 10,000
Marketable Securities	20,000
Accounts Receivable	25,000
Merchandise Inventory	30,000
Prepayments for Miscellaneous Services	3,000
Land, Buildings, and Equipment	40,000
Total Debits	$128,000

CREDITS

Accounts Payable (for merchandise)	$ 25,000
Interest Payable	300
Taxes Payable	4,000
Notes Payable (6 percent, long-term)	20,000
Accumulated Depreciation	16,000
Capital Stock	50,000
Retained Earnings	12,700
Total Credits	$128,000

(2) Income and retained earnings data for 1982:

Sales		$200,000
Less Expenses:		
Cost of Goods Sold	$130,000	
Depreciation Expense	3,000	
Taxes Expense	8,000	
Other Operating Expenses	48,700	
Interest Expense	1,200	
Total Expenses		190,900
Net Income		$ 9,100
Less Dividends		5,000
Increase in Retained Earnings		$ 4,100

(3) Summary of cash receipts and disbursements in 1982:

Cash Receipts

Cash Sales	$ 47,000	
Collection from Credit Customers	150,000	
Total Receipts		$197,000

Cash Disbursements

Payment to Suppliers of Merchandise	$128,000	
Payment to Suppliers of Miscellaneous Services	49,000	
Payment of Taxes	7,500	
Payment of Interest	1,200	
Payment of Dividends	5,000	
Purchase of Marketable Securities	8,000	
Total Disbursements		198,700

Excess of Disbursements over Receipts .... $ 1,700

(4) Purchases of merchandise during the period, all on account, were $127,000. All "Other Operating Expenses" were credited to Prepayments.

Prepare a balance sheet for January 1, 1982. (Hint: Set up T-accounts for each of the accounts in the trial balance and enter the *ending* balances in the T-accounts. Starting with information from the income statement and statement of cash receipts and disbursements, reconstruct the transactions that took place during the year and enter the amounts in the appropriate T-accounts.)

42 The Secunda Company's trial balance at the beginning of 1982 and the adjusted, preclosing trial balance at the end of 1982 appear on the next page.

All goods and services acquired during the year were purchased on account. The Other Operating Expenses account includes depreciation charges and expirations of prepayments. Dividends declared during the year were debited to Retained Earnings.

Prepare a schedule showing all cash transactions for the year 1982. (Hint: Set up T-accounts for each of the accounts listed in the trial balance and enter the amounts shown

DEBITS	1/1/82	12/31/82
Cash	$ 20,000	$ 9,000
Accounts Receivable	36,000	51,000
Merchandise Inventory	45,000	60,000
Prepayments	2,000	1,000
Land, Buildings, and Equipment	40,000	40,000
Cost of Goods Sold	—	50,000
Interest Expense	—	3,000
Other Operating Expenses	—	29,000
Total Debits	$143,000	$243,000
CREDITS		
Accumulated Depreciation	$ 16,000	$ 18,000
Interest Payable	1,000	2,000
Accounts Payable	30,000	40,000
Mortgage Payable	20,000	17,000
Capital Stock	50,000	50,000
Retained Earnings	26,000	16,000
Sales	—	100,000
Total Credits	$143,000	$243,000

as of January 1, 1982, and December 31, 1982. Starting with the entries in revenue and expense accounts, reconstruct the transactions which took place during the year and enter the amounts in the appropriate T-accounts. The effect of earnings activities is not yet reflected in the Retained Earnings account because the trial balance is pre-closing.)

43 Tertia Company presents the following incomplete post-closing trial balances, as well as a statement of cash receipts and disbursements:

DEBITS	1/1/82	12/31/82
Cash	$?	$?
Accounts and Notes Receivable	36,000	41,000
Merchandise Inventory	55,000	49,500
Interest Receivable	1,000	700
Prepaid Miscellaneous Services	4,000	5,200
Building, Machinery, and Equipment	47,000	47,000
Total Debits	$?	$?
CREDITS		
Accounts Payable (miscellaneous services)	$ 2,000	$ 2,500
Accounts Payable (merchandise)	34,000	41,000
Property Taxes Payable	1,000	1,500
Accumulated Depreciation	10,000	12,000
Mortgage Payable	35,000	30,000
Capital Stock	25,000	25,000
Retained Earnings	76,000	?
Total Credits	$183,000	$211,200

126

Cash Receipts	Year of 1982
1 Collection from Credit Customers	$144,000
2 Cash Sales	63,000
3 Collection of Interest	1,000
	$208,000

Less: Cash Disbursements	
4 Payment to Suppliers of Merchandise	$114,000
5 Repayment on Mortgage	5,000
6 Payment of Interest	500
7 Payment to Suppliers of Miscellaneous Services	57,500
8 Payment of Property Taxes	1,200
9 Payment of Dividends	2,000
	$180,200
Increase in Cash Balance for Year	$ 27,800

Prepare a combined statement of income and retained earnings for the year 1982. (Hint: Set up T-accounts for each of the balance sheet accounts listed in the trial balance and enter the amounts shown as of January 1, 1982, and December 31, 1982. Starting with the cash receipts and disbursements for the year, reconstruct the transactions that took place during the year and enter them in the appropriate T-accounts. The effect of earnings activities for the year is already reflected in the Retained Earnings account, because the trial balance shown is post closing.)

44 Refer to the Consolidated Statements of Income and Retained Earnings and the Consolidated Balance Sheet for General Products Company in Appendix A at the back of the book. Respond to each of the following questions. Be sure to show supporting computations for your responses.

a Assume that marketable securities with a cost of $95.6 million were sold during 1982. Compute the acquisition cost of marketable securities purchased during the year.

b Assuming that all sales during 1982 were made on account and that $44 million of accounts receivable were written off as uncollectible during 1982, calculate the amount of cash collections from customers during the year.

c Refer to the assumptions made in part **b**. Calculate the provision for estimated uncollectible accounts during 1982.

d Compute the amount of dividends paid in cash during 1982.

e Prepare a common-size (see Glossary) income statement for each of the years 1980, 1981, and 1982 in which each income statement account is expressed as a percentage of sales revenue (that is, sales revenue equals 100%). What changes in the profitability of General Products Company can be observed over this 3-year period?

127

Chapter 4   *Income Statement—Extensions of the Accrual Concept*

Chapter 3 points out that most business firms use an accrual, rather than a cash, basis of accounting. The two distinguishing features of the accrual basis are:

1 Revenue is recognized when all, or a substantial portion, of the services to be provided have been performed and cash, a receivable, or some other asset susceptible to reasonably precise measurement, has been received.
2 Expenses are recognized in the period when related revenues are recognized or, if an association with a particular revenue stream is not evident, expenses are recognized in the period when goods or services are consumed in operations.

For most merchandising firms, revenue is recognized in the period when goods are sold. Expenses are then matched either directly with the revenue or with the period when goods or services are consumed. This chapter explores the application of the accrual concept to other types of businesses. Particular attention is given to firms involved in manufacturing, to firms involved in long-term contract activities, and to firms selling goods on an installment basis.

Accrual Basis for Manufacturers

A manufacturing firm incurs various costs in changing the physical form of the goods it produces. The earnings process for a typical manufacturing firm is depicted in Figure 4.1. Productive facilities (plant and equipment) are acquired to provide a firm with a capacity to manufacture goods. Raw materials for use in production are also acquired. During the period of production, labor and other manufacturing serv-

128

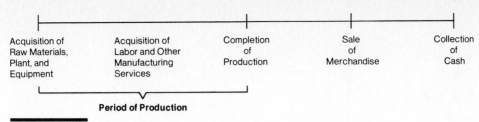

Figure 4.1
Earnings Process for Manufacturing Firm

ices (for example, utilities, insurance, taxes, and depreciation on production facilities) are used in converting the raw materials into a salable product. The finished product is held in inventory until sold. When the good is sold, either cash is collected or a receivable from the customer arises.

Most manufacturing firms recognize revenue at the time goods are sold. At this time, the production activity has been completed, a customer has been identified and a selling price agreed upon, and an assessment of the customer's credit standing provides a reasonable basis for estimating the amount of cash that will be collected.

Accounting for Manufacturing Costs

As Chapter 3 points out, a merchandising firm acquires inventory items in finished form ready for sale. The acquisition cost of these items remains in the asset account, Merchandise Inventory, until the units are sold. At the time of sale, the cost of the items sold is transferred from the asset account, Merchandise Inventory, to the expense account, Cost of Goods Sold.

A manufacturing firm, on the other hand, incurs various costs in transforming raw materials into finished products. These manufacturing costs are generally classified into direct material (or raw material), direct labor, and manufacturing overhead. Manufacturing overhead includes a variety of indirect costs that provide a firm with productive capacity (depreciation, insurance, and taxes on manufacturing facilities, supervisory labor, and supplies for factory equipment). Until the units are sold and revenue is recognized, manufacturing costs are treated as product costs—assets—and accumulated in various inventory accounts.

A manufacturing firm, like a merchandising firm, also incurs various selling costs (commissions for the sales staff, depreciation, insurance and taxes on the sales staff's automobiles) and administrative costs (salary of president, depreciation on computer facilities). Selling and administrative costs are treated as period expenses by both merchandising and manufacturing firms. Figures 4.2 and 4.3 summarize the nature and flow of various costs for a manufacturing firm.

Separate inventory accounts are maintained by a manufacturing firm for product costs incurred at various stages of completion. The Raw Materials Inventory account includes the cost of raw materials purchased but not yet transferred to production. The balance in the Raw Materials Inventory account indicates the cost of raw mate-

129

Figure 4.2
Flow of Manufacturing Costs through the Accounts

Raw Materials Inventory (A)

Cost of Raw Materials Purchased | Raw Materials Costs Incurred in Manufacturing

Cash (A) or Wages Payable (L)

| Direct Labor Costs Incurred in Manufacturing

Cash (A), Accumulated Depreciation (XA), Other Accounts

| Overhead Costs Incurred in Manufacturing

Work-in-Process Inventory (A)

Raw Materials → Costs Incurred in Manufacturing

Direct Labor → Costs Incurred in Manufacturing

Overhead Costs → Incurred in Manufacturing

| Manufacturing Cost of Units Completed and Transferred to Storeroom

Finished Goods Inventory (A)

Manufacturing → Cost of Units Transferred from Factory

| Manufacturing Cost of Units Sold

Cost of Goods Sold (OE)

Manufacturing → Cost of Units Sold

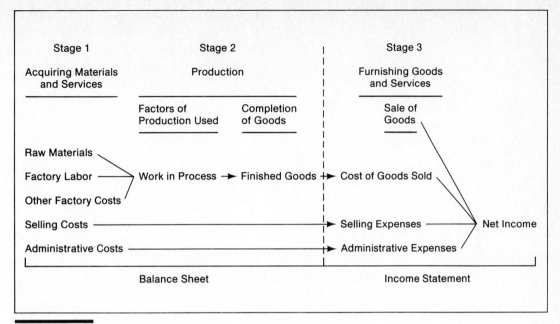

Figure 4.3
Diagram of Cost Flows

rials on hand in the raw materials storeroom or warehouse. When raw materials are issued to producing departments, the cost of the materials is transferred from the Raw Materials Inventory account to the Work-in-Process Inventory account. The Work-in-Process Inventory account accumulates the costs incurred in producing units during the period. The Work-in-Process Inventory account is debited for the cost of raw materials transferred from the raw materials storeroom, the cost of direct labor services used, and the manufacturing overhead costs incurred. The Work-in-Process Inventory account is credited for the total manufacturing cost of units completed in the factory and transferred to the finished goods storeroom. The Finished Goods Inventory account includes the total manufacturing cost of units completed but not yet sold. The cost of units sold during the period is transferred from the Finished Goods Inventory account to the Cost-of-Goods-Sold account.

Illustration of the Accounting Process for a Manufacturing Firm

The accounting process for a manufacturing firm is illustrated with information about the operations of the Moon Manufacturing Company. The Company was formed on December 31, 1981, with the issuance of 10,000 shares of $10-par value common stock for $30 per share. The firm began business on January 1, 1982. Transactions during January 1982 are described below, and the appropriate journal entries are provided:

1 A building costing $200,000 and equipment costing $50,000 are acquired for cash.

(1) Building (A)	200,000	
Equipment (A)	50,000	
Cash (A)		250,000

2 Raw materials costing $25,000 are purchased on account.

(2) Raw Materials Inventory (A)	25,000	
Accounts Payable (L)		25,000

3 Raw materials costing $20,000 are issued to producing departments.

(3) Work-in-Process Inventory (A)	20,000	
Raw Materials Inventory (A)		20,000

4 The total payroll for January is $60,000. Of this amount, $40,000 is paid to factory workers, and $20,000 is paid to selling and administrative personnel.

(4) Work-in-Process Inventory (A)	40,000	
Salaries Expense (OE)	20,000	
Cash (A)		60,000

Recall that nonmanufacturing costs are recorded as expenses of the period in which the services are consumed, because these costs rarely create assets with future benefits. Journal entry (4) illustrates the difference between the recording of a product cost and a period expense.

5 The expenditures for utilities during January are $1,200. Of this amount, $1,000 is attributable to manufacturing, and $200 to selling and administrative activities.

(5) Work-in-Process Inventory (A)	1,000	
Utilities Expense (OE)	200	
Cash (A)		1,200

6 Depreciation on building and equipment during January is as follows: factory, $8,000; selling and administrative, $2,000.

(6) Work-in-Process Inventory (A)	8,000	
Depreciation Expense (OE)	2,000	
Accumulated Depreciation (XA)		10,000

7 The manufacturing cost of units completed during January and transferred to the finished goods storeroom is $48,500.

| (7) Finished Goods Inventory (A) | 48,500 | |
| Work-in-Process Inventory (A) | | 48,500 |

8 Sales during January total $75,000, of which $25,000 is on account.

(8) Cash (A)	50,000	
Accounts Receivable (A)	25,000	
Sales Revenue (OE)		75,000

9 The manufacturing cost of the goods sold during January is $42,600.

| (9) Cost of Goods Sold (OE) | 42,600 | |
| Finished Goods Inventory (A) | | 42,600 |

The manner in which the various costs incurred flow through the accounts may be further illustrated by entering these journal entries in T-accounts as shown in Exhibit 4.1.

Exhibit 4.1
**Moon Manufacturing Company
T-Accounts Showing Transactions
during January 1982**

Raw Materials Inventory (A)			Work-in-Process Inventory (A)	
(2) 25,000	20,000 (3)		(3) 20,000	48,500 (7)
			(4) 40,000	
			(5) 1,000	
			(6) 8,000	
Bal. 1/31 5,000			Bal. 1/31 20,500	

Finished Goods Inventory (A)			Cost of Goods Sold (OE)	
(7) 48,500	42,600 (9)		(9) 42,600	
Bal. 1/31 5,900			Bal. 1/31 42,600	

Cash (A)

Bal. 1/1	300,000	250,000	(1)
(8)	50,000	60,000	(4)
		1,200	(5)
Bal. 1/31	38,800		

Accounts Receivable (A)

(8)	25,000	
Bal. 1/31	25,000	

Building (A)

(1) 200,000		
Bal. 1/31	200,000	

Equipment (A)

(1)	50,000	
Bal. 1/31	50,000	

Accumulated Depreciation (XA)

	10,000	(6)	
	10,000	Bal. 1/31	

Salaries Expense (OE)

(4)	20,000	
Bal. 1/31	20,000	

Sales Revenue (OE)

	75,000	(8)
	75,000	Bal. 1/31

Accounts Payable (L)

	25,000	(2)
	25,000	Bal. 1/31

Utilities Expense (OE)

(5)	200	
Bal. 1/31	200	

Depreciation Expense (OE)

(6)	2,000	
Bal. 1/31	2,000	

Exhibit 4.2 presents an income statement for Moon Manufacturing Company for January 1982.

Exhibit 4.2
**Moon Manufacturing Company
Income Statement
for the Month of January 1982**

Sales Revenue		$75,000
Less Expenses:		
Cost of Goods Sold	$42,600	
Salaries Expense	20,000	
Utilities Expense	200	
Depreciation Expense	2,000	
Total Expenses		64,800
Net Income		$10,200

Summary of the Accounting
for Manufacturing Operations

The accounting procedures for the selling and administrative costs of manufacturing firms are similar to those for merchandising firms. These costs are treated as expenses of the period in which services are consumed. The accounting procedures for a manufacturing firm differ from those of a merchandising firm primarily in the treatment of inventories. A manufacturing firm incurs various costs in transforming raw materials into finished products. Until the units produced are sold, manufacturing costs are accumulated in inventory accounts—the Work-in-Process Inventory account or the Finished Goods Inventory account—depending on the stage of completion of each unit being produced. Product costs are therefore debited to inventory (asset) accounts until the time of sale.

Accrual Basis for Long-Term Contractors

The earnings process for a long-term contractor (for example, building construction, ship-building) differs from that of a manufacturing firm (depicted in Figure 4.1) in three important respects:

1 The period of construction (production) may span several accounting periods.
2 A customer is identified and a contract price agreed upon in advance (or at least in the early stages of construction).
3 Periodic payments of the contract price are often made by the buyer as work progresses.

Revenue from these long-term contracts is often recognized during the period of construction. The existence of a contract indicates that a buyer has been identified and a price agreed upon. Either cash is collected in advance or an assessment of the customer's credit standing leads to a reasonable expectation that the contract price will be received in cash after construction is completed. Although future services required on these long-term construction contracts can be substantial at any given time, the costs to be incurred in providing these services can often be estimated with reasonable precision. In agreeing to a contract price, the firm must have some confidence in its estimates of the total costs to be incurred on the contract. Construction activities are, therefore, the critical revenue-generating events.

Revenue is often recognized by these contractors using the *percentage-of-completion method.* A portion of the total contract price, based on the degree of completion of the work, is recognized as revenue each period. This proportion is based either on engineers' or architects' estimates of the degree of completion or the ratio of costs incurred to date to the total expected costs for the contract. The actual schedule of cash collections is *not* significant for the revenue recognition process when the percentage-of-completion method is used. Even if all of the contract price is collected at completion of construction, the percentage-of-completion method may still be used as long as reasonable estimates of the amount of cash to be collected and of the costs remaining to be incurred can be made as construction progresses.

As portions of the contract price are recognized as revenues, corresponding proportions of the total estimated costs of the contract are recognized as expenses. Thus, the percentage-of-completion method is an accrual basis of accounting, because expenses are matched with related revenues.

Some firms involved with construction contracts postpone the recognition of revenue until the construction project and the sale are completed. This method is the same as the completed-sale basis, but is often referred to as the *completed-contract method* of recognizing revenue. In some cases, the completed-contract method is used because the contracts are of such short duration (such as 3 or 6 months) that earnings reported with the percentage-of-completion method and the completed-contract method are not significantly different. In these cases, the completed-contract method is used because it is generally easier to implement. Some firms use the completed-contract method in situations when a specific buyer has not been obtained during the periods while construction is progressing, as is sometimes the case in constructing residential housing. In these cases, future selling efforts are required and substantial uncertainty may exist regarding the contract price ultimately to be established and the amount of cash to be received.

The primary reason for a contractor's not using the percentage-of-completion method when a contract exists is the uncertainty of total costs to be incurred in carrying out the project. If total costs cannot be reasonably estimated, the percentage of total costs incurred by a given date also cannot be estimated, and the percentage of services already rendered (revenue) cannot be determined.

Accrual Basis When Cash Collectibility Is Extremely Uncertain

Occasionally, estimating the amount of cash or other assets that will be received from customers is difficult. This may occur because the future financial condition of the buyer is highly uncertain or because the payments are spread over so long a time that assessing future uncertainties is difficult. Therefore, an objective measure of the present value of the services rendered and the benefits to be received cannot be made at the time of the sale. Under these circumstances, revenue is recognized at the time of cash collection. But, unlike the cash method of accounting, there is an attempt to match expenses with revenues.

Installment Method

The recognition of revenue at the time of cash collection is sometimes followed by land development companies. These companies typically sell undeveloped land and promise to develop it over several future years. The buyer makes a nominal down payment and agrees to pay the remainder of the purchase price in installments over 10, 20, or more years. In these cases, future development of the land is a significant aspect of the earnings process. Also, substantial uncertainty often exists as to the ultimate collectibility of the installment notes, particularly those not due until several years in the future. The customer can always elect to stop making payments, merely losing the right to own the land.

Under these circumstances, the critical revenue-generating event is the collection

136

of cash. In such cases, the firm may use the *installment method*. In the installment method, revenue is recognized as the periodic cash collections are received, and costs incurred in generating the revenue are matched as closely as possible with the revenue. (For example, if 40 percent of the purchase price is collected, then 40 percent of the cost of the land is recognized as an expense.) The installment method is similar to the cash basis of accounting, in that revenue is recognized as cash is received. In the installment method, however, an effort is made to match expenses with associated revenues.

Cost-Recovery-First Method

Under circumstances where there is such great uncertainty about cash collection, the *cost-recovery-first method* of income recognition can also be used. (It is, in our opinion, preferable under these circumstances.) Under this method, costs of generating revenues are matched dollar for dollar with cash receipts until all such costs are recovered. Revenues and total expenses are equal in each period until all costs are recovered. Only when cumulative cash receipts exceed total costs will profit (that is, revenue without any matching expenses) be shown in the income statement.

Use of Installment and Cost-Recovery-First Methods

The installment method and the cost-recovery-first method are permitted under generally accepted accounting principles when great uncertainty exists about cash collection. For most sales of goods and services, past experience and an assessment of customers' credit standings provide a sufficient basis for estimating the amount of cash to be received. If a reasonable estimate of the amount of cash to be received can be made, the installment method and the cost-recovery-first method are not allowed for financial reporting and revenue must be recognized no later than the time of sale.[1]

The installment method is allowable for income tax reporting under certain circumstances, even when cash collections are assured. Retailers and other firms selling on extended payment plans often use the installment method for income tax reporting (while recognizing revenue at the time of sale for financial reporting). The cost-recovery-first method is not permitted for income tax reporting.

Recognition of Revenue between Purchase and Sale

The period between the acquisition, or production, and the sale of merchandise and other salable goods is referred to as a *holding period*. The current market prices of these assets could change during this holding period. Such changes are described as *unrealized holding gains and losses*, because a transaction or exchange has not taken place.

Unrealized holding gains could be recognized as they occur. Accountants typically wait, however, until the asset is sold or exchanged in an arm's length transaction before recognizing any gain. At that time, an inflow of net assets subject to objective measurement is presumed to have taken place. Because the accountant

---

[1]Accounting Principles Board, *Opinion No. 10*, "Omnibus Opinion-1966," 1966, par. 12, footnote 8.

assumes that the firm is a going concern, the unrealized gain will eventually be recognized as revenue in the ordinary course of business in a future period. The recognition of revenue and the valuation of assets are therefore closely associated. Nonmonetary assets are typically stated at acquisition cost until sold. At the time of sale, an inflow of net assets occurs (for example, cash, accounts receivable), and revenue reflecting the previously unreported unrealized gain is recognized. This treatment of unrealized holding gains has the effect of shifting income from periods when the asset is held and the market price increases to the later period of sale. The longer the holding period (as, for example, land held for several decades), the more is reported income likely to be shifted to later periods.

Current accounting practices do not treat all unrealized holding losses in the same way as unrealized holding gains. If the current market prices of inventory items or marketable securities decrease below acquisition cost during the holding period, the asset is usually written down. As a result, the unrealized loss is recognized in the period of price decline. This treatment of losses rests on the convention that earnings should be reported conservatively. Considering the estimates and predictions required in measuring revenues and expenses, some accountants feel it is desirable to provide a conservative measure of earnings so statement users will not be misled into thinking the firm is doing better than it really is.

The inconsistent treatment of unrealized gains and unrealized losses does not seem warranted. The arguments used against recognizing unrealized gains apply equally well to unrealized losses. If gains cannot be determined objectively prior to sale, then how can losses be measured prior to sale? If losses can be measured objectively prior to sale, then why cannot gains? We consider the accounting treatment of unrealized holding gains and losses further in Chapters 7, 8, and 13.

Summary Illustration of Income Recognition Methods

Exhibit 4.3 illustrates various methods of income recognition. The illustration relates to a contract for the construction of a bridge for $12 million. The expected and actual pattern of cash receipts and disbursements under the contract is as follows:

Period	Expected and Actual Cash Receipts	Expected and Actual Cash Expenditures
1	$ 1,000,000	$1,600,000
2	1,000,000	4,000,000
3	2,000,000	4,000,000
4	4,000,000	—
5	4,000,000	—
Total	$12,000,000	$9,600,000

The bridge was completed in period 3. Exhibit 4.3 indicates the revenues, expenses, and income recognized each period under the contract using the cash method, the percentage-of-completion method, the completed-contract (completed-sale) method,

138

Exhibit 4.3
Comprehensive Illustration of
Revenue and Expense Recognition
(All Dollar Amounts in Thousands)

Period		Cash Basis of Accounting[a]		
		Revenue	Expense	Income
1		$ 1,000	$1,600	$ (600)
2		1,000	4,000	(3,000)
3		2,000	4,000	(2,000)
4		4,000	—	4,000
5		4,000	—	4,000
Total		$12,000	$9,600	$2,400

Period	Percentage-of-Completion Method			Completed-Contract Method		
	Revenue	Expense	Income	Revenue	Expense	Income
1	$ 2,000[d]	$1,600	$ 400	$ —	$ —	$ —
2	5,000[e]	4,000	1,000	—	—	—
3	5,000[e]	4,000	1,000	12,000	9,600	2,400
4	—	—	—	—	—	—
5	—	—	—	—	—	—
Total	$12,000	$9,600	$2,400	$12,000	$9,600	$2,400

Period	Installment Method[b]			Cost-Recovery-First Method[c]		
	Revenue	Expense	Income	Revenue	Expense	Income
1	$ 1,000	$ 800[f]	$ 200	$ 1,000	$1,000	$ 0
2	1,000	800[f]	200	1,000	1,000	0
3	2,000	1,600[g]	400	2,000	2,000	0
4	4,000	3,200[h]	800	4,000	4,000	0
5	4,000	3,200[h]	800	4,000	1,600	2,400
Total	$12,000	$9,600	$2,400	$12,000	$9,600	$2,400

[a]The cash basis is not allowed for tax or financial reporting if inventories are a material factor in generating income.
[b]The installment method is allowed for financial reporting only if extreme uncertainty exists as to the amount of cash to be collected from customers. Its use for tax purposes is not affected by the collectibility of cash.
[c]The cost-recovery-first method is allowed for financial reporting only if extreme uncertainty exists as to the amount of cash to be collected from customers. It is not permitted for tax purposes.
[d]$1,600/$9,600 × $12,000.
[e]$4,000/$9,600 × $12,000.
[f]$1,000/$12,000 × $9,600.
[g]$2,000/$12,000 × $9,600.
[h]$4,000/$12,000 × $9,600.

the installment method, and the cost-recovery-first method. Not all five methods of income recognition could be justified for financial reporting, nor could they all be used on the tax return in this case. They are presented merely for illustrative purposes. Note that the total revenues, expenses, and income recognized for the 5 years

139

are the same for all methods. In historical cost accounting over long enough time periods, income is equal to cash inflows less cash outflows. There is, however, a significant difference in the patterns of annual income, depending on the accounting method.

Format and Classification within the Income Statement

The income statement might contain some or all of the following sections or categories, depending on the nature of the firm's income for the period:

1 Income from continuing operations.
2 Income, gains, and losses from discontinued operations.
3 Adjustments for changes in accounting principles.
4 Extraordinary gains and losses.
5 Earnings per share.

The great majority of income statements include only the first section. The other sections are added if necessary.

Income from Continuing Operations   Revenues, gains, expenses, and losses from the continuing areas of business activity of a firm are presented in the first section of the income statement.

Income, Gains, and Losses from Discontinued Operations   If a firm sells a major division or segment of its business during the year or contemplates its sale within a short time after the end of the accounting period, Accounting Principles Board *Opinion No. 30* requires that any income, gains, and losses related to that segment be disclosed separately from ordinary, continuing operations in a section of the income statement entitled "Income, Gains, and Losses from Discontinued Operations."[2] This section follows the section presenting Income from Continuing Operations.

Adjustments for Changes in Accounting Principles   A firm that changes its principles, or methods, of accounting during the period is required in some cases to disclose the effects of the change on current and prior years' net income.[3] This information is presented in a separate section, after Income, Gains, and Losses from Discontinued Operations.

Extraordinary Gains and Losses   Extraordinary gains and losses are presented in a separate section of the income statement. For an item to be extraordinary, it must generally meet both of the following criteria:

1 Unusual in nature.
2 Infrequent in occurrence.[4]

---

[2]Accounting Principles Board, *Opinion No. 30,* "Reporting the Results of Operations," 1973.
[3]Accounting Principles Board, *Opinion No. 20,* "Accounting Changes," 1971.
[4]Accounting Principles Board, *Opinion No. 30,* "Reporting the Results of Operations," 1973.

140

An example of an item likely to be extraordinary for most firms would be a loss from expropriation or confiscation of assets by a foreign government. Such items are likely to be rare. Since 1973, when Accounting Principles Board *Opinion No. 30* was issued, extraordinary items have seldom been seen in published annual reports (except for gains or losses on bond retirements[5] which are discussed in Chapter 10).

Earnings per Share Earnings-per-share data must be shown in the body of the income statement by publicly-held firms in order to receive an unqualified accountant's opinion.[6] Earnings per common share is conventionally calculated by dividing net income minus preferred stock dividends by the average number of outstanding common shares during the accounting period. For example, assume that a firm had net income of $500,000 during the year 1982. Dividends declared and paid on outstanding preferred stock were $100,000. The average number of shares of outstanding common stock during 1982 was 1 million shares. Earnings per common share would be $.40 [=($500,000 − $100,000)/1,000,000].

If a firm has securities outstanding that can be converted into common stock (for example, convertible bonds) or exchanged for common stock (for example, stock options), it may be required to present two sets of earnings-per-share amounts: primary earnings per share and fully diluted earnings per share.[7] The calculation of primary and fully diluted earnings per share is discussed in Chapter 6.

Problem 1 for Self-Study

The following data relate to the manufacturing activities of the Haskell Corporation during March 1982.

	March 1	March 31
Raw Materials Inventory	$42,400	$ 46,900
Work-in-Process Inventory	75,800	63,200
Finished Goods Inventory	44,200	46,300
Factory Costs Incurred during the Month:		
Raw Materials Purchased		$ 60,700
Labor Services Received		137,900
Heat, Light, and Power		1,260
Rent		4,100
Expirations of Previous Factory Acquisitions and Prepayments:		
Depreciation of Factory Equipment		$ 1,800
Prepaid Insurance Expired		1,440
Other Data Relating to the Month:		
Sales		$400,000
Selling and Administrative Expenses		125,000

[5]Financial Accounting Standards Board, *Statement of Financial Accounting Standards No. 4,* "Reporting Gains and Losses from Extinguishment of Debt," 1975.
[6]Accounting Principles Board, *Opinion No. 15,* "Earnings Per Share," 1969.
[7]*Ibid.*

141

a Calculate the cost of raw materials used during March.

b Calculate the cost of units completed during March and transferred to the finished goods storeroom.

c Calculate the cost of goods sold during March.

d Calculate income before taxes for March.

Suggested Solution

The transactions and events relating to manufacturing activities are shown in the appropriate T-accounts in Exhibit 4.4.

Exhibit 4.4
**T-Accounts and Transactions
for Haskell Corporation**

Raw Materials Inventory				Work-in-Process Inventory			
Bal.	42,400			Bal.	75,800	215,300	(8)*
(1)	60,700	56,200	(2)*	(2)	56,200		
Bal.	46,900			(3)	137,900		
				(4)	1,260		
Finished Goods Inventory				(5)	4,100		
				(6)	1,800		
Bal.	44,200			(7)	1,440		
(8)	215,300	213,200	(9)*	Bal.	63,200		
Bal.	46,300						
				Cost of Goods Sold			
Cash or Various Liabilities				(9)	213,200		
		60,700	(1)	**Prepaid Insurance**			
		137,900	(3)			1,440	(7)
		1,260	(4)				
		4,100	(5)	**Accumulated Depreciation**			
						1,800	(6)

* Amounts calculated by plugging.

a The cost of raw materials used is $56,200.

b The cost of units completed during March is $215,300.

c The cost of units sold during March is $213,200.

d Income before taxes is $61,800 (= $400,000 − $213,200 − $125,000).

Problem 2 for Self-Study

The Brennan Construction Company contracted on May 15, 1982, to build a bridge for the city for $4,500,000. Brennan estimated the cost of constructing the bridge would be $3,600,000. Brennan incurred $1,200,000 in construction costs during 1982, $2,000,000 during 1983, and $400,000 during 1984 in completing the bridge. The city paid $1,000,000 during

1982, $1,500,000 during 1983, and the remaining $2,000,000 of the contract price at the time the bridge was completed and approved in 1984.

a Calculate the net income (revenue less expenses) of Brennan on the contract during 1982, 1983, and 1984, assuming that the percentage-of-completion method is used.

b Repeat part a, assuming that the completed-contract method is used.

c Repeat part a, assuming that the installment method is used.

d Repeat part a, assuming that the cost-recovery-first method is used.

Suggested Solution

a Percentage-of-Completion Method.

Year	Incremental Percentage Complete	Revenue Recognized	Expenses Recognized	Net Income
1982	12/36 (.333)	$1,500,000	$1,200,000	$300,000
1983	20/36 (.556)	2,500,000	2,000,000	500,000
1984	4/36 (.111)	500,000	400,000	100,000
Total	36/36 (1.000)	$4,500,000	$3,600,000	$900,000

b Completed-Contract Method.

Year	Revenue Recognized	Expenses Recognized	Net Income
1982	$ 0	$ 0	$ 0
1983	0	0	0
1984	$4,500,000	$3,600,000	$900,000
Total	$4,500,000	$3,600,000	$900,000

c Installment Method.

Year	Cash Collected (= Revenue)	Fraction of Cash Collected	Expenses (= Fraction × Total Cost)	Net Income
1982	$1,000,000	2/9	$ 800,000	$200,000
1983	1,500,000	3/9	1,200,000	300,000
1984	2,000,000	4/9	1,600,000	400,000
Total	$4,500,000	1.0	$3,600,000	$900,000

d Cost-Recovery-First Method.

Year	Cash Collected (= Revenue)	Expenses Recognized	Net Income
1982	$1,000,000	$1,000,000	$ 0
1983	1,500,000	1,500,000	0
1984	2,000,000	1,100,000	900,000
Total	$4,500,000	$3,600,000	$900,000

Questions and Problems

1 Review the meaning of the following concepts or terms discussed in this chapter.
   a Product cost.
   b Period expense.
   c Direct material.
   d Direct labor.
   e Manufacturing overhead.
   f "Flow of Costs."
   g Raw Materials Inventory.
   h Work-in-Process Inventory.
   i Finished Goods Inventory.
   j Percentage-of-completion method.
   k Completed-sales, or completed-contract, method.
   l Installment method.
   m Cost-recovery-first method.
   n Unrealized holding gain or loss.
   o Conservatism.
   p Income from Continuing Operations.
   q Income, Gains, and Losses from Discontinued Operations.
   r Adjustments for Changes in Accounting Principles.
   s Extraordinary Gains and Losses.
   t Primary earnings per share.
   u Fully diluted earnings per share.

2 "Depreciation on equipment may be a product cost or a period expense, depending on the type of equipment." Explain.

3 Compare and contrast the Merchandise Inventory account of a merchandising firm and the Finished Goods Inventory account of a manufacturing firm.

4 Indicate whether each of the following types of wages and salaries are (1) product costs or (2) period expenses:
   a Cutting-machine operators.
   b Delivery labor.
   c Factory janitors.
   d Factory payroll clerks.
   e Factory superintendent.
   f General office secretaries.
   g Guards at factory gate.
   h Inspectors in factory.
   i Maintenance workers who service factory machinery.
   j Night watch force at the factory.
   k General office clerks.
   l Operator of a lift truck in the shipping room.
   m President of the firm.
   n Sales manager.
   o Shipping room workers.
   p Sweepers who clean retail store.
   q Traveling salespersons.

5 Indicate whether each of the following types of materials and supplies are (1) product costs or (2) period expenses:
a Cleaning lubricants for factory machines.
b Paper for central office computer.
c Glue used in assembling products.
d Supplies used by factory janitor.
e Gasoline used by salespersons.
f Sales promotion pamphlets distributed.
g Materials used in training production workers.

6 Indicate whether each of the following costs are (1) period expenses, (2) product costs, or (3) some balance sheet account other than those for product costs.
a Office supplies used.
b Salary of factory supervisor.
c Purchase of a fire insurance policy on the store building for the 3-year period beginning next month.
d Expiration of 1 month's protection of the insurance in **c**.
e Property taxes for the current year on the factory building.
f Wages of truck drivers who deliver finished goods to customers.
g Wages of factory workers who install a new machine.
h Wages of mechanics who repair and service factory machines.
i Salary of the president of the company.
j Depreciation of office equipment.
k Factory supplies used.

7 Westside Products showed the following amounts in its inventory accounts on January 1, 1982:

Raw Materials Inventory	$15,000
Work-in-Process Inventory	65,000
Finished Goods Inventory	32,000

The following transactions occurred during January:
(1) Raw materials costing $28,500 were acquired on account.
(2) Raw materials costing $31,600 were issued to producing departments.
(3) Salaries and wages paid during January for services received during the month were as follows:

Factory Workers	$46,900
Sales Personnel	14,300
Administrative Officers	20,900

(4) Depreciation on buildings and equipment during January were as follows:

Manufacturing Facilities	$12,900
Selling Facilities	2,300
Administrative Facilities	1,800

145

(5) Other operating costs incurred and paid in cash were as follows:

Manufacturing	$15,600
Selling	4,900
Administrative	3,700

(6) The cost of goods manufactured and transferred to the finished goods storeroom totaled $85,100.

(7) Sales on account during January totaled $150,000.

(8) A physical inventory taken on January 31 revealed a finished goods inventory of $35,200.

a Present journal entries to record the transactions and events during January.

b Prepare an income statement for Westside Products for January.

8 On July 1, 1982, the accounts of the Tampa Manufacturing Company contained the following balances:

Debit Balances		Credit Balances	
Cash	$ 110,000	Accumulated Depreciation	$ 30,000
Accounts Receivable	220,000	Accounts Payable	56,000
Raw Materials Inventory	80,000	Wages Payable	24,000
Work-in-Process Inventory	230,000	Capital Stock	1,000,000
Finished Goods Inventory	170,000	Retained Earnings	200,000
Factory Supplies Inventory	20,000		
Manufacturing Equipment	480,000		
Total	$1,310,000	Total	$1,310,000

Transactions for the month of July are listed below in summary form:

(1) Sales, all on account, were $310,000.

(2) Labor services furnished by employees during the period (but as yet unpaid) amounted to $80,000. All labor is employed in the factory.

(3) Factory supplies were purchased for $8,500; payment was made by check.

(4) Raw materials purchased on account, $100,000.

(5) Collections from customers, $335,000.

(6) Payment of $108,000 was made to raw materials suppliers.

(7) Payments to employees total $78,500.

(8) Rent of the factory building for the month, $8,000, was paid.

(9) Depreciation of manufacturing equipment for the month, $12,000.

(10) Other manufacturing costs incurred and paid, $40,000.

(11) All selling and administrative services are furnished by Clark and Company for $10,000 per month. Their bill was paid by check.

(12) Raw materials used during month, $115,000.

(13) Factory supplies used during month, $8,000.

(14) Cost of goods completed during month, $258,000.

(15) Goods costing $261,500 were shipped to customers during the month.

a Open T-accounts and record the July 1, 1982, amounts. Record transactions (1) through (15) in the T-accounts, opening additional accounts as needed.
b Prepare an adjusted, preclosing trial balance as of July 31, 1982.
c Prepare a combined statement of income and retained earnings for July 1982.
d Enter closing entries in the T-accounts using an Income Summary account.
e Prepare a balance sheet as of July 31, 1982.

9 Melton Plastics Company was incorporated on September 16, 1982. By September 30, 1982, the firm was ready to begin operations. The trial balance at that date was as follows:

Cash	$387,200	
Raw Materials Inventory	19,200	
Factory Equipment	136,000	
Accounts Payable		$ 22,400
Capital Stock		520,000
	$542,400	$542,400

The following data relate only to the manufacturing operations of the firm during October:

(1) Materials purchased on account, $161,600.
(2) Wages and salaries earned during the month, $148,000.
(3) Raw materials requisitioned and put into process during the month, $168,800.
(4) Equipment was acquired during the month at a cost of $112,000. A check for $40,000 was issued, and an equipment contract payable in eight equal monthly installments was signed for the remainder.
(5) Additional payments by check:

Raw Materials Suppliers	$140,000
Payrolls	112,420
Building Rent	6,000
Utilities	2,920
Insurance Premiums (for 1 year from October 1, 1982)	9,600
Miscellaneous Factory Costs	26,400
	$297,340

(6) Invoices received but unpaid at October 31, 1982:

City Water Department	$ 120
Hoster Machine Supply Company, for additional equipment	2,400

(7) Depreciation on equipment for the month, $1,200.
(8) One month's insurance expiration is recorded.
(9) The cost of parts finished during October was $281,750.

a Open T-accounts and enter the amounts from the opening trial balance.
b Record the transactions during the month in the T-accounts, opening additional accounts as needed.
c Prepare an adjusted trial balance at October 31, 1982.

147

10 This problem is a continuation of Problem **9**, Melton Plastics Company. In addition to the manufacturing activities described in that problem, the following transactions relating to selling and administrative activities occurred during October 1982.

(10) Sales, on account, $340,600.

(11) Collections from customers, $330,000.

(12) Salaries earned during the month: sales, $30,800; office, $31,200.

(13) Payments by check:

Sales Salaries	$27,630
Office Salaries	27,550
Advertising during October	7,200
Rent of Office and Office Equipment for October	2,200
Office Supplies	1,600
Miscellaneous Office Costs	1,400
Miscellaneous Selling Costs	2,800
Total	$70,380

(14) The inventory of office supplies on October 31, 1982, is $800.

(15) The inventory of finished goods on October 31, 1982, is $59,000.

a Employing the T-accounts of Problem **9** and additional accounts as needed, record the selling and administrative activities for the month in the T-accounts.

b Enter closing entries in the T-accounts, using an Income Summary account.

c Prepare a combined statement of income and retained earnings for the month.

d Prepare a balance sheet as of October 31, 1982.

11 The following data relate to the manufacturing activities of the Cornell Company during June 1982.

	June 1	June 30
Raw Materials Inventory	$ 46,900	$ 43,600
Factory Supplies Inventory	7,600	7,700
Work-in-Process Inventory	110,900	115,200
Finished Goods Inventory	76,700	71,400

Factory costs incurred during the month:

Raw Materials Purchased	$429,000
Supplies Purchased	22,300
Labor Service Received	362,100
Heat, Light, and Power	10,300
Insurance	4,200

Expirations of previous factory acquisitions and prepayments:

Depreciation on Factory Equipment	$36,900
Prepaid Rent Expired	3,600

a Calculate the cost of raw materials and factory supplies used during June.

b Calculate the cost of units completed during June and transferred to the finished goods storeroom.

c Calculate the cost of goods sold during June.

12 The following data relate to the activities of Myers Corporation during April 1982.

	April 1	April 30
Raw Materials Inventory	$18,700	$16,400
Work-in-Process Inventory	66,800	72,400
Finished Goods Inventory	32,900	29,800

Factory costs incurred during the month:

Raw Materials Purchased	$87,300
Labor Services Received	66,100
Heat, Light and Power	2,700
Depreciation	15,600

Other data relating to the month:

Sales	$250,000
Selling and Administrative Expenses	38,100

a Calculate the cost of raw materials used during April.

b Calculate the cost of units completed during April and transferred to the finished goods storeroom.

c Calculate net income for April.

13 Discuss when revenue is likely to be recognized by firms in each of the following types of businesses:

a A shoe store.

b A ship-building firm constructing an aircraft carrier under a government contract.

c A real estate developer selling lots on long-term contracts with small down payments.

d A clothing manufacturer.

e A citrus-growing firm.

f A producer of television movies, where the rights to the movies for the first 3 years are sold to a television network and all rights thereafter revert to the producer.

g A residential real estate developer who constructs only "speculative" houses and then later sells the houses to buyers.

h A producer of fine whiskey that ages from 6 to 12 years before sale.

i A savings and loan association lending money for home mortgages.

j A travel agency.

k A printer who prints only custom-order stationery.

l A seller of trading stamps to food stores redeemable by food store customers for various household products.

m A wholesale food distributor.

n A livestock rancher.

o A shipping company that loads cargo in one accounting period, carries cargo across the ocean in a second accounting period, and unloads the cargo in a third period. The shipping is all done under contract, and cash collection of shipping charges is relatively certain.

14 R and D Corporation conducts research and development services for several business clients. In most cases, R and D Corporation contracts with clients for specific development work on existing products. In other cases, R and D Corporation conducts basic research in an area and then attempts to market any new technologies or designs that are developed.

In January 1982, scientists at R and D Corporation began work developing a synthetic energy source. During 1982, $780,000 of costs were incurred in this effort. Late in July 1983, potentially promising results emerged in the form of a substance the scientists called Energitol. Costs incurred through the end of July 1983 were $420,000. At this point, R and D Corporation attempted to sell the formulas and rights of Energitol to Diversified Industries, Incorporated, for $5,000,000. Diversified Industries, Incorporated, however, was reluctant to sign before further testing was done. It did wish, though, to have the first option to acquire the formulas and rights to Energitol if future testing showed that the product would be profitable. It therefore paid R and D Corporation $20,000 for an option to be able to acquire the formulas and rights to Energitol anytime before December 31, 1983. Costs incurred during the remainder of 1983 in testing the product were $540,000.

On December 28, 1983, Diversified Industries, Incorporated, exercised its option and agreed to purchase the formulas and rights to Energitol for $5,000,000. Diversified Industries, Incorporated, paid $500,000 immediately, with the remainder payable in five equal annual installments on December 31, 1984, to December 31, 1988.

On March 15, 1984, R and D Corporation delivered the formulas and samples of Energitol to Diversified Industries, Incorporated. Additional costs incurred during 1984 by R and D Corporation totaled $240,000.

a When do you feel that revenue should be recognized by R and D Corporation from its work on Energitol? Why?

b You may assume that the total costs of $1,980,000 actually incurred over the years 1982–84 were accurately estimated during 1982. Determine the amount of revenue and expense for each year from 1982 to 1988, assuming that the accrual basis of accounting is used and revenue is recognized:

(1) At the time the option is sold.

(2) At the time the option is exercised.

(3) At the time the formulas are delivered.

(4) As cash is collected using the installment method.

15 Pickin Chicken, Incorporated, and Country Delight, Incorporated, both sell franchises for their chicken restaurants. The franchisee receives the right to use the franchisor's products and to benefit from national training and advertising programs. The franchisee agrees to pay $50,000 for exclusive franchise rights in a particular city. Of this amount, $20,000 is paid upon signing the franchise agreement and the remainder is payable in five equal annual installments of $6,000 each.

Pickin Chicken, Incorporated, recognizes franchise revenue as franchise agreements are signed, whereas Country Delight, Incorporated, recognizes franchise revenue on an installment basis. In 1982, both companies sold eight franchises. In 1983, they both sold five franchises. In 1984, neither company sold a franchise.

a Determine the amount of revenue recognized by each company during 1982, 1983, 1984, 1985, 1986, 1987, and 1988.

b When do you feel that franchise revenue should be recognized? Why?

16 Maine Shipbuilding Company agreed on June 15, 1982 to construct an oil tanker for Global Petroleum Company. The contract price of $80 million is to be paid as follows: at the time of signing, $8 million; December 31, 1983, $32 million; at completion on June 30, 1984, $40 million. Maine Shipbuilding Company incurred the following costs in constructing the tanker: 1982: $21.6 million; 1983: $36 million; 1984: $14.4 million. These amounts conformed to original expectations.

Calculate the amount of revenue, expense, and net income for 1982, 1983, and 1984 under each of the following revenue recognition methods.

a Percentage-of-completion method.

b Completed-contract method.

c Installment method.

d Cost-recovery-first method.

e Which method do you feel provides the best measure of Maine Shipbuilding Company's performance under the contract? Why?

17 The Humbolt Electric Company received a contract late in 1981 to build a small electricity-generating unit. The contract price was $700,000 and it was estimated that total costs would be $600,000. Estimated and actual construction time was 15 months and it was agreed that payments would be made by the purchaser as follows:

March 31, 1982	$ 70,000
June 30, 1982	105,000
September 30, 1982	203,000
December 31, 1982	161,000
March 31, 1983	161,000
	$700,000

Estimated and actual costs of construction incurred by the Humbolt Electric Company were as follows:

January 1–March 31, 1982	$120,000
April 1–June 30, 1982	120,000
July 1–September 30, 1982	180,000
October 1–December 31, 1982	120,000
January 1–March 31, 1983	60,000
	$600,000

The Humbolt Electric Company prepares financial statements quarterly at March 31, June 30, and so forth.

Calculate the amount of revenue, expense, and net income for each quarter under each of the following methods of revenue recognition:

a Percentage-of-completion method.

b Completed-contract method.

151

c Installment method.

d Cost-recovery-first method.

e Which method do you feel provides the best measure of Humbolt's performance under this contract? Why?

f Under what circumstances would the methods not selected in part **e** provide a better measure of performance?

18 The Webster Corporation produces a single product at a cost of $5 each, all of which is paid in cash when the unit is produced. The selling cost consists of a sales commission of $3 a unit and is paid in cash at the time of shipment. The selling price is $10 a unit; all sales are made on account. No uncollectible accounts are expected, and no costs are incurred at the time of collection.

During 1982, the firm produced 200,000 units, shipped 150,000 units, and collected $1 million from customers. During 1983, the firm produced 125,000 units, shipped 160,000 units, and collected $2 million from customers.

Determine the amount of net income for 1982 and 1983:

a If revenue and expense are recognized at the time of production.

b If revenue and expense are recognized at the time of shipment.

c If revenue and expense are recognized at the time of cash collection.

d A firm experiencing growth in its sales volume will often produce more units during a particular period than it sells. In this way, inventories can be built up in anticipation of an even larger sales volume during the next period. Under these circumstances, will recognition of revenue and expense at the time of production, shipment, or cash collection generally result in the largest reported net income for the period? Explain.

e A firm experiencing decreases in its sales volume will often produce fewer units during a period than it sells in an effort to reduce the amount of inventory on hand for next period. Under these circumstances, will recognition of revenue and expense at the time of production, shipment, or cash collection generally result in the largest reported net income for a period? Explain.

19 The results of various transactions and events are usually classified within the income statement in one of the following three sections: (1) income from continuing operations, (2) income, gains, and losses from discontinued operations, and (3) extraordinary items. Using the appropriate number, identify the classification of each of the transactions or events below. State any assumptions you feel are necessary.

a Depreciation expense for the year on a company's automobile used by its president.

b Uninsured loss of a factory complex in Louisiana as a result of a hurricane.

c Gain from the sale of marketable securities.

d Loss from the sale of a delivery truck.

e Loss from the sale of a division that conducted all of the firm's research activities.

f Earnings during the year up to the time of sale of the division in part **e**.

g Loss in excess of insurance proceeds on an automobile destroyed during an accident.

h Loss of plant, equipment, and inventory held in a South American country when confiscated by the government of that country.

20 Comment on any unusual features of the following income statement of Nordic Enterprises, Inc.

152

Nordic Enterprises, Inc.
Income Statement
December 31, 1982

Revenues and Gains:

Sales Revenue	$1,964,800	
Rental Revenue	366,900	
Interest Revenue	4,600	
Gain on Sale of Equipment	2,500	
Gain on Sale of Subsidiary	643,200	$2,982,000

Expenses and Losses:

Cost of Goods Sold	$1,432,900	
Depreciation Expense	226,800	
Salaries Expense	296,900	
Interest Expense	6,600	
Loss of Plant Due to Fire	368,800	
Income Tax Expense	200,000	
Dividends Expense	100,000	2,632,000
Net Income		$ 350,000

21 The Freda Company begins business on January 1, 1982. Activities of the company for the first 2 years are summarized below.

	1982	1983
Sales, All on Account	$100,000	$150,000
Collections from Customers		
On 1982 Sales	45,000	55,000
On 1983 Sales		60,000
Purchases of Merchandise	90,000	120,000
Inventory of Merchandise at 12/31	30,000	57,000
All Expenses Other than Merchandise, Paid in Cash	16,000	22,000

a Prepare income statements for 1982 and 1983, assuming the company uses the accrual method of accounting.

b Prepare income statements for 1982 and 1983, assuming the company uses the installment method of accounting.

Chapter 5 Flows of Funds and the Statement of Changes in Financial Position

Chapter 1 pointed out that three major financial statements are useful to those interested in understanding the financial activities of a business. Chapter 2 discussed the balance sheet, a snapshot of financial position at a given time. Chapters 3 and 4 considered the income statement, a report on revenues and expenses for a period. This chapter discusses a third major statement, the statement of changes in financial position, which reports the flows of funds into and out of a business during a period. The discussion includes the rationale for the statement, the alternative meanings of the term *funds,* and the accounting procedures for preparing the statement. Example statements of changes in financial position appear in Exhibits 1.3, 5.7, 5.13, and A.3 (Appendix A at the back of the book).

Rationale for the Statement of Changes in Financial Position

Solinger Electric Corporation was formed during January 1979 to operate a retail electrical supply business. The net income from operating the business has increased each year since opening, from $3,000 in 1979 to $20,000 in 1982. The firm has had increasing difficulty, however, paying its monthly bills as they become due. Management is puzzled as to how net income could be increasing while, at the same time, the firm continually finds itself strapped for cash.

The experience of Solinger Electric Corporation is not unusual. Many firms, particularly those experiencing rapid growth, discover that their cash position is deteriorating despite an excellent earnings record. The statement of changes in financial

154

position provides information that is useful in assessing changes in a firm's *liquidity* (its holdings of cash and other assets that could be readily turned into cash), by reporting on the flows of funds into and out of the business during a period.

Relationship between Income Flows and Cash Flows

Revenues and expenses reported in the income statement for a period differ in amount from cash receipts and disbursements for the period. The differences arise for two principal reasons.

1 The accrual basis of accounting is used in measuring net income. Thus, the recognition of revenues does not necessarily coincide with receipts of cash from customers. Likewise, the recognition of expenses does not necessarily coincide with disbursements of cash to suppliers, employees, and other creditors. As Chapter 3 points out, the accrual basis of accounting focuses on the use of assets in generating earnings and not on their financing (that is, their associated cash receipts and disbursements).

2 The firm receives cash from sources that are not related directly to the earnings process, such as issuing capital stock or bonds. Similarly, the firm makes cash disbursements for such things as dividends and the acquisition of equipment that are not related directly to generating earnings during the current period.

To illustrate the differences between income flows and cash flows, refer to the data for Solinger Electric Corporation for 1982 in Exhibit 5.1. Sales revenue reported in the income statement totaled $125,000. However, only $90,000 was collected in cash from customers. The remaining amount of sales was not collected by the end of the year and is reflected in the increase in the Accounts Receivable account on the balance sheet.[1] Likewise, the cost of goods sold shown on the income statement totaled $60,000. Only $50,000 cash was disbursed to suppliers during the year. Similar differences between income flows and cash flows can be seen for salaries and for other expenses. Note that there is no specific cash flow associated with depreciation expense during 1982. Cash was used in some earlier periods for the acquisition of buildings and equipment, but the amount of cash spent earlier was not reported then as an expense in accrual accounting. Rather, it was reflected in the balance sheet as an increase in the asset account for buildings and equipment and shown in the statement of changes in financial position as a nonoperating use of funds. Now that the buildings and equipment are being used, the cost of the assets' services used is reported as expense of the period. Although the operating activities generated $20,000 in net income, these activities led to an increase in cash of only $8,000 during 1982.

---

[1] We have simplified the illustration. In a realistic situation, some of the receipts would have been from collection of receivables existing at the start of the year. Similarly, some of the payments would have been for liabilities existing at the start of the year.

Exhibit 5.1
Solinger Electric Corporation Income Statement and Statement of Cash Receipts and Disbursements for the Year 1982

	Income Statement	Statement of Cash Receipts and Disbursements	
Sales Revenue	$125,000	$ 90,000	Collections from Customers
			Less Disbursements:
Less Expenses:			
Cost of Goods Sold	$ 60,000	$ 50,000	To Merchandise Suppliers
Salaries	20,000	19,000	To Employees
Depreciation	10,000	0	—
Other	15,000	13,000	To Other Suppliers
Total Expenses	$105,000	$ 82,000	Total Disbursements to Suppliers and Employees
Net Income	$ 20,000	$ 8,000	Net Cash Inflow from Operations
		100,000	Receipts from Issuing Long-Term Bonds
		$108,000	Total Receipts from Operations and Bond Issue
		$ 10,000	Disbursements for Dividends
		125,000	Disbursements for Equipment
		$135,000	Total Disbursements for Dividends and Equipment
		$ 27,000	Net Decrease in Cash

156

The firm engaged in other activities affecting cash during 1982, as is reported near the bottom of Exhibit 5.1. Cash in the amount of $100,000 was received from the issue of bonds, $10,000 was disbursed for dividends, and $125,000 was disbursed for the acquisition of new equipment. The result of all of the firm's activities is a decrease in cash of $27,000. Whereas earnings led to an increase in net assets of $20,000, the firm finds itself with $27,000 less cash.

Objective of the Statement of Changes in Financial Position

The statement of changes in financial position reports the major sources and uses of funds flowing through a firm during a period of time. The major sources and uses are depicted graphically in Figure 5.1 and are described below.

1 *Sources—Operations* The net amount of funds generated from selling goods and providing services is one of the most important sources of funds for a financially healthy company. When assessed over several years, funds provided by operations indicate the extent to which the operating or earnings activities have generated more liquid resources than are used up. The excess from operations can then be used for dividends, acquisition of buildings and equipment, or repayment of long-term debt as necessary.

Figure 5.1
Sources and Uses of Funds

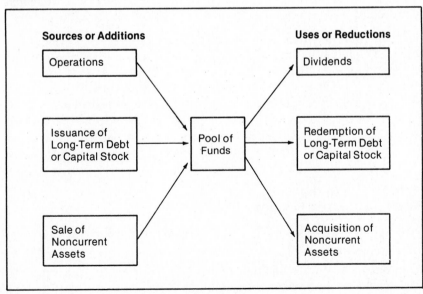

157

2 *Sources—Issuance of Long-Term Debt or Capital Stock* In the long run, a firm must generate most of its funds from operating activities. Potential shareholders are not willing to invest in unprofitable firms. Neither are banks willing to lend large amounts of funds to firms that do not generate profits. A potentially profitable firm finds that it can raise funds by issuing shares to owners or by borrowing. The amount of funds that can be generated by issuing stock or by borrowing is limited, however, by the marketplace's assessment of the firm's prospects.

3 *Sources—Sales of Noncurrent Assets* The sale of buildings, equipment, and other noncurrent assets results in an increase in funds. These sales generally are not a major source of financing for an ongoing firm. The amounts received from the sales are not likely to be sufficient to replace the assets sold.

4 *Uses—Dividends* Dividends are generally a recurring use of funds. Most publicly-held firms are reluctant to omit the payment of dividends, even during a year of poor earnings performance.

5 *Uses—Redemption of Long-Term Debt or Capital Stock* In most instances, publicly-held firms redeem or pay long-term debt at maturity with the proceeds of another debt issue. Thus, these redemptions often have little effect on the *net* change in funds. Some firms also occasionally reacquire, or redeem, their own capital stock for various reasons (discussed in Chapter 12).

6 *Uses—Acquisition of Noncurrent Assets* The acquisition of noncurrent assets, such as buildings and equipment, usually represents the most important ongoing use of funds. Such assets must be replaced as they wear out, and additional noncurrent assets must be acquired if a firm is to grow.

Firms sometimes issue long-term debt or capital stock directly to the vendor, or seller, in acquiring buildings, equipment, or other noncurrent assets. These transactions technically do not affect funds. However, the transaction is reported in the statement of changes in financial position as though two transactions took place: the issuance of long-term debt or capital stock for cash and the immediate use of that cash in the acquisition of noncurrent assets. This is called the *dual transactions assumption*. Such a transaction would normally be disclosed in the statement of changes in financial position as both a source and use of funds of equal amounts.

Uses of Information in the Statement of Changes in Financial Position

The statement of changes in financial position provides information that may be used in:

1 Assessing changes in a firm's liquidity, and
2 Assessing changes in the structure of a firm's assets and equities.

Liquidity Perhaps the most important factor not reported on either the balance sheet or income statement is how the operations of a period affected the liquidity of a firm. It is easy to conclude that increased earnings mean increased cash or other liquid assets. Such a conclusion may not be valid. The successful firm may acquire a new plant, so that it has less funds after a good year than before. On the other hand, increased liquidity can accompany reduced earnings. Consider, for example, a firm that is gradually reducing the scope of its operations. Such a firm is likely to report reduced net income or even losses over time. But because it is not replacing plant and equipment, it is likely to be accumulating cash or other liquid assets.

Structure of Assets and Equities In addition to providing information about changes in a firm's liquidity during a period, the statement of changes in financial position also indicates the major transactions causing changes in the structure of a firm's assets and equities. For example, acquisitions and sales of specific types of assets (buildings, equipment, patents) are reported. Likewise, issues and redemptions of long-term debt and capital stock are disclosed. These transactions are difficult to observe by looking at the income statement or the balance sheet or both. For example, the change in the account, Buildings and Equipment—Net of Accumulated Depreciation, could be attributable to depreciation charges, to acquisition of new buildings and equipment, to disposition of old buildings and equipment, or to a combination of these. The income statement and comparative balance sheets do not provide sufficient information about these three items individually for the reader to disaggregate the net change in the account during the period. A statement of changes in financial position is required to report this information.

Alternative Definitions of Funds

Funds were viewed as "cash" in Exhibit 5.1. The term "funds" is, however, a general one which can have different meanings, depending on the circumstances. Consider the following two questions which the management of Solinger Electric Corporation might raise:

1 Does the firm have sufficient funds to acquire new equipment tomorrow?
2 Will the firm have sufficient funds to acquire new equipment within the next 6 months?

In answering the first question, management is likely to consider the amount of cash on hand and in its bank account. It would also consider if the equipment could be acquired on account from one of its regular suppliers. In answering the second question, management would, in addition, consider if the firm had marketable securities or other assets that could be sold for cash during the next 6 months. It should be clear, however, that *time is the important factor* in answering the questions about available funds. When the time horizon is short, the meaning of funds must be more restrictive than when the time horizon is longer.

Exhibit 5.2
Solinger Electric Corporation Statements of Cash Receipts and Disbursements and Increases and Decreases in Working Capital for the Year 1982

	Statement of Cash Receipts and Disbursements	Statement of Increases and Decreases in Working Capital	
			Increase in Working Capital from Operations:
Collections from Customers	$ 90,000	$125,000	... Sales Revenue (Cash or Receivable)
			Less Decreases in Working Capital from Operations:
Less Disbursements:			
To Merchandise Suppliers	$ 50,000	$ 60,000	... Inventory Sold
To Employees	19,000	20,000	... Salaries Paid or Earned and Accrued
To Other Suppliers	13,000	15,000	... Other Expenses Paid or Accrued
Total Disbursements to Suppliers and Employees	$ 82,000	$ 95,000	... Total Decreases in Working Capital from Operations
Net Cash Inflow from Operations	$ 8,000	$ 30,000	... Net Increase in Working Capital from Operations
			Increases in Working Capital from Issuing Long-Term Bonds
Receipts from Issuing Long-Term Bonds	100,000	100,000	
Total Receipts from Operations and Bond Issue	$108,000	$130,000	... Total Increases in Working Capital from Operations and Bond Issue
Disbursements for Dividends	$ 10,000	$ 10,000	... Decrease in Working Capital for Dividends Declared
Disbursements for Equipment	125,000	125,000	... Decrease in Working Capital for Equipment Acquired
Total Disbursements for Dividends and Equipment	$135,000	$135,000	... Total Decreases in Working Capital for Dividends Declared and Equipment Acquired
Net Decrease in Cash	$ 27,000	$ 5,000	... Net Decrease in Working Capital

The statements of changes in financial position of most publicly-held firms use a definition of funds broader than cash. In most published annual reports, the statement explains the change in the net current asset, or *working capital*, position of the firm. That is, funds are defined as the difference between current assets (cash, readily marketable securities, accounts receivable, inventories, and current prepayments) and current liabilities (accounts payable, salaries payable, and other short-term obligations). Current assets are those assets that are either cash or are expected to be turned into cash, or sold, or consumed within the operating cycle, usually 1 year. Current liabilities are obligations expected to be discharged or paid within approximately 1 year. Thus, the amount of working capital at a particular time represents the excess of cash and near-cash assets over near-term claims on these liquid assets. This broader definition of funds is considered by many to provide more useful information to investors and other users of a firm's financial statements than does the more restrictive definition of funds as cash alone. Still, many financial analysts find cash, or cash plus marketable securities, to be more useful definitions of funds.

Exhibit 5.2 shows the relationship between the cash receipts or disbursements and the increases or decreases in working capital of Solinger Electric Corporation during 1982. Some revenues, $90,000, are collected in cash, but others, $35,000, are not. The $35,000 of revenues not collected in cash results in an increase in the amount of accounts receivable. Because accounts receivable is a current asset, the effect of revenues is to increase the amount of working capital by $125,000 (= $90,000 + $35,000). Most firms collect their accounts receivable shortly after sale, so the working capital definition of funds may give a more meaningful indication of the effect of revenues on the firm's liquidity.

On the other hand, liquidity is decreased not only when salaries are actually paid, but when obligations to workers are incurred that must be discharged within a short time. Using a working capital definition of funds, rather than a cash definition, may give the reader of financial statements more insight about decreases in a firm's current and near-term liquidity than does a cash definition. For example, the Solinger Electric Corporation's Salaries Expense and Other Operating Expenses resulted in a $32,000 (= $19,000 + $13,000) decrease in cash but a $35,000 reduction in working capital. The current liabilities for these items (for example, Salaries Payable and Accounts Payable to Other Suppliers) must therefore have increased by $3,000 (= $35,000 − $32,000). The firm's liquidity is affected by the need to pay current obligations in the near future, and the obligations should be considered in assessing liquidity.

Note that depreciation expense does not affect either cash flows or working capital flows. Whereas operations generated a net cash inflow of $8,000, working capital from operations increased by $30,000. An increase in accounts receivable caused most of the $22,000 difference.

This chapter discusses the procedures for preparing the statement of changes in financial position using both a cash and a working capital definition of funds. We begin by considering a cash definition of funds because the procedures are a direct extension of the dual entry recording framework discussed in Chapters 2–4.

Analysis of the Effects of Transactions on Cash

Algebraic Formulation

The effects of various transactions on cash might be seen by reexamining the accounting equation. In doing so, we use the following notation:

C—cash
NCA—noncash assets
L—liabilities
OE—owners' equity
Δ—the change in an item, whether positive (an increase) or negative (a decrease) from the beginning of a period to the end of the period.

The accounting equation states that:

$$\text{Assets} = \text{Liabilities} + \text{Owners' Equity}$$
$$C + NCA = L + OE.$$

Furthermore, this equation must be true for balance sheets constructed at both the start of the period and the end of the period. If the start-of-the-period and end-of-the-period balance sheets maintain the accounting equation, then the following equation must also be valid:

$$\Delta C + \Delta NCA = \Delta L + \Delta OE.$$

Rearranging terms in this equation, we obtain the equation for changes in cash:

$$\Delta C = \Delta L + \Delta OE - \Delta NCA.$$

The left-hand side of the above equation represents the change in cash. The right-hand side of the equation, reflecting changes in all noncash accounts, must also be equal in amount to the net change in cash. The equation states that increases in cash (left-hand side) are equal to, or caused by, the increases in liabilities plus the increases in owners' equity less the increases in noncash assets (right-hand side). Next, we illustrate how the changes in the accounts on the right-hand side bring about the change in cash on the left-hand side.

Illustration of Transactions Analysis

We can analyze some typical transactions to demonstrate how the equation is maintained and how cash is affected.

Assume that the following events occur during 1982 for the Solinger Electric Corporation, considered earlier in Exhibits 5.1 and 5.2.

1 Merchandise costing $70,000 is acquired on account.
2 Merchandise costing $60,000 is sold to customers on account for $125,000.
3 Salaries of $19,000 are paid in cash.
4 Other expenses of $13,000 are paid in cash.
5 Cash collections of customers' accounts total $90,000.
6 Cash payments to suppliers of merchandise total $50,000.
7 Salaries earned but not paid as of December 31, 1982, are accrued, $1,000.
8 Other expenses not paid as of December 31, 1982, are accrued, $2,000.
9 Depreciation for 1982 is recorded, $10,000.
10 Long-term debt is issued for cash, $100,000.
11 Dividends of $10,000 are declared and paid.
12 Equipment costing $125,000 is acquired for cash.

The effects of these transactions on cash are analyzed in Exhibit 5.3. Cash decreased by $27,000 during 1982. Both sides of the equation show this net change. The net change in cash during a period (left-hand side of the equation) can therefore be explained, or analyzed, by focusing on the changes in noncash accounts (right-hand side of the equation). For Solinger Electric Corporation, the net decrease in cash of $27,000 is explained as follows:

Increases in Cash:	
From Operations	$ 8,000
From Issuing Long-Term Debt	100,000
Total Increases	$108,000
Decreases in Cash:	
For Dividends	$ 10,000
For Acquisition of Equipment	125,000
Total Decreases	$135,000
Net Decrease in Cash	$ 27,000

Note that the recording of depreciation for the period does not affect cash. A noncash asset is decreased and owners' equity is decreased. Cash is not affected. (Cash was reduced in the period when the noncurrent asset was purchased.)

The information necessary to prepare the statement of changes in financial position could be generated, or developed, using the transactions analysis approach illustrated in Exhibit 5.3. This approach quickly becomes cumbersome, however, as the number of transactions increases. In the next section, we describe an alternative procedure for preparing the statement of changes in financial position which uses the T-account discussed in previous chapters.

Exhibit 5.3
Analysis of the Effects of Solinger Electric Corporation's Transactions during 1982 on Cash and Noncash Accounts

Transactions	Changes in Cash ΔC		ΔL		Changes in Noncash Accounts ΔOE		ΔNCA
(1) Merchandise costing $70,000 is acquired on account, increasing a noncash asset and a noncash liability	$ 0	=	$ 70,000	+	0	—	(+$ 70,000)
(2) Merchandise costing $60,000 is sold to customers on account for $125,000, increasing a noncash asset, accounts receivable, by $125,000, decreasing the noncash asset, inventory, by $60,000, and increasing owners' equity by $65,000	0	=	0	+	$65,000	—	(+$125,000) (−$ 60,000)
(3) Salaries of $19,000 are paid in cash, decreasing cash and owners' equity	(−$ 19,000)	=	0	+	(−$19,000)	—	0
(4) Other expenses of $13,000 are paid in cash, decreasing cash and owners' equity	(−$ 13,000)	=	0	+	(−$13,000)	—	0
(5) Cash collections of customers' accounts total $90,000, increasing cash and decreasing the noncash asset, accounts receivable	$ 90,000	=	0	+	0	—	(−$ 90,000)
(6) Payments to suppliers of merchandise total $50,000, decreasing cash and a liability	(−$ 50,000)	=	(−$ 50,000)	+	0	—	0
(7) Salaries of $1,000 earned but not paid as of December 31, 1982, are accrued, increasing a liability and decreasing owners' equity	0	=	$ 1,000	+	(−$ 1,000)	—	0
(8) Other expenses of $2,000 not paid as of December 31, 1982, are accrued, increasing a liability and decreasing owners' equity	0	=	$ 2,000	+	(−$ 2,000)	—	0
(9) Depreciation for 1982 of $10,000 is recorded, decreasing owners' equity and noncash assets	0	=	0	+	(−$10,000)	—	(−$ 10,000)
Total from Operations	$ 8,000	=	$ 23,000	+	$20,000	—	($ 35,000)
(10) Long-term debt is issued for $100,000, increasing cash and a liability	$100,000	=	$100,000	+	0	—	0
(11) Dividends of $10,000 are declared and paid, decreasing cash and owners' equity	(−$ 10,000)	=	0	+	(−$10,000)	—	0
(12) Equipment costing $125,000 is acquired for cash, decreasing cash and increasing noncash assets	(−$125,000)	=	0	+	0	—	$125,000
Net Change in Cash and Noncash Accounts	−$ 27,000	=	$123,000	+	$10,000	—	$160,000

Preparation of the Statement of Changes in Financial Position: Funds Defined as Cash

As with the balance sheet and income statement, it is not essential that you know how to prepare a statement of changes in financial position in order to use it effectively. Nevertheless, learning how to construct this statement facilitates understanding its rationale and content. In this section, we present a step-by-step procedure for preparing the statement of changes in financial position with funds defined as cash. We then illustrate this procedure, using the transactions of Solinger Electric Corporation for 1982.

The Procedure and an Illustration

Step 1 Obtain balance sheets for the beginning and end of the period covered by the statement of changes in financial position. The comparative balance sheets of Solinger Electric Corporation for December 31, 1981 and 1982, are presented in Exhibit 5.4.

Step 2 Prepare a T-account *work sheet*. An example of such a T-account work sheet is shown in Exhibit 5.5. At the top of the work sheet is a master T-account titled Cash. Note that this T-account has sections labeled From Operations and Other (Nonoperating) Sources and Uses. Transactions affecting cash during the period are classified under one of these headings to aid in the preparation of the statement of changes in financial position. This procedure is explained later in this section. The beginning and ending amounts of cash are then entered in the master T-account. The beginning and ending amounts of cash for Solinger Electric Corporation are $30,000 and $3,000 respectively. The check marks indicate that the figures are balances. The number at the top of the T-account is the opening balance; the one at the bottom is the closing balance. Note that the master T-account, Cash, is another means of expressing the left-hand side of the equation for changes in cash in Exhibit 5.3.

After the master T-account for Cash has been prepared (as at the top of Exhibit 5.5), the work sheet is completed by preparing T-accounts for *each* noncash asset and liability and owners' equity account. Enter the beginning and ending balances in each account for the period as given in Exhibit 5.4. The lower portion of Exhibit 5.5 shows the T-accounts for each noncash account. Note that the sum of the changes in these individual T-accounts is another means of expressing the right-hand side of the equation for changes in cash in Exhibit 5.3.

Step 3 Explain the change in the master cash account between the beginning and end of the period by explaining, or accounting for, the change in the balance of each noncash account during the period. This step is accomplished by *reconstructing the entries originally recorded in the accounts during the period.* The reconstructed entries are written in the appropriate T-accounts. You will see that once the net change in

Exhibit 5.4
Solinger Electric Corporation
Comparative Balance Sheets for
December 31, 1981 and 1982

ASSETS	December 31, 1981	1982
Current Assets:		
Cash	$ 30,000	$ 3,000
Accounts Receivable	20,000	55,000
Merchandise Inventory	40,000	50,000
Total Current Assets	$ 90,000	$108,000
Noncurrent Assets:		
Buildings and Equipment (Cost)	$100,000	$225,000
Accumulated Depreciation	(30,000)	(40,000)
Total Noncurrent Assets	$ 70,000	$185,000
Total Assets	$160,000	$293,000
EQUITIES		
Current Liabilities:		
Accounts Payable—Merchandise Suppliers	$ 30,000	$ 50,000
Accounts Payable—Other Suppliers	10,000	12,000
Salaries Payable	5,000	6,000
Total Current Liabilities	$ 45,000	$ 68,000
Noncurrent Liabilities:		
Bonds Payable	$ 0	$100,000
Owners' Equity:		
Capital Stock	$100,000	$100,000
Retained Earnings	15,000	25,000
Total Owners' Equity	$115,000	$125,000
Total Equities	$160,000	$293,000

each of the noncash accounts has been accounted for, sufficient information will have been generated to account for the net change in cash. That is, if you have explained the changes in the right-hand side of the cash equation, you will also have explained the causes of the changes in cash itself on the left-hand side.

The process of reconstructing the transactions during the year is usually easiest if information supplementary to the balance sheet is accounted for first. Assume the following information concerning the Solinger Electric Corporation for 1982:

1 Net income is $20,000.
2 Depreciation expense is $10,000.
3 Dividends declared and paid total $10,000.

Exhibit 5.5
T-Account Work Sheet for
Solinger Electric Corporation
(Using Cash as Funds)

Cash

✔ 30,000
From Operations

Net Income and Additions   Net Loss and Subtractions

Other (Nonoperating)

Sources   Uses

✔ 3,000

Accounts Receivable	**Merchandise Inventory**	**Buildings and Equipment (Cost)**
✔ 20,000	✔ 40,000	✔ 100,000
✔ 55,000	✔ 50,000	✔ 225,000

Accumulated Depreciation	**Accounts Payable— Merchandise Suppliers**	**Accounts Payable— Other Suppliers**
30,000 ✔	30,000 ✔	10,000 ✔
40,000 ✔	50,000 ✔	12,000 ✔

Salaries Payable	**Bonds Payable**	**Retained Earnings**
5,000 ✔	0 ✔	15,000 ✔
6,000 ✔	100,000 ✔	25,000 ✔

The analytical entry to record the information concerning net income is:

(1) Cash (Operations—Net Income)	20,000	
Retained Earnings		20,000
Entry recorded in T-account work sheet.		

167

To understand this entry, review the process of recording revenues and expenses and the closing entries for those temporary accounts from Chapter 3. All of the journal entries that together record the process of earning $20,000 net income are equivalent to the following single journal entry:

Net Assets (= All Assets − All Liabilities)	20,000	
Retained Earnings		20,000
Summary entry equivalent to recording earnings of $20,000.		

In the summary journal entry, we debit Net Assets. The initial assumption at this stage of preparing the statement of changes in financial position is that all of the net assets generated by the earnings process were cash. Thus, in the analytic entry (1) above, the debit results in showing a provisional increase in cash from operations in an amount equal to net income for the period.

Some portion of the items recognized as expenses and deducted in calculating net income does not, however, decrease cash (refer to Exhibit 5.1). The portion of the expenses that does not affect cash is added to the provisional increase in cash to calculate the net amount of cash from operations. Such an adjustment for an expense not using cash is illustrated for depreciation expense in entry (2).

(2) Cash (Operations—Depreciation Expense Addback)	10,000	
Accumulated Depreciation		10,000
Entry recorded in T-account work sheet.		

Because depreciation expense was deducted in calculating net income but did not reduce cash, the amount of depreciation expense must be added back to net income in calculating the amount of cash provided by operations.

The supplementary information concerning dividends of $10,000 declared and paid is recorded as follows:

(3) Retained Earnings	10,000	
Cash (Other Uses—Dividends)		10,000
Entry recorded in T-account work sheet. Dividends reduce retained earnings and cash.		

Once the supplementary information has been reflected in the T-accounts, it is necessary to make inferences about the reasons for the remaining changes in the noncash accounts on the balance sheet. (If the statement of changes in financial position were being prepared for an actual firm, such inferences might not be necessary, because sufficient information regarding the change in each account is likely to be available from the firm's accounting records.) The changes in noncash accounts are explained in the order of their appearance.

The Accounts Receivable account shows an increase of $35,000. The analytical entry to record this assumed information in the work sheet is:

(4) Accounts Receivable	35,000	
Cash (Operations—Subtractions)		35,000
Entry recorded in T-account work sheet.		

The operations of the period generated sales. Not all of these sales resulted in an increase in cash. Some of the sales resulted in an increase in Accounts Receivable. Because we start the statement of changes in financial position with net income, in deriving the amount of cash from operations we must *subtract that portion of revenues not producing cash* (that is, the excess of sales on account over cash collections from customers).

The next noncash account showing a change is that for Merchandise Inventory. That account shows an increase during the year of $10,000. As the operations of the firm have expanded, so has the amount carried in inventory. The analytical entry in the work sheet to explain the change in Merchandise Inventory is:

(5) Merchandise Inventory	10,000	
Cash (Operations—Subtractions)		10,000
Entry recorded in T-account work sheet.		

Solinger Electric Corporation found it necessary to increase the amount of inventory carried to make possible increased future sales. An increase in inventory is ordinarily an operating use of cash. Because we start the statement of changes in financial position with net income, in deriving cash from operations we must subtract from net income the incremental investment in inventories during the year (that is, the excess of purchases over the cost of goods sold).

The next noncash account showing a change is that for Buildings and Equipment (Cost). The Buildings and Equipment (Cost) account shows a net increase of $125,000 ($= \$225,000 - \$100,000$). Because we have no other information, we must assume or deduce that buildings and equipment costing $125,000 were acquired during the year. The analytical entry is:

(6) Buildings and Equipment (Cost)	125,000	
Cash (Other Uses—Acquisitions of Buildings and Equipment)		125,000
Entry recorded in T-account work sheet.		

Acquisition of buildings and equipment is a nonoperating use of cash.

The next noncash account showing a change is that for Accounts Payable—Merchandise Suppliers. As the amounts carried in inventory have increased, so have the amounts owed to suppliers of inventory. The analytical entry to explain the increase in the amount of Accounts Payable—Merchandise Suppliers is:

(7) Cash (Operations—Net Income and Additions)	20,000	
Accounts Payable—Merchandise Suppliers		20,000
Entry recorded in T-account work sheet.		

Ordinarily, one thinks of using cash to acquire inventory. Suppliers who allow us to pay later for goods and services received now are effectively supplying us with cash. Thus an increase in the amount of accounts payable for inventory results from a transaction where inventory increased but cash did not decrease, which is equivalent to saying that an increase in payables is a source of cash, even if only a temporary one.[2] The increase in cash resulting from increased payables for inventory is an operating source of funds.

The next noncash account showing a change is Accounts Payable—Other Suppliers. As the scope of operations has increased, so has the amount owed to others. The analytical entry to explain the increase in the amount of Accounts Payable—Other Suppliers is:

(8) Cash (Operations—Net Income and Additions)	2,000	
Accounts Payable—Other Suppliers		2,000
Entry recorded in T-account work sheet.		

The reasoning behind this entry is the same as for entry (7), just above. Creditors who permit a firm to owe them more are effectively a source of cash. The same reasoning applies to our own employees who are owed an increased amount of Salaries Payable, the next noncash account showing a change. The analytic entry to record the increase in Salaries Payable is:

(9) Cash (Operations—Net Income and Additions)	1,000	
Salaries Payable		1,000
Entry recorded in T-account work sheet.		

Employees who do not demand immediate payment for salaries earned have provided their employer with cash, at least temporarily.

The final noncash account showing a change not yet explained is Bonds Payable. It shows a net increase of $100,000 for the year. Because we have no other informa-

---

[2] The actual degree to which such a source is temporary is controversial. We are inclined to argue that when a growing business increases the amount of accounts payable, that increase is likely to result in a relatively permanent increase in funds provided by creditors. A growing firm is likely to increase the amount of payables even more in subsequent periods as operations continue to increase. Arguments of this sort are beyond the current discussion; we return to them in Chapter 11.

170

Exhibit 5.6
**T-Account Work Sheet for
Solinger Electric Corporation
(Using Cash as Funds)**

Cash

✔ 30,000

From Operations

Net Income and Additions			Net Loss and Subtractions		
Net Income	(1)	20,000	35,000	(4)	Increased Accounts Receivable
Depreciation Expense	(2)	10,000	10,000	(5)	Increased Merchandise Inventory
Increased Accounts Payable to Merchandise Suppliers	(7)	20,000			
Increased Accounts Payable to Other Suppliers	(8)	2,000			
Increased Salaries Payable	(9)	1,000			

Other (Nonoperating)

Sources			Uses		
Long-Term Bonds Issued	(10)	100,000	10,000	(3)	Dividends Declared and Paid
			125,000	(6)	Buildings and Equipment Acquired

✔ 3,000

Accounts Receivable		**Merchandise Inventory**		**Buildings and Equipment (Cost)**	
✔ 20,000		✔ 40,000		✔ 100,000	
(4) 35,000		(5) 10,000		(6) 125,000	
✔ 55,000		✔ 50,000		✔ 225,000	

Accumulated Depreciation		**Accounts Payable Merchandise Suppliers**		**Accounts Payable Other Suppliers**	
	30,000 ✔		30,000 ✔		10,000 ✔
	10,000 (2)		20,000 (7)		2,000 (8)
	40,000 ✔		50,000 ✔		12,000 ✔

Salaries Payable		**Bonds Payable**		**Retained Earnings**	
	5,000 ✔		0 ✔		15,000 ✔
	1,000 (9)		100,000 (10)	(3) 10,000	20,000 (1)
	6,000 ✔		100,000 ✔		25,000 ✔

171

tion, we must assume or deduce that long-term bonds were issued during the year. The analytic entry is:

(10) Cash (Other Sources—Long-Term Bond Issue) 100,000	
Bonds Payable	100,000

Exhibit 5.6 presents the T-account work sheet for a cash definition of funds for Solinger Electric Corporation for 1982. All changes in the noncash T-accounts have been explained with the 10 entries. If the work is correct, the causes of the change in the Cash account have been presented in the entries in the master Cash account.

Step 4 The final step is the preparation of a formal statement of changes in financial position. The statement for Solinger Electric Corporation is presented in Exhibit 5.7. It is prepared directly from the information provided in the master T-account for Cash in the completed work sheet.

Exhibit 5.7
Solinger Electric Corporation Statement of Changes in Financial Position Cash Definition of Funds for the Year 1982

Sources of Cash
Operations:

Net Income	$20,000	
Additions:		
Depreciation Expense Not Using Cash	10,000	
Increased Accounts Payable:		
To Suppliers of Merchandise	20,000	
To Other Suppliers	2,000	
Increased Salaries Payable	1,000	
Subtractions:		
Increased Accounts Receivable	(35,000)	
Increased Merchandise Inventory	(10,000)	
Cash Provided by Operations		$ 8,000
Proceeds of Long-Term Bonds Issue		100,000
Total Sources of Cash		$108,000
Uses of Cash		
Dividends		$ 10,000
Acquisition of Buildings and Equipment		125,000
Total Uses of Cash		$135,000
Net (Decrease) in Cash for Year: Sources — Uses		($ 27,000)
Net (Decrease) in Cash Account for Year: From Balance Sheet		($ 27,000)

The first item disclosed in the statement is the amount of cash generated by operations. In deriving cash from operations, published annual reports typically start with net income. Expenses not using cash are then added to net income, and revenues not providing cash are subtracted to obtain cash from operations. This format is illustrated in Exhibit 5.7. Because depreciation expense is added to net income to determine cash provided by operations, some readers of financial statements incorrectly conclude that depreciation expense is a source of cash. As Exhibit 5.3 illustrated, the recording of depreciation expense does not affect cash. A noncash asset is decreased and an owners' equity account is decreased. Cash is not affected. Cash from operations results from selling goods and services to customers. If no sales are made, then there will be no cash provided by operations regardless of how large the depreciation charge may be.

Depreciation Is Not a Source of Funds To demonstrate that depreciation is not a source of funds, refer to the income statement of Solinger Electric Corporation (Exhibit 5.1) and the cash flow from the operations section of the statement of changes

---

Exhibit 5.8
Solinger Electric Corporation
Year 1982
Depreciation $10,000

Income Statement		Cash Flow from Operations	
Revenues	$125,000	Net Income	$20,000
Expenses Except Depreciation	(95,000)	Additions:	
	$ 30,000	Depreciation	10,000
Depreciation Expense	(10,000)	Other	23,000
		Subtractions:	(45,000)
		Cash Flow Provided by	
Net Income	$ 20,000	Operations	$ 8,000

Exhibit 5.9
Solinger Electric Corporation
Year 1982
Depreciation $25,000

Income Statement		Cash Flow from Operations	
Revenues	$125,000	Net Income	$ 5,000
Expenses Except Depreciation	(95,000)	Additions:	
	$ 30,000	Depreciation	25,000
		Other	23,000
Depreciation Expense	(25,000)	Subtractions:	(45,000)
		Cash Flow Provided by	
Net Income	$ 5,000	Operations	$ 8,000

173

in financial position (Exhibit 5.7). These are reproduced in condensed form in Exhibit 5.8. Ignore income taxes for a moment. Suppose that depreciation for 1982 had been $25,000 rather than $10,000. Then the condensed income statement and cash flow from operations would appear as in Exhibit 5.9. Note that the total cash flow from operations remains $8,000, which is the difference between receipts from revenues and all expenses that did use cash. The only effects on cash of transactions involving long-term assets are that: (1) cash is typically used when a long-term asset is acquired, and (2) cash is provided when the asset is sold. In interpreting the statement of changes in financial position, do not commit the common error of thinking that depreciation is a source of funds.

At a more sophisticated level, however, when income taxes are a factor, depreciation does affect funds flow. Depreciation is a factor in the calculation of net income reported in the financial statements. Depreciation is also a deduction from otherwise taxable income on tax returns. The larger is depreciation on tax returns, the smaller is taxable income, and the smaller is the current payment for income taxes. We discuss the effect of depreciation on income taxes in Chapters 9 and 11.

An alternative procedure for deriving cash flow from operations is to list all revenue items that provide cash and then to subtract all expense items that use cash. This approach is illustrated in the left-hand column of Exhibit 5.2 (and in Exhibit 1.3). This alternative presentation is appealing to us because depreciation expense does not appear as an element in the calculation of cash flow provided by operations. The latter presentation, although acceptable, is rarely used in published financial statements.

Extension of the Illustration

The illustration for Solinger Electric Corporation considered so far in this chapter is simpler than the typical published statement of changes in financial position in at least four respects:

1 There are only a few balance sheet accounts whose changes are to be explained.
2 Several types of more complex transactions that affect the sources of cash from operations are not involved.
3 Each transaction recorded in step **3** involves only one debit and one credit.
4 Each explanation of a noncash account change involves only one analytic entry on the work sheet, except for the Retained Earnings account.

Most of the complications that arise in interpreting published statements of changes in financial position relate to accounting events that are not discussed until later chapters. As these transactions are discussed, their effects on the statement of changes in financial position will be illustrated. We can illustrate now one complication caused by a supplementary disclosure. Suppose that the firm sold some of its buildings and equipment during the year. For now, and until we address the issue again in Chapter 9, we assume that the firm disposes of existing buildings and equipment at their book value; the cash proceeds from disposition are equal to acquisition cost less accumulated depreciation of the assets. With this assumption, there will be no gain or loss on disposition.

Let us reconsider Solinger Electric Corporation with the following new information. Solinger Electric Corporation sold some equipment during 1982. This equipment cost $10,000 and was sold for $3,000 at a time when accumulated depreciation on the equipment sold was $7,000. The actual entry made during the year to record the sale of the equipment was as follows:

Cash	3,000	
Accumulated Depreciation	7,000	
Buildings and Equipment (Cost)		10,000
Journal entry for sale of equipment.		

Assume that the comparative balance sheets as shown in Exhibit 5.4 are correct and thus that the net decrease in cash for 1982 is still $27,000. The entries in the T-accounts must be altered to reflect this new information. The following entry in the T-accounts is required to recognize the effect of the sale of equipment:

(1a) Cash (Other Sources—Proceeds from Sale of Equipment)	3,000	
Accumulated Depreciation	7,000	
Buildings and Equipment (Cost)		10,000
Entry recorded in T-account work sheet.		

The debit to Cash (Other Sources—Proceeds from Sale of Equipment) shows the proceeds of the sale.

As a result of entry (1a), the T-accounts for Buildings and Equipment (Cost) and Accumulated Depreciation would appear as follows:

Buildings and Equipment (Cost)		Accumulated Depreciation	
✔ 100,000			30,000 ✔
	10,000 (1a)	(1a) 7,000	
✔ 225,000			40,000 ✔

When the time comes to explain the change in the account, Buildings and Equipment (Cost), the T-account indicates that there is an increase of $125,000 and a credit entry (1a) of $10,000 to recognize the sale of equipment. The net increase in the Buildings and Equipment (Cost) account can be accounted for, given the decrease already entered, only by assuming that new buildings and equipment have been acquired during the period for $135,000.

The reconstructed entry to complete the explanation of the change in this account would be as follows:

(6a) Buildings and Equipment (Cost)	135,000	
Cash (Other Uses—Acquisition of Buildings and Equipment)		135,000
Entry recorded in T-account work sheet.		

Likewise, when the change in the T-account for Accumulated Depreciation is explained, there is a net credit change of $10,000 and a debit entry (1a) of $7,000 to recognize the sale. Thus, the depreciation charge for 1982 must have been $17,000. The reconstructed entry to complete the explanation of the change in the Accumulated Depreciation account would be as follows:

(2a) Cash (Operations—Depreciation Expense Addback)	17,000	
Accumulated Depreciation		17,000
Entry recorded in T-account work sheet.		

A revised T-account work sheet for Solinger Electric Corporation incorporating the new information on the sale of equipment is presented in Exhibit 5.10.

Preparation of the Statement of Changes in Financial Position: Funds Defined as Working Capital

The procedure for preparing the statement of changes in financial position illustrated earlier in this chapter for a cash definition of funds can be easily adapted to any other definition of funds. In this section, we show the procedures for preparing the statement using a working capital definition of funds.

Algebraic Formulation

Working capital is equal to current assets minus current liabilities. The effects of various transactions on working capital might be seen by reexamining the accounting equation. In doing so, we use the following notation:

CA—current assets
CL—current liabilities
NCA—noncurrent assets
NCL—noncurrent liabilities
OE—owners' equity
Δ—the change in an item, whether positive (an increase) or negative (a decrease) from the beginning of a period to the end of the period.

Exhibit 5.10
**Revised T-Account Work Sheet for
Solinger Electric Corporation
(Using Cash as Funds)**

Cash

✔30,000

From Operations

Net Income and Additions			Net Loss and Subtractions	
Net Income	(1)	20,000	35,000 (4)	Increased Accounts Receivable
Depreciation Expense	(2a)	17,000	10,000 (5)	Increased Merchandise Inventory
Increased Accounts Payable to Merchandise Suppliers	(7)	20,000		
Increased Accounts Payable to Other Suppliers	(8)	2,000		
Increased Salaries Payable	(9)	1,000		

Other (Nonoperating)

Sources			Uses	
Sale of Equipment	(1a)	3,000	10,000 (3)	Dividends Declared and Paid
Long-Term Bonds Issued	(10)	100,000	135,000 (6a)	Buildings and Equipment Acquired

✔ 3,000

Accounts Receivable		**Merchandise Inventory**		**Buildings and Equipment (Cost)**	
✔ 20,000		✔ 40,000		✔ 100,000	
(4) 35,000		(5) 10,000		(6a) 135,000	10,000 (1a)
✔ 55,000		✔ 50,000		✔ 225,000	

Accumulated Depreciation		**Accounts Payable Merchandise Suppliers**		**Accounts Payable Other Suppliers**	
	30,000 ✔		30,000 ✔		10,000 ✔
(1a) 7,000	17,000 (2a)		20,000 (7)		2,000 (8)
	40,000 ✔		50,000 ✔		12,000 ✔

Salaries Payable		**Bonds Payable**		**Retained Earnings**	
	5,000 ✔		0 ✔		15,000 ✔
	1,000 (9)		100,000 (10)	(3) 10,000	20,000 (1)
	6,000 ✔		100,000 ✔		25,000 ✔

177

The accounting equation states that:

$$\text{Assets} = \text{Liabilities} + \text{Owners' Equity}$$
$$CA + NCA = CL + NCL + \quad OE.$$

Furthermore, this equation must be true for balance sheets constructed at both the start of the period and the end of the period. If the start-of-the-period and end-of-the-period balance sheets maintain the accounting equation, then the following equation must also be valid:

$$\Delta CA + \Delta NCA = \Delta CL + \Delta NCL + \Delta OE.$$

Rearranging terms in this equation, we get the working capital equation:

$$\Delta CA - \Delta CL = \Delta NCL + \Delta OE - \Delta NCA.$$

Working capital is equal to current assets minus current liabilities, so the left-hand side of the above equation represents the net change in working capital. The right-hand side of the equation, reflecting changes in all *non*working capital accounts, must also be equal in amount to the net change in working capital. The equation states that increases in working capital (left-hand side) are equal to, or caused by, the increases in noncurrent liabilities plus the increase in owners' equity less the increase in noncurrent assets (right-hand side).

The Procedure and an Illustration

We illustrate next the construction of a statement of changes in financial position using a working capital definition of funds for the Solinger Electric Corporation for 1982. The steps outlined below parallel those described earlier for a cash definition of funds.

Step 1 Obtain balance sheets for the beginning and end of the period. The comparative balance sheets of Solinger Electric Corporation for December 31, 1981 and 1982, are presented in Exhibit 5.4.

Step 2 Prepare a T-account work sheet. First prepare a master account titled Working Capital. This master account is merely an aggregation of individual current asset and current liability accounts into a single summary account. This account will show the change in working capital for the period, and after the work sheet is complete, it will show the causes of that change in working capital. The master account will show sections From Operations and Other (Nonoperating) to separate the two kinds of transactions affecting working capital.

After the master T-account for Working Capital has been prepared (as at the top of Exhibit 5.11), the work sheet is completed by preparing T-accounts for *each nonworking capital account*. These accounts are shown at the bottom of Exhibit 5.11 for

178

the Solinger Electric Corporation. The beginning and ending balances in the accounts for the period are entered in each of the separate T-accounts. The T-account work sheet for Solinger Electric Corporation after completion of step **2** is shown in Exhibit 5.11.

Exhibit 5.11
T-Account Work Sheet for Solinger Electric Corporation

Working Capital

✔ 45,000

From Operations

Net Income and Addbacks | Net Loss and Subtractions

Other (Nonoperating)

Sources | Uses

✔ 40,000

Buildings and Equipment (Cost)	**Accumulated Depreciation**	**Bonds Payable**
✔ 100,000	30,000 ✔	0 ✔
✔ 225,000	40,000 ✔	100,000 ✔

Capital Stock	**Retained Earnings**
100,000 ✔	15,000 ✔
100,000 ✔	25,000 ✔

179

Step 3 Explain the change in the master Working Capital account by explaining the changes in the nonworking capital accounts. This step is accomplished by reconstructing on the work sheet the entries originally recorded in the accounts during the period. The reconstructed entries are written in the appropriate T-accounts. Once the net change in each of the nonworking capital accounts has been explained, then sufficient information will have been generated to explain the net change in working capital. We start with the supplementary information, which, for the Solinger Electric Corporation for 1982, is:

1 Net income is $20,000.
2 Depreciation expense is $10,000.
3 Dividends declared and paid total $10,000.

The analytical entry to record the information concerning net income is:

(1) Working Capital (Operations—Net Income)	20,000	
Retained Earnings		20,000
Entry recorded in T-account work sheet.		

Working capital is provisionally assumed to increase by the amount of net income for the period. Some portion of the items recognized as expenses and deducted in determining net income does not, however, decrease working capital. The portion of the expenses that does not affect working capital is added to the provisional increase in working capital to calculate the net amount of working capital from operations. Such an adjustment for an expense not using working capital is illustrated for depreciation expense in entry (2).

(2) Working Capital (Operations—Depreciation Expense Addback)	10,000	
Accumulated Depreciation		10,000
Entry recorded in T-account work sheet.		

Because depreciation expense was deducted in calculating net income but did not reduce working capital, the amount of depreciation expense must be added back to net income in determining the amount of working capital provided by operations. The results of entries (1) and (2) on the T-account work sheet might be summarized as follows:

Working Capital (Operations—Net Income and Addbacks)	30,000	
Retained Earnings		20,000
Accumulated Depreciation		10,000

180

This combined entry shows that the operating activities of Solinger Electric Corporation resulted in a $30,000 increase in working capital during 1982. That is, revenues increasing working capital exceeded expenses using working capital (total expenses less depreciation expense) by $30,000.

The supplementary information concerning dividends of $10,000 declared and paid is recorded as follows:

(3) Retained Earnings	10,000	
Working Capital (Other Uses—Dividends)		10,000
Entry recorded in T-account work sheet.		

Once the supplementary information has been reflected in the T-accounts, inferences must be made about the reasons for the remaining changes in the nonworking capital accounts. The Buildings and Equipment (Cost) account shows a net increase of $125,000 (= $225,000 − $100,000). Because we have no other information, we must assume or deduce that buildings and equipment costing $125,000 were acquired during the year. The analytical entry is:

(4) Buildings and Equipment (Cost)	125,000	
Working Capital (Other Uses—Acquisitions of Buildings and Equipment)		125,000
Entry recorded in T-account work sheet.		

The Bonds Payable account increased $100,000 during 1982. Because we have no other information, we must assume or deduce that long-term bonds were issued during the year. The analytical entry is:

(5) Working Capital (Other Sources—Long-Term Bond Issue)	100,000	
Bonds Payable		100,000
Entry recorded in T-account work sheet.		

Exhibit 5.12 presents the T-account work sheet for Solinger Electric Corporation for 1982 after analytic entry (5). All changes in the nonworking capital T-accounts have been explained. If the work has been done correctly, the change in the Working Capital account has also been explained by the entries in the master Working Capital account.

Exhibit 5.12
**T-Account Work Sheet for
Solinger Electric Corporation**

Working Capital

✔ 45,000

From Operations

Net Income and Addbacks			Net Loss and Subtractions
Net Income	(1)	20,000	
Depreciation Expense	(2)	10,000	

Other (Nonoperating)

Sources			Uses
Long-Term Bonds Issued	(5)	100,000	10,000 (3) Dividends Declared and Paid
			125,000 (4) Buildings and Equipment Acquired

✔ 40,000

Buildings and Equipment (Cost)	**Accumulated Depreciation**	**Bonds Payable**
✔ 100,000	30,000 ✔	0 ✔
(4) 125,000	10,000 (2)	100,000 (5)
✔ 225,000	40,000 ✔	100,000 ✔

Capital Stock	**Retained Earnings**
100,000 ✔	15,000 ✔
	(3) 10,000 20,000 (1)
100,000 ✔	25,000 ✔

Exhibit 5.12 shows the sum of the debit entries in the Working Capital account to be $130,000, whereas the sum of the credit entries is $135,000. There is an excess of credits over debits in the account of $5,000, which accounts for the decrease in working capital from $45,000 to $40,000 during the year.

182

We can see in Exhibit 5.12 that operations provided working capital of $30,000 (= $20,000 + $10,000), whereas new bond issues provided $100,000 of working capital. Working capital of $135,000 was used: $10,000 for dividends and $125,000 for new buildings and equipment.

Step 4 The final step is the preparation of the formal statement of changes in financial position. The statement for Solinger Electric Corporation is shown in Exhibit 5.13. Section I presents the sources and uses of working capital. This section of the statement is prepared directly from information in the master Working Capital account. Section II of the Statement of Changes in Financial Position analyzes the

---

Exhibit 5.13
Solinger Electric Corporation Statement of Changes in Financial Position for the Year 1982

SECTION I. SOURCES AND USES OF WORKING CAPITAL

Sources of Working Capital

Operations:

Net Income	$20,000	
Add Back Expenses Not Using Working Capital:		
Depreciation	10,000	
Total Sources from Operations		$ 30,000
Proceeds from Long-Term Bonds Issued		100,000
Total Sources of Working Capital		$130,000

Uses of Working Capital

Dividends		$ 10,000
Acquisition of Buildings and Equipment		125,000
Total Uses of Working Capital		$135,000
Net Decrease in Working Capital During the Year (Sources Minus Uses)		$ 5,000

SECTION II. ANALYSIS OF CHANGES IN WORKING CAPITAL ACCOUNTS

Current Asset Item Increases (Decreases)

Cash	$(27,000)	
Accounts Receivable	35,000	
Merchandise Inventory	10,000	
Net Increase (Decrease) in Current Asset Items		$ 18,000

Current Liability Increases (Decreases)

Accounts Payable—Merchandise Suppliers	$20,000	
Accounts Payable—Other Suppliers	2,000	
Salaries Payable	1,000	
Net Increase (Decrease) in Current Liability Items		23,000
Net Decrease in Working Capital During the Year (Net Increases in Current Liability Items Minus Net Increase in Current Asset Items)		$ 5,000

changes in the individual current asset and current liability accounts. That is, the manner in which the net change in working capital (explained in Section I of the statement) affects the various working capital accounts is analyzed in Section II. The information needed for preparing Section II is obtained from the comparative balance sheets in Exhibit 5.4.

The information in Section II of the statement is necessary for a complete assessment of a firm's liquidity and changes in the structure of its assets and equities. The net change explained in Section I can result from the offsetting of much larger increases and decreases in individual current asset and current liability accounts.

For example, cash decreased by $27,000, whereas accounts receivable increased by $35,000 during the year. Together, this represents an increase of $8,000 in the firm's most liquid assets. However, most of the increased liquidity does not reflect cash immediately available to pay liabilities or to make purchases. Instead, cash must first be collected from customers. Financial statement readers interested in assessing changes in the structure of the firm's working capital would find the information in Section II of the statement of changes in financial position to be useful.

Converting Working Capital Provided by Operations to Cash Provided by Operations

The preceding sections have illustrated the construction of the statement of changes in financial position, first using a cash definition of funds and then using a working capital definition of funds. Most published financial statements use working capital as the definition of funds. If the analyst wishes to convert such a statement to one using a cash definition, then the analyst can use the procedures illustrated earlier or the following shortcuts.

1 Begin with the amount of working capital provided by operations as previously determined.
2 Add the amount of the change in current operating accounts (other than cash) that experienced a net credit change during the period. These are decreases in receivables, inventories, and prepayments and increases in current operating liability accounts.
3 Subtract the amount of the change in current operating accounts (other than cash) that experienced a net debit change during the period. These are increases in receivables, inventories, and prepayments and decreases in current operating liability accounts.
4 The result is the cash flow provided by operations.

We saw in Exhibit 5.2 that the working capital provided by operations during 1982 by Solinger Electric Corporation was $30,000, whereas the cash flow provided by operations was $8,000. Exhibit 5.14 illustrates the procedure for converting working capital to cash flow provided by operations.

Exhibit 5.14
**Solinger Electric Corporation Conversion of Working Capital
Provided by Operations to Cash Flow Provided by Operations**

Working Capital Provided by Operations		$30,000
Add the Net Change in Current Operating Asset Accounts (Except Cash) That Decreased and Current Operating Liability Accounts That Increased During the Period (Credit Changes):		
Accounts Payable—Merchandise Suppliers	$20,000	
Accounts Payable—Other Suppliers	2,000	
Salaries Payable	1,000	
Total Additions		23,000
Subtract the Net Change in Current Operating Asset Accounts (Except Cash) That Increased and Current Operating Liability Accounts That Decreased During the Period (Debit Changes):		
Accounts Receivable	$35,000	
Merchandise Inventory	10,000	
Total Subtractions		(45,000)
Cash Provided by Operations		$ 8,000

The rationale for the additions and the subtractions in this procedure may be better understood by considering Salaries Payable and Accounts Receivable.

The change in the Salaries Payable account is explained as follows:

Salaries Payable, December 31, 1981	$ 5,000
Plus Salaries Expense—1982	20,000
Less Salaries Paid in Cash—1982	(19,000)
Salaries Payable, December 31, 1982	$ 6,000

The amount of working capital provided by operations reflects a $20,000 use of working capital relating to salary expense during the period. Because only $19,000 was disbursed to employees, $1,000 (= $20,000 − $19,000) must be added back to working capital from operations to determine cash flow from operations.

The change in the Accounts Receivable account is explained as follows:

Accounts Receivable, December 31, 1981	$ 20,000
Plus Sales on Account—1982	125,000
Less Cash Collections from Customers—1982	(90,000)
Accounts Receivable, December 31, 1982	$ 55,000

The amount of working capital provided by operations reflects a $125,000 source of working capital relating to sales on account during the period. Since only $90,000 was collected in cash, $35,000 (= $125,000 − $90,000) must be subtracted from working capital provided by operations to determine cash flow provided by operations.

Summary

Generally accepted accounting principles require that a statement of changes in financial position be presented whenever a firm presents an income statement and a balance sheet. The statement of changes in financial position reports on flows of funds into and out of a business during a period. The critical element in defining funds is the time horizon relevant for measuring liquidity. The shorter the time horizon, the more restrictive the definition. Funds are usually defined as working capital (current assets minus current liabilities), but occasionally funds may be defined simply as cash.

The statement of changes in financial position discloses the sources of funds from operations separately from the nonoperating sources and uses. The primary source of funds is usually operations. Understanding the notion of funds provided by operations is particularly important to understanding the statement of changes in financial position. Net income is derived from revenues and expenses computed on an accrual basis. The statement of changes in financial position converts net income from the accrual basis to a report of funds flows. Funds provided by operations are rarely equal to net income.

The statement of changes in financial position is basically derived from an analysis of changes in balance sheet accounts during the accounting period. If the double-entry recording process has been applied properly, the net change in funds (working capital or cash or whatever) accounts during the period will equal the net change in all nonfunds accounts. By reconstructing the entries made in nonfunds accounts and explaining their net change during the period, the net change in the funds accounts is also explained.

The format of the statement of changes in financial position is organized in two sections. The sources and uses of funds are presented first, followed by an analysis of the changes in the individual funds accounts. Most published statements of changes in financial position show the derivation of funds provided by operations by beginning with net income and then adding expenses that do not use funds and subtracting revenues that do not provide funds.

Problem for Self-Study

Exhibit 5.15 presents a comparative balance sheet for Gordon Corporation as of December 31, 1981 and 1982. The following information pertains to Gordon Corporation for 1982.

1 Net income was $200,000.
2 Dividends declared and paid were $120,000.
3 Depreciation expense totaled $80,000.
4 Buildings and equipment originally costing $50,000 and with accumulated depreciation of $40,000 were sold for $10,000.

   a Prepare a T-account work sheet for the preparation of a statement of changes in financial position, defining funds as cash.

Exhibit 5.15
Gordon Corporation
Comparative Balance Sheet
December 31, 1981 and 1982
(amounts in OOO's)

	December 31, 1981	December 31, 1982
ASSETS		
Current Assets:		
Cash	$ 70	$ 40
Accounts Receivable	320	420
Merchandise Inventories	360	470
Prepayments	50	70
Total Current Assets	$ 800	$1,000
Property, Plant, and Equipment:		
Land	$ 200	$ 250
Buildings and Equipment (net of accumulated depreciation of $800 and $840)	1,000	1,150
Total Property, Plant, and Equipment	$1,200	$1,400
Total Assets	$2,000	$2,400
LIABILITIES AND SHAREHOLDERS' EQUITY		
Current Liabilities:		
Accounts Payable	$ 320	$ 440
Income Taxes Payable	60	80
Other Current Liabilities	170	360
Total Current Liabilities	$ 550	$ 880
Noncurrent Liabilities:		
Bonds Payable	$ 250	$ 200
Total Liabilities	$ 800	$1,080
Shareholders' Equity:		
Common Stock	$ 500	$ 540
Retained Earnings	700	780
Total Shareholders' Equity	$1,200	$1,320
Total Liabilities and Shareholders' Equity	$2,000	$2,400

b Prepare a T-account work sheet for the preparation of a statement of changes in financial position, defining funds as working capital.

c Convert working capital provided by operations to cash flow provided by operations.

Suggested Solution

Exhibit 5.16 presents a completed T-account work sheet for Gordon Corporation with funds defined as cash. Exhibit 5.17 presents a completed T-account work sheet with funds defined as working capital. Exhibit 5.18 shows the conversion of working capital provided by operations to cash flow provided by operations.

Exhibit 5.16
T-Account Work Sheet for Gordon Corporation
Funds Defined as Cash
(amounts in 000's)

Cash

✔ 70

From Operations

Net Income and Addbacks | Net Loss and Subtractions

(1)	200	100	(5)
(3)	80	110	(6)
(10)	120	20	(7)
(11)	20		
(12)	190		

Other (Nonoperating)

(4)	10	120	(2)
(14)	40	50	(8)
		240	(9)
		50	(13)

✔ 40

Accounts Receivable

✔	320	
(5)	100	
✔	420	

Merchandise Inventories

✔	360	
(6)	110	
✔	470	

Prepayments

✔	50	
(7)	20	
✔	70	

Land

✔	200	
(8)	50	
✔	250	

Buildings and Equipment—Net

✔	1,000		
(4)	40	80	(3)
(9)	240	50	(4)
✔	1,150		

Accounts Payable

	320	✔
	120	(10)
	440	✔

Income Taxes Payable

	60	✔
	20	(11)
	80	✔

Other Current Liabilities

	170	✔
	190	(12)
	360	✔

Bonds Payable

		250	✔
(13)	50		
		200	✔

Common Stock

	500	✔
	40	(14)
	540	✔

Retained Earnings

(2)	120	700	✔
		200	(1)
		780	✔

188

Exhibit 5.17

T-Account Work Sheet for Gordon Corporation
Funds Defined as Working Capital
(amounts in 000's)

Working Capital

✔ 250

From Operations

Net Income and Additions | Net Loss and Subtractions

(1) 200
(3) 80

Other (Nonoperating)

(4) 10 | 120 (2)
(8) 40 | 50 (5)
| 240 (6)
| 50 (7)

✔ 120

Land	Buildings and Equipment—Net	Bonds Payable
✔ 200	✔ 1,000	250 ✔
(5) 50	(4) 40 80 (3)	(7) 50
	(6) 240 50 (4)	
✔ 250	✔ 1,150	200 ✔

Common Stock	Retained Earnings
500 ✔	700 ✔
40 (8)	(2) 120 200 (1)
540 ✔	780 ✔

Exhibit 5.18

Gordon Corporation Conversion
of Working Capital Provided by
Operations To Cash Flow Provided by Operations
(amounts in 000's)

Working Capital Provided by Operations	$280
Plus:	
Increase in Accounts Payable	120
Increase in Income Taxes Payable	20
Increase in Other Current Liabilities	190
Less:	
Increase in Accounts Receivable	(100)
Increase in Merchandise Inventories	(110)
Increase in Prepayments	(20)
Cash Provided by Operations	$380

Questions and Problems

1 Review the meaning of the following concepts or terms discussed in this chapter.
   a Funds flow.
   b Liquidity.
   c Cash as funds.
   d Working capital as funds.
   e Cash provided by operations.
   f Working capital provided by operations.
   g Dual transactions assumption.
   h Depreciation is not a source of funds.
   i Analysis of changes in working capital accounts.

2 "The reporting objective of the income statement under the accrual basis of accounting and the reporting objective of the statement of changes in financial position could be more easily accomplished by issuing a single income statement using the cash basis of accounting." Evaluate this proposal.

3 The text indicates that the statement of changes in financial position provides information about changes in the structure of a firm's assets and equities. Of what value is information about the structure of a firm's assets and equities?

4 One writer stated that:

   Depreciation expense was the chief source of funds for growth in industries.
   A reader criticized this statement by replying:

   The fact remains that if the companies listed had elected, in any year, to charge off $10 million more depreciation than they did charge off, they would not thereby have added one dime to the total of their funds available for plant expansion or for increasing inventories or receivables. Therefore, to speak of depreciation expense as a source of funds has no significance in a discussion of fundamentals.

   Comment on these statements, including income tax effects.

5 Refer to the discussion in Chapter 4 of the accounting for a manufacturing firm. A manufacturing firm records depreciation on factory machinery (or equipment or buildings) with an entry such as the following:

Work-in-Process Inventory	10,000	
Accumulated Depreciation (Factory Machinery)		10,000

   Assume that none of the work-in-process was completed during the current accounting period. All sales were made from Finished Goods Inventory and there were no transfers from Work-in-Process Inventory to Finished Goods Inventory.
   a Under these unrealistic assumptions, trace the effects of the above entry on the balance sheet accounts. Think about the totals of current assets, all assets, liabilities, and all equities.
   b What is the effect of the above entry on working capital?
   c Aside from income tax effects, can depreciation be a source of funds? Explain.
   d What can you generalize from the above answers to a more realistic situation where part of the goods produced during the current period were sold?

6 Exhibit 5.19 shows a simplified statement of changes in financial position for a period. Nine of the lines in the statement are numbered. Other lines are various subtotals and grand totals; these are to be ignored in the remainder of the problem. Assume that the accounting cycle is complete for the period and that all of the financial statements have been prepared. Then it is discovered that a transaction has been overlooked. That transaction is recorded in the accounts and all of the financial statements are corrected. For each of the following transactions, indicate which of the numbered lines of the funds statement is affected. Define funds as working capital. If net income, line (1), is affected, be sure to indicate whether it decreases or increases. Ignore income tax effects.

a Depreciation expense on cash register.

b Purchase of machinery for cash.

c Declaration of a cash dividend on common stock; the dividend has not been paid at the close of the fiscal year.

d Issue of preferred stock for cash.

e Issue of common stock for cash.

f Proceeds of sale of common stock investment, a noncurrent asset, for cash. The investment was sold for book value.

g Merchandise Inventory is sold for a price in excess of cost, but payment is received in the form of a long-term note receivable.

Exhibit 5.19
**Simplified Statement of Changes
in Financial Position for a Period**
(*Problems 6, 7, and 8*)

Sources of Funds

From Operations:

Net Income	(1)
Additions for Expenses Not Using Funds	+ (2)
Subtractions for Revenues Not Producing Funds	− (3)
Total Funds Provided by Operations	S1

Other Sources:

Issues of Long-Term Debt and Owners' Equity	(4)
Proceeds from Dispositions of Noncurrent Assets	(5)
	S2
Total Sources of Funds	S1 + S2

Uses of Funds

Dividends	(6)
Acquisition of Noncurrent Assets	(7)
Retirement of Noncurrent Debt and Equity Securities	(8)
Total Uses of Funds	S3
Sources of Funds Minus Uses of Funds = Change in Funds for Year, (S1 + S2 − S3)	T

Analysis of Changes in Funds Accounts

Change in Funds Accounts	(9)
Increases in Funds Minus Decreases in Funds = Change in Funds for Year, (9) = (S1 + S2 − S3)	T

---

7 Refer to the instructions in the preceding question. Repeat those instructions for the following transactions.
  a Amortization of patent, treated as an expense.
  b Amortization of patent, charged to production activities. The items being produced have not yet been completed.
  c Acquisition of a factory site by issue of capital stock.
  d Purchase of inventory on account.
  e Uninsured fire loss of merchandise inventory.
  f Collection of an account receivable.
  g Issue of bonds for cash.

8 Refer to Exhibit 5.19 and to the instructions in Problem **6**. Now define funds as cash only. Expand the meanings of lines (2) and (3) of Exhibit 5.19 as follows:

Line (2): Additions for Expenses Not Using Cash; for Decreases in Current Asset Accounts Other than Cash; and for Increases in Current Liabilities.

Line (3): Subtractions for Revenues Not Producing Cash; for Increases in Current Asset Accounts Other than Cash; and for Decreases in Current Liabilities.

Analyze the effects of the transactions on the funds statement for the period.

  a Use transactions **a–g** of Problem **6**.
  b Use transactions **a–g** of Problem **7**.

9 The following items were found in the financial statements of Maher Company for 1982:

Sales	$90,000
Depreciation Expense	45,000
Income Taxes	10,000
Other Expenses	20,000
Common Stock Issued During Year	17,500

Prepare a portion of the statement of changes in financial position (working capital definition of funds) to present working capital from operations for the year 1982.

10 Refer to the preceding problem. Assuming the following changes in working capital accounts other than cash:

Accounts Receivable	$45,000 Increase
Merchandise Inventories	30,000 Increase
Prepayments	5,000 Decrease
Accounts Payable	15,000 Increase
Income Taxes Payable	7,500 Decrease

Compute the amount of cash provided by operations.

11 The comparative balance sheet of the Kanodia Company showed a balance in the Buildings and Equipment account at December 31, 1982, of $24,600,000; at December 31, 1981, the balance was $24,000,000. The Accumulated Depreciation account showed a balance of $8,600,000 at December 31, 1982, and $7,600,000 at December 31, 1981. The Statement of Changes in Financial Position reports that expenditures for buildings and equipment for the year totaled $1,300,000. The income statement indicates a depreciation charge of $1,200,000 for the year. Buildings and equipment were sold during the year at their book value.

192

Calculate the acquisition cost and accumulated depreciation of the buildings and equipment retired during the year and the proceeds from their disposition.

12 Condensed financial statement data for the Harris Company are shown in Exhibits 5.20 and 5.21. During 1982, equipment costing $10,000 and with $8,000 of accumulated depreciation was sold for $2,000.

Exhibit 5.20
Harris Company
Comparative Balance Sheets
(Problems 12, 13, and 14)

ASSETS	January 1, 1982	December 31, 1982
Cash	$ 20,000	$ 24,000
Accounts Receivable	52,000	58,000
Inventory	79,000	81,000
Land	15,000	15,000
Buildings and Equipment (Cost)	400,000	415,000
Less Accumulated Depreciation	(240,000)	(252,000)
Total Assets	$326,000	$341,000
LIABILITIES AND SHAREHOLDERS' EQUITY		
Accounts Payable	$ 62,000	$ 65,000
Notes Payable (Current)	16,000	14,000
Mortgage Payable	60,000	60,000
Common Stock	120,000	125,000
Retained Earnings	68,000	77,000
Total Liabilities and Shareholders' Equity	$326,000	$341,000

Exhibit 5.21
Harris Company Statement of Income
and Retained Earnings for the Year 1982

Revenues		$200,000
Expenses:		
Cost of Goods Sold	$100,000	
Wages and Salaries	30,000	
Depreciation	20,000	
Income Taxes	11,000	
Total		161,000
Net Income		$ 39,000
Dividends on Common Stock		30,000
Addition to Retained Earnings for Year		$ 9,000
Retained Earnings, January 1, 1982		68,000
Retained Earnings, December 31, 1982		$ 77,000

193

a Prepare a T-account work sheet for the statement of changes in financial position for the year 1982. Use a working capital definition of funds.

b Prepare a statement of changes in financial position for the year 1982. Use a working capital definition of funds.

13 (This problem should not be attempted until Problem **12** has been worked.) Refer to Problem **12** concerning Harris Company. Convert working capital provided by operations to cash flow provided by operations.

14 Refer to Problem **12** concerning Harris Company. Work parts **a** and **b**, defining funds as cash.

15 Condensed financial statement data for the Victoria Company for the year are shown in Exhibit 5.22.

Exhibit 5.22
Victoria Company
Postclosing Trial Balance
Comparative Data
(*Problems 15, 16, and 17*)

Debits:	January 1	December 31
Cash	$ 62,000	$ 55,000
Accounts Receivable	135,000	163,000
Merchandise Inventory	247,000	262,000
Plant and Equipment (Cost)	1,362,000	1,389,000
Total Debits	$1,806,000	$1,869,000
Credits:		
Accounts Payable	$ 72,000	$ 75,000
Accumulated Depreciation	508,000	573,000
Long-Term Debt	200,000	215,000
Capital Stock	509,000	509,000
Retained Earnings	517,000	497,000
Total Credits	$1,806,000	$1,869,000

INCOME STATEMENT DATA	
Sales	$1,338,000
Cost of Goods Sold (excluding depreciation)	932,000
Selling and Administrative Expenses	298,000
Depreciation Expense	93,000
Interest Expense	20,000
Other Expenses	15,000

Expenditures on new plant and equipment for the year amounted to $121,000. Old plant and equipment that had cost $94,000 were sold during the year. It was sold for cash at book value.

a Prepare an income statement (including a reconciliation of retained earnings) for the year.

b Prepare a statement of changes in financial position for the Victoria Company for the year, defining funds as working capital. Support the Statement of Changes in Financial Position with a T-account work sheet.

16 (This problem should not be attempted until Problem **15** has been worked.) Refer to the data of Problem **15** for the Victoria Company. Convert working capital provided by operations to cash provided by operations.

17 Refer to the data of Problem **15** for the Victoria Company. Work part **b**, defining funds as cash.

18 Condensed financial statement data of the Alberta Company for the years ending December 31, 1981, 1982, and 1983, are presented in Exhibits 5.23 and 5.24.

Exhibit 5.23
Alberta Company
Postclosing Trial Balance
Comparative Data
(*Problems 18 and 19*)

Debits:	12/31/81	12/31/82	12/31/83
Current Assets	$ 290,000	$ 322,000	$ 342,000
Noncurrent Assets	1,616,000	1,679,000	1,875,000
Total Debits	$1,906,000	$2,001,000	$2,217,000
Credits:			
Current Liabilities	$ 81,000	$ 80,000	$ 83,000
Accumulated Depreciation	697,000	720,000	745,000
Long-Term Debt	106,000	90,000	135,000
Capital Stock	377,000	423,000	514,000
Retained Earnings	645,000	688,000	740,000
Total Credits	$1,906,000	$2,001,000	$2,217,000

Exhibit 5.24
Alberta Company
Income and Retained Earnings
Statement Data

	1982	1983
Sales	$910,000	$970,000
Interest and Other Revenue	5,000	7,000
Cost of Goods Sold (Excluding Depreciation)	370,000	413,000
Selling and Administrative Expenses	320,000	301,000
Depreciation	87,000	98,000
Federal Income Taxes	55,000	66,000
Dividends Declared	40,000	47,000

The original cost of the noncurrent assets sold during 1982 was $108,000. These assets were sold for cash at their net book value. Prepare a statement of changes in financial position for the year 1982 with funds defined as working capital. Support the statement with a T-account work sheet.

19 Refer to the data of Problem **18**. Prepare a T-account work sheet and a statement of changes in financial position for 1983 with funds defined as working capital. Noncurrent assets were sold during the year at book value. Expenditures on new noncurrent assets amounted to $318,000 during 1983.

20 Financial statement data for the Perkerson Supply Company for the years ending December, 31, 1981, and December 31, 1982, are presented in Exhibit 5.25.

Exhibit 5.25
Perkerson Supply Company
Comparative Balance Sheets
(*Problems 20, 21, and 22*)

ASSETS

	December 31 1981	1982
Current Assets:		
Cash	$ 179,000	$ 162,000
Accounts Receivable	473,000	526,000
Inventory	502,000	604,000
Total Current Assets	$1,154,000	$1,292,000
Noncurrent Assets:		
Land	$ 297,000	$ 315,000
Buildings and Machinery	4,339,000	4,773,000
Less Accumulated Depreciation	(1,987,000)	(2,182,000)
Total Noncurrent Assets	$2,649,000	$2,906,000
Total Assets	$3,803,000	$4,198,000

LIABILITIES AND SHAREHOLDERS' EQUITY

Current Liabilities:		
Accounts Payable	$ 206,000	$ 279,000
Taxes Payable	137,000	145,000
Other Short-Term Payables	294,000	363,000
Total Current Liabilities	$ 637,000	$ 787,000
Noncurrent Liabilities:		
Bonds Payable	992,000	967,000
Total Liabilities	$1,629,000	$1,754,000
Shareholders' Equity:		
Common Stock	$ 836,000	$ 852,000
Retained Earnings	1,338,000	1,592,000
Total Shareholders' Equity	$2,174,000	$2,444,000
Total Liabilities and Shareholders' Equity	$3,803,000	$4,198,000

Additional information:

(1) Net income for the year was $324,000; dividends declared and paid were $70,000.

(2) Depreciation expense for the year was $305,000 on buildings and machinery.

(3) Machinery originally costing $125,000 and with accumulated depreciation of $110,000 was sold for $15,000.

Prepare a statement of changes in financial position for the Perkerson Supply Company for 1982 with funds defined as working capital. Support the statement with a T-account work sheet.

21 (This problem should not be attempted until Problem **20** has been worked.) Refer to Problem **20** concerning the Perkerson Supply Company. Convert working capital provided by operations to cash provided by operations.

22 Refer to Problem **20** concerning the Perkerson Supply Company. Work the problem using a definition of funds as only cash.

23 The Quinta Company presents the postclosing trial balance shown in Exhibit 5.26 and statement of changes in financial position shown in Exhibit 5.27 for the year 1982.

Investment, equipment, and land were sold for cash at their net book value. The accumulated depreciation of the equipment sold was $20,000. Current liabilities were $75,000 at the start of the year and $125,000 at the end of the year.

Prepare a balance sheet for the beginning of the year, January 1, 1982.

Exhibit 5.26
Quinta Company
Postclosing Trial Balance,
December 31, 1982
(*Problem 23*)

Debit Balances:

Working Capital (= Current Assets − Current Liabilities)	$200,000
Land	40,000
Buildings and Equipment	500,000
Investments (Noncurrent)	100,000
Total Debits	$840,000

Credit Balances:

Accumulated Depreciation	$200,000
Bonds Payable	100,000
Common Stock	200,000
Retained Earnings	340,000
Total Credits	$840,000

Exhibit 5.27
Quinta Company
Statement of Changes in
Financial Position
for the Year 1982

SOURCES OF WORKING CAPITAL
From Operations:

Net Income		$200,000
Addbacks for Depreciation Expense Not Using Working Capital		60,000
Total Sources from Operations		$260,000

Proceeds from Issues of Securities and Debit:

Capital Stock Issue	$60,000	
Bond Issue	40,000	
Total Proceeds		100,000

Proceeds of Disposition of Noncurrent Assets:

Sale of Investments	$40,000	
Sale of Buildings and Equipment	15,000	
Sale of Land	10,000	
Total Proceeds		65,000

Total Sources of Working Capital $425,000

USES OF WORKING CAPITAL

Dividends	$200,000
Acquisition of Buildings and Equipment	130,000

Total Uses of Working Capital $330,000

Increase in Working Capital During the Year
(Sources Minus Uses) .... $ 95,000

Net Increase in Working Capital Items
(Net Current Asset Item Increases Minus
Net Current Liability Item Increases) .... $ 95,000

24 The purpose of this problem is to convince you that depreciation expense uses no funds and that depreciation is not a source of funds. To carry out this exercise, get one writing pen, a dollar's worth of change, and a piece of paper. Put 40 cents, the writing pen, and the piece of paper on the other side of the desk and put 60 cents on your side of the desk. **(1)** Your balance sheet now looks like the one shown below.

My Balance Sheet as of Now
(*Problem 24*)

Assets		Equities	
Cash	$0.60	Contributed Capital	$0.60

198

(2) You are about to acquire a *noncurrent* asset, one long-lived writing pen. The pen costs 40 cents.

(3) Acquire the pen by exchanging 40 cents for the pen which is now across the desk. Record the following journal entry:

Noncurrent Assets	0.40	
Cash		0.40

(4) Acquire the piece of paper, a current asset item, by trading 5 cents for the paper which is now across the desk. Record the following journal entry:

Current Asset—Paper Inventory	0.05	
Cash		0.05

(5) Sign your name on the piece of paper you now have with the pen you acquired. (No journal entry required.)

(6) Because of a sudden surge in your popularity, your autograph has become valuable. Sell your autograph to the other side of the table for 80 cents. Record the following journal entry:

Cash	0.80	
Sales		0.80

(7) The accounting period is over. Record an adjusting entry to recognize 10 cents depreciation for the period on the writing pen:

Depreciation on Noncurrent Assets	0.10	
Accumulated Depreciation on Noncurrent Assets		0.10

(8) Depreciation on Noncurrent Assets is, in this case, a cost of work-in-process inventory that is to be counted as part of Cost of Goods Sold. Record the following journal entry to measure Cost of Goods Sold.

Cost of Goods Sold	0.15	
Depreciation on Noncurrent Assets		0.10
Current Asset—Paper Inventory		0.05

(9) Close all temporary accounts with the following entry:

Sales	0.80	
Cost of Goods Sold		0.15
Retained Earnings		0.65

a Ignore income taxes. Prepare an income statement for the period just ended and a balance sheet as of the end of the period.

b Prepare a statement of changes in financial position for the period just ended. Start with net income and adjustments thereto.

Note: Observe that depreciation used no funds not otherwise counted in the nonoperating sources and uses. Funds were provided by selling one autograph. Notice that your funds on hand at the end of the period do not depend on the amount of depreciation on the pen for the period. If this is not clear, repeat **a** and **b** assuming depreciation of $0.30 or $0.00 in step **(7)**.

25 Refer to Exhibit A.3 in Appendix A, the Statement of Changes in Financial Position for General Products Company for the years 1980, 1981, and 1982. Respond to each of the following questions.

a What was the total amount of working capital provided by operations during 1980? During 1981? During 1982?

b Calculate the amount of cash and marketable securities provided by operations during 1980, during 1981, and during 1982. Assume that changes in short-term borrowings are considered *nonoperating* sources and uses of cash.

c How would you assess the change in liquidity of General Products during 1980, 1981, and 1982?

26 (Adapted from a problem by Professor Leonard Morrissey.)

RV Suppliers, Incorporated, founded in July 1976, manufactures "Kaps." A "Kap" is a relatively low-cost camping unit attached to a pickup truck. Most units consist of an extruded aluminum frame and a fiberglass skin.

After a loss in its initial (1976–77) year, the Company was barely profitable in fiscal years 1978 and 1979. More substantial profits were realized in fiscal years 1980 and 1981, as indicated in the financial statements shown in Exhibits 5.28 and 5.29.

Exhibit 5.28
RV Suppliers, Incorporated
Income Statements
(amounts in 000's)

	Fiscal Years Ended June 30		
	1980	**1981**	**1982**
Net Sales	$266.4	$424.0	$247.4
Cost of Goods Sold	191.4	314.6	210.6
Gross Margin	$ 75.0	$109.4	$ 36.8
Operating Expenses[a]	35.5	58.4	55.2
Income (Loss) Before Income Taxes	$ 39.5	$51.0	$(18.4)
Income Taxes	12.3	16.4	(5.0)
Net Income (Loss)	$ 27.2	$ 34.6	$(13.4)

[a]Includes depreciation expense of $1.7 in 1980, $4.8 in 1981, and $7.6 in 1982.

However, in fiscal 1982, ended just last month, the Company suffered a loss of $13,400. Sales dropped from $424,000 in fiscal 1981 to $247,000 in fiscal 1982. The outlook for fiscal 1983 is not encouraging. Potential buyers continue to shun pickup trucks in preference to more energy-efficient small foreign and domestic automobiles.

Exhibit 5.29
RV Suppliers, Incorporated
Balance Sheet
(amounts in 000's)

ASSETS	June 30, 1980	June 30, 1981	June 30, 1982
Current Assets:			
Cash	$ 14.0	$ 12.0	$ 5.2
Accounts Receivable	28.8	55.6	24.2
Inventories	54.0	85.6	81.0
Tax Refund Receivable	0	0	5.0
Prepayments	4.8	7.4	5.6
Total Current Assets	$101.6	$160.6	$121.0
Property, Plant, Equipment—Net[a]	30.2	73.4	72.2
Total Assets	$131.8	$234.0	$193.2

LIABILITIES AND SHAREHOLDERS' EQUITY			
Current Liabilities:			
Bank Notes Payable	$ 10.0	$ 52.0	$ 70.0
Accounts Payable	31.6	53.4	17.4
Income Taxes Payable	5.8	7.0	0
Other Current Liabilities	4.2	6.8	4.4
Total Current Liabilities	$ 51.6	$119.2	$ 91.8
Shareholders' Equity:			
Capital Stock	$ 44.6	$ 44.6	$ 44.6
Retained Earnings	35.6	70.2	56.8
Total Shareholders' Equity	$ 80.2	$114.8	$101.4
Total Liabilities and Shareholders' Equity	$131.8	$234.0	$193.2

	1980	1981	1982
[a]Acquisitions	$ 13.4	$ 48.4	$ 11.8
Depreciation Expense	(1.7)	(4.8)	(7.6)
Book Value and Sales Proceeds from Retirements	(.4)	(.4)	(5.4)
Net Change in Property, Plant, and Equipment	$ 11.3	$ 43.2	$ (1.2)

How did the Company finance its rapid growth during the year ended June 30, 1981? What were the sources and uses of cash during the year? Similarly, how did the Company manage its financial affairs during the abrupt contraction in business during the year just ended last month?

Chapter 6　Introduction to Financial Statement Analysis

A major function of accounting and financial reporting is helping investors make investment decisions. For example, assume that you recently inherited $25,000 and must decide what to do with the bequest. You have narrowed the investment decision to either purchasing a certificate of deposit at a local bank or purchasing shares of common stock of Horrigan Corporation, currently selling for $40 per share. Your decision will be based on the *return* anticipated from each investment and the *risk* associated with that return.

The bank is currently paying interest at the rate of 12 percent annually on certificates of deposit. Because it is unlikely that the bank will go out of business, you are virtually certain of earning 12 percent each year.

The return from investing in the shares of common stock of Horrigan Corporation has two components. First, the firm paid a cash dividend in 1982, their most recent year, of $.625 per share, and it is anticipated that this dividend will continue in the future. Second, the market price of the stock is likely to change between the date the shares are purchased and the date in the future when they are sold. The difference between the eventual selling price per share and the $40 purchase price, often called a *capital gain,* is a second component of the return from buying the stock.

Compared to the interest on the certificate of deposit, the return from the common stock investment is more risky. Future dividends and market price changes are likely to be associated, at least partially, with the profitability of the firm. Future income might be less than is currently anticipated if competitors introduce new

202

products that erode Horrigan Corporation's share of its sales market. Future income might be greater than currently anticipated if Horrigan Corporation makes important discoveries or introduces successful new products.

The market price of Horrigan Corporation's shares will probably also be affected by economy-wide factors such as inflation and unemployment. Also, specific industry factors, such as raw materials shortages or government antitrust actions, may influence the market price of the shares. Because most individuals prefer less risk to more risk, you will probably demand a higher expected return from the purchase of Horrigan Corporation's shares than if you invest the inheritance in a certificate of deposit.

There are numerous sources of information that might be consulted in assessing the return and risk of investment alternatives. One such source is the financial statements prepared by firms and distributed periodically to shareholders and potential investors as part of the firm's annual report. These financial statements, based on the results of past activities, can be analyzed in order to obtain useful information for predicting future rates of return and for assessing risk.

In this chapter, we introduce some of the basic concepts and methods of financial statement analysis. Comprehensive analysis and interpretation require an understanding of specific, generally accepted accounting principles discussed in Chapters 7 through 13. Thus, this chapter provides a bridge between the preceding introductory chapters and the more advanced ones that follow.

Objectives of Financial Statement Analysis

The first question likely to be raised in analyzing a set of financial statements is "What do I look for?" Most financial statement analysis is directed at some aspect of a firm's *profitability* or its *risk*.

For example, assume that you are interested in acquiring a firm's common stock and wish to predict future dividends and market price changes for the stock. Dividends and market price changes are likely to be affected, at least partially, by the future profitability of the firm. The firm's past earnings performance can be analyzed as a basis for predicting its future profitability.

Suppose instead that you wished to acquire a firm's long-term bonds. Your return will be primarily in the form of periodic contractual interest receipts. Of particular concern here is the likelihood (risk) that the firm will have sufficient cash available to make the required periodic interest payments when due and to repay the principal at maturity. The focus of financial statement analysis in this case is the long-term solvency risk, or long-run cash-generating ability, of the firm.

Finally, assume that you plan to extend a loan to a firm, expecting repayment of the loan with interest in 6 months. The focus of financial statement analysis in this case is the short-term liquidity risk of the firm.

Before analyzing a set of financial statements, it is important that the objective of the analysis be clearly specified. The analytical techniques used will differ, as we show in this chapter, depending on the purpose of the analysis.

Usefulness of Ratios

The various items in financial statements may be difficult to interpret in the form in which they are presented. For example, the profitability of a firm may be difficult to assess by looking at the amount of net income alone. It is helpful to compare earnings with the assets or capital required to generate those earnings. This relationship, and other important ones between various items in the financial statements, can be expressed in the form of ratios. Some ratios compare items within the income statement; some use only balance sheet data; others relate items from more than one statement. Ratios are useful tools of financial statement analysis because they conveniently summarize data in a form that is more easily understood, interpreted, and compared.

Exhibit 6.1
Horrigan Corporation
Comparative Balance Sheets
(amounts in millions)

	December 31			
ASSETS	**1979**	**1980**	**1981**	**1982**
Cash	$ 10	$ 10	$ 8	$ 10
Marketable Securities	—	4	—	2
Accounts Receivable (net)	26	36	46	76
Inventories	14	30	46	83
Total Current Assets	$ 50	$ 80	$100	$171
Land	$ 20	$ 30	$ 60	$ 60
Building	150	150	150	190
Equipment	70	192	276	313
Less Accumulated Depreciation	(40)	(52)	(66)	(84)
Total Noncurrent Assets	$200	$320	$420	$479
Total Assets	$250	$400	$520	$650
LIABILITIES AND SHAREHOLDERS' EQUITY				
Accounts Payable	$ 25	$ 30	$ 35	$ 50
Salaries Payable	10	13	15	20
Income Taxes Payable	5	7	10	20
Total Current Liabilities	$ 40	$ 50	$ 60	$ 90
Bonds Payable	50	50	100	150
Total Liabilities	$ 90	$100	$160	$240
Common Stock ($10-par value)	$100	$150	$160	$160
Additional Paid-in Capital	20	100	120	120
Retained Earnings	40	50	80	130
Total Shareholders' Equity	$160	$300	$360	$410
Total Liabilities and Shareholders' Equity	$250	$400	$520	$650

Ratios are, by themselves, difficult to interpret. For example, does a rate of return on common stock of 8.6 percent reflect a good performance? Once calculated, the ratios must be compared with some standard. Several possible standards might be used:

1 The planned ratio for the period being analyzed.
2 The corresponding ratio during the preceding period for the same firm.
3 The corresponding ratio for a similar firm in the same industry.
4 The average ratio for other firms in the same industry.

Difficulties encountered in using each of these bases for comparison are discussed later.

In the sections that follow, we describe several ratios that are useful for assessing profitability, short-term liquidity, and long-term solvency risk. To demonstrate the calculation of various ratios, we use data for Horrigan Corporation for the years 1980 through 1982 as shown in Exhibit 6.1 (comparative balance sheets), Exhibit 6.2 (comparative income statements), and Exhibit 6.3 (comparative statements of changes in financial position). Our analysis for Horrigan Corporation is based on a study of the changes in its various ratios over the 3-year period. Such an analysis is referred to as *time-series analysis*. Comparison of a given firm's ratios with those of other firms for a particular period is referred to as *cross-section analysis*. Cross-section analysis requires an understanding of the accounting principles used by different firms and is considered in Chapter 15.

Exhibit 6.2
Horrigan Corporation
Comparative Income Statements
(amounts in millions)

	Years Ended December 31		
	1980	**1981**	**1982**
Sales	$210	$310	$475
Less Expenses:			
Cost of Goods Sold	$119	$179	$280
Selling	36	38	46
Administrative	12	13	15
Depreciation	12	14	18
Interest	5	10	16
Total	$184	$254	$375
Net Income before Taxes	$ 26	$ 56	$100
Income Tax Expense	10	22	40
Net Income	$ 16	$ 34	$ 60

Exhibit 6.3
Horrigan Corporation
Comparative Statements of
Changes in Financial Position
(amounts in millions)

	For the Year Ended December 31		
Sources of Working Capital	**1980**	**1981**	**1982**
Operations:			
Net Income	$ 16	$ 34	$ 60
Add Back Expenses Not Using Working Capital:			
Depreciation	12	14	18
Working Capital Provided by Operations	$ 28	$ 48	$ 78
Other Sources:			
Issuance of Bonds	—	50	50
Issuance of Common Stock	130	30	—
Total Sources	$158	$128	$128
Uses of Working Capital			
Dividends	$ 6	$ 4	$ 10
Purchase of Land	10	30	—
Purchase of Building	—	—	40
Purchase of Equipment	122	84	37
Total Uses	$138	$118	$ 87
Net Increase in Working Capital	$ 20	$ 10	$ 41
Analysis of Effects of Increases (Decreases) in Working Capital			
Cash	$ —	$ (2)	$ 2
Marketable Securities	4	(4)	2
Accounts Receivable	10	10	30
Inventories	16	16	37
Accounts Payable	(5)	(5)	(15)
Salaries Payable	(3)	(2)	(5)
Income Taxes Payable	(2)	(3)	(10)
Net Increase in Working Capital	$ 20	$ 10	$ 41

Measures of Profitability

Usually the most important question asked about a business is "How profitable is it?" Most financial statement analysis is directed at various aspects of this question. Some measures of profitability relate earnings to resources or capital employed; other computations relate earnings and various expenses to sales; whereas a third group seeks to explain profitability by measuring the efficiency with which inventories, receivables, or other assets have been managed.

Rate of Return on Assets

The most important profitability ratio for assessing management's performance in using assets to generate earnings is the *rate of return on assets*. This ratio is often called the *return on investment,* or *ROI,* or the *all-capital earnings rate*. It is calculated as follows:

$$\frac{\text{Net Income Plus Interest Expense Net of Income Tax Savings}}{\text{Average Total Assets}}.$$

The rate of return on assets measures management's performance in using assets independent of the financing of those assets. Thus, the earnings figure used in calculating the rate of return on assets is income before deducting any payments or distributions to the providers of capital. Because interest is a payment to a furnisher of capital, interest expense should not be deducted in measuring the return on total assets. To derive income before interest charges, it is usually easier to start with net income and add to that figure. The amount added to net income is not, however, the interest expense shown on the income statement. Because interest expense is deductible in calculating taxable income, interest expense does not reduce *aftertax* net income by the full amount of interest expense. The amount added back to net income is interest expense reduced by income tax savings.

For example, interest expense for Horrigan Corporation for 1982, as shown in Exhibit 6.2, is $16 million. The income tax rate is assumed to be 40 percent of pretax income. The income taxes saved, because interest is deductible in computing taxable income, is $6.4 million ($= .40 \times \$16$ million). The amount of interest expense net of income tax savings that is added back to net income is therefore $9.6 million ($= \$16$ million–$6.4 million). There is no need to add back dividends paid to shareholders, because they are not deducted as an expense in calculating net income.

Because the earnings rate *during the year* is being computed, the measure of investment should reflect the average amount of assets in use during the year. A crude, but usually satisfactory, figure for average total assets is one-half the sum of total assets at the beginning and at the end of the year.

The calculation of rate of return on assets for Horrigan Corporation for 1982 is as follows:[1]

$$\frac{\text{Net Income Plus Interest Expense Net of Income Tax Savings}}{\text{Average Total Assets}} = \frac{\$60 + (\$16 - \$6.4)}{\frac{1}{2}(\$520 + \$650)} = 11.9 \text{ percent.}$$

---

[1]Throughout the remainder of this chapter, we omit reference to the fact that the amounts for Horrigan Corporation are in millions of dollars.

Thus, for each dollar of assets used, the management of Horrigan Corporation was able to earn $.119 during 1982 before payments to the suppliers of capital. The rate of return on assets was 5.8 percent in 1980 and 8.7 percent in 1981. Thus, the rate of return has increased steadily during this 3-year period.

Disaggregating the Rate of Return on Assets

One means of studying changes in the rate of return on assets is to disaggregate the ratio into two other ratios as follows:

$$\begin{array}{c}\text{Rate of}\\\text{Return}\\\text{on Assets}\end{array} = \begin{array}{c}\text{Profit Margin Ratio}\\\text{(before interest expense}\\\text{and related income tax effects)}\end{array} \times \begin{array}{c}\text{Total Assets}\\\text{Turnover}\\\text{Ratio.}\end{array}$$

or

$$\frac{\begin{array}{c}\text{Net Income Plus}\\\text{Interest Expense}\\\text{Net of Income}\\\text{Tax Savings}\end{array}}{\begin{array}{c}\text{Average Total}\\\text{Assets}\end{array}} = \frac{\begin{array}{c}\text{Net Income Plus}\\\text{Interest Expense}\\\text{Net of Income}\\\text{Tax Savings}\end{array}}{\text{Sales}} \times \frac{\text{Sales}}{\begin{array}{c}\text{Average Total}\\\text{Assets}\end{array}}.$$

The profit margin ratio is a measure of a firm's ability to control the level of costs, or expenses, relative to revenues generated. By holding down costs, a firm will be able to increase the profits from a given amount of revenue and thereby improve its profit margin ratio. The total assets turnover ratio is a measure of a firm's ability to generate revenues from a particular level of investment in assets.

Exhibit 6.4 shows the disaggregation of the rate of return on assets for Horrigan Corporation for 1980, 1981, and 1982 into profit margin and total assets turnover ratios. Much of the improvement in the rate of return on assets between 1980 and 1981 can be attributed to an increase in the profit margin ratio from 9.05 percent to 12.90 percent. The total assets turnover ratio remained relatively stable between these two years. On the other hand, most of the improvement in the rate of return on assets between 1981 and 1982 can be attributed to the increased total assets turnover. The firm was able to generate $.812 of sales from each dollar invested in assets during 1982 as compared to $.674 of sales per dollar of assets in 1981. The increased total assets turnover, coupled with an improvement in the profit margin ratio, permitted Horrigan Corporation to increase its rate of return on assets during 1982. We must analyze the changes in the profit margin ratio and total assets turnover ratio in greater depth to pinpoint the causes of the changes in Horrigan Corporation's profitability over this 3-year period. We return to this analysis shortly.

Improving the rate of return on assets can be accomplished by increasing the profit margin ratio, the rate of asset turnover, or both. Some firms, however, may

Exhibit 6.4
**Disaggregation of Rate of Return
on Assets for Horrigan Corporation
for the Years 1980, 1981, and 1982**

$$\frac{\text{Net Income Plus Interest Expense Net of Income Tax Savings}}{\text{Average Total Assets}} = \frac{\text{Net Income Plus Interest Expense Net of Income Tax Savings}}{\text{Sales}} \times \frac{\text{Sales}}{\text{Average Total Assets}}$$

$$1980: \frac{\$16 + (\$5 - \$2)}{\frac{1}{2}(\$250 + \$400)} = \frac{\$16 + (\$5 - \$2)}{\$210} \times \frac{\$210}{\frac{1}{2}(\$250 + \$400)}$$

$$5.8 \text{ percent} = 9.05 \text{ percent} \times .646$$

$$1981: \frac{\$34 + (\$10 - \$4)}{\frac{1}{2}(\$400 + \$520)} = \frac{\$34 + (\$10 - \$4)}{\$310} \times \frac{\$310}{\frac{1}{2}(\$400 + \$520)}$$

$$8.7 \text{ percent} = 12.90 \text{ percent} \times .674$$

$$1982: \frac{\$60 + (\$16 - \$6.4)}{\frac{1}{2}(\$520 + \$650)} = \frac{\$60 + (\$16 - \$6.4)}{\$475} \times \frac{\$475}{\frac{1}{2}(\$520 + \$650)}$$

$$11.9 \text{ percent} = 14.65 \text{ percent} \times .812$$

have little flexibility in altering one of these components. For example, a firm committed under a 3-year labor union contract may have little control over wage rates paid. Or a firm operating under market- or government-imposed price controls may not be able to increase the prices of its products. In these cases, the opportunities for improving the profit margin ratio may be limited. In order to increase the rate of return on assets, the level of investment in assets such as inventory, plant, and equipment must be reduced or, to put it another way, revenues per dollar of assets must be increased.

Analyzing Changes in the Profit Margin Ratio

Profit, or net income, is measured by subtracting various expenses from revenues. To identify the reasons for a change in the profit margin ratio, changes in a firm's expenses relative to sales must be examined. One approach is to express individual expenses and net income as a percentage of sales. Such an analysis is presented in Exhibit 6.5 for Horrigan Corporation. Note that we have altered somewhat the conventional income statement format in this analysis by subtracting interest expense (net of its related income tax effects) as the last expense item. The percentages on the line, Income before Interest and Related Income Tax Effect, correspond (except for rounding) to the profit margin ratios (before interest and related tax effects) shown in Exhibit 6.4.

209

Exhibit 6.5
Net Income and Expenses as a Percentage of Sales for Horrigan Corporation for 1980, 1981, and 1982

	Years Ended December 31		
	1980	**1981**	**1982**
Sales	100.0%	100.0%	100.0%
Less Operating Expenses:			
Cost of Goods Sold	56.7%	57.7%	58.9%
Selling	17.1	12.3	9.7
Administrative	5.7	4.2	3.2
Depreciation	5.7	4.5	3.8
Total	85.2%	78.7%	75.6%
Income before Income Taxes and Interest	14.8%	21.3%	24.4%
Income Taxes at 40 percent	5.7	8.4	9.7
Income before Interest and Related Income Tax Effect	9.1%	12.9%	14.7%
Interest Expense Net of Income Tax Effect	1.5	1.9	2.1
Net Income	7.6%	11.0%	12.6%

The analysis in Exhibit 6.5 indicates that the improvement in the profit margin ratio over the 3 years for Horrigan Corporation can be attributed primarily to decreases in selling, administrative, and depreciation expenses as a percentage of sales. The reasons for these decreasing percentages should be explored further with management. Does the decrease in selling expenses as a percentage of sales reflect a reduction in the rate of advertising expenditures that could hurt future sales? Does the decrease in depreciation expense as a percentage of sales reflect a failure to expand plant and equipment as sales have increased? On the other hand, do these decreasing percentages merely reflect the realization of economies of scale as fixed selling, administrative, and depreciation expenses are being spread over a larger number of units?[2] The amount or trend in a particular ratio cannot, by itself, be the basis for investing or not investing in a firm. Ratios merely indicate areas where additional analysis is required. For example, the increasing percentage of cost of goods sold to sales should be explored further. It may reflect a successful, planned pricing policy of reducing gross margin (selling price less cost of goods sold) in order to increase the volume of sales. On the other hand, the replacement cost of inventory items may be increasing without corresponding increases being made in selling prices. Or, the firm may be accumulating excess inventories that are physically deteriorating or becoming obsolete.

---

[2]This phenomenon is called *operating leverage* and is discussed more fully in managerial accounting textbooks.

Analyzing Changes in the Total Assets Turnover Ratio

The total assets turnover ratio depends on the turnover ratios for its individual asset components. Three turnover ratios are commonly calculated: accounts receivable turnover, inventory turnover, and fixed asset turnover.

Accounts Receivable Turnover The rate at which accounts receivable turn over gives an indication of their nearness to being converted into cash. The accounts receivable turnover is calculated by dividing net sales on account by average accounts receivable. For Horrigan Corporation, the accounts receivable turnover for 1982, assuming all sales are on account (that is, none are for immediate cash), is calculated as follows:

$$\frac{\text{Net Sales on Account}}{\text{Average Accounts Receivable}} = \frac{\$475}{\frac{1}{2}(\$46 + \$76)} = 7.79 \text{ times per year.}$$

The concept of accounts receivable turnover is often expressed in terms of the average number of days receivables are outstanding before cash is collected. The calculation is to divide the accounts receivable turnover ratio into 365 days. The average number of days that accounts receivable are outstanding for Horrigan Corporation for 1982 is 46.9 days (= 365 days/7.79 times per year). Thus, on average, accounts receivable are collected approximately $1\frac{1}{2}$ months after the date of sale. The interpretation of this average collection period depends on the terms of sale. If the terms of sale are "net 30 days," the accounts receivable turnover indicates that collections are not being made in accordance with the stated terms. Such a ratio would warrant a review of the credit and collection activity for an explanation and for possible corrective action. If the firm offers terms of "net 45 days," then the results indicate that accounts receivable are being handled better.

Inventory Turnover The inventory turnover ratio is considered to be a significant indicator of the efficiency of operations for many businesses. It is calculated by dividing cost of goods sold by the average inventory during the period. The inventory turnover for Horrigan Corporation for 1982 is calculated as follows:

$$\frac{\text{Cost of Goods Sold}}{\text{Average Inventory}} = \frac{\$280}{\frac{1}{2}(\$46 + \$83)} = 4.34 \text{ times per year.}$$

Thus, inventory is typically on hand an average of 84.1 days (= 365 days/4.34 times per year) before it is sold.

The interpretation of the inventory turnover figure involves two opposing considerations. Management would like to sell as many goods as possible with a minimum of capital tied up in inventories. An increase in the rate of inventory turnover between periods would seem to indicate more profitable use of the investment in inventory. On the other hand, management does not want to have so little inventory on hand that shortages result and customers are turned away. An increase in the rate of

211

inventory turnover in this case may mean a loss of customers and thereby offset any advantage gained by decreased investment in inventory. Some trade-offs are therefore required in deciding the optimum level of inventory for each firm, and thus the desirable rate of inventory turnover.

The inventory turnover ratio is sometimes calculated by dividing sales, rather than cost of goods sold, by the average inventory. As long as there is a relatively constant relationship between selling prices and cost of goods sold, changes in the *trend* of the inventory turnover can usually be identified with either measure. It is inappropriate to use sales in the numerator if the inventory turnover ratio is to be used to calculate the average number of days inventory is on hand until sale.

Plant Asset Turnover The plant asset turnover ratio is a measure of the relationship between sales and the investment in plant assets such as property, plant, and equipment. It is calculated by dividing sales by average plant assets during the year. The plant assets turnover ratio for Horrigan Corporation for 1982 is:

$$\frac{\text{Sales}}{\text{Average Plant Assets}} = \frac{\$475}{\frac{1}{2}(\$420 + \$479)} = 1.06 \text{ times per year.}$$

Thus, for each dollar invested in plant assets during 1982, $1.06 was generated in sales.

Changes in the plant asset turnover ratio must be interpreted carefully. Investments in plant assets (for example, production facilities) are often made several periods before the time when sales are generated from products manufactured in the plant. Thus, a low or decreasing rate of plant asset turnover may be indicative of an expanding firm preparing for future growth. On the other hand, a firm may cut back its capital expenditures if the near-term outlook for its products is poor. Such action could lead to an increase in the plant asset turnover ratio.

We noted earlier that the total assets turnover for Horrigan Corporation was relatively steady between 1980 and 1981 but increased dramatically in 1982. Exhibit 6.6 presents the four turnover ratios we have discussed for Horrigan Corporation over this 3-year period. The accounts receivable turnover ratio increased steadily over the 3 years, indicating either more careful screening of credit applications or more effective collection efforts. The inventory turnover ratio decreased during the 3

Exhibit 6.6
**Asset Turnover Ratios for
Horrigan Corporation for the 3
Years 1980, 1981, and 1982**

	1980	1981	1982
Total Assets Turnover	.646	.674	.812
Accounts Receivable Turnover	6.77	7.56	7.79
Inventory Turnover	5.41	4.71	4.34
Plant Asset Turnover	.81	.84	1.06

years. Coupling this result with the increasing percentage of cost of goods sold to sales shown in Exhibit 6.5 indicates that there may be excessive investments in inventories that are physically deteriorating or becoming obsolete.

Most of the increase in the total assets turnover between 1981 and 1982 can be attributed to an increase in the plant assets turnover. We note in the statement of changes in financial position for Horrigan Corporation in Exhibit 6.3 that total capital expenditures on land, building, and equipment have decreased over the 3-year period. The reasons for this decrease should be investigated.

Summary of the Analysis of the Rate of Return on Assets This section began by stating that the rate of return on assets is a useful measure for assessing management's performance in using assets. The rate of return on assets was then disaggregated into profit margin and total assets turnover components. The profit margin ratio was, in turn, disaggregated by relating various expenses and net income to sales. The total assets turnover was further analyzed by calculating turnover ratios for accounts receivable, inventory, and plant assets.

The analysis revealed the following:

1 The rate of return on assets increased steadily over the 3-year period from 1980 to 1982.
2 The improved rate of return on assets can be attributed to an increasing profit margin over all 3 years and an improved total asset turnover during 1982.
3 The improved profit margin is in large measure attributable to a decrease in the percentage of selling expenses to sales. The reason for this decrease should be explored further to ascertain whether advertising and selling efforts are being curtailed currently that might adversely affect future sales.
4 The changes in the total assets turnover reflect the effects of increasing accounts receivable and plant asset turnover and a decreasing inventory turnover. The increasing plant asset turnover might be attributable to a reduction in the level of investment in new property, plant, and equipment that could hurt future productive capacity and should be explored further. The decreasing rate of inventory turnover coupled with the increasing percentage of cost of goods sold to sales may be indicative of inventory control problems (build-up of obsolete inventory) and should likewise be explored further.

Rate of Return on Common Stock Equity

The investor in a firm's common stock is probably more interested in the *rate of return on common stock equity* than the rate of return on assets. The rate of return on common stock equity is calculated as follows:

$$\frac{\text{Net Income} - \text{Dividends on Preferred Stock}}{\text{Average Common Shareholders' Equity}}.$$

Exhibit 6.7
**Effects of Leverage on Rate of
Return of Shareholders' Equity
(Income Tax Rate Is 40 Percent of
Pretax Income)**

	Long-Term Equities		Income after Taxes but before Interest Charges[a]	Aftertax Interest Charges[b]	Net Income	Rate of Return on Total Assets[c] (Percent)	Rate of Return on Common Shareholders' Equity (Percent)
	Long-Term Borrowing at 10 Percent per Year	Shareholders' Equity					
Good Earnings Year							
Leveraged Company	$40,000	$ 60,000	$10,000	$2,400	$ 7,600	10.0%	12.7%
No-Debt Company	—	100,000	10,000	—	10,000	10.0	10.0
Neutral Earnings Year							
Leveraged Company	40,000	60,000	6,000	2,400	3,600	6.0	6.0
No-Debt Company	—	100,000	6,000	—	6,000	6.0	6.0
Bad Earnings Year							
Leveraged Company	40,000	60,000	4,000	2,400	1,600	4.0	2.7
No-Debt Company	—	100,000	4,000	—	4,000	4.0	4.0

[a]But not including any income tax savings caused by interest charges. Income before taxes and interest for *good* year is $16,667; for *neutral* year is $10,000; for *bad* year is $6,667.
[b]$40,000 (borrowed) × .10(interest rate) × [1 − .40(income tax rate)]. The numbers shown in the preceding column for aftertax income do not include the effects of interest charges on taxes.
[c]In each year, the rate of return on assets is the same for both companies as the rate of return on common shareholders' equity for No-Debt-Company: 10 percent, 6 percent, and 4 percent, respectively.

To calculate the amount of earnings assignable to common stock equity, the earnings allocable to any preferred stock equity—usually the dividends on preferred stock declared during the period—must be deducted from net income. The capital provided during the period by common shareholders can be calculated by averaging the aggregate par value of common stock, capital contributed in excess of par value on common stock, and retained earnings (or by deducting the equity of preferred shareholders from total shareholders' equity) at the beginning and end of the period.

The rate of return on common stock equity of Horrigan Corporation for 1982 is calculated as:

$$\frac{\text{Net Income} - \text{Dividends on Preferred Stock}}{\text{Average Common Shareholders' Equity}} = \frac{\$60 - \$0}{\frac{1}{2}(\$360 + \$410)} = 15.6 \text{ percent.}$$

The rate of return on common stock equity of Horrigan Corporation, 15.6 percent, is larger than the rate of return on assets (11.9 percent). The return to the common stock equity is larger than the rate of return on assets because the payments to the other suppliers of capital (for example, creditors and bondholders) are less than the overall 11.9-percent rate of return generated from capital that they provided. Observe that current liabilities carry no explicit interest payment and bonds carry an average interest rate of less than 11 percent ($= \$16/\$150$).

The common stock equity earned a higher rate of return only because the shareholders undertook more risk in their investment. They were placed in a riskier position because the firm incurred debt obligations with fixed payment dates. In each of the years 1980 through 1982, the rate of return on assets exceeded the average cost of debt, so that the rate of return on common stock equity exceeded the rate of return on assets. The phenomenon of common shareholders trading extra risk for a potentially higher return is called *financial leverage* and is described next.

Financial Leverage: Trading on the Equity

Financing with debt and preferred stock to increase the potential return to the residual common shareholders' equity is referred to as *financial leverage* or *trading on the equity*. So long as a higher rate of return can be earned on assets than is paid for the capital used to acquire those assets, then the rate of return to common shareholders can be increased. Exhibit 6.7 explores this phenomenon. Leveraged Company and No-Debt Company both have $100,000 of assets. Leveraged Company borrows $40,000 at a 10-percent annual rate. No-Debt Company raises all its capital from common shareholders. Both companies pay income taxes at the rate of 40 percent.

Consider first a "good" earnings year. Both companies earn $10,000 before interest charges (but after taxes except for tax effects of interest charges).[3] This represents a rate of return on assets for both companies of 10 percent ($= \$10,000/\$100,000$). Leveraged Company's net income is $7,600 [$= \$10,000 - (1 - .40 \text{ tax rate}) \times (.10$ interest rate $\times \$40,000$ borrowed)], representing a rate of return on common share-

---

[3] That is, income before taxes and before interest charges is $16,667; $10,000 = (1 - .40) \times \$16,667$.

215

holders' equity of 12.7 percent (= $7,600/$60,000). Net income of No-Debt Company is $10,000, representing a rate of return on shareholders' equity of 10 percent. Leverage increased the rate of return to shareholders of Leveraged Company, because the capital contributed by the long-term debtors earned 10 percent but required an aftertax interest payment of only 6 percent [= (1 − .40 tax rate) × (.10 interest rate)]. This additional 4-percent return on each dollar of assets increases the return to the common shareholders.

Although leverage increased the return to the common stock equity during the "good" earnings year, the increase would be larger if a larger proportion of the assets were financed with long-term borrowing and the firm were made more risky. For example, assume that the assets of $100,000 were financed with $50,000 of long-term borrowing and $50,000 of shareholders' equity. Net income of Leveraged Company in this case would be $7,000 [= $10,000 − (1 − .40 tax rate) × (.10 × $50,000 borrowed)]. The rate of return on common stock equity would be 14 percent (= $7,000/$50,000). This rate compares with a rate of return on common stock equity of 12.7 percent when long-term debt was only 40 percent of the total capital provided.

Financial leverage increases the rate of return on common stock equity when the rate of return on assets is higher than the aftertax cost of debt. The greater the proportion of debt in the capital structure, however, the greater the risk borne by the common shareholders. Debt cannot, of course, be increased without limit. As more debt is added to the capital structure, the risk of default or insolvency becomes greater. Lenders, including investors in a firm's bonds, will require a higher and higher return (interest rate) to compensate for this additional risk. A point will be reached when the aftertax cost of debt will exceed the rate of return that can be earned on assets. At this point, leverage can no longer increase the potential rate of return to common stock equity. For most large manufacturing firms, liabilities represent between 30 percent and 60 percent of total capital.

Exhibit 6.7 also demonstrates the effect of leverage in a "neutral" earnings year and in a "bad" earnings year. In the "neutral" earnings year, the rate of return to common shareholders is neither increased nor decreased by leverage, because the return on assets is 6 percent and the aftertax cost of long-term debt is 6 percent. In the "bad" earnings year, the return on assets of 4 percent is less than the aftertax cost of debt of 6 percent. The return on common stock equity therefore drops—to only 2.7 percent—below the rate of return on assets. Clearly, financial leverage can work in two ways. It can enhance owners' rate of return in good years, but owners run the risk that bad earnings years will be even worse than they would be without the borrowing.

Earnings per Share of Common Stock

Earnings per share of common stock is calculated by dividing net income applicable to common shareholders by the average number of common shares outstanding during the period.

216

Earnings per share for Horrigan Corporation for 1982 is calculated as follows:

$$\frac{\text{Net Income} - \text{Preferred Stock Dividend}}{\text{Weighted Average Number of Common Shares Outstanding during the Period}} = \frac{\$60 - \$0}{16 \text{ shares}^4} = \$3.75 \text{ per share.}$$

Earnings per share were $1.28 (= $16/12.5) for 1980 and $2.19 (= $34/15.5) for 1981.

If a firm has securities outstanding that can be converted into or exchanged for common stock, it may be required to present two earnings-per-share amounts: *primary earnings per share* and *fully diluted earnings per share*. For example, some firms issue convertible bonds or convertible preferred stock that can be exchanged directly for shares of common stock. Also, many firms have employee stock option plans under which shares of the company's common stock may be acquired by employees under special arrangements. If these convertible securities were converted or stock options were exercised and additional shares of common stock were issued, the amount conventionally shown as earnings per share would probably decrease, or become *diluted*. When a firm has outstanding securities that, if exchanged for shares of common stock, would decrease earnings per share by 3 percent or more, a dual presentation of primary and fully diluted earnings per share is required.[5]

Primary Earnings per Share In calculating earnings per share, adjustments may be made to the conventionally calculated amount for securities that are nearly the same as common stock. These securities are called *common stock equivalents*. Common stock equivalents are securities whose principal value arises from their capability of being exchanged for, or converted into, common stock rather than only for their own periodic cash yields over time. Stock options and warrants are always common stock equivalents. Convertible bonds and convertible preferred stock may or may not be common stock equivalents. A test is employed to ascertain if the return from these convertible securities at the date of their issue is substantially below the return available from other debt or preferred stock investments. If so, the presumption is that the securities derived their value primarily from their conversion privileges and are therefore common stock equivalents. Adjustments are made in calculating primary earnings per share for the dilutive effects of securities classified as common stock equivalents.

Fully Diluted Earnings per Share As the title implies, fully diluted earnings per share indicates the maximum possible dilution that would occur if all options, warrants, and convertible securities outstanding at the end of the accounting period were

---

[4] Exhibit 6.1 indicates that the par value of a common share is $10 and that the common stock account has a balance of $160 million throughout 1982. The shares outstanding were therefore 16 million.

[5] Accounting Principles Board, *Opinion No. 15,* "Earnings per Share," 1969.

217

exchanged for common stock. This amount, therefore, represents the maximum limit of possible dilution that could take place on the date of the balance sheet. All securities convertible into or exchangeable for common stock, whether or not classified as common stock equivalents, enter into the calculation of fully diluted earnings per share.

Firms that do not have convertible or other potentially dilutive securities outstanding compute earnings per share in the conventional manner. Firms with outstanding securities that have the potential for materially diluting earnings per share, as conventionally computed, must present dual earnings-per-share amounts.

Interpreting Earnings per Share Earnings per share has been criticized as a measure of profitability because it does not consider the amount of assets or capital required to generate that level of earnings. Two firms with the same earnings and earnings per share will not be equally profitable if one of the firms requires twice the amount of assets or capital to generate that earnings than does the other firm.

Earnings-per-share amounts are also difficult to interpret when comparing firms. For example, assume that two firms have identical earnings, common shareholders' equity, and rates of return on common shareholders' equity. One firm may have a lower earnings per share simply because it has a larger number of shares outstanding (due perhaps to the use of a lower par value for its shares or to different earnings retention policies; see Problem 15 at the end of this chapter).

Price-Earnings Ratio

Earnings-per-share amounts are often compared with the market price of the stock. This is usually expressed as a *price-earnings ratio* (= market price per share/earnings per share). For example, the common stock of Horrigan Corporation is selling for $40 per share at the end of 1982. The price-earnings ratio, often called the P/E ratio, is 10.67 to 1 (= $40/$3.75). This ratio is often presented in tables of stock market prices and in financial periodicals. The relationship is sometimes expressed by saying that "the stock is selling at 10.7 times earnings."

The relation between earnings and market price per share might be expressed as a rate (= earnings per share/market price per share). This calculation, 9.4 percent (= $3.75/$40) for Horrigan Corporation, is seen less often than the price-earnings ratio.

Measures of Short-Term Liquidity Risk

Investors or creditors whose claims will become payable in the near future are interested in the short-term liquidity or "nearness to cash" of a firm's assets. One tool for predicting whether or not cash will be available when the claims become due is a budget of cash receipts and disbursements for several months or quarters in the future. Such budgets are often prepared for management and used internally for planning cash requirements. Budgets of cash receipts and disbursements are not generally available for use by persons outside a firm. Investors must, therefore, use other tools in assessing short-term liquidity.

The statement of changes in financial position is one published source of information for assessing liquidity. The amount of working capital provided by operations indicates the extent to which the operating activities have generated sufficient working capital for the payment of dividends and the acquisition of fixed assets. The statement also discloses the extent to which additional financing has been used for those purposes. Exhibit 6.3 indicated that working capital provided by operations for Horrigan Corporation increased each year between 1980 and 1982.

Additional insights into the impact of operations on liquidity can be obtained by converting working capital provided by operations to cash flow provided by operations. Exhibit 6.8 presents the analysis for Horrigan Corporation. Cash flow provided by operations increased each year but by a smaller amount than working capital provided by operations. A substantial portion of the cash flow generated each year by operations was reinvested in receivables and inventory. Nevertheless, operations produced substantial and increasing cash flows each year.

Exhibit 6.8
Horrigan Corporation Conversion of Working Capital Provided by Operations to Cash Flow Provided by Operations for the Years 1980, 1981, and 1982 (amounts in millions)

	1980	1981	1982
Working Capital Provided by Operations	$28	$48	$78
Add Increases in Current Liabilities:			
Accounts Payable	5	5	15
Salaries Payable	3	2	5
Income Taxes Payable	2	3	10
Subtract Increases in Current Asset Accounts Other Than Cash and Marketable Securities:			
Accounts Receivable	(10)	(10)	(30)
Inventories	(16)	(16)	(37)
Cash Flow Provided by Operations	$12	$32	$41

Several ratios are also useful in assessing the short-term liquidity risk of a firm. The most popular ones are the current ratio, the quick ratio, and the accounts receivable turnover ratio.

Current Ratio

The *current ratio* is calculated by dividing current assets by current liabilities. It is commonly expressed as a ratio such as "2 to 1" or "2 : 1," meaning that current assets are twice as large as current liabilities. The current ratio of Horrigan Corporation on

219

December 31, 1979, 1980, 1981, and 1982, is:

$$\frac{\text{Current}}{\text{Ratio}} = \frac{\text{Current Assets}}{\text{Current Liabilities}}$$

December 31, 1979: $\dfrac{\$\ 50}{\$\ 40} =$ 1.25 to 1.0

December 31, 1980: $\dfrac{\$\ 80}{\$\ 50} =$ 1.60 to 1.0

December 31, 1981: $\dfrac{\$100}{\$\ 60} =$ 1.67 to 1.0

December 31, 1982: $\dfrac{\$171}{\$\ 90} =$ 1.90 to 1.0.

This ratio is presumed to indicate the ability of the concern to meet its current obligations, and is therefore of particular significance to short-term creditors. Although an excess of current assets over current liabilities is generally considered desirable from the creditor's viewpoint, changes in the trend of the ratio may be difficult to interpret. For example, when the current ratio is larger than 1 to 1, an increase of equal amount in both current assets and current liabilities results in a decline in the ratio, whereas equal decreases result in an increased current ratio.

If a corporation has a particularly profitable year, the large current liability for income taxes may cause a decline in the current ratio. In a recession period, business is contracting, current liabilities are paid, and even though the current assets may be at a low point, the ratio may go to high levels. In a boom period, just the reverse effect might occur. In other words, a very high current ratio may accompany unsatisfactory business conditions, whereas a falling ratio may accompany profitable operations.

Furthermore, the current ratio is susceptible to "window dressing"; that is, management can take deliberate steps to produce a financial statement that presents a better current ratio at the balance sheet date than the average or normal current ratio. For example, toward the close of a fiscal year normal purchases on account may be delayed. Or loans to officers, classified as noncurrent assets, may be collected and the proceeds used to reduce current liabilities. These actions may be taken so that the current ratio will appear as favorable as possible in the annual financial statements at the balance sheet date.

Although the current ratio is probably the most common ratio presented in statement analysis, there are limitations in its use as discussed above. Its trends are difficult to interpret and, if overemphasized, it can easily lead to undesirable business practices as well as misinterpretation of financial condition.

Quick Ratio

A variation of the current ratio, usually known as the *quick ratio* or *acid-test ratio,* is computed by including in the numerator of the fraction only those current assets that could be converted quickly into cash. The numerator customarily includes cash, marketable securities, and receivables, but it would be better to make a study of the facts in each case before deciding whether or not to include receivables and to exclude inventories. In some businesses, the inventory of merchandise might be converted into cash more quickly than the receivables of other businesses.

Assuming that the accounts receivable of Horrigan Corporation are included but that inventory is excluded, the quick ratio on December 31, 1979, 1980, 1981, and 1982, is:

$$\frac{\text{Quick}}{\text{Ratio}} = \frac{\text{Cash, Marketable Securities, Accounts Receivable}}{\text{Current Liabilities}}$$

December 31, 1979: $\dfrac{\$36}{\$40} =$ .90 to 1.0

December 31, 1980: $\dfrac{\$50}{\$50} =$ 1.0 to 1.0

December 31, 1981: $\dfrac{\$54}{\$60} =$ .90 to 1.0

December 31, 1982: $\dfrac{\$88}{\$90} =$ .98 to 1.0.

Whereas the current ratio increased steadily over the period, the quick ratio remained relatively constant. The increase in the current ratio results primarily from a buildup of inventories.

Accounts Receivable Turnover Ratio

The accounts receivable turnover ratio, discussed earlier in the section on profitability ratios, also provides useful information about a firm's liquidity. The ratio is calculated by dividing net sales on account by the average amount of accounts receivable during the period. In assessing short-term liquidity, it is helpful to reexpress the ratio in terms of the average number of days accounts receivable are outstanding. Using the accounts receivable turnover amounts from Exhibit 6.6, the average number of days Horrigan Corporation's receivables were outstanding during 1980, 1981, and 1982, were:

$$\frac{\text{Average Number of Days Accounts Receivable Are Outstanding}}{} = \frac{365}{\text{Accounts Receivable Turnover Ratio}}$$

1980: $\dfrac{365}{6.77} =$ 53.9 days

1981: $\dfrac{365}{7.56} =$ 48.3 days

1982: $\dfrac{365}{7.79} =$ 46.9 days.

Over the 3-year period, the accounts receivable of Horrigan Corporation have become more liquid.

Other Short-Term Liquidity Ratios

Several other ratios are sometimes used to assess short-term liquidity. One ratio relates cash *inflow* from operations to the average amount of current liabilities during a period. This ratio is intended to provide information similar to the current ratio but is not as susceptible to year-end window dressing. Another ratio sometimes encountered is the *defensive interval*.[6] It is calculated by dividing the average daily cash expenditures for operating expenses into a firm's most liquid assets, generally cash, marketable securities, and accounts receivable. The defensive interval is the number of days the firm could theoretically remain in business without additional sales or new financing. This ratio has been found to be a good predictor of bond default and bankruptcy.

Summarizing the analysis of Horrigan Corporation's short-term liquidity, we have noted the following:

1 Working capital and cash flow provided by operations have been positive and growing at a reasonably stable rate with sales and net income. Operations are now the primary source of liquid assets for the firm.
2 The current ratio has been improving over the last 3 years, but most of the improvement is explained by a buildup of inventories.
3 The average collection period for accounts receivable has been decreasing during the past 3 years, indicating that they are becoming more liquid, or that collection policy has been more stringent, or both.

Measures of Long-Term Solvency Risk

Measures of long-term solvency are used in assessing the firm's ability to meet interest and principal payments on long-term debt and similar obligations as they become due. If the payments cannot be made on time, the firm becomes *insolvent* and may have to be reorganized or liquidated.

Perhaps the best indicator of long-term solvency is a firm's ability to generate profits over a period of years. If a firm is profitable, it will either generate sufficient capital from operations or be able to obtain needed capital from creditors and owners. The measures of profitability discussed previously are therefore applicable for this purpose as well. Two other commonly used measures of long-term solvency are debt ratios and the number of times that interest charges are earned.

---

[6]George H. Sorter and George Benston, "Appraising the Defensive Position of a Firm: The Interval Measure," *The Accounting Review*, (October 1960): 633–640.

Debt Ratios

There are several variations of the debt ratio, but the one most commonly encountered in financial analysis is the *long-term debt ratio*. It reports the portion of the firm's long-term capital that is furnished by debt holders. To calculate this ratio, divide total noncurrent liabilities by the sum of total noncurrent liabilities and total shareholders' equity.

Another form of the debt ratio is the *debt-equity ratio*. To calculate the debt-equity ratio, divide total liabilities (current and noncurrent) by total equities (liabilities plus shareholders' equity = total assets).

The two forms of the debt ratio for Horrigan Corporation on December 31, 1979, 1980, 1981, and 1982, are shown in Exhibit 6.9. In general, the higher these ratios, the higher the likelihood that the firm may be unable to meet fixed interest and principal payments in the future. The decision for most firms is how much financial leverage with its attendant risk they can afford to assume. Funds obtained from issuing bonds or borrowing from a bank have a relatively low interest cost but require fixed, periodic payments that increase the likelihood of bankruptcy.

Exhibit 6.9
Horrigan Corporation
Debt Ratios

$$\text{Long-Term Debt Ratio} = \frac{\text{Total Noncurrent Liabilities}}{\text{Total Noncurrent Liabilities Plus Shareholders' Equity}}$$

$$\text{Debt-Equity Ratio} = \frac{\text{Total Liabilities}}{\text{Total Liabilities Plus Shareholders' Equity}}$$

Dec. 31, 1979: $\dfrac{\$50}{\$210} = 24$ percent

Dec. 31, 1980: $\dfrac{\$50}{\$350} = 14$ percent

Dec. 31, 1981: $\dfrac{\$100}{\$460} = 22$ percent

Dec. 31, 1982: $\dfrac{\$150}{\$560} = 27$ percent

Dec. 31, 1979: $\dfrac{\$90}{\$250} = 36$ percent

Dec. 31, 1980: $\dfrac{\$100}{\$400} = 25$ percent

Dec. 31, 1981: $\dfrac{\$160}{\$520} = 31$ percent

Dec. 31, 1982: $\dfrac{\$240}{\$650} = 37$ percent

In assessing the debt ratios, analysts customarily vary the standard in direct relation to the stability of the firm's earnings. The more stable the earnings, the higher the debt ratio that is considered acceptable or safe. The debt ratios of public utilities are customarily high, frequently on the order of 60 to 70 percent. The stability of public utility earnings makes these ratios acceptable to many investors who would be dissatisfied with such large leverage for firms with less stable earnings.

Because several variations of the debt ratio appear in corporate annual reports, care in making comparisons of debt ratios among firms is necessary.

Interest Coverage: Times Interest Charges Earned

Another measure of long-term solvency is the *number of times that interest charges are earned*, or covered. This ratio is calculated by dividing net income before interest and income tax expenses by interest expense. For Horrigan Corporation, the times interest earned ratios for 1980, 1981, and 1982, are:

$$\frac{\text{Times Interest}}{\text{Charges Earned}} = \frac{\text{Net Income before Interest and Income Taxes}}{\text{Interest Expense}}$$

$$1980: \quad \frac{\$16 + \$5 + \$10}{\$5} = 6.2 \text{ times}$$

$$1981: \quad \frac{\$34 + \$10 + \$22}{\$10} = 6.6 \text{ times}$$

$$1982: \quad \frac{\$60 + \$16 + \$40}{\$16} = 7.3 \text{ times.}$$

Thus, whereas the bonded indebtedness increased sharply during the 3-year period, the growth in net income before interest and income taxes was sufficient to provide increasing coverage of the fixed interest charges.

The purpose of this ratio is to indicate the relative protection of bondholders and to assess the probability that the firm will be forced into bankruptcy by a failure to meet required interest payments. If periodic repayments of principal on long-term liabilities are also required, the repayments might also be included in the denominator of the ratio. The ratio would then be described as the *number of times that fixed charges were earned*, or covered.

The times interest or fixed charges earned ratios can be criticized as measures for assessing long-term solvency because the ratios use earnings rather than cash flows in the numerator. Interest and other fixed payment obligations are paid with cash, and not with earnings. When the value of the ratio is relatively low (for example, two to three times), some measure of cash flows, such as cash flows from operations, may be preferable in the numerator.

Limitations of Ratio Analysis

For convenient reference, Exhibit 6.10 summarizes the calculation of the ratios discussed in this chapter.

The analytical computations discussed in this chapter have a number of limitations that should be kept in mind by anyone preparing or using them. Several of the more important limitations are the following:

1 The ratios are based on financial statement data and are therefore subject to the same criticisms as the financial statements (for example, use of acquisition cost rather than current replacement cost or net realizable value; the latitude permitted firms in selecting from among various generally accepted accounting principles).

2 Changes in many ratios are highly associated with each other. For example, the changes in the current ratio and quick ratio between two different times are often in the same direction and approximately proportional. It is therefore not necessary to compute all the ratios to assess a particular factor.

3 When comparing the size of a ratio between periods for the same firm, one must recognize conditions that have changed between the periods being compared (for example, different product lines or geographical markets served, changes in economic conditions, changes in prices).

4 When comparing ratios of a particular firm with those of similar firms, one must recognize differences between the firms (for example, use of different methods of accounting, differences in the method of operations, type of financing, and so on).

Exhibit 6.10
Summary of Financial Statement Ratios

Ratio	Numerator	Denominator
Rate of Return on Assets	Net Income + Interest Expense (net of tax effects)[a]	Average Total Assets During the Period
Profit Margin Ratio (before interest effects)	Net Income + Interest Expense (net of tax effects)[a]	Sales
Various Expense Ratios	Various Expenses	Sales
Total Assets Turnover Ratio	Sales	Average Total Assets During the Period
Accounts Receivable Turnover Ratio	Net Sales on Accounts	Average Accounts Receivable During the Period
Inventory Turnover Ratio	Cost of Goods Sold	Average Inventory During the Period
Plant Asset Turnover Ratio	Sales	Average Plant Assets During the Period
Rate of Return on Common Stock Equity	Net Income − Preferred Stock Dividends	Average Common Shareholders' Equity During the Period
Earnings per Share of Stock[b]	Net Income − Preferred Stock Dividends	Weighted Average Number of Common Shares Outstanding During the Period
Current Ratio	Current Assets	Current Liabilities
Quick or Acid-Test Ratio	Highly Liquid Assets (ordinarily, cash, marketable securities, and receivables)[c]	Current Liabilities
Long-Term Debt Ratio	Total Noncurrent Liabilities	Total Noncurrent Liabilities Plus Shareholders' Equity
Debt-Equity Ratio	Total Liabilities	Total Equities (liabilities plus shareholders' equity)
Times Interest Charges Earned	Net Income Before Interest and Income Taxes	Interest Expense

[a]If a consolidated subsidiary is not owned entirely by the parent corporation, the minority interest share of earnings must also be added back to net income. See the description in Chapter 13.
[b]This calculation can be more complicated when there are convertible securities, options, or warrants outstanding.
[c]Receivables could conceivably be excluded for some firms and inventories included for others. Such refinements are seldom employed in practice.

Results of financial statement analyses cannot be used by themselves as direct indications of good or poor management. Such analyses merely indicate areas that might be investigated further. For example, a decrease in the turnover of raw materials inventory, ordinarily considered to be an undesirable trend, may reflect the accumulation of scarce materials that will keep the plant operating at full capacity during shortages when competitors have been forced to restrict operations or to close down. Ratios derived from financial statements must be combined with an investigation of other facts before valid conclusions can be drawn.

Exhibit 6.11
Cox Corporation
Comparative Balance Sheet
December 31, 1981 and 1982

	December 31 1981	December 31 1982
ASSETS		
Current Assets:		
Cash	$ 600	$ 750
Accounts Receivable	3,600	4,300
Merchandise Inventories	5,600	7,900
Prepayments	300	380
Total Current Assets	$10,100	$13,330
Property, Plant, and Equipment:		
Land	$ 500	$ 600
Buildings and Equipment (Net)	9,400	10,070
Total Property, Plant, and Equipment	$ 9,900	$10,670
Total Assets	$20,000	$24,000
LIABILITIES AND SHAREHOLDERS' EQUITY		
Current Liabilities:		
Notes Payable	$ 2,000	$ 4,000
Accounts Payable	3,500	3,300
Other Current Liabilities	1,500	1,900
Total Current Liabilities	$ 7,000	$ 9,200
Noncurrent Liabilities:		
Bonds Payable	4,000	2,800
Total Liabilities	$11,000	$12,000
Shareholders' Equity:		
Preferred Stock	$ 1,000	$ 1,000
Common Stock	2,000	2,500
Additional Paid-in Capital	1,500	1,800
Retained Earnings	4,500	6,700
Total Shareholders' Equity	$ 9,000	$12,000
Total Liabilities and Shareholders' Equity	$20,000	$24,000

Summary

We began this chapter by raising the question, "Should you invest your inheritance in a certificate of deposit or in the shares of common stock of Horrigan Corporation?" Our analysis of Horrigan Corporation's financial statements indicates that it has been a growing, profitable company with few indications of either short-term liquidity or long-term solvency problems. At least three additional inputs are necessary before making the investment decisions. First, you must consider other sources of information besides the financial statements to determine if relevant information for projecting rates of return or for assessing risk needs to be considered. Second, you must decide your attitude toward, or willingness to assume, risk. Third, you must decide if you think the stock market price of the shares makes them an attractive purchase.[7] It is at this stage in the investment decision that the analysis becomes particularly subjective.

Problem for Self-Study

Exhibit 6.11 presents a comparative balance sheet for Cox Corporation as of December 31, 1981 and 1982, and Exhibit 6.12 presents an income statement for the year 1982. Using information from these financial statements, compute the following ratios. The income tax rate is 40 percent.

Exhibit 6.12
Cox Corporation
Income and Retained Earnings Statement
for the Year Ended December 31, 1982

Sales Revenue		$30,000
Less Expenses:		
Cost of Goods Sold	$18,000	
Selling	4,500	
Administrative	1,800	
Interest	700	
Income Taxes	2,000	
Total Expenses		27,000
Net Income		$ 3,000
Less Dividends:		
Preferred	$ 100	
Common	700	800
Increase in Retained Earnings for 1982		$ 2,200
Retained Earnings, December 31, 1981		4,500
Retained Earnings, December 31, 1982		$ 6,700

---

[7] Other important factors cannot be discussed here, but are in finance texts. Perhaps the most important question of all is how a particular investment fits in with the investor's entire portfolio. Modern research suggests that the suitability of a potential investment depends more on the attributes of the other components of an investment portfolio and the risk attitude of the investor than it does on the attributes of the potential investment itself.

a Rate of return on assets.
b Profit margin ratio (before interest and related tax effects).
c Cost of goods sold to sales percentage.
d Selling expense to sales percentage.
e Total assets turnover.
f Accounts receivable turnover.
g Inventory turnover.

h Plant asset turnover.
i Rate of return on common stock equity.
j Current ratio (both dates).
k Quick ratio (both dates).
l Long-term debt ratio (both dates).
m Debt-equity ratio (both dates).
n Times interest charges earned.

Suggested Solution

a Rate of return on assets $= \dfrac{\$3,000 + (1 - .40)(\$700)}{.5(\$20,000 + \$24,000)} = 15.5\%.$

b Profit margin ratio $= \dfrac{\$3,000 + (1 - .40)(\$700)}{\$30,000} = 11.4\%.$

c Cost of goods sold to sales percentage $= \$18,000/\$30,000 = 60.0\%.$

d Selling expense to sales percentage $= \$4,500/\$30,000 = 15.0\%.$

e Total assets turnover $= \dfrac{\$30,000}{.5(\$20,000 + \$24,000)} = 1.4$ times per year.

f Accounts receivable turnover $= \dfrac{\$30,000}{.5(\$3,600 + \$4,300)} = 7.6$ times per year.

g Inventory turnover $= \dfrac{\$18,000}{.5(\$5,600 + \$7,900)} = 2.7$ times per year.

h Plant asset turnover $= \dfrac{\$30,000}{.5(\$9,900 + \$10,670)} = 2.9$ times per year.

i Rate of return on common stock equity $= \dfrac{\$3,000 - \$100}{.5(\$8,000 + \$11,000)} = 30.5\%.$

j Current ratio
   December 31, 1981: $\$10,100/\$7,000 = 1.4:1.$
   December 31, 1982: $\$13,330/\$9,200 = 1.4:1.$

k Quick ratio
   December 31, 1981: $\$4,200/\$7,000 = .6:1.$
   December 31, 1982: $\$5,050/\$9,200 = .5:1.$

l Long-term debt ratio
   December 31, 1981: $\$4,000/\$13,000 = 30.8\%.$
   December 31, 1982: $\$2,800/\$14,800 = 18.9\%.$

m Debt-equity ratio
   December 31, 1981: $\$11,000/\$20,000 = 55.0\%.$
   December 31, 1982: $\$12,000/\$24,000 = 50.0\%.$

n Times interest charges earned $= \dfrac{\$3,000 + \$2,000 + \$700}{\$700} = 8.1$ times.

Questions and Problems

1 Review the meaning of the following concepts or terms discussed in this chapter.

a Risk and return.
b Profitability.
c Short-term liquidity risk.
d Long-term solvency risk.
e Time-series analysis.
f Cross-section analysis.
g Rate of return on assets.
h Profit margin and expense ratios.
i Total assets turnover ratio.
j Accounts receivable turnover ratio.
k Inventory turnover ratio.
l Plant asset turnover ratio.
m Rate of return on common stock equity.
n Operating leverage.
o Financial leverage.
p Earnings per share.
q Primary earnings per share.
r Fully diluted earnings per share.
s Price-earnings ratio.
t Current ratio.
u Quick ratio.
v Long-term debt ratio.
w Debt-equity ratio.
x Times interest charges earned.

2 Describe several factors that might limit the comparability of a firm's current ratio over several periods.

3 Describe several factors that might limit the comparability of one firm's current ratio with that of another firm in the same industry.

4 Under what circumstances will the rate of return on the common stock equity be more than the rate of return on assets? Under what circumstances will it be less?

5 In calculating the inventory turnover, when might the use of the average of the beginning and ending inventories lead to an inaccurate result?

6 Illustrate with amounts how a decrease in working capital can accompany an increase in the current ratio.

7 It has been suggested that for any given firm at a particular time there is an optimal inventory turnover ratio. Explain.

8 A company president recently stated: "The operations of our company are such that we can use effectively only a small amount of financial leverage." Explain.

9 The following data are taken from the 1982 annual reports of Alabama Company and Carolina Company.

	Alabama Co.	Carolina Co.
Sales	$2,000,000	$2,400,000
Expenses Other Than Interest and Income Taxes	1,700,000	2,150,000
Interest Expense	100,000	50,000
Income Tax Expense at 40 Percent	80,000	80,000
Net Income	120,000	120,000
Average Total Assets During the Year	1,500,000	1,000,000

a Calculate the rate of return on assets for each company.

b Disaggregate the rate of return in part **a** into profit margin and total assets turnover components.

c Comment on the relative performance of the two companies.

10 Net income attributable to common shareholders' equity of Florida Corporation during 1982 was $250,000. Earnings per share were $.50 during the period. The average common shareholders' equity during 1982 was $2,500,000. The market price at year-end was $6.00 per share.

a Calculate the rate of return on common shareholders' equity for 1982.

b Calculate the rate of return currently being earned on the market price of the stock (the ratio of earnings per common share to market price per common share).

c Why is there a difference between the rates of return calculated in parts **a** and **b**?

11 The revenues of Lev Company were $1,000 for the year. A financial analyst computed the following ratios for Lev Company, using the year-end balances for balance sheet amounts.

Debt-Equity Ratio (all liabilities/all equities)	$73\frac{1}{3}\%$
Income Tax Expense as a Percentage of Pretax Income	40%
Net Income as a Percentage of Revenue	12%
Rate of Return on Shareholders' Equity	10%
Rate of Return on Assets	6%

From this information, compute each of the following items.

a Interest expense.

b Income tax expense.

c Total expenses.

d Net income.

e Total assets.

f Total liabilities.

12 Refer to the data below for the Adelsman Company.

	Year 1	Year 2	Year 3
Rate of Return on Common Shareholders' Equity	8%	10%	11%
Earnings per Share	$3.00	$4.00	$4.40
Net Income/Total Interest Expense[a]	10	5	4
Debt-Equity Ratio (liabilities/all equities)	20%	50%	60%

[a]Note that this computation does not represent "times interest earned" as defined in the chapter.

The income tax rate was 40 percent in each year and 100,000 common shares were outstanding throughout the period.

a Did the company's profitability increase over the 3-year period? How can you tell? (Hint: Compute the rate of return on assets.)

b Did risk increase? How can you tell?

c Are shareholders better off in year 3 than in year 1?

13 The following information is taken from the annual reports of two companies, one of which is a retailer of quality men's clothes and the other of which is a discount household goods store. Neither company had any interest-bearing debt during the year. Identify which of these companies is likely to be the clothing retailer and which is likely to be the discount store. Explain.

	Company A	Company B
Sales	$3,000,000	$3,000,000
Net Income	60,000	300,000
Average Total Assets	600,000	3,000,000

14 The Borrowing Company has total assets of $100,000 during the year. It has borrowed $20,000 at a 10-percent annual rate and pays income taxes at a rate of 40 percent of pretax income. Shareholders' equity is $80,000.

a What must net income be for the rate of return on shareholders' equity to equal the rate of return on assets (the all capital earnings rate)?

b What is the rate of return on shareholders' equity for the net income determined above in part **a**?

c What must income before interest and income taxes be to achieve this net income?

d Repeat parts **a, b,** and **c** assuming borrowing of $80,000 and shareholders' equity of $20,000.

e Compare the results from the two different debt-equity relations. What generalizations can be made?

15 Company A and Company B both start the year 1981 with $1 million of shareholders' equity and 100,000 shares of common stock outstanding. During 1981 both companies earn net income of $100,000, a rate of return of 10 percent on shareholders' equity. Company A declares and pays $100,000 of dividends to common shareholders at the end of 1981, whereas Company B retains all its earnings, declaring no dividends. During 1982, both companies earn net income equal to 10 percent of shareholders' equity at the beginning of 1982.

a Compute earnings per share for Company A and for Company B for 1981 and for 1982.

b Compute the rate of growth in earnings per share for Company A and Company B, comparing earnings per share in 1982 with earnings per share in 1981.

c Using the rate of growth in earnings per share as the criterion, which company's management appears to be doing a better job for its shareholders? Comment on this result.

16 (CMA adapted.) The Virgil Company is planning to invest $10 million in an expansion program that is expected to increase income before interest and taxes by $2.5 million. Currently, Virgil Company has total equities of $40 million, 25 percent of which is debt and 75 percent of which is shareholders' equity, represented by 1 million shares. The expansion can be financed with the issuance of 200,000 new shares at $50 each or by issuing long-term debt at an annual interest rate of 10 percent. The following is an excerpt from the most recent income statement.

Earnings Before Interest and Taxes	$10,500,000
Less: Interest Charges	500,000
Earnings Before Income Taxes	$10,000,000
Income Taxes (at 40 percent)	4,000,000
Net Income	$ 6,000,000

231

Assume that Virgil Company maintains its current earnings on its present assets, achieves the planned earnings from the new program, and that the tax rate remains at 40 percent.

a What will be earnings per share if the expansion is financed with debt?

b What will be earnings per share if the expansion is financed by issuing new shares?

c At what level of earnings before interest and taxes will earnings per share be the same, whichever of the two financing programs is used?

d At what level of earnings before interest and taxes will the rate of return on shareholders' equity be the same, whichever of the two financing plans is used?

17 Merchandise inventory costing $30,000 is purchased on account. Indicate the effect (increase, decrease, no effect) of this transaction on (1) working capital and (2) the current ratio, assuming that current assets and current liabilities immediately prior to the transaction were as follows:

a Current assets, $120,000; current liabilities, $120,000.

b Current assets, $120,000; current liabilities, $150,000.

c Current assets, $120,000; current liabilities, $80,000.

18 a Compute the ratio of return on common shareholders' equity in each of the independent cases below.

Case	Total Assets	Interest-Bearing Debt	Common Shareholders' Equity	Rate of Return on Assets	Aftertax Cost of Interest-Bearing Debt
A	$200	$100	$100	6%	6%
B	$200	$100	$100	8%	6%
C	$200	$120	$ 80	8%	6%
D	$200	$100	$100	4%	6%
E	$200	$ 50	$100	6%	6%
F	$200	$ 50	$100	5%	6%

b In which cases is leverage working to the advantage of the common shareholders?

19 Assuming an excess of current assets over current liabilities, indicate the effect of the following upon the current ratio:

a Collection of an account receivable.

b Payment of an account payable.

c Acquisition of merchandise on account.

d Acquisition of merchandise for cash.

e Acquisition of machinery on account.

f Acquisition of machinery for cash.

g Sale of marketable securities at less than book value.

h Sale of an investment at less than book value.

20 Following is a schedule of the current assets and current liabilities of the Lewis Company:

232

	December 31	
Current Assets:	**1982**	**1981**
Cash	$ 355,890	$ 212,790
Accounts Receivable	389,210	646,010
Inventories	799,100	1,118,200
Prepayments	21,600	30,000
Total Current Assets	$1,565,800	$2,007,000
Current Liabilities:		
Accounts Payable	$ 152,760	$ 217,240
Accrued Payroll, Taxes, etc.	126,340	318,760
Notes Payable	69,500	330,000
Total Current Liabilities	$ 348,600	$ 866,000

The Lewis Company operated at a loss during 1982.

a Calculate the current ratio for each date.

b Explain how the improved current ratio is possible under the 1982 operating conditions.

21 The following information relates to the activities of Tennessee Corporation and Kentucky Corporation for 1982.

	Tennessee Corp.	Kentucky Corp.
Sales on Account, 1982	$4,050,000	$2,560,000
Accounts Receivable, December 31, 1981	960,000	500,000
Accounts Receivable, December 31, 1982	840,000	780,000

a Compute the accounts receivable turnover of each company.

b Compute the average number of days that accounts receivable are outstanding for each company.

c Which company is managing its accounts receivable more efficiently?

22 Indicate the effects (increase, decrease, no effect) of each of the independent transactions below on (1) rate of return on common stock equity, (2) current ratio, and (3) debt-equity ratio. State any necessary assumptions.

a Merchandise inventory costing $120,000 is sold on account for $150,000.

b Collections from customers on accounts receivable total $100,000.

c A provision is made for estimated uncollectible accounts, $15,000.

d Specific customers' accounts totaling $10,000 are written off as uncollectible.

e Merchandise inventory costing $205,000 is purchased on account.

f A machine costing $40,000, on which $30,000 depreciation had been taken, is sold for $8,000.

g Dividends of $80,000 are declared. The dividends will be paid during the next accounting period.

23 Indicate the effects (increase, decrease, no effect) of the independent transactions below on (1) earnings per share, (2) working capital, and (3) quick ratio, where accounts receivable are *included* but merchandise inventory is *excluded* from "quick assets." State any necessary assumptions.

a Merchandise inventory costing $240,000 is sold on account for $300,000.

b Dividends of $160,000 are declared. The dividends will be paid during the next accounting period.

c Merchandise inventory costing $410,000 is purchased on account.

d A machine costing $80,000, on which $60,000 depreciation had been taken, is sold for $16,000.

e Merchandise inventory purchased for cash in the amount of $7,000 is returned to the supplier because it is defective. A cash reimbursement is received.

f 10,000 shares of $10-par value common stock were issued on the last day of the accounting period for $15 per share. The proceeds were used to acquire the assets of another firm composed of the following: accounts receivable, $30,000; merchandise inventory, $60,000; plant and equipment, $100,000. The acquiring firm also agreed to assume current liabilities of $40,000 of the acquired company.

g Marketable securities costing $16,000 are sold for $20,000.

24 The following data are taken from the financial statements of the Press Company:

	December 31	
	1982	**1981**
Current Assets	$210,000	$180,000
Noncurrent Assets	275,000	255,000
Current Liabilities	78,000	85,000
Long-Term Liabilities	75,000	30,000
Common Stock (10,000 shares)	300,000	300,000
Retained Earnings	32,000	20,000
	1982 Operations	
Net Income	$72,000	
Interest Expense	3,000	
Income Taxes (40% rate)	48,000	
Dividends Declared	60,000	

Calculate the following ratios:

a Rate of return on assets.

b Rate of return on shareholders' equity.

c Earnings per share of common stock.

d Current ratio (both dates).

e Times interest earned.

f Debt-equity ratio (both dates).

25 Refer to the financial statements of Jonathan Electronics Corporation in Chapter 1 and calculate the following:

a Rate of return on assets. The income tax rate is 40 percent.

b Rate of return on shareholders' equity.

c Earnings per share. (500,000 shares were outstanding throughout the year.)

d Profit margin ratio (based on total revenues).

e Inventory turnover.

234

f Current ratio (both dates).
g Debt-equity ratio (both dates).
h Times interest earned.

26 The income statements and balance sheets of Illinois Corporation and Ohio Corporation are presented in Exhibits 6.13 and 6.14.

Exhibit 6.13
Income Statements
for the Year 1982
(*Problem 26*)

	Illinois Corp.	Ohio Corp.
Sales	$4,300,000	$3,000,000
Less Expenses:		
Costs of Goods Sold	$2,800,000	$1,400,000
Selling and Administrative Expenses	330,000	580,000
Interest Expense	100,000	200,000
Income Tax Expense	428,000	328,000
Total Expenses	$3,658,000	$2,508,000
Net Income	$ 642,000	$ 492,000

Exhibit 6.14
Balance Sheets
December 31, 1982
(*Problem 26*)

	Illinois Corp.	Ohio Corp.
Assets:		
Cash	$ 100,000	$ 50,000
Accounts Receivable (net)	700,000	400,000
Merchandise Inventory	1,200,000	750,000
Plant and Equipment (net)	4,000,000	4,800,000
Total Assets	$6,000,000	$6,000,000
Equities:		
Accounts Payable	$ 572,000	$ 172,000
Income Taxes Payable	428,000	328,000
Long-Term Bonds Payable (10 percent)	1,000,000	2,000,000
Capital Stock	2,000,000	2,000,000
Retained Earnings	2,000,000	1,500,000
Total Equities	$6,000,000	$6,000,000

Assume that the balances in asset and equity accounts at year-end approximate the average balances during the period. The income tax rate is 40 percent. On the basis of this information, which company is:
a More profitable?
b More liquid?
c More secure in terms of long-term solvency?
Use financial ratios, as appropriate, in doing your analysis.

235

27 Exhibits 6.15 and 6.16 present information taken from the financial statements of the Eastern Oil Company for the years ending December 31, 1981 and 1982.

Exhibit 6.15
Eastern Oil Company
Consolidated Statement of
Financial Position
(Problem 27)

	(in millions of dollars)	
	December 31, 1982	December 31, 1981
Assets:		
Cash	$ 921.0	$ 866.1
Receivables (net)	1,198.3	1,173.2
Inventories	1,676.0	1,566.0
Plant and Equipment (net)	11,930.4	11,305.3
Other Noncurrent Assets	4,589.5	4,331.2
Total Assets	$20,315.2	$19,241.8
Equities:		
Current Liabilities	$ 3,329.7	$ 3,240.1
Long-Term Liabilities	5,392.6	5,051.0
Capital Stock (average shares outstanding in 1982: 224,100,000; in 1981: 221,000,000)	2,640.5	2,608.4
Retained Earnings	8,952.4	8,342.3
Total Equities	$20,315.2	$19,241.8

Exhibit 6.16
Eastern Oil Company
Statement of Income for the
Years 1982 and 1981
(Problem 27)

	(in millions of dollars)	
	1982	1981
Revenues:		
Sales	$20,361.7	$18,143.3
Other Revenue	801.4	553.4
Total Revenues	$21,163.1	$18,696.7
Expenses:		
Crude Oil and Product Costs	$ 6,283.8	$ 5,520.7
Selling and Administrative Expenses	11,806.8	10,415.2
Interest Expenses	261.7	241.6
Income Taxes Expense	1,349.2	1,209.2
Total Expenses	$19,701.5	$17,386.7
Net Income to Shareholders	$ 1,461.6	$ 1,310.0

236

On the basis of this information, assess the relative **(1)** profitability, **(2)** liquidity, and **(3)** solvency of the firm as between 1981 and 1982. Assume that the balances in the asset and equity accounts at year-end approximate the average balances during the period. Also assume an income tax rate of 40 percent.

28 The comparative balance sheets, income statement, and statement of changes in financial position of Solinger Electric Corporation for 1982 are shown in Exhibits 6.17, 6.18, and 6.19 respectively. Income taxes are 40 percent of pretax income.

Exhibit 6.17
Solinger Electric Corporation
Comparative Balance Sheets
for December 31, 1981 and 1982
(*Problem 28*)

ASSETS	December 31	
Current Assets:	**1981**	**1982**
Cash	$ 30,000	$ 3,000
Accounts Receivable	20,000	55,000
Merchandise Inventory	40,000	50,000
Total Current Assets	$ 90,000	$108,000
Noncurrent Assets:		
Buildings and Equipment (cost)	$100,000	$225,000
Accumulated Depreciation	(30,000)	(40,000)
Total Noncurrent Assets	$ 70,000	$185,000
Total Assets	$160,000	$293,000
EQUITIES		
Current Liabilities:		
Accounts Payable—Merchandise Suppliers	$ 30,000	$ 50,000
Accounts Payable—Other Suppliers	10,000	12,000
Salaries Payable	5,000	6,000
Total Current Liabilities	$ 45,000	$ 68,000
Noncurrent Liabilities:		
Bonds Payable	0	100,000
Total Liabilities	$ 45,000	$168,000
Owners' Equity:		
Capital Stock ($10 par value)	$100,000	$100,000
Retained Earnings	15,000	25,000
Total Owners' Equity	$115,000	$125,000
Total Equities	$160,000	$293,000

Exhibit 6.18
Solinger Electric Corporation
Income Statement
for the Year 1982
(Problem 28)

Sales Revenue	$125,000
Less Expenses:	
Cost of Goods Sold	$ 60,000
Salaries	19,667
Depreciation	10,000
Interest	2,000
Income Taxes	13,333
Total Expenses	$105,000
Net Income	$ 20,000

a Calculate the following ratios for Solinger Electric Corporation for 1982.
  (1) Rate of return on assets.
  (2) Rate of return on common shareholders' equity.
  (3) Earnings per share.
  (4) Accounts receivable turnover (assuming that all sales are made on account).
  (5) Inventory turnover.
  (6) Plant asset turnover.
  (7) Current ratio on December 31, 1981, and December 31, 1982.
  (8) Quick ratio on December 31, 1981, and December 31, 1982 (assuming that merchandise inventories are excluded from quick assets).
  (9) Debt-equity ratio on December 31, 1981, and December 31, 1982.
  (10) Times interest charges earned ratio.
b Was Solinger Electric Corporation successfully leveraged during 1982?
c Assume that the bonds were issued on November 1, 1982. At what annual interest rate were the bonds apparently issued?
d If Solinger Electric Corporation earns the same rate of return on assets in 1983 as it realized in 1982, and issues no more debt, will the firm be successfully leveraged in 1983?
e Calculate the amount of cash flow provided by operations during 1982.

29 Comparative balance sheets, income statement, and statement of changes in financial position of Nykerk Electronics Corporation for 1982 are presented in Exhibits 6.20, 6.21, and 6.22 respectively.
  a Calculate the following ratios for Nykerk Electronics Corporation for 1982.
    (1) Rate of return on assets.
    (2) Rate of return on common shareholders' equity.
    (3) Earnings per share.
    (4) Accounts receivable turnover (assuming that all sales are made on account).
    (5) Inventory turnover.
    (6) Plant asset turnover.

238

Exhibit 6.19
Solinger Electric Corporation
Statement of Changes in
Financial Position
for the Year 1982
(Problem 28)

SECTION I. SOURCES AND USES OF WORKING CAPITAL
Sources of Working Capital

Operations:

Net Income.	$20,000	
Addback Expenses Not Using Working Capital:		
Depreciation	10,000	
Total Sources from Operations		$ 30,000
Proceeds from Long-Term Bonds Issued		100,000
Total Sources of Working Capital		$130,000

Uses of Working Capital

Dividends		$ 10,000
Acquisition of Buildings and Equipment		125,000
Total Uses of Working Capital		$135,000
Net Decrease in Working Capital during the Year (Sources Minus Uses)		$ 5,000

SECTION II. ANALYSIS OF CHANGES IN WORKING CAPITAL ACCOUNTS
Current Asset Item Increases (Decreases)

Cash	$(27,000)	
Accounts Receivable	35,000	
Merchandise Inventory	10,000	
Net Increase (Decrease) in Current Asset Items		$ 18,000

Current Liability Increases (Decreases)

Accounts Payable—Merchandise Suppliers	$20,000	
Accounts Payable—Other Suppliers	2,000	
Salaries Payable	1,000	
Net Increase (Decrease) in Current Liability Items		23,000
Net Decrease in Working Capital During the Year (Net Increase in Current Liability Items Minus Net Increase in Current Asset Items)		$ 5,000

(7) Current ratio on December 31, 1981, and December 31, 1982.

(8) Quick ratio on December 31, 1981, and December 31, 1982.

(9) Debt-equity ratio on December 31, 1981, and December 31, 1982.

(10) Times interest charges earned ratio.

b Calculate the amount of cash flow provided by operations for 1982. For this purpose, do not include the change in Notes Payable in the analysis.

c Was Nykerk Electronics Corporation successfully leveraged during 1982?

Exhibit 6.20
Nykerk Electronics Corporation
Comparative Balance Sheets
(*Problem 29*)

	(in 000's of dollars)	
ASSETS	**December 31**	
Current Assets:	**1982**	**1981**
Cash	$ 1,300	$ 1,100
Marketable Securities	300	300
Accounts Receivable (net)	2,600	2,500
Inventories	7,300	6,900
Total Current Assets	$11,500	$10,800
Noncurrent Assets:		
Plant and Equipment	$ 5,200	$ 4,500
Less Accumulated Depreciation	1,300	1,000
Net Plant and Equipment	$ 3,900	$ 3,500
Land	1,200	1,200
Total Noncurrent Assets	$ 5,100	$ 4,700
Total Assets	$16,600	$15,500
LIABILITIES AND SHAREHOLDERS' EQUITY		
Current Liabilities:		
Accounts Payable	$ 1,600	$ 1,700
Accrued Payables	800	900
Income Taxes Payable	300	200
Notes Payable	1,900	1,200
Total Current Liabilities	$ 4,600	$ 4,000
Long-Term Liabilities:		
Bonds Payable (8 percent)	$ 2,000	$ 2,100
Mortgage Payable	200	200
Total Long-Term Liabilities	$ 2,200	$ 2,300
Total Liabilities	$ 6,800	$ 6,300
Shareholders' Equity:		
Preferred Stock (6 percent, $100 par)	$ 2,000	$ 2,000
Common Stock ($1 par)	500	500
Additional Paid-in Capital	2,500	2,500
Total Contributed Capital	$ 5,000	$ 5,000
Retained Earnings	4,800	4,200
Total Shareholders' Equity	$ 9,800	$ 9,200
Total Liabilities and Shareholders' Equity	$16,600	$15,500

Exhibit 6.21
Nykerk Electronics Corporation
Statement of Income
and Retained Earnings
Year of 1982
(Problem 29)

	(in 000's of dollars)
Revenues:	
Sales	$26,500
Less Sales Allowances, Returns, and Discounts	600
Net Sales	$25,900
Interest and Other Revenues	200
Total Revenues	$26,100
Expenses:	
Cost of Goods Sold	$20,500
Selling and Administrative Expenses:	
Selling Expenses	$2,120
Administrative Expenses	1,000
Depreciation	300
Total Selling and Administrative Expenses	3,420
Interest Expense	180
Income Tax Expense	800
Total Expenses	$24,900
Net Income to Shareholders	$ 1,200
Dividends:	
Dividends on Preferred Shares	$ 120
Dividends on Common Shares	480
Total Dividends	600
Addition to Retained Earnings for Year	$ 600
Retained Earnings, January 1, 1982	4,200
Retained Earnings, December 31, 1982	$ 4,800

30 Refer to the financial statements of General Products Company in Appendix A at the back
of the book.

Calculate the amount of the following ratios for 1982.

a Rate of return on assets. Assume an income tax rate of 46 percent in computing aftertax interest charges. In computing income before charges to suppliers of capital, add to
net income the $21 million shown as the minority interest in earnings of consolidated
affiliates. Minority interest is explained in Chapter 13.

b Rate of return on common stock equity.

c Accounts receivable turnover (assuming that all sales are made on account).

d Inventory turnover.

e Plant asset turnover.

f Current ratio on December 31, 1981, and December 31, 1982.

Exhibit 6.22
Nykerk Electronics Corporation
Statement of Changes in Financial Position
Year of 1982 (amounts in 000's)
(Problem 29)

Sources of Working Capital:		
Net Income	$1,200	
Addback Expenses Not Using Working Capital:		
Depreciation Expense	300	
Working Capital Provided by Operations		$1,500
Uses of Working Capital:		
Preferred Stock Dividend	$ 120	
Common Stock Dividend	480	
Purchase of Plant and Equipment	700	
Redemption of Bonds Payable	100	1,400
Increase in Working Capital for the Year		$ 100

Analysis of Increases (Decreases) in Working Capital Amounts:	
Cash	$ 200
Marketable Securities	0
Accounts Receivable (Net)	100
Inventories	400
Accounts Payable	100
Accrued Payables	100
Income Taxes Payable	(100)
Notes Payable	(700)
Increase in Working Capital for the Year	$ 100

g Quick ratio on December 31, 1981, and December 31, 1982 (assuming that quick assets includes cash, marketable securities, and current receivables).

h Debt-equity ratio on December 31, 1981, and December 31, 1982 (assuming that minority interest is considered to be part of shareholders' equity).

i Times interest charges earned ratio (also add back the minority interest in net income of consolidated affiliates).

31 One approach to financial statement analysis is to prepare common-size statements. These statements express each financial statement item as a percentage of some base, such as total assets, total equities, or total revenues. Presented in Exhibit 6.23 are common-sized balance sheets for Horrigan Corporation as discussed in the chapter.

    a Assuming that the ratio analysis presented in the chapter had not yet been performed, what significant changes in the structure of Horrigan Corporation's assets and equities can you observe from the common-size statement above?

    b In what respects are the changes observed in part **a** consistent with the ratio analysis presented in the chapter?

    c In what respects are the changes observed in part **a** inconsistent with the ratio analysis presented in the chapter?

Exhibit 6.23
Horrigan Corporation
Common-Size Balance Sheets
(Problem 31)

	December 31			
	1979	1980	1981	1982
ASSETS				
Cash	4.0%	2.5%	1.5%	1.5%
Marketable Securities	—	1.0	—	.3
Accounts Receivable (net)	10.4	9.0	8.8	11.7
Inventories	5.6	7.5	8.9	12.8
Total Current Assets	20.0%	20.0%	19.2%	26.3%
Land	8.0%	7.5%	11.5%	9.2%
Building	60.0	37.5	28.9	29.2
Equipment	28.0	48.0	53.1	48.2
Less Accumulated Depreciation	(16.0)	(13.0)	(12.7)	(12.9)
Total Noncurrent Assets	80.0%	80.0%	80.8%	73.7%
Total Assets	100.0%	100.0%	100.0%	100.0%
LIABILITIES AND SHAREHOLDERS' EQUITY				
Accounts Payable	10.0%	7.5%	6.8%	7.7%
Salaries Payable	4.0	3.3	2.9	3.1
Income Taxes Payable	2.0	1.7	1.9	3.0
Total Current Liabilities	16.0%	12.5%	11.6%	13.8%
Bonds Payable	20.0	12.5	19.2	23.1
Total Liabilities	36.0%	25.0%	30.8%	36.9%
Common Stock	40.0%	37.5%	30.8%	24.6%
Additional Paid-in Capital	8.0	25.0	23.0	18.5
Retained Earnings	16.0	12.5	15.4	20.0
Total Shareholders' Equity	64.0%	75.0%	69.2%	63.1%
Total Liabilities and Shareholders' Equity	100.0%	100.0%	100.0%	100.0%

32 Exhibit 6.24 shows five items from the financial statements for three companies for a recent year.

a Compute the income to sales (or income to operating revenues) ratio for each company. Which company seems to be the most successful according to this ratio?

b How many dollars of sales on average does each of the companies make for each dollar's worth of average assets held during the year?

c Compute the rate of return on assets for each company. Which company seems to be the most successful according to this ratio?

d Compute the rate of return on common shareholders' equity for each company. Which company seems to be the most successful according to this ratio?

e The three companies are American Telephone & Telegraph, Safeway Stores, and Sears, Roebuck and Company. (Dollar amounts shown are actually in thousands.) Which of the companies corresponds to A, B, and C? What clues did you use in reaching your conclusion?

Exhibit 6.24
**Comparison of Operations
and Investment**
(Problem 32)

	Company A	Company B	Company C
For Year			
Operating Revenues	$28,947,200	$13,639,900	$9,716,900
Income Before Interest and Dividends[a]	4,295,800	824,600	156,400
Net Income to Common Shareholders[b]	2,915,800	522,600	148,600
Average During Year			
Total Assets	77,107,200	10,885,000	1,532,400
Common Shareholders' Equity	29,769,200	5,118,800	743,830

[a]Net Income + Interest Charges × (1 − Tax Rate).
[b]Net Income − Preferred Stock Dividends.

Exhibit 6.25
Data for Ratio Detective Exercise
(Problem 33)

Balance Sheet at End of Year	Company Numbers						
	(1)	(2)	(3)	(4)	(5)	(6)	(7)
Current Receivables	0.31%	29.11%	6.81%	25.25%	3.45%	38.78%	17.64%
Inventories	7.80	0.00	3.14	0.00	6.45	14.94	20.57
Net Plant and Equipment*	8.50	9.63	11.13	19.88	49.87	15.59	37.60
All Other Assets	2.16	7.02	25.59	32.93	24.05	15.54	30.07
Total Assets	18.78%	45.76%	46.67%	78.06%	83.83%	84.85%	105.88%
*Cost of Plant and Equipment (gross) . . .	14.64%	14.80%	19.57%	29.03%	79.03%	24.80%	59.73%
Current Liabilities	6.08%	9.82%	6.41%	17.49%	14.83%	35.28%	27.68%
Long-Term Liabilities	2.12	7.96	0.00	0.00	0.00	8.33	1.33
Owners' Equity	10.58	27.98	40.25	60.57	69.00	41.24	76.86
Total Equities	18.78%	45.76%	46.67%	78.06%	83.83%	84.85%	105.88%
Income Statement for Year							
Revenues	100.00%	100.00%	100.00%	100.00%	100.00%	100.00%	100.00%
Cost of Goods Sold (Excluding Depreciation) or Operating Expenses[a] . .	78.97	53.77	48.21	59.07	68.62	60.88	33.29
Depreciation	1.04	1.39	1.72	2.07	4.07	1.09	3.02
Interest Expense	0.16	.52	0.00	0.08	0.02	1.35	0.73
Advertising Expense	3.72	0.00	11.43	0.06	4.39	2.93	2.28
Research and Development Expense . . .	0.00	1.00	0.00	0.00	0.15	0.00	9.06
Income Taxes	1.28	.53	9.59	6.52	7.87	3.78	8.55
All Other Items (net)	13.34	18.88	18.58	24.52	6.40	24.39	27.66
Total Expenses	98.50%	76.08%	89.53%	92.32%	91.51%	94.41%	84.59%
Net Income	1.50%	23.92%	10.47%	7.68%	8.49%	5.59%	15.41%

[a]Represents operating expenses for the following companies: Advertising/public opinion survey firm, insurance company, finance company, and the public accounting partnership.

33 In this problem, you become a financial analyst/detective. The condensed financial statements in Exhibit 6.25 are constructed on a percentage basis. In all cases, total sales revenues are shown as 100.00%. All other numbers were divided by sales revenue for the year. The 13 companies (all corporations except for the accounting firm) shown here represent the following industries:

(1) Advertising and public opinion survey firm.

(2) Beer brewery.

(3) Department store chain (that carries its own receivables).

(4) Distiller of hard liquor.

(5) Drug manufacturer.

(6) Finance company (lends money to consumers).

(7) Grocery store chain.

(8) Insurance company.

(9) Manufacturer of tobacco products, mainly cigarettes.

(10) Public accounting (CPA) partnership.

(11) Soft drink bottler.

(12) Steel manufacturer.

(13) Utility company.

	Company Numbers					
Balance Sheet at End of Year	**(8)**	**(9)**	**(10)**	**(11)**	**(12)**	**(13)**
Current Receivables	12.94%	9.16%	25.18%	27.07%	13.10%	653.94%
Inventories	15.47	56.89	79.53	0.00	1.62	0.00
Net Plant and Equipment*	70.29	28.36	19.22	2.64	251.62	2.88
All Other Assets	18.37	26.42	24.72	223.91	23.68	200.37
Total Assets	117.08%	120.82%	148.65%	253.63%	290.01%	857.18%
*Cost of Plant and Equipment (gross)	167.16%	42.40%	35.08%	4.45%	320.90%	3.81%
Current Liabilities	19.37%	33.01%	20.42%	161.37%	28.01%	377.56%
Long-Term Liabilities	20.62	34.07	36.09	10.62	115.50	280.79
Owners' Equity	77.09	53.74	92.13	81.63	146.51	198.83
Total Equities	117.08%	120.82%	148.65%	253.63%	290.01%	857.18%
Income Statement for Year						
Revenues	100.00%	100.00%	100.00%	100.00%	100.00%	100.00%
Cost of Goods Sold (Excluding Depreciation) or Operating Expenses^a	81.92	57.35	42.92	82.61	45.23	47.69
Depreciation	5.81	1.90	1.97	0.05	14.55	0.00
Interest Expense	1.23	2.69	3.11	1.07	7.15	24.33
Advertising Expense	0.00	6.93	13.04	0.00	0.00	0.00
Research and Development Expense	0.76	0.00	0.00	0.00	0.71	0.00
Income Taxes	2.15	7.47	10.63	3.92	8.73	12.89
All Other Items (net)	3.81	14.82	17.99	2.97	11.51	−5.57
Total Expenses	95.68%	91.16%	89.66%	90.62%	87.89%	79.35%
Net Income	4.32%	8.84%	10.34%	9.38%	12.11%	20.65%

245

Use whatever clues you can to match the companies in Exhibit 6.25 with the industries listed above. You may find it useful to refer to average industry ratios compiled by Dun & Bradstreet, Prentice-Hall, Robert Morris Associates, and the Federal Trade Commission. Copies of these documents can be found in most libraries.

34 On October 2, 1975, W. T. Grant Company filed for bankruptcy protection under Chapter XI of the Bankruptcy Act. At that time, it reported assets of $1.02 billion and liabilities of $1.03 billion. The company had operated at a profit for most years prior to 1974, but reported an operating loss of $177 million for its fiscal year January 31, 1974, to January 31, 1975.

Exhibit 6.26
W. T. Grant Company
Comparative Balance Sheets
(*Problem 34*)

	January 31				
	1971	**1972**	**1973**	**1974**	**1975**
ASSETS					
Cash and Marketable Securities	$ 34,009	$ 49,851	$ 30,943	$ 45,951	$ 79,642
Accounts Receivable	419,731	477,324	542,751	598,799	431,201
Inventories	260,492	298,676	399,533	450,637	407,357
Other Current Assets	5,246	5,378	6,649	7,299	6,581
Total Current Assets	$719,478	$831,229	$ 979,876	$1,102,686	$ 924,781
Investments	23,936	32,367	35,581	45,451	49,764
Property, Plant, and Equipment (net)	61,832	77,173	91,420	100,984	101,932
Other Assets	2,382	3,901	3,821	3,862	5,790
Total Assets	$807,628	$944,670	$1,110,698	$1,252,983	$1,082,267
EQUITIES					
Short-term Debt	$246,420	$237,741	$ 390,034	$ 453,097	$ 600,695
Accounts Payable	118,091	124,990	112,896	103,910	147,211
Current Deferred Taxes	94,489	112,846	130,137	133,057	2,000
Total Current Liabilities	$459,000	$475,577	$ 633,067	$ 690,064	$ 749,906
Long-term Debt	32,301	128,432	126,672	220,336	216,341
Noncurrent Deferred Taxes	8,518	9,664	11,926	14,649	—
Other Long-term Liabilities	5,773	5,252	4,694	4,195	2,183
Total Liabilities	$505,592	$618,925	$ 776,359	$ 929,244	$ 968,430
Preferred Stock	$ 9,600	$ 9,053	$ 8,600	$ 7,465	$ 7,465
Common Stock	18,180	18,529	18,588	18,599	18,599
Additional Paid-in Capital	78,116	85,195	86,146	85,910	83,914
Retained Earnings	230,435	244,508	261,154	248,461	37,674
Total	$336,331	$357,285	$ 374,488	$ 360,435	$ 147,652
Less Cost of Treasury Stock	(34,295)	(31,540)	(40,149)	(36,696)	(33,815)
Total Shareholders' Equity	$302,036	$325,745	$ 334,339	$ 323,739	$ 113,837
Total Equities	$807,628	$944,670	$1,110,698	$1,252,983	$1,082,267

The accompanying Exhibits 6.26–6.29 contain:

(1) Balance sheets, income statements, and statements of changes in financial position for W. T. Grant Company for the 1971 through 1975 fiscal periods.

(2) Additional financial information about W. T. Grant Company, the retail industry, and the economy for the same period as above.

Prepare an analysis which explains the major causes of Grant's collapse. You may find it useful to refer to financial and nonfinancial data presented in other sources, such as the *Wall Street Journal*, in addition to that presented here. Assume an income tax rate of 48 percent.

Exhibit 6.27
W. T. Grant Company
Statement of Income and Retained Earnings
(*Problem 34*)

	Years Ended January 31				
	1971	**1972**	**1973**	**1974**	**1975**
Sales	$1,254,131	$1,374,811	$1,644,747	$1,849,802	$1,761,952
Concessions	4,986	3,439	3,753	3,971	4,238
Equity in Earnings	2,777	2,383	5,116	4,651	3,086
Other Income	2,874	3,102	1,188	3,063	3,376
Total Revenues	$1,264,768	$1,383,735	$1,654,804	$1,861,487	$1,772,652
Cost of Goods Sold	$ 843,192	$ 931,237	$1,125,261	$1,282,945	$1,303,267
Selling, General, & Administration	329,768	373,816	444,377	518,280	540,953
Interest	18,874	16,452	21,127	51,047	199,238
Taxes: Current	21,140	13,487	9,588	(6,021)	(19,439)
Deferred	11,660	13,013	16,162	6,807	(98,027)
Other Expenses	557	518	502	—	24,000
Total Expenses	$1,225,191	$1,348,523	$1,617,017	$1,853,058	$1,949,992
Net Income	$ 39,577	$ 35,212	$ 37,787	$ 8,429	$ (177,340)
Dividends	(20,821)	(21,139)	(21,141)	(21,122)	(4,457)
Other	—	—	—	—	(28,990)
Change in Retained Earnings	$ 18,756	$ 14,073	$ 16,646	$ (12,693)	$ (210,787)
Retained Earnings—Beg. of Period	211,679	230,435	244,508	261,154	248,461
Retained Earnings—End of Period	$ 230,435	$ 244,508	$ 261,154	$ 248,461	$ 37,674

Exhibit 6.28
W. T. Grant Company
Statement of Changes in
Financial Position
(*Problem 34*)

	Years Ended January 31				
	1971	**1972**	**1973**	**1974**	**1975**
Sources of Working Capital					
Operations:					
Net Income.	$39,577	$ 35,212	$ 37,787	$ 8,429	$(177,340)
Plus Depreciation	9,619	10,577	12,004	13,579	14,587
Deferred Taxes	233	1,145	2,262	2,723	(14,649)
Other	74	(520)	(558)	(497)	(2,013)
Less Equity in Earnings.	(2,777)	(2,383)	(3,403)	(3,570)	(331)
Total from Operations.	$46,726	$ 44,031	$ 48,092	$ 20,664	$(179,746)
Sale of Common to Employees	5,218	7,715	3,492	2,584	886
on Open Market	—	2,229	174	260	—
Issue of Long-Term Debt.	—	100,000	—	100,000	—
Other	—	—	2,307	—	—
Total Sources	$51,944	$153,975	$ 54,065	$ 123,508	$(178,860)
Uses of Working Capital					
Dividends	$20,821	$ 21,138	$ 21,141	$ 21,122	$ 4,457
Acquisition of Prop., Plant, & Equipment	16,141	25,918	26,250	23,143	15,535
Acquisition of Treasury Stock	13,224	—	11,466	133	—
Reacquisition of Preferred Stock	948	308	252	618	—
Retirement of Long-Term Debt	1,538	5,143	1,760	6,336	3,995
Investment in Securities	436	5,951	2,040	5,700	5,182
Other	47	47	—	642	727
Total Uses	$53,155	$ 58,505	$ 62,909	$ 57,694	$ (29,898)
Net Change in Working Capital	$(1,211)	$ 95,470	$ (8,844)	$ 65,814	$(208,756)
Analysis of Increase (Decrease)					
in Working Capital					
Cash and Short-Term Securities	$ 1,032	$ 15,842	$ (18,908)	$ 15,008	$ 33,691
Accounts Receivable	51,464	57,593	65,427	56,047	(121,351)
Merchandise Inventories	38,365	38,184	100,857	51,104	(43,280)
Prepayments	209	428	1,271	651	11,032
Short-Term Debt	(64,288)	8,680	(152,293)	(63,063)	(147,898)
Accounts Payable	(13,947)	(6,900)	12,093	8,987	(42,028)
Deferred Taxes (Installment Sales)	(14,046)	(18,357)	(17,291)	(2,920)	101,078
Net Change in Working Capital	$(1,211)	$ 95,470	$ (8,844)	$ 65,814	$(208,756)

Exhibit 6.29
Additional Information
(*Problem 34*)

	Fiscals Years Ending January 31				
	1971	1972	1973	1974	1975
W. T. Grant Company					
Range of Stock Price, Dollar per Share[a]	$41\frac{7}{8}$–$70\frac{5}{8}$	$34\frac{3}{4}$–$48\frac{3}{4}$	$9\frac{7}{8}$–$44\frac{3}{8}$	$9\frac{5}{8}$–41	$1\frac{1}{2}$–$11\frac{3}{8}$
Earnings per Share in Dollars	$2.64	$2.25	$2.49	$ .76	$(12.74)
Dividends per Share in Dollars	$1.50	$1.50	$1.50	$1.50	$ .30
Number of Stores	1,116	1,168	1,208	1,189	1,152
Total Store Area, Thousands of Square Feet	38,157	44,718	50,619	53,719	54,770
Retail Industry[b]	**1970**	**1971**	**1972**	**1973**	**1974**
Total Chain Store Industry Sales in Millions of Dollars	$364,571	$408,850	$443,379	$503,317	$537,782
Number of Variety Stores (such as W. T. Grant)	7,056	6,972	7,498	8,212	8,714
Aggregate Economy[c]	**1970**	**1971**	**1972**	**1973**	**1974**
Gross National Product in Millions of Dollars	$1,075.3	$1,107.5	$1,171.1	$1,233.4	$1,210
Bank Short-Term Lending Rate	8.48%	6.32%	5.82%	8.30%	11.28%

[a]Source: Standard and Poor's Stock Reports.
[b]Source: Standard Industry Surveys.
[c]Source: Survey of Current Business.

Part Three Measuring and Reporting Assets and Equities

Chapter 7 *Cash, Marketable Securities, and Receivables*

By now, you have been exposed to all of the basic concepts and procedures of financial accounting. We have discussed the purpose of accounting, its theoretical framework, some of its procedures, and have introduced financial statement analysis. From this point onward, we shall be concerned with the application of generally accepted accounting principles to individual assets and equities. The chapters are arranged in approximate balance sheet order. Current assets are the subject of Chapters 7 and 8. This chapter emphasizes liquid, cash-like, or "quick" assets, and Chapter 8 emphasizes inventories. Chapter 9 discusses noncurrent assets. Chapters 10, 11, and 12 consider the right-hand side of the balance sheet—liabilities and owners' equity. Chapter 13, somewhat out of "balance sheet order," focuses on accounting for certain long-term investments in securities of other companies.

Liquidity and Money-like Assets

Chapters 5 and 6 pointed out that liquidity is essential for business operations. An insolvent company, one that cannot pay its bills and meet its commitments as they mature, will not survive no matter how large its owners' equity. Most bankrupt companies show positive owners' equity on their balance sheets at the time of bankruptcy. Bankruptcy is usually caused by an inability to meet debts as they become due. One of the largest bankruptcies occurred in 1970 when the Penn Central Transportation Company was placed into bankruptcy by its parent holding company, the Penn Central Company. At that time, Penn Central Transportation Company had almost $2 billion of shareholders' equity, including some $500 million of retained

252

earnings. Nevertheless, the company became insolvent because it could not meet "only" a few hundred million dollars in current obligations at that time.

Money-like assets are an important determinant of a firm's liquidity. Cash, marketable securities, accounts receivable, and notes receivable are the principal liquid assets of a business. In previous chapters, we have seen that these assets are generally stated at their current cash, or cash-equivalent, values on the balance sheet. This chapter explores in greater depth various inclusion and valuation questions related to each of these liquid assets. It also considers liquidity management. The objective of the chapter is to develop a sufficient understanding of the methods of accounting and reporting for money-like assets so that an assessment can be made of a firm's liquidity at a moment in time and changes in that liquidity over time.

Cash

Cash is the most liquid asset. It is also the most vulnerable because of its susceptibility to theft or embezzlement. This section considers cash inclusions and valuation as well as cash management and control.

Cash Inclusions and Valuation

To be included in Cash on the balance sheet, items should be freely available for use as a medium of exchange. Included in this category are coins, currency, travelers' checks, undeposited checks, and other cash on hand. Most cash is cash in the bank in the form of demand deposits, savings accounts, and certificates of deposit. Although there are generally certain restrictions on the immediate withdrawal of funds from savings accounts and certificates of deposit, they are considered to be sufficiently available for use as a medium of exchange to be included in cash. Foreign currency is also included unless there are restrictions on a firm's ability to use the currency. For example, foreign currency held by a division located in a country that significantly restricts the outflow of funds would probably not be included. Also, funds set aside or restricted for a particular purpose would not be included. For example, firms are often required to establish "sinking funds" to retire outstanding debt. The cash in a sinking fund would be reported under Investments, rather than in Cash, on the balance sheet.

Compensating balances are frequently excluded from Cash. A compensating balance generally takes the form of a minimum checking account balance that must be maintained in connection with a borrowing arrangement with a bank. For example, a firm might borrow $5 million from a bank and agree to maintain a 10-percent ($= \$500,000$) compensating balance in an interest-free checking account. This arrangement results in a reduction of the amount effectively borrowed and an increase in the interest rate effectively paid by the borrower. Unless compensating balances are adequately disclosed, incorrect assessments of a firm's liquidity can occur.

The SEC requires that legally restricted deposits held as compensating balances against short-term borrowing arrangements be stated separately from Cash but included among Current Assets. Similar compensating balances held against long-term borrowing arrangements should be included under noncurrent assets, preferably Investments. In cases where compensating balance arrangements exist but the firm is not legally precluded from using the cash, the nature of the arrangements and the amounts involved should be disclosed in a footnote to the financial statements.[1]

Once an item meets the criteria to be included in cash, there are few valuation problems. Cash is normally stated at its face amount. Foreign currency must be translated to its U.S. dollar-equivalent amount using the exchange rate in effect on the date of the balance sheet.

Cash Management

The management of cash involves two primary considerations. First, a firm must establish a system of internal controls to ensure that cash is properly safeguarded from theft or embezzlement. Typical internal control procedures include the separation of duties of individuals handling various cash receipt and disbursement tasks, the immediate depositing of cash receipts, the disbursement of cash only by authorized checks, and the regular preparation of bank account reconciliations. The appendix to this chapter describes some of the internal control procedures for cash.

A second management concern is that cash balances be regulated in such a way that neither too much nor too little cash is available at any time. Cash on hand or in checking accounts generally does not earn interest. In fact, during inflationary periods, idle cash loses purchasing power and thus decreases in real value. A firm, therefore, does not want to maintain excessive cash balances. On the other hand, a firm does not want to find itself so short of cash that it is unable to meet its obligations as they become due or unable to take advantage of cash discounts.

One effective tool in cash management is the preparation of a weekly or monthly budget of cash receipts and disbursements. Such a budget will indicate both the amounts and times when excess cash will be available for investment or when additional borrowing will become necessary.

Marketable Securities

A business may find itself with more cash than it needs for current and near-term business purposes. Rather than allow cash to remain unproductive, the business may invest some of its currently excess cash in income-yielding securities, such as U.S. government bonds or stocks or bonds of other companies. Such uses of liquid assets are recorded under the caption of *marketable securities* or *temporary investments* and are alternatives to putting cash in savings accounts or certificates of deposit. A business may acquire marketable securities intending to hold them for a longer period.

---

[1]Securities and Exchange Commission, *Accounting Series Release No. 148,* "Amendments to Regulations S-X and Related Interpretations and Guidelines Regarding the Disclosure of Compensating Balances and Short-Term Borrowing Arrangements," Securities and Exchange Commission, 1973.

Such securities are treated as long-term investments. This section considers the classification and valuation of marketable securities held either temporarily as current assets or as long-term investments.

Classification of Marketable Securities

Securities are classified as "marketable securities" and shown among current assets as long as they can be readily converted into cash *and* management intends to do so when it needs cash. Securities that do not meet both of these criteria are included under Investments on the balance sheet.

Example 1 Morrissey Manufacturing Corporation invested $150,000 of temporarily excess funds in U.S. Treasury notes. The notes mature in 3 months. This investment is properly classified among marketable securities because the notes can be sold at any time and even if not sold, the cash will be collected within 3 months.

Example 2 Suppose that Morrissey Manufacturing Corporation in **Example 1** above had acquired 20-year bonds of Greer Electronics Company instead of the U.S. Treasury notes. Its intent in acquiring the bonds was the same as before, the investment of temporarily excess cash. These bonds would similarly be classified as marketable securities, because they can be traded in an established marketplace.

Example 3 West Corporation acquired 10 percent of the outstanding shares of Haskell Corporation on the open market for $10 million. West Corporation plans to hold these shares as a long-term investment. Even though the shares of Haskell Corporation are readily marketable, they would not be classified as marketable securities, because West Corporation does not intend to turn the securities into cash within a reasonably short period. These securities would be classified under Investments on the balance sheet.

In published financial statements, all securities properly classified as the current asset Marketable Securities are grouped together and shown on a single line on the balance sheet. As discussed below, however, a distinction is made for accounting purposes between *marketable debt securities* and *marketable equity securities*.

Valuation of Marketable Securities as Temporary Investments

Marketable securities, like other assets, are initially recorded at acquisition cost. Acquisition cost includes the purchase price plus any commissions, taxes, and other costs incurred. For example, if marketable securities are acquired for $10,000 and $300 is paid in commissions and taxes, the entry is:

Marketable Securities	10,300	
Cash		10,300

Dividends on marketable securities are recognized as revenue when the dividends are declared. Interest revenue is recognized when earned. Assuming that $250 of dividends were declared and $300 of interest was earned on the marketable securities above and these amounts were immediately received in cash, the entry is:

Cash	550	
Dividend Revenue		250
Interest Revenue		300

There is nothing unusual about the valuation of marketable securities at date of acquisition or the recording of dividends and interest. The valuation of marketable securities after acquisition may, however, depart from strict historical cost accounting.

Marketable Equity Securities Financial Accounting Standards Board *Statement of Financial Accounting Standards No. 12* (1975) requires that the *portfolio* of marketable equity securities (that is, common stock, preferred stock, stock options, and warrants classified as current assets) be stated at the lower of acquisition cost or market at the end of each period.[2] Under the *lower-of-cost-or-market method,* decreases in the market value of a portfolio of marketable equity securities are recognized as holding losses each period as the decreases occur, even though a market transaction or exchange has not taken place. The credit to reduce the carrying amount of the current asset Marketable (Equity) Securities is made to an account contra to Marketable (Equity) Securities usually called the Allowance for Excess of Cost of Marketable Securities over Market Value.

Using a separate contra account enables the simultaneous identification of both the acquisition cost and the amount of decline, if any, in the market value of the portfolio. Separate identification of the cost and current market value, when below cost, are required, because any subsequent increase in the market value of the portfolio up to the original acquisition cost is recognized as a holding gain. The portfolio cannot be stated at an amount greater than the original acquisition cost; that is, the allowance account can never have a debit balance. The procedures for applying the lower-of-cost-or-market method are illustrated next.

Example 4 Wolfson Company acquired various marketable equity securities during 1979 as shown in Exhibit 7.1.[3] The entry to record the acquisition of securities during 1979 is:

Marketable Securities	100,000	
Cash		100,000

---

[2] "Market value," as defined by Financial Accounting Standards Board, *Statement No. 12,* "Accounting for Certain Marketable Securities", is the quoted market price for both buyers and sellers excluding brokerage commissions, taxes, and similar costs.

[3] In reality, a firm holding these securities for 4 years would likely classify them as investments, not as current assets. For purposes of illustration, we have shown the accounting for a portfolio of marketable securities over several years.

Exhibit 7.1
**Data for Illustration of Accounting
for Marketable Securities of Wolfson Company**

			Market Value			
Security	Date Acquired	Acquisition Cost	Dec. 31, 1979	Dec. 31, 1980	Dec. 31, 1981	Dec. 31, 1982
A Company	4/1/1979	$50,000	$53,000	$54,000	$52,000	$43,000
B Company	6/1/1979	30,000	27,000	22,000	—[a]	—
C Company	8/1/1979	20,000	16,000	23,000	24,000	—[b]
Total		$100,000	$96,000	$99,000	$76,000	$43,000

[a]Holdings of Company B sold during 1981 for $32,000.
[b]Holdings of Company C sold during 1982 for $17,000.

Unrealized Holding Loss At the end of 1979, the portfolio of marketable equity securities had an aggregate acquisition cost of $100,000 (=$50,000 + $30,000 + $20,000) and an aggregate market value of $96,000 (=$53,000 + $27,000 + $16,000). A write-down of $4,000 is required to recognize the unrealized holding loss.

Unrealized Holding Loss on Valuation of Marketable Securities	4,000	
Allowance for Excess of Cost of Marketable Securities over Market Value		4,000
Entry to adjust credit balance in allowance account to $4,000.		

The loss account appears in the income statement for 1979 among the expenses. The allowance account is shown as a contra account to marketable securities on the balance sheet at the end of 1979. Exhibit 7.2 and 7.7 illustrate the required disclosures.

Because the lower-of-cost-or-market method is applied to the entire portfolio, rather than security by security, the amount of the decline in market value below cost is not recorded separately for each security. In many cases, as in this example, gains on some securities offset losses on others.

Recovery of Unrealized Holding Loss Taking the example one step further, assume that there were no acquisitions or dispositions of marketable equity securities during 1980 and that the market value of the portfolio at the end of 1980 was $99,000. The valuation of the portfolio of securities is increased (but never to an amount greater than original acquisition cost). The entry is:

Allowance for Excess of Cost of Marketable Securities over Market Value	3,000	
Recovery of Unrealized Holding Loss on Valuation of Marketable Securities		3,000
To increase valuation of marketable securities by reducing allowance account.		

The debit entry above decreases the credit balance in the allowance account to $1,000. The Recovery of Unrealized Holding Loss on Valuation of Marketable Securities account is included in the income statement for 1980 as a revenue, or gain. See Exhibit 7.2 for illustrative disclosures.

Exhibit 7.2
**Items in Income Statement and
Balance Sheet of Wolfson Company Illustrating Transactions in
Marketable Securities as Temporary Investments—Current Assets**

	1979	1980	1981	1982
Excerpts from Income Statement for Year				
Other Items (Assumed) Before Taxes	$300,000	$300,000	$300,000	$300,000
Realized Gain (Loss) on Sale of Marketable Securities	—	—	2,000	(3,000)
Unrealized Holding Loss on Valuation of Marketable Securities	(4,000)	—	—	(7,000)
Recovery of Unrealized Holding Loss on Valuation of Marketable Securities	—	3,000	1,000	—
Income Before Taxes	$296,000	$303,000	$303,000	$290,000
Balance Sheet Items at Year-End				
Marketable Securities at Cost	$100,000	$100,000	$ 70,000	$ 50,000
Less Allowance for Excess of Cost of Marketable Securities over Market Value . .	(4,000)	(1,000)	—	(7,000)
Marketable Securities at Lower-of-Cost-or-Market[a]	$ 96,000	$ 99,000	$ 70,000	$ 43,000

[a]Notes to the financial statements must disclose separately the unrealized gains on all securities with gains and the unrealized losses on securities with losses. These disclosures are illustrated later in Exhibit 7.7 for the Alexis Company. Consider, for example, the first column shown here and the underlying data reported in the preceding exhibit. Unrealized gains on securities with gains (A Company) total $3,000, while unrealized losses on securities with losses (B Company and C Company) total $7,000 [= ($30,000—$27,000) + ($20,000 − $16,000)]. Both the amounts of the unrealized gains of $3,000 and the unrealized losses of $7,000 appear in notes, while the net unrealized loss of $4,000 (= $7,000—$3,000) appears in the Allowance account for the year. For the third year shown here, the notes disclose that the aggregate market value of the securities exceeds their cost by $6,000.

Realized Gain or Loss through Sale When an individual marketable equity security is sold, the realized gain or loss is the difference between the selling price and the original acquisition cost of the individual security, regardless of the related balance in the allowance account. For example, assume that the securities of B Company were sold during 1981 for $32,000. The entry to record the sale during 1981 is:

Cash	32,000	
Realized Holding Gain on Sale of Marketable Securities		2,000
Marketable Securities		30,000

To recognize realized holding gain of $2,000 (= $32,000 proceeds of sale − $30,000 original cost).

Exhibit 7.3
Items in Income Statement and Balance Sheet of Wolfson Company
Illustrating Transactions in Long-Term Investments in
Marketable Equity Securities

	1979	1980	1981	1982
Excerpts from Income Statement for Year				
Other Items (Assumed) Before Taxes	$300,000	$300,000	$300,000	$300,000
Realized Gain (Loss) on Sale of Investments in Marketable Equity Securities	—	—	2,000	(3,000)
Income Before Taxes	$300,000	$300,000	$302,000	$297,000
Excerpts from Balance Sheet Items at Year-End Asset Section				
Investments in Marketable Equity Securities at Cost	$100,000	$100,000	$ 70,000	$ 50,000
Less Allowance for Excess of Cost of Investments in Marketable Equity Securities over Market Value	(4,000)	(1,000)	—	(7,000)
Marketable Securities at Lower-of-Cost-or-Market	$ 96,000	$ 99,000	$ 70,000[a]	$ 43,000
Owners' Equity Section				
Net Unrealized Loss on Investments in Marketable Equity Securities (Debit Balance)	($ 4,000)	($ 1,000)	—	($ 7,000)

[a]The captions on the balance sheet or the notes must disclose that the market value on December 31, 1981, is $76,000.

The realized holding gain would be included in the calculation of net income for 1981, as shown in Exhibit 7.2. The aggregate acquisition cost of the portfolio at the end of 1981 is now $70,000 (= $50,000 + $20,000). The aggregate market value of the portfolio at the end of 1981 is $76,000 (= $52,000 + $24,000). Thus the allowance account should have a zero balance so that the portfolio appears at cost on the balance sheet. Because the allowance account has a $1,000 credit balance carried over from 1980, the following entry is necessary at the end of 1981 to reduce the allowance account to zero.

Allowance for Excess of Cost of Marketable Securities over Market Value 1,000
   Recovery of Unrealized Holding Loss on Valuation of Marketable Securities . . .   1,000
To increase valuation of marketable securities by reducing the allowance.

The securities are shown at $70,000 on the December 31, 1981, balance sheet in Exhibit 7.2. Income for 1981 is increased by $1,000 as well as by the realized gain of $2,000.

Realized Loss and Unrealized Loss The data for 1982 illustrate the simultaneous realization of a loss on sale of one security and further unrealized holding losses on securities still held. Holdings of Company C that had cost $20,000 are sold for $17,000. The journal entry is:

Cash	17,000	
Realized Holding Loss on Sale of Marketable Securities	3,000	
Marketable Securities		20,000
Sale of holding of Company C for $3,000 less than original cost.		

Securities held at the end of 1982 have an aggregate cost of $50,000 and an aggregate market value of $43,000. Thus, the balance in the allowance account must be $7,000. The journal entry is:

Unrealized Holding Loss on Valuation of Marketable Securities	7,000	
Allowance for Excess of Cost of Marketable Securities over Market Value		7,000
Adjustment of balance in allowance account from zero to $7,000.		

Income for 1982 is decreased by the realized loss of $3,000 and by the unrealized holding loss of $7,000. See Exhibit 7.2.

Marketable Debt Securities FASB *Statement No. 12* addressed only marketable equity securities. The accounting for marketable debt securities follows *Accounting Research Bulletin No. 43* (Chapter 3A), which prescribes acquisition cost as the valuation method except "where market value is less than cost by a substantial amount . . . , the amount to be included as a current asset should not exceed the market value."

As a practical matter, many firms have adopted the lower-of-cost-or-market method for marketable debt securities during the past decade. The issuance of FASB *Statement No. 12* has made this practice even more acceptable. The lower-of-cost-or-market method is usually applied to the portfolio of marketable debt securities separately from the portfolio of marketable equity securities.

Valuation of Marketable Securities as Long-term Investments

Businesses may acquire marketable equity securities of another firm as a long-term investment. Long-term investments in equity securities are generally intended to be either passive or active. A passive investment is one where the owning firm hopes to accumulate wealth by sharing in the good fortunes and good management of another firm but where the owning firm does not actively control or significantly influence the activities of the other firm. (In this sense, an individual's purchase of shares of stock is usually passive.) In other cases, a firm will acquire shares of another company with the notion of controlling or significantly influencing the other company's activities for purposes thought advantageous to the investor firm.

260

The accounting for passive investments differs from the accounting for active investments. Passive investments, over which no control or significant influence is sought or exercised, are accounted for with the lower-of-cost-or-market method similar to that explained above for temporary holdings. There are, however, important differences. The decrease in the market value of a portfolio of equity securities classified as investments is not recognized as a loss in calculating net income during the period when the decrease occurs, as is done for marketable securities classified as current assets. Instead, the debit is to an account such as Net Unrealized Loss on Investments in Marketable Equity Securities, which is an owners' equity contra account. The account appears in the owners' equity section, usually between Additional Paid-in Capital and Retained Earnings. The account always has a debit balance and is, thus, subtracted from the other amounts (credit balances) of owners' equity.

Exhibit 7.3 illustrates the accounting for long-term investments in marketable securities. It is based on the same data used in illustrating the accounting for temporary investments. The principal difference between the amounts shown in Exhibit 7.2 and 7.3 is the treatment of unrealized holding losses and recoveries of unrealized holding losses. In Exhibit 7.2, these items enter into the calculation of net income as they arise. In Exhibit 7.3, these items do not affect net income as they arise but are shown in the owners' equity section of the balance sheet.

Transfer of Securities between Current and Noncurrent Portfolios

The same holding of marketable equity securities may be classified either as a current asset or as a noncurrent asset, depending on the intentions of the owning company. A security can be transferred from the current asset portfolio to the noncurrent asset portfolio or vice versa. If the market price of the security is less than cost on the date of transfer, generally accepted accounting principles require a "dual transaction assumption." FASB *Statement No. 12* (paragraph 10) requires under these conditions that a transfer of a security between portfolios be treated as though the security were sold for cash at the time of transfer and immediately repurchased at the same price. Thus, the transfer between portfolios establishes a realized loss and a new cost basis. Assume, for example, that equity securities had been purchased for $50,000 and held as a current asset while the market price declined to $40,000. The investment has been accounted for using the lower-of-cost-or-market basis. If the firm decides to reclassify the investment as a long-term investment, the following entry is made:

Realized Loss on Reclassification of Marketable Security as a Noncurrent Asset	10,000	
Investments (Noncurrent Asset)	40,000	
Marketable Securities (Current Asset)		50,000

The loss appears on the income statement for the year; the cost basis of the noncurrent asset is $40,000; subsequent increases in market value, even to $50,000, are not recognized in the accounts.

Order of Procedures for Lower-of-Cost-or-Market Method

Students often find the treatment of the various events relating to investments in marketable securities confusing: the recording of realized gains or losses (through sale or reclassification from current to noncurrent or vice versa), the recording of unrealized losses, the recovery of unrealized losses, and the valuation of the allowance account. Confusion will be minimized and the final answer will more likely be correct if the transactions are analyzed and recorded in the following order:

1 Record any realized gains or losses, from whatever source (sale, reclassification from current to noncurrent portfolio, or vice versa).
2 Compare the market value of the portfolio at the end of the period with its cost to ascertain the required credit balance in the Allowance account (= cost less market value if cost exceeds market value and zero otherwise).
3 Prepare a journal entry to adjust the Allowance account from its zero or credit balance at the start of the period to its required credit or zero balance at the end of the period.
   a If the adjustment requires a credit to the Allowance account, then the debit is to the Unrealized Loss account, which appears in the income statement for current assets but only in the owners' equity section of the balance sheet for long-term investments.
   b If the adjustment requires a debit to the Allowance account, the credit for current assets is to the Recovery of Unrealized Loss account, which appears on the income statement, and for long-term investments is to the Unrealized Loss account, which appears only on the balance sheet.

Individual securities are valued at cost, not at the lower of cost or market with separate valuation allowances; only the portfolio is valued at lower of cost or market.

The Investment account is a "controlling account" showing the sum of all of the recorded acquisition costs of all the individual securities in the portfolio. When a security is removed from the portfolio, its acquisition cost must be taken out of the Investment account.

Evaluation of Lower of Cost or Market

The lower-of-cost-or-market valuation method provides only a partial solution to the problem of accounting for marketable securities. For many years, some accounting theorists have argued that marketable securities should be shown at market value, whether greater or less than cost. Their very marketability makes valuing them on a current basis reasonably objective. The market value of the securities is the most relevant value for assessing a firm's liquidity. The FASB has taken the position, however, that permitting the write-up of marketable securities to an amount greater than acquisition cost would be a departure from historical cost accounting, a move that the FASB does not feel is appropriate yet. The case for market values for marketable securities is so strong that upward revaluations from acquisition cost may soon become part of generally accepted accounting principles. Keep in mind that the total gain (or loss) on the holding of a security is the difference between the cash received on disposal less the original cash cost; over long enough time periods, income equals cash-in less cash-out. The write-downs and write-ups, if any, merely allocate that income to the various accounting periods between the dates of purchase and sale as market conditions change.

Accounts Receivable

The third liquid asset considered in this chapter is accounts receivable. Trade accounts receivable typically arise when sales of goods or services are made on account. The entry is:

Accounts Receivable	250	
Sales Revenue		250

Receivables sometimes also arise from transactions other than sales. For example, advances might be made to officers or employees, deposits might be made to guarantee performance or cover potential damages, or claims may be made against insurance companies, governmental bodies, common carriers, or others. These receivables are classified as either current assets or investments, depending on the expected collection date. In this section, we focus on trade accounts receivable, considering both their valuation and their management.

Accounts Receivable Valuation

Accounts receivable are initially recorded at the amount owed by customers. This amount is reduced for estimated uncollectible accounts, sales discounts, and sales returns and allowances. The reporting objective is to state accounts receivable at the amount expected to be collected in cash. The charge against income for expected uncollectible amounts, sales discounts, and sales returns and allowances should be made in the period when the related revenue is recognized. In this way, a proper periodic measurement of revenue will be achieved.

Uncollectible Accounts

Whenever credit is extended to customers, there will almost certainly be some accounts that will never be collected. The uncollectible amount will vary among different types of businesses both as to its relative significance and as to its regularity. There are two methods of accounting for uncollectible accounts: (1) the direct charge-off method and (2) the allowance method.

Direct Charge-off Method

The direct charge-off method recognizes losses from uncollectible accounts in the period in which a specific customer's account is determined to be uncollectible. The method is sometimes called the "direct write-off method." For example, if it is decided that the account receivable of John Mahoney for $200 has become uncollectible, the following entry would be made:

Bad Debt Expense	200	
Accounts Receivable		200
To record loss from an uncollectible customer's account.		

The direct charge-off method has three important shortcomings. First, the loss from uncollectible accounts is usually not recognized in the period in which the sale occurs and revenue is recognized. Too much income is recognized in the period of sale and too little in the period of write-off. Second, the amount of losses from uncollectible accounts recognized in any period is susceptible to intentional misrepresentation, because it is difficult to decide when a particular account becomes uncollectible. Third, the amount of accounts receivable on the balance sheet does not reflect the amount of cash expected to be collected. The direct charge-off method is not appropriate when such losses are significant in amount, occur frequently, and are reasonably predictable, as in retail stores.

Allowance Method

An alternative procedure is the allowance method. The allowance method involves:

1 Estimating the amount of uncollectible accounts that will occur over time in connection with the sales of each period.
2 Making an adjusting entry reducing the reported revenue of the period for the estimated uncollectible amount.
3 Making a corresponding adjustment to the amount of accounts receivable so that the balance sheet figure reports the amount expected to be collected.

The entry involves a debit to Sales Contra, Estimated Uncollectibles, which is an account contra to Sales, and a credit to Allowance for Uncollectible Accounts, which is an account contra to the total of Accounts Receivable. The credit must be made to a contra account rather than to Accounts Receivable because no specific, individual account is being written off at the time of entry.[4] Because the Allowance for Uncollectible Accounts is a contra to Accounts Receivable, its balance at the end of the period appears on the balance sheet as a deduction from Accounts Receivable. The Sales Contra, Estimated Uncollectibles account, as a revenue contra, is deducted from sales revenue on the income statement.

To illustrate the allowance method, assume that 2 percent of the credit sales made during the present period are estimated never to be collected. If sales on account are $90,000, then the entry to reduce revenue and reduce the amount of Accounts Receivable to the amount expected to be collected would be:

---

[4]Recall that Accounts Receivable is a master, or "control," account showing the total of all amounts receivable from specific customers. There is a separate account for each customer in a subsidiary ledger; the Accounts Receivable account merely records their total.

264

Sales Contra, Estimated Uncollectibles	1,800	
Allowance for Uncollectible Accounts		1,800

To record estimate of uncollectible accounts arising from current period's sales (.02 × $90,000).

When a particular customer's account is judged uncollectible, it is written off against the Allowance for Uncollectible Accounts. If, for example, it is decided that a balance of $200 due from John Mahoney will not be collected, the entry to charge off the account is:

Allowance for Uncollectible Accounts	200	
Accounts Receivable		200

To write off John Mahoney's account.

Under the allowance method, the revenue for the period of sale is reduced by the amount of uncollectibles that is estimated to arise from that period's sales. Some time later, when the attempts at collection are finally abandoned, the specific account is written off. Net assets are not affected by writing off the specific account. The reduction in net assets took place earlier, when the Allowance for Uncollectible Accounts was credited in the entry recognizing the estimated amount of eventual uncollectibles.

Rationale for the Revenue Contra Presentation

In practice, many firms do not treat the adjustment for estimated uncollectibles as a reduction in revenue. Instead the adjustment is treated as an administrative or selling expense, reported in the income statement as Bad Debt Expense. Net income for the period is the same whether the uncollectibles charge is treated as a revenue contra or as an expense provided that the same method for estimating the *amount* of uncollectibles is used.

We prefer to treat the adjustment for estimated uncollectibles as a reduction in revenue, not as an expense. To justify this preference, we ask, "What is the optimal amount of uncollectible accounts for a firm?" For most firms, the optimal amount of uncollectibles is not zero. If a firm is to have no uncollectible accounts, it must screen credit customers carefully, which is costly. Furthermore, the firm would deny credit to many customers who would pay their bills even though they could not pass a more stringent credit check. Some of the customers who are denied credit will take their business elsewhere and sales will be lost. So long as the amount *collected* from credit sales to a given class of customers exceeds the cost of goods sold and the other costs of serving that class of customers, the firm will be better off selling to that class rather than losing the sales. The rational firm should prefer granting credit to a class of customers who have a high probability of paying their bills, rather than losing their business, even though there may be some uncollectible accounts.

For example, if gross margin—selling price less cost of goods sold—on new credit sales is 20 percent of credit sales, then a firm could afford uncollectible accounts of

265

up to 20 percent of the new credit sales and still show increased net income, so long as all other costs of serving those customers remain constant.

An expense is a "gone asset." Accounts that prove uncollectible are not assets, because the rational firm made credit sales expecting that a small percentage of those sales would never be collected. Hence, the amount of uncollectibles was never an asset or revenue in the first place. Thus we prefer to treat the amount of estimated uncollectible accounts as an adjustment in determining revenue, not as a "gone asset" or expense.

We do not suggest, of course, that a firm grant credit indiscriminately or ignore collection efforts for uncollected accounts receivable. We do suggest that a cost/benefit analysis of credit policy will probably dictate a strategy that results in some amount of uncollectible accounts, an amount that is reasonably predictable before any sales are made.

Estimating Uncollectibles

There are two basic methods used for calculating the amount of the adjustment for uncollectible accounts. These are the *percentage-of-sales method* and the *aging-of-accounts-receivable method.*

Percentage-of-Sales Method   The easiest method in most cases is to multiply the total sales on account during the period by an appropriate percentage, because it seems reasonable to assume that uncollectible account amounts will vary directly with the volume of credit business. (The example on page 264 used the percentage-of-sales method.) The percentage to be used can be found by studying the experience of the business or by an inquiry into the experience of similar enterprises. The rates found in use will generally be within the range of $\frac{1}{4}$ percent to 2 percent of credit sales.

To illustrate, assume that sales on account total $1,500,000, and experience indicates that the appropriate percentage of uncollectible accounts is 2 percent. The entry is:

Sales Contra, Estimated Uncollectibles.	30,000	
Allowance for Uncollectible Accounts		30,000
To provide for estimate of uncollectibles computed as a percentage of sales.		

If cash sales occur in a relatively constant proportion to credit sales, the estimated uncollectibles percentage, proportionately reduced, can be applied to the total sales for the period. The total amount of all sales may be more readily available than that for sales on account.

Aging-of-Accounts-Receivable Method   Another method of calculating the amount of the adjustment, often called *aging the accounts,* involves classifying each customer's account as to the length of time for which the account has been uncollected. Common intervals used for classifying individual accounts receivable are:

1 Not yet due.
2 Past due 30 days or less.
3 Past due 31 to 60 days.
4 Past due 61 to 180 days.
5 Past due more than 180 days.

The presumption is that the balance in the Allowance for Uncollectible Accounts should be large enough to cover substantially all accounts receivable past due for more than 6 months and smaller portions of the more recent accounts. The actual portions are estimated from past experience.

As an example of the adjustment to be made, assume that the present balance in the Accounts Receivable account is $850,000 and the balance in the Allowance for Uncollectible Accounts before the adjusting entry for the period is $36,000. An aging of the accounts receivable balance ($850,000), shown in Exhibit 7.4, results in an estimate that $68,000 of the accounts will probably become uncollectible. The adjustment requires that the Allowance for Uncollectible Accounts balance be $68,000, an increase of $32,000. The adjusting entry at the end of the period is:

Sales Contra, Estimated Uncollectibles.	32,000	
Allowance for Uncollectible Accounts		32,000
To increase Allowance account to $68,000 computed by an aging analysis; $68,000 − $36,000 = $32,000.		

Exhibit 7.4
Illustration of Aging Accounts Receivable

Classification of Accounts	Amount	Estimated Uncollectible Percentage	Estimated Uncollectible Amounts
Not yet due	$680,000	0.5%	$ 3,400
1–30 days past due.	60,000	6.0	3,600
31–60 days past due	30,000	25.0	7,500
61–180 days past due	50,000	50.0	25,000
Over 180 days past due	30,000	95.0	28,500
	$850,000		$68,000

Even when the percentage method is used, aging the accounts should be done periodically as an occasional check on the accuracy of the percentage being used. If the aging analysis shows that the balance in the Allowance for Uncollectible Accounts is apparently too large or too small, the percentage of sales to be charged to the contra-revenue account can be lowered or raised so that the apparent error will work itself out through future adjustments.

When the percentage-of-sales method is used, the periodic provision for uncollectible accounts (for example, $30,000) is merely added to the amounts provided in previous periods in the account, Allowance for Uncollectible Accounts. When the aging method is used, the balance in the account, Allowance for Uncollectible Accounts, is adjusted (for example, by $32,000) to reflect the desired ending balance. If the percentage used under the percentage-of-sales method is reasonably accurate, the *balance* in the allowance account should be approximately the same at the end of each period under these two methods of estimating uncollectible accounts.

Exhibit 7.5 illustrates the operation of the allowance method for uncollectibles over two periods. In the first period the percentage method is used. In the second period the aging method is used. Normally, a firm would use the same method in all periods.

Sales Discounts

Often the seller of merchandise offers a reduction from its invoice price for prompt payment. Such reductions are called *sales discounts* or *cash discounts.*[5] Discounts should be considered as a reduction in sales revenue in the period of the sale. There is nothing incongruous in the proposition that goods may have two prices: a cash price or a higher price if goods are sold on credit. The cash discount is offered, not only as an interest allowance on funds paid before the bill is due—the implied interest rate is unreasonably large—but also as an incentive for prompt payment so that additional bookkeeping and collection costs can be avoided. To state it more realistically, the goods are sold for a certain price if prompt payment is made, and a penalty is added in the form of a higher price if the payment is delayed. The bills rendered by many public utilities illustrate this more realistic approach. The amount of sales discount made available to customers, then, should be considered as one of the adjustments in the measurement of net sales revenue.

The need to prepare operating statements for relatively short periods leads to alternative possibilities for recording sales discounts and computing the amount of sales discounts reported for a period. The theoretical issue is whether the amount of cash discount should be deducted from sales revenue in the period when the sales revenue is recognized or in the period of cash collection. In computing the amount of sales discounts recognized for a period, the major alternatives are the following:

1 To recognize discounts when taken by the customer, without regard to the period of sale (called the *gross price method*).
2 To estimate the total amount of discounts that will be taken on the sales made during the period (called the *allowance method*).
3 To record sales amounts reduced by all discounts made available to customers and to recognize additional revenue when a discount lapses (called the *net price method*).

These methods are discussed in intermediate accounting texts.

---

[5] See Glossary at the back of the book for the definition of a *discount* and a summary of the various contexts where this word is used in accounting.

Exhibit 7.5
Review of the Allowance Method
of Accounting for Uncollectible Accounts

Transactions in the First Period:

(1) Sales are $1,000,000.

(2) Cash of $937,000 is collected from customers in payment of their accounts.

(3) At the end of the first period, it is estimated that uncollectibles will be 2 percent of sales; $.02 \times \$1,000,000 = \$20,000$.

(4) Specific accounts totaling $7,000 are written off as uncollectible.

(5) The revenue, revenue contra, and other temporary accounts are closed.

Transactions in the Second Period:

(6) Sales are $1,200,000.

(7) Specific accounts totaling $22,000 are written off during the period as information on their uncollectibility becomes known. The debit balance of $9,000 will remain in the Allowance account until the adjusting entry is made at the end of the period; see (9).

(8) Cash of $1,100,000 is collected from customers in payment of their accounts.

(9) An aging of the accounts receivable shows that the amount in the Allowance account should be $16,000. The amount of the adjustment is $25,000. It is computed as the difference between the desired $16,000 credit balance and the current $9,000 debit balance in the Allowance account.

(10) The revenue, revenue contra, and other temporary accounts are closed.

Cash		Accounts Receivable		Allowance for Uncollectible Accounts	
(2) 937,000		(1) 1,000,000	937,000 (2)		20,000 (3)
			7,000 (4)	(4) 7,000	
Bal. ?		Bal. 56,000			13,000 Bal.
		(6) 1,200.000			
(8) 1,100,000			22,000 (7)	(7) 22,000	
			1,100,000 (8)		25,000 (9)
Bal. ?		Bal. 134,000			16,000 Bal.

Sales Contra, Estimated Uncollectibles		Sales Revenue	
(3) 20,000			1,000,000 (1)
	Closed (5)	(5) Closed	
(9) 25,000			1,200,000 (6)
	Closed (10)	(10) Closed	

Sales Returns

When a customer returns merchandise, the sale has, in effect, been canceled, and an entry that reverses the recording of the sale would be appropriate. In analyzing sales activities, however, management may be interested in the amount of goods returned.

269

If so, a sales contra account is used to accumulate the amount of returns for a particular period.

A cash refund, such as might be made in a retail store when a customer returns merchandise that had been purchased for cash, would be entered as:

Sales Contra, Returns	23	
Cash on Hand		23

Return of goods by a customer who buys "on account" would usually involve the preparation of a credit memorandum, which is, in effect, the reverse of a sales invoice. The credit memorandum lists the goods that have been returned and indicates the amount that is to be allowed the customer. The entry to record the issuance of the credit would normally be a debit to the sales contra account for returns and a credit to the Accounts Receivable account. The net amount of sales for the period will have been reduced by the amount of such returns.

Somewhat misleading sales and income amounts can result if goods are returned in a period after the one of sale. If there is no adjustment, the sales and income amounts for the period of sale are overstated, because they reflect transactions that are later canceled. Further, sales and revenue amounts are correspondingly understated in the period when the goods are returned. It would be possible to use the same type of estimated allowance procedure for returns that was illustrated for uncollectible accounts, but because the amounts involved are usually relatively small, it is not customary to do so.

Sales Allowances

A *sales allowance* is a reduction in price granted to a customer, usually after the goods have been delivered and found to be unsatisfactory or damaged. Again, as in the case of sales returns, the effect is a reduction in the sales revenue, but it may be desirable to accumulate the amount of such adjustments as a separate item. A revenue contra account, Sales Contra, Allowances, may be used for this purpose, or a combined account title, Sales Contra, Returns and Allowances, may be used. The record-keeping problems are similar to those caused by sales returns.

Presentation of Sales Adjustments in the Income Statement

In discussing the complications that accompany accounts receivable, we have introduced several adjustments to sales that are accumulated in revenue contra accounts. All these adjustments—for uncollectible accounts, for discounts, for returns, and for allowances—are illustrated in the Alexis Company's income statement, Exhibit 7.6. Alexis Company uses the gross price method for recording sales-related transactions. Exhibit 7.6 appears later in this chapter.

270

Turning Receivables into Cash

In some cases, a firm may find itself temporarily short of cash and unable to obtain financing from its usual sources. In such instances, accounts receivable can be used to obtain financing. A firm may *assign* its accounts receivable to a bank or finance company to obtain a loan. The borrowing company physically maintains control of the accounts receivable, collects amounts remitted by customers, and then forwards the proceeds to the lending institution. Alternatively, the firm may *pledge* its accounts receivable to the lending agency. If the borrowing firm is unable to make loan repayments when due, the lending agency has the power to sell the accounts receivable in order to obtain payment. Finally, the accounts receivable may be *factored* to a bank or finance company to obtain cash. In this case, the accounts receivable are, in effect, sold to the lending institution, and it physically controls the receivables and collects payments from customers. If accounts receivable have been assigned or pledged, a footnote to the financial statements should indicate this fact. The collection of such accounts receivable will not increase the liquid resources available to the firm to pay general trade creditors. Accounts receivable that have been factored will not appear on the balance sheet, because they have been sold.

Notes Receivable

Many business transactions involve written promises to pay sums of money at a future date. These written promises are called promissory notes. The holder of a promissory note has a liquid asset, notes receivable. A promissory note is a written contract in which one person, known as the *maker,* promises to pay to another person, known as the *payee,* a definite sum of money. The money may be payable either on demand or at a definite future date. A note may or may not provide for the payment of interest in addition to the principal amount.

Promissory notes are used most commonly in connection with obtaining loans at banks or other institutions, the purchase of various kinds of property, and as a temporary settlement of an open or charge-account balance when payment cannot be made within the usual credit period. A note may be *secured* by a mortgage on real estate (land and buildings) or personal property (machinery and merchandise), or by the deposit of specific collateral (stock certificates, bonds, and so forth). If the secured note is not collected at maturity, the lender can take possession of the real estate, personal property, or other collateral, sell it, and apply the proceeds to the repayment of the note. Any proceeds in excess of the amount due under the note are then paid to the borrower. Alternatively, the note may be *unsecured,* in which case it has about the same legal position as an account receivable.

Calculation of Interest Revenue

Interest is the price paid for the use of borrowed funds. From the lender's point of view, it is a type of revenue. The interest price is usually expressed as a percentage rate of the principal, with the rate being stated on an annual basis. Thus, a 2-month, 12-percent note would have interest equal to 2 percent of the principal; a 4-month,

15-percent note would have interest equal to 5 percent of principal, and so on. Because interest is a payment for the use of borrowed funds for a period of time, it accrues with the passage of time. Although interest accrues every day (indeed, every time the clock ticks), firms usually record interest only at the time of payment or at the end of an accounting period.

Most short-term notes receivable from customers are based on *simple interest* calculations.[6] The general formula for the calculation of simple interest is:

$$\text{Interest} = \text{Base (Principal or Face)} \times \text{Interest Rate} \times \text{Elapsed Time.}$$

The calculation of simple interest for a year or for any multiple or fraction of a year is an elementary arithmetic computation. For example, the interest at the rate of 12 percent a year on $20,000 is $200 for 1 month, $400 for 2 months, $1,200 for 6 months, and so on. The calculation for shorter periods, although still not an involved mathematical problem, is complicated by the odd number of days in a year and the variations in the number of days in a month. Simple interest at the rate of 12 percent a year on $20,000 for 90 days would be $20,000 \times .12 \times 90/365$, or $592, if an exact computation were made. For many purposes, especially the calculation of accrued interest, a satisfactory approximation of the correct interest can be obtained by assuming that the year has 360 days and that each month is one-twelfth of a year. Thus, 30 days is the equivalent of 1 month, and 60 days is the equivalent of 2 months, or one-sixth of a year. Under this method, the interest at 12 percent on $20,000 for 90 days would be the same as the interest for 3 months, or one-quarter of a year, or $600. Keep in mind that nearly all quotations of simple interest rates state the rate per year, unless some other period is specifically mentioned. In the formula for simple interest, Principal $\times$ Rate $\times$ Elapsed Time, "time" should be expressed in terms of years, or portions of a year, because the rate is the rate per year.

For the sake of uniformity and simplicity, we shall use the following rules in connection with the calculation of interest throughout the text and problems:

1 When the maturity terms are given in months, consider 1 month to be one-twelfth of a year; 3 months to be one-fourth of a year; 6 months to be one-half of a year, and so on, regardless of the actual number of days in the period. This is equivalent to regarding any 1-month period as being 30 days in a 360-day year.

2 When the maturity terms are given in days, use the 360-day year. Consider 30 days to be one-twelfth of a year, 60 days to be one-sixth of a year, 17 days to be 17/360 of a year, and so on. Calculate maturity dates and elapsed time by using the actual number of days.

Accounting for Interest-Bearing Notes Receivable

The notes to be discussed in this section, so-called interest-bearing notes, are those that indicate a face, or principal, amount together with explicit interest at a stated rate for the time period stated in the note.[7] For example, the basic elements of such a

---

[6] Most long-term notes involve *compound interest,* which is discussed in Appendix B.

[7] Non-interest-bearing notes, those for which the face amount is the same as the maturity value and implicit interest is included in the principal, involve compound interest calculations and are discussed in Chapters 10 and 11.

note might read: "Two months after date (June 30, 1982), the Suren Company promises to pay to the order of the Mullen Company $3,000 with interest from date at the rate of 12 percent per annum." At the maturity date, August 31, 1982, the maturity value would be the face amount of $3,000 plus interest of $60 calculated in accordance with the preceding discussion ($60 = $3,000 $\times$ .12 $\times$ 2/12), or a total of $3,060.

Among the types of transactions related to a note receivable discussed in this section are the following: receipt of note, interest recognition at an interim date, transfer prior to maturity, and collection at maturity date.

Receipt of Notes and Collection at Maturity Promissory notes usually are received from customers in connection with sales or with the settlement of an open account receivable. The customer is usually the maker, but the customer may transfer a note that has been received from another. It is common practice to allow the customer full credit for the face value and accrued interest, if any, although a different value might be agreed upon in some instances.

If, on June 30, 1982, the Mullen Company were to receive a 60-day, 12-percent note for $3,000, dated June 30, 1982, from the Suren Company, to apply on its account, the entry would be:

June 30 Notes Receivable	3,000	
Accounts Receivable—Suren Company		3,000

Assuming the accounting period of the Mullen Company to be the calendar year, the entry upon collection at maturity would be:

Aug. 31 Cash	3,060	
Notes Receivable		3,000
Interest Revenue		60

Assuming the accounting period of the Mullen Company to be 1 month, the interest adjustment at the interim date, July 31, would be:

July 31 Interest Receivable	30	
Interest Revenue		30
($3,000 $\times$ .12 $\times$ 30/360 = $30.)		

The entry upon collection at maturity would then be:

Aug. 31 Cash	3,060	
Notes Receivable		3,000
Interest Receivable		30
Interest Revenue		30

At the maturity date, the note may be collected, as illustrated above, renewed, partially collected with renewal of the balance, or dishonored by the maker. These other possibilities involve more advanced accounting procedures and are not discussed in this book.

Transfer of Notes Receivable To obtain cash, a note may be transferred to another party *without recourse.* This procedure is equivalent to a sale of the note, because the transferor has no further liability even if the maker fails to pay at maturity.

If Mullen Company transferred without recourse the 2-month, 12-percent, $3,000 note to Lane Trust Company for $3,030 one month after the date of the note, the entry would be:

July 31 Cash	3,030	
Notes Receivable		3,000
Interest Revenue		30
To record transfer of note without recourse.		

Most businesses that "purchase" notes are, however, unwilling to acquire them without recourse. Such firms do not want to be responsible for investigating the creditworthiness of the maker or for any collection efforts required for dishonored notes. Consequently, most notes that are transferred are done so *with recourse.*

A transfer with recourse places a potential or "contingent" obligation on the transferor if the maker fails to pay at maturity. This contingent obligation is assumed when the transferor signs or "endorses" the note with only a signature or with a signature together with wording such as "pay to the order of . . . ." Such a transfer

---

Exhibit 7.6
**Income Statement Illustration of Sales and
Sales Adjustments Alexis Company
Partial Income Statement
for the Year Ended June 30, 1982**

Revenues:		
Sales—Gross		$515,200
Less Sales Adjustments:		
Discounts Taken[a]	$23,600	
Allowances	11,000	
Estimated Uncollectibles	10,300	
Returns	8,600	
Total Sales Adjustments		53,500
Net Sales		$461,700

[a]The gross price method is used. If the net price method were used, discounts taken would not be shown and there would be an *addition* to revenue for the amount of sales discounts that lapsed.

274

is not a completed transaction because of the possibility that the endorser will have to pay the note in case the maker defaults at maturity.

Contingent obligations, such as those for notes transferred with recourse or for the potential loss arising from an unsettled damage suit, are discussed in Chapter 10. Contingent obligations are not shown directly in the accounts, but are merely disclosed in notes to the balance sheet.

If Mullen Company transferred with recourse the 60-day, 12-percent $3,000 note to Lane Trust Company 1 month after the date of the note, the entry would be the same as if the note was transferred without recourse. If Mullen Company prepared

Exhibit 7.7
Detailed Illustration of Current Assets on the Balance Sheet
Alexis Company Balance Sheet (Excerpts)
June 30, 1982 and 1981

	June 30, 1982		June 30, 1981	
Current Assets:				
Cash in Change and Petty Cash Funds		$ 1,000		$ 800
Cash in Bank		13,000		11,000
Cash Held as Compensating Balances		1,500		1,500
Certificates of Deposit		8,000		7,500
Marketable Securities Acquisition Cost	$30,000		$25,000	
Less: Allowance for Excess of Cost of Marketable Securities over Market Value (On June 30, 1981, market value of $31,000 exceeds cost)	(3,000)		—	
Marketable Securities at Lower of Cost or Market (See Note A)		27,000		25,000
Notes Receivable (See Note B)		12,000		10,000
Interest and Dividends Receivable		500		400
Accounts Receivable, Gross	$58,100		$57,200	
Less: Allowance for Uncollectible Accounts	(3,600)		(3,500)	
Accounts Receivable, Net		54,500		53,700
Merchandise Inventory[a]		72,000		67,000
Prepayments		4,800		4,300
Total Current Assets		$194,300		$181,200

Note A. Gross unrealized holding gains and gross unrealized holding losses on Marketable Securities are as follows:

	June 30, 1982	June 30, 1981
Gross Unrealized Holding Gains	$7,000	$7,000
Gross Unrealized Holding Losses	(10,000)	(1,000)
Net Unrealized Holding Gain (Loss)	($3,000)	$6,000

Note B. The amount shown for Notes Receivable does not include notes with a face amount of $2,000 that have been discounted with recourse at The First National Bank. The company is contingently liable for these notes, should the makers not honor them at maturity. The estimated amount of our liability is zero.

[a] Additional, required disclosures for this item omitted here. See Chapter 8.

275

financial statements before Lane Trust Company collected from the maker, however, the notes to Mullen's balance sheet would contain a statement such as the following:

Contingencies. The firm is contingently liable for a note transferred and accrued interest thereon to the Lane Trust Company. The face value of the transferred note is $3,000.

Illustration of Balance Sheet Presentation

The balance sheet accounts discussed in this chapter include Cash, Certificates of Deposit, Marketable Securities, Notes Receivable, and Accounts Receivable. The presentation of these items in the balance sheet is illustrated in Exhibit 7.7, which includes all of the current assets, not just the liquid assets, for the Alexis Company as of June 30, 1982.

Summary

This chapter has examined the accounting for cash and other liquid, or cash-like, assets. Among the questions addressed were the following:

1 What items are included in each of the liquid asset accounts?
2 At what amount are they stated?
3 Are there any restrictions on the use of particular liquid assets?

The appendix to this chapter discusses internal control procedures for protecting cash.

Appendix 7.1
Controlling Cash

Of all assets, cash is the most vulnerable—the most difficult to safeguard from theft. This appendix discusses the usual procedures of accounting for and controlling cash. For internal control purposes, most firms maintain two cash accounts, Cash on Hand and Cash in Bank.

Controlling Cash Receipts and Disbursements

The system for controlling cash receipts should be designed to ensure that all money collected for the firm benefits the firm. In most businesses, collections are received primarily through the mail in the form of bank checks or in currency for cash sales. The need to control the collections of currency and coins is obvious. All collections for cash sales should be recorded promptly, either in a cash register or some other device that both records the receipts and locks in the amount of the collection. Other kinds of collections are more susceptible to mishandling because they occur less often. These include receipts from the sale of assets not normally intended to be sold, receipts from dividends and interest on investments, collections on notes receivable, proceeds of bank loans, and proceeds of stock or bond issues.

One way to provide effective control of cash receipts would be to maintain duplicate sets of records, each under separate supervision. But doing so would be expensive. The business need not undertake this expensive control device, however, if it (1) designs its cash-handling techniques so that the monthly statement received from its bank effectively serves as a duplicate record and (2) separates the functions of cash handling and record keeping. To use the bank statement as an effective cash-controlling device requires prompt depositing of all receipts and making all disbursements by check.

Undeposited Cash

If a firm follows the desirable practice of depositing all receipts intact each day, disbursements will usually be made only from checking accounts. Any balance in the Cash on Hand account will represent cash received since the last deposit. A daily record of cash on hand is desirable. Cash registers facilitate the accumulation of such cash data. There are many types, but the usual cash register is a combination of a cash drawer and a multiple-register adding machine. The transactions are entered by hand. Then they are recorded and accumulated by the register so that at the end of the day the totals are available for each of several divisions of the day's activities— the total cash sales (sometimes classified according to products or departments), total collections on account, and total sales of each salesperson.

Cash in Bank—Deposits

A deposit ticket provides the information for preparing the journal entry to record the deposit of cash funds in the checking account. The deposit ticket should be prepared in duplicate; the bank keeps the original and the firm keeps the duplicate. The duplicate is often initialed by the bank teller and used as a receipt for the deposit of the funds. The total on the deposit ticket is entered in a journal as a debit to Cash in Bank and a credit to Cash on Hand.

Cash in Bank—Issuance of Checks

The information for the entry to record checks drawn in payment of bills comes from the document authorizing the disbursement. The customary entry will be a debit to Accounts Payable and a credit to Cash in Bank.

Control of Disbursements by Check

All cash payments except for those of very small amounts should be made by check. The firm can thereby restrict the authority for payments to a few employees. Firms often provide further control by requiring that all checks be signed by two employees. Another control device is the use of a Cash Disbursements Journal or Check Register in which all checks issued are recorded. Using such a journal provides control because a single person, who is not allowed to authorize payments or to sign checks, is responsible for recording all payments.

In any case, control over disbursements should ensure that:

1 Disbursements are made only by authorized persons.
2 Adequate records support each disbursement. Such records attest that disbursement was for goods and services procured by proper authority and actually received by the business. The records attest that payment is made in accordance with the purchase contract.
3 The transaction is entered properly in the formal account records.
4 Authorization of payment is separate from making payment, and record keeping is separate from both.

Exhibit 7.8
Lipscomb Company
Bank Reconciliation Schedule—
State National Bank
April 1, 1982

Balance shown on bank statement, April 1, 1982		$3,941.43
Deposits of March 30 and 31, not yet recorded by bank		753.25
Check of F. Lipscomb deducted by bank in error		102.00
		$4,796.68
Outstanding checks:		
#2443	$ 79.67	
#2459	242.53	
#2471	131.26	
#2472	32.44	
#2473	243.55	
Less: Total outstanding checks		(729.45)
Adjusted bank balancea		$4,067.23
Balance shown on books, April 1, 1982		$3,588.23
Items unrecorded on books:		
Collection of note of J. B. Ball:		
Face amount of note	$500.00	
Less collection charge	(15.00)	485.00
Less: Bank service charge for March		(24.00)
Adjusted book balance before correction of errors		$4,049.23
Check #2467 for $268.81 was entered in the check register as $286.81. It was issued in March 1982, to pay a bill for office equipment		18.00
Adjusted book balancea		$4,067.23

aThis is the amount that would be shown in the Cash in Bank account if a balance sheet were prepared as of April 1, 1982.

The Bank Statement

At the end of each month (or other regular interval), the bank sends a statement together with the canceled checks that have been paid and deducted from the depositor's account, and memorandums of any other additions or deductions that have been made by the bank. When the bank statement is received, it should be compared promptly with the record of deposits, checks drawn, and other bank items on the records of the firm.

The balance shown on the bank statement will rarely correspond to the balance of the Cash in Bank account. The two basic causes of the difference are time lag and errors. In the normal course of business activities, some items will have been recorded by either the bank or the firm without having reached the recording point on the other set of records, hence a *time lag* difference. Causes of such differences include: checks outstanding (that is, checks recorded by the drawing firm but not yet received by the bank on which they were drawn), deposits made just before the bank statement date that do not appear on the bank statement, and transactions (such as service charges and collections of notes or drafts) that have not been recorded on the firm's books. The other basic difference is caused by errors in record keeping by either the firm or the bank. The process of comparing the bank statement with the books is known as *reconciling* the bank account, and the schedule that is prepared to demonstrate the results of the comparing is called a *bank reconciliation*. Exhibit 7.8 shows a typical reconciliation schedule. The preparation of the bank reconciliation schedule is explained below.

Preparing the Bank Reconciliation Schedule

The bank reconciliation explains the difference between the book balance of Cash in Bank and the bank's statement of the firm's cash on deposit. It indicates the required adjustments of the firm's accounts. If the bank statement is used as a control device, the bank reconciliation is the final step in the monthly procedure for controlling cash receipts and disbursements. The bank reconciliation provides a convenient summary of the adjusting entries that must be made by the firm to account for previous errors in recording cash-related transactions or for cash transactions that have not yet been recorded.

Preparing the bank reconciliation schedule typically involves the following steps.

1 Enter at the top of the reconciliation schedule the balance as shown on the bank statement.
2 Enter next any deposits that have not been recorded on the bank statement. Such items usually occur because the bank has prepared the statement before the deposits for the last day or two have been recorded. If there are any time or date breaks in the list of deposits for the period, the bank should be notified promptly.
3 Enter any other adjustments of the bank's balance, such as errors in recording canceled checks or deposits, or the return of checks belonging to some other customer of the bank. Errors on bank statements are infrequent.

4 Obtain a total.
5 List the outstanding checks. A list should be prepared, beginning with the checks still outstanding from the previous period and continuing with the checks outstanding which were drawn during the current period.
6 Deduct the sum of the outstanding checks from the total obtained in step 4. The balance is the adjusted bank balance—the balance that would be shown on the bank statement if all deposits had been entered, all checks written had been returned, and no errors had been made; it is the final figure for this first section of the statement.

These steps will frequently conclude the reconciliation because this balance should correspond to the balance of the Cash in Bank account as of the bank statement date when there are no unrecorded transactions or errors. If these two amounts are not equal at this point, the following steps must be taken and shown in a second section of the reconciliation schedule.

7 Enter the Cash in Bank account balance as shown on the books as of the bank statement date.
8 Add or deduct any errors or omissions that have been disclosed in the process of reviewing the items returned by the bank. These will include such items as errors in recording deposits or checks, unnumbered checks that have not been entered in the check register, and service charges and collection fees deducted by the bank.
9 The net result is the adjusted book balance, and it must correspond to the adjusted bank balance derived in the first section. If it does not, the search must be continued for other items that have been overlooked.

Adjusting Entries from Bank Reconciliation Schedule

The bank reconciliation schedule shows two distinct kinds of differences:

1 Differences between the balance shown on the bank statement and the adjusted bank balance.
2 Differences between the account balance on the firm's books and the adjusted book balance.

Only the second type of difference requires entries on the firm's books. Any deposits not credited by the bank will presumably have been recorded by the time the reconciliation is prepared and, in any event, represent funds that the depositor may assume are in the bank and available for disbursement by check.

Entries must be made for all of the differences between the firm's account balance on the books and the adjusted book balance, since they represent errors or omissions that must be corrected. The reconciliation illustrated in Exhibit 7.8 requires adjustments for bank service charges, for the collection of a note, and for the check whose amount was incorrectly recorded. (The bank must, of course, correct any error on its books when the mistake is called to its attention.) The entries would be:

Bank Service Charge Expense	24	
Cash in Bank		24
Service charges for month of March.		
Cash in Bank	485	
Collection Expense	15	
Note Receivable, J. B. Ball		500
Note collected by bank.		
Cash in Bank	18	
Accounts Payable		18
To correct entry of check #2467.		

Summary of Accounting for Cash

Cash is an enterprise's most vulnerable resource. An internal control system is essential to the proper management of cash. One way to provide control is to maintain duplicate and independent records of cash flows, but this is not necessary if an enterprise uses the monthly bank statement as a duplicate record. Using the bank statement as an effective control device requires depositing receipts daily and making all disbursements by check or through petty cash funds. By this means the bank reconciliation serves as a control device, because the bank record will reflect the cash inflows and outflows of the enterprise.

Problem 1 for Self-Study

Refer to the data in Exhibit 7.1 showing transactions in marketable securities for the Wolfson Company over four years. Assume that in addition to those transactions, Wolfson Company purchased 1,000 shares of D Company on October 1, 1979, for $40 per share, $40,000 in total. Shares of D Company had a market value of $45 per share at the end of 1979, $35 per share at the end of 1980, $30 per share at the end of 1981, and $50 per share at the end of 1982.

a What are the amounts of each of the following at the end of each of the four years: Marketable Securities at Cost, Allowance for Excess of Cost of Marketable Securities over Market Value, and Marketable Securities at Lower of Cost or Market? What is the Unrealized Loss (or Recovery of Unrealized Loss) for each of the four years, 1979, 1980, 1981, and 1982?

b If, early in 1980, Wolfson Company sells 900 shares at $30 each, $27,000 in total, what is the realized gain or loss for the year 1980 and the Unrealized Holding Loss or Recovery of Unrealized Holding Loss for the year 1980?

c Ignore the information in Part b. During 1980, Wolfson Company transferred all 1,000 shares of D Company to its noncurrent asset portfolio of Investments at a time when these

281

shares had an aggregate market value of $38,000. What is income before taxes for the year 1980?

d Ignore information in **b** and **c**. Now assume that the securities of all four companies have been classified as the noncurrent asset Investments from the time of acquisition. During 1980 Wolfson Company sold 400 shares of D Company for $38 per share and transferred the remaining 600 shares to a current asset account, Marketable Securities, at a time when the share price was $35 each. What is income before taxes for the year 1980?

e Ignore information in **b, c,** and **d**. Assume, now, that Wolfson Company left its holdings of D Company intact until the last day of 1980, when it sold some shares for $35 per share. If the correct balance on the balance sheet at the end of 1980 for marketable securities valued at lower of cost or market is $109,500, how many shares were sold on December 31, 1980?

Suggested Solution

a See Exhibit 7.9.

Exhibit 7.9
Self-Study Problem 1
(Suggested Solution to Part a)

Marketable Securities	1979	1980	1981	1982
At Cost	$140,000	$140,000	$110,000	$90,000
Allowance	—	(6,000)	(4,000)	—
At Lower of Cost or Market	$140,000	$134,000	$106,000	$90,000
Unrealized Loss for Year	—	$ (6,000)	—	—
Recovery of Unrealized Loss for Year	—	—	$ 2,000	$ 4,000

---

b Realized Loss = $900 \times (\$40 - \$30) = \$9,000$.
December 31 valuation of remaining portfolio is:

At Cost	$\$100,000 + 100 \times \$40 = \$104,000$
At Market	$\$ 99,000 + 100 \times \$35 = \$102,500$
Required Allowance	$ 1,500
Allowance at Start of Year	$ 0
Unrealized Holding Loss for Year	$ 1,500

c Other Items Before Taxes $300,000
Realized Loss on Transfer of Securities
 Between Portfolios (= $40,000 − $38,000) ..... (2,000)
Unrealized Holding Loss of Securities A, B, and C ..... (1,000)
Income Before Taxes $297,000

d Other Items Before Taxes $300,000
Realized Loss on Sales 400 × ($40 − $38) ..... (800)
Realized Loss on Transfer 600 × ($40 − $35) ..... (3,000)
Income Before Taxes $296,200

e Let x represent number of shares of D Company remaining, so that:

Marketable Securities (12/31/80)

At Cost.	$100,000 + $40x
Allowance	(1,000 + 5x)
At Lower of Cost or Market.	$ 99,000 + $35x

If the correct balance is $109,500, then $35x$ is $10,500 and x is 300 shares; 700 ($= 1,000 - 300$) shares were sold.

Problem 2 for Self-Study

Refer to the data in Exhibit 7.5 showing sales and collection activities for two periods. At the end of the third period, the *unadjusted* trial balance included the following accounts and amounts: Accounts Receivable—$75,000 debit; Allowance for Uncollectible Accounts—$8,000 debit; Sales Contra, Estimated Uncollectibles—zero (adjusting entries have not yet been made); Sales Revenue—$1,300,000. No further specific accounts receivable need be written off for the period.

a Reconstruct the transactions of the third period, assuming all sales were made on account.

b What were the total cash collections for the third period from customers who paid their accounts?

c Reconstruct the transactions of the third period, assuming that only $1 million of the $1.3 million total sales were made on account.

d What were the total cash collections for the third period, including collections both from customers who paid cash and from customers who paid their accounts?

e Does one need to know the actual split of sales between cash sales and sales on account to know the total amount of cash collected from customers, that is, the sum of cash sales and collections on account? Why or why not?

f Assume that 2 percent of all sales for the third period is estimated to be uncollectible. What is the adjusting entry to be made at the end of the third period for estimated uncollectibles? What net balance of Accounts Receivable will appear on the balance sheet at the end of the third period?

g Independent of the answer to the preceding part, assume that an aging of accounts receivable indicates that the amount in the Allowance for Uncollectibles appropriate for the status of outstanding accounts at the end of the third period is $20,000. What is the adjusting entry to be made at the end of the third period for estimated uncollectibles? What amount of net sales will be reported for the third period?

Suggested Solution

a Sales were $1,300,000, debited to Accounts Receivable. Specific accounts receivable of $24,000 ($= $16,000 credit at start of period plus $8,000 debit by the end of period) were written off with debits to the Allowance for Uncollectibles account and credits to Accounts Receivable. Thus, the balance in accounts receivable before cash collections was $1,410,000 ($= $134,000 + $1,300,000 - $24,000). Because the ending balance is actually

283

$75,000, the cash collections from customers who bought on account are $1,335,000 (= $1,410,000 − $75,000).

b $1,335,000, as derived above.

c Sales were $1,300,000, debited $300,000 to Cash and $1,000,000 to Accounts Receivable. Specific accounts receivable of $24,000 were written off with debits to the Allowance for Uncollectibles account and credits to Accounts Receivable. The amount is derived as in part **a** above. The write-off of specific accounts left a balance of $1,110,000 (= $134,000 + $1,000,000 − $24,000), but the actual ending balance was $75,000, so $1,035,000 (= $1,110,000 − $75,000) of accounts must have been collected in cash.

d $1,335,000 = $300,000 cash sales plus $1,035,000 from collections on account.

e No. Once cash from a sale on account has been collected, the overall effect of the sale on the financial statements is identical with a cash sale. Thus, cash sales and collected credit sales have the same effects on the financial statements.

f Sales Contra, Estimated Uncollectibles	26,000	
Allowance for Uncollectibles		26,000

Amount is equal to .02 × $1,300,000. Ending balance in the allowance account is $18,000 (= $26,000 credit less $8,000 debit).

The net Accounts Receivable balance at the end of the third period is $57,000 (= $75,000 − $18,000).

g Sales Contra, Estimated Uncollectibles	28,000	
Allowance for Uncollectibles		28,000

A $28,000 credit is required to establish a $20,000 credit balance in an account with a tentative $8,000 debit balance.

Net sales for the third period will be reported as $1,272,000 (= $1,300,000 gross sales less $28,000 adjustment for uncollectibles). The net Accounts Receivable balance at the end of the third period is $55,000 (= $75,000 − $20,000).

Questions and Problems

1 Review the meaning of the following concepts or terms discussed in this chapter.

a Liquidity.

b Quick assets.

c Insolvent.

d Cash.

e Demand deposits.

f Certificate of deposit.

g Foreign currency.

h Compensating balance.

i Marketable securities.

j Investments (noncurrent).

k Marketable debt securities.

l Marketable equity securities.

m Lower of cost or market.

n Unrealized loss on marketable securities.

o Recovery of unrealized loss on marketable securities.

p Realized gain or loss on marketable securities.

q Sales Contra, Estimated Uncollectibles.

r Aging of accounts receivable.

s Sales Contra, Discounts.

t Sales Contra, Returns and Allowances.

u Simple interest.

v Recourse.

w Factoring.

x Contingent liability.

2 What evidence of cash control have you observed in a cafeteria? A department store? A theater? A gasoline station?

3 The Tastee Delight ice cream stores prominently advertise on signs in the stores that the customer's purchase is free if the clerk does not present a receipt. Oakland's Original hot dog stand says that the customer's purchase is free if the cash register receipt contains a red star. What control purposes do such policies serve?

4 Current assets are defined as those assets that are expected to be turned into cash, or sold, or consumed within the next operating cycle. Cash is not always classified as a current asset, however. Explain.

5 Does application of the lower-of-cost-or-market valuation method to the portfolio of marketable equity securities or to each marketable equity security individually result in the most conservative asset values and net income amounts?

6 Which of the two methods for treating uncollectible accounts (direct write-off and allowance) implies recognizing revenue reductions earlier rather than later? Why?

7 a An old wisdom in tennis holds that if your first serves are always good, then you are not hitting them hard enough. An analogous statement in business might be that if you have no uncollectible accounts, then you probably are not selling enough on credit. Comment on the validity of this statement.
  b When are more uncollectible accounts better than fewer uncollectible accounts?
  c When is a higher percentage of uncollectible accounts better than a lower one?

8 The customary method of accounting for sales returns results in adequate reporting for the returned sales when the goods are returned in the same period in which they are sold. If the goods are returned in a period subsequent to that of the sale, distortion of the reported revenue figures results. Explain how sales returns may produce each of the described effects.

9 Under what circumstances will the Allowance for Uncollectible Accounts have a debit balance during the accounting period? The balance sheet figure for the Allowance for Uncollectible Accounts at the end of the period should never show a debit balance. Why?

10 What is the effect on the financial statements of discounting, or transferring, a note with recourse versus without recourse?

11 Indicate if each of the following items should be included in "cash" on the balance sheet. If not, indicate how the item should be reported.
  a Cash that has been collected from customers and is awaiting deposit in the firm's checking account.
  b Cash left in cash registers each day which serves as a change fund.
  c Cash set aside in a special savings account to accumulate funds to replace equipment as it wears out. The firm is not legally obligated to use the funds for this purpose.
  d Cash set aside in a special savings account to accumulate funds to retire debt as it becomes due. The firm is legally obligated to use the funds for this purpose.
  e A postdated check received from a customer. The check is dated 60 days after the date of the balance sheet.
  f A money order received from a customer.
  g Postage stamps.

h Cash in a petty cash fund which is used for small miscellaneous expenditures, such as freight charges and executive lunches.

i Cash in a checking account which must be maintained at a certain minimum level in accordance with a written loan agreement for a 6-month loan.

12 You are asked to compute the amount that should be shown as "Cash" on the balance sheet as of December 31, 1982, for Zeff Transportation Company. The following information is obtained.

a Coins, currency, and checks received from customers on December 31, 1982, but not yet deposited, $6,500.

b Amount in a petty cash fund which is maintained for making small miscellaneous cash expenditures. The fund normally has a balance of $100, but expenditures of $22 were made on December 31, 1982.

c The firm's postage meter was "filled" on December 31, 1982, and contains $500 of postage.

d The books indicate that the balance in the firm's checking account on December 31, 1982, is $45,800. When the bank statement is received on January 10, 1983, it is learned that one customer's check for $800, which was deposited on December 28, 1982, was returned for insufficient funds. In addition, the bank collected, during December 1982, a note receivable from one of Zeff's customers and added the amount to Zeff's bank account. The note had a face value of $2,000 and interest of $200.

e Certificate of deposit for a face value of $10,000. The certificate was acquired on July 1, 1982, and matures on June 30, 1983. Simple interest of 12 percent per year accumulates on the note and is payable at maturity with the principal.

f British sterling currency, £10,000. The exchange rate on December 31, 1982, is $2.50 per pound sterling.

13 Refer to the Simplified Statement of Changes in Financial Position Statement for a Period in Exhibit 5.19 on page 191. Nine of the lines in the statement are numbered. Line (2) should be expanded to say "Additions for Expense and Other Charges Against Income Not Using Funds from Operations" and line (3) should be expanded to say "Subtractions for Revenue and Other Credits to Income Not Producing Funds from Operations." Ignore the unnumbered lines in responding to the questions below.

Assume that the accounting cycle is complete for the period and that all of the financial statements have been prepared. Then, it is discovered that a transaction has been overlooked. That transaction is recorded in the accounts, and all of the financial statements are corrected. Define *funds* as *working capital*. For each of the following transactions or events indicate which of the numbered lines of the funds statement is affected and by how much. Ignore income tax effects.

a Estimated uncollectibles equal to 1 percent of the year's sales of $1 million are recognized. An entry is made increasing the Allowance for Uncollectible Accounts.

b The specific account receivable of Eli Worman in the amount of $2,000 is written off by a firm using the allowance method.

c The specific account receivable of Eli Worman in the amount of $3,000 is written off by a firm using the direct write-off method.

d A firm owns marketable securities. Dividends of $30,000 are declared on the shares owned.

e The portfolio of marketable securities acquired this period has a market value of $60,000 less than their net amount shown on the balance sheet at the end of the current accounting period. An entry is made changing the allowance account contra to marketable securities.

286

f The market value of the same portfolio of marketable securities referred to in part **e** has increased $40,000 by the end of the next period. An entry is made changing the allowance account for marketable securities.

14 Davidoff Corporation borrowed $1 million from the local bank on July 1, 1982. The bank charged Davidoff Corporation interest at its prime lending rate of 13.5 percent. The principal and interest on the loan are repayable on June 30, 1983. Davidoff Corporation must maintain a $100,000 compensating balance in an interest-free checking account at the bank during the term of the loan.

    a What is the effective annual interest rate that Davidoff Corporation is paying on this loan?

    b What message to Davidoff Corporation is implicit in the bank's requirement that a compensating balance be maintained?

15 a Arrange the following data related to the Antle Company in bank reconciliation form.

Adjusted bank balance	$6,713
Adjusted book balance	6,713
Balance per bank statement, October 31, 1982	7,873
Balance per books, October 31, 1982	6,028
Error in deposit of October 28; $457 deposit entered on books as $547	90
Outstanding checks	1,305
Payroll account check deducted from this account in error	145
Proceeds on note of W. Y. Smith, taken by the bank for collection, less collection fee of $25	775

    b Present journal entries on the books of the Antle Company to record the adjustments indicated in the bank reconciliation schedule.

16 a Prepare a bank reconciliation schedule at July 31, 1982, for the Home Appliance Company from the following information:

Balance per bank statement, July 29	$1,240
Balance per ledger, July 31	714
Deposit of July 30 not recorded by bank	280
Debit memo—service charges	8
Credit memo—collection of note by bank	300

An analysis of canceled checks returned with the bank statement reveals the following:

Check #901 for purchase of supplies was drawn for $58 but was recorded as $85.

The manager wrote a check for traveling expenses of $95 while out of town. The check was not recorded. The following checks are outstanding:

#650	$120
#721	162
#728	300
	$582

b Journalize the adjusting entries required by the information revealed in the bank reconciliation schedule.

17 On May 31, 1982, the books of the Griffin Company show a debit balance in the Cash in Bank account of $4,720. The bank statement at that date shows a balance of $6,000. The deposit of May 31 of $250 is not included in the bank statement. Notice of collections made by the bank on mortgages of the company in the amount of $350, including interest of $250, and of bank service charges of $20 have not previously been received. Outstanding checks at May 31 total $1,200.

a Prepare a bank reconciliation for the Griffin Company at May 31, 1982.
b Journalize the entries required upon preparation of the bank reconciliation schedule.

18 The following items are taken from the April 30, 1982, bank reconciliation schedule of the Porter Company. Present a journal entry required on the books of the company for each item; indicate if no adjustment is required.

(a) Outstanding checks total $1,650.
(b) A check drawn as $196 for office supplies was recorded in the appropriate journal as $169.
(c) Included among the checks returned by the bank was one for $150 drawn by the Peter Company and charged to this company in error.
(d) The deposit of April 30 of $420 was not included on the bank statement.
(e) A debit memorandum was included for service charges for April in the amount of $10.
(f) The bank collected a note of $1,750, including $50 of interest, for the company.
(g) Checks for traveling expenses of $250 had not been entered in the journal.
(h) A check was written and recorded on April 29 for the regular monthly salary of an office employee who had resigned on March 31. The check has been voided, but an entry to record the voiding has not been made. The monthly salary was $600; deductions of $60 for payroll taxes and $120 for withheld income taxes were made.

19 The bank reconciliation of the Clovis Company at March 31, 1982, was as follows:

Balance per bank statement, March 31, 1982	$3,965
Unrecorded deposit	475
Outstanding checks	820
Adjusted bank and book balance, March 31, 1982	3,620

The bank statement, returned checks, and other documents received from the bank at the end of April provide the following information:

Balance, April 29, 1982	$ 3,800
Deposit of March 31, 1982	475
Deposits of April 1–29 including a credit memo for a collection of a note, $860	16,160
Canceled checks issued prior to April 1, 1982	600
Canceled checks issued during April, 1982	16,200

The Cash in Bank account of the Clovis Company for the month of April shows deposits of $16,140 and checks drawn of $17,015. The credit memo has not as yet been recorded on

288

the books of the company; it represents the collection of a note with $800 face value on which $40 interest had been accrued as of March 31, 1982.

a Prepare a bank reconciliation for the Clovis Company at April 30, 1982.

b Present in journal entry form any adjustment of the company's books resulting from the information determined in the bank reconciliation.

20 Indicate the classification of each of the securities below in the balance sheet of Bower Corporation on December 31, 1982.

a U.S. Treasury Bills, acquired on October 15, 1982. The bills mature on April 15, 1983.

b Shares of Brazil Coffee Corporation, a major supplier of raw materials for Bower Corporation's products.

c Shares of Overland Transportation Company. The shares were originally acquired as a temporary investment of excess cash. Overland Transportation Company has been so profitable that Bower Corporation plans to increase its ownership percentage, eventually obtaining 51 percent of the outstanding shares.

d American Telephone and Telegraph Company bonds that mature in 1985. The bonds were acquired with a cash advance from a customer on a contract for the manufacture of machinery and will be sold, as needed, to pay costs of manufacturing. The manufacturing process will take 3 years.

21 The aggregate cost and aggregate market value of the portfolio of marketable equity securities of Elson Corporation at various dates are shown below:

Date	Aggregate Cost	Aggregate Market Value
December 31, 1980.	$150,000	$130,000
December 31, 1981.	160,000	144,000
December 31, 1982.	170,000	185,000
December 31, 1983.	180,000	168,000

Give the journal entry required at the end of each year, assuming that the accounting period is the calendar year.

22 Information relating to the marketable equity securities of Albion Corporation is summarized below:

					Market Value	
Security	Date Acquired	Acquisition Cost	Date Sold	Selling Price	Dec. 31, 1982	Dec. 31, 1983
A	1/5/82	$40,000	11/5/83	$50,000	$45,000	—
B	6/12/82	85,000	—	—	75,000	$82,000
C	2/22/83	48,000	—	—	—	46,000
D	3/25/83	25,000	11/5/83	18,000	—	—
E	4/25/83	36,000	—	—	—	40,000

a Give all journal entries relating to these marketable equity securities during 1982 and 1983, assuming that the calendar year is the accounting period.

289

b Indicate the manner in which marketable securities would be presented in the balance sheet and related notes on December 31, 1982.

c Indicate the manner in which marketable securities would be presented in the balance sheet and related notes on December 31, 1983.

23 Exhibit 7.10 gives data on holdings of marketable securities of Sprouse Company for the years 1981 and 1982. There were no sales of securities during 1981. During 1982, Sprouse Company purchased new shares in Security F. During 1982, the following sales of securities took place:

	Net Proceeds of Sale	Cost	Realized Gain (Loss)
Security A	$125,000	$100,000	$ 25,000
Security B	65,000	100,000	(35,000)
	$190,000	$200,000	$(10,000)

The valuation allowances required at December 31, 1982, are as follows:

	Charged Against Income	Charged Against Equity
In Current Assets:		
Cost $900,000 less market $850,000	$50,000	
In Noncurrent Assets:		
Cost $650,000 less market $540,000		$110,000

Exhibit 7.10
Data on Marketable Securities for Sprouse Company
(*Problem 23*)

	1982		1981	
	Cost	Market	Cost	Market
In Current Assets:				
Security A	$100,000	$100,000	$200,000	$250,000
B	200,000	150,000	300,000	250,000
C	200,000	175,000	200,000	150,000
D	150,000	100,000	150,000	200,000
E	50,000	100,000	50,000	75,000
F	200,000	225,000	—	—
Total of Portfolio	$900,000	$850,000	$900,000	$925,000
In Noncurrent Assets:				
Security G	$300,000	$200,000	$300,000	$200,000
H	100,000	190,000	100,000	250,000
I	250,000	150,000	250,000	250,000
Total of Portfolio	$650,000	$540,000	$650,000	$700,000

Ignore income taxes.

a Prepare in parallel columns for year-end 1982 and 1981 the data that appear in the December 31, 1982, balance sheet.

b Prepare a suitable footnote to accompany the balance sheet for December 31, 1982.

24 Information relating to the marketable equity securities of TSS Company is shown below:

Security	Date Acquired	Acquisition Cost	Date Sold	Selling Price	Market Value Dec. 31, 1981	Dec. 31, 1982
H	4/26/81	$18,000	2/9/82	$15,000	$16,000	—
I	5/25/81	25,000	8/10/82	26,000	24,000	
J	11/24/81	12,000	—	—	14,000	$15,000
K	2/26/82	34,000	—	—		33,500
L	12/17/82	8,000	—	—	—	7,800

a Compute both the realized and the unrealized gain or loss for 1981.

b Compute both the realized and the unrealized gain or loss for 1982.

c Repeat steps **a** and **b**, but assume that lower of cost or market is applied individually to each security, rather than to the portfolio of securities.

d Does application of lower of cost or market at the level of the portfolio or at the level of individual securities result in the more conservative asset values and measures of earnings?

25 The sales, all on account, of the Needles Company in 1981, its first year of operations, were $600,000. Collections totaled $500,000. On December 31, 1981, it was estimated that 1.5 percent of all sales would probably be uncollectible. On that date, specific accounts in the amount of $3,000 were written off.

The company's *unadjusted* trial balance (but after all *non*-adjusting entries were made) on December 31, 1982, included the following accounts and balances:

Accounts Receivable (Dr.)	$60,000
Allowance for Uncollectible Accounts (Dr.)	4,000
Sales Contra, Estimated Uncollectibles	—
Sales (Cr.)	$700,000

It was estimated that the 1982 ending balance of accounts receivable contained $12,000 of probable uncollectibles.

Present journal entries to portray the following:

a Transactions and adjustments of 1981 related to sales and customers' accounts.

b Transactions of 1982 resulting in the above trial balance amounts.

c Adjustment for estimated uncollectibles for 1982.

26 The trial balance of the Walker Company at the end of 1981, its first year of operations, included $20,000 of outstanding customers' accounts. An analysis reveals that 80 percent of the total credit sales of the year had been collected and that no accounts had been charged off as uncollectible.

The auditor estimated that 2 percent of the total credit sales would be uncollectible.

On January 31, 1982, it was concluded that the account of H. J. Williams, who had owed a balance of $300 for 6 months, was uncollectible and should be written off at that time.

On July 1, 1982, the amount owed by H. J. Williams, previously written off, was collected in full.

Present dated journal entries to record the following:

a Adjustment for estimated uncollectible accounts on December 31, 1981.

b Write-off of the H. J. Williams account on January 31, 1982.

c Collection of the H. J. Williams account on July 1, 1982. Assume that it is felt that there is evidence that the account should never have been written off as uncollectible, but that total uncollectibles are likely not to be different from the original estimates.

27 The amounts in certain accounts on January 1, 1982, and before adjusting entries on December 31, 1982, are shown below:

	January 1, 1982	December 31, 1982
Accounts Receivable	$400,000 Dr.	$ 500,000 Dr.
Allowance for Uncollectible Accounts	30,000 Cr.	20,000 Dr.
Sales Contra, Estimated Uncollectibles	0	0
Sales	0	2,000,000 Cr.

During 1982, 90 percent of sales were on account. It was estimated that 3 percent of credit sales would become uncollectible. During 1982, one account for $1,500 was collected, although it had been written off as uncollectible during 1981. When the written-off account was reinstated, the credit was to the allowance account.

a Give the journal entries made during 1982 that explain the changes in the four accounts as listed above.

b Give any adjusting entries required on December 31, 1982.

28 The balance sheets of Wilton Corporation on December 31, 1981 and 1982, showed accounts receivable of $8,300,000 and $9,700,000, respectively. A footnote indicates that the balances in the Allowance for Uncollectible Accounts account at the beginning and end of 1982, after closing entries, were credits of $750,000 and $930,000, respectively. The income statement for 1982 shows that the provision for estimated uncollectible accounts was $300,000, which was 1 percent of sales. All sales are made on account. There were no recoveries during 1982 of accounts written off in previous years.

Give all the journal entries made during 1982 that have an effect on Accounts Receivable and Allowance for Uncollectible Accounts.

29 The data in the following schedule pertain to the first 8 years of the Glidden Company's credit sales and experiences with uncollectible accounts.

292

Year	Credit Sales	Related Uncollectible Accounts	Year	Credit Sales	Related Uncollectible Accounts
1	$200,000	$5,100	5	$500,000	$6,000
2	300,000	6,450	6	550,000	5,400
3	400,000	7,450	7	560,000	5,750
4	450,000	8,000	8	580,000	5,950

Glidden Company has not previously used an Allowance for Uncollectible Accounts but has merely charged accounts written off directly to Uncollectible Accounts Expense.

What percentage of credit sales for a year would you recommend that Glidden Company charge to the sales contra account if the allowance method were to be adopted at the end of year 8?

30 Love Company's accounts receivable show the following balances by ages:

Age of Accounts	Balance Receivable
0–30 days	300,000
31–60 days	75,000
61–120 days	30,000
More than 120 days	15,000

The credit balance in the Allowance for Uncollectible Accounts is now $6,000.

Love Company's independent auditors suggest that the following percentages be used to compute the estimates of amounts that will eventually prove uncollectible: 0–30 days, .5 of 1 percent; 31–60 days, 1 percent; 61–120 days, 10 percent; more than 120 days, 60 percent.

Prepare a journal entry that will carry out the auditor's suggestion.

31 The Feldman Company has a gross margin on credit sales of 30 percent. That is, cost of goods sold on account is 70 percent of sales on account. Uncollectible accounts amount to 2 percent of credit sales. If credit is extended to a new class of customers, credit sales will increase by $10,000, 8 percent of the new credit sales will be uncollectible, and selling expenses will increase by $1,000.

a Would Feldman Company be better or worse off if it extended credit to the new class of customer and by how much?

b How would your answer to part **a** differ if $3,000 of the $10,000 increase in credit sales had been made anyway as sales for cash? (Assume that the uncollectible amount on new credit sales is $800.)

32 The Hanrahan Company has credit sales of $100,000, a gross margin on those sales of 25 percent, with 3 percent of the credit sales uncollectible. If credit is extended to a new class of customers, sales will increase by $40,000, selling expenses will increase by $2,500, and uncollectibles will be 5 percent of *all* credit sales. Verify that Hanrahan Company will be $3,500 better off if it extends credit to the new customers. What percentage of the new credit sales are uncollectible?

33 Calculate simple interest on a base of $6,000 for the following intervals and rates, using a 360-day year.

a 60 days at 12 percent.
b 90 days at 9 percent.
c 60 days at 16 percent.
d 15 days at 16 percent.
e 5 months, 15 days at 12 percent.

34 On May 10, 1982, the Dukes Company receives a note from one of its customers, Salk Builders, Inc., to apply on its account. The 6-month, 12-percent note for $6,000, issued on May 10, 1982, is valued at its face amount, $6,000.

On July 25, 1982, the Dukes Company endorses the note and transfers it with recourse to the Beaver Company to settle an account payable. The note is valued at its face amount plus accrued interest.

On November 12, 1982, the Dukes Company is notified that the note was paid at maturity.

a Present dated entries on the books of the Dukes Company, assuming that it closes its books quarterly on March 31, June 30, and so on.
b Present dated entries on the books of the Beaver Company, assuming that it closes its books quarterly on March 31, June 30, and so on.

35 On November 1, 1982, the Atlas Company receives a note from one of its customers to apply on its open account receivable. The 9-month, 18-percent note for $8,000, issued November 1, 1982, is valued at its face amount.

On January 31, 1983, the Atlas Company endorses the note and transfers it with recourse to First National Bank in return for a cash payment of $8,100. The company's checking account at this bank is increased for the proceeds, $8,100.

On August 1, 1983, the Atlas Company is notified by the bank that the note was collected from the customer at maturity.

Atlas Company closes its books annually on December 31.

Present dated journal entries on the books of Atlas Company relating to this note.

36 Give the likely transaction or event that would result in making each of the independent journal entries below:

a	Notes Receivable	300	
	Accounts Receivable		300
b	Marketable Securities	10,000	
	Cash		10,000
c	Sales Contra, Estimated Uncollectibles	2,300	
	Allowance for Uncollectible Accounts		2,300
d	Unrealized Loss on Valuation of Marketable Equity Securities	4,000	
	Allowance for Excess of Cost of Marketable Equity Securities over Market Value		4,000
e	Cash	295	
	Notes Receivable		285
	Interest Revenue		10
f	Cash	1,200	
	Loss on Sale of Marketable Securities	200	
	Marketable Securities		1,400

294

g	Allowance for Uncollectible Accounts	450	
	Accounts Receivable		450
h	Allowance for Excess of Cost of Marketable Equity Securities over Market Value	1,000	
	Recovery of Unrealized Loss on Valuation of Marketable Equity Securities		1,000
i	Bad Debt Expense	495	
	Accounts Receivable		495
j	Accounts Receivable	285	
	Allowance for Uncollectible Accounts		285

Chapter 8 *Inventories and Cost of Goods Sold*

In the last decade many major U.S. corporations changed their method of accounting for inventories and cost of goods sold. As a result of the change in methods, these corporations reported net income that was smaller by hundreds of millions of dollars than would have been reported without the change. Paradoxically, perhaps, these firms were actually better off as a result of the change. This chapter shows how a firm can be better off reporting smaller, rather than larger, net income. We introduce the choices that a firm must make in accounting for inventories. Then, we show how the decisions made can affect reported expenses and net income for the period. The choices made in accounting for inventories can make two companies that are basically alike appear to be quite different.

Inventory Terminology

The term *inventory,* as used in accounting and in this chapter, means a stock of goods or other items owned by a firm and held for sale, or for processing before being sold, as part of a firm's ordinary business operations. Tools, for example, are inventory in the hands of a tool manufacturer or hardware store, but not in the hands of a carpenter. Marketable securities are inventory in the hands of a securities broker or dealer, but not in the hands of a manufacturer.

Goods held for sale by a retail or wholesale business are referred to as *merchandise* or *merchandise inventory;* goods held for sale by a manufacturing concern are referred to as *finished goods.* The inventories of manufacturing firms also include *work in process* (partially completed products in the factory) and *raw materials* (ma-

296

terials being stored which will become part of goods to be produced). Various types of supplies that will be consumed in administrative, selling, and manufacturing operations are also frequently included in inventories on the balance sheet.

The term *inventory* is sometimes used as a verb. To "inventory" a stock of goods means to prepare a list of the items on hand at some specified date, to assign a unit price to each item, and to calculate the total cost of the goods.

Significance of Accounting for Inventories

One major objective of financial accounting is to measure periodic income. The role of accounting for inventories in measuring income is the assignment of cost to various accounting periods as expenses. The total cost of goods available for sale or use during a period must be allocated between the current period's usage (cost of goods sold, an expense) and the amounts carried forward to future periods (end-of-period inventory, an asset).

Inventory Equation

One equation applies to all inventory situations and facilitates our discussion of accounting for inventory. In the following equation, all quantities are measured in physical units.

$$\underbrace{\begin{array}{c} \text{Beginning} \\ \text{Inventory} \end{array} + \text{Additions}}_{\substack{\text{Goods Available for} \\ \text{Use or Sale}}} - \text{Withdrawals} = \begin{array}{c} \text{Ending} \\ \text{Inventory.} \end{array}$$

If we begin a period with 2,000 lb of sugar (beginning inventory) and if we purchase (add) 4,500 lb during the period, then there are 6,500 (= 2,000 + 4,500) lb available for use. If we use (withdraw) 5,300 lb during the period, then there should be 1,200 lb of sugar left at the end of the period (ending inventory). The inventory equation can also be rewritten as:

$$\underbrace{\begin{array}{c} \text{Beginning} \\ \text{Inventory} \end{array} + \text{Additions}}_{\substack{\text{Goods Available for} \\ \text{Use or Sale}}} - \begin{array}{c} \text{Ending} \\ \text{Inventory} \end{array} = \text{Withdrawals.}$$

If we begin the period with 2,000 lb of sugar, if we purchase 4,500 lb of sugar, and if we observe 1,200 lb of sugar on hand at the end of the period, then we know that 5,300 (= 2,000 + 4,500 − 1,200) lb of sugar were used, or otherwise withdrawn from inventory, during the period. The sum of Beginning Inventory plus Additions is usually called "Goods Available for Use or Sale." In this example, there are 6,500 lb of sugar available for use or sale.

If accounting were concerned merely with keeping a record of physical quantities, there would be few problems in accounting for inventories. But, of course, accounting reports are stated in dollar amounts, not physical quantities. If all prices remained constant, inventory accounting problems would be minor, because all items would be valued at the same per-unit cost. Any variation in values of inventories would be attributable solely to changes in quantities. The major problems in inventory accounting arise from fluctuations over time in the unit acquisition costs of inventory items.

Consider the inventory of goods for sale in a merchandising firm. The inventory equation can be written as follows, with all quantities measured in dollars of cost:

$$\text{Beginning Inventory} + \text{Net Purchases} - \text{Cost of Goods Sold} = \text{Ending Inventory}.$$

Rearranging terms, the equation becomes:

$$\text{Beginning Inventory} + \text{Net Purchases} - \text{Ending Inventory} = \text{Cost of Goods Sold}.$$

The valuation for the ending inventory will appear on the balance sheet as the asset, Merchandise Inventory; the amount of Cost of Goods Sold will appear on the income statement as an expense of generating the sales revenue.

To illustrate, suppose that a merchandising firm (appliance store) had a beginning inventory of one T.V. set, "T.V. set 1," which cost $250. Suppose, further, that two T.V. sets are purchased during the period, T.V. set 2 for $290 and T.V. set 3 for $300, and that one T.V. set is sold for $550. The three T.V. sets are exactly alike in all physical respects; only their costs differ. Assume that there is no way to know which T.V. set was sold.

If financial statements are prepared with amounts measured in dollar terms, then some assumption must be made about which T.V. set was sold. The total cost of the three T.V. sets available for sale is $840 (= $250 + $290 + $300), and the average cost of a T.V. set is $280 (= $840/3). There are at least four assumptions that can be made in applying the inventory equation to determine the Cost of Goods Sold expense for the income statement and the ending inventory for the balance sheet. Exhibit 8.1 shows these assumptions. As the inventory equation and the T.V. set example both show, the higher the Cost of Goods Sold, the lower must be the Ending Inventory. The choice of which particular pair of numbers to use—one for the income statement and one for the balance sheet—is determined by the *cost-flow assumption*. Making a cost-flow assumption is a major problem in accounting for inventories.

Problems of Inventory Accounting

Discussion of inventory accounting can be conveniently split into consideration of individual problems, considered more or less separately. The remainder of this chapter discusses four such problems:

1 Periodic and perpetual systems for keeping track of items in inventory.

298

Exhibit 8.1
**Assumptions for Inventory
Illustrations**

Assumed Item Sold	Cost of Goods Available for Sale (Beginning Inventory Plus Purchases)[a]	=	Cost of Goods Sold (for Income Statement)	+	Ending Inventory (for Balance Sheet)
T.V. Set 1	$840		$250		$590
T.V. Set 2	840		290		550
T.V. Set 3	840		300		540
"Average" T.V. Set	840		280		560

[a]Cost of goods available for sale = cost of (T.V. Set 1 + T.V. Set 2 + T.V. Set 3) = ($250 + $290 + $300) = $840.

2 Valuation basis for items in inventory.
3 Costs included in acquisition cost.
4 Cost-flow assumptions for the movement of goods and prices into and out of inventory.

The income tax laws affect some of the firm's choices in accounting for inventories. We discuss the impact of income taxes at the appropriate places.

Inventory Systems

There are two principal systems for calculating the physical quantity and dollar amount of an inventory. One is known as the *periodic* inventory system and the other as the *perpetual* inventory system. The periodic system is less expensive to use than the perpetual system, but the perpetual system provides useful information not provided by the periodic system.

Periodic Inventory System

In a periodic inventory system, the ending inventory figure is calculated by taking a physical count of units on hand at the end of an accounting period and multiplying the quantity on hand by the cost per unit. Then the inventory equation calculates the withdrawals that represent the cost-of-goods-sold expense. The following form of the inventory equation computes the cost of goods sold under a periodic system:

$$\underbrace{\begin{array}{l}\text{Beginning} \\ \text{Inventory} \\ \text{(known)}\end{array} + \begin{array}{l}\text{Purchases} \\ \text{(known)}\end{array}}_{\begin{array}{c}\text{Goods Available} \\ \text{for Use or Sale}\end{array}} - \begin{array}{l}\text{Ending} \\ \text{Inventory} \\ \text{(counted} \\ \text{and valued)}\end{array} = \begin{array}{l}\text{Cost of} \\ \text{Goods Sold.} \\ \text{(solved for)}\end{array}$$

When a periodic system is used, no entry is made for withdrawals (cost of goods sold) until the inventory on hand at the end of the accounting period is counted and valued. To illustrate the application of a periodic system, assume that sales during the year amounted to $350,000. The entries made to record sales during the year would have the combined effect of the following entry:

Cash and Accounts Receivable	350,000	
Sales		350,000
Sales recorded for the entire year have this effect.		

At the end of the year, a physical count is taken, an inventory valuation is made, and the cost of the withdrawals is determined from the inventory equation. For example:

Cost of Merchandise Inventory, January 1	$ 40,000
Plus Merchandise Purchased (Net) During the Year	215,000
Cost of Goods Available for Sale During the Year	$255,000
Less Cost of Merchandise Inventory, December 31	(45,000)
Cost of Goods Sold During the Year	$210,000

We assume that all purchases have been debited to the Merchandise Inventory account. The cost-of-goods-sold expense is recognized in a single entry:

Cost of Goods Sold	210,000	
Merchandise Inventory		210,000
Cost of Goods Sold recognized under a periodic inventory system.		

The principal disadvantage of a periodic inventory system is that no information is generated to aid in controlling the amount of inventory shrinkage (the general name for losses from such causes as breakage, theft, evaporation, and waste). All goods not accounted for by the physical inventory count are assumed to have been either sold or used. Any losses from shrinkage are buried in the cost of goods sold. Furthermore, physically counting the inventory at the end of the accounting period can seriously interfere with normal business operations for several days. Some firms using the periodic inventory method even close down and engage practically the entire staff on the physical count and measurement of the items on hand. Preparing income statements more frequently than once a year is expensive when the inventory figures are obtained only by physically counting inventories.

Perpetual Inventory System

In a *perpetual* (*continuous*) inventory system, the cost of withdrawals is calculated and recorded at the time that items are taken from inventory. A perpetual inventory system requires a constant tracing of costs as items move into and out of inventory.

300

Such entries as the following may be made from day to day:

Accounts Receivable	800	
Sales		800
Cost of Goods Sold	475	
Finished Goods Inventory		475
To record the cost of goods withdrawn from inventory and sold for $800.		

The balance in the Merchandise Inventory account when postings for a period have been completed is the cost of the goods still on hand. Statements can be prepared without carrying out a physical count of inventory. In a perpetual inventory system, the following form of the inventory equation is used to compute what should be in the ending inventory after each acquisition or withdrawal:

$$\underbrace{\substack{\text{Beginning} \\ \text{Inventory} \\ \text{(known)}} + \substack{\text{Purchases} \\ \text{(known)}}}_{\substack{\text{Goods Available} \\ \text{for Use or Sale}}} - \substack{\text{Withdrawals} \\ \text{(recorded)}} = \substack{\text{Ending} \\ \text{Inventory.} \\ \text{(solved for)}}$$

Using a perpetual inventory system does not eliminate the need to take a physical inventory in which the items of inventory on hand are counted and valued. A physical count and valuation must be done to check the accuracy of the book figures and to gauge the loss from shrinkages. The loss is the difference between the amounts in the Inventory account and the cost of the goods actually on hand. The loss would be recorded as follows, assuming a book balance for inventory of $10,000 and a valuation, based on a physical count, of $9,200:

Cost of Goods Sold (or Loss)	800	
Merchandise Inventory		800
To write down inventory.		

The credit reduces the book amount of inventory from its recorded amount, $10,000, to the correct amount, $9,200. The debit is to the usual Cost of Goods Sold account or to a Loss account, such as Loss from Inventory Shrinkages. In either case, it reduces net income for the current period.

Some businesses using a perpetual system make a complete physical check at the end of the accounting period, in the same way as when a periodic inventory system is used. A more effective procedure is available. Rather than taking the inventory of all items at one time, the count may be staggered throughout the period. For example, a college bookstore may check actual physical amounts of textbooks and inventory account amounts at the end of the school year, whereas the comparison for T-shirts might be done in November. All items should be counted at least once during every year, but not all items need be counted at the same time. The count of a particular item should be scheduled for a time when the stock on hand is near its low point for the year.

301

Choosing between Periodic and Perpetual Inventory Systems

A perpetual system helps maintain up-to-date information on quantities actually on hand. Thus, its use is justified when being "out of stock" may lead to costly consequences, such as customer dissatisfaction or the need to shut down production lines. In such cases, a perpetual inventory system might keep track of the physical quantities of inventory but not the dollar amounts. Further, controlling losses is easier under a perpetual system because inventory records continuously indicate the goods that should be on hand. A periodic inventory system usually costs less to administer than a perpetual inventory system, but it provides no data on losses, shrinkages, and deterioration.

As with other choices that have to be made in accounting, the costs of any system have to be compared with its benefits. A periodic inventory system is likely to be cost-effective when being out of stock will not be extremely costly, when there is a large volume of items with a small value per unit, or when items are hard to steal or pilfer. Perpetual systems are cost-effective when there is a small volume of high-value items or when running out of stock is costly.

As the cost of record keeping with computers declines, the cost of perpetual systems declines. Their use, therefore, increases over time.

Bases of Inventory Valuation

The basis of valuation for inventories significantly affects both net income and the amount at which inventories are shown on the balance sheet. At least five bases of valuation are used for one purpose or another. The most common ones, discussed below, are acquisition cost, current cost as measured either by replacement cost or net realizable value, lower of (acquisition) cost or market, and standard cost. Some of the following is review of fundamentals discussed in Chapter 2. Generally accepted accounting principles require the use of the lower-of-cost-or-market basis for most purposes.

Acquisition Cost Basis

When the acquisition cost basis is used, units in inventory are carried at their historical cost until sold. In accounting, the terms *acquisition cost* and *historical cost* are used to mean the same thing.

Use of historical or acquisition costs in accounting implies the use of the *realization convention*: increases (or decreases) in the market value of individual assets, including items of inventory, are not recognized as holding gains (or losses) until the particular assets are sold. Thus, when the acquisition cost basis is used for items in inventory, only sales transactions affect income. Any changes in the value of inventory items occurring between the time of acquisition and the time of sale are not recognized. The figure shown on the balance sheet for inventory will be more or less out of date depending on how much prices have changed since the items were acquired. The longer the time elapsed since acquisition, the more likely is the current value of the inventory to differ from its acquisition cost.

Current Value Basis

When a current cost, or current value, basis is used, units in inventory are stated at a current market price. Two current-value bases are discussed below: current entry value, often called *replacement cost;* and current exit value, often called *net realizable value.*

When inventories are stated at current cost, gains and losses from changes in prices of inventory items are recognized during the holding period that elapses between acquisition (or production) and the time of sale.

Whereas an acquisition cost basis for inventory shows objective, verifiable information that may be out of date, a current value basis shows current information that can be more useful but the amount shown may be more difficult to ascertain and to audit.

Replacement Cost The replacement cost of an inventory item at a given time is the amount the firm would have to pay to acquire the item at that time. In computing replacement cost, one assumes that a fair market (or arms'-length) transaction between a willing buyer and a willing seller takes place. One also assumes that the inventory is bought in the customary fashion in the customary quantities. Replacement cost does not imply the forced purchase of inventory by a frantic buyer from a hoarding seller (which probably implies a premium price) or purchases of abnormally large quantities (which often can be bought at a lower-than-normal price) or purchases of abnormally small quantities (which usually cost more per unit to acquire).

Net Realizable Value The amount that a firm could realize as a willing seller (not a "distressed seller") in an arms'-length transaction with a willing buyer in the ordinary course of business is *net realizable value,* an exit value. Not all items of inventory are in a form ready for sale (there may be partially complete inventory in a manufacturing firm, for example). Also, a sales commission and other selling costs must often be incurred in ordinary sales transactions. For these reasons, net realizable value is defined as the estimated selling price of the inventory less any estimated costs necessary to make the item ready for sale and to sell it. Consider as examples, agricultural products and precious metals on hand at the close of an accounting period. These are often stated at net realizable value. It may be easier to estimate a market price less selling costs than it is to determine the historical cost of a bushel of apples that has been harvested from an orchard.

Lower-of-Cost-or-Market Basis

The lower-of-cost-or-market valuation basis is the lesser of the two amounts: acquisition cost or "market value." Market value is generally replacement cost.[1]

---

[1] Actually, the definition of "market value" in the computation of lower of cost or market is more complex than mere replacement cost. Market value is replacement cost but no more than net realizable value nor less than the quantity net realizable value reduced by a "normal profit margin" on sales of items of this type.

A decline of $5,000 in the market value of inventory might be recognized with the following entry:

Loss from Decline in Value of Inventory	5,000	
Inventory		5,000

The credit is made directly to the Inventory account, not to a contra account as is done for marketable securities (explained in Chapter 7), because subsequent recoveries in market value are not recorded as gains. When a periodic inventory system is used, the above entry is not recorded explicitly, but the loss is reflected in a higher cost of goods sold. Consider, for example, the periodic calculation in Exhibit 8.2 of cost of goods sold when beginning inventory is $19,000, purchases are $100,000, and ending inventory has a cost of $22,000 but has a market value of $20,000.

Exhibit 8.2
Calculating Cost of Goods Sold Illustrating Different Bases of Inventory Valuation

	Cost Basis	Lower-of-Cost-or Market Basis
Beginning Inventory	$ 19,000	$ 19,000
Purchases	100,000	100,000
Goods Available for Sale	$119,000	$119,000
Less Ending Inventory	(22,000)	(20,000)
Cost of Goods Sold	$ 97,000	$ 99,000

Note that cost of goods sold is $2,000 larger under the lower-of-cost-or-market basis than under the acquisition cost basis. The loss of $2,000 is not reported separately, but income will be $2,000 smaller than when the acquisition cost basis is used. If the amount of the writedown to market is so large that the reader of the statements will be misled without separate disclosure of the decline in market value, then the writedown can be shown as an adjustment to cost of goods sold or as a loss, separately reported as part of operating activities.

The lower-of-cost-or-market basis for inventory valuation is thought to be a "conservative" policy because (1) losses from decreases in market value are recognized before goods are sold, but gains from increases in market value are not recorded before a sale takes place and (2) inventory figures on the balance sheet are never greater, but may be less, than acquisition cost. That is, *holding losses* are reported currently, whereas *holding gains* are not reported until the goods are sold.

An examination of the effects of using the lower-of-cost-or-market basis over a series of accounting periods shows why the "conservatism" argument is questionable. Over long-enough time spans, income equals cash-in less cash-out. For any one unit, there is only one total gain or loss figure—the difference between its selling price and its acquisition cost; the valuation rule merely determines how this amount of gain or loss is to be spread over the accounting periods between acquisition and final disposition. When the lower-of-cost-or-market basis is used, the net income of the present period may be "conservatively" lower than if the acquisition cost basis were used, but if so, the net income of a later period, when the unit is sold, will be higher.

Standard Costs

Standard cost is a predetermined estimate of what items of manufactured inventory *should* cost. Studies of past and estimated future cost data provide the basis for standard costs. Standard cost systems are frequently used by manufacturing firms for internal performance measurement and control. These are discussed in managerial and cost accounting texts. Standard cost is also used occasionally as the valuation basis for preparing financial statements. Units in inventory may be valued at standard cost, especially in the preparation of monthly or quarterly statements. If so, any excess of actual cost over standard cost (called an *unfavorable variance*) is usually debited to cost of goods sold or to other expenses of the period. If actual cost is less than standard cost, the favorable variance is usually credited to cost of goods sold.

Generally Accepted Accounting Basis for Inventory Valuation

Generally, accounting uses a historical cost basis. Because the "market value" of some inventory items can be significantly less than acquisition cost, either because of price changes for this kind of inventory generally or because of physical deterioration of the particular items in an inventory, generally accepted accounting principles require the use of lower of cost or market.[2] This is the same thing as saying that "market values" must be used in some cases. Computing market value requires both replacement cost and net realizable value amounts. Thus, generally accepted accounting principles for inventory valuation and measurement of cost of goods sold require a combination of three valuation bases: acquisition cost, replacement cost, and net realizable value. In a period of rising prices, replacement cost and net realizable value are likely to be higher than acquisition cost, so valuation at cost and the lower of cost or market usually give the same valuation.

The FASB requires disclosure by large firms of the current replacement cost of beginning inventory, ending inventory, and cost of goods sold in notes to the financial statements even though the financial statements are based on lower-of-cost-or-market values.[3] Chapter 14 discusses these disclosures more fully.

---

[2]Committee on Accounting Procedure, *Accounting Research Bulletin No. 43,* "Inventory Pricing," Chapter 4, statements 5 and 6, 1953.

[3]Financial Accounting Standards Board, *Statement of Financial Accounting Standards No. 33,* "Financial Reporting and Changing Prices," 1979.

Acquisition of Inventory

Components of Inventory Cost

All costs incurred to acquire goods and prepare them for sale should enter into the valuation of the goods as assets. For a merchandising firm, such costs include purchasing, transportation, receiving, unpacking, inspecting, and shelving costs as well as that portion of the bookkeeping and office cost which relates to the recording of purchases.[4] The example on page 42 (in Chapter 2), showing the computation of the cost of some equipment, applies to inventory as well.

For a manufacturing firm, inventory costs include direct materials, direct labor, and manufacturing overhead. In the illustrations for manufacturing firms considered so far in this book, *all* production costs were debited to Work-in-Process Inventory. This procedure, called *absorption* (or *full*) *costing,* is the one most commonly used in accounting practice. An alternative procedure, known as *direct costing* (or more properly, *variable costing*), has received substantial attention in recent years.

In the direct costing procedure, product costs are classified into variable manufacturing costs (those that tend to vary with output) and fixed manufacturing costs (those that tend to be relatively unaffected in the short run by the number of units produced). Non-variable (fixed) manufacturing costs are treated in the same way as selling and administrative costs; that is, they are treated as expenses assigned to the period of incurrence rather than as costs assignable to the product produced. Non-variable manufacturing costs are charged in their entirety against revenues in calculating net income for the period. In the direct costing procedure, only variable manufacturing costs are classified as product costs, to be assigned to Work-in-Process Inventory and, later, to Finished Goods Inventory. Direct labor and direct materials are variable costs. Most manufacturing overhead items, such as property taxes and depreciation of equipment, are non-variable costs.

When the absorption costing method is used, reported net income from one year to the next can display strange patterns if the number of units produced differs from the number of units sold. These unusual changes in net income could lead some statement users to make incorrect interpretations about the operating performance of a firm. The direct costing procedure does not result in these unusual patterns of income. It has been suggested, therefore, that the direct costing method should be used so that more useful information will be provided for assessing operating performance.

Generally accepted accounting principles, however, do not permit a firm to issue financial statements based on direct costing. We suspect that direct costing is not generally acceptable for financial reporting primarily because it is not allowed for

---

[4] Because the amounts involved are often relatively small, and because it is difficult to assign a definite dollar amount for many of these costs to specific purchases, the tendency in practice is to restrict the actual additions to a few significant items that can easily be identified with particular goods, such as transportation costs. The costs of operating a purchasing department, the salaries and expenses of buyers, the costs of the receiving and warehousing departments, and the costs of handling and shelving are usually treated as expenses of the period in which they are incurred, although they are logically part of the total cost of merchandise made ready for sale.

tax reporting. Because direct costing is not a generally accepted accounting principle, we defer to managerial accounting courses the discussion of criticism of the absorption costing method and suggested benefits of the direct costing method for internal management uses.

The Purchase Transaction

The procedures for recording purchases of merchandise, raw materials, and supplies vary from one business to another. Purchase transactions culminate when the goods are received and inspected and the purchase is entered into the records. From the legal point of view, purchases should be recorded in the formal accounting records when title to the goods passes. The question of when title passes is often a technical, legal matter, and the precise answer depends on a consideration of all of the circumstances of the transaction. As a convenience, the accountant usually recognizes purchases only after both the invoice and the goods are received and inspected. Adjustments may be made at the end of the accounting period to reflect the legal formalities for goods in transit that belong to the purchaser.

Merchandise Purchases Account

During the accounting period, acquisitions of merchandise can be debited either to the appropriate inventory account, such as Merchandise Inventory, or to a Merchandise Purchases account. (The shorter title Purchases is used in practice, but the full title is used here to avoid ambiguity.) The Merchandise Purchases account is a temporary, asset adjunct account. That is, at the end of each accounting period, the balance in Merchandise Purchases is added to the appropriate inventory account and does not itself appear in the balance sheet. The typical entry to record a specific purchase of merchandise is:

Merchandise Purchases	950	
Accounts Payable (or Cash)		950
To record purchase of merchandise.		

At the end of the period, the closing entry, assuming that merchandise costing $7,675 was purchased during the period, is:

Merchandise Inventory	7,675	
Merchandise Purchases		7,675
To close purchases account, adding its balance to the inventory account.		

The special account to record purchases is used to give more complete information about purchase transactions during the period than is provided when all purchases are debited directly to the Merchandise (or Raw Materials) Inventory account.

Merchandise Purchases Adjustments

The invoice price of goods purchased will seldom measure the total acquisition cost correctly. Additional costs may be incurred in transporting and handling the goods, and deductions may be required for cash discounts, goods returned, and other allowances or adjustments of the invoice price. All of these adjustments could be handled through the one Merchandise Purchases account. Frequently, however, a number of contra and adjunct accounts are used for these adjustments so that a more complete analysis of the cost of purchases is available. Purchase Discounts, Freight-in, Purchase Returns, and Purchase Allowances accounts are used to provide the needed detail. The accounting for purchase adjustments closely parallels the accounting for sales adjustments discussed in Chapter 7.

Merchandise Purchases Discounts

The largest adjustment to the invoice price of merchandise purchases is likely to be that for purchase discounts. Sellers often offer a discount from the invoice price for prompt payment. For example, the terms of sale "2/10, net/30" mean that a 2-percent discount from invoice price is offered if payment is made within 10 days and the full invoice price is due in any case within 30 days.[5] The amount of discounts taken during a period is sometimes shown as a special or "other" revenue item on the income statement. Some supporters of this treatment argue that the discounts represent interest earned on cash and so should be viewed as a revenue item.

A more appropriate interpretation, however, is to treat purchase discounts as a reduction in the purchase price. Purchases have a cash price, and if payment is delayed there is an additional charge for the delay and for the other additional services the seller is compelled to render. To view purchase discounts as revenue to the purchaser would indicate that revenue may be earned simply by buying goods and paying for them with cash within a specified time even though the goods have not been sold to others. Discounts should therefore be treated as a reduction in the cost of merchandise purchased, thereby deferring their effect on net income until the goods have been sold.

Manufactured Inventories

Amounts for manufactured inventories include raw material costs and all other costs incurred in changing the physical form of the raw materials into finished goods. Manufactured inventories typically include three types of costs:

1 Direct material.
2 Direct labor.
3 Manufacturing overhead (sometimes called "indirect manufacturing costs").

---

[5] Problem 4 at the end of Appendix B attempts to help you understand that the interest rate implied in these terms of sales is about *45 percent per year.* That is, a purchaser who does not take such a discount is borrowing money at an interest rate of about 45 percent per year. Most purchasers find it advantageous to take such discounts and to borrow elsewhere at lower rates.

Costs included in manufactured inventories are called *product costs,* in contrast to period expenses.

Figure 4.2 (page 130) shows how various costs are classified as product costs or period expenses in a manufacturing firm.

Cost-Flow Assumptions

Specific Identification and the Need for a Cost-Flow Assumption

Individual units of an item can sometimes be physically identified as coming from a specific purchase. If so, then there is no special problem in ascertaining the acquisition cost of the units withdrawn from inventory and the cost of the units still on hand. For example, cost can be marked on the unit or on its container, or the unit can be traced back to its purchase invoice or cost record. The inventory and cost of goods sold of an automobile dealer or of a dealer in diamonds or fur coats would probably be computed using specific identification of costs.

In most cases, however, new items are mixed with old units on shelves, in bins, or in other ways, and physical identification is impracticable. Moreover, it may be desirable (for reasons to be discussed in this section) to assume that cost flows differ from physical flows of goods.

Flow of Historical Costs

The inventory *valuation* problem arises because there are *two* unknowns in the inventory equation:

$$\underbrace{\underset{\text{(known)}}{\text{Beginning}\atop\text{Inventory}} + \underset{\text{(known)}}{\text{Net}\atop\text{Purchases}}}_{\substack{\text{Goods Available}\\ \text{for Use or Sale}}} = \underset{\text{(unknown)}}{\text{Cost of}\atop\text{Goods Sold}} + \underset{\text{(unknown)}}{\text{Ending}\atop\text{Inventory}}.$$

The values of the beginning inventory and net purchases are known; the values of the cost of goods sold and of ending inventory are not known. The question is whether to value the units in ending inventory using the most recent costs, the oldest costs, the average cost, or some other alternative. Of course, the question could have been put in terms of valuing the cost of goods sold, for once we place a value on one unknown quantity, the inventory equation automatically determines the value of the other. The sum of the two unknowns, Cost of Goods Sold and Ending Inventory, in the inventory equation for historical costs must equal the cost of goods available for sale ($=$ beginning inventory plus net purchases). The higher the value assigned to one unknown, the lower must be the value assigned to the other.

When prices are changing, no historical cost-based accounting method for valuing both ending inventory and cost of goods sold allows the accountant to show current values on both the income statement and the balance sheet. For example, in a period of rising prices, if recent, higher acquisition prices are used in measuring cost of goods sold shown on the income statement, then older, lower acquisition prices must be used in valuing the ending inventory shown on the balance sheet. As long as cost of goods sold and ending inventory are based on acquisition costs, financial statements can present current values in the income statement or the balance sheet, but not in both. Of course, combinations of current and out-of-date information can be shown in both statements.

If more than one purchase is made of the same item at different prices, and specific identification is not feasible, then some assumption must be made as to the flow of costs. From the cost-flow assumption, the accountant computes the acquisition cost applicable to the units remaining in the inventory. One of three cost-flow assumptions is typically used for this purpose. These cost-flow assumptions are:

1 First-in, first-out (FIFO).
2 Last-in, first-out (LIFO).
3 Weighted average.

The demonstrations of each of these methods that follow are based on the T.V. set example introduced earlier in the chapter and repeated at the top of Exhibit 8.3. The example of the three T.V. sets illustrates most of the important points about the cost-flow assumption required in accounting for inventories and cost of goods sold. The first problem for self-study at the end of this chapter is a more computationally complex illustration, but it contains no new concepts.

First-In, First-Out

The first-in, first-out cost-flow assumption, abbreviated FIFO, assigns the cost of the earliest units acquired to the withdrawals and the cost of the most recent acquisitions to the ending inventory. This cost flow assumes that the oldest materials and goods are used first. This cost-flow assumption conforms to good business practice in managing physical flows, especially in the case of items that deteriorate or become obsolete. Column (1) of Exhibit 8.3 illustrates FIFO. T.V. set 1 is assumed to be sold, whereas T.V. sets 2 and 3 are assumed to remain in inventory. The designation FIFO refers to the cost flow of units sold. A parallel description for ending inventory is last-in, still-here, or LISH.

Last-In, First-Out

The last-in, first-out cost-flow assumption, abbreviated LIFO, assigns the cost of the latest units acquired to the withdrawals and the cost of the oldest units to the ending inventory. Some theorists argue that LIFO matches current costs to current revenues and therefore that LIFO better measures income. Column (3) of Exhibit 8.3 illustrates LIFO. The $300 cost of T.V. set 3 is assumed to leave, whereas the costs of T.V. sets 1 and 2 are assumed to remain in inventory. The designation of LIFO refers to the cost flow for units sold. A parallel description for ending inventory is first-in, still-here, or FISH.

Exhibit 8.3
Comparison of Cost-Flow
Assumptions Historical Cost Basis

Assumed Data

Beginning Inventory: T.V. Set 1 Cost	$250
Purchases: T.V. Set 2 Cost	290
T.V. Set 3 Cost	300
Cost of Goods Available for Sale	$840
Sales: One T.V. Set	$550

	Cost-Flow Assumption		
Financial Statements	**FIFO**	**Weighted Average**	**LIFO**
	(1)	(2)	(3)
Sales	$550	$550	$550
Cost of Goods Sold	250^a	280^b	300^c
Gross Margin on Sales	$300	$270	$250
Ending Inventory	590^d	560^e	540^f

^{a}T.V. Set 1 costs $250
^{b}Average T.V. set costs $280 (= $840/3).
^{c}T.V. Set 3 costs $300.
^{d}T.V. Sets 2 and 3 cost $290 + $300 = $590.
^{e}Two average T.V. sets cost 2 × $280 = $560.
^{f}T.V. Sets 1 and 2 cost $250 + $290 = $540.

LIFO has been increasingly used since 1939, when it first became acceptable for income tax reporting. In a period of consistently rising prices, LIFO results in a higher cost of goods sold, a lower reported periodic income, and lower current income taxes than either FIFO or weighted-average cost-flow assumptions.

LIFO cannot usually be justified in terms of physical flows but is used because it produces a cost-of-goods-sold figure that is based on more up-to-date prices. In a period of rising prices, LIFO's higher (than FIFO's) cost-of-goods-sold figure reduces reported income and income taxes.

Weighted Average

Under the weighted-average cost-flow assumption, the average of the costs of all goods available for sale (or use) during the accounting period, including the cost applicable to the beginning inventory, must be calculated.[6] The weighted-average cost is applied to the units on hand at the end of the month. Column (2) in Exhibit 8.3 illustrates the weighted-average cost-flow assumption. The weighted-average cost of T.V. sets available for sale during the period is $280 [$=\frac{1}{3}$ × ($250 + $290 + $300)]. Cost of Goods Sold is thus $280 and ending inventory is $560 (= 2 × $280).

[6]This description is technically correct only when a periodic inventory method is used. The first problem for self-study at the end of this chapter explores the procedures for applying the weighted-average method in a perpetual inventory system.

311

Comparison of Cost-Flow Assumptions

FIFO results in balance sheet figures that are closest to current cost, because the latest purchases dominate the ending inventory valuation. The cost-of-goods-sold expense tends to be out of date, however, because it assumes that the earlier prices of the beginning inventory and the earliest purchases are charged to expense. When prices change, FIFO usually leads to the highest reported net income of the three methods when prices are rising and the smallest when prices are falling.

Because LIFO ending inventory can contain costs of items acquired many years previously, LIFO produces balance sheet figures usually far removed from current costs. LIFO's cost-of-goods-sold figure closely approximates current costs. Exhibit 8.4 summarizes the differences between FIFO and LIFO. Of the cost-flow assumptions, LIFO usually implies the smallest net income when prices are rising (highest cost of goods sold), and the largest when prices are falling (lowest cost of goods sold). Also, LIFO results in the least fluctuation in reported income in businesses where selling prices tend to change as current prices of inventory items change.

The weighted-average cost-flow assumption falls between the other two in its effect on both the balance sheet and the income statement. It is, however, much more like FIFO than like LIFO in its effects on the balance sheet. When inventory turns over rapidly, the weighted-average inventory values are almost as close to present prices as FIFO. Weighted averages reflect all of the prices during the period in proportion to the quantities purchased at those prices as well as beginning inventory costs carried over from the previous period.

Exhibit 8.4
Age of Information about Inventory Items

Cost-Flow Assumption	Income Statement	Balance Sheet	Inventory-on-Hand Assumption
FIFO	Old Prices	Current Prices	LISH
LIFO	Current Prices	Very[a] Old Prices	FISH

[a]The oldest prices on the FIFO income statement are just over 1 year old in nearly all cases and the *average* price on the FIFO income statement (for a year) is slightly more than ½ year old. The larger the rate of inventory turnover, the closer the average age on the income statement is to ½ year. LIFO balance sheet items are generally much older than the FIFO income statement items, with some costs from the 1940s in many cases.

A Closer Look at LIFO's Effects on Financial Statements

As we discussed above, LIFO usually presents a cost-of-goods-sold figure that is closely related to current costs. It also generally has the practical advantage of deferring income taxes. If a firm uses a LIFO flow assumption in its income tax return, it must also use LIFO in its financial reports to shareholders. This "LIFO conformity rule" of the Internal Revenue Service is under attack in Congress, by some members of the U.S. Treasury Department, and by the federal courts. The outcome is uncertain. By the time you read this, LIFO conformity may no longer be required. Because LIFO conformity is required as this book goes to press, our discussions and illustrations assume it.

In the last decade, many firms, such as Du Pont, General Motors, Eastman Kodak, and Sears Roebuck, have switched from FIFO to LIFO. Given the rapid rate of price increases over the past decade, the switch from FIFO to LIFO has resulted in substantially lower cash payments for income taxes. For example, when Du Pont and General Motors switched from FIFO to LIFO, they each lowered current income taxes by about $150 million. At the same time, these firms reported lower net income to shareholders than would have been reported if FIFO had still been used.[7]

LIFO Layers In any year when purchases exceed sales, the quantity of units in inventory increases. The amount added to inventory for that year is called a *LIFO layer.* For example, assume a firm acquires ten T.V. sets each year and sells eight T.V. sets each year for 4 years. Then, its inventory at the end of the fourth year would be 8 units. The cost of the 8 units under LIFO is the costs of sets numbered 1 and 2 (from the first year), 11 and 12 (from the second year), 21 and 22 (from the third year), and 31 and 32 (from the fourth year). Common terminology would say this firm has four LIFO layers and each is labeled with its year of acquisition. The physical units on hand would almost certainly be the most recently acquired units in year four, but they would be valued on the balance sheet at prices paid during each of the 4 years.

Dipping into LIFO Layers One criticism of LIFO relates to dipping into old LIFO layers. A major objective of using LIFO is to reduce current taxes in periods of rising prices and rising inventory quantities. Usually LIFO produces this result. If inventory quantities decline, however, the opposite effect can occur in the year of the decline, because older, lower costs per unit of prior years' LIFO layers leave the balance sheet and are charged to expense.

For example, if under LIFO a firm must for some reason reduce end-of-period physical inventory quantities below what they were at the beginning of the period, then cost of goods sold will be based on the current period's purchases plus a portion of the older and lower costs in the beginning inventory. Such a firm will have larger reported income and income taxes in that period than if the firm had been able to maintain its ending inventory at beginning-of-period levels.

Example of Dip into LIFO Layers Assume that LIFO inventory at the beginning of 1982 consists of 460 units with a total cost of $34,200 as shown in Exhibit 8.5. Assume that the cost at the end of 1982 is $120 per unit. If, however, the 1982 ending inventory drops to 100 units, then all the 360 units purchased in 1979 through 1981 will also enter cost of goods sold. These 360 units cost $29,200 (= $6,600 + $9,600 + $13,000), but the current cost of comparable units is $43,200 (= 360 units × $120 per unit). Cost of goods sold will be $14,000 (= $43,200 − $29,200) smaller because of the "dip into old LIFO layers" of inventory. Income before taxes will be $14,000 larger than if inventory quantities had not declined from 460 to 100 units.

---

[7] Thus, the apparent "paradox" in the introduction to this chapter is explained.

Exhibit 8.5
**Data for Illustration of LIFO Dips
(Inventory at January 1, 1982)**

LIFO Layers		Cost	
Number of Units	Year Purchased	Per Unit	Total Cost
100	1978	$ 50	$ 5,000
110	1979	60	6,600
120	1980	80	9,600
130	1981	100	13,000
460			$34,200

Annual Report of Disclosure of Dip into LIFO Layers In reality, many LIFO firms have inventory layers built up since the 1940s, and the costs of the early units are often as little as 10 percent of the current cost. For these firms, a dip into old layers will substantially increase income. A footnote from an earlier annual report of the U.S. Steel Corporation illustrates this phenomenon:

> Because of the continuing high demand throughout the year, inventories of many steel-making materials and steel products were unavoidably reduced and could not be replaced during the year. Under the LIFO system of accounting, used for many years by U.S. Steel, the net effect of all the inventory changes [reductions] was to increase income for the year by about $16 million.

In recent years, U.S. Steel has not explained the cause of the increase in income; a recent annual report merely said:

> Included in the Cost of Sales and Income [before taxes] are estimated credits of . . . $124.5 . . . from LIFO liquidations.

LIFO's Effects on Purchasing Behavior Consider the quandary faced by a purchasing manager of a LIFO firm nearing the end of a year when the quantity sold for the year has exceeded the quantity purchased for the year. If the year ends with sales greater than purchases, the firm will dip into old LIFO layers and will have to pay increased taxes. Assume that the purchasing manager thinks current prices for the goods are abnormally high and prefers to delay purchasing until prices drop, presumably in the next period. Waiting implies, however, dips into old LIFO layers during this period and higher taxes. Buying now may entail higher inventory and carrying costs. One disadvantage of LIFO is that it can induce behavior on the part of a firm attempting to manage its LIFO layers and cost of goods sold that would be unwise in the absence of tax effects. Some criticize LIFO because it gives management the opportunity to manipulate income: under LIFO, end-of-year purchases, which can be manipulated, affect net income for the year.

LIFO Balance Sheet LIFO usually leads to a balance sheet figure for inventory so far removed from current values as possibly to delude and confuse readers of financial statements. For example, in recent years U.S. Steel has reported that the cost of its ending inventory based on LIFO is about one-third of what it would have been had FIFO been used. U.S. Steel's inventory on the balance sheet, reported assuming LIFO, makes up about 10 percent of total assets. Using a FIFO cost-flow, inventory would be about 25 percent of total assets.

Consider the current ratio (= current assets/current liabilities). The current ratio is often used by readers of financial statements to assess the liquidity of a company. If LIFO is used in periods of rising prices while inventory quantities are increasing, the amount of inventory included in the numerator will be much smaller than if the inventory were valued at current prices. Hence, the unwary reader may underestimate the liquidity of a company that uses a LIFO cost-flow assumption.

Similarly, the calculation of inventory turnover (= cost of goods sold/average inventory during the period) can be drastically affected by using LIFO. Again referring to the U.S. Steel example, the inventory turnover ratio from the financial statements constructed assuming LIFO cost-flow is about twice as large as would result from FIFO cost flow. One of the self-study problems at the end of this chapter explores this phenomenon.

Supplementary LIFO Disclosure When a company uses LIFO, the SEC requires that it disclose in notes the current value of beginning and ending inventory. These disclosures are illustrated in Appendix A for the General Products Company. See Note 10 in Appendix Exhibit A.4.

FIFO Versus LIFO Impact on Financial Statements: An Illustration

No accounting method for inventories based on historical cost can simultaneously report current data in both the income statement and the balance sheet. If a firm reports current prices in the income statement under LIFO, then its balance sheet amount for ending inventory contains *very* old data. The SEC is concerned that readers of financial statements not be misled by out-of-date information. It requires firms using LIFO to disclose in notes to the financial statements the amounts by which LIFO inventories would have increased if they had been recorded at FIFO or current cost.[8] From this disclosure and the inventory equation, we can compute what a LIFO firm's income would have been had it been using FIFO instead. In this way, the financial statements of firms using LIFO can be made more comparable with the financial statements of firms using FIFO.

---

[8] The excess of current cost over LIFO cost of inventories is referred to by some managers as the "LIFO reserve." Of all the terms in accounting, *reserve* is the most objectionable. The Glossary at the back of this book explains the reasons. Although a term like "inventory valuation allowance" is perhaps more cumbersome than "LIFO reserve," it is less likely to mislead.

Note 10 to the financial statements of General Products Company in Appendix A states, in part:

> If the FIFO method of inventory accounting had been used to value all inventories, they would have been $2,240 [million] higher than reported at December 31, 1982 ($1,950 [million] higher at year-end 1981).

General Product's beginning inventories under LIFO (see Note 10) amounted to $3,161 million, its ending inventory amounted to $3,343 million, and its cost of goods sold totaled $17,751 million. Exhibit 8.6 demonstrates the calculation of cost of goods sold on a FIFO basis. Recall from the inventory equation:

$$\text{Beginning Inventory} + \text{Purchases} - \text{Ending Inventory} = \text{Cost of Goods Sold}.$$

FIFO's higher beginning inventory increases the reported cost of goods available for sale and the cost of goods sold by $1,950 million, relative to LIFO. FIFO's higher ending inventory decreases cost of goods sold by $2,240 million, relative to LIFO. Hence, the cost of goods sold is $2,240 million minus $1,950 million, or $290 million less under FIFO than it was under LIFO. General Products pretax income would be $290 million more under FIFO than under the LIFO flow assumption actually used.

Exhibit 8.6
General Products Company Inventory Data from Financial Statements and Footnotes (amounts in millions)

(Amounts shown in **boldface** are given in General Products Company's financial statements. Other amounts are computed as indicated.)

	LIFO Cost-Flow Assumption (Actually Used)	+	Excess of FIFO over LIFO Amount	=	FIFO Cost-Flow Assumption (Hypothetical)
Beginning Inventory	**$ 3,161**		**$ 1,950**		$ 5,111
Purchases	17,933[a]		0		17,933
Cost of Goods Available for Sale	$21,094		**$ 1,950**		$23,044
Less Ending Inventory	**3,343**		**2,240**		5,583
Cost of Goods Sold	**$17,751**		$ (290)		17,461
Sales	**$24,959**		0		**$24,959**
Less Cost of Goods Sold	**17,751**		$ (290)		**17,461**
Gross Margin on Sales	$ 7,208		$ 290		$ 7,498

---

[a]Computation of Purchases not presented in GP's financial statements:

Purchases = Cost of Goods Sold + Ending Inventory − Beginning Inventory

$17,933 = **$17,751** + **$3,343** − **$3,161**

The choice of cost-flow assumption can have an important effect on financial statements and their interpretation. During periods of substantial price change, no other choice between generally accepted financial accounting principles affects financial statements for most companies as much as the cost-flow assumption for inventory.

Identifying Operating Margin and Holding Gains

The reported net income under FIFO is generally larger than under LIFO during periods of rising prices. This higher reported net income is caused by including a larger *realized holding gain* in reported net income under FIFO than under LIFO. The significance of holding gains in the calculation of net income under FIFO and LIFO is illustrated in this section.

The conventionally reported gross margin (sales minus cost of goods sold) can be split into:

1 An operating margin.
2 A realized holding gain.

In addition, there is usually an unrealized holding gain that is not currently included in income, but is disclosed in notes to the financial statements.

The difference between the selling price of an item and its replacement cost at the time of sale is called an *operating margin.* This operating margin gives some indication of the relative advantage that a particular firm has in the market for its goods, such as a reputation for quality or service. The difference between the current replacement cost of an item and its acquisition cost is called a *holding gain* (or *loss*). The holding gain (or loss) reflects the change in cost of an item during the period while the inventory item is held.

To illustrate the calculation of the operating margin and holding gain, consider the example of the T.V. sets discussed in this chapter. The acquisition cost of the 3 items available for sale during the period is $840. Assume that 1 T.V. set is sold for $550. The replacement cost of the T.V. set at the time it was sold is assumed to be $320. The current replacement cost at the end of the period for each item in ending inventory is $350. The top portion of Exhibit 8.7 illustrates the separation of the conventionally reported gross margin into the operating margin and the realized holding gain.

The operating margin is the difference between the $550 selling price and the $320 replacement cost at the time of sale. The operating margin of $230 is the same under both the FIFO and LIFO cost-flow assumptions. The *realized holding gain* is the difference between cost of goods sold based on replacement cost and cost of goods sold based on acquisition cost. The realized holding gain under FIFO is larger than under LIFO, because the earlier purchases at lower costs are charged to cost of goods sold under FIFO. This larger realized holding gain under FIFO is the principal reason why net income under FIFO is typically larger than under LIFO during periods of rising prices. In conventional financial statements, the realized holding gain is *not* disclosed separately, as it is in Exhibit 8.7. Sometimes the realized holding gain on inventory is called *inventory profit*.

Exhibit 8.7
**Reporting of Operating Margins
and Holding Gains for T.V. Sets
Using the Periodic Inventory Method**

	Cost-Flow Assumption			
	FIFO		LIFO	
Sales Revenue	$550		$550	
Less Replacement Cost of Goods Sold	320		320	
Operating Margin on Sales		$230		$230
Realized Holding Gain on T.V. Sets:				
Replacement Cost (at Time of Sale) of Goods Sold	$320		$320	
Less Acquisition Cost of Goods Sold				
(FIFO—T.V. Set 1; LIFO—T.V. Set 3)	250		300	
Realized Holding Gain on T.V. Sets		70		20
Conventionally Reported Gross Margin[a]		$300		$250
Unrealized Holding Gain:				
Replacement Cost of Ending Inventory (2 × $350)	$700		$700	
Less Acquisition Cost of Ending Inventory				
(FIFO—T.V. Sets 2 & 3; LIFO—T.V. Sets 1 & 2)	590		540	
Unrealized Holding Gain on T.V. Sets		110		160
Economic Profit on Sales and Holding Inventory of T.V. Sets				
(not reported in financial statements)		$410		$410

[a]Note that Exhibit 8.3 stops here.

The calculation of an unrealized holding gain on units in ending inventory is also shown in Exhibit 8.7. The *unrealized holding gain* is the difference between the current replacement cost of the ending inventory and its acquisition cost. This unrealized holding gain on ending inventory is not reported in the income statement as presently prepared. The unrealized holding gain under LIFO is larger than under FIFO, because earlier purchases with lower costs are assumed to remain in ending inventory under LIFO. The sum of the operating margin plus all holding gains (both realized and unrealized) is the same under FIFO and LIFO. Most of the holding gain under FIFO, i.e., the realized portion, is recognized in computing net income each period, whereas most of the holding gain under LIFO, i.e. the unrealized portion, is not currently recognized in the income statement. Instead, under LIFO the unrealized holding gain remains unreported, so long as the older acquisition costs are shown on the balance sheet as ending inventory.

The total increase in wealth for a period includes both realized and unrealized holding gains. That total increase, $410 in the example, is independent of the cost-flow assumption, but is not reported in financial statements under currently accepted accounting principles.

The FASB requires disclosure in notes of the realized and unrealized holding gains on inventory (and plant) under certain conditions. See the discussion in Chapter 14.

Current Cost Basis Removes the Need for a Cost-Flow Assumption

The preceding sections illustrate the difficulty in constructing useful financial statements in historical cost accounting for inventory in times of changing prices. If a FIFO cost-flow assumption is used, then the income statement reports out-of-date cost of goods sold. If a LIFO cost-flow assumption is used, then the balance sheet reports out-of-date ending inventory. (See Exhibit 8.4.)

If a current cost basis for inventory is used, then up-to-date information can be shown on both statements. Using a current cost basis eliminates the realization convention in accounting and requires the accountant to make estimates of current costs. Some accountants think that the benefits of current data outweigh the costs of having less auditable numbers.

Exhibit 8.8 illustrates how the T.V. set example would look when both cost of goods sold and ending inventory are valued at replacement cost.

The first income figure, $230, is labeled *Operating Margin*. This figure shows selling price less replacement cost of goods sold at the time of sale. This number has significance for companies operating in unregulated environments. The significance can perhaps be understood by considering the following assertion. If the retailer of the T.V. sets pays out more than $230 in other expenses, taxes and dividends, then there will be insufficient funds retained in the firm for it to replace inventory and to allow it to continue in business carrying out the same operations next period as it did this period. On the date of sale, a new T.V. set costs $320; the historical cost of the T.V. set sold, whether $250 or $320 or whatever amount in between, is irrelevant to understanding the current economic conditions facing the retailer.

The second income item shown in Exhibit 8.8 is called *Holding Gains*. Holding gains of $180 occurred during the period on the T.V. sets held in inventory. At the time of sale, the replacement cost of T.V. sets had increased to $320. Thus, the holding gain on three T.V. sets, on the date of sale of one of them, was $120 [= 3 \times $320 - ($250 + $290 + $300)]. By the end of the accounting period there was another $60 [= 2 \times ($350 - $320)] holding gain on the two T.V. sets still held in inventory as the replacement cost increased to $350 from $320.

The $410 income figure shown after the inclusion of holding gains is also significant. It represents the increase in wealth of the firm without regard to the realization convention. To the economist, income is the change in wealth during the period. The economist thinks it unimportant that a part of the gain has not been realized in an arms'-length transaction. So long as a firm's wealth has increased (through holding gains), then that firm is better off at the end of the period than at the start, and the firm has had income. To the economist and some accountants, income should be

319

measured whether or not it has been realized in arms'-length transactions. Economic income, including all holding gains, is $410 in the example.

Exhibit 8.8
Using Replacement Cost Data to Analyze Components of Income

ASSUMED DATA

Beginning Inventory: T.V. Set 1 Cost		$250
Purchases:	T.V. Set 2 Cost	290
	T.V. Set 3 Cost	300
Historical Cost of Goods Available for Sale		$840
Sales: One T.V. Set for		$550
Replacement Cost of T.V. Sets on:		
Date of Sale		$320
At End of Period		$350

INCOME STATEMENT

Sales	$550
Replacement Cost of Goods Sold	320
Operating Margin	$230
Holding Gains for Year[a] (see calculation below)	180
Economic Income	$410

Calculation of Holding Gains for Year:

Replacement Cost at Time of Sale[a]	$ 320
Replacement Cost of Ending Inventory (2 × $350)	700
Total Replacement Cost	$1,020
Historical Cost of Goods Available for Sale	840
Total Holding Gains for Year	$ 180
Ending Inventory (2 T.V. sets, $350 current cost each)	$ 700

[a] To give some recognition to the realization convention, the total holding gain might be divided into realized and unrealized portions. To do so requires knowing the acquisition cost of the T.V. set sold, and that requires a cost-flow assumption. As Exhibit 8.7 indicates, if a LIFO assumption is made, then the realized holding gain is $20 and the realized income of $250 could be shown intermediate between the operating margin of $230 and the economic income of $410.

In recent years, generally accepted accounting principles have required major corporations to disclose the current cost of goods sold computed at the time of sale and the current cost of ending inventory. With such information, it is possible to measure operating margin and holding gains and to assess the economic performance of business firms. Chapter 14 discusses current costs more fully.

Summary

Inventory measurements affect both the cost-of-goods-sold expense on the income statement for the period and the amount shown for the asset, inventory, on the balance sheet at the end of the period. The sum of the two must be equal to the beginning inventory plus the cost of purchases, at least in accounting based on acquisition costs and market transactions. The allocation between expense and asset depends primarily on three factors:

1 The inventory system used.
2 The valuation basis used.
3 The cost-flow assumption used.

The first factor involves a choice between periodic and perpetual inventory systems. The second factor involves a choice among the acquisition-cost basis, the lower-of-cost-or-market basis, or some current cost basis. Lower of cost or market is most often used. The third factor concerns a choice among the FIFO, LIFO, and weighted-average cost-flow assumptions. When a current cost basis is used, there is no need to use a cost-flow assumption, except to separate realized from unrealized holding gains.

Problem 1 for Self-Study

Exhibit 8.9 presents data on beginning amounts of, additions to, and withdrawals from the inventory of item X during June. Beginning inventory is assumed to be 100 units, costing $10 each, in all cases.[9]

a Compute cost of goods sold and ending inventory using a FIFO cost-flow assumption. Note that periodic and perpetual methods give the same results.
b Compute cost of goods sold and ending inventory using a LIFO cost-flow assumption in a periodic inventory system.

Exhibit 8.9
Data for Illustration
of Inventory Calculations

Item X	Units	Unit Cost	Total Cost
Beginning Inventory, June 1	100	$10.00	$1,000
Purchases, June 7	400	11.00	4,400
Purchases, June 12	100	12.50	1,250
Total Goods Available for Sale at Cost	600		$6,650
Withdrawals, June 5	25		?
Withdrawals, June 10	10		?
Withdrawals, June 15	200		?
Withdrawals, June 25	260		?
Total Withdrawals During June	495		?
Ending Inventory, June 30	105		?
Replacement Cost Per Unit, June 30		$13.60	

[9]To simplify the problem, beginning inventory is shown as having the same opening valuation of $1,000 under all cost-flow assumptions. If costs had varied in the past, then the opening unit costs would have differed for each cost-flow assumption.

c Compute cost of goods sold and ending inventory using a LIFO cost-flow assumption in a perpetual inventory system.

d Compute cost of goods sold and ending inventory using a weighted-average cost-flow assumption in a periodic inventory system.

e Compute cost of goods sold and ending inventory using a weighted-average cost-flow assumption in a perpetual inventory system.

Exhibit 8.10
Ending Inventory and Cost-of-Goods-Sold Computation Using a Periodic Inventory System and a FIFO Cost-Flow Assumption

ITEM X

Ending Inventory Computation

100 units @ $12.50 (from June 12 purchase)	$1,250
5 units @ $11.00 (from June 7 purchase)	55
Ending Inventory, June 30	$1,305

Cost-of-Goods-Sold Computation

Cost of Goods Available for Sale	$6,650
Less Ending Inventory	1,305
Cost of Goods Sold	$5,345

Exhibit 8.11
Ending Inventory and Cost-of-Goods-Sold Computation Using a Periodic Inventory System and a LIFO Cost-Flow Assumption

ITEM X

Ending Inventory Computation

100 units @ $10.00 (from beginning inventory)	$1,000
5 units @ $11.00 (from first purchase, June 7)	55
Ending Inventory at Cost	$1,055

Cost-of-Goods-Sold Computation

Cost of Goods Available for Sale	$6,650
Less Ending Inventory	1,055
Cost of Goods Sold	$5,595

Suggested Solution

a See Exhibit 8.10.
b See Exhibit 8.11.
c See Exhibit 8.12.
d See Exhibit 8.13.
e See Exhibit 8.14.

Exhibit 8.12
Ending Inventory and
Cost-of-Goods-Sold Computation
Using a Perpetual Inventory
System and a LIFO Cost-Flow
Assumption

ITEM X
COST-OF-GOODS-SOLD COMPUTATION

		Received			Issued			Balance	
Date	**Units**	**Cost**	**Amount**	**Units**	**Cost**	**Amount**	**Units**	**Cost**	**Amount**
6/1							100	$10.00	$1,000
6/5				25	$10.00	$ 250	75	10.00	750
6/7	400	$11.00	$4,400				75	10.00	750
							400	11.00	4,400
6/10				10	11.00	110	75	10.00	750
							390	11.00	4,290
6/12	100	12.50	1,250				75	10.00	750
							390	11.00	4,290
							100	12.50	1,250
6/15				100	12.50	1,250	75	10.00	750
				100	11.00	1,100	290	11.00	3,190
6/25				260	11.00	2,860	75	10.00	750
							30	11.00	330
Cost of Goods Sold						$5,570			

ENDING INVENTORY COMPUTATION

75 units @ $10.00	$ 750
30 units @ $11.00	330
Ending Inventory	$1,080

ALTERNATIVE COST-OF-GOODS-SOLD COMPUTATION

Cost of Goods Available for Sale	$6,650
Less Ending Inventory	1,080
Cost of Goods Sold	$5,570

Exhibit 8.13
**Ending Inventory and Cost-of-Goods-Sold Computation
Using the Periodic Inventory System and a Weighted-Average
Cost-Flow Assumption**

ENDING INVENTORY COMPUTATION

6/01	100 units @ $10.00	$1,000
6/07	400 units @ $11.00	4,400
6/12	100 units @ $12.50	1,250
	600 units @ $11.08 (= $6,650/600)	$6,650
Ending Inventory (105 units @ $11.08)		$1,163

COST-OF-GOODS-SOLD COMPUTATION

Cost of Goods Available for Sale	$6,650
Less Ending Inventory	1,163
Cost of Goods Sold	$5,487[a]

[a]Because of rounding error, this number is *not* 495 (= 600 − 105) units $\times$ $11.08 = $5,485. In general, the weighted-average unit price should be applied either to ending inventory or to cost of goods sold. After being applied to one, the other is found from the inventory equation.

Exhibit 8.14
**Ending Inventory and Cost-of-Goods-Sold Computation
Using a Perpetual Inventory System and a Moving-Average
Cost-Flow Assumption**

ITEM X
COST-OF-GOODS-SOLD AND ENDING INVENTORY COMPUTATION

Date	Received			Issued			Balance		
	Units	Cost	Amount	Units	Cost	Amount	Units	Total Cost	Unit Cost[a]
6/1							100	$1,000	$10.00
6/5				25	$10.00	$ 250	75	750	10.00
6/7	400	$11.00	$4,400				475	5,150	10.84
6/10				10	10.84	108	465	5,042	10.84
6/12	100	12.50	1,250				565	6,292	11.14
6/15				200	11.14	2,228	365	4,064	11.13[b]
6/25				260	11.13	2,894	105	1,170	11.14
Cost of Goods Sold						$5,480			

ALTERNATIVE COST-OF-GOODS-SOLD COMPUTATION

Cost of Goods Available for Sale	$6,650
Less Ending Inventory	1,170
Cost of Goods Sold	$5,480

[a]Unit Cost = Total Cost/Units.
[b]Note how the rounding effects change the unit cost even though no new units were acquired.

324

Problem 2 for Self-Study

Refer to the data for item X in Exhibits 8.10 and 8.11, showing cost of goods sold and ending inventory in a periodic inventory system, using FIFO and LIFO cost-flow assumptions, respectively. Assume that the 495 units withdrawn from inventory were sold for $15 each, $7,425 in total. Construct a schedule that both separates operating margin from holding gains and separates *realized* holding gains from *unrealized* holding gains. Show the results for FIFO and LIFO in parallel columns. The total of operating margin and realized holding gain should be equal to the gross margin reported in historical cost income statements. The total of operating margin and all holding gains should be the same for LIFO as for FIFO.

Suggested Solution

See Exhibit 8.15.

Exhibit 8.15
Reporting of Operating Margins and Holding Gains for Item X

PERIODIC INVENTORY METHOD	Cost-Flow Assumption			
	FIFO		**LIFO**	
Sales Revenue from Item X (495 × $15.00)	$7,425		$7,425	
Less Replacement Cost of Goods Sold [(25 × $10.00) + (10 × $11.00) + (460 × $12.50)]	6,110		6,110	
Operating Margin on Sales of Item X		$1,315		$1,315
Realized Holding Gain on Item X:				
Replacement Cost of Goods Sold	$6,110		$6,110	
Less Acquisition Cost of Goods Sold (FIFO—Exhibit 8.10; LIFO—Exhibit 8.11)	5,345		5,595	
Realized Holding Gain on Item X		765		515
Conventionally Reported Gross Margin		$2,080		$1,830
Unrealized Holding Gain on Item X:				
Replacement Cost of Ending Inventory (105 × $13.60; see Exhibit 8.9)	$1,428		$1,428	
Less Acquisition Cost of Ending Inventory (FIFO—Exhibit 8.10; LIFO—Exhibit 8.11)	1,305		1,055	
Unrealized Holding Gain on Item X		123		373
Economic Profit on Sales and Holding Inventory of Item X		$2,203		$2,203

Problem 3 for Self-Study

American Steel Company uses a LIFO cost-flow assumption for inventories. Its year-end financial statements show the following amounts.

325

Balance Sheet Inventories:
Beginning of Year $1,500,000
End of Year $1,700,000
Income Statement Amounts:
Cost of Goods Sold $8,000,000
Income Before Taxes   800,000
Net Income (40 percent tax rate)   480,000
Supplementary Information in Notes on Inventory Provide Data on
the Excess of FIFO Cost Over Reported LIFO Cost of Inventory:
Beginning of Year $1,650,000
End of Year $1,850,000

a Compute the inventory-turnover ratio from the published financial statements based on LIFO cost flow.

b Compute the income before taxes assuming FIFO cost flow.

c Compute the net income assuming FIFO cost flow and an income tax rate of 40 percent.

d Compute the inventory-turnover ratio computed from the financial statements as they would appear using FIFO cost flow.

Suggested Solution

a Inventory Turnover $= \dfrac{\text{Cost of Goods Sold}}{\text{Average Inventory During Year}}$

$= \dfrac{\$8,000,000}{.5(\$1,500,000 + \$1,700,000)}$

$= 5$ times per year.

b Pretax income would be larger by the amount that cost of goods sold would be smaller. Cost of goods sold would be smaller by $200,000 = $1,850,000 − $1,650,000. See Exhibit 8.6.

c Net income would be larger by the amount found in **b** multiplied by (1 − income tax rate) = $200,000 × .60 = $120,000.

d Inventory Turnover $= \dfrac{\text{Cost of Goods Sold}}{\text{Average Inventory During Year}}$

$= \dfrac{\$8,000,000 - \$200,000}{.5[(\$1,500,000 + \$1,650,000) + (\$1,700,000 + \$1,850,000)]}$

$= \dfrac{\$7,800,000}{\$3,350,000}$

$= 2.33$ times per year.

Questions and Problems

1 Review the meaning of the following concepts or terms discussed in this chapter.

  a Inventory (both as a noun and as a verb).

  b Inventory equation.

326

c Purchases.
d Purchase returns.
e Purchase discounts.
f Shrinkages.
g Periodic inventory system.
h Perpetual inventory system.
i Acquisition-cost basis.
j Replacement cost.
k Net realizable value.
l Lower-of-cost-or-market basis.
m Standard cost.
n Absorption (full) costing.
o Direct (variable) costing.
p Cost-flow assumption.
q FIFO.
r LIFO.
s Weighted average.
t LIFO inventory layer contrasted to LIFO reserve.
u LIFO conformity.
v Realized holding gain.
w Unrealized holding gain.
x Inventory profit.

2 Goods that cost $1,500 are sold for $2,000 cash. Present the normal journal entries at the time of the sale:

 a When a periodic inventory system is used.
 b When a perpetual inventory system is used.

3 Which of the two inventory systems, periodic or perpetual, would you expect to find used in each of the following situations?

 a The greeting card department of a retail store.
 b The fur coat department of a retail store.
 c Supplies storeroom for an automated production line.
 d Automobile dealership.
 e Wholesale dealer in bulk salad oil.
 f Grocery store.
 g College bookstore.
 h Diamond ring department of a jewelry store.
 i Ballpoint pen department of a jewelry store.

4 Under what circumstances would the perpetual and periodic inventory systems both yield the same inventory amount if the weighted-average flow assumption were used?

5 A noted accountant once claimed that firms which use a LIFO cost-flow assumption will find that historical cost of goods sold is *greater than* replacement cost of goods sold computed as of the time of sale. Under what circumstances is this assertion likely to be true? (Hint: Compare the effects of periodic and perpetual systems on LIFO cost of goods sold.) Do you agree that the assertion is likely to be true?

6 During a period of rising prices, will the FIFO or LIFO cost-flow assumption result in the higher ending inventory amount? The lower inventory amount? Assume no changes in physical quantities during the period.

7 Refer to the preceding question. Which cost-flow assumption will result in the higher ending inventory amount during a period of declining prices? The lower inventory amount?

8 a During a period of rising prices, will a FIFO or LIFO cost-flow assumption result in the higher cost of goods sold? The lower cost of goods sold? Assume no changes in physical quantities during the period.

b Which cost-flow assumption, LIFO or FIFO, will result in the higher cost of goods sold during a period of declining prices? The lower cost of goods sold?

9 On December 30, 1982, merchandise amounting to $1,000 was received by the Warren Company and was counted in its December 31 listing of all inventory items on hand. The invoice was not received until January 4, 1983, at which time the acquisition was recorded as a 1983 acquisition. The acquisition should have been recorded for 1982. Assume that the error was not ever discovered by the firm. Warren Company uses a periodic inventory system. Indicate the effect (overstatement, understatement, none) on each of the following amounts. Ignore income taxes.

a Inventory, 12/31/82.
b Inventory, 12/31/83.
c Cost of goods sold, 1982.
d Cost of goods sold, 1983.
e Net income, 1982.
f Net income, 1983.
g Accounts payable, 12/31/82.
h Accounts payable, 12/31/83.
i Retained earnings, 12/31/83.

10 Indicate the effect on Working Capital Provided by Operations of the following independent transactions. Include the effects of income taxes, assuming a rate of 40 percent of pretax income and that the accounting methods used on the tax return are the same as on the financial statements.

a A firm using the lower-of-cost-or-market basis for inventories writes ending inventory down by $100,000.

b A firm has been using FIFO. It switches to LIFO during the current year and finds that the cost of goods sold is $200,000 larger than it would have been under FIFO.

11 The chapter points out that two alternatives for treating discounts on merchandise purchases are often used in practice: (1) the gross price method, which recognizes the amount of discounts taken on payments made during the period, without regard to the period of purchase, and (2) the net price method, which deducts all discounts made available from the gross purchase invoice prices at the time of purchases. This problem explains the two methods.

Alternative 1: Gross Price Method The gross price method of accounting for purchases records invoices at the gross price and accumulates the amount of discounts taken on payments made. Suppose that goods with a gross invoice price of $1,000 are purchased, 2/10, net/30. (That is, a 2-percent discount from invoice price is offered if payment is made within 10 days and the full invoice price is due, in any case, within 30 days.) The entries to record the purchase and the payment (1) under the assumption that the payment is made in time to take the discount, and (2) under the assumption that the payment is too late to take advantage of the discount, are as follows:

	(1) Discount Taken		(2) Discount Not Taken	
Gross Price Method				
Purchases (or Inventory)................	1,000		1,000	
Accounts Payable		1,000		1,000
To record purchase.				
Accounts Payable.....................	1,000		1,000	
Cash		980		1,000
Purchase Discounts (or Inventory)...........		20		—
To record payment.				

The balance in the Purchase Discounts account is deducted from the balance in the Purchases account in calculating net purchases for a period. Such a deduction merely approximates the results achieved by treating purchase discounts as a reduction in purchase price at the time of purchase. It is only an approximation because the total adjustment includes discounts taken on payments made this period, without regard to the period of purchase.

An accurate adjustment would require eliminating the discounts taken related to purchases of previous periods while including the amount of discounts available at the end of the accounting period that are expected to be taken during the following period. This refinement in the treatment of purchase discounts is seldom employed in practice.

Alternative 2: Net Price Method In recording purchases, the purchase discount is deducted from the gross purchase price immediately upon receipt of the invoice, and the net invoice price is used in the entries. The example used previously of a $1,000 invoice price for goods subject to a 2-percent cash discount would be recorded as follows under the net price method:

	(1) Discount Taken		(2) Discount Not Taken	
Net Price Method				
Purchases (or Inventory)................	980		980	
Accounts Payable		980		980
To record purchase.				
Accounts Payable.....................	980		980	
Purchase Discounts Lost................	—		20	
Cash		980		1,000
To record payment.				

The balance in the Purchase Discounts Lost account could be added to the cost of the merchandise purchased and, therefore, viewed as an additional component of goods available for sale. We believe, however, that discounts lost should be shown as a general operating expense rather than as an addition to the cost of purchases, because lost dis-

329

counts may indicate an inefficient office force or inadequate financing. In this text, we treat purchase discounts lost as an expense unless an explicit contrary statement is made.

a Attempt to decide which of these two alternatives is preferable and why. You might find working part **b**, below, helpful in making your decision.

b Prepare a journal form with two pairs of columns, one headed Net Price Method and the other headed Gross Price Method. Using this journal form, show summary entries for the following events in the history of Evans and Foster, furniture manufacturers.

(1) During the first year of operations, materials with a gross invoice price of $60,000 are purchased. All invoices are subject to a 2-percent cash discount if paid within 10 days.

(2) Payments to creditors during the year amount to $53,000, settling $54,000 of accounts payable at gross prices.

(3) Of the $6,000, gross, in unpaid accounts at the end of the year, the discount time has expired on one invoice amounting to $400. It is expected that all other discounts will be taken. This expectation is reflected in the year-end adjustment.

(4) During the first few days of the next period, all invoices are paid in accordance with expectations.

12 The accounts listed below might appear in the records of a retail store. Their use is never required, but accounts such as these are often a convenience. From the name of the account and your understanding of the accounting for purchases and sales, indicate:

a Whether the account is a permanent account (to appear as such on the balance sheet) or a temporary account (to be closed at the end of the accounting period).

b The normal balance, debit or credit, in the account. If the account is a temporary one, then give the normal balance prior to closing.

c If the account is a temporary one, the kind of account it is closed to—balance sheet asset, balance sheet liability, balance sheet owners' equity through a revenue account, or balance sheet owners' equity through an expense (or revenue contra) account.

(1) Merchandise Purchases.

(2) Merchandise Purchase Allowances.

(3) Merchandise Purchase Returns.

(4) Purchase Returns.

(5) Sales Tax on Purchases.

(6) Freight-in on Purchases.

(7) Sales Allowances.

(8) Allowance for Sales Discounts.

(9) Federal Excise Taxes Payable on Sales.

(The next two items should not be attempted until Problem **11** has been read.)

(10) Purchase Discounts.

(11) Purchase Discounts Taken.

(12) Purchase Discounts Lost.

13 (This problem should not be attempted until Problem **11** has been read.) The following are selected transactions of the Skousen Appliance Store:

a A shipment of refrigerators is received from the Standard Electric Company, $15,000. Terms 2/30, n/60.

b Part of the shipment of **a** is returned. The gross invoice price of the returned goods is $1,200, and a credit memorandum for this amount is received from the Standard Electric Company.

c The invoice of the Standard Electric Company is paid in time to take the discount.
   (1) Give entries on the books of the Skousen Appliance Store, assuming that the net price method is used.
   (2) Give entries on the books of the Skousen Appliance Store, assuming that the gross price method is used.

14 The Salem Company began business on January 1, 1980. The information concerning merchandise inventories, purchases, and sales for the first 3 years of operations is as follows:

	1980	1981	1982
Sales	$300,000	$330,000	$450,000
Purchases	280,000	260,000	350,000
Inventories, Dec. 31:			
At cost	80,000	95,000	95,000
At market	75,000	80,000	100,000

a Compute the gross margin on sales (sales minus cost of goods sold) for each year, using the lower-of-cost-or-market basis in valuing inventories.
b Compute the gross margin on sales (sales minus cost of goods sold) for each year, using the acquisition-cost basis in valuing inventories.
c Indicate your conclusion whether the lower-of-cost-or-market basis of valuing inventories is "conservative" in all situations where it is applied.

15 The merchandise inventory of Parks Store was destroyed by fire on July 4. The accounting records were saved. They provided the following information:

Cost of Merchandise Inventory on Hand, January 1	$ 45,000
Purchases of Merchandise, January 1 to July 4	125,000
Sales, January 1 to July 4	180,000

The average retail markup over cost of the goods sold during the year before the fire was 50 percent of the acquisition cost. That is, selling price equals 150 percent of cost.

a Estimate the cost of the goods on hand at the time of the fire.
b Give the journal entry to record the loss, assuming that it was uninsured.
c Give the journal entry to record the loss, assuming that all goods were fully insured for their acquisition cost.

16 Refer to the data in the preceding problem. Assume that the store owner does not know the average retail markup over cost for the destroyed goods. The accounting records show that the total sales revenue during the 4 years preceding the fire amounted to $1,000,000 and the total cost of goods sold over the same period was $650,000.

a Assuming that the ratio of sales prices to cost of goods sold for the last 4 years holds for this year, estimate the cost of the goods destroyed in the fire.
b Assume the same facts as above, except that the $1,000,000 represents the original selling price of the goods sold during the last 4 years. Certain goods were marked down before sale so that the actual sales revenue was only $975,000. Assuming that the same

331

percentage of goods were marked down by the same price percentage during the first 6 months of this year, as in the previous 4 years, estimate the cost of the goods destroyed by the fire.

17 The inventory footnote to the 1982 annual report of the Alcher Company reads in part as follows:

Because of continuing high demand throughout the year, inventories were unavoidably reduced and could not be replaced. Under the LIFO system of accounting, used for many years by Alcher Company, the net effect of all the inventory changes was to increase pretax income by $600,000 over what it would have been had inventories been maintained at their physical levels at the start of the year.

The price of Alcher Company's merchandise purchases was $11 per unit during 1982 after having risen steadily for many years. Alcher Company uses a periodic inventory method. Alcher Company's inventory positions at the beginning and end of the year are summarized below:

Date	Physical Count of Inventory	LIFO Cost of Inventory
January 1, 1982	300,000 units	$?
December 31, 1982	200,000 units	$2,600,000

a What was the average cost per unit of the 100,000 units removed from the January 1, 1982, LIFO inventory?
b What was the January 1, 1982, LIFO cost of inventory?

18 The inventory at September 1 and the purchases during September of Hanna Company's raw material were as follows:

9/1 Inventory	1,000 lbs.	$ 4,500
9/5 Purchased	3,000 lbs.	13,500
9/14 Purchased	3,500 lbs.	17,500
9/27 Purchased	3,000 lbs.	16,500
9/29 Purchased	1,000 lbs.	8,000

The inventory at September 30 is 1,800 pounds.

Assume a periodic inventory system. Compute the cost of the inventory on September 30 under each of the following cost-flow assumptions:

a FIFO.
b Weighted average.
c LIFO.

19 The following information concerning Arpesfeld Company's inventory of raw materials is available:

Nov. 2 Inventory.	4,000 lbs. @ $5
9 Issued	3,000 lbs.
16 Purchased.	7,000 lbs. @ $6
23 Issued	3,000 lbs.
30 Issued	3,000 lbs.

Compute the cost of goods sold and the cost of ending inventory on November 30 for each of the following combinations of inventory systems and cost-flow assumptions.

a Periodic FIFO.
b Periodic weighted average.
c Periodic LIFO.
d Perpetual FIFO.
e Perpetual weighted average.
f Perpetual LIFO.

20 The Central Supply Company has in its inventory on May 1 three units of item K, all purchased on the same date at a price of $60 per unit. Information relative to item K is as follows:

Date	Explanation	Units	Unit Cost	Tag Number
May 1	Inventory	3	$60	K–515,516,517
3	Purchase	2	65	K–518,519
12	Sale	3		K–515,518,519
19	Purchase	2	76	K–520,521
25	Sale	1		K–516

Compute the cost of units sold in accordance with the following:

a Specific identification of units sold.
b FIFO cost-flow assumption and periodic inventory system.
c FIFO cost-flow assumption and perpetual inventory system.
d LIFO cost-flow assumption and periodic inventory system.
e LIFO cost-flow assumption and perpetual inventory system.
f Weighted-average cost-flow assumption and perpetual inventory system.
g Weighted-average cost-flow assumption and periodic inventory system.

21 The Harrison Corporation was organized and began retailing operations on January 1, 1981. Purchases of merchandise inventory during 1981 and 1982 were as follows:

	Quantity Purchased	Unit Price	Acquisition Cost
1/10/81	1,000	$10	$10,000
6/30/81	400	15	6,000
10/20/81	200	16	3,200
Total 1981	1,600		$19,200

	Quantity Purchased	Unit Price	Acquisition Cost
2/18/82	300	$18	$ 5,400
7/15/82	100	20	2,000
12/15/82	500	22	11,000
Total 1982	900		$18,400

The number of units sold during 1981 and 1982 was 900 units and 1,100 units, respectively. Harrison Corporation uses a periodic inventory system.

a Calculate the cost of goods sold during 1981 under the FIFO cost-flow assumption.

b Calculate the cost of goods sold during 1981 under the LIFO cost-flow assumption.

c Calculate the cost of goods sold during 1981 under the weighted-average cost-flow assumption.

d Calculate the cost of goods sold during 1982 under the FIFO cost-flow assumption.

e Calculate the cost of goods sold during 1982 under the LIFO cost-flow assumption.

f Calculate the cost of goods sold during 1982 under the weighted-average cost-flow assumption.

g For the 2 years, 1981 and 1982, taken as a whole, will FIFO or LIFO result in reporting the larger net income? What is the difference in net income for the 2-year period under FIFO as compared to LIFO? Assume an income tax rate of 40 percent for both years.

h Which method, LIFO or FIFO, should Harrison Corporation probably prefer and why?

22 (This problem should not be attempted until Problem **21** has been done.) Assume the same data for the Harrison Corporation as given in the previous problem. In addition, assume the following:

Selling Price per Unit:	
1981	$25
1982	30
Average Current Replacement Cost:	
1981	$15
1982	20
Current Replacement Cost:	
December 31, 1981.	$17
December 31, 1982.	22

a Prepare an analysis for 1981 that identifies operating margins, realized holding gains and losses, and unrealized holding gains and losses for the FIFO, LIFO, and weighted-average cost-flow assumptions.

b Repeat part **a** for 1982.

c Demonstrate that over the 2-year period, the economic profits before taxes of Harrison Corporation are independent of the cost-flow assumption.

23 On January 1, the merchandise inventory of Revsine Appliance Store consisted of 1,000 units acquired for $450 each. During the year, 2,500 additional units were acquired at an average price of $600 each while 2,300 units were sold for $900 each. The replacement cost of these units at the time they were sold averaged $600 during the year. The replacement cost of units on December 31 was $750 per unit.

a Calculate cost of goods sold under both FIFO and LIFO cost-flow assumptions.

b Prepare partial statements of income showing gross margin on sales as revenues less cost of goods sold with both FIFO and LIFO cost-flow assumptions.

c Prepare partial income statements separating the gross margin on sales into operating margins and realized holding gains under both FIFO and LIFO.

d Append to the bottom of the statements prepared in part **c** a statement showing the amount of unrealized holding gains and the total of realized income plus unrealized holding gains.

e If you did the above steps correctly, the totals in part **d** are the same for both FIFO and LIFO. Is this equality a coincidence? Why or why not?

24 The Sanlex Company started the year with no inventories on hand. It manufactured two batches of inventory, 100 units each, which were identical except that the variable costs of producing the first batch were $120 and the variable costs of producing the second batch were $200 because of rising prices. By the end of the year, Sanlex Company had sold 75 units from the first batch for $300 and none of the second batch. The ending inventory had a market value of $305. Total fixed manufacturing costs for the year were $160. Under the absorption costing procedure, $100 of fixed manufacturing costs allocated to units produced remained in inventory at the close of the year. Selling and administrative expenses for the year were $40.

Prepare a statement of pretax income for the Sanlex Company for the year under each of the following sets of assumptions.

a FIFO, acquisition-cost basis.

b LIFO, acquisition-cost basis.

c FIFO, lower-of-cost-or-market basis.

25 This problem tries to make clear the difference between the impact on financial statements of the choice between a FIFO and a LIFO flow assumption. Take 12 pieces of paper and mark each one with a number between 1 and 12 inclusive. Sort the pieces of paper into a pile with the numbers in consecutive order facing up, so that number 1 is on top and number 12 is on bottom. These 12 pieces of paper are to represent 12 identical units of merchandise purchased at prices increasing from $1 to $12. Assume that four of the units are purchased each period for three periods, that three units are sold each period, and that the periodic inventory method is used.

a Compute the cost-of-goods-sold and ending-inventory amounts for each of the three periods under a FIFO flow assumption.

b Compute the cost-of-goods-sold and ending-inventory amounts for each of the three periods under a LIFO flow assumption.

c Re-sort the 12 pieces of paper into decreasing order to represent declining prices for successive purchases. Compute the cost-of-goods-sold and ending-inventory amounts for each of the three periods under a FIFO flow assumption.

d Repeat part **c** using a LIFO flow assumption.

e If you are not convinced that the following are all true statements, then repeat parts **a–d** until you are.

(1) In periods of rising prises and increasing physical inventories, FIFO implies higher reported income than does LIFO.

335

(2) In periods of declining prices and increasing physical inventories, LIFO implies higher reported income than does FIFO.

(3) Under FIFO, current prices are reported on the balance sheet and old prices are reported on the income statement.

(4) Under LIFO, current prices are reported on the income statement and very old prices are reported on the balance sheet.

(5) The difference between FIFO and LIFO balance sheet amounts for inventory at the end of each period after the first one is larger than the differences between FIFO and LIFO reported net income for each period after the first one.

f Assume that in period 4, only one unit (number 13) is purchased for $13, but three are sold. What additional "truth" can you deduce from comparing LIFO and FIFO cost of goods sold when physical quantities are declining?

g The LIFO portion of Figure 8.1 represents a periodic inventory method. In this part of the question, assume that in each period the first item is acquired before any sales occur. Then one item is sold; then the two items are purchased; then one more item is sold; then the last purchase is made and the last sale occurs. (If P represents purchase and S represents sale, the events of each period are PSPPSPS.) Draw a figure similar to those in Figure 8.1 to represent a LIFO cost-flow assumption coupled with a perpetual inventory system. Convince yourself that in times of rising prices the LIFO cost-

Figure 8.1
To Aid in Understanding Problem 25

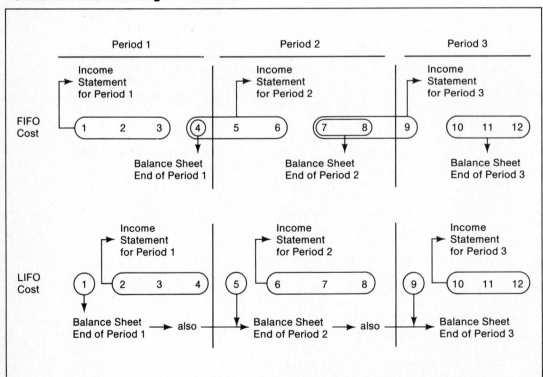

336

of-goods-sold figure with a periodic method exceeds LIFO cost of goods sold computed under a perpetual method.

26 The purpose of this problem is to help you explore the relationship between replacement cost of goods sold and historical LIFO cost of goods sold. The points to note are as follows:

(1) LIFO cost of goods sold is generally larger in a periodic system than in a perpetual system.

(2) LIFO cost of goods sold for most companies is insignificantly different from replacement cost of goods sold using replacement costs as of the time of sale.

(3) Historical LIFO cost of goods sold in a periodic inventory system is likely to be larger (although not significantly) than the replacement cost of goods sold using replacement cost at the time of sale.

Exhibit 8.16
Data for Problem 26

	Replacement Cost of Goods Measured at	
	Sales Dates (Mid-Month)	Purchases Dates (End of Month)
December 1981	—	$ 300,000
January 1982	$ 201,000	202,000
February 1982	203,000	204,000
March 1982	205,000	206,000
April 1982	207,000	208,000
May 1982.	209,000	210,000
June 1982	211,000	212,000
July 1982.	213,000	214,000
August 1982	215,000	216,000
September 1982.	217,000	218,000
October 1982	219,000	220,000
November 1982	221,000	222,000
December 1982	223,000	224,000
Replacement Cost of Goods Sold at Times of Sale	$2,544,000	
Cost of Goods Available for Sale		$2,856,000

The accompanying data are hypothetical. They are constructed from ratios of an actual retailing firm selling grocery products. Sales revenue for the year is $2,820,000. All expenses (including income taxes) other than cost of goods sold are $144,000 for the year. Exhibit 8.16 shows cost of goods available for sale. The costs of the grocery items for this company increase during the year at a steady rate of about 1 percent per month. The company starts the year with an inventory equal to $1\frac{1}{2}$ months' sales. These items were acquired at the end of December 1981 for $300,000. At the end of each month during 1982, the firm is assumed to acquire inventory in physical quantities equal to the next month's sales requirements. We assume that all sales occur at mid-month during each month and that all purchases occur at the end of a month to be sold during the next month. (These artificial assumptions capture the reality of a firm acquiring inventory on average $\frac{1}{2}$ month before it is sold and inventory-turnover rate of about eight times per year.) Identical physical quantities are purchased and sold each month.

Exhibit 8.16 shows the actual cost of the items purchased at the end of each month and the replacement cost of those items if they had been acquired at mid-month.

At the end of the year, ending physical inventory is equal in amount to $1\frac{1}{2}$ months' sales, which is the same as the physical quantity on hand at the start of the year.

a Compute LIFO historical cost of goods sold and net income for 1982 using a periodic inventory system.

b Compute LIFO historical cost of goods sold and net income for 1982 using a perpetual inventory system.

c Compute net income for 1982 using replacement cost of goods sold at the time of sale.

d What is the percentage difference between the largest and smallest cost-of-goods-sold figures computed in the preceding 3 parts?

e What is the percentage error in using LIFO costs of goods sold to approximate replacement cost of goods sold? (Compute percentage errors for both LIFO periodic and LIFO perpetual calculations.)

f Would you expect that most companies that use LIFO for tax purposes do so with a periodic inventory system or with a perpetual inventory system? Why?

27 The LIFO Company and the FIFO Company both manufacture paper and cardboard products. Prices of timber, paper pulp, and finished paper products have generally increased by about 5 percent per year through the *start of this year.* Inventory data for the beginning and end of the year are shown below:

	January 1	December 31
LIFO Company Inventory (last-in, first-out)	$19,695,000	$15,870,000
FIFO Company Inventory (first-in, first-out, lower of cost or market)	46,284,000	38,250,000

Income statements for the two companies for the year ending December 31 are as follows:

	LIFO Company	FIFO Company
Sales	$57,000,000	$129,000,000
Expenses:		
Cost of Goods Sold	$44,580,000	$108,000,000
Depreciation	5,400,000	12,000,000
General Expenses	2,220,000	5,400,000
Income Taxes (40 percent of pretax income)	1,920,000	1,440,000
Total Expenses	$54,120,000	$126,840,000
Net Income	$ 2,880,000	$ 2,160,000

a Assuming that the prices for timber, paper pulp, and finished paper had remained unchanged during the year, how would the two companies' respective inventory valuation methods affect the interpretation of their financial statements for the year?

b How would the answer to part **a** differ if prices at the end of the year had been lower than at the beginning of the year?

c How would the answer to part **a** differ if prices at the end of the year had been higher than at the beginning of the year?

28 The Wilson Company sells chemical compounds made from expensium. The company has used a LIFO inventory-flow assumption for many years. The inventory of expensium on January 1, 1976 consisted of 2,000 pounds from the inventory bought in 1972 for $30 a pound. The following schedule shows purchases and physical ending inventories of expensium for the years 1976 through 1981.

Year	Purchase Price per Pound during Year	Cost of Units Purchased	End-of-Year Inventory in Pounds
1976	$48	$240,000	2,000
1977	46	296,000	2,200
1978	48	368,000	3,000
1979	50	384,000	3,600
1980	50	352,000	2,600
1981	52	448,000	4,000

Because of temporary scarcities, expensium is expected to cost $62 per pound during 1982 but to fall back to $52 per pound in 1983. Sales for 1982 are expected to require 7,000 pounds of expensium. The purchasing agent suggests that the inventory of expensium be allowed to decrease from 4,000 to 600 pounds by the end of 1982 and to be replenished to the desired level of 4,000 pounds early in 1983.

The controller argues that such a policy would be foolish. If inventories are allowed to decrease to 600 pounds, then the cost of goods sold will be extraordinarily low (because the older LIFO purchases will be consumed) and income taxes will be extraordinarily high. Furthermore, he points out that the diseconomies of smaller orders during 1982, as required by the purchasing agent's plan, would lead to about $4,000 of extra costs for record keeping. These costs would be treated as an expense for 1982. He suggests that 1982 purchases should be planned to maintain an end-of-year inventory of 4,000 pounds.

Assume that sales for 1982 do require 7,000 pounds of expensium, that the prices for 1982 and 1983 are as forecast, and that the income tax rate for Wilson Company is 40 percent.

Calculate the cost of goods sold and end-of-year LIFO inventory:

a For each of the years 1976 through 1981.

b For 1982, assuming that the controller's advice is followed so that inventory at the end of 1982 is 4,000 pounds.

c For 1982, assuming that the purchasing agent's advice is followed and inventory at the end of 1982 is 600 pounds.

Assuming that the controller's, not the purchasing agent's, advice is followed, calculate:

d The tax savings for 1982.

e The extra cash costs for inventory.

f Using the results derived so far, what should Wilson Company do?

g Would your advice be different if Wilson Company used a FIFO cost-flow assumption?

29 The Burch Corporation began a merchandising business on January 1, 1980. It acquired merchandise costing $100,000 in 1980, $125,000 in 1981, and $135,000 in 1982. Exhibit 8.17

339

shows information about Burch Corporation's inventory, as it would appear on the balance sheet under different inventory methods.

Exhibit 8.17
Burch Corporation
Inventory Valuations for Balance
Sheet under Various Assumptions (Problem 29)

Date	LIFO Cost	FIFO Cost	Lower FIFO Cost or Market
12/31/80	$40,200	$40,000	$37,000
12/31/81	36,400	36,000	34,000
12/31/82	41,800	44,000	44,000

In answering each of the following questions, indicate how the answer is deduced. You may assume that in any one year, prices moved only up or down, but not both, in the same year.

a Did prices go up or down in 1980?

b Did prices go up or down in 1982?

c Which inventory method would show the highest income for 1980?

d Which inventory method would show the highest income for 1982?

e Which inventory method would show the highest income for 1981?

f Which inventory method would show the lowest income for all three years combined?

g For 1982 how much higher or lower would income be on the FIFO cost basis than it would be on the lower-of-cost-or-market basis?

30 The notes to the financial statements in an annual report of the Westinghouse Electric Corporation contain the following statement. "The excess of current cost [or inventories] ... over the cost of inventories valued on the LIFO basis was $230 million at [year-end] and $163 million at [the beginning of the year]."

a How much higher or lower would Westinghouse's pretax reported income have been if its inventories had been valued at current costs, rather than with a LIFO cost-flow assumption?

b Westinghouse reported $28 million net income for the year. Assume tax expense equal to 46 percent of pretax income. By what percentage would Westinghouse's net income increase if a FIFO flow assumption had been used?

31 Exhibit 8.18 shows data for the General Electric Company's inventories (excluding uranium subsidiaries) for a period of years under the LIFO assumption as actually used and under FIFO, as they would have been if it had been used.

a Compute the pretax income for years 2 through 6, assuming that a FIFO cost-flow assumption had been used.

b Calculate the percentage change in pretax income for each of the years 3 through 6 under both LIFO and FIFO (that is, the increase in pretax income in year 3 relative to year 2, the increase in pretax income in year 4 relative to year 3, and so on).

Exhibit 8.18
**General Electric Company
(amounts in millions)**
(Problem 31)

End of Year	LIFO Ending Inventory	FIFO Ending Inventory
1	$1,611.7	$1,884.5
2	1,759.0	2,063.1
3	1,986.2	2,415.9
4	2,257.0	3,040.7
5	2,202.9	3,166.6
6	2,354.4	3,515.2

For the Year	Pretax Operating Income Using LIFO
2	$ 897.2
3	1,011.6
4	1,000.7
5	1,174.0
6	1,627.5

	Amounts in Millions	
End of Year	Current Assets	Current Liabilities
2	$3,979.3	$2,869.7
3	4,485.4	3,492.4
4	5,222.6	3,879.5
5	5,750.4	4,163.0
6	6,685.0	4,604.9

c Calculate the percentage change in pretax income between year 2 and year 6 (that is, the 5-year period taken as a whole) under both LIFO and FIFO.

d Did the quantity of items in inventory increase or decrease during each of the years 3 through 6? How can you tell?

e Did the acquisition cost of items in inventory increase or decrease during each of the years 3 through 6? How can you tell?

f Assume for this part that the inventory value under LIFO at the end of year 1 of $1,611.7 is the initial LIFO layer. This layer may be viewed as the bottom layer on a cake. Construct a figure showing the addition or subtraction of LIFO layers for each of the years 2 through 6.

g The current assets and current liabilities of the General Electric Company at the end of years 2 through 6 using a LIFO cost-flow assumption are shown in Exhibit 8.18. Compute General Electric's current ratio for each year using the data given.

h Recompute General Electric's current ratio for each year using a FIFO cost-flow assumption for inventories. Although it is unrealistic to do so, assume for this part that there are no changes in income taxes payable or in current liabilities. (To make the figures realistic after taxes, ending LIFO inventory should be increased by about *one-half* the difference between FIFO and LIFO ending inventory amounts. Why?)

32 The financial statements of the General Products Company (GP) are included in Appendix A at the back of this book. Refer to the data for 1982.

a GP uses a LIFO cost-flow assumption. There is sufficient information given in the notes for you to construct hypothetical financial statements assuming both that GP used a FIFO cost-flow assumption and that GP used a current-cost basis for inventories, without any cost-flow assumption. Some of this is done in Exhibit 8.6. For each of these treatments—LIFO, FIFO, current cost—compute each of the following ratios (ignoring income tax effects):

(1) Current ratio.
(2) Inventory turnover ratio.
(3) Rate of return on shareholders' equity.

(Make current cost adjustments only for effects on inventory, ignoring effects for property, plant, and equipment. When assuming a FIFO cost-flow assumption or a current-value basis for inventory, be sure to increase owners' equity by the same amount that you increase ending inventory. When you hypothetically debit ending inventory to increase it, you must also credit owners' equity.)

b What inferences can you draw from the computations done in part **a** about comparing the financial statements of a company using LIFO with ones of a company using FIFO? What inferences can you draw about the comparison of financial statements using historical-cost accounting for inventories with those based on current values measured by replacement cost?

33 Data for companies A, B, and C shown in Exhibit 8.19 are taken from the annual reports of three actual companies in the same industry for a recent year. One of these companies uses a LIFO cost-flow assumption for 100 percent of its inventories, another uses LIFO for about 60 percent of its inventories, and the other uses LIFO for about 45 percent of its

---

Exhibit 8.19
Data for Analysis of
LIFO and FIFO
Effects on Financial Statements
(*Problems 33 and 34*)

	Dollar Amounts in Millions				
			Company		
	A	**B**	**C**	**D**	**E**
Sales Revenue	$14,950	$10,445	$5,152	$15,697	$5,042
Cost of Goods Sold:ᵃ					
Historical Cost Basis	13,497	8,318	3,638	10,852	3,720
Replacement Cost Basis	13,432	8,322	3,675	11,110	3,720
Net Income.	695	106	108	931	383
Ending Inventory:					
Historical Cost Basis	2,215	756	1,026	2,265	1,245
Replacement Cost Basis	2,303	875	1,056	3,540	2,169
Ratio of Net Income					
to Revenue	4.6%	1.0%	2.1%	5.9%	7.6%

ᵃExcludes depreciation charges.

inventories. From these data and the lessons of this chapter, answer the following questions, making explicit the reasoning used in each case.

a From the cost-of-goods-sold data alone, which of the companies appears to be the 100-percent LIFO company? The 60-percent LIFO company? The 45-percent LIFO company?

b From the ending-inventory data alone, which of the companies appears to be the 100-percent LIFO company? The 60-percent LIFO company? The 45-percent LIFO company?

c From your answers to parts **a** and **b**, draw a conclusion as to which of the companies appears to be which.

d Note that Company A earned net income equal to 4.6 percent of sales, where Company B earned net income equal to 1.0 percent of sales. Can you conclude that Company A is more profitable than Company B? Why or why not?

e Although all three of these companies are in the same industry, the nature of the goods sold and the operations of two of the companies are somewhat different from the nature of the goods sold and the operations of the third. Which of the three appears to be the one that is different from the other two?

34 (This question should not be attempted until the preceding question has been read.) Data for Company D and Company E shown in Exhibit 8.19 are taken from the annual reports of two actual companies for a recent year. One of these companies uses a LIFO cost-flow assumption for all of its inventories, whereas the other uses LIFO for only a portion. From these data and the lessons of this chapter, answer the following questions, making explicit the reasoning you used.

a Which of the two companies is more likely to be the 100-percent LIFO company?

b Data for companies A, B, and C are also shown in Exhibit 8.19. These three companies are in an industry much different from the industries that include Company D and Company E. Which of the two industries is more likely to be related to retailing and which is more likely to be related to manufacturing?

Chapter 9 *Long-lived Assets and Amortization Expense*

Assets are future benefits. Assets are either short-lived or long-lived. A business acquires a short-lived asset, such as cash, in one period and can use up its benefits in the same period. A long-lived asset is different: To enjoy all its benefits, the owner must use it for many years. In these cases, the accountant must apportion, or allocate, the cost of the asset over the several accounting periods of benefit. This general process is called *amortization*. Amortization of *plant assets,* which include the fixtures, machinery, equipment, and physical structures of a business, is called *depreciation.*

In addition to its plant assets, a company such as Gulf Oil has other long-lived assets. Oil companies own natural gas and oil wells. These natural resources are called *wasting assets.* Oil wells, coal mines, uranium deposits, and other natural resources are eventually used up, and amortization of the cost of these wasting assets is called *depletion.*

Businesses may also acquire *intangible assets* and, although there are many examples of them, some of the best-known ones are everyday words such as *Coca-Cola, Kleenex,* and *Kodak,* all famous trademarks. A local operator may pay several thousand dollars to acquire a McDonald's or Kentucky Fried Chicken franchise. Such franchises frequently do not have a perpetual life; the accountant must amortize their costs.

Most of this chapter treats depreciation because plant assets[1] are the most com-

---

[1] The terms *plant assets* and *fixed assets* are often used interchangeably. They refer to long-lived assets used in the operations of trading, service, and manufacturing enterprises, and include land, buildings, machinery, and equipment. The ordinary usage of the terms *plant assets* and *fixed assets* often does not adequately encompass the class of long-lived assets that includes all land, buildings, machinery, and equipment. *Plant assets* is sometimes used too narrowly to mean only items in a factory or plant. *Fixed assets* is sometimes used too narrowly to mean only items such as land and buildings that are immovable and tend to have very long service lives.

344

mon long-lived assets, and depreciation problems are typical of almost all other amortization problems.

The problems of plant asset valuation and depreciation expense measurement can be conveniently separated into the consideration of four separate kinds of events:

1 Recording the acquisition of the asset.
2 Recording its use over time.
3 Recording adjustments for changes in capacity or efficiency and for repairs or improvements.
4 Recording its retirement or other disposal.

Acquisition of Plant Assets

The cost of a plant asset includes all charges necessary to prepare it for rendering services, and it is often recorded in a series of transactions. Thus, the cost of a piece of equipment will be the sum of the entries to recognize the invoice price (less any discounts), transportation costs, installation charges, and any other costs necessary before the equipment is ready for use. When a firm acquires a new asset in exchange for an old one, such as in a trade-in transaction or a bartered transaction, the fair market value of the assets given up plus any cash disbursed in the transaction should be used as the cost of the new asset. Trade-in transactions are discussed later in this chapter.

Improvements versus Repairs

Repair and maintenance *costs* will almost certainly occur during the life of the asset These costs are required to *maintain* the service level anticipated from the asset and are treated as expenses of the period. Once an asset is in service, certain costs may be incurred to *improve* the asset and should be "capitalized," or added to its cost. Improvements are defined as those costs that extend the life of the asset, increase the asset's output, or reduce the cost of operating the asset. It is often difficult to decide whether a particular expenditure is a repair to be treated as a period expense or is an improvement to be treated as an asset. The line between maintaining service and improving or extending it is not a distinct one. Some expenditures seem to meet the criteria to be either a repair expense or an improvement cost. There is frequent disagreement between Internal Revenue Service and taxpayers, as well as among accountants, over this question in specific situations.

Fundamental Concepts

Depreciation

Most plant assets can be kept intact and in usable operating condition for more than a year, but, except for land, eventually they must be retired from service. The central purpose of the depreciation accounting process is to allocate the cost of these assets to the periods of their use in a reasonable and orderly fashion.

345

It is useful to think of the cost of an asset with a limited life as the price paid for a series of future services—a purchase of so many hours or other units of service. When deciding to purchase a building or machine, the purchaser need not make elaborate calculations to arrive at the present value of a series of precisely appraised future benefits, but the purchaser must at least roughly approximate those procedures. It would be irrational to purchase an asset if the present value of the services expected to be received from it were known to be less than the required investment.

The investment in a depreciating asset is the price paid for a series of future services. The asset account may well be considered as a prepayment, similar in many respects to prepaid rent or insurance—a payment in advance for services to be received. As the asset is used in each accounting period, an appropriate portion of the investment in the asset is treated as the cost of the service received and is recognized as an expense of the period or as part of the cost of goods produced during the period.

The Causes of Depreciation

The causes of depreciation are the causes of decline in an asset's service-rendering potential and of its ultimate retirement. Unless the asset must eventually be retired from its planned use, there is no depreciation. The services or benefits provided by land do not ordinarily diminish over time, so land is not depreciated. Many factors lead to the retirement of assets from service, but the causes of decline in service potential can be classified as either *physical* or *functional.* The physical factors include such things as ordinary wear and tear from use, chemical action such as rust or electrolysis, and the effects of wind and rain. The most important functional or nonphysical cause is *obsolescence.* Inventions, for example, may result in new equipment, the use of which reduces the unit cost of production to the point where continued operation of the old asset is not economical, even though it may be relatively unimpaired physically. Retail stores often replace display cases and storefronts long before they are worn out in order to keep the appearance of the store as attractive as their competitors'. Changed economic conditions may also become functional causes of depreciation, such as when an old airport becomes inadequate and must be abandoned, and a new, larger one is built to meet the requirements of heavier traffic, or when an increase in the cost of gasoline causes a reduction in demand for automobile products, which results in a reduced scale of operations in automobile manufacturing.

Identifying the specific causes of depreciation is not essential for considering the fundamental problem of its measurement. It is enough to know that almost any physical asset will eventually have to be retired from service and that in some cases the retirement will become necessary at a time when physical deterioration is negligible. The specific causes do become important, however, when the attempt is made to estimate the useful life of an asset.

Depreciation as a Decline in Value

Depreciation is frequently used in ordinary conversation to mean a decline in value. Such an interpretation may be fundamentally sound when applied to the entire service life of a plant asset; there certainly is a decline in the value of an asset from the time it is acquired until it is retired from service. However, a decline in asset values is an unsatisfactory description of the charge made to the operations of each accounting period. One incorrect inference from such a description is that if, in a given period of time, there has been an increase in the value of an asset, such as an increase arising from increasing prices for the asset, then there has been no depreciation during that period. Rather, there have been two partially offsetting processes: (1) a holding gain on the asset, which usually is not recognized in historical cost-based accounting, and (2) depreciation of the asset's historical cost. As the previous chapter indicated, a holding gain is an increase in the market price of an asset since the time the asset was acquired or last revalued.

Further, the word *value* has so many uses and connotations that it is not a serviceable term for a definition. (The noun *value* should seldom be used in accounting without a qualifying adjective.) If depreciation is defined as a decline in value and the undepreciated balance of an asset account as a "present" value, it is usually necessary to explain that under generally accepted accounting principles, it is value to the going concern based on historical cost, not on selling price, not on second-hand value, nor on replacement cost. The word *value* is not entirely inappropriate in describing an element of depreciation, but it is not helpful in isolating its essence.

Summary of Depreciation Concepts

Depreciation is a process of cost allocation, not one of valuation. This chapter discusses the problems of *allocating* assets' costs to the periods of benefits. A depreciation problem will exist whenever (1) capital is invested in services to be rendered by a plant asset, and (2) when, at some reasonably predictable date in the future, the asset has to be retired from service with a residual value less than its cost because of a decline in service potential. The problem is to interpret and account satisfactorily for this diminution of the investment in the asset.

Note especially that replacing the asset is *not* essential to the existence of depreciation. Depreciation is the expiration or disappearance of investment from the time the plant asset is put into use until the time it is retired from service. Whether or not the asset is replaced is completely independent of the amount or treatment of its depreciation.

Depreciation Accounting Problems

There are three principal accounting problems in allocating the cost of an asset over time:

1 Determining the depreciable basis of the asset.

2 Estimating its useful service life.

3 Deciding on the pattern of expiration of services over the useful service life.

Calculating the Periodic Charge

Determining the amount of the periodic charge for depreciation is not an exact process. The cost of the plant asset is a *joint cost* of the several benefited periods. That is, each of the periods of the asset's use benefits from its services. There is usually no logically correct way to allocate a joint cost. The depreciation process seeks to assign reasonable periodic charges that reflect a careful and systematic method of calculation.

Whenever it is feasible to do so, depreciation should be computed for individual items such as a single building, machine, or truck. Where many similar items are in use and each one has a relatively small cost, individual calculations may be impracticable and the depreciation charge is usually calculated for the group as a whole. Furniture and fixtures, tools, and telephone poles are examples of assets that are usually depreciated in groups. Group depreciation techniques are treated in advanced financial accounting courses. The basic principles of depreciating individual items discussed here apply in a similar manner, however, to group depreciation situations.

Depreciable Basis of Plant Assets

Depreciation charges have traditionally been based on the acquisition cost of the asset less (except for declining-balance methods described later) the estimated residual value—the amount to be received when the asset is retired from service. As inflation has become recognized as a major economic problem, there has been increasing recognition that basing depreciation charges on acquisition costs will not, in most cases, charge amounts to expense that are sufficient for maintaining the productive capacity of the business. Basing depreciation on acquisition costs will enable a business to provide for maintenance of its financial position measured in historical dollars but not of its physical productive capacity in periods of rising prices.

FASB *Statement No. 33*[2] requires major corporations to disclose as supplemental information depreciation charges both measured in constant dollars and based on current costs. The formal financial statements retain acquisition cost measured in nominal dollars as the basis for depreciation calculations and reporting. Chapter 14 describes the calculation and reporting of depreciation to reflect the effect of changing prices.

Interest during Construction

When a firm constructs its own buildings or equipment, many entries to record the labor, material, and overhead costs will normally be required before the total cost is

---

[2] Financial Accounting Standards Board, *Statement of Financial Accounting Standards No. 33,* "Financial Reporting and Changing Prices," 1979.

recorded on the books. FASB *Statement No. 34*[3] requires the firm to capitalize interest paid during the construction period as part of the cost of the asset being constructed. The amount of interest to be capitalized is based on the entity's actual borrowings and interest payments. It is intended to be that portion of interest cost incurred during the assets' acquisition periods that theoretically could have been avoided if the assets had not been acquired. If there is a specific new borrowing in connection with the asset being constructed, the interest rate on that borrowing is used. If the expenditures on plant exceed such specific new borrowings, the interest rate to be applied to such excess is the weighted average of rates applicable to other borrowings of the enterprise. In some cases, there may not be specific new borrowings; then the average interest rate on old borrowings is used to compute the total amount to be capitalized. The amount of interest capitalized is recorded as a reduction of interest expense for the period. The total amount of interest capitalized cannot exceed total interest costs for the period. The reduction in interest expense increases net income during the construction period.

Example Assume the following long-term debt structure:

Construction Loan at 15 Percent on Building under Construction	$1,000,000
Other Recent Borrowings (Bond Issues) at 12 Percent	600,000
Other, Older Borrowings at Average Rate of 10 Percent	3,000,000
Total Long-Term Debt	$4,600,000

The account for Land and Building under Construction has an average balance during the year of $2,000,000. The amount of interest to be capitalized is based on all of the new construction-related borrowings, $1,000,000, all of the recent other borrowings, $600,000, and enough of the older borrowings, $400,000, to bring the total to $2,000,000. The interest capitalized is computed as:

$1,000,000 \times .15$	$150,000
$600,000 \times .12$	72,000
$400,000 \times .10$	40,000
$2,000,000	$262,000

The entries to record interest and then to capitalize the required amounts might be:

Interest Expense	522,000	
Interest Payable		522,000

To record all interest as expense: $522,000 = (.15 \times \$1,000,000) + (.12 \times \$600,000) + (.10 \times \$3,000,000) = \$150,000 + \$72,000 + \$300,000$.

---

[3] Financial Accounting Standards Board, *Statement of Financial Accounting Standards No. 34,* "Capitalization of Interest Cost," 1979.

Building under Construction	262,000
Interest Expense	262,000

The amount capitalized reduces interest expense and increases the recorded cost of the building.

The preceding two entries might be combined as one:

Interest Expense	260,000
Building under Construction	262,000
Interest Payable	522,000

The amount for Interest Expense is a plug.

Both total interest for the year, $522,000, and the amount capitalized, $262,000, must be disclosed in notes. The income statement will report interest expense, $260,000, in the example. The amount shown in future years for depreciation of the plant will be larger than otherwise because of interest capitalization into the plant accounts in earlier years.

Estimating Residual Value

Depreciation charges are based on the difference between acquisition cost and the asset's estimated *salvage value* or *net residual value.* Estimates of residual value are necessary for making the depreciation calculation. (The terms *salvage value* and *net residual value* refer to estimated proceeds on disposition of an asset less all removal and selling costs. Salvage value must be an estimate at any time before the asset is retired. Hence, before retirement, the terms *salvage value* and *estimated salvage value* are synonymous.)

For buildings, common practice assumes a zero salvage value. This treatment rests on the assumption that the cost to be incurred in tearing down the building will approximate the sales value of the scrap materials recovered. For other assets, however, the salvage value may be substantial, and should be estimated and taken into account in making the periodic depreciation charge. This is particularly true where it is planned to retire an asset while it still has substantial value. For example, a car rental firm will replace its automobiles at a time when other owners can use the cars for several years more. The rental firm will be able to realize a substantial part of acquisition cost from the sale of used cars. Past experience usually forms the best basis for estimating salvage value.

Estimates of salvage value are necessarily subjective. Disputes over estimated salvage value have led to many disagreements between Internal Revenue Service agents and taxpayers. Partly to reduce such controversy, the Internal Revenue Code was amended to provide that, starting in 1962, salvage value of up to 10 percent of the cost of assets such as machinery and equipment may be ignored in depreciation calculations for tax purposes. The Internal Revenue Code was amended again in 1971 to provide that salvage value may be ignored entirely in calculating depreciation if a procedure known in the Code as the *asset depreciation range system* is used.

The asset may not be depreciated below its estimated salvage value, however. The same rule is frequently followed in making calculations for financial records. In calculating depreciation in problems in this text, the entire salvage value is to be taken into account unless explicit contrary instructions are given.

Estimating Service Life

The second factor in the depreciation calculation is the estimated economic service life of the asset. In making the estimate, both the physical and the functional causes of depreciation must be taken into account. Experience with similar assets, corrected for differences in the planned intensity of use or alterations in maintenance policy, is usually the best guide for this estimate. Income tax laws allow shorter lives to be used in computing depreciation for tax reporting, but these tax-related lives need *not* be used for financial reporting.

In 1962, the Internal Revenue Service published guidelines of suggested useful lives. The guidelines provide estimated useful lives based on categories of assets by broad classes. Examples of guideline lives were as follows:

Warehouses	60 years
Factory Buildings	45 years
Land Improvements	20 years
Office Furniture, Fixtures, Machines, and Equipment	10 years
Heavy Trucks	6 years
Light Trucks	4 years
Automobiles	3 years

In 1971, the Internal Revenue Service ruled that the guideline lives need not be strictly followed. Rather, the IRS said that taxpayers may use a life anywhere in the range from 80 percent to 120 percent of the guideline life. Such ranges were called *asset depreciation ranges*.

In 1981, Congress passed new income tax legislation that changed the laws for computing depreciation on tax returns. The system is referred to as an Accelerated Cost Recovery System (ACRS). Almost all assets are grouped into one of three classes: those to be depreciated over 3 years for tax purposes (such as autos and light trucks), those to be depreciated over 5 years for tax purposes (such as most machinery and equipment), and those to be depreciated over 10 years for tax purposes. Because almost all assets have service lives for tax purposes of 3, 5, or 10 years, the rule has come to be known as the "3-5-10 rule."

Despite the abundance of data from experience, estimation of service lives is the most difficult task in the entire depreciation calculation. Making proper allowances for obsolescence is particularly difficult because obsolescence results, for the most part, from forces external to the firm. Unless the estimator possesses prophetic powers, it is likely that the estimates will prove to be incorrect. For this reason, it is wise to reconsider the estimates of useful service life of important assets or groups of assets every few years.

Pattern of Expiration of Services

Once the cost has been determined and both salvage value and service life have been estimated, the total of depreciation charges for the whole life of the asset has been determined. There then remains the problem of selecting the pattern for allocating those charges to the specific years of the life. There are five basic patterns for such allocations when depreciation is based on the passage of time. They are labeled *E, A, S, D,* and *N* in Figure 9.1.

If salvage value is assumed to be zero, then, of course, the salvage value line coincides with the horizontal axis and the entire cost will be depreciated.

The patterns are discussed in more detail in the next section. A represents *accelerated* depreciation; S, *uniform* or *straight-line* depreciation; D, *decelerated* depreciation. (Understanding the terms "accelerated" and "decelerated" is easier if you compare the depreciation charges in the early years to straight-line depreciation.) Patterns A and S are much more commonly used than D. Pattern E, of course, represents immediate expensing of the item. All costs are charged to the period when the cost is incurred. This pattern is discussed further in the section on intangibles. Pattern N represents the situation, such as for land, where there are no periodic amortization charges. The asset is shown on the books at acquisition cost until it is sold or otherwise retired.

Figure 9.1
**Patterns of Depreciation:
Book Value over Life of Asset**

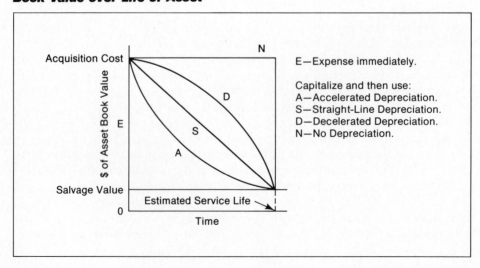

Depreciation Methods

All depreciation methods should aim to allocate, reasonably and systematically, the cost of the asset minus its estimated salvage value to the periods in which it is used. The methods discussed here are as follows:

1 Straight-line (time) method (Pattern S).
2 Production or use (straight-line use) method.
3 Declining-balance methods (Pattern A).
4 Sum-of-the-years'-digits method (Pattern A).

When a depreciable asset is acquired or retired during an accounting period, depreciation should be calculated only for that portion of the period during which the asset is used.

The Straight-Line (Time) Method

The allocation method that is used most commonly for financial reporting is known as the *straight-line* method. It was used almost exclusively until 1954, when the income tax laws were revised to recognize accelerated depreciation methods for general use. Under the straight-line method, the cost of the asset, less any estimated salvage value, is divided by the number of years of its expected life in order to arrive at the annual depreciation:

$$\text{Annual Depreciation} = \frac{\text{Cost Less Estimated Salvage Value}}{\text{Estimated Life in Years}}.$$

For example, if a machine costs $12,000, has an estimated salvage value of $1,000, and has an expected useful life of 5 years, the annual depreciation will be $2,200 [$= (\$12,000 - \$1,000)/5$]. Occasionally, instead of a positive salvage value, the cost of removal exceeds the gross proceeds on disposition. This excess of removal costs over gross proceeds should be added to the cost of the asset in making the calculation. Thus, if a building is constructed for $37,000, and it is estimated that it will cost $5,000 to remove it at the end of 25 years, the annual depreciation would be $1,680 [$= (\$37,000 + \$5,000)/25$].

A common practice, especially when the salvage value is assumed to be zero, is to apply an appropriate percentage, known as the depreciation rate, to the *acquisition cost* in order to calculate the annual charge. The rate is chosen so that it will charge the entire acquisition cost off over the estimated life. A rate of 10 percent will write off the cost of an asset in 10 years, a rate of 25 percent in 4 years, and so on. The machine referred to in the preceding paragraph would be depreciated annually at the rate of 20 percent of acquisition cost less salvage value for 5 years.

Production or Use (Straight-Line Use) Method

Although the straight-line (time) method is widely used, it is justifiable only because it frequently corresponds roughly to the amount of use that can be made of the asset, and because it requires only simple arithmetic. Many assets are not, however, used uniformly over time. Manufacturing plants often have seasonal variations in operation so that certain machines may be used 24 hours a day at one time and 8 hours or less a day at another time of year. Trucks are not likely to receive the same amount of use in each month or year of their lives. The straight-line (time) method of depreciation may, then, result in an illogical depreciation charge for such assets.

When the rate of usage varies from period to period and when the total usage of an asset over its life can be estimated reliably, a depreciation charge based on actual usage during the period may be justified. For example, depreciation of a truck for a period could be based on the ratio of miles driven during the period to total miles expected to be driven over the truck's life. The depreciation cost per unit (mile) of use is:

$$\text{Depreciation Cost per Unit} = \frac{\text{Cost Less Estimated Salvage Value}}{\text{Estimated Number of Units}}.$$

The arithmetic of the calculation is simple, but it is necessary to keep a special record of the units of operation of each asset or of the number of units produced. If a truck that costs $12,000 and has an estimated salvage value of $600 is expected to be driven 100,000 miles before it is retired from service, then the depreciation per mile is $.114 [=($12,000 − $600)/100,000]. Then, if the truck is operated 2,000 miles in a given month, the depreciation charge for the month is 2,000 × $.114 = $228.

Accelerated Depreciation

The efficiency and earning power of many plant assets decline as the assets grow older. Cutting tools lose some of their precision; printing presses are shut down more frequently for repairs; rentals in an old office building are lower than those in its gleaming new neighbor. These examples show the tendency of some assets to provide more and better services in the early years of their lives while requiring increasing amounts of maintenance as they grow older. Where this is the case, methods that recognize progressively smaller depreciation charges in successive periods may be justified. Such methods are referred to as *accelerated depreciation* methods because the depreciation charges in the early years of the asset's life are larger than in later years. Accelerated depreciation leads to a pattern such as A in Figure 9.1.

For convenience, the depreciation charges for a year, however they are determined, are allocated on a straight-line basis to periods *within* the year.

Declining-Balance Methods

The *declining-balance* method is one accelerated depreciation method. In this method, the depreciation charge is calculated by multiplying the *net book value* of the asset (cost less accumulated depreciation) at the start of each period by a fixed rate. The estimated salvage value is not subtracted from the cost in making the depreciation calculation, as is the case with other depreciation methods. Because the net book value declines from period to period, the result is a declining periodic charge for depreciation throughout the life of the asset.[4] The rate most commonly used is the maximum one permitted for income tax purposes, which ordinarily is twice the straight-line rate. When this rate is used, the method is called the *double-declining-balance* method. Thus, for example, an asset with an estimated 10-year life would be depreciated at a rate of 20 percent ($= \frac{1}{10} \times 2$) per year of the book value at the start of the year. To take another example, if a machine costing $5,000 is purchased on January 1, 1982, and it is estimated to have a 5-year life, a 40 percent ($= \frac{1}{5} \times 2$) rate would be used. The depreciation charges would be calculated as shown in Exhibit 9.1.

Exhibit 9.1
Double-Declining-Balance
Depreciation
Asset with 5-Year Life

Year	Acquisition Cost (1)	Accumulated Depreciation as of Jan. 1 (2)	Net Book Value as of Jan. 1 = (1) − (2) (3)	Depreciation Rate (4)	Depreciation Charge for the Year = (3) × (4) (5)
1982	$5,000	$ 0	$5,000	.40	$2,000
1983	5,000	2,000	3,000	.40	1,200
1984	5,000	3,200	1,800	.40	720
1985	5,000	3,920	1,080[a]	.40	432
1986	5,000	4,352	648	.40	259
1987	5,000	4,611	389	—	—

[a]If the asset had a zero salvage value, the firm would switch to straight-line write-off of the remaining balance over the remaining life, or $540 ($= \$1,080/2$) a year for the last 2 years.

The undepreciated cost as of December 31, 1986, as shown in Exhibit 9.1, is $389 ($= \$648 - \$259$). This amount is unlikely to equal the salvage value at that time. The problem is usually anticipated and solved by adjusting the depreciation charge in one or more of the later years. Under income tax rules, the asset cannot be depreciated below salvage value. If the salvage value is large, the asset is likely to be depreciated to that amount before the end of the estimated service life and the last

---

[4]Under the declining-balance method, as strictly applied, the fixed depreciation rate used is one that will charge the cost less salvage value of the asset over its service life. The formula for computing the rate is:

$$\text{Depreciation Rate} = 1 - \sqrt[n]{\frac{s}{c}} = 1 - \left(\frac{s}{c}\right)^{1/n}$$

In this formula $n =$ estimated periods of service life, $s =$ estimated salvage value, and $c =$ cost.

Estimates of salvage value have a profound effect on the rate. Unless a positive salvage value is assumed, the rate is 100 percent—that is, all depreciation is charged in the first period. For an asset costing $10,000, with an estimated life of 5 years, the depreciation rate is 40 percent per period if salvage value is $778, but it is 60 percent if salvage value is $102.

The effect of small changes in salvage value on the rate and the seeming mathematical complexity of the formula have resulted in widespread use of approximations or rules of thumb instead of the formula.

period(s) will have no depreciation charges. If the salvage value is small, the firm can switch in the last years of asset life to writing off the undepreciated cost minus salvage value in straight-line fashion over the remaining life.

Refer again to Exhibit 9.1. If the asset had an estimated salvage value of $200, the depreciation charges in 1985 and 1986 could be $440 a year (net book value at January 1, 1985, of $1,080 less the estimated salvage value of $200 divided by the 2 years of remaining life). In general, the switch to the straight-line method for the remaining life is made when the switch will produce a greater depreciation charge than the one resulting from continued application of the double-declining-balance method. For assets with zero scrap value, this ordinarily occurs in the period following the midpoint of the service life.

Sum-of-the-Years'-Digits Method

The other accelerated depreciation method mentioned in the Internal Revenue Code is the *sum-of-the-years'-digits* method. Under this method, the depreciation charge is calculated by applying a fraction, which diminishes from year to year, to the cost less estimated salvage value of the asset. The numerator of the fraction is the number of years of remaining life at the beginning of the year for which the depreciation calculation is being made. The denominator is the sum of all such numbers, one for each year of estimated service life; if the service life is n years, the denominator for the sum-of-the-years'-digits method is $1 + 2 + \cdots + n.$[5]

The method is illustrated by again considering an asset costing $5,000 purchased January 1, 1982, which has an estimated service life of 5 years and an estimated salvage value of $200. The sum of the years' digits is 15 ($= 1 + 2 + 3 + 4 + 5$).[6] The depreciation charges are calculated in Exhibit 9.2.

Exhibit 9.2
Sum-of-the-Years'-Digits Depreciation
Asset with 5-Year Life, $5,000 Cost,
and $200 Estimated Salvage Value

Year	Acquisition Cost Less Salvage Value (1)	Remaining Life in Years (2)	Fraction = (2)/15 (3)	Depreciation Charge for the Year = (3) × (1) (4)
1982	$4,800	5	5/15	$1,600
1983	4,800	4	4/15	1,280
1984	4,800	3	3/15	960
1985	4,800	2	2/15	640
1986	4,800	1	1/15	320
				$4,800

---

[5] A useful formula for summing the numbers 1 through n is $1 + 2 + \cdots + n = n(n + 1)/2$.
[6] That is, according to the formula given in the previous footnote: $1 + 2 + 3 + 4 + 5 = 5 \times 6/2 = 15$.

Compound Interest Methods

Compound interest methods are not widely used in financial accounting, but they are theoretically sound for many management decisions. For plant assets producing equal annual net inflows of cash, compound interest depreciation leads to a pattern like D in Figure 9.1. Compound interest methods are not illustrated in this text.

Factors to Consider in Choosing the Depreciation Method

To the individual firm, depreciation is a factor in the computation of income reported on the financial statements as well as a deduction from otherwise taxable income on tax returns. The firm need not choose the same depreciation method for both financial and tax reporting purposes. If it chooses different methods for the two purposes, the difference between income on the financial statements and taxable income requires a reconciliation in the financial statements. This reconciliation leads to a liability for deferred taxes, which is discussed in Chapter 11.

Financial Reporting The goal in financial reporting for long-lived assets is to seek a statement of income that realistically measures the expiration of these assets. The only difficulty is that no one knows, in any satisfactory sense, just what portion of the service potential of a long-lived asset expires in any one period. The cost of the plant asset is a joint cost of the several periods of use and there is no logical way of allocating joint costs. All that can be said is that financial statements should report depreciation charges based on reasonable estimates of asset expirations so that the goal of fair presentation can more nearly be achieved. The firm's selection from alternative accounting principles, including the choice of depreciation methods, is discussed more fully in Chapter 15.

Tax Reporting We are relatively confident about the depreciation method to be used for tax purposes. It seems clear that the goal of the firm should be to maximize the present value of the reductions in tax payments from claiming depreciation. When tax rates remain constant over time and there is a flat tax rate (for example, all income taxed at a 46-percent rate), this goal can usually be achieved by maximizing the present value of the depreciation deductions from otherwise taxable income. That is, for tax purposes the asset should be written off as quickly as possible. Of course, a firm can deduct only the acquisition cost, less salvage value, from otherwise taxable income over the life of the asset. Earlier deductions are, however, worth more than later ones, because a dollar saved today is worth more than a dollar saved tomorrow.

Congress has presented business firms with several permissible alternatives to follow in determining the amount of depreciation to be deducted each year. The firm can choose double-declining-balance, sum-of-the-years'-digits, straight-line, or various combinations of these methods. It seems clear to us that the firm should choose that alternative which meets the general goal of paying the least amount of tax, as late as possible, within the law. This goal is sometimes called the *least and latest rule*.

We can put this more strongly by saying that management has an affirmative obligation in a competitive economy to carry on operations so as to minimize all costs—that is, to minimize the present value of those costs over the long run. Failure to minimize costs hinders the attempt of the competitive market economy to allocate resources efficiently. Management's obligation to reduce costs applies to taxes as well as to other costs, and, in most circumstances, the present value of taxes is minimized by taking depreciation as rapidly as is legally possible. It is clear that either the double-declining-balance or the sum-of-the-years'-digits method will give a more rapid rate of charge-off than the straight-line method. However, the choice between the two accelerated methods depends on the specific circumstances of the firm. In general, the way to maximize the present value of the depreciation charges is to start with the double-declining-balance method and to switch to the sum-of-the-years'-digits method sometime during the asset's life. There are, however, some limitations on the kinds of changes in methods a firm can make for income tax purposes. The intricacies of the optimal depreciation method are beyond the scope of an introductory accounting course.[7] All problems in this text that require an accelerated depreciation method will specify which method is to be used.

Accounting for Periodic Depreciation

The debit made in the entry to record periodic depreciation is usually either to an expense account or to a production cost account. In a manufacturing concern, the depreciation of factory buildings and equipment is a production cost, a part of the work-in-process and finished product cost. Depreciation on sales equipment is a selling expense. Depreciation on office equipment is a general or administrative expense. The matching credit for periodic depreciation could logically be made directly to the asset account affected, such as buildings or equipment. Although such an entry is sometimes made, it is customary to credit a special contra-asset account so that the acquisition cost of the asset will be left undisturbed and the total amount written off through depreciation can be readily observed. The effect, however, is precisely the same as a direct credit to the asset account. We have used Accumulated Depreciation as the title of the account to be credited.

The entry to record periodic depreciation of office facilities, a period expense, is:

Depreciation Expense	1,500	
Accumulated Depreciation		1,500

The entry to record periodic depreciation of manufacturing facilities, a product cost, is:

Work-in-Process Inventory	1,500	
Accumulated Depreciation		1,500

---

[7] For a complete analysis of these problems, see Clyde P. Stickney and Jeffrey B. Wallace, "A Guide to Increasing the Maximum Available Depreciation Deduction Under the ADR System," *Taxation for Accountants* (July 1975): 42–48; and Clyde P. Stickney and Jeffrey B. Wallace, *The Class Life (ADR) System* (Tucson: Lawyers & Judges Publishing Co., 1977).

The Depreciation Expense account is closed at the end of the accounting period as a part of the regular closing-entry procedure. The Work-in-Process Inventory account is an asset. Product costs, such as depreciation on manufacturing facilities, are accumulated in the Work-in-Process account until the goods being produced are completed and transferred to Finished Goods Inventory. The Accumulated Depreciation account remains open at the end of the period and is shown on the balance sheet as a deduction from the asset account to which it refers. The balance in the Accumulated Depreciation account usually represents the total charges to accounting periods prior to the balance sheet date for the depreciation on assets currently in use. The difference between the balance of the asset account and the balance of its accumulated depreciation account (with possibly an adjustment for salvage value) represents the amount that will presumably be charged to future accounting periods. This difference is called the *book value* of the asset.

In preparing a statement of changes in financial position, the periodic depreciation charge is an addback in the "operations" section. It represents an expense that does not use funds but instead uses a noncurrent asset.

Changes in Periodic Depreciation

The original depreciation schedule for a particular asset may require changing. The original or previous estimate of useful life (and possibly of salvage value as well) may have been incorrect as judged in the light of new information. To change the depreciation plan because of previous misestimates of useful life or salvage value is a relatively common and desirable accounting practice.

Misestimates of the useful life of an asset may become apparent at any time during its life. It is usually possible to improve the degree of accuracy of the estimates as the time of retirement approaches. If it appears that the misestimate will be relatively minor, an adjustment usually is not made. If the misestimate appears to be material, corrective action must be taken if the effect of the previous estimation error is to be kept at a minimum. The generally accepted procedure for handling this problem is to make no adjustment for the past misestimate, but to spread the remaining undepreciated balance less the revised estimate of salvage value over the new estimate of remaining service life of the asset. We feel that a more logical procedure would be to make an adjustment of past periods' earnings for the misestimate of the past periods, and use the revised rate of depreciation for the remaining portion of the life of the asset. Such an adjustment is not permitted under generally accepted accounting principles, however.[8]

To illustrate the accounting for changes in periodic depreciation, assume the following facts. An office machine was purchased on January 1, 1977, for $9,200. It was estimated that the machine would be operated for 10 years with a salvage value of $200. On December 31, 1982, before the books are closed for the year, it is decided that, in light of the evidence presently available, a total useful life of 15 years with

---

[8]Accounting Principles Board, *Opinion No. 20,* "Accounting Changes," 1971; Financial Accounting Standards Board, *Statement of Financial Accounting Standards No. 16,* "Prior Period Adjustments," 1977.

359

the same salvage estimate of $200 would be a more reasonable estimate. The depreciation charge recorded for each of the years from 1977 through 1981 under the straight-line method would have been $900 [= ($9,200 − $200)/10].

If the revised estimate of service life were ignored, the original annual depreciation charge of $900 would be continued through 1986. The years 1987 to 1991 would receive no charge to operations for the use of the machine. The Accumulated Depreciation account would remain undisturbed for those years until the machine was retired from service. Thus, during the last 5 years that the machine was in service, no charge for depreciation would be made.

The accepted procedure for recognizing this substantial increase in service life is to revise the future depreciation so that the correct total will presumably be accumulated in the Accumulated Depreciation account at the end of the revised service life. In our example, the total amount of acquisition cost yet to be depreciated before the 1982 adjustments is $4,500 [= ($9,200 − $200) − $4,500]. The new estimate of the *remaining* life is 10 years, so the new annual depreciation charge is $450 (= $4,500/10). The only change in the accounting procedure is to substitute the new amount of $450 for the former annual depreciation of $900. The depreciation entry on December 31, 1982, and each year thereafter would be:

Depreciation Expense	450
Accumulated Depreciation	450
To record depreciation for 1982 on revised basis.	

The revised depreciation path is illustrated in Figure 9.2.

Depreciation and Repairs

Depreciation is not the only cost of using a plant asset. There will almost always be some repair and maintenance costs during the life of the asset. The repair policy adopted by the business will often affect the depreciation rate. If, for example, machinery, trucks, and other plant assets are checked frequently and repaired as soon as any difficulty develops, such assets will have a longer useful life, and, therefore, a lower depreciation rate than would otherwise be the case. The more commonly used estimates of service life and depreciation rates assume that normal repairs will be made during the life of an asset.

Although some major parts of an asset may have shorter lives than the asset as a whole, it is frequently impracticable to account for them with separate depreciation accounts. Thus, the cost of a replacement set of tires is usually charged to repairs expense, although it would be possible to treat the tires as a separate asset subject to depreciation. It may be useful, though, in some cases to disaggregate assets for the purposes of depreciation. For example, specifying single machines instead of a group of machines, or dealing with engines in aircraft separately from the rest of the asset, may be a practicable and logical procedure.

360

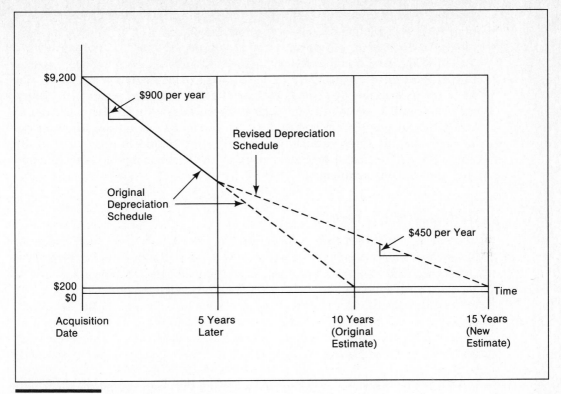

Figure 9.2
Illustration of Revised Depreciation Schedule. Asset's Service Life Estimate Is Increased from 10 to 15 Years at the Start of Year 6. The Straight-Line Method Is Used. Asset Cost Is $9,200 and Has Estimated Salvage Value of $200.

Repairs must be distinguished from improvements and from rehabilitation. *Repairs* are the small adjustments and replacements of parts whose effect does not extend estimated service life materially or otherwise increase productive capacity. *Improvements* involve adding a part or installing a new part that is substantially better than the old one. The benefit from the improvement will be received for a significant time over the future, but the total useful life of the asset will not ordinarily be extended. *Rehabilitation* involves major construction so that the asset can provide a broader range of services or so that the life of the asset is extended considerably beyond the originally estimated date of retirement.

For example, the replacement of shingles that have blown off a roof would be treated as a repair. The replacement of a shingled roof with a metal roof, or the construction of an addition to the building, would be an improvement. The reconstruction of the interior, the constuction of a new front, or the reinforcement of the foundation would in most cases come under the definition of rehabilitation.

Repairs are charged to expense as expenditures are made. Improvements are debited to the asset account. Rehabilitations are merely extensive improvements. They are normally treated in the same way as improvements even though a rehabilitation may extend the life of an asset. Rehabilitations or improvements could logically be viewed, however, as a replacement of the old asset and entries made just as though the old asset were retired from service and a new one acquired. In any case, the accounting for improvements and rehabilitations results in a net debit to the asset account. The total depreciation charges for the remaining life of the original asset are increased accordingly.

Retirement of Assets

When an asset is retired from service, the cost of the asset and the related amount of accumulated depreciation must be removed from the books. As part of this entry, the amount received from the sale or trade-in and any difference between that amount and book value must be recorded. The difference between the proceeds received on retirement and book value is a gain (if positive) or a loss (if negative). Before making the entry to write off the asset and its accumulated depreciation, an entry should be made to bring the depreciation up to date; that is, the depreciation that has occurred between the start of the current accounting period and the date of disposition must be recorded.

To illustrate the retirement of an asset, assume that sales equipment which cost $5,000, was expected to last 4 years, and had an estimated salvage value of $200, is depreciated on a straight-line basis. Depreciation has been recorded for 2 years, and the equipment is sold at mid-year in the third year. The depreciation from the start of the accounting period to the date of sale of $600 $[= \frac{1}{2} \times (\$5,000 - \$200)/4]$ is recorded:

Depreciation Expense	600	
Accumulated Depreciation		600
To record depreciation charges up to the date of sale.		

The book value of the asset is now its cost less $2\frac{1}{2}$ years of straight-line depreciation of $100 per month or $2,000 $(= \$5,000 - \$3,000)$. The entry to record the retirement of the assets depends on the amount of the selling price.

1 Suppose that the equipment were sold for $2,000 cash. The entry to record the sale would be:

Cash	2,000	
Accumulated Depreciation	3,000	
Equipment		5,000

362

2 Suppose that the equipment were sold for $2,300. The entry to record the sale would be:

Cash	2,300	
Accumulated Depreciation	3,000	
Equipment		5,000
Gain on Retirement of Equipment		300

3 Suppose that the equipment were sold for $1,500. The entry to record the sale would be:

Cash	1,500	
Accumulated Depreciation	3,000	
Loss on Retirement of Equipment	500	
Equipment		5,000

Retirement Entries in the Statement of Changes in Financial Position The cash received from the disposition of a plant asset is a nonoperating source of funds. It is shown on the funds statement as a nonoperating source, "Proceeds from Disposition of Noncurrent Assets." The Loss on Retirement of Equipment is an item that reduces net income but does not use funds. Thus, in deriving funds from operations, the amount of the loss is an addback in determining funds from operations. Its presentation is similar to that for depreciation expense.

If there is a Gain on Retirement of Equipment, two alternative treatments are possible and are found in practice. One shows the entire proceeds from disposition of the asset as a nonoperating source of funds and thus requires treating the Gain on Retirement as a subtraction in determining funds from operations. The subtraction would be classified under the general heading of revenues not producing funds from operations, because the funds produced are shown under the heading of proceeds from disposition of plant assets. The alternative treatment shows only the book value of the asset disposed of as a nonoperating source of funds and includes the gain in funds from operations. (That is, there is no subtraction in the operating section.) We prefer the first approach and follow it throughout this book.

Trade-in Transactions

Instead of selling the asset when it is retired from service, it is more common for the asset to be traded in on a new unit. This is a particularly common practice for automobiles. The trade-in transaction can best be viewed as a sale of the old asset followed by a purchase of the new asset. The accounting for trade-in transactions depends on the data available about the value of the asset traded in and the cost of the new asset. The cash-equivalent cost of the new asset acquired is the important information for recording all trade-in transactions.

If the fair market value of the used asset traded in can be found, that amount plus the cash given up determines the valuation of the new asset. Assume in the preceding illustration that the used equipment had a fair market value of $1,300 and was traded in on a new piece of equipment, along with an additional $5,500 of cash. The entries, using a two-step approach, would be:

Accumulated Depreciation	3,000	
Trade-in Allowance	1,300	
Loss on Disposition of Equipment	700	
Equipment		5,000
To record disposition of old equipment; plug for loss.		
Equipment	6,800	
Trade-in Allowance		1,300
Cash		5,500
To record acquisition of new equipment; plug for cost of new equipment.		

The entries shown above would not be affected by information about the list price of the new equipment. Valuation of the used asset in established second-hand markets almost always offers more reliable information than quoted list prices. However, if a reliable valuation of the used asset is not available, then the lowest cash price for the new asset, which is frequently the list price, will determine the valuation of the new asset as well as the gain or loss on disposition of the old asset. If the list price of the new equipment in the preceding example were $7,000 and there were no other reliable information available, the entries would be:

Equipment	7,000	
Cash		5,500
Trade-in Allowance		1,500
To record acquisition at list price; plug for trade-in allowance.		
Accumulated Depreciation	3,000	
Trade-in Allowance	1,500	
Loss on Disposition of Equipment	500	
Equipment		5,000
To record disposition of old equipment. Loss is determined by list price of new equipment.		

The income tax regulations do not permit the recognition of a gain or loss on the trade-in of an old asset in acquiring a new, similar asset. Instead, the cost of the new asset is assumed to be the book value of the used asset plus the cash paid. In the illustration used in this section, the entries would be:

Accumulated Depreciation	3,000	
Trade-in Allowance	2,000	
Equipment		5,000
To record disposition of old equipment at book value.		

Equipment	7,500	
Cash		5,500
Trade-in Allowance		2,000
To record acquisition of new equipment. Cost of new equipment is a plug.		

The recording of all three methods has been illustrated with a two-step approach. The two entries could be combined into one, removing the need for a Trade-in Allowance account.

The same analysis and same type of entries would be made if there were a gain on disposition. The one exception, in generally accepted accounting principles, to the concept that the cash-equivalent price of the new asset is recorded occurs where this would result in a gain from the trade-in of a *similar* asset. In that case, no gain is recognized and the new asset is recorded at the book value of the old asset plus the cash paid in the trade-in transaction.[9]

The Investment Tax Credit

In order to stimulate investment in machinery and equipment, Congress has passed tax laws that permit the purchaser of machinery and equipment to claim a credit based on new investment. The credit is applied to reduce the purchaser's income tax liability to the federal government. The rate of the credit and the property eligible for the credit have varied through the years as Congress has amended the tax laws. In the examples in this section, we will assume a 10-percent tax credit on all equipment purchases.[10]

If a firm buys $900,000 of equipment with an estimated service life of 8 years this year, it will receive a $90,000 (= .10 × $900,000) investment tax credit. If its income tax liability shown on the tax return before the investment tax credit is $600,000, the following entry would be made:

Income Tax Expense	600,000	
Income Tax Payable		600,000
To record income taxes before the investment tax credit.		

---

[9] In the highly unlikely situation where cash is received by the party making the trade-in, some gain is recognized; Accounting Principles Board, *Opinion No. 29,* "Accounting for Nonmonetary Transactions," 1973. (See *trade-in transaction* in the Glossary at the back of the book.)

[10] The investment credit provisions are much more complex. The eligibility of property for the credit depends on its service life. One-third of the cost of equipment with an estimated service life of 3 years but less than 5 years is eligible, whereas two-thirds of the cost of equipment with an estimated service life of 5 years but less than 7 years is eligible. Only if the estimated service life is 7 years or more is the entire cost of the asset fully eligible for the investment tax credit. The credit may not exceed a stated percentage (recently 90 percent) of the tax liability with appropriate carrybacks and carryforwards.

There are two generally accepted methods of recording the investment tax credit—the flow-through method and the deferral method.[11] Under the flow-through method, the entire investment credit earned during the year by all asset acquisitions is recorded as a reduction in income tax expense of the year. (It all flows through to income this year). The entry would be:

Income Tax Payable	90,000	
Income Tax Expense		90,000
To record the investment credit (= .10 × $900,000) for the year.		

If the deferral approach is used, the reduction in income tax expense is spread over the years of the service life of the equipment acquired. The entire investment credit reduces the amount of income taxes payable in the year of acquisition, even though the reported reductions in income tax expense are spread over the years of service life. In the example, the entry in the year of acquisition, using the deferral method, would be:

Income Tax Payable	90,000	
Income Tax Expense		11,250
Deferred Investment Credit		78,750
Part ($\frac{1}{8}$ × $90,000) of investment credit reduces expense in first year. The remaining portion will reduce expense in later years.		

The Deferred Investment Credit account appears on the balance sheet among the noncurrent liabilities. At the end of each of the 7 following years, the following entry would be made:

Deferred Investment Credit	11,250	
Income Tax Expense		11,250
To amortize the deferred investment credit. Recorded income tax expense is reduced by $11,250 in each year 2 through 8.		

Income tax expense is reduced by the full amount of the investment credit under both methods, but over different time periods.

If the deferral approach is used, the credit to income tax expense includes not only a part of this year's investment credit but also portions of the investment credit relating to earlier years that are still being amortized. For a firm in equilibrium (and assuming no recent change in the tax law with regard to the investment credit), income tax expense and net income will be the same under the flow-through and deferral approaches. For a growing firm, the flow-through method produces higher reported net income in all years during the growth period.

---

[11] Accounting Principles Board, *Opinion No. 4*, "Accounting for the 'Investment Credit,'" 1964. Problem 31 at the end of this chapter explores the theoretical possibilities one ought to consider in choosing the methods in practice.

If the deferral method is used, income tax expense for a growing firm will be greater than taxes paid or taxes currently payable. This excess represents an expense that does not use funds. It thus results in an addback in the operating section of the statement of changes in financial position.

Wasting Assets and Depletion

The costs of finding natural resources and preparing to extract them from the earth should be capitalized and amortized. Amortization of wasting assets, or natural resources, is called *depletion.* The depletion method most often used is the *units-of-production* method. For example, if $4.5 million in costs are incurred to discover an oil well that contains an estimated 1.5 million barrels of oil, then the costs of $4.5 million would be amortized (depleted) at the rate of $3 (= $4,500,000/1,500,000) for each barrel of oil removed from the well. The major accounting problem of extractive industries stems from the uncertainty of the benefits from exploratory efforts.

Percentage Depletion Allowances

In some special circumstances, the tax laws permit computation of depletion in measuring taxable income as a percentage of the revenues secured from the sale of the minerals each year. The total of depletion charges over the life of the asset is not limited to costs incurred if this method, known as *percentage depletion,* is used. In financial accounting, depletion allocates the cost of natural resources to the periods when the resources are used. The percentage depletion allowances are a device instituted by the Congress to make the search for natural resources more attractive than it otherwise would be. The effect of percentage depletion is to allow some firms to deduct, on income tax returns over the life of the asset, amounts larger than the total of costs incurred. Financial statement expense over the life of the asset must be equal to the acquisition cost of the asset in a historical-cost system.

Intangible Assets and Amortization

Assets can provide future benefits without having physical form. Such assets are called *intangibles.* Examples are research costs, advertising costs, patents, trade secrets, know-how, trademarks, and copyrights. The first problem with intangibles is to decide whether the expenditures have future benefits and can be quantified with a sufficient degree of precision so that they should be "capitalized" (set up as assets) and amortized over time, or whether they have no future benefits and thus are expenses of the period in which the costs are incurred. In this latter case, the immediate expensing of the asset's cost is represented by Pattern E in Figure 9.1. The second problem to solve is how to amortize the costs if they have been capitalized. Deciding the period of amortization (= estimated service life) is a difficult question. Amortization of capitalized intangibles is usually recorded using the straight-line method, but

367

other methods can be used if they seem appropriate. This section discusses some common intangibles and the issues involved in deciding whether to expense or to capitalize their costs.

Research and Development

One common intangible cost is that for research and development (R&D). This type of cost is incurred for various reasons. Perhaps the firm seeks to develop a technological or marketing advance in order to have an edge on competition. Or it might wish to explore possible applications of existing technology to design a new product or improve an old one. Other research may be undertaken in response to a government contract, in preparing for bids on potential contracts, or in pursuit of "discoveries," with no specific product in mind. Whatever the reason, practically all research costs will yield their benefits, if any, in future periods. Herein lies the accounting issue: should research and development costs be charged to expense immediately as they are incurred, or should they be capitalized and amortized over future periods?

Generally accepted accounting principles[12] require immediate expensing of research and development costs. (Note 2 of the financial statements of General Products Company in Appendix Exhibit A.4 illustrates the required disclosures.) This requirement is based on arguments that the future benefits from most R&D efforts are too uncertain to warrant capitalization and that writing them off as soon as possible is more conservative. Nevertheless, others feel that there must be future benefits in many cases or else R&D efforts would not be pursued. Theoretically, R&D costs should be matched with the benefits produced by the R&D expenditures through the capitalization procedure with amortization over the benefited periods.

If R&D costs were to be capitalized, there would be a number of problems. The first would be to determine and analyze R&D costs. Direct costs for each research project would have to be segregated for management control purposes. General R&D overhead costs could either be expensed in total or spread to specific projects and treated just as the rest of the specific project costs are treated. The second problem would be deciding which projects should be capitalized. Where it is obvious that no foreseeable benefits are forthcoming from a certain line of research, its costs might be expensed. Costs of projects that result in future benefits should be capitalized. A third accounting problem would be to determine the period over which capitalized R&D costs should be amortized. Usually, the life span of benefits is uncertain, and the benefits are unevenly distributed over the years. As a consequence, it would usually be necessary to select an arbitrary time period, such as 5 years, over which to amortize the costs.

Advertising

The case for capitalizing and then amortizing advertising costs may not be as strong as that for R&D. Advertising expenditures are designed to increase sales of the period in which they are made, but there is a lag between the incurrence of these

---

[12] Financial Accounting Standards Board, *Statement of Financial Accounting Standards No. 2,* "Accounting for Research and Development Costs," 1974.

costs and their impact. The impact of advertising probably extends into subsequent periods.

Common practice immediately expenses (Pattern E in Figure 9.1) all advertising and sales promotion costs, regardless of the timing of their impact. Those supporting this practice argue that: (1) it is more conservative to do so; (2) it is almost impossible to quantify the future effects and timing of benefits derived from these costs; and (3) when these costs remain stable from year to year, income is not affected by the capitalization policy after the first few years. Nevertheless, we support the capitalization treatment. Doing so will better match costs and resulting benefits.

Patents

A patent is a right obtained from the federal government to exclude others from the benefits from an invention. The legal life of patent protection may be as long as 17 years, although the economic life of the patent may be considerably less. The accounting for patent costs depends on whether the patent was purchased from another party or developed internally. If the former, the purchase price is capitalized. If the latter, the total cost of product development and patent application is expensed as required for all R&D costs. Purchased patent costs are usually amortized over the shorter of: (1) the remaining legal life, or (2) its estimated economic life. If for some reason the patent becomes worthless, the remaining capitalized cost is recognized immediately as an expense of that period.

Goodwill

Goodwill is an intangible asset that will be mentioned here only briefly. A more detailed discussion follows in Chapter 13. Goodwill arises from the purchase of one company or operating unit by another company and is measured as the difference between the amount paid for the acquired company as a whole and the sum of the current value of its individual assets and net of its liabilities. Thus, goodwill will appear in the financial statements of the company making the acquisition. Under present practice, goodwill (and other intangibles) acquired after October, 1970, must be amortized over a time period not longer than 40 years.[13] It is generally not recognized by a company that develops the goodwill itself, even though large expenditures for advertising and other publicity may be made annually. All such expenditures are charged to expense as incurred. Notes 2 and 13 of the General Products Company in Appendix Exhibit A.4 illustrates the typical disclosure for amortization of intangibles.

Summary

Although there are three major classes of long-lived operating assets—plant assets, wasting assets (natural resources), and intangibles—the major accounting problems for each class are the same: (1) calculate the cost of the asset to be capitalized as an

---

[13] Accounting Principles Board, *Opinion No. 17,* "Intangible Assets," 1970.

asset, (2) estimate the total period of benefit or the amount of expected benefits, and (3) assign the cost among the benefited periods or units of benefit in a systematic and reasonable fashion.

We have focused our attention on depreciable plant assets and their depreciation. For these assets, the cost figure to be charged off is frequently reduced by salvage value. The period (or number of units) of benefit is determined by judgment based on experience or by relying on guidelines set down by the Internal Revenue Service. The pattern of depreciation charges over the asset's life is usually based on some conventional method—the most common methods in practice are straight-line, double-declining-balance, and sum-of-the-years'-digits.

If the asset is retired before the end of the estimated service life for an amount different from its book value, a gain or loss will be recognized. If the asset is traded in on another asset, a gain or loss may or may not be recognized depending on the terms of the transaction.

Intangibles such as trademarks, copyrights, patents, and computer programs are the most valuable resources owned by some firms. The accounting treatment of purchased intangibles is the same as for tangible assets. For intangibles developed by a firm, accounting requires the immediate expensing of the developmental costs. This accounting drastically alters the look of some financial statements. The firms most likely to be affected are service, rather than manufacturing, companies.

Problem 1 for Self-Study

Purdy Company acquires two used trucks from Foster Company. Although the trucks are not identical, they both cost $15,000. Purdy Company knew when it negotiated the purchase price that the first truck required extensive engine repair, expected to cost about $4,000. The repair was made the week after acquisition and actually cost $4,200. Purdy Company thought the second truck was in normal operating condition when it negotiated the purchase price but discovered on using the truck that certain bearings needed replacing. The cost of this repair, made the week after acquisition, was $4,200.

a What costs should be recorded in the accounts for the two trucks?
b If the amounts recorded above are different, then distinguish between the two "repairs."

Suggested Solution

a First truck recorded at $19,200. Second truck recorded at $15,000, with $4,200 debited to expense or loss.
b At the time the first truck was acquired, Purdy Company knew it would have to make the "repair." The purchase price was presumably reduced because of the known cost to be incurred. At the time of acquisition, the cost was anticipated to be required in order to produce the expected service potential of the asset. The fact that the cost is $4,200, rather than "about $4,000," seems not to violate the Purdy Company's expectations at the time it acquired the truck. If the repair had cost significantly more than $4,000, say $7,000, then the excess would be loss or expense.

The second truck was assumed to be operable when the purchase price was agreed. The cost of the repair is incurred to bring about the level of service potential already thought to have been acquired. There are no more future benefits after the repair than had been anticipated at the time of acquisition. Therefore, the $4,200 is expense or loss.

Problem 2 for Self-Study

Jensen Company purchased land with a building standing on it as the site for a new plant it planned to construct. The company received bids from several independent contractors for demolition of the old building and construction of the new one. It rejected all bids and undertook demolition and construction using company labor, facilities, and equipment.

All transactions relating to these properties were debited or credited to a single account, Real Estate. Various items in the Real Estate account are described below. The Real Estate account is to be closed. All amounts in it should be taken out and reclassified into one of the following accounts:

(1) Land account.
(2) Buildings account.
(3) Revenue, gain, or expense contra account.
(4) Expense, loss, or revenue contra account.
(5) Some other account.

You may reclassify amounts of the following transactions into two or more of the above. If you use **(5)**, some other account, indicate the nature of the account.

a Cost of land, including old building.
b Legal fees paid to bring about purchase of land and to transfer its title.
c Invoice cost of materials and supplies used in construction.
d Direct labor and materials cost incurred in demolition of old building.
e Direct costs of excavating raw land to prepare it for the foundation of the new building.
f Discounts earned for prompt payment of item **c**.
g Interest for year on notes issued to finance construction.
h Amounts equivalent to interest on Jensen Company's own funds used in construction that would have been invested in marketable securities if an independent contractor had been used. The amount was debited to Real Estate and credited to Interest Revenue so that the cost of the real estate would be comparable to its cost if it had been built by an independent contractor.
i Depreciation for period of construction on trucks that were used both in construction and regular company operations.
j Proceeds of sale of materials salvaged from old buildings were debited to Cash and credited to Real Estate.
k Cost of building permits.
l Salaries of certain corporate engineering executives can be allocated between Salary Expense and Real Estate. The portion debited to Real Estate represents an estimate of the portion of the time spent during the year on planning and construction activities for the new building.
m Payments for property taxes on plant site owed by its former owner but assumed by Jensen Company.
n Payments for property taxes on plant site for construction period.
o Insurance premiums to cover workers engaged in demolition and construction activities.

The insurance policy contains various deductible clauses, requiring the company to pay the first $5,000 of damages from any accident.

p Cost of injury claims for $2,000 paid by the company because the amount was less than the deductible amount in the policy.

q Costs of new machinery to be installed in building.

r Installation costs for the machinery above.

s Profit on construction of new building (computed as the difference between lowest independent contractor's bid and the actual construction cost) was debited to Real Estate and credited to Construction Revenue.

Suggested Solution

(1) a, b, d, j, l, m, o.
(2) c, e, f, g, i, k, l, n, o, p.
(3) —.
(4) h, i, s.
(5) i, q, r.

Comments and Explanations

f If the net price method is used for recording acquisition, then no entry is required at the time the discounts are taken. If the gross price method is used, then the credits for the discount will be to the Building account, reducing its cost.

h Although one capitalizes explicit interest, one may not capitalize opportunity-cost interest or interest imputed on one's own funds used. The adjusting entry credits Real Estate and debits Interest Revenue or its contra. In any case, the debit reduces income, removing the revenue that had been recognized by the company.

i Computation of the amounts to be allocated requires an estimate. Once the amounts are estimated, they are debited to Building or to Depreciation Expense and Work-in-Process Inventory, as appropriate for the regular company operations.

j Credit to Land account, reducing its cost.

l Allocate to Land and Building based on estimate of how time was spent. Given the description, most of these costs are probably for the building. If all of the salaries had been debited to Real Estate, then some must be reclassified as Salary Expense.

m Part of the cost of the land.

n Capitalized as part of the Building account for the same reasons that interest during construction is capitalized. Some accountants would treat this item as expense. In any case, this item can be an expense for tax reporting.

p Although many would treat this as an expense or loss for the period, we think it is part of the cost of the building for the same reason that the explicit insurance cost is capitalized. If, however, the company was irrational in acquiring insurance policies with deductible clauses, then this item is expense or loss. We assume, as is reasonable for most managements most of the time, that management made a rational decision. In any case, it can be treated as an expense or loss for tax reporting.

q Debit to Machine and Equipment account, an asset account separate from Building.

r Treat the same as preceding item; installation costs are part of the cost of the asset. See Chapter 2.

s The effect of recognizing revenue is reversed. The Real Estate account is credited and Construction Revenue or its contra is debited.

Problem 3 for Self-Study

Central States Electric Company constructed a nuclear generating power plant at a cost of $200 million. The plant is expected to last 50 years before being retired from service. The company estimates that at the time the plant is retired from service, $20 million in "decommissioning costs" (costs to dismantle the plant and dispose of the radioactive materials) will be incurred. Straight-line depreciation is computed and charged once per year, at year-end.

During the eleventh year of operation, new regulations governing nuclear waste disposal are enacted. The estimated decommissioning costs increase from $20 million to $24 million.

During the thirty-first year of operation, the life of the plant is revised. It will last 60 years in total, not 50 years.

At the end of the thirty-fifth year, the plant is sold to another utility company for $80 million.

a What is the depreciation charge for the first year?
b What is the depreciation charge for the eleventh year?
c What is the depreciation charge for the thirty-first year?
d Record the journal entry for the sale of the plant at the end of the thirty-fifth year.

Suggested Solution

(Dollar amounts in millions.)

a $4.4 per year = ($200 + $20)/50 years.
b $4.5 per year = ($200 + $20 + $4 − $4.4 per year × 10 years)/40 years remaining life.
   = ($224 − $44)/40.
   = $180/40.
c $3.0 per year = ($180 − $4.5 × 20 years)/30 years remaining life.
   = ($180 − $90)/30.
   = $90/30.
d Book value at
   time of sale = $200 − $4.4 × 10 − $4.5 × 20 − $3.0 × 5
   = $51.

December 31 of Year 35		
Cash	80.0	
Accumulated Depreciation on Power Plant	149.0	
Power Plant		200.0
Gain on Disposal of Plant		29.0
Accumulated Depreciation = $4.4 × 10 + $4.5 × 20 + $3.0 × 5		

Problem 4 for Self-Study

Widdicomb Company is considering changing from the flow-through method to the deferral method of accounting for the investment credit. It expects to acquire assets subject to increasing dollar amounts of investment credits each year for the foreseeable future. Indicate the effect on each of the following items in the financial statements 2 years hence if the deferral, rather than flow-through, method is used, starting now and continuing for the indefinite future.

a Recorded Cost of Assets Acquired.
b Income Taxes Payable.
c Income Tax Expense.
d Deferred Investment Credits on balance sheet.
e Depreciation Expense.
f Net Income for year.
g Retained Earnings.
h Total Equities.

Suggested Solution

Larger under the deferral method than under the flow-through method: **c, d**.
Smaller under the deferral method than under the flow-through method: **f, g**.
The same under both methods: **a, b, e, h**.

Questions and Problems

1 Review the meaning of the following concepts or terms discussed in this chapter.

a Amortization.
b Plant assets and depreciation.
c Interest during construction.
d Wasting assets and depletion.
e Percentage depletion allowance.
f Intangibles.
g Capitalize.
h Improvements.
i Repairs.
j Maintenance.
k Joint cost.
l Value.
m Residual or salvage value.
n Service or depreciable life.
o Asset depreciation range.
p Straight-line (time and use) methods.
q Declining- and double-declining-balance methods.
r Sum-of-the-years'-digits method.
s Book value.
t Treatment of changes in estimates of useful lives and residual values of long-lived assets.
u Trade-in transaction.
v Research and development.
w Goodwill.
x Investment credit.
y Flow-through method.
z Deferral method.

2 a "Accounting for depreciating assets would be greatly simplified if accounting periods were only long enough or the life of the assets short enough." What is the point of the quotation?

b "The major purpose of depreciation accounting is to provide funds for the replacement of assets as they wear out." Do you agree? Explain.

3 "Showing both acquisition cost and accumulated depreciation amounts separately provides a rough indication of the relative age of the firm's long-lived assets."

a Assume that the Abril Company acquired an asset with a depreciable cost of $100,000 several years ago. Accumulated depreciation as of December 31, recorded on a straight-line basis, is $60,000. The depreciation charge for the year is $10,000. What is the asset's depreciable life? How old is the asset?

b Assume straight-line depreciation. Devise a formula that, given the depreciation charge for the year and the asset's accumulated depreciation, can be used to determine the age of the asset.

4 For each of the following expenditures or acquisitions, indicate the type of account debited. Classify the accounts as asset other than product cost, product cost (Work-in-Process Inventory), or expense. If the account debited is an asset account, then specify whether it is current or noncurrent.

a $150 for repairs of office machines.

b $1,500 for emergency repairs to an office machine.

c $250 for maintenance of delivery trucks.

d $5,000 for a machine acquired in return for a 3-year note.

e $4,200 for research and development staff salaries.

f $3,100 for newspaper ads.

g $6,400 for wages of factory workers engaged in production.

h $3,500 for wages of factory workers engaged in installing equipment.

i $2,500 for salaries of office work force.

j $1,000 for legal fees in acquiring an ore deposit.

k $1,200 for a 1-year insurance policy beginning next month.

l $1,800 for U.S. Treasury Notes, to be sold to pay the next installment due on income taxes.

m $4,000 for royalty payment on a patent used in manufacturing.

n $10,000 for purchase of a trademark.

o $100 filing fee for copyright registration application.

5 Refer to the Simplified Statement of Changes in Financial Position for a Period in Exhibit 5.19 on page 191. Nine of the lines in the statement are numbered. Line (2) should be expanded to say "Additions for Expenses and Other Charges Against Income Not Using Funds," and line (3) should be expanded to say "Subtractions for Revenues and Other Credits to Income Not Producing Funds from Operations." Ignore the unnumbered lines in responding to the questions below.

Assume that the accounting cycle is complete for the period and that all of the financial statements have been prepared. Then, it is discovered that a transaction has been overlooked. That transaction is recorded in the accounts and all of the financial statements are corrected. Define *funds* as *working capital*. For each of the following transactions, indicate which of the numbered lines of the funds statement is affected and by how much. Ignore income tax effects.

a A machine that cost $10,000 and that has $7,000 of accumulated depreciation is sold for $4,000 cash.

b A machine that cost $10,000 and that has $7,000 of accumulated depreciation is sold for $2,000 cash.

c A machine that cost $10,000 and that has $7,000 of accumulated depreciation is traded in on a new machine. The new machine has a cash price of $12,000. A trade-in allowance for the old machine of $4,000 is given, so that $8,000 cash is paid.

d A fire destroys a warehouse. The loss is uninsured. The warehouse cost $80,000 and at the time of the fire had accumulated depreciation of $30,000.

e Refer to the facts of part **d**. Inventory costing $70,000 was also destroyed. The loss was uninsured.

6 Refer to the instructions in the preceding question. Follow the instructions for the following transactions or events relating to the investment credit. During the year, qualifying assets with a 10-year depreciable life are acquired, and investment credits of $10,000 are realized.

a The flow-through method of accounting is used. Record the effects for the year the assets are acquired.

b The flow-through method of accounting is used. Record the effects for the year after the assets are acquired.

c The deferral method is used. Record the effects for the year the assets are acquired.

d The deferral method is used. Record the effects for the year after the assets are acquired.

7 a What is the effect of capitalizing interest on reported net income summed over all the periods of the life of a given self-constructed asset, from building through use, until eventual retirement? Contrast with a policy of expensing interest as incurred.

b Consider a company engaging in increasing dollar amounts of self-construction activity each period over periods when interest rates do not decline. What is the effect on reported income each year of capitalizing interest in contrast to expensing interest as incurred?

8 On April 30, 1982, the Tico Wholesale Company acquired a new machine with a fair market value of $14,000. The seller agreed to accept the company's old machine, $7,000 in cash, and a 12-percent, 1-year note for $4,000 in payment.

The old machine was purchased on January 1, 1977, for $10,000. It was estimated that the old machine would be useful for 8 years, after which it would have a salvage value of $400. It is estimated that the new machine will have a service life of 10 years and a salvage value of $800.

Assuming that the Tico Company uses the straight-line method of depreciation and closes its books annually on December 31, give the entries that were made in 1982.

9 On July 1, 1959, a building and site were purchased for $96,000 by The Hub, a retail clothing store. Of this amount, $40,000 was allocated to the land and the remainder to the building. The building is depreciated on a straight-line basis.

On July 1, 1981 (no additions or retirements having been recorded in the meanwhile), the net book value of the building was $25,200. On March 31, 1982, the building and site were sold for $60,000. The fair market value of the land was $50,000 on this date.

The firm closes its books annually at June 30. Give the entries required on March 31, 1982. (Hint: First compute what the annual depreciation charges must be, based on the facts given.)

10 Journalize the following transactions:

(1) A piece of office equipment is purchased for $850 cash.

(2) Depreciation for 1 year of $170 is recorded.

(3) The equipment is sold for $400. At the time of the sale, the Accumulated Depreciation shows a balance of $340. Depreciation of $170 for the year of the sale has not yet been recorded.

11 Give the journal entries for the following selected transactions of the Eagle Manufacturing Company. The company uses the straight-line method of calculating depreciation and closes its books annually on December 31.

(1) A machine is purchased on November 1, 1976, for $30,000. It is estimated that it will be used for 10 years and that it will have a salvage value of $600 at the end of that time. Give the journal entry for the depreciation at December 31, 1976.

(2) Record the depreciation for the year ending December 31, 1977.

(3) In August, 1982, it is decided that the machine will probably be used for a total of 12 years and that its scrap value will be $400. Record the depreciation for the year ending December 31, 1982.

(4) The machine is sold for $1,000 on March 31, 1987. Record the entries of that date, assuming that depreciation is recorded as indicated in **(3)**.

12 The Alexander Company acquired three used machine tools for a total price of $49,000. Costs to transport the machine tools from the seller to Alexander Company's factory were $1,000. The machine tools were renovated, installed, and put to use in manufacturing the firm's products. The costs of renovation and installation were as follows:

	Machine Tool A	Machine Tool B	Machine Tool C
Renovation Costs	$1,700	$800	$950
Installation Costs	300	550	250

The machine tools have the following estimate lives: tool A—4 years; tool B—10 years; tool C—6 years.

a Assume that each machine tool is capitalized in a separate asset account and that the remaining life of each machine tool is used as the basis for allocating the joint costs of acquisition. Compute the depreciable cost of each of the three machine tools.

b Present journal entries to record depreciation charges for years 1, 5, and 8, given the assumption in part **a**. Use the straight-line method.

c Assume that the three machine tools are treated as one composite asset in the accounts. If management decides to depreciate the entire cost of the composite asset on a straight-line basis over 10 years, what is the depreciation charge for each year?

d Which treatment, **a** or **c**, should management of the Alexander Company probably prefer for tax purposes and why?

13 On March 1, 1982, one of the buildings owned by the Metropolitan Storage Company was destroyed by fire. The cost of the building was $100,000; the balance in the Accumulated Depreciation account at January 1, 1982, was $38,125. A service life of 40 years with a zero salvage value had been estimated for the building. The company uses the straight-line method. The building was not insured.

a Give the journal entries made at March 1.

b If there have been no alterations in the service life estimate, when was the building acquired?

14 Give correcting entries for the following situations. In each case, the firm uses the straight-line method of depreciation and closes its books annually on December 31. Recognize all gains and losses currently.

a A cash register was purchased for $300 on January 1, 1977. It was depreciated at a rate of 10 percent. On June 30, 1982, it was sold for $200 and a new cash register was acquired for $500. The bookkeeper made the following entry to record the transaction:

Store Equipment	300	
Cash in Bank		300

b A used truck was acquired in May 1982 for $4,000. Its cost, when new, was $6,000, and the bookkeeper made the following entry to record the purchase:

Truck	6,000	
Accumulated Depreciation		2,000
Cash		4,000

c A testing mechanism was purchased on April 1, 1980 for $600. It was depreciated at a 10-percent annual rate. On June 30, 1982, it was stolen. The loss was not insured, and the bookkeeper made the following entry:

Theft Loss	600	
Testing Mechanism		600

15 The Grogan Manufacturing Company started business on January 1, 1980. At that time it acquired machine A for $20,000, payment being made by check.

Due to an expansion in the volume of business, machine B, costing $25,000, was acquired on September 30, 1981. A check for $15,000 was issued, with the balance to be paid in annual installments of $2,000 plus interest at the rate of 6 percent on the unpaid balance. The first installment is due on September 30, 1982.

On June 30, 1982, machine A was sold for $13,000 and a larger model, machine C, was acquired for $30,000.

All installments are paid on time.

All machines have an estimated life of 10 years with an estimated salvage value equal to 10 percent of acquisition cost. The company closes its books on December 31. The straight-line method is used.

Prepare dated journal entries to record all transactions through December 31, 1982, including year-end adjustments but excluding closing entries.

16 The Dickhaut Manufacturing Company purchased a plot of land for $90,000 as a plant site. There was a small office building on the plot, conservatively appraised at $20,000, which the company will continue to use with some modification and renovation. The company had plans drawn for a factory and received bids for its construction. It rejected all bids and decided to construct the plant itself. Below are listed additional items that management feels should be included in plant asset accounts.

(1) Materials and supplies	$200,000
(2) Excavation	12,000
(3) Labor on construction	140,000
(4) Cost of remodeling old building into office building	13,000
(5) Interest on money borrowed by Dickhaut*	6,000

*This interest is the entire amount of interest paid during the construction period.

(6) Interest on Dickhaut's own money used 9,000
(7) Cash discounts on materials purchased 7,000
(8) Supervision by management 10,000
(9) Workman's compensation insurance premiums 8,000
(10) Payment of claims for injuries not covered by insurance 3,000
(11) Clerical and other expenses of construction 8,000
(12) Paving of streets and sidewalks 5,000
(13) Architect's plans and specifications 4,000
(14) Legal costs of conveying land 2,000
(15) Legal costs of injury claim 1,000
(16) Income credited to Retained Earnings account, being the difference between
the foregoing cost and the lowest contractor's bid 11,000

Show in detail the items to be included in the following accounts: Land, Factory Building, Office Building, and Site Improvements. Explain why you excluded any items that you did not include in the four accounts.

17 Calculate the depreciation charge for the first and second years of the asset's life in the following cases.

Asset	Cost	Estimated Salvage Value	Life (Years)	Depreciation Method
a. Blast Furnace	$800,000	$25,000	20	Double-Declining-Balance
b. Hotel	500,000	50,000	45	Straight-Line
c. Typewriter	800	80	8	Sum-of-the-Years'-Digits
d. Tractor	18,000	1,500	10	Double-Declining-Balance
e. Delivery Truck	22,000	5,200	6	Sum-of-the-Years'-Digits

18 On January 1, 1982, the Central Production Company acquired a new turret lathe for $36,000. It was estimated to have a useful life of 4 years and no salvage value. The company closes its books annually on December 31. Indicate the amount of the depreciation charge for each of the 4 years under:

a The straight-line method.
b The declining-balance method at twice the straight-line rate.
c The sum-of-the-years'-digits method.
d Assume now that the lathe was acquired on April 1, 1982. Indicate the amount of the depreciation charge for each of the years from 1982 to 1986, using the sum-of-the-years'-digits method. (Hint: Depreciation charges for a year, however they are determined, are allocated on a straight-line basis to periods *within* a year.)

19 Chan Company builds some of its own chemical processing plants. At the start of the year the Construction in Process account had a balance of $1 million. Construction activity occurred uniformly throughout the year. At the end of the year the balance was $5 million. The borrowings of the company during the year were:

New Construction Loans at 20 Percent per Year	$ 2,000,000
Old Bond Issues Maturing at Various Times, Averaging 10-Percent Rate	8,000,000
Total Interest-Bearing Debt	$10,000,000

   a Compute the amount of interest to be capitalized into the Construction in Process account for the year.

   b Present journal entries for interest for the year.

20 A machine is acquired for $8,900. It is expected to last 8 years and to be operated for 25,000 hours during that time. It is estimated that its salvage value will be $1,700 at the end of that time. Calculate the depreciation charge for each of the first 3 years using:

   a The straight-line (time) method.

   b The sum-of-the-years'-digits method.

   c The declining-balance method using a 25-percent rate (the maximum rate allowed).

   d The units-of-production method. Operating times are as follows: first year, 3,500 hours; second year, 2,000 hours; third year, 5,000 hours.

21 The Slowpoke Shipping Company buys a new car for $10,000 on January 1, 1981. It is estimated that it will last 6 years and have a salvage value of $1,000. Early in 1983, it is determined that the car will last only an additional 2 years, or 4 years in total. The company closes its books on December 31. Present a table showing the depreciation charges for each year from 1981 to 1984 and give the adjusting entry made in 1983. Follow the instructions for each of the following methods:

   a The straight-line method.

   b The sum-of-the-years'-digits method.

   c The declining-balance method with depreciation at twice the straight-line rate. The remaining undepreciated cost less salvage value is to be written off in the last year.

22 The Linder Manufacturing Company acquires a new machine for $7,200 on July 1, 1978. It is estimated that it will have a service life of 6 years and then have a salvage value of $900. The company closes its books annually on June 30.

   a Compute the depreciation charges for each year of the asset's life assuming the use of:

     (1) The straight-line method.

     (2) The sum-of-the-years'-digits method.

     (3) The declining-balance method, with a rate twice the straight-line rate.

   b If the machine were sold for $700 on October 30, 1983, give the journal entries that would be made on that date under each of the methods in part **a**.

23 The Twombly Company purchased a new panel truck in May 1980. The truck cost $18,600. It was estimated that the truck would be driven for 100,000 miles before being traded in and that its salvage value at that time would be $2,600.

   Odometer readings are as follows:

December 31, 1980	12,000
December 31, 1981	50,000
December 31, 1982	82,000
June 16, 1983	98,000

On June 16, 1983, the truck was traded in for a new one with a list price of $22,000. The old truck had a fair market value of $2,600, but the dealer allowed $3,000 on it toward the list price of the new one. The balance of the purchase price was paid by check.

a Determine the depreciation charges for each year through 1982, using a "production" or "use" method.

b Record the entries for June 16, 1983, assuming that the list price of the new truck is unreliable, whereas the fair market value of the old is reliable.

c Record the entries for June 16, 1983, assuming that there were no reliable estimates for the fair market value of the old truck.

24 Refer to the data in Problem 12 at the end of Chapter 5 on page 193 for the Harris Company. Assume in the supplementary information, item (2), that the proceeds of sale of the equipment amount to $400, rather than $2,000. As a result, net income declines from $39,000 to $37,400, and dividends are reduced from $30,000 to $28,400. All other items remain unchanged. Prepare a statement of changes in financial position for the year 1982, using a working capital definition of funds.

25 Refer to the data in Problem 12 at the end of Chapter 5 on page 193 for the Harris Company. Assume in the supplementary information, item (2), that the proceeds of sale of the equipment amount to $3,000, rather than $2,000. As a result, net income increases from $39,000 to $40,000, and dividends are increased from $30,000 to $31,000. All other items remain unchanged. Prepare a statement of changes in financial position for the year 1982, using a working capital definition of funds.

26 The balance sheet of Woolf's Department Store shows a building with an original cost of $800,000 and accumulated depreciation of $660,000. The building is being depreciated on a straight-line basis over 40 years. The remaining depreciable life of the building is 7 years. On January 2 of the current year, an expenditure of $28,000 was made on the street-level displays of the store. Indicate the accounting for the current year if the expenditure of $28,000 was made under each of the following circumstances. Each of these cases is to be considered independently of the others, except where noted. Ignore income tax effects.

a Management decided that improved displays would make the store's merchandise seem more attractive. The displays are a worthwhile investment.

b A violent hailstorm on New Year's Day destroyed the display windows previously installed. There was no insurance coverage for this sort of destruction. The new windows installed are physically identical to the old windows. The old windows had a book value of $28,000 at the time of the storm.

c Vandals destroyed the display windows on New Year's Day. There was no insurance coverage for this sort of destruction. The new windows installed are physically identical to the old windows. The old windows had a book value of $28,000 at the time of the destruction.

d The old displays contained windows constructed of nonshatterproof glass. Management had previously considered replacing its old nonshatterproof windows with new ones but had decided that there was *zero* benefit to the firm in doing so. New shatterproof windows are installed because a new law was passed requiring that all stores must have shatterproof windows on the street level. The alternative to installing the new windows was to shut down the store. In responding to this part, assume *zero* benefits result from the new windows. Part **e** below considers the more realistic case of some benefits.

e Management had previously considered replacing its old, nonshatterproof windows with new ones, but decided that the new windows would produce future benefits of

381

only $7,000 and so were not a worthwhile investment. However, a new law (see part **d**) now requires them to do so (or else shut down) and the new windows are installed.

27 In each of the following situations, compute the amounts of revenue, gain, expense, and loss to be shown on the income statement for the year and the amount of asset to be shown on the balance sheet as of the end of the year. Show the journal entry or entries required, and provide reasons for your decisions. Straight-line amortization is used. The reporting period is the calendar year. The situations are independent of each other, except where noted.

a Because of a new fire code, a department store must install additional fire escapes on its building. The fire escapes are acquired for $28,000 cash on January 1. The building is expected to be demolished 7 years from the date the fire escapes were installed.

b Many years ago, a firm acquired shares of stock in the General Electric Company for $100,000. On December 31, the firm acquired a building with an appraised value of $1 million. The company paid for the building by giving up its shares in the General Electric Company at a time when equivalent shares traded on the New York Stock Exchange for $1,050,000.

c Same data as part **b**, except that the shares of stock represent ownership in Small Timers, Inc., whose shares are traded on a regional stock exchange. The last transaction in shares of Small Timers, Inc., occurred on December 27. Using the prices of the most recent trades, the shares of stock of Small Timers, Inc. given in exchange for the building have a market value of $1,050,000.

d A company decides that it can save $3,500 a year for at least a decade by switching from small panel trucks to larger delivery vans. To do so requires remodeling costs of $18,000 for various garages. The first fleet of delivery vans will last for 5 years, and the garages will last for 20 years. The garages are remodeled on January 1.

e A company drills for oil. It sinks 10 holes during the year at a cost of $1 million each. Nine of the holes are dry, but the tenth is a gusher. By the end of the year, the oil known to be recoverable from the gusher has a net realizable value of $40 million. No oil was extracted during the year.

f A company manufactures aircraft. During the current year, all sales were to the government under defense contracts. The company spent $400,000 on institutional advertising to keep its name before the business community. It expects to resume sales of small jet planes to corporate buyers in 2 years.

g A company runs a large laboratory that has, over the years, found marketable ideas and products worth tens of millions of dollars. On average, the successful products have a life of 10 years. Expenditures for the laboratory this year were $1,500,000.

h A textile manufacturer gives $250,000 to the Textile Engineering Department of a local university for basic research in fibers. The results of the research, if any, will belong to the general public.

i On January 1, an automobile company incurs costs of $6 million for specialized machine tools necessary for producing a new model automobile. Such tools last for 6 years, on average, but the new model automobile is expected to be produced for only 3 years.

j On January 1, an airline purchased a fleet of airbuses for $100 million cash. The airbuses have an expected useful life of 10 years and no salvage value. At the same time the airline purchased for cash $20 million of spare parts for use with those airbuses. The spare parts have no use, now or in the future, other than replacing broken or worn-out airbus parts. During the first year of operation, no spare parts were used.

382

k Refer to the data in the preceding part. In the second year of operation, $1 million of spare parts were used.

28 In each of the following situations, compute the amounts of gain or loss to be shown on the income statement for the year, as well as the amount of asset to be shown on the balance sheet as of the end of the year. Show the journal entry or entries required, and provide reasons for your decisions.

    a A company wishes to acquire a 5-acre site for a new warehouse. The land it wants is part of a 10-acre site that the owner insists be purchased as a whole for $18,000. The company purchases the land, spends $2,000 in legal fees for rights to divide the site into two 5-acre plots, and immediately offers half of the land for resale. The two best offers are
    (1) $12,000 for the east half, and
    (2) $13,000 for the west half.
    The company sells the east half.

    b The same data as in part **a**, except the two best offers are
    (1) $5,000 for the east half, and
    (2) $12,000 for the west half.
    The company sells the west half.

29 The Libby Company has income tax expense, before any investment credits, of $50,000 each year. At the start of the first year, it acquires an asset with a depreciable life of 4 years. Assume that the asset qualifies for an investment credit of $4,000.

    a Record income taxes and the entries related to the investment credit for the 4 years of the asset's life using the flow-through method.

    b Record entries related to income taxes and the investment credit for the 4 years of the asset's life using the deferral method.

30 Refer to the data in the preceding problem for the Libby Company. Assume that each year the Libby Equilibrium Company acquires an asset with a depreciable life of 4 years. Each year the asset acquired qualifies for an investment credit of $4,000, and income tax expense before any investment credits is $50,000.

    a Record entries related to income taxes and the investment credit for each of the first 5 years using the flow-through method.

    b Record entries related to income taxes and the investment credit for each of the first 5 years using the deferral method.

    c Assuming that Libby Equilibrium Company's income taxes, asset acquisitions, and investment credits continue in the following years as in the first 4 years, describe the effects on the financial statements of the two methods of accounting for the investment credit.

    d Assume the same data as in part **c**, but that the new asset's cost increases by 10 percent each year and that the amount of the investment credit earned increases by 10 percent each year. Describe the effects on the financial statements of the two methods of accounting for the investment credit.

31 Three companies have each recently made investments in equipment designed to save fuel. The equipment purchased by each company costs $200,000 and has a 10-year service life. In all three cases, the company was entitled to a $20,000 investment tax credit when it purchased the asset during the current year. The income taxes otherwise payable of all three companies were reduced by $20,000 during the current year. In all three companies, management had made careful studies of the costs and benefits of acquiring the new equipment.

Management of Company A decided that the equipment purchased would provide operating cost savings with a present value of $250,000. The company is delighted to acquire the asset.

Management of Company B decided that the equipment it purchased would provide operating cost savings with a present value of $180,000. The equipment was worth acquiring only because of the investment credit.

Management of Company C decided that the equipment it purchased provided operating cost savings with a present value of $195,000. The equipment was acquired only because the investment credit made the investment worthwhile.

a Discuss the considerations the management of each of these companies might give to accounting for the investment credit.

b What can you conclude from this question about the appropriate method of accounting for the investment credit?

32 The Consumer Products Company has $300,000 of total assets. The Consumer Products Company has been earning $45,000 per year and generating $45,000 per year of cash flow from operations. Each year the Consumer Products Company distributes its earnings by paying cash of $45,000 to owners. Management of the Consumer Products Company believes that a new advertising campaign now will lead to increased sales over the next 4 years. The anticipated net cash flows of the project are as follows:

Beginning of Year	Net Cash (Outflow) Inflow
1	($24,000)
2, 3, and 4	10,000 each year

Assume that the advertising campaign is undertaken, that cash flows are as planned, and that the Consumer Products Company makes payments to owners of $45,000 at the end of the first year and $47,000 at the end of each of the next 3 years. Assume that there are no interest expenses in any year. Ignore any income tax effects.

a Compute net income and the rate of return on assets of the Consumer Products Company for each of the 4 years, assuming that advertising expenditures are expensed as they occur. Use the year-end balance of total assets in the denominator of the rate-of-return calculation.

b Compute net income and the rate of return on assets of the Consumer Products Company for each year of the project, assuming that advertising costs are capitalized and then amortized on a straight-line basis over the last 3 years. Use the year-end balance of total assets in the denominator of the rate of return on assets.

c How well has the management of the Consumer Products Company carried out its responsibility to its owners? On what basis do you make this judgment? Which method of accounting seems to reflect performance more adequately?

33 In 1982, Epstein Company acquired the assets of Falk Company. The assets of Falk Company included various intangibles. Discuss the accounting for the acquisition in 1982, and in later years, for each of the items described below.

384

a Registration of the trademark Thyrom® for thyristors expires in 3 years. Epstein Company thought that the trademark had a fair market value of $100,000. It expects to continue making and selling Thyrom thyristors indefinitely.

b The design patent covering the ornamentation of the containers for displaying Thyrom thyristors expires in 5 years. The Epstein Company thought that the design patent had a fair market value of $30,000 and expects to continue making the containers indefinitely.

c An unpatented trade secret on a special material used in manufacturing thyristors was viewed as having a fair market value of $200,000.

d Refer to the trade secret in part **c**. Suppose that in 1983 a competitor discovers the trade secret, but does not disclose the secret to other competitors. How should the plans for accounting be changed?

e During 1982, the Epstein Company produced a sales promotion film, *Using Thyristors for Fun and Profit,* at a cost of $45,000. The film is licensed to purchasers of thyristors for use in training their employees and customers. The film is copyrighted.

34 Equilibrium Company plans to spend $60,000 at the beginning of each of the next several years advertising the Company's brand names and trademarks. As a result of the advertising expenditure for a given year, aftertax income (not counting advertising expense) is expected to increase by $24,000 a year for 3 years, including the year of the expenditure itself. Equilibrium Company has other aftertax income of $20,000 per year. The controller of Equilibrium Company wonders what the effect on the financial statements will be of following one of two accounting policies with respect to advertising expenditures:

(1) Expensing the advertising costs in the year of expenditures.

(2) Capitalizing the advertising costs and amortizing them over 3 years, including the year of the expenditure itself.

Assume that the Company does spend $60,000 at the beginning of each of 4 years and that the planned increase in income occurs. Ignore income tax effects.

a Prepare a 4-year condensed summary of net income, assuming that policy **(1)** is followed and advertising costs are expensed as incurred.

b Prepare a 4-year condensed summary of net income, assuming that policy **(2)** is followed and advertising costs are capitalized and amortized over 3 years. Compute also the amount of Deferred Advertising Costs (asset) to be shown on the balance sheet at the end of each of the 4 years.

c In what sense is policy **(1)** a conservative policy?

d What will be the effect on net income and on the balance sheet if Equilibrium Company continues to spend $60,000 each year and the effects on aftertax income continue as in the first 4 years?

Chapter 10 *Liabilities: Introduction*

This chapter and the next two examine the accounting concepts and procedures for the right-hand side of the balance sheet, which shows the sources of a firm's financing. The funds used to acquire assets come from two sources: owners and non-owners. Owners' equity is the subject of Chapter 12. This chapter and Chapter 11 discuss obligations incurred by a business that result from raising funds from non-owners. Banks and creditors providing debt on a long-term basis are aware of their role as providers of funds. Suppliers and employees who do not require immediate cash payment for goods provided or services rendered usually do not think of themselves as contributing to a firm's funds, even though they do. Likewise, customers who advance cash to a firm prior to delivery of a good or service provide funds to the firm. The obligations that a business incurs to these non-owning contributors of funds are called *liabilities*.

Basic Concepts of Liabilities

In accounting, an obligation is generally recognized as a liability of an entity if it has three essential characteristics:[1]

1 The obligation involves a probable future sacrifice of resources—a future transfer of cash, goods, or services or the forgoing of a future cash receipt—at a specified or determinable date.

---

[1] Financial Accounting Standards Board, *Statement of Financial Accounting Concepts No. 3,* "Elements of Financial Statements of Business Enterprises," 1980, par. 29.

386

2 The entity has little or no discretion to avoid the transfer.

3 The transaction or event giving rise to the entity's obligation has already occurred.

A thorough understanding of liabilities requires knowledge of compound-interest and present-value computations. In these computations, payments made at different times are made comparable by taking into account the interest that cash can earn over time. Appendix B at the back of the book introduces the computations. Although Appendix B can be omitted without losing continuity with the rest of the book, much of the discussion in this chapter and the next will be easier to follow if you understand present-value analysis.

Example 1 Miller Corporation's employees have earned wages and salaries that will not be paid until the next payday, 2 weeks after the end of the current accounting period. Miller Corporation's suppliers are owed substantial amounts for goods sold to Miller Corporation, but these debts are not due for 10 to 30 days after the end of the period. Miller Corporation owes the federal and state governments for taxes, but the payments are not due until the 15th of next month. Each of these items meets the three criteria to be a liability. Thus, they are shown as liabilities under titles such as Wages Payable, Salaries Payable, Accounts Payable, and Taxes Payable.

Example 2 When Miller Corporation sells television sets, it gives a warranty to repair or replace any faulty parts or faulty sets within 1 year after sale. This obligation meets the three criteria of a liability. Because some television sets will surely need repair, the future sacrifice of resources is probable. The obligation to make repairs is Miller Corporation's. The transaction giving rise to the obligation, the sale of the television set, has already occurred.

The amount is not known with certainty, but Miller Corporation has had sufficient experience with its own television sets to be able to estimate with reasonable precision what the expected costs of repairs or replacements will be. The repairs or replacements will occur within a time span, 1 year, known with reasonable precision. Miller Corporation will thus show Estimated Liability for Warranty Payments on its balance sheet.

Example 3 Miller Corporation signs a binding contract to supply certain goods to a customer within the next 6 months. In this case, there is an obligation, definite time, and definite amount (of goods, if not cash), but there has been no past or current transaction. Chapter 2 pointed out that accounting does not recognize assets or liabilities in events where there is no mutual performance. Without some mutual performance, there is no current or past benefit. Thus no liability is shown in this case.

Example 4 Facts are the same as in Example 3, except that the customer has made a $10,000 cash deposit on signing the order. Here Miller Corporation engaged in a transaction, accepting cash. It will show a liability called Advances from Customers in the amount of $10,000.

Example 5 Miller Corporation has signed a 3-year, noncancelable lease with the IBM Corporation to make payments of $3,000 per month for the use of a computer system with a 3-year life. Definite amounts are due at definite times, and a transaction has occurred—a computer system has been received. Thus Miller Corporation should show a liability called Present Value of Future Payments under Capital Leases on its balance sheet.

Example 6 Miller Corporation is defendant in a class-action lawsuit alleging damages of $10 million. The lawsuit was filed by customers who claim to have been injured by misleading advertising about Miller Corporation's television sets. Lawyers retained by the Corporation think that there is an adequate defense to the charges. Because there is no obligation to make a payment at a reasonably definite time, there is no liability. The notes to the financial statements will disclose the existence of the lawsuit, but no liability will be shown on the balance sheet.

Example 7 Miller Corporation has signed a contract promising to employ its president for the next 5 years and to pay the president a salary of $250,000 per year. The salary is to be increased in future years at the same rate as the Consumer Price Index, published by the U.S. Government, increases. Miller Corporation has an obligation to make payments (although the president may quit at any time without penalty). The payments are of reasonably certain amounts and are to be made at definite times. At the time the contract is signed, no mutual performance has occurred. Because a transaction is not deemed to have taken place, no liability is shown on the balance sheet. A liability will, of course, arise as the president performs services over time.

Example 8 Miller Corporation has signed a contract with Interstate Oil Pipe Line Company to ship at least 10,000 barrels of crude oil per month for the next 3 years. Miller Corporation must pay for the shipping services, whether or not it actually ships oil. An arrangement such as this, called a *throughput contract,* is not recorded as a liability, because the event giving rise to the obligation is viewed as being actual shipment, which has not yet occurred. Such an obligation is merely disclosed in notes. Similarly, long-term obligations for so-called "take or pay contracts," where the "purchaser" is obligated to pay for certain quantities or goods, whether or not the purchaser actually takes delivery to the goods, is not a formal liability, but must be disclosed.[2]

Valuation

In *historical*-cost accounting, liabilities are shown on the balance sheet as the present value of payments to be made in the future. The interest rate used in computing the present-value amount throughout the life of a liability is the interest rate that the

[2] Financial Accounting Standards Board, *Statement of Financial Accounting Standards No. 47,* "Disclosure of Long-Term Obligations," 1981.

388

specific borrower was required to pay at the time the liability was initially incurred. That is, the *historical* interest rate is used.

As mentioned in Chapter 2, most current liabilities are stated at the amount payable because the difference between the amount ultimately payable and its present value is immaterial.

Classification

Liabilities are generally classified on the balance sheet as *current* or *noncurrent*. The criterion generally used for dividing current from noncurrent liabilities is the length of time that will elapse before payment must be made. The dividing line between the two is usually 1 year.

Contingencies— Potential Obligations

One of the criteria used by the accountant to recognize a liability is that there be a probable future sacrifice of resources. The world of business and law is full of uncertainties. At any given time a firm may find itself potentially liable for events that have occurred in the past. This so-called contingency (or "loss contingency") is, in fact, not an accounting liability. It is not currently an obligation but is a potential, future obligation. It arises from an event that has occurred in the past but whose outcome is not now known. Whether or not the item becomes a liability, and how large a liability it will become, depends on a future event, such as the outcome of a lawsuit.

Suppose that the company is sued for damages in a formal court proceeding for an accident involving a customer who was visiting the company. The suit is not scheduled for trial until after the close of the accounting period. If the company's lawyers and auditors agree that the outcome is likely to be favorable for the company or that, if unfavorable, the amount of the damage settlement will not be large, then no liability will be recognized on the balance sheet. The notes to the financial statements must disclose, however, significant contingencies.

The FASB has said that an estimated loss from a contingency should be recognized in the accounts only if both of the following conditions are met:[3]

(a) Information available prior to the issuance of the financial statements indicates that it is probable that an asset had been impaired or that a liability had been incurred. . . .

(b) The amount of the loss can be reasonably estimated.

---

[3] Financial Accounting Standards Board, *Statement of Financial Accounting Standards No. 5,* "Accounting for Contingencies," 1975. When information indicates that it is probable that an asset has been impaired or a liability has been incurred and an estimate of the amount has been made, but the estimate is a range, then the lower end of the range is to be used. For example, if the estimated loss is a range from $1 million to $1.5 million, then the amount $1 million would be used.

An example suggested by the FASB Statement is that of a toy manufacturer who has sold products for which a safety hazard has been discovered. The toy manufacturer thinks it likely that liabilities have been incurred. Test (b), on the preceding page, would be met if experience or other information enabled the manufacturer to make a reasonable estimate of the loss. The journal entry would be:

Loss on Damage Claim	50,000	
Estimated Liability for Damages		50,000
To recognize estimated liability for expected damage arising from safety hazard of toys sold.		

The debit in the above entry is to a loss account (presented among other expenses on the income statement), and the credit is to an estimated liability which should be treated as a current liability, similar to the Estimated Warranty Liability account, on the balance sheet. In practice, an account with the title "Estimated Liability for Damages" would seldom, if ever, appear in published financial statements, because it would be perceived as an admission of guilt. Such an admission is likely to adversely affect the outcome of the lawsuit. The liability account would be combined with others for financial statement presentation.

The term *contingency,* or sometimes *contingent liability,* is used only when the item is not recognized in the accounts but, rather, in the footnotes. (Notes receivable sold *with* recourse, described in Chapter 7, are another example of a contingency.) A recent annual report of General Motors illustrates the disclosure of contingencies as follows.

Note 14. Contingent Liabilities

There are various claims and pending actions against the Corporation and its subsidiaries with respect to commercial matters, including warranties and product liability, governmental regulations including environmental and safety matters, civil rights, patent matters, taxes and other matters arising out of the conduct of business. Certain of these actions purport to be class actions, seeking damages in very large amounts. The amounts of liability on these claims and actions at . . . [year-end] were not determinable but, in the opinion of the management, the ultimate liability resulting will not materially affect the consolidated financial position or results of operations of the Corporation and its consolidated subsidiaries.

Current Liabilities

Current liabilities are normally those due within 1 year. They include accounts payable to creditors, payroll accruals, short-term notes payable, taxes payable, and a few others. Current liabilities are continually discharged and replaced with new ones in the course of business operations.

These obligations will not be paid for several weeks or months after the current balance sheet date. Their present value is therefore less than the amount that will be

390

paid. Nevertheless, these items are shown at the full amount to be paid, because the difference is usually so small that separate accounting for the difference and subsequent interest expense is judged not worth the trouble.

Accounts Payable to Creditors

Companies seldom pay for goods and services when received. Payment is usually deferred until a bill is received from the supplier. Even then, the bill might not be paid immediately, but instead, accumulated with other bills until a specified time of the month when all bills are paid. Because explicit interest is not paid on these accounts, management tries to obtain as much capital as possible from its creditors by delaying payment as long as possible. Failure to pay creditors according to schedule can, however, lead to poor credit ratings and to restrictions on future credit.

Payroll Items

Deductions are taken from an employee's gross pay to cover federal income taxes, payroll (FICA or social security) taxes, medical plans, pension plans, insurance plans, and other items.[4] The accounting for these deductions is relatively simple, although time-consuming. Instead of showing the gross pay as being entirely payable to employees, the employer shows the net, or "take-home," pay as being payable to employees, and deductions, or withholdings, as being payable to the various recipients. For example, gross wages of $2,000 in a merchandising firm might be shown as follows:

Wage Expense	2,000	
Wages Payable		1,460
Federal Withholding Taxes Payable		240
State Withholding Taxes Payable		80
Payroll Taxes Payable		160
Medical Plan Payable		20
Pension Plan Payable		30
Insurance Plan Payable		10

In addition, the employer is required to pay a FICA tax for each worker. Assuming in this example that the labor contract requires the employer also to match the medical and pension plan contributions of the workers and that those contributions

---

[4]FICA is the Federal Insurance Contribution Act. The actual deduction depends on several factors and has steadily increased over time. For the purpose of illustrations and problems in this text, it will be assumed that the employee's and employer's shares of the tax are each calculated at 8 percent of the first $30,000 of gross income for each employee.

are judged to be a component of wage expense, the additional journal entry would be:

Wage Expense	210	
Payroll Taxes Payable		160
Medical Plan Payable		20
Pension Plan Payable		30

Short-Term Notes and Interest Payable

Businesses obtain interim financing for less than a year from banks or other creditors in return for a short-term note called a *note payable*. Such notes are discussed in Chapter 7 from the point of view of the lender, or note holder. The treatment of these notes by the borrower is the mirror image of the treatment by the lender. Where the lender records an asset, the borrower records a liability. When the lender records interest receivable and revenue, the borrower records interest payable and expense.

Income Taxes Payable

The corporation is the only major form of business organization on which a separate federal income tax is levied. An income tax must be paid each year by corporations on their taxable income from business activities. In contrast, business entities organized as partnerships or sole proprietorships do not pay income taxes. Instead, the income of the business entity is taxed to the individual partners or sole proprietor. Each partner or sole proprietor adds his or her share of business income to income from all other (nonbusiness) sources in preparing an individual income tax return.

The details of the income tax on corporations are subject to change. The rates and schedules of payments mentioned below should not be taken as an indication of the exact procedure in force at any particular time, but rather as an indication of the type of accounting procedures that are involved. Throughout the remainder of the text, an income tax rate of 40 percent is used in almost all illustrations for ease of calculation. The accounting for state and local income taxes follows the same general pattern as that for federal income taxes, except for rates and dates of payment.

Corporations must make an estimate of the amount of taxes that will be due for the year and make quarterly payments equal to one-fourth of the estimated tax. This is frequently described as "pay-as-you-go" taxation. For a corporation on a calendar-year basis, and using 1982 as an example, 25 percent of the estimated tax for 1982 must be paid by April 15, 1982, 50 percent by June 15, 1982, 75 percent by September 15, 1982, and the entire estimated tax for 1982 must be paid by December 15, 1982.

The estimated income and, hence, the estimated tax may change as the year passes. The corporation must report such changed estimates quarterly. The amount of the quarterly payment is revised to reflect the new estimated tax and takes into account the cumulative payments made during previous quarters of the year. The final income tax return for the year is due by March 15, 1983. Any difference between the actual tax liability for 1982 and the cumulative tax payments during 1982 must be paid, one-half by March 15, 1983, and one-half by June 15, 1983. The law provides for penalties if the amount estimated is substantially less than the actual tax liability.

If income statements are prepared more often than quarterly, or the end of the reporting period does not coincide with the tax payment period, it is necessary to estimate the income tax for the reporting period so that a more accurate measurement can be made of the net income for the period. Monthly or other short-period estimates of the tax are likely to be far from dependable, because there are various special provisions in the tax law. During the first quarters of the year, it is not clear how many of the special provisions the corporation will ultimately be able to use. All that can be done is to set up the best possible estimate of tax in the light of earnings of the year to date and the prospects for the remainder of the year.

Exhibit 10.1
Estimating Quarterly Income Tax Payments and Final Payments of Actual Taxes

Date	Estimates of Taxable Income for	Amounts Payable for Income Taxes of
	Year 1	Year 1
Year 1		
April 15	$1,000,000	$100,000[a]
June 15	1,000,000	100,000[b]
September 15	1,000,000	100,000[c]
December 15	1,000,000	100,000[d]
Year 2		
March 15	1,100,000*	20,000[e]
April 15	—	—[f]
June 15	1,100,000*	20,000[e]
September 15	—	—
December 15	—	—

[a] $.25 \times [.40 \times (\$1,000,000)]$.
[b] $.50 \times [.40 \times (\$1,000,000)] - \$100,000$.
[c] $.75 \times [.40 \times (\$1,000,000)] - \$200,000$.
[d] $1.00 \times [.40 \times (\$1,000,000)] - \$300,000$.
[e] $.50 \times [.40 \times (\$1,100,000) - \$400,000]$.
[f] First quarterly payment for Year 2 taxes paid at this time, although this amount and subsequent quarterly payments are not illustrated.

*Actual income for Year 1 was $1,100,000.

Illustration of Income Tax Computations Exhibit 10.1 illustrates the procedures over several quarterly payments. The related journal entries are of two kinds:

Income Tax Expense	100,000	
Income Taxes Payable		100,000
To accrue quarterly payment.		
Income Taxes Payable	100,000	
Cash		100,000
To make payment.		

Deferred Performance Liabilities

Another current liability arises when customers make advance payments for goods or services to be delivered or provided in the future. This liability, unlike the preceding ones, is discharged by delivering goods or services, rather than by paying cash. This liability represents "unearned" and, therefore, unrecognized, revenue; that is, cash is received before the goods or services are furnished to the customer.

An example of this type of liability is the advance sale of theater tickets, say, for $200. Upon the sale, the following entry is made:

Cash	200	
Advances from Customers		200
Tickets are sold for cash, but there is no revenue until service is rendered.		

These deferred performance obligations qualify as liabilities. The account credited is called Advances from Customers or Liability for Advance Sales. After the theater performance, or after the tickets have expired, revenue is recognized and the liability is removed:

Advances from Customers	200	
Performance Revenue		200
Service has been rendered and revenue is recognized.		

Deferred performance liabilities also arise in connection with the sale of magazine subscriptions, transportation tickets, and service contracts.

A related type of deferred performance liability arises when a firm provides a warranty for free service or repairs for some period after the sale. At the time of sale, the firm can only estimate the likely amount of warranty liability. If sales during the accounting period were $28,000, and the firm estimated that an amount equal to 4 percent of the sales revenue will eventually be used to satisfy warranty claims, the entry is:

Accounts Receivable	28,000	
Warranty Expense	1,120	
Sales		28,000
Estimated Warranty Liability		1,120
To record sales and estimated payment to be made for warranties on items sold.		

Note that this entry recognizes the warranty expense in the period when revenue is recognized, even though the repairs may be made in a later period. Thus, warranty expense is matched with associated revenues. Because the expense is recognized, the liability is created. In this case, neither the amount nor the due date of the liability is definite, but they are reasonably certain. FASB *Statement No. 5,* discussed earlier, requires the accrual of the expense and related warranty liability when the amounts can be "reasonably estimated."

As expenditures of, say, $175 are made next period for repairs under the warranty, the entry is:

Estimated Warranty Liability	175	
Cash (or other assets consumed for repairs)		175
Repairs made. No expense is recognized now; all expense was recognized on date of sale.		

With experience, the firm will adjust the percentage of sales it charges to Warranty Expense. Its goal is to achieve a credit balance in the Estimated Warranty Liability account at each balance sheet date that reasonably estimates the actual cost of repairs to be made under warranties outstanding at that time.

Long-Term Liabilities

The principal long-term liabilities are mortgages, notes, bonds, and leases. The significant differences between long-term and short-term, or current, liabilities are that: (1) interest on long-term liabilities is ordinarily paid at regular intervals during the life of a long-term obligation, whereas interest on short-term debt is usually paid in a lump sum at maturity; (2a) the principal of long-term obligations is often paid back in installments, or (2b) special funds are accumulated by the borrower for retiring long-term liabilities.

Accounting for all long-term liabilities generally follows the same procedures. Those procedures are outlined next. We illustrate their application to the various long-term liabilities throughout the rest of this chapter and the next.

Procedures for Recording Long-Term Liabilities

Long-term liabilities are initially recorded at the present value of all payments to be made using the market interest rate at the time the liability is incurred. This market interest rate is also used to compute the amount of interest expense throughout the life of the liability. A portion (perhaps all) of each cash payment represents interest expense. Any excess of cash payment over interest expense is used to reduce the liability itself (often called the *principal*). If a given payment is not sufficient to discharge the entire interest expense that has accrued since the last payment date, then the liability principal is increased by the amount of the deficiency.

Retirement of long-term liabilities can occur in several ways, but the process is the same. The net amount shown on the books for the obligation is debited, the asset given up in return (usually cash) is credited, and any difference is recognized as a gain or loss on retirement of the debt.

Mortgages and Interest-Bearing Notes

A mortgage is a contract in which the lender is awarded legal title to certain property of the borrower, with the provision that the title reverts to the borrower when the loan is repaid in full. (In a few states, the lender merely acquires a lien on the borrower's property rather than legal title to it.) The mortgaged property is security for the loan. The customary terminology designates the lender as the "mortgagee" and the borrower as the "mortgagor."[5]

As long as the mortgagor meets the obligations under the mortgage agreement, the mortgagee does not have the ordinary rights of an owner to possess and use the property. If the mortgagor defaults on either the principal or interest payments, the mortgagee can usually arrange to have the property sold for his or her benefit through a process called *foreclosure*. The mortgagee has first rights to the proceeds from the foreclosure sale for satisfying any unpaid claim. If there is an excess, it is paid to the mortgagor. If the proceeds are insufficient to pay the remaining loan, the lender becomes an unsecured creditor of the borrower for the unpaid balance.

A note is similar to a mortgage except that no property is typically given (mortgaged) as collateral.

Accounting for Mortgages and Interest-Bearing Notes

Some of the more common problems in accounting for mortgages are presented in the following illustration.

On October 1, 1982, the Western Company borrows $125,000 for 5 years from the Home Savings and Finance Company to obtain funds for additional working capital. As security, Western Company gives Home Savings and Finance Company title to

---

[5] When you borrow money to finance your home purchase, you give the bank a mortgage, not vice versa.

several parcels of land that it owns and that are on its books at a cost of $50,000. Interest is charged on the unpaid balance of the loan principal at an interest rate of 12 percent per year compounded semiannually. Payments are due on April 1 and October 1 of each year. Western agrees to make 10 payments over the 5 years of the mortgage so that when the last payment is made on October 1, 1987, the loan and all interest will have been paid. The first nine payments are to be $17,000 each. The tenth payment is to be just large enough to discharge the balance of the loan. The Western Company closes its books annually on December 31. (The derivation of the semiannual payment of $17,000 is shown in Example 11 in Appendix B at the end of the book.)

The entries from the time the mortgage is issued through December 31, 1983, are as follows:

10/1/82	Cash	125,000	
	Mortgage Payable		125,000
	Loan obtained from Home Savings and Finance Company for 5 years at 12 percent compounded semiannually.		

As Example 11 in Appendix B shows, $125,000 is approximately equal to the present value of 10 semiannual cash payments of $17,000, each discounted at 12 percent compounded semiannually.

12/31/82	Interest Expense	3,750	
	Interest Payable		3,750
	Adjusting entry: Interest expense on mortgage from 10/1/82 to 12/31/82.		

Interest expense on the loan for the first 6 months is $7,500 ($= .06 \times \$125,000$). To simplify the calculations, accounting typically assumes that the interest accrues evenly over the 6-month period. Thus, interest expense for October, November, and December is one-half of the $7,500, or $3,750.

4/1/83	Interest Expense	3,750	
	Interest Payable	3,750	
	Mortgage Payable	9,500	
	Cash		17,000
	Cash payment made requires an entry. Interest expense on mortgage from 1/1/83 to 4/1/83, payment of 6 months' interest, and reduction of loan by the difference, $17,000 − $7,500 = $9,500.		

After the cash payment on April 1, 1983, the unpaid principal of the loan is $115,500 ($= \$125,000 - \$9,500$). Interest expense during the second 6-month period is based on this unpaid principal amount.

10/01/83	Interest Expense	6,930	
	Mortgage Payable	10,070	
	Cash		17,000

Cash payment made requires an entry. Interest expense for the period 4/1/83 to 10/1/83 is $6,930$ [$= .12 \times (\$125,000 - \$9,500) \times \frac{1}{2}$]. The loan is reduced by the difference, $\$17,000 - \$6,930 = \$10,070$.

Exhibit 10.2
Amortization Schedule for $125,000 Mortgage (or Note), Repaid in 10 Semiannual Installments of $17,000, Interest Rate of 12 Percent, Compounded Semiannually

SEMIANNUAL JOURNAL ENTRY

Dr. Interest Expense . . . . Amount in Column (3)
Dr. Mortgage (or Note) Payable . . . . Amount in Column (5)
  Cr. Cash . . . . Amount in Column (4)

6-Month Period (1)	Loan Balance Start of Period (2)	Interest Expense for Period (3)	Payment (4)	Portion of Payment Reducing Principal (5)	Loan Balance End of Period (6)
0					$125,000
1	$125,000	$7,500	$17,000	$ 9,500	115,500
2	115,500	6,930	17,000	10,070	105,430
3	105,430	6,326	17,000	10,674	94,756
4	94,756	5,685	17,000	11,315	83,441
5	83,441	5,006	17,000	11,994	71,448
6	71,448	4,287	17,000	12,713	58,734
7	58,734	3,524	17,000	13,476	45,259
8	45,259	2,715	17,000	14,285	30,974
9	30,974	1,858	17,000	15,142	15,832
10	15,832	950	16,782	15,832	0

Note: In preparing this table, calculations were rounded to the nearest cent. Then, for presentation, results are rounded to the nearest dollar.
Column (2) = Column (6) from Previous Period.
Column (3) = .06 × Column (2).
Column (4)   Given, except row 10, where it is the amount such that Column (4) = Column (2) + Column (3).
Column (5) = Column (4) − Column (3).
Column (6) = Column (2) − Column (5).

12/31/83	Interest Expense.	3,163	
	Interest Payable.		3,163

Adjusting entry: Interest expense from 10/1/83 to 12/31/83 = $[.12 \times (\$125,000 - \$9,500 - \$10,070) \times \frac{3}{12}]$.

Exhibit 10.2 presents an "amortization schedule" for this mortgage. It shows the allocation of each $17,000 payment between interest and repayment of principal. (The last payment, $16,782 in this case, often differs slightly from the others because of the cumulative effect of rounding errors.) Amortization schedules indicate both the numbers that are recorded each period and the amount of the outstanding loan at the end of each period.

Bonds

Mortgages or notes are used whenever funds can be borrowed from one lender. When large amounts are needed, the firm may have to borrow from the general investing public through a bond issue. Bonds are used primarily by corporations and governmental units. The distinctive features of a bond issue are as follows:

1 A *bond indenture,* or agreement, is drawn up which shows in detail the terms of the loan and the rights and duties of the borrower and other parties to the contract.
2 *Bond certificates* are used. Engraved certificates are prepared, each one representing a portion of the total loan. The usual minimum denomination in business practice is $1,000, although smaller denominations are occasionally used. Government bonds are issued in denominations as small as $50.
3 If property is pledged as security for the loan (as in a mortgage bond), then a *trustee* is named to hold title to the property serving as security. The trustee acts as the representative of the bondholders and is usually a bank or trust company.
4 An agent is appointed, usually a bank or trust company, to act as *registrar* and *disbursing agent.* The borrower deposits interest and principal payments with the disbursing agent, who distributes the funds to the bondholders.
5 Most bonds are *coupon bonds.* Coupons are attached to the bond certificate covering the interest payments throughout the life of the bond. When a coupon comes due, the bondholder cuts it off and deposits it with a bank. The bank sends the coupon through the bank clearing system to the disbursing agent for payment, which is deposited in the bondholder's account at the bank.
6 Bonds are frequently *registered as to principal,* which means that the holder's name appears on the bond certificate and on the records of the registrar. Sometimes both the principal and interest of bonds are registered, in which case the interest payments are mailed directly to the bondholder and coupons are not used. Registered bonds are easily replaced if lost, but the transfer from one holder to another is cumbersome. Unregistered bonds may be transferred merely by delivery, whereas registered bonds have to be assigned formally from one holder to another.

7 The entire bond issue is usually issued by the borrower to an investment banking firm, or to a group of investment bankers known as a *syndicate,* which takes over the responsibility of reselling the bonds to the investing public. Members of the syndicate usually bear the risks and rewards of interest-rate fluctuations during the period while the bonds are being sold to the public.

Types of Bonds

Mortgage bonds carry a mortgage on real estate as security for the repayment of the loan. *Collateral trust bonds* are usually secured by stocks and bonds of other corporations. The most common type of corporate bond, except in the railroad and public utility industries, is the *debenture bond.* This type carries no special security or collateral; instead, it is issued on the general credit of the business. To give added protection to the bondholders, provisions are usually included in the bond indenture that limit the amount of subsequent long-term debt that can be incurred. *Convertible bonds* are debentures that the holder can exchange, possibly after some specific period of time has elapsed, for a specific number of shares of capital stock.

Almost all bonds provide for the payment of interest at regular intervals, usually semiannually. The amount of interest is typically expressed as a percentage of the principal. For example, a 12-percent, 10-year semiannual coupon bond with face or principal amount of $1,000 promises to pay $60 every 6 months. Here, we assume, the first payment occurs 6 months after the issue date. A total of 20 payments are made. At the time of the final $60 coupon payment, the $1,000 principal is also due. The coupon rate is 12 percent in this case. The principal amount of a bond is its face, or par, value. The terms *face value* and *par value* are synonymous in this context. In general, the par amount multiplied by the coupon rate equals the amount of cash paid per *year,* whether in quarterly, semiannual, or annual installments. By far the majority of corporate bonds provide for semiannual coupon payments. A bond can be issued and subsequently traded in the marketplace for amounts below par, at par, or above par.

Proceeds of a Bond Issue

The amount received by the borrower may be more or less than the par value of the bonds issued. The difference arises primarily because there is a difference between the coupon rate printed on the bond certificates and the interest rate the market requires given the risk of the borrower, the general level of interest rates in the economy, and other factors. If the coupon rate is less than the rate the market requires the firm to pay, then the bonds will sell for less than par. The difference between par and selling price is called the *discount* on the bond. If the coupon rate is larger than the rate the market requires, then the bonds will sell above par. The difference between selling price and par is called the *premium* on the bond.

The presence of a discount or premium in and of itself indicates nothing about the credit standing of the borrower. A firm with a credit standing that would enable it to borrow funds at 11 percent might issue 10-percent bonds that would sell at a discount, whereas another firm with a lower credit standing, that would require it to pay 12 percent on loans, might issue bonds at 15 percent that would sell at a premium.

The following illustrations cover the calculations of the proceeds of a bond issue when the market interest rate is equal to, more than, and less than the coupon rate.

Issued at Par The Macaulay Corporation issues $100,000 face value of 12-percent semiannual coupon debenture bonds. The bonds are dated July 1, 1982. The face, or principal, amount is repayable on July 1, 1987, 5 years later. Interest payments (coupons) are due on July 1 and January 1 of each year. The coupon payments promised at each interest payment date total $6,000. Figure 10.1 presents a time line for the two sets of cash flows associated with this bond. Assuming that the issue was

+$100,000									−$100,000
−$6,000	−$6,000	−$6,000	−$6,000	−$6,000	−$6,000	−$6,000	−$6,000	−$6,000	−$6,000
7/1/82	1/1/83	7/1/83	1/1/84	7/1/84	1/1/85	7/1/85	1/1/86	7/1/86	1/1/87	7/1/87

Figure 10.1
**Time Line for 5-Year Semiannual
Coupon Bonds, 12-Percent Annual
Coupons. $100,000 Par Value
Issued at Par.**

taken by Penman & Company, investment banker, on July 1, 1982, at a rate to yield 12 percent compounded semiannually, the calculation of the proceeds to Macaulay would be as follows. (The present-value calculations are explained in Appendix B at the back of the book.)

(a) Present value of $100,000 to be paid at the end of 5 years. . . . . $ 55,839
   (Appendix Table 2 at the back of the book shows the present value of $1 to be received
   in 10 periods at 6 percent per period to be $.55839; $100,000 × .55839 = $55,839.)

(b) Present value of $6,000 to be paid each 6 months for 5 years 44,161
   (Appendix Table 4 shows the present value of an ordinary annuity of $1 per period for
   10 periods discounted at 6 percent to be $7.36009; $6,000 × 7.36009 = $44,161.)

Total Proceeds. $100,000

The issue price would be stated as 100.0 (that is, 100 percent of par), which implies that the market interest rate was 12 percent compounded semiannually, the same as the coupon rate.

Issued at Less than Par Assume that these same bonds were issued at a price to yield 14 percent compounded semiannually. The cash flows after July 1, 1982, associated with these bonds (payment of periodic interest plus repayment of principal) are identical to those in the time line shown in Figure 10.1. These future cash flows

401

would be discounted to their present value, however, using a 14-percent discount rate compounded semiannually. The calculation of the issue proceeds (that is, initial market price) would be as follows. (Why it is that "12-percent" bonds can be issued to yield 14 percent is discussed below on pages 404 and 405.)

(a) Present value of $100,000 to be paid at the end of 5 years $50,835
  (Present value of $1 to be received in 10 periods at 7 percent per period is $0.50835; $100,000 × 0.50835 = $50,835.)

(b) Present value of $6,000 to be paid each 6 months for 5 years 42,141
  (Present value of an ordinary annuity of $1 per period for 10 periods, discounted at 7 percent per period = $7.02348; $6,000 × 7.02358 = $42,141.)

Total Proceeds $92,976

If the issue price were stated on a conventional pricing basis in the market at 92.98 (92.98 percent of par), the issuing price would be $92,980. This amount implies a market yield of slightly less than 14 percent compounded semiannually.

Issued at More than Par Assume that the bonds were issued at a price to yield 10 percent compounded semiannually. The cash flows, after July 1, 1982, would again be identical to those shown in Figure 10.1. They would be discounted, however, at 10 percent compounded semiannually to calculate their present value. The calculation of the proceeds would be as follows:

(a) Present value of $100,000 to be paid at the end of 5 years. . . . . $ 61,391
  (Present value of $1 to be received in 10 periods at 5 percent per period is $0.61391; $100,000 × 0.61391 = $61,391.)

(b) Present value of $6,000 to be paid each 6 months for 5 years 46,330
  (Present value of an ordinary annuity at $1 per period for 10 periods, discounted at 5 percent per period = $7.72173; $6,000 × 7.72173 = $46,330.)

Total Proceeds $107,721

If the issue price were stated on a conventional pricing basis in the market at 107.72 (107.72 percent of par), the issuing price would be $107.720.[6] The price would imply a market yield of slightly more than 10 percent compounded semiannually.

---

[6] In many contexts, bond prices are quoted in dollars plus thirty-seconds of a dollar. A bond selling for about 107.721 percent of par would be quoted at $107\frac{23}{32}$, which would be written as 107.23. In order to read published bond prices, you must know whether the information after the "decimal" point refers to fractions expressed in one-hundredths or in thirty-seconds. (If you are reading published bond prices and see any number larger than 31 after the decimal point, then you can be sure that one-hundredths are being used. If you see many prices, but none of the numbers shown after the point is larger than 31, then you can be reasonably sure that thirty-seconds are being used.)

Bond Tables

These tedious calculations need not be made every time a bond issue is analyzed. Bond tables have been prepared to show the results of calculations like those just described. Examples of such tables are included in Tables 5 and 6 at the back of the book. Table 5 shows the price for 10-percent, semiannual coupon bonds as a percent of par for various market interest rates (yields) and years to maturity. Table 6 shows market rates and implied prices for 12-percent, semiannual coupon bonds. (Some modern electronic calculators are capable of making the calculations represented by these tables in a few seconds.)

The percentages of par shown in these tables represent the present value of the bond indicated. Because the factors are expressed as a percent of par, they have to be multiplied by 10 to find the price of a $1,000 bond. If you have never used bond tables before now, turn to Table 6 after Appendix B at the back of the book and find in the 5th-year row the three different prices for the three different market yields used in the preceding examples. Notice further that a bond will sell at par if, and only if, it has a market yield equal to its coupon rate.

These tables are useful whether a bond is being issued by a corporation or resold later by an investor. The approach to computing the market price will be the same in either case, although the years to maturity will be less than the original term of the bond when it is resold. The following generalizations can be made regarding bond prices:

1 When the market interest rate equals the coupon rate, the market price will equal par.
2 When the market interest rate is greater than the coupon rate, the market price will be less than par.
3 When the market interest rate is less than the coupon rate, the market price will be greater than par.

Accounting for Bonds Issued at Par

The following illustration covers the more common problems associated with bonds issued at par.

We use the data presented in the previous sections for the Macaulay Corporation, where the bonds were issued at par and we assume that the books are closed semiannually on June 30 and December 31. The entry at the time of issue would be:

7/1/82	Cash	100,000	
	Debenture Bonds Payable		100,000
	$100,000 of 12-percent, 5-year bonds issued at par.		

The entries for interest would be made at the end of the accounting period and on the interest payment dates. Entries through January 2, 1983, would be:

12/31/82	Interest Expense	6,000	
	Interest Payable		6,000
1/2/83	Interest Payable	6,000	
	Cash		6,000
	To record payment of 6 months' interest.		

Bond Issued between Interest Payment Dates The actual date that a bond is issued seldom coincides with one of the payment dates. Assuming these same bonds were actually brought to market on August 1, rather than July 1, and were issued at par, the purchaser of the bond would be expected to pay Macaulay Corporation for 1 month's interest in advance. After all, on the first coupon Macaulay Corporation promises a full $60, for 6 months' interest, but would have had the use of the borrowed funds for only 5 months. The purchasers of the bonds would pay $100,000 plus 1 month's interest of $1,000 ($= .12 \times \$100,000 \times \frac{1}{12}$) and would get the $1,000 back when the first coupons are redeemed. The journal entries made by Macaulay Corporation, the issuer, would be:

8/1/82	Cash	101,000	
	Bonds Payable		100,000
	Interest Payable		1,000
	To record issue of bonds at par between interest payment dates. The purchasers pay an amount equal to interest for the first month but will get it back when the first coupons are redeemed.		

Accounting for Bonds Issued at Less than Par

The following illustrates the more common problems associated with bonds issued for less than par.

Assume the data presented for the Macaulay Corporation, where 12-percent, $100,000-par value, 5-year bonds were issued to yield approximately 14 percent compounded semiannually. The issue price was shown previously to be $92,976. The journal entry at the time of issue would be:

7/1/82	Cash	92,976	
	Debenture Bonds Payable		92,976

The issuance of these bonds for $92,976, instead of the $100,000 par value, indicates that 12 percent is not a sufficiently high rate of interest for the bonds to induce purchasers to pay the full par value in the open market. If purchasers of these bonds paid the full $100,000 par value, they would earn only 12 percent compounded semiannually, the coupon rate. Purchasers desiring a rate of return of 14 percent will postpone their purchases until the market price drops to $92,976. At this price, purchasers of the bonds will earn the 14 percent required return. The return will be composed of ten $6,000 coupon payments over the next 5 years plus $7,024 (= $100,000 − $92,976) as part of the payment at maturity.

For Macaulay Corporation, the total interest expense over the life of the bonds is equal to $67,024 (periodic interest payments totaling $60,000 plus $7,024 paid at maturity). Two methods of allocating the total interest expense of $67,024 to the periods of the loan are the effective-interest method and the straight-line method.

Interest Expense under the Effective-Interest Method

Under the effective interest method, interest *expense* each period is equal to the market interest rate at the time the bonds were initially issued (14 percent compounded semiannually in this example) times the total recorded liability at the beginning of the interest period. For example, interest expense for the period from July 1, 1982, to December 31, 1982, the first 6-month period, is $6,508 (= .07 × $92,976). The bond indenture provides that only $6,000 (= .06 × $100,000) need be paid on January 2, 1983. This amount is equal to the coupon rate times the par value of the bonds. The difference between the interest expense of $6,508 and the interest currently payable of $6,000 is added to the principal amount to be paid at maturity. The journal entry made on December 31, 1982, to recognize interest for the last 6 months of 1982 is:

12/31/82	Interest Expense	$6,508	
	Interest Payable		6,000
	Debenture Bonds Payable		508
	To recognize interest expense for 6 months.		

The Interest Payable account would be shown as a current liability on the balance sheet at the end of 1982. Debenture Bonds Payable of $93,484 (= $92,976 + $508) would be reported as a noncurrent liability.

On January 2, 1983, the first periodic cash payment is made.

1/2/83	Interest Payable	$6,000	
	Cash		6,000
	To record payment of interest for 6 months.		

Interest expense for the second 6 months, from January 1, 1983, through June 30, 1983, is $6,544 (= .07 × $93,484). Interest expense for the second 6 months of $6,544 is larger than the $6,508 for the first 6 months because the recorded balance of the liability at the beginning of the second 6 months is larger. The journal entry on June 30, 1983, to record interest expense is:

6/30/83	Interest Expense	$6,544	
	Interest Payable		6,000
	Debenture Bonds Payable		544
	To recognize interest expense for 6 months.		

An amortization schedule for these bonds over their 5-year life is shown in Exhibit 10.3.

Exhibit 10.3

Effective-Interest Amortization Schedule for $100,000 of 12-Percent, 5-Year Bonds Issued for 92.976 Percent of Par to Yield 14 Percent, Interest Payable Semiannually

SEMIANNUAL JOURNAL ENTRY
Dr. Interest Expense . . . . Amount in Column (3)
  Cr. Cash . . . . Amount in Column (4)
  Cr. Debenture Bonds Payable . . . . Amount in Column (5)

Period (6-month intervals) (1)	Liability at Start of Period (2)	Effective Interest: 7 Percent per Period (3)	Coupon Rate: 6 Percent of Par (4)	Increase in Principal Amount Payable (5)	Liability at End of Period (6)
0					$92,976
1	$92,976	$ 6,508	$ 6,000	$508	93,484
2	93,484	6,544	6,000	544	94,028
3	94,028	6,582	6,000	582	94,610
4	94,610	6,623	6,000	623	95,233
5	95,233	6,666	6,000	666	95,899
6	95,899	6,713	6,000	713	96,612
7	96,612	6,763	6,000	763	97,375
8	97,375	6,816	6,000	816	98,191
9	98,191	6,873	6,000	873	99,064
10	99,064	6,936	6,000	936	100,000
Total		$67,024	$60,000	$7,024	

Note: In preparing this table, calculations were rounded to the nearest cent. Then, for presentation, results were rounded to the nearest dollar.

Column (2) = Column (6) from Previous Period.
Column (3) = .07 × Column (2).
Column (4)   Given.
Column (5) = Column (3) − Column (4).
Column (6) = Column (2) + Column (5).

The effective interest method of recognizing interest expense on a bond has the following financial statement effects.

1 On the income statement, interest expense will be a constant percentage of the recorded liability at the beginning of each interest period. This percentage will be equal to the market interest rate for these bonds when they were initially issued. When bonds are issued for less than par value, the *dollar amount* of interest expense will increase each period as the recorded principal amount increases toward the maturity value.

2 On the balance sheet at the end of each period, the bonds will be stated at the present value of the *remaining* cash outflows discounted at the market rate of interest when the bonds were initially issued. For example, on June 30, 1983, the present value of the remaining cash payments is as follows:

Present Value of July 1, 1983, Interest Payment	$ 6,000
Present Value of eight remaining semiannual interest payments discounted at 14 percent, compounded semiannually (Appendix Table 4 shows the present value of an ordinary annuity of $1 per period for 8 periods discounted at 7 percent to be $5.97130; $6,000 × 5.97130 = $35,827)	35,827
Present value of $100,000 to be paid at the end of 4 years (Appendix Table 2 shows the present value of $1 to be paid at the end of 8 periods discounted at 7 percent to be $.58201; $100,000 × .58201 = $58,201)	58,201
Total Present Value	$100,028
Less Amount Shown as Current Liability	6,000
Equals Amount Shown for Debenture Bonds Payable	$ 94,028

The amount $94,028 appears in column (6) of Exhibit 10.3 for the liability at the end of the second 6-month period.

Discount on Bonds Payable Account

The preceding description of the recording of bonds issued below par value shows the book value of the bonds directly in the Bonds Payable account. Accounting has traditionally shown Bonds Payable at par value with a liability contra account, Discount on Bonds Payable, carrying the amount by which par value must be reduced to book value. If the Discount on Bonds Payable account were used, the balance sheet on June 30, 1983, after two semiannual interest periods would show:

Bonds Payable—Par Value	$100,000
Less: Discount on Bonds Payable	(5,972)
Bonds Payable—Net Book Value	$ 94,028

Interest Expense under the Straight-Line Method

Under the straight-line method, total interest expense (periodic coupon payments plus any amount paid at the time of maturity) is spread evenly over the life of the bonds. In the example for Macaulay Corporation, total interest expense is $67,024 [= ($6,000 × 10) + ($100,000 − $92,976)]. Interest expense each 6 months will therefore be $6,702.40 (= $67,024/10). The journal entry to record interest expense at the end of each 6 months is:

Interest Expense.	6,702.40	
Interest Payable.		6,000.00
Debenture Bonds Payable.		702.40
To recognize interest expense for 6 months.		

The straight-line method of computing interest expense is computationally easier than the effective-interest method. It has two theoretical weaknesses, however.

1 When bonds are issued for less than par value, interest expense will be a decreasing percentage of the bond liability at the beginning of each period. That is, interest expense (numerator) will be constant but the bond liability (denominator) will increase as the maturity date approaches. In contrast, the effective interest method provides an amount for interest expense that is a constant percentage of the beginning-of-the-period liability.
2 The amount at which the bonds are stated on the balance sheet each period will not equal the present value of the remaining cash flows relating to the bond discounted at the historical-interest rate.

Preferred Method of Recognizing Interest Expense

Generally accepted accounting principles require the effective interest method.[7] The straight-line method is allowed only when its results do not differ materially from the effective interest method.

Interest on Bonds Issued for Less than Par and the Statement of Changes in Financial Position

Recognizing interest expense on bonds issued for less than par requires special treatment in the statement of changes in financial position. Interest expense reported for the first 6 months is $6,508: $6,000 in coupon payments and $508 in increased principal amount. Notice that only $6,000 of working capital was used for the expense. There was an increase in Interest Payable of $6,000 followed by discharge of that current liability with cash payment. The remainder of the interest expense, $508, is an increase in the noncurrent liability, Debenture Bonds Payable. Consequently, there must be an *addback* to net income in computing "funds provided by opera-

---

[7] Accounting Principles Board, *Opinion No. 21,* "Interest on Receivables and Payables," 1971, par. 15.

tions" in the statement of changes in financial position. The amount of the addback is the amount of the expense that did not use working capital, $508.

Accounting for Bonds Issued for More than Par

The following discussion illustrates the more common problems associated with bonds issued for more than par.

Assume the data presented for the Macaulay Corporation, in which 12 percent, $100,000-par value, 5-year bonds were issued to yield approximately 10 percent compounded semiannually. The issue price was shown previously to be $107,721. The journal entry at the time of issue would be:

7/1/82	Cash	107,721
	Debenture Bonds Payable	107,721

The issuance of these bonds for $107,721, instead of the $100,000 par value, indicates that 12 percent is a higher rate of interest for the bonds than the purchasers demand. If purchasers of these bonds paid the $100,000 par value, they would earn 12 percent compounded semiannually, the coupon rate. Purchasers requiring a rate of return of only 10 percent will bid up the market price to $107,721. At this price, purchasers of the bonds will earn only the 10 percent demanded return. The return will be composed of ten $6,000 coupon payments over the next 5 years reduced by $7,721 (= $107,721 − $100,000) principal lent but not repaid at maturity.

For Macaulay Corporation, the total interest expense over the life of the bonds is equal to $52,279 (periodic interest payments totaling $60,000 less $7,721 of principal not repaid at maturity). Two methods of allocating the total interest expense of $52,279 to the periods of the loan are the effective-interest method and the straight-line method.

Interest Expense under the Effective-Interest Method

Under the effective-interest method, interest *expense* each period is equal to the market interest rate at the time the bonds were initially issued (10 percent compounded semiannually in this example) times the recorded principal of the liability at the beginning of the interest period. For example, interest expense for the period from July 1, 1982, to December 31, 1982, the first 6-month period, is $5,386 (= .05 × $107,721). The bond indenture provides that $6,000 (= .06 × $100,000) be paid on January 2, 1983. This amount is equal to the coupon rate times the par value of the bonds. The difference between the payment of $6,000 and the interest expense of $5,386 reduces the principal amount to be paid at maturity. The journal

409

entry made on December 31, 1982, to recognize interest for the last 6 months of 1982 is:

12/31/82	Interest Expense.	5,386	
	Debenture Bonds Payable	614	
	Interest Payable.		6,000
	To recognize interest expense for 6 months.		

The Interest Payable account would be shown as a current liability on the balance sheet at the end of 1982. Debenture Bonds Payable of $107,107 (= $107,721 − $614) would be reported as a noncurrent liability.

Exhibit 10.4

Effective-Interest Amortization Schedule for $100,000 of 12-Percent, 5-Year Bonds Issued for 107.721 Percent of Par to Yield 10 Percent, Interest Payable Semiannually

SEMIANNUAL JOURNAL ENTRY

Dr. Interest Expense . . . . Amount in Column (3)
Dr. Debenture Bonds Payable . . . . Amount in Column (5)
   Cr. Cash . . . . Amount in Column (4)

Period (6-month Intervals) (1)	Liability at Start of Period (2)	Effective Interest: 5 Percent per Period (3)	Coupon Rate: 6 Percent of Par (4)	Decrease in Principal Amount (5)	Liability at End of Period (6)
0					$107,721
1	$107,721	$ 5,386	$ 6,000	$ 614	107,107
2	107,107	5,355	6,000	645	106,462
3	106,462	5,323	6,000	677	105,785
4	105,785	5,289	6,000	711	105,074
5	105,074	5,254	6,000	746	104,328
6	104,328	5,216	6,000	784	103,544
7	103,544	5,177	6,000	823	102,721
8	102,721	5,136	6,000	864	101,857
9	101,857	5,093	6,000	907	100,950
10	100,950	5,050	6,000	950	100,000
Total		$52,279	$60,000	$7,721	

Column (2) = Column (6) from Previous Period.
Column (3) = .05 × Column (2).
Column (4)   Given.
Column (5) = Column (4) − Column (3).
Column (6) = Column (2) − Column (5).

On January 2, 1983, the first periodic cash payment is made.

1/02/83	Interest Payable	6,000	
	Cash		6,000
	To record payment of interest for 6 months.		

Interest expense for the second 6 months, from January 1, 1983, through June 30, 1983, is $5,355 (= .05 × $107,107). Interest expense for the second 6 months of $5,355 is smaller than the $5,386 for the first 6 months because the unpaid balance of the liability at the beginning of the second 6 months is smaller. The journal entry on June 30, 1983, to record interest expense is:

6/30/83	Interest Expense	5,355	
	Debenture Bonds Payable	645	
	Interest Payable		6,000
	To recognize interest expense for 6 months.		

An amortization schedule for these bonds over their 5-year life appears in Exhibit 10.4.

The effective-interest method of recognizing interest expense on a bond has the following financial statement effects.

1 On the income statement interest expense will be a constant percentage of the recorded liability at the beginning of each interest period. This percentage will be equal to the market interest rate when the bonds were initially issued. When bonds are issued for more than par value, the *dollar amount* of interest expense will decrease each period as the unpaid principal amount decreases to the maturity value.

2 On the balance sheet at the end of each period, the bonds will be stated at the present value of the *remaining* cash flow discounted at the market rate of interest when the bonds were initially issued. For example, on June 30, 1983, the present value of the remaining cash payments is as follows:

Present Value of July 1, 1983, Interest Payment	$ 6,000
Present Value of 8 remaining semiannual interest payments discounted at 10 percent, compounded semiannually (Appendix Table 4 shows the present value of an ordinary annuity of $1 per period for 8 periods discounted at 5 percent to be $6.46321; $6,000 × 6.46321 = $38,779)	38,779
Present value of $100,000 to be paid at the end of 4 years (Appendix Table 2 shows the present value of $1 to be paid at the end of 8 periods discounted at 5 percent to be $.67684; $100,000 × .67684 = $67,684)	67,684
Total Present Value	$112,463
Less Amount Shown as Current Liability.	6,000
Equals Amount Shown for Debenture Bonds Payable	$106,463

The amount $106,462, different because of rounding effects, appears in column (6) of Exhibit 10.4 for the liability at the end of the second 6-month period.

Premium on Bonds Payable Account

The preceding description of the recording of bonds issued above par value shows the book value of the bonds directly in the Bonds Payable account. Accounting has traditionally shown Bonds Payable at par value with a liability adjunct account, Premium on Bonds Payable, carrying the amount to add to par value to show book value. If the Premium on Bonds Payable account were used, the balance sheet on June 30, 1983, after two semiannual interest periods would show:

Bonds Payable—Par Value	$100,000
Plus: Premium on Bonds Payable	6,462
Bonds Payable—Net Book Value	$106,462

Interest Expense under the Straight-Line Method

Under the straight-line method, total interest expense (periodic coupon payments plus any amount paid at the time of maturity) is spread evenly over the life of the bonds. In the example for Macaulay Corporation, total interest expense is $52,279 [= ($6,000 × 10) + ($100,000 − $107,721)]. Interest expense each 6 months will therefore be $5,227.90 (= $52,279/10). The journal entry to record interest expense at the end of each 6 months is:

Interest Expense	5,227.90	
Debenture Bonds Payable	772.10	
Interest Payable		6,000.00
To recognize interest expense for 6 months.		

The straight-line method of computing interest expense is computationally easier than the effective-interest method. It has two theoretical weaknesses however.

1 When bonds are issued for more than par value, interest expense will be an increasing percentage of the bond liability at the beginning of each period. That is, interest expense (numerator) will be constant but the bond liability (denominator) will decrease as the maturity date approaches. In contrast, the effective-interest method provides an amount for interest expense that is a constant percentage of the beginning-of-the-period liability.

2 The amount at which the bonds are stated on the balance sheet each period will not equal the present value of the remaining cash flows relating to the bond discounted at the historical-interest rate.

Effects on Statement of Changes in Financial Position

Interest expense on bonds originally issued above par is less than the periodic amounts of cash disbursed for interest coupons. The excess of cash disbursed (or current liability for Interest Payable recorded) over interest is a return of principal to the lenders. This excess is an operating use of cash that does not reduce net income. Thus, there must be a subtraction in the statement of changes in financial position in deriving "funds provided by operations" for the excess of cash disbursed over interest expense for periodic interest entries on bonds issued above par.

Bond Retirement

Many bonds remain outstanding until the stated maturity date. If that were done in the Macaulay example, the company would pay the final coupon, $6,000, and the face amount, $100,000, on the stated maturity date. (The entry recognizing expense and payment is combined here for convenience.)

7/1/87	Interest Expense	6,000	
	Debenture Bonds Payable	100,000	
	Cash		106,000
	Retirement at maturity of bonds originally issued along with payment for final coupons and recognition of interest expense.		

Retirement before Maturity It is not unusual for a firm to enter the marketplace and to purchase its own bonds before maturity. Interest rates constantly change. Assume that Macaulay Corporation originally issued its bonds at par to yield 12 percent compounded semiannually. Assume that 3 years later, on July 1, 1985, interest rates in the marketplace have increased so that the market then requires a 15-percent interest rate to be paid by Macaulay Corporation. Refer to Table 6 at the back of the book, 2-year row, 15-percent column, where you will see that 12-percent bonds with 2 years until maturity will sell in the marketplace for 94.9760 percent of par if the current interest rate is 15 percent compounded semiannually.

The marketplace is not constrained by the principles of historical-cost accounting. Even though Macaulay Corporation continues to show the Debenture Bonds Payable on the balance sheet at $100,000, the marketplace puts a price of only $94,976 on the entire bond issue. From the point of view of the marketplace, these bonds are the same as 2-year bonds issued on July 1, 1985, at an effective yield of 15 percent and, so, carry a discount of $5,024 (= $100,000 − $94,976).

If Macaulay Corporation goes into the marketplace on July 1, 1985, to purchase, say, $10,000 of par value of its own bonds, it would have to pay only $9,498 (= .94976 × $10,000) for those bonds. The journal entries it would make at the time of purchase are:

7/1/85	Interest Payable	6,000	
	Cash		6,000
	To record payment of coupons, as usual.		
	Debenture Bonds Payable	10,000	
	Cash		9,498
	Gain on Retirement of Bonds		502
	To record purchase of bonds for less than the current amount shown in the accounting records.		

The adjustment to give equal debits and credits in the second journal entry is recorded as a gain. The gain arises because the firm is able to retire a liability recorded at one amount, $10,000, for a smaller cash payment, $9,498. This gain actually occurred as interest rates increased between 1982 and 1985. In historical-cost accounting, the gain is reported only when realized—in the period of bond retirement. This phenomenon is analogous to a firm's purchasing marketable securities, holding those securities as prices increase, selling the securities in a subsequent year, and reporting all the gain in the year of sale. It is caused by the historical-cost accounting convention of recording amounts at historical cost and not recording increases in wealth until those increases are realized in arm's-length transactions with outsiders.

During the 1970s, interest rates jumped upward from their levels in the 1960s. Many companies had issued bonds at prices near par with coupon rates of only 3 or 4 percent per year in the 1960s. When interest rates in the 1970s jumped to 12 or 15 percent per year, these bonds sold in the marketplace for substantial discounts. Many companies went into the marketplace and repurchased their own bonds, recording substantial gains in the process. (In one year Pan American World Airlines was able to report profits after 7 consecutive years of losses. Pan Am had gains on bond retirement that year in excess of the entire amount of reported net income.)

Because there is no alternative in historical-cost accounting to showing a gain (or loss) on bond retirement (the debits must equal the credits) and because the FASB is reluctant to let companies manage their own reported income by repurchasing bonds, it requires that gains and losses on bond retirements be reported in the income statement, generally as *extraordinary* items.[8] Such items are included in net income, but with a separate caption. See the discussion in Chapter 4.

---

[8] Financial Accounting Standards Board, *Statement of Financial Accounting Standards No. 4*, "Reporting Gains and Losses from Extinguishment of Debt," 1975. An exception is mentioned in the next footnote.

Special Provisions for Bond Retirement

Serial Bonds If the issuing firm is required to make a special provision for retiring the bond issue, the details of that requirement will be spelled out in the bond indenture. There are two major types of retirement provisions. One provides that certain portions of the principal amount will come due on a succession of maturity dates; the bonds of such issues are known as *serial bonds*. (The bonds considered so far in this chapter are not serial bonds.)

Sinking-Fund Bonds The other major type of retirement provision stipulates that the firm must accumulate a fund of cash or other assets that will be used to pay the bonds when the maturity date arrives or to reacquire and retire portions of the bond issue from time to time. Funds of this type are commonly known as *sinking funds,* although *bond-retirement funds* would be a more descriptive term. The sinking fund is usually held by the trustee of the bond issue. It is shown on the balance sheet as a noncurrent asset in the "Investments" section.

Refunded Bonds Some bond issues make no provision for installment repayment or for accumulating sinking funds for the payment of the bonds when they come due. Such bonds are usually well protected with property held by the trustees as security or by the high credit standing of the issuer. Under these circumstances, the entire bond liability may be paid at maturity out of cash in the bank at that time. Quite commonly, however, this procedure is not followed. Instead the bond issue is *refunded*—a new set of bonds is issued to obtain the funds to retire the old ones when they come due.

Callable Bonds A common provision gives the issuing company the right to retire portions of the bond issue before maturity if it so desires, but does not require it do so. In order to facilitate such reacquisition and retirement of a part of the bond issue, the bond indenture usually provides that the bonds shall be *callable*. That is, the issuing company will have the right to reacquire its bonds at prices specified in the bond indenture. The *call price* is usually set a few percentage points above the par value and declines as the maturity date approaches. Because the call provision may be exercised by the issuing company at a time when the market rate of interest is less than the coupon rate, callable bonds usually are sold in the marketplace for something less than otherwise similar, but noncallable, bonds.

Assume, for example, that a firm had issued 12-percent semiannual coupon bonds at par, but market interest rates and the firm's credit standing at a later date would currently allow it to borrow at 10 percent. The firm would be paying more to borrow the face value than it would have to pay if the bonds were issued currently. If

415

$100,000-par value bonds issued at par are called at 105, the entry, in addition to the one to record the accrued interest expense, would be:

Debenture Bonds Payable	100,000	
Loss on Retirement of Bonds	5,000	
Cash		105,000
Bonds called and retired.		

This loss recognized on bond retirement, like the analogous gain, is generally classified as an extraordinary item in the income statement.[9]

When bonds are retired, the book value of the bonds at the time of retirement must be removed from the accounting records. Suppose that $100,000-par value bonds were issued for more than par value several years ago and that the book value of the bonds is now $103,500. If $10,000-par value bonds are called at 105, the entry to record the retirement would be:

Bonds Payable	10,350	
Loss on Retirement of Bonds	150	
Cash		10,500
Partial retirement of bonds originally issued for more than par value. The Loss is an extraordinary item.		

The market rate of interest a firm must pay depends on two factors: the general level of interest rates and its own creditworthiness. If the market rate of interest has risen since bonds were issued (or the firm's credit rating has declined), the bonds will sell in the market at less than issue price. A firm that wanted to retire such bonds would not *call* them, because the call price is typically greater than the issue price. Instead the firm would purchase its bonds in the open market and realize a gain on the retirement of bonds.

Unifying Principles of Accounting for Long-Term Liabilities

Long-term liabilities are obligations to pay fixed amounts at definite future times extending beyond 1 year. The obligations are shown at the present value of the future payments. The present value is computed in calculations using the historical rate of interest—the market interest rate on the date the obligation was incurred.

The method of accounting for all long-term liabilities and related expenses is conceptually and procedurally identical—the effective-interest method. The liability is initially recorded at the present value of the future contractual payments using the

---

[9] Gain or loss on bond retirement is part of ordinary income from operations when it results from bond retirement in accord with sinking fund provisions; *ibid.*

interest rate relevant for the borrower on the date the loan begins. At any subsequent interest-accrual or interest-payment date, Interest Expense is computed by multiplying the book value of the liability by the historical interest rate. The amount of interest expense increases liabilities. The amount of any cash payment made reduces the liabilities. The difference between interest expense and the cash payment increases or decreases the book value of the liability for the next accounting period.

Summary

A liability is an obligation by an entity involving a probable future sacrifice of resources. The amount of the obligation and the timing of its payment can be estimated with reasonable certainty. The transaction causing the obligation to arise has already occurred.

Accounting for long-term liabilities is accomplished by recording these obligations at their present value at the date the obligation is incurred and then showing the change in that present value as the maturity date of the obligation approaches. In historical-cost accounting, the interest rate used throughout the life of the liability is the appropriate market rate at the time the liability was originally incurred. Retirement of long-term liabilities can be brought about in a variety of ways, but in each case, the process is the same. The net obligation is offset against what is given in return, usually cash, with gain or loss on retirement recognized as appropriate.

Problem 1 for Self-Study

Avner Company issues a 3-year, $100,000 note bearing interest at the rate of 15 percent per year. That is, Avner Company promises to pay $15,000 at the end of 1 year, $15,000 at the end of 2 years, and $115,000 at the end of 3 years. The market rate of interest on the date the note is issued is 10 percent.

a Compute the proceeds Avner Company receives for its note.
b Prepare an amortization schedule similar to Exhibit 10.2 for the life of the note.
c Prepare journal entries that would be made on the date of issue, 6 months after the date of issue (assuming the books were closed then), and 1 year after the date of issue, assuming an interest payment is made then.

Suggested Solution

a Present value of 3 payments of $15,000, discounted at 10 percent; see Table 4, 3-period row, 10-percent column: $15,000 × 2.48685 . . . . $ 37,303

Present value of 1 payment of $100,000 discounted at 10 percent for 3 periods; see Table 2, 3-period row, 10-percent column: $100,000 × .75131   75,131

Net Proceeds from Issue of Note $112,434

b See Exhibit 10.5.

Exhibit 10.5
**Amortization Schedule for Note with Face Value
of $100,000 Issued for $112,434, Bearing Interest at the
Rate of 15 Percent of Face Value per Year, Issued to Yield 10
Percent**
(Problem 1 for Self-Study)

Yearly Periods (1)	Loan Balance Start of Period (2)	Interest Expense for Period (3)	Payment (4)	Portion of Payment Reducing Principal (5)	Loan Balance End of Period (6)
0					$112,434
1	$112,434	$11,243	$ 15,000	$ 3,757	108,677
2	108,677	10,868	15,000	4,132	104,545
3	104,545	10,455	115,000	104,545	0

Column (2) = Column (6) from Previous Period.
Column (3) = .10 × Column (2).
Column (4)   Given.
Column (5) = Column (4) − Column (3).
Column (6) = Column (2) − Column (5).

c Cash.	112,434	
Note Payable.		112,434

Proceeds of issue of note.

Interest Expense.	5,622	
Interest Payable.		5,622

See Exhibit 10.5; accrual of 6 months' interest = $11,243/2.

Interest Expense.	5,621	
Interest Payable	5,622	
Note Payable.	3,757	
Cash		15,000

Interest expense for the remainder of the first year and cash payment made.
Excess of cash payment over interest expense reduces note principal.

Problem 2 for Self-Study

Generally accepted accounting principles require that long-term monetary liabilities be stated at the present value of the future cash flows discounted at the market rate of interest appropriate to the monetary items at the time they were initially recorded. APB *Opinion No. 21* specifically excludes from present-value valuation those obligations that are under warranties. Warranties, being nonmonetary liabilities, are stated at the estimated cost of providing warranty goods and services in the future.

Assume that the estimated future costs of a 3-year warranty plan on products sold during 1982 are as follows:

Year	Expected Cost
1983	$ 500,000
1984	600,000
1985	900,000
Total	$2,000,000

Actual costs coincided with expectations both as to timing and amount.

a Prepare the journal entries for each of the years 1982 through 1985 for this warranty plan following current generally accepted accounting principles.

b Now, assume that generally accepted accounting principles allow these liabilities to be shown at their present value. Prepare the journal entries for each of the years 1982 through 1985 for this warranty plan assuming that the warranty liability is stated at the present value of the future costs discounted at 10 percent. To simplify the calculations, assume that all warranty costs are incurred on December 31 of each year.

c What theoretical arguments can be offered for the valuation basis in part **b**?

Suggested Solution

a	1982	Warranty Expense	2,000,000	
		Estimated Warranty Liability		2,000,000
	1983	Estimated Warranty Liability	500,000	
		Cash and Other Accounts		500,000
	1984	Estimated Warranty Liability	600,000	
		Cash and Other Accounts		600,000
	1985	Estimated Warranty Liability	900,000	
		Cash and Other Accounts		900,000

b The present value of the future cost amounts on December 31, 1982, discounted at 10 percent, is:

1983	$500,000 × .90909	$ 454,545
1984	$600,000 × .82645	495,870
1985	$900,000 × .75131	676,179
	Total	$1,626,594

	1982	Warranty Expense	1,626,594	
		Estimated Warranty Liability		1,626,594
	1983	Interest Expense	162,659	
		Estimated Warranty Liability		162,659
		.10 × $1,626,594 = $162,659.		

419

| 1983 | Estimated Warranty Liability . . . . | 500,000 | |
| | Cash and Other Accounts. . . . . | | 500,000 |

| 1984 | Interest Expense. . . . . | 128,925 | |
| | Estimated Warranty Liability . . . . | | 128,925 |

.10 × ($1,626,594 + $162,659 − $500,000) = $128,925.

| 1984 | Estimated Warranty Liability . . . . | 600,000 | |
| | Cash and Other Accounts. . . . . | | 600,000 |

| 1985 | Interest Expense. . . . . | 81,818 | |
| | Estimated Warranty Liability . . . . | | 81,818 |

.10 × (1,626,594 + $162,659 − $500,000 + $128,925 − $600,000) = .10 × $818,178 = $81,818.

1985	Estimated Warranty Liability	899,996	
	Interest Expense.	4	
	Cash		900,000

There is a rounding error of $4 in the Estimated Warranty Liability account at the end of 1985. Interest expense for 1985 is, therefore, increased by $4.

c The goods and services provided under the warranty plan must first be acquired for cash. Thus, even though customers will receive goods and services, the firm must expend cash at some point. To be consistent with monetary liabilities, these amounts would be discounted to their present value.

Questions and Problems

1 Review the meaning of the following concepts or terms discussed in this chapter.
   a Liability.
   b FICA.
   c Contingent liability and estimated liability.
   d Mortgage, mortgagee, mortgagor.
   e Bond indenture.
   f Coupon bond.
   g Debenture bond.
   h Convertible bond.
   i Yield or effective rate of bond.
   j Bond tables.
   k Amortization of bonds using the straight-line and effective-interest methods.
   l Sinking fund.
   m Serial bonds.
   n Bond refunding.
   o Call price.

2 What factors determine the amount of money a firm actually receives when it offers a bond issue to the market?

3 A call premium is the difference between the call price of a bond and its par value. What is the purpose of such a premium?

4 Why does a company that gives trading stamps to its customers usually not have a problem of estimating a liability for the cost of goods to be given to customers who redeem their stamps?

420

5 A noted accountant once remarked that the optimal number of faulty TV sets for the General Electric Company to sell is "not zero," even if GE promises to repair all faulty GE sets that break down, for whatever reason, within 2 years of purchase. Why is the optimal number "not zero"?

6 Refer to the discussion in Chapter 7, where the reductions in income for expected uncollectibles are shown as a revenue contra for the period of sale, not as an expense for the later period when uncollectibility becomes known. Estimated warranty costs are subtracted from income for the period of sale, not in the later period when the repair is made. Why is this item called "warranty expenses" rather than being treated as a revenue contra?

7 What are the relative advantages and disadvantages of the straight-line method versus the effective-interest method of accounting for interest expense on a bond?

8 For each of the following items, indicate:

(1) Does the item meet all of the criteria of the accountant's usual definition of a liability?
(2) Is the item shown as a liability?
(3) If the item is recognized as a liability, how is the amount of the liability computed?

   a Interest accrued but not paid on a note.
   b Advances from customers for goods and services to be delivered later.
   c Firm orders from customers for goods and services to be delivered later.
   d Mortgages payable.
   e Bonds payable.
   f Product warranties.
   g Fifteen-year cancelable lease on an office building.
   h Damages the company must pay if a pending lawsuit is lost.
   i Cost of restoring strip-mining sites after mining operations are completed.

9 While shopping in a store on July 5, 1980, a customer slipped on the floor and sustained back injuries. On January 15, 1981, the customer sued the store for $1 million. The case came to trial on April 30, 1981. The jury's verdict was rendered on June 15, 1981, with the store found guilty of gross negligence. A damage award of $400,000 was granted to the customer. The store, on June 25, 1981, appealed the decision to a higher court on the grounds that certain evidence had not been admitted by the lower court. The higher court ruled on November 1, 1981, that the evidence should have been admitted. The lower court reheard the case beginning on March 21, 1982. Another jury, on April 20, 1982, again found the store guilty of gross negligence and awarded $500,000. On May 15, 1982, the store paid the $500,000 judgment. When should a loss from these events be recognized by the supermarket? Explain your reasoning.

10 A private school has a reporting year ending June 30. It hires teachers for the 10-month period, September of one year through June of the following year. It contracts to pay teachers in 12 monthly installments over the period September of one year through August of the next year. For the current academic year, the total contractual salaries to be paid to teachers is $360,000. How should this amount be accounted for in the financial statements issued June 30, at the end of the academic year?

11 The following questions compare the effective-interest method and the straight-line method of accounting for interest expense on bonds.

421

a Which method gives higher interest expense in the first year for a bond issued at less than par value?

b Which method gives higher interest expense in the first year for a bond issued at more than par value?

c Which method gives higher interest expense in the last year for a bond issued at less than par value?

d Which method gives higher interest expense in the last year for a bond issued at more than par value?

e Which method involves the larger adjustment to net income in deriving funds provided by operations in the first year for a bond issued at more than par value?

f Which method involves the larger adjustment to net income in deriving funds provided by operations in the first year for a bond issued at less than par value?

12 The Gonedes Company issues 12-percent semiannual coupon bonds maturing in 10 years. The face amount of the bonds is $1 million. The net cash proceeds to Gonedes Company from the bond issue amounts to $944,907.

What interest rate will be used in applying the effective-interest method over the life of this bond issue?

13 Colantoni Company sells appliances, all for cash. All acquisitions of appliances during a year are debited to the Merchandise Inventory account. The company provides warranties on all its products, guaranteeing to make repairs within 1 year of the date of sale as required for any of its appliances that break down. The company has many years of experience with its products and warranties.

The schedule shown in Exhibit 10.6 contains trial balances for the Colantoni Company at the ends of 1982 and 1983. The trial balances for the end of 1982 are the Adjusted Preclosing Trial Balance (after all adjusting entries have been properly made) and the final Postclosing Trial Balance. The trial balance shown for the end of 1983 is taken before any adjusting entries of any kind, although entries have been made to the Estimated Liability for Warranty Repairs account during the year 1983, as repairs have been made. Colantoni Company closes its books once each year.

At the end of 1983, the management of Colantoni Company analyzes the appliances sold within the preceding 12 months. All appliances in the hands of customers that are still covered by warranty are classified as follows: those sold on or before June 30 (more than 6 months old), those sold after June 30, but on or before November 30 (more than 1 month, but less than 6 months old), and those sold on or after December 1. One-half of 1 percent of the appliances sold more than 6 months ago are estimated to require repair, 5 percent of the appliances sold 1 to 6 months before the end of the year are estimated to require repair, and 8 percent of the appliances sold within the last month are assumed to require repair. From this analysis, management estimated that $5,000 of repairs still would have to be made in 1984 on the appliances sold in 1983. Ending inventory on December 31, 1983, is $120,000.

a What were the total acquisitions of merchandise inventory during 1983?

b What is the cost of goods sold for 1983?

c What was the dollar amount of repairs made during the year 1983?

d What is the Warranty Expense for 1983?

e Give journal entries for repairs made during 1983, for the warranty expense for 1983, and for cost of goods sold for 1983.

Exhibit 10.6
Colantoni Company
(Problem 13)

TRIAL BALANCES—END OF 1982	Adjusted Preclosing		Postclosing	
	Dr.	Cr.	Dr.	Cr.
Estimated Liability for Warranty Repairs . .		$ 6,000		$ 6,000
Merchandise Inventory	$ 100,000		$100,000	
Sales		800,000		
Warranty Expense	18,000			
All Other Accounts	882,000	194,000	110,000	204,000
Totals	$1,000,000	$1,000,000	$210,000	$210,000

TRIAL BALANCES—END OF 1983	Unadjusted Trial Balance	
	Dr.	Cr.
Estimated Liability for Warranty Repairs	$ 15,000	
Merchandise Inventory	820,000	
Sales		$1,000,000
Warranty Expense	—	—
All Other Accounts	265,000	100,000
Totals	$1,100,000	$1,100,000

14 If a company borrows $1,000,000 by issuing, at par, 20-year, 10-percent bonds with semi-annual coupons, the total interest expense over the life of the issue is $2,000,000 (= 20 × .10 × $1,000,000). If a company undertakes a 20-year mortgage or note with an implicit borrowing rate of 10 percent, the annual payments are $1,000,000/8.51356 = $117,460. (See Table 4 at the end of the book, 20-period row, 10-percent column.) The total mortgage payments are $2,349,200 (= 20 × $117,460), and the total interest expense over the life of the note or mortgage is $1,349,200 (= $2,349,200 − $1,000,000).

Why are the amounts of interest expense different for these two means of borrowing for the same length of time at identical interest rates?

15 Refer to the Simplified Statement of Changes in Financial Position for a Period in Exhibit 5.19 on page 191. Nine of the lines in the statement are numbered. Line (2) should be expanded to say "Additions for Expenses and Other Charges Against Income Not Using Funds from Operations," and line (3) should be expanded to say "Subtractions for Revenues and Other Credits to Income Not Producing Funds from Operations." Ignore the unnumbered lines in responding to the questions below.

Assume that the accounting cycle is complete for the period and that all of the financial statements have been prepared. Then it is discovered that a transaction has been overlooked. That transaction is recorded in the accounts and all of the financial statements are corrected. Define *funds* as *working capital*. For each of the following transactions, indicate which of the numbered lines of the funds statement is affected and by how much. Ignore income tax effects.

a Bonds are issued for $100,000 cash.
b Bonds with a fair market value of $100,000 are issued for a building.
c Bonds with a book value of $100,000 are retired for $90,000 cash.
d Bonds with a book value of $100,000 are called for $105,000 cash and retired.
e Interest expense on bonds is recorded using the effective-interest method. The bonds have a face value of $100,000 and a current book value of $90,000. The coupon rate is 10 percent, paid semiannually, and the bonds were originally issued to yield 12 percent, compounded semiannually.
f Interest expense on bonds is recorded using the effective-interest method. The bonds have a face value of $100,000 and a book value of $105,000. The coupon rate is 12 percent paid semiannually, and the bonds were originally issued to yield 10 percent, compounded semiannually.

16 On December 1, 1982, the O'Brien Company obtained a 90-day loan for $15,000 from the Twin City State Bank at an annual interest rate of 12 percent. On the maturity date the note was renewed for another 30 days, with a check being issued to the bank for the accrued interest. The O'Brien Company closes its books annually at December 31.

a Present entries on the books of the O'Brien Company to record the issue of the note, the year-end adjustment, the renewal of the note, and the payment of cash at maturity of the renewed note.
b Present entries at maturity date of the original note for the following variations in the settlement of the note of the O'Brien Company.

(1) The original note is paid at maturity.
(2) The note is renewed for 30 days; the new note bears interest at 15 percent per annum. Interest on the old note was not paid at maturity.

17 The Myrtle Lunch sells coupon books that patrons may use later to purchase meals. Each coupon book sells for $17 and has a face value of $20. That is, each book can be used to purchase meals with menu prices of $20. On July 1, redeemable unused coupons with face value of $1,500 were outstanding. During July, 250 coupon books were sold; during August, 100; during September, 100. Cash receipts exclusive of coupons were $1,200 in July, $1,300 in August, and $1,250 in September. Coupons with a face value of $2,700 were redeemed by patrons during the 3 months.

a If the Myrtle Lunch had a net income of $500 for the quarter ending September 30, how large were expenses?
b What effect, if any, do the July, August, and September coupon sales and redemptions have on the right-hand side of the September 30 balance sheet?

18 The Lindahl Company sells service contracts to repair copiers at $300 per year. When the contract is signed, the $300 fee is collected and the Service Contact Fees Received in Advance account is credited. Revenues on contracts are recognized on a quarterly basis during the year in which the coverage is in effect. On January 1, 1,000 service contracts were outstanding. Of these, 500 expired at the end of the first quarter, 300 at the end of the second quarter, 150 at the end of the third quarter, and 50 at the end of the fourth quarter. Sales and service during the year came to these amounts (assume that all sales occurred at the beginning of the quarter):

	Sales of Contracts	Service Expenses
First Quarter	$120,000 (400 contracts)	$50,000
Second Quarter	240,000 (800 contracts)	60,000
Third Quarter	90,000 (300 contracts)	45,000
Fourth Quarter	60,000 (200 contracts)	55,000

a Prepare journal entries for the first three quarters of the year for the Lindahl Company. Assume that quarterly reports are prepared on March 31, June 30, and September 30.

b What is the balance in the Service Contract Fees Received in Advance account on December 31?

19 The Holmes Sales Company sells a building lot to N. Wolfe on September 1, 1982, for $27,000. The down payment is $3,000, and minimum payments of $265 a month are to be made on the contract. Interest at the rate of 12 percent per annum on the unpaid balance is deducted from each payment, and the balance is applied on the principal. Payments are made as follows: October 1, $265; November 1, $265; December 1, $600; January 2, $265.

Prepare a schedule showing payments, interest and principal, and remaining liability at each of these dates. Round amounts to the nearest dollar.

20 Lynne Michals secures a mortgage loan of $112,000 from the Oakley National Bank. The terms of the mortgage require monthly payments of $1,660. The interest rate to be applied to the unpaid balance is 9 percent per year.

Calculate the distribution of payments for the first 4 months between principal and interest and present the new balance figures. Prepare a table showing payments, interest and principal, and remaining liability at each of these dates. Round amounts to the nearest dollar.

21 On June 1, the Loebbecke Company purchases a warehouse from F. S. Brandon for $600,000, of which $100,000 is assigned to the land and $500,000 to the building. There is a mortgage on the property payable to the Dixie National Bank, which, together with the accrued interest, will be assumed by the purchaser. It bears interest at the rate of 12 percent per year. The balance due on the mortgage is $240,000. The principal of the mortgage will be paid on April 1 and October 1 of each year. A 10-year second mortgage for $150,000 is issued to F. S. Brandon; it bears interest at the rate of 15 percent per year, payable on June 1 and December 1. A check is drawn to complete the purchase.

Prepare journal entries for the Loebbecke Company, which closes its books once a year on December 31, for June 1, October 1, and December 1.

22 On October 1, 1982, Howell Stores, Inc., issues 20-year, first mortgage bonds with a face value of $1,000,000. The proceeds of the issue are $1,060,000. The bonds bear interest at the rate of 10 percent per year, payable semiannually at April 1 and October 1. Howell Stores, Inc., closes its books annually at December 31. Round amounts to the nearest dollar.

a Present dated journal entries related to the bonds from October 1, 1982, through October 1, 1983, inclusive. Assume that Howell Stores, Inc., uses the straight-line method to recognize interest expense.

b Repeat instructions for part **a**, but assume that the company uses the effective-

425

interest method. The effective-interest rate to be used is 9.3 percent, compounded semiannually.

23 On May 1, 1982, the Oliver Company acquired $1,000,000 par value of bonds of the Bret Company for $1,398,000 plus accrued interest. Costs of acquisition amounted to an additional $2,000. The bonds bear interest at 15 percent per year payable on March 31 and September 30 and mature on March 31, 1992. Use the straight-line method to recognize interest expense.

a Present journal entries on the books of the Oliver Company from May 1, 1982, through March 31, 1983, inclusive. Assume that the books are closed annually on December 31.
b Present the journal entry (or entries) for the sale of the bonds on August 1, 1985, at 103.5 plus accrued interest.

24 In 1982, the Central Power Company issued $2 million bonds in two series, A and B. Each series had face amount of $1 million and was issued at prices to yield 11 percent. Issue A contained semiannual 10-percent coupons. Issue B contained 12-percent semiannual coupons. Issues A and B both mature 30 years from issue date.

Answer the following questions for issue A. Round amounts to the nearest dollar.

a What is the issuing price of the bonds?
b Make the journal entry for the date of bond issue.
c Using the effective-interest method, show the journal entries made on the first semiannual interest payment date.
d Repeat part **c** for the second and third payment dates.
e Show the semiannual entry if straight-line method is used.

25 Refer to the data in Problem **24**. Work the problem for issue B.

26 Hanouille Company issues 10-percent semiannual coupon bonds maturing five years from the date of issue. Interest of 5 percent of the face value of $100,000 is payable January 1 and July 1. The bonds are issued to yield 12 percent, compounded semiannually.

a What are the initial issue proceeds received by Hanouille Company?
b Construct an amortization schedule for this bond issue, similar to Exhibit 10.3.
c By how much does interest expense for the first year (note *year,* not first 6-month period) of the bond's life under the effective-interest method differ from that under the straight-line method?
d Assume that at the end of the third year of the bond's life, $10,000 face value of bonds are called and retired for 103 percent of par. Give the journal entry to record the retirement.

27 The Siegal Company files its income tax returns on a calendar-year basis and issues financial statements quarterly as of March 31, June 30, and so on. All income taxes are estimated or paid at the rate of 40 percent of taxable income. The following data are applicable to the company's income tax for year 1.

Year 1

March 31	It is estimated that total taxable income for year 1 will be about $15 million. The first quarter's financial statements are prepared.
April 15	The first payment on estimated taxes is made.
June 15	It is now estimated that total taxable income for the year will be about $17 million. The second payment on estimated taxes is made.
June 30	The second quarter's financial statements are prepared.
Sept. 15	It is now estimated that total taxable income for the year will be about $16 million. The third payment on estimated taxes is made.
Sept. 30	The third quarter's financial statements are prepared.
Dec. 15	It is now estimated that total taxable income for the year will be about $17.5 million. The fourth payment on estimated taxes is made.
Dec. 31	Income for the year is $17,750,000. Financial statements for the year are prepared.

Year 2

March 15	The first payment of the balance of taxes for year 1 is made.
June 15	The second payment of tax balance for year 1 is made.

a Prepare schedules showing
  (1) For tax returns: estimated taxes for year, cumulative payments due, and payment made for each payment date.
  (2) For financial statements: tax expenses for the quarterly reports and annual report.
b Record the transactions related to year 1 income taxes in journal-entry form.
c Present the T-accounts for Cash, Prepaid Income Taxes (if necessary), Income Taxes Payable, and Income Tax Expense.

Chapter 11   *Liabilities: A Closer Look*

The preceding chapter discussed the concept of an accounting liability and described the accounting for current liabilities, long-term bonds, and long-term notes. This chapter examines more controversial issues in liability recognition, valuation, and accounting. The chapter treats the accounting for long-term notes payable where the historical interest rate must be imputed, the accounting for leases and pensions, and problems in accounting for income taxes caused by differences in accounting principles between financial reports and income tax returns.

Contracts and Long-Term Notes: Interest Imputation

Real estate is often purchased on a *land contract*. Equipment is frequently acquired on the installment plan, and the liability is called an *equipment contract*. Payments on such contracts are usually made monthly. Sometimes an explicit interest rate is provided in the contract. The accounting for contracts, or notes, with explicit interest is similar to the accounting for bonds discussed in Chapter 10. In other cases, an explicit interest rate is not stated. Instead, so-called *carrying charges* are added to the purchase price, and the total is divided over a certain number of months without any specific charge being indicated for interest. The "principal" or "face" in this case actually includes *implicit* interest.

Generally accepted accounting principles require that long-term liabilities carrying no explicit interest be stated at the present value of the future cash payments. The interest rate used in discounting is that rate appropriate to the particular bor-

428

rower given the amount and terms of the borrowing arrangement. The interest rate so determined is referred to as an *imputed interest rate*. The difference between the present value and the face value of the liability represents interest to be recognized over the period of the loan. If the note is recorded at its maturity value, then the interest, or discount, must be recorded in a contra account. The next two sections discuss two acceptable ways to compute the present value of the liability and the amount of imputed interest.

Base Interest Rate on Market Value of Asset

The first approach uses the market value of the assets acquired as a basis for computing the present value of the liability. For example, assume that a piece of equipment can be bought for $10,500 cash. The equipment is purchased in return for a single-payment note with face amount of $16,000 payable in 3 years. The implied interest rate is about 15 percent per year. (That is, $1.15^3 \times \$10,500$ is approximately equal to $16,000.) The journal entry using this approach would be:

Equipment	10,500	
Note Payable		10,500
To record purchase of equipment using the known cash price. The amount for the note is inferred from the known cash price of the equipment.		

At the end of each accounting period that intervenes between the acquisition of the equipment and repayment of the note, journal entries would be made to recognize interest expense. In addition, each period there would be entries for depreciation of the equipment. These are not shown. Assume that the note was issued at the beginning of a year. The entries for the 3 years would be:

(1) Interest Expense	1,575	
Note Payable		1,575
Entry made 1 year after issuance of note. Interest is .15 × $10,500. The amount is not paid in cash but is added to the principal amount of the liability.		
(2) Interest Expense	1,811	
Note Payable		1,811
Entry made 1 year after entry above, 2 years after issuance of note. Interest is .15 × ($10,500 + $1,575).		
(3) Interest Expense	2,114	
Note Payable		2,114
Entry made 1 year after entry (2) at maturity of note to increase liability to its maturity amount, $16,000. Interest = $16,000 − ($10,500 + $1,575 + $1,811) which is approximately equal to .15 × ($10,500 + $1,575 + $1,811); the difference is the accumulated rounding error caused by using 15 percent as the implicit interest rate, rather than the exact rate, which is 15.074 percent.		
(4) Note Payable	16,000	
Cash		16,000
To repay note at maturity.		

Of the $16,000 paid at maturity, $5,500 represents interest accumulated on the note since its issue.

Use of Market Interest Rate to
Establish Market Value of Asset
and Present Value of Note

If undeveloped land had been purchased with the same 3-year note, the firm might not be able to establish the current market value of the asset acquired. The firm would then use the interest rate it would have to pay for a similar loan in the open market to find the present value of the note. This is the second acceptable method for quantifying the amount of the liability and computing the imputed interest. Suppose that the market rate for notes such as the one above is 12 percent compounded annually, rather than 15 percent. The present value at 12 percent per year of the $16,000 note due in 3 years is $11,388 (= $16,000 $\times$ .71178; Appendix Table 2 at the back of the book, 3-period row, 12-percent column). The entry to record the purchase of land and payment with the note would be:

Land.	11,388	
Note Payable		11,388
To record purchase of land. Cost of land is inferred from known interest rate.		

Entries would be made at the end of each period to recognize interest expense and to increase the principal amount of the liability. After the third period, the principal amount of the liability would be $16,000.

Funds Statement Effects of Interest Imputation

The process just described for imputing interest on long-term notes results in the recognition of interest expense even though no cash is disbursed (at least until the last period when the note is discharged). In deriving funds provided by continuing operations there must be an addback to net income in the amount of expense that is credited to the long-term liability account, rather than to a working capital account.

Total Expense Is
Independent of Interest Rate

In the first case, the equipment is recorded at $10,500 and there is $5,500 of imputed interest. In the second case, the equipment is recorded at $11,388 and there is $4,612 of imputed interest. The total expense over the combined lives of the note and the equipment—interest plus depreciation—is the same, $16,000, no matter which interest rate is used. Over long-enough time periods in accounting, total expense equals the total cash expenditure; accrual accounting changes only the timing of the expense recognition.

430

Long-Term Notes Held as Receivables

A note that is the long-term liability of the borrower is a long-term asset of the lender. Generally accepted accounting principles require the lender to show the asset in the Long-Term Note Receivable account at its present value. The rate at which the lender discounts the note should in theory be the same as that used by the borrower, but in practice the two rates sometimes differ. The lender's accounting mirrors the borrower's: the lender has interest revenue where the borrower has interest expense.

Leases

Many firms acquire rights to use assets through long-term noncancelable leases. A company might, for example, agree to lease an airplane for 15 years, or a building for 40 years, promising to pay a fixed periodic fee for the duration of the lease. Promising to make an irrevocable series of lease payments commits the firm just as surely as a bond indenture or mortgage, and the accounting is similar.

Here we examine the accounting for long-term, noncancelable leases, how the accounting treatments for short-term and long-term leases differ, and the effects on the financial statements of both treatments.

Suppose that the Myers Company wants to acquire a computer that has a 3-year life and costs $45,000. Assume that Myers Company can borrow money for 3 years at 15 percent per year. The computer manufacturer is willing to sell the equipment for $45,000 or to lease it for 3 years. Myers Company is responsible for property taxes, maintenance, and repairs of the computer whether leased or purchased.

Assume that the lease is signed on January 1, 1982, and that payments on the lease are due on December 31, 1982, 1983, and 1984. In practice, lease payments are usually made in advance, but the computations in the example are simpler if we assume payments at the end of the year. Compound-interest computations show that each lease payment must be $19,709. (The present value of $1 paid at the end of this year and each of the next 2 years is $2.28323 when the interest rate is 15 percent per year. See Table 4 at the end of the book. Because the lease payments must have present value of $45,000, each payment must be $45,000/2.28323 = $19,709.)

Operating-Lease Method

In an *operating lease,* the owner, or lessor, merely transfers the rights to use the property to the lessee for specified periods of time. At the end of the lease period, the property is returned to the lessor. The telephone company leases telephones by the month. Car rental companies lease cars by the day or week on an operating basis. If the Myers Company lease is cancelable and Myers Company can stop making payments and return the computer at any time, then the lease is considered an *operating lease.* No entry would be made on January 1, 1982, when the lease is signed, and the following entry would be made on December 31, 1982, 1983, and 1984:

Rent Expense	19,709	
Cash		19,709
To recognize annual expense of leasing computer.		

Capital-Lease Method

If this lease is noncancelable, then the lease arrangement would be viewed as a form of borrowing to purchase the computer. It would be accounted for as a *capital lease.*[1] This treatment recognizes the signing of the lease as the simultaneous acquisition of a long-term asset, called a *leasehold,* and the incurring of a long-term liability for lease payments. At the time the lease is signed, both the leasehold and the liability are recorded on the books at the present value of the liability, $45,000 in the example.

The entry made at the time Myers Company signed its 3-year noncancelable lease would be:

Asset—Computer Leasehold	45,000	
Liability—Present Value of Lease Obligations		45,000
To recognize acquisition of asset and the related liability.		

At the end of the year, two separate entries must be made. The leasehold is a long-term asset and, like most long-term assets, it must be amortized over its useful life. The first entry made at the end of each year recognizes the amortization of the leasehold asset. Assuming that Myers Company uses straight-line amortization of its leasehold, the entries made at the end of 1982, 1983, and 1984 would be:

Amortization Expense (on Computer Leasehold)	15,000	
Asset—Computer Leasehold		15,000

(An alternative treatment is to credit a contra-asset account, Accumulated Amortization of Computer Leasehold.) The second entry made at the end of each year recognizes the lease payment, which is part payment of interest on the liability and part reduction in the liability itself. The entries made at the end of each of the 3 years would be:

December 31, 1982:		
Interest Expense	6,750	
Liability—Present Value of Lease Obligations	12,959	
Cash		19,709
To recognize lease payment, interest on liability for year (.15 × $45,000 = $6,750) and the plug for reduction in the liability. The present value of the liability after this entry is $32,041 = $45,000 − $12,959.		

---

[1] Financial Accounting Standards Board, *Statement of Financial Accounting Standards No. 13,* "Accounting for Leases," 1976, reissued and reinterpreted, 1980.

432

December 31, 1983:

Interest Expense. 4,806

Liability—Present Value of Lease Obligations 14,903

  Cash 19,709

To recognize lease payment, interest on liability for year (.15 ×
$32,041 = $4,806) and the plug for reduction in the liability. The present value
of the liability after this entry is $17,138 = $32,041 − $14,903.

December 31, 1984:

Interest Expense. 2,571

Liability—Present Value of Lease Obligations 17,138

  Cash 19,709

To recognize lease payment, interest on liability for year (.15 ×
$17,138 = $2,571) and the plug for reduction in the liability. The present value
of the liability after this entry is zero (= $17,138 − $17,138).

Exhibit 11.1 shows the amortization schedule for this lease. Note that its form is
exactly the same as in the mortgage amortization schedule shown in Exhibit 10.2.
The underlying principle uses the effective-interest method of computing interest
each period.

Exhibit 11.1
**Amortization Schedule for $45,000 Lease Liability,
Repaid in Three Annual Installments of $19,709 Each,
Interest Rate 15 Percent, Compounded Annually**

ANNUAL JOURNAL ENTRY

Dr. Interest Expense . . . .   Amount in Column (3)

Dr. Liability—Present Value

  of Lease Obligations . . . .   Amount in Column (5)

    Cr. Cash . . . .   Amount in Column (4)

Year (1)	Lease Liability Start of Year (2)	Interest Expense for Year (3)	Payment (4)	Portion of Payment Reducing Lease Liability (5)	Lease Liabilty End of Year (6)
0					$45,000
1	$45,000	$6,750	$19,709	$12,959	32,041
2	32,041	4,806	19,709	14,903	17,138
3	17,138	2,571	19,709	17,138	0

Column (2) = Column (6), Previous Period.

Column (3) = .15 × Column (2).

Column (4)   Given.

Column (5) = Column (4) − Column (3).

Column (6) = Column (2) − Column (5).

433

Notice that, in the capital-lease method, the total expense over the 3 years is $59,127, consisting of $45,000 (= $15,000 + $15,000 + $15,000) for amortization expense and $14,127 (= $6,750 + $4,806 + $2,571) for interest expense. This is exactly the same as the total expense recognized under the operating-lease method described above ($19,709 × 3 = $59,127). Over long-enough time periods, expense is equal to the cash expenditure. The difference between the operating-lease method and the capital method is the *timing* of the expense recognition and the entries in income statement and balance sheet accounts. The capital-lease method recognizes both the asset (leasehold) and the liability. It also recognizes expense sooner than does the operating-lease method, as summarized in Exhibit 11.2.

Exhibit 11.2
Comparison of Expense Recognized under Operating and Capital-Lease Methods

	Expense Recognized Each Year under	
Year	Operating-Lease Method	Capital Lease Method
1982	$19,709	$21,750 (= $15,000 + $6,750)
1983	19,709	19,806 (= 15,000 + 4,806)
1984	19,709	17,571 (= 15,000 + 2,571)
Total	$59,127[a]	$59,127 (= $45,000[b] + $14,127[c])

[a] Rent expense.
[b] Amortization expense.
[c] Interest expense.

Choosing the Accounting Method

When a journal entry results in a debit to an asset account and a credit to a liability account, there is no increase in owners' equity. Note, however, that the debt-equity ratio increases, making the company appear more risky. Thus, given a choice, most managements would prefer not to show an asset and a related liability on the balance sheet. This preference has led managements to structure asset acquisitions so that the financing takes the form of operating leases. These managements prefer an operating lease to either an installment purchase or capital lease, where both the asset and liability are put onto the balance sheet.

Moreover, the operating lease treatment delays expense recognition by the lessee. In the simple example used here, expense under the capital-lease method is only slightly larger than expense under the operating-lease method in the first year. In more realistic cases where the lease extends over 20 years, the expense in the first year under the capital-lease method may be 25 percent larger than under the operating-lease method.

The FASB has established relatively stringent requirements for accounting for long-term noncancelable leases. A lease must be accounted for as a capital lease if it meets any one of four conditions.[2]

The most stringent of these conditions compares the contractual lease payments discounted at an "appropriate" market interest rate with 90 percent of the fair market value of the asset at the time the lease is signed. (The interest rate must be appropriate, given the creditworthiness of the lessee.) When the present value of lease payments exceeds 90 percent of the fair market value, then the capital lease method must be used. The major risks and rewards of ownership have been transferred from the lessor (landlord) to the lessee. Thus, in economic substance, the lessee has acquired an asset and agreed to pay for it under a long-term contract, to be recognized as a liability. Another criterion is that the capital-lease method must be used if the lease period is 75 percent or more of the asset's expected remaining economic life.

Effects on Lessor

The lessor (landlord) generally uses the same criteria for classifying a lease as a capital lease or an operating lease as does the lessee (tenant). In capital-lease accounting, the lessor recognizes revenue in an amount equal to the present value of all future lease payments and expense in an amount equal to the book value of the leased asset. The difference between the revenue and expense is the lessor's gain on the "sale" of the asset. The lease receivable is recorded like any other long-term receivable at the present value of the future cash flows. Interest revenue is then recognized over the collection period of the payments. Lessors tend to prefer capital-lease accounting because it enables the recognition of a gain on the "sale" of the asset on the date the lease is signed. Under the operating-lease method, all lease revenue is recognized gradually over time as lease payments are received.

Deferred Income Taxes

As we have indicated at various points in this book, there are some areas where there are alternative generally accepted accounting principles. The income tax laws similarly allow a choice of alternative treatments for the same event. One example is in the calculation of depreciation charges. Both generally accepted accounting principles and the tax law allow a firm to choose from among straight-line, sum-of-the-years'-digits, and double-declining-balance methods of depreciation.

In selecting among alternative methods for tax purposes, management usually tries to minimize the present value of the firm's tax liabilities. The principles of income tax management are summarized conveniently by the expression, "Pay the least amount of tax, as late as possible, within the law." This is sometimes known as the *least and latest* rule. It is, however, difficult to generalize about which of the alternative accounting principles management selects, or should select, for financial reporting. This question is discussed more fully in Chapters 9 and 15.

---

[2]Financial Accounting Standards Board. *op. cit.,* par. 7.

435

Suppose that, for whatever reasons it deems appropriate, management decides to use straight-line depreciation for a given plant asset for financial reporting. Suppose, further, that management has calculated that the present value of taxes paid will be smallest if the sum-of-the-years'-digits method is used for tax purposes. The firm is allowed to use straight-line for financial reporting and sum-of-the-years'-digits for taxes. The firm will thereby show a higher pretax "book" income in its financial reports than in its tax return in the early years of the asset's life.[3] In later years, book depreciation for this asset exceeds the tax depreciation. This is permissible, but the firm must report as income tax expense in its income statement the amount of taxes that would have resulted had it used the straight-line method for tax reporting.[4] The goal is to report aftertax book income as though taxes were based on pretax book income. The difference between the actual tax payment that results from using the accelerated method and the tax payment that *would have* resulted had it used the straight-line method for tax reporting is credited to a Deferred Income Tax Liability account.

Illustration

The problems of deferred income taxes can perhaps be best understood by examining an example. Assume that Burns, Inc. pays income taxes at the rate of 40 percent of taxable income. Suppose that Burns purchased a plant asset for $150,000 that has a 5-year life and an estimated salvage value of zero. Suppose further that this asset produces an excess of revenues over operating expenses (other than depreciation and taxes) of $44,000 a year. That is, after paying for the costs of running and maintaining the asset, the firm enjoys a $44,000-per-year excess of revenue over expenses (except depreciation and taxes). Burns uses straight-line depreciation for financial reporting and the sum-of-the-years'-digits method for calculating its taxes. Thus, in the first year the new plant asset is used, depreciation on the financial records will be $30,000 (= $150,000/5) and on the tax return will be $50,000 (= $150,000 \times 5/15). Suppose that in addition to the $44,000 from the plant asset, other pretax income for each year is $80,000. Exhibit 11.3 summarizes the computation of taxes for tax purposes and for financial reporting.

The first column in Exhibit 11.3 shows the tax return for the first year and for the fifth year. Note that nothing changes over time other than the depreciation deduction and taxes payable. Depreciation decreases and taxes payable increase. The middle column shows book income resulting from an accounting where income tax expense is equal to income taxes payable. Note that pretax book income is the same, $94,000, in both the first and fifth years but that aftertax net income declines from $64,400 in the first year to $48,400 in the fifth year. The decline results from income

---

[3]The term *financial statement income,* although descriptive, is somewhat cumbersome. Throughout this section, we use the term *book income* to refer to net income before taxes reported in the financial statements and *taxable income* to refer to the amount reported on the income tax return. Similarly, the terms *book purposes* and *tax purposes* differentiate the financial statements from the income tax return.

[4]Accounting Principles Board, *Opinion No. 11,* "Accounting for Income Taxes," 1967.

Exhibit 11.3
**Deferred Income Tax
Computations for Burns, Inc.**

	Tax Return	Book Income Using Taxes Payable (Not Acceptable)	Financial Reporting (Required)
First Year			
Other Pretax Income	$ 80,000	$80,000	$80,000
Excess of Revenues over Expenses			
Except Depreciation from Plant Asset	44,000	44,000	44,000
Depreciation	(50,000)	(30,000)	(30,000)
Income Before Taxes	$ 74,000	$94,000	$94,000
Income Taxes Currently Payable (at 40 percent). . .	$ 29,600		
Income Tax Expense (at 40 percent):			
on Taxable Income		(29,600)	
on Pretax Book Income			(37,600)
Net Income		$64,400	$56,400
Fifth Year			
Other Pretax Income	$ 80,000	$80,000	$80,000
Excess of Revenues over Expenses			
Except Depreciation from Plant Asset	44,000	44,000	44,000
Depreciation	(10,000)	(30,000)	(30,000)
Income Before Taxes	$114,000	$94,000	$94,000
Income Taxes Currently Payable (at 40 percent). . .	$ 45,600		
Income Tax Expense (at 40 percent):			
on Taxable Income		(45,600)	
on Pretax Book Income			(37,600)
Net Income		$48,400	$56,400

taxes payable increasing from $29,600 to $45,600. Those who set generally accepted accounting principles are uncomfortable with the notion that reported income (as in the middle column) will decline merely because different accounting methods are used for tax and for book purposes.

Consequently, in this case, generally accepted accounting principles require that the income tax expense used in book reporting be based on pretax *book* income, not on actual taxes payable. The third column of Exhibit 11.3 shows the required accounting. Note that aftertax net income in the fifth year equals that of the first year, just as pretax income in the fifth year equals that of the first year.

Rationale for Deferred Tax Accounting

Relative to straight-line depreciation, accelerated depreciation "borrows" income tax deductions in the early years from later years (as we demonstrate in Exhibit 11.4). The reason for the decline in taxable income is predictable during the first year,

437

Exhibit 11.4
Summary of Deferred Income Tax
Liability Account for Burns, Inc.

ANNUAL JOURNAL ENTRY

Dr. Income Tax Expense. . . . . Amount in Column (5)

or { Dr. Deferred Income Tax Liability. . . . . Amount in Column (9)
    { Cr. Deferred Income Tax Liability . . . . Amount in Column (10)
      Cr. Income Taxes Payable . . . . Amount in Column (8)

		Financial Statements				Tax Returns			Deferred Income Tax Liability Account		
Year (1)	Income Before Depreciation and Tax Expenses (2)	Depreciation Expense (3)	Pretax Income (4)	Tax Expense (5)ᵃ	Depreciation Deduction (6)ᵇ	Pretax Income (7)ᶜ	Taxes Payable (8)ᵈ	Debit (9)	Credit (10)	Credit Balance at Year-End (11)
1	$124,000	$ 30,000	$ 94,000	$ 37,600	$ 50,000	$ 74,000	$ 29,600		$8,000	$ 8,000
2	124,000	30,000	94,000	37,600	40,000	84,000	33,600		4,000	12,000
3	124,000	30,000	94,000	37,600	30,000	94,000	37,600	—	—	12,000
4	124,000	30,000	94,000	37,600	20,000	104,000	41,600	$4,000		8,000
5	124,000	30,000	94,000	37,600	10,000	114,000	45,600	8,000		0
		$150,000	$470,000	$188,000	$150,000	$470,000	$188,000			

ᵃ .40 × $94,000.
ᵇ $150,000 × t/15, where t = 5, 4, 3, 2, 1 for the years, in order.
ᶜ $124,000 − (6).
ᵈ (7) × .40.

because it results from a difference in the depreciation methods used in financial statements and the tax return. The tax reduction in the first year, relative to the fifth, is a difference that will reverse with the mere passage of time. Generally accepted accounting principles prefer that the reported net income be the same in each year because pretax income on the financial statements is the same each year. The required accounting matches income tax expense and pretax book income rather than income tax expense and taxable income. The rationale is that income taxes will become payable in future years when the difference between book and taxable income reverses. This future cash outflow is an expense of the current period to be matched against pretax book income much the same as future warranty costs are an expense of the period when the warranteed product is sold.

Procedures

Generally accepted accounting principles require that income tax expense under these conditions be computed as though straight-line depreciation were used on the tax return. Under such an assumption, income tax expense would be $37,600 each year. Because only $29,600 is payable in the first year, the following entry would be made:

Income Tax Expense	37,600	
Income Tax Payable		29,600
Deferred Income Tax Liability		8,000
First year income tax entry; expense is larger than cash payment; liability is created.		

If only one asset is considered, the $8,000 tax not paid—but credited to the Deferred Income Tax Liability account—is not forgiven by the government. Instead, these payments are merely delayed. If Burns had only this one asset, the additional taxes would be paid in the fifth year. The bottom panel of Exhibit 11.3 shows the computation of Income Taxes Payable in the fifth year to be $45,600. Because the financial statements will have Income Tax Expense computed under the assumption that straight-line depreciation is used on the tax return, the reported Income Tax Expense will remain $37,600. Because the actual tax payment must be $45,600, however, the journal entry to recognize the income tax expense for the fifth year is:

Income Tax Expense	37,600	
Deferred Income Tax Liability	8,000	
Income Tax Payable		45,600
Fifth-year income tax entry; expense is less than cash payment; liability is discharged.		

Exhibit 11.4 shows a summary of the entries in Burns' Deferred Income Tax Liability account for the 5 years during which it uses the plant asset. Observe that the total tax expense shown on the financial statements over the asset's life is the same as the

total taxes payable, but that using the accelerated method on the tax returns defers payment and thus leads to a lower present value of taxes paid.

Funds Statement Effects In the first year, income tax expense exceeds income taxes payable by $8,000. That $8,000 of tax expense did not use working capital, so an addback to net income is required in the statement of changes in financial position in deriving "funds provided by operations." The $8,000 of expense increases the noncurrent liability for deferred income taxes. The statement of changes in financial position of General Products Company for 1982, in Exhibit A.3, illustrates the addback to net income for deferred taxes in arriving at working capital provided by operations.

In the fifth year more working capital ($45,600) is used than the amount of the expense ($37,600) reported in the income statement. Consequently, there must be a subtraction of $8,000 in the statement of changes in financial position to derive "working capital provided by operations." See also the 1981 column of Exhibit A.3 for General Products Company.

Timing Differences and Permanent Differences

In general, the deferred income tax liability arises from differences in timing between financial reporting of revenues and expenses and tax reporting of these items. The following list shows some of the ways in which the timing differences can arise.

1 Depreciation for tax purposes is different from that shown in the financial records in a given period either because different depreciation methods or different asset lives, or both, are used for the two purposes. Total depreciation over the asset's entire life is the same for book and for tax purposes.
2 Income from credit sales is recognized in the financial records in the year of sale, but recognized for tax purposes in the year when cash is collected from customers. Total income from the credit sales is the same for book and for tax; merely their timing of recognition differs.
3 Income from long-term construction projects is recognized in financial records on the percentage-of-completion basis but on tax returns under the completed-contract basis. Total income is again the same for book and for tax but its timing of recognition differs.

Some differences between reported income and taxable income will never reverse. These include items of revenue that are never taxed or expenses that are never deductible in computing income taxes payable. An example is interest revenue on tax-exempt municipal bonds held as assets. Such tax-exempt interest is part of reported income but is never part of taxable income. Differences between reported income and taxable income that never reverse are called *permanent differences.* Permanent differences do not require recognition of deferred income taxes.

Income Tax Accounting Summarized

Income taxes payable computed on the tax return are based on accounting principles selected by the firm, generally to minimize the present value of the cash burden for income taxes. Income tax expense shown in the financial statements is computed from a measure of taxable income determined using the financial statement's accounting principles for timing differences, rather than the tax return's accounting principles. The excess of income tax expense over income taxes payable, if any, is credited to the Deferred Income Taxes balance sheet account. The excess of income taxes payable over income tax expense, if any, is debited to the Deferred Income Taxes balance sheet account. If the Deferred Income Taxes account has a credit balance, then it appears on the balance sheet among the equities, usually as a liability. If the Deferred Income Taxes account has a debit balance, then it appears on the balance sheet among the assets.

Disclosure of Deferred Income Taxes in Financial Statements

Notes to financial statements contain a wealth of information about income taxes. Among the items of information included is the amount of deferred tax expense for the year caused by each of the several important timing differences. This disclosure is illustrated in Note 6 of Exhibit A.4 in Appendix A for General Products Company.

Typically, the financial statements do not disclose the amount of deductions claimed on the tax return. The information in the notes about deferred taxes can be used to deduce many of them. For example, the financial statements of Burns, Inc., for the first year in our example, show depreciation expense of $30,000. The notes disclose both that the deferred tax expense caused by depreciation timing differences is $8,000 and that the income tax rate is 40 percent of pretax income. From these data, we can deduce that depreciation claimed on the tax return exceeded depreciation expense on the financial statements by $20,000 (= $8,000/.40). Thus, depreciation claimed on the tax return must have been $50,000 (= $30,000 + $20,000).

Weakness of the Accounting for Deferred Income Taxes

As the example for Burns, Inc., shows, if the deferred income tax liability arises from the depreciation of one asset, it will eventually be paid. But the tax law, by granting the general use of accelerated depreciation methods, has in effect offered to delay tax payments by certain firms. These firms are the going concerns who choose to use the accelerated method on the tax return but who believe that the straight-line method properly reflects depreciation and so use it in financial reporting.

Benefits Ignored The first weakness of deferred tax accounting is that the benefit of accepting the government's offer to delay taxes is not explicitly reported in the conventional financial statements. Note that the income statements of Burns, Inc. would

441

look the same as the third column in Exhibit 11.3 if it were to use straight-line depreciation on the tax return. (In fact, Income Tax Expense on Burns' financial statement is computed making the assumption that straight-line depreciation is used on the tax return.) Taxes paid later are less burdensome than taxes paid sooner. The conventional financial statements of most firms fail to recognize this fact of economic life.

Payments Deferred Indefinitely In reality, a going concern using accelerated depreciation on the tax return may be able to defer payment of the so-called liability indefinitely. If the firm continues to acquire depreciable assets each year (in dollar amounts no less than it acquired in the preceding year), then in every year Income Taxes Payable will *be less than or equal to* Income Tax Expense computed as generally accepted accounting principles require. In no year will there be a debit entry to the Deferred Income Tax account on the balance sheet. Tax payments will exceed tax expense (as in years 4 and 5 of the Burns example) only when the firm stops acquiring new assets while it continues to earn taxable income. It is difficult to visualize a firm that actually shrinks in size (as is required for the income taxes payable to exceed income tax expense) and at the same time remains profitable. Most shrinking firms owe no taxes because they fail to earn taxable income.

The deferred tax is probably not going to be paid, and if it is, the time when payment is finally made is not certain.[5]

Not a Legal Liability The third weakness of deferred tax accounting is that the amount shown on the balance sheet is not a legal obligation (to the federal government or to anyone else). The government levies taxes on taxable income as shown on the tax return and only as it is earned. It does not automatically levy a tax because depreciation deductions decline. The government does not suggest to Burns, Inc. in year 1 that the firm will also be profitable in year 5 and that it has in year 1 a liability for $8,000 due in year 5.

---

[5] Whether timing differences actually reverse remains a controversial question among accounting writers. A majority agree with generally accepted accounting principles on the matter of computing and recognizing deferred income taxes. They argue that the reasons offered against recognizing deferred income tax liabilities also support a conclusion that Accounts Payable are not liabilities either. After all, accounts payable are never paid off in the aggregate for a going concern; in fact, the amount of Accounts Payable usually grows over time.

The critical difference between accounts payable and income taxes, however, is that income taxes are levied on the income of a firm as a whole. Losses or deductions from one project can offset gains or income from another. The government does not tax a firm asset by asset. If a firm shrinks and becomes bankrupt, having no taxable income, then the government does not ask for income tax payments; creditors (those who are due to be paid for the Accounts Payable) will be entitled to payment (or partial payment) from the remaining assets as the firm winds down its business. Accounts Payable do have significance as liabilities even though they may increase year after year. There has been empirical work on this issue of whether there are any, many, or few firms that find taxes payable exceeding tax expense because of reversals of depreciation timing differences. The interested reader can refer to the interchange in the *Journal of Accountancy,* April 1977, pages 53–59, where we and others engage in a debate over some actual data. We think the data show that in an examination of 3,100 companies over 19 years (nearly 60,000 company-years), there are about 700 cases (slightly over 1 percent) of a firm's remaining profitable while its depreciable assets shrink in size for the year.

To avoid facing the question of whether the liability will ever be paid, Accounting Principles Board *Opinion No. 11* refers to the item as a "deferred credit" rather than as a liability.

442

Uncertain Amount Still another, but less important, weakness of deferred tax accounting is that if the firm does find at some future date that it has income taxes payable larger than income tax expense, it is unlikely that the tax rate on the income will be the same as the rate at the time the deferred tax expense was originally computed. Tax rates change periodically. Even if the amount does eventually come due, it is not an amount that is currently known with reasonable certainty.

Undiscounted Amount Finally, note that obligations for deferred income taxes are shown as undiscounted amounts, not at the present value of those amounts. All other long-term obligations reported on the balance sheet are shown at the present value of the future cash payments. The present value is computed using the historical interest rate appropriate for the firm, as borrower, on the date the obligation is first recorded. The different valuation methodology for deferred income taxes is, in our opinion, another weakness in the accounting for income taxes.

Pensions

Under a pension plan, an employer promises to make payments to employees after retirement. Private pension plan systems have grown in number and size over the last several decades so rapidly that the major asset of many individuals is the present value of their pension benefits. The basic operations of a pension plan are simple, but the concepts can be lost in a variety of details. In a pension plan:

1 The employer sets up a pension plan, specifying the eligibility of employees, the types of promises to employees, the method of funding, and the pension plan administrator.[6]
2 The employer computes a pension expense each period according to some formula. The employer debits Pension Expense for that amount and credits Pension Liability. This process is called "expensing pension obligations."
3 The employer transfers cash to the plan each period according to some formula. The employer debits Pension Liability (or, in some cases, an asset account) and credits Cash. This process is called "funding pension liabilities." The amounts expensed each period in Step 2 are usually, but *not* necessarily, the same as the amounts funded in this step.

The preceding steps comprise the employer's accounting for pensions. The employer is sometimes called the "plan sponsor." The following steps are carried out by the pension plan.

1 The plan receives cash each period from the plan sponsor. In the accounting records of the pension plan, Cash is debited and Liability for Payments to Employees is credited.

---

[6] Pension law distinguishes the *plan administrator* (who has the fiduciary responsibility for the plan) from the *funding agent* (which receives cash payments and invests them). This discussion does not distinguish between the functions of these two agents in the pension process.

443

2 Funds received are invested to generate income. The income is not part of the employer's (sponsor's) income for the period, but is reported in separate financial statements of the pension plan.

3 The plan makes payments to those entitled to receive them. The plan debits Liability for Payments to Employees and credits Cash.

Accounting Principles Board *Opinion No. 8* (1966) and FASB *Statement No. 36* (1980) govern the *employer's* accounting and reporting for the pension plan. FASB *Statement No. 35* (1980) governs the *administrator's* accounting and reporting for the pension plan.

Introduction to Pension Plans

There are almost as many different kinds of pension plans as there are employers who have them. The basic variables of a pension plan are the following:

1 Its requirement for contributions by employers and employees.
2 Vesting provisions.
3 Funding provisions.
4 The kinds of promises made by the employer.
5 Treatment of "accrued actuarial liability," if any.

Each of these variables is explained and discussed.

Contributions Under a *noncontributory* plan, the employee makes no explicit contribution of funds to the pension plan; only the employer contributes. Under a *contributory* plan both the employee and the employer contribute, but they do not necessarily contribute equal amounts. Employees retain a claim to their explicit contributions under virtually all plans. The employee's rights to the employer's contributions are determined by the *vesting* provisions. The rest of this section considers noncontributory plans or, if the plan is contributory, only the employer's contributions.

Vesting Provisions An employee's rights under a pension plan may be fully vested or partially vested. When the rights are *fully vested,* the pension benefits purchased with the employer's contributions cannot be taken away from the employee. (These benefits are partially insured by an agency of the federal government.) If the rights are not vested, the employee will lose rights to the employer's contributions if he or she leaves the company. Under *partially vested* (or "graded vesting") plans, rights vest gradually. For example, an employee in the fifth year of work might have no vested rights, but by the time he or she has been employed for 15 years, all rights will be vested. The nature of vesting provisions will influence the present value of the expected pension liabilities generated during an accounting period. If employees leave their jobs, then their rights, and therefore the employer's liabilities, are less if the benefits are only partially vested than when the benefits are fully vested.

Federal pension law (the Pension Reform Act of 1974, called the *Employee Retirement Income and Security Act* or *ERISA*) requires that an employee's benefits from contributions by the employer must become vested according to one of several formulas. These generally provide for full vesting by the time the employee has worked for the employer for 15 years.

Funding Provisions A pension plan may be *fully funded* or *partially funded.* Under a fully funded plan, the employer sets aside cash, or pays cash to an outside trustee, such as an insurance company, equal to the present value of all expected pension liabilities. Partially funded plans have cash available in an amount less than the present value of all pension obligations. ERISA mandates certain minimum funding requirements for corporate pension plans.

Employer Promises

Employers make essentially two different kinds of pension promises to employees:

1 A few employers make promises about the amounts to be contributed to the pension plan without specifying the benefits to be received by retired employees. Such plans are referred to as *defined-contribution* plans. Employer inputs, or contributions to the plan, are defined. The amounts eventually received by employees depend on the investment performance of the pension fund.
2 Most employers make promises about the amount each employee will receive during retirement without specifying the amounts the employer will contribute to the plan, referred to as *defined-benefit* plans. Outputs to employees are defined. The employer must make contributions to the plan so that those amounts plus their earnings are large enough to make the payments promised to the pensioners.

Defined-Contribution Plans In a defined-contribution plan, the employer promises to contribute an amount determined by formula to each employee's pension account. Zenith Radio Corporation, for example, promises to contribute between 6 and 12 percent of income before the contribution (the exact amount depending on some other factors) to the pension plan each year. An employee's share in the company's pension fund depends on his or her annual compensation. Another employer might agree to contribute an amount equal to 5 percent of an employee's salary to a pension fund. Subject to reasonable investment risks, the funds are managed to produce as large a series of payments as is possible during the employee's retirement. No specific promises are made to employees about the amount of the eventual pension. Inputs are defined; total outputs depend on investment performance.

The accounting for defined-contribution plans is particularly simple. If the employer contributes $75,000 to a trustee to be managed for employees' retirement benefits, the journal entry under generally accepted accounting principles is:

Pension Expense	75,000	
Cash		75,000

445

Other than periodically overseeing the activities of the plan administrator to insure that investment policies are being prudently carried out, the employer's obligation under the pension plan is largely completed once the cash is paid to the plan administrator. Neither the assets of the pension plan nor the amounts expected to be paid to retired employees appear in the employer's financial statements. The income from pension fund investments each period is not included in the net income of the employer, but in separate financial statements of the plan.

Defined-Benefit Plans Under a defined-benefit plan, the employer promises the employee a series of payments at retirement based on a formula. The typical formula takes into account the employee's length of service and some measure of average earnings. For example, the employer might promise to pay during retirement an annual pension equal to 20 percent of the average annual salary earned during the 5 highest-paid working years for all employees. The percentage might increase by one percent point for each year of service, so that an employee with 40 years of service would get a pension equal to 60 percent of his or her average salary during the 5 highest-paid working years. The defined-benefit formula is

$$\begin{array}{c}\text{Pension Benefit} \\ \text{per Year During} \\ \text{Retirement}\end{array} = (.20 + .01\, n) \times \begin{array}{c}\text{Average Salary for} \\ \text{the 5 Highest-Paid} \\ \text{Years of} \\ \text{Employment}\end{array}$$

where n is the number of years of the employee's employment. Outputs are defined by formula; the exact amount to be paid later to employees is not known currently and therefore must be estimated. This amount depends on factors such as mortality, inflation, and future wages.

The employer must set aside funds currently and in the future to fulfill its pension obligations to employees. The amount set aside depends, among other factors, on the rate of return to be earned on pension fund investments. Because defined-benefit pension plans are based on numerous estimates, such plans must be able to cope with misestimates as they become apparent.

Comparison of Types of Promises Most corporate pension plans are defined-benefit plans. ERISA makes defined-contribution plans relatively more attractive than they had been previously. The number of defined-contribution plans is increasing, but such plans remain a minority. Some employees prefer a defined-benefit plan because it reduces the employee's risk in planning for retirement. Employers tend to prefer defined-contribution plans because of the reduced uncertainty of pension expenses and contributions. The plan used in any given firm is likely to be the result of labor-management negotiations.

Later sections discuss defined-benefit plans in more detail.

Generally Accepted Accounting Principles by Employers for Defined-Benefit Plans

Current Service Benefits: Normal Costs Generally accepted accounting principles[7] require the employer with a defined-benefit plan to show as a cost of the period the present value of the pension liabilities generated by employee's service during the period. The expense for pensions earned during a given period is called the *normal cost* of that period. ERISA generally requires that the liabilities generated during the period for normal costs be funded in the current period. For example, if actuarial calculations show the expected present value of pension obligations arising from labor services for the year to be $500,000, the entry to recognize the expense is:[8]

Pension Expense (Normal Costs)	500,000	
Pension Liability		500,000
To recognize pension expense for current service and related liability.		

When the pension plan is funded, the entry, assuming that $500,000 is paid to the plan administrator, is:

Pension Liability	500,000	
Cash		500,000
To fund pension liability.		

Because federal law generally requires companies to fund pension expense for normal costs in the same year that it is recognized, most companies show no Pension Liability account for current service on their balance sheets. In these cases, the effect of the two entries shown above is often recorded in a single entry:

Pension Expense (Normal Costs)	500,000	
Cash		500,000
To recognize pension expense for current service and its immediate funding.		

Prior-Service Benefits: Actuarial Accrued Liability

When a pension plan is adopted, current employees will usually receive retroactive benefits for services rendered before the plan's adoption. Moreover, from time to time, the pension plan may be made more generous; that is, the benefits promised to

---

[7] Accounting Principles Board, *Opinion No. 8*, "Accounting for the Cost of Pension Plans," 1966.

[8] If the wages of the workers involved were debited to product cost accounts (such as Work-in-Process Inventory), then the pension costs would be product costs, not period expenses. In the rest of this chapter we assume that all pension costs are debited to Pension Expense to simplify the illustrations.

employees during retirement may be "sweetened." At the time the plan is made more generous, there will usually be retroactive benefits that are given to employees who have been working for several years. Consequently, at any given time, the total expected present value of benefits arising from employees' services may include amounts relating to services rendered during past accounting periods. The amount is called *actuarial accrued liability.*[9]

The present value of the unfunded obligation for actuarial accrued liability is not recognized as a liability in the accounting records, but its amount must be disclosed in the notes to the financial statements.

The obligation for actuarial accrued liability is disclosed in notes on the date the obligation is incurred either because of a plan's adoption or a plan's sweetening. In subsequent periods, the obligation is gradually recognized in the formal accounting records. The recognition takes the form of a journal entry debiting Pension Expense and crediting Pension Liability. (The liability is usually funded in the same period, with cash paid to the pension plan administrator.)

This process of gradually recognizing the obligations as a formal liability is called *amortizing* actuarial accrued liability. The amortizing results in debits to expense—decreasing owners' equity—and credits to liability—creating (or increasing) a balance sheet liability. Eventually a cash payment discharges the liability.

Generally accepted accounting principles and federal law permit amortization and funding of actuarial accrued liability over a time span chosen by the individual firm, subject to minimum and maximum limitations.

At a minimum, the firm must amortize and fund actuarial accrued liability over 30 or 40 years, depending on the circumstances. That is, the firm must make a series of no more than 30 or 40 annual payments that have a present value equal to the amount of the original actuarial accrued liability. The resulting amounts are the smallest annual payments that can be made for actuarial accrued liability.

The maximum rate at which a firm may amortize actuarial accrued liability under generally accepted accounting principles has been somewhat less than the maximum rate allowed under federal pension law. The issues are beyond the scope of this discussion, but in all cases the supplemental actuarial accrued liability may not be amortized over a period shorter than 10 years.

Illustration If actuarial accrued liability of $1,000,000 is to be amortized and funded over 30 years using a discount rate of 8 percent, then the annual expense and funding payment for actuarial accrued liability would be $88,827.[10] The journal entry to recognize the expense would be:

---

[9]*Actuarial accrued liability* has been used since 1981. Before that time, the terms *past service cost, prior service cost,* and *supplemental actuarial value* were used. These terms had different meanings depending on the context. See the discussion in the Glossary at "actuarial accrued liability."

[10]The present value of a $1 annuity for 30 years discounted at 8 percent per year is $11.25778; $1,000,000/11.25778 = $88,827.

| Pension Expense (Actuarial Accrued Liability) | 88,827 | |
| Pension Liability | | 88,827 |

To recognize pension expense for actuarial accrued liability of $1,000,000 being amortized and funded over 30 years.

The above entry recognizes the pension expense. Its effect is to remove the obligation for pension payments from the footnotes, where it is not recognized as a liability, and to transfer the obligation to the balance sheet where it is shown as an actual long-term liability. When the revenue and expense accounts for the period are closed, the Pension Expense account is closed to income, reducing it, and then to the Retained Earnings account, reducing it. The overall balance sheet effect of this entry is to recognize an increase in a liability and a decrease in owners' equity.

Most corporate pension plans provide for funding of pension liabilities as they are recognized. Thus the corporation making the journal entry just above is likely to make a funding payment of cash of $88,827 to a pension fund and to make the following journal entry:

| Pension Liability | 88,827 | |
| Cash | | 88,827 |

To fund liability.

Note that the entries recognizing the liability and then funding it could be combined as follows:

| Pension Expense (Actuarial Accrued Liability) | 88,827 | |
| Cash | | 88,827 |

To recognize and fund pension expense for actuarial accrued liability of $1,000,000 being amortized and funded over 30 years.

From the point of view of accrual accounting, the funding via cash payment is not required. Accounting merely requires that the obligation for both normal costs and actuarial accrued liability be recognized as expense and recognized as liabilities on a systematic basis. As the obligation is funded, the liability is reduced. ERISA, however, requires periodic funding of these liabilities.

Funds Statement Effects When pension expense is recorded, income decreases and a long-term liability for pensions increases. When pension liabilities are funded, cash and long-term liabilities are both reduced. Thus, when pension funding is the same amount each period as pension expense, no pension-related adjustments to net income are required in deriving funds provided by continuing operations. If pension

449

expense exceeds pension funding, an addback of the excess is required in deriving funds provided by continuing operations. If pension expense is less than pension funding, a subtraction of the excess is required in deriving funds provided by continuing operations. (Some accountants would show the excess as a reduction in long-term liabilities in the section below funds provided by operations.)

Shortcomings in Generally Accepted Accounting Principles for Actuarial Accrued Liability in Corporate Pension Plans

Recall that a liability results from a past transaction that creates an obligation to make a payment at a future time. The obligation to employees for benefits based on their prior work meets these criteria. The timing of payments can be reasonably estimated because of demographic data on retirement ages and actuarial data on length of life. The amounts of payments can also be estimated. Actuaries can estimate mortality (both before and after retirement) as well as wage rates. The obligation is usually present because of employment contracts and federal law. Thus when a pension plan is brought into existence with retroactive benefits promised for past service or when a plan is sweetened with the sweetenings applying retroactively for prior service, then we think that a liability has been created. Generally accepted accounting principles recognize the amount, but allow it to be merely disclosed in the footnotes as an obligation until amortized, rather than shown in the balance sheet as a liability. That treatment is based on a premise that benefits received for the payments are to be received in the future as employees work.

Summary of Corporate Pension Accounting by Employer

Total corporate pension expense for a period under a defined-benefit plan is made up of the sum of the charge for current-service benefits earned during the period (normal cost) plus the charge for the gradual recognition of accrued actuarial value.

Generally accepted accounting principles require certain minimum disclosures for pension plans by the employer. The notes to the balance sheet must disclose:

1 The amount of actuarial accrued liability, if there is any, and the time over which it is being funded.
2 The amount of vested but unfunded benefits, almost always an amount less than (1).
3 Actuarial methods used and the impact of vesting provisions on the expected present value of liabilities.

The required disclosure is illustrated in Note 3 of Exhibit A.4 in Appendix A at the back of the book for the General Products Company.

Generally Accepted Accounting Principles by the *Plan* for Defined-Benefit Pensions

The pension plan receives the cash paid by the employer/sponsor and invests it until paid to retired employees. The plan keeps its own accounting records and makes disclosures according to rules in FASB *Statement No. 35*. Note 3 of Exhibit A.4 in Appendix A illustrates the required disclosures for General Products Company.

Plan Assets Accounted for at Market Value

The plan reports its assets, usually investments of various sorts, at fair market value, a laudable departure from the accounting required for most investments described in Chapters 7 and 13. The fluctuations in market value each year are part of the earnings or losses of the pension plan.

Problem 1 for Self-Study

The Chang Company purchased a truck from Guttman's Auto Agency. The truck had a list price of $25,000, but discounts of 10 to 15 percent from list price are common in purchases of this sort. Chang Company paid for the truck by giving a noninterest-bearing note due 2 years from the date of purchase. The note had a face value of $28,730. The rate of interest that Chang Company paid to borrow on secured 2-year loans ranged from 10 to 15 percent during the period when the purchase occurred.

a Record the acquisition of the truck on Chang Company's books assuming that the fair market value of the truck was computed using a 10-percent discount from list price.

b What imputed interest rate will be used throughout the loan for computing interest expense if the acquisition is recorded as in **a**?

c Record the acquisition of the truck on Chang Company's books, assuming that the estimated interest rate Chang Company must pay to borrow is deemed reliable and is 12 percent per year.

d Record the acquisition of the truck on Chang Company's books, assuming that the interest rate Chang Company must pay to borrow is 1 percent per month.

e Prepare journal entries to record the loan and to record interest over 2 years, assuming that the truck is recorded at $23,744 and the interest rate implicit in the loan is 10 percent per year.

f Throughout, this book has stressed that over long-enough time periods, total expense is equal to cash outflow. In what sense is the total expense for this transaction the same, independent of the interest rate (and, therefore, the interest expense)?

Suggested Solution

a	Truck	22,500	
	Note Payable		22,500

.90 × $25,000 = $22,500.

451

b $28,730/$22,500 = 1.27689. $(1 + r)^2 = 1.27689$ implies that $r = \sqrt{1.27689} - 1 = .13$ or 13 percent per year. That is, $22,500 grows to $28,730 in 2 years when the interest rate is 13 percent per period.

c

Truck	22,903	
Note Payable		22,903

$(1.12)^{-2} = .79719; .79719 \times \$28,730 = \$22,903.$

d $(1.01)^{-24} = .78757.$ (See Table 2, 24-column row, 1-percent column.) $.78757 \times \$28,730 = \$22,627.$

Truck	22,627	
Note Payable		22,627

e

Truck	23,744	
Note Payable		23,744
Year 1 Interest Expense $(= .10 \times \$23,744)$	2,374	
Note Payable		2,374
Year 2 Interest Expense $[= .10 \times (\$23,744 + \$2,374)]$	2,612	
Note Payable		2,612
Balance in Note Payable Account at End of Year 2		$28,730

f Total expense equals interest expense on note *and* depreciation on truck. Interest expense is $28,730 less the amount at which the truck is recorded. Depreciation expense is equal to the amount at which the truck is recorded less estimated salvage value. Thus, over the life of the truck, or 2 years, whichever is longer, the total expense equals $28,730 less salvage value of the truck.

Problem 2 for Self-Study

Landlord Company, as lessor, entered into a long-term lease agreement with Tenant Company, as lessee. The present value of the lease payments exceeded the lessor's cost of manufacturing the asset. Both companies accounted for the lease as an operating lease, whereas both companies should have accounted for it as a capital lease. What effect—understated, overstated, or none—does this error have on each of the following items in the financial statements of each of the companies for the first year of the lease?

a Current assets.
b Liabilities.
c Revenue.
d Expense.
e Net income.
f Retained earnings.

452

Suggested Solution

		Tenant Company	Landlord Company
a	Current Assets	None	Understated*
b	Liabilities	Understated	None
c	Revenue	None	Understated**
d	Expense	Understated	Understated**
e	Net Income	Overstated	Understated**
f	Retained Earnings	Overstated	Understated**

* Lease receivables are part current and part noncurrent. Asset is all noncurrent.

** In a capital lease, the lessor treats the signing of the lease as an installment sale. The lessor has sales revenue, cost of goods sold, and a new asset, the long-term receivable.

Problem 3 for Self-Study

The accounting records of Wilson Company disclose the following data on book and taxable income for the years 1980 through 1983.

	1980	1981	1982	1983
(1) Pretax Book Income	$90,000	$90,000	$90,000	$90,000
(2) Timing Differences (Reducing) or Increasing Book Income to Taxable Income	($20,000)	($10,000)	$15,000	$ 5,000
(3) Permanent Differences Increasing (or Decreasing) Taxable Income	($ 8,000)	$ 6,000	($ 4,000)	$ 2,000

The income tax rate is 40 percent of taxable income.

a Compute taxable income on which income taxes are payable.

b Compute the book amount on which income tax expense is based for each year.

c Give the journal entries to record income tax expense, income taxes payable and deferred income taxes for each year.

d Compute aftertax net income for each year.

e What is the balance in the Deferred Income Taxes account on the balance sheet at the end of 1983?

Suggested Solution

a Taxable income on the tax return each year is Line (1) plus or minus Line (2) plus or minus Line (3). 1980—$62,000; 1981—$86,000; 1982—$101,000; 1983—$97,000.

b Income tax expense for each year is based on Line (1) plus or minus Line (3). 1980—$82,000; 1981—$96,000; 1982—$86,000; 1983—$92,000.

c See Exhibit 11.5.

Exhibit 11.5
Wilson Company
(Suggested Solution to Problem 3 for Self-Study)

Journal Entries

	1980	1981	1982	1983
Income Tax Expense*	32,800	38,400	34,400	36,800
Deferred Income Taxes	—	—	6,000	2,000
Income Taxes Payable**	24,800	34,400	40,400	38,800
Deferred Income Taxes	8,000	4,000	—	—

* .40 of amounts in answer to part **b**.
** .40 of amounts in answer to part **a**.

Income Statement

	1980	1981	1982	1983
Pretax Book Income	$90,000	$90,000	$90,000	$90,000
Income Tax Expense	(32,800)	(38,400)	(34,400)	(36,800)
Net Income	$57,200	$51,600	$55,600	$53,200

454

d See Exhibit 11.5.

e $4,000 credit = $8,000 credit + $4,000 credit − $6,000 debit − $2,000 debit.

Problem 4 for Self-Study

The Dominiak Company reports the following information about its financial statements and tax return for a year:

Depreciation Expense from Financial Statements.	$270,000
Financial Statement Pretax Income.	160,000
Income Tax Expense from Financial Statements	36,000
Income Taxes Payable from Tax Returns	24,000

Taxable income is taxed at a rate of 40 percent. Permanent differences result from interest on municipal bonds that is revenue in the financial statements but is exempt from income taxes. Timing differences result from the use of accelerated depreciation for tax returns and straight-line depreciation for financial reporting.

Reconstruct the financial statements and the tax return for the year, identifying the components of timing differences and permanent differences.

Suggested Solution

See Exhibit 11.6.

Problem 5 for Self-Study

Edwards Company adopted a pension plan at the beginning of 1982. It is a noncontributory, defined-benefit plan and provides immediate, full vesting for all employees. The normal pension costs for 1982 and 1983 are $40,000 and $45,000, respectively. These amounts are expensed and funded in full each year.

The plan grants retroactive benefits to all employees for their years of work preceding 1982. The present value of the actuarial accrued liability created on adoption of the pension plan was $324,000. This amount is to be recognized as an expense and a liability over 20 years. The interest rate used in computing the actuarial accrued liability is 8 percent per year. Pension expenses are recognized and funded on the last day of each year. The amounts paid to the pension plan are equal to the amounts expensed. Assume that the pension fund actually earns 9 percent during 1983.

a Give journal entries made by Edwards Company for 1982 and 1983.

b What is the dollar value of the investments in the pension fund at the end of 1983 before the 1983 contribution is recorded?

c Assuming that the pension fund was expected to earn only 8 percent in each year, what is the dollar amount of actual earnings in excess of the projected earnings for the year 1983?

455

Exhibit 11.6
Illustration of Timing Differences and Permanent Differences
Dominiak Company
(*Suggested Solution to Problem 4 for Self-Study*)

	Financial Statements	Type of Difference	Income Tax Return
Operating Income Except Depreciation	$360,000 (6)	—	$360,000 (4)
Depreciation	(270,000) (g)	Timing	(300,000) (3)
Municipal Bond Interest	70,000 (5)	Permanent	—
Taxable Income	—		$ 60,000 (2)
Pretax Income	$160,000 (g)		
Income Taxes Payable at 40 Percent			$ 24,000 (g)
Income Tax Expense at 40 Percent of $90,000 = $160,000 − $70,000, Which Is Book Income Excluding Permanent Differences.	(36,000) (g)		
Net Income.	$124,000 (1)		

Order and derivation of computations:

(g) Given.

(1) $124,000 = $160,000 − $36,000.

(2) $60,000 = $24,000/.40.

(3) Timing difference for depreciation is ($36,000 − $24,000)/.40 = $30,000. Because income taxes payable are less than income tax expense, we know that depreciation deducted on tax return exceeds depreciation expense on financial statements. Thus, the depreciation deduction on the tax return is $300,000 = $270,000 + $30,000.

(4) $360,000 = $300,000 + $60,000.

(5) Taxable income on financial statements is $90,000 = $36,000/.40. Total financial statement income before taxes, including permanent differences, is $160,000. Hence permanent differences are $160,000 − $90,000 = $70,000.

(6) $160,000 + $270,000 − $70,000 = $360,000. See also (4), for check.

Suggested Solution

a The present value of $1 paid at the end of each of the next twenty years is $9.81815 when the discount rate is 8 percent per year; see Table 4, 20-payment row, 8-percent column. The annual amount to amortize $324,000 over 20 years at 8 percent is $33,000 (= $324,000/9.81815). Thus, the journal entries are:

	1982		1983	
Pension Expense (Normal Costs)	40,000		45,000	
Pension Expense (Actuarial Accrued Liability)	33,000		33,000	
Pension Liability.		73,000		78,000
To recognize expense.				
Pension Liability	73,000		78,000	
Cash		73,000		78,000
To fund liability with payments to pension plan.				

b $79,570 = 1.09 \times $73,000.

c $730 = $73,000 \times (1.09 - 1.08).

Questions and Problems

1 Review the meaning of the following concepts or terms discussed in this chapter.

   a Interest-bearing note.
   b Noninterest-bearing note.
   c Implicit interest.
   d Imputed interest rate.
   e Capital lease.
   f Operating lease.
   g Deferred income tax expense and liability.
   h Timing difference.
   i Permanent difference.
   j Pension plan.
   k Defined-benefit plan.
   l Defined-contribution plan.
   m Contributory versus noncontributory plan.
   n Fully funded versus partially funded plan.
   o Fully vested versus partially vested benefits.
   p Normal costs.
   q Actuarial accrued liability.

2 In what sense is the historical-cost accounting for noncurrent liabilities subsequent to the date of issuance based on historical costs?

3 Brealey Company negotiated a 5-year loan for $1 million with its bank. The terms of the loan require that the interest rate can be changed as the bank chooses, but that the company can repay the loan at any time. Interest is to be paid quarterly. How should Brealey Company classify this note on its balance sheet?

4 Why is the question, "Who bears the risks and enjoys the potential rewards of an asset?" important for lease accounting?

5 In what ways is the economic substance of a capital lease similar to, and different from, that of an installment purchase?

6 Distinguish between the lessee's accounting for a capital lease and for an installment purchase.

7 In what sense is the total expense from a lease independent of the method of accounting for it by the lessee?

8 "Deferred income taxes might be viewed as an interest-free loan from the government." Do you agree? Why or why not?

9 How should the deferred income tax liability be treated by an analyst who wishes to study the debt-equity ratio of a business?

10 Under what circumstances will the Deferred Income Taxes account be reduced to a zero balance?

11 You have been called to testify before a Congressional committee on income taxation. One committee member states: "My staff has added up the amounts shown for Deferred Income Taxes on the balance sheets of the largest 500 U.S. Corporations. If we collected these amounts immediately, we could reduce the national deficit by billions of dollars. After all, I have to pay my taxes as they become due each year. Why shouldn't corporations have to do the same?" How would you respond?

12 What are the economic and accounting differences between a defined-benefit pension plan and a defined-contribution plan?

13 Why does the amendment ("sweetening") of a defined-benefit plan increase accrued actuarial value, whereas a change with the same cost in a defined-contribution plan does not increase accrued actuarial value?

14 When a company adopts a defined-benefit pension plan giving credit to current employees for past service, accrued actuarial value, perhaps in large amounts, arises. This amount is merely disclosed in notes and is only gradually recognized in the balance sheet. This chapter criticizes the nonrecognition of accrued actuarial value as a liability.

Assume, contrary to generally accepted accounting principles, that the amount was immediately credited to liability when it came into existence. What accounts might be debited? Give justifications that might be used to justify debiting an asset account, an expense account, or a direct debit to Retained Earnings.

15 For each of the following items indicate:

(1) Does the item meet all of the criteria of the accountant's usual definition of a liability?
(2) Is the item shown as a liability?
(3) If the item is recognized as a liability, how is the amount of the liability determined?

a Fifteen-year cancelable lease on an office building.
b Twenty-year noncancelable lease on a factory building.
c Deferred income taxes.
d Anticipated future cost of restoring strip mining sites after mining operations are completed.
e Obligation to pay pensions under defined-benefit formula for labor services during current year.
f Obligation to pay pensions under defined-benefit formula for labor services provided before the plan had been adopted.

16 Refer to the Simplified Statement of Changes in Financial Position for a Period in Exhibit 5.19. Nine of the lines in the statement are numbered. Line (2) should be expanded to say "Additions for Expenses, Losses, and Other Charges Against Income Not Using Funds from Operations," and line (3) should be expanded to say "Subtractions for Revenues, Gains, and Other Credits to Income Not Producing Funds from Operations." Ignore the unnumbered lines in responding to the questions below.

Assume that the accounting cycle is complete for the period and that all of the financial statements have been prepared. Then it is discovered that a transaction has been overlooked. That transaction is recorded in the accounts and all of the financial statements are corrected. Define *funds* as *working capital*. For each of the following transactions, indicate

458

which of the numbered lines of the funds statement is affected and by how much. Ignore income tax effects except where taxes are explicitly mentioned.

For the following questions, assume that an asset with an economic life of 10 years costing $100,000 is leased for $19,925 per year, paid at the end of each year.

a The lessor, using the operating lease method, records depreciation for the year.

b The lessor, using the operating lease method, records receipt of a cash payment for the year.

c The lessee, using the operating lease method, records payment of cash for the year.

d The lessor, using the capital lease method, records receipt of cash at the end of the first year and uses an interest rate of 15 percent per year. $15,000 is interest and $4,925 is receipt of principal.

e The lessee, using the capital lease method, records payment of cash for the first year and uses an interest rate of 15 percent per year. $15,000 is interest and $4,925 is payment of principal.

17 Refer to the instructions in the preceding question. Define *funds* as *working capital*. For each of the following transactions, indicate which of the numbered lines of the funds statement is affected and by how much. Assume an income tax rate of 40 percent of taxable income.

a Pretax financial statement income is $200,000. Depreciation claimed on the tax return exceeds depreciation expense on the financial statements by $50,000. An entry is made to record income tax expense.

b Pretax financial statement income is $300,000 and the income tax rate is 40 percent of taxable income. Warranty deductions allowed on the tax return are less than warranty expense on the financial statements by $40,000. An entry is made to record income tax expense.

c Nontaxable municipal bond interest of $10,000 is received. No previous entry had been made for this interest. All effects of this transaction, including income tax effects, if any, are recorded.

18 Refer to the instructions in the two preceding questions. Define *funds* as *working capital*. For each of the following transactions, indicate which of the numbered lines of the funds statement is affected and by how much. Ignore income tax effects except where taxes are explicitly mentioned.

Make clear any assumptions you think are necessary to answer the questions clearly.

a A pension plan is adopted; accrued actuarial liability of $100,000 arises.

b Actuarial accrued liability is expensed and credited to liability in the amount of $50,000.

c Actuarial accrued liability is funded in the amount of $80,000.

d Normal costs of $40,000 are recognized.

e Actuarial accrued liability of $60,000 is recognized as expense and $40,000 of that amount is funded.

19 Garstka Company acquires a computer from Berney's Computer Store. The cash price (fair market value) of the computer is $50,568. Garstka Company gives a 3-year, interest-bearing note with maturity value of $60,000. The note requires annual interest payments of 9 percent of face value, $5,400 per year. The interest rate implicit in the note is 16 percent per year.

a Prepare an amortization schedule for the note.

b Prepare journal entries for Garstka Company over the life of the note.

459

20 (Adapted from CPA Examination.) The Jackson Company manufactured a piece of equipment at a cost of $7 million, which is held for resale from January 1 to June 30 at a price of $8 million. On July 1, Jackson leased the equipment to the Crystal Company. The lease is appropriately recorded as an operating lease for accounting purposes. The lease is for a 3-year period. Equal monthly payments under the lease are $115,000 and are due on the first of the month. The first payment was made on July 1. The equipment is being depreciated on a straight-line basis over an 8-year period with no residual value expected.

a What expense should Crystal record as a result of the above facts for the current year ended December 31? Show supporting computations in good form.

b What income or loss before income taxes should Jackson record as a result of the above facts for the year ended December 31? Show supporting computations in good form.

21 Maher Company has calculated that the annual payment in arrears to amortize a $1 million loan over 25 years at 15-percent interest is $154,700.

a What is rent expense for the first year of an operating lease when the rent payment is $154,700.

b What is lease expense for the first year of a 25-year capital lease for use of an asset costing $1 million requiring annual payments in arrears of $154,700? Use straight-line amortization of leasehold.

c How much larger in percentage terms is the lessee's expense in the first year under the capital lease than under the operating lease?

22 Assume that Rich's Department Stores is about to sign four separate leases for stores in four separate shopping centers. Each of the stores would cost $20 million if purchased outright and has an economic life of 20 years. Assume that the company currently must pay interest at the rate of 15 percent per year on long-term borrowing when sound collateral backs the loan. The lease payments are to be made at the end of each year in all four cases.

Based on the information given here, decide whether each of the four leases requires accounting as operating leases or as capital leases. Give your reasoning.

	Lease Term	Annual Lease Payment
a Cumberland Mall	16 Years	$2,500,000
b Normandale Center	16 Years	2,600,000
c Eastbrook Haven	12 Years	3,300,000
d Peachtree Parkview	12 Years	3,400,000

23 The Carom Company plans to acquire, as of January 1, 1982, a computerized cash register system that costs $100,000 and that has a 5-year life and no salvage value. The company is considering two plans for acquiring the system.

(1) Outright purchase. To finance the purchase, $100,000 of par-value 10-percent semiannual coupon bonds will be issued January 1, 1982, at par.

(2) Lease. The lease requires five annual payments to be made on December 31, 1982, 1983, 1984, 1985, and 1986. The lease payments are such that they have a present value of $100,000 on January 1, 1982, when discounted at 10 percent per year.

460

Straight-line amortization methods will be used for all depreciation and amortization computations.

a Verify that the amount of the required lease payment is $26,380 by constructing an amortization schedule for the five payments. Note that there will be a $2 rounding error in the fifth year. Nevertheless, you may treat each payment as being $26,380 in the rest of the problem.

b What balance sheet amounts will be affected if plan **(1)** is selected? If plan **(2)** is selected, the lease is cancelable, and the operating lease treatment is used? If plan **(2)** is selected, the lease is noncancelable, and the capital lease treatment is used?

c What will be the total depreciation and interest expenses for the 5 years under plan **(1)**?

d What will be the total expenses for the 5 years under plan **(2)** if the lease is accounted for as an operating lease? As a capital lease?

e Why are the answers in part **d** the same? Why are the answers in part **c** different from those in part **d**?

f What will be the total expenses for the first year, 1982, under plan **(1)**? Under plan **(2)** accounted for as an operating lease? Under plan **(2)** accounted for as a capital lease?

g Repeat part **f** for the fifth year, 1986.

24 Pan American World Air Lines (Pan Am) leased three Boeing 707 aircraft in 1963 from Sally Leasing Company (Sally). The aircraft had a purchase price of $6.64 million each. The leases covered 13-year terms, were noncancelable, contained no purchase options, and required monthly payments of $71,115. The rental cost per month of $71,115 was several hundred dollars less than Pan Am would have had to pay for conventional financing at the then-prevalent interest rate.

a What, if anything, did Pan Am give up in return for its savings of several hundred dollars per month for 13 years? What, if anything, did Sally Leasing Company get for giving up several hundred dollars per month for 13 years?

b Who bore the risks and rewards of ownership in these leases?

c Verify that the interest rate implicit in the lease contract is about three-fourths of 1 percent per month.

d Assume that FASB *Statement No. 13* had been in effect when these leases were signed. How would the leases be accounted for?

25 Joyce Company reported the following amounts for book and tax purposes for its first 3 years of operations:

	1981	1982	1983
Pretax Book Income	$300,000	$280,000	$440,000
Taxable Income	240,000	320,000	340,000

The differences between book and taxable income are attributable to the use of different depreciation methods. The income tax rate was 40 percent during all years.

a Give the journal entry to record income tax expense for each year.

b Assume, for this part, that $10,000 of interest on state and municipal bonds was included in the pretax book income amounts shown above for each year but properly excluded from taxable income. Give the journal entry to record income tax expense for each year.

26 Refer to the data in Exhibit 4.3 on page 139 showing income over a 5-year period under various methods of revenue and income recognition. Use the methods of accounting indicated below for financial statements and for tax returns. Assume an income tax rate of 40 percent. Compute income tax expense, income taxes payable, and deferred income taxes for each period. Put this information into journal-entry form.

a Use the percentage-of-completion method on the financial statements and the completed contract method on the tax return.

b Use the cost-recovery-first method on the financial statements and the installment method on the tax return.

27 Equilibrium Company adopted a program of purchasing a new machine each year. It uses the sum-of-the-years'-digits method of depreciation on its income tax return and straight-line depreciation on its financial statements. Each machine costs $15,000 installed and has a depreciable life of 5 years.

a Calculate depreciation for each of the first 7 years in accordance with the sum-of-the-years'-digits method of depreciation.

b Calculate depreciation for each year using straight-line method of depreciation.

c Calculate the annual difference in depreciation charges using the results from parts **a** and **b**.

d Calculate the annual increase or decrease in the Deferred Income Taxes account for the balance sheet. Assume a 40-percent tax rate and straight-line depreciation in financial reports.

e Calculate year-end balances for the Deferred Income Taxes account on the balance sheet.

f If Equilibrium Company continues to follow its policy of buying a new machine every year, what will happen to the balance in the Deferred Income Taxes account on the balance sheet?

28 The Strawcab Company owns one depreciable asset. The asset originally had a depreciable life of 6 years. It is 4 years old at the end of the current year. It had an estimated salvage value of $4,000 when new. This estimate has not changed. The company uses sum-of-the-years'-digits depreciation on its tax return and straight-line depreciation on its financial statements. The company's income tax rate is 40 percent of pretax taxable income. The footnotes to the financial statements indicate that the only cause of timing differences between the financial statements and tax returns is depreciation and that the income tax expense differs from income taxes payable by $1,200.

a Which is larger this year, income taxes payable or income tax expense, and by how much?

b What is the acquisition cost of the asset?

c Assume the same general facts as above except the asset had an original depreciable life of 8 years, is 2 years old at the end of the current year, and has an estimated salvage value of $2,000. The difference between income tax expense and income taxes payable this year was reported to be $1,600. Repeat parts **a** and **b**.

29 The numbers in this problem are hypothetical, but the size relation between them is adapted from recent financial statements of Sears, Roebuck & Co. The purpose of this problem is to demonstrate the effects of deferred income tax accounting in a retailing operation.

Sears reports income on a charge account sale in the year when the sale is made, but

462

reports the income on the tax return in the year when the cash is collected from the customer. Every Christmas season, Sears makes hundreds of millions of dollars of sales that are not collected until the next tax year. Each year, the Christmas sales exceed the previous year's Christmas sales. The tax on these sales is not paid until the next year, but Sears must report the tax on the current year's income statement. In recent years, the amount of the deferred tax expense for these charge sales alone has been larger than 10 percent of Sears' entire aftertax net income. The balance sheet amount of Sears' deferred tax liability for charge sales alone is over $1 billion and has never declined. That $1 billion would be part of its Retained Earnings account if Sears were not required to report deferred income taxes on those charge sales. Retained Earnings would be about 20 percent larger.

Sears will have to pay its deferred taxes for charge sales only when its dollar sales shrink in amount while it remains profitable. This is unlikely ever to happen. When W. T. Grant, another large retailer, went bankrupt in the mid-1970s, it had a large credit balance in its deferred tax account that disappeared in one year. But not a single penny was paid to the government for deferred taxes.

Assume (for parts **a–d**) that Rosenwald Stores makes all of its sales on account, that the physical amount sold remains constant each year, and that prices are stable from year to year. Of those sales, five-sixths are collected in the year of sale and one-sixth is collected in the next. Exhibit 11.7 shows the financial statements of Rosenwald Stores in each year.

Exhibit 11.7
Rosenwald Stores
(*Problem 29*)

**INCOME STATEMENT EACH YEAR
(ALSO TAX RETURN PRIOR TO 1982)**

Sales	$120,000
Cost of Goods Sold	$ 72,000
All Other Expenses Except Income Taxes	36,000
Total	$108,000
Pretax Income	$ 12,000
Income Tax Expense at 40 Percent	4,800
Net Income	$ 7,200

INCOME TAX RETURNS	1982	Subsequent Years
Collections on Sales Made in Current Year	$100,000	$100,000
Collections on Sales Made in Previous Year	—	20,000
Total Revenue	$100,000	$120,000
Costs of Goods Sold and Collected for in Current Year	$ 60,000	$ 60,000
Cost of Goods Sold in Previous Year and Collected for This Year	—	12,000
All Other Expenses Except Income Taxes	36,000	36,000
Total Deductions	$ 96,000	$108,000
Taxable Income	$ 4,000	$ 12,000
Income Taxes Payable at 40 Percent	$ 1,600	$ 4,800

Rosenwald Stores has been using the sales basis of revenue recognition on its tax returns, so that there have been no timing differences. In 1982, Rosenwald Stores, following the rule of least and latest, switches to the installment method of revenue recognition on its income tax returns. Its tax returns for 1982 differ from tax returns for all subsequent years. These tax returns are also shown in Exhibit 11.7. The income tax rate is 40 percent.

a Prepare a journal entry that recognizes income tax expense and income taxes payable for each of the years before 1982.

b Prepare a journal entry that recognizes income tax expense and income taxes payable for 1982.

c Prepare a journal entry that recognizes income tax expense and income taxes payable for each year after 1982.

d What will happen in subsequent years to the Deferred Income Taxes balance sheet account created in 1982?

e Now, assume that because of expanding physical volume of sales and general inflation, all pretax figures on the financial statements grow at the rate of 10 percent per year. What will happen to the balance in the Deferred Income Taxes account on the balance sheet?

f Return to the steady-state, stable-price environment of parts **a–d.** Now assume that in a later year, say 1990, Rosenwald Stores declares bankruptcy. (This is not representative of Sears, Roebuck & Co., but other retailers have gone bankrupt.) In 1990, collections of all sales made in 1989 are completed, but sales for 1990 fall to $40,000, all of which are collected in 1990. Cost of Goods Sold is $24,000 and All Other Expenses Except Taxes fall to $30,000. Prepare a schedule computing income taxes payable and an income statement for 1990.

g What conclusions can you draw from this exercise about deferred income tax accounting? If you can find them, obtain financial statements for a recent year for Sears, Roebuck & Co. What is the current balance in the Deferred Tax account for installment sales? What fraction of shareholders' equity does this represent? By what percentage would Sears' income increase if deferred tax expense from installment sales were not deducted in computing net income? Discuss.

30 The Hicks Company is adopting a pension plan. Two plans are being considered. Both of the proposed pension plans are defined-benefit plans. The benefits actually paid to a given retired ex-employee who actually qualifies for benefits are to be the same for whichever of the two proposed plans is adopted.

a Who, the employee or The Hicks Company, is more likely to bear the risks and rewards of fluctuating market returns on funds invested to pay the pensions?

In each of the parts below, explain which of the two plans is likely to be less costly from the standpoint of The Hicks Company and why. If the costs are likely to be the same in both of the plans, then explain why.

b Contributory plan or noncontributory plan.

c Plan with benefits fully vested in 5 years or plan with benefits fully vested in 10 years.

d Fully funded plan or partially funded plan.

e Plan that amortizes actuarial accrued liability over 20 years or plan that amortizes actuarial accrued liability over 30 years. Assume that funding is unaffected by this choice.

31 On January 1, 1982, Kayco Company instituted a pension plan. The actuarial accrued liability—the present value of the past service benefits awarded to current employees—is $1,200,000. The present value of the benefits earned by employees during both 1982 and

464

1983 is $700,000 at the end of each of those years. Kayco Company designates the Retirement Insurance Company as the trustee of the pension plan and deposits all funding payments with the insurance company at the end of each year. Interest on unfunded liabilities is accrued at a rate of 8 percent per year. Kayco Company plans to fund an amount each year equal to the pension expense recognized for the year.

Show the journal entries that Kayco Company would make on December 31, 1982 and 1983, for its pension plan and related expenses under the following two assumptions:

a Actuarial accrued liability is amortized over 10 years.

b Actuarial accrued liability is amortized over 30 years.

32 (This problem should not be attempted until the previous one has been worked.) Refer to the actuarial accrued liability data for Kayco Company presented in the preceding problem. Assume that the amount is amortized over 10 years, that all expenses are funded as recognized, and that interest on the unfunded amount of actuarial accrued liability is charged at the rate of 8 percent per year.

a What amount of unfunded obligation for accrued actuarial value would be disclosed in the footnotes to Kayco Company's financial statements issued for December 31, 1982?

b What amount of unfunded obligation for accrued actuarial value would be disclosed in the footnotes to Kayco Company's financial statements issued for December 31, 1983?

33 Refer to Note 5 of the financial statements of General Products Company shown in Appendix A at the back of the book.

a What is the combined average federal, state, and local income tax rate that General Products Company appeared to pay in 1982? That is, if General Products Company were to earn another $1, how much of that $1 would be paid in income taxes to federal, state, and local governments?

In the remainder of this problem, assume that the marginal income tax rate is 40 percent of pretax income.

b By how much did depreciation claimed on the tax return exceed depreciation expense reported in the financial statements for the year 1982?

c Warranty costs are not deductible on the tax return until actual repairs or replacements are made. Estimated warranty expenses are shown in the financial statements whenever they can be computed with a reasonable degree of precision. Did warranty expense on the financial statements exceed deductions for warranty costs on the tax return or vice versa in 1982? How can you tell? By how much?

Chapter 12 *Owners' Equity*

The economic resources of a firm come, essentially, from two major sources. Nonowners provide funds to a firm; the sources of these funds are shown on the balance sheet as *liabilities,* discussed in Chapters 10 and 11. Owners provide funds; the sources of these funds are shown on the balance sheet as *owners' equity.* This chapter discusses owners' equity.

The accounting equation states that:

$$\text{Assets} = \text{Liabilities} + \text{Owners' Equity}$$

or

$$\text{Assets} - \text{Liabilities} = \text{Owners' Equity}.$$

Many readers of financial statements think of owners' equity as being calculated from the excess of assets over liabilities. Double-entry record keeping provides, however, a continuous, independent calculation of owners' equity.

This chapter discusses corporate owners' equity. The corporation is a widely used form of business organization in the United States for at least three reasons:

1 The corporate form provides the owner, or shareholder, with limited liability. That is, should the corporation become insolvent, creditors' claims are limited to the assets of the corporate entity. The assets of the individual owners are not subject to the claims of the corporation's creditors. On the other hand, creditors of partnerships and sole proprietorships have a claim on both the owners' personal and business assets in settlement of such firms' debts.

466

2 The corporate form facilitates the raising of large amounts of funds through the issue of shares by the corporation. The general public can acquire the shares in varying amounts. Individual investments can range from a few dollars to hundreds of millions of dollars.

3 The corporate form makes transfer of ownership interests relatively easy, because individual shares can be sold by current owners to others without interfering with the ongoing operations of the business. The continuity of the management and of operations is not affected by these ongoing changes in ownership.

This chapter discusses three separate kinds of problems in accounting for owners' equity in corporations: the accounting for capital contributed by owners, the accounting for income earned by the firm which may be retained or distributed to owners, and other changes in owners' equity accounts.

Capital Contributions

The corporation is a legal entity separate from its owners. Capital contributions are made by individuals or other entities under a contract between themselves and the corporation.[1] Because those who contribute funds are usually issued certificates for shares of stock, they are known as "stockholders" or "shareholders." The rights and obligations of a shareholder are governed by:

1 The corporation laws of the state in which incorporation takes place.

2 The articles of incorporation or *charter*. This is a contract between the firm and the state in which the business is incorporated. The enterprise is granted the privilege of operating as a corporation for certain stated purposes and of obtaining its capital through the issue of shares of stock.

3 The bylaws of the corporation. Bylaws are adopted by the board of directors and act as the rules and regulations under which the internal affairs of the corporation are conducted.

4 The stock contract. Each type of capital stock has its own provisions as to such matters as voting, sharing in earnings, distribution of earnings, and sharing in assets in case of dissolution.

Some "closely held" corporations have a small number of shareholders and operate much the same as a partnership. The few people involved agree to the amount of capital to be contributed, elect each other to be members of the board of directors and officials of the firm, and agree on policies regarding dividends and salaries. They may restrict the transfer of shares to outsiders, and may even become liable for debts of the corporation by endorsing its notes and bonds.

In the case of large, widely owned corporations, the effect of the corporation's being a separate legal entity is more pronounced. Officials and directors may own

---

[1] In accounting for owners' equity, the term *contribution* almost never means a gift; capital given to the corporation as a gift is specifically called *donated capital.*

little or no stock in the corporation. Actual control is likely to be in the hands of a few individuals or a group who own or control enough shares to elect a majority of the board of directors. Most "minority" shareholders think of their stock holdings merely as passive investments, and they participate little, if at all, in the conduct of the affairs of the corporation. The shareholders assume no obligation for the debts of the business. Shares of stock change hands at the will of the shareholders, and the record may not show the change for some time after it has occurred. The record of who owns shares is usually kept by a bank or trust company.

Issue of Shares of Stock

The accounting for the initial issue of shares of stock is normally a routine matter. The usual entry, where the shares are issued for cash, is:

Cash	1,250,000	
Capital Stock		1,250,000
Issue of shares of capital stock.		

In addition to exchanges for cash, stock is sometimes issued in exchange for property, for personal services rendered, or in settlement of a liability. The form of the entry in these cases is the same as the one illustrated above, but the debit will be made to the accounts for property or services received or the liability settled. The amount for the entry should be the fair market value of the product, property, or services received, or, if this amount is not reasonably estimable, the fair market value of the stock issued.[2]

Classes of Shares

Corporations are often authorized to issue more than one class of shares, each representing ownership in the business. Most shares issued are either *common* or *preferred*. Occasionally, there may be several classes of common or preferred shares, each with different rights and privileges. All corporations must have at least one class of shares. They are usually called "common shares," but they may be designated by another name, such as Class A shares. Preferred shares may, but need not be, issued by a corporation.

Common shares have the claim to earnings of the corporation after commitments to preferred shareholders have been satisfied. Frequently, common shares are the only voting shares of the company. In the event of corporate dissolution, all of the proceeds of asset disposition, after settling the claims of creditors and required distributions to preferred shareholders, are distributable to the common shareholders.

Preferred shares have special privileges. Although these privileges vary considerably from issue to issue, a preferred share usually entitles its holder to dividends at a

---

[2] Accounting Principles Board, *Opinion No. 29*, "Accounting for Nonmonetary Transactions," 1973.

certain rate, which must be paid before dividends can be paid to common shareholders. Sometimes, though, these dividends may be postponed or omitted. If the provisions of the stock contract designate the preferred dividends as *cumulative,* then all current and previously postponed dividends must be paid before any dividends on common shares can be paid.

Many preferred shares issued by corporations in recent years have been *callable.* Callable preferred shares can be reacquired by the corporation at a specified price, which may vary according to a preset time schedule. Callability is commonly thought to be for the benefit of the corporation. If financing becomes available at a lower cost than the rate fixed for the preferred shares, a corporation may wish to reduce the relatively fixed commitment of preferred dividends (as compared to common). It can do so by exercising its option to call the preferred shares. This option is valuable to the corporation but makes the shares less attractive to potential owners. Other things being equal, noncallable shares will be issued for a higher price than will callable shares. Thus, the degree to which the corporation benefits by making shares callable is not clear-cut.

Preferred shares with a conversion feature have also become increasingly popular. Convertible preferred shares may be converted into a specified amount of common shares at specified times by their owner. The conversion privilege may appear advantageous to both the individual shareholder and the corporation. The preferred shareholder enjoys the security of a relatively assured dividend as long as the shares are held. The shareholder also has the opportunity to realize capital appreciation by converting the shares into common stock if the market price of the common shares rises sufficiently. Because of this feature, the change in the market price of convertible preferred shares will often parallel changes in the market price of the common shares.

The firm may also benefit from the conversion option. By including it in the issue, the company is usually able to specify a lower dividend rate on the preferred than otherwise would have been required to issue the shares for a given price.

A major consideration in the issue of preferred shares is that dividends are not deductible in calculating taxable income. However, bond interest is deductible. Thus, the aftertax cost of borrowing may be less than the aftertax cost of issuing preferred shares, even though the interest rate on the bonds is higher than the preferred stock dividend rate.

In recent years, some firms have issued redeemable preferred shares. The holder of these shares is allowed under specified conditions to trade these shares in for cash. Because such shares have some characteristics of debt, the SEC requires separate disclosure of them.[3]

Separate accounts are used for each class of shares. On the balance sheet, each class of shares is shown separately, many times with a short description of the major features of the shares. Customarily, preferred shares are listed before common shares on the balance sheet.

---

[3] Securities and Exchange Commission, *Accounting Series Release No. 268,* "Presentation in Financial Statements of 'Redeemable Preferred Stocks'," 1979.

469

Par Value and No-Par Shares

Shares of capital stock often have a *par,* or nominal, value. The articles of incorporation specify the amount, which is printed on the face of the stock certificates. The par value of common stock has some legal significance but little economic significance. For legal reasons, accountants separate par value from other contributed capital amounts. The par value rarely denotes the worth of the shares, except perhaps at the date of original issue. Readers of financial statements can usually assume merely that the par value of all common shares is the minimum investment that has been made by the shareholders in the corporation. Par value of preferred stock is more meaningful. The dividend rate specified in the preferred stock contract (for example, 9 percent) is almost always based on par value. Any preference as to assets in liquidation that preferred stockholders may have is usually related to the par value of the preferred shares.

Although preferred shares usually have a par value, common shares without a par value are widely used. When no-par-value shares are issued, the amount actually contributed can be credited directly to the capital stock account. Customary practice, however, assigns a *stated* value to the no-par shares, which has much the same effect as assigning the shares a par value. Some state corporation laws require the directors to assign a stated value to each no-par share. The stated value can usually be changed from time to time at the discretion of the directors. Shares assigned a certain par or stated value will almost always sell on the stock market at a price different from par or stated value. Also, *the book value of a share of common stock*—the total common shareholders' equity divided by the number of shares outstanding—is almost always greater than the par value of the shares. The excess results from retained earnings and from capital contributions in excess of par or stated value.

Contributions in Excess of Par or Stated Value

The corporation credits its capital stock account with only the par or stated value of the shares issued. Shares are usually issued for amounts greater than par. Typically, individuals who purchase newly issued shares from the corporation some years after the corporation began operations pay a higher price per share to compensate current shareholders for the additional capital assets provided by the retention of earnings. The excess of issue proceeds over par (or stated) value is credited to an account called Additional Paid-in Capital. The title "Capital Contributed in Excess of Par (Stated) Value" is more descriptive but is too cumbersome to be widely used. Sometimes the title used is "Premium on Capital Stock."

The entries to record additional paid-in capital involve nothing new. If par-value shares are used, the credit to the Additional Paid-in Capital account is always the difference between the amount received and the par value of the shares issued to the shareholders. For shares with no par value, the additional paid-in capital is the excess of the amount received over the stated value. Thus, the entry to record the issue of 100 shares of no-par-value stock, with a stated value of $10 per share, for $10,000, would be the same as the entry to record the issuance of a like number

470

of $10 par-value shares for the same proceeds:

Cash	10,000	
Capital Stock—Stated (or Par) Value		1,000
Additional Paid-in Capital		9,000
Issue of shares for amount greater than stated (or par) value.		

Treasury Shares

Shares of stock reacquired by the issuing corporation are called *treasury stock* or *treasury shares*. Treasury shares may be acquired for a variety of purposes. The firm may reacquire its own shares for later distribution under stock option plans or for stock dividends. (Stock option plans and stock dividends are discussed later in this chapter.) The firm may also consider treasury shares a worthwhile use for idle funds. Treasury shares are not entitled to dividends nor to vote, because they are not considered to be "outstanding" shares for these purposes. Treasury shares held may be reissued, or resold, on the market.

Accounting for Treasury Shares The fundamental principle of accounting for treasury shares is that a corporation does not report profit or loss on transactions involving its own shares. Even though the firm may "sell" (actually, reissue) the shares for more than their acquisition cost, the "gain" is not reported in income. Similarly, the firm may subsequently reissue shares for less than their acquisition cost. Even so, it will not report a loss as part of net income. The adjustments for reissue of treasury shares are made directly to the contributed capital accounts, bypassing the income statement and, generally, the Retained Earnings account.

When common shares are reacquired, a Treasury Shares—Common account is debited with the total amount paid to reacquire the shares.

Treasury Shares—Common	11,000	
Cash		11,000
$11,000 paid to reacquire 1,000 common shares.		

If the treasury shares are later reissued by the corporation, Cash is debited with the amount received and the Treasury Shares account credited with the cost of the shares. It is unlikely, of course, that the reissue price will precisely equal the amount paid to acquire the treasury shares. If the reissue price is greater than the acquisition price, the Additional Paid-in Capital account is credited to make the entry balance. Assuming that the 1,000 shares reacquired in the entry illustrated above were reissued for $14,000, the entry would be:

Cash	14,000	
Treasury Shares—Common		11,000
Additional Paid-in Capital		3,000
Reissue of 1,000 shares of treasury stock at a price greater than acquisition cost.		

If the reissue price is less than the amount paid, the debit to make the entry balance is usually to Additional Paid-in Capital, as long as there is a sufficient credit balance in that account. If there is not, the additional balancing debit is made directly to Retained Earnings. This debit to Retained Earnings is viewed similarly to a dividend, not an expense or loss reported in the income statement.

Disclosure of Treasury Shares   The Treasury Shares account is a contra account to owners' equity. Note that it is contra to total shareholders' equity. Chapter 7 introduced the direct debits to shareholders' equity required for declines in market value of the portfolio of investments in marketable equity securities. Those debits are generally shown as a negative number either before or after Retained Earnings. A recent annual report of Warner Communications Inc. illustrates the disclosures of these two deductions from shareholders' equity; see Exhibit 12.1.

Exhibit 12.1
**Presentation of Owners' Equity in Balance Sheet for
Warner Communications Inc.
(Amounts in 000's)**

Shareholders' Equity:	
Convertible preferred shares issued, par value $1 per share, 20,000,000 shares authorized	—
Common shares issued, par value $1 per share, 40,000,000 shares authorized.	$ 28,407
Paid-in capital	136,373
Retained earnings.	487,568
Net unrealized loss on marketable equity securities	(3,887)
	$ 648,461
Less common shares in treasury, at cost	33,540
Total shareholders' equity.	$ 614,921

Retention of Earnings

After a new business has established itself and is profitable, it usually generates additional owners' equity from undistributed earnings. These undistributed earnings are the accumulated periodic net income that remains after dividends have been declared. Retention of earnings increases shareholders' equity and provides a main source of capital for expansion.

Net Income and Cash Position

One misconception about net income is that it represents a fund of cash available for distribution or expansion. Earnings from operations usually involve cash at some stage: goods are sold to customers, the cash is collected, more goods are acquired, bills are paid, more sales are made, and so on. Assets generated by earnings do not, however, remain in the form of cash.[4] Only under most unrealistic conditions, with net plant and equipment, inventories, receivables, and liabilities remaining at constant amounts, would earnings correspond to the increase in cash. The statement of changes in financial position shows how the funds provided by operations and other sources are used during a period.

A well-managed firm keeps its cash at a reasonable minimum. If cash starts to accumulate, the firm may pay some obligations, increase its inventory, buy more equipment, declare dividends, or use the funds in some other way. Thus, there is no way of knowing how the retention of earnings affects the individual asset and liability accounts at any particular time. The only certain statement is that an increase in retained earnings results in increased *net assets* (that is, an increase in the excess of all assets over all liabilities).

Cash Dividends

The shareholders of a corporation do not directly control distributions of corporate net income. State laws and corporation bylaws almost always delegate the authority to declare dividends to the board of directors. When a dividend is declared, the entry is:

Retained Earnings	150,000	
Dividends Payable		150,000

To record declaration of dividends. (Sometimes an account called Dividends or Dividends Declared is debited. The Dividends account is a temporary account and is closed to Retained Earnings at the end of the period.)

Once the board of directors declares a dividend, the dividend becomes a legal liability of the corporation. Dividends Payable is shown as a current liability on the balance sheet if the dividends have not been paid at the end of the accounting period. When the dividends are paid, the entry is:

Dividends Payable	150,000	
Cash		150,000

Stock Dividends

The previous section indicated that the retention of earnings may generate a substantial increase in the amount of shareholders' equity that represents a relatively permanent commitment to the business. To indicate such a permanent commitment

---

[4] For many businesses, increased net income is frequently associated with decreased cash, whereas contraction of net income may be accompanied by an increase in cash. In the first stages of a business decline, cash may start to build up from the liquidation of inventories and receivables that have not been replaced, as well as from postponing replacement or expansion of plant. When conditions improve, inventories and receivables are expanded, new plant acquired, and a cash shortage may develop.

of reinvested earnings, a *stock dividend* may be issued. The accounting involves a debit to Retained Earnings and a credit to the contributed capital accounts. When a stock dividend is issued, shareholders receive additional shares of stock in proportion to their existing holdings without making any additional contributions. If a 5-percent stock dividend is issued, each shareholder receives one additional share for every 20 shares held before the dividend. Generally accepted accounting principles require that the valuation of the newly issued shares be based on the market value of the shares issued. For example, the directors of a corporation may decide to issue a stock dividend of 10,000 additional shares of common stock with a par value of $10 per share at a time when the market price of a share is $38. The entry would be:

Retained Earnings	380,000	
Common Stock—Par		100,000
Additional Paid-in Capital		280,000

Declaration of a stock dividend—recorded using market price of shares to quantify the amounts: $38 \times 10,000$ shares = $380,000.

The stock dividend relabels a portion of the retained earnings that had been legally available for dividend declarations as a more permanent form of owners' equity. A stock dividend formalizes the fact that some of the funds represented by past earnings have been used for plant expansion, to replace assets at increased prices, or to retire bonds. Such funds are therefore unavailable for cash dividends.

Stock dividends have little economic substance for shareholders: the same ownership is spread over more pieces of paper. If the distributed shares are of the same type as those held before, each shareholder's proportionate interest in the capital of the corporation and proportionate voting power have not changed. Although the book value per common share (total common shareholders' equity divided by number of common shares outstanding) decreases, the total book value of each shareholder's interest will remain unchanged, because a proportionately larger number of shares will be held. The market value per share should decline, but, all else being equal, the total market value of an individual's shares will not change. To describe such a distribution of shares as a "dividend"—meaning a distribution of earnings—is, therefore, misleading. It is, nevertheless, generally accepted terminology.

Dividend in Kind

The distribution of shares of stock issued by another, unrelated corporation to shareholders as a dividend is not called a stock dividend. It is described as a *dividend in kind* or a *property dividend.* Another dividend in kind is a systematic distribution of a corporation's products to its shareholders. Such dividends are accounted for just like cash dividends, except that when the dividend is paid, the asset given up, rather than cash, is credited.

474

Dividend Policy

The directors, in considering whether or not to declare cash dividends, must conclude both (1) that the declaration of a dividend is legal and (2) that it would be financially expedient.

Legal Restrictions on Dividends: Statutory

State corporation laws impose certain restrictions on the directors' freedom to declare dividends. These restrictions are thought to protect creditors, who otherwise might be in a precarious position because neither shareholders nor directors are liable for debts of the corporation.

Generally, the laws provide that dividends "may not be paid out of capital" but must be "paid out of earnings." The wording and interpretation of this rule varies among states. "Capital" is sometimes defined to be equal to the total amount paid in by shareholders. "Capital" is occasionally defined to be the amount shown in the Capital Stock account, freeing the amount in the Additional Paid-in Capital account for certain kinds of dividend declarations. In some states, the corporation must indicate a certain amount of stated capital below which shareholders' equity may not be reduced through dividend declarations. This stated capital amount may be less than the total paid-in capital. Some states allow dividends to be declared out of the earnings of the current period even though Retained Earnings are negative because of accumulated losses from previous periods. There are other specialized features and variations among the state statutes.

For most companies, these legal restrictions have little influence on the accounting for shareholders' equity and dividends. A balance sheet does not spell out all the legal niceties of amounts available for dividends, but it ought to disclose information necessary for the user to apply the legal rules of the state in which the business is incorporated. For example, state statutes can provide that "treasury shares may be acquired only with retained earnings." That is, dividends cannot exceed the amount of Retained Earnings reduced by the cost of treasury shares. If shares of stock are reacquired by the issuing corporation under these circumstances, then the amount of this restriction on dividends should be indicated by a footnote to the balance sheet.[5]

The statutory requirements for declaring dividends can be met by building up a balance in retained earnings. Such a balance does not mean that a fund of cash is available for the dividends. Managing cash is a specialized problem of corporate finance; cash for dividends must be anticipated just as well as cash for the purchase of equipment, the retirement of debts, and so on. Borrowing from the bank to pay the regular dividend is not unsound if the corporation's financial condition justifies the increase in liabilities that results.

---

[5] Accounting Principles Board, *Opinion No. 6,* "Status of Accounting Research Bulletins," 1965.

Legal Restrictions on Dividends: Contractual

Contracts with bondholders, other lenders, and preferred shareholders often restrict dividend payments and thereby compel the retention of earnings. For example, a recent balance sheet of the Caterpillar Tractor Company contains the following footnote:

> There are varying restrictions on the payment of cash dividends under the indentures relating to the long-term debt. . . . [U]nder the terms of the most restrictive indenture, approximately $695 million of "profit employed in the business" [retained earnings of $1.8 billion] was not available for the payment of dividends.

Bond contracts often provide that the retirement of the debt be made "out of earnings." Such a provision involves curtailing dividends so that the necessary debt service payments plus any dividends will not exceed the amount of net income for the period. Such a provision forces the shareholders to increase their investment in the business by restricting the amount of dividends that might otherwise be made available to them.

Dividends and Corporate Financial Policy

Dividends are seldom declared up to the maximum legal limit. The directors may allow the retained earnings to increase as a matter of corporate financial policy for several reasons:

1 Earnings are not reflected in a corresponding increase of available cash.
2 Restricting dividends in prosperous years may permit continued dividend payments in poor years.
3 Funds may be needed for expansion of working capital or plant and equipment.
4 Reducing the amount of borrowings, rather than paying dividends, may seem prudent.

Earnings Are Not Cash Although there are substantial earnings, the directors might decide that cash could not be spared for dividends equal to the net income of the period. Such factors as a maturing bank loan, an increase in the replacement cost of inventory, or the need for new machinery could easily consume all available cash. The statement of changes in financial position, introduced in Chapter 5, helps the reader understand how funds provided by earnings and other sources have been used during the year.

Equalization of Dividends Many corporate shareholders want to receive a regular minimum cash return. To accommodate such shareholders and to create a general impression of stability, directors commonly attempt to declare a regular dividend.

They try to maintain the regular dividend through good years and bad. When earnings and financial policy permit, they may declare "extra" dividends.

Financing Expansion Many corporations have financed substantial increases in their receivables, inventories, or plant and equipment without issuing bonds or additional shares of stock. Cash provided by operations that is not paid out as dividends may be used to acquire additional assets. Increased retained earnings cannot be associated with any particular item or group of items in the balance sheet, but it can be correct to say that, as a matter of policy, expansion is financed through the retention of earnings. From the corporation's standpoint, the overall financial result is much the same as if a substantial amount of cash had been distributed as dividends and an equal amount of cash had been obtained through issuing additional shares of stock. It has, however, saved the trouble and cost of finding buyers and issuing the additional stock certificates.

Voluntary Reduction of Indebtedness Contractual arrangements for reducing long-term debt may impose legal restrictions on the directors' dividend-paying powers. Even when there is no contractual obligation to do so, the directors may decide to reduce the amount of the liabilities and use the funds provided by operations for this purpose, rather than paying dividends.

Financial Policy Shareholders who want to maintain or increase their ownership percentage in a growing firm will prefer a policy that restricts dividends in order to finance expansion. If dividends are declared, such shareholders will use the funds received to acquire an equivalent amount of the new shares issued to finance the expansion. These shareholders will be saved transaction costs and will be able to defer individual income taxes if earnings are retained. If the corporation pays dividends, the shareholders must pay income taxes on the receipts before they can be reinvested. If the funds are reinvested directly by the corporation, there is a deferral of, and possibly a permanent avoidance of, personal income taxes.

Other shareholders may want a steady flow of cash and are unable, for contractual or psychological reasons, to sell a portion of their shares to raise cash if regular dividends are not declared. Such shareholders will resent being forced to reinvest in the corporation when expansion is financed through the retention of earnings. They may attempt to force the board of directors to adopt a more liberal dividend policy or change their investment to corporations that have more liberal dividend policies.

The degree to which expansion should be financed through retention of earnings is basically a problem of managerial finance, not accounting. Recent research in finance suggests that, within wide limits, what a firm does makes little difference so long as it tends to follow the same policy over time. Shareholders who want earnings reinvested can invest in shares of firms that finance expansion with earnings, whereas others who want a flow of cash can invest in shares of firms that pay out most of their net income in dividends.

Other Changes in Owners' Equity Accounts

Stock Splits

Stock splits (or, more technically, *split-ups*) are similar to stock dividends. Additional shares of stock are issued to shareholders in proportion to existing holdings. No additional assets are brought into the firm. In a stock split, the par or stated value of all the stock in the issued class is reduced in proportion to the additional shares issued. A corporation may, for example, have 1,000 shares of $10-par-value stock outstanding, and, by a stock split, exchange those shares for 2,000 shares of $5-par-value stock (a two-for-one split), or 4,000 shares of $2.50-par-value stock (a four-for-one split), or any number of shares of no-par stock. If the shares outstanding have no par or stated value, then the shareholders are merely issued additional stock certificates.

A stock split generally does not require a journal entry. The amount of retained earnings is not reduced. The amount shown in the capital stock account is merely represented by a larger number of shares. Of course, the additional number of shares held by each stockholder must be recorded in the subsidiary capital stock records.

It is customary to limit stock dividends to a maximum of 20 to 25 percent (that is, one share for every five or four shares held). Distributions in a greater ratio (for example, one share for every two shares held) are treated as stock splits.

A stock split (or a stock dividend) usually reduces the market value per share, all other factors remaining constant, in inverse proportion to the split (or dividend). Thus a two-for-one split could be expected to result in a 50-percent reduction in the market price per share. Stock splits have, therefore, usually been used to keep the market prices per share from rising to a price level unacceptable to management. For example, the board of directors might think that a market price of $30 to $40 is an effective trading range for its stock. This is a purely subjective estimate, and it is almost never supported by convincing evidence. If the share prices have risen to $60 in the market, then the board of directors may declare a two-for-one split. The only certain result of stock splits and dividends is increased record-keeping costs. Stock splits and stock dividends are seldom used by corporations whose stocks are not currently or soon to be traded on a stock exchange or in a public over-the-counter market.

Stock Options

Stock options are often a part of employee compensation plans. Under such plans, employees are granted an option to purchase shares in their company. Stock options present two kinds of accounting problems: (1) recording the granting of the option and (2) recording its exercise or lapse.

Granting the Option The generally accepted accounting treatment[6] for options usually results in no entry being made at the time the options are granted. The

---

[6]Accounting Principles Board, *Opinion No. 25,* "Accounting for Stock Issued to Employees," 1972.

exercise price of an option is the price the option holder will have to pay to acquire a share of stock. If the exercise price is equal to the market price of the stock on the date the option is granted, then the granting of the option is not viewed as resulting in compensation to the employee or expense to the employer and no entry is made. If the exercise price is less than the market price of the stock on the date of the grant, then compensation expense may have to be recognized under some circumstances.

Exercise or Lapse When the option is exercised, the conventional entry treats the transaction simply as an issue of shares at the option price.

Cash	35,000	
Common Shares—Par		5,000
Additional Paid-in Capital		30,000
To record issue of 1,000 shares of $5-par-value stock upon exercise of options and receipt of $35,000 cash.		

If the option lapses or expires without being exercised, no entry is required.

Disclosure of Options Generally accepted accounting principles require that the terms of options granted, outstanding, and exercised during a period be disclosed in text or notes accompanying the financial statements. For example, Note 20 to the financial statements of General Products Company in Appendix A, Exhibit A.4, discloses data on stock options.

Stock Appreciation Rights

Because of changes in the income tax laws and because of lackluster performance of the stock market in recent years, many executives have found stock option plans less attractive as a form of compensation than before. Corporations have in many cases substituted stock appreciation rights for stock options. A *stock appreciation right* is a promise made to an employee to pay cash to that employee at a future date. The amount is the difference between the market price of a certain number of shares on a given future date and some base price designated on the date the rights are granted. The granting of stock appreciation rights is a form of compensation. Generally accepted accounting principles (FASB *Interpretation No. 28,* 1978)[7] measure the amount of compensation as the excess of the market value of the shares over the base price set when the rights were granted. Subsequent changes, either increases or decreases, in the market value of the shares after the date of the grant result in a change in the measure of compensation. The amount of compensation is charged to expense over the period (during which the employee performs the services) that must elapse before the stock appreciation right can be exercised.

---

[7]FASB *Interpretation No. 28,* "Accounting for Stock Appreciation Rights and Other Variable Stock Option or Award Plans," 1978.

Stock Rights and Warrants

Opportunities to buy shares of stock may be granted through *stock rights.* Although stock rights are similar to stock options, there are some differences. Stock options are granted to employees, are nontransferable, and are a form of compensation. In contrast, stock rights are granted to current shareholders, are usually transferable, and can be traded in public markets. Stock rights are ordinarily associated with attempts to raise new capital for a firm from current shareholders.

Stock rights entitle the owner to purchase shares at a specified price. They are generally exercisable for only a limited period but occasionally are good indefinitely. Journal entries are not necessary when stock rights are granted to current shareholders. When the rights are exercised, the entry is like the one to record the issue of new shares at the price paid.

Stock warrants are issued to the general investing public for cash or used as a "bonus" with other security issues. They are exercisable for a limited period in most cases. Assume a corporation issues warrants to the public containing rights to purchase 10,000 shares for $20 each and receives $15,000 cash for the warrants. The entry would be:

Cash	15,000	
Common Stock Warrants		15,000
To record issue of warrants to the public. The Common Stock Warrants account would normally be included with Additional Paid-in Capital for balance sheet presentation.		

When the rights contained in these warrants are exercised and 10,000 shares of $5-par-value common stock are issued in exchange for the warrants plus $200,000, the entry would be:

Cash	200,000	
Common Stock Warrants	15,000	
Common Stock—Par Value		50,000
Additional Paid-in Capital		165,000
To record the issue of 10,000 shares for $200,000 cash and the redemption of warrants. (The amount originally received for the warrants is transferred to Additional Paid-in Capital.)		

If the warrants expire without having been exercised, the entry would be:

Common Stock Warrants	15,000	
Additional Paid-in Capital		15,000
To record expiration of common stock warrants and the transfer to permanent contributed capital.		

Convertible Bonds

Convertible bonds are, typically, semiannual coupon bonds like the ones discussed in Chapter 10—with one added feature. The holder of the bond can *convert,* or "trade in," the bond into shares of stock. The number of shares to be received when the bond is converted into stock, the dates when conversion can occur, and other details are specified in the bond indenture. Convertible bonds are usually callable.

Investors often find convertible bonds attractive. The owner is promised a regular interest payment. In addition, should the company business be so successful that its share prices rise on the stock market, then the holder of the bond can convert the investment from debt into equity. The creditor has become an owner and can share in the good fortune of the company.[8] Of course, an investor does not get something for nothing. Because of the potential participation in the earnings of the company once the bonds are converted into common shares, an investor in the bonds must accept a lower interest rate than would be received if the bonds were not convertible into stock. From the company's point of view, convertible bonds allow borrowing at lower rates of interest than is required on ordinary debt, but the company must promise to give up an equity interest if the bonds are converted. The purchaser of the convertible bond is paying something for the option to acquire common stock later. Thus, a portion of the proceeds from the issue of convertible bonds actually represents a form of capital contribution, even though it is not so recorded.

Issue of Convertible Bonds Suppose, for example, that the Johnson Company's credit rating would allow it to issue $100,000 of ordinary 10-year, 14-percent semiannual coupon bonds at par. The firm prefers to issue convertible bonds with a lower coupon rate. Assume that Johnson Company issues at par $100,000 of 10-year, 10 percent semiannual coupon bonds, but each $1,000 bond is convertible into 50 shares of Johnson Company $5-par-value common stock. (The entire issue is convertible into 5,000 shares.) The following entry is required:

Cash	100,000	
Convertible Bonds Payable		100,000
Issue of convertible bonds at par.		

This entry effectively treats convertible bonds just like ordinary, nonconvertible bonds and records the value of the conversion feature at zero. (Generally accepted accounting principles do recognize the potential issue of common stock implied by the conversion feature in the calculations of earnings-per-share figures.)

More Logical Treatment Appendix Table 5 (for 10-percent coupon bonds) indicates that 10-percent, 10-year semiannual (nonconvertible) coupon bonds sell for about 79 percent of par when the market rate of interest is 14 percent. Thus, if the

---

[8] In recent years the brokerage commission fees on convertible bonds have often been less than those for comparable dollar amounts of investments in the underlying common shares.

10-percent convertible bonds can be issued at par, then the conversion feature must be worth about 21 ($= 100 - 79$) percent of par. Then 21 percent of the proceeds from the bond issue is actually a capital contribution by the bond buyers for the right to acquire common stock later. The logical entry to record the issue of these 10-percent convertible bonds at par would be:

Cash	100,000	
Convertible Bonds Payable		79,000
Additional Paid-in Capital		21,000
Issue of 10-percent semiannual coupon convertible bonds at a time when ordinary 10-percent bonds could be issued for 79 percent of par.		

Notice that the calculation of the amounts for this entry requires that we know what the proceeds would be of an issue of nonconvertible bonds that are otherwise similar to the convertible bonds. Because auditors are often unable to ascertain this information in a reasonably objective manner, generally acceptable accounting principles do not allow the logical journal entry above.[9]

Conversion of Bonds To carry the illustration under generally accepted accounting principles further, assume that the common stock of the Johnson Company increases in the market to $30 a share so that one $1,000 bond, which is convertible into 50 shares of stock, can be converted into stock with a market value of $1,500. If the entire convertible issue were converted into common stock at this time, then 5,000 shares of $5-par-value stock would be issued on conversion.

The usual entry to record the conversion of bonds into stock ignores current market prices in the interest of simplicity and merely shows the swap of stocks for bonds at their book value.

Convertible Bonds Payable	100,000	
Common Stock—$5 Par		25,000
Additional Paid-in Capital		75,000
To record conversion of 100 convertible bonds with book value of $100,000 into 5,000 shares of $5-par-value stock.		

An allowable alternative treatment recognizes that market prices provide information useful in quantifying the market value of the shares issued. Under the alternative treatment, when the market price of a share is $30 and the fair market value of the 5,000 shares issued on conversion is $150,000, then the journal entry made would be:

---

[9] Accounting Principles Board, *Opinion No. 14,* "Accounting for Convertible Debt and Debt Issued with Stock Purchase Warrants," 1969. The Accounting Principles Board stated that, in reaching its conclusions, less weight was given to the practical difficulties than to some other considerations, spelled out in the Opinion. We concur with the dissent to this Opinion expressed by several members of the Board.

Convertible Bonds Payable	100,000	
Loss on Conversion of Bonds	50,000	
Common Stock—$5 Par		25,000
Additional Paid-in Capital		125,000

To record conversion of 100 convertible bonds into 5,000 shares of $5-par-value stock at a time when the market price of a share is $30.

The alternative entry results in the same total owners' equity: smaller retained earnings (because the Loss on Conversion of Bonds will reduce current net income and thus Retained Earnings), but larger contributed capital. It is the equivalent of the following two entries:

Cash	150,000	
Common Stock—$5 Par		25,000
Additional Paid-in Capital		125,000

To record issue of 5,000 shares of $5-par-value stock at $30 per share.

Convertible Bonds Payable	100,000	
Loss on Retirement of Bonds	50,000	
Cash		150,000

Retirement by purchase for $150,000 of 100 convertible bonds carried on the books at $100,000.

Earnings per Share

Chapter 6 explained that earnings per share of common stock is conventionally calculated by dividing net income attributable to the common stockholders by the weighted-average number of shares of common stock outstanding during the period. When a firm has outstanding securities that, if exchanged for common stock, would decrease earnings per share as conventionally calculated, then the earnings-per-share calculations become somewhat more complicated. Stock options, stock rights, warrants, and convertible bonds all have the potential of reducing earnings per share and must be taken into account in calculating earnings per share. These complications are discussed in intermediate accounting books.

Retained Earnings Adjustments

Nearly all items that cause the total of retained earnings to change during a period result from transactions reported in the income statement for that period. The only common exception to this general rule—dividend declarations—has been mentioned throughout the book. Dividend declarations are distributions that reduce the balance in the Retained Earnings account but do not affect reported income. There are two other exceptions to the general rule that changes in retained earnings arise from transactions reported in the income statement. These are *corrections of errors* and

483

prior-period adjustments for items significant enough that they are not reported as part of, or "buried in," the current year's income statement.

Errors result from such actions as miscounting inventories, arithmetic mistakes, and misapplications of accounting principles. Such errors, if they are material, are corrected with debits or credits to the Retained Earnings account. Assume, for example, that merchandise inventory is discovered to be $10,000 less than was reported at the end of the previous period, and that cost of goods sold was computed last period using a periodic inventory method:

$$\text{Cost of Goods Sold} = \text{Beginning Inventory} + \text{Purchases} - \text{Ending Inventory}.$$

Then, the following entry (ignoring income tax effects) would be made this period:

Retained Earnings.	10,000	
Merchandise Inventory.		10,000
Correction of inventory error. Last period's cost of goods sold was too small; income was overstated.		

Since FASB *Statement No. 16* was issued in 1977, prior-period adjustments are even rarer than they were before. There is only one transaction that qualifies for prior-period adjustment. It is esoteric, and we do not discuss it here.[10]

Disclosure of Changes in Owners' Equity

The changes in all owners' equity accounts must be explained in the annual reports to shareholders.[11] As previous chapters have pointed out, the reconciliation of retained earnings may appear in the balance sheet, in a statement of income and retained earnings, or in a separate statement. The financial statements of General Products Company in Appendix A show the reconciliation of retained earnings at the bottom of the combined statement of income and retained earnings (Exhibit A.1) and the causes of all other changes in owners' equity accounts in a separate schedule in Note 18.

Journal Entries for Changes in Owners' Equity

To review the accounting for owners' equity, we reconstruct the journal entries made for 1981 and 1982 which resulted in the changes in owners' equity disclosed for

---

[10] For the sake of completeness we shall state that a prior-period adjustment is recorded only when a firm receives an income tax benefit associated with using an operating loss carryforward of a subsidiary acquired in a purchase.

[11] Accounting Principles Board, *Opinion No. 12*, "Omnibus Opinion—1967," 1967.

484

General Products Company in Exhibits A.1 and Note 18 of Exhibit A.4. The amounts in the entries in Exhibit 12.2 represent millions of dollars.

Exhibit 12.2
Journal Entries Illustrating Transaction Involving Owners' Equity for General Products Company, 1981–82

Entry and Explanation	Millions of Dollars			
	1982		**1981**	
(1) Income Summary	1,514		1,409	
Retained Earnings		1,514		1,409
Net income for the year, recorded assuming that an Income Summary account is used. This entry, in effect, closes all temporary revenue and expense accounts, with the credit balance being reported as income for the year.				
(2) Retained Earnings	670		624	
Dividends Payable—Common Stock		670		624
Cash dividends declared on preferred and common stock.				
(3) Treasury Shares, at Cost	145		156	
Cash		145		156
Acquisitions of treasury shares in market transactions with outsiders.				
(4) Cash	139		146	
Capital in Excess of Par Value ("Loss")			2	
Treasury Shares, at Cost		136		148
Capital in Excess of Par Value ("Gain")		3		—
Issue of shares to employees under stock plan and savings and stock ownership, incentive compensation and stock option plans. The shares issued in 1981 had market value on date of re-issue of $2 million less than their cost. The "loss" is debited to the Capital in Excess of Par Value account. The shares issued in 1982 had market value on date of re-issue of $3 million more than their cost. The "gain" is credited to the Capital in Excess of Par Value account, which GP calls "Amounts Received for Stock in Excess of Par Value."				

Changes in Owners' Equity Reported in the Statement of Changes in Financial Position

The transactions affecting owners' equity generally affect funds and are reported in the statement of changes in financial position. Exhibit A.3 in Appendix A presents the statement of changes in financial position for General Products Company. The effects of net income can be seen in the statement of changes in financial position. The "Sources" section also shows the amounts for "Newly Issued Common Shares" and "Disposition of Treasury Shares" for the various compensation and savings plans. The section "Application of Funds" shows lines for Dividend Declarations and Purchase of Treasury Shares.

Summary

Accounting for owners' equity in a corporation is based on the premise that there should be a separate account for each source of capital contributed by owners. The sources of capital from shareholders include:

1 Receipts from issues of stock at par or stated value.
2 Receipts in excess of par or stated value of stock issues.
3 Earnings retentions.

Owners' equity is reduced when the corporation experiences losses from business operations, declares dividends, or acquires treasury stock.

Problem for Self-Study

Exhibit 12.3 shows the owners' equity accounts for Lorla Corporation at the ends of 1981 and 1982. During 1982 Lorla Corporation issued new shares of stock for $40 a share and reacquired 60 shares for the treasury at $42 per share. Still later in the year, it sold some of the treasury shares. Revenues for 1982 were $90,000 and net income was $10,000.

Exhibit 12.3
Lorla Corporation Owners' Equity Accounts
(Problem for Self-Study)

	December 31	
	1981	1982
Common Stock ($5 par value)	$ 5,000	$ 5,500
Additional Paid-in Capital	30,000	33,620
Net Unrealized Loss on Investments in Marketable Equity Securities	(900)	(800)
Retained Earnings	60,000	67,300
	$94,100	$105,620
Less: Cost of Treasury Shares	—	(840)
Total Owners' Equity	$94,100	$104,780

Reconstruct all of the transactions involving owners' equity accounts for the year 1982, and show the journal entries for those transactions.

Suggested Solution

Cash	4,000	
Common Stock ($5 par value)		500
Additional Paid-in Capital		3,500

Because the Common Stock account went up by $500 and the par value is $5 per share, 100 shares (= $500/$5 per share) must have been issued. The issue price was $40 per share; hence the cash raised was $4,000 (= $40 × 100 shares).

Treasury Shares	2,520	
Cash		2,520

Acquisition of 60 shares for the treasury at $42 per share; $60 \times \$42 = \$2,520$.

Cash	1,800	
Treasury Shares		1,680
Additional Paid-in Capital		120

Because the year-end balance in the treasury shares account is $840, 20 shares ($= \$840/\$42$ per share) must remain in the treasury. Thus, 40 ($= 60 - 20$) shares were re-sold. Because the year-end Additional Paid-in Capital account is $120 [$= \$33,620 - (\$30,000 + \$3,500)$] larger than is explained by the issue of new shares, a "gain" of $120 must have been realized on the resale of the shares from the treasury. Because 40 shares were re-sold, the total "gain" was $120, and the "gain" per share must have been $3 ($= \$120/40$ shares). Thus, the total resale price per share must have been $45 ($= \$42 + \$3$). Cash raised must have been $1,800 $= \$45$ per share $\times$ 40 shares.

Allowance for Excess of Cost Over Market Value of Investments in Marketable		
Equity Securities	100	
Recovery of Unrealized Loss on Investment in Marketable Equity Securities.		100

Market Value of the portfolio of investments in marketable equity securities has increased by $100 during the year.

Revenue Accounts	90,000	
Expense Accounts		80,000
Retained Earnings		10,000

Closing entries for revenue and expense accounts, given that revenues were $90,000 and net income was $10,000 for the year.

Retained Earnings	2,700	
Dividends Payable		2,700

The Retained Earnings account increased by only $7,300 for the year. Dividends must have been $10,000 - \$7,300 = \$2,700$.

Questions and Problems

1 Review the meaning of the following concepts or terms discussed in this chapter.

  a Corporation.
  b Corporate charter.
  c Corporate bylaws.
  d Capital stock, common stock, preferred shares.
  e Cumulative preferred shares.
  f Callable preferred shares.
  g Convertible preferred shares.
  h Par value.
  i Stated value.
  j Additional paid-in capital.
  k Treasury shares.
  l Earnings are not cash.
  m Convertible bond.
  n Stock dividend.

o Stock split.
p Stock option.
q Stock appreciation right.
r Stock right.
s Stock warrant.
t Correction of error.
u Prior-period adjustment.

2 Under what circumstances would you expect par-value stock to be issued at a price in excess of par? What is the entry to record such an issue?

3 A construction corporation is attempting to borrow money on a note secured by some of its property. A bank agrees to accept the note, provided that the president of the corporation will personally endorse it. What is the point of this requirement?

4 "Par value of preferred stock is frequently a significant figure, but par value of common stock possesses little significance." Why may par value of preferred stock be significant?

5 In what way is the par value of common stock with a par value different from the stated value of no-par common stock?

6 What is treasury stock? How is it reported on the balance sheet?

7 A certain corporation retained almost all of its earnings, only rarely paying a cash dividend. When some of the shareholders objected, the reply of the president was: "Why do you want cash dividends? You would just have to go to the trouble of reinvesting them. Where can you possibly find a better investment than our own company?" Comment.

8 Compare the position of a shareholder who receives a cash dividend with that of one who receives a stock dividend.

9 At the annual shareholders' meeting, the president of the Santa Cris Corporation made the following statement: "The net income for the year, after taxes, was $1,096,000. The directors have decided that the corporation can afford to distribute only $500,000 as a cash dividend." Are the two sentences of this statement compatible?

10 The text says, "Convertible bonds are usually callable." The call feature is included so that the issuer can force conversion of the bonds. Explain.

11 a Assume that accounting were to require recognition of compensation expense on the date that stock options were granted to an employee. A precise measure of the amount of the compensation expense would not be possible, but various approximations could be made. How might the accountant put a dollar amount on the compensation expense granted through stock options? You may assume that the exercise price is the market price on the date the option is granted.

b Assume that accounting were to require recognition of compensation expense on the date a stock appreciation right were granted to an employee. A precise measure of the amount of the compensation expense would not be possible, but various approximations could be made. How might the accountant put a dollar amount on the compensation expense granted through stock appreciation rights?

12 Indicate whether each of the following statements is true or false and justify your response. Ignore the effects of income taxes.

488

a Cash dividends reduce the book value per share of capital stock.

b A stock dividend does not affect the Retained Earnings account.

c Investing 50 percent of net income in government bonds has no effect on the amount legally available for dividends.

d Stock dividends reduce the book value per share of capital stock.

e The declaration of a cash dividend does not reduce the amount of the shareholders' equity.

f The distribution of a stock dividend tends to reduce the market value per share of capital stock.

g A stock split generally does not affect the Retained Earnings account.

h A stock-dividend declaration is usually accompanied by a reduction in par or stated value per share.

13 Indicate the effect of each of the following transactions on **(1)** the balance in the Retained Earnings and **(2)** the total shareholders' equity.

a Bonds are issued at a discount.

b A check is written to the Internal Revenue Service for additional income taxes levied on past years' income (no previous entry).

c A stock split is voted by the directors. The par value per share is reduced from $200 to $50 and each shareholder is given four new shares in exchange for each old share.

d The manager is voted a bonus of $3,500 by the directors.

e Notes payable in the face amount of $50,000 are paid by check.

f A dividend in preferred stock is issued to common shareholders (no previous entry).

g Securities held as a long-term investment are sold at book value.

h A building site is received as a donation by the company from the local chamber of commerce.

i A building is sold for less than its book value.

14 Refer to the Simplified Statement of Changes in Financial Position for a Period in Exhibit 5.19 on page 191. Nine of the lines in the statement are numbered. Line (2) should be expanded to say "Additions for Expenses and Other Charges Against Income Not Using Funds," and line (3) should be expanded to say "Subtractions for Revenues and Other Credits to Income Not Producing Funds from Operations." Ignore the unnumbered lines in responding to the questions below.

Assume that the accounting cycle is complete for the period and that all of the financial statements have been prepared. Then it is discovered that a transaction has been overlooked. That transaction is recorded in the accounts and all of the financial statements are corrected. Define *funds* as *working capital.* For each of the following transactions, indicate which of the numbered lines of the funds statement is affected and by how much. Ignore income tax effects.

a Common shares are issued for $200,000.

b Common shares originally issued for $50,000 are repurchased for $75,000 and retired.

c Convertible bonds with a book value of $100,000 and a market value of $240,000 are converted into common shares with a par value of $10,000 and a market value of $240,000.

d Treasury shares acquired for $20,000 are reissued for $15,000.

e A stock dividend is declared. The par value of the shares issued is $1,000 and their market value is $300,000.

f A cash dividend of $70,000 is declared.

489

g A previously declared cash dividend of $70,000 is paid.

h Stock rights are exercised. The shares have a par value of $1,000 and market value of $35,000 on the date of exercise. The exercise price is $20,000, and $20,000 cash is received.

15 For each of the following transactions, present the journal entries in two-column form. These transactions do not relate to the same set of records.

a The shares of no-par stock of a corporation are selling on the market at $100 a share. In order to bring the market value down to a "more popular" figure, the board of directors votes to issue four shares to shareholders in exchange for each share already held by them. The shares are issued.

b The treasurer of the corporation reports that cash on hand exceeds normal requirements by $300,000. Pending a decision by the board of directors on the final disposition of the funds, investments in marketable securities in the amount of $299,600 are made.

c The net income for the year is $150,000. The directors vote to issue 1,000 shares of 10-percent, $100-par-value preferred stock as a stock dividend on the 2,500 shares of no-par common stock outstanding. The preferred's market price is $102 a share. The common's market price is $50 a share.

d After the books are closed and the financial statements are issued, it is discovered that an arithmetic error was made in calculating depreciation on office equipment for the preceding period. The depreciation expense was $8,000 too large.

16 The comparative balance sheet of the Forty-Misty Company shows the following data:

	Dec. 31, 1981	Dec. 31, 1982
Common Stock	$1,200,000	$1,320,000
Retained Earnings	460,000	400,000
Total Shareholders' Equity	$1,660,000	$1,720,000

During 1982, common shareholders received $60,000 in cash dividends and $120,000 in stock dividends. A refund on 1980 taxes of $30,000 was received on March 1, 1982, and was credited directly to Retained Earnings. A loss on retirement of plant assets of $5,600 occurred during the year and was debited directly to Retained Earnings.

a What net income is reported for 1982, after the accounting was done as described?

b What net income should actually be reported for 1982? Show your calculations.

17 The comparative balance sheet of the Royal Corporation shows the following information:

	Dec. 31, 1981	Dec. 31, 1982
Preferred Stock (6%)	$ 750,000	$ 600,000
Common Stock	1,400,000	1,540,000
Retained Earnings	324,000	372,000
Total Shareholders' Equity	$2,474,000	$2,512,000

During 1982 stock dividends of $150,000 were issued to common shareholders. In addition, common shareholders received $70,000 in cash dividends; the preferred shareholders received $36,000 in cash dividends. On July 1, 1982, preferred stock with a par value of

490

$150,000 was called at 104; that is, $156,000 was paid to retire the shares. The call premium was debited to the Retained Earnings account. What net income is reported to shareholders for 1982?

18 The Chelex Company began business on January 1. Its balance sheet on December 31 contains the shareholders' equity section shown below.

Exhibit 12.4
Chelex Company
Shareholders' Equity as of December 31

Capital Stock ($10 par value)	$ 50,000
Additional Paid-in Capital	78,000
Retained Earnings	10,000
Less: 300 Shares Held in Treasury	(6,000)
Total Shareholders' Equity	$132,000

During the year, Chelex Company engaged in the following capital stock transactions:

(1) Issued shares for $25 each.
(2) Acquired a block of 500 shares for the treasury in a single transaction.
(3) Reissued some of the treasury shares.

Assuming that these were all of the capital stock transactions during the year, answer the following questions:

a How many shares were issued for $25?
b What was the price at which the treasury shares were acquired?
c How many shares were reissued from the block of treasury shares?
d What was the price at which the treasury shares were issued?
e What journal entries must have been made during the year?

19 The Worman Company began business on January 1. Its balance sheet on December 31 contains the shareholders' equity section shown below.

Exhibit 12.5
Worman Company
Shareholders' Equity as of December 31

Capital Stock ($5 par value)	$ 50,000
Additional Paid-in Capital	254,800
Retained Earnings	25,000
Less: 600 Shares Held in Treasury	(16,800)
Total Shareholders' Equity	$313,000

During the year, Worman Company engaged in the following capital stock transactions:

(1) Issued shares for $30 each.
(2) Acquired a block of 1,000 shares for the treasury in a single transaction.
(3) Reissued some of the treasury shares.

Assuming that these were the only capital stock transactions during the year, answer the following questions:

a How many shares were issued for $30 each?
b What was the price at which the treasury shares were acquired?
c How many shares were reissued from the block of treasury shares?
d What was the price at which the treasury shares were reissued?
e What journal entries must have been made during the year?

20 Give journal entries for the following transactions.

a Outstanding shares of stock are acquired by the issuing corporation for its treasury at a cost of $100,000.
b Dividends are declared on preferred stock, $220,000.
c A dividend is paid to common shareholders consisting of shares of preferred stock in the same corporation with a par value of $200,000.
d A dividend is paid to common shareholders consisting of shares of no-par common stock in the same corporation. The amount assigned to these shares of stock is $600,000.
e The building is mortgaged for $100,000, and this amount is distributed to the common shareholders as a cash dividend.

21 Give journal entries, if required, for the following transactions, which are unrelated unless otherwise specified:

a The regular quarterly dividend is declared on the 10-percent, $100-par-value preferred stock. There are 10,000 shares authorized, 8,000 shares issued, and 1,600 shares reacquired and held in the treasury.
b The dividend on the preferred stock (see part a) is paid.
c A stock dividend of $250,000 of no-par common stock is issued to common shareholders.
d A building replacement fund of $125,000 is created. The fund is to be used to purchase a new building when the present one becomes inadequate.
e Bonds with $500,000 par value are retired at par out of the sinking fund created for that purpose.
f The shares of no-par stock of the corporation are selling on the market at $300 a share. In order to bring the market value down to a more popular price and thereby broaden the distribution of its stockholdings, the board of directors votes to issue four extra shares to shareholders for each share already held by them. The shares are issued.

22 Journalize the following transactions:

a A cash dividend of $2 a share is declared on the outstanding preferred stock. There are 5,000 shares authorized, 3,000 shares issued, and 100 shares reacquired and held in the treasury.
b A cash dividend of $1 a share is declared on the no-par common stock, of which there are 10,000 shares authorized, 7,000 shares issued, and 1,000 shares reacquired and held in the treasury.
c The dividend on the preferred stock is paid.
d The dividend on the common stock is paid.

23 The following events relate to shareholders' equity transaction of the Richardson Copper Company during the first year of its existence. Present journal entries for each of the transactions.

492

a January 2. Articles of incorporation are filed with the State Corporation Commission. The authorized capital stock consists of 5,000 shares of $100-par-value, preferred stock which offers an 8-percent annual dividend, and 50,000 shares of no-par common stock. The original incorporators are issued 100 shares of common stock at $20 per share; cash is collected for the shares. A stated value of $20 per share is assigned to the common stock.

b January 6. 1,600 shares of common stock are issued for cash at $20 per share.

c January 8. 3,000 shares of preferred stock are issued at par.

d January 9. Certificates for the shares of preferred stock are issued.

e January 12. The tangible assets and goodwill of Richardson Copper Works, a partnership, are acquired in exchange for 600 shares of preferred stock and 10,000 shares of common stock. The tangible assets acquired are valued as follows: inventories, $40,000; land, $45,000; buildings, $80,000; and equipment, $95,000.

f July 3. The semiannual dividend on the preferred stock outstanding is declared, payable July 25, to shareholders of record on July 12.

g July 5. Operations for the first 6 months have been profitable, and it is decided to expand. The company issues 20,000 shares of common stock for cash at $33 per share.

h July 25. The preferred stock dividend declared July 3 is paid.

i October 2. The directors declare a dividend of $1 per share on the common stock, payable October 25, to shareholders of record on October 12.

j October 25. The dividend on common stock declared on October 2 is paid.

24 The following data are selected from the records of capital stock and retained earnings of the Wheellock Company. Present journal entries for these transactions.

a July 5, 1982. Articles of incorporation are filed with the secretary of state. The authorized capital stock consists of 1,000 shares of 6-percent preferred stock with a par value of $100 per share and 10,000 shares of no-par common stock.

b July 8, 1982. The company issues 3,000 shares of common stock for cash at $60 per share.

c July 9, 1982. The company issues 6,000 shares of common stock for the assets of the partnership of Wheellock and Wheellock. Their assets are valued as follows: accounts receivable, $30,000; inventories, $60,000; land, $80,000; buildings, $90,000; and equipment, $100,000.

d July 13, 1982. 750 shares of preferred stock are issued at par for cash.

e December 31, 1982. The balance in the Income Summary account, after closing all expense and revenue accounts, is $300,000. That account is to be closed to the Retained Earnings account.

f January 4, 1983. The regular semiannual dividend on the preferred stock and a dividend of $2 per share on the common stock are declared. The dividends are payable on February 1.

g February 1, 1983. The dividends declared on January 4 are paid.

h July 2, 1983. The regular semiannual dividend on the preferred stock is declared. The dividend is payable on August 1.

i August 1, 1983. The dividend declared on July 2 is paid.

25 The following transactions all relate to the same set of records. Use the straight-line method for calculating bond interest. Journalize these transactions.

a The company issues 23,000 shares of common stock (par value, $1 per share) for cash at $40 per share.

493

b Twenty-year, 8-percent bonds with $500,000 par value are issued for $492,000.

c Interest expense on the bond is recognized at the time the first semiannual interest payment is made.

d The bond indenture requires a sinking fund to be built up to pay the principal of the bonds at maturity. The company deposits $18,600 with the sinking fund trustee.

e A cash dividend of $2 per share of common stock is declared.

f At the end of the twentieth year of the life of the bonds, the final semiannual interest payment is made and the bonds are retired. There are sufficient funds in the sinking fund to accomplish the retirement.

g A fund of $50,000 is created for future expansion.

h An additional 7,000 shares of common stock are issued for cash at $11 a share.

26 Refer to the schedule reproduced here, which shows employee stock option data for the International Products Company (IP). At December 31, 1983, there were 2.7 million options outstanding to purchase shares at an average of $54 per share. Total shareholders' equity at December 31, 1983, was about $2.5 billion.

Exhibit 12.6
**International Products Company
Disclosure of Employee
Stock Options**

		Average per Share	
Stock Options	Shares Subject to Option	Option Price	Market Price
Balance at December 31, 1981	2,388,931	$45	$72
Options granted	475,286	77	77
Options exercised	(297,244)	42	76
Options terminated	(90,062)	45	—
Balance at December 31, 1982	2,476,911	50	83
Options granted	554,965	75	75
Options exercised	(273,569)	42	74
Options terminated	(58,307)	52	—
Balance at December 31, 1983	2,700,000	54	77

a If IP were to issue 2.7 million shares in a public offering at the market price per share on December 31, 1983, what would be the proceeds of the issue?

b If IP were to issue 2.7 million shares to employees who exercised all outstanding stock options, what would be the proceeds of the issue?

c Are IP's shareholders better off under **a** or under **b**?

d The text accompanying the stock option data in the IP annual report reads, in part, as follows:

> Option price under these plans is the full market value of International Products common stock on date of grant. Therefore, participants in the plans do not benefit unless the stock's market price rises, thus benefiting all share owners. . . .

IP seems to be saying that stockholders are not harmed by these options, whereas your answers to parts **a** and **b** show shareholders are worse off when options are exercised than when shares are issued to the public. Attempt to reconcile IP's statement with your own analysis in parts **a** and **b**.

27 On January 2, 1979, the Oklahoma Corporation issues $1 million of 20-year, $1,000-par-value, 10-percent semiannual coupon bonds at par. Each $1,000 bond is convertible into 40 shares of $1-par-value common stock. The Oklahoma Corporation's credit rating is such that it would have to issue 15-percent semiannual coupon bonds if the bonds were not convertible and if they were to be issued at par. On January 2, 1983, the bond issue is converted into common stock. The common stock has a market price of $45 a share on January 2, 1983. Present the journal entries made on January 2, 1979 and 1983, under generally accepted accounting principles, to record the issue and conversion of the issue.

28 In May 1978, the A-Tat Company issued 100,000 shares of no-par, convertible preferred stock for $50 a share. The shares promised a dividend of $6. All shares were issued for cash. These shares were convertible into common stock (par value, $1 a share) at a rate of 5 shares of common stock for each share of preferred. The preferred shares were issued when the prime interest rate was 10 percent, and they are not regarded as equivalent to common shares in the calculation of earnings per share.

The company's earnings increased sharply during the next 4 years, and during January, 1982, all shares of preferred were converted into common shares. One million common shares were outstanding before conversion of the shares. If the conversion had not taken place, the net income to common for the year 1982 would have been $3,000,000. Other data are as follows:

Market Prices:	May 1978	January 1982
A-Tat Common Stock.	$10	$ 20
A-Tat $6 Preferred Stock.	50	100
Book Value per A-Tat Common Share (before conversion of preferred).	14	18

  a Prepare journal entries to record the issuance and conversion of the preferred stock.
  b Compute earnings per common share before conversion of the shares. What was the effect of the conversion on book values and on earnings per common share?
  c Did the conversion of the preferred shares into common stock lead to a dilution of the common shareholders' equity? Explain your reasoning.

29 After several years of rapid expansion, the Alcher Company approached the State National Bank for a $1 million loan. The bank was willing to lend the money at an interest rate of 12 percent per year. Alcher Company then approached an individual investor who was willing to provide the same funds for only 8 percent per year, provided that the Alcher Company gave the investor an option to purchase 20,000 shares of Alcher Company $5-par-value common stock for $20 per share at any time within 5 years of the initial date of the loan.

Alcher weighed both opportunities and decided to borrow from the investor. At the time of the loan, the common shares had a market price of $15 per share. Five years after the initial date of the loan, the investor exercised the option and purchased 20,000 shares for $20 each. At that time, the market price of the common shares was $45 each.

  a Did the use of the "detachable warrants" (the technical name for the option granted to the investor) reduce the Alcher Company's cost of borrowing?

495

b How should the loan and annual interest payments of $80,000 be recorded in the books of the Alcher Company to reflect the economic reality of the transaction?

c How might the exercise of the warrants (and the purchase of the 20,000 shares) be recorded?

d Did exercise of the option dilute the owners' equity of the other shareholders on the date the option was exercised?

e What disclosures during the life of the loan do you think appropriate? Why?

30 The shareholders' equity section of the balance sheet of the Lipscomb Corporation at December 31 is shown below.

Shareholders' Equity

Common Stock—$10 Par Value, 500,000 Shares Authorized and 100,000 Shares Outstanding	$1,000,000
Additional Paid-in Capital	500,000
Retained Earnings	3,000,000
Total Shareholders' Equity	$4,500,000

---

a Calculate the total book value and the book value per common share as of December 31.

b For each of the following transactions or events, give the appropriate journal entry and determine the total book value and the book value per common share of the Lipscomb Corporation after the transaction. The transactions and events are independent of each other, except where noted.

(1) A 10-percent stock dividend is declared when the market price of Lipscomb Corporation's common stock is $60 per share.

(2) A two-for-one stock split is declared, and the par value of the common stock is reduced from $10 to $5 per share. The new shares are issued immediately.

(3) Ten thousand shares of Lipscomb Corporation's common stock are purchased on the open market for $50 per share and held as treasury stock.

(4) Ten thousand shares of Lipscomb Corporation's common stock are purchased on the open market for $30 per share and held as treasury stock.

(5) The shares acquired in **(3)** are sold for $70 per share.

(6) The shares acquired in **(3)** are sold for $40 per share.

(7) The shares acquired in **(3)** are sold for $30 per share.

(8) Options to acquire 10,000 shares of Lipscomb Corporation stock are exercised by officers for $15 per share.

(9) Same as **(8)**, except that the exercise price is $50 per share.

(10) Convertible bonds with a book value of $300,000 and a market value of $340,000 are exchanged for 10,000 shares of common stock having a market value of $34 per share. No gain or loss is recognized on the conversion of bonds.

(11) Same as **(10)**, except that gain or loss is recognized on the conversion of bonds into stock. Ignore income tax effects.

c Using the results from **b**, summarize the transactions and events that result in a reduction in:

(1) total book value.

(2) book value per share.

496

31 (Case introducing earnings-per-share calculations for companies with a complicated capital structure.) The Layton Ball Corporation has a relatively complicated capital structure. In addition to common shares, it has issued stock options, warrants, and convertible bonds. Exhibit 12.7 summarizes some pertinent information about these items. Net income for the year 1982 is $9,500, and the income tax rate used in computing income tax expense is 40 percent of pretax income.

Exhibit 12.7
Layton Ball Corporation
Information on Capital Structure
for Earnings-per-Share Calculation
(*Problem 31*)

Assume the following data about the capital structure and earnings for the Layton Ball Corporation for the year 1982:

Number of Common Shares Outstanding Throughout 1982	2,500 shares
Market Price per Common Share Throughout 1982	$25
Options Outstanding During 1982:	
Number of Shares Issuable on Exercise of Options	1,000 shares
Exercise Warrants Price per Share	$15
Warrants Outstanding During 1982:	
Number of Shares Issuable on Exercise of Warrants	2,000 shares
Exercise Price per Share	$30
Convertible Bonds Outstanding:	
Number (Issued in December 1968)	100 bonds
Proceeds per Bond at Time of Issue (= par value)	$1,000
Shares of Common Issuable on Conversion (per bond)	10 shares
Coupon Rate (per year)	$4\frac{1}{6}\%$

---

a First, ignore all items of capital except for the common shares. Calculate earnings per common share.

b In past years, employees have been issued options to purchase shares of stock. Exhibit 12.7 indicates that the price of the common stock throughout 1982 was $25, but that the stock options could be exercised at any time for $15 each. The holder of an option is allowed to surrender it along with $15 cash and receive one share in return. Thus the number of shares would be increased, which would decrease the earnings-per-share figure. The company would, however, have more cash. We could assume that the company would use the cash to go out and buy outstanding shares for the treasury, which would reduce the number of shares outstanding and increase earnings per share. Assume that the holders of warrants were to tender their warrants, along with $15 each, to purchase shares. Assume that the company would use the cash to purchase shares for the treasury at a price of $25 each. Compute a new earnings-per-share figure. (Treasury shares are *not* counted in the denominator of the earnings-per-share calculation.)

c Exhibit 12.7 indicates that there are also warrants outstanding in the hands of the public. Anyone who owns such a warrant is allowed to turn in that warrant along with $30 cash and to purchase one share. If the warrants are exercised, then there would be more shares outstanding, which would reduce earnings per share. The company would, however, have more cash, which it could use to purchase shares for the treasury, reducing the number of shares outstanding. Assume that all holders of warrants were to exercise them. Assume that the company were to use the cash to purchase outstanding shares for the treasury. Compute a new earnings-per-share figure. (Ignore the information about options and the calculations in part **b** at this point.)

d There are convertible bonds outstanding. A holder of a convertible bond is entitled to trade in that bond for 10 shares. If a bond is converted, the number of shares would increase, which would tend to reduce earnings per share. On the other hand, the company would not have to pay interest and thus would have no interest expense on the bond, because it would no longer be outstanding. This would tend to increase income and earnings per share. Assume that all holders of convertible bonds were to convert their bonds into shares. Compute a new net income figure (do not forget income tax effects on income of the interest saved) and a new earnings-per-share figure. (Ignore the information about options and warrants and the calculations in parts **b** and **c** at this point.)

e Now consider all the above calculations. Which sets of assumptions from parts **b**, **c**, and **d** would lead to the lowest possible earnings per share when they are all made simultaneously? Compute a new earnings per share under the most restrictive set of assumptions about reductions in earnings per share.

f Accountants publish several earnings-per-share figures for companies with complicated capital structures and complicated events during the year. *The Wall Street Journal,* however, publishes only one figure in its daily columns (where it reports the price-earnings ratio—the price of a share of stock divided by its earnings per share). Which of the figures computed above for earnings per share do you think should be reported by *The Wall Street Journal* as *the* earnings-per-share figure? Why?

Chapter 13 *Long-Term Investments in Corporate Securities*

For a variety of reasons, corporations often acquire the capital stock of other corporations. For example, a corporation may temporarily hold excess cash that is not needed in regular operations. Rather than permit the cash to remain idle in its bank account, the corporation may invest in the common stock of another corporation. Relatively short-term investments of excess cash in corporate securities are usually classified as Marketable Securities and are shown in the Current Assets section of the balance sheet. Chapter 7 discusses the accounting for short-term investments in marketable securities.

A corporation may acquire another corporation's capital stock for some more long-term purpose. For example, a firm may acquire shares of capital stock of a major raw materials supplier to help assure continued availability of raw materials. Or, a firm may wish to diversify its operations by acquiring a controlling interest in an established firm in some new area of business. Long-term investments in corporate securities are typically classified on the asset side of the balance sheet in a separate section called "Investments." The accounting for long-term investments is discussed in both Chapter 7 and this chapter.

Types of Long-Term Investments

The accounting for long-term investments depends on the purpose of the investment and on the percentage of voting stock that one corporation owns of another. Refer to Figure 13.1. Three types of long-term investments can be identified:

499

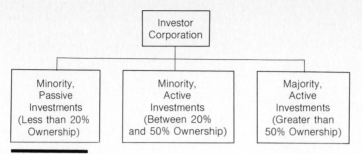

Figure 13.1
Types of Intercorporate Investments in Securities

1 Minority, Passive Investments—Shares of capital stock of another corporation are viewed as a good long-term investment and are acquired for the dividends and capital gains (increases in the market price of the shares) anticipated from owning the shares. The percentage owned of the other corporation's shares is not so large that the acquiring company can control or exert significant influence over the other company. Generally accepted accounting principles view investments of less than 20 percent of the voting stock of another company as minority, passive investments, in most cases.[1]

2 Minority, Active Investments—Shares of another corporation are acquired so that the acquiring corporation can exert significant influence over the other company's activities. This significant influence is usually at a broad policy-making level through representation on the other corporation's board of directors. Because the shares of capital stock of most publicly-held corporations are widely dispersed among numerous individuals, many of whom do not vote their shares, it is possible to exert significant influence over another corporation with ownership of less than a majority of the voting stock. Generally accepted accounting principles view investments of between 20 percent and 50 percent of the voting stock of another company as minority, active investments "unless evidence indicates that significant influence cannot be exercised."[2]

3 Majority, Active Investments—Shares of another corporation are acquired so that the acquiring corporation can control the other company. This control is typically at both the broad policy-making level and at the day-to-day operational level. Ownership of more than 50 percent of the voting stock of another company implies an ability to control, unless there is evidence to the contrary.[3]

---

[1] Accounting Principles Board, *Opinion No. 18,* "The Equity Method of Accounting for Investments in Common Stock," 1971.

[2] Accounting Principles Board, *Opinion No. 18,* "The Equity Method of Accounting for Investments in Common Stock," 1971; Financial Accounting Standards Board, *Interpretation No. 35,* "Criteria for Applying the Equity Method of Accounting for Investments in Common Stock," 1981.

[3] A corporation may be unable to exercise its control over another corporation, despite the ownership of a majority of the voting stock, if the other corporation is in bankruptcy proceedings and under the control of a court.

500

The accounting for these three types of investments is discussed in the sections which follow. Throughout the chapter, we call the acquiring corporation P, for *purchaser* or for *parent,* depending on the context, whereas S stands for *seller* or for *subsidiary.*

Minority, Passive Investments

If a firm does not own a sufficient percentage of the voting stock of another corporation to control or significantly influence it (assumed to be 20 percent or more under generally accepted accounting principles), the management of the investment involves two activities: (1) awaiting the receipt of dividends and (2) deciding when the investment should be sold for a capital gain or loss. Minority, passive investments must be accounted for by using the *lower-of-cost-or-market method.* Chapter 7 describes and illustrates the lower-of-cost-or-market method for both marketable securities classified as Current Assets (that is, those planned to be sold within a short period when cash is needed) and minority, passive investments classified as Investments (that is, those held for some long-term purpose). To summarize the lower-of-cost-or-market method for minority, passive investments:

1 Investments are initially recorded at acquisition cost.
2 Dividends received or receivable each period are recognized as dividend revenue.
3 At the end of each period, the market value of the portfolio of noncurrent marketable equity securities is compared to the acquisition cost of the portfolio. The amount shown on the balance sheet for these investments is the lower-of-acquisition-cost or current-market value.

Assume that a portfolio of marketable equity securities held as long-term investments had an acquisition cost of $100,000. The portfolio has a market value of $95,000 at the end of a firm's first year of operations. The following entry would be made at year-end:

Unrealized Holding Loss on Valuation of Marketable Equity Investments 5,000
   Allowance for Excess of Cost of Investments over Market Value   5,000

The account debited, Unrealized Holding Loss on Valuation of Marketable Equity Investments, is included in the shareholders' equity section of the balance sheet, typically between Additional Paid-in Capital and Retained Earnings. See Exhibit 12.1 on page 472. The unrealized loss is not included in the calculation of net income for the period. The suggested rationale is that these investments are acquired for their long-term capital gains (plus dividends). Short-term changes in market value, therefore, should not affect periodic earnings. The account credited, Allowance for Excess of Cost of Investments over Market Value, is a contra account to the Investments in Securities account. Using it permits the investments to be shown at the lower of cost or market while retaining the amount of acquisition cost in the accounts.

Subsequent increases in price up to, but not exceeding, the original cost of the investment are debited to the asset contra and credited to the balance sheet shareholders' equity account for unrealized losses.

4 When a particular minority, passive investment is sold, the difference between the selling price and the acquisition cost of the investment is recognized as a gain or loss. Thus, all changes in market value between the time an investment is acquired and when it is sold are reflected in net income in the period of sale. The net amount shown for investments on the asset side of the balance sheet reflects the *potential* future holding loss on the portfolio of such investments.

You may find it helpful to review the illustration of the lower-of-cost-or-market method for minority, passive investments in Chapter 7.

Minority, Active Investments

Judgment is required in ascertaining when significant influence can be exercised over another company when less than a majority of the voting stock is owned. For the sake of uniformity, generally accepted accounting principles presume that one company can significantly influence another company when 20 percent or more of the voting stock of the other company is owned. Significant influence may be present when less than 20 percent is owned, but in these cases management must demonstrate to the independent accountants that it exists.

Minority, active investments, those where ownership is between 20 percent and 50 percent, must be accounted for using the *equity method.* Under the equity method, the firm owning shares in another firm recognizes as revenue (expense) each period its share of the net income (loss) of the other firm. Dividends received from S are not recognized as income but as a return of capital. In the discusssion that follows, we designate the firm owning shares as P and the firm whose shares are owned as S.

Equity Method: Rationale

The rationale for the equity method when significant influence is present can be best understood by considering the financial statement effects of using the lower-of-cost-or-market method in these circumstances. Under the lower-of-cost-or-market method, P recognizes income or loss on the income statement only when it receives a dividend or sells all or part of the investment. Suppose, as often happens, that S follows a policy of financing its own growing operations through retention of earnings and consistently declares dividends significantly less than its net income. The market price of S's shares will probably increase to reflect the retention of assets generated by earnings. Under the lower-of-cost-or-market method, P will continue to show the investment at acquisition cost and P's only reported income from the in-

502

vestment will be the modest dividends received. P, because of its ownership percentage, can influence the dividend policy of S and thereby the amount of income recognized under the lower-of-cost-or-market method. Under these conditions, the lower-of-cost-or-market method may not reasonably reflect the earnings of S generated under P's influence. The equity method is designed to provide a better measure of a firm's earnings and of its investment when, because of its ownership interest, significant influence can be exerted over the operations of another firm.

Equity Method: Procedures

Under the equity method, the initial purchase of an investment is recorded at acquisition cost, the same as under the lower-of-cost-or-market method. Company P treats as revenue, each period, its proportionate share of the periodic earnings, not the dividends, of Company S. Dividends declared by S are then treated by P as a reduction in its Investment in S.

Suppose that P acquires 30 percent of the outstanding shares of S for $600,000. The entry to record the acquisition would be:

(1) Investment in Stock of S.	600,000	
Cash		600,000
Investment made in 30 percent of Company S.		

Between the time of the acquisition and the end of P's next accounting period, S reports income of $80,000. P, using the equity method, would record:

(2) Investment in Stock of S.	24,000	
Revenue from Investments		24,000
To record 30 percent of income earned by investee, accounted for using the equity method. Revenue account title often used in practice is Equity in Earnings of Unconsolidated Affiliates.		

If S declares a dividend of $30,000 to holders of common stock, P would be entitled to receive $9,000 and would record:

(3) Dividends Receivable.	9,000	
Investment in Stock of S		9,000
To record dividends receivable from investee, accounted for using the equity method, and the resulting reduction in the investment account.		

Notice that the credit is to the Investment in S account. P records income earned by S as an *increase* in investment. The dividend becomes a return of capital or a *decrease* in investment.[4]

Suppose that S subsequently reports earnings of $100,000 and also declares dividends of $40,000. P's entries would be:

(4) Investment in Stock of S.	30,000	
Revenue from Investments		30,000
(5) Dividends Receivable.	12,000	
Investment in Stock of S		12,000
To record revenue and dividends from investee, accounted for using equity method.		

P's Investment in S account now has a balance of $633,000 as follows:

**Investment in
Stock of S**

(1)	600,000	9,000 (3)
(2)	24,000	12,000 (5)
(4)	30,000	
Bal.	633,000	

If P now sells one-fourth of its shares for $165,000, P's entry to record the sale would be:

Cash	165,000	
Investment in Stock of S.		158,250
Gain on Sale of Investment in S		6,750
($\frac{1}{4}$ × $633,000 = $158,250.)		

The equity method as described above is simple enough to use. To make financial reports that use the equity method more realistic, generally accepted accounting principles require some modification of the entries under certain circumstances, described next.

---

[4] Students often have difficulty understanding journal entry (3), particularly the credit by the investor when a dividend is declared by the investee company. The transactions and entries are analogous to an individual's ordinary savings account at a local bank. Assume that you put $600,000 in a savings account, that later interest of 4 percent (or $24,000) is added by the bank to the account, and that still later you ask the bank to withdraw $9,000 from the savings account, depositing the $9,000 in your checking account. Journal entries (1)–(3) in the text could be recorded for these three events, with slight changes in the account titles: Investment in S changes to Savings Account, Revenue from Investments changes to Interest Revenue, and Dividends Receivable changes to Cash in Bank. The cash withdrawal reduces the amount invested in the savings account. Similarly, the declaration of a cash dividend by an investee company accounted for with the equity method reduces the investor's investment in the company.

504

Even though S does not declare all of its earnings in dividends, P reports its proportionate share of S's earnings as income. But this income to P is not currently taxable. Consequently, there will sometimes be an entry in the deferred tax account. Calculating the amount of the deferred tax charge presents issues too complex for this introductory text.

An additional complication in using the equity method arises when the acquisition cost of P's shares exceeds P's proportionate share of the book value of the net assets (= assets minus liabilities), or shareholders' equity, of S at the date of acquisition. For example, assume that P acquires 25 percent of the stock of S for $400,000, when the total shareholders' equity of S is $1 million. The excess of P's cost over book value acquired is $150,000 (= $400,000 − .25 × $1,000,000) and generally represents *goodwill.* Goodwill must be amortized over a period not greater than 40 years.[5] Accounting for goodwill, including its amortization, is discussed later in the appendix to this chapter.

On the balance sheet, an investment accounted for on the equity method is shown in the Investments section. The amount shown will generally be equal to the acquisition cost of the shares plus P's share of S's undistributed earnings since the date the shares were acquired. On the income statement, P shows its share of S's income as a revenue each period. (The financial statements of the investee, S, are not affected by the accounting method used by the investor, P.)

Equity Method and the Statement of Changes in Financial Position

When Company P uses the lower-of-cost-or-market method to account for its investment in Company S, all dividend revenues recognized in computing net income also produce working capital. No adjustment to net income is therefore required in calculating Working Capital Provided by Operations.

Accounting for investments using the equity method requires, however, an adjustment to net income to compute Working Capital Provided by Operations. Suppose that Company P prepares its financial statements at the end of a year during which transactions (1)–(5), above, occurred. P's revenue from its investment in S is $54,000. This amount is the sum of the revenue recognized in transactions (2) and (4). P's income (ignoring income tax effects) increased $54,000 because of its investment. However, P's working capital increased by only $21,000 [transactions (3) and (5)] as a result of S's dividend declarations. Consequently, there must be a *subtraction* from net income of $33,000 (= $54,000 − $21,000) in computing Working Capital Provided by Operations to show that working capital did not increase by as much as the amount of revenue recognized under the equity method.

In preparing P's statement of changes in financial position using the T-account method, the following change in a noncurrent asset account would have to be explained:

---

[5] Accounting Principles Board, *Opinion No. 17,* "Intangible Assets," 1970.

505

**Investment in
Stock of S**

Bal.	0	
Bal.	633,000	

The entries to explain this debit change of $633,000 would be:

Investment in Stock of S   600,000
   Working Capital (Use—Acquisition of Investment)   600,000
To recognize use of funds for an investment in a noncurrent asset.

Investment in Stock of S   33,000
   Working Capital (Subtraction—Undistributed Income Under Equity Method) . .   33,000
To recognize that working capital was not increased by the full amount of reve-
nue recognized under the equity method.

Keep in mind that these two entries are not formally made in the accounting records, but are made only in the work sheet used for preparing the statement of changes in financial position.

Equity Method Illustrated

The equity method can be illustrated using information for General Products Company found in Appendix A. The balance sheet (Exhibit A.2) indicates that investments were $1,691 million on December 31, 1981, and $1,820 million on December 31, 1982. Note 12 to the financial statements indicates that the investment in General Products Credit Corporation, a wholly-owned, unconsolidated finance affiliate, is included in investments on the balance sheet. Because General Products Company owns all of General Products Credit Corporation's outstanding common stock, but chooses not to consolidate it, the equity method of accounting is used.

The change in the Investment in General Products Credit Corporation account during 1982 is as follows (amounts in millions):

Investment in General Products Credit Corporation, December 31, 1981 (Note 12) $817
Plus: Equity in Earnings of General Products Credit Corporation for 1982 (Note 4)   115
     Additional Investments (change in capital stock account of General Products Credit
     Corporation (Note 12))   92

Less: Dividends Received (Note 12) . . . .   (93)

Investment in General Products Credit Corporation, December 31, 1982 (Note 12) $931

Income generated from this investment totaled $115 million during 1982. However, only $93 million was received in cash. Thus, the statement of changes in financial position must show a subtraction of $22 (= $115 − $93) million for income that did not produce working capital. Also included among other uses of working capital will be $92 million for additional investments in the credit subsidiary. (For an explanation as to why a subsidiary would pay a dividend of $93 million and require the parent to reinvest $92 million immediately, see Authors' Note 61, in Appendix A.)

Majority, Active Investments

When one firm, P, owns more than 50 percent of the voting stock of another company, S, P can control the activities of S. This control can be both at a broad policy-making level and at a day-to-day operational level. The majority investor in this case is called the *parent* and the majority-owned company is called the *subsidiary*. Generally accepted accounting principles permit majority-owned active investments to be accounted for in one of two ways. In most cases, the financial statements of the majority-owned *subsidiary* are combined, or *consolidated,* with those of the parent. In some instances, however, consolidated financial statements are not prepared. Instead, the investment is reported using the equity method. Whether consolidated statements are prepared or the equity method is used depends on the consolidation policy of the firm, which is discussed later in this section.

Reasons for Legally Separate Corporations

There are many reasons why a business firm prefers to operate as a group of legally separate corporations, rather than as a single legal entity. From the standpoint of the parent company, the more important reasons for maintaining legally separate subsidiary companies include the following:

1 To reduce the financial risk. Separate corporations may be used for mining raw materials, transporting them to a manufacturing plant, producing the product, and selling the finished product to the public. If any one part of the total process proves to be unprofitable or inefficient, losses from insolvency will fall only on the owners and creditors of the one subsidiary corporation.

2 To meet more effectively the requirements of state corporation laws and tax legislation. If an organization does business in a number of states, it is often faced with overlapping and inconsistent taxation, regulations, and requirements. Organizing separate corporations to conduct the operations in the various states may be more economical.

3 To expand or diversify with a minimum of capital investment. A firm may absorb another company by acquiring a controlling interest in its voting stock. The result may be accomplished with a substantially smaller capital investment, as well as with less difficulty, inconvenience, and risk, than if a new plant had been constructed or the firm had geared up for a new line of business.

Purpose of Consolidated Statements

For a variety of reasons, then, a single *economic entity* may exist in the form of a parent and several legally separate subsidiaries. (The General Electric Company, for example, consists of about 150 legally separate companies.) A consolidation of the financial statements of the parent and each of its subsidiaries presents the results of operations, financial position, and changes in financial position of an affiliated group of companies under the control of a parent, essentially as if the group of companies were a single entity. The parent and each subsidiary are legally separate entities, but they operate as one centrally controlled *economic* entity. Consolidated financial statements generally provide more useful information to the shareholders of the parent corporation than would separate financial statements of the parent as investor and each subsidiary as an operating company.

Consolidated financial statements also generally provide more useful information than does use of the equity method. The parent, because of its voting interest, can effectively control the use of all of the subsidiary's assets. Consolidation of the individual assets and equities of both the parent and the subsidiary provides a more realistic picture of the operations and financial position of the single economic entity.

In a legal sense, consolidated statements merely supplement, and do not replace, the separate statements of the individual corporations, although it is common practice to present only the consolidated statements in published annual reports.

Consolidation Policy

Consolidated financial statements are generally prepared when all of the following three criteria are met:

1 The parent owns more than 50 percent of the voting stock of the subsidiary.
2 There are no important restrictions on the ability of the parent to exercise control of the subsidiary.
3 The asset and equity structure of the subsidiary is not significantly different from that of the parent.

Ownership of more than 50 percent of the subsidiary's voting stock implies an ability to exert control over the activities of the subsidiary. For example, the parent can control the subsidiary's corporate policies and dividend declarations. There may be situations, however, where control of the subsidiary's activities cannot be carried out effectively, despite the ownership of a majority of the voting stock. For example, the subsidiary may be located in a foreign country that has severely restricted the withdrawal of funds from that country. Or the subsidiary may be in bankruptcy and under the control of a court-appointed group of trustees. In these cases, the financial statements of the subsidiary probably will not be consolidated with those of the parent. When the parent owns more than 50 percent of the shares and can exercise control, but consolidated statements are not prepared, then the equity method must be used.

If the asset and equity structure of the subsidiary is significantly different from that of the parent, the subsidiary's financial statements are frequently not consolidated with those of the parent and the equity method is used. For example, a consolidated statement might not be prepared if the parent is a manufacturing concern with heavy investments in property, plant, and equipment, whereas the subsidiary is a finance or insurance company with large holdings of cash, receivables, and marketable securities. The presentation of consolidated financial statements of corporations with significantly different asset and equity structures is sometimes thought to submerge potentially important information about the individual corporations. This is particularly true when the assets of the subsidiary are not, by law, fully available for use by the parent, such as when the subsidiary is a bank or an insurance company.

Example 1 American Telephone and Telegraph Company (AT&T) conducts its activities through many subsidiaries organized under the laws of various states (for example, Illinois Bell, Southern Bell, Pacific Telephone and Telegraph). AT&T owns all, or a significant percentage, of the common shares of each of these subsidiaries. It can, therefore, exert control over the activities of the subsidiaries much the same as if the subsidiaries were branches or divisions. AT&T often raises capital in the debt and equity markets and distributes it to the subsidiaries. In evaluating the operations and financial position of AT&T, it is more useful to consider all of the assets under its control, not just those of the parent, many of whose assets are investments. Consolidated statements are also easier to comprehend than separate statements for each of its many operating subsidiaries. AT&T also owns Western Electric, the manufacturer of most of AT&T's telephone equipment. Because Western Electric is a manufacturing company (whereas most of the other subsidiaries operate telephone systems), AT&T chooses not to consolidate Western Electric, but to use the equity method for it.

Example 2 General Motors, General Electric, and Westinghouse, among others, have wholly owned finance subsidiaries. These subsidiaries make many of their loans to customers who wish to purchase the products of the parent company. The financial statements of these subsidiaries are not consolidated with those of the parent company. The assets of these subsidiaries are largely receivables. It is argued that statement readers might be misled as to the relative liquidity of these firms if consolidated statements were prepared and the assets of the parent—largely noncurrent manufacturing plant and equipment—were combined with the more liquid assets of the finance subsidiary.

Example 3 Sears, Roebuck & Co. and J. C. Penney Company are large retailers. Each has organized a separate subsidiary to finance customers' purchases and another separate subsidiary to sell insurance. Sears consolidates both its finance subsidiary and its insurance subsidiary. Penney's consolidates neither, but uses the equity method for both.

Example 4 A major mining corporation owns a mining subsidiary in South America. The government of the country enforces stringent control over cash payments outside the country. The company is not able to control the use of all the assets, despite the ownership of a majority of the voting shares. Therefore, it does not prepare consolidated statements with the subsidiary.

Disclosure of Consolidation Policy The summary of significant accounting principles in financial statements includes a statement about the consolidation policy of the parent. If a significant majority-owned subsidiary is not consolidated, then its financial statements are often included in the notes to the financial statements. For example, the note on page 632 for the General Products Company indicates that all significant majority-owned subsidiaries are consolidated, with the exception of its finance company. For this subsidiary, the equity method is required and used. The financial statements of the finance company are themselves presented in Note 12 on pages 644 and 646.

Understanding Consolidated Statements

This section discusses three concepts essential for understanding consolidated financial statements:

1 The need for intercompany eliminations.
2 The meaning of consolidated net income.
3 The nature of the external minority interest.

Need for Intercompany Eliminations State corporation laws typically require each legally separate corporation to maintain its own set of books. Thus, during the accounting period, the accounting records of each corporation will record transactions of that entity with all other entities (both affiliated and non-affiliated). At the end of the period, each corporation will prepare its own set of financial statements. The consolidation of these financial statements basically involves summing the amounts for various financial statement items across the separate company statements. The amounts resulting from the summation must be adjusted, however, to eliminate double counting resulting from intercompany transactions. Consolidated financial statements are intended to reflect the results that would be achieved if the affiliated group of companies were a single company. Consolidated financial statements reflect transactions only between the group of consolidated companies and other entities.

The eliminations to remove intercompany transactions are typically made on a consolidation work sheet and are not recorded on the books of any of the legal entities being consolidated. The consolidated financial statements are then prepared directly from the work sheet. There are generally no separate books for the consolidated entity.

To illustrate the need for, and the nature of, elimination entries, refer to the data for Company P and Company S in Exhibit 13.1. Column (1) shows the balance sheet and income statement data for Company P taken from its separate company books. Column (2) shows similar data for Company S. Column (3) sums the amounts from Columns (1) and (2). The amounts in Column (3) include the effects of several

510

Exhibit 13.1
Illustrative Data for
Preparation of Consolidated
Financial Statements

	Single-Company Statements		
CONDENSED BALANCE SHEETS FOR DECEMBER 31, 1982	**Company P (1)**	**Company S (2)**	**Combined (3) = (1) + (2)**
Assets:			
Accounts Receivable	$ 200,000	$ 25,000	$ 225,000
Investment in Stock of Company S (at equity)	705,000	—	705,000
Other Assets	2,150,000	975,000	3,125,000
Total Assets	$3,055,000	$1,000,000	$4,055,000
Equities:			
Accounts Payable	$ 75,000	$ 15,000	$ 90,000
Other Liabilities	70,000	280,000	350,000
Common Stock	2,500,000	500,000	3,000,000
Retained Earnings	410,000	205,000	615,000
Total Equities	$3,055,000	$1,000,000	$4,055,000
CONDENSED INCOME STATEMENT FOR 1982			
Revenues:			
Sales	$ 900,000	$ 250,000	$1,150,000
Equity in Earnings of Company S	48,000	—	48,000
Total Revenues	$ 948,000	$ 250,000	$1,198,000
Expenses:			
Cost of Goods Sold (excluding depreciation)	$ 440,000	$ 80,000	$ 520,000
Depreciation Expense	120,000	50,000	170,000
Administrative Expenses	80,000	40,000	120,000
Income Tax Expense	104,000	32,000	136,000
Total Expenses	$ 744,000	$ 202,000	$ 946,000
Net Income	$ 204,000	$ 48,000	$ 252,000
Dividend Declarations	50,000	13,000	63,000
Increase in Retained Earnings for the Year	$ 154,000	$ 35,000	$ 189,000

intercompany items and, therefore, do not represent the correct amounts for *consolidated* assets, equities, revenues, or expenses.

For example, separate company records indicate that $12,000 of Company S's accounts receivable represent amounts payable by Company P. The funds underlying this transaction are effectively counted twice in Column (3): once as part of Accounts Receivable on Company S's books and a second time as Cash (Other Assets) on Company P's books. Also, the liability shown on Company P's books is included in the combined amount for Accounts Payable in Column (3), even though

511

the amount is not payable to an entity external to the consolidated group. To eliminate double counting on the asset side and to report Accounts Payable at the amount payable to external entities, an elimination entry must be made to reduce the amounts for Accounts Receivable and Accounts Payable in Column (3) by $12,000.

To take a more complex example, Company P's balance sheet shows an asset, Investment in Stock of Company S. The subsidiary's balance sheet shows its individual assets. When the two balance sheets are added together in Column (3), the sum shows both Company P's investment in Company S's assets and the assets themselves. Company P's account, Investment in Stock of Company S, must therefore be eliminated from the sum of the balance sheets. Because the consolidated balance sheet must maintain the accounting equation, corresponding eliminations must be made on the right-hand, or equities, side in this case.

To understand the eliminations from the right-hand side of the balance sheet, recall that the right-hand side shows the sources of the firm's financing. Company S is financed by creditors (liabilities) and by owners (shareholders' equity). In this case, Company P owns 100 percent of Company S's voting shares. Thus, the assets on the consolidated balance sheet of the single economic entity are financed by the creditors of both companies and by Company P's shareholders. That is, the equities of the consolidated entity are the liabilities of both companies but the shareholders' equity of Company P alone. If the shareholders' equity accounts of Company S were added to those of Company P, then the financing from Company P's shareholders would be counted twice (once on the parent's books and once on the subsidiary's books). Hence, when Company P's investment account is eliminated from the sum of the two companies' assets, the accounting equation is maintained by eliminating the shareholders' equity accounts of Company S.

Similarly, certain intercompany items must be eliminated from the sum of income statement accounts, so that the operating performance of the consolidated entity can be meaningfully presented. Company P's accounts show Equity in Earnings of Company S of $48,000. Company S's records show individual revenues and expenses which net to $48,000. If the revenues and expenses of the two companies were merely summed, as is done in Column (3) of Exhibit 13.1, the earnings of Company S would be double-counted. The account, Equity in Earnings of Company S, must, therefore, be eliminated in preparing consolidated statements (illustrated later in the chapter).

Another example of an intercompany item involves intercompany sales of inventory. Separate company records indicate that Company S sold merchandise to Company P for $40,000 during the year. None of this inventory remains in Company P's inventory on December 31, 1982. The merchandise inventory items sold are included in Sales Revenue on both Company S's books (sale to Company P) and on Company P's books (sale to external entity). Thus, sales are overstated from the standpoint of the consolidated entity. Likewise, Cost of Goods Sold of both companies includes the separate company cost of the goods sold. To eliminate double counting, the intercompany sale from Company S to Company P must be eliminated (illustrated later).

To complete the above example, suppose that the subsidiary sells to the parent but that the parent has not yet sold the goods to the public. The subsidiary will have

512

recorded profits on the sale, but from the standpoint of the overall economic entity, no profits for shareholders have actually been realized, because the items are still in the inventory of the overall economic entity. Consequently, profits from the subsidiary's sales to the parent, that have not been realized by subsequent sales to outsiders, are eliminated from consolidated net income and balance sheet amounts. The consolidated income statement attempts to show sales, expenses, and net income figures that report the results of operations of the group of companies as though they were a single company.

Consolidated Income The amount of consolidated net income for a period is the same as the amount that the parent would show on its separate company books from applying the equity method. That is, consolidated net income is equal to:

$$
\begin{array}{llll}
\text{Parent Company's} & & \text{Parent Company's} & & \text{Profit (or Plus Loss)} \\
\text{Net Income from} & + & \text{Share of Subsidiary's} & - & \text{on Intercompany} \\
\text{Its Own Activities} & & \text{Net Income} & & \text{Transactions.}
\end{array}
$$

The principal difference between the consolidated income statement and the income statement, where the subsidiary is accounted for using the equity method, is the components of the income presented. When the equity method is used for an unconsolidated subsidiary, the parent's share of the subsidiary's net income minus gain (or plus loss) on intercompany transactions is shown on a single line, Equity in Earnings of Unconsolidated Subsidiary. When a consolidated income statement is prepared, the individual revenues and expenses of the subsidiary (less intercompany adjustments) are combined with those of the parent, and the account, Equity in Earnings of Unconsolidated Subsidiary, shown on the parent's books, is eliminated.[6]

External Minority Interest in Consolidated Subsidiary In many cases, the parent will not own 100 percent of the voting stock of a consolidated subsidiary. The owners of the remaining shares of voting stock are called *external minority shareholders,* or the *minority interest.*[7] These shareholders continue to have a proportionate interest in the net assets (= total assets minus total liabilities) of the subsidiary as shown on the subsidiary's separate corporate records. They also have a proportionate interest in the earnings of the subsidiary.

An issue in the generally accepted accounting principles for consolidated statements is whether the statements should show only the parent's share of the assets and liabilities of the subsidiary or whether they should show all of the subsidiary's assets and liabilities along with the minority interests in them. The generally accepted accounting principle is to show all of the assets and liabilities of the subsidiary, because the parent, with its controlling voting interest, can effectively direct the use of all the assets and liabilities, not merely an amount equal to the parent's percent-

---

[6] The equity method is sometimes referred to as a "one-line consolidation" because the individual revenues and expenses of the subsidiary are netted in the one account, Equity in Earnings of Unconsolidated Subsidiary.

[7] Do not confuse this minority interest in a consolidated subsidiary with a firm's own minority investments, discussed earlier. The minority *interest* belongs to others outside the parent and its economic entity. The parent's minority *investments* are merely those for which the parent owns less than 50 percent of the shares.

age of ownership. The consolidated balance sheet and income statement in these instances must, however, disclose the interest of the minority shareholders in the subsidiary that has been consolidated.

The amount of the minority interest shown on the balance sheet is generally the result of multiplying the common stockholders' equity of the subsidiary by the minority's percentage of ownership. For example, if the common shareholders' equity (or assets minus liabilities) of a consolidated subsidiary totals $500,000 and the minority owns 20 percent of the common stock, then the minority interest shown on the consolidated balance sheet is $100,000 (= .20 × $500,000).

The minority interest is typically presented among the equities on the consolidated balance sheet between the liabilities and shareholders' equity. See, for example, the General Products Company's consolidated balance sheet in Exhibit A.2 on page 628. Note that "Minority Interest" is shown among the liabilities but is not clearly labeled as one. This presentation is typical of many published financial statements. We think that the right-hand side of the balance sheet should contain only liabilities and owners' equity items, so that the minority interest should be classified as one or the other. The minority interest does not meet the criteria to be a liability discussed in Chapter 10, because there is no maturity date. We therefore prefer to classify it as part of owners' equity.

The amount of the minority interest in the subsidiary's income, shown on the consolidated income statement, is generally the result of multiplying the *subsidiary's* net income by the minority's percentage of ownership. The consolidated income is allocated to show the portions applicable to the parent company and the portion of the subsidiary's income applicable to the minority interest. Refer again to General Products Company's consolidated income statement, shown in Exhibit A.1. Notice the deduction of $21 million for the "Minority Interest in Earnings of Consolidated Affiliates" before the consolidated net income figure for 1982. The consolidated net income includes only that portion of net income of subsidiary companies allocable to the shareholders of General Products Company. Typically, the minority interest in the subsidiary's income is shown as a deduction in calculating consolidated net income.

The minority interest share of earnings is deducted in calculating consolidated net income. This deduction did not require the use of working capital. Consequently, there must be an addback to derive working capital provided by operations. General Products Company shows the addback of $21 million in its statement of changes in financial position, Exhibit A.3, as "Minority Interest in Earnings of Consolidated Affiliate."

Limitations of Consolidated Statements

The consolidated statements do not replace those of individual corporations; rather, they supplement those statements and aid in their interpretation. Creditors must rely on the resources of one corporation and may be misled if forced to rely entirely on a consolidated statement that combines the data of a company in good financial condition with those of one verging on insolvency. Dividends can legally be declared only from the retained earnings of one corporation. Where the parent company does not own all of the shares of the subsidiary, the outside or minority stockholders can judge the dividend constraints, both legal and financial, only by an inspection of the subsidiary's statements.

Preparing Consolidated Financial Statements

This section illustrates the preparation of consolidated financial statements for Company P and Company S. Knowing how to construct consolidated financial statements is not essential for learning how to interpret and to analyze them. Nevertheless, we think it helps.

Data for the Illustration

The single-company financial statements of Company P and Company S are shown in Exhibit 13.1 on page 511. The following additional information is to be considered in preparing the consolidated financial statements.

1 Company P acquired 100 percent of the outstanding shares of Company S for $650,000 cash on January 1, 1979. At the time of acquisition, the book value of the shareholders' equity of Company S was $650,000, comprised of the following balances:

Company S, January 1, 1979	
Common Stock	$500,000
Retained Earnings	150,000
Total Shareholders' Equity	$650,000

Company P made the following journal entry on its books at the time of acquisition:

Investment in Stock of Company S	650,000	
Cash		650,000

2 Company P records its investment in the shares of Company S using the equity method. The increase in Retained Earnings of Company S since January 1, 1979, the date of acquisition, has been $55,000 (= $205,000 − $150,000). This increase has been reflected in the Investment in Company S account on Company P's books: $705,000 = $650,000 + $55,000.

3 At December 31, 1982, $12,000 of Company S's accounts receivable represent amounts payable by Company P.

4 During 1982, Company S sold merchandise to Company P for $40,000. None of that merchandise remains in Company P's inventory as of December 31, 1982.

515

Exhibit 13.2
Work Sheet to Derive Consolidated Financial Statements for Company P and Company S Based on Data from Preclosing Trial Balances

Trial Balance Accounts	Company P Debit	Company P Credit	Company S Debit	Company S Credit	Adjustments and Eliminations Debit	Adjustments and Eliminations Credit	P and S Consolidated Debit	P and S Consolidated Credit
Accounts Receivable	$ 200,000		$ 25,000			(2) $ 12,000	$ 213,000	
Investment in Stock of Company S	705,000		—			(1) 705,000	—	
Other Assets	2,150,000		975,000				3,125,000	
Accounts Payable		$ 75,000		$ 15,000	(2) $ 12,000			$ 78,000
Other Liabilities		70,000		280,000				350,000
Common Stock		2,500,000		500,000	(1) 500,000			2,500,000
Retained Earnings, January 1, 1982:								
Company P		256,000						256,000
Company S				170,000	(1) 170,000			
Sales		900,000		250,000	(3) 40,000			1,110,000
Equity in Earnings of Company S		48,000		—	(1) 48,000			
Cost of Goods Sold	440,000		80,000			(3) 40,000	480,000	
Depreciation Expense	120,000		50,000				170,000	
Administrative Expenses	80,000		40,000				120,000	
Income Taxes	104,000		32,000				136,000	
Dividends Declared	50,000		13,000			(1) 13,000	50,000	
Totals	$3,849,000	$3,849,000	$1,215,000	$1,215,000	$770,000	$770,000	$4,294,000	$4,294,000

Work Sheet Preparation

In preparing consolidated statements for Company P and Company S, the following steps, characteristic of the consolidation procedure, are illustrated.

A Elimination of the parent company's investment account.
B Elimination of intercompany receivables and payables.
C Elimination of intercompany sales and purchases.

The preparation of consolidated statements illustrated here starts with single-company, preclosing trial balances. These data are shown in the first two pairs of columns of the work sheet in Exhibit 13.2. Note that the amounts shown for Retained Earnings are the balances as of January 1, 1982. Revenue, expense, and dividend declaration accounts for 1982 have not yet been closed to Retained Earnings. The fourth pair of columns in Exhibit 13.2 shows the amounts on a consolidated basis for Company P and Company S. The amounts in the last pair of columns are merely the horizontal sum of the amounts in the other columns—Company P items, Company S items, as well as adjustments and eliminations. The adjustments and eliminations are discussed below. Keep in mind that these adjustments and eliminations are recorded only on a work sheet to prepare consolidated statements—not in the accounting records of either company.

A Elimination of Parent Company's Investment Account Company P acquired the shares of Company S for a price equal to their book value ($650,000). Since acquisition, Company P has used the equity method and has recorded the increase in Retained Earnings of Company S ($55,000) in its investment account. To avoid double counting the net assets of Company S, the investment account must be eliminated. The elimination is as follows:

(1) Common Stock (Company S)	500,000	
Retained Earnings, January 1, 1982 (Company S)	170,000	
Equity in Earnings of Company S (Company P)	48,000	
Dividends Declared (Company S)		13,000
Investment in Stock of Company S (Company P)		705,000

Aside from the minority interest, if any, the owners' equity of the consolidated entity is provided by the shareholders of the parent. There is no minority interest in this example. Thus, the owners' equity of the subsidiary is provided entirely by financing from the parent. If the owners' equity of the parent and of the subsidiary were merely added together, then equities would be counted twice. When the investment account is eliminated to avoid double counting of net assets, the subsidiary's owners' equity accounts—corresponding to the parent's investment—are eliminated to avoid double counting of the equities. The total amount eliminated is equal to the balance in the investment account ($705,000). This amount is also equal to the total shareholders' equity of Company S on December 31, 1982 ($500,000 + $205,000; see Exhibit 13.1). Because the elimination is being made to a preclosing trial balance, the revenue, expense, and dividend declaration accounts of Company S have not yet been closed to Company S's Retained Earnings. Thus, in addition to eliminating the capital stock of Company S ($500,000), the balance in Retained Earnings of Company S on January 1, 1982 ($170,000), the Equity in Earnings of Company S for 1982 ($48,000), and the Dividends Declared by Company S during 1982 ($13,000) are eliminated. The balance in the account, Equity in Earnings of Company S, is replaced with the individual revenues and expenses of Company S in the consolidated income statement.

B Elimination of Intercompany Receivables and Payables A parent may sell goods on account or buy goods on account from a subsidiary and treat the resulting obligation as an account receivable or an account payable. The subsidiary will treat the obligation as an account payable or an account receivable. A parent often makes loans to subsidiaries that appear on the parent's books as Notes Receivable, Investment in Bonds, or Advances to Subsidiary. The subsidiary would show Notes Payable, Bonds Payable, or Advances from Parent on its books. A single company would not show Accounts Receivable and Accounts Payable for departments within the company. These transactions must be eliminated from the consolidated balance sheet so that the resulting statement will appear as that of a single company.

In the illustration, Company S's accounts receivable include $12,000 due it from Company P. The entry to record the elimination of the intercompany receivables and payables in Exhibit 13.2 is:

(2) Accounts Payable	12,000	
Accounts Receivable		12,000
To eliminate intercompany payables and receivables.		

C Elimination of Intercompany Sales and Purchases Sales between consolidated companies should not be reported in a consolidated income statement, any more than transfers from Work-in-Process Inventory to Finished Goods Inventory should be reported as sales within a single company. During 1982, Company P acquired $40,000 of merchandise inventory from Company S. To eliminate intercompany sales requires a debit to Sales (selling corporation) and a credit to Purchases or to Goods Available for Sale (purchasing corporation). In the illustration we are working with, there are no Purchases or Goods Available for Sale accounts. As part of its regular adjusting entries, Company P computed its cost of goods sold from the inventory equation:

$$\text{Cost of Goods Sold} = \text{Beginning Inventory} + \text{Purchases} - \text{Ending Inventory}$$
$$= \quad \text{Goods Available for Sale} \quad - \text{Ending Inventory}.$$

Therefore, the offsetting credit to eliminate intercompany sales must be to the Cost of Goods Sold account.

518

(3) Sales	40,000	
Cost of Goods Sold		40,000
To eliminate intercompany sales and purchases.		

Company S sold goods to Company P and Company P sold the goods outside the consolidated pair of companies. In the absence of the elimination of intercompany sales, these sales would be counted twice. The profits on the sales would be computed properly, but the amount of gross sales and purchases (Cost of Goods Sold) would be inflated. To see that profits are computed properly, even without the elimination, assume that the goods cost Company S $30,000 and that Company P sold them for $45,000. In the single-company income statements, Company S profits are $10,000 (= $40,000 − $30,000) as a result of the sale to Company P. Company P profits are $5,000 (= $45,000 − $40,000) as a result of its sales to others. Total profits of the consolidated group from these transactions are $15,000, or Company P's revenue of $45,000 less Company S's cost of $30,000. The elimination of intercompany sales does not change the consolidated sales to outsiders or the consolidated cost of goods sold to outsiders.

If either company holds bonds or long-term notes of the other, then there would be a similar elimination of the "borrower's" interest expense and of the "lender's" interest revenue.

Statement Preparation

Once the consolidation work sheet has been completed, the consolidated statements can be prepared. Column (2) of Exhibit 13.3 presents a consolidated balance sheet on December 31, 1982, and a consolidated income statement for 1982 for Company P and Company S. As a basis for comparison, Column (1) of Exhibit 13.3 repeats the balance sheet and income statement for Company P alone (assuming that Company S is not consolidated and the Investment in Stock of Company S is accounted for using the equity method). Note the following aspects of using the equity method for an unconsolidated subsidiary versus fully consolidating that subsidiary.

1 When a subsidiary is not consolidated, the parent's balance sheet will show the investment in the subsidiary's net assets in a single investment account. When the subsidiary is consolidated, the investment account is replaced with the individual assets and liabilities of the subsidiary.
2 Consolidated retained earnings is equal to the amount of Retained Earnings on the parent's books that results from using the equity method for an unconsolidated subsidiary.
3 When a subsidiary is not consolidated, the parent's interest in the earnings of the subsidiary is shown on the single line, Equity in Earnings of Company S, on the parent's income statement. When the subsidiary is consolidated, the Equity in Earnings of Company S account is replaced with the individual revenues and expenses of the subsidiary.

519

4 Consolidated net income is equal to the amount of net income on the parent's books that results from using the equity method for an unconsolidated subsidiary.

Exhibit 13.3
Balance Sheet and Income Statement Assuming that Company S Is Not Consolidated and that Company S Is Consolidated

	Company P Unconsolidated (Equity Method)	Company P and Company S Consolidated
	(1)	(2)
BALANCE SHEET		
Assets:		
Accounts Receivable	$ 200,000	$ 213,000
Investment in Stock of S Company	705,000	—
Other Assets	2,150,000	3,125,000
Total Assets	$3,055,000	$3,338,000
Equities:		
Accounts Payable	$ 75,000	$ 78,000
Other Liabilities	70,000	350,000
Common Stock	2,500,000	2,500,000
Retained Earnings	410,000	410,000
Total Equities	$3,055,000	$3,338,000
INCOME STATEMENT		
Revenues:		
Sales	$ 900,000	$1,110,000
Equity in Earnings of Company S	48,000	—
Total Revenues	$ 948,000	$1,110,000
Expenses:		
Cost of Goods Sold	$ 440,000	$ 480,000
Depreciation Expense	120,000	170,000
Administrative Expenses	80,000	120,000
Income Taxes	104,000	136,000
Total Expenses	$ 744,000	$ 906,000
Net Income	$ 204,000	$ 204,000

Consolidated Statement of Changes in Financial Position

The consolidated statement of changes in financial position is prepared from consolidated balance sheets for the beginning and end of the period, plus additional information from the consolidated income statement. In the illustration, the consolidated statement of changes in financial position is particularly simple. It starts with consolidated net income of $204,000, shows an addback for depreciation expense of $170,000, shows dividends of $50,000, and reports other details of changes in current asset and current liability items.

The illustration, now complete, for Company P and Company S is simpler than typical consolidation problems in several respects. More complex consolidation problems are discussed in Appendix 13.1.

Summary

Businesses acquire stock in other businesses for a variety of reasons and in a variety of ways. The acquisition of stock of another company as a long-term investment is generally recorded as follows:

Investment in S	X	
Cash or Other Consideration Given		X

The investment account is recorded at the amount of cash given or the market value of other consideration exchanged.

The accounting for the investment subsequent to acquisition depends on the ownership percentage. The lower-of-cost-or-market method is used when the parent owns less than 20 percent. The equity method is used when the parent owns at least 20 percent, but not more than 50 percent, of the stock of another company. Consolidated statements are generally prepared when the parent owns more than 50 percent of the voting shares of another company, but the equity method may be used. Exhibit 13.4 summarizes the accounting for investments subsequent to the acquisition.

Under the lower-of-cost-or-market method, income is recognized only when dividends become receivable by the investor or when the securities are sold.

Consolidated statements and the equity method both have the same effect on net income. The parent shows as income its proportional share of the acquired firm's periodic income after acquisition. Income statement amounts of revenues and expenses will be larger under the consolidation method, however, because the revenues and expenses of the acquired company are combined with those of the parent. Balance sheet components will be larger under the consolidation method than under the equity method, because the individual assets and liabilities of the acquired company will be substituted for the investment balance on the parent company's books.

Problem for Self-Study

Reynolds Corporation acquired shares of common stock of Company R, Company S, and Company T on January 2, 1982, as long-term investments. These are the only long-term investments in securities of Reynolds Corporation. Data relating to the acquisitions are shown below.

Company	Percentage Acquired	Book Value and Market Value of Total Net Assets on January 2, 1982	Acquisition Cost	Net Income for 1982	Dividends Declared for 1982	Market Value of Shares Owned on December 31, 1982
R	10%	$5,000,000	$ 540,000	$1,000,000	$400,000	$ 520,000
S	30	5,000,000	1,700,000	1,000,000	400,000	1,710,000
T	100	5,000,000	5,000,000	1,000,000	400,000	5,200,000

Any goodwill arising from the acquisitions is amortized over 10 years.

a Give the journal entries made during 1982 to acquire the shares of Company R and to account for the investment, using the lower-of-cost-or-market method.

b Give the journal entries made during 1982 to acquire the shares of Company S and to account for the investment, using the equity method.

Exhibit 13.4
**Effects of Various Methods
of Accounting for Long-Term Investments
in Corporate Securities**

Method of Accounting	Balance Sheet	Income Statement	Statement of Changes in Financial Position
Lower-of-cost-or-market method (generally when ownership percentage is less than 20 percent).	Investment account shown at lower of acquisition cost or current market value as a noncurrent asset. Unrealized losses resulting from decline in market value below cost are credited to an asset contra and debited to an unrealized loss account that is shown as a negative component of owners' equity.	Dividends declared by investee shown as revenue of investor. Gains and losses (from original cost) are reported in income only as realized in arm's-length transactions with outsiders.	Dividends declared by investee included in working capital provided by operations of investor.
Equity method (generally when ownership percentage is at least 20 percent but not more than 50 percent).	Investment account shown at cost plus share of investee's net income less share of investee's dividends since acquisition.	Equity in investee's net income shown as revenue in period that investee earns income.	Equity in investee's undistributed earnings is subtracted from net income to derive working capital provided by operations of investor. Working capital from operations is thus increased only by the amount of dividend declarations.
Consolidation (generally when ownership percentage is greater than 50 percent).	Investment account is eliminated and replaced with individual assets and liabilities of subsidiary. Minority interest in subsidiary's net assets shown among equities.	Individual revenues and expenses of subsidiary are combined with those of parent. Minority interest in subsidiary's net income shown as a subtraction.	Individual sources and uses of working capital of subsidiary are combined with those of parent. Minority interest in net income is added to net income to obtain working capital provided by operations.

c Give the journal entries made during 1982 to acquire the shares of Company T and to account for the investment, using the equity method.

d Give the consolidation work sheet entry to eliminate the Investment in Stock of Company T account at the end of 1982, assuming that the equity method is used and that the work sheet is based on preclosing trial balance amounts. Company T had $2,000,000 in its Common Stock account throughout 1982 and a zero balance in Additional Paid-in Capital.

e Repeat part **d**, but assume that the work sheet is based on postclosing trial balance amounts.

Parts **f** through **i** should not be worked until Appendix 13.1 has been read.

f Assume that the shares of Company T had been acquired for $5,500,000, instead of $5,000,000. Give the journal entries made during 1982 to acquire the shares of Company T and to account for the investment, using the equity method. Any excess of cost over book value is considered goodwill and is amortized over 10 years.

g Refer to Part **f**, above. Give the consolidation work sheet entry to eliminate the Investment in Stock of Company T account, assuming the work sheet is based on preclosing trial balance data.

h Assume that Reynolds Corporation had paid $4,000,000 for 80 percent of the shares of Company T on January 2, 1982. Give the journal entries made during 1982 to acquire the shares of Company T and to account for the investment, using the equity method.

i Refer to Part **h**, above. Give the consolidation work sheet entries to eliminate the Investment in Stock of Company T account and to recognize the external minority interest in Company T, assuming the work sheet is based on preclosing trial balance data.

Suggested Solution

a Investment in Stock of Company R.   540,000

   Cash   540,000

To record acquisition of shares of Company R.

Cash and Dividends Receivable.   40,000

   Dividend Revenue   40,000

To record dividends received or receivable for 1982.

Unrealized Holding Loss on Valuation of Marketable Equity Investments .   20,000

   Allowance for Excess of Cost of Investments over Market Value   20,000

To write down portfolio (Company R only) of minority, passive investments to market value; $20,000 = $540,000 − $520,000.

b Investment in Stock of Company S.   1,700,000

   Cash   1,700,000

To record acquisition of shares of Company S.

Investment in Stock of Company S.   300,000

   Equity in Earnings of Company S   300,000

To accrue share of Company S's earnings for 1982; $300,000 = .30 × $1,000,000.

Cash and Dividend Receivable 120,000
   Investment in Stock of Company S 120,000
To record dividends received or receivable for 1982.

Amortization Expense 20,000
   Investment in Stock of Company S 20,000
To record amortization of goodwill implicit in purchase price, $20,000 = ($1,700,000 − $1,500,000)/10.

---

c Investment in Stock of Company T 5,000,000
   Cash 5,000,000
To record acquisition of shares of Company T.

Investment in Stock of Company T 1,000,000
   Equity in Earnings of Company T 1,000,000
To accrue earnings of Company T for 1982; $1,000,000 = 100% × $1,000,000.

Cash or Dividends Receivable 400,000
   Investment in Stock of Company T 400,000
To record dividends received or receivable for 1982.

---

d Common Stock 2,000,000
Retained Earnings (January 2) 3,000,000
Equity in Earnings of Company T 1,000,000
   Dividends Declared 400,000
   Investment in Stock of Company T 5,600,000
To eliminate investment account on consolidation work sheet.

---

e Common Stock 2,000,000
Retained Earnings (December 31) 3,600,000
   Investment in Stock of Company T 5,600,000
To eliminate investment account on consolidation work sheet.

---

f Investment in Stock of Company T 5,500,000
   Cash 5,500,000
To record acquisition of shares of Company T.

Investment in Stock of Company T 1,000,000
   Equity in Earnings of Company T 1,000,000
To accrue earnings of Company T for 1982.

Cash and Dividends Receivable 400,000
   Investment in Stock of Company T 400,000
To record dividends received or receivable for 1982.

Amortization Expense 50,000
   Investment in Stock of Company T 50,000
To record amortization of goodwill implicit in purchase price; $50,000 = ($5,500,000 − $5,000,000)/10.

524

g	Common Stock	2,000,000	
	Retained Earnings	3,000,000	
	Equity in Earnings of Company T	1,000,000	
	Goodwill	450,000	
	Dividends Declared		400,000
	Investment in Stock of Company T		6,050,000

To eliminate investment account on consolidation work sheet;
$6,050,000 = $5,500,000 + $1,000,000 − $400,000 − $50,000.

h	Investment in Stock of Company T	4,000,000	
	Cash		4,000,000

To record acquisition of shares of Company T.

Investment in Stock of Company T	800,000	
Equity in Earnings of Company T		800,000

To accrue share of Company T's earnings for 1982; $800,000 =
.80 × $1,000,000.

Cash or Dividends Receivable	320,000	
Investment in Stock of Company T		320,000

To record dividends received or receivable for 1982; $320,000 =
.80 × $400,000.

i	Common Stock	1,600,000	
	Retained Earnings	2,400,000	
	Equity in Earnings of Company T	800,000	
	Dividends Declared		320,000
	Investment in Stock of Company T		4,480,000

To eliminate investment account on consolidation work sheet;
$4,480,000 = $4,000,000 + $800,000 − $320,000.

Common Stock	400,000	
Retained Earnings	600,000	
Minority Interest in Earnings of Company T	200,000	
Dividends Declared		80,000
Minority Interest in Net Assets of Company T		1,120,000

To recognize external minority interest in Company T.

Appendix 13.1
Some Complexities in Consolidation

The illustrations in Exhibits 13.1 and 13.2 were simplified. This appendix considers two situations encountered in consolidated statements not illustrated in this chapter. These are:

1 Acquisition price of subsidiary exceeds book value acquired.

525

2 Less than 100 percent of the subsidiary's stock is acquired, resulting in a minority interest.

Refer to the data in Exhibits 13.1 and 13.2, and to steps **A–C** listed on pages 517–519.

Acquisition Price
Exceeds Book Value Acquired

Suppose that Company P had paid $700,000, rather than $650,000, for its 100-percent investment in Company S. The $50,000 difference in purchase price represents the amount paid for Company S's assets in excess of their book value, for goodwill, or for both. Assume that on the date of acquisition, January 1, 1979, the book value of Company S's recorded assets and liabilities equaled their market values at that time. The fact that Company P was willing to pay $700,000 for recorded assets having book values and market values equal to $650,000 means that Company S must have had *unrecorded* assets of $50,000 on January 1, 1979. The $50,000 of unrecorded assets represents goodwill. Generally accepted accounting principles[8] require that goodwill be amortized over a period not exceeding 40 years. Assume that Company P chose a 40-year amortization period. On its separate company books, Company P would have made the following entry during each of the years 1979 through 1982.

Amortization Expense	1,250	
Investment in Stock of Company S		1,250
To recognize amortization of goodwill; $1,250 = ($700,000 − $650,000)/40.		

In preparing the consolidation work sheet at the end of 1982, Entry (1) would be the same as that shown in Exhibit 13.2. After Entry (1), the Investment in Stock of Company S would still have a debit balance of $45,000 [= $50,000 − (4 × $1,250)]. This amount represents the unamortized goodwill arising from the acquisition. A work sheet entry should be made to reclassify this amount from the investment account to goodwill. The entry is:

Goodwill	45,000	
Investment in Stock of Company S		45,000
To reclassify goodwill.		

The consolidated balance sheet on December 31, 1982, will show goodwill of $45,000 [= $50,000 − (4 × $1,250)]. Consolidated net income for 1982 will now be $202,750 (= $204,000 − $1,250) to reflect amortization expense for 1982. Consolidated retained earnings will be $405,000 [= $410,000 − (4 × $1,250)]. The statement of

---

[8] Accounting Principles Board, *Opinion No. 17,* "Intangible Assets," 1970.

changes in financial position will show an addback of $1,250 for amortization expense which did not use cash or working capital.

Recognizing External, Minority Interest

Now assume that Company P had acquired only 90 percent of the capital stock of Company S on January 1, 1979, at its book value. In this case, other individuals or entities own the remaining 10 percent of the shares. These individuals or entities represent an external minority interest in the earnings and net assets of Company S.

The net assets, or shareholders' equity, of Company S is allocable to Company P and to the minority shareholders as shown in Exhibit 13.5.

Exhibit 13.5
**Allocation of Shareholders' Equity of Company S
to Company P and Minority Interest Shareholders**

	Total	To Company P (90%)	To Minority Shareholders (10%)
	(1)	(2)	(3)
January 1, 1979: Common Stock	$500,000	$450,000	$50,000
Retained Earnings	150,000	135,000	15,000
Increase in Retained Earnings, January 1, 1979—January 1, 1982	20,000	18,000	2,000
Subtotal	$670,000	$603,000	$67,000
Net Income for 1982	48,000	43,200	4,800
Dividends Declared for 1982	(13,000)	(11,700)	(1,300)
December 31, 1982	$705,000	$634,500	$70,500

Assuming that Company P has acquired its 90-percent interest in Company S for book value, it would have paid $585,000 (= .90 × $650,000) on January 1, 1979. The Investment in Stock of Company S account would have been recorded initially at this amount on Company P's books. Between 1979 and 1982, Company P would have increased the investment account for 90 percent of Company S's earnings and decreased the investment account for 90 percent of Company S's dividends. Thus, the Investment in Stock of Company S account would show a balance of $634,500 on December 31, 1982 [see Column (2) of Exhibit 13.5]. The work sheet elimination entry for the investment account would be as follows:

Common Stock (Company S)	450,000	
Retained Earnings, January 1 (Company S)	153,000	
Equity in Earnings of Company S (Company P)	43,200	
Dividends Declared (Company S)		11,700
Investment in Stock of Company S (Company P)		634,500

The remaining balances in Company S's shareholders' equity accounts are the minority interest. The work sheet entry to recognize the minority interest is:

Common Stock (Company S)	50,000	
Retained Earnings (Company S)	17,000	
Minority Interest in Earnings of Company S	4,800	
Dividends Declared (Company S)		1,300
Minority Interest in Net Assets of Company S		70,500

The account, Minority Interest in Earnings of Company S, is "created" on the consolidation work sheet. It does not appear as an account on either of the separate-company books. It represents the external minority interest in the earnings of Company S and is shown as a deduction in calculating consolidated net income. Consolidated net income is, therefore, $199,200 (= $204,000 − $4,800).

The account Minority Interest in Net Assets of Company S is, likewise, created on the consolidation work sheet. It represents the external minority interest in the net assets of Company S, a *consolidated* subsidiary. It is shown on the right-hand side of the consolidated balance sheet, usually between liabilities and shareholders' equity.

The consolidated statement of changes in financial position starts with the net income of $199,200 to shareholders of Company P. Amounts are added back for the minority interest in S's undistributed earnings for the year: of $3,500 (= $4,800 − $1,300) and for depreciation ($170,000), neither of which uses working capital. The only use of working capital shown is the $50,000 of dividends declared by the parent. Parts f through i of the Problem for Self-Study on page 523 review the material in this appendix.

Questions and Problems

1 Review the meaning of the following concepts or terms discussed in this chapter.
  a Marketable securities classified as current assets or as long-term investments.
  b Minority, passive investments.
  c Minority, active investments.
  d Majority, active investments.
  e Lower-of-cost-or-market method for long-term investments.
  f Significant influence by an investor over an investee.
  g Equity method.
  h Parent.
  i Subsidiary.
  j Consolidated financial statements.
  k Consolidation policy.
  l Economic entity versus legal entity.
  m Adjustments and eliminations in a consolidation work sheet.
  n Intercompany transactions.
  o Minority interest in a consolidated subsidiary.
  p Goodwill.

2 Unrealized holding losses from price declines of marketable equity securities classified as current assets are recognized as they arise in calculating net income. Similar unrealized holding losses from long-term investments accounted for using the lower-of-cost-or-market method are not recognized as they arise in calculating net income. What is the rationale for this difference in accounting treatment?

3 Compare and contrast each of the following pairs of accounts.
  a Unrealized Holding Loss on Valuation of Marketable Equity Securities, and Unrealized Holding Loss on Valuation of Marketable Equity Investments.
  b Allowance for Excess of Cost of Marketable Securities over Market Value, and Allowance for Excess of Cost of Investments over Market Value.
  c Dividend Revenue, and Equity in Earnings of Unconsolidated Affiliates.
  d Equity in Earnings of Unconsolidated Affiliate, and Minority Interest in Earnings of Consolidated Subsidiary.
  e Minority Interest in Earnings of Consolidated Subsidiary, and Minority Interest in Net Assets of Consolidated Subsidiary.

4 "Dividends received or receivable from another company may be either an item of revenue in calculating net income or a return of capital, depending on the method of accounting used." Explain.

5 Why is the equity method sometimes called a *one-line consolidation*? Consider both the balance sheet and the income statement in your response.

6 Distinguish between minority investments in other companies and the minority interest in a consolidated subsidiary.

7 "Net income will be the same regardless of whether an investment in a subsidiary is accounted for using the equity method and not consolidated or whether the subsidiary is consolidated. Total assets will be different, however, depending on whether or not the subsidiary is consolidated." Explain.

8 Refer to the Simplified Statement of Changes in Financial Position for a Period in Exhibit 5.19 on page 191. Nine of the lines in the statement are numbered. Line (2) should be expanded to say "Additions for Expenses and Other Charges Against Income Not Using Funds," and line (3) should be expanded to say "Subtractions for Revenue and Other Credits to Income Not Producing Funds from Operations." Ignore the unnumbered lines in responding to the questions below.
  Assume that the accounting cycle is complete for the period and that all of the financial statements have been prepared. Then it is discovered that a transaction has been overlooked. The transaction is recorded in the accounts, and all of the financial statements are corrected. Define *funds* as *working capital*. For each of the following transactions or events, indicate which of the numbered lines of the funds statement is affected and by how much. Ignore income tax effects.
  a A 100-percent-owned affiliate accounted for on the equity method earns $10,000 and declares dividends of $4,000.
  b A 100-percent-owned affiliate accounted for on the equity method reports a loss for the year of $5,000.
  c Minority interest in income of a consolidated subsidiary is recognized in the amount of $20,000.

d Minority interest in the losses of a consolidated subsidiary is recognized in the amount of $8,000.

e A 100-percent-owned consolidated subsidiary sold merchandise to the parent company for $10,000. The subsidiary's cost of the goods sold was $6,000. The parent sold the merchandise for $12,000. An elimination of the intercompany transactions is made.

f The *investment* in the portfolio of equity securities accounted for with the lower-of-cost-or-market method is written down from $10,000 to $8,000.

g A dividend of $7,000 is declared on shares held as an *investment* and accounted for with the lower-of-cost-or-market method.

h The market value of the portfolio of equity securities accounted for as *current assets* (Marketable Securities) is $5,000 less than the net amount shown for the same portfolio on the balance sheet at the end of the previous accounting period. The amount in the allowance contra to the Marketable Securities account is changed.

i The market value of the portfolio of marketable equity securities in the preceding part **h** increases $3,000 by the end of the next accounting period. The amount in the allowance contra to the Marketable Securities account is changed.

9 On January 1, Buyer Company acquired common stock of X Company. At the time of acquisition, the book value and fair market value of X Company's net assets were $200,000. During the year, X Company earned $50,000 and declared dividends of $40,000. How much income would Buyer Company report for the year from its investment under the assumption that Buyer Company:

a Paid $30,000 for 15 percent of the common stock and uses the lower-of-cost-or-market method for its investment in X Company?

b Paid $40,000 for 15 percent of the common stock and uses the lower-of-cost-or-market method for its investment in X Company?

c Paid $60,000 for 30 percent of the common stock and uses the equity method to account for its investment in X Company?

d Paid $80,000 for 30 percent of the common stock and uses the equity method to account for its investment in X Company? Give the maximum income that Buyer Company can report from the investment.

10 Maddox Corporation made three long-term intercorporate investments on January 2, 1982. Data relating to these investments are as follows:

Company	Percentage Acquired	Book Value and Market Value of Net Assets on January 2, 1982	Acquisition Cost	Net Income for 1982	Dividends Declared during 1982	Market Value of Shares Held on December 31, 1982
A	10%	$1,800,000	$ 200,000	$100,000	$40,000	$ 180,000
B	25	1,800,000	500,000	100,000	40,000	510,000
C	60	1,800,000	1,400,000	100,000	40,000	1,431,000

Assume that these were the only three intercorporate investments of Maddox Corporation. Goodwill is amortized over 40 years.

a Give the journal entries on Maddox Corporation's books to record these acquisitions of common stock and to account for the intercorporate investments during 1982 under

530

generally accepted accounting principles. The investment in Company C is not consolidated. Be sure to include any required year-end adjusting entries.

b Assuming that the financial statements of Company C are consolidated with those of Maddox Corporation, that the investment in Company C is accounted for using the equity method, and that the consolidation work sheet is based on preclosing trial balance data, give the work sheet entry to eliminate the Investment in Stock of Company C account on December 31, 1982. The Common Stock account of Company C has a balance of $1,000,000, and Additional Paid-in Capital has a zero balance.

c Refer to Part **b** above. Give the consolidation work sheet entry to recognize the minority interest in Company C on December 31, 1982.

11 Johnson Corporation made three long-term intercorporate investments on January 2, 1982. Data relating to these investments are as follows:

Company	Percentage Acquired	Book Value and Market Value of Net Assets on January 2, 1982	Acquisition Cost	Net Income for 1982	Dividends Declared during 1982
X	20%	$2,000,000	$ 400,000	$200,000	$ 80,000
Y	25	3,000,000	800,000	300,000	120,000
Z	30	4,000,000	1,300,000	400,000	160,000

Give the journal entries to record the acquisition of these investments and to apply the equity method during 1982. Goodwill is amortized over 20 years.

12 The CAR Corporation manufactures computers in the United States. It owns 75 percent of the voting stock of Charles of Canada, 80 percent of the voting stock of Alexandre de France (in France), and 90 percent of the voting stock of R Credit Corporation (a finance company). The CAR Corporation prepares consolidated financial statements consolidating Charles of Canada, using the equity method for R Credit Corporation, and using the lower-of-cost-or-market method for its investment in Alexandre de France. Data from the annual reports of these companies are given below.

	Percentage Owned	Net Income	Dividends	Accounting Method
CAR Corporation Consolidated . .	—	$1,000,000	$ 70,000	—
Charles of Canada	75%	100,000	40,000	Consolidated
Alexandre de France	80	80,000	50,000	Lower of Cost or Market
R Credit Corporation . . . . ·. . . .	90	120,000	100,000	Equity

a Which, if any, of the companies is incorrectly accounted for by CAR according to generally accepted accounting principles?

Assuming the accounting for the three subsidiaries shown above to be correct, answer the following questions.

b How much of the net income reported by CAR Corporation Consolidated is attributable to the operations of the three subsidiaries?

c What is the amount of the minority interest now shown on the income statement and how does it affect net income of CAR Corporation Consolidated?

d If all three subsidiaries had been consolidated, what would have been the net income of CAR Corporation Consolidated?

e If all three subsidiaries had been consolidated, what would be the minority interest shown on the income statement?

13 The Roe Company purchased 80 percent of the common stock of Danver Company on January 2 at book value, $480,000. The total common stock of Danver Company at this date was $450,000, and the retained earnings balance was $150,000. During the year, net income of the Danver Company was $90,000; dividends declared were $36,000. The Roe Company uses the equity method to account for the investment.

a Give the journal entry made by Roe Company during the year to account for its investment in Danver Company.

b Give the elimination entry for the investment account, assuming that the consolidation work sheet is based on preclosing trial balance data.

14 Company P owns 70 percent of a consolidated subsidiary, Company S. During the year, Company P's sales to Company S amounted to $50,000. The cost of those sales was $35,000. The following data are taken from the two companies' income statements:

	Company P	Company S
Sales	$120,000	$250,000
Cost of Goods Sold	70,000	150,000

a Compute consolidated sales and consolidated cost of goods sold for the year, assuming that Company S sold all the goods purchased from Company P.

b Compare the consolidated sales, cost of goods sold, and gross margin on sales to the sum of the sales, cost of goods sold, and gross margins of the separate companies.

15 The Hart Company acquired control of the Keller Company on January 2, 1982, by purchasing 80 percent of its outstanding stock for $700,000. The entire excess of cost over book value acquired is attributed to goodwill, which is amortized over 40 years. The shareholders' equity accounts of the Keller Company appeared as follows on January 2, 1982, and December 31, 1982:

	Jan. 2, 1982	Dec. 31, 1982
Common Stock	$600,000	$600,000
Retained Earnings	200,000	420,000

Keller Company had earnings of $250,000 and declared dividends of $30,000 during 1982. The accounts receivable of the Hart Company at December 31, 1982, include $4,500 which is due it from the Keller Company. Hart Company accounts for its investment in Keller Company on its single-company books using the equity method.

a Give the journal entries to record the acquisition of the shares of Keller Company and to apply the equity method during 1982 on the books of Hart Company.

b Give the required elimination entries for a consolidation work sheet at the end of 1982, assuming that the work sheet is based on preclosing trial balance data.

16 The Little Company is a subsidiary of the Butler Company and is accounted for using the equity method on the single-company books of the Butler Company.

a Present journal entries for the following selected transactions. Record the set of entries on the books of the Little Company separately from the set of entries on the books of the Butler Company.

(1) On January 2, the Butler Company acquired on the market, for cash, 80 percent of all the common stock of the Little Company. The outlay was $325,000. The total contributed capital of the stock outstanding was $300,000; the retained earnings balance was $80,000. The excess of cost over book value acquired is all attributed to goodwill and is amortized over 10 years.

(2) The Little Company purchased materials from the Butler Company on account at the latter's cost, $23,000.

(3) The Little Company obtained an advance of $9,000 from the Butler Company. The funds were deposited in the bank.

(4) The Little Company paid $19,000 on the purchases in **(2)**.

(5) The Little Company repaid $7,500 of the loan received from the Butler Company in **(3)**.

(6) The Little Company declared and paid a dividend of $24,000 during the year.

(7) The net income of the Little Company for the year was $40,000.

b Prepare the adjustment and elimination entries which would be necessary in the preparation of the December 31 consolidated balance sheet, recognizing the effects of only the above transactions. Assume that the work sheet is based on preclosing financial statement data.

17 Lesala Corporation purchased most of the common stock of its subsidiary in 1980. The subsidiary earned $1 million in 1982 but declared no dividends. The following is an excerpt from Lesala Corporation's financial statements issued for 1982.

Lesala Corporation
Consolidated Statement of
Changes in Financial Position
for the Year 1982

Sources of Working Capital:

Consolidated Net Income.		$3,000,000
Addback Charges Not Requiring Working Capital:		
Depreciation of Plant	$150,000	
Amortization of Goodwill Arising from Acquisition of Consolidated Subsidiary	10,000	
Minority Interest in Earnings of Consolidated Subsidiary	200,000	360,000
Total Working Capital from Operations		$3,360,000

---

a What percentage of the consolidated subsidiary does Lesala Corporation own?

b Goodwill arising from the acquisition of the consolidated subsidiary is being amortized, using the straight-line method, to show the minimum charges allowed by generally accepted accounting principles. What was the excess of the subsidiary's market

533

value as a going concern over the market value of the actual assets shown on its books as of the date of acquisition? Assume that the acquisition occurred on January 1, 1980.

18 The trial balances of High Company and Low Company on December 31, 1982, are shown in Exhibit 13.6.

The High Company acquired all of the common stock of Low Company on January 1, 1982, for $80,000. The receivables of High Company and the liabilities of Low Company contain $5,000 of advances from High Company to Low Company.

Exhibit 13.6
High Company and Low Company
Preclosing Trial Balances
(Problems 18 and 19)

Debits:	High Company	Low Company
Cash	$ 50,000	$ 5,000
Accounts Receivable	80,000	15,000
Investment in Stock of Low Company (at equity)	90,000	—
Other Assets	360,000	100,000
Cost of Goods Sold	160,000	60,000
Selling and Administrative Expenses	50,000	20,000
Income Tax Expense	40,000	10,000
Totals	$830,000	$210,000
Credits:		
Accounts Payable	$ 70,000	$ 30,000
Bonds Payable	100,000	—
Common Stock	150,000	50,000
Retained Earnings	200,000	30,000
Sales Revenue	300,000	100,000
Equity in Earnings of Low Company	10,000	—
Totals	$830,000	$210,000

Prepare a consolidation work sheet for High Company and Low Company for 1982. The adjustments and eliminations columns should contain entries to:

(1) Eliminate the investment account.
(2) Eliminate intercompany receivables and payables.

19 Refer to the data for High Company and Low Company in Problem 18. Give the consolidation work sheet adjustment and elimination entries under each of the following independent situations:

a The High Company paid $100,000, instead of $80,000, for all of the common stock of Low Company on January 1, 1982. The market values of Low Company's recorded assets and liabilities equaled their book values. Goodwill is amortized over 10 years.

b The High Company paid $64,000 for 80 percent of the common stock of Low Company on January 1, 1982. The Investment in Stock of Low Company account showed a balance of $72,000 on December 31, 1982.

20 The preclosing trial balances of Company L and Company M on December 31, 1982, are shown in Exhibit 13.7. Company L acquired 90 percent of the common stock of Company M on January 2, 1981, for $270,000. On this date, the shareholders' equity accounts of Company M were as follows:

Common Stock	$100,000
Retained Earnings	200,000
Total	$300,000

Exhibit 13.7
Company L and Company M
Preclosing Trial Balances
(Problem 20)

	Company L	Company M
Debits:		
Receivables	$ 60,000	$130,000
Investment in Stock of Company M	319,500	—
Other Assets	761,500	285,000
Cost of Goods Sold	550,000	150,000
Other Expenses	120,000	10,000
Dividends Declared	30,000	15,000
Totals	$1,841,000	$590,000
Credits:		
Accounts Payable	$ 80,000	$ 20,000
Other Liabilities	90,000	40,000
Common Stock	400,000	100,000
Retained Earnings	435,000	230,000
Sales Revenue	800,000	200,000
Equity in Earnings of Company M	36,000	—
Totals	$1,841,000	$590,000

During 1982, Company L sold merchandise costing $30,000, on account, to Company M for $40,000. Of the amount, $10,000 remains unpaid at year-end. Company M sold all of the merchandise during 1982.

a Prepare a consolidation work sheet for Company L and Company M for 1982. The adjustments and eliminations columns should contain entries to:

(1) Eliminate the investment account.
(2) Eliminate intercompany sales.
(3) Eliminate intercompany receivables and payables.
(4) Recognize the minority interest.

b Prepare a consolidated statement of income and retained earnings for 1982 and a consolidated balance sheet as of December 31, 1982.

535

21 The condensed balance sheets of the Ely Company and the Sims Company at December 31 are shown in Exhibit 13.8.

Exhibit 13.8
Ely Company and Sims Company
Balance Sheet Data
(Problem 21)

	Ely Company	Sims Company
ASSETS		
Cash	$ 60,000	$ 5,000
Receivables.	120,000	15,000
Investment in Sims Company Stock (at equity)	88,200	—
Other Assets	540,000	100,000
	$808,200	$120,000
LIABILITIES AND SHAREHOLDERS' EQUITY		
Current Liabilities	$250,000	$ 30,000
Common Stock	400,000	50,000
Retained Earnings	158,200	40,000
	$808,200	$120,000

The receivables of the Ely Company and the liabilities of the Sims Company contain an advance from the Ely Company to the Sims Company of $5,500. The Ely Company acquired 85 percent of the capital stock of the Sims Company on the market at January 2 of this year for $80,000. At that date, the balance in the Retained Earnings account of the Sims Company was $30,000. Amortize goodwill, if any, over 40 years.

Prepare a consolidation work sheet for Ely Company and Sims Company. The adjustment and elimination columns should contain entries to:

(1) Eliminate the Investment in the Sims Company account.
(2) Eliminate intercompany obligations.
(3) Recognize the minority interest.

22 The condensed balance sheets of Companies R and S on December 31, 1982, are shown in Exhibit 13.9.
Additional information:

Company R owns 90 percent of the capital stock of Company S. The stock of Company S was acquired on January 1, 1981, when Company S's retained earnings amounted to $20,000.

Company R holds a note issued by Company S in the amount of $8,200.

Excess of cost over book value acquired is all attributable to goodwill, to be amortized over 40 years.

Prepare a work sheet for a consolidated balance sheet.

23 Sealco Enterprises published the consolidated income statement for the year that is shown in Exhibit 13.10.

The unconsolidated affiliate retained 20 percent of its earnings of $100,000 during the year, having paid out the rest as dividends. The consolidated subsidiary earned $200,000 during the year and declared no dividends.

Exhibit 13.9
Company R and Company S
Balance Sheet Data
(Problem 22)

ASSETS	Company R	Company S
Cash	$ 18,000	$ 13,000
Accounts and Notes Receivable	90,000	25,000
Inventories	220,000	125,000
Investment in Stock of Company S (at equity)	312,450	—
Plant Assets	300,000	212,000
Total Assets	$940,450	$375,000
LIABILITIES AND SHAREHOLDERS' EQUITY		
Accounts and Notes Payable	$ 55,000	$ 17,000
Dividends Payable	—	12,500
Other Liabilities	143,000	11,000
Common Stock	600,000	250,000
Capital Contributed in Excess of Stated Value	—	50,000
Retained Earnings	142,450	34,500
Total Liabilities and Shareholders' Equity	$940,450	$375,000

Exhibit 13.10
Sealco Enterprises
Consolidated Income Statement
(Problem 23)

Revenues:

Sales		$1,000,000
Equity in Earnings of Unconsolidated Affiliate		40,000
Total Revenues		$1,040,000

Expenses:

Cost of Goods Sold (Excluding Depreciation)		$ 650,000
Administrative Expenses		100,000
Depreciation Expense		115,000
Amortization of Goodwill		5,000
Income Tax Expenses:		
Currently Payable	$42,000	
Deferred	10,000	52,000
Total Expenses		$ 922,000
Income of the Consolidated Group		$ 118,000
Less Minority Interest in Earnings of Consolidated Subsidiary		30,000
Net Income to Shareholders		$ 88,000

a What percentage of the unconsolidated affiliate does Sealco Enterprises own?

b What dividends did Sealco Enterprises receive from the unconsolidated affiliate during the year?

c What percentage of the consolidated subsidiary does Sealco Enterprises own?

d Prepare the "working capital provided by operations" section of the Sealco Enterprises Consolidated Statement of Changes in Financial Position for the year, assuming that

(i) The statement starts with net income to shareholders.

(ii) The statement shows only revenues and expenses that involve working capital.

24 General Manufacturing (G.M.) Company manufactures heavy-duty industrial equipment and consumer durable goods. In order to enable its customers to make convenient credit arrangements, G.M. Company organized General Manufacturing Credit Corporation several years ago. G.M. Credit Corporation is 100-percent owned by G.M. Company. G.M. Company accounts for its investment in G.M. Credit Corporation using the *equity method.* G.M. owns shares of many other companies, and consolidates several of them in its financial statements. Refer to the comparative balance sheets and income statements for the two companies in Exhibits 13.11 and 13.12.

a Given that G.M. Company accounted for its investment in G.M. Credit Corporation on the equity method, identify, for 1982, the components of G.M. Company's income that are attributable to the Credit Corporation's dividends and earnings.

b Assume that G.M. Company had accounted for its investment in the Credit Corporation using the lower-of-cost-or-market method, and market value has exceeded acquisition cost at all times since acquisition.

(i) Show the components of G.M. Company's income from the Credit Corporation, and compute how much larger or smaller G.M. Company's income would have been for 1982 than was reported.

(ii) Identify any G.M. Company balance sheet accounts that would have different balances, and calculate the differences from what is shown in the actual statements and what would be shown had the alternative treatment been used.

c Assume that G.M. Company had accounted for its investment in the Credit Corporation by *consolidating* it. Perform the same computations as required in **(i)** and **(ii)** of part **b**, above, for 1982. Notice that when a 100-percent-owned affiliate—accounted for with the equity method—is consolidated, the effect on balance sheet totals and subtotals can be summarized as follows:

1 Total owners' equity on the parent's books remain unchanged.

2 Total liabilities on the parent's books increases by the amount of the affiliate's total liabilities (assuming there are no intercompany receivables and payables).

3 Total assets on the parent's books increases net by an amount equal to the affiliate's liabilities. (All of the affiliate's assets are put onto the parent's books, but the parent's investment in the affiliate, an amount equal to the affiliate's owners' equity, is removed. The net effect is to increase assets by the amount of the affiliate's total assets − affiliate's owners' equity = affiliate's liabilities.)

d Compute the following ratios for G.M. from the annual report as published for 1982. (Refer to Exhibit 6.10 if you have forgotten how to compute these ratios.)

(i) Rate of return on assets. (Insufficient information is given to allow an addback to the numerator for interest payments net of tax effects; ignore that adjustment to net income which is ordinarily required. Use the year-end balance of total assets for the year's average.)

(ii) Debt-equity ratio.

Exhibit 13.11
General Manufacturing Company and Consolidated Affiliates
(Problems 24, 25, 26)

	(In millions of $) December 31		
BALANCE SHEET	**1982**	**1981**	**1980**
Investment in G. M. Credit Corporation	$ 260.0	$ 231.9	$ 190.0
Other Assets	7,141.8	6,655.9	6,008.5
Total Assets	$ 7,401.8	$6,887.8	$6,198.5
Total Liabilities	$ 4,317.2	$4,086.0	$3,644.9
Shareholders' Equity	3,084.6	2,801.8	2,553.6
Total Equities	$ 7,401.8	$6,887.8	$6,198.5

	For the Years		
INCOME STATEMENT	**1982**	**1981**	**1980**
Sales	$10,387.6	$9,546.4	$8,813.6
Equity in Net Earnings of Credit Corporation	41.1	30.9	19.9
Total Revenues	$10,428.7	$9,577.3	$8,833.5
Expenses	(9,898.7)	(9,105.5)	(8,505.0)
Net Income	$ 530.0	$ 471.8	$ 328.5

Exhibit 13.12
General Manufacturing Credit Corporation
(Problems 24, 25, 26)

	(In millions of $) December 31		
BALANCE SHEET	**1982**	**1981**	**1980**
Total Assets	$2,789.5	$2,358.7	$2,157.0
Total Liabilities	$2,529.5	$2,126.8	$1,967.0
Capital Stock	$ 110.0	$ 90.0	$ 55.0
Retained Earnings	150.0	141.9	135.0
Shareholders' Equity	$ 260.0	$ 231.9	$ 190.0
Total Equities	$2,789.5	$2,358.7	$2,157.0

	For the Year		
STATEMENT OF INCOME AND RETAINED EARNINGS	**1982**	**1981**	**1980**
Revenues	$ 319.8	$ 280.0	$ 247.5
Less: Expenses	278.7	249.1	227.6
Net Income	$ 41.1	$ 30.9	$ 19.9
Less: Dividends	33.0	24.0	15.0
Earnings Retained for Year	$ 8.1	$ 6.9	$ 4.9
Retained Earnings at January 1	141.9	135.0	130.1
Retained Earnings at December 31	$ 150.0	$ 141.9	$ 135.0

e For 1982, compute the two ratios required in part **d**, assuming that G.M. had consolidated the Credit Corporation, rather than accounting for it with the equity method. Use the information derived in part **c**.

f Compare the results in parts **d** and **e**. What conclusions can you draw from this exercise about comparing financial ratios for companies that consolidate their subsidiaries with those of companies that do not?

25 Repeat Problem **24** for 1981.

26 Repeat Problem **24** for 1980.

27 This problem illustrates the impact that consolidation policy can have on financial statements and financial statement analysis. Sears, Roebuck & Co. and J.C. Penney Company are large retailers who have similar operations. Both companies have organized financing subsidiaries. Each subsidiary borrows funds in credit markets and lends the funds to customers who purchase goods or services from the retailers. Each subsidiary is 100-percent owned by its parent company. Sears consolidates its financing subsidiary (Sears, Roebuck Acceptance Corp.) in published financial statements. Penney's uses the equity method for its financing subsidiary (J.C. Penney Financial Corporation) and shows the separate financial statements of the financing subsidiary in notes to the published financial statements.

In this problem we focus on the debt ratio, because the effects are easy to illustrate. Other ratios could be used as well. Throughout this text, we have defined the debt-equity ratio as

$$\text{Debt-Equity Ratio} = \frac{\text{Total Liabilities}}{\text{Total Equities}}.$$

Many financial analysts prefer to use a form of the debt ratio such as

$$\text{Debt Ratio} = \frac{\text{Total } \textit{Long-Term} \text{ Debt}}{\text{Total Shareholders' Equity}}.$$

Such analysts feel that this version of the debt ratio focuses more attention on the risk of companies being analyzed. (The notion is that the percentage of current liabilities to total equities is, to a large degree, determined by the nature of the business and that so long as current assets are as large as current liabilities, the percentage of current liabilities in total equities is not important.)

The accompanying Exhibit 13.13 shows pertinent data from recent financial statements for both Sears and Penney's. Both versions of the debt ratio mentioned above are presented. The data for Sears are taken directly from the financial statements. For Penney's, the exhibit shows data from the published balance sheet in column (1), data from the statements of the financing subsidiary in column (2), and presents a column for Penney's hypothetical financial statements, assuming consolidation of the financing subsidiary. Column (3) represents the accounting for Penney's that is analogous to Sears' accounting.

a Complete column (3) for Penney's. (The ratios shown are correct; you can check your work from them.) You may find the summary in part **c** of Problem 24 above to be useful.

540

Exhibit 13.13
**Effect of Consolidation Policy
(All Dollar Amounts in Millions)**
(Problem 27)

	J. C. Penney Company			Sears, Roebuck & Co.
	Financial Statements as Issued (1)	Financing Subsidiary Statements as Shown in Notes (2)	Hypothetical Financial Statements if Subsidiary Were Consolidated (3)	Financial Statements as Issued (4)
Total Assets	$3,483.8	$1,458.1	?	$12,711.5
Total Liabilities	1,567.2	1,078.9	?	6,774.6
Long-Term Debt	355.5	517.0	?	1,563.5
Shareholders' Equity	1,916.6	379.2	?	5,936.9
Debt-Equity Ratio (Total Liabilities/Total Equities)	45.0%	72.3%	58.0%	53.3%
Long-Term Debt/Shareholders' Equity	18.5%	136.3%	45.5%	26.3%

b As measured by the debt ratios (and ignoring other factors—see Problem 15 in Chapter 15), which company appears to be the more risky? Which company do you think is more risky and why?

c Assume that the managements of Penney's and Sears are both considering additional long-term financing to raise funds. Managements of both companies are concerned about how the marketplace will react to new debt financing on the one hand or new common share issues on the other. How are financial analysts who are concerned with risk (as measured in part by debt ratios) likely to react to these two companies? How are managements of the two companies likely to react in making their financing decisions if they anticipate the reaction of financial analysts?

28 When one corporation acquires all, or substantially all, of another corporation's common stock in a single transaction, the transaction is referred to as a *corporate acquisition.* Two methods of accounting for corporate acquisitions are permitted under generally accepted accounting principles, depending on the manner in which the acquisition is structured.

Purchase Method The purchase method is a direct extension of acquisition-cost accounting. The Investment in Subsidiary account on the parent's books is recorded initially at the amount of cash or market value of other consideration given in the exchange. When the consolidation work sheet is prepared, any difference between the amount in the investment account on the date of acquisition and the book value of the net assets acquired is allocated to individual assets and liabilities, based on their market values. Thus, under the purchase method, the assets and liabilities of the acquired company are reported in the consolidated balance sheet based on their market value at the date of acquisition. The consolidated income statement will show expenses (depreciation and amortization) based on these market values. The principles of the purchase method have implicitly been used throughout this chapter.

Exhibit 13.14
**Consolidated Statements
Comparing Purchase and
Pooling-of-Interests Methods**
(*Problem 28*)

BALANCE SHEETS	Historical Cost		Company S Shown at Current Values (3)	Companies P & S Consolidated at Date of Acquisition	
	P (1)	S (2)		Purchase (4)	Pooling of Interests (5)
Assets:					
Current Assets	$1,500,000	$450,000	$ 450,000	$1,950,000	$1,950,000
Long-Term Assets Less Accumulated Depreciation	1,700,000	450,000	850,000	?	?
Goodwill	—	—	830,000	?	—
Total Assets	$3,200,000	$900,000	$2,130,000	$5,330,000	$4,100,000
Equities:					
Liabilities	$1,300,000	$450,000	$ 450,000	$1,750,000	$1,750,000
Common Stock ($5 par)	500,000	100,000	100,000	?	?
Additional Paid-in Capital	200,000	150,000	150,000	?	?
Retained Earnings	1,200,000	200,000	200,000	?	?
Unrecorded Equity at Current Valuation . .	—	—	1,230,000	—	—
Total Liabilities and Shareholders' Equity .	$3,200,000	$900,000	$2,130,000	$5,330,000	$4,100,000

INCOME STATEMENTS (IGNORING INCOME TAXES)	Actual			Projected	
Precombination Income from Combination	$ 300,000	$160,000		$ 460,000	$ 460,000
Cost Savings (Projected)	—	—		50,000	50,000
Extra Depreciation Expense	—	—		?	—
Amortization of Goodwill	—	—		?	—
Net Income	$ 300,000	$160,000		$ 409,250	$ 510,000
Number of Common Shares Outstanding . .	100,000	20,000		?	?
Earnings per Share	$3.00	$8.00		?	?
Rate of Return on Assets (Using Balances at Merger Date)				?	?
Rate of Return on Owners' Equity (Using Balances at Merger Date)				?	?

Assumptions: (1) Company S has 20,000 shares outstanding that sell for $84 each
in the market.
(2) Company P's shares sell for $42 each in the market. Company P
issues 40,000 shares for the purpose of acquiring Company S.

Pooling of Interests Method The pooling of interests method accounts for a corporate acquisition as the uniting of ownership interests of two companies by exchange of equity (common stock) securities. The exchange of equity interests is viewed as a change in *form*, not in *substance*. That is, the shareholders of the predecessor companies become shareholders in the new combined enterprise. Each of the predecessor companies continues carrying out its operations as before. Because there is no change in the substance of either the ownership interest or the nature of the activities of the enterprises involved, no new

542

basis of accountability arises. That is, the book values of the assets and liabilities of the predecessor companies are carried over to the new combined, or consolidated, enterprise. Unlike the purchase method, assets and liabilities do not reflect market values at the date of acquisition on the consolidated balance sheet.

This problem demonstrates the impact of the purchase method versus the pooling of interests method on the consolidated balance sheet and income statement.

Company P and Company S decide to combine operations. Management estimates that the combination will save $50,000 a year in expenses of running the combined businesses. Columns (1) and (2) in Exhibit 13.14 show abbreviated single-company financial statements for Company P and Company S before combination. Company S has 20,000 shares of stock outstanding that sell for $84 per share in the market. The market value of Company S as a going concern is, then, $1,680,000. As shown in Column (3), S's shareholders have $1,230,000 of equity not recorded on the books. Of this $1,230,000, $400,000 is attributable to undervalued noncurrent assets, and $830,000 is attributable to goodwill. Company P has 100,000 shares outstanding, which have a $5 par value and sell for $42 each in the market. Ignore income taxes throughout this problem.

a Assume that Company P purchases Company S to combine their operations. Company P issues (sells) 40,000 additional shares on the market for $42 each, or $1,680,000 in total, and uses the proceeds to purchase all shares of Company S for $84 each. (Each share of Company S is, in effect, "sold" for two shares of Company P.) Company P has acquired 100 percent of the shares of Company S and now owns Company S. Company P's acquisition of Company S would be accounted for as a purchase. Company P decides to amortize the revalued asset costs over 5 years and to amortize the goodwill over 40 years. Complete column (4) to show the effects of purchase accounting.

b Assume that Company P issued the 40,000 shares of stock directly to the owners of Company S in return for their shares. The merger is treated as a pooling of interests. Complete column (5) to show the effects of pooling accounting.

c Suggest reasons why managers of business firms involved in corporate acquisition might prefer the pooling of interests method.

Chapter 14   Accounting for the Effects of Changing Prices

The most persistent and significant criticism of the conventional accounting model based on historical, or acquisition, costs is that it ignores the economic facts of life. Throughout the world, a steady and rapid upward movement in prices has been occurring during the last decade. Yet, until recently, this important economic phenomenon largely went unrecognized under generally accepted accounting principles. FASB *Statement No. 33* (1979), however, now requires that the conventional financial statements be supplemented with certain information about the impact of changing prices on larger firms. This chapter discusses the accounting problems associated with changing prices and illustrates techniques for dealing with them.

Impact of Changing Prices on Conventional Financial Statements

The accounting problems associated with changing prices might be separated into those related to *changes in general price levels* and those associated with *changes in prices of specific goods and services.* This distinction might be grasped most easily by considering the manner in which a price index is constructed.

Nature and Construction of Price Indices

A *price index* is a measure of the prices of a group, or "basket," of goods and services between two dates. For example, assume that we wish to construct a price index for food to measure the change in overall prices between January 1 and December 31 of

544

a particular year. We begin by constructing a typical market basket of food items. To keep the illustration simple, suppose we specify that a typical market basket includes meat, starch, vegetable, beverage, and bread. We ascertain the price of a specific commodity in each of these food groupings at the beginning and end of a year. The prices of the individual commodities at each date are summed to obtain the aggregate market price of the basket of goods. The aggregate market price at one date is then compared to the aggregate price at the other date to obtain a price index. Exhibit 14.1 illustrates the construction of such a price index.[1]

Exhibit 14.1
Illustration of the Construction of a Price Index

Commodity	January 1	December 31	Percentage Change in Market Price of Individual Commodities
Sirloin Steak (pound)	$3.00	$3.30	+10%
Rice (32 ounces)	1.20	1.10	−8
Frozen Vegetables (package)	.60	.69	+15
Beer (six-pack)	1.90	2.32	+22
Bread (loaf)	.60	.62	+3
Total	$7.30	$8.03	
Price index, where January 1 prices equal 100% (in percent).	100	110 (= $8.03/$7.30)	

Prices for this group of commodities increased an average of 10 percent between the beginning and end of the year. The prices of the individual commodities, however, changed at different rates. The price of bread remained relatively stable, while the price of rice decreased. The prices of sirloin steak, frozen vegetables, and beer increased significantly, but only that of the frozen vegetables and the beer increased more than the average 10 percent for the group.

Price indices are constructed by the federal government for many different groupings, or baskets, of commodities. Some of these indices are based on a wide assortment of goods and services and are intended as measures of price changes in general. The two most important *general price indices* are the Gross National Product Implicit Price Deflator Index (issued quarterly) and the Consumer Price Index (issued monthly). Indices are constructed for many specific groupings of goods and services, such as women's apparel, men's shoes, automobiles, and refrigerators. Even these

---

[1] A price series is a set of index numbers, such as 100 and 110 in Exhibit 14.1, that represent the price levels at different times. The absolute numbers are not important. The percentage change in the numbers from one period to the next provides the information about the change in relative prices. Thus, a price index series of 50 and 55 represents the same price increase, of 10 percent, as does a price index series of 100 and 110. Similarly a price index series of 200 and 220 represents a price increase of 10 percent. By convention, the time period for which the price index is 100 is called the "base period" of a given price series.

more *specific price indices,* however, contain an assortment of goods of various qualities, dimensions, and styles within the particular product category.

Accounting Problems Associated with General Price Changes

The conventional accounting model uses as a measuring unit the *actual,* or *nominal,* dollars expended or received over time in recording transactions or events in the accounts. Implicit in the use of nominal dollars is the assumption that the dollar represents a constant, or uniform, measuring unit over time. That is, the measuring unit (the dollar) used in recording the acquisition of a machine costing $10,000 five years ago is assumed to have the same economic significance as the measuring unit used in recording the acquisition of merchandise inventory one week ago for $10,000.

As general price levels change, however, the purchasing power of the dollar, or its command over goods and services, changes. The general purchasing power sacrificed to acquire the machine five years ago is not equivalent to the purchasing power sacrificed last week to acquire the merchandise inventory. In terms of general purchasing power, therefore, the dollar does not represent a constant, or uniform, measuring unit through time. The amounts assigned to individual assets in the conventional financial statements cannot be summed to measure the total purchasing power sacrificed to acquire total assets. Likewise, the dollars sacrificed to acquire the various assets consumed as expenses differ in purchasing power from the dollars generated by the revenues of the period, because the dollars used to acquire the assets that were consumed as expenses were spent at times different from the date of revenue recognition.

Accounting Problems Associated with Specific Price Changes

The conventional accounting model also rests on *acquisition,* or *historical, cost valuations.* Increases in the market prices of individual assets are not reflected in the valuation of assets on the balance sheet or as gains in measuring net income until the assets are sold. Only at the time of sale is the measurement of the gain considered to be sufficiently objective to warrant recognition in the accounts.

Management, however, bases many decisions on information about changes in the prices of individual assets and liabilities. In pricing decisions, management considers the current cost of replacing the goods and services sold. In plant asset replacement decisions, management considers the current market values of individual assets held relative to the acquisition prices of assets with similar operating characteristics. In refinancing decisions, management considers the current market value of outstanding debt relative to the cost of issuing new debt. By using historical-cost valuations and the realization convention, the conventional financial statements fail to reflect properly the results of management's decisions in the firm's current economic environment.

Official Pronouncement on Accounting for Changing Prices

Recognizing the deficiencies of the conventional accounting model based on nominal dollars and historical-cost valuations, the FASB requires large, publicly-held firms to report certain supplementary information about the impact of changing prices.[2] The types of information disclosed are described and illustrated in the remaining sections of the chapter under the following headings:

1 Historical cost/constant dollar accounting—Conventional financial statement data is restated to a constant-dollar basis to obtain a uniform measuring unit.
2 Current cost/nominal dollar accounting—Historical-cost valuations are replaced with current-cost valuations.
3 Current cost/constant dollar accounting—Current-cost valuations are restated to a constant-dollar basis.

To illustrate each of these three approaches to reporting the effects of changing prices, data for Aliber Corporation for 1982 are used. The data are summarized in Exhibit 14.2. The firm is organized on January 2, 1982, by issuing common stock for $400 cash. The Consumer Price Index (CPI), a measure of the general price level, is assumed to be 200 on this date. Aliber Corporation immediately acquires two widgets for $100 each and equipment with a 5-year life for $100. During the first 6 months of 1982, the CPI increases 5 percent from 200 to 210. On June 30, 1982, the firm sells one widget for $240 and replaces it with a new widget costing $115. It also pays other operating expenses of $100. During the second 6 months of the year, the CPI increases 10 percent, from 210 to 231. At the end of 1982, the current cost of replacing one widget is $140, and the current cost of replacing the equipment in new condition is $120.

Historical Cost/Constant Dollar Accounting

Objective of Historical Cost/Constant Dollar Accounting

The objective of historical cost/constant dollar accounting is to state all financial statement amounts in dollars of uniform general purchasing power, thereby obtaining a constant, or uniform, measuring unit. The general approach is to convert the actual, or nominal, dollars received or expended over time to an equivalent number of dollars on some constant-dollar date. For example, consider the equipment acquired on January 2, 1982, by Aliber Corporation for $100. This acquisition-cost amount represents a sacrifice of 100 January 2, 1982, dollars. That sacrifice in purchasing power can be stated in several different ways, as illustrated next.

---

[2]Financial Accounting Standards Board, *Statement of Financial Standards No. 33,* "Financial Reporting and Changing Prices," 1979.

547

Exhibit 14.2
Data for Inflation
Accounting Illustration—Aliber Corporation

Balance Sheet as of January 2, 1982

Cash: $400   Contributed Capital: $400

	January 2, 1982		**June 30, 1982**		**December 31, 1982**
Consumer Price Index (CPI)	200	(5% Increase)→	210	(10% Increase)→	231
Cost of One Widget	$100		$115		$140
Cost of Equipment	$100		$110		$120
Transactions	1) Buy 2 widgets at $100 each, $200.		1) Sell 1 widget for $240; replace widget at $115.		1) Close books and prepare statements.
	2) Purchase equipment (5-year life) for $100.		2) Pay other expenses of $100.		

548

1 The purchasing power of $100 on January 2, 1982, is equal to the purchasing power of 50.00 base-year dollars because

$$\$100 \times 100/200 = \$50.00.$$

2 The purchasing power of $100 on January 2, 1982, is equal to the purchasing power of 105.00 June 30, 1982, dollars because

$$\$100 \times 210/200 = \$105.00.$$

3 The purchasing power of $100 on January 2, 1982, is equal to the purchasing power of 115.50 December 31, 1982, dollars because

$$\$100 \times 231/200 = \$115.50.$$

In words, 100 dollars of January 2, 1982, purchasing power have 50.00 dollars of base-year purchasing power or 105 dollars of June 30, 1982, purchasing power or 115.50 dollars of December 31, 1982, purchasing power.

Using the constant dollar notation, we can write

$$C\$_{1/2/82}100.00 = C\$_{Base}50.00 = C\$_{6/30/82}105.00 = C\$_{12/31/82}115.50.$$

These four amounts are economically equivalent because they represent equal amounts of general purchasing power. The notation "C$" denotes that constant, instead of nominal, dollars underlie the measurements made.[3]

The constant-dollar date used for restating financial statement amounts is an arbitrary choice. Some have suggested that the date ought to be the base year of the price index used for restatement. Others have suggested using the end of the current year. Still others, including the FASB for certain disclosures, advocate mid-year dollars of the most recent year being reported. The restatement procedures are analogous, whatever date is used. In the illustrations in this chapter, constant dollars of December 31, 1982, purchasing power are used.

It should be noted that the historical cost/constant dollar amounts do not reflect changes over time in the market prices of individual assets. The market price of the equipment of Aliber Corporation, for example, could have changed in an entirely different direction and pattern from that of the general price change. The focus of historical cost/constant dollar accounting is on making the measuring unit used in acquisition cost-based accounting systems more comparable over time. It is not intended as a technique for reflecting current market prices of individual assets and equities.

---

[3] In principle, the notation "C$" is incomplete. To be completely unambiguous, there should be a subscript indicating which date's purchasing power is being used as the numéraire. Because the numéraire is fixed for a given set of financial statements; the typical accounting disclosure indicates the constant dollar date in some fashion less clumsy than by putting subscript on the C$. (See, for example, the notes of General Products Company in Exhibit A.4. near our notations "81" and "84," on page 663.) In this paragraph, however, we have had to use the subscripts on the C$ notation to indicate the different dates that might be used in stating the purchasing power given up to acquire the asset.

Restatement of Monetary and Nonmonetary Items

An important distinction is made in the constant-dollar restatement procedure between monetary items and nonmonetary items.

Monetary Items A *monetary item* is a claim receivable or payable in a specified number of dollars, regardless of changes in the general purchasing power of the dollar. Examples of monetary items are cash; accounts, notes, and interest receivable; accounts, notes, and interest payable; income taxes payable; and bonds. In preparing a constant-dollar restated balance sheet, the valuation of monetary items at the number of dollars due on the date of the balance sheet automatically states them in terms of the general purchasing power of the dollar at that time. No restatement is therefore necessary, and the conventionally reported and restated amounts are the same. For example, Aliber Corporation has $125 of cash on December 31, 1982. On the conventionally prepared balance sheet, this item would be stated at $125, the amount of cash on hand. On the constant-dollar restated balance sheet, this item would also be reported at C$125, representing $125 of December 31, 1982, general purchasing power.

Because monetary items are receivable or payable in a specified number of dollars rather than in terms of a given amount of general purchasing power, holding monetary items over time while the general purchasing power of the dollar changes gives rise to *purchasing power gains and losses.* During a period of inflation, holders of monetary assets lose general purchasing power. For example, a firm with outstanding notes receivable incurs a purchasing-power loss, because the dollars loaned out are worth more in terms of general purchasing power than the dollars to be received when the account is collected. Likewise, a holder of monetary liabilities gains in general purchasing power during periods of inflation, because the dollars required to repay the debt represent less purchasing power than the dollars originally borrowed.[4] The gain or loss from holding monetary items is reported as an element of constant-dollar net income but is not included in conventionally reported nominal-dollar net income.

Nonmonetary Items A *nonmonetary item* is an asset or equity that does not represent a claim to or for a specified number of dollars. That is, if an item is not a monetary item, then it must be nonmonetary. Examples of nonmonetary items are inventory, land, buildings, equipment, capital stock, revenues, and expenses. In conventionally prepared financial statements, nonmonetary items are stated in terms of varying amounts of general purchasing power depending on the date the nonmone-

---

[4] The purchasing power gain on long-term debt, for example, is conceptually an offset to interest expense. In setting an interest rate on long-term borrowing, lenders recognize that the dollars to be received when the debt is repaid will be worth less in terms of general purchasing power than the dollars loaned out. Lenders will, therefore, set a higher interest rate to compensate for this expected purchasing power loss. To the borrower, the purchasing power gain has effectively been "paid for" as part of the higher interest cost on the debt. As long as the actual rate of inflation coincides with that anticipated in setting the interest rate, the borrower is not better off as a result of reporting a purchasing power gain. The borrower is better (worse) off only if the actual rate of inflation is greater (less) than the anticipated rate.

tary assets were acquired and nonmonetary equities arose. These conventionally reported amounts must be restated to an equivalent number of dollars as of the constant-dollar restatement date. The amount of this restatement does not represent a gain or loss to be included in net income, but is merely an adjustment to change the measuring unit.

Illustration of the Restatement Procedure

Column (1) of Exhibit 14.3 presents an income statement for 1982 and a balance sheet on December 31, 1982, for Aliber Corporation as conventionally reported, based on historical cost/nominal dollars. Column (2) shows these historical-cost amounts restated to constant dollars of December 31, 1982, purchasing power.

Income Statement Consider first the income statement. The sale of the widget for $240 occurred on June 30, 1982, when the CPI was 210. The equivalent number of constant December 31, 1982, dollars is C$264 (= $240 × 231/210). The widget that was sold had a historical cost in nominal dollars of $100 on January 2, 1982, when the CPI was 200. The equivalent number of constant December 31, 1982, dollars is C$115.50 (= $100 × 231/200). The restatement of depreciation and other operating expenses likewise reflects the cumulative change in the CPI between the date the original historical-cost measurements were made (January 2, 1982, and June 30, 1982, respectively) and the end of the year.

Operating income measured in constant-dollars will typically be less than operating income measured in nominal dollars, as is the case for Aliber Corporation. Sales and operating expenses will typically be restated for approximately one-half year of general price change. Cost of goods sold will usually reflect either somewhat less (LIFO cost-flow assumption) or somewhat more (FIFO cost-flow assumption) than one-half year of price change. Depreciation expense, however, will reflect cumulative inflation since the depreciable assets were acquired. The restatement of depreciation expense for 1982 for Aliber Corporation reflects only 1 year of general price change. The restatement of depreciation expense on the equipment for 1983 will reflect changes in the general price level for both 1982 and 1983. In later years, still more cumulative inflation will be reflected in the restatements. Firms with relatively large amounts of old depreciable assets find that depreciation expense stated in constant dollars is much larger than depreciation expense stated in nominal dollars.

Also shown in Column (2) is the purchasing power loss for the year. Aliber Corporation held cash during the year, its only monetary item, and incurred a loss in general purchasing power of C$18. The calculation of this loss is as follows:

Purchasing Power Loss on $100 (= $400 − $200 − $100) held during first 6 months when CPI increased 5 percent; $100 × 10/200 = $5. Restatement of purchasing power loss to constant December 31, 1982, dollars; $5 × 231/210	C$ 5.50
Purchasing Power Loss on $125 (= $100 + $240 − $115 − $100) held during second 6 months when CPI increased 10 percent; $125 × 21/210	12.50
Total Purchasing Power Loss	C$18.00

Exhibit 14.3
Aliber Corporation
Financial Statements Reflecting Accounting for Changing Prices

	(1) Historical-Cost/ Nominal Dollars	(2) Historical-Cost/ Constant 12/31/82 Dollars	(3) Current-Cost/ Nominal Dollars	(4) Current-Cost/ Constant 12/31/82 Dollars
INCOME STATEMENT				
Sales	$240	C$264.0^a	$240	C$264.0^a
Cost of Goods Sold	$100	C$115.5^b	$115	C$126.5^n
Depreciation	20	23.1^c	22^j	24.2^o
Other Expenses	100	110.0^d	100	110.0^d
Operating Income	$ 20	C$ 15.4	$ 3	C$ 3.3
Realized Holding Gains:				
Goods Sold	—	—	15^j	11.0^p
Depreciable Assets Used	—	—	2^k	1.1^q
Unrealized Holding Gains:				
Inventory	—	—	65^l	38.0^r
Depreciable Assets	—	—	16^m	3.6^s
Purchasing Power Loss		(18.0)^e	—	(18.0)^e
Net Income	$ 20	C$ (2.6)	$101	C$ 39.0
BALANCE SHEET				
Cash	$125	C$125.0	$125	C$125
Inventory	215	242.0^f	280	280
Equipment	$100	C$115.5^g	$120	C$120
Accumulated Depreciation	(20)	(23.1)	(24)^t	(24)^t
Total Assets	$420	92.4	96	96
		C$459.4	$501	C$501
Contributed Capital	$400	C$462.0^h	$400	C$462^h
Retained Earnings	20	(2.6)	101	39
Total Equities	$420	C$459.4	$501	C$501

Notes for Exhibit 14.3 on page 553.

552

Most publicly-held firms are in a net monetary liability position because of outstanding long-term debt. Therefore, they experience purchasing power gains instead of losses. These purchasing power gains sometimes more than offset the lower operating income resulting from the restatement of depreciation.

Balance Sheet Column (2) also shows the restatement of the balance sheet to a constant-dollar basis. Cash is the only monetary item. It is shown at C$125, the same amount as in the nominal-dollar balance sheet. Ending inventory is composed of two units, one purchased for $100 on January 2, 1982, and the other purchased for $115 on June 30, 1982. The December 31, 1982, constant-dollar equivalent of these amounts is:

January 2, 1982, Purchase: $100 \times 231/200$	C$115.50
June 30, 1982, Purchase: $115 \times 231/210$	126.50
Total	C$242.00

The cost of the equipment purchased for $100 on January 31, 1982, is restated to C$115.50 December 31, 1982, dollars ($= \$100 \times 231/200$). Accumulated depreciation is equal to one-fifth of the constant-dollar cost, or C$23.10. Contributed capital is likewise restated for 1 year of general price change; $\$400 \times 231/200 = C\$462$. Constant-dollar retained earnings is equal to the constant-dollar net loss for the year.

Notes to Exhibit 14.3: [a]$240 \times (231/210) = C\$264.0$.
[b]$100 \times (231/200) = C\$115.5$.
[c]$100 \times (231/200) = C\$115.5$; $C\$115.5/5 = C\$23.1$.
[d]$100 \times (231/210) = C\$110$.
[e]$[\$100 \times (10/200) \times (231/210) + \$125 \times (21/210)] =$
    $C\$5.50 + C\$12.50 = C\$18$.
[f]$100 \times (231/200) + \$115 \times (231/210) = C\$242$.
[g]$100 \times (231/200) = C\$115.5$.
[h]$400 \times (231/200) = C\$462$.
[i]$110/5 = \$22$.
[j]$115 - \$100 = \$15$.
[k]$22 - \$20 = \$2$.
[l]$280 - \$215 = \$65$.
[m]$96 - \$80 = \$16$.
[n]$115 \times (231/210) = C\$126.5$.
[o]$22 \times (231/210) = C\$24.2$.
[p]$C\$126.5 - \$115.5 = C\$11$.
[q]$C\$24.2 - \$23.1 = C\$1.1$.
[r]$C\$280 - \$242 = C\$38$.
[s]$C\$96 - \$92.4 = C\$3.6$.
[t]The amount shown for accumulated depreciation differs from the amount shown for depreciation expense at the end of Aliber Corporation's first year of operations. The difference arises because depreciation expense is measured in terms of *average* current cost and accumulated depreciation is measured in terms of *end-of-year* current cost, as required by FASB *Statement No. 33*. Because a full set of financial statements adjusted for the effect of changing prices is not required by *Statement No. 33,* this articulation problem between the income statement and balance sheet was not dealt with by the FASB.

Summary of Constant-Dollar Restatement Procedure The constant-dollar restatement procedure can be summarized as follows:

1 Select the constant-dollar date to which all financial statement items will be restated.
2 Restate revenues and expenses on the income statement from the nominal dollars underlying their measurement in the conventional income statement to dollars of the desired constant general purchasing power. The numerator of the restatement factor is the Consumer Price Index on the desired constant-dollar date. The denominator is the Consumer Price Index on the date of the underlying nominal dollar measurements.
3 Calculate the purchasing power gain or loss. Monetary assets held and monetary liabilities outstanding during the year are multiplied by the change in the general purchasing power of the dollar while they are held or outstanding. This purchasing power gain or loss is then restated to dollars of the desired constant general purchasing power.
4 Restate each balance sheet item to its constant-dollar equivalent. If dollars of end-of-the-year purchasing power are selected as the constant-dollar, monetary items are automatically stated in year-end dollars, and no restatement is required. Nonmonetary items must be restated from the nominal dollars underlying their measurement in the conventional financial statements to the equivalent number of constant dollars.

Evaluation of Historical Cost/ Constant-Dollar Accounting

The procedures for restating financial statements to a constant-dollar basis can be traced back to before 1920.[5] Yet it was not until 1979 that disclosure of constant-dollar information became a part of generally accepted accounting principles. The usefulness of constant-dollar information has been, and continues to be, controversial.

The Case for Constant-Dollar Accounting Proponents of constant-dollar accounting offer the following arguments:

1 Constant-dollar accounting makes the results of arithmetic operations more meaningful. If the measuring unit (the dollar) varies over time because of changes in the general purchasing power of the dollar, then additions and subtractions of recorded amounts cannot be made meaningfully.
2 Constant-dollar accounting makes inter-period comparisons more meaningful.

---

[5] See Livingston Middleditch, Jr., "Should Accounts Reflect the Changing Value of the Dollar?" *Journal of Accountancy* (February 1918): 114–120. This article was "rediscovered" and reprinted by Stephen A. Zeff (ed.) in *Asset Appreciation, Business Income and Price-Level Accounting: 1918–1935* (New York: Arno Press, 1976). Generally, however, the credit for developing constant-dollar accounting is given to Henry W. Sweeney for his *Stabilized Accounting* (New York: Harper & Brothers, 1936).

554

Changes in the amount of an item (sales, cost of goods sold) are difficult to interpret if the measuring unit used is not the same over time.

3 Constant-dollar accounting improves the meaning and measurement of net income. Revenues and expenses are matched in terms of a constant measuring unit. Also, a gain or loss is explicitly recognized for the change in the general purchasing power of monetary assets and liabilities held. Income before the purchasing-power gain or loss must exceed any loss of purchasing power of monetary assets and equities if the purchasing power of the monetary, or financial, capital of the firm is to be maintained.

4 Constant-dollar accounting is relatively objective in that government-prepared price indices are used to restate audited historical cost amounts.

The Case against Constant-Dollar Accounting Opponents of constant-dollar accounting argue that it fails to measure the economically significant effects of changing prices on a firm. They argue as follows:

1 With respect to nonmonetary items, the strategies that firms follow in coping with inflation focus on changes in the prices of the specific goods and services that the firm normally acquires and not on changes in the prices of a broad market basket of consumer goods and services. Raw materials are purchased early in anticipation of increased acquisition costs. A capital-intensive plant is constructed in anticipation of increased labor costs. Yet, under constant-dollar accounting, the results of these decisions are judged against a standard based on changes in the general purchasing power of the dollar.

2 With respect to monetary items, the purchasing-power gain or loss is based on an inappropriate index of purchasing power. Users of financial statements are interested in a firm's ability to maintain the purchasing power of its monetary assets for the particular kinds of goods and services that it normally purchases.

Current Cost/Nominal Dollar Accounting

Objective of Current Cost/Nominal Dollar Accounting

The objective of current cost/nominal dollar accounting is to report the effects of specific price changes on the operating performance and financial position of a firm. Current cost is generally defined as the amount a firm would have to pay currently to replace the service potential embodied in its specific assets. It takes into account the inherent technological capabilities and levels of obsolescence of the existing assets. For example, if a firm owned a 2-year-old automobile, it would base its current replacement-cost valuation on the prices of similar 2-year-old automobiles in the used car market. If replacement-cost amounts for identical, used assets are not available, then the replacement cost of new assets with similar service potential would be used. The replacement cost of the new asset would be adjusted downward, however, for both the used condition of the existing asset and any technological changes that have occurred.

Measuring Current-Cost Amounts

There are several sources of information that might be consulted in ascertaining the current cost of a particular asset.

1 Used Asset Market For automobiles, furniture, office machines, and similar items, active used-asset markets exist that can help to measure the current cost of such assets.

2 Suppliers Catalogs For inventories of raw materials, supplies, and standardized equipment, suppliers catalogs can be consulted.

3 Appraisals The current cost of land and building might be determined from real estate appraisers.

4 Specific Price Indices The federal government prepares specific price indices for a wide assortment of goods and services. These price indices indicate the change over time in the price of particular classes of items. These indices typically indicate the current cost of items in new condition. To use the price indices to measure the current cost of existing assets, some recognition must be given to their used condition.

Illustration of Current Cost/ Nominal Dollar Accounting

Column (3) of Exhibit 14.3 on page 552 shows the income statement and balance sheet of Aliber Corporation for 1982 on a current cost/nominal dollar basis.

Income Statement Sales revenue is stated at the amount of cash received (or expected to be received) from the sale of inventory items; the amount is the same as in the conventional financial statements. Matched against sales revenue is the current cost of inventory sold, equipment services used, and other goods and services consumed. When the widget was sold on June 30, 1982, it had a replacement cost of $115. The current cost of goods sold is, therefore, stated at this amount. The equipment of Aliber Corporation had an average current cost of $110 during 1982. Based on a 5-year life and the straight-line depreciation method, depreciation expense on a current-cost basis is $22 (= $110/5). Other expenses incurred during the year are already stated in terms of current cost.

Operating income indicates the extent to which selling prices were set sufficiently high to cover the current cost of replacing goods and services sold or consumed during the period. If a firm is to maintain its operating capacity, it must be able to replace assets as they are used up. Cash generated from sales is the primary means

556

for doing so. Thus, operating income on a current cost basis indicates the extent to which a firm has maintained its operating capacity during the period.

The income statement also shows realized and unrealized holding gains and losses on nonmonetary assets. Recall from the discussion of inventories in Chapter 8 that a holding gain arises when an asset is held while its current cost increases. Consider, for example, the widget purchased on January 1, 1982, for $100 and sold on June 30, 1982, for $240. The current cost of replacing the widget on June 30, 1982, was $115. While the widget was held, its current cost increased $15 (= $115 − $100). Because this widget was sold during the year, the holding gain has been realized. The conventional gross margin on the sale of $140 (= $240 − $100) is separated in Column (3) into an operating margin of $125 (= selling price − current cost of goods sold = $240 − $115) and a realized holding gain of $15 (= current cost of goods sold − historical cost of goods sold = $115 − $100). There is also a realized holding gain of $2 on the equipment used. The gain is equal to the difference between the current cost of the equipment's services used during the year of $22 and the historical cost of those services of $20. Note that operating income plus realized holding gains on a current cost/nominal dollar basis are equal to net income in the conventional financial statements: $3 + $15 + $2 = $20.

The income statement in Column (3) also includes unrealized holding gains on inventory and equipment not yet sold or used. The current cost of replacing the two widgets at the end of 1982 is $280 (= $140 × 2). The historical cost of these widgets is $215 (= $100 + $115). Thus, the unrealized holding gain is $65 (= $280 − $215). Similarly, the current cost of replacing the equipment in new condition at the end of 1982 is $120. If the equipment has a 5-year life, the current cost of replacing the equipment in its existing 1-year-old condition is $96 (= $\frac{4}{5}$ × $120). The difference between the current cost of the equipment of $96 and the historical cost of the same service potential of $80 (= $\frac{4}{5}$ × $100) is an unrealized holding gain.

Net income on a current cost/nominal dollar basis is composed of operating income, realized holding gains and losses, and unrealized holdings gains and losses.

Balance Sheet   Cash is stated at its face amount in the current-cost balance sheet. If Aliber Corporation had other monetary items (accounts receivable, accounts payable, bonds payable), they should, at least theoretically, also be revalued to a current-cost basis. The approach is to ascertain the current interest rate appropriate to the monetary item. The future cash flows associated with the monetary item should be discounted to their present value using the current interest rate. As a practical matter, probably only *long-term* receivables and *long-term* debt would be revalued. *Statement No. 33* does not currently require the revaluation of monetary items in its current-cost disclosures.

The inventory and equipment, both nonmonetary items, are stated at their current cost on December 31, 1982. Contributed capital is stated at its historical cost/nominal dollar amount, because it is not feasible to measure the current cost of such contributed capital at the end of the year. The current market value of the outstanding capital stock might appear to be an appropriate basis for such a current-cost valuation. This market value is for the firm's entire net assets (contributed

557

capital plus retained earnings), not just the contributed capital portion. Retained earnings for Aliber Corporation is equal to current-cost net income for 1982.

Evaluation of Current Cost/ Nominal Dollar Accounting

Current cost/nominal dollar accounting continues to be controversial.

The Case for Current Cost/Nominal Dollar Accounting Advocates of current cost/nominal dollar accounting offer the following arguments.

1 Management's actions to cope with changing prices are based on expected changes in the prices of the particular goods and services normally acquired by a firm. Current-cost financial statements provide a consistent basis on which to evaluate management's actions and performance.
2 Current-cost income is separated into operating margin and holding gains and losses, permitting statement users to assess the impact of changing prices on the profitability of the firm.
3 Current-cost balance sheets provide a more realistic indication of the current economic value of assets and liabilities than do the balance sheets based on historical costs.

The Case against Current Cost/Nominal Dollar Accounting Opponents of current cost/nominal dollar accounting offer the following arguments.

1 Current-cost amounts are often difficult to calculate, particularly for specialized used assets, raising questions about the reliability and comparability of current-cost data between firms.
2 Current-cost net income must be interpreted cautiously. Unrealized holding gains do not produce cash or claims to cash. Basing dividends on current cost net income, including realized and unrealized holding gains, may result in impairing the operating capacity of the firm.
3 Current-cost accounting in nominal dollars fails to recognize that the measuring unit used to calculate current-cost amounts is not of the same dimension over time. Changes in the general purchasing power of the dollar make current-cost amounts on the balance sheet at the beginning and end of the period noncomparable. Likewise, net income amounts over time, using current costs, are not based on a constant measuring unit.
4 Changes in current costs relative to changes in the general price level are not considered in measuring holding gains and losses under current cost/nominal dollar accounting. A holding gain of 8 percent on a tract of land on a current cost basis has one meaning when the general price level increases 6 percent and another meaning when general prices increase by 10 percent.
5 Current-cost accounting fails to recognize purchasing-power, or inflation, gains or

losses on monetary items. As discussed earlier in this chapter, monetary items gain or lose purchasing power as they are held over time. These gains and losses are often equally as important as holding gains and losses on inventories, depreciable assets, and similar items.

Current Cost/Constant Dollar Accounting

Objective of Current Cost/Constant Dollar Accounting

The objective of current cost/constant dollar accounting is to report in a constant measuring unit the effects of specific price changes on the operating performance and financial position of a firm. Because constant-dollar accounting deals with the measuring unit and current-cost accounting deals with the valuation basis, there are no theoretical obstacles to combining the two approaches.

Illustration of Current Cost/Constant Dollar Accounting

Column (4) of Exhibit 14.3 on page 552 shows the income statement and balance sheet of Aliber Corporation on a current cost/constant dollar basis. The constant dollar date is December 31, 1982.

Income Statement Sales revenue, cost of goods sold, depreciation, and other expenses are stated in Column (3) at their current cost on June 30, 1982, measured in terms of June 30, 1982, dollars. To measure them in terms of December 31, 1982, dollars requires that they be restated using the factor, 231/210.

The realized holding gains must be recomputed to reflect a constant measuring unit. Recall that the realized holding gain on the widget sold in Column (3) is equal to the current cost of the widget on June 30, 1982, of $115 less the historical cost on January 1, 1982, of $100. These two amounts are expressed in different measuring units. Both amounts must be restated to constant December 31, 1982, dollars as follows:

Current Cost of Widget Sold: $115 × 231/210	C$126.50
Historical Cost of Widget Sold: $100 × 231/200	115.50
Realized Holding Gain on Inventory Sold	C$ 11.00

Similarly, the realized holding gain on depreciable assets used in Column (3) is the difference between the average current cost of the services used during the year of $22 and the historical cost of the services of $20. Both amounts must be expressed in constant December 31, 1982, dollars as follows:

Current Cost of Depreciable Assets Used: $22 \times 231/210$	C$24.2
Historical Cost of Depreciable Assets Used: $20 \times 231/200$	23.1
Realized Holding Gain on Depreciable Assets Used	C$ 1.1

The unrealized holding gains must also be recalculated to place all measurements in terms of constant December 31, 1982, dollars.

Current cost/constant dollar net income is composed of operating income, realized and unrealized holding gains and losses on nonmonetary items, and purchasing power gains and losses on monetary items.

Balance Sheet　The amounts on the asset side of the balance sheet in Column (3) reflect current costs on December 31, 1982. Because these amounts are already stated in terms of December 31, 1982, dollars, no restatement is necessary. Contributed capital is restated from January 1, 1982, to December 31, 1982, dollars using the factor, 231/200.

Evaluation of Current Cost/ Constant Dollar Accounting

A careful reading of the arguments for and against historical cost/constant dollar accounting and current cost/nominal dollar accounting reveals that most of the criticisms of these two approaches are overcome by combining them. An added difficulty arises, however. The computations may be so complex that readers of the financial statements will be unable to understand and interpret the disclosures made. An educational effort is required to inform statement readers as to the kinds of interpretations that should and should not be made.

Required Disclosures under Statement No. 33

The FASB recognizes that opinions vary widely on the usefulness of information generated by each of the three approaches to accounting for changing prices discussed in this chapter (that is, the information of Columns (2), (3), and (4) of Exhibit 14.3). Rather than require that a full set of supplemental financial statements be prepared under only one of these three approaches, the FASB in *Statement No. 33* requires certain minimum disclosures using each of the three approaches. This approach provides statement users with time to educate themselves as to the nature of the disclosures made and to assess their relative usefulness. The FASB will continually monitor the reporting process to determine if the required disclosures should be altered.

The following minimum disclosures are required by *Statement No. 33.*

1 Income from continuing operations for the current fiscal year on an historical cost/constant dollar basis. This amount is analogous to Operating Income in Column (2) of Exhibit 14.3.

2 The purchasing power gain or loss on net monetary items for the current fiscal year. *Statement No. 33* requires that the purchasing power gain or loss be excluded from income from continuing operations. Thus, unlike the presentation in Column (2) of Exhibit 14.3, the income from continuing operations of C$15.4 would not be netted with the purchasing power loss of $18 to obtain a constant-dollar net income figure.

3 Income from continuing operations for the current fiscal year on a current cost/nominal dollar basis. This amount is analogous to Operating Income in Column (3) of Exhibit 14.3.

4 Increases or decreases for the current fiscal year in the current cost amounts of inventory and property, plant, and equipment, net of inflation. We have referred to these as holding gains and losses in Exhibit 14.3. The amounts to be disclosed are those in Column (4), the amounts net of general price inflation. These holding gains and losses must be disclosed separately. They need not be added to income from continuing operations to obtain a current-cost net income.

5 Current cost of inventory and property, plant, and equipment at the end of the current fiscal year. Other assets and equities on the balance sheet need not be stated at current cost.

6 For each of the five most recent fiscal years, the following items must be disclosed:
   a Net sales and other operating revenue.
   b Historical cost/constant dollar information:
      (1) Income from continuing operations.
      (2) Income per common share from continuing operations.
      (3) Purchasing power gain or loss on monetary items.
      (4) Net assets at fiscal year-end.
   c Current-cost information:
      (5) Income from continuing operations.
      (6) Income per common share from continuing operations.
      (7) Increases or decreases in current-cost amounts of inventory and property, plant, and equipment, net of inflation.
      (8) Net assets at fiscal year-end.
   d Other information:
      (9) Cash dividends declared per common share.
      (10) Market price per common share at fiscal year-end.

The notes to the financial statements of General Products Company in Appendix A illustrate the supplementary disclosures required by FASB *Statement No. 33.*

Changing Prices and the Statement of Changes in Financial Position

Of the three principal financial statements, the statement of changes in financial position is the least affected by changing prices. Most transactions affecting the flow of funds occur during the period being reported. Any adjustment of these amounts for either general or specific price changes would reflect price changes for approximately 1 year or less.

As is the case in preparing the statement of changes in financial position in historical cost/nominal dollars, the restated statement reflecting either general or specific price changes can be most easily prepared after the balance sheet and income statement have been restated for price changes. The amounts included in the restated statement of changes in financial position can usually be obtained from either the restated balance sheet or the restated income statement.

FASB *Statement No. 33* does not require the disclosure of information about the effects of inflation on the statement of changes in financial position.

Summary

Accounting for changing prices is currently in a period of transition and experimentation. Financial statement preparers and users have recognized for many years that changing prices, either in general or for specific goods and services, bring to question the validity and meaningfulness of conventional financial statements based on historical cost and nominal dollars. The pronouncement by the Financial Accounting Standards Board allows firms considerable flexibility in the way changing prices are accounted for and disclosed. Whether constant-dollar accounting, current-cost accounting, or some other approach replaces or regularly supplements the historical cost/nominal dollars financial statements will depend on the benefits of the disclosures as perceived by users, relative to the cost of generating the necessary data. It is, as yet, too early to evaluate effectively these benefits and costs.

Problem for Self-Study

The Whitmyer Corporation was formed on January 2, 1982, to conduct an office rental business. Listed below are various transactions and other events of the firm during 1982. The assumed values of the Consumer Price Index (CPI) are shown in parentheses.

(1) January 2, 1982 (CPI = 200): Common stock is issued at par value, $1,000,000.
(2) January 2, 1982 (CPI = 200): Land costing $100,000 and a building costing $1,500,000 are acquired. A cash payment of $900,000 is made for the land and building with a long-term, 10-percent note signed for the remainder of the purchase price. Interest on the note is payable on December 31 of each year, and the principal is repayable in 10 years.
(3) January 2, 1982 to December 31, 1982 (average CPI = 212): Rentals totaling $300,000 for the year are collected in cash.

562

(4) January 2, 1982 to December 31, 1982 (average CPI = 212): Operating costs incurred evenly over the year total $60,000, of which $40,000 are paid in cash and the remainder are on account. All of these costs are expenses of 1982.

(5) January 2, 1982 to December 31, 1982 (average CPI = 212): Interest costs are accrued monthly on the mortgage payable and are paid on December 31, 1982.

(6) December 31, 1982 (CPI = 224): Depreciation on the building is calculated using the straight-line method, a 30-year life, and zero salvage value.

(7) December 31, 1982 (CPI = 224): A cash dividend of $75,000 is declared and paid.

On December 31, 1982, the land had a current cost of $150,000. A similar new office building had a current cost in new condition of $1,560,000, while a similar 1-year-old office building had a current cost of $1,508,000. The amounts reported as operating and interest expenses in the conventional financial statements closely approximate their average current costs during the year.

Prepare an income statement for 1982 and a balance sheet as of December 31, 1982, for Whitmyer Corporation under each of the following (round all amounts to the nearest dollar).

a Historical cost/nominal dollars.
b Historical cost/constant dollars of December 31, 1982, purchasing power.
c Current cost/nominal dollars.
d Current cost/constant dollars of December 31, 1982, purchasing power.

Suggested Solution

Exhibit 14.4 presents income statements and balance sheets for Whitmyer Corporation for 1982. The computations are shown in the notes to Exhibit 14.4 and in Exhibit 14.5.

Questions and Problems

1 Review the meaning of the following concepts or terms discussed in this chapter.
  a General price level changes.
  b Specific price level changes.
  c Price index.
  d Nominal dollars.
  e Constant dollars.
  f Acquisition cost.
  g Current cost.
  h Constant-dollar date.
  i Monetary item.
  j Nonmonetary item.
  k Purchasing power gain or loss on monetary items.
  l Current cost.
  m Realized holding gain or loss on nonmonetary items.
  n Unrealized holding gain or loss on nonmonetary items.
  o Holding gains and losses net of inflation.

Exhibit 14.4
Whitmyer Corporation
Financial Statements Reflecting Accounting for Changing Prices

	Historical-Cost/ Nominal Dollars	Historical-Cost/ Constant Dollars	Current-Cost/ Nominal Dollars	Current-Cost/ Constant Dollars
INCOME STATEMENT				
Rent Revenue	$ 300,000	C$ 316,981[a]	$ 300,000	C$ 316,981[a]
Depreciation Expense	(50,000)	(56,000)[b]	(51,000)[j]	(53,887)[o]
Operating Expenses	(60,000)	(63,396)[c]	(60,000)	(63,396)[c]
Interest Expense	(70,000)	(73,962)[d]	(70,000)	(73,962)[d]
Operating Income	$ 120,000	C$ 123,623	$ 119,000	C$ 125,736
Realized Holding Gain:				
Building	—	—	1,000[k]	(2,113)[p]
Unrealized Holding Gain:				
Land	—	—	50,000[l]	38,000[q]
Building	—	—	58,000[m]	(116,000)[r]
Purchasing Power Gain	—	62,377[e]	—	62,377[e]
Net Income	$ 120,000	C$ 186,000	$ 228,000	C$ 108,000
Less Dividends Declared	(75,000)	(75,000)	(75,000)	(75,000)
Retained Earnings, December 31, 1982	$ 45,000	C$ 111,000	$ 153,000	C$ 33,000
BALANCE SHEET				
Assets:				
Cash	$ 215,000	C$ 215,000	$ 215,000	C$ 215,000
Land	100,000	112,000[f]	150,000	150,000
Building—Cost	1,500,000	1,680,000[g]	1,560,000	1,560,000
Less Accumulated Depreciation	(50,000)	(56,000)[h]	(52,000)[n]	(52,000)
Total Assets	$1,765,000	C$1,951,000	$1,873,000	C$1,873,000
Liabilities and Shareholders' Equity:				
Accounts Payable	$ 20,000	C$ 20,000	$ 20,000	C$ 20,000
Note Payable	700,000	700,000	700,000	700,000
Common Stock	1,000,000	1,120,000[i]	1,000,000	1,120,000[i]
Retained Earnings	45,000	111,000	153,000	33,000
Total Equities	$1,765,000	C$1,951,000	$1,873,000	C$1,873,000

Notes for Exhibit 14.4 on page 565.

564

Exhibit 14.5
Whitmyer Corporation
Calculation of Purchasing Power Gain or Loss
for The Year 1982

	Historical-Cost/ Nominal Dollars	Restatement	Historical-Cost/ Constant Dollars
Net Monetary Position, January 1, 1982.	—	—	—
Increases in Net Monetary Assets:			
Issue of Common Stock for Cash . . .	$1,000,000	224/200	C$1,120,000
Accrual of Rent Receivable	300,000	224/212	316,981
Decreases in Net Monetary Assets:			
Disbursement of Cash in Acquisition of Land and Building	(900,000)	224/200	(1,008,000)
Issuance of Note Payable in Acquisition of Land and Building	(700,000)	224/200	(784,000)
Accrual of Operating Costs	(60,000)	224/212	(63,396)
Accrual of Interest Costs	(70,000)	224/212	(73,962)
Declaration of Dividend	(75,000)	224/224	(75,000)
Net Monetary Liability Position, December 31, 1982	$(505,000)		C$(567,377)

Purchasing Power Gain: C$567,377 − C$505,000 = C$62,377.

2 Refer to the income statements and balance sheets of Aliber Corporation in Exhibit 14.3 in the chapter.

   a Under what conditions will the amounts in Column (1) (historical cost/nominal dollars) and Column (3) (current cost/nominal dollars) be the same?

   b Under what conditions will the amounts in Column (2) (historical cost/constant dollars) and Column (4) (current cost/constant dollars) be the same?

   c Under what conditions will the amounts in Column (2) (historical cost/constant dollars) and Column (3) (current cost/nominal dollars) be the same?

Notes to Exhibit 14.4: [a]$300,000 × 224/212 = C$316,981.
[b]$50,000 × 224/200 = C$56,000.
[c]$60,000 × 224/212 = C$63,396.
[d]$70,000 × 224/212 = C$73,962.
[e]See Exhibit 14.5.
[f]$100,000 × 224/200 = C$112,000.
[g]$1,500,000 × 224/200 = C$1,680,000.
[h]C$1,680,000/30 = C$56,000.
[i]$1,000,000 × 224/200 = C$1,120,000.
[j]($1,500,000 + $1,560,000)/2 = $1,530,000; $1,530,000/30 = $51,000.
[k]$51,000 − $50,000 = $1,000.
[l]$150,000 − $100,000 = $50,000.
[m]($1,560,000 − $52,000) − ($1,500,000 − $50,000) = $1,508.000 − $1,450,000 = $58,000.
[n]$1,560,000/30 = $52,000.
[o]$51,000 × 224/212 = C$53,887.
[p]($51,000 × 224/212) − ($50,000 × 224/200) = C$53,887 − C$56,000 = C$(2,113).
[q]$150,000 − ($100,000 × 224/200) = C$150,000 − C$112,000 = C$38,000.
[r]C$1,508,000 − C$1,624,000 = C$(116,000).

3 When historical cost/constant dollar financial statements are prepared, under what conditions will a firm incur:
  a A purchasing power gain?
  b A purchasing power loss?
  c Neither a purchasing power gain nor a purchasing power loss?

4 Why is there no purchasing power gain or loss on nonmonetary items in historical cost/constant dollar financial statements?

5 "Financial statements prepared under the conventional accounting model reflect dollars of mixed purchasing power." Explain the meaning of this statement in relation to the balance sheet, income statement, and statement of changes in financial position.

6 For which types of asset and equity structures would you expect:
  a Significant differences between net income as conventionally reported and as restated to a constant dollar basis (including the purchasing power gain or loss)?
  b Insignificant differences between the two earnings measures?

7 "The amount of income from continuing operations for any given year on a historical cost/constant dollar basis will differ depending on which constant-dollar date is selected." Explain.

8 "Operating income on a current cost/nominal dollar basis indicates the extent to which a firm has maintained its operating capacity during a period." Explain.

9 "All realized holding gains or losses were once unrealized holding gains or losses." Do you agree? Why or why not?

10 A firm reports a realized holding gain on land in its current cost/nominal dollar income statement but a realized holding loss in its current cost/constant dollar income statement. What is the likely explanation for this difference?

11 "The LIFO cost-flow assumption for inventories and accelerated depreciation methods for plant and equipment are only partial solutions to the accounting problems associated with specific price changes." Explain.

12 Rockness Corporation acquired a parcel of land on January 2, 1982, for $50,000. The parcel was sold on July 1, 1982, for $65,000. An index of the general price level and the current cost of the land on various dates are as follows:

	General Price Index	Current Cost
January 2, 1982	160	$50,000
July 1, 1982	185	65,000
December 31, 1982	200	75,000

Calculate the amount of income or loss relating to this land for 1982 under each of the following bases (round amounts to the nearest dollar).
  a Historical cost/nominal dollars.
  b Historical cost/constant dollars of December 31, 1982, purchasing power.
  c Current cost/nominal dollars.
  d Current cost/constant dollars of December 31, 1982, purchasing power.

566

13 The merchandise inventory of Scoggin's Appliance Store on January 1, 1982, consists of 1,000 units acquired for $250 each. During 1982, 2,500 units are purchased at a unit price of $300, while 2,400 units are sold for $400 each. The average current cost per unit during 1982 is $300, while the current cost on December 31, 1982, is $360 per unit.

a Using historical-cost and nominal dollars, calculate the gross margin (sales minus cost of goods sold) for 1982 using the FIFO and the LIFO cost-flow assumptions.

b Using current-cost and nominal dollars, disaggregate the gross margin in Part **a** into the operating margin and realized holding gain.

14 Sunder Equipment Corporation depreciates its machinery using the straight-line method over a 10-year life with zero estimated salvage value. A full year's depreciation is taken in the year of acquisition and none in the year of disposal. Acquisitions, which took place evenly over the appropriate years, were as follows: 1980, $400,000; 1981, $200,000; 1982, $300,000. An index of the average general price level during 1980 was 180, during 1981 was 220, and during 1982 was 240. The general price index on December 31, 1982, is 250.

a Calculate the amount of depreciation expense for 1982 and the book value of the machinery on December 31, 1982, using the historical costs and nominal dollars.

b Repeat Part **a**, using the historical costs and constant dollars of December 31, 1982, purchasing power. Round all amounts to the nearest dollar.

15 The Cunningham Hardware Store had a net monetary asset position of $300,000 on January 1, 1982, at which time an index of the general price level was 200. Transactions during 1982 and associated indices of the general price level (GPI) are listed below.

(1) Purchases, all on account, totaled $400,000 (GPI = 210).
(2) Sales, all on account, totaled $600,000 (GPI = 210).
(3) Collections from customers for sales on account, $450,000 (GPI = 215).
(4) Payments to suppliers for purchases on account, $300,000 (GPI = 215).
(5) Declaration of a $200,000 dividend, payable during January 1983 (GPI = 250). The general price index on December 31, 1982, is 230.

a Calculate the amount of the purchasing power gain or loss for 1982 stated in terms of constant December 31, 1982, dollars. Round all amounts to the nearest dollar.

b Repeat Part **a**, assuming a net monetary liability position of $300,000 on January 1, 1982.

16 On January 1, 1982, the Bill Langston family had $800 in its checking account and $4,000 in a savings account. The unpaid balance for the mortgage on their home totaled $25,000, and unpaid bills relating to purchases during December 1981 amounted to $600. An index of the general price level on January 1, 1982, was 210. During 1982, the following transactions occurred (general price index is shown in parentheses):

(1) Bill Langston's take-home salary during 1982 was $25,000 (average GPI = 225).
(2) The unpaid bills of $600 on January 1, 1982, were paid (GPI = 213).
(3) Principal repayments of $2,000 were made during 1982 on the home mortgage loan (average GPI = 225).
(4) Food, clothing, interest, and other costs incurred by the family during 1982 totaled $20,500, of which $19,700 was paid in cash (average GPI = 225).
(5) Interest earned and added to the savings account totaled $300 (average GPI = 225).
(6) In addition to the interest earned in **(5)**, $1,500 was transferred from the checking to the savings account during 1982 (GPI = 158). The general price index on December 31, 1982, is 240.

Calculate the purchasing power gain or loss for 1982 for the family stated in terms of constant December 31, 1982, dollars. Round conversion factors used to two decimal places; for example, 240/225 = 1.07.

17 Sprouse Corporation is organized on January 2, 1982, with the issuance of common stock for $200. The following transactions occur during 1982.

(1) January 2, 1982: Two widgets are purchased for $50 each.

(2) January 2, 1982: Furniture with a 5-year life and zero estimated salvage value is acquired for $50. The straight-line depreciation method is used.

(3) June 30, 1982: One widget is sold for $120.

(4) June 30, 1982: One new widget is purchased for $80.

(5) June 30, 1982: Other expenses of $50 are paid in cash.

An index of the general price level was 100 on January 1, 1982, 120 on June 30, 1982, and 132 on December 31, 1982. On December 31, 1982, the current cost of a widget was $90. On this same date, the current cost of replacing the furniture in new condition was $60.

a Prepare a four-column income statement for 1982 and balance sheet as of December 31, 1982, for Sprouse Corporation using the following headings:

1 Historical cost/nominal dollars.

2 Historical cost/constant dollars of December 31, 1982, purchasing power.

3 Current cost/nominal dollars.

4 Current cost/constant dollars of December 31, 1982, purchasing power.

b How successful was Sprouse Corporation in coping with inflation during 1982?

18 The financial statements of the Hargrave Corporation for 1982, its first year of operations, are presented in Exhibits 14.6 and 14.7.

Exhibit 14.6
Hargrave Corporation
Balance Sheet
December 31, 1982
(Problem 18)

ASSETS

Cash	$ 70,000
Accounts Receivable	200,000
Merchandise Inventory	350,000
Store Equipment	400,000
Less Accumulated Depreciation	(40,000)
Total Assets	$980,000

EQUITIES

Accounts Payable	$480,000
Common Stock	250,000
Additional Paid-in Capital	50,000
Retained Earnings	200,000
Total Equities	$980,000

Exhibit 14.7
Hargrave Corporation
Income Statement
for The Year 1982
(Problem 18)

Sales Revenue	$800,000
Less Expenses:	
Cost of Goods Sold	$450,000
Depreciation Expense	40,000
Selling and Administrative Expenses	110,000
Total Expenses	$600,000
Net Income	$200,000

Indices of the general price level on various dates were as follows (round dollar amounts to the nearest dollar).

(1) On January 1, 1982, when common stock was issued	200
(2) When store equipment was acquired	205
(3) When merchandise inventory was acquired	210
(4) When sales were made	220
(5) When selling and administrative costs were incurred	215
(6) On December 31, 1982	240

a Restate the balance sheet on December 31, 1982, to the general purchasing power of the dollar on December 31, 1982.

b Restate the income statement for the year 1982, to the general purchasing power of the dollar on December 31, 1982. Include a separate calculation of the monetary gain or loss.

19 Refer to the data for Hargrave Corporation in Problem **18**. Assuming the following additional information about current cost for 1982:

	December 31, 1982
Merchandise Inventory	$410,000
Store Equipment (net)	396,000

	For the Year 1982
Cost of Goods Sold	$490,000
Depreciation Expense	42,000
Selling and Administrative Expenses	110,000

a Prepare an income statement for 1982 and a balance sheet as of December 31, 1982, for Hargrave Corporation in terms of current-cost and nominal dollars.

b Repeat Part **a**, but state all amounts in terms of constant December 31, 1982, dollars. Assume that sales were made evenly over the year.

20 The financial statements of the Hargrave Corporation (see Problem **18**) for 1983, its second year of operations, are presented in Exhibits 14.8 and 14.9.

Exhibit 14.8
Hargrave Corporation
Balance Sheet
December 31, 1983
(Problem 20)

ASSETS

Cash	$ 110,000
Accounts Receivable	210,000
Merchandise Inventory (based on FIFO)	500,000
Store Equipment	400,000
Accumulated Depreciation	(80,000)
Total Assets	$1,140,000

EQUITIES

Accounts Payable	$ 490,000
Common Stock	250,000
Additional Paid-in Capital	50,000
Retained Earnings	350,000
Total Equities	$1,140,000

Exhibit 14.9
Hargrave Corporation
Income Statement
For the Year 1983
(Problem 20)

Sales Revenue	$1,000,000
Less Expenses:	
Cost of Goods Sold	$ 550,000
Depreciation Expenses	40,000
Selling and Administrative Expenses	150,000
Total Expenses	$ 740,000
Net Income	$ 260,000

Indices of the general price level on various dates during 1983 were as follows (round conversion factors to two decimal places; for example, $225/200 = 1.13$).

(1) On January 1, 1983	240
(2) When merchandise inventory was acquired	245
(3) When sales were made	260
(4) When selling and administrative costs were incurred	255
(5) When dividend was declared and paid	280
(6) On December 31, 1983	280

a Restate the balance sheet on December 31, 1983, in terms of constant dollars of December 31, 1983, purchasing power.

b Restate the income statement for the year ending December 31, 1983, in terms of constant dollars of December 31, 1983, purchasing power. Include a separate calculation of the purchasing power gain or loss.

c Prepare an analysis of changes in retained earnings for the year ending December 31, 1983, before and after restatement to a constant-dollar basis. The January 1, 1983, balance in retained earnings, restated to constant dollars of December 31, 1983, purchasing power is C$293,375.

21 The Bulova Corporation acquired two tables on January 1, 1982. One of these tables was sold on June 30, 1982. The other table was still in inventory on December 31, 1982. Figure 14.1 depicts various selling price and cost relationships relating to these tables during 1982. Point A is the acquisition cost of each table.

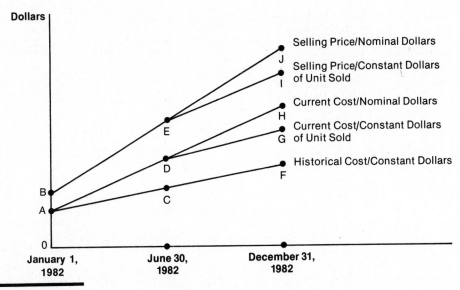

Figure 14.1
Selling Price and Cost Relationship for Bulova Corporation

Using the letters shown in Figure 14.1, indicate the computation of the following items.

a Gross margin on sale in historical cost/nominal dollars.

b Gross margin on sale in historical cost/constant dollars of June 30, 1982, purchasing power.

c Gross margin on sale in historical cost/constant dollars of December 31, 1982, purchasing power.

d Operating margin before holding gains and losses in current cost/nominal dollars.

e Realized holding gain in current cost/nominal dollars.

f Unrealized holding gain in current cost/nominal dollars.

g Operating margin before holding gains and losses in current cost/constant dollars of June 30, 1982, purchasing power.

h Operating margin before holding gains and losses in current cost/constant dollars of December 31, 1982, purchasing power.

i Realized holding gain or loss in current cost/constant dollars of June 30, 1982, purchasing power.

j Realized holding gain or loss in current cost/constant dollars of December 31, 1982, purchasing power.

k Unrealized holding gain or loss in current cost/constant dollars of December 31, 1982, purchasing power.

22 Exhibit 14.10 presents a skeleton four-column income statement under four accounting valuation and measurement bases. Various lines of these income statements are denoted by letter. Using these letters, identify the line or lines on the income statement being described in each of the following cases.

Exhibit 14.10
(*Problem 22*)

	Historical-Cost/ Nominal Dollars (1)	Historical-Cost/ Constant Dollars (2)	Current-Cost/ Nominal Dollars (3)	Current-Cost/ Constant Dollars (4)
Sales	A	E	J	P
Expenses	B	F	K	Q
Operating Income	C	G	L	R
Realized Holding Gains and Losses	—	—	M	S
Unrealized Holding Gains and Losses	—	—	N	T
Purchasing Power Gain or Loss.	—	H	—	U
Net Income.	D	I	O	V

a A firm wishes to know whether its selling prices are sufficiently high to cover the cost of replacing goods and services consumed during the period.

b A firm wishes to know how much of its conventional net income is due to operating advantages in the markets it serves and how much is due to acquiring assets prior to increases in their replacement cost.

c A firm wishes to know whether the costs of replacing its inventory and depreciable assets have increased faster or slower during the current period than changes in the general price level.

d A firm's dividend policy is to pay out the maximum dividend without impairing operating capacity. Which item in Exhibit 14.10 should form the basis for this firm's dividend decisions?

e When there have been no changes in either specific or general prices, these net income amounts will be the same.

f When specific prices have changed at the same rate as the general price level, these measures of operating income will be the same.

g When specific prices of inventory, property, plant, and equipment have increased at a faster rate than the general price level, what will be the relationship between M and S?

h Respond to Part **g**, assuming that specific prices have increased at a slower rate than the general price level.

i Respond to Part **g**, assuming that specific prices have increased at the same rate as the general price level.

j If sales and cost incurrences occur evenly over the year and the constant-dollar date is mid-year dollars, what should be the relationship between L and R?

k If sales and cost incurrences occur evenly over the year and the constant-dollar date is year-end dollars, what should be the relationship between L and R?

l During inflation, a firm with a relatively large net debt-to-equity ratio will find this item to be a positive amount.

23 Refer to the supplementary information on the impact of changing prices presented for General Products Company in Appendix A. Respond to each of the following questions.

a Was General Products Company likely to have been in a net monetary asset position or a net monetary liability position during 1982? Explain.

b How much of the conventional income before income taxes, as reported in historical cost/nominal dollars of $2,493 million for 1982, is composed of realized holding gains on inventory items sold and depreciable assets used?

c With respect to inventory items sold during 1982, did the general price level increase at a faster or a slower rate than the specific prices of the inventory items since the inventory items were acquired? Explain.

d With respect to depreciable assets used during 1982, did the general price level increase at a faster or a slower rate than the specific prices of depreciable assets since the depreciable assets were acquired? Explain.

e What is the amount of unrealized holding gain or loss for the year 1982 on inventory, property, plant, and equipment measured in current cost/nominal dollars?

f What is the amount of unrealized holding gain or loss for the year 1982 on inventory, property, plant, and equipment measured in current cost/constant average 1982 dollars?

Part Four **Synthesis**

Chapter 15 *Significance and Implications of Alternative Accounting Principles*

The independent accountant expresses an unqualified opinion on a firm's financial statements by stating that the statements were prepared in accordance with "generally accepted accounting principles." In previous chapters, we have described and illustrated most of the important accounting principles currently employed in preparing financial statements. In this chapter, we focus on the following questions:

1 What criteria should a firm employ in selecting its accounting principles from among those that are considered "generally acceptable"?
2 What are the effects of using alternative accounting principles on the principal financial statements?
3 What are the effects of using alternative accounting principles on investors' decisions to invest their capital resources?

One who understands the significance and implications of alternative generally accepted accounting principles is a more effective reader and interpreter of published financial statements. Throughout this chapter, we use the terms *accounting principles, methods,* and *procedures* interchangeably.

Summary of Generally Accepted Accounting Principles

In this section, we list the major currently acceptable accounting principles, most of which have been discussed in previous chapters. These accounting principles might be classified into three broad groups based on the flexibility permitted to firms in

576

selecting alternative methods of accounting for a specific item. In some instances, the firm has wide flexibility in choosing among alternative methods, such as in the selection of depreciation methods. In other instances, the specific conditions associated with a transaction or event dictate the method of accounting that must be used. For example, the method of accounting for investments in the common stock of other firms depends on the ownership percentage. In a third category are instances where the firm has wide flexibility in selecting accounting principles for purposes of preparing its income tax return but limited flexibility in selecting methods for its financial statements. For example, a retail merchandising firm selling goods or services on an installment basis is permitted to use the installment basis of recognizing revenue in its tax return but generally cannot use this method in its financial statements. Although a list of major currently acceptable accounting principles is given below, remember that a particular firm does not have wide flexibility in selecting its accounting methods in all instances.

Revenue Recognition Revenue may be recognized at the time goods are sold or services are rendered, as is typically done under the accrual basis of accounting, at the time cash is collected (installment method or cost-recovery-first method), or as production progresses (percentage-of-completion method for long-term contracts).

Uncollectible Accounts A provision for uncollectible accounts can be made in the period when revenue is recognized (allowance method) or, if the amount of uncollectibles is not material, in the period when specific accounts are found to be uncollectible (direct write-off method).

Inventories Inventories can be valued on one of several bases: acquisition cost, lower of acquisition cost or market, standard cost, and, in the case of some by-products and precious minerals, net realizable value. When the cost of the specific goods sold cannot be, or is not, determined, a cost-flow assumption must be made. The cost-flow assumption may be FIFO, LIFO, or weighted average, although LIFO must be used for financial reports if it is used for income tax returns.[1]

Investments in Securities Investments in the common stock securities of other firms are accounted for using either the lower-of-cost-or-market method or the equity method, or else consolidated statements are prepared. The method used depends primarily on the percentage of outstanding shares that are held.

Machinery, Equipment, and Other Depreciable Assets These plant assets may be depreciated using the straight-line, double-declining-balance, sum-of-the-years'-digits, or units-of-production method. Estimates of service lives of similar assets may differ among firms.

---

[1]As this book goes to press, the "LIFO conformity rule" of the IRS, which requires that LIFO be used in financial reports if it is used in tax reporting, is under attack in Congress, by some members of the U.S. Treasury Department, and by the federal courts. The outcome is uncertain. By the time you read this, LIFO conformity may no longer be required. Because LIFO conformity is required as this book goes to press, our discussions and illustrations assume it.

Intangible Resources Development Cost The costs incurred in creating intangible resources, such as a well-trained labor force or a good reputation among customers, can be treated as an expense in the year the costs are incurred, or capitalized and amortized over some period of years. Thus, advertising costs may be either capitalized when incurred and subsequently amortized, or expensed when incurred. Research and development costs, however, must be recognized as an expense in the year in which the costs are incurred.

Leases Rights to the use of property acquired under lease may be set up as an asset and subsequently amortized (capital-lease method), or no recognition can be given to the lease except at the time that lease payments are made or due each period (operating-lease method). Likewise, the lessor can set up the rights to receive future lease payments as a receivable at the inception of the lease (capital-lease method), or no recognition can be given to the lease except to the extent that lease payments are received or due each period (operating-lease method). Whether the capital- or operating-lease method is used depends on such factors as the life of the lease relative to the life of the leased asset and the present value of the lease payments relative to the market value of the leased property. The facts of each lease agreement determine the method to be used. The same method will generally be used for any one lease by both the lessor and the lessee.

Interest Revenue and Expense on Long-Term Investments and Debt Interest or expense on long-term investments and debt is recognized using the effective-interest method, although the straight-line method can be used if the results are not materially different.

Investment Tax Credits A credit, or reduction, in income taxes is permitted for investments in certain depreciable assets, such as equipment, furniture, automobiles, and similar property. The credit is currently 10 percent of the cost of the property, although the rate has been changed several times by Congress. The credit reduces the amount of income tax that the firm must pay in the year the assets are acquired. For financial reporting purposes, the firm can recognize the credit as an immediate reduction in income tax expense (flow-through method), or the credit can be deferred and amortized over the life of the property that gave rise to the credit (deferral method).

The preceding list of alternative acceptable accounting principles is not intended to be exhaustive. Also, it should be remembered that a firm does not always have a choice in the methods which can be used. The factors that a firm might consider in selecting its accounting principles are discussed next.

The Firm's Selection of Alternative Accounting Principles

The methods of accounting used for income tax and financial reporting purposes generally do not have to be the same. (An exception is the requirement that if LIFO is used for income tax purposes, it must also be used for financial reporting.) Because the firm might pursue different objectives for financial and tax reporting, we discuss separately the selection of accounting principles for the two types of reports.

Financial Reporting Purposes

Accurate Presentation One of the criteria that might be used in assessing the usefulness of accounting information is *accuracy in presentation* of the underlying events and transactions. This criterion might be used by the firm as a basis for selecting its methods of accounting. For example, assets have been defined as resources having future service potential and expenses as a measurement of the services consumed during the period. In applying the accuracy criterion, the firm would select the inventory cost-flow assumption and depreciation method that most accurately measured the pattern of services consumed during the period and the amount of services still available at the end of the period. As a basis for selecting accounting methods, this approach has at least one serious limitation. The notions of service potential and services consumed are seldom observable and therefore difficult to measure. Without this information, it is virtually impossible to ascertain which accounting principles lead to the most accurate presentation of the underlying events. This criterion might serve as a normative criterion toward which the development and selection of accounting principles should be directed.

Conservatism In choosing among alternative, generally acceptable, methods, the firm might select the set that provides the most conservative measure of net income. Considering the uncertainties involved in measuring benefits received as revenues and services consumed as expenses, others have suggested that a conservative measure of earnings should be provided, thereby reducing the possibility of unwarranted optimism by users of financial statements. As a criterion for selecting accounting principles, *conservatism* implies that methods should be chosen that minimize cumulative reported earnings. That is, expenses should be recognized as quickly as possible, and the recognition of revenue should be postponed as long as possible. This reporting objective would lead to selecting the double-declining-balance or sum-of-the-years'-digits depreciation method, selecting the LIFO cost-flow assumption if periods of rising prices are anticipated, and expensing of intangible development costs in the year incurred.

The rationale for conservatism as a reporting objective has been challenged. Over the whole life of the firm, income is equal to cash receipts minus cash expenditures. Thus, to the extent that net income of earlier periods is smaller, earnings of later periods must be larger. The "later" periods when income must be larger may, however, be many periods later, sometimes even the last period of the firm's existence. Also, some statement users may be misled by earnings reports based on conservative reporting principles. Consider, for example, investors who sell shares because they feel that the firm is not operating in a sufficiently profitable manner with the resources available, when earnings reported in a less conservative manner would not have induced the sale. Or consider the potential investors who do not purchase securities because they are misled by the published "conservative" statement of earnings.

Profit Maximization A reporting objective having an effect opposite to conservatism might be employed in selecting among alternative generally accepted accounting principles. Somewhat loosely termed *reported profit maximization,*[2] this criterion suggests the selection of accounting methods that maximize cumulative reported earnings. That is, revenue should be recognized as quickly as possible, and the recognition of expense should be postponed as long as possible. For example, the straight-line method of depreciation would be used and, when periods of rising prices were anticipated, the FIFO cost-flow assumption would be selected. The use of profit maximization as a reporting objective is an extension of the notion that the firm is in business to generate profits and the firm should present as favorable a report on performance as possible within currently acceptable accounting methods. Profit maximization is subject to a similar, but mirror-image, criticism as the use of conservatism as a reporting objective. Reporting income earlier under the profit maximization criterion must mean that smaller income will be reported in some later period.

Income Smoothing A final reporting objective that might be used in selecting accounting principles is referred to as *income smoothing.* This criterion suggests the selection of accounting methods that result in the smoothest earnings trend over time. As discussed later in this chapter, empirical research has shown that a relationship exists between changes in earnings and changes in stock prices. Advocates of income smoothing suggest that if a company can minimize fluctuations in earnings, then the perceived risk of investing in shares of its stock will be reduced and, all else equal, its stock price will be higher. Note that this reporting criterion suggests that net income, not revenues and expenses individually, is the object of smoothing. As a result, the firm must consider the total pattern of its operations before selecting the appropriate accounting methods. For example, the straight-line method of depreciation may provide the smoothest amount of depreciation expense on a machine over its life. If, however, the productivity of the machine declines with age so that revenues decrease in later years, net income using the straight-line method may not provide the smoothest net income stream. In this case, perhaps the double-declining-balance or sum-of-the-years'-digits method should be used.

Summary The principal message of this section is that accurate presentation, although perhaps a desirable reporting objective, is not an operational goal in selecting accounting principles. As a result, firms are free to select from among the methods included in the set of generally acceptable accounting principles using whatever reporting criterion they choose.

Where does this flexibility permitted in selecting accounting principles leave the user of financial statements? Accounting Principles Board *Opinion No. 22*[3] requires firms to disclose the accounting principles used in preparing financial statements,

---

[2] The concept of profit maximization as a reporting objective is not the same as the profit-maximization dictum of microeconomics.

[3] Accounting Principles Board, *Opinion No. 22,* "Disclosure of Accounting Policies," 1972.

either in a separate statement or as a note to the principal statements. An example of such disclosure for General Products Company is presented at the beginning of Exhibit A.4 in Appendix A. The effect of alternative accounting principles on investment decisions is discussed later in the chapter.

Income Tax Reporting Purposes

In selecting accounting procedures for income tax purposes, the corporation's objective should be to select those methods that minimize the present value of the stream of income tax payments. The operational rule, sometimes called the *least and latest rule,* is to pay the least amount of taxes as late as possible within the law. The desirability of this rule was discussed at somewhat greater length in Chapter 9. The least and latest rule generally translates into a policy of recognizing expenses as quickly as possible and postponing the recognition of revenue as long as possible. This policy might be altered somewhat if income tax rates are expected to change, if the firm had losses in earlier years, or if the firm is a sole proprietorship or partnership where earnings of the firm are subject to graduated income tax rates of the owners.

The desire to recognize expenses as quickly as possible suggests the adoption of the LIFO inventory cost-flow assumption, accelerated depreciation methods (either double-declining-balance or sum-of-the-years'-digits), and immediate expensing of research and development, advertising, and similar costs. Using the installment basis of recognizing revenue is generally desirable for income tax purposes where permitted by the Internal Revenue Code and Regulations, because it results in postponing the recognition of revenue and the resulting income tax payments until cash is collected.

An Illustration of the Effects of Alternative Accounting Principles on a Set of Financial Statements

In this section, we illustrate the effects of using different accounting principles on a set of financial statements. The illustration has been constructed so that the accounting principles used create significant differences in the financial statements. Therefore, inferences should not be drawn about the usual magnitude of the effects of alternative methods from this example.

The Scenario

On January 1, 1982, two corporations are formed to operate merchandising businesses. The two firms are alike in all respects except for their methods of accounting. Conservative Company chooses the accounting principles that will minimize its reported net income. High Flyer Company chooses the accounting principles that will maximize its reported net income. The following events occur during 1982.

1 Both corporations issue 2 million shares of $10-par value stock on January 1, for $20 million cash.

2 Both firms acquire equipment on January 1, 1982, for $14 million cash. The equipment is estimated to have a 10-year life and zero salvage value.

3 Both firms make the following purchases of merchandise inventory:

Date	Units Purchased	Unit Price	Cost of Purchases
January 1	170,000	@$60	$10,200,000
May 1	190,000	@$63	11,970,000
September 1	200,000	@$66	13,200,000
Total	560,000		$35,370,000

4 During the year, both firms sell 420,000 units at an average price of $100 each. All sales are made for cash.

5 During the year, both firms have selling, general, and administrative expenses, excluding depreciation, of $7.3 million.

6 The income tax rate is assumed to be 46 percent.

Accounting Principles Used

The methods of accounting used by each firm in preparing its financial statements are described below.

Inventory Cost-Flow Assumption Conservative Company makes a LIFO cost-flow assumption, whereas High Flyer Company makes a FIFO assumption. The method chosen by each firm is used for both its financial reports and income tax returns. Because the beginning inventory is zero, the cost of goods available for sale by each firm is equal to the purchases during the year of $35,370,000. Both firms have 140,000 units in ending inventory. Conservative Company therefore reports a cost of goods sold of $26,970,000 [= $35,370,000 − (140,000 × $60)], whereas High Flyer Company reports a cost of goods sold of $26,130,000 [= $35,370,000 − (140,000 × $66)]. Income tax regulations require a firm to use LIFO in its financial reports if it uses LIFO for its tax return. High Flyer Company desires not to use LIFO in its financial reports and therefore forgoes the tax savings opportunities from using it for tax purposes.

Depreciation Conservative Company decides to depreciate its equipment using the double-declining-balance method both on its tax return and in its financial statements. High Flyer Company decides to use the straight-line method in reporting income to shareholders but the double-declining-balance method in its tax return. Conservative Company therefore reports depreciation expense of $2.8 million $(= 2 \times \frac{1}{10} \times \$14,000,000)$, whereas High Flyer Company reports depreciation expense of $1.4 million $(= \frac{1}{10} \times \$14,000,000)$ to shareholders and $2.8 million on its tax return.

582

Investment Tax Credit Because both firms purchased long-term, depreciable equipment costing $14 million, each is entitled to a tax reduction or credit of $1.4 million (= .10 × $14,000,000) in the taxes otherwise payable for 1982. On its financial statements to shareholders, Conservative Company chooses to report the benefits of the tax reduction over the 10-year life of the equipment that gave rise to the tax reduction (deferral method), while High Flyer Company reports the entire benefit of the tax reduction in computing net income reported to shareholders (flow-through method) for 1982.

Comparative Income Statements

Exhibit 15.1 presents comparative income statements for Conservative Company and High Flyer Company for the year ending December 31, 1982. Because Conservative Company reports the same revenues and expenses on both its financial statements and income tax returns, its taxable income is the same as reported income

Exhibit 15.1
Comparative Income Statements Based on Different Accounting Principles for the Year Ending December 31, 1982 (amounts in 000's, except for per-share amounts)

	Conservative Company		High Flyer Company	
	Financial Statement	**Tax Return**	**Financial Statement**	**Tax Return**
Sales Revenue	$42,000.0	$42,000.0	$42,000.0	$42,000.0
Expenses:				
Cost of Goods Sold	$26,970.0	$26,970.0	$26,130.0	$26,130.0
Depreciation on Equipment	2,800.0	2,800.0	1,400.0[b]	2,800.0[b]
Other Selling, General, and Administrative	7,300.0	7,300.0	7,300.0	7,300.0
Expenses Before Income Taxes	$37,070.0	$37,070.0	$34,830.0	$36,230.0
Net Income Before Income Taxes	$ 4,930.0	$ 4,930.0	$ 7,170.0	$ 5,770.0
Income Tax Expense[a]	2,127.8		1,898.2	
Net Income	$ 2,802.2		$ 5,271.8	
Earnings per Share (2,000,000 shares outstanding)	$1.40		$2.64	
[a]Computation of Income Tax Expense:				
Income before Taxes	$ 4,930.0	$ 4,930.0	$ 7,170.0	$ 5,770.0
Income Tax on Current Income (at 46 percent)	$ 2,267.8	$ 2,267.8	$ 3,298.2	$ 2,654.2
Less: Tax Credit for Investment in Equipment	140.0	1,400.0	1,400.0	1,400.0
Income Tax Expense	$ 2,127.8		$ 1,898.2	
Income Tax Currently Payable		$ 867.8		$ 1,254.2
Deferred Investment Tax Credit ($1,400 − $140)	$ 1,260.0			
[b]Income Taxes Deferred by Timing Differences for Depreciation [.46 × ($2,800 − $1,400)]			$ 644.0	

583

before taxes. High Flyer Company reports larger deductions from revenues on the income tax return than it reports to shareholders. The difference for depreciation on equipment is viewed as a timing difference. A portion of the income tax expense shown on the income statement of High Flyer Company is not payable currently, and therefore a deferred tax liability will appear on the balance sheet. In this illustration, net income and earnings per share of High Flyer Company are almost double the amounts shown for Conservative Company.

Comparative Balance Sheets

Exhibit 15.2 presents comparative balance sheets for Conservative Company and High Flyer Company as of December 31, 1982. The individual asset accounts as well as total assets of Conservative Company are stated at lower amounts than those of High Flyer Company. The only real difference between the economic positions of each company is the amount of cash. The difference in the amount of cash is attributable to the payment of different amounts of income taxes by the two firms. Note that Conservative Company has more cash because it paid smaller income taxes. We would argue that it is better off than High Flyer Company.

The differences in the amounts at which the remaining assets are stated are attributable to the different accounting methods used by the two companies. The amounts shown for merchandise inventory and equipment net of depreciation of Conservative Company are smaller than the corresponding amounts for High Flyer Company because a larger portion of the costs incurred during the period by Conservative Company has been recognized as an expense.

In the equities portion of the balance sheet, Conservative Company shows deferred investment tax credits, reflecting its decision to recognize the current reduc-

Exhibit 15.2
Comparative Balance Sheets Based on Alternative Accounting Principles, December 31, 1982 (amounts in 000's)

ASSETS	Conservative Company	High Flyer Company
Cash	$ 4,462.2	$ 4,075.8
Merchandise Inventory	8,400.0	9,240.0
Equipment (at acquisition cost)	14,000.0	14,000.0
Less: Accumulated Depreciation	(2,800.0)	(1,400.0)
Total Assets	$24,062.2	$25,915.8
EQUITIES		
Deferred Investment Tax Credits	$ 1,260.0	—
Deferred Income Taxes	—	$ 644.0
Common Stock	20,000.0	20,000.0
Retained Earnings	2,802.2	5,271.8
Total Equities	$24,062.2	$25,915.8

tion in income taxes payable as an element of income over the life of the property. Each year $140,000 (= $1,400,000/10) will be amortized and shown as a reduction in income tax expense. (Income taxes *payable* in future years are not affected.) High Flyer Company used the flow-through method and recognized the full $1.4 million of tax savings in the determination of net income for 1982. High Flyer Company also reports deferred income taxes on the balance sheet resulting from differences in the timing of depreciation on equipment in the financial statements and income tax return.

Note the effect of using alternative accounting principles on the ratio, rate of return on total assets. Conservative Company reports a smaller amount of net income but also a smaller amount of total assets. One might expect, then, the rate of return on total assets of the two firms to approximate each other more closely than either net income or total assets individually. Significant differences in the ratio for the two firms are still observable, however, in this illustration. The rate of return on total assets of Conservative Company is 12.7 percent [= $2,802,200/($20,000,000 + $24,062,200)/2] and of High Flyer Company is 23.0 percent [= $5,271,800/ ($20,000,000 + $25,915,800)/2].

Comparative Statements of Changes in Financial Position

Exhibit 15.3 presents comparative statements of changes in financial position for Conservative Company and High Flyer Company. The amount of working capital provided by operations of High Flyer Company is larger than for Conservative Company. The difference is more than accounted for by the difference in inventory cost-flow assumptions used. High Flyer Company, using FIFO, reported a smaller amount for cost of goods sold and thereby used a smaller amount of working capital in generating revenues. The remaining difference between the amounts reported as working capital provided by operations of the two firms is attributable to the differing amount of income taxes paid. Unlike the income statement and balance sheet, the accounting principles that create differences between the amounts of working capital provided by operations and in the increases or decreases in working capital for the year are only those principles affecting working capital accounts (for example, inventory-valuation method and cost-flow assumption, treatment of uncollectible accounts).

The effects of using different accounting principles for nonworking capital accounts are eliminated from this statement through the process of adding and subtracting amounts to net income to obtain working capital provided by operations. The use of alternative accounting principles generally creates smaller differences in the amounts of working capital provided by operations than in the amounts reported as net income.

Moral of the Illustration

In order to interpret published financial statements, you must be aware of which accounting principles from the set of alternative generally accepted accounting principles are used. When reports of several companies are compared, the amounts

Exhibit 15.3
**Comparative Statements of Changes
in Financial Position for the Year Ending December 31, 1982
(amounts in 000's)**

	Conservative Company		High Flyer Company	
Sources of Working Capital:				
Net Income.	$ 2,802.2		$ 5,271.8	
Add Depreciation Expense Not Using Working Capital	2,800.0		1,400.0	
Add Excess of Investment Tax Credit Reducing Current Taxes Payable Over Credit Recognized in Computing Net Income ($1,400 − $140)	1,260.0		—	
Add Portion of Income Tax Expense Not Payable Currently	—		644.0	
Working Capital Provided by Operations . .	$ 6,862.2		$ 7,315.8	
Issuance of Common Shares	20,000.0		20,000.0	
Total Sources of Working Capital		$26,862.2		$27,315.8
Uses of Working Capital:				
Purchase of Equipment.		14,000.0		14,000.0
Increase in Working Capital		$12,862.2		$13,315.8
Analysis of Increases in Working Capital:				
Cash		$ 4,462.2		$ 4,075.8
Merchandise Inventory		8,400.0		9,240.0
Increase in Working Capital		$12,862.2		$13,315.8

shown should be adjusted where possible for the different accounting methods used. The techniques for making some of these adjustments were illustrated in previous chapters (for example, LIFO to FIFO cost-flow assumption, equity method to consolidated statements). The notes to the financial statements will disclose the accounting methods used, but not necessarily the data required to make appropriate adjustments.

Assessing the Effects of Alternative Accounting Principles on Investment Decisions

In previous sections of this chapter, emphasis has been given to the flexibility that firms have in selecting accounting procedures and to the possible effects of using different accounting procedures on the financial statements. We now focus briefly on a related and important question: Do investors accept financial statement information as presented, or do they somehow filter out all or most of the differences in the financial statements of various firms resulting from differences in the methods of accounting employed? If investors accept financial statement information in the form presented, without adjustments for the methods of accounting used, then two firms, otherwise identical except for the accounting procedures employed, might receive a disproportionate amount of capital funds. Thus, the use of alternative accounting principles could lead to a misallocation of resources in the economy. On the other hand, if investors make adjustments for the different accounting procedures in analyzing the financial statements of various firms, then perhaps the concern over the variety of acceptable accounting principles is excessive. If investors do make such adjustments, then increased disclosure of the procedures followed may be more important than greater uniformity in accounting principles.

The question as to the effect of alternative accounting principles on investment decisions has been the subject of extensive debate among public accountants, academicians, personnel in government agencies, and financial statement users.

Those who believe that investors can be misled point to examples where the market prices of particular firms' shares of stock have decreased dramatically after the effects of using specific accounting procedures have been carefully analyzed and reported in the financial press.[4] In these examples it is often difficult, however, to judge if the price change is attributable to the disclosure of the effects of using particular accounting procedures or to other, more temporary factors affecting the specific firm, its industry, or all firms in the economy. Also, it is difficult to generalize on the effects of using alternative accounting principles on investment decisions from isolated and anecdotal examples.

An expanding number of empirical research studies, on the other hand, have provided support for the view that investors at the aggregate market level are rarely misled by the accounting methods employed. This research has developed from the theory and empirical evidence that the stock market is efficient, in the sense that market prices adjust quickly and in an unbiased manner to new information.[5] Unlike the examples supporting the view that investors are misled, these empirical studies have been based on data for a large number of firms over long time periods. Also, an effort is made in these studies to control for the effects of economy-wide and industry effects on market price changes.

Several studies have shown that changes in earnings and changes in market prices are associated and, therefore, indicate that information contained in the financial statements is used by investors in making their resource allocation decisions.[6] Several studies have examined the effects of *changes* in the methods of accounting on

---

[4] For several examples, see Abraham J. Briloff, *More Debits Than Credits* (New York: Harper & Row, 1976). For an analysis of these examples see George Foster, "Briloff and the Capital Market," *Journal of Accounting Research* (Spring 1979): 262–274.

[5] See Eugene F. Fama, "Efficient Capital Markets: A Review of Theory and Empirical Work," *Journal of Finance* (May 1970): 383–417.

[6] See, for example, Ray Ball and Philip Brown, "An Empirical Evaluation of Accounting Income Numbers," *Journal of Accounting Research* (Autumn 1968): 159–178; William H. Beaver, "The Information Content of Annual Earnings Announcements," *Empirical Research in Accounting: Selected Studies, 1968,* Supplement to Vol. 6, *Journal of Accounting Research* (Autumn 1968): 67–92; Robert G. May, "The Influence of Quarterly Earnings Announcements on Investor Decisions as Reflected in Common Stock Price Changes," *Empirical Research in Accounting: Selected Studies, 1971,* Supplement to Vol. 9, *Journal of Accounting Research:* 119–163.

market prices. Changes in accounting methods that have no real or economic effects have been shown to have little influence on market prices.[7] A third group of studies looked at *differences* in the methods of accounting across firms to assess the effects on investment decisions. The results of this last group of studies have been mixed, with several studies supporting the position that investors are misled and several studies supporting the position that they are not misled.[8] The methodology employed in most studies in this third group has been extensively criticized, so the full implications are not clear, at least to us.

Research into the question regarding the effects of alternative accounting principles on investment decisions has not progressed sufficiently for any consensus to have been reached. We have briefly described some of the research that has been conducted to emphasize an important point. It is not obvious, as it might first appear, that the current flexibility permitted firms in selecting accounting principles necessarily misleads investors and results in a misallocation of resources. In fact, there is a growing amount of evidence to the contrary.[9]

Development of Principles in Accounting

In Chapter 1, we indicated that the development of "generally accepted accounting principles" is essentially a political process. Various persons or groups have power or authority in the decision process, including Congress and the Securities and Exchange Commission, the courts, professional accounting organizations and their members, business firms, and financial statement users. Although Congress has the ultimate authority to specify acceptable accounting methods, it has delegated that authority in almost all cases to the Securities and Exchange Commission. The Commission has indicated that it will generally accept the pronouncements of the Financial Accounting Standards Board on accounting principles. The role of the private

---

[7] See, for example, Ray Ball, "Changes in Accounting Techniques and Stock Prices," *Empirical Research in Accounting: Selected Studies, 1972,* Supplement to Vol. 10, *Journal of Accounting Research* (Autumn 1968): 1–38; Robert S. Kaplan and Richard Roll, "Investor Evaluation of Accounting Information: Some Empirical Evidence," *Journal of Business* (April 1972): 225–257; Shyam Sunder, "Relationships Between Accounting Changes and Stock Prices: Problems of Measurement and Some Empirical Evidence," *Empirical Research in Accounting: Selected Studies, 1973,* Supplement to Vol. 11, *Journal of Accounting Research:* 1–45.

[8] See, for example, Robert E. Jensen, "An Experimental Design for Study of Effects of Accounting Variations in Decision Making," *Journal of Accounting Research* (Autumn 1966): 224–238; Thomas R. Dyckman, "On the Investment Decision," *The Accounting Review* (April 1964): 285–295; John L. O'Donnell, "Relationships Between Reported Earnings and Stock Prices in the Electric Utility Industry," *The Accounting Review* (January 1965): 135–143.

[9] For a description of the theoretical framework and a summary of the empirical work behind this position, see Nicholas J. Gonedes and Nicholas Dopuch, "Capital Market Equilibrium, Information-Production, and Selecting Accounting Techniques: Theoretical Framework and Review of Empirical Work," *Studies on Financial Accounting Objectives: 1974,* Supplement to Vol. 12, *Journal of Accounting Research* (Autumn 1968): 48–129; and Robert S. Kaplan, "Information Content of Financial Accounting Numbers: A Survey of Empirical Evidence," in: *Symposium of Impact of Accounting Research in Financial Accounting and Disclosure on Accounting Practice,* ed. by T. Keller and R. Abdel-khalik (Durham: Duke University Press, 1978).

sector versus the public sector in setting accounting principles and regulating professional accounting practice continues, however, to be the subject of extensive debate.

Summary

The structure of accounting principles might be depicted as shown in Figure 15.1. The *universe* of possible accounting principles is encircled by a dashed line because of the difficulty in defining the relative size, or boundaries, of circle A. The process of specifying the principles designated as *generally acceptable* (the subset of principles from circle A represented by circle B) is political in nature. Congress and the Securities and Exchange Commission have the legal authority to make the selection, but most of the responsibility for doing so has, in effect, been delegated to the Financial Accounting Standards Board. The individual firm's selection of accounting principles (the subset of principles from circle B represented by circle C) might be based on a criterion of accurate presentation. However, because benefits received and services consumed are seldom observable events and are therefore difficult to measure, consensus on which generally accepted accounting principles provide an accurate or fair presentation is difficult to obtain. This chapter suggests that a firm might pursue a specific reporting objective, such as conservatism, profit maximization, or income smoothing, in selecting its accounting principles.

Before we can know whether circle B should be widened or narrowed, we must learn whether investors accept financial statement information as presented or whether investors make adjustments to recognize the effects of using alternative accounting principles. This question has been, and continues to be, the subject of extensive research.

Figure 15.1
Structure of Accounting Principles

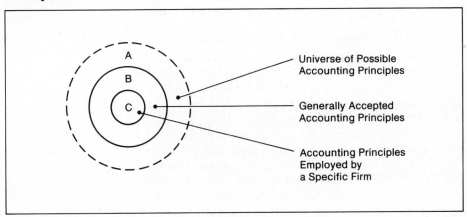

589

Master Review Problem for Self-Study

Presented below are a set of financial statements for Kaplan Corporation, including a consolidated income statement (Exhibit 15.4) and a consolidated statement of changes in financial position (Exhibit 15.6) for 1982, and a comparative consolidated balance sheet (Exhibit 15.5) on December 31, 1981 and 1982. Following the financial statements is a series of notes providing additional information on certain items in the financial statements. Respond to each of the questions on page 595, using information from the financial statements and notes. It is suggested that you study the statements and notes carefully before attempting to respond to the questions.

Exhibit 15.4
Kaplan Corporation
Consolidated Income Statement for the Year 1982
(amounts in 000's)

Revenues:

Sales	$12,000
Less: Sales Contra, Estimated Uncollectibles	120
Net Sales	$11,880
Equity in Earnings of Unconsolidated Affiliates	300
Dividend Revenue	20
Gain on Sale of Marketable Securities	30
Total Revenues	$12,230

Expenses:

Cost of Goods Sold	$ 7,200
Selling and Administrative	2,569
Loss on Sale of Equipment	80
Unrealized Loss from Price Decline of Marketable Equity Securities	20
Interest (Notes 7 and 8)	561
Total Expenses	$10,430
Net Income Before Income Taxes and Minority Interest	$ 1,800
Income Tax Expense	720
Net Income Before Minority Interest	$ 1,080
Minority Interest in Earnings of Heimann Corporation	40
Net Income	$ 1,040

Note 1: Summary of Accounting Policies

Basis of Consolidation The financial statements of Kaplan Corporation are consolidated with Heimann Corporation, an 80-percent-owned subsidiary acquired on January 2, 1981.

Marketable Securities Marketable securities are stated at the lower of acquisition cost or market.

Exhibit 15.5
Kaplan Corporation
Consolidated Balance Sheets
December 31, 1981 and 1982
(amounts in 000's)

	December 31, 1981	December 31, 1982
ASSETS		
Current Assets:		
Cash	$ 1,470	$ 2,739
Marketable Securities (Note 2)	450	550
Accounts Receivable (net; Note 3)	2,300	2,850
Inventories (Note 4)	2,590	3,110
Prepayments	800	970
Total Current Assets	$ 7,610	$10,219
Investments (Note 5):		
Investment in Maher Corporation (10 percent)	$ 200	$ 185
Investment in Johnson Corporation (30 percent)	310	410
Investment in Burton Credit Corporation (100 percent)	800	930
Total Investments	$ 1,310	$ 1,525
Property, Plant, and Equipment:		
Land	$ 400	$ 500
Buildings	800	940
Equipment	3,300	3,800
Total Cost	$ 4,500	$ 5,240
Less Accumulated Depreciation	(1,200)	(930)
Net Property, Plant, and Equipment	$ 3,300	$ 4,310
Goodwill (Note 6)	90	80
Total Assets	$12,310	$16,134
LIABILITIES AND SHAREHOLDERS' EQUITY		
Current Liabilities:		
Note Payable (Note 7)	$ —	$ 1,000
Accounts Payable	1,070	2,425
Salaries Payable	800	600
Interest Payable	300	400
Income Taxes Payable	250	375
Total Current Liabilities	$ 2,420	$ 4,800
Long-Term Liabilities:		
Bonds Payable (Note 8)	$ 6,209	$ 6,209
Deferred Income Taxes	820	940
Total Long-Term Liabilities	$ 7,029	$ 7,149
Minority Interest	$ 180	$ 214
Shareholders' Equity:		
Common Shares ($10-par value)	$ 500	$ 600
Additional Paid-in Capital	800	1,205
Unrealized Loss on Valuation of Investments	(25)	(40)
Retained Earnings	1,436	2,226
Total	$ 2,711	$ 3,991
Less Treasury Shares (at cost)	(30)	(20)
Total Shareholders' Equity	$ 2,681	$ 3,971
Total Liabilities and Shareholders' Equity	$12,310	$16,134

Exhibit 15.6
**Kaplan Corporation Consolidated Statement of Changes
in Financial Position for the Year 1982
(amounts in 000's)**

Sources of Working Capital:

Operations:

Net Income. $1,040

Plus Expenses and Losses Not Using Working Capital:

  Depreciation 560

  Deferred Taxes 120

  Loss on Sale of Equipment 80

  Minority Interest in Undistributed Earnings of Consolidated Subsidiaries 34

  Amortization of Discount on Bonds 28

  Amortization of Goodwill 10

Less Revenues and Gains Not Providing Working Capital:

  Equity in Earnings of Affiliates and Subsidiaries in Excess of Dividends Received . . . . (180)

  Amortization of Premium on Bonds . . . . (28)

Working Capital Provided by Operations $1,664

Equipment Sold 150

Common Shares Issued 500

Treasury Shares Sold 15

  Total Sources $2,329

Uses of Working Capital:

Dividends . . . . $ 250

Investments in Securities (Johnson Corporation) 50

Acquisition of Land 100

Acquisition of Building 300

Acquisition of Equipment 1,400

  Total Uses $2,100

Net Change in Working Capital . . . . $ 229

Increases in Working Capital:

Cash $1,269

Marketable Securities 100

Accounts Receivable 550

Inventories 520

Prepayments 170

Salaries Payable 200

  Total Increases $2,809

Decreases in Working Capital:

Notes Payable $1,000

Accounts Payable 1,355

Interest Payable 100

Income Taxes Payable 125

  Total Decreases $2,580

Net Change in Working Capital . . . . $ 229

Accounts Receivable Uncollectible accounts of customers are accounted for using the allowance method.

Inventories Inventories are determined using a last-in, first-out (LIFO) cost-flow assumption.

Investments Investments of less than 20 percent of the outstanding common stock of other companies are accounted for using the lower-of-cost-or-market method. Investments of greater than or equal to 20 percent of the outstanding common stock of unconsolidated affiliates and subsidiaries are accounted for using the equity method.

Buildings and Equipment Depreciation for financial reporting purposes is calculated using the straight-line method. For income tax purposes, the sum-of-the-years'-digits method is used.

Goodwill Goodwill is amortized over a period of 10 years.

Interest on Long-Term Debt Interest expense on bonds payable is recognized using the effective-interest method.

Deferred Income Taxes Deferred income taxes are provided for timing differences between book income and taxable income.

Investment Tax Credit The investment tax credit is accounted for using the flow-through method.

Note 2: Marketable securities are shown net of an allowance for market price declines below acquisition cost of $50,000 on December 31, 1981, and $70,000 on December 31, 1982.

Note 3: Accounts receivable are shown net of an allowance for uncollectible accounts of $200,000 on December 31, 1981, and $250,000 on December 31, 1982.

Note 4: Inventories consist of the following:

	December 31, 1981	December 31, 1982
Raw Materials	$ 330,000	$ 380,000
Work in Process	460,000	530,000
Finished Goods	1,800,000	2,200,000
Total	$2,590,000	$3,110,000

The current cost of inventories exceeded the amounts determined on a LIFO basis by $420,000 on December 31, 1981, and $730,000 on December 31, 1982.

Note 5: Condensed financial statements for Burton Credit Corporation, a wholly owned, unconsolidated subsidiary, are shown on the following page.

Burton Credit Corporation
(amounts in OOO's)

BALANCE SHEET	December 31, 1981	December 31, 1982
Cash and Marketable Securities	$ 760	$ 840
Accounts Receivable (net)	6,590	7,400
Other Assets	1,050	1,260
Total Assets	$8,400	$9,500
Notes Payable Due Within 1 Year	$3,900	$4,300
Long-Term Note Payable	2,620	3,100
Other Liabilities	1,080	1,170
Common Stock	100	100
Additional Paid-in Capital	300	300
Retained Earnings	400	530
Total Equities	$8,400	$9,500

STATEMENT OF INCOME AND RETAINED EARNINGS	1982
Revenues	$680
Expenses	520
Net Income	$160
Less: Dividends	(30)
Retained Earnings, December 31, 1981	400
Retained Earnings, December 31, 1982	$530

Note 6: On January 2, 1981, Kaplan Corporation acquired 80 percent of the outstanding common shares of Heimann Corporation by issuing 20,000 shares of Kaplan Corporation common stock. The Kaplan Corporation shares were selling on January 2, 1981, for $40 a share. Any difference between the acquisition price and the book value of the net assets acquired was considered goodwill and is being amortized over a period of 10 years from the date of acquisition.

Note 7: The note payable included under current liabilities is a 1-year note due on January 2, 1983. The note requires annual interest payments on December 31 of each year.

Note 8: Bonds payable are the following:

	December 31, 1981	December 31, 1982
4-percent, $2,000,000 bonds due December 31, 1987, with interest payable semiannually	$1,800,920	$1,829,390
10-percent, $3,000,000 bonds due December 31, 1991, with interest payable semiannually	3,407,720	3,379,790
8-percent, $1,000,000 bonds due on December 31, 1997, with interest payable semiannually	1,000,000	1,000,000
Total	$6,208,640	$6,209,180

a Marketable securities costing $180,000 were sold during 1982. Determine the price at which these securities were sold.

b Refer to part **a.** Compute the cost of marketable securities purchased during 1982.

c What was the amount of specific customers' accounts written off as uncollectible during 1982?

d Assume that all sales are made on account. Compute the amount of cash collected from customers during the year.

e Compute the cost of units completed and transferred to the finished goods storeroom during 1982.

f Direct labor and overhead costs incurred in manufacturing during the year totaled $4,500,000. Determine the cost of raw materials purchased during 1982.

g Assume that the amounts disclosed in Note 4 for the current cost of inventories represent the amounts that would be obtained from using a first-in, first-out (FIFO) cost-flow assumption. What would cost of goods sold have been if FIFO rather than LIFO had been used?

h Prepare an analysis that explains the causes of the changes in each of the three intercorporate investment accounts.

i Assume that Burton Credit Corporation has been consolidated with Kaplan Corporation instead of being treated as an unconsolidated subsidiary. Prepare a condensed consolidated balance sheet on December 31, 1982, and a condensed consolidated income statement for 1982 for Kaplan Corporation and Burton Credit Corporation.

j Prepare an analysis that explains the change in each of the following four accounts during 1982: Land, Building, Equipment, and Accumulated Depreciation.

k Give the journal entry made on Kaplan Corporation's books on January 2, 1981, when it acquired Heimann Corporation.

l Compute the book value of the net assets of Heimann Corporation on January 2, 1981.

m Compute the total amount of dividends declared by Heimann Corporation during 1982.

n The 4-percent bonds payable were initially priced to yield 6 percent compounded semiannually. The 10-percent bonds were initially priced to yield 8 percent compounded semiannually. Using the appropriate present value tables at the back of the book, demonstrate that $1,800,920 and $3,407,720 (see Note 8) were the correct valuations of these two bond issues on December 31, 1981.

o Calculate the amount of interest expense and any change in the valuation of the bond liability for 1982 on each of the three long-term bond issues (see Note 8).

p Compute the amount of income taxes actually paid during 1982.

q On July 1, 1982, Kaplan Corporation sold 10,000 shares of its common stock on the open market for $50 a share. Prepare an analysis explaining the change during 1982 in each of the following accounts: Common Share, Additional Paid-in Capital, Retained Earnings, Treasury Shares.

Suggested Solution

a	Cost of Marketable Securities Sold	$180,000
	Gain on Sale (from Income Statement)	30,000
	Selling Price	$210,000

b Marketable Securities at Cost on December 31, 1981 ($450,000 + $50,000) . . $500,000
Plus Purchases . . . . ?
Less Cost of Marketable Securities Sold . . . . (180,000)
Marketable Securities at Cost on December 31, 1982 ($550,000 + $70,000) . . $620;000

The cost of marketable securities purchased during 1982 was $300,000.

c Allowance for Uncollectible Accounts, December 31, 1981 . . . . $200,000
Plus Provision for Uncollectible Accounts during 1982 120,000
Less: Specific Customers' Accounts Written Off as Uncollectible during 1981 . . (?)
Allowance for Uncollectible Accounts, December 31, 1982 . . . . $250,000

Specific customers' accounts written off as uncollectible during 1982 totaled $70,000.

d Gross Accounts Receivable December 31, 1981[a] . . . . $ 2,500
Plus Sales during the Year 12,000
Less Gross Accounts Receivable December 31, 1982[b] . . . . (3,100)
Accounts Collected or Written Off $11,400
Less Write-Offs . . . . (70)
Cash Collected during Year $11,330

[a]$2,300 + $200.
[b]$2,850 + $250.

e Finished Goods Inventory, December 31, 1981 . . . . $1,800,000
Plus Cost of Units Completed during the Year . . . . ?
Less Cost of Units Sold during the Year . . . . (7,200,000)
Finished Goods Inventory, December 31, 1982 . . . . $2,200,000

The cost of units completed was $7,600,000.

f Work in Process Inventory, December 31, 1981 . . . . $ 460,000
Plus Cost of Raw Materials Used . . . . ?
Plus Direct Labor and Manufacturing Overhead Costs Incurred 4,500,000
Less Cost of Units Completed . . . . (7,600,000)
Work-in-Process Inventory, December 31, 1982 . . . . $ 530,000

The cost of raw materials used during 1982 was $3,170,000.

Raw Materials Inventory, December 31, 1981 . . . . $ 330,000
Plus Cost of Raw Materials Purchased . . . . ?
Less Cost of Raw Materials Used . . . . (3,170,000)
Raw Materials Inventory, December 31, 1982 . . . . $ 380,000

The cost of raw materials purchased was $3,220,000.

g

	LIFO	Difference	FIFO
Inventory, December 31, 1981	$ 2,590,000	$420,000	$ 3,010,000
Purchases Plus Costs Incurred	7,720,000	—	7,720,000
Goods Available	$10,310,000	$420,000	$10,730,000
Less Inventory, December 31, 1982	3,110,000	730,000	3,840,000
Cost of Goods Sold	$ 7,200,000	$310,000	$ 6,890,000

Cost of goods sold under FIFO would have been $6,890,000.

h Investment in Maher Corporation (lower-of-cost-or-market method)

Balance, December 31, 1981	$200,000
Plus Additional Investments	-0-
Less Sale of Investments	-0-
Less Increase in Unrealized Loss on Valuation of Investments	15,000
Balance, December 31, 1982	$185,000

Investment in Johnson Corporation (equity method)

Balance, December 31, 1981	$310,000
Plus Additional Investments	50,000
Plus Equity in Earnings (total equity in earnings of $300,000 from income statement minus equity in earnings of Burton Credit Corporation of $160,000)	140,000
Less Sale of Investments	-0-
Less Dividend Received (plug)	(90,000)
Balance, December 31, 1982	$410,000

Investment in Burton Credit Corporation (equity method)

Balance, December 31, 1981	$800,000
Plus Additional Investments	-0-
Plus Equity in Earnings	160,000
Less Sale of Investments	-0-
Less Dividends Received	(30,000)
Balance, December 31, 1982	$930,000

i

Balance Sheet	Kaplan Corp.	Burton Credit Corp.	Eliminations	Consolidated
Cash and Marketable Securities .	$ 3,289	$ 840		$ 4,129
Accounts Receivable	2,850	7,400		10,250
Investment in Burton Credit Corporation	930	—	$930	—
Other Assets	9,065	1,260		10,325
Total Assets	$16,134	$9,500		$24,704
Notes Payable:				
Due Within 1 Year	$ 1,000	$4,300		$ 5,300
Long-Term	6,209	3,100		9,309
Other Liabilities	4,740	1,170		5,910

Balance Sheet	Kaplan Corp.	Burton Credit Corp.	Eliminations	Consolidated
Minority Interest	214			214
Common Shares	600	100	$100	600
Additional Paid-in Capital	1,205	300	300	1,205
Unrealized Loss on Valuation of Investments	(40)	—		(40)
Retained Earnings	2,226	530	530	2,226
Treasury Shares	(20)	—		(20)
Total Equities	$16,134	$9,500		$24,704

Income Statement				
Revenues	$11,930	$ 680		$12,610
Equity in Earnings of Unconsolidated Affiliate	300	—	$160ᵃ	140
Expenses	(11,190)	(520)		(11,170)
Net Income	$ 1,040	$ 160		$ 1,040

ᵃThe credit entry for $160 would be made to the Investment account in Burton Credit Corporation. Because the entry above—to eliminate the investment account—was made to *postclosing* trial balance data, this $160 debit is implicitly included in the debit of $530 made to the Retained Earnings account.

j Land

Balance, December 31, 1981	$ 400,000
Plus Acquisitions	100,000
Less Disposals	-0-
Balance, December 31, 1982	$ 500,000

Building

Balance, December 31, 1981	$ 800,000
Plus Acquisition	300,000
Less Disposals (plug)	(160,000)
Balance, December 31, 1982	$ 940,000

Equipment

Balance, December 31, 1981	$3,300,000
Plus Acquisitions	1,400,000
Less Disposals (plug)	(900,000)
Balance, December 31, 1982	$3,800,000

Accumulated Depreciation

Balance, December 31, 1981	$1,200,000
Plus Depreciation for 1982	560,000
Less Accumulated Depreciation on Building (plug)	(160,000)
Less Accumulated Depreciation on Equipment Sold (see below)	(670,000)
Balance, December 31, 1982	$ 930,000

Selling Price of Equipment Sold . . . . $ 150,000
Loss on Sale of Equipment 80,000
Book Value of Equipment Sold . . . . $ 230,000

Cost of Equipment Sold (from above) . . . . $ 900,000
Less Accumulated Depreciation on Equipment Sold . . . . (670,000)
Book Value of Equipment Sold . . . . $ 230,000

k Investment in Heimann Corporation 800,000
    Common Stock (20,000 × $10) 200,000
    Additional Paid-in Capital (20,000 × $30) 600,000

l Cost of Investment in Heimann Corporation . . . . $ 800,000
Goodwill $80,000 + (2 × $10,000) . . . . (100,000)
Book Value of Net Assets Acquired . . . . $ 700,000

80 percent acquired; so book value of Heimann on date of acquisition is $700,000/.80 = $875,000.

m Plus Minority Interest in Heimann Corporation, January 2, 1982 . . . . $180,000
Plus Minority Interest in Earnings of Heimann Corporation (from income statement) . 40,000
Less Minority Interest in Dividends of Heimann Corporation (plug) . . . . (6,000)
Minority Interest in Heimann Corporation, December 31, 1982 (from balance sheet) . $214,000

Total dividends declared were $30,000 (= $6,000/.20).

n **4–Percent Bond Issue**
$40,000 × 9.9540 . . . . $ 398,160
$2,000,000 × .70138 1,402,760
   Total $1,800,920

10–Percent Bond Issue
$150,000 × 13.59033 . . . . $2,038,550
$3,000,000 × .45639 1,369,170
   Total $3,407,720

o 4-Percent Bond Issue	Liability Beginning of the Period	Market Interest Rate	Interest Expense	Interest Payable	Addition to or Reduction in Liability	Liability End of the Period
January 1, 1982	$1,800,920	.03	$ 54,028	$ 40,000	$14,028	$1,814,948
July 1, 1982	1,814,948	.03	54,448	40,000	14,448	1,829,390
Total			$108,476	$ 80,000	$28,476	
10-Percent Bond Issue						
January 1, 1982	3,407,720	.04	$136,309	$150,000	$13,691	$3,394,029
July 1, 1982	3,394,029	.04	135,761	150,000	14,239	3,379,790
Total			$272,070	$300,000	$27,930	
8-Percent Bond Issue						
January 1, 1982	1,000,000	.04	$ 40,000	$ 40,000	$ -0-	$1,000,000
July 1, 1982	1,000,000	.04	40,000	40,000	-0-	1,000,000
Total			$ 80,000	$ 80,000	$ -0-	

p		
Income Taxes Payable, December 31, 1981	$250,000
Plus Current Income Tax Expense for 1982 (see below)	600,000
Less Cash Payment during 1982	?
Income Taxes Payable, December 31, 1982	$375,000
Total Income Tax Expense	$720,000
Less Increase in Deferred Income Taxes	(120,000)
Current Income Tax Expense	$600,000

Cash payments for income taxes totaled $475,000 during 1982.

		Common Shares		Additional Paid-in Capital	Retained Earnings	Treasury Shares
		Number of Shares	Amount			
q	Balance, December 31, 1981 . .	50,000	$500,000	$ 800,000	$1,436,000	$30,000
	Common Stock Issued on the Open Market	10,000	100,000	400,000	—	—
	Treasury Stock Sold	—	—	5,000	—	(10,000)
	Net Income	—	—	—	1,040,000	—
	Dividends (plug)*	—	—	—	(250,000)	—
	Balance, December 31, 1982 . .	60,000	$600,000	$1,205,000	$2,226,000	$20,000

* Or, see funds statement.

Questions and Problems

1 Review the meaning of the following concepts or terms discussed in this chapter.
   a Generally accepted accounting principles.
   b Accurate presentation.

600

    c Fair presentation.

    d Conservatism.

    e Profit maximization.

    f Income smoothing.

    g Least and latest rule.

    h Statement of accounting policies.

    i Development of accounting principles is a political process.

2 Indicate the generally accepted accounting principle, or method, described in each of the following statements. Explain your reasoning.

    a This inventory cost-flow assumption results in reporting the largest net income during periods of rising prices.

    b This method of accounting for uncollectible accounts recognizes the implied income reduction in the period of sale.

    c This method of accounting for long-term investments in the securities of unconsolidated subsidiaries or other corporations usually requires an adjustment to net income to calculate working capital provided by operations in the statement of changes in financial position.

    d This method of accounting for long-term leases by the lessee gives rise to a noncurrent liability.

    e This inventory cost-flow assumption results in approximately the same balance sheet amount as the FIFO flow assumption.

    f This method of recognizing interest expense on bonds provides a uniform annual rate of interest expense over the life of the bond.

    g During periods of rising prices, this inventory valuation basis produces approximately the same results as the acquisition-cost valuation basis.

    h When specific customers' accounts are deemed uncollectible and written off, this method of accounting results in a decrease in the current ratio.

    i This method of depreciation generally provides the largest amounts of depreciation expense during the first several years of an asset's life.

    j This method of accounting for intercorporate investments in securities can result in a decrease in the investor's total shareholders' equity without affecting retained earnings.

    k This method of recognizing income from long-term contracts generally results in the least fluctuation in earnings over several periods.

    l When specific customers' accounts are deemed uncollectible and are written off, this method of accounting has no effect on working capital.

    m When used in calculating taxable income, this inventory cost-flow assumption must also be used in calculating net income reported to shareholders.

    n Under this method of accounting for long-term leases of equipment by the lessor, an amount for depreciation expense on the leased equipment will appear on the income statement.

    o This method of recognizing interest expense on bonds provides a uniform annual amount of interest expense over the life of the bonds.

3 Indicate the accounting principle, or procedure, apparently being used to record each of the following independent transactions. Indicate your reasoning.

    a Losses from Uncollectible Accounts X

       Accounts Receivable X

b Cash X

Dividend Income X

c Income Taxes Payable—Current X

Deferred Investment Tax Credits X

d Unrealized Loss from Price Declines in Marketable Securities X

Allowance to Reduce Marketable Securities to Market X

e Cash X

Investment in Unconsolidated Subsidiary X

Dividend declared and received from unconsolidated subsidiary.

f Sales Contra, Estimated Uncollectibles X

Allowance for Uncollectible Accounts X

4 Indicate the accounting principle, or procedure, apparently being used to record each of the following independent transactions. Give your reasoning.

a Rent Expense (for Lease Contract) X

Cash X

b Advertising Expense X

Deferred Advertising Costs X

c Investment in Unconsolidated Subsidiary X

Equity in Earnings of Unconsolidated Subsidiary X

d Allowance for Uncollectible Accounts X

Accounts Receivable X

e Loss from Price Decline for Inventories X

Merchandise Inventories X

f Income Taxes Payable—Current X

Income Tax Expense (from Investment Credit) X

g Liability under Long-Term Lease X

Interest Expense X

Cash X

5 Indicate the accounting principle that provides the most conservative measure of earnings in each of the following cases.

a FIFO, LIFO, or weighted-average cost-flow assumption for inventories during periods of rising prices.

b FIFO, LIFO, or weighted-average cost-flow assumption for inventories during periods of declining prices.

c Lower-of-cost-or-market or equity method of accounting for long-term investments in the securities of unconsolidated subsidiaries where dividends declared by the subsidiary are less than its earnings.

d Sum-of-the-years'-digits or straight-line depreciation method during the first one-third of an asset's life.

e Sum-of-the-years'-digits or straight-line depreciation method during the last one-third of an asset's life.

f Deferral or flow-through method of accounting for the investment tax credit in the year qualifying assets are acquired.

g The valuation of inventories at acquisition cost or lower of cost or market.

h Lower-of-cost-or-market or equity method of accounting for long-term investments in the securities of unconsolidated subsidiaries where the investee realizes net losses and does not pay dividends.

i Effective-interest or straight-line method of recognizing interest expense on bonds in the first year that bonds originally issued at a discount are outstanding.

j Effective-interest or straight-line method of recognizing interest expense on bonds in the last year that bonds originally issued at a discount are outstanding.

6 South Company and North Company incur $50,000 of advertising costs each year. South Company expenses these costs immediately, whereas North Company capitalizes the costs and amortizes them over 5 years.

a Compute the amount of advertising expense and deferred advertising costs each firm would report beginning in the first year that advertising costs are incurred and continuing for 6 years.

b For this part, assume that the amount of advertising costs incurred by each firm increases by $10,000 each year. Repeat part a.

c Comment on the differences noted in parts a and b.

7 On January 1, 1982, two corporations are formed to operate merchandising businesses. The firms are alike in all respects except for their methods of accounting. Ruzicka Company chooses the accounting principles that will minimize its reported net income. Murphy Company chooses the accounting principles that will maximize its reported net income but, where different procedures are permitted, will use accounting methods that minimize its taxable income. The following events occur during 1982.

(1) Both companies issue 500,000 shares of $1-par value common shares for $6 per share on January 2, 1982.

(2) Both firms acquire equipment on January 2, 1982, for $1,650,000 cash. The equipment is estimated to have a 10-year life and zero salvage value. An investment tax credit of 10 percent is applicable to this equipment.

(3) Both firms engage in extensive sales promotion activities during 1982, incurring costs of $400,000.

(4) The two firms make the following purchases of merchandise inventory.

Date	Units Purchased	Unit Price	Cost of Purchase
January 2	50,000	$6.00	$ 300,000
April 1	60,000	6.20	372,000
August 15	40,000	6.25	250,000
November 30	50,000	6.50	325,000
Total	200,000		$1,247,000

(5) During the year, both firms sell 140,000 units at an average price of $15 each.

(6) Selling, general, and administrative expenses, other than advertising, total $100,000 during the year.

The Ruzicka Company uses the following accounting methods (for both book and tax purposes): LIFO inventory cost-flow assumption, sum-of-the-years'-digits depreciation method, immediate expensing of the costs of sales promotion, and the deferral method of accounting for the investment credit.

603

The Murphy Company uses the following accounting methods: FIFO inventory cost-flow assumption for both book and tax purposes, the straight-line depreciation method for book and the double-declining-balance method for tax purposes, capitalization and amortization of the costs of the sales promotion campaign over 4 years for book and immediate expensing for tax purposes, and the flow-through method of accounting for the investment credit.

a Prepare comparative income statements for the two firms for the year 1982. Include separate computations of income tax expense. The income tax rate is 46 percent.

b Prepare comparative balance sheets for the two firms as of December 31, 1982. Both firms have $1 million of outstanding accounts receivable on this date and a single current liability for income taxes payable for the year.

c Prepare comparative statements of changes in financial position for the two firms for the year 1982.

8 The Langston Corporation is formed on January 2, 1982, with the issuance at par of 100,000 shares of $10-par value common stock for cash. During 1982, the following transactions occur.

(1) The assets of the Dee's Department Store are acquired on January 2, 1982, for $800,000 cash. The market values of the identifiable assets received are as follows: accounts receivable, $200,000; merchandise inventory, $400,000 (200,000 units); store equipment, $150,000; goodwill, $50,000.

(2) Merchandise inventory is purchased during 1982 as follows:

Date	Units Purchased	Unit Price	Cost of Purchase
April 1	30,000	$2.10	$ 63,000
August 1	20,000	2.20	44,000
October 1	50,000	2.40	120,000
Total	100,000		$227,000

(3) During the year, 210,000 units are sold at an average price of $3.20.

(4) Extensive training programs are held during the year to acquaint previous employees of Dee's Department Store with the merchandising policies and procedures of Langston Corporation. The costs incurred in the training programs total $50,000.

(5) Selling, general, and administrative costs incurred and recognized as an expense during 1982 are $80,000.

(6) The store equipment is estimated to have a 5-year useful life and zero salvage value.

(7) The income tax rate is 46 percent. Goodwill arising from a corporate acquisition is not deductible in computing taxable income and the difference is a permanent difference, not a timing difference. Ignore investment tax credit provisions in this problem.

The management of Langston Corporation is uncertain about the accounting methods that should be used in preparing its financial statements. The choice has been narrowed to two sets of accounting methods, and you have been asked to determine net income for 1982 using each set.

a Set A consists of the following accounting methods (for book and tax purposes): LIFO inventory cost-flow assumption, double-declining-balance depreciation method, immediate expensing of the costs of the training program, and amortization of goodwill over 10 years.

604

b Set B consists of the following accounting methods: FIFO inventory-costing assumption, straight-line depreciation for book and double-declining-balance for tax purposes, capitalization and amortization of the costs of the training program over 5 years for book and immediate expensing for tax purposes, and amortization of goodwill over 40 years.

9 Refer to Problem **8**. Calculate working capital provided by operations under both Set A and Set B accounting principles. Prepare a separate analysis that explains the difference in the amount of working capital provided by operations under Set A and Set B.

10 Net income of Miller Corporation for the year ending December 31, 1982, is $600,000 based on the accounting methods actually used by the firm. You have been asked to determine the amount of net income that would have been reported under several alternative accounting methods. The income tax rate is 40 percent, and the same accounting methods are used for financial reporting and income tax purposes unless otherwise indicated. Each of the following questions should be considered independently.

a Miller Corporation acquired a machine costing $300,000 on January 1, 1982. The machine was depreciated during 1982 using the straight-line method based on a 5-year useful life and zero salvage value. What would net income have been if the sum-of-the-years'-digits depreciation method had been used? Ignore the investment tax credit.

b Miller Corporation obtained an investment tax credit of $10,000 on the machine acquired in part **a**. It accounted for the investment credit using the flow-through method. What would net income have been if the deferral method had been used? In responding to this question, assume that the machine was depreciated using the straight-line method based on a 5-year life and zero salvage value. Also assume that this is the first year that investment tax credits have been realized by Miller Corporation.

c Miller Corporation used the lower-of-cost-or-market method of accounting for its 18-percent investment in the common shares of General Tools Corporation. During 1982, General Tools Corporation earned $200,000 and paid dividends of $50,000. The market value of General Tools Corporation was the same at the end of 1982 as it was at the beginning of 1982. What would net income have been during 1982 if Miller Corporation continued to account for the investment under the lower-of-cost-or-market method for income tax purposes but used the equity method for financial reporting purposes?

d Miller Corporation used the FIFO inventory cost-flow assumption. Under FIFO, the January 1, 1982, inventory was $300,000, and the December 31, 1982, inventory was $320,000. Under LIFO, the January 1, 1982, inventory would have been $240,000 and the December 31, 1982, inventory would have been $230,000. What would net income have been if the LIFO inventory-costing assumption had been used?

11 Refer to Problem **26** in Chapter 6. Illinois Corporation and Ohio Corporation are in an industry that experienced a 10-percent increase in prices during 1982. Illinois Corporation uses the LIFO inventory cost-flow assumption and straight-line depreciation method. Ohio Corporation uses the FIFO inventory cost-flow assumption and the double-declining-balance depreciation method. Reassess the relative profitability and liquidity of the two firms in light of the information concerning their accounting procedures.

12 The income statement of Garrett Corporation for 1982 appears in Exhibit 15.7.
Current income tax expense has been reduced by $40,000 for amortization of deferred

investment tax credits. The investment credit realized during 1982 and added to the Deferred Investment Tax Credit account on the balance sheet is $60,000.

Determine the amount of working capital provided by operations for Garrett Corporation during 1982. Your analysis should begin with net income of $630,000.

Exhibit 15.7
Garrett Corporation
Income Statement
for the Year Ended
December 31, 1982
(*Problem 12*)

Revenues:

Sales	$5,000,000
Interest	100,000
Dividends (Note 1)	60,000
Equity in Earnings of Unconsolidated Affiliate (Note 2)	300,000
Recovery of Loss on Valuation of Marketable Equity Securities	30,000
Total Revenue	$5,490,000
Expenses:	
Cost of Goods Sold (Note 3)	$3,000,000
Selling and Administrative (Note 3)	800,000
Interest	200,000
Total Expenses	$4,000,000
Income Before Income Taxes	$1,490,000
Income Tax Expense (Note 4)	700,000
Income Before Minority Interest	$ 790,000
Less Minority Interest in Earnings of Consolidated Subsidiary	160,000
Net Income	$ 630,000

Note 1: Garrett Corporation owns 10 percent of the outstanding common shares of Williams Corporation. During 1982, Williams Corporation earned $2,000,000 and declared dividends of $600,000.

Note 2: Garrett Corporation owns 30 percent of the outstanding common shares of Knowles Corporation. During 1982, Knowles Corporation earned $1,000,000 and declared dividends of $400,000.

Note 3: Depreciation charges of $200,000 and $100,000 are included in Cost of Goods Sold and Selling and Administrative Expenses, respectively.

Note 4: Income Tax Expense is composed of the following:

Current	$500,000
Deferred	200,000
Total	$700,000

---

13 The data in Exhibit 15.8 are taken from the adjusted trial balances of the Hickory Merchandising Company as of December 31, 1981 and 1982. The brackets indicate amounts to be found in the solution of the problem.

Exhibit 15.8
Hickory Merchandising Company
Adjusted Trial Balance
(*Problem 13*)

	December 31, 1981		December 31, 1982	
Accounts Payable		$ 97,320		$ 98,715
Accounts Receivable—Net	$ 580,335		$ 617,530	
Accruals and Withholdings Payable		99,800		99,700
Administrative Expenses	449,160		447,260	
Bonds Payable (6%)		275,000		277,000
Cash	114,080		149,485	
Common Stock		100,000		[ ]
Cost of Goods Sold	3,207,840		3,220,390	
Depreciation Expense	45,710		48,825	
Dividends on Common Shares— Cash and Stock	50,000		[ ]	
Dividends on Preferred Shares—Cash	6,000		6,000	
Dividends Payable		—		[ ]
Federal and State Income Tax Expense	104,975		122,675	
Federal and State Income Tax Payable		104,975		111,675
Gain on Sale of Plant		—		[ ]
Interest Expense on Notes	2,900		3,100	
Interest Expense on Bonds	20,000		[ ]	
Interest and Dividend Revenue		16,010		18,070
Inventories	616,120		633,690	
Investments in Subsidiaries	162,000		162,000	
Notes Payable		51,500		53,400
Notes Receivable	65,600		68,400	
Plant and Equipment—Net	391,880		[ ]	
Preferred Stock		100,000		100,000
Premium on Common Stock		700,000		[ ]
Prepaid Insurance	8,240		7,640	
Retained Earnings		[ ]		[ ]
Royalties Revenue		37,020		44,285
Sales		4,552,320		4,605,275
Selling Expenses	642,530		656,230	
	$6,467,370	$6,467,370	$6,739,860	$6,739,860

Additional data:
(1) Preferred shares: 6-percent, cumulative, $100-par value; 2,000 shares authorized.
(2) Common shares: $1-par value; 150,000 shares authorized.
(3) On January 10, 1982, a 10-percent stock dividend was declared on common stock, issuable in common stock. The market price per share was $10 and the dividend was capitalized at $10 per share.
(4) On March 31 and September 30, 1982, dividends of 25 cents per share were declared. The dividends were payable on April 20 and October 20, 1982, respectively. On December 31, 1982, an extra dividend of $12\frac{1}{2}$ cents per share was declared payable on

January 20, 1983. Note that all dividends, in cash and in shares, have been debited to Dividends accounts, not to Retained Earnings.

(5) Plant and equipment items having a cost of $39,240 and accumulated depreciation of $32,570 were retired and sold for $15,000. Acquisitions during 1982 amounted to $71,500.

Exhibit 15.9
Barr Sales Company
Trial Balance Data
(*Problem 14*)

	December 31	
	1982 Adjusted Trial Balance	**1981 Postclosing Trial Balance**
Accounts Payable—Merchandise	$ 8,400	$ 9,160
Accounts Receivable	25,100	25,900
Accumulated Depreciation	4,600	5,600
Allowance for Uncollectible Accounts	400	430
Cash	27,802	21,810
Common Stock ($10-par value)	55,000	50,000
Cost of Goods Sold	155,000	
Deposits by Customers	420	
Depreciation	1,000	
Dividends on Common Shares (both in cash and in shares)	8,125	
Dividends Payable	2,750	2,500
Federal Income Tax Expense	3,600	
Federal Income Tax Payable	3,600	2,400
Furniture and Fixtures	21,000	20,000
Gain on Sale of Land	1,500	
Installment Contracts Payable	2,000	
Interest Expense on Mortgage	482	
Interest Revenue on Investments	500	
Interest Payable on Mortgage	50	
Interest Receivable	50	30
Investments	14,000	15,000
Loss on Sale of Investments	300	
Merchandise Inventory	33,450	31,150
Mortgage Payable (5 percent)	10,122	10,140
Other Expenses	26,293	
Premium on Common Shares	4,500	4,000
Prepaid Rent	300	
Rent Expense	3,600	
Retained Earnings	28,860	28,860
Sales	210,000	
Sales Commissions	12,400	
Sales Commissions Payable	600	800
Sales Contra, Estimated Uncollectibles	800	

---

(6) The bonds were issued on June 30, 1964, and mature on June 30, 1994. All bonds issued remain outstanding; straight-line amortization is used.

a Prepare a well-organized comparative statement of income and retained earnings.
b Prepare a well-organized comparative balance sheet.
c Prepare a well-organized statement of changes in financial position.

14 The data in Exhibit 15.9 are taken from the records of the Barr Sales Company. Additional information:

(1) During the year the company retired fully depreciated fixtures that had cost $2,000. These were the only dispositions of furniture and fixtures.

(2) Furniture and fixtures acquired on May 10, 1982, were financed one-third down, one-third due May 10, 1983, and one-third due May 10, 1984.

(3) On December 9, 1982, the company sold a parcel of land it had purchased on January 14, 1982, at a cost of $8,000.

(4) On June 15, 1982, the company purchased additional investments at a cost of $3,200. This was the only acquisition during the year. All investments are shown at cost, since market value exceeds cost.

(5) Merchandise was delivered during the year on customers' deposits in the amount of $1,200. All other deliveries were on account.

(6) On January 2, 1982, the board of directors declared a 5-percent stock dividend. The dividend was capitalized at $11 per share.

(7) On June 20, 1982, and December 20, 1982, the board of directors declared the regular semiannual cash dividends of $0.50 per share.

(8) On June 30, 1982, the company issued 250 shares of stock for cash.

(9) Note that all dividends, both in cash and in shares, were debited to Dividends on Common Shares, not to Retained Earnings.

a Prepare a well-organized statement of income and retained earnings for 1982.
b Prepare a well-organized comparative balance sheet.
c Prepare a well-organized statement of changes in financial position for 1982.

15 Two conventional calculations of the debt-equity ratio were introduced in Chapter 6. In this problem we focus on the following definition:

$$\text{Debt Ratio} = \frac{\text{Total Long-Term External Financing}}{\text{Owners' Equity}}.$$

Many analysts use this ratio to assess the risk in the financial structure of a corporation. The higher the debt-equity ratio, other things being equal, the greater the risk. Many analysts construct ratios from the conventional, historical-cost financial statements without adjustment. This problem illustrates how the assessment of the relative risk of companies can change as more sophisticated analysis of the financial statements is undertaken. In this problem, various adjustments to the conventional financial statements are made and new versions of the debt-equity ratio are compared.

The problem may be worked all at once at the end of the course as a review, or it may be worked part by part as the various topics in the course are covered. Each part contains guidance as to when in the course the reader should be ready to work that part.

Data for four companies are presented in Exhibit 15.10. The methods are illustrated with the data for General Products Company (from Appendix A). The reader is to prepare answers for the three other companies. All data are taken from the financial statements of the various companies for the same year. All dollar amounts are in millions. Income tax effects are ignored, except where noted.

Exhibit 15.10
(Dollar amounts in millions)
(Problem 15)

	General Products Company	Eastman Kodak	General Motors	Zenith
1. Long-Term Debt	$1,000	$ 152.4	$ 1,668.7	$ 50.0
2. Deferred Tax Credits (Balance Sheet)	—a	144.0	472.5	18.3
3. Owners' Equity	8,200	4,026.3	14,385.2	292.4
4. Excess of Current (FIFO) Cost over LIFO Cost of Ending Inventory	2,240	330.3	299.5	9.2
5. Unrecognized Pension Cost (Unamortized Prior-Service Costs or Unfunded Vested Costs, if larger)	2,046	520.0	3,000.0b	None
6. Long-Term Debt of Financing Subsidiary.	2,384	None	6,509.2b	None

aGeneral Products Company reports only deferred tax debits (assets).
bExcludes $2 billion of unfunded pension obligations of subsidiary.

a (After Chapter 6.) Compute the debt ratio for each of the companies. Include deferred income taxes with long-term financing in the numerator. For General Products Company the debt ratio is

$$= \frac{\$1,000 + \$0}{\$8,200}$$

$$= 12.2\%.$$

Which companies appear to be significantly different from the others in terms of financial structure and risk? Discuss.

b (After Chapter 8.) Chapter 8 pointed out that LIFO companies show old, out-of-date inventory amounts on their balance sheets. The LIFO cost-flow assumption has the effect of understating total assets and understating owners' equity. (Owners' equity is understated because the unrealized holding gains on the inventory are not included in the balance sheet.) We can make the financial statements more realistic by adjusting them with the following entry, which ignores income tax effects:

Inventory	2,240	
Owners' Equity		2,240

$2,240 million is the amount shown in General Products Company's notes as the excess of current cost, or FIFO cost, over the balance sheet amount of ending inventory.

The debt-equity ratio for General Products Company after making this inventory adjustment is

$$\frac{\$1,000 + \$0}{\$8,200 + \$2,240} = \frac{\$1,000}{\$10,440} = 9.6\%.$$

Compute the debt ratio for each of the companies and the percentage change in the ratio from part **a** for each of the firms. On which companies did this adjustment have the most impact?

c (After Chapter 11.) Chapter 11 suggests that certain items shown as liabilities should not be, whereas certain other items not shown as liabilities should be. These two "errors" do not necessarily cancel each other out.

(i) First, note that in most cases Deferred Income Taxes are not likely even to be paid and ought, in our opinion, to be reclassified as owners' equity. We can reflect this reclassification in the financial statements by making the following entry:

Deferred Income Taxes (Balance Sheet) . . . . a

   Owners' Equity . . . . a

Amount is that shown in line 2 of Exhibit 15.10. The amount for General Products Company is zero because Deferred Income Taxes has a debit, or asset, balance.

Case-by-case analysis might be required in practice to find out if some of the companies' timing differences are likely to reverse in the foreseeable future. Our analysis of these companies' items does not reveal any such significant potential reversals.

(ii) The unrecognized prior-service cost for pension plans meets all of the criteria to be a (long-term) liability, but is not shown as such. The amount is merely disclosed in the notes. To bring this number onto the balance sheet, the financial statements are adjusted with the following entry, which ignores income tax effects:

Owners' Equity 2,046

   Pension Liability 2,046

$2,046 million is the amount shown in General Products Company's notes to the financial statements for unamortized prior-service costs.

After adjusting for the pension liability only, General Products Company's debt-equity ratio is

$$\frac{\$1,000 + \$0 + \$2,046}{\$8,200 - \$2,046} = \frac{\$3,046}{\$6,154} = 49.5\%.$$

If all adjustments in parts **a**, **b**, and **c** are made, General Products Company's debt-equity ratio is

$$\frac{\$1,000 + \$2,046}{\$8,200 + 0 + \$2,240 - \$2,046} = \frac{\$3,046}{\$8,394} = 36.3\%.$$

Make the adjustments suggested above and recompute the debt ratio for each of the other three companies. Compute the ratios on a cumulative and noncumulative basis; that is, compute the debt ratio after making each individual adjustment to the ratios computed in part **a**, and then after taking all the adjustments together, compute the percentage change in the ratio for each company. On which of the companies did each of these adjustments have the most impact?

d (After Chapter 13.) Chapter 13 illustrated that various companies use different consolidation policies with respect to a wholly owned subsidiary engaged in the financing of customer purchases of the company's goods. For example (see Chapter 13, Problem 27), Sears consolidates its financial subsidiary, but J. C. Penney does not. To make comparisons of debt ratios more valid, the same consolidation policy should be used for all companies. The following entry has the effect of consolidating an unconsolidated, but 100-percent-owned, subsidiary:

Assets of Subsidiary	9,344	
Investment of Parent in Subsidiary		931
Liabilities of Subsidiary		8,413

See Note 12 of General Products Company's financial statements. $9,344 million represents the total amount of the subsidiary's assets; $931 million represents General Products Company's investment in the subsidiary (which is equal to the subsidiary's total owners' equity); $8,413 million represents the subsidiary's total liabilities.

Once this entry is made, there may be another entry eliminating intercompany receivables and payables, if any. These eliminating entries are immaterial, and their effect has been taken into account in showing the data above.

For purposes of this problem, we are interested in examining the effect of bringing the financing subsidiary's long-term liabilities onto the parent company's balance sheet. The effect of the preceding entry on long-term liabilities can be accomplished with the following entry:

Assets	2,384	
Long-Term Liabilities		2,384

$2,384 million represents the amount of General Products Company's financial subsidiary's total long-term liabilities.

After consolidating General Products Company's financing subsidiary, the debt ratio becomes

$$\frac{\$1,000 + \$0 + \$2,384}{\$8,200} = \frac{\$3,384}{\$8,200} = 41.3\%.$$

If all adjustments to General Products Company's balance sheet are taken into account, the debt ratio is

$$\frac{\$1,000 + \$2,046 + \$2,384}{\$8,200 + \$0 + \$2,240 - \$2,046} = \frac{\$5,430}{\$8,394} = 64.7\%.$$

Make the adjustments suggested here for General Motors, the only company of the three that does not consolidate its financing subsidiary. Recompute the debt ratio for this company both cumulatively and noncumulatively. Calculate the percentage change in the debt ratio. Comment on any apparent changes in the debt ratio from those computed in parts **a**, **b**, and **c**.

e What can you infer from this exercise about the debt ratio computed from published financial statements?

16 The principal objective of this book has been to help you develop a sufficient understanding of the accounting process that generates financial statements for external users so that the resulting statements can then be (1) interpreted, (2) analyzed, and (3) evaluated. This problem has been designed partly as a review of the material covered in the book and partly as a means of assessing your progress toward this objective. A partial set of financial statements of Calmes Corporation for 1982, including consolidated comparative balance sheets at December 31, 1981 and 1982, and a consolidated statement of income and retained earnings for the year 1982 is presented in Exhibits 15.11 and 15.12. A series of discussion questions and short problems relating to the financial statements of Calmes Corporation are then presented. It is suggested that you study the financial statements before responding to these questions and problems.

Exhibit 15.11
Calmes Corporation Consolidated Statement of Income and Retained Earnings for the Year Ended December 31, 1982
(Problem 16)

Revenues:

Sales		$6,000,000
Less Estimated Uncollectible Accounts		60,000
Net Sales		$5,940,000
Gain on Sale of Machinery and Equipment		100,000
Income from Completed Contracts		960,000
Equity in Earnings of Unconsolidated Subsidiaries and Affiliates:		
Calmes Finance Corporation	$900,000	
Richardson Company	50,000	
Anthony Corporation	50,000	1,000,000
Total Revenues		$8,000,000

Expenses:

Cost of Goods Sold		$2,500,000
Employee Payroll		1,500,000
Depreciation of Plant and Equipment and Amortization of Leased Property Rights		500,000
Amortization of Intangibles		100,000
Interest		300,000
General Corporate		100,000
Income Taxes—Current		700,000
Income Taxes—Deferred		100,000
Total Expenses		$5,800,000
Net Income Before Minority Interest		$2,200,000
Minority Interest in Earnings		200,000
Net Income		$2,000,000
Less: Dividends on Preferred Shares		60,000
Dividends on Common Shares		840,000
Increase in Retained Earnings		$1,100,000
Retained Earnings, January 1, 1982		1,400,000
Retained Earnings, December 31, 1982		$2,500,000
Primary Earnings per Common Share (based on 1,000,000 average shares outstanding)		$1.94
Fully Diluted Earnings per Share (assuming conversion of preferred stock)		$1.25

Exhibit 15.12
Calmes Corporation Consolidated Balance Sheets
December 31
(*Problem 16*)

ASSETS	1982	1981
Current Assets:		
Cash	$ 50,000	$ 100,000
Marketable Securities at Lower of Cost of Market (market value, $160,000)	150,000	—
Accounts Receivable (net of estimated uncollectibles of $80,000 in 1982 and $50,000 in 1981)	300,000	250,000
Merchandise Inventory	700,000	600,000
Accumulated Costs under Contracts in Process in Excess of Progress Billings	200,000	150,000
Prepayments	100,000	100,000
Total Current Assets	$ 1,500,000	$1,200,000
Investments (at equity):		
Calmes Finance Corporation (100% owned)	$ 2,000,000	$1,100,000
Richardson Company (50% owned)	500,000	450,000
Anthony Company (25% owned)	100,000	50,000
Total Investments	$ 2,600,000	$1,600,000
Property, Plant, and Equipment:		
Land	$ 250,000	$ 200,000
Building	2,000,000	2,000,000
Machinery and Equipment	4,000,000	3,650,000
Property Rights Acquired under Lease	750,000	750,000
Total	$ 7,000,000	$6,600,000
Less Accumulated Depreciation and Amortization	(2,000,000)	(1,900,000)
Total Property, Plant, and Equipment	$ 5,000,000	$4,700,000
Intangibles (at net book value):		
Patent	$ 200,000	$ 250,000
Goodwill	700,000	750,000
Total Intangibles	$ 900,000	$1,000,000
Total Assets	$10,000,000	$8,500,000

Part I—Financial Statement Interpretation

For each of the accounts or items listed below and appearing on the consolidated balance sheets and income statement of the Calmes Corporation, describe **(1)** the nature of the account or item (that is, the transaction or conditions that resulted in its recognition) and **(2)** the valuation method used in determining its amount. Respond in descriptive terms rather than using specific numbers from the financial statements of the Calmes Corporation. The first one is provided as an example.

a Accumulated Costs under Contracts in Progress in Excess of Progress Billings—
The Calmes Corporation is providing services of some type to specific customers under

Exhibit 15.12 (continued)

LIABILITIES AND SHAREHOLDERS' EQUITY	1982	1981
Current Liabilities:		
Notes Payable	$ 250,000	$ 200,000
Accounts Payable	350,000	330,000
Salaries Payable	150,000	120,000
Income Taxes Payable	200,000	150,000
Rent Received in Advance	50,000	—
Other Current Liabilities	200,000	100,000
Total Current Liabilities	$ 1,200,000	$ 900,000
Long-Term Debt:		
Bonds Payable	$ 1,824,000	$1,800,000
Equipment Mortgage Indebtedness	176,000	650,000
Capitalized Lease Obligations	500,000	550,000
Total Long-Term Debt	$ 2,500,000	$3,000,000
Deferred Income Taxes	$ 800,000	$ 700,000
Minority Interest in Subsidiary	$ 500,000	$ 300,000
Shareholders' Equity:		
Convertible Preferred Stock	$ 1,000,000	$1,000,000
Common Stock	1,000,000	1,000,000
Additional Paid-in Capital	1,000,000	900,000
Retained Earnings	2,500,000	1,400,000
Total	$ 5,500,000	$4,300,000
Less Cost of Treasury Shares	(500,000)	(700,000)
Total Shareholders' Equity	$ 5,000,000	$3,600,000
Total Liabilities and Shareholders' Equity	$10,000,000	$8,500,000

contract. All costs incurred under the contracts are accumulated in this current asset account. When customers are billed periodically for a portion of the contract price, this account is credited. The account, therefore, reflects the excess of costs incurred to date on uncompleted contracts over the amounts billed to customers. Since the account does not include any income or profit from the contracts (that is, "accumulated costs"), the firm is apparently using the completed-contract method rather than the percentage-of-completion method of recognizing revenues.

b Investment in Calmes Finance Corporation.
c Property Rights Acquired Under Lease.
d Goodwill.
e Rent Received in Advance.
f Deferred Income Taxes (Balance Sheet).
g Minority Interest in Subsidiary (Balance Sheet).
h Treasury Shares.
i Estimated Uncollectible Accounts (Income Statement).

Additional Information:

(1) Machinery and equipment costing $500,000, and with a book value of $100,000, were sold for cash during 1982.

(2) The only transaction affecting common or preferred stocks during 1982 was the sale of treasury stock.

(3) The bonds payable have a maturity value of $2 million.

Part II—Financial Statement Analysis

a Determine the amount of specific customers' accounts written off as uncollectible during 1982, assuming that there were no recoveries during 1982 of accounts written off in years prior to 1982.

b The Calmes Corporation used the LIFO cost-flow assumption in determining its cost of goods sold and beginning and ending merchandise inventory amounts. If the FIFO cost-flow assumption had been used, the beginning inventory would have been $900,000 and the ending inventory would have been $850,000. Compute the actual gross profit (net sales less cost of goods sold) of the Calmes Corporation for 1982 under LIFO and the corresponding amount of gross profit if FIFO had been used (ignore income tax effects). Calmes Corporation used the periodic inventory method.

c Refer to part **b**. What can be said about the quantity of merchandise inventory at the beginning and end of 1982 and the direction of price changes during 1982? Explain.

d The Calmes Corporation accounts for its three intercorporate investments in unconsolidated subsidiaries under the equity method. The shares in each of these companies were acquired at book value at the time of acquisition. What were the total dividends declared by these three companies during 1982? How can you tell?

e The Calmes Corporation accounts for its three intercorporate investments in unconsolidated subsidiaries under the equity method. The shares in each of these companies were acquired at book value at the time of acquisition. Give the journal entry (entries) that was (were) made during 1982 in applying the equity method.

f The building was acquired on January 1, 1981. It was estimated to have a 40-year useful life and zero salvage value at that time. Determine the amount of depreciation expense on this building for 1982, assuming that the double-declining-balance method is used.

g Machinery and equipment costing $500,000, and with a book value of $100,000, were sold for cash during 1982. Give the journal entry to record the disposition.

h The bonds payable carry 6-percent annual coupons. Interest is paid on December 31 of each year. Give the journal entry made on December 31, 1982, to recognize interest expense for 1982, assuming that Calmes Corporation uses the effective-interest method.

i Refer to part **h**. What was the effective or market interest rate on these bonds on the date they were issued? Explain.

j The only timing difference between net income and taxable income during 1982 was in the amount of depreciation expense. If the income tax rate was 40 percent, determine the difference between the depreciation deduction reported on the tax return and the depreciation expense reported on the income statement.

k Give the journal entry that explains the change in the treasury shares account assuming that there were no other transactions affecting common or preferred shares during 1982.

l If the original amount of the patent acquired was $500,000 and the patent is being amortized on a straight-line basis, when was the patent acquired?

m The stock of the Anthony Company was acquired on December 31, 1981. If the same amount of stock in the Anthony Company were held during the year, but the amount represented only *15-percent* ownership of the Anthony Company, how would the financial statements have differed? Disregard income tax effects.

n During 1982, Calmes paid $85,000 to the lessor of property represented on the balance sheet by "Property Rights Acquired under Lease." Property rights acquired under lease have a 10-year life and are being amortized on a straight-line basis. What was the total expense reported by Calmes Corporation during 1982 from using the leased property?

o How would the financial statements have differed if the Calmes Corporation accounted for marketable securities on the lower-of-cost-or-market basis and the market value of these securities had been $130,000 instead of $160,000 at the end of 1982? Disregard income tax effects.

p If the Minority Interest in Subsidiary represents a 20-percent interest in Calmes Corporation's only consolidated subsidiary, what was the *total* amount of dividends declared by this subsidiary during 1982? How can you tell?

Exhibit 15.13
Calmes Corporation
Consolidated Statement of Changes in Financial
Position for the Year Ended December 31, 1982
(*Problem 16*)

Sources of Working Capital:

Operations

(3) _____ . . . . $ _____

Add Back Expenses and Deductions Not
Using Working Capital for Operations:

(4) _____ . . . . _____

(5) _____ . . . . _____

(6) _____ . . . . _____

(7) _____ . . . . _____

(8) _____ . . . . _____

Subtract Revenues and Additions Not
Providing Working Capital for Operations:

(9) _____ . . . . (_____)

(10) _____ . . . . (_____)

Working Capital Provided by Operations. $1,824,000

Other Sources of Working Capital:

(11) _____ . . . . _____

(12) _____ . . . . _____

Total Sources of Working Capital . . . . (2) $ _____

Uses of Working Capital:

(13) _____ . . . . $ _____

(14) _____ . . . . _____

(15) _____ . . . . _____

(16) _____ . . . . _____

(17) _____ . . . . _____

Total Uses of Working Capital $2,324,000

Net Change in Working Capital . . . . (1) $ _____

617

q Refer to the earnings-per-share amounts in the income statement of Calmes Corporation. How many shares of common stock would be issued if all of the outstanding shares of preferred stock were converted into common stock?

r Insert the missing items of information numbered (1)–(17) in the statement of changes in financial position of the Calmes Corporation in Exhibit 15.13. Be sure to include both descriptions of the missing items and their amounts. Provide supporting calculations for each of the missing items in the statement.

s As indicated in the statement of changes in financial position, working capital provided by operations of Calmes Corporation during 1982 was $1,824,000. Convert this figure to cash flow provided by operations.

t On January 2, 1983, the Calmes Corporation requested its bank to grant a 6-month loan for $300,000. If approved, the loan would be granted on January 10, 1983. As the bank's senior credit analyst, you have been asked to assess the liquidity of the Calmes Corporation and present a memorandum summarizing your conclusions. Include any ratios and any other information from the financial statements that you feel are relevant. Also include a summary of information not disclosed in the financial statements that you feel the loan officer should consider before making a final decision.

Part III—Financial Statement Evaluation

a The treasurer of the Calmes Corporation recently remarked, "The value or worth of our company on December 31, 1982, is $5,000,000, as measured by total stockholders' equity." Describe briefly at least three reasons why the difference between recorded total assets and recorded total liabilities on the balance sheet does not represent the firm's value or worth.

b The accounting profession has been criticized for permitting several "generally accepted accounting principles" for the same or similar transactions. What are the major arguments for **(1)** narrowing the range of acceptable and **(2)** continuing the present system of permitting business firms some degree of flexibility in selecting their accounting methods?

17 Partial financial statements of Tuck Corporation for 1982 are presented in Exhibit 15.14 (comparative statement of income and retained earnings), and Exhibit 15.15 (consolidated balance sheet). Also shown are a statement of accounting policies and a set of notes to the financial statements. After studying these financial statements and notes, respond to each of the following questions.

a Prepare an analysis that explains the change in Marketable Equity Securities—Net account during 1982.

b Calculate the proceeds from sales of marketable equity securities classified as a current asset during 1982.

c Calculate the amount of the provision for estimated uncollectible accounts made during 1982.

d Calculate the amount of cost of goods sold assuming a FIFO cost-flow assumption had been used.

e Give the journal entry(s) to account for the change in the Investment in Thayer Corporation—Net account during 1982.

f Calculate the amount of income or loss from the Investment in Thayer Corporation during 1982.

g Give the journal entry(s) to account for the change in the Investment in Tuck Credit Corporation account during 1982.

618

Exhibit 15.14
Tuck Corporation
Consolidated Statement of Income and Retained Earnings
for the Year Ended December 31, 1982
(Problem 17)

Revenues and Gains:

Sales—Net of Estimated Uncollectible Accounts	$4,000,000	
Gain on Sale of Equipment	3,000	
Recovery of Unrealized Loss on Valuation of Marketable Equity Securities	4,000	
Rental Revenue	240,000	
Dividend Revenue	8,000	
Equity in Earnings of Unconsolidated Subsidiary and Affiliate	102,000	
Total Revenues and Gains		$4,357,000

Expenses, Losses, and Deductions:

Cost of Goods Sold (including depreciation and amortization)	$2,530,000	
Selling and Administrative Expenses (including depreciation and amortization)	1,096,205	
Warranty Expense	46,800	
Interest Expense	165,995	
Loss on Sale of Marketable Equity Securities	8,000	
Income Tax Expense	200,000	
Minority Interest in Earnings of Consolidated Subsidiary	10,000	
Total Expenses, Losses, and Deductions		4,057,000
Consolidated Net Income		$ 300,000
Less Dividends Declared		(120,000)
Increase in Retained Earnings for 1982		$ 180,000
Retained Earnings, December 31, 1981		220,000
Retained Earnings, December 31, 1982		$ 400,000

h Assume that Tuck Credit Corporation had been consolidated with Tuck Corporation on December 31, 1982. Calculate the amount of (1) Total Assets, (2) Total Liabilities, and (3) Net Income.

i Prepare an analysis that identifies the factors and the amounts that explain the change in the Minority Interest in Subsidiary account on the balance sheet.

j Calculate the balance in the Investment in Harvard Corporation account on Tuck Corporation's books on December 31, 1982, assuming that the equity method had been used.

k Calculate the amount of cash received during 1982 for rental fees.

l Calculate the actual cost of goods and services required to service customers' warranties during 1982.

m Refer to Note 7. Calculate the amount of interest expense on the $1 million, 6-percent bonds for 1982.

n Give the journal entry(s) that accounts for the change in the Mortgage Payable account during 1982.

o The income tax rate is 40 percent. Calculate the difference between the amount of depreciation recognized for financial reporting purposes and the amount recognized for tax reporting.

Exhibit 15.15
Tuck Corporation
Consolidated Comparative Balance Sheets
(Problem 17)

	December 31, 1981	December 31, 1982
ASSETS		
Current Assets:		
Cash	$ 240,000	$ 280,000
Marketable Equity Securities—Net (Note 1)	125,000	141,000
Accounts Receivable—Net (Note 2)	1,431,200	1,509,600
Inventories (Note 3)	1,257,261	1,525,315
Prepayments	28,000	32,000
Total Current Assets	$3,081,461	$3,487,915
Investments: (Note 4)		
Investment in Thayer Corporation—Net (15 percent owned)	$ 92,000	$ 87,000
Investment in Hitchcock Corporation (30 percent owned)	120,000	135,000
Investment in Tuck Credit Corporation (100 percent owned)	215,000	298,000
Total Investments	$ 427,000	$ 520,000
Property, Plant, and Equipment: (Note 5)		
Land	$ 82,000	$ 82,000
Building	843,000	843,000
Equipment	497,818	1,848,418
Leasehold	98,182	98,182
Total Plant Assets at Cost	$1,521,000	$2,871,600
Less Accumulated Depreciation and Amortization	(376,000)	(413,000)
Total Plant Assets—Net	$1,145,000	$2,458,600
Intangibles:		
Goodwill—Net	$ 36,000	$ 34,000
Total Assets	$4,689,461	$6,500,515

p Give the journal entry made on July 1, 1982 upon conversion of the preferred stock.
q Give the journal entry(s) to account for the change in the Treasury Stock account during 1982.
r Prepare a T-account work sheet for the preparation of a statement of changes in financial position, defining funds as working capital.

Statement of Accounting Policies

Basis of Consolidation The financial statements of Tuck Corporation are consolidated with Harvard Corporation, a 90-percent-owned subsidiary acquired on January 2, 1980.

Marketable Equity Securities Marketable equity securities are stated at lower of acquisition cost or market.

Accounts Receivable Uncollectible accounts of customers are accounted for using the allowance method.

Exhibit 15.15 (continued)
LIABILITIES AND SHAREHOLDERS' EQUITY

Current Liabilities:	**1981**	**1982**
Note Payable (Note 6)	$ 100,000	$ 200,000
Accounts Payable	666,100	723,700
Rental Fees Received in Advance	46,000	58,000
Estimated Warranty Liability	75,200	78,600
Interest Payable on Notes	1,500	2,000
Dividends Payable	25,000	30,000
Income Taxes Payable—Current	140,000	160,000
Total Current Liabilities	$1,053,800	$1,252,300
Noncurrent Liabilities:		
Bonds Payable (Note 7)	$1,104,650	$1,931,143
Mortgage Payable (Note 8)	299,947	280,943
Capitalized Lease Obligation (Note 9)	62,064	56,229
Deferred Income Taxes	130,000	145,000
Total Noncurrent Liabilities	$1,596,661	$2,413,315
Total Liabilities	$2,650,461	$3,665,615
Shareholders' Equity:		
Minority Interest in Subsidiary	$ 32,000	$ 36,500
Convertible Preferred Stock, $100 par Value (Note 10)	700,000	200,000
Common Stock, $10 par Value (Note 11)	1,000,000	1,650,000
Additional Paid-in Capital—Common	130,000	583,600
Unrealized Loss from Price Declines of Marketable Equity Investments	(16,000)	(21,000)
Retained Earnings	220,000	400,000
Total	$2,066,000	$2,849,100
Less Cost of Treasury Stock (Note 12)	(27,000)	(14,200)
Total Shareholders' Equity	$2,039,000	$2,834,900
Total Liabilities and Shareholders' Equity	$4,689,461	$6,500,515

Inventories Inventories are measured using a last-in, first-out cost-flow assumption.

Investments Investments of less than 20 percent of the outstanding common stock of other companies are accounted for using the lower-of-cost-or-market method. Investments of greater than or equal to 20 percent of the outstanding common stock of unconsolidated affiliates and subsidiaries are accounted for using the equity method.

Building, Equipment, and Leaseholds Depreciation for financial reporting purposes is calculated using the straight-line method. For income tax purposes, the declining-balance method is used.

Goodwill Goodwill arising from investments in Harvard Corporation is amortized over a period of 20 years.

Interest Expense on Long-term Debt Interest expense on long-term debt is recognized using the effective-interest method.

Deferred Income Taxes Deferred income taxes are provided for timing differences between book and taxable income. All timing differences relate to depreciation.

Notes to the Financial Statements

Note 1: Marketable equity securities are shown net of an allowance for price declines below acquisition cost of $25,000 on December 31, 1981, and $21,000 on December 31, 1982. Marketable equity securities costing $35,000 were sold during 1982. No dividends were received from marketable equity securities during 1982.

Note 2: Accounts receivable are shown net of an allowance for uncollectible accounts of $128,800 on December 31, 1981, and $210,400 on December 31, 1982. A total of $63,000 of accounts were written off as uncollectible during 1982.

Note 3: The valuation of inventories on a FIFO basis exceeded the amounts on a LIFO basis by $430,000 on December 31, 1981, and by $410,000 on December 31, 1982.

Note 4: Condensed balance sheet data for Tuck Credit Corporation, a wholly owned, unconsolidated credit subsidiary, are shown below:

	December 31, 1981	December 31, 1982
Total Assets	$375,000	$478,000
Total Liabilities	$160,000	$180,000
Shareholders' Equity	$215,000	$298,000

Net income of Tuck Credit Corporation for 1982 was $87,000. Dividends declared and paid during 1982 totaled $24,000.

Note 5: Equipment with a cost of $23,000 and a book value of $4,000 was sold during 1982. This was the only disposition of property, plant, or equipment during the year.

Note 6: A 90-day, 9-percent note with a face amount of $100,000 was paid with interest at maturity on January 30, 1982. On December 1, 1982, Tuck Corporation borrowed $200,000 from its local bank, promising to repay the principal plus interest at 12 percent in 6 months.

Note 7: Bonds Payable on the balance sheet is composed of the following:

	December 31, 1981	December 31, 1982
$1,000,000, 6-percent, semiannual coupon bonds, due December 31, 1996, priced at $1,125,510 to yield 5 percent, compounded semiannually, at the time of issue on January 2, 1977	$1,104,650	$1,099,823
$1,000,000, 8-percent, semiannual coupon bonds, due December 31, 2001, priced at $828,409 to yield 10 percent, compounded semiannually, at the time of issue on January 2, 1982	—	831,320
Total	$1,104,650	$1,931,143

Note 8: Mortgage Payable represents a mortgage on buildings requiring equal installment payments of $40,000 on December 31 of each year. The loan underlying the mortgage bears interest of 7 percent, compounded annually. The final installment payment is due on December 31, 1992.

Note 9: The Capitalized Lease Obligation represents a 20-year, noncancelable lease on certain equipment. The lease requires annual payments in advance of $10,000 on January 2 of each year. The last lease payment will be made on January 2, 1988. The lease is capitalized at the lessee's borrowing rate (at the inception of the lease) of 8 percent.

Note 10: Each share of preferred stock is convertible into 5 shares of common stock. On July 1, 1982, holders of 5,000 shares of preferred stock exercised their options. The conversion was recorded using book values.

Note 11: On October 1, 1982, 40,000 shares of common stock were issued on the open market for $15 per share.

Note 12: Treasury Stock is composed of the following:

December 31, 1981:	2,250 shares at $12 per share	$27,000
December 31, 1982:	450 shares at $12 per share	$ 5,400
	550 shares at $16 per share	8,800
		$14,200

During 1982, 1,800 shares of treasury stock were sold and 550 shares were acquired.

18 In the 1960s, Chrysler switched its inventory cost-flow assumption from FIFO to LIFO. It was the only one of the big-three auto makers to do so at that time. By 1970, Chrysler's inventories had grown and prices of its acquisition for inventory had increased so much that it had saved over $50 million in income taxes by using LIFO. Then, in the 1970s, Chrysler switched from LIFO back to FIFO. To comply with government tax regulations on inventory accounting, Chrysler paid to the government all of the taxes that it had saved from using LIFO over the entire time it had used LIFO. Chrysler paid the federal government over $50 million for the privilege of switching from LIFO back to FIFO.

Investigation of why Chrysler would send the government $50 million for the privilege of switching back to FIFO suggests that Chrysler was in danger of violating a covenant in some of its bond indentures with respect to the debt-equity ratio. If the debt-equity ratio rose above a critical value, certain bonds would become due immediately that otherwise would not mature for a decade or more.

Under what conditions would a company not want its old bonds suddenly to come due for immediate payment? Explain. Under what conditions would switching from LIFO to FIFO and incurring an immediate $50 million liability improve Chrysler's position? Explain. What is the purpose of bond indentures such as the one Chrysler had agreed to? Were the bondholders made better off by Chrysler's actions? Discuss.

Appendix A **Corporate Financial Statements Illustrated and Annotated**

This appendix illustrates current financial reporting with a comprehensive set of corporate financial statements prepared in accordance with generally accepted accounting principles.

The financial statements for the General Products Company, shown here, are adapted from those of the General Electric Company. General Electric will send you a copy of its actual, current annual report. Write Investor Relations; General Electric Company; Fairfield, Connecticut 06431.

This appendix is organized as follows. We have split the annual report of General Products Company into 4 exhibits, numbered Exhibit A.1 to A.4. These exhibits generally appear on the left-hand pages that follow. In the margins of those exhibits are circled numbers (which do not appear in the original). On nearby pages are authors' comments that explain various features of the accounting appearing in the financial statements. Questions and problems appear at the end of the appendix.

Exhibit A.1
Statement of income and retained earnings
General Products Company and consolidated affiliates

For the years ended December 31 (In millions)	1982	1981	1980
Sales Sales of products and services to customers (note 1) .	$24,959	$22,461	$19,654
Operating Cost of goods sold	17,751	15,991	13,915
expenses Selling, general and administrative expense	4,258	3,716	3,205
Depreciation, depletion and amortization	707	624	576
Operating expenses (notes 2 and 3)	22,716	20,331	17,696
Operating margin	2,243	2,130	1,958
Other income (note 4)	564	519	419
Interest and other financial charges (note 5)	(314)	(258)	(224)
Earnings Earnings before income taxes and minority interest .	2,493	2,391	2,153
(1) Provision for income taxes (note 6).	(958)	(953)	(894)
(2) Minority interest in earnings of consolidated affiliates.	(21)	(29)	(29)
Net income applicable to common stock	$ 1,514	$ 1,409	$ 1,230
(3) Earnings per common share (in dollars) (note 7). . .	$6.65	$6.20	$5.39
Dividends declared per common share (in dollars) . .	$2.95	$2.75	$2.50
Operating margin as a percentage of sales	9.0%	9.5%	10.0%
Net earnings as a percentage of sales	6.1%	6.3%	6.3%
For the years ended December 31 (In millions)	**1982**	**1981**	**1980**
(4) **Retained** Balance January 1	$6,307	$5,522	$4,862
earnings Net earnings	1,514	1,409	1,230
Dividends declared on common stock	(670)	(624)	(570)
Balance December 31	$7,151	$6,307	$5,522

The information in the notes is an integral part of these statements.

(5) Report of independent certified public accountants

To Share Owners and Board of Directors of General Products Company

We have examined the statement of financial position of General Products Company and consolidated affiliates as of December 31, 1982 and 1981, and the related statements of earnings, retained earnings and changes in financial position for each of the three years in the period ended December 31, 1982. Our examinations were made in accordance with generally accepted auditing standards, and accordingly included such tests of the accounting records and such other auditing procedures as we considered necessary in the circumstances.

In our opinion, the aforementioned financial statements present fairly the financial position of General Products Company and consolidated affiliates at December 31, 1982 and 1981, and the results of their operations and the changes in their financial position for each of the three years in the period ended December 31, 1982, in conformity with generally accepted accounting principles applied on a consistent basis.

Stuckey, Wells & Co.
1101 E. 58th Street
Chicago, IL 60637   *Stuckey Wells & Co.*   February 20, 1983

626

Authors' Comments

(1) Provision usually means "estimated expense" in this country; see the Glossary at *provision* for the contrast in this word's meanings in the U.S. and the U.K.

(2) GP does not own all the shares in all of its consolidated subsidiaries. Some of the shares belong to outsiders, called the *minority interest*. The minority interest's share of the earnings of the subsidiary companies does not belong to GP's shareholders. Hence, in deriving income to GP's shareholders, the minority interest's share in earnings is subtracted from the earnings of the consolidated group of companies. Note, however, that this reduction in income uses no cash or other funds, so that there is an adjustment on the Statement of Changes in Financial Position for this charge against income. See our comment 15.

(3) This is primary earnings per share, as called for by APB *Opinion No. 15*. See GP's Note 7 for a discussion of fully diluted earnings per share. Fully diluted earnings per share is not separately shown here because the amount is within one percent of the primary earnings per share amount. (In general, fully diluted earnings per share need not be separately shown if it is within 3 percent of primary earnings per share.)

(4) Generally accepted accounting principles call for a reconciliation of changes in all of the owners' equity accounts during the year. The only major changes in GP's retained earnings account are caused by the earning of income and the declaration of dividends. GP's Note 18 explains other changes in owners' equity.

(5) This is the auditors' report. This particular report is both nonqualified ("clean") and in standard format. The first paragraph of the auditors' report is the scope paragraph—telling the work done—and the last paragraph is the opinion. The auditors' report usually precedes or follows the annual report, but is reproduced here for convenience.

(6) GP uses the completed contract method of recognizing revenue from long-term construction contracts; see GP's Summary of Significant Accounting Policies at "Sales." As GP incurs costs on these contracts it makes journal entries such as:

Work-in-Process Inventory for Long-term Contracts	X
Various Assets and Liabilities	X
To record cost of construction activity.	

Some of GP's long-term construction contracts provide that the customer shall make progress payments to GP as the work is done. GP does not recognize revenue until the work is completed, so the journal entry made at the time cash is received is one such as:

Cash	Y
Advances from Customers on Long-term Contracts	Y
To record cash received and to set up the corresponding liability.	

When the balance sheet is prepared, the amounts in the inventory accounts, X (debit balance), are netted against the amounts in the liability accounts, Y (credit balance). If there is a net credit balance, as here, with Y greater than X, then the difference, $Y - X$, is recorded as a liability. GP shows this liability under the title "Progress collections." On contracts where the amounts in the inventory account exceed the cash collections, then the

627

Exhibit A.2
Statement of financial position
General Products Company and consolidated affiliates

At December 31 (In millions)	1982	1981
Assets		
Cash (note 8)	$ 1,601	$ 1,904
Marketable securities (note 8)	600	672
Current receivables (note 9)	4,339	3,647
Inventories (note 10)	3,343	3,161
Current assets	9,883	9,384
Property, plant and equipment—net (note 11)	5,780	4,613
Investments (note 12)	1,820	1,691
Other assets (note 13)	1,028	956
Total assets	$18,511	$16,644
Liabilities and equity		
(6) Short-term borrowings (note 14)	$ 1,093	$ 871
Accounts payable (note 15)	1,671	1,477
Progress collections and price adjustments accrued	2,084	1,957
Dividends payable	170	159
Taxes payable	628	655
Other payables (note 16)	1,946	1,753
Current liabilities	7,592	6,872
Long-term borrowings (note 17)	1,000	947
Other liabilities	1,565	1,311
Total liabilities	10,157	9,130
(7) Minority interest in equity of consolidated affiliates	154	152
Preferred stock ($1 par value; 2,000,000 shares authorized; none issued)	—	—
Common stock ($2.50 par value; 251,500,000 shares authorized; 231,463,949 shares issued 1982 and 1981)	579	579
Amounts received for stock in excess of par value	659	656
Retained earnings	7,151	6,307
	8,389	7,542
(8) Deduct common stock held in treasury	(189)	(180)
Total share owners' equity (notes 18, 19, and 20)	8,200	7,362
Total liabilities and equity	$18,511	$16,644
Commitments and contingent liabilities (note 21)		

The information in the notes is an integral part of this statement.

628

difference, $X - Y$, is shown as an asset under a title such as "Costs Incurred on Long-term Contracts in Excess of Billings." This netting of costs incurred against cash collections and the separate showing of the excesses are required by ARB *No. 45.*

On many of GP's contracts the only cash collected before completion of construction is for engineering costs incurred in preparation to undertake construction. GP expenses these engineering costs, rather than accumulating them in Work-in-Process inventory accounts. Thus, there is no asset account to net against the liability. The "Progress collections" title is appropriate because it tends to represent gross "advances from customers," rather than a netting of work-in-process inventory against advances from customers.

(7) (Refer to our comment 2 for a description of "minority interest" on the income statement.) This account represents the equity of the minority shareholders in the consolidated affiliates. From the point of view of GP's shareholders, this equity belonging to the minority is a liability. From the point of view of the consolidated entity, the minority shareholders' interest is part of total owners' equity. Thus whether one believes that minority interest is a liability or an item of owners' equity depends upon whether one views the financial statements as being prepared for the shareholders of GP (the proprietorship theory) or for all potential readers (the entity theory). Note that GP avoids the issue by not classifying "minority interest" either with liabilities or with owners' equity.

(8) GP uses the cost method of accounting for treasury stock and shows the cost of its own shares acquired on the market as contra to all of owners' equity. Refer to our comment 69.

(9) Most companies define funds as working capital = current assets − current liabilities. GP uses a more restrictive definition of funds; for GP, funds = cash + marketable securities − short-term borrowings.

(10) This statement, as is customary, starts with net income as shown in the income statement in Exhibit A.1. The next few lines show subtractions for revenues and other credits to income that did not produce funds and additions for expenses and other charges against income that did not use funds. Total funds produced by operations appears after these adjustments to income. An acceptable alternative format, but one that is seldom used, shows only those revenues that produce funds and subtracts only those expenses that use funds in deriving funds produced by operations.

(11) Depreciation is *not* a source of funds. Rather, it is an expense that reduces net income without using any funds. The funds were used some time in the past when the depreciable assets were acquired.

(12) See our comment 48. GP earns investment credits in the year it acquires new qualifying assets. Because it uses the conservative deferral method for investment credits, it recognizes the effect on income over the lives of the assets acquired. More funds are provided by the investment credit than are recognized in income in the year of acquisition. On the other hand, income is increased somewhat because of the effect of amounts deferred in prior years that are used to reduce reported tax expense in the current year. The net difference is added to net income in deriving funds provided by operations.

629

Exhibit A.3
Statement of changes in financial position
General Products Company and consolidated affiliates

For the years ended December 31 (In millions)	1982	1981	1980
(9) Source of funds *From operations* **(10)**			
Net earnings	$ 1,514	$1,409	$1,230
Items of income not requiring (or producing) funds from operating activities			
(11) Depreciation, depletion and amortization	707	624	576
(12) Investment tax credit deferred—net	56	45	25
(13) Income tax timing differences	63	(37)	32
(14) Earnings retained by nonconsolidated finance affiliate	(22)	(18)	(15)
(15) Minority interest in earnings of consolidated affiliates	21	29	29
Total from operations	2,339	2,052	1,877
(16) Increase in long-term borrowings	122	50	96
Newly issued common stock	—	—	3
Disposition of treasury shares	136	148	190
(17) Increase in current payables other than short-term borrowings	498	786	570
Decrease in investments	—	—	24
Other—net	143	102	149
Total source of funds	3,238	3,138	2,909
Application of funds Additions to property, plant and equipment	1,948	1,262	1,055
Dividends declared on common stock	670	624	570
Increase in investments	129	281	—
(16) Reduction in long-term borrowings	69	97	386
Purchase of treasury shares	145	156	196
(18) Increase in current receivables	692	358	306
(19) Increase in inventories	182	158	399
Total application of funds	3,835	2,936	2,912
Net change Net change in cash plus marketable securities **(20)** less short-term borrowings = net liquid assets	$ (597)	$ 202	$ (3)
Analysis of net change Increase (decrease) in cash and marketable securities	$ (375)	$ 113	$ 185
Decrease (increase) in short-term borrowings	(222)	89	(188)
Increase (decrease) in net liquid assets **(20)**	$ (597)	$ 202	$ (3)

The information in the notes is an integral part of this statement.

630

(13) In 1982 and 1980, income tax expense for the year exceeded the amount of income taxes payable. See the discussion at GP's Note 6 and our comments 49–53. Because fewer funds were used for income taxes than were reported as income tax expense, there has to be an addition for the amount of expense not using funds in deriving funds from operations. The results for 1981 show that taxes payable exceeded tax expense.

(14) All earnings of the GP Credit Corporation ($115 million in 1982) are included in income under the equity method. See "Other income," GP's Note 4. Only $93 million of dividends were declared by the Credit Corporation; see the "Current and retained earnings statement" of the Credit Company in GP's note 12. The difference, $22 (= $115 − $93) million, provided no funds to GP and must be subtracted from net income to derive GP's funds from operations. That is, the entire $115 million is included in the $1,514 million shown as net earnings by GP, but dividend declarations of the Credit Corporation provided funds of only $93 million.

(15) See our comment 2. The charge on the income statement for the minority's interest in earnings (of $21 million in 1982) reduces the income reported to GP's shareholders, but does not reduce the amount of funds provided by operations of the consolidated entity. Thus, there is an addback to net income for $21 million in 1981 in deriving funds produced by operations.

(16) As is preferable, GP shows separately funds provided by new borrowings and funds used to reduce old borrowings. Some companies show only the net effect either as a source or as an application of funds; they provide no information about the amount of actual borrowings and repayments during the period.

(17) GP's definition of funds does not include current payables. Thus, an increase in current payables provides funds just as new long-term borrowing provides funds. Some might call this an operating source of funds.

(18) GP's definition of funds does not include current receivables. An increase in receivables uses funds just as any increase in investments uses funds. Some might call this an operating use of funds.

(19) GP's definition of funds does not include inventories. Increases in inventories use funds. Some might call this an operating use of funds.

(20) Notice the self-balancing nature of this statement. The actual decrease in funds (= cash + marketable securities − short-term borrowings) of $597 million in 1982 is exactly explained in the top part of the statement with the various sources and applications of funds. Some companies do not place the "Analysis" section at the bottom of the statement, thus losing the elegance of the statement; these companies show the "Analysis" in a footnote.

631

(21) *Exhibit A.4*
**Summary of significant
accounting policies**

(22) **Basis of consolidation**

The financial statements consolidate the accounts of the parent General Products Company and those of all majority-owned and controlled companies ("affiliated companies"), except the finance company (23) whose operations are not similar to those of the consolidated group. All significant items relating to transactions among the parent and affiliated companies are eliminated from the consolidated state- (24) ments.

(25) The nonconsolidated finance company is included in the statement of financial position under invest- ments and is valued at equity plus advances. In addition, companies in which GP and/or its consoli- dated affiliates own 20% to 50% of the voting stock ("associated companies") are included under investments, valued at the appropriate share of equity plus advances. After-tax earnings of nonconsoli- dated finance companies and associated companies are included in the statement of earnings under other income.

(26) **Sales**

The Company and its consolidated affiliates record a transaction as a sale only when title to products passes to the customer.

(27) **Vacation expense**

Most employees earn credits during the current year for vacations to be taken in the following year. The expense for this liability is accrued during the year vacations are earned rather than in the year vacations are taken.

Pensions

Investments of the General Products Pension Trust, which funds the obligations of the General Products Pension Plan, are carried at amortized cost plus programmed appreciation in the common stock portfo- (28) lio. The funding program and Company cost determination for the Pension Plan use 6% as the estimated rate of future Trust income. Trust income includes recognition of appreciation in the common stock portfolio on a systematic basis which does not give undue weight to short-term market fluctuations. Programmed appreciation will not be recognized if average carrying value exceeds average market value, calculated on a moving basis over a multiyear period.

Changes in accrued actuarial liabilities for prior service are amortized over 20 years. Net actuarial gains and losses are amortized over 15 years.

Costs of separate, supplementary pension plan, primarily affecting long-service professional and managerial employees, are not funded. Current service costs and amortization of actuarial liabilities for prior service over a period of 20 years are being charged to operating expenses currently.

Investment tax credit

(29) The investment tax credit is recorded by the "deferral method" and is amortized as a reduction of the provision for taxes over the lives of the facilities to which the credit applies, rather than being "flowed through" to income in the year the asset is acquired.

Inventories

Substantially all manufacturing inventories located in the U.S. are valued on a last-in first-out, or LIFO, (30) basis. Manufacturing inventories outside the U.S. are generally valued on a first-in first-out, or FIFO, basis. Valuations are based on the cost of material, direct labor and manufacturing overhead, and do not (31) exceed net realizable values. Certain indirect manufacturing expenses are charged directly to operating costs during the period incurred, rather than being inventoried.

Mining inventories, which include principally mined ore and coal, metal concentrates and mining supplies, are stated at the lower of average cost or market. The cost of mining inventories includes both direct and indirect costs consisting of labor, purchased supplies and services, and depreciation, deple- tion and amortization of property, plant and equipment.

Property, plant and equipment

Manufacturing plant and equipment includes the original cost of land, buildings and equipment less depreciation, which is the estimated cost consumed by wear and obsolescence. An accelerated depre- ciation method, based principally on a sum-of-the-years-digits formula, is used to record depreciation of the original cost of manufacturing plant and equipment purchased and installed in the U.S. subsequent to 1960. Most manufacturing plant and equipment located outside the U.S. is depreciated on a straight- line basis. If manufacturing plant and equipment is subject to abnormal economic conditions or obsoles- cence, additional depreciation is provided. Expenditures for maintenance and repairs of manufacturing plant and equipment are charged to operations as incurred.

(21) APB *Opinion No. 22* requires that all annual reports include a summary of significant accounting principles used so that the reader can know which accounting alternatives have been chosen by the company.

(22) A parent, such as GP, usually consolidates a subsidiary when all three of the following criteria are met:

(i) The parent owns more than 50 percent of the voting shares of the subsidiary.
(ii) There are no important restrictions on the ability of the parent to exercise control of the subsidiary.
(iii) The asset and equity structure of the subsidiary is not significantly different from that of the parent.

(23) GP tells us here that it consolidates all "majority-owned" (greater than 50 percent) and "controlled" companies except the finance company which is not similar to the others in the consolidated group. Instead, the finance affiliate is accounted for under the equity method. As can be seen from GP Credit Corporation's balance sheet in note 12, most (90 percent at year end 1982) of the Credit Corporation's assets are receivables and most (80 percent) of its equities are debt, rather than owner's equity. In this sense, the operations of the finance affiliate "are not similar to those of the consolidated group." As our comment 61 points out, the nonconsolidation of the finance company makes GP's balance sheet differ substantially from its appearance if the finance affiliates were consolidated. Although there is no effect on final net income, the components of income are affected.

(24) Consolidated financial statements present information about a group of affiliated companies as if the group were one economic entity. Consequently, gains or losses on sales of assets between companies in the consolidated group must be eliminated from reported financial statements. The recognition of such gains or losses is postponed until the assets are sold by one company of the consolidated group to a buyer outside of the consolidated group.

(25) GP tells us that it uses the equity method for the nonconsolidated finance affiliate. Under the equity method, GP's net earnings include its share of the earnings, not just the dividends, of this company. See our comment 14.

(26) GP uses the completed contract method of recognizing revenue on long-term construction projects. See our comment 6.

(27) GP tells us that (as required by *SFAS No. 43*) it charges vacation pay to expense (or product cost) accounts as employees earn vacations, rather than charging income when employees take their vacations.

(28) That is, in computing future values of pension fund investments and interest on unfunded obligations for prior service costs, a 6-percent rate is used. GP's note 3 indicates that the rate earned in 1982 was 8.4 percent.

(29) See our comment 48 for a discussion of the investment credit and the effect of GP's using the conservative deferral method.

(30) Most foreign governments do not allow LIFO for tax purposes.

(31) GP tells us it will not show an item of inventory on the balance sheet at an amount greater than net realizable value; we can deduce that it must be using a lower-of-cost-or-market valuation basis.

633

The cost of mining properties includes initial expenditures and cost of major rebuilding projects which substantially increase the useful lives of existing assets. The cost of mining properties is depreciated, depleted or amortized over the useful lives of the related assets by use of unit-of-production, straight-line or declining-balance methods.

Mining exploration costs are expensed until it is determined that the development of a mineral deposit is likely to be economically feasible. After this determination is made, all costs related to further development are capitalized. Amortization of such costs begins upon commencement of production and is over ten years or the productive life of the property, whichever is less.

(32) Oil and gas properties are accounted for by use of the full-cost method.

Notes to financial statements

1 Sales

(33) Approximately one-eighth of sales were to agencies of the U.S. government, which is the Company's largest single customer. The principal source of these sales was the Technical Systems and Materials segment of the Company's business.

2 Operating expenses

Operating costs by major categories are shown below: (In millions)	1982	1981	1980
Employee compensation, including benefits	$ 9,196	$ 8,286	$ 7,401
Materials, supplies, services and other costs	12,696	11,320	9,867
Depreciation, depletion and amortization	707	624	576
Taxes, except Social Security and those on income	299	259	251
Increase in inventories during the year	(182)	(158)	(399)
Operating expenses.	$22,716	$20,331	$17,696

(34)

Supplemental details are as follows: (In millions)	1982	1981	1980
Maintenance and repairs	$784	$775	$672
Company-funded research and development	760	640	521
Social Security taxes	484	471	397
Advertising	315	282	247
Mineral royalties and export duties	80	82	79

(35)

(36) Foreign currency translation gains, after recognizing related income tax effects and minority interest share, were $40 million in 1982 and $12 million in 1981 and 1980.

3 Pensions

Total pension costs of General Products and consolidated affiliates were $478 million in 1982, $413 million in 1981, and $381 million in 1980. General Products and its affiliates have a number of pension plans. The most significant of these plans is the General Products Pension Plan (the "Plan"), in which substantially all employees in the U.S. are participating. Approximately 80,800 persons were receiving benefits at year-end 1982 (75,700 and 72.100 at year-end 1981 and 1980, respectively).

Pension benefits under the Plan are funded through the General Products Pension Trust. Earnings of the Trust, including the programmed recognition of common stock appreciation, as a percentage of the carrying value of the portfolio, were 8.4% for 1982 and 1981, and 7.8% for 1980. The limitation on recognition of programmed appreciation of common stock was not exceeded in any year.

Condensed information for the General Products Pension Trust appears below.

(32) GP uses "full cost" accounting for its oil and gas operations. See the Glossary at *reserve recognition accounting* for discussion of the options. The U.S. Congress passed a law that required the SEC (and FASB) to set uniform accounting in the petroleum industry by the end of 1977. *FASB Statement No. 19* was issued in 1977 to comply. The statement required successful efforts accounting and forbade full cost accounting. In 1978, the SEC said it would allow either successful efforts or full cost accounting until it could write rules for "reserve recognition accounting." In 1981, the SEC indicated that it was delaying indefinitely use of reserve recognition accounting in the principal financial statements; either successful efforts or full cost can be used. GP's reported income is probably slightly larger because it uses full cost accounting rather than successful efforts accounting.

(33) *SFAS No. 14* requires disclosure of this information about customers whose purchases represent 10 percent or more of a firm's revenues.

(34) All manufacturing costs incurred during the year are shown as components of operating costs. If inventories have increased (ending inventory $>$ beginning inventory), then some of those costs have not expired and are not expenses. Hence, the increase in inventories is deducted from total operating costs to derive operating *expenses.*

(35) *SFAS No. 2* requires the expensing of research and development costs, and the disclosure, such as GP's here, of the costs incurred during the year for R & D. *SFAS No. 2* allows the capitalizing of R & D costs that are incurred under contract and that are reimbursable. GP is making clear that these costs ($760 million in 1982) do not qualify for capitalization.

(36) *SFAS No. 8* requires separate disclosure of these amounts.

General Products Pension Trust
Change in net assets at current value

(In millions) For the year	1982	1981	1980
Net assets at January 1	$4,968	$4,202	$3,734
Company contributions	404	341	317
Employee contributions	86	94	83
Investment income	435	383	312
Pensions paid	(254)	(225)	(201)
⃝37 Unrecognized portion of change in current value	779	173	(43)
Net assets at December 31	$6,418	$4,968	$4,202

Net assets at current value

(In millions) December 31	1982	1981	1980
U.S. government obligations and guarantees	$ 44	$ 118	$ 93
Corporate bonds and notes	727	496	340
Real estate and mortgages	825	713	725
Common stocks and other equity securities	4,181	3,193	2,726
	5,777	4,520	3,884
Cash and short-term investments	553	371	240
Other assets—net	88	77	78
Current value of net assets	$6,418	$4,968	$4,202
Carrying value of net assets	$5,593	$4,922	$4,329

The actuarial present value of accumulated plan benefits for the General Products Pension Plan and the supplementary pension plan together represent over 90% of accumulated pension plan benefits for General Products and its consolidated affiliates. These present values have been calculated using a 6% interest rate assumption as of December 31 for each of the years in the table below. The table also sets forth the total of the current value of Pension Trust assets and the relevant accruals in the Company's accounts.

⃝38 **General Products Pension Plan and Supplementary Pension Plan**

(In millions) December 31	1982	1981	1980
Estimated actuarial present value of accumulated plan benefits:			
Vested benefits	$6,027	$5,426	$4,732
Non-vested benefits	415	382	331
Total benefits	$6,442	$5,808	$5,063
Current value of trust assets plus accruals	$6,580	$5,075	$4,273

For pension plans not included above, there was no significant difference between accumulated benefits and the relevant fund assets plus accruals.

⃝39 The foregoing amounts are based on FASB standards which differ from those used by the Company for funding and cost determination purposes. Based on the actuarial method used by the Company, and with assets at carrying value, unfunded and unamortized liabilities for the two principal pension plans totaled $964 million, $1,082 million and $882 million at year-end 1982, 1981, and 1980, respectively.

636

(37) The "unrecognized portion of changes in current value" is analogous to unrealized holding gains.

(38) *SFAS No. 36* requires that the assets and liabilities of the pension plan be disclosed in notes to the employer's financial statements. *SFAS No. 36* requires that the same actuarial cost method be used by all companies in their disclosures about their pension plans. See Chapter 11. In the paragraph following the schedule GP discloses the results of applying the more conservative actuarial cost method it uses for its own purposes.

(39) GP discloses that the present value of the expected payments to current and retired employees exceeds the carrying value ($5,593 million in 1981) of pension plan assets by $964 million at the end of 1982.

(40) GP uses the equity method of accounting for its 100-percent ownership of the GP Credit Corporation. Hence it shows 100 percent of the earnings of the Credit Corporation as "Other income." See our comments 14 and 61.

(41) "Customer financing" is interest on receivables held by GP arising from some of its sales.

(42) *SFAS No. 34* requires separate disclosure of amounts of interest capitalized into plant under construction. See the discussion in Chapter 9.

(43) This first schedule shows the details of income tax expense, called a "provision." The bottom line of the first schedule is the total expense reported on the statement of earnings. It is the sum of U.S. federal, foreign and other income tax expenses. The U.S. federal and foreign income tax expense amounts are derived in essentially two steps: first is shown the amount of taxes payable; then there is an adjustment for timing differences. GP also shows the effect of the investment credit, which is discussed below in our comment 48.

(44) In 1982 income expenses exceeded income taxes payable because of timing differences. The details of the U.S. federal timing differences are shown in the next schedule.

(45) GP uses the deferral method of accounting for the investment credit; see our comment 48 and Chapter 9.

(46) The Internal Revenue Service has not completed its audit of GP's tax returns for years after 1974.

(47) APB *Opinion No. 23* says that income of affiliates that is expected to be indefinitely reinvested in the affiliate need not be subject to income tax provisions by the parent. If the parent expects to receive dividends from the affiliate in the foreseeable future, then the parent must make an income tax provision.

(48) GP uses the deferral method of accounting for the investment credit, rather than the less conservative flow-through method. (Most U.S. corporations use the flow-through method.) GP earned $92 million of investment credits during 1982. A portion (which cannot be computed from the published data) of this $92 million reduced reported tax expense in 1982; the remainder is shown as a deferred investment credit on the balance sheet (under "Other liabilities"). A portion of previous years' investment credits, which had been deferred, also served to reduce 1982 reported tax expense. The total of these two reductions of reported tax expense in 1982 was $36 million. If GP had used the flow-through method, income tax expense would have been reduced by an additional $56 (= $92 − $36) million and 1982 net income would have been $56 million larger. Under

An increase in pensions of retired employees effective February 1, 1983, will increase the actuarial present value of accumulated vested benefits by an estimated $196 million.

4 Other income

(In millions)	1982	1981	1980
Net earnings of General Products Credit Corporation..	$115	$ 90	$ 77
Income from:			
Marketable securities and bank deposits	229	229	140
Customer financing	72	70	49
Royalty and technical agreements	52	50	44
Associated companies and nonconsolidated uranium mining affiliate	22	11	34
Other investments:			
Interest	21	20	19
Dividends	13	11	10
Other sundry items.	40	38	46
	$564	$519	$419

5 Interest and other financial charges

Interest capitalized on major property, plant and equipment projects was $21 million, $18 million, and $15 million in 1982, 1981, and 1980, respectively.

6 Provision for income taxes

(In millions)	1982	1981	1980
U.S. federal income taxes:			
Estimated amount payable	$574	$599	$590
Effect of timing differences	14	(31)	(13)
Investment credit deferred—net	56	45	25
	644	613	602
Foreign income taxes:			
Estimated amount payable	238	323	221
Effect of timing differences	39	(6)	45
	277	317	266
Other (principally state and local income taxes)	37	23	26
	$958	$953	$894

All General Products consolidated U.S. federal income tax returns have been closed through 1974.

Provision has been made for federal income taxes to be paid on that portion of the undistributed earnings of affiliates and associated companies expected to be remitted to the parent company. Undistributed earnings intended to be reinvested indefinitely in affiliates and associated companies totaled $1,111 million at the end of 1982, $944 million at the end of 1981, and $815 million at the end of 1980.

Changes in estimated foreign income taxes payable and in the effect of timing differences result principally from fluctuations in foreign earnings and tax rates, and from recognizing in the current year for tax payment purposes the results of transactions in Australia recorded for financial reporting purposes in other years.

Investment credit amounted to $92 million in 1982, compared with $76 million in 1981 and $51 million in 1980. In 1982, $36 million were included in net earnings, compared with $31 million in 1981 and $26 million in 1980. At the end of 1980, the amount still deferred and to be included in net earnings in future years was $262 million.

638

the flow-through method, retained earnings at the end of 1982 would have been $262 million larger. Total deferred investment credits of $262 million are part of "Other liabilities" on the balance sheet.

(49) This schedule shows the components of the timing differences on U.S. federal income taxes.

(50) Depreciation on the tax return exceeded the amount included in cost of goods sold and other expenses on the financial statements. For most companies, tax depreciation exceeds book depreciation because an accelerated method is used for taxes and the straight-line method is used for financial reporting. GP, however, uses an accelerated method (based on the sum-of-the-years' digits) in its financial statements; see the Summary of Significant Accounting Policies. The excess of tax deductions for depreciation over book depreciation expenses for GP arises from GP's using shorter depreciable lives for tax than for book calculations. See the Glossary at *3-5-10 rule*. We can compute the excess of tax depreciation deductions over the book depreciation expense reported in the financial statements by using the $48 million timing difference shown here for 1982. If income tax expense exceeds income taxes payable by $48 million because of depreciation timing differences and if the marginal income tax rate is 46 percent of pretax income, then depreciation on the tax return must have exceeded depreciation on the financial statements by x where

$$.46x = \$48 \text{ million or}$$
$$x = \$48 \text{ million}/.46, \text{ or}$$
$$x = \$104 \text{ million}.$$

(51) Revenues from subsidiaries ("affiliates") shown on the financial statements under the equity method exceeded taxable revenue from these subsidiaries. Taxable revenue from this source is based primarily on the amount of dividends received. (Note that 85 percent of dividends received by one corporation from another corporation are not taxed. This is, however, a permanent difference that would not appear here.)

(52) GP makes sales on credit, with cash payments from the customer to GP spread over time. Such sales are called "installment sales." APB *Opinion No. 10* requires that revenue from most such sales be recognized in the financial statements for the period of sale. For tax purposes, GP recognizes revenue when the cash payments are collected. Thus a timing difference is created. The amount shown here for GP is relatively small because GP tends not to have large percentages of its sales on the installment method.

(53) Estimated warranty expense recognized by the "allowance method" does not qualify as a tax deduction. GP uses the "allowance method" of recognizing warranty expense for financial reporting. As products carrying warranties are sold, GP makes the following entry recognizing the estimated liability for future repairs and replacements:

Estimated Warranty Expense (Provision)   X
   Estimated Warranty Liability   X
Entry made in the period of sale for expected warranty costs.

---

(49) **Effect of timing differences on U.S. federal income taxes (In millions)**

Increase (decrease) in provision for income taxes	1982	1981	1980
(50) Tax over book depreciation	$ 48	$ 23	$ 26
(51) Undistributed earnings of affiliates and associated companies	29	(2)	8
(52) Margin on installment sales	1	(10)	(10)
(53) Provision for warranties	(46)	(36)	(31)
Other—net	(18)	(6)	(6)
	$ 14	$(31)	$(13)

(54) The cumulative net effect of timing differences has resulted in a deferred-tax asset which is shown under other assets.

(55) **Reconciliation from statutory to effective income tax rates**

	1982	1981	1980
U.S. federal statutory rate	46.0%	46.0%	46.0%
Reduction in taxes resulting from:			
Varying tax rates of consolidated affiliates (including DISC)	(4.7)	(3.3)	(2.4)
Inclusion of earnings of the Credit Corporation in before-tax income on an after-tax basis	(2.1)	(1.7)	(1.5)
Investment credit	(1.5)	(1.3)	(1.2)
Income tax at capital gains rate	(0.1)	—	(0.6)
Other—net	0.8	0.2	1.2
Effective tax rate	38.4%	39.9%	41.5%

(56) Based on the location of the component furnishing goods or services, domestic income before taxes was $1,854 million in 1982 ($1,706 million in 1981, and $1,592 million in 1980). The corresponding amounts for foreign-based operations were $639 million, $685 million and $561 million in each of the last three years, respectively. Provision for income taxes is determined on the basis of the jurisdiction imposing the tax liability. Therefore, U.S. and foreign taxes shown at the left do not compare directly with these segregations.

(57) **7 Earnings per common share**

Earnings per share are based on the average number of shares outstanding. Any dilution which would result from the potential exercise or conversion of such items as stock options or convertible debt outstanding is insignificant (less than 1% in 1982, 1981, and 1980).

8 Cash and marketable securities

(58) Deposits restricted as to usage and withdrawal or used as partial compensation for short-term borrowing arrangements were not material.

(59) Marketable securities (none of which are equity securities) are carried at the lower of amortized cost or market value. Carrying value was substantially the same as market value at year-end 1982 and 1981.

640

Later, when repairs are made, and warranty costs are incurred, the entry is:

Estimated Warranty Liability . . . . Y
   Assets Used and Liabilities Incurred . . . . Y
To recognize cost of actual repairs and replacements.

The repair and, therefore, the second entry often occur in a year subsequent to the year of sale. The cost of providing the warranty services does not become a tax deduction until the repair is actually made. Thus timing differences are created: an expense is subtracted on the financial statements in one year but is deducted on the tax return in a later year. We can make the following statements about all three years reported on. The provision for warranties (the estimated expense) results in income taxes payable being larger than income tax expense. Therefore, it must be true that the estimated expense of rendering warranty service in future years for sales in the current year is greater than the actual costs of warranty repairs made in current years, most of which related to sales of earlier years.

(54) Primarily because of the accounting (explained just above) for warranties, GP's cumulative income tax payments have exceeded cumulative income tax expense reported in the financial statements although this cumulative excess was reduced in 1982. This has resulted in a "deferred tax debit" (whereas most companies have the reverse situation and a "deferred tax credit") which GP reports among its "Other assets"; see GP's Note 13.

(55) Most readers of financial statements are aware that the U.S. federal tax rate on most corporate income is 46 percent of pretax income. The SEC requires that companies report in their notes why the reported income tax expense rate differs from 46 percent. The $115 million of income in 1982 for GP Credit reported in GP's note 4 is after taxes. Yet it appears in GP's income statement before the income tax calculation. GP need pay no further taxes on the income from GP Credit; this accounts for part of the difference between GP's effective tax rate on "pretax income," 38.4 percent in 1982, and the statutory rate, 46 percent. The investment credit reduces taxes otherwise payable and this accounts for another part of the difference.

(56) The SEC requires disclosure of the disaggregation of pretax income into domestic and foreign sources.

(57) GP reports only primary earnings per share. Because it has so few dilutive securities outstanding, fully diluted earnings per share would be less than one percent below the primary earnings per share. A dual presentation of earnings per share is required only when fully diluted earnings per share is 97 percent or less of primary earnings per share.

(58) See *compensating balance* in the Glossary. Compensating balances increase the stated cost of borrowing; accordingly, the SEC requires disclosure of such amounts, if they are significant. GP states that its compensating balances are not significant.

(59) *ARB No. 43* requires disclosure of aggregate cost and aggregate market value of these nonequity, marketable securities.

641

9 Current receivables

(In millions) December 31	1982	1981
Customers' accounts and notes	$3,816	$3,254
Associated companies	25	36
Nonconsolidated affiliates	17	7
Other	584	439
	4,442	3,736
Less allowances for uncollectibles	(103)	(89)
	$4,339	$3,647

10 Inventories

(In millions) December 31	1982	1981
Raw materials and work in process	$2,082	$1,943
Finished goods	961	966
Unbilled shipments	300	252
	$3,343	$3,161

About 84% of total inventories are valued using the LIFO method of inventory accounting.

 If the FIFO method of inventory accounting had been used to value all inventories, they would have been $2,240 million higher than reported at December 31, 1982 ($1,950 million higher at year-end 1981).

11 Property, plant and equipment

(In millions)	1982	1981
Major classes at December 31:		
Manufacturing plant and equipment		
Land and improvements	$ 139	$ 125
Buildings, structures and related equipment	2,329	2,098
Machinery and equipment	6,197	5,324
Leasehold costs and manufacturing plant under construction	453	372
Mineral property, plant and equipment	1,917	1,456
	$11,035	$9,365
Cost at January 1	$ 9,365	$8,328
Additions	1,948	1,262
Dispositions	(278)	(225)
Cost at December 31	$11,035	$9,365
Accumulated depreciation, depletion and amortization		
Balance at January 1	$ 4,752	$4,305
Current-year provision	707	624
Dispositions	(214)	(188)
Other changes	10	11
Balance at December 31	$ 5,255	$4,752
Property, plant and equipment less depreciation, depletion and amortization at December 31	$ 5,780	$4,613

(60) GP provides information that allows us to calculate what the operating income would have been if a FIFO cost flow assumption had been used. (See Chapter 8 for an explanation of why LIFO leads to lower reported net income in periods of rising prices.) The IRS does not allow companies using LIFO for tax purposes to disclose directly on the income statement what income would have been under FIFO. The SEC requires the disclosure of beginning and ending inventories as they would have been under FIFO, if these amounts are significantly different from the LIFO amounts. The SEC's required disclosure of inventory differences allows the reader to compute the income difference. As of December 31, 1982, cumulative pretax income is $2,240 million less than it would have been under FIFO. As of January 1, 1982, cumulative pretax income is $1,950 million less than it would have been under FIFO. This difference increased by $290 (= $2,240 − $1,950) million during the year 1982. Hence 1982 pretax income would have been $290 million, or about 19 percent, larger if FIFO had been used.

This calculation may be seen more clearly in Exhibit 8.6 on page 316.

12 Investments

(In millions) December 31	1982	1981
Nonconsolidated finance affiliate	$ 931	$ 817
Nonconsolidated uranium mining affiliate	188	157
Miscellaneous investments (at cost):		
Government and government guaranteed securities	187	233
Other	143	155
	330	388
Marketable equity securities	44	44
Associated companies	342	301
Less allowance for losses	(15)	(16)
	$1,820	$1,691

Condensed consolidated financial statements for the nonconsolidated finance affiliate, General Products Credit Corporation (GPCC), follow. During the normal course of business, (GPCC) has transactions with the parent General Products Company and certain of its consolidated affiliates, and GPCC results are included in General Products' consolidated U.S. federal income tax return. However, virtually all products financed by GPCC are manufactured by companies other than General Products.

General Products Credit Corporation
Current and retained earnings

(In millions) For the year	1982	1981	1980
Earned income	$1,389	$1,102	$813
Expenses:			
Interest and discount	719	528	337
Operating and administrative	451	396	315
Provision for losses			
—receivables	75	69	56
—other assets	3	(2)	8
Provision for income taxes	26	21	20
	1,274	1,012	736
Net earnings	115	90	77
Less dividends	(93)	(72)	(62)
Retained earnings at January 1	239	221	206
Retained earnings at December 31	$ 261	$ 239	$221

(61)

644

(61) Note that the following two events both occurred during 1982:

(i) GP required GPCC to declare dividends (payable to GP) in the amount of $93 million, and

(ii) GP invested an additional $92 ($= \$658 - \$566$) million in GPCC through the purchase of "Capital stock."

One might wonder why the parent bothers to have the subsidiary declare dividends and then turn right around and reinvest that cash in the same subsidiary. The executive compensation plan for the top managers of GP contains bonus clauses tying total pay to the reported income of the parent company as computed with a special formula. In that formula, the income from the Credit Company is based on accounting using the cost method, not the equity method. (One of the questions at the end of this Appendix explores why this fact might explain the otherwise-puzzling phenomenon.)

General Products Credit Corporation Financial position (In millions) December 31	1982	1981
Cash and marketable securities	$ 531	$ 374
Receivables:		
Time sales and loans	8,159	7,480
Deferred income	(1,380)	(1,124)
	6,779	6,356
	1,643	1,207
Investment in leases	197	141
Sundry receivables	8,619	7,704
Total receivables	(249)	(231)
Allowance for losses	8,370	7,473
Net receivables	443	321
Other assets	$9,344	$8,168
(62) Total assets		
Notes payable:		
Due within one year	$4,425	$3,921
Long-term—senior	1,984	1,743
—subordinated	400	325
Other liabilities	707	631
Total liabilities	7,516	6,620
Deferred income taxes	876	718
Deferred investment tax credit	21	13
(61) Capital stock	658	566
Additional paid-in capital	12	12
Retained earnings	261	239
Equity	931	817
Total liabilities, deferred tax items and equity	$9,344	$8,168

646

(62) If the Credit Corporation were consolidated, rather than accounted for on the equity method, all these assets, liabilities and deferred credits would be shown on GP's balance sheet. GP's consolidated retained earnings would be no different, however, because the equity method records income of unconsolidated subsidiaries as earned. The $931

Exhibit A.5
General Products and GP Credit Corporation, 1982
(*for Authors' Comment 62*)

Income Statement	Equity Method (as Reported)	Adjustment		Consolidated
		Debit	Credit	
Revenues (other than from Credit Corporation)^a	$25,408	$	$ 1,389 (1)	$26,797
Equity Method Revenues from Credit Corporation	115	115 (1)		
Total Revenues^b	$25,523			
Total Expenses^c	24,009	1,274 (1)		25,283
Net Income	$ 1,514			$ 1,514
Balance Sheet				
All Assets Except Investment in Credit Corporation	$17,580	9,344 (2)		$26,924
Investment in Credit Corporation.	931		931 (2)	
Total Assets	$18,511			$26,924
Liabilities (including Minority Interest)	$10,311		8,413^d (2)	$18,724
Owner's Equity	8,200			8,200
Total Equities	$18,511	$10,733	$10,733	$26,924

Rate of Return on Assets:

$$\frac{\$1,514 + \$21^e + (.54 \times \$314^f)}{\$18,511} \qquad \frac{\$1,514 + \$21^e + .54 \times (\$314^f + \$719^g)}{\$26,924}$$

$$= \frac{\$1,705}{\$18,511} = 9.2\% \qquad\qquad = \frac{\$2,093}{\$26,924} = 7.8\%$$

Debt-Equity Ratio:

$$\frac{\$10,311}{\$18,511} = 56\% \qquad\qquad \frac{\$18,724}{\$26,924} = 68\%$$

a $24,959 + $564 − $115; a plug.
b $24,959 shown as Sales in Exhibit A.1 plus $564 of Other income.
c $22,716 (operating expense) + $314 (interest) + $958 (income taxes) + $21 (minority interest).
d GP Credit's "liabilities" ($7,516) plus "deferred income taxes" ($876) plus "deferred investment credit" ($21).
e Minority interest in net income from income statement.
f GP's interest expense. Multiply by 0.54 to state on aftertax basis.
g GP Credit's interest expense. Multiply by 0.54 to state on aftertax basis.

Adjusting entry (1) adds the revenues and expenses of the Credit Corporation to the consolidated totals, while removing the equity method revenue reported by GP.

Adjusting entry (2) adds the assets and liabilities of the Credit Corporation to the consolidated totals, while removing GP's net investment from the asset account for Investments.

647

(63) The nonconsolidated uranium mining company is valued at lower of cost or equity, plus advances. The estimated realizable value of miscellaneous investments was $287 million at December 31, 1982 ($350 million at December 31, 1981).

(64) Marketable equity securities are valued at the lower of cost or market. Aggregate market value of marketable equity securities was $242 million and $181 million at year-end 1982 and 1981, respectively. At December 31, 1982, gross unrealized gains on marketable equity securities were $198 million.

Investments in nonconsolidated affiliates and associated companies included advances of $180 million at December 31, 1982 ($123 million at December 31, 1981).

13 Other assets

(In millions) December 31	1982	1981
Long-term receivables	$340	$307
Deferred charges	198	145
Real estate development projects	132	81
Recoverable engineering costs on government contracts	113	121
Customer financing	103	107
(65) Licenses and other intangibles—net	75	52
(66) Deferred income taxes	21	98
Other	46	45
	$1,028	$956

Licenses and other intangibles acquired after October 1970 are being amortized over appropriate periods of time.

14 Short-term borrowings

The average balance of short-term borrowings, excluding the current portion of long-term borrowings, was $822 million during 1982 (calculated by averaging all month-end balances for the year) compared with an average balance of $705 million in 1981. The maximum balance included in these calculations was $962 million and $727 million at the end of October 1982 and March 1981, respectively. The average effective interest rate for the year 1982 was 18.9%, and for 1981 was 17.6%. These average rates represent total short-term interest incurred divided by the average balance outstanding. A summary of short-term borrowings and the applicable interest rates is shown below.

Short-term borrowings (In millions) December 31	1982		1981	
	Amount	Average rate at Dec. 31	Amount	Average rate at Dec. 31
Parent notes with trust departments	$ 353	15.05%	$290	12.62%
Consolidated affiliate bank borrowings	539	30.83	389	27.10
Other, including current portion of long-term borrowings	201		192	
	$1,093		$871	

Parent borrowings are from U.S. sources. Borrowings of consolidated affiliated companies are primarily from foreign sources. Other borrowings include amounts from nonconsolidated affiliate of $95 million in 1982 ($65 million in 1981).

Although the total unused credit available to the Company through banks and commercial credit markets is not readily quantifiable, informal credit lines in excess of $1 billion had been extended by approximately 100 U.S. banks at year end.

(= \$9,344 − \$7,516 − \$876 − \$21) million of net assets added to GP's balance sheet would be offset with the elimination of \$931 shown on the balance sheet and detailed in GP's Note 12.

If GP were to consolidate GP Credit Corporation, the results would be as shown in the Exhibit A.5. It shows the income statement and balance sheet as reported and as they would appear if GP Credit Corporation were consolidated. We also show two key financial ratios, as they would be calculated from year-end account balances. The consolidation policy with respect to GP Credit Corporation affects the appearance of the financial statements. For an even larger effect, refer to the financial statements of General Motors Corporation and go through the exercise of consolidating GMAC (General Motors Acceptance Corporation), which GM accounts for by the equity method.

(63) The disclosure of both historical cost and current market values follows the requirement of *SFAS No. 12.* The net realizable value of these securities at year-end 1982 is \$287 million; the cost (see GP's Note 12) was \$330 million. Thus GP has an unrealized holding loss on these securities of \$43 (= \$287 value − \$330 cost) million at year-end 1982. At year-end 1981, the unrealized holding loss was \$38 (= \$350 − \$388) million. Thus the unrealized holding loss increased during the year by \$5 million, from \$38 million to \$43 million. GP therefore had unrealized holding loss during 1982 of \$5 million on these securities.

(64) The aggregate market value of these securities at year-end 1982 is \$242 million; the cost is \$44 million. Thus, the unrealized holding gain at the end of 1982 is \$198 (= \$242 − \$44) million. At year-end 1981, the unrealized holding gain was \$137 (= \$181 value − \$44 cost) million. Thus, the unrealized holding gain increased by \$61 (= \$198 − \$137) million during the year 1982. GP had an increase in wealth of \$61 million which is not reported in the conventional financial statements which are based on historical costs.

(65) Licenses and other intangibles acquired before October 1970 need not be amortized. APB *Opinion No. 17* requires that licenses and intangibles acquired after October 1970 be amortized over a period of not more than 40 years.

(66) See our comments 53 and 54.

15 Accounts payable

(In millions) December 31	1982	1981
Trade accounts	$1,402	$1,259
Collected for the account of others	203	172
Nonconsolidated affiliates	66	46
	$1,671	$1,477

16 Other payables

The balances at year-end 1982 and 1981 included compensation and benefit costs accrued of $703 million and $641 million, respectively.

17 Long-term borrowings

(In millions) Outstanding December 31	1982	1981	Due date	Sinking fund prepayment period
General Products Company:				
$5\frac{3}{4}$% Notes	$ 62	$ 69	1993	1974–92
5.30% Debentures	70	80	1994	1975–93
$7\frac{1}{2}$% Debentures	135	149	1998	1979–97
$8\frac{1}{2}$% Debentures	288	295	2006	1987–03
Coal International Inc.:				
Notes with banks	37	5	1995	1983–95
8% Guaranteed Sinking Fund Debentures	15	17	1989	1979–89
7.6% Notes	28	32	1990	1976–90
Other	32	25		
General Products Overseas Capital Corporation:				
$4\frac{1}{4}$% Bonds	23	24	1987	1978–86
$4\frac{1}{4}$% Debentures	50	50	1989	None
$5\frac{1}{2}$% Sterling/ Dollar Guaranteed Loan Stock	9	8	1995	None
Other	34	37		
All other	217	156		
	$1,000	$947		

The amounts shown above are after deduction of the face value of securities held in treasury as shown on the next page.

Face value of long-term borrowings in treasury (In millions) December 31	1982	1981
General Products Company:		
5.30% Debentures	$50	$50
$7\frac{1}{2}$% Debentures	35	29
$8\frac{1}{2}$% Debentures	12	5
General Products Overseas Capital Corporation:		
$4\frac{1}{4}$% Bonds	6	7

Coal International Inc. notes with banks were subject to average interest rates at year-end 1982 and 1981 of 11.3% and 7.9%, respectively.

Borrowings of General Products Overseas Capital Corporation are unconditionally guaranteed by General Products as to payment of principal, premium if any, and interest. This Corporation primarily assists in financing capital requirements of foreign companies in which General Products has an equity interest, as well as financing certain customer purchases.

Borrowings include $4\frac{1}{4}$% Guaranteed Debentures due in 1989, which are convertible into General Products common stock at $80.75 a share, and $5\frac{1}{2}$% Sterling/Dollar Guaranteed Loan Stock due in 1995 in the amount of £3.6 million ($9 million), convertible into GP common stock at $73.50 a share. During 1982 and 1981, General Products Overseas Capital Corporation $4\frac{1}{4}$% Guaranteed Bonds having a face value and a reacquired cost of $2 million were retired in accordance with sinking fund provisions.

All other long-term borrowings were largely by foreign and real estate development affiliates with various interest rates and maturities and included amounts due to nonconsolidated affiliate of $7 million in 1982 and 1981.

(67) Long-term borrowing maturities during the next five years, including the portion classified as current, are $91 million in 1983, $130 million in 1984, $62 million in 1985, $42 million in 1986, and $68 million in 1987. These amounts are after deducting reacquired debentures held in treasury for sinking fund requirements.

(68) **18 Common stock**

At December 31, 1982 and December 31, 1981, respectively, 227,765,000 and 227,839,000 common shares were outstanding. Common stock held in treasury at December 31, 1982, included 1,921,706 shares for the deferred compensation provisions of incentive compensation plans (1,785,656 shares at December 31, 1981). These shares are carried at market value at the time of allotment, which amounted to $96 million and $88 million at December 31, 1982 and 1981, respectively. The liability is recorded under other liabilities.

Other common stock in treasury, which is carried at cost, aggregated 1,777,382 and 1,839,762 shares at December 31, 1982 and 1981, respectively. These shares are held for future corporate requirements, including distributions under employee savings plans, incentive compensation awards and possible conversion of General Products Overseas Capital Corporation convertible indebtedness. The maximum number of shares required for conversions was 736,079 at December 3, 1982 (737,725 at December 31, 1981). Corporate requirements of shares for benefit plans and conversions may be met either from unissued shares or from shares in treasury.

	1982	1981	1982	1981
	(In millions)		(Thousands of shares)	
Common stock issued				
Balance January 1 and December 31	$ 579	$ 579	231,464	231,464
Amounts received for stock in excess of par value				
Balance January 1	$ 656	$ 658		
Gain/(loss) on disposition of treasury stock . .	3	(2)		
Balance December 31	$659	$ 656		
Common stock held in treasury				
Balance January. 1.	$ 180	$ 172	3,625	3,428
Purchases	145	156	2,684	3,155
Dispositions:				
Employee savings plans	(99)	(124)	(1,879)	(2,492)
Employee stock ownership plan	(16)	(11)	(296)	(213)
Incentive compensation plans	(7)	(8)	(158)	(152)
Stock options and appreciation rights	(14)	(5)	(275)	(101)
Conversion of Overseas Capital Corporation loan stock.	—	—	(2)	—
Balance December 31	$ 189	$ 180	3,699	3,625

(69)

During 1980, the balance in common stock issued did not change, amounts received for common stock in excess of par value decreased by $10 million, and the balance of common stock held in treasury increased by $6 million.

19 Retained earnings

Retained earnings at year-end 1982 included approximately $251 million ($246 million at December 31, 1981), representing the excess of earnings of nonconsolidated affiliates over dividends received since their formation. In addition, retained earnings have been increased by $10 million ($5 million reduction at December 31, 1981), which represents the change in equity in associated companies since acquisition.

(70)

(71) 20 Stock option information

Stock option plans, appreciation rights and performance units are described in the Company's current Proxy Statement. A summary of stock option transactions during the last two years is shown below.

652

(67) GP's Note 14 gives the details of its short-term borrowings. GP's Note 16 gives the details of its long-term borrowings. This paragraph helps the analyst to understand GP's intermediate-term borrowings. From these data, the analyst can estimate cash requirements for debt retirement over the next several years.

(68) APB *Opinion No. 12* (1966) requires the disclosure of all changes in owners' equity accounts. GP shows the sources of the changes in the retained earnings account below the income statement, in Exhibit A.1. The schedule in Note 18 shows the sources of the changes in the other owners' equity accounts.

(69) Neither gain nor loss can be recognized on transactions by a company in its own shares (called *treasury shares*). GP's accounting is correct, but the use of the terms *gain* and *loss* may be misleading. When GP reissues previously-acquired treasury shares, the adjustment to achieve equal debits and credits is not to a gain or loss account (to appear on the income statement), but to the account "Amounts received for stock in excess of par value." If treasury shares are acquired for an outlay of $1,000 and then are reissued for $1,200, then the entries would be:

Common Stock Held in Treasury	1,000	
Cash		1,000
To record acquisition of treasury shares.		
Cash	1,200	
Common Stock Held in Treasury		1,000
Amounts Received for Stock in Excess of Par Value (not Gain on Disposition of Treasury Shares)		200
To record reissue of treasury shares for an amount greater than outlay to acquire them.		

If proceeds of reissue are $800, not $1,200, then in the second entry the $200 is debited, not credited, to the account "Amounts Received for Stock in Excess of Par Value."

(70) Associated companies are 20-percent to 50-percent owned by GP. APB *Opinion No. 18* requires GP to use the equity method for its investment in those companies.

(71) *Accounting Research Bulletin No. 43* (1953) requires the disclosure of the details of stock option plans and of the currently outstanding options. At the end of 1982, the market price of a share of GP common stock was $61.25. The average price of the 4,303,322 options exercisable at the end of 1982 was $51.56. Thus, if all the options were exercised, the present owners' equity would be diluted by approximately $42 million [= ($61.25 − $51.56) × 4,303,322 shares] in comparison to the issue of new shares at the current market price.

653

Stock options	Shares subject to option	Average per share Option price	Market price
Balance at January 1, 1981.	4,088,853	$51.37	$47.13
Options granted.	1,023,122	46.25	46.25
Options exercised	(98,145)	40.63	50.14
Options surrendered on exercise of appreciation rights	(68,834)	40.52	49.17
Options terminated	(186,068)	50.77	—
Balance at December 31, 1981.	4,758,928	50.67	50.63
Options granted	98,100	61.50	61.50
Options exercised	(273,193)	44.13	56.16
Options surrendered on exercise of appreciation rights	(123,350)	41.93	54.92
Options terminated	(157,163)	51.02	—
Balance at December 31, 1982	4,303,322	51.56	61.25

The number of shares available for granting additional options at the end of 1982 was 1,862,756 (1,831,456 at the end of 1981).

21 Commitments and contingent liabilities

 Lease commitments and contingent liabilities, consisting of guarantees, pending litigation, taxes and other claims, in the opinion of management, are not considered to be material in relation to the Company's financial position.

(73) Industry segment information

Consumer Products and Services consists of major appliances, air conditioning equipment, lighting products, housewares and audio products, television receivers, and broadcasting and cablevision services. It also includes service operations for major appliances, air conditioners, TV receivers, and housewares and audio products.

General Products Credit Corporation, a wholly owned nonconsolidated finance affiliate, engages primarily in consumer, commercial and industrial financing, principally in the U.S. It also participates, to a lesser degree, in life insurance and fire and casualty insurance activities. Products of companies other than GP constitute virtually all products financed by GPCC.

Industrial Products and Components includes components (appliance controls, small motors and electronic components); industrial capital equipment (construction, automation and transportation); maintenance, inspection, repair and rebuilding of electric, electronic and mechanical apparatus; and a network of supply houses offering products of General Products and other manufacturers.

Power Systems includes steam turbine-generators, gas turbines, nuclear power reactors and nuclear fuel assemblies, transformers, switchgear, meters, and installation and maintenance engineering services.

Technical Systems and Materials consists of jet engines for aircraft, industrial and marine applications; electronic and other high-technology products and services primarily for aerospace applications and defense; materials (engineered plastics, silicones, industrial cutting materials, laminated and insulating materials, and batteries); medical and communications equipment; and time sharing, computing, and remote data processing.

Natural Resources includes the mining of coking coal (principally in Australia), uranium, steam coal, iron and copper. In addition, it includes oil and natural gas production, ocean shipping (primarily in support of mining operations) and land acquisition and development.

654

(72) Both the SEC and the FASB (*SFAS No. 13*) require disclosure of material commitments under long-term noncancelable leases. GP has no such material commitments. In general, the disclosures must include the effects on both the income statement and the balance sheet of capitalizing such leases.

(73) *SFAS 14* requires disclosure of segment data. Segments are required to be defined both by kind of operation (consumer products, industrial power, etc.) and by location (United States, Far East, etc.).

(In millions) — **Revenues** For the years ended December 31

	Total revenues			Intersegment sales			External sales and other income		
	1982	1981	1980	1982	1981	1980	1982	1981	1980
Consumer products and services...	$ 5,599	$ 5,358	$ 4,788	$ 201	$ 199	$ 188	$ 5,398	$ 5,159	$ 4,600
Net earnings of GP Credit Corp. ...	115	90	77	—	—	—	115	90	77
Total consumer products and services	5,714	5,448	4,865	201	199	188	5,513	5,249	4,677
Industrial products and components.	5,157	4,803	4,124	565	508	468	4,592	4,295	3,656
Power systems	4,023	3,564	3,486	175	210	174	3,848	3,354	3,312
Technical systems and materials ...	7,128	6,061	4,745	258	255	190	6,870	5,806	4,555
Natural resources	1,374	1,260	1,032	—	—	—	1,374	1,260	1,032
Foreign multi-industry operations ...	3,234	2,901	2,767	75	64	55	3,159	2,837	2,712
Corporate items and eliminations...	(1,107)	(1,057)	(946)	(1,274)	(1,236)	(1,075)	167	179	129
Total	$25,523	$22,980	$20,073	$ —	$ —	$ —	$25,523	$22,980	$20,073

(74)

	Operating profit			Net earnings		
	For the years ended December 31			For the years ended December 31		
	1982	1981	1980	1982	1981	1980
Consumer products and services ..	$ 558	$ 568	$ 574	$ 292	$ 311	$ 300
Net earnings of GP Credit Corp. .	115	90	77	115	90	77
Total consumer products and services	673	658	651	407	401	377
Industrial products and components.	568	485	426	315	272	223
Power systems	194	174	196	141	114	93
Technical systems and materials ...	774	672	545	373	356	278
Natural resources	404	431	372	224	208	180
Foreign multi-industry operations ...	285	241	245	68	65	76
Total segment operating profit ..	2,898	2,661	2,435			
Interest and other financial charges .	(314)	(258)	(224)			
Corporate items and eliminations ...	(91)	(12)	(58)	(14)	(7)	3
Total	$ 2,493	$ 2,391	$ 2,153	$ 1,514	$ 1,409	$ 1,230

(74)

	Assets			Property, plant and equipment					
	At December 31			For the years ended December 31					
					Additions			Depreciation, depletion and amortization	
	1982	1981	1980	1982	1981	1980	1982	1981	1980
Consumer products and services...	$ 2,325	$ 2,157	$ 2,018	$ 238	$ 208	$ 169	$ 133	$ 115	$ 104
Investment in GP Credit Corp. ...	931	817	677	—	—	—	—	—	—
Total consumer products and services	3,256	2,974	2,695	238	208	169	133	115	104
Industrial products and components .	2,595	2,329	2,125	224	176	166	109	106	91
Power systems	2,289	2,135	2,105	129	101	84	91	84	79
Technical systems and materials ...	4,475	3,422	2,683	693	444	289	200	163	150
Natural resources	2,109	1,679	1,489	446	201	212	94	83	77
Foreign multi-industry operations ...	2,564	2,259	2,100	161	109	119	66	61	64
Corporate items and eliminations ...	1,223	1,846	1,839	57	23	16	14	12	11
Total	$18,511	$16,644	$15,036	$ 1,948	$ 1,262	$ 1,055	$ 707	$ 624	$ 576

656

(74) Earnings of the individual segments sum to an amount larger than net income for 1982 of $1,514 by $14 million. Assets of the individual segments sum to an amount smaller than total assets by $1,223 million. Hence rates of return computed for individual segments will overstate true rate of return. If a "true" rate of return for the company as a whole is defined to be net income over total assets, then GP's rate of return is 8.2 percent (= $1,514/18,511). The incomes of the individual segments total $1,528 million and the sum of the segments assets is $17,288 (= $18,511 − $1,223) million. If one were computing rates of return for individual segments, then, the aggregate rate of return might be computed as 8.8 percent (= $1,528/$17,288). For GP, the resulting overstatement of the combined segment rates of return is not as dramatic as it is for some other companies. Some who criticize segment reporting have in mind the misleading inferences the unwary analyst (or politician or government regulator) might draw from computing rates of return for individual segments.

Foreign Multi-industry Operations consists principally of foreign affiliates which manufacture products primarily for sale in their respective home markets.

(75) **Net earnings for industry segments** include allocation of corporate interest income, expense and other financial charges to parent company components based on change in individual component average nonfixed investment. Interest and other financial charges of affiliated companies recognize that such companies generally service their own debt.

General corporate expenses are allocated principally on the basis of cost of operations, with certain exceptions and reductions which recognize the varying degrees to which affiliated companies maintain their own corporate structures.

In addition, provision for income taxes ($958 million in 1982, $953 million in 1981, and $894 million in 1980) is allocated based on the total corporate effective tax rate, except for GPCC and Natural Resources, whose income taxes are calculated separately.

Minority interest ($21 million in 1982 and $29 million in both 1981 and 1980) is allocated to operating components having responsibility for investments in consolidated affiliates.

In general, it is GP's policy to price internal sales as nearly as practiable to equivalent commercial selling prices.

(In millions)	Revenues For the years ended December 31								
	Total revenues			Intersegment sales			External sales and other income		
	1982	1981	1980	1982	1981	1980	1982	1981	1980
United States	$20,750	$18,859	$16,443	$ 484	$ 467	$ 362	$20,266	$18,392	$16,081
Far East including Australia	1,277	1,183	1,109	355	280	242	922	903	867
Other areas of the world	4,459	3,814	3,270	124	129	145	4,335	3,685	3,125
Elimination of intracompany transactions	(963)	(876)	(749)	(963)	(876)	(749)	—	—	—
Total	$25,523	$22,980	$20,073	$ —	$ —	$ —	$25,523	$22,980	$20,073

	Net Earnings For the years ended December 31			Assets At December 31		
	1982	1981	1980	1982	1981	1980
United States	$ 1,175	$ 1,120	$ 961	$13,732	$12,693	$11,410
Far East including Australia	169	174	170	1,090	842	889
Other areas of the world	181	120	104	3,808	3,207	2,827
Elimination of intracompany transactions	(11)	(5)	(5)	(119)	(98)	(90)
Total	$ 1,514	$ 1,409	$ 1,230	$18,511	$16,644	$15,036

658

Geographic segment information (including allocation of income taxes and minority interest in earnings of consolidated affiliates) is based on the location of the operation furnishing goods or services. Included in United States revenues were export sales to unaffiliated customers of $3,781 million in 1982, $2,772 million in 1981, and $2,571 million in 1980. Of such sales, $2,089 million in 1982 ($1,581 million in 1981 and $1,662 million in 1980) were to customers in Europe, Africa and the Middle East; and $926 million in 1982 ($741 million in 1981 and $498 million in 1980) were to customers in the Far East including Australia. U.S. revenues also include royalty and licensing income from unaffiliated foreign sources.

Revenues, net earnings and assets associated with foreign operations are shown in the tabulations above. At December 31, 1982, foreign operation liabilities, minority interest in equity and GP interest in equity were $2,562 million, $141 million and $2,195 million, respectively. On a comparable basis, the amounts were $2,101 million, $139 million and $1,809 million, respectively, at December 31, 1981, and $1,910 million, $150 million and $1,656 million, respectively, at December 31, 1980.

(76) *Six-year summary (a)*
Selected financial data

(Dollar amounts in millions; per-share amounts in dollars)	1982	1981	1980	1979	1978	1977
Summary of operations						
Sales of products and services to customers	$24,959	$22,461	$19,654	$17,519	$15,697	$14,105
Cost of goods sold	17,751	15,991	13,915	12,288	11,048	10,210
Selling, general and administrative expense	4,258	3,716	3,205	3,011	2,635	2,238
Depreciation, depletion and amortization	707	624	576	522	486	470
Operating costs	22,716	20,331	17,696	15,821	14,169	12,918
Operating margin	2,243	2,130	1,958	1,698	1,528	1,187
Other income	564	519	419	390	274	174
Interest and other financial charges	(314)	(258)	(224)	(199)	(175)	(187)
Earnings before income taxes and minority interest	2,493	2,391	2,153	1,889	1,627	1,174
Provision for income taxes	(958)	(953)	(894)	(773)	(668)	(460)
Minority interest	(21)	(29)	(29)	(28)	(28)	(26)
Net earnings	$ 1,514	$ 1,409	$ 1,230	$ 1,088	$ 931	$ 688
Earnings per common share (b)	$ 6.65	$ 6.20	$ 5.39	$ 4.79	$ 4.12	$ 3.07
Dividends declared per common share (c)	$ 2.95	$ 2.75	$ 2.50	$ 2.10	$ 1.70	$ 1.60
Earnings as a percentage of sales	6.1%	6.3%	6.3%	6.2%	5.9%	4.9%
Earned on average share owners' equity	19.5%	20.2%	19.6%	19.4%	18.9%	15.7%
Dividends—General Products	$ 670	$ 624	$ 570	$ 477	$ 333	$ 293
Dividends—Coal International Inc. (d)	—	—	—	—	$ 28	$ 33
Shares outstanding—average (in thousands) (e)	227,541	227,173	227,985	227,154	225,791	224,262
Share owner accounts—average	524,000	540,000	552,000	553,000	566,000	582,000
Market price range per share (c)	63-44	$55\frac{1}{8}$-45	$57\frac{5}{8}$-$43\frac{5}{8}$	$57\frac{1}{4}$-$47\frac{3}{8}$	$59\frac{1}{4}$-46	$52\frac{7}{8}$-$32\frac{3}{8}$
Price/earnings ratio range (c)	9-7	9-7	11-8	12-10	14-11	17-10
Current assets	$ 9,883	$ 9,384	$ 8,755	$ 7,865	$ 6,685	$ 5,750
Current liabilities	7,592	6,872	6,175	5,417	4,605	4,163
Working capital	$ 2,291	$ 2,512	$ 2,580	$ 2,448	$ 2,080	$ 1,587
Short-term borrowings	$ 1,093	$ 871	$ 960	$ 772	$ 611	$ 667
Long-term borrowings	1,000	947	994	1,284	1,322	1,239
Minority interest in equity of consolidated affiliates	154	152	151	132	119	105
Share owners' equity	8,200	7,362	6,587	5,943	5,253	4,617
Total capital invested	$10,447	$ 9,332	$ 8,692	$ 8,131	$ 7,305	$ 6,628
Earned on average total capital invested	17.3%	17.6%	16.3%	15.8%	15.1%	12.5%
Share owners' equity per common share—year end (b)	$ 36.00	$ 32.31	$ 28.88	$ 26.05	$ 23.18	$ 20.49
Total assets	$18,511	$16,644	$15,036	$13,697	$12,050	$10,741
Property, plant and equipment additions	$ 1,948	$ 1,262	$ 1,055	$ 823	$ 740	$ 588
Employees—average worldwide	402,000	405,000	401,000	384,000	380,000	380,000

(a) Unless specifically noted, all years are adjusted to include Coal International Inc., which became a wholly owned affiliate of General Products on December 20, 1978, through the exchange of 41,002,034 shares of General Products common stock for all of the outstanding shares of Coal.
(b) Computed using outstanding shares as described in note (e).
(c) For General Products common stock as reported in the years shown.

(d) Reflects transactions prior to merger date.
(e) Includes General Products outstanding average shares or year-end shares as appropriate, plus, in 1978 and prior years, outstanding shares previously reported by Coal multiplied by 1.3. Adjustments have been made for the two-for-one Coal stock split effected in the form of stock dividends in 1975.

(77) **Other information (unaudited)**

Quarterly dividend and stock market information

	Dividends declared		Common stock market price range	
	1982	**1981**	**1982**	**1981**
First quarter	70¢	65¢	$57\frac{1}{2}$–$44	$50\frac{3}{8}$–$45\frac{1}{2}$
Second quarter	75	70	52 – $44\frac{1}{2}$	$51\frac{5}{8}$– $46\frac{7}{8}$
Third quarter	75	70	$58\frac{1}{8}$– $51\frac{1}{8}$	$55\frac{1}{8}$– $49\frac{1}{8}$
Fourth quarter	75	70	63 – $51\frac{1}{2}$	$52\frac{1}{4}$– 45

The New York Stock Exchange is the principal market on which GP common stock is traded and, as of December 8, 1982, there were approximately 512,282 share owners of record.

(78) **Operations by quarter for 1982 and 1981**

(Dollar amounts in millions; per share amounts in dollars)	First quarter	Second quarter	Third quarter	Fourth quarter
1982				
Sales of products and services to customers . .	$5,881	$6,197	$5,963	$6,918
Operating margin	527	556	513	647
Net earnings	342	403	358	411
Net earnings per common share	1.50	1.77	1.58	1.80
1981				
Sales of products and services to customers . .	$5,082	$5,642	$5,609	$6,128
Operating margin	470	598	511	551
Net earnings	303	382	341	383
Net earnings per common share	1.33	1.69	1.50	1.68

(79) ## Changing Prices

Your Company's financial results are not immune to the distorting effects of inflation. Financial data elsewhere in this Annual Report, including the audited financial statements, are presented using the traditional basis of financial reporting which does not fully identify the effects of inflation. The following table presents information which supplements the traditional financial statements in order to gauge the effect of changing prices on results for 1982.

(80) **Supplementary Information**
Effect of Changing Prices

For the year
ended December 31, 1982

(in millions; except per-share amounts)	As reported	Adjusted for (a) general inflation	current costs
Sales of products and services to customers	$24,959	C$24,959	C$24,959
Cost of goods sold	17,751	17,904	17,892
Selling, general and administrative expense	4,258	4,258	4,258
Depreciation, depletion and amortization	707	1,052	1,092
Operating costs	22,716	23,214	23,242
Operating margin	2,243	1,745	1,717
Other income	564	564	564
Interest and other financial charges	(314)	(314)	(314)
Earnings before income taxes	2,493	1,995	1,967
Provision for income taxes	(958)	(958)	(958)
Minority interest	(21)	(8)	(8)
Net earnings	$ 1,514	C$ 1,029	C$ 1,001
Earnings per share	$ 6.65	C$ 4.52	C$ 4.40
Effective tax rate	38.4%	48.0%	48.7%
Share owners' equity at Dec. 31	$ 8,200	C$12,377	C$12,913

(81) (a) In dollars of average 1982 purchasing power based on the CPI-H (82) (83)

This table shows two different ways of attempting to remove inflationary impacts from financial results as traditionally reported. In both "adjusted for" columns, restatements are made to (1) cost of goods sold (82) for the current cost of replacing inventories, and (2) depreciation for the current cost of plant and equipment. The column headed "general inflation" uses only a broad index to calculate the restatement, (83) while the column headed "current costs" uses data more specifically applicable to GP.

The restatements to cost of goods sold are relatively small for GP because extensive use of last-in, first-out inventory accounting already largely reflects current costs in the traditional earnings statement. However, restatements to depreciation, which allocates plant and equipment costs to expenses over time, are relatively large because of the high rate of inflation, particularly in the last three years. This is because traditional reporting of depreciation based on original cost does not adequately reflect higher prices for replacement of productive capacity of fixed assets which were purchased a number of years ago. Both of these methods of adjusting for inflation result in lower earnings than traditionally reported.

Significantly, because inflation adjustments are not allowable for tax purposes, the "real" tax rate was about 10 points higher than in traditional statements.

Your management believes the "current cost" method is more representative of GP's results, but emphasizes the considerable subjectivity involved in the calculations. These types of adjusted data are likely to be more useful in reviewing trends over a period of time, rather than in making comparisons of restatements for any one period or in specific analyses of one period compared with another. GP's after-tax earnings on the traditional basis of accounting have been higher each year from 1978 through 1982. Since 1977, the average annual growth rate for earnings as reported was about 16%. Using the "current cost" method of removing the effects of inflation, earnings grew at an average annual rate since 1977 of about 24%. However, the purchasing power of a dollar in 1982 had diminished by more than one-third since 1977. To reflect this deterioration of the dollar's purchasing power, current-cost earnings for the years since 1977 can be expressed in dollars of 1977 purchasing power. On this basis, the data indicate a real average annual growth rate in earnings since 1977 of about 14%.

(84) **Current cost information in average dollars of 1982 purchasing power(a)**

(In millions except per-share amounts)

	Sales	Net earnings (b)	Share owners' equity Dec. 31 (b)	Earnings (b)	Dividends	Market price Dec. 31	Purchasing power gain (loss) (c)
				Per common share			
1982	C$24,959	C$1,001	C$12,913	C$4.40	C$2.95	C$59	C$(198)
1981	25,493	1,119	12,659	4.93	3.12	54	(237)
1980	24,819	1,092	12,508	4.79	3.16	57	(145)
1979	23,817	1,001	12,095	4.40	2.86	66	(69)
1978	22,717	885	11,947	3.92	2.46	79	(23)
1977	21,590	479	11,414	2.13	2.45	68	22

(a) Average 1982 dollars, using the U.S. Consumer Price Index—Hypothetical (1967 = 100): 1977—201.5; 1978—213.1; 1979—226.9; 1980—244.3; 1981—271.8; and 1982—308.5.
(b) Current cost basis.
(c) On net monetary items.

Proper use of supplementary information concerning the effect of changing prices requires an understanding of certain basic concepts and definitions.

In the table showing details for 1982, "as reported"refers to information drawn directly from the financial statements and notes. This information is prepared using generally accepted accounting principles which render an accounting based on the number of actual dollars involved in transactions, with no recognition given to the fact that the value of the dollar changes over time.

"Adjusted for general inflation" refers to information prepared using a different approach to transactions involving inventory and property, plant and equipment assets. Under this procedure, the number of dollars involved in transactions at different dates are all restated to equivalent amounts in terms of the general purchasing power of the dollar as it is measured by the Consumer Price Index—Hypothetical. (CPI—H). For example, $1,000 invested in a building in 1967 would be restated to its 1982 dollar purchasing power equivalent of $3,085 to value the asset and calculate depreciation charges. Similarly, the 1981 purchases of non-LIFO inventory sold in 1982 would be accounted for at their equivalent in terms of 1982 dollars, rather than in terms of the actual number of dollars spent. Using this method, earnings for 1981 in 1982 dollars were $1,208 million ($5.31 per share) and share owners' equity at December 31, 1981, was $11,845 million.

"Adjusted for current costs" refers to information prepared using a third approach to inventory and property, plant and equipment transactions. In this case, rather than restating to dollars of the same general purchasing power, estimates of specific current costs of the assets are used. Principal types of information used to adjust for changes in specific prices (current costs) are: for inventory costs, GP-generated indices of price changes for specific goods and services; and for property, plant and equipment, externally generated indices of price changes for major classes of assets. Data for mineral resource assets have been adjusted by applying internally generated indices to reflect current costs. Adjustments for oil and gas properties are based on industry indices.

At December 31, 1982, the current cost of inventory was $5,701 million, and of property, plant and equipment was $8,797 million ($5,251 million and $7,004 million, respectively, at December 31, 1981).

(85) In dollars of average 1982 purchasing power, estimated current costs applicable to such assets increased during 1982, or during the part of the year the assets were held, by approximately $1,356 million, which was $196 million less than the $1,552 million increase which could be expected because of general inflation. The comparable increase for 1981 in dollars of average 1982 purchasing power was approximately $1,261 million, which was $373 million less than the $1,634 million increase which could be expected because of general inflation.

In presenting results of either of the supplementary accounting methods for more than one year, real trends are more evident when results for all years are expressed in terms of the general purchasing power of the dollar for a designated period. Results of such restatements are generally called "constant dollar" presentations. In the six-year presentations shown here, dollar results for earlier periods have been restated to their equivalent number of constant dollars of 1982 general purchasing power (CPI—H basis).

Because none of these restatements is allowable for tax purposes under existing laws, income tax amounts are the same as in the traditional statements (but expressed in constant dollars).

All average annual growth rates in this Report use the "least squares" method of calculation.

662

(86) **Form 10-K and other supplemental information**
The financial information in this Report, in the opinion of management, substantially conforms with or exceeds the information required in the "10-K Report" submitted to the Securities and Exchange Commission. Certain supplemental information, considered nonsubstantive, is included in that report, however, and copies will be available without charge, on or about May 1.

(75) The major difficulty in constructing meaningful and useful segment reports is the allocation of these "corporate items" to the major categories. They are truly common or joint costs of running the entire corporation but must be allocated to the various segments in order to present subtotals for segment earnings that add up to the total earnings, $1,514 million for 1982.

(76) The detail shown here by GP goes beyond that required by the SEC in its 1980 *ASR Nos. 279–281*. GP shows six years of data so that one can construct time series analysis for at least five years in all cases. Note that if only five columns are shown, then growth rates for items like sales can be computed for only four years.

(77) During 1976 the SEC defined a new class of footnotes with which the auditor is "associated" (to use the SEC's term), but which are not audited.

(78) During the year, GP (and other companies) are required to send quarterly (interim) financial statements to shareholders. The SEC requires companies to show in the annual statements the amounts of the interim earnings *after* all information for the year is available. If there is a difference, the company must explain why its interim reported numbers differ from the corresponding numbers shown in the annual report.

(79) *SFAS No. 33* requires these disclosures which are discussed in Chapter 14.

(80) The first column of the supplementary income statement shows the conventional financial statements based on nominal dollar measures of historical cost. The second column shows constant dollar measures of historical cost. The third column shows current costs. The measuring unit in the third column can be interpreted either as nominal dollars or as constant dollars of 1982 year-average purchasing power. One of the reasons that the FASB allows using year-average dollars as the measuring unit is that the numbers that appear in the third column of this statement will be essentially the same whether the current costs are measured using constant average-year dollars or nominal dollars. The FASB requires supplementary data on income from continuing operations only; GP's disclosure for individual revenues and expenses goes beyond the minimum requirement.

(81) Note that there is no such price index as the CPI—H (which stands for CPI—Hypothetical). The FASB requires use of the CPI—U (Consumer *Price Index* for all *Urban* consumers). Because the price index for 1982 cannot be known until after the end of 1982 and this book goes to press before then, we have constructed a hypothetical price index for use in this example disclosure.

(82) *Constant-Dollar Accounting Disclosures.* The numbers shown in the middle column are based on historical costs measured in constant dollars of general purchasing power. The notation "C$" denotes constant dollars. The FASB allows use of the notation "$" and most companies use the simpler, if less precise, "$" symbol.

(83) *Current-Cost Accounting Disclosures.* The items in the current-cost column are measured in constant dollars (of mid-year purchasing power of the specific items), but because these appear the same as when they are measured in nominal dollars, *SFAS No. 33* allows the symbol "$" to be used in the third column, instead of "C$."

(84) *Multi-Year Summary.* The FASB requires a five-year summary. GP shows data for six years so that trends can be seen for five years of operations. The summary shows data in a format useful for following the trend of items over time. *SFAS No. 33* permits the use in this summary of either current 1982 dollars or dollars of some base period, such as 1967, which is the base period for the CPI. Using current dollars expresses the data in units that reflect current experience, but it requires the data of the earlier years in the summary to be restated each year to reflect the change in the measuring unit. When the summary is stated in base-period dollars, there is no need for annual revision of those data.

Excerpts from the constant-dollar summary and from the nominal dollar six-year summary on page 662 are instructive. Observe, for example, that the market price of a share of GP common stock is shown as C$68 for 1977. Its actual market price at the end of 1977 was $44.40. (The amount shown is derived from C$68 = $44.40 × 308.5/201.5.) Whereas the nominal dollar amount of a share has increased over 34 percent (from $44 to $59) over the five-year period from the end of 1977 to the end of 1982, the general purchasing power represented by an investment in that share has declined by about 13 percent, from C$68 to C$59. Similarly, although nominal dollar sales have increased over the years shown at about 12 percent per year, from $14 billion to nearly $25 billion, sales measured in constant dollars have risen by only 3 percent per year, from C$21.6 to C$25.0 billion.

Note in the last column of the multi-year summary that GP reports purchasing power losses on net monetary items for each of the years 1978 through 1982 and a gain only for 1977. From this we can infer that GP's average balance of monetary assets exceeded the average balance of monetary liabilities in each of the years 1978 through 1982.

(85) Exhibit A.6 summarizes some of the information in this paragraph. Exhibit A.6 derives the total holding gain for 1982 in nominal dollars of $1,420 million. GP reports the total holding gains as $1,356 million. The difference between the two amounts of $64 (= $1,420 − $1,356) million reflects the increase in current cost of inventories and plant between mid-year and December 31.

(86) The SEC requires that firms make the Form 10-K available to shareholders and tell them of its availability.

664

Exhibit A.6
**Summary of Data on Realized
and Unrealized Holding Gains
for 1982 in Nominal Dollars**
(*for Authors' Comment 85*)

	Inventory and Cost of Goods Sold	Property, Plant Equipment and Depreciation
ASSET BALANCES:		
December 31, 1982		
Current Cost^a	$ 5,701	$ 8,797
Historical Cost^b	(3,343)	(5,780)
Unrealized Holding Gain, End of Year . . . . (1)	$ 2,358	$ 3,017
December 31, 1981		
Current Cost^a	$ 5,251	$ 7,004
Historical Cost^b	(3,161)	(4,613)
Unrealized Holding Gain, Start of Year . . . (2)	2,090	2,391
Unrealized Holding Gain		
During 1982 = (2) − (1)	$ 268	$ 626
Expense Totals:		
Based on		
Current Cost^c	$17,892	$ 1,092
Historical Costs^d	(17,751)	(707)
Realized Holding Gains	141	385
Total Holding Gains of $1,420 (= $409 + $1,011).	$ 409	$ 1,011

a See Exhibit A.4 at Authors' Comment 85.
b From Statement of Financial Position, Exhibit A.2.
c See Exhibit A.4 at Authors' Comment 80.
d From Statement of Income and Retained Earnings, Exhibit A.1.

Questions and Problems

1 Review the meaning of the following concepts or terms discussed in this appendix.

  a Allowance method.
  b Central corporate expenses and central corporate assets hinder measures of segment rates of return.
  c Compensating balance.
  d Consolidated financial statements.
  e Deferred income tax debit.
  f Installment sales.
  g Minority interest on income statement vs. minority interest on balance sheet.
  h Progress billings.
  i Provision.
  j Statutory vs. effective income tax rate.

2 Assume that all sales of General Products Company and consolidated affiliates for the year 1982 were made on account. How much cash was collected from customers?

3 What amount of cash was disbursed during 1982 by GP and consolidated affiliates for dividends?

4 Refer to Note 9 of the GP annual report. Observe there receivables labeled "Associated companies" and "Nonconsolidated affiliates." Are these receivables more likely to represent amounts owed to GP by these "Associated companies" and "Nonconsolidated affiliates" or are they amounts owed by customers to "Associated companies" and "Nonconsolidated affiliates?" Explain your reasoning.

5 Refer to the data in GP's Note 15 on accounts payable. Are the amounts shown for "nonconsolidated affiliates" more likely amounts owed by GP to these "nonconsolidated affiliates" or amounts owed by them to others? Explain your reasoning.

6 Refer to the data in GP's Note 14 on short-term borrowings. Compute the dollar amount of interest expense on these borrowings for 1982.

7 Assume that GP prepared the statement of changes in financial position using funds defined as working capital, rather than as cash plus marketable securities less short-term borrowings. Prepare an analysis of changes in net change in funds for the year 1982.

8 Refer to GP's Note 19 on retained earnings. What are the retained earnings of the nonconsolidated affiliates *other* than those of GP Credit Company at the end of 1982?

9 Assuming a marginal income tax rate of 46 percent, by what amount did depreciation claimed on the tax return for 1981 differ from the depreciation expense reported in the financial statements for 1981?

10 Refer to author's comment 62. Explain why the compensation agreement described there might help one understand the simultaneous dividend declaration and common stock issue of GP Credit Company.

11 Assume that GP Credit Corporation were consolidated, rather than accounted for on the equity method.
  a By how much would GP's consolidated revenue and other income for 1981 differ from the amounts reported?
  b By how much would GP's consolidated expenses for 1981 differ from the amounts reported?
  c By how much would GP's consolidated income for 1981 differ from the amount reported?
  d By how much would GP's consolidated assets differ from the amount reported?
  e By how much would GP's consolidated owners' equity differ from the amount reported?

12 Refer to GP's multi-year summary of data on the effects of changing prices. What was the market price per share in nominal dollars of a share of GP's stock at the end of 1978?

Appendix B — Compound Interest Concepts and Applications

Money is a scarce resource, which its owner can use to command other resources. Like owners of other scarce resources, owners of money can permit others (borrowers) to rent the use of their money for a period of time. Payment for the use of money differs little from other rental payments, such as those made to a landlord for the use of property or to a car rental agency for the use of a car. Payment for the use of money is called *interest*. Accounting is concerned with interest because it must record transactions in which the use of money is bought and sold.

Accountants and managers are concerned with interest calculations for another, equally important, reason. Expenditures for an asset most often do not occur at the same time as the receipts for services produced by that asset. Money received sooner is more valuable than money received later. The difference in timing can affect whether or not acquiring an asset is profitable. Amounts of money received at different times are different commodities. Managers use interest calculations to make amounts of money to be paid or received at different times comparable. For example, an analyst might compare two amounts to be received at two different times by using interest calculations to find the equivalent value of one amount at the time the other is due.

Contracts involving a series of money payments over time, such as bonds, mortgages, notes, and leases, are evaluated by finding the *present value* of the stream of

667

payments. The present value of a stream of payments is a single amount of money at the present time that is the economic equivalent of the entire stream.

Compound Interest Concepts

The quotation of interest "cost" is typically specified as a percentage of the amount borrowed per unit of time. Examples are 12 percent per year and 1 percent per month, which are not the same. Another example occurs in the context of discounts on purchases. The terms of sale "2/10, net/30" is equivalent to 2 percent for 20 days because if the discount is not taken, payment can be delayed and the money can be used for up to an extra 20 (= 30 − 10) days.

The amount borrowed or loaned is called the *principal.* To *compound* interest means that the amount of interest earned during a period is added to the principal and the principal for the next interest period is larger.

For example, if you deposit $1,000 in a savings account that pays compound interest at the rate of 6 percent per year, you will earn $60 by the end of 1 year. If you do not withdraw the $60, then $1,060 will be earning interest during the second year. During the second year your principal of $1,060 will earn $63.60 interest, $60 on the initial deposit of $1,000 and $3.60 on the $60 earned the first year. By the end of the second year, you will have $1,123.60.

When only the original principal earns interest during the entire life of the loan, the interest due at the time the loan is repaid is called *simple* interest. In simple interest calculations, interest on previously earned interest is ignored. The use of simple interest calculations in accounting arises in the following way. If you borrow $10,000 at a rate of 12 percent per year, but compute interest for any month as $100 (= $10,000 $\times$ .12 $\times \frac{1}{12}$), then you are using a simple interest calculation.

The "force," or effect, of compound interest is more substantial than many people realize. For example, compounded annually at 6 percent, money "doubles itself" in less than 12 years. Put another way, if you invest $49.70 in a savings account that pays 6 percent compounded annually, you will have $100 in 12 years. If the Indians who sold Manhattan Island for $24 in May 1626 had been able to invest that principal at 8 percent compounded annually, the principal would have grown to $17.6 *trillion* by May 1981, 355 years later. The rate of interest affects the amount of accumulation more than you might expect. If the investment earned 6 percent rather than 8 percent, the $24 would have grown to $23 *billion* in 355 years; if the rate were 4 percent, the $24 would have grown to a mere $27 *million.*

At simple interest of 6 percent per year, the Indians' $24 would have grown to only $535 in 355 years, $24 of principal and $511 of simple interest (= $24 $\times$ .06 $\times$ 355). Nearly all economic calculations involve compound interest.

Problems involving compound interest generally fall into two groups with respect to time: first, there are the problems for which we want to know the future value of money invested or loaned today; second, there are the problems for which we want to know the present value, or today's value, of money to be received or paid at later dates. In addition, the accountant must sometimes compute the interest rate implicit in certain payment streams.

Future Value

When $1.00 is invested today at 12 percent compounded annually, it will grow to $1.12000 at the end of 1 year, $1.25440 at the end of 2 years, $1.40493 at the end of 3 years, and so on according to the formula

$$F_n = P(1 + r)^n$$

where

F_n represents the accumulation or future value,
P represents the one-time investment today,
r is the interest rate per period, and
n is the number of periods from today.

The amount F_n is the future value of the present payment, P, compounded at r percent per period for n periods. Table 1, following this section of the book, shows the future values of $P = \$1$ for various numbers of periods and for various interest rates. Extracts from that table are shown here in Table B.1.

Table B.1 (Excerpt from Table 1)
Future Value of $1 at 6 Percent and 12 Percent per Period
$F_n = (1 + r)^n$

Number of Periods = n	Rate = r	
	6%	12%
1	1.06000	1.12000
2	1.12360	1.25440
3	1.19102	1.40493
10	1.79085	3.10585
20	3.20714	9.64629

Example Problems in Computing Future Value

Example 1 How much will $1,000 deposited today at 6 percent compounded annually be worth 10 years from now?

One dollar deposited today at 6 percent will grow to $1.79085; therefore $1,000 will grow to $1,000(1.06)^{10} = \$1,000 \times 1.79085 = \$1,790.85$.

Example 2 Macaulay Corporation deposits $10,000 in an expansion fund today. The fund will earn 12 percent per year. How much will the $10,000 grow to in 20 years if the entire fund and all interest earned on it are left on deposit in the fund?

One dollar deposited today at 12 percent will grow to $9.64629 in 20 years. Therefore, $10,000 will grow to $96,463 (= \$10,000 \times 9.64629)$ in 20 years.

Present Value

The preceding section developed the tools for computing the future value, F_n, of a sum of money, P, deposited or invested today. P is known; F_n is calculated. This section deals with the problems of calculating how much principal, P, has to be invested today in order to have a specified amount, F_n, at the end of n periods. The future amount, F_n, the interest rate, r, and the number of periods, n, are known; P is to be found. In order to have \$1 one year from today when interest is earned at 6 percent, P of \$.94340 must be invested today. That is, $F_1 = P(1.06)^1$ or \$1 = \$.94340 \times 1.06$. Because $F_n = P(1 + r)^n$, dividing both sides of the equation by $(1 + r)^n$ yields

$$\frac{F_n}{(1 + r)^n} = P$$

or

$$P = \frac{F_n}{(1 + r)^n} = F_n(1 + r)^{-n}.$$

Present-Value Terminology

The number $(1 + r)^{-n}$ is the present value of \$1 to be received after n periods when interest is earned at r percent per period. The term *discount* is used in this context as follows: The *discounted* present value of \$1 to be received n periods in the future is $(1 + r)^{-n}$ when the *discount* rate is r percent per period for n periods. The number r is the discount *rate* and the number $(1 + r)^{-n}$ is the discount *factor* for n periods. A discount factor $(1 + r)^{-n}$ is merely the reciprocal, or inverse, of a number, $(1 + r)^n$, in Table B.1. Therefore, tables of discount factors are not necessary for present-value calculations if tables of future values are at hand. But present-value calculations are so frequently needed, and division is so onerous, that tables of discount factors are as widely available as tables of future values. Portions of Table 2, which shows discount factors or, equivalently, present values of \$1 for various interest (or discount) rates for various numbers of periods, are shown in Table B.2.

Table B.2 (Excerpt from Table 2)
Present Value of \$1 at 6 Percent and 12 Percent per Period
$$P = F_n(1 + r)^{-n}$$

Number of Periods = n	Rate = r	
	6%	12%
1	.94340	.89286
2	.89000	.79719
3	.83962	.71178
10	.55839	.32197
20	.31180	.10367

Example Problems in Determining Present Values

Example 3 What is the present value of $1 due 10 years from now if the interest (equivalently, the discount) rate r is 6 percent per year?

From Table B.2, 6-percent column, 10-period row, the present value of $1 to be received 10 periods hence at 6 percent is $.55839.

Example 4 (This example is used in Chapter 11.) You issue a noninterest-bearing note that promises to pay $16,000 3 years from today in exchange for undeveloped land. How much is that promise worth today if the discount rate appropriate for such notes is 12 percent per period?

One dollar received three years hence discounted at 12 percent has a present value of $.71178. Thus, the promise is worth $16,000 \times .71178 = $11,388.

Changing the Compounding Period: Nominal and Effective Rates

"Twelve percent, compounded annually" is the price for a loan; this means that interest is added to or *converted* into principal once a year at the rate of 12 percent. Often, however, the price for a loan states that compounding is to take place more than once a year. A savings bank may advertise that it pays 6 percent, compounded quarterly. This means that at the end of each quarter the bank credits savings accounts with interest calculated at the rate 1.5 percent ($= 6$ percent/4). The interest payment can be withdrawn or left on deposit to earn more interest.

If $10,000 is invested today at 12 percent compounded annually, its future value 1 year later is $11,200. If the rate of interest is stated as 12 percent compounded semiannually, then 6 percent interest is added to the principal every 6 months. At the end of the first 6 months, $10,000 will have grown to $10,600, so that the accumulation will be $10,600 \times 1.06 = $11,236 by the end of the year. Notice that 12 percent compounded *semiannually* is equivalent to 12.36 percent compounded *annually*.

Suppose that the price is quoted as 12 percent, compounded quarterly. Then an additional 3 percent of the principal will be added to, or converted into, principal every 3 months. By the end of the year, $10,000 will grow to $10,000 \times (1.03)^4 = $10,000 \times 1.12551 = $11,255. Twelve percent compounded quarterly is equivalent to 12.55 percent compounded annually. If 12 percent is compounded monthly, then $1 will grow to $1 \times (1.01)^{12} = $1.12683 and $10,000 will grow to $11,268. Thus, 12 percent compounded monthly is equivalent to 12.68 percent compounded annually.

For a given *nominal* rate, such as the 12 percent in the examples above, the more often interest is compounded or converted into principal, the higher the *effective* rate of interest paid. If a nominal rate, r, is compounded m times per year, then the effective rate is $(1 + r/m)^m - 1$.

In practice, to solve problems that require computation of interest quoted at a nominal rate of r percent per period compounded m times per period for n periods, merely use the tables for rate r/m and $m \times n$ periods. For example, 12 percent compounded quarterly for five years is equivalent to the rate found in the interest tables for $r = 12/4 = 3$ percent for $m \times n = 4 \times 5 = 20$ periods.

Some savings banks advertise that they compound interest daily or even continuously. The mathematics of calculus provides a mechanism for finding the effective rate when interest is compounded continuously. We shall not go into details but merely state that if interest is compounded continuously at nominal rate r per year, then the effective annual rate is $e^r - 1$, where e is the base of the natural logarithms. Tables of values of e^r are widely available.[1] Six percent per year compounded continuously is equivalent to 6.1837 percent compounded annually; 12 percent per year compounded continuously is equivalent to 12.75 percent compounded annually. Do not confuse the compounding period with the payment period. Some banks, for example, compound interest daily but pay interest quarterly. You can be sure that such banks do not employ clerks or even computers to calculate interest every day. They merely use tables to derive an equivalent effective rate to apply at the end of each quarter.

Example Problems in Changing the Compounding Period

Example 5 What is the future value five years hence of $600 invested at 12 percent compounded semiannually?

Twelve percent compounded two times per year for five years is equivalent to six percent per period compounded for ten periods. Table B.1 shows the value of $F_{10} = (1.06)^{10}$ to be 1.79085. Six hundred dollars, then, would grow to $600 \times 1.79085 = \$1,074.51$.

Example 6 How much money must be invested today at 12 percent compounded semiannually in order to have $10,000 ten years from today?

Twelve percent compounded two times a year for ten years is equivalent to six percent per period compounded for 20 periods. The *present* value, Table B.2, of $1 received 20 periods hence at 6 percent per period is $.31180. That is, $.31180 invested today for 20 periods at an interest rate of 6 percent per period will grow to $1. To have $10,000 in 20 periods (10 years), $3,118 ($= \$10,000 \times \$.31180$) must be invested today.

Example 7 If prices increased at the rate of 6 percent during each of two consecutive 6-month periods, how much did prices increase during the entire year?

If a price index is 100.00 at the start of the year, it will be $100.00 \times (1.06)^2 = 112.36$ at the end of the year. The price change for the entire year is $(112.36/100.00) - 1 = 12.36$ percent.

---

[1] See, for example, Sidney Davidson and Roman L. Weil (eds.), *Handbook of Modern Accounting,* 2nd ed. (New York: McGraw-Hill Book Company, 1977), chap. 8, Exhibit 1.

Annuities

An *annuity* is a series of equal payments made at the beginning or end of equal periods of time. Examples of annuities include monthly rental payments, semiannual corporate bond coupon (or interest) payments, and annual payments to a retired employee under a pension plan. Armed with an understanding of the tables for future and present values, you can solve any annuity problem. Annuities arise so often, however, and their solution is so tedious without special tables that annuity problems warrant special study and the use of special tables.

Terminology for Annuities

The terminology used for annuities can be confusing because not all writers use the same terms. Definitions of the terms used in this text follow.

An annuity whose payments occur at the *end* of each period is called an *ordinary annuity* or an *annuity in arrears.* Corporate bond coupon payments are usually paid in arrears or, equivalently, the first payment does not occur until after the bond has been outstanding for six months.

An annuity whose payments occur at the *beginning* of each period is called an *annuity due* or an *annuity in advance.* Rent is usually paid in advance, so that a series of rental payments is an annuity due.

A *deferred* annuity is one whose first payment is at some time later than the end of the first period.

Annuities can be paid forever. Such annuities are called *perpetuities.* Bonds that promise payments forever are called *consols.* The British and Canadian governments have, from time to time, issued consols. A perpetuity can be in arrears or in advance. The only difference between the two is the timing of the first payment.

Annuities can be confusing. Their study is made easier with a *time line* such as the one shown below.

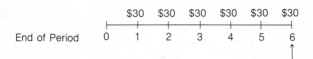

A time line marks the end of each period, numbers the period, shows the payments to be received or paid, and shows the time at which the annuity is valued. The time line just pictured represents an ordinary annuity (in arrears) for six periods of $30 to be valued at the end of period 6. The end of period 0 is "now." The first payment is to be received one period from now.

Ordinary Annuities (Annuities in Arrears)

The future values of ordinary annuities are shown in the back of the book in Table 3, portions of which are reproduced in Table B.3.

673

Table B.3 (Excerpt from Table 3)
Future Value of an Ordinary Annuity of $1 per Period at 6 Percent and 12 Percent

$$F_A = \frac{[(1 + r)^n - 1]}{r}$$

	Rate = r	
Number of Periods = n	**6%**	**12%**
1	1.00000	1.00000
2	2.06000	2.12000
3	3.18360	3.37440
5	5.63709	6.35285
10	13.18079	17.54874
20	36.78559	72.05244

Consider an ordinary annuity for three periods at 6 percent. The time line for the future value of such an annuity is

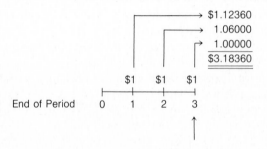

The $1 received at the end of the first period earns interest for two periods, so it is worth $1.12360 at the end of period 3. (See Table B.1.) The $1 received at the end of the second period grows to $1.06 by the end of period 3, and the $1 received at the end of period 3 is, of course, worth $1 at the end of period 3. The entire annuity is worth $3.18360 at the end of period 3. This is the amount shown in Table B.3 for the future value of an ordinary annuity for three periods at 6 percent. The mathematical expression for the future value, F_A, of an annuity of A per period compounded at r percent per period for n periods is

$$F_A = \frac{A[(1 + r)^n - 1]}{r}.$$

The future value of an ordinary annuity is calculated as follows:

$$\text{Future Value of Ordinary Annuity} = \text{Periodic Payment} \times \text{Factor for the Future Value of an Ordinary Annuity}$$

674

Thus,

$$\$3.18360 \quad = \quad \$1 \quad \times \quad 3.18360.$$

The present values of ordinary annuities are shown in Table 4, portions of which are reproduced in Table B.4.

Table B.4 (Excerpt from Table 4)
Present Value of an Ordinary Annuity of $1 per Period at 6 Percent and 12 Percent

$$P_A = \frac{[1 - (1 + r)^{-n}]}{r}$$

Number of Periods = n	Rate = r	
	6%	12%
1	.94340	.89286
2	1.83339	1.69005
3	2.67301	2.40183
5	4.21236	3.60478
10	7.36009	5.65022
20	11.46992	7.46944

The time line for the present value of an ordinary annuity of $1 per period for three periods, discounted at 6 percent, is

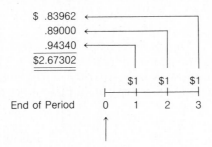

The $1 to be received at the end of period 1 has a present value of $.94340, the $1 to be received at the end of period 2 has a present value of $.89000, and the dollar to be received at the end of the third period has a present value of $.83962. Each of these numbers comes from Table B.2. The present value of the annuity is the sum of these individual present values, $2.67302, shown in Table B.4 as 2.67301 (our calculation differs because of roundings).

The present value of an ordinary annuity for n periods is the sum of the present value of $1 received one period from now plus the present value of $1 received two periods from now, and so on until we add on the present value of $1 received n

675

periods from now. The mathematical expression for the present value, P_A, of an annuity of A per period, for n periods, compounded at r percent per period, is

$$P_A = \frac{A[1 - (1 + r)^{-n}]}{r}.$$

The present value of an ordinary annuity is calculated as follows:

$$\begin{matrix} \text{Present Value} \\ \text{of an} \\ \text{Ordinary Annuity} \end{matrix} = \begin{matrix} \text{Periodic} \\ \text{Payment} \end{matrix} \times \begin{matrix} \text{Factor for the} \\ \text{Present} \\ \text{Value of an Ordinary} \\ \text{Annuity} \end{matrix}$$

Thus,

$$\$2.67302 = \$1 \times 2.67302.$$

Example Problems Involving Ordinary Annuities

Example 8 An individual plans to invest $1,000 at the end of each of the next ten years in a savings account. The savings account accumulates interest of 12 percent compounded annually. What will be the balance in the savings account at the end of ten years?

The time line for this problem is

	$1,000	$1,000	$1,000	$1.000	$\cdots$	$1,000
End of Period 0	1	2	3	4	$\cdots$	10
						x ↑

The symbol x denotes the amount to be calculated. Table B.3 indicates that the factor for the future value of an annuity at 12 percent for ten periods is 17.54874. Thus,

$$\begin{matrix} \text{Future Value} \\ \text{of an} \\ \text{Ordinary Annuity} \end{matrix} = \begin{matrix} \text{Periodic} \\ \text{Payment} \end{matrix} \times \begin{matrix} \text{Factor for} \\ \text{the Future} \\ \text{Value of an} \\ \text{Ordinary Annuity} \end{matrix}$$

$$x = \$1,000 \times 17.54874$$

$$x = \$17,549.$$

Example 9 Parents are accumulating a fund to send their child to college. The parents will invest a fixed amount at the end of each calendar quarter for the next 10 years. The funds will accumulate in a savings certificate that promises to pay 8 percent interest compounded quarterly. What amount must be invested to accumulate a fund of $20,000.

The time line for this problem is

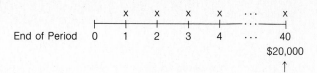

This problem is similar to Example 8 because both involve periodic investments of cash that accumulate interest over time until a specific time in the future. In Example 8, the periodic investment is given and the future value is computed. In Example 9, the future value is given and the periodic investment is computed. Table 3 indicates that the future value of an annuity at 2 percent ($= 8$ percent per year/4 quarters per year) per period for 40 ($= 4$ quarters per year $\times$ 10 years) periods is 60.40198. Thus,

$$\begin{matrix} \text{Future Value} \\ \text{of an} \\ \text{Ordinary Annuity} \end{matrix} = \begin{matrix} \text{Periodic} \\ \text{Payment} \end{matrix} \times \begin{matrix} \text{Factor for} \\ \text{the Future} \\ \text{Value of an} \\ \text{Ordinary Annuity} \end{matrix}$$

$$\$20,000 = x \times 60.40198$$

$$x = \frac{\$20,000}{60.40198}$$

$$x = \$331.$$

Because the periodic payment is being calculated, the future value amount of $20,000 is divided by the future value factor.

Example 10 An individual wishes to receive $60 every six months, starting six months hence, for the next five years. How much must be invested today in a savings account if the interest rate on the savings account is 12 percent compounded semiannually?

The time line is

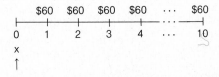

The factor from Table B.4 for the present value of an annuity at 6 percent ($= 12$ percent per year/2 semiannual periods per year) for 10 ($= 2$ periods per year $\times$ 5

677

years) periods is 7.36009. Thus,

$$\begin{array}{ccc} \text{Present Value} & \text{Periodic} & \text{Factor for the Present} \\ \text{of an} & = \text{Payment} \times & \text{Value of an} \\ \text{Ordinary Annuity} & & \text{Ordinary Annuity} \end{array}$$

$$x = \$60 \times 7.36009$$
$$x = \$441.61.$$

If \$441.61 is invested today, the principal plus interest compounded on the principal will provide sufficient funds so that \$60 can be withdrawn every six months for the next five years. (This example illustrates the calculations that would be made to find the present value at the time of issue of 12-percent semiannual coupon payments on bonds with a face value of \$1,000 maturing in five years and issued at par; see the discussion in Chapter 10.)

Example 11 (Western Company mortgage example, from Chapter 10.) A company borrows \$125,000 from a savings-and-loan association. The interest rate on the loan is 12 percent compounded semiannually. The company agrees to repay the loan in equal semiannual installments over the next five years. The first payment is to be made six months from now. What is the amount of the required semiannual payment?

The time line is

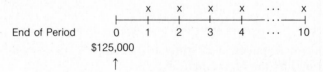

This problem is similar to Example 10 because both involve periodic payments in the future that are discounted to today. In Example 10, the periodic payments were given and the present value was computed. In Example 11, the present value is given and the periodic payment is computed. Table B.4 indicates that the present value of annuity at 6 percent (= 12 percent per year/2 semiannual periods per year) for 10 (= 2 periods per year $\times$ 5 years) periods is 7.36009. Thus,

$$\begin{array}{ccc} \text{Present Value} & \text{Periodic} & \text{Factor for the Present} \\ \text{of an} & = \text{Payment} \times & \text{Value of an} \\ \text{Ordinary Annuity} & & \text{Ordinary Annuity} \end{array}$$

$$\$125,000 = x \times 7.36009$$
$$x = \frac{\$125,000}{7.36009}$$
$$x = \$16,983.$$

Because the periodic payment is being calculated, the present value amount of $125,000 must be divided by the present value factor. (You may wish to turn to Exhibit 10.2 to study the amortization table for this loan. The amount of each semiannual payment shown there is $17,000 rather than $16,983, but the last payment is less than $17,000.)

Example 12 (Myers Company lease example, from Chapter 11.) A company signs a lease acquiring the right to use property for three years. Lease payments of $19,709 are to be made annually at the end of this and the next two years. The discount, or interest, rate is 15 percent per year. What is the present value of the lease payments?

The time line is

$$\begin{array}{ccccc} & & \$19{,}709 & \$19{,}709 & \$19{,}709 \\ \text{End of Period} & 0 & 1 & 2 & 3 \\ & x & & & \\ & \uparrow & & & \end{array}$$

The factor from Table 4 for the present value of an annuity at 15 percent for three periods is 2.28323. Thus,

$$\begin{array}{rcl} \text{Present Value of an Ordinary Annuity} & = & \text{Periodic Payment} \times \begin{array}{c} \text{Factor for the Present Value of an Ordinary Annuity} \end{array} \\ x & = & \$19{,}709 \times 2.28323 \\ x & = & \$45{,}000. \end{array}$$

In the Myers Company example in Chapter 11 the cost of the equipment is given at $45,000 and the periodic rental payment is computed with an annuity factor. Thus,

$$\begin{array}{rcl} \text{Present Value of an Ordinary Annuity} & = & \text{Periodic Payment} \times \begin{array}{c} \text{Factor for the Present Value of an Annuity} \end{array} \\ \$45{,}000 & = & x \times 2.28323 \\ x & = & \dfrac{\$45{,}000}{2.28323} \\ x & = & \$19{,}709. \end{array}$$

Example 13 (Pension funding example.) A company is obligated to make annual payments to a pension fund at the end of the next 30 years. The present value of those payments is to be $100,000. What must the annual payment be if the fund is projected to earn interest at the rate of 8 percent per year?

679

The time line is

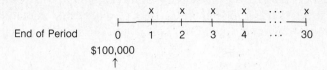

Table 4 indicates that the factor for the present value of $1 paid at the end of the next 30 periods at 8 percent per period is 11.25778. Thus,

$$\begin{array}{c}\text{Present Value} \\ \text{of an} \\ \text{Ordinary Annuity}\end{array} = \begin{array}{c}\text{Periodic} \\ \text{Payment}\end{array} \times \begin{array}{c}\text{Factor for} \\ \text{the Present} \\ \text{Value of an} \\ \text{Ordinary Annuity}\end{array}$$

$$\$100,000 = x \times 11.25778$$

$$x = \frac{\$100,000}{11.25778}$$

$$x = \$8,883.$$

Example 14 Mr. Mason is 62 years old. He wishes to invest equal amounts on his sixty-third, sixty-fourth and sixty-fifth birthdays so that starting on his sixty-sixth birthday he can withdraw $5,000 on each birthday for 10 years. His investments will earn 8 percent per year. How much should be invested on the sixty-third through sixty-fifth birthdays?

The time line for this problem is

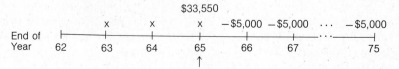

On his sixty-fifth birthday, Mr. Mason needs to have accumulated a fund equal to the present value of an annuity of $5,000 per period for 10 periods, discounted at 8 percent per period. The factor from Table 4 for 8 percent and 10 periods is 6.71008. Thus,

$$\begin{array}{c}\text{Present Value} \\ \text{of an} \\ \text{Ordinary Annuity}\end{array} = \begin{array}{c}\text{Period} \\ \text{Payment}\end{array} \times \begin{array}{c}\text{Factor for} \\ \text{the Present} \\ \text{Value of an} \\ \text{Ordinary Annuity}\end{array}$$

$$x = \$ 5,000 \times 6.71008$$

$$x = \$33,550.$$

The time line now appears as follows:

The question now becomes: How much must be invested on Mr. Mason's sixty-third, sixty-fourth and sixty-fifth birthdays to accumulate to a fund of $33,550 on his sixty-fifth birthday? The factor for the future value of an annuity for three periods at 8 percent is 3.24640. Thus,

$$\begin{array}{ccc} \text{Future Value} & & \text{Factor for} \\ \text{of an} & = \text{Periodic} \times & \text{the Future} \\ \text{Ordinary Annuity} & \text{Payment} & \text{Value of an} \\ & & \text{Ordinary Annuity} \end{array}$$

$$\$33{,}550 = x \times 3.24640$$

$$x = \frac{\$33{,}550}{3.24640}$$

$$x = \$10{,}335.$$

In the solution above, all calculations are expressed in terms of equivalent amounts on Mr. Mason's sixty-fifth birthday. That is, the present value of an annuity of $5,000 per period for 10 periods at 8 percent is equal to the future value of an annuity of $10,335 per period for 3 periods at 8 percent and both of these amounts are equal to $33,550. The problem could have been worked by selecting any common time period between Mr. Mason's sixty-second and seventy-fifth birthdays.

One possibility would be to express all calculations in terms of equivalent amounts on Mr. Mason's sixty-second birthday. To solve the problem in this way, first find the present value on Mr. Mason's *sixty-fifth* birthday of an annuity of $5,000 per period for 10 periods ($33,550 = $5,000 × 6.71008). Discount $33,550 back three periods using Table 2 for the present value of $1 ($26,633 = $33,550 × .79383). The result is the present value of the payments to be made to Mr. Mason *measured as of his sixty-second birthday.* Then find the amounts that must be invested by Mr. Mason on his sixty-third, sixty-fourth and sixty-fifth birthdays that have a *present value* on his sixty-second birthday equal to $26,633. The calculation is as follows:

$$\begin{array}{ccc} \text{Present Value} & & \text{Factor for} \\ \text{of an} & = \text{Periodic} \times & \text{the Present} \\ \text{Ordinary Annuity} & \text{Payment} & \text{Value of an} \\ & & \text{Ordinary Annuity} \end{array}$$

$$\$26{,}633 = x \times 2.57710$$

$$x = \$10{,}335.$$

The amount $10,335 is the same as that found above.

Perpetuities

A periodic payment to be received forever is called a *perpetuity.* Future values of perpetuities are undefined. If $1 is to be received at the end of every period and the discount rate is r percent, then the present value of the perpetuity is $\$1/r$. This

681

expression can be derived with algebra or by observing what happens in the expression for the present value of an ordinary annuity of $\$A$ per payment as n, the number of payments, approaches infinity:

$$P_A = \frac{A[1 - (1 + r)^{-n}]}{r}.$$

As n approaches infinity, $(1 + r)^{-n}$ approaches zero, so that P_A approaches $A(1/r)$. If the first payment of the perpetuity occurs now, the present value is $A[1 + 1/r]$.

Examples of Perpetuities

Example 15 The Canadian government offers to pay $30 every six months forever in the form of a perpetual bond. What is that bond worth if the discount rate is 15 percent compounded semiannually?

Fifteen percent compounded semiannually is equivalent to 7.5 percent per six-month period. If the first payment occurs 6 months from now, the present value is $30/.075 = $400. If the first payment occurs today, the present value is $30 + $400 = $430.

Example 16 Every two years, Ms. Young gives $10,000 to the University to provide a scholarship for an entering student in a two-year business administration course. If the University credits 6 percent per year to its investment accounts, how much must Ms. Young give to the University to provide such a scholarship every two years forever, starting two years hence?

A perpetuity in arrears assumes one payment at the end of each period. Here, the period is two years; 6 percent compounded once a year over two years is equivalent to a rate of $(1.06)^2 - 1 = .12360$ or 12.36 percent compounded once per two-year period. Consequently, the present value of the perpetuity paid in arrears every two years is $80,906 (= $10,000/.12360). A gift of $80,906 will be sufficient to provide a $10,000 scholarship forever. A gift of $90,906 (= $80,906 + $10,000) is required if the first scholarship is to be awarded now.

Combinations of Cash Flows

Financial instruments may combine annuities and single payments. Bonds typically pay a specified sum every six months and a single, lump-sum payment along with the final periodic payment. Here is a simple example: The Macaulay Corporation promises to pay $60 every six months for five years, the first payment to occur six months from now, and an additional $1,000, five years from now. If payments are discounted at 12 percent, compounded semiannually, then the $1,000 single payment has a present value of $1,000 × .55839 = $558.39 (Table B.2, 10 periods, 6 percent) and the present value of the annuity is $60 × 7.36009 = $441.61 (Table B.4, 10 periods, 6 percent). The sum of the two components is $1,000. (This is a $1,000 par-value, five-year bond with 12-percent semiannual coupons issued at par to yield 12 percent compounded semiannually.)

Life-Contingent Annuities

The annuities discussed above all last for a certain or specified number of payments. Such annuities are sometimes called *certain annuities* to distinguish them from *contingent annuities,* for which the number of payments depends on an event to occur at an uncertain date. For example, businesses often want to know the cost of an annuity (pension) that will be paid only so long as the annuitant (retired employee) lives. Such annuities are called *life-contingent* or *life annuities.* Some texts show an incorrect calculation for the cost of a life annuity. The details of life-annuity calculations are beyond the scope of this text, but an unrealistic, hypothetical example is shown below so that our readers will be properly warned about the subtleties of life annuities.

Mr. Caplan is 65 years old today, and he has an unusual disease. He will die either one and a half years from today or ten and a half years from today. Mr. Caplan has no family, and his employer wishes to purchase an ordinary life annuity for Mr. Caplan that will pay him $10,000 on his sixty-sixth birthday and $10,000 on every birthday thereafter on which Mr. Caplan is still alive. Funds invested in the annuity will earn 10 percent per year. How much should Mr. Caplan's life annuity cost?

The Wrong Calculation Mr. Caplan's life expectancy is six years: one-half chance of his living one and a half years plus one-half chance of his living ten and a half years. The employer expects that six payments will be made to Mr. Caplan. The present value of an ordinary annuity of $1 for 6 years at 10 percent is $4.35526 (Table 4). Therefore the annuity will cost $43,553.

When a series of payments has uncertain length, the expected value of those payments is *not* the present value of an annuity for the expected life, but is the weighted average of the present values of the separate payments where the weights are the probabilities of the payment's being made.

The Right Calculation Mr. Caplan will receive one payment for certain. The present value of that payment of $10,000 at 10 percent is $9,091 (Table 2). Mr. Caplan will receive nine further payments if he survives the critical second year. Those nine payments have present value $52,355; which is equal to the present value of a nine-year ordinary annuity that is deferred for 1 year, $61,446 − $9,091 (Table 4). The probability is one-half that Mr. Caplan will survive to receive those nine payments. Thus, their *expected* present value is $26,178 (= .5 × $52,355), and the *expected* present value of the entire life annuity is $9,091 + $26,178 = $35,269.

Implicit Interest Rates: Finding Internal Rates of Return

In the preceding examples, we knew the interest rate and computed a future value or a present value given stated cash payments. Or we computed the required payments given their known future value or their known present value. In some calculations, we know the present or future value and the periodic payments; we must find the implicit interest rate. For example, Chapter 11 illustrates a case in which we know that the cash price of some equipment is $10,500 and that the asset was acquired

683

using a note. The note is noninterest-bearing, has a face value of $16,000 and matures in three years. In order to compute interest expense over the three-year period, the implicit interest rate must be known. The time line for this problem is

$$+\$10,500 \quad\quad 0 \quad\quad 0 \quad\quad \$16,000$$

End of Year $\quad$ 0 $\quad$ 1 $\quad$ 2 $\quad$ 3

The implicit interest rate is r, such that

(I) $$\$10,500 = \frac{\$16,000}{(1 + r)^3}$$

(II) $$0 = \$10,500 - \frac{\$16,000}{(1 + r)^3}.$$

That is, the present value of $16,000 discounted three periods at r percent per period is $10,500. The present value of all current and future cash flows nets to zero when future flows are discounted at r per period. In general, the only way to find such an r is a trial-and-error procedure. In cases where r appears only in one term, as here, r can be found analytically. Here, $r = (\$16,000/\$10,500)^{1/3} - 1 = .1507 = 15.1$ percent.

The general procedure is called "finding the internal rate of return" of a series of cash flows. The *internal rate of return* of a series of cash flows is the discount rate that equates the net present value of that series of cash flows to zero. The steps in finding the internal rate of return are as follows:

1. Make an educated guess, called the "trial rate," at the internal rate of return. If you have no idea what to guess, try zero.
2. Calculate the present value of all the cash flows (including the one at the end of year 0).
3. If the present value of the cash flows is zero, stop. The current trial rate is the internal rate of return.
4. If the amount found in step 2 is less than zero, try a larger interest rate as the trial rate and go back to step 2.
5. If the amount found in step 2 is greater than zero, try a smaller interest rate as the new trial rate and go back to step 2.

The iterations below illustrate the process for the example in equation (II).

Iteration Number	Trial Rate $= r$	Net Present Value: Right-Hand Side of (II)
1	0.0%	−$5,500
2	10.0	− 1,521
3	15.0	− 20
4	15.5	116
5	15.2	34
6	15.1	7

684

With a trial rate of 15.1 percent, the right-hand side is close enough to zero so that 15.1 percent can be used as the implicit interest rate. Continued iterations would find trial rates even closer to the true rate, which is about 15.0739 percent.

Finding the internal rate of return for a series of cash flows can be tedious and should not be attempted unless one has at least a desk calculator. An exponential feature, the feature that allows the computation of $(1 + r)$ raised to various powers, helps.[2]

Example Problem Involving Implicit Interest Rates

Example 17 The Alexis Company acquires a machine with a cash price of $10,500. It pays for the machine by giving a note promising to make payments equal to 7 percent of the face value, $840, at the end of each of the next three years and a single payment of $12,000 in three years. What is the implicit interest rate in the loan?

The time line for this problem is

$$\begin{array}{c c c c c}
\$10,500 & -\$840 & -\$840 & -\$12,840 \\
\vdash & + & + & \dashv \\
\text{End of Period} \quad 0 & 1 & 2 & 3
\end{array}$$

The implicit interest rate is r, such that[3]

(III) $$\$10,500 = \frac{\$840}{(1 + r)} + \frac{\$840}{(1 + r)^2} + \frac{\$12,840}{(1 + r)^3}.$$

The internal rate of return is found to the nearest tenth of 1 percent to be 12.2 percent:

Iteration Number	Trial Rate	Right-Hand Side of (III)
1	7.0%	$12,000
2	15.0	9,808
3	11.0	10,827
4	13.0	10,300
5	12.0	10,559
6	12.5	10,428
7	12.3	10,480
8	12.2	10,506
9	12.1	10,532

[2]There are ways to guess the trial rate that will approximate the true rate in fewer iterations than the method described here. If you want to find internal rates of return efficiently with successive trial rates, then refer to a mathematical reference book to learn about the "Newton search" method, sometimes called the "method of false position."

[3]Compare this formulation to that in equation (II), above. Note that the left-hand side is zero in one case but not in the other. The left-hand side can be either a nonzero number or zero, depending on what seems convenient for the particular context.

Summary

Accountants typically use one of four kinds of compound interest calculations: the present or future value of a single payment or of a series of payments. In working annuity problems, you will find drawing a time line helpful in deciding which particular kind of annuity is involved.

Questions and Problems

1 Review the following concepts or terms discussed in this Appendix.

    a Compound interest.
    b Principal.
    c Simple interest.
    d Future value.
    e Present value.
    f Discounted value.
    g Discount factor.
    h Discount rate.
    i Ordinary annuity (annuity in arrears).
    j Contingent annuity.
    k Perpetuity.
    l Implicit interest rate.
    m Internal rate of return.

2 Does the present value of a given amount to be paid in ten years increase or decrease if the interest rate increases? Suppose that the amount were due in five years? 20 years? Does the present value of an annuity to be paid for ten years increase or decrease if the discount rate decreases? Suppose that the annuity were for five years? 20 years?

3 Rather than pay you $100 a month for the next 20 years, the person who injured you in an automobile accident is willing to pay a single amount now to settle your claim for injuries. Would you rather an interest rate of 6 percent or 12 percent be used in computing the present value of the lump-sum settlement? Comment or explain.

4 The terms of sale "2/10, net/30" mean that a discount of 2 percent from gross invoice price can be taken if the invoice is paid within ten days and that otherwise the full amount is due within 30 days.

    a Write an expression for the implied annual rate of interest being offered, if the entire discount is viewed as being interest for funds received sooner rather than later. (Note that 98 percent of the gross invoice price is being borrowed for 20 days.)
    b The tables at the back of the book do not permit the exact evaluation of the expression derived in part **a**. The rate of interest implied is 44.59 percent per year. Use the tables to convince yourself that this astounding (to some) answer must be close to correct.

5 State the rate per period and the number of periods, in each of the following:

    a 12 percent per annum, for five years, compounded annually.
    b 12 percent per annum, for five years, compounded semiannually.
    c 12 percent per annum, for five years, compounded quarterly.
    d 12 percent per annum, for five years, compounded monthly.

6 Compute the future value of:

  a $100 invested for five years at 4 percent compounded annually.

  b $500 invested for 15 periods at 2 percent compounded once per period.

  c $200 invested for eight years at 3 percent compounded semiannually.

  d $2,500 invested for 14 years at 8 percent compounded quarterly.

  e $600 invested for three years at 12 percent compounded monthly.

7 Compute the present value of:

  a $100 due in 30 years at 4 percent compounded annually.

  b $250 due in eight years at 8 percent compounded quarterly.

  c $1,000 due in two years at 12 percent compounded monthly.

8 Compute the amount (future value) of an ordinary annuity (an annuity in arrears) of:

  a 13 rents of $100 at $1\frac{1}{2}$ percent per period.

  b 8 rents of $850 at 6 percent per period.

  c 28 rents of $400 at 4 percent per period.

9 Mr. Adams has $500 to invest. He wishes to know how much it will amount to if he invests it at

  a 6 percent per year for 21 years.

  b 8 percent per year for 33 years.

10 Ms. Black wishes to have $15,000 at the end of eight years. How much must she invest today to accomplish this purpose if the interest rate is

  a 6 percent per year?

  b 8 percent per year?

11 Mr. Case plans to set aside $4,000 each year, the first payment to be made on January 1, 1982 and the last on January 1, 1987. How much will he have accumulated by January 1, 1987 if the interest rate is

  a 6 percent per year?

  b 8 percent per year?

12 Ms. David wants to have $450,000 on her sixty-fifth birthday. She asks you to tell her how much she must deposit on each birthday from her fifty-eighth to sixty-fifth, inclusive, in order to receive this amount. Assume an interest rate of

  a 8 percent per year.

  b 12 percent per year.

13 If Mr. Edwards invests $900 on June 1 of each year from 1982 to 1992, inclusive, how much will he have accumulated on June 1, 1993 (note that 1 year elapses after last payment) if the interest rate is

  a 5 percent per year?

  b 10 percent per year?

14 Mr. Frank has $145,000 with which he purchases an annuity on February 1, 1982. The annuity consists of six annual payments, the first to be made on February 1, 1983. How much will he receive in each payment? Assume an interest rate of

  a 8 percent per year.

  b 12 percent per year.

15 In the preceding Questions **6–14**, you have been asked to compute a number. First you must decide what factor from the tables is appropriate and then you use that factor in the appropriate calculation. Notice that the last step could be omitted. You could write an arithmetic expression showing the factor you want to use without actually copying down the number and doing the arithmetic. For example, define the following notation: $T(i, p, r)$ means Table i (1, 2, 3, or 4), row p (periods 1 to 20, 22, 24, . . . , 40, 45, 50, 100), and column r (interest rates from $\frac{1}{2}$ percent up to 20 percent). Thus, $T(3, 16, 12)$ would be the factor in Table 3 for 16 periods and an interest rate of 12 percent per period, which is 42.75328. Using this notation, you can write an expression for any compound interest problem. Any clerk can evaluate the expression.

You can check that you understand this notation by observing that the following are true statements:

$T(1, 20, 8) = 4.66096$
$T(2, 12, 5) = 0.55684$
$T(3, 16, 12) = 42.75328$
$T(4, 10, 20) = 4.19247.$

In the following questions, write an expression for the correct answer using the notation introduced here, but do not attempt to evaluate the expression.

a Work the **a** parts of Questions **6–10**, above.
b Work the **b** parts of Questions **11–14**, above.
c How might the use of this notation make it easier for your instructor to write examination questions on compound interest?

16 Ms. Grady agrees to lease a certain property for ten years, at the following annual rentals, payable in advance:

years 1 and 2—$1,000 per year.
years 3 to 6—$2,000 per year.
years 7 to 10—$2,500 per year.

What single immediate sum will pay all of these rents if they are discounted at

a 6 percent per year?
b 8 percent per year?
c 10 percent per year?

17 In order to establish a fund that will provide a scholarship of $3,000 a year indefinitely, with the first award to occur now, how much must be deposited if the fund earns:

a 6 percent per period?
b 8 percent per period?

18 Consider the scholarship fund in the preceding question. Suppose that the first scholarship is not to be awarded until one year from now. How much should be deposited if the fund earns:

a 6 percent per period?
b 8 percent per period?
Suppose that the first scholarship is not to be awarded until 5 years from now. How much should be deposited if the fund earns:

c 6 percent per year?
d 8 percent per year?

19 The state helps a rural county maintain a bridge and has agreed to pay $6,000 now and every two years thereafter forever toward the expenses. The state wishes to discharge its obligation by paying a single sum to the county now in lieu of the payment due and all future payments. How much should the state pay the county if the discount rate is

a 8 percent per year?
b 12 percent per year?

20 Find the interest rate implicit in a loan of $100,000 which is discharged with the two annual installments of $55,307 each paid at the ends of years one and two.

21 A single-payment note has a face value of $140,493, to be paid in three years. The note is exchanged for equipment having a fair market value of $100,000 three years before the maturity date on the note.

What interest rate will be imputed in accounting for the single-payment note?

22 A single-payment note has a face value of $67,280, due on maturity of the note. The note is exchanged for land with a fair market value of $50,000 two years before the maturity date on the note.

a What interest rate will be imputed in accounting for this single-payment note?
b Construct an amortization schedule for the note using the interest rate imputed. Show book value of the note at the start of each year, interest for each year, amount reducing or increasing book value each year, and book value at the end of the year.

23 Berman Company purchased a plot of land for possible future development. The land had fair market value of $86,000. Berman Company gave a three-year interest-bearing note. The note had face value of $100,000 and provided for interest at a stated rate of 8 percent—payments of $8,000 were due at the ends of each of three years, the last payment coinciding with the maturity date of the note's face value of $100,000.

a What is the interest rate implicit in the note accurate to the nearest tenth of one percent?
b Construct an amortization schedule for the note for each year, showing the book value of the note at the start of the year, interest for the year, payment for the year, amount reducing or increasing the book value of the note for each payment, and the book value of the note at the end of each year. Use the interest rate found in part **a**.

24 An oil-drilling company figures that $300 must be spent for an initial supply of drill bits and that $100 must be spent every month to replace the worn-out bits. What is the present value of the cost of the bits if the company plans to be in business indefinitely and discounts payments at 1 percent per month?

25 If you promise to leave $25,000 on deposit at the Quarter Savings Bank for four years, the bank will give you a new car today and your $25,000 back at the end of four years. How much are you, in effect, paying today for the car if the bank pays 8 percent interest compounded quarterly (2 percent paid four times per year)?

26 When Mr. Shafer died, his estate after taxes amounted to $300,000. His will provided that Widow Shafer would receive $24,000 per year starting immediately from the principal of the estate and that the balance of the principal would pass to the Shafers' son on Widow Shafer's death. The state law governing this estate provided for a *dower* option. If Widow Shafer elects the dower option, she renounces the will and can have one-third of the estate in cash now. The remainder will then pass immediately to their son. Widow Shafer wants to maximize the present value of her bequest. Should she take the annuity or elect the dower option if she will receive five payments and discounts payments at:

a 8 percent per year?

b 12 percent per year?

27 Mrs. Heileman occasionally drinks beer. She consumes one case in 20 weeks. She can buy beer in disposable bottles for $6.60 per case or for $6.00 a case of returnable bottles if a $1.50 refundable deposit is paid at the time of purchase. If her discount rate is $\frac{1}{4}$ percent per week, how much in present-value dollars does she save by buying the returnables and thereby losing the use of the $1.50 deposit for 20 weeks?

28 When the General Electric Company first introduced the Lucalox ceramic, screw-in light bulb, the bulb cost three and one half times as much as an ordinary bulb but lasted five times as long. An ordinary bulb cost $.50 and lasted about eight months. If a firm has a discount rate of 12 percent compounded three times a year, how much would it save in present-value dollars by using one Lucalox bulb?

29 The Roberts Dairy Company switched from delivery trucks with regular gasoline engines to ones with diesel engines. The diesel trucks cost $2,000 more than the ordinary gasoline trucks, but $600 per year less to operate. Assume that the operating costs are saved at the end of each month. If Roberts Dairy uses a discount rate of 1 percent per month, approximately how many months, at a minimum, must the diesel trucks remain in service for the switch to save money?

30 On January 1, 1981, Outergarments, Inc., opened a new textile plant for the production of synthetic fabrics. The plant is on leased land; 20 years remain on the nonrenewable lease.

The cost of the plant was $2 million. Net cash flow to be derived from the project is estimated to be $300,000 per year. The company does not normally invest in such projects unless the anticipated yield is at least 12 percent.

On December 31, 1981, the company finds cash flows from the plant to be $280,000 for the year. On the same day, farm experts predict cotton production to be unusually low for the next two years. Outergarments estimates the resulting increase in demand for synthetic fabrics to boost cash flows to $350,000 for each of the next two years. Subsequent years' estimates remain unchanged. Ignore tax considerations.

a Calculate the present value of the future expected cash flows from the plant when it was opened.

b What is the present value of the plant on January 1, 1982 after the reestimation of future incomes?

c On January, 1982, the day following the cotton production news release. Overalls Company announces plans to build a synthetic fabrics plant to be opened in three years. Outergarments, Inc., keeps its 1982–1984 estimates, but reduces the estimated annual cash flows for subsequent years to $200,000. What is the value of the Outergarments' present plant on January 1, 1982, after the new projections?

d On January 2, 1982, an investor contacts Outergarments about purchasing a 20-percent share of the plant. If the investor expects to earn at least a 12-percent annual return on the investment, what is the maximum amount that the investor can pay? Assume that the investor and Outergarments, Inc., use the same estimates of annual cash flows.

Compound Interest, Annuity, and Bond Tables

Table 1
Future Value of $1

$$F_n = P(1 + r)^n$$

r = interest rate; n = number of periods until valuation; $P = \$1$

Periods = n	1/4%	1/2%	3/4%	1%	1 1/2%	2%	3%	4%	5%	6%	7%	8%	10%	12%	15%	20%
1	1.00250	1.00500	1.00750	1.01000	1.01500	1.02000	1.03000	1.04000	1.05000	1.06000	1.07000	1.08000	1.10000	1.12000	1.15000	1.20000
2	1.00501	1.01003	1.01506	1.02010	1.03023	1.04040	1.06090	1.08160	1.10250	1.12360	1.14490	1.16640	1.21000	1.25440	1.32250	1.44000
3	1.00752	1.01508	1.02267	1.03030	1.04568	1.06121	1.09273	1.12486	1.15763	1.19102	1.22504	1.25971	1.33100	1.40493	1.52088	1.72800
4	1.01004	1.02015	1.03034	1.04060	1.06136	1.08243	1.12551	1.16986	1.21551	1.26248	1.31080	1.36049	1.46410	1.57352	1.74901	2.07360
5	1.01256	1.02525	1.03807	1.05101	1.07728	1.10408	1.15927	1.21665	1.27628	1.33823	1.40255	1.46933	1.61051	1.76234	2.01136	2.48832
6	1.01509	1.03038	1.04585	1.06152	1.09344	1.12616	1.19405	1.26532	1.34010	1.41852	1.50073	1.58687	1.77156	1.97382	2.31306	2.98598
7	1.01763	1.03553	1.05370	1.07214	1.10984	1.14869	1.22987	1.31593	1.40710	1.50363	1.60578	1.71382	1.94872	2.21068	2.66002	3.58318
8	1.02018	1.04071	1.06160	1.08286	1.12649	1.17166	1.26677	1.36857	1.47746	1.59385	1.71819	1.85093	2.14359	2.47596	3.05902	4.29982
9	1.02273	1.04591	1.06956	1.09369	1.14339	1.19509	1.30477	1.42331	1.55133	1.68948	1.83846	1.99900	2.35795	2.77308	3.51788	5.15978
10	1.02528	1.05114	1.07758	1.10462	1.16054	1.21899	1.34392	1.48024	1.62889	1.79085	1.96715	2.15892	2.59374	3.10585	4.04556	6.19174
11	1.02785	1.05640	1.08566	1.11567	1.17795	1.24337	1.38423	1.53945	1.71034	1.89830	2.10485	2.33164	2.85312	3.47855	4.65239	7.43008
12	1.03042	1.06168	1.09381	1.12683	1.19562	1.26824	1.42576	1.60103	1.79586	2.01220	2.25219	2.51817	3.13843	3.89598	5.35025	8.91610
13	1.03299	1.06699	1.10201	1.13809	1.21355	1.29361	1.46853	1.66507	1.88565	2.13293	2.40985	2.71962	3.45227	4.36349	6.15279	10.69932
14	1.03557	1.07232	1.11028	1.14947	1.23176	1.31948	1.51259	1.73168	1.97993	2.26090	2.57853	2.93719	3.79750	4.88711	7.07571	12.83918
15	1.03816	1.07768	1.11860	1.16097	1.25023	1.34587	1.55797	1.80094	2.07893	2.39656	2.75903	3.17217	4.17725	5.47357	8.13706	15.40702
16	1.04076	1.08307	1.12699	1.17258	1.26899	1.37279	1.60471	1.87298	2.18287	2.54035	2.95216	3.42594	4.59497	6.13039	9.35762	18.48843
17	1.04336	1.08849	1.13544	1.18430	1.28802	1.40024	1.65285	1.94790	2.29202	2.69277	3.15882	3.70002	5.05447	6.86604	10.76126	22.18611
18	1.04597	1.09393	1.14396	1.19615	1.30734	1.42825	1.70243	2.02582	2.40662	2.85434	3.37993	3.99602	5.55992	7.68997	12.37545	26.62333
19	1.04858	1.09940	1.15254	1.20811	1.32695	1.45681	1.75351	2.10685	2.52695	3.02560	3.61653	4.31570	6.11591	8.61276	14.23177	31.94800
20	1.05121	1.10490	1.16118	1.22019	1.34686	1.48595	1.80611	2.19112	2.65330	3.20714	3.86968	4.66096	6.72750	9.64629	16.36654	38.33760
22	1.05647	1.11597	1.17867	1.24472	1.38756	1.54598	1.91610	2.36992	2.92526	3.60354	4.43040	5.43654	8.14027	12.10031	21.64475	55.20614
24	1.06176	1.12716	1.19641	1.26973	1.42950	1.60844	2.03279	2.56330	3.22510	4.04893	5.07237	6.34118	9.84973	15.17863	28.62518	79.49685
26	1.06707	1.13846	1.21443	1.29526	1.47271	1.67342	2.15659	2.77247	3.55567	4.54938	5.80735	7.39635	11.91818	19.04007	37.85680	114.4755
28	1.07241	1.14987	1.23271	1.32129	1.51722	1.74102	2.28793	2.99870	3.92013	5.11169	6.64884	8.62711	14.42099	23.88387	50.06561	164.8447
30	1.07778	1.16140	1.25127	1.34785	1.56308	1.81136	2.42726	3.24340	4.32194	5.74349	7.61226	10.06266	17.44940	29.95992	66.21177	237.3763
32	1.08318	1.17304	1.27011	1.37494	1.61032	1.88454	2.57508	3.50806	4.76494	6.45339	8.71527	11.73708	21.11378	37.58173	87.56507	341.8219
34	1.08860	1.18480	1.28923	1.40258	1.65900	1.96068	2.73191	3.79432	5.25335	7.25103	9.97811	13.69013	25.54767	47.14252	115.80480	492.2235
36	1.09405	1.19668	1.30865	1.43077	1.70914	2.03989	2.89828	4.10393	5.79182	8.14725	11.42394	15.96817	30.91268	59.13557	153.15185	708.8019
38	1.09953	1.20868	1.32835	1.45953	1.76080	2.12230	3.07478	4.43881	6.38548	9.15425	13.07927	18.62528	37.40434	74.17966	202.54332	1020.675
40	1.10503	1.22079	1.34835	1.48886	1.81402	2.20804	3.26204	4.80102	7.03999	10.28572	14.97446	21.72452	45.25926	93.05097	267.86355	1469.772
45	1.11892	1.25162	1.39968	1.56481	1.95421	2.43785	3.78160	5.84118	8.98501	13.76461	21.00245	31.92045	72.89048	163.9876	538.76927	3657.262
50	1.13297	1.28323	1.45296	1.64463	2.10524	2.69159	4.38391	7.10668	11.46740	18.42015	29.45703	46.90161	117.3909	289.0022	1083.65744	9100.438
100	1.28362	1.64667	2.11108	2.70481	4.43205	7.24465	19.21863	50.50495	131.5013	339.3021	867.7163	2199.761	13780.61	83522.27	117×10^4	828×10^6

Table 2
Present Value of $1

$$P = F_n (1 + r)^{-n}$$

r = discount rate; n = number of periods until payment; F_n = $1

Periods = n	1/4%	1/2%	3/4%	1%	1 1/2%	2%	3%	4%	5%	6%	7%	8%	10%	12%	15%	20%
1	.99751	.99502	.99256	.99010	.98522	.98039	.97087	.96154	.95238	.94340	.93458	.92593	.90909	.89286	.86957	.83333
2	.99502	.99007	.98517	.98030	.97066	.96117	.94260	.92456	.90703	.89000	.87344	.85734	.82645	.79719	.75614	.69444
3	.99254	.98515	.97783	.97059	.95632	.94232	.91514	.88900	.86384	.83962	.81630	.79383	.75131	.71178	.65752	.57870
4	.99006	.98025	.97055	.96098	.94218	.92385	.88849	.85480	.82270	.79209	.76290	.73503	.68301	.63552	.57175	.48225
5	.98759	.97537	.96333	.95147	.92826	.90573	.86261	.82193	.78353	.74726	.71299	.68058	.62092	.56743	.49718	.40188
6	.98513	.97052	.95416	.94205	.91454	.88797	.83748	.79031	.74622	.70496	.66634	.63017	.56447	.50663	.43233	.33490
7	.98267	.96569	.94904	.93272	.90103	.87056	.81309	.75992	.71068	.66506	.62275	.58349	.51316	.45235	.37594	.27908
8	.98022	.96089	.94198	.92348	.88771	.85349	.78941	.73069	.67684	.62741	.58201	.54027	.46651	.40388	.32690	.23257
9	.97778	.95610	.93496	.91434	.87459	.83676	.76642	.70259	.64461	.59190	.54393	.50025	.42410	.36061	.28426	.19381
10	.97534	.95135	.92800	.90529	.86167	.82035	.74409	.67556	.61391	.55839	.50835	.46319	.38554	.32197	.24718	.16151
11	.97291	.94661	.92109	.89632	.84893	.80426	.72242	.64958	.58468	.52679	.47509	.42888	.35049	.28748	.21494	.13459
12	.97048	.94191	.91424	.88745	.83639	.78849	.70138	.62460	.55684	.49697	.44401	.39711	.31863	.25668	.18691	.11216
13	.96806	.93722	.90743	.87866	.82403	.77303	.68095	.60057	.53032	.46884	.41496	.36770	.28966	.22917	.16253	.09346
14	.96565	.93256	.90068	.86996	.81185	.75788	.66112	.57748	.50507	.44230	.38782	.34046	.26333	.20462	.14133	.07789
15	.96324	.92792	.89397	.86135	.79985	.74301	.64186	.55526	.48102	.41727	.36245	.31524	.23939	.18270	.12289	.06491
16	.96084	.92330	.88732	.85282	.78803	.72845	.62317	.53391	.45811	.39365	.33873	.29189	.21763	.16312	.10686	.05409
17	.95844	.91871	.88071	.84438	.77639	.71416	.60502	.51337	.43630	.37136	.31657	.27027	.19784	.14564	.09293	.04507
18	.95605	.91414	.87416	.83602	.76491	.70016	.58739	.49363	.41552	.35034	.29586	.25025	.17986	.13004	.08081	.03756
19	.95367	.90959	.86765	.82774	.75361	.68643	.57029	.47464	.39573	.33051	.27651	.23171	.16351	.11611	.07027	.03130
20	.95129	.90506	.86119	.81954	.74247	.67297	.55368	.45639	.37689	.31180	.25842	.21455	.14864	.10367	.06110	.02608
22	.94655	.89608	.84842	.80340	.72069	.64684	.52189	.42196	.34185	.27751	.22571	.18394	.12285	.08264	.04620	.01811
24	.94184	.88719	.83583	.78757	.69954	.62172	.49193	.39012	.31007	.24698	.19715	.15770	.10153	.06588	.03493	.01258
26	.93714	.87838	.82343	.77205	.67902	.59758	.46369	.36069	.28124	.21981	.17220	.13520	.08391	.05252	.02642	.00874
28	.93248	.86966	.81122	.75684	.65910	.57437	.43708	.33348	.25509	.19563	.15040	.11591	.06934	.04187	.01997	.00607
30	.92783	.86103	.79919	.74192	.63976	.55207	.41199	.30832	.23138	.17411	.13137	.09938	.05731	.03338	.01510	.00421
32	.92321	.85248	.78733	.72730	.62099	.53063	.38834	.28506	.20987	.15496	.11474	.08520	.04736	.02661	.01142	.00293
34	.91861	.84402	.77565	.71297	.60277	.51003	.36604	.26355	.19035	.13791	.10022	.07305	.03914	.02121	.00864	.00203
36	.91403	.83564	.76415	.69892	.58509	.49022	.34503	.24367	.17266	.12274	.08754	.06262	.03235	.01691	.00653	.00141
38	.90948	.82735	.75281	.68515	.56792	.47119	.32523	.22529	.15661	.10924	.07646	.05369	.02673	.01348	.00494	.00098
40	.90495	.81914	.74165	.67165	.55126	.45289	.30656	.20829	.14205	.09722	.06678	.04603	.02209	.01075	.00373	.00068
45	.89372	.79896	.71445	.63905	.51171	.41020	.26444	.17120	.11130	.07265	.04761	.03133	.01372	.00610	.00186	.00027
50	.88263	.77929	.68825	.60804	.47500	.37153	.22811	.14071	.08720	.05429	.03395	.02132	.00852	.00346	.00092	.00011
100	.77904	.60729	.47369	.36971	.22563	.13803	.05203	.01980	.00760	.00295	.00115	.00045	.00007	.00001	.00000	.00000

Table 3
Future Value of Annuity of $1 in Arrears

$$F = \frac{(1 + r)^n - 1}{r}$$

r = interest rate; n = number of payments

No. of Payments = n	¼%	½%	¾%	1%	1½%	2%	3%	4%	5%	6%	7%	8%	10%	12%	15%	20%
1	1.00000	1.00000	1.00000	1.00000	1.00000	1.00000	1.00000	1.00000	1.00000	1.00000	1.00000	1.00000	1.00000	1.00000	1.00000	1.00000
2	2.00250	2.00500	2.00750	2.01000	2.01500	2.02000	2.03000	2.04000	2.05000	2.06000	2.07000	2.08000	2.10000	2.12000	2.15000	2.20000
3	3.00751	3.01503	3.02256	3.03010	3.04523	3.06040	3.09090	3.12160	3.15250	3.18360	3.21490	3.24640	3.31000	3.37440	3.47250	3.64000
4	4.01503	4.03010	4.04523	4.06040	4.09090	4.12161	4.18363	4.24646	4.31013	4.37462	4.43994	4.50611	4.64100	4.77933	4.99338	5.36800
5	5.02506	5.05025	5.07556	5.10101	5.15227	5.20404	5.30914	5.41632	5.52563	5.63709	5.75074	5.86660	6.10510	6.35285	6.74238	7.44160
6	6.03763	6.07550	6.11363	6.15202	6.22955	6.30812	6.46841	6.63298	6.80191	6.97532	7.15329	7.33593	7.71561	8.11519	8.75374	9.92992
7	7.05272	7.10588	7.15948	7.21354	7.32299	7.43428	7.66246	7.89829	8.14201	8.39384	8.65402	8.92280	9.48717	10.08901	11.06680	12.91590
8	8.07035	8.14141	8.21318	8.28567	8.43284	8.58297	8.89234	9.21423	9.54911	9.89747	10.25980	10.63663	11.43589	12.29969	13.72682	16.49908
9	9.09053	9.18212	9.27478	9.36853	9.55933	9.75463	10.15911	10.58280	11.02656	11.49132	11.97799	12.48756	13.57948	14.77566	16.78584	20.79890
10	10.11325	10.22803	10.34434	10.46221	10.70272	10.94972	11.46388	12.00611	12.57789	13.18079	13.81645	14.48656	15.93742	17.54874	20.30372	25.95868
11	11.13854	11.27917	11.42192	11.56683	11.86326	12.16872	12.80780	13.48635	14.20679	14.97164	15.78360	16.64549	18.53117	20.65458	24.34928	32.15042
12	12.16638	12.33556	12.50759	12.68250	13.04121	13.41209	14.19203	15.02581	15.91713	16.86994	17.88845	18.97713	21.38428	24.13313	29.00167	39.58050
13	13.19680	13.39724	13.60139	13.80933	14.23683	14.68033	15.61779	16.62684	17.71298	18.88214	20.14064	21.49530	24.52271	28.02911	34.35192	48.49660
14	14.22979	14.46423	14.70340	14.94742	15.45038	15.97394	17.08632	18.29191	19.59863	21.01507	22.55049	24.21492	27.97498	32.39260	40.50471	59.19592
15	15.26537	15.53655	15.81368	16.09690	16.68214	17.29342	18.59891	20.02359	21.57856	23.27597	25.12902	27.15211	31.77248	37.27971	47.58041	72.03511
16	16.30353	16.61423	16.93228	17.25786	17.93237	18.63929	20.15688	21.82453	23.65749	25.67253	27.88805	30.32428	35.94973	42.75328	55.71747	87.44213
17	17.34429	17.69730	18.05927	18.43044	19.20136	20.01207	21.76159	23.69751	25.84037	28.21288	30.84022	33.75023	40.54470	48.88367	65.07509	105.9306
18	18.38765	18.78579	19.19472	19.61475	20.48938	21.41231	23.41444	25.64541	28.13238	30.90565	33.99903	37.45024	45.59917	55.74971	75.83636	128.1167
19	19.43362	19.87972	20.33868	20.81090	21.79672	22.84056	25.11687	27.67123	30.53900	33.75999	37.37896	41.44626	51.15909	63.43968	88.21181	154.7400
20	20.48220	20.97912	21.49122	22.01900	23.12367	24.29737	26.87037	29.77808	33.06595	36.78559	40.99549	45.76196	57.27500	72.05244	102.44358	186.6880
22	22.58724	23.19443	23.82230	24.47159	25.83758	27.29898	30.53678	34.24797	38.50521	43.39229	49.00574	55.45676	71.40275	92.50258	137.63164	271.0307
24	24.70282	25.43196	26.18847	26.97346	28.63352	30.42186	34.42647	39.08260	44.50200	50.81558	58.17667	66.76476	88.49733	118.1552	184.16784	392.4842
26	26.82899	27.69191	28.59027	29.52563	31.51397	33.67091	38.55304	44.31174	51.11345	59.15638	68.67647	79.95442	109.1818	150.3339	245.71197	567.3773
28	28.96580	29.97452	31.02823	32.12910	34.48148	37.05121	42.93092	49.96758	58.40258	68.52811	80.69769	95.33883	134.2099	190.6989	327.10408	819.2233
30	31.11331	32.28002	33.50290	34.78489	37.53868	40.56808	47.57542	56.08494	66.43885	79.05819	94.46079	113.2832	164.4940	241.3327	434.74515	1181.881
32	33.27157	34.60862	36.01483	37.49407	40.68829	44.22703	52.50276	62.70147	75.29883	90.88978	110.2181	134.2135	201.1378	304.8477	577.10046	1704.109
34	35.44064	36.96058	38.56458	40.25770	43.93309	48.03380	57.73018	69.85791	85.06696	104.1838	128.2588	158.6267	245.4767	384.5210	765.36535	2456.118
36	37.62056	39.33610	41.15272	43.07688	47.27597	51.99437	63.27594	77.59831	95.83632	119.1209	148.9135	187.1022	299.1268	484.4631	1014.34568	3539.009
38	39.81140	41.73545	43.77982	45.95272	50.71989	56.11494	69.15945	85.97034	107.7095	135.9042	172.5610	220.3159	364.0434	609.8305	1343.62216	5098.373
40	42.01320	44.15885	46.44648	48.86637	54.26789	60.40198	75.40126	95.02552	120.7998	154.7620	199.6351	259.0565	442.5926	767.0914	1779.09031	7343.858
45	47.56606	50.32416	53.29011	56.48107	63.61420	71.89271	92.71986	121.0294	159.7002	212.7435	285.7493	386.5056	718.9048	1358.230	3585.12846	18281.31
50	53.18868	56.64516	60.39426	64.46318	73.68283	84.57940	112.7969	152.6671	209.3480	290.3359	406.5289	573.7702	1163.909	2400.018	7217.71628	45497.19
100	113.44996	129.33370	148.14451	170.4814	228.8030	312.2323	607.2877	1237.624	2610.025	5638.368	12381.66	27484.52	137796.1	696010.5	783 × 10⁴	414 × 10⁶

Note: To convert from this table to values of an annuity in advance, determine the annuity in arrears above for one more period and subtract 1.00000.

less payments

Table 4
Present Value of an Annuity of $1 in Arrears

$$P_A = \frac{1 - (1 + r)^{-n}}{r}$$

r = discount rate; n = number of payments

No. of Payments = n	1/4%	1/2%	3/4%	1%	1½%	2%	3%	4%	5%	6%	7%	8%	10%	12%	15%	20%
1	0.99751	0.99502	0.99256	0.99010	.98522	.98039	.97087	.96154	.95238	.94340	.93458	.92593	.90909	.89286	0.86957	.83333
2	1.99252	1.98510	1.97772	1.97040	1.95588	1.94156	1.91347	1.88609	1.85941	1.83339	1.80802	1.78326	1.73554	1.69005	1.62571	1.52778
3	2.98506	2.97025	2.95556	2.94099	2.91220	2.88388	2.82861	2.77509	2.72325	2.67301	2.62432	2.57710	2.48685	2.40183	2.28323	2.10648
4	3.97512	3.95050	3.92611	3.90197	3.85438	3.80773	3.71710	3.62990	3.54595	3.46511	3.38721	3.31213	3.16987	3.03735	2.85498	2.58873
5	4.96272	4.92587	4.88944	4.85343	4.78264	4.71346	4.57971	4.45182	4.32948	4.21236	4.10020	3.99271	3.79079	3.60478	3.35216	2.99061
6	5.94785	5.89638	5.84560	5.79548	5.69719	5.60143	5.41719	5.24212	5.07569	4.91732	4.76654	4.62288	4.35526	4.11141	3.78448	3.32551
7	6.93052	6.86207	6.79464	6.72819	6.59821	6.47199	6.23028	6.00205	5.78637	5.58238	5.38929	5.20637	4.86842	4.56376	4.16042	3.60459
8	7.91074	7.82296	7.73661	7.65168	7.48593	7.32548	7.01969	6.73274	6.46321	6.20979	5.97130	5.74664	5.33493	4.96764	4.48732	3.83716
9	8.88852	8.77906	8.67158	8.56602	8.36052	8.16224	7.78611	7.43533	7.10782	6.80169	6.51523	6.24689	5.75902	5.32825	4.77158	4.03097
10	9.86386	9.73041	9.59958	9.47130	9.22218	8.98259	8.53020	8.11090	7.72173	7.36009	7.02358	6.71008	6.14457	5.65022	5.01887	4.19247
11	10.83677	10.67703	10.52067	10.36763	10.07112	9.78685	9.25262	8.76048	8.30641	7.88687	7.49867	7.13896	6.49506	5.93770	5.23371	4.32706
12	11.80725	11.61893	11.43491	11.25508	10.90751	10.57534	9.95400	9.38507	8.86325	8.38384	7.94269	7.53608	6.81369	6.19437	5.42062	4.43922
13	12.77532	12.55615	12.34235	12.13374	11.73153	11.34837	10.63496	9.98565	9.39357	8.85268	8.35765	7.90378	7.10336	6.42355	5.58315	4.53268
14	13.74096	13.48871	13.24302	13.00370	12.54338	12.10625	11.29607	10.56312	9.89864	9.29498	8.74547	8.24424	7.36669	6.62817	5.72448	4.61057
15	14.70420	14.41662	14.13699	13.86505	13.34323	12.84926	11.93794	11.11839	10.37966	9.71225	9.10791	8.55948	7.60608	6.81086	5.84737	4.67547
16	15.66504	15.33993	15.02431	14.71787	14.13126	13.57771	12.56110	11.65230	10.83777	10.10590	9.44665	8.85137	7.82371	6.97399	5.95423	4.72956
17	16.62348	16.25863	15.90502	15.56225	14.90765	14.29187	13.16612	12.16567	11.27407	10.47726	9.76322	9.12164	8.02155	7.11963	6.04716	4.77463
18	17.57953	17.17277	16.77918	16.39827	15.67256	14.99203	13.75351	12.65930	11.68959	10.82760	10.05909	9.37189	8.20141	7.24967	6.12797	4.81219
19	18.53320	18.08236	17.64683	17.22601	16.42617	15.67846	14.32380	13.13394	12.08532	11.15812	10.33560	9.60360	8.36492	7.36578	6.19823	4.84350
20	19.48449	18.98742	18.50802	18.04555	17.16864	16.35143	14.87747	13.59033	12.46221	11.46992	10.59401	9.81815	8.51356	7.46944	6.25933	4.86958
22	21.37995	20.78406	20.21121	19.66038	18.62082	17.65805	15.93692	14.45112	13.16300	12.04158	11.06124	10.20074	8.77154	7.64465	6.35866	4.90943
24	23.26598	22.56287	21.88915	21.24339	20.03041	18.91393	16.93554	15.24696	13.79864	12.55036	11.46933	10.52876	8.98474	7.78432	6.43377	4.93710
26	25.14261	24.32402	23.54219	22.79520	21.39863	20.12104	17.87684	15.98277	14.37519	13.00317	11.82578	10.80998	9.16095	7.89566	6.49056	4.95632
28	27.00989	26.06769	25.17071	24.31644	22.72672	21.28127	18.76411	16.66306	14.89813	13.40616	12.13711	11.05108	9.30657	7.98442	6.53351	4.96967
30	28.86787	27.79405	26.77508	25.80771	24.01584	22.39646	19.60044	17.29203	15.37245	13.76483	12.40904	11.25778	9.42691	8.05518	6.56598	4.97894
32	30.71660	29.50328	28.35565	27.26959	25.26714	23.46833	20.38877	17.87355	15.80268	14.08404	12.64656	11.43500	9.52638	8.11159	6.59053	4.98537
34	32.55611	31.19555	29.91278	28.70267	26.48173	24.49859	21.13184	18.41120	16.19290	14.36814	12.85401	11.58693	9.60857	8.15656	6.60910	4.98984
36	34.38647	32.87102	31.44681	30.10751	27.66068	25.48884	21.83225	18.90828	16.54685	14.62099	13.03521	11.71719	9.67651	8.19241	6.62314	4.99295
38	36.20770	34.52985	32.95808	31.48466	28.80505	26.44064	22.49246	19.36786	16.86789	14.84602	13.19347	11.82887	9.73265	8.22099	6.63375	4.99510
40	38.01986	36.17223	34.44694	32.83469	29.91585	27.35548	23.11477	19.79277	17.15909	15.04630	13.33171	11.92461	9.77905	8.24378	6.64178	4.99660
45	42.51088	40.20720	38.07318	36.09451	32.55234	29.49016	24.51871	20.72004	17.77407	15.45583	13.60552	12.10840	9.86281	8.28252	6.65429	4.99863
50	46.94617	44.14279	41.56645	39.19612	34.99969	31.42361	25.72976	21.48218	18.25593	15.76186	13.80075	12.23348	9.91481	8.30450	6.66051	4.99945
100	88.38248	78.54264	70.17462	63.02888	51.62470	43.09835	31.59891	24.50500	19.84791	16.61755	14.26925	12.49432	9.99927	8.33323	6.66666	5.00000

Note: To convert from this table to values of an annuity in advance, determine the annuity in arrears above for one less period and add 1.00000.

695

Table 5
**Bond Values in Percent of Par:
10-Percent Semiannual Coupons**

Bond value $= 10/r + (100 - 10/r)(1 + r/2)^{-2n}$
$r =$ yield to maturity; $n =$ years to maturity

Market Yield Percent per Year Compounded Semiannually

Years to Maturity	8.0	9.0	9.5	10.0	10.5	11.0	12.0	13.0	14.0	15.0	20.0
0.5	100.9615	100.4785	100.2387	100.0	99.7625	99.5261	99.0566	98.5915	98.1308	97.6744	95.4545
1.0	101.8861	100.9363	100.4665	100.0	99.5368	99.0768	98.1666	97.2691	96.3840	95.5111	91.3223
1.5	102.7751	101.3745	100.6840	100.0	99.3224	98.6510	97.3270	96.0273	94.7514	93.4987	87.5657
2.0	103.6299	101.7938	100.8917	100.0	99.1186	98.2474	96.5349	94.8613	93.2256	91.6267	84.1507
2.5	104.4518	102.1950	101.0899	100.0	98.9251	97.8649	95.7876	93.7665	91.7996	89.8853	81.0461
5.0	108.1109	103.9564	101.9541	100.0	98.0928	96.2312	92.6399	89.2168	85.9528	82.8398	69.2772
9.0	112.6593	106.0800	102.9803	100.0	97.1339	94.3770	89.1724	84.3513	79.8818	75.7350	58.9929
9.5	113.1339	106.2966	103.0838	100.0	97.0393	94.1962	88.8419	83.8979	79.3288	75.1023	58.1754
10.0	113.5903	106.5040	103.1827	100.0	96.9494	94.0248	88.5301	83.4722	78.8120	74.5138	57.4322
15.0	117.2920	108.1444	103.9551	100.0	96.2640	92.7331	86.2352	80.4120	75.1819	70.4740	52.8654
19.0	119.3679	109.0250	104.3608	100.0	95.9194	92.0976	85.1540	79.0312	73.6131	68.8015	51.3367
19.5	119.5845	109.1148	104.4017	100.0	95.8854	92.0357	85.0509	78.9025	73.4701	68.6525	51.2152
20.0	119.7928	109.2008	104.4408	100.0	95.8531	91.9769	84.9537	78.7817	73.3366	68.5140	51.1047
25.0	121.4822	109.8810	104.7461	100.0	95.6068	91.5342	84.2381	77.9132	72.3985	67.5630	50.4259
30.0	122.6235	110.3190	104.9381	100.0	95.4591	91.2751	83.8386	77.4506	71.9216	67.1015	50.1642
40.0	123.9154	110.7827	105.1347	100.0	95.3175	91.0345	83.4909	77.0728	71.5560	66.7690	50.0244
50.0	124.5050	110.9749	105.2124	100.0	95.2666	90.9521	83.3825	76.9656	71.4615	66.6908	50.0036

Table 6
Bond Values in Percent of Par:
12-Percent Semiannual Coupons

Bond value $= 12/r + (100 - 12/r)(1 + r/2)^{-2n}$

$r =$ yield to maturity; $n =$ years to maturity

Market Yield Percent per Year Compounded Semiannually

Years to Maturity	8.0	9.0	10.0	11.0	11.5	12.0	12.5	13.0	14.0	15.0	20.0
0.5	101.9231	101.4354	100.9524	100.4739	100.2364	100.0	99.7647	99.5305	99.0654	98.6047	96.3636
1.0	103.7722	102.8090	101.8594	100.9232	100.4600	100.0	99.5433	99.0897	98.1920	97.3067	93.0579
1.5	105.5502	104.1234	102.7232	101.3490	100.6714	100.0	99.3348	98.6758	97.3757	96.0992	90.0526
2.0	107.2598	105.3813	103.5459	101.7526	100.8713	100.0	99.1387	98.2871	96.6128	94.9760	87.3205
2.5	108.9036	106.5850	104.3295	102.1351	101.0603	100.0	98.9540	97.9222	95.8998	93.9312	84.8369
5.0	116.2218	111.8691	107.7217	103.7688	101.8620	100.0	98.1816	96.4056	92.9764	89.7039	75.4217
9.0	125.3186	118.2400	111.6896	105.6230	102.7585	100.0	97.3432	94.7838	89.9409	85.4410	67.1944
9.5	126.2679	118.8899	112.0853	105.8038	102.8449	100.0	97.2642	94.6326	89.6644	85.0614	66.5403
10.0	127.1807	119.5119	112.4622	105.9752	102.9266	100.0	97.1898	94.4907	89.4060	84.7083	65.9457
15.0	134.5841	124.4333	115.3724	107.2669	103.5353	100.0	96.6489	93.4707	87.5910	82.2844	62.2923
19.0	138.7357	127.0750	116.8679	107.9024	103.8283	100.0	96.3995	93.0104	86.8065	81.2809	61.0694
19.5	139.1690	127.3445	117.0170	107.9643	103.8565	100.0	96.3760	92.9675	86.7351	81.1915	60.9722
20.0	139.5855	127.6024	117.1591	108.0231	103.8832	100.0	96.3539	92.9272	86.6683	81.1084	60.8838
25.0	142.9644	129.6430	118.2559	108.4658	104.0822	100.0	96.1930	92.6377	86.1993	80.5378	60.3407
30.0	145.2470	130.9570	118.9293	108.7249	104.1960	100.0	96.1053	92.4835	85.9608	80.2609	60.1314
40.0	147.8308	132.3480	119.5965	108.9655	104.2982	100.0	96.0313	92.3576	85.7780	80.0614	60.0195
50.0	149.0100	132.9248	119.8479	109.0479	104.3316	100.0	96.0093	92.3219	85.7307	80.0145	60.0029

Glossary

A

AAA. *American Accounting Association.*

Abacus. A scholarly journal containing articles on theoretical aspects of accounting. Published twice a year by the Sydney University Press, Sydney, Australia.

abatement. A complete or partial cancellation of a levy imposed by a government unit.

abnormal spoilage. Actual spoilage exceeding that expected to occur if operations are normally efficient. Usual practice treats this cost as an *expense* of the period rather than as a *product cost*. Contrast with *normal spoilage*

aboriginal cost. In public utility accounting, the *acquisition cost* of an *asset* incurred by the first *entity* devoting that asset to public use. Most public utility regulation is based on aboriginal cost. If it were not, then public utilities could exchange assets among themselves at ever-increasing prices in order to raise the rate base and, then, prices based thereon.

absorption costing. The generally accepted method of *costing* that assigns all types of *manufacturing costs* (direct material and labor as well as fixed and variable overhead) to units produced. Sometimes called "full costing." Contrast with *direct costing*.

Accelerated Cost Recovery System. See *3-5-10 rule*.

accelerated depreciation. Any method of calculating *depreciation* charges where the charges become progressively smaller each period. Examples are *double-declining-balance* and *sum-of-the-years'-digits* methods.

acceptance. A written promise to pay that is equivalent to a promissory *note*.

account. Any device for accumulating additions and subtractions relating to a single *asset, liability, owners' equity* item, including *revenues* and *expenses*.

account form. The form of *balance sheet* where *assets* are shown on the left and *equities* are shown on the right. Contrast with *report form*. See also *T-account*.

account payable. A *liability* representing an amount owed to a *creditor*, usually arising from purchase of *merchandise* or materials and supplies; not necessarily due or past due. Normally, a *current* liability.

account receivable. A claim against a *debtor* usually arising from sales or services rendered; not necessarily due or past due. Normally, a *current* asset.

accountancy. The British word for *accounting*. In the United States, it means the theory and practice of accounting.

Accountants' Index. A publication of the *AICPA* that indexes, in detail, the accounting literature of the period.

accountant's opinion. *Auditor's report.*

accountant's report. *Auditor's report.*

accounting. An *information system* conveying information about a specific *entity*. The information is in financial terms and is restricted to information that can be made reasonably precise. The *AICPA* defines accounting as a service activity

699

whose "function is to provide quantitative information, primarily financial in nature, about economic entities that is intended to be useful in making economic decisions."

accounting changes. As defined by *APB Opinion* No. 20, a change in (a) an *accounting principle* (such as a switch from *FIFO* to *LIFO* or from *sum-of-the-years'-digits* to *straight-line depreciation*), (b) an accounting estimate (such as estimated useful lives or salvage value of depreciable assets and estimates of *warranty* costs or *uncollectible accounts*), and (c) the reporting *entity*. Changes of type (a) should be disclosed. The cumulative effect of the change on *retained earnings* at the start of the period during which the change was made should be included in reported earnings for the period of change. Changes of type (b) should be treated as affecting only the period of change and, if necessary, future periods. The reasons for changes of type (c) should be disclosed and, in statements reporting on operations of the period of the change, the effect of the change on all other periods reported on for comparative purposes should also be shown. In some cases (such as a change from *LIFO* to other inventory *flow assumptions* or in the method of accounting for long-term construction contracts), changes of type (a) are treated like changes of type (c). That is, for these changes all statements shown for prior periods must be restated to show the effect of adopting the change for those periods as well. See *all-inclusive concept* and *accounting errors*.

accounting conventions. Methods or procedures used in accounting. This term tends to be used when the method or procedure has not been given official authoritative sanction by a pronouncement of a group such as the *APB, FASB,* or *SEC*. Contrast with *accounting principles*.

accounting cycle. The sequence of accounting procedures starting with *journal entries* for various transactions and events and ending with the *financial statements* or, perhaps, the *post-closing trial balance*.

accounting entity. See *entity*.

accounting equation. *Assets = Equities. Assets = Liabilities + Owners' Equity.*

accounting errors. Arithmetic errors and misapplications of *accounting principles* in previously published financial statements that are corrected in the current period with direct *debits* or *credits* to *retained earnings*. In this regard, they are treated like *prior-period adjustments*, but, technically, they are not classified by *APB Opinion* No. 9 as prior-period adjustments. See *accounting changes* and contrast with changes in accounting estimates as described there.

accounting event. Any occurrence that is recorded in the accounting records.

accounting methods. *Accounting principles*. Procedures for carrying out accounting principles.

accounting period. The time period for which *financial statements* that measure *flows*, such as the *income statement* and the *statement of changes in financial position*, are prepared. Should be clearly identified on the financial statements. See *interim statements*.

accounting policies. *Accounting principles* adopted by a specific *entity*.

accounting principles. The methods or procedures used in accounting for events reported in the *financial statements*. This term tends to be used when the method or procedure has been given official authoritative sanction by a pronouncement of a group such as the *APB, FASB,* or *SEC*. Contrast with *accounting conventions* and *conceptual framework*.

Accounting Principles Board. See *APB*.

accounting procedures. See *accounting principles*, but usually this term refers to the methods for implementing accounting principles.

accounting rate of return. Income for a period divided by average investment during the period. Based on income, rather than discounted cash flows and, hence, is a poor decision-making aid or tool. See *ratio*.

Accounting Research Bulletin. ARB. The name of the official pronouncements of the former *Committee on Accounting Procedure* of the *AICPA*. Fifty-one bulletins were issued between 1939 and 1959. ARB No. 43 summarizes the first forty-two bulletins.

Accounting Research Study. ARS. One of a series of studies published by the Director of Accounting Research of the *AICPA* "designed to provide professional accountants and others interested in the development of accounting with a discussion and documentation of accounting problems." Fifteen such studies were published between 1961 and 1974.

The Accounting Review. Scholarly publication of the *American Accounting Association*.

Accounting Series Release. ASR. See *SEC*.

accounting standards. *Accounting principles*.

Accounting Standards Executive Committee. AcSEC. The senior technical committee of the *AICPA* authorized to speak for the *AICPA* in the areas of *financial accounting* and reporting as well as *cost accounting*.

Accounting Trends and Techniques. An annual publication of the *AICPA* that surveys the reporting practices of 600 large corporations. It presents tabulations of specific practices, terminology, and disclosures along with illustrations taken from individual annual reports.

accounts receivable turnover. *Net sales* on account for a period divided by the average balance of net accounts receivable. See *ratio*.

accretion. Increase in economic worth through physical change, usually said of a natural resource such as an orchard, caused by natural growth. Contrast with *appreciation*.

accrual. Recognition of an *expense (or revenue)* and the related *liability (or asset)* that is caused by an *accounting event*, frequently by the passage of time, and that is not signaled by an explicit cash transaction. For example, the recognition of interest expense or revenue (or wages, salaries, or rent) at the end of a period even though no explicit cash transaction is made at that time. Cash flow follows accounting recognition; contrast with *deferral.* See *anortization.*

accrual basis of accounting. The method of recognizing *revenues* as *goods* are sold (or delivered) and as *services* are rendered, independent of the time when cash is received. *Expenses* are recognized in the period when the related revenue is recognized independent of the time when cash is paid out. *SFAC No. 1* says "accrual accounting attempts to record the financial effects on an enterprise of transactions and other events and circumstances that have cash consequences for the enterprise in the periods in which those transactions, events, and circumstances occur rather than only in the periods in which cash is received or paid by the enterprise." Contrast with the *cash basis of accounting.* See *accrual* and *deferral.* The basis would more correctly be called "accrual/deferral" accounting.

accrued. Said of a *revenue* (*expense*) that has been earned (recognized) even though the related *receivable* (*payable*) is not yet due. This adjective should not be used as part of an account title. Thus, we prefer to use Interest Receivable (Payable) as the account title, rather than Accrued Interest Receivable (Payable). See *matching convention.* See *accrual.*

accrued depreciation. An incorrect term for *accumulated depreciation.* Acquiring an asset with cash, capitalizing it, and then amortizing its cost over periods of use is a process of *deferral* and allocation, not of *accrual.*

accrued payable. A *payable* usually resulting from the passage of time. For example, *salaries* and *interest* accrue as time passes. See *accrued.*

accrued receivable. A *receivable* usually resulting from the passage of time. See *accrued.*

accumulated depreciation. A preferred title for the *contra-asset* account that shows the sum of *depreciation* charges on an asset since it was acquired. Other titles used are *allowance* for *depreciation* (acceptable term) and *reserve* for *depreciation* (unacceptable term).

accurate presentation. The qualitative accounting objective suggesting that information reported in financial statements should correspond as precisely as possible with the economic effects underlying transactions and events. See *fair presentation* and *full disclosure.*

acid test ratio. *Quick ratio.*

acquisition cost. Of an *asset,* the net *invoice* price plus all *expenditures* to place and ready the asset for its intended use. The other expenditures might include legal fees, transportation charges, and installation costs.

ACRS. Accelerated Cost Recovery System. See *3-5-10 rule.*

AcSEC. *Accounting Standards Executive Committee of the AICPA.*

activity accounting. *Responsibility accounting.*

activity-based depreciation. *Production method of depreciation.*

actual cost (basis). *Acquisition* or *historical cost.* Also contrast with *standard* cost.

actuarial. Usually said of computations or analyses that involve both *compound interest* and probabilities, such as the computation of the *present value* of a life-contingent *annuity.* Sometimes the term is used if only one of the two is involved.

actuarial accrued liability. A 1981 report of the Joint Committee on Pension Terminology (of various actuarial societies) stated that the term *supplemental actuarial value* is no longer recommended and that this term be used instead. It will take a few years for this term to become standard in accounting. The Joint Committee defines this term as "the portion . . . of the actuarial present value of pension plan benefits . . . not provided for by future normal costs."

additional paid-in capital. An alternative acceptable title for the *capital contributed in excess of par* (*or state*) *value account.*

adequate disclosure. *Fair presentation* of *financial statements* requires *disclosure* of *material* items. This *auditing standard* does not, however, require publicizing all information detrimental to a company. For example, the company may be threatened with a lawsuit and disclosure might seem to require a *debit* to a *loss* account and a *credit* to an *estimated liability.* But the mere making of this entry might adversely affect the actual outcome of the suit. Such entries need not be made although impending suits should be disclosed.

adjunct account. An *account* that accumulates additions to another account. For example, Premium on Bonds Payable is adjunct to the liability Bonds Payable; the effective liability is the sum of the two account balances at a given date. Contrast with *contra account.*

adjusted acquisition (historical) cost. Cost adjusted to a *constant dollar amount* to reflect *general price level changes.* See also *book value.*

adjusted bank balance of cash. The *balance* shown on the statement from the bank plus or minus amounts, such as for unrecorded deposits or outstanding checks, to reconcile the bank's balance with the correct cash balance. See *adjusted book balance of cash.*

adjusted basis. The *basis* used to compute gain or loss on disposition of an *asset* for tax purposes. Also, see *book value.*

adjusted book balance of cash. The *balance* shown in the firm's account for cash in bank plus or minus amounts, such as for *notes* collected by the bank or bank service charges, to reconcile the account balance with the correct cash balance. See *adjusted book balance of cash.*

adjusted trial balance. *Trial balance* taken after *adjusting entries* but before *closing entries.* Contrast with *pre-* and *post-closing trial balances.* See *unadjusted trial balance* and *post-closing trial balance.* See also *work sheet.*

adjusting entry. An entry made at the end of an *accounting period* to record a *transaction* or other *accounting event,* which for some reason has not been recorded or has been improperly recorded during the accounting period. An entry to update the accounts. See *work sheet.*

adjustment. A change in an *account* produced by an *ad-*

justing entry. Sometimes the term is used to refer to the process of restating *financial statement* amounts to *constant dollars*.

administrative expense. An *expense* related to the enterprise as a whole as contrasted to expenses related to more specific functions such as manufacturing or selling.

admission of partner. Legally, when a new partner joins a *partnership*, the old partnership is dissolved and a new one comes into being. In practice, however, the old accounting records may be kept in use and the accounting entries reflect the manner in which the new partner joined the firm. If the new partner merely purchases the interest of another partner, the only accounting is to change the name for one capital account. If the new partner contributes *assets* and *liabilities* to the partnership, then the new assets must be recognized with debits and the liabilities and other source of capital, with credits. See *bonus method*.

ADR. See *asset depreciation range*.

advances from (by) customers. A preferred title for the *liability* account representing *receipts* of *cash* in advance of delivering the *goods* or rendering the *service* (that will cause *revenue* to be recognized). Sometimes called "deferred revenue" or "deferred income."

advances to affiliates. *Loans* by a parent company to a *subsidiary*. Frequently combined with "investment in subsidiary" as "investments and advances to subsidiary" and shown as a *noncurrent asset* on the parent's *balance sheet*. These advances are eliminated in *consolidated financial statements*.

advances to suppliers. A preferred term for *disbursements* of cash in advance of receiving *assets* or *services*.

adverse opinion. An *auditor's report* stating that the financial statements are not fair or are not in accord with *GAAP*.

affiliated company. Said of a company controlling or controlled by another company.

after closing. *Postclosing*; said of a *trial balance* at the end of the period.

after cost. Said of *expenditures* to be made subsequent to *revenue* recognition. For example, *expenditures* for *repairs* under warranty are after costs. Proper recognition of after costs involves a debit to expense at the time of the sale and a credit to an *estimated liability*. When the liability is discharged, the debit is to the estimated liability and the credit is to the assets consumed.

agency fund. An account for *assets* received by governmental units in the capacity of trustee or agent.

agent. One authorized to transact business, including executing contracts, for another.

aging accounts receivable. The process of classifying *accounts receivable* by the time elapsed since the claim came into existence for the purpose of estimating the amount of uncollectible accounts receivable as of a given date. See *sales contra, estimated uncollectibles* and *allowance for uncollectibles*.

aging schedule. A listing of *accounts receivable*, classified by age, used in *aging accounts receivable*.

AICPA. American Institute of Certified Public Accountants. The national organization that represents *CPA*s. See *AcSEC*. It oversees the writing and grading of the Uniform CPA Examination. Each state, however, sets its own requirements for becoming a CPA in that state. See *certified public accountant*.

all capital earnings rate. *Rate of return on assets*.

all financial resources. All *assets* less all *liabilities*. Sometimes the *statement of changes in financial position* explains the changes in all financial resources rather than only the changes in *working capital*.

all-inclusive (income) concept. Under this concept, no distinction is drawn between *operating* and *nonoperating revenues* and *expenses*; thus the only entries to retained earnings are for *net income* and *dividends*. Under this concept all income, *gains*, and *losses* are reported in the *income statement*; thus, events usually reported as *prior-period adjustments* and as *corrections of errors* are included in net income. This concept in its pure form is not the basis of *GAAP*, but *APB Opinions* Nos. 9 and 30 move very far in this direction. They do permit retained earnings entries for prior-period adjustments and correction of errors.

allocate. To spread a *cost* from one *account* to several accounts, to several products, or activities, or to several periods.

allocation of income taxes. See *deferred income tax*.

allowance. A balance sheet *contra account* generally used for *receivables* and depreciable assets. See *sales* (or *purchase*) *allowance* for another use of this term.

allowance for funds used during construction. One principle of public utility regulation and rate setting is that customers should pay the full costs of producing the services (e.g., electricity) that they use—nothing more and nothing less. Thus an electric utility is even more careful than other businesses to capitalize into an *asset account* the full costs, but no more, of producing a new electric power generating plant. One of the costs of building a new plant is the *interest* cost on money tied up during construction. If *funds* are explicitly borrowed by an ordinary business, the journal entry for interest of $1,000 is typically:

```
Interest Expense . . . . . . . . . . . . . .  1,000
    Interest Payable . . . . . . . . . . . .          1,000
Interest expense for the period.
```

If the firm is constructing a new plant, then another entry would be made capitalizing interest into the plant-under-construction account:

```
Construction Work in Progress . . . . . . . . . 750
    Interest Expense . . . . . . . . . . . . . . . .      750
Capitalize relevant portion of interest relating to
construction work in progress into the asset
account.
```

The cost of the *plant asset* is increased; when the plant is used, *depreciation* is charged; the interest will become an

702

expense through the depreciation process in the later periods of use, not currently as the interest is paid. Thus the full cost of the electricity generated during a given period is reported as expense in that period.

But suppose, as is common, that the electric utility does not explicitly borrow the funds, but uses some of its own funds, including funds raised from equity shares as well as from debt. Even though there is not explicit interest expense, there is the *opportunity cost* of the funds. Put another way, the cost of the plant under construction is not less in an economic sense just because the firm used its own cash, rather than borrowing. The public utility using its own funds, on which $750 of interest would be payable if the funds had been explicitly borrowed, will make the following entry:

```
Construction Work in Progress  . . . . . . . . 750
    Allowance for Funds Used
        During Construction . . . . . . . . . . . .     750
Recognition of interest, an opportunity cost, on
own funds used.
```

The allowance account is a form of *revenue*, to appear on the income statement, and will be closed to Retained Earnings, increasing it. On the *funds statement*, it is an income or revenue item not producing funds and so must be subtracted from net income in deriving *funds provided by operations*. *SFAS No. 34* specifically prohibits non-utility companies from capitalizing the opportunity cost (interest) on own funds used into plant under construction.

allowance for uncollectibles (accounts receivable). A *contra* to Accounts Receivable that shows the estimated amount of *accounts receivable* that will not be collected. When such an allowance is used, the actual *write-off* of specific accounts receivable (*debit* allowance, *credit* specific account) does not affect *revenue* or *expense* at the time of the write-off. The revenue reduction is recognized when the allowance is credited; the amount of the credit to the allowance may be based on a percentage of sales on account for a period of time or computed from *aging accounts receivable*. This contra account enables an estimate to be shown of the amount of receivables that will be collected without identifying specific uncollectible accounts. See *allowance method*.

allowance method. A method of attempting to *match* all *expenses* of a transaction with its associated *revenues*. Usually involves a debit to expense and a credit to an *estimated liability*, such as for estimated warranty expenditures, or a debit to a revenue (*contra*) account and a credit to an asset (*contra*) account, such as for uncollectible accounts. See *allowance for uncollectibles* for further explanation. When the allowance method is used for *sales discounts*, sales are recorded at *gross invoice* prices (not reduced by the amounts of discounts made available). An estimate of the amount of discounts to be taken is debited to a *revenue contra account* and *credited* to an allowance account, shown contra to *accounts receivable*.

American Accounting Association. AAA. An organization primarily for academic accountants, but open to all interested in accounting. It publishes *The Accounting Review*.

American Institute of Certified Public Accountants. See *AICPA*.

American Stock Exchange. AMEX. ASE. A public market where various corporate *securities* are traded.

AMEX. *American Stock Exchange*.

amortization. Strictly speaking, the process of liquidating or extinguishing ("bringing to death") a *debt* with a series of payments to the *creditor* (or to a *sinking fund*). From that usage has evolved a related use involving the accounting for the payments themselves: "amortization schedule" for a mortgage which is a table showing the allocation between *interest* and *principal*. The term has come to mean writing off ("liquidating") the cost of an asset. In this context it means the general process of *allocating acquisition cost* of an asset to either the periods of benefit as *expenses* or to *inventory* accounts as *product costs*. Called *depreciation* for *plant assets, depletion* for *wasting assets* (natural resources), and "amortization" for *intangibles. SFAC No. 3* refers to amortization as "the accounting process of reducing an amount by periodic payments or write-downs." The expressions "unamortized debt discount or premium" and "to amortize debt discount or premium" relate to *accruals*, not to *deferrals*. The expressions "amortization of long-term assets" and "to amortize long-term assets" refer to deferrals, not accruals.

analysis of changes in working capital accounts. The *statement of changes in financial position* explains the causes of the changes in *working capital* during a period. This part of the statement, which may appear in footnotes, shows the net changes in the specific working capital accounts that have been explained in the main section of the statement.

analysis of variances. See *variance analysis*.

annual report. A report for shareholders and other interested parties prepared once a year, includes a *balance sheet*, an *income statement*, a *statement of changes in financial position*, a reconciliation of changes in *owners' equity* accounts, a *summary of significant accounting principles*, other explanatory *notes*, the *auditor's report*, and, comments from management about the year's events. See *10-K* and *financial statements*.

annuitant. One who receives an *annuity*.

annuity. A series of payments, usually made at equally spaced time intervals.

annuity certain. An *annuity* payable for a definite number of periods. Contrast with *contingent annuity*.

annuity due. An *annuity* whose first payment is made at the start of period 1 (or at the end of period 0). Contrast with *annuity in arrears*.

annuity in advance. An *annuity due*.

annuity in arrears. An *ordinary annuity* whose first payment occurs at the end of the first period.

annuity method of depreciation. See *compound interest depreciation*.

antidilutive. Said of a *potentially dilutive security* that will increase *earnings per share* if it is *exercised* or *converted into*

703

common stock. In computing *primary* and *fully diluted earnings per share*, antidilutive securities may not be assumed to be exercised or converted and hence do not affect reported earnings per share in a given period.

APB. Accounting Principles Board of the *AICPA*. It set *accounting principles* from 1959 through 1973, issuing 31 *APB Opinions*. It was superseded by the *FASB*.

APB Opinion. The name given to pronouncements of the APB that make up much of *generally accepted accounting principles*; there are 31 APB Opinions, issued from 1962 through 1973.

APB Statement. The *APB* issued four Statements between 1962 and 1970. The Statements were approved by at least two-thirds of the Board, but they are recommendations, not requirements. For example, Statement No. 3 (1969) suggested the publication of *constant dollar financial statements* but did not require them.

APBs. An abbreviation used for *APB Opinions*.

application of funds. Any transaction that reduces *funds* (however "funds" is defined). A *use of funds*.

applied cost. A *cost* that has been *allocated* to a department, product, or activity; need not be based on actual costs incurred.

applied overhead. *Overhead costs* charged to departments, products or activities.

appraisal. The process of obtaining a valuation for an *asset* or *liability* that involves expert opinion rather than evaluation of explicit market transactions.

appraisal method of depreciation. The periodic *depreciation* charge is the difference between the beginning and end-of-period appraised value of the *asset* if that difference is positive. If negative, there is no charge. Not generally accepted.

appreciation. An increase in economic worth caused by rising market prices for an *asset*. Contrast with *accretion*.

appropriated retained earnings. See *retained earnings, appropriated*.

appropriation. In governmental accounting, an *expenditure* authorized for a specified amount, purpose, and time.

appropriation account. In governmental accounting, an account set up to record specific authorizations to spend; it is credited with appropriation amounts. *Expenditures* during the period and *encumbrances* outstanding at the end of the period are closed (debited) to this account at the end of the period.

ARB. Accounting Research Bulletin.

arbitrage. Strictly speaking, the simultaneous purchase in one market and sale in another of a *security* or commodity in hope of making a *profit* on price differences in the different markets. Often this term is loosely used when the item sold is somewhat different from the item purchased; for example, the sale of shares of *common stock* and the simultaneous purchase of a *convertible bond* that is convertible into identical common shares.

arm's length. Said of a transaction negotiated by unrelated parties, each acting in his or her own self interest; the basis for a *fair market value* determination.

arrears. Said of *cumulative preferred stock dividends* that have not been declared up to the current date. See *annuity in arrears* for another context.

ARS. *Accounting Research Study*.

articles of incorporation. Document filed with state authorities by persons forming a corporation. When the document is returned with a certificate of incorporation, it becomes the corporation's *charter*.

articulate. Said of the relationship between any operating statement (for example, *income statement* or *statement of changes in financial position*) and *comparative balance sheets*, where the operating statement explains (or reconciles) the change in some major balance sheet category (for example, *retained earnings* or *working capital*).

ASE. *American Stock Exchange*.

ASR. *Accounting Series Release*.

assess. To value property for the purpose of property taxation; the assessment is computed by the taxing authority. To levy a charge on the owner of property for improvements thereto, such as for sewers or sidewalks.

assessed valuation. A dollar amount for real estate or other property used by a government as a basis for levying taxes. The amount may or may not bear some relation to *market value*.

asset. *SFAC No. 3* defines assets as "probable future economic benefits obtained or controlled by a particular entity as a result of past transactions. An asset has three essential characteristics: (a) it embodies a probable future benefit that involves a capacity, singly or in combination with other assets, to contribute directly or indirectly to future net cash inflows, (b) a particular enterprise can obtain the benefit and control others' access to it, and (c) the transaction or other event giving rise to the enterprise's right to or control of the benefit has already occurred." A footnote points out that "probable" means that which can be reasonably expected or believed but is neither certain nor proved. May be *tangible* or *intangible*, *short-term* (current) or *long-term* (noncurrent).

asset depreciation range. ADR. The range of *depreciable lives* allowed by the *Internal Revenue Service* for a specific depreciable *asset*.

asset turnover. Net sales divided by average assets. See *ratio*.

assignment of accounts receivable. Transfer of the legal ownership of an *account receivable* through its sale. Contrast with *pledging* accounts receivable where the receivables serve as *collateral* for a *loan*.

at par. Said of a *bond* or *preferred stock* issued or selling at its *face amount*.

attachment. The laying claim to the *assets* of a borrower or debtor by a lender or creditor when the borrower has failed to pay debts on time.

704

attest. Rendering of an *opinion* by an auditor that the *financial statements* are fair. This procedure is called the "attest function" of the CPA. See *fair presentation*.

attribute measured. When making physical measurements, such as of a person, one needs to decide the units with which to measure, such as inches or centimeters or pounds or grams. One chooses the attribute—height or weight—independently of the measuring unit—English or metric. In conventional accounting the attribute measured is *historical cost* and the measuring unit is *nominal dollars*. Some theorists argue that accounting is more useful when the attribute measured is *current cost*. Others argue that accounting is more useful when the measuring unit is *constant dollars*. Some, including us, think both changes from conventional accounting should be made. The attribute historhical cost can be measured in nominal dollars or in constant dollars. The attribute current cost can also be measured in nominal dollars or constant dollars. Choosing between two attributes and two measuring units implies four different accounting systems. Each of these four has its uses.

audit. Systematic inspection of accounting records involving analyses, tests, and *confirmations*. See *internal audit*.

audit committee. A committee of the board of directors of a *corporation* usually consisting of outside directors who nominate the independent auditors and discuss the auditors' work with them. If the auditors believe certain matters should be brought to the attention of shareholders, the auditors first bring these matters to the attention of the audit committee.

Audit Guides. See *Industry Audit Guides*.

audit program. The procedures followed by the *auditor* in carrying out the *audit*.

audit trail. A reference accompanying an *entry*, or *posting*, to an underlying source record or document. A good audit trail is essential for efficiently checking the accuracy of accounting entries. See *cross-reference*.

auditing standards. A set of ten standards promulgated by the *AICPA*, including three general standards, three standards of field work, and four standards of reporting. According to the AICPA, these standards "deal with the measures of the quality of the performance and the objectives to be attained," rather than with specific auditing procedures.

Auditing Standards Advisory Council. An *AICPA* committee.

Auditing Standards Board. Operating committee of the *AICPA* promulgating auditing rules.

auditor. One who checks the accuracy, fairness, and general acceptability of accounting records and statements and then *attests* to them.

auditor's opinion. *Auditor's report*.

auditor's report. The auditor's statement of the work done and an opinion of the *financial statements*. Opinions are usually unqualified ("clean"), but may be *qualified*, or the auditor may disclaim an opinion in the report. Often called the "accountant's report." See *adverse opinion*.

AudSEC. The former Auditing Standards Executive Committee of the *AICPA*, now functioning as the *Auditing Standards Board*.

authorized capital stock. The number of *shares* of stock that can be issued by a corporation; specified by the *articles of incorporation*.

average. The arithmetic mean of a set of numbers; obtained by summing the items and dividing by the number of items.

average collection period of receivables. See *ratio*.

average-cost flow assumption. An *inventory flow assumption* where the cost of units is the *weighted average* cost of the *beginning inventory* and purchases. See *inventory equation*.

average tax rate. The rate found by dividing *income tax expense* by *net income* before taxes. Contrast with *marginal tax rate, statutory tax rate*.

avoidable cost. An *incremental* or *variable cost*. See *programmed cost*.

B

bad debt. An *uncollectible account receivable*; see *sales contra, estimated uncollectibles*.

bad debt expense. See *sales contra, estimated uncollectibles*.

bad debt recovery. Collection, perhaps partial, of a specific account receivable previously written off as uncollectible. If the *allowance method* is used, the *credit* is usually to the *allowance* account. If the direct write-off method is used, the credit is to a *revenue account*.

bailout period. In a *capital budgeting* context, the total time that must elapse before net accumulated cash inflows from a project including potential *salvage value* of assets at various times equal or exceed the accumulated cash outflows. Contrast with *payback period*, which assumes completion of the project and uses terminal salvage value. Bailout is superior to payback because bailout takes into account, at least to some degree, the *present value* of the cash flows after the termination date being considered. The potential salvage value at any time includes some estimate of the flows that can occur after that time.

balance. The sum of *debit* entries minus the sum of *credit* entries in an *account*. If positive, the difference is called a debit balance; if negative, a credit balance.

balance sheet. Statement of financial position that shows *total assets = total liabilities + owners' equity*.

balance sheet account. An account that can appear on a balance sheet. A *permanent account*; contrast with *temporary account*.

bank balance. The amount of the balance in a checking account shown on the *bank statement*. Compare with *adjusted bank balance* and see *bank reconciliation schedule*.

bank prime rate. See *prime rate*.

bank reconciliation schedule. A schedule that shows

how the difference between the book balance of the cash in bank account and the bank's statement can be explained. Takes into account the amount of such items as checks issued that have not cleared or deposits that have not been recorded by the bank as well as errors made by the bank or the firm.

bank statement. A statement sent by the bank to a checking account customer showing deposits, checks cleared, and service charges for a period, usually one month.

bankrupt. Said of a company whose *liabilities* exceed its *assets* where a legal petition has been filed and accepted under the bankruptcy law. A bankrupt firm is usually, but need not be, *insolvent*.

base stock method. A method of inventory valuation that assumes that there is a minimum normal or base stock of goods that must be kept on hand at all times for effective continuity of operations. This base quantity is valued at *acquisition cost* of the inventory on hand in the earliest period when inventory was on hand. The method is not allowable for income tax purposes and is no longer used, but is generally considered to be the forerunner of the *LIFO* method.

basis. *Acquisition cost*, or some substitute therefor, of an asset used in computing gain or loss on disposition or retirement. *Attribute measured*.

basket purchase. Purchase of a group of assets for a single price; *costs* must be assigned to each of the assets so that the individual items can be recorded in the *accounts*.

bear. One who believes that security prices will fall. A "bear market" refers to a time when stock prices are generally declining. Contrast with *bull*.

bearer bond. See *registered bond* for contrast and definition.

beginning inventory. Valuation of *inventory* on hand at the beginning of the accounting period.

betterment. An *improvement*, usually *capitalized*.

bid. An offer to purchase, or the amount of the offer.

big bath. A *write-off* of a substantial amount of costs previously treated as *assets*. Usually caused when a corporation drops a line of business that required a large investment but that proved to be unprofitable. Sometimes used to describe a situation where a corporation takes a large write-off in one period in order to free later periods of gradual write-offs of those amounts. In this sense it frequently occurs when there is a change in top management.

Big Eight. The eight largest U.S. *public accounting (CPA)* partnerships; in alphabetical order: Arthur Andersen & Co.; Coopers & Lybrand; Deloitte Haskins & Sells; Ernst & Whinney; Peat, Marwick, Mitchell & Co.; Price Waterhouse & Co.; Touche Ross & Co.; and Arthur Young & Company. A ninth firm, Klynveld Main Goerdeler, is actually larger than many of these when world-wide operations are measured.

Big Nine. See *Big Eight*.

bill. An *invoice* of charges and *terms of sale* for *goods and services*. Also, a piece of currency.

bill of materials. A specification of the quantities of *direct materials* expected to be used to produce a given job or quantity of output.

board of directors. The governing body of a corporation elected by the shareholders.

bond. A certificate to show evidence of debt. The *par value* is the *principal* or face amount of the bond payable at maturity. The *coupon rate* is the amount of interest payable in one year divided by the principal amount. Coupon bonds have attached to them coupons that can be redeemed at stated dates for interest payments. Normally, bonds carry semiannual coupons.

bond conversion. The act of exchanging *convertible bonds* for *preferred* or *common stock*.

bond discount. From the standpoint of the issuer of a *bond* at the issue date, the excess of the *par value* of a bond over its initial sales price; at later dates the excess of par over the sum of (initial issue price plus the portion of discount already amortized). From the standpoint of a bondholder, the difference between par value and selling price when the bond sells below par.

bond indenture. The contract between an issuer of *bonds* and the bondholders.

bond premium. Exactly parallel to *bond discount* except that the issue price (or current selling price) is higher than *par value*.

bond ratings. Ratings of corporate and *municipal bond* issues by Moody's Investors Service and by Standard & Poor's Corporation, based on the issuer's existing *debt* level, its previous record of payment, the *coupon rate* on the bonds, and the safety of the *assets* or *revenues* that are committed to paying off *principal* and *interest*. Moody's top rating is Aaa; Standard & Poor's is AAA.

bond redemption. Retirement of *bonds*.

bond refunding. To incur *debt*, usually through the issue of new *bonds*, intending to use the proceeds to retire an *outstanding* bond issue.

bond sinking fund. See *sinking fund*.

bond table. A table showing the current price of a *bond* as a function of the *coupon rate*, years to *maturity*, and effective *yield to maturity* (or *effective rate*).

bonus. Premium over normal *wage* or *salary*, paid usually for meritorious performance.

bonus method. When a new partner is admitted to a *partnership* and the new partner is to be credited with *capital* in excess proportion to the amount of *tangible* assets he or she contributes, two methods may be used to recognize this excess, say $10,000. First, $10,000 may be transferred from the old partners to the new one. This is the bonus method. Second, goodwill in the amount of $10,000 may be recognized as an asset with the credit to the new partner's capital account. This is the *goodwill method*. (Notice that the new partner's percentage of total ownership is not the same under the two methods.) If the new partner is to be credited with capital in smaller proportion than the amount of con-

706

tribution, then there will be bonus or goodwill for the old partners.

book. As a verb, to record a transaction. As a noun, usually plural, the *journals* and *ledgers*. As an adjective, see *book value*.

book inventory. An *inventory* amount that results, not from physical count, but from the amount of beginning inventory plus *invoice* amounts of net purchases less invoice amounts of *requisitions* or withdrawals; implies a *perpetual* method.

book of original entry. A *journal*.

book value. The amount shown in the books or in the *accounts* for an *asset, liability*, or *owners' equity* item. Generally used to refer to the net amount of an *asset* or group of assets shown in the account which records the asset and reductions, such as for *amortization*, in its cost. Of a firm, the excess of total assets over total liabilities. *Net assets*.

book value per share of common stock. Common *shareholders' equity* divided by the number of shares of *common stock outstanding*. See *ratio*.

bookkeeping. The process of analyzing and recording transactions in the accounting records.

boot. The additional money paid or received along with a used item in a trade-in or exchange transaction for another item. See *trade-in transaction*.

borrower. See *loan*.

branch. A sales office or other unit of an enterprise physically separated from the home office of the enterprise but not organized as a legally separate *subsidiary*. The term is rarely used to refer to manufacturing units.

branch accounting. An accounting procedure that enables the financial position and operations of each *branch* to be reported separately but later combined for published statements.

breakeven analysis. See *breakeven chart*.

breakeven chart. A graph presenting the relationship of changes in volume to the amount of *profit*, or *income*. On such a graph, total *revenue* and total *costs* for each volume level are indicated and profit or loss at any volume can be read directly from the chart.

breakeven point. The volume of sales required so that total *revenues* and total *costs* are equal. May be expressed in units (*fixed costs/contribution per unit*) or in sales dollars [selling price per unit $\times$ (fixed costs/contribution per unit)].

budget. A financial plan that is used to estimate the results of future operations. Frequently used to help control future operations.

budgetary accounts. In governmental accounting, the accounts that reflect estimated operations and financial condition, as affected by estimated *revenues, appropriations*, and *encumbrances*. In contrast to *proprietary accounts* that record the transactions.

budgetary control. Management of governmental (nongovernmental) unit in accordance with an official (ap-

proved) *budget* in order to keep total expenditures within authorized (planned) limits.

budgeted cost. See *standard cost* for definition and contrast.

budgeted statements. *Pro forma* statements prepared before the event or period occurs.

bull. One who believes that security prices will rise. A "bull market" refers to a time when stock prices are generally rising. Contrast with *bear*.

burden. See *overhead costs*.

business combination. As defined in APB *Opinion* No. 16, the bringing together into a single accounting *entity* of two or more incorporated or unincorporated businesses. The *merger* will be accounted for either with the *purchase method* or the *pooling-of-interests method*. See *conglomerate*.

business entity. *Entity. Accounting entity*.

bylaws. The rules adopted by the shareholders of a corporation that specify the general methods for carrying out the functions of the corporation.

byproduct. A *joint product* whose sales value is so small relative to the sales value of the other joint product(s) that it does not receive normal accounting treatment. The costs assigned to byproducts reduce the costs of the main product(s). Byproducts are allocated a share of joint costs such that the expected gain or loss upon their sale is zero. Thus, byproducts are shown in the *accounts* at *net realizable value*.

C

CA. *Chartered accountant*.

call premium. See *callable bond*.

call price. See *callable bond*.

callable bond. A *bond* for which the issuer reserves the right to pay a specific amount, the call price, to retire the obligation before *maturity* date. If the issuer agrees to pay more than the *face amount* of the bond when called the excess of the payment over the face amount is the "call premium."

Canadian Institute of Chartered Accountants. The national organization that represents *chartered accountants* in Canada.

cancelable lease. See *lease*.

capacity. Stated in units of product, the amount that can be produced per unit of time. Stated in units of input, such as *direct labor* hours, the amount of input that can be used in production per unit of time. This measure of output or input is used in allocating *fixed costs* if the amounts producible are normal, rather than maximum, amounts.

capacity costs. A *fixed cost* incurred to provide a firm with the capacity to produce or to sell. Consists of *standby costs* and *enabling costs*. Contrast with *programmed costs*.

capacity variance. Standard fixed *overhead* rate per unit of normal *capacity* (or base activity) times (units of base activity budgeted or planned for a period minus actual units of base activity worked or assigned to product during the period). Often called a "volume variance."

capital. *Owners' equity* in a business. Often used, equally correctly, to mean the total assets of a business. Sometimes used to mean *capital assets*.

capital asset. Properly used, a designation for income tax purposes that describes property held by a taxpayer, except *cash*, inventoriable *assets*, goods held primarily for sale, most depreciable property, *real estate, receivables*, certain *intangibles*, and a few other items. Sometimes this term is imprecisely used to describe *plant* and *equipment*, which are clearly not capital assets under the income tax definition. Often the term is used to refer to an *investment* in *securities*.

capital budget. Plan of proposed outlays for acquiring long-term *assets* and the means of *financing* the acquisition.

capital budgeting. The process of choosing *investment* projects for an enterprise by considering the *present value* of cash flows and deciding how to raise the funds required by the investment.

capital consumption allowance. The term used for *depreciation expense* in national income accounting and the reporting of funds in the economy.

capital contributed in excess of par (or stated) value. A preferred title for the account that shows the amount received by the issuer for *capital stock* in excess of *par (or stated)* value.

capital expenditure (outlay). An *expenditure* to acquire long-term *assets*.

capital gain. The excess of proceeds over *cost*, or other *basis*, from the sale of a *capital asset* as defined by the Internal Revenue Code. If the capital asset has been held for a sufficiently long time before sale, then the tax on the gain is computed at a rate lower than is used for other gains and ordinary income.

capital lease. A *lease* treated by the *lessee* as both the borrowing of funds and the acquisition of an *asset* to be *amortized*. Both the *liability* and the asset are recognized on the balance sheet. Expenses consist of *interest* on the *debt* and *amortization* of the asset. The *lessor* treats the lease as the sale of the asset in return for a series of future cash receipts. Contrast with *operating lease*.

capital loss. A negative capital gain; see *capital gain*.

capital rationing. In a *capital budgeting* context, the imposing of constraints on the amounts of total capital expenditures in each period.

capital stock. The ownership shares of a corporation. Consists of all classes of *common* and *preferred stock*.

capital structure. The composition of a corporation's equities; the relative proportions of *short-term debt, long-term debt*, and *owners' equity*.

capital surplus. An inferior term for *capital contributed in excess of par (or stated) value*.

capitalization of a corporation. A term used by investment analysts to indicate *shareholders' equity* plus *bonds outstanding*.

capitalization of earnings. The process of estimating the economic worth of a firm by computing the *net present value* of the predicted *net income* (not *cash flows*) of the firm for the future.

capitalization rate. An *interest rate* used to convert a series of payments or receipts or earnings into a single *present value*.

capitalize. To record an *expenditure* that may benefit a future period as an *asset* rather than to treat the expenditure as an *expense* of the period of its occurrence. Whether or not expenditures for advertising or for research and development should be capitalized is controversial, but *SFAS No. 2* requires expensing of *R&D* costs. We believe expenditures should be capitalized if they lead to future benefits and thus meet the criterion to be an asset.

carryback, carryforward, carryover. The use of losses or tax credits in one period to reduce income taxes payable in other periods. There are three common kinds of carrybacks: for net operating losses, for *capital losses*, and for the *investment credit*. The first two are applied against taxable income and the third against the actual tax. In general, carrybacks are for three years with the earliest year first. Operating losses and the investment credit can be carried forward for seven years. Corporate capital loss carryforwards are for five years. The capital loss for individuals can be carried forward indefinitely.

carrying cost. Costs (such as property taxes and insurance) of holding, or storing, *inventory* from the time of purchase until the time of sale or use.

carrying value (amount). *Book value*.

CASB. Cost Accounting Standards Board. A board of five members authorized by the U.S. Congress to "promulgate cost-accounting standards designed to achieve uniformity and consistency in the cost-accounting principles followed by defense contractors and subcontractors under federal contracts." The *principles* promulgated by the CASB are likely to have considerable weight in practice where the *FASB* has not established a standard. Although the Congress allowed the CASB to go out of existence in 1980, its standards have the same force as before.

cash. Currency and coins, negotiable checks, and balances in bank accounts.

cash basis of accounting. In contrast to the *accrual basis of accounting*, a system of accounting in which *revenues* are recognized when *cash* is received and *expenses* are recognized as *disbursements* are made. No attempt is made to *match revenues* and *expenses* in determining *income*. See *modified cash basis*.

cash budget. A schedule of expected cash *receipts* and *disbursements*.

cash collection basis. The *installment method* for recognizing *revenue*. Not to be confused with the *cash basis of accounting*.

cash cycle. The period of time that elapses during which *cash* is converted into *inventories*, inventories are converted

708

into *accounts receivable*, and receivables are converted back into cash. *Earnings cycle*.

cash disbursements journal. A specialized *journal* used to record *expenditures* by *cash* and by *check*. If a *check register* is also used, a cash disbursements journal records only expenditures of currency and coins.

cash discount. A reduction in sales or purchase price allowed for prompt payment.

cash dividend. See *dividend*.

cash equivalent value. A term used to describe the amount for which an *asset* could be sold. *Market value. Fair market price (value)*.

cash flow. Cash *receipts* minus *disbursements* from a given *asset*, or group of assets, for a given period.

cash flow statement. A statement similar to the typical *statement of changes in financial position* where the flows of cash, rather than of *working capital*, are explained.

cash receipts journal. A specialized *journal* used to record all *receipts* of *cash*.

cash (surrender) value of life insurance. An amount equal, not to the face value of the policy to be paid in event of death, but to the amount that could be realized if the policy were immediately canceled and traded with the insurance company for cash. If a firm owns a life insurance policy, the policy is reported as an asset at an amount equal to this value.

cash yield. See *yield*.

cashier's check. A bank's own *check* drawn on itself and signed by the cashier or other authorized official. It is a direct obligation of the bank. Compare with *certified check*.

CCA. *Current cost accounting; current-value accounting*.

central corporate expenses. General *overhead expenses* incurred in running the corporate headquarters and related supporting activities of a corporation. These expenses are treated as *period expenses*. Contrast with *manufacturing overhead*. A major problem in *line-of-business reporting* is the treatment of these expenses.

certificate. The document that is the physical embodiment of a *bond* or a *share of stock*. A term sometimes used for the *auditor's report*.

certificate of deposit. Federal law constrains the *rate of interest* that banks can pay. Under current law banks are allowed to pay a rate higher than the one allowed on a *time deposit* if the depositor promises to leave funds on deposit for several months or more. When the bank receives such funds, it issues a certificate of deposit. The depositor can withdraw the funds before maturity if a penalty is paid.

certified check. The *check* of a depositor drawn on a bank on the face of which the bank has inserted the words "accepted" or "certified" with the date and signature of a bank official. The check then becomes an obligation of the bank. Compare with *cashier's check*.

certified financial statement. A financial statement attested to by an independent *auditor* who is a *CPA*.

certified internal auditor. See *CIA*.

certified public accountant. CPA. An accountant who has satisfied the statutory and administrative requirements of his or her jurisdiction to be registered or licensed as a public accountant. In addition to passing the Uniform CPA Examination administered by the *AICPA*, the CPA must meet certain educational, experience, and moral requirements that differ from jurisdiction to jurisdiction. The jurisdictions are the 50 states, the District of Columbia, Guam, Puerto Rico, and the Virgin Islands.

chain discount. A series of *discount* percentages; for example, if a chain discount of 10 and 5 percent is quoted, then the actual, or *invoice*, price is the nominal, or list, price times .90 times .95, or 85.5% of invoice price.

change fund. Coins and currency issued to cashiers, delivery drivers, and so on.

changes, accounting. See *accounting changes*.

changes in financial position. See *statement of changes in financial position*.

charge. As a noun, a *debit* to an account; as a verb, to debit.

charge off. To treat as a *loss* or *expense* an amount originally recorded as an *asset*; use of this term implies that the charge is not in accord with original expectations.

chart of accounts. A list of names and numbers of *accounts* systematically organized.

charter. Document issued by a state government authorizing the creation of a corporation.

chartered accountant. CA. The title used in Australia, Canada, and the United Kingdom for an accountant who has satisfied the requirements of the institute of his or her jurisdiction to be qualified to serve as a *public accountant*. In Canada, each provincial institute or order has the right to administer the examination and set the standards of performance and ethics for Chartered Accountants in its province. For a number of years, however, the provincial organizations have pooled their rights to qualify new members through the Inter-provincial Education Committee and the result is that there are nationally-set and graded examinations given in English and French. The pass/fail grade awarded by the Board of Examiners (a subcommittee of the Inter-provincial Education Committee) is rarely deviated from.

check. You know what a check is. The Federal Reserve Board defines a check as "a *draft* or order upon a bank or banking house purporting to be drawn upon a deposit of funds for the payment at all events of a certain sum of money to a certain person therein named or to him or his order or to bearer and payable instantly on demand." It must contain the phrase "pay to the order of." The amount shown on the check's face must be clearly readable and it must have the signature of the drawer. Checks need not be dated, although they usually are. The *balance* in the *cash account* is usually reduced when a check is issued, not later when it clears the bank and reduces cash in bank.

check register. A *journal* to record *checks* issued.

CIA. Certified Internal Auditor. One who has satisfied certain requirements of the *Institute of Internal Auditors* including experience, ethics, education, and passing examinations.

CICA. *Canadian Institute of Chartered Accountants.*

CIF. Cost, insurance, and freight; a term used in contracts along with the name of a given port to indicate that the quoted price includes insurance, handling, and freight charges up to delivery by the seller at the given port.

circulating capital. *Working capital.*

clean opinion. See *auditor's report.*

clean surplus concept. The notion that the only entries to the *retained earnings* account are to record *net income* and dividends. See *comprehensive income*. Contrast with *current operating performance concept*. This concept, with minor exceptions, is now controlling in *GAAP*. (See *APB Opinions* Nos. 9 and 30.)

clearing account. An account containing amounts to be transferred to another account(s) before the end of the *accounting period*. Examples are the *income summary* account (whose balance is transferred to retained earnings) and the purchases account (whose balance is transferred to *inventory* or to *cost of goods sold*).

close. As a verb, to transfer the *balance* of a *temporary* or *contra* or *adjunct* account to the main account to which it relates; for example, to transfer *revenue* and *expense* accounts directly, or through the *income summary* account, to an *owner's equity* account, or to transfer *purchase discounts* to purchases.

closed account. An account with equal debits and credits, usually as a result of a closing entry. See *ruling an account.*

closing entries. The entries that accomplish the transfer of balances in temporary accounts to the related balance sheet accounts. See *work sheet.*

closing inventory. *Ending inventory.*

COLA. Cost of living adjustment. See *indexation.*

CMA. Certificate in Management Accounting. Awarded by the Institute of Management Accounting of the *National Association of Accountants* to those who pass a set of examinations and meet certain experience and continuing education requirements.

CoCoA. *Continuously contemporary accounting.*

coding of accounts. The numbering of *accounts*, as for a *chart of accounts*, which is particularly necessary for computerized accounting.

coinsurance. Insurance policies that protect against hazards such as fire or water damage often specify that the owner of the property may not collect the full amount of insurance for a loss unless the insurance policy covers at least some specified "coinsurance" percentage, usually about 80 percent, of the *replacement cost* of the property.

Coinsurance clauses induce the owner to carry full, or nearly-full, coverage.

collateral. Assets pledged by a *borrower* that will be given up if the *loan* is not paid.

collectible. Capable of being converted into cash; now, if due; later, otherwise.

combination. See *business combination.*

commercial paper. *Short-term notes* issued by corporate borrowers.

commission. Remuneration, usually expressed as a percentage, to employees based upon an activity rate, such as sales.

Committee on Accounting Procedure. CAP. Predecessor of the *APB*. The *AICPA's* principles-promulgating body from 1939 through 1959. Its 51 pronouncements are called *Accounting Research Bulletins.*

common cost. *Cost* resulting from use of *raw materials*, a facility (for example, plant or machines), or a service (for example, fire insurance) that benefits several products or departments and must be allocated to those products or departments. Common costs result when multiple products are produced together although they could be produced separately; joint costs occur when multiple products are of necessity produced together. Many writers use common costs and *joint costs* synonymously. See *joint costs, indirect costs, and overhead*. See *sterilized allocation.*

common dollar accounting. *Constant dollar accounting.*

common monetary measuring unit. For U.S. corporations, the dollar. See also *stable monetary unit assumption* and *constant dollar accounting.*

common shares. *Shares* representing the class of owners who have residual claims on the assets and earnings of a corporation after all debt and preferred shareholders' claims have been met.

common-size statement. A *percentage statement* usually based on total *assets* or *net sales* or *revenues.*

common stock equivalent. A *security* whose primary value arises from its ability to be exchanged for *common shares*; includes *stock options, warrants*, and also *convertible bonds* or *convertible preferred stock* whose cash *yield* for any year within five years of issue is less than two-thirds the *prime rate* at the time of issue.

company-wide control. See *control system.*

comparative (financial) statements. Financial statements showing information for the same company for different times, usually two successive years. Nearly all published financial statements are in this form. Contrast with *historical summary.*

compensating balance. When a bank lends funds to a customer, it often requires that the customer keep on deposit in his or her checking account an amount equal to some percentage, say 20 percent, of the loan. The amount required to be left on deposit is the compensating balance. Such amounts effectively increase the *interest rate*. The

710

amounts of such balances must be disclosed in *notes* to the *financial statements*.

completed contract method. Recognizing *revenues* and *expenses* for a job or order only when it is finished, except that when a loss on the contract is expected, revenues and expenses are recognized in the period when the loss is first forecast. This term is generally used only for long-term contracts. It is otherwise equivalent to the *sales basis* of *revenue recognition*.

completed sales basis. See *sales basis of revenue recognition*.

composite depreciation. *Group depreciation* of dissimilar items.

composite life method. *Group depreciation*, which see, for items of unlike kind. The term may be used when a single item, such as a crane, which consists of separate units with differing service lives, such as the chassis, the motor, the lifting mechanism, and so on, is depreciated as a whole rather than treating each of the components separately.

compound entry. A *journal entry* with more than one *debit* or more than one *credit*, or both. See *trade-in transaction* for an example.

compound interest. *Interest* calculated on *principal* plus previously undistributed interest.

compound interest depreciation. A method designed to hold the *rate of return* on an asset constant. First find the *internal rate of return* on the cash inflows and outflows of the asset. The periodic depreciation charge is the cash flow for the period less the internal rate of return multiplied by the asset's book value at the beginning of the period. When the cash flows from the asset are constant over time, the method is sometimes called the "annuity method" of depreciation.

compounding period. The time period for which *interest* is calculated. At the end of the period, the interest may be paid to the lender or added (that is, converted) to principal for the next interest-earning period, which is usually a year or some portion of a year.

comprehensive budget. *Master budget*.

comprehensive income. Defined in *SFAS No. 3* as "the change in equity (net assets) of an entity during a period from transactions and other events and circumstances from nonowner sources. It includes all changes in equity during a period except those resulting from investments by owners and distributions to owners." In this definition, "equity" means *owners' equity*.

comptroller. Same meaning and pronunciation as *controller*.

conceptual framework. A coherent system of interrelated objectives and fundamentals, promulgated by the *FASB* primarily through its *SFAC* publications, expected to lead to consistent standards for *financial accounting* and reporting.

confirmation. A formal memorandum delivered by the customers or suppliers of a company to its independent *auditor* verifying the amounts shown as receivable or payable. The confirmation document is originally sent by the

auditor to the customer. If the auditor asks that the document be returned whether the *balance* is correct or incorrect, then it is called a "positive confirmation." If the auditor asks that the document be returned only if there is an error, it is called a "negative confirmation."

conglomerate. *Holding company*. This term is used when the owned companies are in dissimilar lines of business.

conservatism. A *reporting objective* that calls for anticipation of all *losses* and *expenses* but defers recognition of *gains* or *profits* until they are *realized* in *arm's length* transactions. In the absence of certainty, events are to be reported in a way that tends to minimize cumulative income.

consignee. See *on consignment*.

consignment. See *on consignment*.

consignor. See *on consignment*.

consistency. Treatment of like *transactions* in the same way in consecutive periods so that financial statements will be more comparable than otherwise. The reporting policy implying that procedures, once adopted, should be followed from period to period by a reporting *entity*. See *accounting changes* for the treatment of inconsistencies.

consol. A *bond* that never matures; a *perpetuity* in the form of a bond. Originally issued by Great Britain after the Napoleonic wars to consolidate debt issues of that period. The term arose as an abbreviation for "consolidated annuities."

consolidated financial statements. Statements issued by legally separate companies that show financial position and income as they would appear if the companies were one economic *entity*.

constant dollar. A hypothetical unit of *general purchasing power*, denoted "C$" by the *FASB*.

constant dollar accounting. Accounting where items are measured in *constant dollars*. See *historical-cost/constant-dollar accounting* and *current-cost/constant-dollar accounting*.

constant dollar date. The time at which the *general purchasing power* of one *constant dollar* is exactly equal to the *general purchasing power* of one *nominal dollar*; that is, the date when C$1 = $1. When the constant dollar date is mid-period, then the nominal amounts of *revenues* and *expenses* spread evenly throughout the period are equal to their constant dollar amounts, but end-of-period *balance sheet* amounts measured in constant mid-period dollars differ from their nominal dollar amounts. When the constant dollar date is at the end of the period, then the constant dollar and nominal dollar amounts on a balance sheet for that date are identical.

constructive receipt. An item is included in taxable income when the taxpayer can control funds whether or not cash has been received. For example, *interest* added to *principal* in a savings account is deemed by the *IRS* to be constructively received.

Consumer Price Index. CPI. A *price index* computed and issued monthly by the Bureau of Labor Statistics of the U.S.

711

Department of Labor. The index attempts to track the price level of a group of goods and services purchased by the average consumer. The *FASB* requires use of the CPI in *constant dollar accounting*. Contrast with *GNP Implicit Price Deflator*.

contingency. A potential *liability*; if a specified event were to occur, such as losing a lawsuit, a liability would be recognized. The contingency is merely disclosed in notes, rather than shown in the balance sheet. *SFAS No. 5* requires treatment as a contingency until the outcome is "probable" and the amount of payment can be reasonably estimated, perhaps within a range. When the outcome becomes probable (the future event is "likely" to occur) and the amount can be reasonably estimated (using the lower end of a range if only a range can be estimated), then the liability is recognized in the accounts, rather than being disclosed in the notes. A *material* contingency may lead to a qualified, *"subject to,"* auditor's opinion. *Gain* contingencies are not recorded in the accounts, but are merely disclosed in notes.

contingent annuity. An *annuity* whose number of payments depends upon the outcome of an event whose timing is uncertain at the time the annuity is set up; for example, an annuity payable for the life of the *annuitant*. Contrast with *annuity certain*.

contingent issue (securities). Securities issuable to specific individuals upon the occurrence of some event, such as the firm's attaining a specified level of earnings.

continuing appropriation. A governmental *appropriation* automatically renewed without further legislative action until it is altered or revoked or expended.

continuing operations. See *income from continuing operations*.

continuity of operations. The assumption in accounting that the business *entity* will continue to operate long enough for current plans to be carried out. The *going-concern assumption*.

continuous compounding. *Compound interest* where the *compounding period* is every instant of time. See *e* for the computation of the equivalent annual or periodic rate.

continuous inventory method. The *perpetual inventory* method.

Continuously Contemporary Accounting. CoCoA. A name coined by the Australian theorist, Raymond J. Chambers, to indicate a combination of *current value accounting* where amounts are measured in *constant dollars* and based on exit values.

contra account. An *account*, such as *accumulated depreciation*, that accumulates subtractions from another account, such as machinery. Contrast with *adjunct account*.

contributed capital. The sum of the balances in *capital stock* accounts plus *capital contributed in excess of par (or stated) value* accounts. Contrast with *donated capital*.

contributed surplus. An inferior term for *capital contributed in excess of par value*.

contribution margin. *Revenue* from *sales* less all variable *expenses*. See *gross margin*.

contribution per unit. Selling price less *variable costs* per unit.

contributory. Said of a *pension plan* where employees, as well as employers, make payments to a pension *fund*. Note that the provisions for *vesting* are applicable only to the employer's payments. Whatever the degree of vesting of the employer's payments, the employee typically gets back all of his or her payments, with interest, in case of death, or other cessation of employment, before retirement.

control (controlling) account. A summary *account* with totals equal to those of entries and balances that appear in individual accounts in a *subsidiary ledger*. Accounts Receivable is a control account backed up with an account for each customer. The balance in a control account should not be changed unless a corresponding change is made in the subsidiary accounts.

control system. A device for ensuring that actions are carried out according to plan or for safeguarding *assets*. A system for ensuring that actions are carried out according to plan can be designed for a single function within the firm, called "operational control," for autonomous segments within the firm that generally have responsibility for both revenues and costs, called "divisional control," or for activities of the firm as a whole, called "company-wide control." Systems designed for safeguarding *assets* are called "internal control" systems.

controllable cost. A *cost* whose amount can be influenced by the way in which operations are carried out, such as advertising costs. These costs can be *fixed* or *variable*. See *programmed costs* and *managed costs*.

controlled company. A company, a majority of whose voting stock is held by an individual or corporation. Effective control can sometimes be exercised when less than 50 percent of the stock is owned.

controller. The title often used for the chief accountant of an organization. Often spelled *comptroller*.

conversion. The act of exchanging a convertible security for another security.

conversion cost. *Direct labor* costs plus factory *overhead* costs incurred in producing a product. That is, the cost to convert raw materials to finished products. *Manufacturing cost*.

conversion period. *Compounding period*. Period during which a *convertible bond* or *convertible preferred stock* can be converted into *common stock*.

convertible bond. A *bond* that may be converted into a specified number of shares of *capital stock* during the *conversion period*.

convertible preferred stock. *Preferred stock* that may be converted into a specified number of shares of *common stock*.

co-product. A product sharing production facilities with another product. For example, if an apparel manufacturer produces shirts and jeans on the same line, these are co-products. Co-products are distinguished from *joint products* and *by-products* which, by their very nature must be produced together, such as the various grades of wood produced in a lumber factory.

copyright. Exclusive right granted by the government to an individual author, composer, playwright, and the like for the life of the individual plus 50 years. If the copyright is granted to a firm, then the right extends 75 years after the original publication. The *economic life* of a copyright may be considerably less than the legal life as, for example, the copyright of this book.

corporation. A legal entity authorized by a state to operate under the rules of the entity's *charter*.

correction of errors. See *accounting errors*.

cost. The sacrifice, measured by the *price* paid or required to be paid, to acquire *goods* or *services*. See *acquisition cost* and *replacement cost*. The term "cost" is often used when referring to the valuation of a good or service acquired. When "cost" is used in this sense, a cost is an *asset*. When the benefits of the acquisition (the goods or services acquired) expire, the cost becomes an *expense* or *loss*. Some writers, however, use cost and expense as synonyms. Contrast with *expense*.

cost accounting. Classifying, summarizing, recording, reporting, and allocating current or predicted *costs*. A subset of *managerial accounting*.

Cost Accounting Standards Board. See *CASB*.

cost center. A unit of activity for which *expenditures* and *expenses* are accumulated.

cost effective. Among alternatives, the one whose benefit, or payoff, per unit of cost is highest. Sometimes said of an action whose expected benefits exceed expected costs whether or not there are other alternatives with larger benefit/cost ratios.

cost flow assumption. See *flow assumption*.

cost flows. Costs passing through various classifications within an entity. See *flow of costs* for a diagram.

cost method (for investments). Accounting for an investment in the *capital stock* or *bonds* of another company where the investment is shown at *acquisition cost*, and only *dividends* declared or *interest receivable* is treated as *revenue*.

cost method (for treasury stock). The method of showing *treasury stock* as a *contra* to all other items of *shareholders' equity* in an amount equal to that paid to reacquire the stock.

cost of capital. *Opportunity cost* of funds invested in a business. The rate of return required to be earned on an asset before the rational owner will devote that asset to a particular purpose. Sometimes measured as the average rate per year a company must pay for its *equities*. In efficient capital markets, the *discount rate* that equates the expected *present value* of all future cash flows to common shareholders with the market value of common stock at a given time.

cost of goods manufactured. The sum of all costs allocated to products completed during a period; includes materials, labor, and *overhead*.

cost of goods purchased. Net purchase price of goods acquired plus costs of storage and delivery to the place where the items can be productively used.

cost of goods sold. Inventoriable *costs* that are expensed because the units are sold; equals beginning inventory plus *cost of goods purchased* or *manufactured* minus *ending inventory*.

cost of sales. Generally refers to *cost of goods sold*; occasionally, to *selling expenses*.

cost or market, whichever is lower. See *lower of cost or market*.

cost percentage. One less *markup percentage*. *Cost of goods available for sale* divided by selling prices of goods available for sale (when *FIFO* is used). With LIFO, *cost of purchases* divided by selling price of purchases. See *markup* for further detail on inclusions in calculation of cost percentage.

cost principle. The *principle* that requires reporting *assets* at *historical* or *acquisition cost*, less accumulated *amortization*. This principle is based on the assumption that cost is equal to *fair market value* at the date of acquisition and subsequent changes are not likely to be significant.

cost recovery first method. A method of *revenue* recognition that *credits cost* as collections are received until all costs are recovered. Only after costs are completely recovered is *income* recognized. To be used in financial reporting only when the total amount of collections is highly uncertain. Can never be used in income tax reporting. Contrast with the *installment method* where *constant proportions* of each collection are credited both to cost and to income.

cost sheet. Statement that shows all the elements comprising the total cost of an item.

cost terminology. The word "cost" appears in many accounting terms. The accompanying exhibit classifies some of these by the distinctions the terms are used to make. Joel Dean was, to our knowledge, the first to attempt such distinctions; we have used some of his ideas here. Some terms have more detailed discussion under their own listings.

cost-to-cost. The *percentage of completion method* where the estimate of completion is the ratio of costs incurred to date divided by total costs expected to be incurred for the entire project.

cost-volume-profit graph (chart). A graph that shows the relation between *fixed costs, contribution per unit, breakeven point*, and *sales*. See *breakeven chart*.

costing. The process of calculating the cost of activities, products, or services. The British word for *cost accounting*.

coupon. That portion of a *bond* document redeemable at a specified date for *interest* payments. Its physical form is much like a ticket; each coupon is dated and is deposited at a bank, just like a check, for collection or is mailed to the issuer's agent for collection.

Cost Terminology: Distinctions Among Terms Containing the Word "Cost"

Terms (Synonyms Given in Parentheses)			Distinctions and Comments
			1. The following pairs of terms distinguish the "attribute" or "basis" measured in accounting.
Historical Cost (Acquisition Cost)	vs.	Current Cost	A distinction used in financial accounting. Current cost can be used more specifically to mean replacement cost, net realizable value, or present value of cash flows. "Current cost" is often used narrowly to mean replacement cost.
Historical Cost (Actual Cost)	vs.	Standard Cost	The distinction between historical and standard costs arises in product costing for inventory valuation. Some systems record actual costs while others record the standard costs.
			2. The following pairs of terms denote various distinctions among historical costs. For each pair of terms, the sum of the two kinds of costs equals total historical cost used in financial reporting.
Variable Cost	vs.	Fixed Cost (Constant Cost)	Distinction used in breakeven analysis and in designing cost accounting systems, particularly for product costing. See (4), below, for a further subdivision of fixed costs and (5), below, for an economic distinction closely paralleling this one.
Traceable Cost	vs.	Common Cost (Joint Cost)	Distinction arises in allocating manufacturing costs to product. Common costs are allocated to product, but the allocations are more-or-less arbitrary. The distinction also arises in segment reporting and in separating manufacturing from nonmanufacturing costs.
Direct Cost	vs.	Indirect Cost	Distinction arises in designing cost accounting systems and in product costing. The distinction generally applies only to manufacturing costs.
Out-of-Pocket Cost (Outlay Cost; Cash Cost)	vs.	Book Cost	Virtually all costs recorded in financial statements require a cash outlay at one time or another. The distinction here separates expenditures to occur in the future from those already made and is used in making decisions. Book costs, such as for depreciation, reduce income without requiring a future outlay of cash. The cash has already been spent. See future vs. past costs in (5), below.
Incremental Cost (Marginal Cost)	vs.	Sunk Cost	Distinction used in making decisions. Incremental costs will be incurred (or saved) if a decision is made to go ahead (or to stop) some activity, but not otherwise. Sunk costs will be reported in financial statements whether the decision is made to go ahead or not, because cash has already been spent or committed. Not all sunk costs are book costs, as, for example, a salary promised but not yet earned, that will be paid even if a no-go decision is made.
Incremental Cost	vs.	Marginal Cost	The economist restricts the term marginal cost to the cost of producing one more unit. Thus the next unit has a marginal cost; the next week's output has an incremental cost. If a firm produces and sells a new product the related new costs would properly be called incremental, not marginal. If a factory is closed, the costs saved are incremental, not marginal.
Escapable Cost	vs.	Inescapable Cost (Unavoidable Cost)	Same distinction as incremental vs. sunk costs, but this pair is used only when the decision maker is considering stopping something—ceasing to produce a product, closing a factory, or the like. See next pair.
Avoidable Cost	vs.	Unavoidable Cost	A distinction sometimes used in discussing the merits of direct and absorption costing. Avoidable costs are treated as product cost and unavoidable costs are treated as period expenses under direct costing.

714

Cost Terminology: Distinctions Among Terms Containing the Word "Cost"

Terms (Synonyms Given in Parentheses)			Distinctions and Comments
Controllable Cost	vs.	Uncontrollable Cost	The distinction here is used in allocating responsibility and in setting bonus or incentive plans. All costs can be affected by someone in the entity; those who design incentive schemes attempt to hold a person responsible for a cost only if that person can influence the amount of the cost.

3. In each of the following pairs, used in historical cost accounting, the word "cost" appears in one of the terms where "expense" is meant.

Expired Cost	vs.	Unexpired Cost	The distinction is between *expense* and *asset*.
Product Cost	vs.	Period Cost	The terms distinguish product cost from period expense. When a given asset is used, is its cost converted into work in process and then finished goods on the balance sheet until the goods are sold or is it an expense shown on this period's income statement? Product costs appear on the income statement as part of cost of goods sold in the period when the goods are sold. Period expenses appear on the income statement with an appropriate caption for the item in the period when the cost is incurred or recognized.

4. The following subdivisions of fixed (historical) costs are used in analyzing operations. The relation between the components of fixed costs is:

Fixed Costs = Capacity Costs + Programmed Costs

Semifixed Costs + "Pure" Fixed Costs	+ Fixed Portions of Semivariable Costs	Standby Costs	+ Enabling Costs

Capacity Cost (Committed Cost)	vs.	Programmed Cost (Managed Cost; Discretionary Cost)	Capacity costs give a firm the capability to produce or to sell. Programmed costs, such as for advertising or research and development, may not be essential, but once a decision to incur them is made, they become fixed costs.
Standby Cost	vs.	Enabling Cost	Standby costs will be incurred whether capacity, once acquired, is used or not, such as property taxes and depreciation on a factory. Enabling costs, such as for security force, can be avoided if the capacity is unused.
Semifixed Cost	vs.	Semivariable Cost	A cost fixed over a wide range but that can change at various levels is a semifixed cost or "step cost." An example is the cost of rail lines from the factory to the main rail line where fixed cost depends on whether there are one or two parallel lines, but are independent of the number of trains run per day. Semivariable costs combine a strictly fixed component cost plus a variable component. Telephone charges usually have a fixed monthly component plus a charge related to usage.

5. The following pairs of terms distinguish among economic uses or decision making uses or regulatory uses of cost terms.

Opportunity Cost	vs.	Outlay Cost (Out-of-Pocket Cost)	Opportunity cost refers to the economic benefit foregone by using a resource for one purpose instead of for another. The outlay cost of the resource will be recorded in financial records. The distinction arises because a resource is already in the possession of the entity with a recorded historical cost. Its economic value to the firm, opportunity cost, generally differs from the historical cost; it can be either larger or smaller.

Cost Terminology: Distinctions Among Terms Containing the Word "Cost"

Terms (Synonyms Given in Parentheses)			Distinctions and Comments
Future Costs	vs.	Past Cost	Effective decision making analyzes only the present and the future outlay costs, out-of-pocket costs, opportunity costs, are relevant for profit maximizing; past costs are used in financial reporting.
Short-Run Cost	vs.	Long-Run Cost	Short-run costs vary as output is varied for a given configuration of plant and equipment. Long-run costs can be incurred to change that configuration. This pair of terms is the accounting analog of the accounting pair, see (2) above, variable and fixed costs. The analogy is not perfect because some short-run costs are fixed, such as property taxes on the factory, from the point of view of breakeven analysis.
Imputed Cost	vs.	Book Cost	In a regulatory setting some costs, for example the cost of owner's equity capital, are calculated and used for various purposes. Imputed costs are not recorded in the historical cost acounting records for financial reporting. Book costs are recorded.
Average Cost	vs.	Marginal Cost	The economic distinction equivalent to fully absorbed cost of product and direct cost of product. Average cost is total cost divided by number of units. Marginal cost is the cost to produce the next unit (or the last unit).

coupon rate. Of a *bond*, the amount of annual coupons divided by par value. Contrast with *effective rate*.

covenant. A promise with legal validity.

CPA. See *certified public accountant*. The *AICPA* suggests that no periods be shown in the abbreviation.

CPI. *Consumer Price Index*.

CPP. Current purchasing power; usually used as an adjective modifying the word "accounting" to mean the accounting that produces *constant dollar financial statements*.

Cr. Abbreviation for *credit*.

credit. As a noun, an entry on the right-hand side of an *account*. As a verb, to make an entry on the right-hand side of an account. Records increases in *liabilities, owner's equity, revenues* and *gains*; records decreases in *assets* and *expenses*. See *debit and credit conventions*. Also the ability or right to buy or borrow in return for a promise to pay later.

credit loss. The amount of *accounts receivable* that is, or is expected to become, *uncollectible*.

credit memorandum. A document used by a seller to inform a buyer that the buyer's *account receivable* is being credited (reduced) because of *errors, returns,* or *allowances*. Also, the document provided by a bank to a depositor to indicate that the depositor's balance is being increased because of some event other than a deposit, such as the collection by the bank of the depositor's *note receivable*.

creditor. One who lends.

cross-reference (index). A number placed by each *account* in a *journal entry* indicating the *ledger* account to which the entry is posted and placing in the ledger the page number of the journal where the entry was made. Used to link the *debit* and *credit* parts of an entry in the ledger accounts back to the original entry in the journal. See *audit trail*.

cross section analysis. Analysis of *financial statements* of various firms for a single period of time, as opposed to time series analysis where statements of a given firm are analyzed over several periods of time.

cumulative dividend. Preferred stock *dividends* that, if not paid, accrue as a commitment that must be paid before dividends to common shareholders can be declared.

cumulative preferred shares. *Preferred* shares with *cumulative dividend* rights.

current asset. *Cash* and other *assets* that are expected to be turned into cash, sold, or exchanged within the normal operating cycle of the firm, usually one year. Current assets include *cash, marketable securities, receivables, inventory,* and *current prepayments*.

current cost. *Cost* stated in terms of current values (of *productive capacity*) rather than in terms of *acquisition cost*. See *net realizable value, current selling price*.

current cost accounting. The *FASB's* term for *financial statements* where the *attribute measured* is *current cost*.

current-cost/nominal-dollar accounting. Accounting based on *current cost* valuations measured in *nominal dollars*. Components of *income* include an *operating margin* and *holding gains and losses*.

716

current fund. In governmental accounting, a synonym for general fund.

current funds. *Cash* and other assets readily convertible into cash. In governmental accounting, funds spent for operating purposes during the current period. Includes *general, special revenue, debt service*, and *enterprise funds*.

current (gross) margin. See *operating margin (based on current costs)*.

current liability. A debt or other obligation that must be discharged within a short time, usually the *earnings cycle* or one year, normally by expending *current assets*.

current operating performance concept. The notion that reported *income* for a period ought to reflect only ordinary, normal, and recurring operations of that period. A consequence is that *extraordinary* and nonrecurring items are entered directly in the Retained Earnings account. Contrast with *clean surplus concept*. This concept is no longer acceptable. (See *APB Opinions* Nos. 9 and 30.)

current ratio. Sum of *current assets* divided by sum of *current liabilities*. See *ratio*.

current replacement cost. Of an *asset*, the amount currently required to acquire an identical asset (in the same condition and with the same service potential) or an asset capable of rendering the same service at a current *fair market price*. If these two amounts differ, the lower is usually used. Contrast with *reproduction cost*.

current selling price. The amount for which an *asset* could be sold as of a given time in an *arm's length* transaction, rather than in a forced sale.

current value accounting. The form of accounting where all assets are shown at *current replacement cost (entry value)* or *current selling price* or *net realizable value (exit value)* and all *liabilities* are shown at *present value*. Entry and exit values may be quite different from each other so there is no general agreement on the precise meaning of current value accounting.

current yield. Of a *bond*, the annual amount of *interest coupons* divided by current market price of the bond. Contrast with *yield to maturity*.

currently attainable standard cost. *Normal standard cost.*

customers' ledger. The *ledger* that shows accounts receivable of individual customers. It is the *subsidiary ledger* for the *controlling account*, Accounts Receivable.

D

days of average inventory on hand. See *ratio*.

DDB. *Double-declining-balance depreciation.*

debenture bond. A *bond* not secured with *collateral*.

debit. As a noun, an entry on the left-hand side of an *account*. As a verb, to make an entry on the left-hand side of an account. Records increases in *assets* and *expenses*; records decreases in *liabilities, owners' equity*, and *revenues*. See *debit and credit conventions*.

debit and credit conventions. The equality of the two

sides of the *accounting equation* is maintained by recording equal amounts of *debits* and *credits* for each *transaction*. The conventional use of the *T-account* form and the rules for debit and credit in *balance sheet accounts* are summarized as follows.

Any Asset Account

Opening Balance Increase + Dr. Ending Balance	Decrease − Cr.

Any Liability Account

Decrease − Dr.	Opening Balance Increase + Cr. Ending Balance

Any Owners' Equity Account

Decrease − Dr.	Opening Balance Increase + Cr. Ending Balance

Revenue and expense accounts belong to the owner's equity group. The relationship and the rules for debit and credit in these accounts can be expressed as follows.

Owner's Equity

Decrease − Dr. Expenses		Increase + Cr. Revenues	
Dr. + *	Cr. −	Dr. −	Cr. + *

Normal balance prior to closing.

debit memorandum. A document used by a seller to inform a buyer that the seller is debiting (increasing) the amount of the buyer's *account receivable*. Also, the document provided by a bank to a depositor to indicate that the depositor's *balance* is being decreased because of some event other than payment for a *check*, such as monthly service charges or the printing of checks.

debt. An amount owed. The general name for *notes, bonds, mortgages*, and the like that are evidence of amounts owed and have definite payment dates.

debt-equity ratio. Total *liabilities* divided by total equities. See *ratio*. Sometimes the denominator is merely total share-

717

holders' equity. Sometimes the numerator is restricted to *long-term debt*.

debt financing. Raising *funds* by issuing *bonds, mortgages,* or *notes*. Contrast with *equity financing. Leverage*.

debt guarantee. See *guarantee*.

debt ratio. *Debt-equity ratio*.

debt service fund. In governmental accounting, a *fund* established to account for payment of *interest* and *principal* on all general obligation *debt* other than that payable from special *assessments*.

debt service requirement. The amount of cash required for payments of *interest*, current maturities of *principal* on outstanding *debt*, and payments to *sinking funds* (corporations) or to the *debt service fund* (governmental).

debtor. One who borrows.

declaration date. Time when a *dividend* is declared by the *board of directors*.

declining-balance depreciation. The method of calculating the periodic *depreciation* charge by multiplying the *book value* at the start of the period by a constant percentage. In pure declining balance depreciation the constant percentage is $1 - \sqrt[n]{s/c}$ where n is the *depreciable life*, s is *salvage value*, and c is *acquisition cost*. See *double-declining-balance depreciation*.

deep discount bonds. Said of *bonds* selling much below (exactly how much is not clear) *par value*

defalcation. Embezzlement.

default. Failure to pay *interest* or *principal* on a *debt* when due.

defensive interval. A financial *ratio* equal to the number of days of normal cash *expenditures* covered by *quick assets*.

It is defined as

$$\frac{quick\ assets}{(all\ expenses\ except\ amortization\ and\ others\ not\ using\ funds/365)}$$

The denominator of the ratio is the cash expenditure per day. This ratio has been found useful in predicting *bankruptcy*.

deferral. The accounting process concerned with past *cash receipts* and *payments*; in contrast to *accrual*. Recognizing a liability resulting from a current cash receipt (as for magazines to be delivered) or recognizing an asset from a current cash payment (or for prepaid insurance or a long-term depreciable asset). See *amortization*.

deferral method. See *flow-through method* (of accounting for the *investment credit*) for definition and contrast.

deferred annuity. An *annuity* whose first payment is made sometime after the end of the first period.

deferred asset. *Deferred charge*.

deferred charge. *Expenditure* not recognized as an *expense* of the period when made but carried forward as an *asset* to be *written off* in future periods, such as for advance rent payments or insurance premiums. See *deferral*.

deferred cost. *Deferred charge*.

deferred credit. Sometimes used to indicate *advances from customers*. Also sometimes used to describe the *deferred income tax liability*.

deferred debit. *Deferred charge*.

deferred expense. *Deferred charge*.

deferred gross margin. *Unrealized gross margin*.

deferred income. *Advances from customers*.

deferred income tax (liability). An *indeterminate-term liability* that arises when the pretax income shown on the tax return is less than what it would have been had the same *accounting principles* been used in tax returns as used for financial reporting. *APB Opinion* No. 11 requires that the firm debit income tax *expense* and credit deferred income tax with the amount of the taxes delayed by using different accounting principles in tax returns from those used in financial reports. See *timing difference* and *permanent difference*. See *installment sales*. If, as a result of timing differences, cumulative taxable income exceeds cumulative reported income before taxes, the deferred income tax account will have a *debit* balance and will be reported as a *deferred charge*.

deferred revenue. Sometimes used to indicate *advances from customers*.

deferred tax. See *deferred income tax*.

deficit. A *debit balance* in the Retained Earnings account; presented on the balance sheet as a *contra* to shareholders' equity. Sometimes used to mean negative *net income* for a period.

defined-benefit plan. A *pension plan* where the employer promises specific dollar amounts to each eligible employee; the amounts usually depend on a formula which takes into account such things as the employee's earnings, years of employment, and age. The employer's cash contributions and pension expense are adjusted in relation to *actuarial* experience in the eligible employee group and investment performance of the pension *fund*. Sometimes called a "fixed-benefit" pension plan. Contrast with *money purchase plan*.

defined-contribution plan. A *money purchase (pension) plan* or other arrangement, based on formula or discretion, where the employer makes cash contributions to eligible individual employee *accounts* under the terms of a written plan document.

deflation. A period of declining *general price changes*.

demand deposit. *Funds* in a *checking account* at a bank.

demand loan. See *term loan* for definition and contrast.

denominator volume. Capacity measured in expected number of units to be produced this period; divided into *budgeted fixed costs* to obtain fixed costs applied per unit of product.

depletion. Exhaustion or *amortization* of a *wasting asset*, or natural resource. Also see *percentage depletion*.

depletion allowance. See *percentage depletion*.

deposit method (of revenue recognition). This method of *revenue* recognition is not distinct from the *completed sale* or *completed contract method*. In some contexts such as retail land sales, the customer must make substantial payments while still having the right to back out of the deal and receive a refund. When there is uncertainty about whether the deal will be completed but a cash collection is made by the seller, the seller must *credit* deposits, a *liability account*, rather than *revenue*. (In this regard, the accounting differs from the completed contract method where the account credited is offset against the *work in process inventory* account.) When the *sale* becomes complete, a revenue account is credited and the deposit account is *debited*.

deposit, sinking fund. Payments made to a *sinking fund*.

deposits in transit. Deposits made by a firm but not yet reflected on the *bank statement*.

depreciable cost. That part of the *cost* of an asset, usually *acquisition cost* less *salvage value*, that is to be charged off over the life of the asset through the process of *depreciation*.

depreciable life. For an *asset*, the time period or units of activity (such as miles driven for a truck) over which *depreciable cost* is to be allocated. For tax returns, depreciable life may be shorter than estimated *service life*.

depreciation. *Amortization of plant assets*; the process of allocating the cost of an asset to the periods of benefit—the *depreciable life*. Classified as a *production cost* or a *period expense*, depending upon the asset and whether *absorption* or *direct costing* is used. Depreciation methods described in this glossary include the *annuity method, appraisal method, composite method, compound interest method, declining-balance method, double-declining-balance method, production method, replacement method, retirement method, straight-line method, sinking fund method, and sum-of-the-years'-digits method*.

depreciation reserve. An inferior term for *accumulated depreciation*. See *reserve*. Do not confuse with a replacement *fund*.

Descartes' rule of signs. In a *capital-budgeting* context, the rule says that a series of cash flows will have a nonnegative number of *internal rates of return*. The number is equal to the number of variations in the sign of the cash flow series or is less than that number by an even integer. Consider the following series of cash flows, the first occurring now and the others at subsequent yearly intervals: $-100, -100, +50, +175, -50, +100$. The internal rates of return are the numbers for r that satisfy the equation

$$-100 - 100/(1 + r) + 50/(1 + r)^2 + 175/(1 + r)^3 - 50/(1 + r)^4 + 100/(1 + r)^5 = 0.$$

The series of cash flows has three variations in sign: a change from minus to plus, a change from plus to minus, and a change from minus to plus. The rule says that this series must have either one or three internal rates of return; in fact, it has only one, about 12 percent. But also see *reinvestment rate*.

development-stage enterprise. As defined in *SFAS No. 7*, a firm whose planned principal *operations* have not commenced or having commenced, have not generated signifi-

cant *revenue*. Such enterprises should be so identified, but no special *accounting principles* apply to them.

differential analysis. Analysis of *incremental costs*.

differential cost. *Incremental cost*. If a total cost curve is smooth (in mathematical terms, differentiable), then the curve graphing the derivative of the total cost curve is often said to show differential costs, the costs increments associated with infinitesimal changes in volume.

dilution. A potential reduction in *earnings per share* or *book value* per share by the potential *conversion* of securities or by the potential exercise of *warrants* or *options*.

dilutive. Said of a *security* that would reduce *earnings per share* if it were exchanged for *common stock*.

dipping into LIFO layers. See *LIFO inventory layer*.

direct cost. Cost of *direct material* and *direct labor* incurred in producing a product. See *prime cost*. In some accounting literature, this term is used to mean the same thing as *variable cost*.

direct costing. This method of allocating costs assigns only *variable manufacturing costs* to product and treats *fixed manufacturing costs* as *period* expenses. A better term for this concept is "variable costing."

direct labor (material) cost. Cost of labor (material) applied and assigned directly to a product; contrast with *indirect labor (material)*.

direct posting. A method of bookkeeping where *entries* are made directly in *ledger accounts*, without the use of a *journal*.

direct write-off method. See *write-off method*.

disbursement. Payment by *cash* or by *check*. See *expenditure*.

DISC. Domestic International Sales Corporation. A U.S. *corporation*, usually a *subsidiary*, whose *income* is primarily attributable to exports. *Income tax* on 50 percent of a DISC's income is usually deferred for a long period. Generally, this results in a lower overall corporate tax for the *parent* than would otherwise be incurred.

disclaimer of opinion. An *auditor's report* stating that an opinion cannot be given on the *financial statements*. Usually results from *material* restrictions on the scope of the audit or from material uncertainties about the accounts which cannot be resolved at the time of the audit.

disclosure. The showing of facts in *financial statements, notes* thereto, or the *auditor's report*.

discontinued operations. See *income from discontinued operations*.

discount. In the context of *compound interest, bonds* and *notes*, the difference between *face* or *future value* and *present value* of a payment. In the context of *sales* and *purchases*, a reduction in price granted for prompt payment. See also *chain discount, quantity discount*, and *trade discount*.

discount factor. The reciprocal of one plus the *discount rate*. If the discount rate is 10 percent per period, the discount factor for three periods is $(1.10)^{-3} = 0.75131$.

discount rate. *Interest rate* used to convert future payments to *present values*.

discounted bailout period. In a *capital budgeting* context, the total time that must elapse before discounted value of net accumulated cash flows from a project, including potential *salvage value* at various times of assets, equals or exceeds the *present value* of net accumulated cash outflows. Contrast with *discounted payback period*.

discounted payback period. Amount of time over which the discounted present value of cash inflows from a project, excluding potential *salvage value* at various times if assets equals the discounted *present value* of the cash outflows.

discounting a note. See *note receivable discounted* and *factoring*.

discounts lapsed (lost). The sum of *discounts* offered for prompt payment that were not taken (or allowed) because of expiration of the discount period. See *terms of sale*.

discovery value accounting. See *reserve recognition accounting*.

Discussion Memorandum. A neutral discussion of all the issues concerning an accounting problem of current concern to the *FASB*. The publication of such a document usually implies that the FASB is considering issuing an *SFAS* or *SFAC* on this particular problem. The discussion memorandum brings together material about the particular problem to facilitate interaction and comment by those interested in the matter. It may lead to an *Exposure Draft*.

dishonored note. A *promissory note* whose maker does not repay the loan at *maturity* for a *term loan*, or on demand, for a *demand loan*.

disintermediation. Federal law regulates the maximum *interest rate* that both banks and savings and loan associations can pay for *time deposits*. When free-market interest rates exceed the regulated interest ceiling for such time deposits, some depositors withdraw their funds and invest them elsewhere at a higher interest rate. This process is known as "disintermediation."

distributable income. The portion of conventional accounting net income that can be distributed to owners (usually in the form of *dividends*) without impairing the physical capacity of the firm to continue operations at current levels. Pretax distributable income is conventional pretax income less the excess of *current cost* of goods sold and *depreciation* charges based on the replacement cost of *productive capacity* over cost of goods sold and depreciation on an *acquisition cost basis*. Contrast with *sustainable income*. See *inventory profit*.

distribution expense. *Expense* of selling, advertising, and delivery activities.

dividend. A distribution of assets generated from *earnings* to owners of a corporation; it may be paid in cash (cash dividend), with stock (stock dividend), with property, or with other securities (dividend in kind). Dividends, except stock dividends, become a legal liability of the corporation when they are declared. Hence, the owner of stock ordinarily recognizes *revenue* when a dividend, other than a stock

dividend, is declared. See also *liquidating dividend* and *stock dividend*.

dividend yield. *Dividends* declared for the year divided by market price of the stock as of a given time of the year.

dividends in arrears. Dividends on *cumulative preferred stock* that have not been declared in accordance with the preferred stock contract. Such arrearages must usually be cleared before dividends on *common stock* can be declared.

dividends in kind. See *dividend*.

divisional control. See *control system*.

divisional reporting. *Line of business reporting*.

dollar sign rules. In presenting accounting statements or schedules, place a dollar sign beside the first figure in each column and beside any figure below a horizontal line drawn under the preceding figure.

dollar value LIFO method. A form of *LIFO* inventory accounting with inventory quantities (*layers*) measured in dollar, rather than physical, terms. Adjustments to account for changing prices are made by use of specific price indexes appropriate for the kinds of items in the inventory.

Domestic International Sales Corporation. See *DISC*.

donated capital. A *shareholders' equity* account credited when contributions, such as land or buildings, are freely given to the company. Do not confuse with *contributed capital*.

double-declining-balance depreciation. DDB. *Declining-balance depreciation*, which see, where the constant percentage used to multiply by book value in determining the depreciation charge for the year is $2/n$ and n is the *depreciable life* in periods. Maximum declining-balance rate permitted in the *income tax* laws. *Salvage value* is omitted from the depreciable amount. Thus if the asset cost $100 and has a depreciable life of 5 years, the depreciation in the first year would be $40 = 2/5 \times \$100$, in the second would be $24 = 2/5 \times (\$100 - \$40)$, and in the third year would be $14.40 = 2/5 \times (\$100 - \$40 - \$24)$. By the fourth year, the remaining undepreciated cost could be depreciated under the straight-line method at $10.80 = 1/2 \times (\$100 - \$40 - \$24 - \$14.40)$ per year for tax purposes.

double entry. The system of recording transactions that maintains the equality of the accounting equation; each entry results in recording equal amounts of *debits* and *credits*.

double T-account. *T-account* with an extra horizontal line showing a change in the account balance to be explained by the subsequent entries into the account, such as:

Plant

42,000	

720

This account shows an increase in the asset account, plant, of $42,000 to be explained. Such accounts are useful in preparing the *statement of changes in financial position*; they are not a part of the formal record keeping process.

double taxation. Corporate income is subject to the corporate income tax and the aftertax income, when distributed to owners, is subject to the personal income tax.

doubtful accounts. *Accounts receivable* estimated to be *uncollectible*.

Dr. The abbreviation for *debit*.

draft. A written order by the first party, called the drawer, instructing a second party, called the drawee (such as a bank) to pay a third party, called the payee. See also *check, cashier's check, certified check, NOW account, sight draft,* and *trade acceptance.*

drawee. See *draft.*

drawer. See *draft.*

drawing account. A *temporary account* used in *sole proprietorships* and *partnerships* to record payments to owners or partners during a period. At the end of the period, the drawing account is closed by crediting it and debiting the owner's or partner's share of income or, perhaps, his or her capital account.

drawings. Payments made to a *sole proprietor* or to a *partner* during a period. See *drawing account.*

dry-hole accounting. See *reserve recognition accounting* for definition and contrast.

dual transactions assumption (fiction). In presenting the *statement of changes in financial position*, some transactions not involving *working capital* accounts are reported as though working capital was generated and then used. For example, the issue of *capital stock* in return for the *asset*, land, is reported in the statement of changes in financial position as though stock were issued for *cash* and cash were used to acquire land. Other examples of transactions that require the dual transaction fiction are the issue of the *mortgage* in return for a noncurrent asset and the issue of stock to bondholders on *conversion* of their *convertible bonds.*

duality. The axiom of *double-entry* record keeping that every *transaction* is broken down into equal *debit* and *credit* amounts.

E

e. The base of natural logarithms; 2.718281828459045.... If *interest* is compounded continuously during a period at stated rate of r per period, then the effective *interest rate* is equivalent to interest compounded once per period at rate i where $i = e^r - 1$. Tables of e^r are widely available. If 12 percent annual interest is compounded continuously, the effective rate is $e^{.12} - 1 = 12.75$ percent.

earned surplus. A term once used, but no longer considered proper, for *retained earnings.*

earnings. *Income*, or sometimes *profit.*

earnings cycle. The period of time that elapses for a given firm, or the series of transactions, during which *cash* is con-

verted into *goods* and *services*, goods and services are sold to customers, and customers pay for their purchases with cash. *Cash cycle.*

earnings per share (of common stock). *Net income* to common shareholders (net income minus *preferred dividends*) divided by the average number of *common shares* outstanding; see also *primary earnings per share* and *fully diluted earnings per share.* See *ratio.*

earnings per share (of preferred stock). *Net income* divided by the average number of *preferred shares* outstanding during the period. This ratio indicates how well the preferred dividends are covered or protected; it does not indicate a legal share of *earnings.* See *ratio.*

earnings, retained. See *retained earnings.*

earn-out. An agreement between two merging firms under which the amount of payment by the acquiring firm to the acquired firm's shareholders depends on the future earnings of the *consolidated entity.*

easement. The acquired right or privilege of one person to use, or have access to, certain property of another. For example, a public utility's right to lay pipes or lines under property of another and to service those facilities.

economic entity. See *entity.*

economic life. The time span over which the benefits of an *asset* are expected to be received. The economic life of a *patent, copyright*, or *franchise* may be less than the legal life. *Service life.*

economic order quantity. In mathematical *inventory* analysis, the optimal amount of stock to order when inventory is reduced to a level called the "reorder point." If A represents the *incremental cost* of placing a single order, D represents the total demand for a period of time in units, and H represents the incremental holding cost during the period per unit of inventory, then the economic order quantity $Q = \sqrt{2AD/H}$. Q is sometimes called the "optimal lot size."

ED. *Exposure Draft.*

effective interest method. A systematic method for computing *interest expense* (or *revenue*) that makes the interest expense for each period divided by the amount of the net *liability* (*asset*) at the beginning of the period equal to the *yield rate* on the bond at the time of issue (acquisition). Interest for a period is yield rate (at time of issue) multiplied by the net liability (asset) at the start of the period. The *amortization* of discount or premium is the *plug* to give equal *debits* and *credits.* (Interest expense is a debit and the amount of coupon payments is a credit.)

effective (interest) rate. Of a bond, the *internal rate of return* or *yield to maturity* at the time of issue. Contrast with *coupon rate.* If the bond is issued for a price below *par*, the effective rate is higher than the coupon rate; if it is issued for a price greater than par, then the effective rate is lower than the coupon rate. In the context of *compound interest*, when the *compounding period* on a *loan* is different from one year, such as a nominal interest rate of 12 percent compounded monthly, then single payment that could be made at the end of a year that is economically equivalent to the series of interest payments exceeds the quoted nominal rate multiplied by the *principal*. If 12 percent per year is compounded monthly, the effective interest rate is 12.683 percent. In general, if the nominal rate is r percent per year and is compounded m times per year, then the effective rate is $(1 + r/m)m - 1$.

efficiency variance. A term used for the *quantity variance* for labor or *variable overhead* in a *standard cost system*.

efficient market hypothesis. The supposition in finance that securities' prices reflect all available information and react nearly instantaneously and in an unbiased fashion to new information.

eliminations. *Work sheet* entries to prepare *consolidated statements* that are made to avoid duplicating the amounts of *assets, liabilities, owners' equity, revenues*, and *expenses* of the consolidated *entity* when the accounts of the *parent* and *subsidiaries* are summed.

employee stock option. See *stock option*.

Employee Stock Ownership Trust (or Plan). See *ESOT*.

employer, employee payroll taxes. See *payroll*.

enabling costs. A type of *capacity cost* that will stop being incurred if operations are shut down completely but must be incurred in full if operations are carried out at any level. Costs of a security force or of a quality control inspector for an assembly line might be examples. Contrast with *standby costs*.

encumbrance. In governmental accounting, an anticipated *expenditure*, or *funds* restricted for anticipated expenditure, such as for outstanding purchase orders. *Appropriations* less expenditures less outstanding encumbrances yields unencumbered balance.

ending inventory. The *cost of inventory* on hand at the end of the *accounting period*, often called "closing inventory." The dollar amount of inventory to be carried to the subsequent period.

endorsee. See *endorser*.

endorsement. See *draft*. The *payee* signs the draft and transfers it to a fourth party, such as the payee's bank.

endorser. The *payee* of a *note* or *draft* signs it, after writing "Pay to the order of X," transfers the note to person X, and presumably receives some benefit, such as cash, in return. The payee who signs over the note is called the endorser and person X is called the endorsee. The endorsee then has the rights of the payee and may in turn become an endorser by endorsing the note to another endorsee.

enterprise. Any business organization, usually defining the accounting *entity*.

enterprise fund. A *fund* established by a governmental unit to account for acquisition, operation, and maintenance of governmental services that are supposed to be self-supporting from user charges, such as for water or airports.

entity. A person, *partnership, corporation*, or other organization. The *accounting entity* for which accounting state-

ments are prepared may not be the same as the entity defined by law. For example, a *sole proprietorship* is an accounting entity but the individual's combined business and personal assets are the legal entity in most jurisdictions. Several affiliated corporations may be separate legal entities while *consolidated financial statements* are prepared for the group of companies operating as a single economic entity.

entity theory. The view of the corporation that emphasizes the form of the *accounting equation* that says *assets = equities*. Contrast with *proprietorship theory*. The entity theory is less concerned with a distinct line between *liabilities* and *shareholders' equity* than is the proprietorship theory. Rather, all equities are provided to the corporation by outsiders who merely have claims of differing legal standings. The entity theory implies using a *multiple-step* income statement.

entry value. The *current cost* of acquiring an asset or service at a *fair-market price. Replacement cost.*

EOQ. *Economic order quantity.*

EPS. *Earnings per share.*

EPVI. *Excess present value index.*

equalization reserve. An inferior title for the allowance account when the *allowance method* is used for such things as maintenance expenses. Periodically, maintenance *expense* is debited and the allowance is credited. As maintenance *expenditures* are actually incurred, the allowance is debited and cash or the other asset expended is credited.

equities. *Liabilities* plus *owners' equity*. See, however, *equity*.

equity. A claim to *assets*; a source of assets. *SFAS No. 3* defines equity as "the residual interest in the assets of an entity that remains after deducting its liabilities." Usage may be changing so that "equity" will exclude liabilities. We prefer to keep the broader definition, including liabilities, because there is no other single word that serves this useful purpose.

equity financing. Raising *funds* by issuance of *capital stock*. Contrast with *debt financing*.

equity method. A method of accounting for an *investment* in the stock of another company in which the proportionate share of the earnings of the other company is debited to the investment account and credited to a *revenue* account as earned. When *dividends* are received, *cash* is debited and the investment account is credited. Used in reporting when the investor owns sufficient shares of stock of an unconsolidated company to exercise significant control over the actions of that company. One of the few instances where revenue is recognized without a change in *working capital*.

equity ratio. *Shareholders' equity* divided by total *assets*. See *ratio*.

equivalent production. *Equivalent units.*

equivalent units (of work). The number of units of completed output that would require the same costs as were actually incurred for production of completed and partially completed units during a period. Used primarily in *process*

722

costing calculations to measure in uniform terms the output of a continuous process.

ERISA. Employee Retirement Income Security Act of 1974. The federal law that sets *pension plan* requirements.

error accounting. See *accounting errors*.

ESOP. Employee Stock Ownership Plan. See *ESOT*.

ESOT. Employee Stock Ownership Trust. A trust *fund* created by a corporate employer that can provide certain tax benefits to the corporation while providing for employee stock ownership. The corporate employer can contribute up to 25 percent of its payroll per year to the trust. The contributions are *deductions* from otherwise taxable income for federal *income tax* purposes. The assets of the trust must be used for the benefit of employees—for example, to fund death or retirement benefits. The assets of the trust are usually the *common stock*, sometimes nonvoting, of the corporate employer. As an example of the potential *tax shelter*, consider the case of a corporation with $1 million of *debt* outstanding, which it wishes to retire, and an annual payroll of $2 million. The corporation sells $1 million of common stock to the ESOT. The ESOT borrows $1 million with the loan guaranteed by, and therefore a *contingency* of, the corporation. The corporation uses the $1 million proceeds of the stock issue to retire its outstanding debt. (The debt of the corporation has been replaced with the debt of the ESOT.) The corporation can contribute $500,000 (= .25 × $2 million payroll) to the ESOT each year and treat the contribution as a deduction for tax purposes. After a little more than two years, the ESOT has received sufficient funds to retire its loan. The corporation has effectively repaid its original $1 million debt with pretax dollars. Assuming an income tax rate of 40 percent, it has saved $400,000 (= .40 × $1 million) of aftertax dollars *if* the $500,000 expense for the contribution to the ESOT for the pension benefits of employees would have been made, in one form or another, anyway. Observe that the corporation could use the proceeds ($1 million in the example) of the stock issue to the ESOT for any of several different purposes: financing expansion, replacing plant assets, or acquiring another company.

Basically this same form of pretax dollar financing through pensions is "almost" available with any corporate pension plan, but with one important exception. The trustees of an ordinary pension trust must invest the assets "prudently" and if they do not, they are personally liable to employees. Current judgment about "prudent" investment requires diversification—pension trust assets should be invested in a wide variety of investment opportunities. (Not more than 10 percent of a pension trust's assets can ordinarily be invested in the parent's common stock.) Thus the ordinary pension trust cannot, in practice, invest all, or even most, of its assets in the parent corporation's stock. This constraint does not apply to the investments of an ESOT. All ESOT assets may be invested in the parent company's stock.

The ESOT also provides a means for closely-held corporations to achieve wider ownership of shares without *going public*. The laws enabling ESOT's provide for independent professional appraisal of shares not traded in public markets and for transactions between the corporation and the ESOT or between the ESOT and the employees to be based on the appraised values of the shares.

estimated expenses. See *after cost*.

estimated liability. The preferred terminology for estimated costs to be incurred for such uncertain things as repairs under *warranty*. An estimated liability is shown in the *balance sheet*. Contrast with *contingency*.

estimated revenue. A term used in governmental accounting to designate revenue expected to accrue during a period whether or not it will be collected during the period. A *budgetary account* is usually established at the beginning of the budget period.

estimated salvage value. Synonymous with *salvage value* of an *asset* before its retirement.

estimates, changes in. See *accounting changes*.

except for. Qualification in *auditor's report*, usually caused by a change, approved by the auditor, from one acceptable accounting principle or procedure to another.

excess present value. In a *capital budgeting* context, *present value* of (anticipated net cash inflows minus cash outflows including initial cash outflow) for a project.

excess present value index. *Present value*, of future *cash* inflows divided by initial cash outlay.

exchange. The generic term for a transaction (or more technically, a reciprocal transfer) between one entity and another. In another context, the name for a market, such as the New York Stock Exchange.

exchange gain or loss. The phrase used by the *FASB* for *foreign exchange gain or loss*.

exchange rate. The *price* of one country's currency in terms of another country's currency. For example, the British pound might be worth $2.25 at a given time. The exchange rate would be stated as "one pound is worth two dollars and twenty-five cents" or "one dollar is worth .4444 (= £1/$2.25) pounds."

excise tax. Tax on the manufacture, sale, or consumption of a commodity.

ex-dividend. Said of a stock at the time when the declared *dividend* becomes the property of the person who owned the stock on the *record date*. The payment date follows the ex-dividend date.

executory contract. An agreement providing for payment by a payor to a payee upon the performance of an act or service by the payee, such as a labor contract. Obligations under such contracts generally are not recognized as *liabilities*.

exemption. A term used for various amounts subtracted from gross income in computing taxable income. Not all such subtractions are called "exemptions." See *tax deduction*.

exercise. When the owner of an *option* or *warrant* purchases the security that the option entitles him or her to purchase, he or she has exercised the option or warrant.

exercise price. See *option*.

exit value. The proceeds that would be received if assets were disposed of in an *arm's-length transaction. Current selling price. Net realizable value.*

expected value. The mean or arithmetic *average* of a statistical distribution or series of numbers.

expendable fund. In governmental accounting, a *fund* whose resources, *principal*, and earnings may be distributed.

expenditure. Payment of *cash* for goods or services received. Payment may be made either at the time the goods or services are received or at a later time. Virtually synonymous with *disbursement* except that disbursement is a broader term and includes all payments for goods or services. Contrast with *expense.*

expense. As a noun, the *cost* of *assets* used up in producing *revenue* or carrying out other activities that are part of the entity's *operations.* A "gone" asset; an expired cost. Do not confuse with *expenditure* or *disbursement*, which may occur before, when, or after the related expense is recognized. Use the word "cost" to refer to an item that still has service potential and is an asset. Use the word "expense" after the asset's service potential has been used. As a verb, to designate a past or current expenditure as a current expense.

expense account. An *account* to accumulate *expenses*; such accounts are closed at the end of the accounting period. A *temporary owners' equity* account. Also used to describe a listing of expenses by an employee submitted to the employer for reimbursement.

experience rating. A term used in insurance, particularly unemployment insurance, to denote changes from ordinary rates to reflect extraordinarily large or small amounts of claims over time by the insured.

expired cost. An *expense* or a *loss.*

Exposure Draft. ED. A preliminary statement of the *FASB* (or *APB* between 1962 and 1973) that shows the contents of a pronouncement the Board is considering making effective.

external reporting. Reporting to shareholders and the public, as opposed to internal reporting for management's benefit. See *financial accounting* and contrast with *managerial accounting.*

extraordinary item. A *material expense* or *revenue* item characterized both by its unusual nature and infrequency of occurrence that is shown along with its income tax effects separately from ordinary income and *income from discontinued operations* on the *income statement.* A *loss* from an earthquake would probably be classified as an extraordinary item. Gain (or loss) on retirement of *bonds* is treated as an extraordinary item under the terms of *SFAS No. 4.*

F

face amount (value). The nominal amount due at *maturity* from a *bond* or *note* not including contractual interest that may also be due on the same date. The corresponding amount of a stock certificate is best called the *par* or *stated value*, whichever is applicable.

factoring. The process of buying *notes* or *accounts receivable* at a *discount* from the holder to whom the debt is owed; from the holder's point of view, the selling of such notes or accounts. When a single note is involved, the process is called "discounting a note."

factory. Used synonymously with *manufacturing* as an adjective.

factory burden. Manufacturing *overhead.*

factory cost. *Manufacturing cost.*

factory expense. Manufacturing *overhead. Expense* is a poor term in this context because the item is a *product cost.*

factory overhead. Usually an item of *manufacturing cost* other than *direct labor* or *direct materials.*

fair market price (value). Price (value) negotiated at *arm's length* between a willing buyer and a willing seller, each acting rationally in his or her own self-interest. May be estimated in the absence of a monetary transaction.

fair presentation (fairness). When the *auditor's report* says that the *financial statements* "present fairly . . . ," the auditor means that the accounting alternatives used by the entity are all in accordance with *GAAP.* In recent years, however, courts are finding that conformity with *generally accepted accounting principles* may be insufficient grounds for an opinion that the statements are fair. *SAS* No. 5 requires that the auditor judge the accounting principles used "appropriate in the circumstances" before attesting to fair presentation.

FASB. Financial Accounting Standards Board. An independent board responsible, since 1973, for establishing *generally accepted accounting principles.* Its official pronouncements are called "Statements of Financial Accounting Concepts" ("SFAC"), "Statements of Financial Accounting Standards" ("SFAS"), and "Interpretations of Financial Accounting Standards." See also *Discussion Memorandum* and *Technical Bulletin.*

FASB Interpretation. An official statement of the *FASB* interpreting the meaning of *Accounting Research Bulletins, APB Opinions*, and *Statements of Financial Accounting Standards.*

FASB Technical Bulletin. See *Technical Bulletin.*

favorable variance. An excess of actual *revenues* over expected revenues. An excess of *standard cost* over actual cost.

federal income tax. *Income tax* levied by the U.S. government on individuals and corporations.

Federal Unemployment Tax Act. See *FUTA.*

feedback. The process of informing employees about how their actual performance compares with the expected or desired level of performance in the hope that the information will reinforce desired behavior and reduce unproductive behavior.

FEI. *Financial Executives Institute.*

FICA. Federal Insurance Contributions Act. The law that sets "*Social Security*" *taxes* and benefits.

fiduciary. Someone responsible for the custody or administration of property belonging to another, such as an executor (of an estate), agent, receiver (in *bankruptcy*), or trustee (of a trust).

FIFO. First-in, first-out; the *inventory flow assumption* by which *ending inventory* cost is computed from most recent purchases and *cost of goods sold* is computed from oldest purchases including beginning inventory. See *LISH*. Contrast with *LIFO*.

finance. As a verb, to supply with *funds* through the *issue* of stocks, bonds, notes, or mortgages, or through the retention of earnings.

financial accounting. The accounting for *assets, equities, revenues*, and *expenses* of a business. Primarily concerned with the historical reporting of the *financial position* and operations of an *entity* to external users on a regular, periodic basis. Contrast with *managerial accounting.*

Financial Accounting Foundation. The independent foundation (committee) that raises funds to support the *FASB*.

Financial Accounting Standards Advisory Council. A committee giving advice to the *FASB* on matters of strategy and emerging issues.

Financial Accounting Standards Board. *FASB.*

Financial Executives Institute. An organization of financial executives, such as chief accountants, *controllers*, and treasurers, of large businesses.

financial expense. An *expense* incurred in raising or managing *funds*.

financial position (condition). Statement of the *assets* and *equities* of a firm displayed as a *balance sheet*.

financial ratio. See *ratio*.

financial reporting objectives. FASB *Statement of Financial Accounting Concepts No. 1* sets out the broad objectives of financial reporting that are intended to guide the development of specific *accounting standards*.

financial statements. The *balance sheet, income statement, statement of retained earnings, statement of changes in financial position*, statement of changes in *owners' equity accounts*, and *notes* thereto.

financial structure. *Capital structure.*

financing lease. *Capital lease.*

finished goods. Manufactured product ready for sale; a *current asset* (*inventory*) account.

firm. Informally, any business entity. (Strictly speaking, a firm is a *partnership*.)

first-in, first-out. See *FIFO*.

fiscal year. A period of 12 consecutive months chosen by a business as the *accounting period* for annual reports. May or may not be a *natural business year* or a calendar year.

FISH. An acronym, conceived by George H. Sorter, for *first-in, still-here*. FISH is the same cost flow assumption as *LIFO*. Many readers of accounting statements find it easier to think about inventory questions in terms of items still on hand. Think of LIFO in connection with *cost of goods sold* but of FISH in connection with *ending inventory*. See *LISH*.

fixed assets. *Plant assets.*

fixed assets turnover. *Sales* divided by average total *fixed assets.*

fixed benefit plan. A *defined-benefit* (*pension*) *plan.*

fixed budget. A plan that provides for specified amounts of *expenditures* and *receipts* that do not vary with activity levels. Sometimes called a "static budget." Contrast with *flexible budget.*

fixed cost (expense). An *expenditure* or *expense* that does not vary with volume of activity, at least in the short run. See *capacity costs*, which include *enabling costs* and *standby costs*, and *programmed costs* for various subdivisions of fixed costs. See *cost terminology.*

fixed liability. *Long-term* liability.

fixed manufacturing overhead applied. The portion of *fixed manufacturing overhead cost* allocated to units produced during a period.

flexible budget. *Budget* that projects receipts and expenditures as a function of activity levels. Contrast with *fixed budget.*

flexible budget allowance. With respect to manufacturing overhead, the total cost that should have been incurred at the level of activity actually experienced during the period.

float. *Checks* whose amounts have been *added* to the depositor's bank account, but not yet subtracted from the *drawer's* bank account.

flow. The change in the amount of an item over time. Contrast with *stock*.

flow assumption. When a *withdrawal* is made from *inventory*, the cost of the withdrawal must be computed by a flow assumption if *specific identification* of units is not used. The usual flow assumptions are *FIFO, LIFO,* and *weighted-average.*

flow of costs. *Costs* passing through various classifications within an *entity*. See the accompanying diagram for a summary of *product* and *period cost* flows.

flow-through method. Accounting for the *investment credit* to show all income statement benefits of the credit in the year of acquisition, rather than spreading them over the life of the asset acquired, called the "deferral method." The *APB* preferred the deferral-method in Opinion No. 2 (1962) but accepted the flow-through method in Opinion No. 4 (1964). The term is also used in connection with *depreciation* accounting where *straight-line method* is used for financial reporting and an *accelerated* method for tax reporting. Followers of the flow-through method would not recognize a *deferred tax liability. APB Opinion* No. 11 prohibits the use of the flow-through approach in financial reporting although it has been used by some regulatory commissions.

FOB. Free on board some location (for example, FOB shipping point; FOB destination); the *invoice* price includes

Flow of Costs (and Sales Revenue)

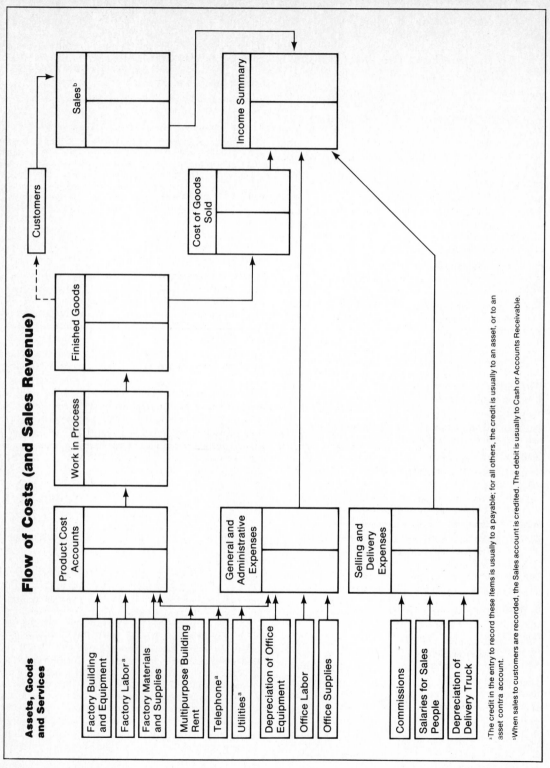

Assets, Goods and Services

Factory Building and Equipment

Factory Labor[a]

Factory Materials and Supplies

Multipurpose Building Rent

Telephone[a]

Utilities[a]

Depreciation of Office Equipment

Office Labor

Office Supplies

Commissions

Salaries for Sales People

Depreciation of Delivery Truck

Product Cost Accounts

Work in Process

Finished Goods

Customers

Sales[b]

Cost of Goods Sold

General and Administrative Expenses

Selling and Delivery Expenses

Income Summary

[a]The credit in the entry to record these items is usually to a payable; for all others, the credit is usually to an asset, or to an asset contra account.

[b]When sales to customers are recorded, the Sales account is credited. The debit is usually to Cash or Accounts Receivable.

726

delivery at seller's expense to that location. Title to goods usually passes from seller to buyer at the FOB location.

footing. Adding a column of figures.

footnotes. More detailed information than that provided in the *income statement, balance sheet, statement of retained earnings,* and *statement of changes in financial position*; these are considered an integral part of the statements and are covered by the *auditor's report*. Sometimes called "notes."

forecast. An estimate or projection of costs or revenues or both.

foreign currency. For *financial statements* prepared in a given currency, any other currency.

foreign exchange gain or loss. Gain or loss from holding *net* foreign *monetary items* during a period when the *exchange rate* changes.

Form 10-K. See *10-K.*

forward exchange contract. An agreement to exchange at a specified future date currencies of different countries at a specified rate called the "forward rate".

franchise. A privilege granted or sold, such as to use a name or to sell products or services.

free on board. *FOB.*

freight-in. The *cost* of freight or shipping incurred in acquiring *inventory*, preferably treated as a part of the cost of *inventory*. Often shown temporarily in an *adjunct account* that is closed at the end of the period with other purchase accounts to the inventory account by the acquirer.

freight-out. The *cost* of freight or shipping incurred in selling *inventory*, treated by the seller as a selling *expense* in the period of sale.

full costing. *Absorption costing.* See *reserve recognition accounting* for another definition in the context of accounting for natural resources.

full disclosure. The reporting policy requiring that all significant or *material* information is to be presented in the financial statements. See *fair presentation.*

fully diluted earnings per share. Smallest *earnings per share* figure on *common stock* that can be obtained by computing an earnings per share for all possible combinations of assumed *exercise* or *conversion* of *potentially dilutive securities.* Must be reported on the *income statement* if it is less than 97 percent of earnings available to common shareholders divided by the average number of common shares outstanding during the period.

fully vested. Said of a *pension plan* when an employee (or his or her estate) has rights to all the benefits purchased with the employer's contributions to the plan even if the employee is not employed by this employer at the time of death or retirement.

function. In governmental accounting, said of a group of related activities for accomplishing a service or regulatory program for which the governmental unit is responsible. In mathematics, a rule for associating a number, called the dependent variable, with another number or numbers, called independent variable(s).

functional classification. *Income statement* reporting form in which *expenses* are reported by functions, that is, cost of goods sold, administrative expenses, financing expenses, selling expenses; contrast with *natural classification.*

fund. An *asset* or group of assets set aside for a specific purpose. See also *fund accounting.*

fund accounting. The accounting for resources, obligations, and *capital* balances, usually of a not-for-profit or governmental *entity*, which have been segregated into *accounts* representing logical groupings based on legal, donor, or administrative restrictions or requirements. The groupings are described as "funds." The accounts of each fund are *self-balancing* and from them a *balance sheet* and an operating statement for each fund can be prepared. See *fund* and *fund balance.*

fund balance. In governmental accounting, the excess of assets of a *fund* over its liabilities and reserves; the not-for-profit equivalent of *owners' equity.*

funded. Said of a *pension plan* or other obligation when *funds* have been set aside for meeting the obligation when it becomes due. The federal law for pension plans requires that all *normal costs* be funded as recognized. In addition, *supplemental actuarial value* of pension plans must be funded over 30 or over 40 years, depending on the circumstances.

funding. Replacing *short-term* liabilities with *long-term* debt.

funds. Generally *working capital*; current assets less current liabilities. Sometimes used to refer to *cash* or to cash and *marketable securities.*

funds provided by operations. An important subtotal in the *statement of changes in financial position*. This amount is the total of revenues producing *funds* less *expenses* requiring funds. Often, the amount is shown as *net income* plus expenses not requiring funds (such as depreciation charges) minus revenues not producing funds (such as revenues recognized under the *equity method* of accounting for a long-term investment). The statement of changes in financial position maintains the same distinctions between *continuing operations, discontinued operations*, and *income* or *loss* from *extraordinary items* as does the *income statement.*

funds statement. An informal name often used for the *statement of changes in financial position.*

funny money. Said of securities such as *convertible preferred stock, convertible bonds, options*, and *warrants* that have aspects of *common stock* equity but that did not reduce reported *earnings per share* prior to the issuance of *APB Opinions* No. 9 in 1967 and No. 15 in 1969.

FUTA. Federal Unemployment Tax Act which provides for taxes to be collected at the federal level, to help subsidize the individual states' administration of their unemployment compensation programs.

G

GAAP. *Generally accepted accounting principles.* A plural noun.

gain. Increase in *owners' equity* caused by a transaction not part of a firm's typical, day-to-day operations and not part of owners' *investment* or *withdrawals*. The term "gain" (or "*loss*") is distinguished in two separate ways from related terms. First, gains (and losses) are generally used for nonoperating, incidental, peripheral, or nonroutine transactions: gain on sale of land in contrast to *gross margin* on *sale of inventory*. Second, gains and losses are *net* concepts, not gross concepts: gain or loss results from subtracting some measure of *cost* from the measure of inflow. *Revenues* and *expenses*, on the other hand, are gross concepts; their difference is a net concept. Gain is nonroutine and net, *profit* or *margin* is routine and net; revenue is routine and gross. Loss is net but can be either routine ("loss on sale of inventory") or not ("loss on disposal of segment of business").

gain contingency. See *contingency*.

general debt. Debt of a governmental unit legally payable from general revenues and backed by the full faith and credit of the governmental unit.

general expenses. *Operating expenses* other than those specifically assigned to cost of goods sold, selling, and administration.

general fixed asset (group of accounts). Accounts showing those long-term assets of a governmental unit not accounted for in *enterprise, trust,* or intragovernmental service funds.

general fund. Assets and liabilities of a nonprofit entity not specifically earmarked for other purposes; the primary operating fund of a governmental unit.

general journal. The formal record where transactions, or summaries of similar transactions, are recorded in *journal entry* form as they occur. Use of the adjective "general" usually implies only two columns for cash amounts or that there are also various *special journals*, such as a *check register* or *sales journal*, in use.

general ledger. The name for the formal *ledger* containing all of the financial statement accounts. It has equal debits and credits as evidenced by the *trial balance*. Some of the accounts in the general ledger may be *controlling accounts*, supported by details contained in *subsidiary ledgers*.

general partner. Member of *partnership* personally liable for all debts of the partnership; contrast with *limited partner*.

general price index. A measure of the aggregate prices of a wide range of goods and services in the economy at one time relative to the prices during a base period. See *consumer price index* and *GNP Implicit Price Deflator*. Contrast with *specific price index*.

general price level adjusted statements. See *constant dollar accounting*.

general price level changes. Changes in the aggregate prices of a wide range of goods and services in the economy. These price changes are measured using a *general price index*. Contrast with *specific price changes*.

general purchasing power. The command of the dollar over a wide range of goods and services in the economy. The general purchasing power of the dollar is inversely related to changes in a general price index. See *general price index*.

general purchasing power accounting. See *constant dollar accounting*.

generally accepted accounting principles. GAAP. As previously defined by the *APB* and now by the *FASB*, the conventions, rules, and procedures necessary to define accepted accounting practice at a particular time; includes both broad guidelines and relatively detailed practices and procedures.

generally accepted auditing standards. The standards, as opposed to particular procedures, promulgated by the *AICPA* (in *Statements on Auditing Standards*) that concern "the auditor's professional quantities" and "the judgment exercised by him in the performance of his examination and in his report." Currently, there are ten such standards: three general ones (concerned with proficiency, independence, and degree of care to be exercised), three standards of field work, and four standards of reporting. The first standard of reporting requires that the *auditor's report* state whether or not the *financial statements* are prepared in accordance with *generally accepted accounting principles*. Thus the typical auditor's report says that the examination was conducted in accordance with generally accepted auditing standards and that the statements are prepared in accordance with generally accepted accounting principles. See *auditor's report*.

GNP Implicit Price Deflator (Index). A *price index* issued quarterly by the Office of Business Economics of the U.S. Department of Commerce. This index attempts to trace the price level of all *goods and services* comprising the *gross national product*. Contrast with *consumer price index*.

going concern assumption. For accounting purposes a business is assumed to remain in operation long enough for all its current plans to be carried out. This assumption is part of the justification for the *acquisition cost* basis, rather than a *liquidation* or *exit value* basis of accounting.

going public. Said of a business when its *shares* become widely traded, rather than being closely held by relatively few shareholders. Issuing shares to the general investing public.

goods. Items of merchandise, supplies, raw materials, or finished goods. Sometimes the meaning of "goods" is extended to include all *tangible* items, as in the phrase "goods and services."

goods available for sale. The sum of *beginning inventory* plus all acquisitions of merchandise or finished goods during an *accounting period*.

goods in process. *Work in process*.

goodwill. The excess of cost of an acquired firm (or operating unit) over the current or *fair market value* of the separately identifiable *net assets* of the acquired unit. Before goodwill is recognized, all identifiable assets, whether or not on the books of the acquired unit, must be given a *fair market value*. For example, a firm has developed a *patent* which is not recognized on its books because of *SFAS No. 2*. If another company acquires the firm, the acquirer will recognize the patent at an amount equal to its estimated fair market value. Informally the term is used to indicate the value of good customer relations, high employee morale, a well-respected business name, and so on, that are expected to result in greater than normal earning power.

goodwill method. A method of accounting for the *admission* of a new partner to a *partnership* when the new partner is to be credited with a portion of capital different from the value of the *tangible* assets contributed as a fraction of tangible assets on the partnership. See *bonus method* for a description and contrast.

GPL. General price level; usually used as an adjective modifying the word "accounting" to mean *constant dollar accounting*.

GPLA. General price level adjusted accounting; *constant dollar accounting*.

GPP. General purchasing power; usually used as an adjective modifying the word "accounting" to mean *constant dollar accounting*.

graded vesting. Said of a *pension plan* where not all employee benefits are currently *vested*. By law, the benefits must become vested according to one of several formulas as time passes

grandfather clause. An exemption in new accounting *pronouncements* exempting transactions that occurred before a given date from the new accounting treatment. For example, *APB Opinion* No. 17, adopted in 1970, exempted *goodwill* acquired before 1970 from required *amortization*. The term "grandfather" appears in the title to *SFAS No. 10*.

gross. Not adjusted or reduced by deductions or subtractions. Contrast with *net*.

gross margin. *Net sales* minus *cost of goods sold*.

gross margin percent. $100 \times (1 - cost\ of\ goods\ sold/net\ sales) = 100 \times (gross\ margin/net\ sales)$.

gross national product. GNP. The market value within a nation for a year of all goods and services produced as measured by final sales of goods and services to individuals, corporations, and governments plus the excess of exports over imports.

gross price method (of recording purchase or sales discounts). The *purchase* (or *sale*) is recorded at its *invoice price*, not deducting the amounts of *discounts* available. Discounts taken are recorded in a *contra* account to purchases (or sales). Information on discounts lapsed is not made available, and for this reason, most firms prefer the *net-price method* of recording purchase discounts.

gross profit. *Gross margin*.

gross profit method. A method of estimating *ending inventory* amounts. *Cost of goods sold* is measured as some fraction of sales; the *inventory equation* is then used to value *ending inventory*.

gross profit ratio. *Gross margin* divided by *net sales*.

gross sales. All *sales* at *invoice* prices, not reduced by *discounts, allowances, returns*, or other adjustments.

group depreciation. A method of calculating *depreciation* charges where similar assets are combined, rather than depreciated separately. No gain or loss is recognized on retire-

ment of items from the group until the last item in the group is sold or retired. See *composite life method*.

guarantee. A promise to answer for payment of debt or performance of some obligation if the person liable for the debt or obligation fails to perform. A guarantee is *contingency* of the *entity* making the promise. Often, the words "guarantee" and "warranty" are used to mean the same thing. In precise usage, however, "guarantee" means promise to fulfill the promise of some person to perform a contractual obligation such as to pay a sum of money, whereas "warranty" is most often used to refer to promises about pieces of machinery or other products. See *warranty*.

H

hidden reserve. The term refers to an amount by which *owners' equity* has been understated, perhaps deliberately. The understatement arises from an undervaluation of *assets* or overvaluation of *liabilities*. By undervaluing assets on this period's *balance sheet, net income* in some future period can be made to look artificially high by disposing of the asset: actual *revenues* less artificially low cost of assets sold yields artificially high net income. There is no *account* that has this title.

historical cost. *Acquisition cost; original cost*; a *sunk cost*.

historical-cost/constant-dollar accounting. Accounting based on *historical cost* valuations measured in *constant dollars. Nonmonetary items* are restated to reflect changes in the *general purchasing power* of the dollar since the time the specific *assets* were acquired or *liabilities* were incurred. A *gain* or *loss* is recognized on *monetary items* as they are held over time periods when the general purchasing power of the dollar changes.

historical summary. A part of the *annual report* to shareholders that shows important items, such as *net income, revenues, expenses, asset* and *equity* totals, *earnings per share*, and the like, for five or ten periods including the current one. Usually not as much detail is shown in the historical summary as in *comparative statements*, which typically report as much detail for the two preceding years as for the current year. Annual reports may contain both comparative statements and a historical summary.

holding company. A company that confines its activities to owning *stock* in, and supervising management of, other companies. A holding company usually owns a controlling interest in, that is more than 50 percent of the voting stock of, the companies whose stock it holds. Contrast with *mutual fund*. See *conglomerate*. In British usage, the term refers to any company with controlling interest in another company.

holding gain or loss. Difference between end-of-period price and beginning-of-period price of an asset held during the period. Realized holding gains and losses are not ordinarily separately reported in financial statements. Unrealized gains are not usually reflected in income at all. Some unrealized losses, such as on inventory or marketable securities, are reflected in income or *owners' equity* as the losses occur; see *lower of cost or market*. See *inventory profit* for further refinement, including *gains* on *assets* sold during the period.

holding gain or loss net of inflation. Increase or decrease in the *current cost* of an asset while it is held measured in units of *constant dollars*.

horizontal analysis. *Time series analysis.*

human resource accounting. A term used to describe a variety of proposals that seek to report and emphasize the importance of human resources—knowledgeable, trained, and loyal employees—in a company's earning process and total assets.

hybrid security. *Security*, such as a *convertible bond*, containing elements of both *debt* and *owners' equity*.

hypothecation. The *pledging* of property, without transfer of title or possession, to secure a loan.

I

I. *Identity matrix.*

ideal standard costs. *Standard costs* set equal to those that would be incurred under the best possible conditions.

identity matrix. A square *matrix* with ones on the main diagonal and zeros elsewhere; a matrix I such that for any other matrix A, IA = AI = A. The matrix equivalent to the number one.

IIA. *Institute of Internal Auditors.*

IMA. Institute of Management Accounting. See *CMA* and *National Association of Accountants*.

imprest fund. *Petty cash fund.*

improvement. An *expenditure* to extend the useful life of an *asset* or to improve its performance (rate of output, cost) over that of the original asset. Such expenditures are *capitalized* as part of the asset's cost. Sometimes called "betterment." Contrast with *maintenance* and *repair*.

imputed cost. A cost that does not appear in accounting records, such as the *interest* that could be earned on cash spent to acquire inventories rather than, say, government bonds. Or, consider a firm that owns the buildings it occupies. This firm has an imputed cost for rent in an amount equal to what it would have to pay to use similar buildings owned by another.

imputed interest. See *interest, imputed*.

income. *Excess of revenues* and *gains* over *expenses* and *losses* for a period; *net income*. Sometimes used with an appropriate modifier to refer to the various intermediate amounts shown in a *multiple-step income statement*. Sometimes used to refer to revenues, as in "rental income." See *comprehensive income*.

income accounts. *Revenue* and *expense accounts*.

income distribution account. *Temporary account* sometimes debited when *dividends* are declared; closed to *retained earnings*.

income from continuing operations. As defined by *APB Opinion* No. 30, all *revenues* less all *expenses* except for the following: results of operations (including income tax effects) that have been or will be discontinued; *gains* or *losses*, including income tax effects, on disposal of segments of the business; gains or losses, including income tax effects, from *extraordinary items*; and the cumulative effect of *accounting changes*.

income from discontinued operations. *Income*, net of tax effects, from parts of the business that have been discontinued during the period or are to be discontinued in the near future. Such items are reported on separate lines of the *income statement* after *income from continuing operations* but before *extraordinary items*.

income (revenue) bond. See *special revenue debt*.

income statement. The statement of *revenues, expenses, gains*, and *losses* for the period ending with *net income* for the period. The *earnings per share* amount is usually shown on the income statement; the *reconciliation* of beginning and ending balances of *retained earnings* may also be shown in a combined statement of income and retained earnings. See *income from continuing operations, income from discontinued operations, extraordinary items, multiple-step, single-step*.

income summary. An *account* used in problem solving that serves as a surrogate for the *income statement*. All *revenues* are closed to the Income Summary as *credits* and all *expenses*, as *debits*. The *balance* in the account, after all other *closing entries* are made, is then closed to the retained earnings or other *owners' equity* account and represents *net income* for the period.

income tax. An annual tax levied by the federal and other governments on the income of an entity.

income tax allocation. See *deferred tax liability* and *tax allocation: intrastatement*.

incremental. An adjective used to describe the change in *cost, expense, investment, cash flow, revenue, profit*, and the like if one or more units are produced or sold or if an activity is undertaken.

indenture. See *bond indenture*.

independence. The mental attitude required of the *CPA* in performing the *attest* function. It implies impartiality and that the members of the auditing CPA firm own no stock in the corporation being audited.

independent accountant. The *CPA* who performs the *attest* function for a firm.

indeterminate-term liability. A *liability* lacking the criterion of being due at a definite time. This term is our own coinage to encompass the *deferred income tax liability* and *minority interest*.

indexation. An attempt by lawmakers or parties to a contract to cope with the effects of *inflation*. Amounts fixed in law or contracts are "indexed" when these amounts change as a given measure of price changes. For example, a so-called escalator clause (*COLA*) in a labor contract might provide that hourly wages will be increased as the *consumer price index* increases. Many economists have suggested the indexation of numbers fixed in the *income tax* laws. If, for example, the personal *exemption* is $1,000 at the start of the period, prices rise by 10 percent during the period, and the personal exemption is indexed, then the personal exemption would automatically rise to $1,100 (= $1,000 + .10 × $1,000) at the end of the period.

indirect costs. Costs of production not easily associated with the production of specific goods and services; *overhead costs.* May be *allocated* on some arbitrary basis to specific products or departments.

indirect labor (material) cost. An *indirect cost* for labor (material) such as for supervisors (supplies).

individual proprietorship. *Sole proprietorship.*

Industry Audit Guide. A series of publications by the *AICPA* providing specific *accounting* and *auditing principles* for specialized situations. Audit guides have been issued covering government contractors, state and local government units, investment companies, finance companies, brokers and dealers in securities, and many others.

inflation. A time of generally rising prices.

inflation accounting. Strictly speaking, *constant dollar accounting.* Some writers use the term, incorrectly, to mean *current cost accounting.*

information system. A system, sometimes formal and sometimes informal, for collecting, processing, and communicating data that are useful for the managerial functions of decision making, planning, and control, and for financial reporting under the *attest* requirement.

insolvent. Unable to pay debts when due. Said of a company even though *assets* exceed *liabilities.*

installment. Partial payment of a debt or collection of a receivable, usually according to a contract.

installment contracts receivable. The name used for *accounts receivable* when the *installment method* of recognizing revenue is used. Its *contra, unrealized gross margin*, is shown on the balance sheet as a subtraction from the amount receivable.

installment (sales) method. Recognizing *revenue* and *expense* (or *gross margin*) from a sales transaction in proportion to the fraction of the selling price collected during a period. Allowed by the *IRS* for income tax reporting, but acceptable in *GAAP* (*APB Opinion* No. 10) only when cash collections are reasonably uncertain. See *realized* (and *unrealized*) *gross margin.*

installment sales. Sales on account where the buyer promises to pay in several separate payments, called *installments.* Sometimes are, but need not be, accounted for on the *installment method.* If installment sales are accounted for with the sales *basis of revenue recognition* for financial reporting but with the installment method for income tax returns, then a *deferred income tax liability* arises.

Institute of Internal Auditors. IIA. The national association of accountants who are engaged in internal auditing and are employed by business firms. Administers a comprehensive professional examination; those who pass qualify to be designated CIA, certified internal auditor.

Institute of Management Accounting. See *CMA.*

insurance. A contract for reimbursement of specific losses; purchased with insurance premiums. Self-insurance

is not insurance but merely the willingness to assume risk of incurring losses while raving the premium.

intangible asset. A nonphysical, *noncurrent* right that gives a firm an exclusive or preferred position in the marketplace. Examples are a *copyright, patent, trademark, goodwill, organization costs, capitalized* advertising cost, computer programs, licenses for any of the preceding, government licenses (e.g., broadcasting or the right to sell liquor), *leases, franchises,* mailing lists, exploration permits, import and export permits, construction permits, and marketing quotas.

intercompany elimination. See *eliminations.*

intercompany profit. If one *affiliated company* sells to another, and the goods remain in the second company's *inventory* at the end of the period, then the first company's *profit* has not been realized by a sale to an outsider. That profit is called "intercompany profit" and is eliminated from net *income* in *consolidated income statements* or when the *equity method* is used.

interest. The charge or cost for using money; expressed as a rate per period, usually one year, called the interest rate. See *effective interest rate* and *nominal interest rate.*

interest, imputed. If a borrower merely promises to pay a single amount, sometime later than the present, then the present value (computed at a *fair market* interest rate, called the "imputed interest rate") of the promise is less than the *face amount* to be paid at *maturity.* The difference between the face amount and the present value of a promise is called imputed interest. See also *imputed cost.*

interest factor. One plus the *interest* rate.

interest method. See *effective interest method.*

interest rate. See *interest.*

interfund accounts. In governmental accounting, the accounts that show transactions between funds, especially interfund receivables and payables.

interim statements. Statements issued for periods less than the regular, annual *accounting period.* Most corporations are required to issue interim statements on a quarterly basis. The basic issue in preparing interim reports is whether their purpose is to report on the interim period (1) as a self-contained accounting period, or (2) as an integral part of the year of which they are a part so that forecasts of annual performance can be made. *APB Opinion* No. 28 and the *SEC* require that interim reports be constructed largely to satisfy the second purpose.

internal audit. An *audit* conducted by employees to ascertain whether or not *internal control* procedures are working, as opposed to an external audit conducted by a *CPA.*

internal control. See *control system.*

internal rate of return. The discount rate that equates the net *present value* of a stream of cash outflows and inflows to zero.

internal reporting. Reporting for management's use in planning and control; contrast with *external reporting* for financial statement users.

Internal Revenue Service. IRS. Agency of the U.S.

731

Treasury Department responsible for administering the Internal Revenue Code and collecting income and certain other taxes.

International Accounting Standards Committee. An organization that promotes the establishment of international accounting standards.

interperiod tax allocation. See *deferred income tax liability*.

interpolation. The estimation of an unknown number intermediate between two (or more) known numbers.

Interpretations of Statements of Financial Accounting Standards. See *FASB Interpretations*.

in the black (red). Operating at a profit (loss).

intrastatement tax allocation. See *tax allocation: intrastatement*.

inventoriable costs. *Costs* incurred that are added to the cost of manufactured products. *Product costs* (*assets*) as opposed to *period expenses*.

inventory. As a noun, the *balance* in an asset *account* such as raw materials, supplies, work in process, and finished goods. As a verb, to calculate the *cost* of goods on hand at a given time or to physically count items on hand.

inventory equation. *Beginning inventory + net addi-*

tions — withdrawals = ending inventory. Ordinarily, additions are net purchases and withdrawals are *cost of goods sold*. Notice that ending inventory, to be shown on the balance sheet, and cost of goods sold, to be shown on the income statement, are not independent of each other. The larger is one, the smaller must be the other. In valuing inventories, beginning inventory and net purchases are usually known. In some inventory methods (for example, some applications of the *retail inventory method*), costs of goods sold is measured and the equation is used to find the cost of ending inventory. In most methods, cost of ending inventory is measured and the equation is used to find the cost of goods sold (withdrawals). In *current cost* (in contrast to *historical cost*) accounting *additions* (in the equation) include holding gains, whether realized or not. Thus the current cost inventory equation is: Beginning Inventory (at Current Cost) + Purchases (where Current Cost is Historical Cost) + Holding Gains (whether Realized or Not) — Ending Inventory (at Current Cost) = Cost of Goods Sold (Current Cost).

inventory holding gains. See *inventory profit*.

inventory layer. See LIFO *inventory layer*.

inventory profit. This term has several possible meanings. Consider the data in the accompanying illustration. The *historical cost* data are derived in the conventional manner; the

Inventory Profit Illustration

Assumed Data	(Historical) Acquisition Cost Assuming FIFO	Current Cost
Inventory, 1/1/82	$ 900	$1,100
Inventory, 12/31/82	1,160	1,550
Cost of Goods Sold for 1982	4,740	4,850
Sales for 1982 . . . . $5,200		
INCOME STATEMENT FOR 1982		
Sales	$5,200	$5,200
Cost of Goods Sold	4,740	4,850
(1) Income from Continuing Operations		$ 350
Realized Holding Gains		110[a]
(2) Realized Income = Conventional Net Income (under FIFO)	$ 460	$ 460
Unrealized Holding Gain		190[b]
(3) Economic income		$ 650

[a]Realized holding gain during a period is current cost of goods sold less historical cost of goods sold; for 1982 the realized holding gain under FIFO is $110 = $4,850 − $4,740. Some refer to this as "inventory profit."

[b]The total unrealized holding gain at any time is current cost of inventory on hand at that time less historical cost of that inventory. The unrealized holding gain during a period is unrealized holding gain at the end of the period less the unrealized holding gain at the beginning of the period. Unrealized holding gain prior to 1982 is $200 = $1,100 − $900. Unrealized holding gain during 1982 = ($1,550 − $1,160) − ($1,100 − $900) = $390 − $200 = $190.

firm uses a *FIFO cost flow assumption*. The *current cost* data are assumed, but are of the kind that the *FASB* requires in *SFAS No. 33*.

The term *income from continuing operations* refers to revenues less expenses based on current, rather than historical, costs. To that subtotal add realized holding gains to arrive at realized (conventional) income. To that, add unrealized holding gains to arrive at *economic income*.

The term "inventory profit" often refers (for example in some *SEC* releases) to the realized holding gain, $110 in the illustration. The amount of inventory profit will usually be material when FIFO is used and prices are rising.

Others, including us, prefer to use the term "inventory profit" to refer to the total *holding gain*, $300 (= $110 + $190, both realized and unrealized), but this appears to be a lost cause.

In periods of rising prices and increasing inventories, the realized holding gains under a FIFO cost-flow assumption will be substantially larger than under LIFO. In the illustration, for example, assume under LIFO that the historical cost of goods sold is $4,800, that historical LIFO cost of beginning inventory is $600, and that historical LIFO cost of ending inventory is $800. Then income from continuing operations, based on current costs, remains $350 (= $5,200 − $4,850), realized holding gains are $50 (= $4,850 − $4,800), realized income is $400 (= $350 + $50), the unrealized holding gain for the year is $250 (= ($1,550 − $800) − ($1,100 − $600)), and economic income is $650 (= $350 + $50 + $250). Because the only real effect of the cost flow assumption is to split the total holding gain into realized and unrealized portions, economic income is the same, independent of the cost flow assumption. The total of holding gains is $300 in the illustration. The choice of cost-flow assumption merely determines the portion reported as realized.

inventory turnover. Number of times the average *inventory* has been sold during a period; *cost of goods sold* for a period divided by average inventory for the period. See *ratio*.

invested capital. *Contributed capital.*

investee. A company whose *stock* is owned by another.

investment. An *expenditure* to acquire property or other assets in order to produce *revenue*; the *asset* so acquired; hence a *current* expenditure made in anticipation of future income. Said of *securities* of other companies held for the long term and shown in a separate section of the *balance sheet*; in this context, contrast with *marketable securities*.

investment credit. A reduction in income tax liability granted by the federal government to firms that buy new equipment. This item is a credit, in that it is deducted from the tax bill, not from pretax income. The tax credit has been a given percentage of the purchase price of certain assets purchased. The actual rules and rates have changed over the years. See *flow-through method* and *carryforward*.

investment tax credit. *Investment credit.*

invoice. A document showing the details of a sale or purchase transaction.

IRS. *Internal Revenue Service.*

issue. When a corporation exchanges its stock (or bonds) for cash or other assets, the corporation is said to issue, not sell, that stock (or bonds). Also used in the context of withdrawing supplies or materials from inventory for use in operations and drawing of a *check*.

issued shares. Those shares of *authorized capital stock* of a *corporation* that have been distributed to the shareholders. See *issue*. Shares of *treasury stock* are legally issued but are not considered to be *outstanding* for the purpose of voting, *dividend declarations* and *earnings per share* calculations.

J

job cost sheet. A schedule showing actual or budgeted inputs for a special order.

job development credit. The name used for the *investment credit* in the 1971 tax law on this subject.

job-order costing. Accumulation of *costs* for a particular identifiable batch of product, known as a job, as it moves through production.

joint cost. Cost of simultaneously producing or otherwise acquiring two or more products, called joint products, that must, by the nature of the process, be produced or acquired together, such as the cost of beef and hides of cattle. Generally, the joint costs of production are allocated to the individual products in proportion to their respective sales value at the *splitoff* point. Other examples include central *corporate expenses, overhead* of a department when several products are manufactured, and *basket purchases*. See *common cost*. See *sterilized allocation*.

joint product. One of two or more outputs with significant value produced by a process that must be produced or acquired simultaneously. See *by-product* and *joint cost*.

journal. The place where transactions are recorded as they occur. The book of original entry.

journal entry. A recording in a *journal*, of equal *debits* and *credits*, with an explanation of the *transaction*, if necessary.

journalize. To make an entry in a *journal*.

Journal of Accountancy. A monthly publication of the *AICPA*.

Journal of Accounting Research. Scholarly journal containing articles on theoretical and empirical aspects of accounting. Published three times a year by the Graduate School of Business of the University of Chicago.

journal voucher. A *voucher* documenting (and sometimes authorizing) a transaction, leading to an entry in the *journal*.

K

kiting. This term means slightly different things in banking and auditing contexts. In both, however, it refers to the wrongful practice of taking advantage of the *float*, the time that elapses between the deposit of a *check* in one bank and its collection at another. In the banking context, an individual deposits in Bank A a check written on Bank B. He (or she) then writes checks against the deposit created in Bank

733

A. Several days later, he deposits in Bank B a check written on Bank A, to cover the original check written on Bank B. Still later, he deposits in Bank A a check written on Bank B. The process of covering the deposit in Bank A with a check written on Bank B and vice versa is continued until an actual deposit of cash can be arranged. In the auditing context, kiting refers to a form of *window dressing* where the amount of the account Cash in Bank is made to appear larger than it actually is by depositing in Bank A a check written on Bank B without recording the check written on Bank B in the *check register* until after the close of the *accounting period*.

know-how. Technical or business information of the type defined under *trade secret*, but that is not maintained as a secret. The rules of accounting for this asset are the same as for other *intangibles*.

L

labor variances. The *price* (or *rate*) and *quantity* (or *usage*) *variances* for *direct labor* inputs in a *standard cost system*.

land. An *asset shown at acquisition cost* plus the *cost* of any nondepreciable *improvements*. In accounting, implies use as a plant or office site, rather than as a *natural resource*, such as timberland or farm land.

lapping (accounts receivable). The theft, by an employee, of cash sent in by a customer to discharge the latter's *payable*. The theft from the first customer is concealed by using cash received from a second customer. The theft from the second customer is concealed by using the cash received from a third customer, and so on. The process is continued until the thief returns the funds or can make the theft permanent by creating a fictitious *expense* or receivable write off, or until the fraud is discovered.

lapse. To expire; said of, for example, an insurance policy or discounts made available for prompt payment that are not taken.

last-in, first-out. See *LIFO*.

layer. See *LIFO inventory layer*.

lead time. The time that elapses between placing an order and receipt of the *goods or services* ordered.

lease. A contract calling for the lessee (user) to pay the lessor (owner) for the use of an asset. A cancelable lease is one the lessee can cancel at any time. A noncancelable lease requires payments from the lessee for the life of the lease and usually has many of the economic characteristics of *debt financing*. Most long-term noncancelable leases meet the usual criteria to be classified as a *liability* but some leases entered into before 1977 need not be shown as a liability. *SFAS No. 13* and the *SEC* require disclosure in notes to the financial statements of the commitments for long-term noncancelable leases. See *capital lease* and *operating lease*.

leasehold. The *asset* representing the right of the *lessee* to use leased property. See *lease* and *leasehold improvement*.

leasehold improvement. An *improvement* to leased property. Should be *amortized* over *service life* or the life of the lease, whichever is shorter.

least and latest rule. Pay the least amount of taxes as late as possible within the law to minimize the *present value* of tax payments for a given set of operations.

ledger. A book of accounts. See *general ledger* and *subsidiary ledger*; contrast with *journal*. Book of final entry.

legal capital. The amount of *contributed capital* that, according to state law, must remain permanently in the firm as protection for creditors.

legal entity. See *entity*.

lender. See *loan*.

lessee. See *lease*.

lessor. See *lease*.

letter stock. Privately placed *common shares*; so called because the *SEC* requires the purchaser to sign a letter of intent not to resell the shares.

leverage. "Operating leverage" refers to the tendency of *net income* to rise at a faster rate than sales when there are *fixed costs*. A doubling of sales, for example, usually implies a more than doubling of net income. "Financial leverage" (or "capital leverage") refers to the increased rate of return on owners' equity (see *ratio*) when an investment earns a return larger than the *interest rate* paid for *debt* financing. Because the interest charges on debt are usually fixed, any *incremental* income benefits owners and none benefits debtors. When "leverage" is used without a qualifying adjective, it usually refers to financial leverage and means the use of *long-term* debt in securing *funds* for the *entity*.

leveraged lease. A special form of lease involving three parties—a *lender*, a *lessor*, and a *lessee*. The lender, such as a bank or insurance company, lends a portion, say 80 percent, of the cash required for acquiring the *asset*. The lessor puts up the remainder, 20 percent, of the cash required. The lessor acquires the asset with the cash, using the asset as security for the loan and leases it to the lessee on a *noncancelable* basis. The lessee makes periodic lease payments to the lessor, who in turn makes payments on the loan to the lender. Typically, the lessor has no obligation for the debt to the lender other than transferring a portion of the receipts from the lessee. If the lessee should default on required lease payments, then the lender can repossess the leased asset. The lessor is usually entitled to deductions for tax purposes for depreciation on the asset, for interest expense on the loan from the lender, and for any investment credit. The lease is leveraged in the sense that the lessor, who enjoys most of the risks and rewards of ownership, usually borrows most of the funds needed to acquire the asset. *See leverage*.

liability. A probable future sacrifice of economic benefits arising from present obligations of a particular *entity* to *transfer assets* or to provide services to other entities in the future as a result of past *transactions* or events. *SFAC No. 3* says that "probable" refers to that which can reasonably be expected or believed but is neither certain nor proved. A liability has three essential characteristics: (1) transfer of assets or services at a specified or determinable date, (2) the entity has little or no discretion to avoid the transfer, and (3) the event causing the obligation has already happened.

lien. The right of person A to satisfy a claim against person B by holding B's property as security or by seizing B's property.

life annuity. A *contingent annuity* in which payments cease at death of a specified person(s), usually the *annuitant(s)*.

LIFO. An *inventory* flow assumption where the *cost of goods sold* is the cost of the most recently acquired units and the *ending inventory cost* is computed from costs of the oldest units; contrast with *FIFO*. In periods of rising prices and increasing inventories, LIFO leads to higher reported expenses and therefore lower reported income and lower balance sheet inventories than does FIFO. See also *FISH* and *inventory profit*.

LIFO conformity rule. The *IRS* requires that companies which use a *LIFO cost flow assumption* for *income taxes* also use LIFO in computing *income* reported in *financial statements* and forbids disclosure of *pro forma* results from using any other cost flow assumption. During 1981, this rule was challenged by a federal court decision. The eventual outcome is not known as this book goes to press; throughout, we have assumed the rule remains in force.

LIFO, dollar value method. See *dollar value LIFO method*.

LIFO inventory layer. The *ending inventory* for a period is likely to be larger than the *beginning inventory*. Under a *LIFO cost flow assumption*, this increase in physical quantities is given a value computed by the prices of the earliest purchases during the year. The LIFO inventory then consists of layers, sometimes called "slices," which typically consist of relatively small amounts of physical quantities from each of the past several years. Each layer carries the prices from near the beginning of the period when it was acquired. The earliest layers will typically (in periods of rising prices) have prices very much less than current prices. If inventory quantities should decline in a subsequent period, the latest layers enter cost of goods sold first.

LIFO reserve. *Unrealized holding gain* in *ending inventory*: current or *FIFO historical* cost of ending inventory less LIFO *historical cost*. See *reserve*.

limited liability. Shareholders of corporations are not personally liable for debts of the company.

limited partner. Member of a *partnership* not personally liable for debts of the partnership; every partnership must have at least one *general partner* who is fully liable.

line of business reporting. See *segment reporting*.

line of credit. An agreement with the bank or set of banks for short-term borrowings on demand.

liquid. Said of a business with a substantial amount (the amount is unspecified) of *working capital*, especially *quick assets*.

liquid assets. *Cash, current marketable securities*, and, sometimes, *current receivables*.

liquidating dividend. *Dividend* declared in the winding up of a business to distribute the assets of the company to the shareholders. Usually treated by recipient as a return of *investment*, not as *revenue*.

liquidation. Payment of a debt. Sale of assets in closing down a business or a segment thereof.

liquidation value per share. The amount each *share* of stock will receive if the corporation is dissolved. For *preferred stock* with a *liquidation preference*, a stated amount per share.

liquidity. Refers to the availability of *cash*, or near cash resources, for meeting a firm's obligations.

LISH. An acronym, conceived by George H. Sorter, for *last-in, still here*. LISH is the same cost flow assumption as *FIFO*. Many readers of accounting statements find it easier to think about inventory questions in terms of items still on hand. Think of FIFO in connection with *cost of goods sold* but of LISH in connection with *ending inventory*. See *FISH*.

list price. The published or nominally quoted price for goods.

list price method. See *trade-in transaction*.

loan. An arrangement where the owner of property, called the lender, allows someone else, called the borrower, the use of the property for a period of time that is usually specified in the agreement setting up the loan. The borrower promises to return the property to the lender and, often, to make a payment for use of the property. Generally used when the property is *cash* and the payment for its use is *interest*.

long-lived (term) asset. An asset whose benefits are expected to be received over several years. A *noncurrent* asset, usually includes *investments, plant assets*, and *intangibles*.

long-term (construction) contract accounting. The *percentage of completion method* of *revenue* recognition. Sometimes used to mean the *completed contract method*.

loss. Excess of *cost* over net proceeds for a single transaction; negative *income* for a period. A cost expiration that produced no *revenue*. See *gain* for a discussion of related and contrasting terms.

loss contingency. See *contingency*.

lower of cost or market. A basis for valuation of *inventory* or *marketable equity securities*. The inventory value is set at the lower of *acquisition cost* or *current replacement cost* (market), subject to the following constraints: First, the market value of an item used in the computation cannot exceed its *net realizable value*—an amount equal to selling price less reasonable costs to complete production and to sell the item. Second, the market value of an item used in the computation cannot be less than the net realizable value minus the normal *profit* ordinarily realized on disposition of completed items of this type. The lower-of-cost-or-market valuation is chosen as the lower of acquisition *cost* or replacement cost (*market*) subject to the upper and lower bounds on replacement cost established in the first two steps. Thus,

Market Value = Midvalue of (Replacement Cost, Net Realizable Value, Net Realizable Value less Normal Profit Margin)

Lower-of-Cost- = Minimum (Acquisition Cost, or-Market Market Value). Valuation

735

The accompanying exhibit illustrates the calculation of the lower-of-cost-or-market valuation for four inventory items. Notice that each of the four possible outcomes occurs once in determining lower of cost or market. Item 1 uses acquisition cost; item 2 uses net realizable value; item 3 uses replacement cost; and item 4 uses net realizable value less normal profit.

		Item		
Calculation of Market Value	1	2	3	4
(a) Replacement Cost	$92	$96	$92	$96
(b) Net Realizable Value	95	95	95	95
(c) Net Realizable Value Less Normal Profit Margin $[= (b) - \$9]$	86	86	86	86
(d) Market = Midvalue [(a), (b), (c)]	92	95	92	86
Calculation of Lower of Cost or Market				
(e) Acquisition Cost	90	97	96	90
(f) Market $[= (d)]$	92	95	92	86
(g) Lower of Cost or Market = Minimum [(e), (f)]	90	95	92	86

Lower of cost or market cannot be used for inventory on tax returns in a combination with a *LIFO* flow assumption.

In the context of inventory, once the asset is written down, a new "original cost" basis is established and subsequent increases in market value are ignored in the accounts.

In the context of *marketable equity securities* the method is applied separately to short-term and long-term portfolios of securities. Losses in market value on the short-term portfolio (and any subsequent recoveries in value up to original cost) are reported as part of *income from continuing operations* for the period. For the long-term portfolio, the losses (and subsequent recoveries, if any) are *debited* (or *credited*) directly to an *owners equity contra account*.

Note that hyphens are not used when the term is used as a noun but hyphens are used when the term is used as an adjectival phrase.

lump-sum acquisition. *Basket purchase*.

M

maintenance. *Expenditures* undertaken to preserve an *asset's* service potential for its originally-intended life; these expenditures are treated as *period expenses* or *product costs*; contrast with *improvement*. See *repair*.

make-or-buy decision. A managerial decision about whether the firm should produce a product internally or purchase it from others. Proper make-or-buy decisions in the short run result when *opportunity costs* are the only costs considered in decision making.

maker (of note) (of check). One who signs a *note* to borrow. One who signs a *check*; in this context synonymous with drawer; see *draft*.

management. Executive authority that operates a business.

Management Accounting. Monthly publication of the *NAA*.

management (managerial) accounting. Reporting designed to enhance the ability of management to do its job of decision making, planning, and control; contrast with *financial accounting*.

management audit. An audit conducted to ascertain whether the objectives, policies, and procedures for a firm or one of its operating units are properly carried out. Generally applies only to activities for which qualitative standards can be specified. See *audit* and *internal audit*.

management by exception. A principle of management where attention is focused only on performance that is significantly different from that expected.

managerial accounting. See *management accounting*.

manufacturing cost. Cost of producing goods, usually in a factory.

manufacturing expense. An imprecise, and generally incorrect, alternative title for *manufacturing overhead*.

manufacturing overhead. General manufacturing *costs* incurred in providing a capacity to carry on productive activities but that are not directly associated with identifiable units of product. *Fixed* manufacturing overhead costs are treated as a *product cost* under *absorption costing* but as an *expense* of the period under *direct costing*.

margin. *Revenue* less specified expenses. See *contribution margin, gross margin*, and *current margin*.

margin of safety. Excess of actual, or budgeted, sales over *breakeven* sales. Usually expressed in dollars; may be expressed in units of product.

marginal cost. The *incremental cost* or *differential cost* of the last unit added to production or the first unit subtracted from production. See *cost terminology*.

marginal costing. *Direct costing*.

marginal revenue. The increment in *revenue* from sale of one additional unit of product.

marginal tax rate. The tax imposed on the next dollar of taxable income generated; contrast with *average tax rate*.

markdown. See *markup* for definition and contrast.

markdown cancellation. See *markup* for definition and contrast.

market price. See *fair market price*.

market rate. The rate of *interest* a company must pay to borrow *funds* currently. See *effective rate*.

marketable equity securities. *Marketable securities* representing *owners' equity* interest in other companies, rather than *loans* to them.

marketable securities. *Stocks* and *bonds* of other companies held that can be readily sold on stock exchanges or over-the-counter markets and that the company plans to sell as cash is needed. Classified as *current assets* and as part of *working capital*. The same securities held for *long-term* purposes would be classified as *noncurrent assets*. *SFAS No. 12* requires the *lower-of-cost-or-market* valuation basis for all marketable equity securities but different accounting treatments (with differing effect on income) depending upon whether the security is a *current* or a *noncurrent asset*.

markon. See *markup* for definition and contrast.

markup. When a retailer acquires items for *inventory*, the items are given a selling price. The difference between the original selling price and cost is most precisely called "markon," although many business people use the term "markup," and because of confusion of this use of "markup" with its precise definition (see below), "original markup" is sometimes used. If the originally-established retail price is increased, the precise term for the amount of price increase is "markup," although "additional markup" is sometimes used. If a selling price is lowered, the terms "markdown" and "markup cancellation" are used. "Markup cancellation" refers to reduction in price following "additional markups" and can, by definition, be no more than the amount of the additional markup; "cancellation of additional markup," although not used, is descriptive. "Markdown" refers to price reductions from the original retail price. A price increase after a markdown is a "markdown cancellation." If original cost is $12 and original selling price is $20, then markon (original markup) is $8; if the price is later increased to $24, the $4 increase is markup (additional markup); if the price is later lowered to $21, the $3 reduction is markup cancellation; if price is lowered further to $17, the $4 reduction is $1 markup cancellation and $3 markdown; if price is later increased to $22, the $5 increase is $3 of markdown cancellation and $2 of markup (additional markup). Markup cancellations and markdowns are separately counted because the former are deducted (while the latter are not) in computing the selling prices of goods available for sale for the denominator of the *cost percentage* used in the conventional *retail inventory method*.

markup cancellation. See *markup* for definition and contrast.

markup percentage. *Markup* divided by (acquisition cost plus *markup*).

master budget. A *budget* projecting all *financial statements* and their components.

matching convention. The concept of recognizing cost expirations (*expenses*) in the same accounting period when the related *revenues* are recognized. Combining or simultaneously recognizing the revenues and expenses that jointly result from the same *transactions* or other events.

material. As an adjective, it means relatively important. See *materiality*. Currently, no operational definition exists. As a noun, *raw material*.

material variances. *Price* and *quantity variances* for *direct materials* in *standard cost systems*. Sometimes used to mean variances that are significant; see *materiality*.

materiality. The concept that accounting should disclose separately only those events that are relatively important (no

operable definition yet exists) for the business or for understanding its statements. *SFAC No. 2* suggests that accounting information is material if "the judgement of a reasonable person relying on the information would have been changed or influenced by the omission or misstatement."

matrix. A rectangular array of numbers or mathematical symbols.

matrix inverse. For a given square *matrix A*, the square matrix inverse is the matrix, A^{-1}, such that $AA^{-1} = A^{-1}A = I$, the *identity matrix*. Not all square matrices have inverses. Those that do not are called singular; those that do are nonsingular.

maturity. The date at which an obligation, such as the *principal* of a *bond* or a *note*, becomes due.

maturity value. The amount expected to be collected when a loan reaches *maturity*. Depending upon the context, the amount may be *principal* or principal and *interest*.

measuring unit. See *attribute measured* for definition and contrast.

merchandise. *Finished goods* bought by a retailer or wholesaler for resale; contrast with finished goods of a manufacturing business.

merchandise turnover. *Inventory turnover* for merchandise; see *ratio*.

merchandising business. As opposed to a manufacturing or service business, one that purchases (rather than manufactures) *finished goods* for resale.

merger. The joining of two or more businesses into a single *economic entity*. See *holding company*.

minority interest. A *balance sheet account* on *consolidated statements* showing the *equity* in a less-than-100-percent-owned *subsidiary* company allocable to those who are not part of the controlling (majority) interest. May be classified either as shareholders' equity or as a liability of *indeterminate term* on the consolidated balance sheet. On the *income statement*, the minority's interest in current period's income of the less-than-100-percent-owned subsidiary must be subtracted to arrive at consolidated *net income* for the period.

minority investment. A holding of less than 50 percent of the *voting stock* in another corporation. Accounted for with the *equity method* when sufficient shares are owned so that the investor can exercise "significant influence," and with the *lower-of-cost-or-market* otherwise. See *mutual fund*.

minutes book. A record of all actions authorized at corporate *board of director's* or shareholders' meetings.

mixed cost. A *semifixed* or a *semivariable* cost.

modified cash basis. The *cash basis of accounting* with long-term assets accounted for with the *accrual basis of accounting*. Most uses of the term "cash basis of accounting" actually mean "modified cash basis."

monetary assets, liabilities. See *monetary items*.

monetary gain or loss. The *gain* or loss *in general purchasing power* as a result of holding *monetary assets* or liabilities during a period when the *general purchasing power of*

737

the dollar changes. During periods of *inflation*, holders of net monetary assets lose, and holders of net monetary liabilities gain, general purchasing power. During periods of *deflation*, holders of net monetary assets gain, and holders of net monetary liabilities lose, general purchasing power. Explicitly reported in *constant dollar accounting*.

monetary items. Amounts fixed in terms of dollars by statute or contract. *Cash, accounts receivable, accounts payable*, and *debt*. The distinction between monetary and nonmonetary items is important for *constant dollar accounting* and for *foreign exchange gain* or *loss* computations. In the foreign exchange context, account amounts denominated in dollars are not monetary items, whereas amounts denominated in any other currency are monetary.

money. A word seldom used with precision in accounting, at least in part because economists have not yet agreed on its definition. Economists use the term to refer to both a medium of exchange and a unit of value. See *cash* and *monetary items*.

money-purchase plan. A *pension plan* where the employer contributes a specified amount of cash each year to each employee's pension fund. Benefits ultimately received by the employee are not specifically defined but depend on the rate of return on the cash invested. Sometimes called a "defined-contribution" pension plan; contrast with *defined-benefit plan*. As of the mid-1970s most corporate pension plans were defined-benefit plans because both the law and *generally accepted accounting principles* for pensions made defined-benefit plans more attractive than money-purchase plans. *ERISA* makes money purchase plans relatively more attractive than they had been. We expect the relative number of money-purchase plans to increase.

mortality table. Data of life expectancies or probabilities of death for persons of specified ages and sex.

mortgage. A claim given by the borrower (mortgagor) to the lender (mortgagee) against the borrower's property in return for a loan.

moving average. An *average* computed on observations over time. As a new observation becomes available, the oldest one is dropped so that the average is always computed for the same number of observations and only the most recent ones. Sometimes, however, this term is used synonymously with *weighted average*.

moving average method. *Weighted-average method.*

multiple-step. Said of an *income statement* where various classes of *expenses* and *losses* are subtracted from *revenues* to show intermediate items such as *operating income*, income of the enterprise (operating income plus *interest* income), income to investors (income of the enterprise less *income taxes*), net income to shareholders (income to investors less interest charges), and income retained (income to shareholders less dividends). See *entity theory*.

municipal bond. A *bond* issued by a village, town, or city. *Interest* on such bonds is generally exempt from federal *income taxes* and from some state income taxes. Because bonds issued by state and county governments often have

these characteristics, such bonds are often called "municipals" as well. Sometimes referred to as "tax exempts."

mutual fund. An investment company that issues its own stock to the public and uses the proceeds to invest in securities of other companies. A mutual fund usually owns less than five or ten percent of the stock of any one company and accounts for its investments using current *market values*; contrast with *holding company*.

mutually exclusive projects. Competing investment projects, where accepting one project eliminates the possibility of undertaking the remaining projects.

N

NAARS. *National Automated Accounting Research System.*

National Association of Accountants. NAA. A national society generally open to all engaged in activities closely associated with *managerial accounting*. Oversees the administration of the *CMA* Examinations through the Institute of Management Accounting.

National Automated Accounting Research System. NAARS. A computer-based information retrieval system containing, among other things, the complete text of most public corporate annual reports and *Forms 10-K*. The system is available to users through the *AICPA*.

natural business year. A 12-month period chosen as the reporting period so that the end of the period coincides with a low point in activity or inventories. See *ratio* for a discussion of analyses of financial statements of companies using a natural business year.

natural classification. *Income statement* reporting form in which *expenses* are classified by nature of items as acquired, that is, materials, wages, salaries, insurance, and taxes, as well as depreciation; contrast with *functional classification*.

natural resources. Timberland, oil and gas wells, ore deposits, and other products of nature that have economic value. The cost of natural resources is subject to *depletion*. Natural resources are "nonrenewable" (for example, oil, coal, gas, ore deposits) or "renewable" (timberland, sod fields); the former are often called "wasting assets." See also *reserve recognition accounting* and *percentage depletion*.

negative confirmation. See *confirmation*.

negative goodwill. Refer to *goodwill*. When the purchase price of the company acquired is less than the sum of the *fair market value* of the *net assets* acquired, *APB Opinion* No. 16 requires that the valuation of noncurrent assets (except *investments* in *marketable securities*) acquired be reduced until the purchase price equals the adjusted valuation of the fair market value of net assets acquired. If after the adjusted valuation of noncurrent assets is reduced to zero and the purchase price is still less than the net assets acquired, then the difference is shown as a credit balance in the balance sheet as negative goodwill and is amortized to income over a period not to exceed forty years. For negative goodwill to exist, someone must be willing to sell a company for less than the fair market value of net current assets and marketable securities. Because such a bargain purchase is rare, negative goodwill is rarely found in the financial statements; when it does appear, it generally signals unrecorded obligations, such as for *pensions*.

negotiable. Legally capable of being transferred by endorsement. Usually said of *checks* and *notes* and sometimes of *stocks* and *bearer bonds*.

net. Reduced by all relevant deductions.

net assets. *Owners' equity*; total *assets* minus total *liabilities*.

net bank position. From a firm's point of view, *cash* in a specific bank less *loans* payable to that bank.

net current assets. *Working capital = current assets − current liabilities*.

net current asset value (per share). *Working capital* divided by the number of common shares outstanding. Many security analysts think that when a common share trades in the market for an amount less than net current asset value, then the shares are undervalued and should be purchased. We find this view naive because it ignores the efficiency of capital markets generally and, specifically, unrecorded obligations such as for *pension plans*, not currently reported as liabilities in the *balance sheet* under *GAAP*.

net income. The excess of all *revenues* and *gains* for a period over all *expenses* and *losses* of the period. See *comprehensive income*.

net loss. The excess of all *expenses* and *losses* for a period over all *revenues* and *gains* of the period. Negative *net income*.

net markup. In the context of *retail inventory methods, markups* less markup cancellations; a figure that usually ignores *markdowns* and markdown cancellations.

net of tax method. A nonsanctioned method for dealing with the problem of income tax allocation; described in *APB Opinion* No. 11. Deferred tax credit items are subtracted from specific asset amounts rather than being shown as a deferred credit or liability.

net of tax reporting. Reporting, such as for *income from discontinued operations, extraordinary items*, and *prior-period adjustments*, where the amounts presented in *financial statements* have been adjusted for all income tax effects. For example, if an extraordinary loss amounted to $10,000 and the marginal tax rate were 40 percent, then the extraordinary item would be reported "net of taxes" as a $6,000 loss. Hence, all income taxes may not be reported on one line of the income statement. The taxes will be allocated to *income from continuing operations, income from discontinued operations, extraordinary items*, cumulative effects of *accounting changes*, and *prior-period adjustments*.

net present value. Discounted or *present value* of all cash inflows and outflows of a project or from an *investment* at a given *discount rate*.

net price method (of recording purchase or sales discounts). The *purchase* (or *sale*) is recorded at its *invoice* price less all *discounts* made available under the assumption

that nearly all discounts will be taken. Discounts lapsed through failure to pay promptly are recorded in an *adjunct account* to purchases (or sales) or in the purchasing context, to an *expense* account. For purchases, management usually prefers to know about the amount of discounts lost because of inefficient operations, not the amounts taken, so that most managers prefer the net price method to the *gross price method*.

net realizable value. Selling price of an item less reasonable further costs to make the item ready for sale and to sell it. See *lower of cost or market*.

net sales. Sales (at gross invoice amount) less *returns, allowances*, freight paid for customers, and *discounts* taken.

net working capital. *Working capital*; the "net" is redundant in accounting. Financial analysts sometimes mean *current* assets when they speak of working capital, so for them the "net" is not redundant.

net worth. A misleading term, to be avoided, that means the same as *owners' equity*.

New York Stock Exchange. NYSE. A public market where various corporate *securities* are traded.

next-in, first-out. See *NIFO*.

NIFO. *Next-in, first-out*. In making decisions, many managers consider *replacement costs* (rather than *historical costs*) and refer to them as NIFO costs.

no par. Said of *stock* without a *par value*.

nominal accounts. *Temporary accounts* as opposed to *balance sheet accounts*. All nominal accounts are *closed* at the end of each *accounting period*.

nominal dollars. The measuring unit giving no consideration to differences in the *general purchasing power of the dollar* over time. The face amount of currency or coin, a *bond*, an *invoice*, a *receivable* is a nominal dollar amount. When that amount is adjusted for changes in *general purchasing power*, it is converted into a *constant dollar* amount.

nominal interest rate. A rate specified on a *debt* instrument, which usually differs from the market or *effective rate*. Also, a rate of *interest* quoted for a year. If the interest is compounded more often than annually, then the *effective interest rate* is higher than the nominal rate.

noncancelable. See *lease*.

noncontributory. Said of a *pension plan* where only the employer makes payments to a pension *fund*; contrast with *contributory*.

noncurrent. Due more than one year (or more than one *operating cycle*) hence.

nonexpendable fund. A governmental fund, whose *principal*, and sometimes earnings, may not be spent.

non-interest-bearing note. A *note* that bears no explicit interest. The *present value* of such a note at any time before *maturity* is less than the *face value* so long as *interest rates* are positive. *APB Opinion* No. 21 requires that the present value, not face value, of long-term non-interest-bearing notes be reported as the *asset* or *liability* amount in financial statements. See *interest, imputed*.

739

nonmonetary items. All items that are not monetary; see *monetary items*.

nonoperating. In the *income statement* context, said of revenues and expenses arising from transactions incidental to the company's main line(s) of business. In the *statement of changes in financial position* context, said of all sources or uses of *working capital* other than working capital provided by operations. See *operations*.

nonprofit corporation. An incorporated *entity*, such as a hospital, with owners who do not share in the earnings. It usually emphasizes providing services rather than maximizing income.

nonrecurring. Said of an event that is not expected to happen often for a given firm. Under *APB Opinion* No. 30, the effects of such events should be disclosed separately, but as part of *ordinary* items unless the event is also unusual. See *extraordinary* item.

normal cost. *Pension plan expenses* incurred during an *accounting period* for employment services performed during that period; contrast with *supplemental actuarial value* and see *funded*.

normal spoilage. Costs incurred because of ordinary amounts of spoilage; such costs should be prorated to units produced as *product costs*; contrast with *abnormal spoilage*.

normal standard cost. The *cost* expected to be incurred under reasonably efficient operating conditions with adequate provision for an average amount of rework, spoilage, and the like.

normal volume. The level of production over a time span, usually 1 year, that will satisfy demand by purchasers.

note. An unconditional written promise by the maker (borrower) to pay a certain amount on demand or at a certain future time. See *footnotes* for another context.

note receivable discounted. A *note* assigned by the holder to another. If the note is assigned with recourse, it is the *contingent liability* of the assignor until the debt is paid. See *factoring*.

NOW account. Negotiable order of withdrawal. A *savings account* on which orders to pay, much like *checks* but technically not checks, can be drawn and given to others who can redeem the order at the savings institution.

number of days sales in inventory (or receivables). Days of average inventory on hand (or average collection period for receivables). See *ratio*.

NYSE. *New York Stock Exchange*.

OASD(H)I. *Old Age, Survivors, Disability, and (Hospital) Insurance*.

objective. See *reporting objective* and *objectivity*.

objectivity. The reporting policy implying that formal recognition will not be given to an event in financial statements until the magnitude of the events can be measured with reasonable accuracy and is subject to independent verification.

obsolescence. A decline in *market value* of an *asset* caused by improved alternatives becoming available that will be more *cost-effective*; the decline in market value is unrelated to physical changes in the asset itself. See *partial obsolescence*.

Occupational Safety and Health Act. *OSHA*.

off balance sheet financing. A description often used for a *long-term, noncancelable lease* accounted for as an *operating lease*.

Old Age, Survivors, Disability, and (Hospital) Insurance. The technical name for Social Security under the Federal Insurance Contribution Act (FICA).

on (open) account. Said of a *purchase* or *sale* when payment is expected sometime after delivery and no *note* evidencing the *debt* is given or received. The purchaser has generally signed an agreement sometime in the past promising to pay for such purchases according to an agreed time schedule. When a sale (purchase) is made on open account, *Accounts Receivable* (*Payable*) is *debited* (*credited*).

on consignment. Said of goods delivered by the owner (the consignor) to another (the consignee) to be sold by the consignee; the owner is entitled to the return of the property or payment of an amount agreed upon in advance. The goods are assets of the consignor.

open account. Any *account* with a nonzero *debit* or *credit balance*. See *on (open) account*.

operating. An adjective used to refer to *revenue* and *expense* items relating to the company's main line(s) of business. See *operations*.

operating accounts. *Revenue, expense,* and *production cost accounts*; contrast with *balance sheet accounts*.

operating cycle. *Earnings cycle*.

operating expenses. *Expenses* incurred in the course of *ordinary* activities of an *entity*. Frequently, a classification including only *selling, general,* and *administrative expenses*, thereby excluding *cost of goods sold, interest,* and *income tax* expenses. See *operations*.

operating lease. A *lease* accounted for by the *lessee* without showing an *asset* for the lease rights (*leasehold*) or a *liability* for the lease payment obligations. Rental payments of the lessee are merely shown as *expenses* of the period. The asset remains on the lessor's *books* where rental collections appear as *revenues*; contrast with *capital lease*.

operating margin (based on current costs). *Revenues* from *sales* minus *current cost* of goods sold. A measure of operating efficiency that is independent of the *cost flow assumption* for *inventory*. Sometimes called "current (gross) margin." See *inventory profit* for illustrative computations.

operating ratio. See *ratio*.

operational control. See *control system*.

operations. A word not precisely defined in *accounting*. Generally, operating activities (producing and selling *goods* or *services*) are distinguished from financing activities (raising funds). Acquiring goods on account and then paying for them in one month, though generally classified as an operating activity, has the characteristics of a financing activity. Or consider the transaction of selling plant assets for a price in excess of book value. On the *income statement*, the gain is part of income from operations (continuing operations or discontinued operations, depending on the circumstances) but on the *statement of changes in financial position*, all of the funds received on disposition are reported below the "funds from operations" section, as a nonoperating source of funds, disposition of noncurrent assets. In income tax accounting an "operating loss" results whenever deductions are greater than taxable revenues.

opinion. The *auditor's report* containing an attestation or lack thereof. Also, *APB Opinion*.

opportunity cost. The *present value* of the *income* (or *costs*) that could be earned (or saved) from using an *asset* in its best alternative use to the one being considered.

option. The legal right to buy something during a specified period at a specified price, called the *exercise* price. Employee stock options should not be confused with put and call options traded in various public markets.

ordinary annuity. An *annuity in arrears*.

ordinary income. For income tax purposes, reportable *income* not qualifying as *capital gains*.

organization costs. The *costs* incurred in planning and establishing an *entity*; example of an *intangible* asset. Often, since the amounts are not *material*, the costs are treated as *expenses* in the period incurred even though the *expenditures* clearly provide future benefits and should be treated as *assets*.

original cost. *Acquisition cost*. In public utility accounting, the acquisition cost of the *entity* first devoting the asset to public use.

original entry. Entry in a *journal*.

OSHA. Occupational Safety and Health Act. The federal law that governs working conditions in commerce and industry.

outlay. The amount of an *expenditure*.

out-of-pocket. Said of an *expenditure* usually paid for with cash. An *incremental* cost.

out-of-stock cost. The estimated decrease in future *profit* as a result of losing customers because insufficient quantities of *inventory* are currently on hand to meet customers' demands.

output. Physical quantity or monetary measurement of *goods* and *services* produced.

outside director. A member of a corporate board of directors who is not a company officer and does not participate in the corporation's day-to-day management.

outstanding. Unpaid or uncollected. When said of *stock*, the shares issued less *treasury stock*. When said of checks, it means a check issued that did not clear the *drawer's* bank prior to the *bank statement* date.

over-and-short. Title for an *expense account* used to account for small differences between book balances of cash and actual cash and vouchers or receipts in *petty cash* or *change funds*.

overapplied (overabsorbed) overhead. An excess of costs applied, or *charged*, to product for a period over actual *overhead* costs during the period. A *credit balance* in an overhead account after overhead is assigned to product.

overdraft. A check written on a checking account that contains funds less than the amount of the check.

overhead costs. Any *cost* not directly associated with the production or sale of identifiable goods and services. Sometimes called "burden" or "indirect costs" and, in Britain, "oncosts." Frequently limited to manufacturing overhead. See *central corporate expenses* and *manufacturing overhead*.

overhead rate. Standard, or other predetermined rate at which *overhead costs* are applied to products or to services.

over-the-counter. Said of a *security* traded in a negotiated transaction, rather than in an auctioned one on an organized stock exchange, such as the *New York Stock Exchange*.

owners' equity. *Proprietorship; assets* minus *liabilities; paid-in capital* plus *retained earnings* of a corporation; partners' capital accounts in a *partnership*; owner's capital account in a *sole proprietorship*.

P

P & L. Profit and loss statement; *income statement*.

paid-in capital. Sum of balances in *capital stock* and *capital contributed in excess of par* (or *stated*) *value* accounts. Same as *contributed capital* (minus *donated capital*). Some use the term to mean only *capital contributed in excess of par* (or *stated value*).

paid-in surplus. See *surplus*.

paper profit. A *gain* not yet realized through a *transaction*. An *unrealized holding gain*.

par. See *at par* and *face amount*.

par value. *Face amount* of a *security*.

par value method. The method of accounting for *treasury stock* that *debits* a common stock account with the *par value* of the shares required and allocates the remaining debits between the *additional paid-in capital* and *retained earnings* accounts; contrast with *cost method*.

parent company. Company owning more than 50 percent of the voting shares of another company, called the *subsidiary*.

partial obsolescence. As technology improves, the economic value of existing *assets* declines. In many cases, however, it will not pay a firm to replace the existing asset with a new one even though the new type, rather than the old, would be acquired if the acquisition were to be made currently. In these cases, the accountant should theoretically recognize a loss from partial obsolescence from the firm's owning an old, out-of-date asset, but *GAAP* does not permit recognition of partial obsolescence. The old asset will be carried at *cost* less *accumulated depreciation* until it is retired from service. See *obsolescence*.

741

partially funded. Said of a *pension plan* where not all earned benefits have been funded. See *funded* for funding requirements.

partially vested. Said of a *pension plan* where not all employee benefits are *vested*. See *graded vesting*.

participating dividend. *Dividend* paid to preferred shareholders in addition to the minimum preferred dividends when the *preferred stock* contract allows such sharing in earnings. Usually applied after dividends on *common stock* have reached a certain level.

participating preferred stock. *Preferred stock* with rights to *participating dividends*.

partner's drawing. A payment to a partner to be charged against his or her share of income or capital. The name of a *temporary account* to record such payments.

partnership. Contractual arrangement between individuals to share resources and operations in a jointly run business. See *general* and *limited partner* and *Uniform Partnership Act*.

par value. *Face amount* of a *security*.

par value method. The method of accounting for *treasury stock* that *debits* a common stock account with the *par value* of the shares reacquired and allocates the remaining debits between the *additional paid-in capital* and *retained earnings* accounts; contrast with *cost method*.

past service cost. *Present value* at a given time of a *pension plan's* unrecognized, and usually unfunded, benefits assigned to employees for their service before the inception of the plan. A part of *supplemental actuarial value*. See *funded*; contrast with *normal cost*.

patent. A right granted for up to 17 years by the federal government to exclude others from manufacturing, using or selling a claimed design, product or plant (e.g., a new breed of rose) or from using a claimed process or method of manufacture. An asset if acquired by purchase. If developed internally, the development costs are *expensed* when incurred under current *GAAP*.

payable. Unpaid but not necessarily due or past due.

pay as you go. Said of an *income tax* scheme where periodic payments of income taxes are made during the period when the income to be taxed is being earned; in contrast to a scheme where no payments are due until the end of, or after, the period whose income is being taxed. (Called PAYE—pay as you earn—in Britain.) Sometimes used to describe an *unfunded pension plan*, where payments to pension plan beneficiaries are made from general corporate funds, not from cash previously contributed to a pension fund. Not acceptable as a method of accounting for pension plans.

payback period. Amount of time that must elapse before the cash inflows from a project equal the cash outflows.

payback reciprocal. One divided by the *payback period*. This number approximates the *internal rate of return* on a project when the project life is more than twice the payback period and the cash inflows are identical in every period after the initial period.

PAYE. See *pay as you go*.

payee. The person or entity to whom a cash payment is made or who will receive the stated amount of money on a check. See *draft*.

payout ratio. *Common stock dividends* declared for a year divided by net *income* to common stock for the year. A term used by financial analysts; contrast with *dividend yield*.

payroll taxes. Taxes levied because salaries or wages are paid; for example, *FICA* and unemployment compensation insurance taxes. Typically, the employer pays a portion and withholds part of the employee's wage fund.

P/E ratio. *Price-earnings ratio*.

Pension Benefit Guarantee Corporation. PBGC. A federal corporation established under *ERISA* to administer terminated pension plans and impose *liens* on corporate assets for certain unfunded pension liabilities.

pension fund. *Fund*, the assets of which are to be paid to retired ex-employees, usually as a *life annuity*. Usually held by an independent trustee and thus is not an *asset* of the employer.

pension plan. Details or provisions of employer's contract with employees for paying retirement *annuities* or other benefits. See *funded, vested, normal cost, past service cost, prior service cost, supplemental actuarial value, money-purchase plan*, and *defined-benefit plan*.

per books. An expression used to refer to the *book value* of an item at a specific time.

percent. Any number, expressed as a decimal, multiplied by 100.

percentage depletion (allowance). Deductible *expense* allowed in some cases by the federal *income tax* regulations; computed as a percentage of gross income from a *natural resource* independent of the unamortized cost of the asset. Because the amount of the total deductions for tax purposes is usually greater than the cost of the asset being *depleted*, many people think the deduction is an unfair tax advantage or "loophole."

percentage-of-completion method. Recognizing *revenues* and *expenses* on a job, order, or contract (a) in proportion to the *costs* incurred for the period divided by total costs expected to be incurred for the job or order ("cost-to-cost"), or (b) in proportion to engineers' or architects' estimates of the incremental degree of completion of the job, order, or contract during the period. Contrast with *completed-contract method*.

percentage statement. A statement containing, in addition to (or instead of) dollar amounts, ratios of dollar amounts to some base. In a percentage *income statement*, the base is usually either *net sales* or total *revenues* and in a percentage *balance sheet*, the base is usually total *assets*.

period. *Accounting period*.

period cost. An inferior term for *period expense*.

period expense (charge). *Expenditure*, usually based upon the passage of time, charged to operations of the ac-

742

counting period rather than *capitalized* as an asset; contrast with *product cost.*

periodic inventory. A method of recording *inventory* that uses data on beginning inventory, additions to inventories, and ending inventory to find the cost of withdrawals from inventory.

periodic procedures. The process of making *adjusting entries, closing entries,* and preparing the *financial statements,* usually by use of *trial balances* and *work sheets.*

permanent account. An account which appears on the *balance sheet;* contrast with *temporary account.*

permanent difference. Difference between reported income and taxable income that will never be reversed and, hence, requires no entry in the *deferred income tax (liability)* account. An example is the difference between taxable and reportable income from interest earned on state and municipal bonds; contrast with *timing difference* and see *deferred income tax liability.*

perpetual annuity. *Perpetuity.*

perpetual inventory. Records on quantities and amounts of *inventory* that are changed or made current with each physical addition to or withdrawal from the stock of goods; an inventory so recorded. The records will show the physical quantities and, frequently, the dollar valuations that should be on hand at any time. Because *cost of goods sold* is explicitly computed, the *inventory equation* can be used to compute *ending inventory.* The computed amount of ending inventory can be compared to the actual amount of ending inventory as a *control* device. Contrast with *periodic inventory.*

perpetuity. An *annuity* whose payments continue forever. The *present value* of a perpetuity in *arrears* is p/r where p is the periodic payment and r is the *interest rate* per period. If $100 is promised each year, in arrears, forever and the interest rate is 20 percent per year, then the value of the perpetuity is $500 = $100/.20.

personal account. *Drawing account.*

petty cash fund. Currency and coins maintained for expenditures that are made with cash on hand.

physical verification. *Verification,* by an *auditor,* performed by actually inspecting items in *inventory, plant assets,* and the like; may be based on statistical sampling procedures; in contrast to mere checking of written records.

plant. *Plant asset.*

plant asset. Buildings, machinery, equipment, land, and natural resources. The phrase "property, plant and equipment" is, therefore, a redundancy. In this context, "plant" means buildings.

plant asset turnover. Number of dollars of *sales* generated per dollar of *plant assets.* Equal to sales divided by average *plant assets.*

pledging. The borrower assigns *assets* as security or *collateral* for repayment of a loan.

pledging of receivables. The process of using expected collections on accounts receivable as *collateral* for a loan. The borrower remains responsible for collecting the receivable but promises to use the proceeds for repaying the debt.

plow back. To retain assets generated by earnings for continued investment in the business.

plug. For any *account,* beginning balance + additions − deductions = ending balance; if any three of the four items are known, the fourth can be found by plugging. In making a *journal entry,* often all *debits* are known, as are all but one of the *credits* (or vice versa). Because *double-entry* bookkeeping requires equal debits and credits, the unknown quantity can be computed by subtracting the sum of the known credits from the sum of all the debits (or vice versa). This process is also known as plugging. The unknown found is called the plug. For example, if a *discount* on *bonds payable* is being *amortized* with the *straight-line method,* then *interest expense* is a plug: interest expense = interest payable + discount amortization. See *trade-in transaction* for an example.

pooling of interests method. Accounting for a *business combination* by merely adding together the *book value* of the *assets* and *equities* of the combined firms. Contrast with *purchase method.* Generally leads to a higher reported *net income* for the combined firms than would be reported had the business combination been accounted for as a purchase because the *market values* of the merged assets are generally larger than their book values. See *APB Opinion* No. 16 for the conditions that must be met before the pooling of interests treatment is acceptable.

positive confirmation. See *confirmation.*

post. To record entries in an *account* in a *ledger;* usually the entries are transferred from a *journal.*

post-closing trial balance. *Trial balance* taken after all *temporary accounts* have been closed.

post-statement events. Events with *material* impact that occur between the end of the *accounting period* and the formal publication of the *financial statements.* Such events must be disclosed in notes for the auditor to give a *clean opinion,* even though the events are subsequent to the period being reported on.

potentially dilutive. A *security* that may be converted into, or exchanged for, common stock and thereby reduce reported *earnings per share: options, warrants, convertible bonds,* and *convertible preferred stock.*

preclosing trial balance. *Trial balance* taken at the end of the period before *closing entries.* In this sense an *adjusted trial balance.* Sometimes taken before *adjusting entries* and then is synonymous with *unadjusted trial balance.*

predetermined (factory) overhead rate. Rate used in applying *overhead* to products or departments developed at the start of a period by dividing estimated overhead cost by the estimated number of units of the overhead allocation base (or *denominator volume*) activity.

preemptive right. The privilege of a shareholder to maintain a proportionate share of ownership by purchasing a proportionate share of any new stock issues.

preference as to assets. The rights of *preferred share-holders* to receive certain payments in case of dissolution before common shareholders receive payments.

preferred shares. *Capital stock* with a claim to *income* or *assets* after *bondholders* but before *common shares*. *Dividends* on preferred shares are *income distributions*, not *expenses*. See *cumulative preferred stock*.

premium. The excess of issue (or market) price over *par value*. For a different context, see *insurance*.

premium on capital stock. Alternative but inferior title for *capital contributed in excess of* (*par*) or stated value.

prepaid expense. An *expenditure* that leads to a *deferred charge* or *prepayment*; strictly speaking, a contradiction in terms for an *expense* is a gone asset and this title refers to past *expenditures*, such as for rent or insurance premiums, that still have future benefits and thus are *assets*.

prepaid income. An inferior alternative title for *advances from customers*. An item should not be called *revenue* or *income* until earned, when goods are delivered or services are rendered.

prepayments. *Deferred charges. Assets* representing *expenditures* for future benefits. Rent and insurance premiums paid in advance are usually classified as *current* prepayments.

present value. Value today of an amount or amounts to be paid or received later, discounted at some *interest* or *discount rate*.

price. The quantity of one *good* or *service*, usually *cash*, asked in return for a unit of another good or service. See *fair market price*.

price-earnings ratio. At a given time, the market value of a company's *common stock*, per share, divided by the *earnings per* common *share* for the past year. See *ratio*.

price index. A series of numbers, one for each period that purports to represent some *average* of prices for a series of periods, relative to a base period.

price level. The number from a *price index* series for a given period or date.

price level adjusted statements. *Financial statements* expressed in terms of dollars of uniform purchasing power. *Nonmonetary* items are restated to reflect changes in general *price levels* since the time specific *assets* were acquired and *liabilities* were incurred. A *gain* or *loss* is recognized on *monetary items* as they are held over time periods when the general *price level changes*. Conventional financial statements show *historical costs* and ignore differences in purchasing power in different periods.

price variance. In accounting for *standard costs*, (actual cost per unit — standard cost per unit) times quantity purchased.

primary earning per share. Net *income* to *common shareholders* plus *interest* (*net of tax* effects) or *dividends* paid on *common stock equivalents* divided by (weighted-average of common share outstanding plus the net increase in the number of common shares that would become *outstanding* if all common stock equivalents were exchanged for common shares with cash proceeds, if any, used to retire common shares).

prime cost. Sum of *direct materials* plus *direct labor* costs assigned to product.

prime rate. The rate for loans charged by commercial banks to their most preferred risks. For the purpose of deciding whether a security is or is not a *common stock equivalent* in calculating *earnings per share*, the corporation should use the rate in effect at the bank at which it does business or an average of such rates if the corporation does business with more than one bank. The *Federal Reserve Bulletin* is considered the authoritative source of information about historical prime rates.

principal. An amount on which *interest* is charged or earned.

principle. See *generally accepted accounting principles*.

prior-period adjustment. A *debit* or *credit* made directly to *retained earnings* (that does not affect *income* for the period) to adjust earnings as calculated for prior periods. Such adjustments are now extremely rare. Theory might suggest that corrections of errors in accounting estimates (such as the *depreciable life* or *salvage value* of an asset) should be treated as adjustments to retained earnings. But *GAAP* require that corrections of such estimates flow through current, and perhaps future, *income statements*. See *accounting changes* and *accounting errors*.

prior service cost. *Supplemental actuarial value.*

pro forma statements. Hypothetical statements. Financial statements as they would appear if some event, such as a *merger* or increased production and sales had occurred or were to occur. Pro forma is often spelled as one word.

proceeds. The *funds* received from disposition of assets or from the issue of securities.

process costing. A method of *cost accounting* based on average costs (total cost divided by the *equivalent units* of work done in a period). Typically used for assembly lines or for products that are produced in a series of steps that are more continuous than discrete.

product. *Goods* or *services* produced.

product cost. Any *manufacturing cost* that can be inventoried. See *flow of costs* for example and contrast with *period expenses*.

production cost. *Manufacturing cost.*

production cost account. A *temporary account* for collecting *manufacturing costs* during a period.

production department. A department producing salable *goods* or *services*; contrast with *service department*.

production method (depreciation). The depreciable asset is given a *depreciable life* measured, not in elapsed time, but in units of output or perhaps in units of time of expected use. Then the *depreciation* charge for a period is a portion of depreciable cost equal to a fraction computed by dividing the actual output produced during the period by

744

the expected total output to be produced over the life of the asset. Sometimes called the "units of production (or output) method."

production method (revenue recognition). *Percentage of completion method* for recognizing *revenue*.

productive capacity. In computing *current cost* of *long-term assets*, we are interested in the cost of reproducing the productive capacity (for example, the ability to manufacture one million units a year), not the cost of reproducing the actual physical assets currently used (see *reproduction cost*). Replacement cost of productive capacity will be the same as reproduction cost of assets only in the unusual case when there has been no technological improvement in production processes and the relative prices of goods and services used in production have remained approximately the same as when the currently used ones were acquired.

profit. Excess of *revenues* over *expenses* for a *transaction*; sometimes used synonymously with *net income* for the period.

profit and loss sharing ratio. The fraction of *net income* or loss allocable to a partner in a *partnership*. Need not be the same fraction as the partner's share of capital.

profit and loss statement. *Income statement.*

profit center. A unit of activity for which both *revenue* and *expenses* are accumulated; contrast with *cost center*.

profit margin. Sales minus all expenses as a single amount. Frequently used to mean ratio of sales minus all *operating* expenses divided by sales.

profit maximization. The doctrine that a given set of operations should be accounted for so as to make reported *net income* as large as possible; contrast with *conservatism*. This concept in accounting is slightly different from the profit maximizing concept in economics where the doctrine states that operations should be managed to maximize the present value of the firm's wealth, generally by equating *marginal costs* and *marginal revenues*.

profit-volume graph. See *breakeven chart*.

profit-volume ratio. *Net income* divided by *net sales* in dollars.

profitability accounting. *Responsibility accounting.*

programmed costs. A *fixed cost* not essential for carrying out operations. Research and development and advertising designed to generate new business are controllable, but once a commitment is made to incur them, they become fixed costs. Sometimes called *managed costs* or *discretionary costs*; contrast with *capacity costs*.

progressive tax. Tax for which the rate increases as the taxed base, such as income, increases; contrast with *regressive tax*.

project financing arrangement. As defined by *SFAS* No. 47, The financing of an investment project in which the lender looks principally to the *cash flows* and *earnings* of the project as the source of funds for repayment and to the *assets* of the project as *collateral* for the loan. The general *credit* of the project entity is usually not a significant factor,

either because the entity is a *corporation* without other assets or because the financing is without direct *recourse* to the entity's owners.

projected financial statement. *Pro forma* financial statement.

promissory note. An unconditional written promise to pay a specified sum of money on demand or at a specified date.

proof of journal. The process of checking arithmetic accuracy of *journal entries* by testing for the equality of all *debits* with all *credits* since the last previous proof.

property dividend. A *dividend in kind.*

proprietary accounts. See *budgetary accounts* for contrast in context of governmental accounting.

proprietorship. *Assets* minus *liabilities* of an *entity*; equals *contributed capital* plus *retained earnings*.

proprietorship theory. The view of the corporation that emphasizes the form of the *accounting equation* that says *assets − liabilities = owners' equity*; contrast with *entity theory*. The major implication of a choice between these theories deals with the treatment of *subsidiaries*. For example, the view that *minority interest* is an *indeterminate-term liability* is based on the proprietorship theory. The proprietorship theory implies using a *single-step income statement*.

prorate. To *allocate* in proportion to some base; for example, allocate *service department* costs in proportion to hours of service used by the benefited department.

prospectus. Formal written document describing *securities* to be issued. See *proxy*.

protest fee. Fee charged by banks or other financial agencies when items (such as checks) presented for collection cannot be collected.

provision. Often the exact amount of an *expense* is uncertain, but must be recognized currently anyway. The entry for the estimated expense, such as for *income taxes* or expected costs under *warranty*, is:

Expense (Estimated) X
　　Liability (Estimated) X

In American usage, the term "provision" is often used in the expense account title of the above entry. Thus, Provision for Income Taxes is used to mean the estimate of income tax expense. (In British usage, the term "provision" is used in the title for the estimated liability of the above entry, so that Provision for Income Taxes is a balance sheet account.)

proxy. Written authorization given by one person to another so that the second person can act for the first, such as to vote shares of stock. Of particular significance to accountants because the *SEC* presumes that financial information is distributed by management along with its proxy solicitations.

public accountant. Generally, this term is synonymous with *certified public accountant*. In some jurisdictions individuals have been licensed as public accountants without being CPAs.

public accounting. That portion of accounting primarily involving the *attest* function, culminating in the *auditor's report*.

PuPU. An acronym for *pu*rchasing *p*ower *u*nit conceived by John C. Burton, former Chief Accountant of the *SEC*. Those who think *constant dollar accounting* is not particularly useful poke fun at it by calling it "PuPU accounting."

purchase allowance. A reduction in sales *invoice price* usually granted because the *goods* received by the purchaser were not exactly as ordered. The goods are not returned to the seller, but are purchased at a price lower than originally agreed upon.

purchase discount. A reduction in purchase *invoice price* granted for prompt payment. See *sales discount* and *terms of sale*.

purchase method. Accounting for a *business combination* by adding the acquired company's assets at the price paid for them to the acquiring company's assets. Contrast with *pooling of interests method*. The acquired assets are put on the books at current values, rather than original costs, the *amortization expenses* are usually larger (and reported income, smaller) than for the same business combination accounted for as a pooling of interests. The purchase method is required unless all criteria to be a pooling are met.

purchase order. Document authorizing a seller to deliver goods with payment to be made later.

Q

qualified report (opinion). *Auditor's report* containing a statement that the auditor was unable to complete a satisfactory examination of all things considered relevant or that the auditor has doubts about the financial impact of some material item reported in the financial statements. See *except for* and *subject to*.

quantity discount. A reduction in purchase price as quantity purchased increases; amount of the discount is constrained by law (Robinson-Patman Act). Not to be confused with *purchase discount*.

quantity variance. In *standard cost* systems, the standard price per unit times (actual quantity used minus standard quantity that should be used).

quasi-reorganization. A *reorganization* where no new company is formed or no court has intervened, as would happen in *bankruptcy*. The primary purpose is to absorb a *deficit* and get a "fresh start."

quick assets. *Assets* readily convertible into *cash*; includes cash, *current marketable securities* and *current receivables*.

quick ratio. Sum of (*cash, current marketable securities*, and *receivables*) divided by *current liabilities*. Some nonliquid receivables may be excluded from the numerator. Often called the "acid test ratio." See *ratio*.

R

Railroad Accounting Principles Board. RAPB. A board brought into existence by the Staggers Rail Act of 1980 to advise the Interstate Commerce Commission on matters of accounting affecting railroads.

RAPB. Railroad Accounting Principles Board.

R & D. See *research* and *development*.

rate of return on assets. *Net income* plus aftertax *interest charges* plus *minority interest* in income divided by average total *assets*. Perhaps the single most useful ratio for assessing management's overall operating performance. See *ratio*.

rate of return on common stock equity. See *ratio*.

rate of return on shareholders' (owners') equity. See *ratio*.

rate of return (on total capital). See *ratio* and *rate of return on assets*.

rate variance. *Price variance*, usually for *direct labor costs*.

ratio. The number resulting when one number is divided by another. Ratios are generally used to assess aspects of profitability, solvency, and liquidity. The commonly used financial ratios are of three kinds:

(1) those that summarize some aspect of *operations* for a period, usually a year, and

(2) those that summarize some aspect of *financial position* at a given moment—the moment for which a balance sheet has been prepared.

(3) those that relate some aspect of operations to some aspect of financial position.

Exhibit 6.10 lists the most common financial ratios and shows separately both the numerator and denominator used to calculate the ratio.

For all ratios that require an average balance during the period, the average is most often derived as one-half the sum of the beginning and ending balances. Sophisticated analysts recognize, however, that when companies use a fiscal year different from the calendar year, this averaging of beginning and ending balances may be misleading. Consider, for example, the *rate of return on assets* of Sears, Roebuck & Company whose fiscal year ends on January 31. Sears chooses a January 31 closing date at least in part because inventories are at a low level and are therefore easy to count—the Christmas merchandise has been sold and the Easter merchandise has not yet all been received. Furthermore, by January 31, most Christmas sales have been collected or returned, so receivable amounts are not unusually large. Thus at January 31, the amount of total assets is lower than at many other times during the year. Consequently, the denominator of the rate of return on assets, total assets, for Sears is more likely to represent a smaller amount of total assets on hand during the year than the average amount. The all capital earnings rate for Sears and other companies who choose a fiscal year-end to coincide with low points in the inventory cycle is likely to be larger than if a more accurate estimate of the average amounts of total assets were used.

raw material. Goods purchased for use in manufacturing a product.

reacquired stock. *Treasury stock*.

real accounts. *Balance sheet accounts*; as opposed to *nominal accounts*. See *permanent accounts*.

real estate. *Land* and its *improvements*, such as landscaping and roads but not buildings.

realizable value. *Market value* or, sometimes, *net realizable value*.

realization convention. The accounting practice of delaying the recognition of *gains* and *losses* from changes in the market price of *assets* until the assets are sold. However, unrealized losses on *inventory* and *marketable securities* classified as *current assets* are recognized prior to sale when the *lower-of-cost-or-market* valuation basis is used.

realize. To convert into *funds*. When applied to a *gain* or *loss*, implies that an *arm's length transaction* has taken place. Contrast with *recognize*; a loss (as for example on *marketable equity securities*) may be recognized in the financial statements even though it has not yet been realized in a transaction.

realized gain (or loss) on marketable equity securities. An income statement account title for the difference between the proceeds of disposition and the *original cost* of *marketable equity securities*.

realized holding gain. See *inventory profit* for definition and an example.

rearrangement costs. Costs of re-installing assets perhaps in a different location. May be *capitalized* as part of the assets cost, just as is original installation cost.

recapitalization. *Reorganization*.

recapture. Various provisions of the *income tax* rules require refund by the taxpayer (recapture by the government) of various tax advantages under certain conditions. For example, the tax savings provided by the *investment credit* or by *accelerated depreciation* must be repaid if the item providing the tax savings is retired prematurely.

receipt. Acquisition of *cash*.

receivable. Any *collectible* whether or not it is currently due.

receivable turnover. See *ratio*.

reciprocal holdings. Company A owns stock of Company B and Company B owns stock of Company A.

recognize. To enter a transaction in the accounts. Not synonymous with *realize*.

reconciliation. A calculation that shows how one balance or figure is derived systematically from another, such as a *reconciliation of retained earnings* or a *bank reconciliation schedule*. See *articulate*.

record date. *Dividends* are paid on payment date to those who own the stock on the record date.

recourse. See *note receivable discounted*.

recovery of unrealized loss on marketable securities. An *income statement account title* for the *gain* during the current period on the current asset portfolio of *marketable equity securities*. This gain will be *recognized* only to the extent that net losses have been recognized in preceding periods in amounts no smaller than the current gain. (The Allowance for Declines in Marketable Equity Securities account can never have a *debit balance*.)

redemption. Retirement by the issuer, usually by a purchase or *call*, of *stocks* or *bonds*.

redemption premium. *Call premium*.

redemption value. The price to be paid by a corporation to retire *bonds* or *preferred stock* if called before *maturity*.

refunding bond issue. Said of a *bond* issue whose proceeds are used to retire bonds already *outstanding*.

register. Collection of consecutive entries, or other information, in chronological order, such as a check register or an insurance register, which lists all insurance policies owned. If entries are recorded, it may serve as a *journal*.

registered bond. *Principal* of such a *bond* and *interest*, if registered as to interest, is paid to the owner listed on the books of the issuer. As opposed to a bearer bond where the possessor of the bond is entitled to interest and principal.

registrar. An *agent*, usually a bank or trust company, appointed by a corporation to keep track of the names of shareholders and distributions of earnings.

registration statement. Statement required by the Securities Act of 1933 of most companies wishing to have its securities traded in public markets. The statement discloses financial data and other items of interest to potential investors.

regressive tax. Tax for which the rate decreases as the taxed base, such as income, increases. Contrast with *progressive tax*.

Regulation S-X. The *SEC*'s regulation specifying the form and content of financial reports to the SEC.

reinvestment rate. In a *capital budgeting* context, the rate at which cash inflows from a project occurring before the project's completion are invested. Once such a rate is assumed, there will never be multiple *internal rates of return*. See *Descartes' rule of signs*.

relative sales value method. A method for *allocating joint costs* in proportion to *realizable values* of the joint products. For example, joint products A and B together cost $100 and A sells for $60 whereas B sells for $90. Then A would be allocated ($60/$150) × $100 = .40 × $100 = $40 of cost while B would be allocated ($90/$150) × $100 = $60 of cost.

relevant cost. *Incremental cost. Opportunity cost.*

relevant range. Activity levels over which costs are linear or for which *flexible budget* estimates and *breakeven charts* will remain valid.

remittance advice. Information on a *check stub*, or on a document attached to a check by the *drawer*, which tells the *payee* why a payment is being made.

rent. A charge for use of land, buildings, or other assets.

reorganization. A major change in the *capital structure* of a corporation that leads to changes in the rights, interests, and implied ownership of the various security owners. Usually results from a *merger* or agreement by senior security holders to take action to forestall *bankruptcy*.

repair. An *expenditure* to restore an *asset's* service potential after damage or after prolonged use. In the second sense, after prolonged use, the difference between repairs and maintenance is one of degree and not of kind. Treated as an *expense* of the period when incurred. Because repairs and maintenance are treated similarly in this regard, the distinction is not important. A repair helps to maintain capacity intact at levels planned when the *asset* was acquired; contrast with *improvement*.

replacement cost. For an asset, the current fair market price to purchase another, similar asset (with the same future benefit or service potential). *Current cost*. See *reproduction cost* and *productive capacity*. See also *distributable income* and *inventory profit*.

replacement cost method of depreciation. The original-cost *depreciation* charge is augmented by an amount based upon a portion of the difference between the *current replacement cost* of the asset and its *original-cost*.

replacement system of depreciation. See *retirement method of depreciation* for definition and contrast.

report. *Financial statement; auditor's report*.

report form. This form of *balance sheet* typically shows *assets* minus *liabilities* as one total. Then below that it shows the components of *owners' equity* summing to the same total. Often, the top section shows *current* assets less current liabilities before *noncurrent assets* less noncurrent liabilities. Contrast with *account form*.

reporting objectives (policies). The general purposes for which financial statements are prepared. The FASB has discussed these in *SFAC No. 1*.

reproduction cost. The *cost* necessary to acquire an *asset* similar in all physical respects to another asset for which a *current value* is wanted. See *replacement cost* and *productive capacity* for further contrast.

requisition. A formal written order or request, such as for withdrawal of supplies from the storeroom.

resale value. *Exit value. Net realizable value*.

research and development. Research is activity aimed at discovering new knowledge in hopes that such activity will be useful in creating a new product, process, or service or improving a present product, process, or service. Development is the translation of research findings or other knowledge into a new or improved product, process, or service. *SFAS No. 2* requires that costs of such activities be *expensed* as incurred on the grounds that the future benefits are too uncertain to warrant *capitalization* as an asset. This treatment seems questionable to us because we wonder why firms would continue to undertake R&D if there were no expectation of future benefit; if future benefits exist, then the *costs* should be assets.

reserve. When properly used in accounting, the term refers to an account that appropriates *retained earnings* and restricts dividend declarations. Appropriating retained earn-

ings is itself a poor and vanishing practice, so the word should seldom be used in accounting. In addition, used in the past to indicate an asset *contra* (for example, "reserve for depreciation") or an *estimated liability* (for example, "reserve for warranty costs"). In any case, reserve accounts have credit balances and are not pools of *funds* as the unwary reader might infer. If a company has set aside a pool of *cash* (*or marketable securities*) then that cash will be called a *fund*.

No other word in accounting is so misunderstood and misused by laymen and "experts" who should know better. A leading unabridged dictionary defines *reserve* as "Cash, or assets readily convertible into cash, held aside, as by a corporation, bank, state or national government, etc. to meet expected or unexpected demands." This definition is absolutely wrong in accounting. Reserves are not funds. For example, a contingency fund of $10,000 is created by depositing cash in a fund and this entry is made:

Dr. Contingency Fund 10,000
  Cr. Cash 10,000

The following entry may accompany this entry, if retained earnings are to be appropriated:

Dr. Retained Earnings. 10,000
  Cr. Reserve for Contingencies 10,000

The transaction leading to the first entry is an event of economic significance. The second entry has little economic impact for most firms. The problem with the word "reserve" arises because the second entry can be made without the first—a company can create a reserve, that is appropriate retained earnings, without creating a fund. The problem is at least in part caused by the fact that in common usage, "reserve" means a pool of assets, as in the phrase "oil reserves." The *Internal Revenue Service* does not help in dispelling confusion about the term *reserve*. The federal *income tax* return for corporations uses the title "Reserve for Bad Debts" to mean the "Allowance for Uncollectible Accounts" and speaks of the "Reserve Method" in referring to the *allowance method* for estimating *revenue* or *income* reductions from estimated *uncollectibles*.

reserve recognition accounting. In exploration for natural resources, there is the problem of what to do with the expenditures for exploration. Suppose that $10 million is spent to drill 10 holes ($1 million each) and that nine of them are dry whereas one is a gusher containing oil with a *net realizable value* of $40 million. Dry-hole, or successful-efforts, accounting would *expense* $9 million and *capitalize* $1 million to be *depleted* as the oil was lifted from the ground. *SFAS No. 19*, now suspended, requires successful-efforts accounting. Full costing would expense nothing but capitalize the $10 million of drilling costs to be depleted as the oil is lifted from the single productive well. Reserve-recognition accounting would capitalize $40 million to be depleted as the oil is lifted, with a $30 million *credit* to *income* or *contributed capital*. The *balance sheet* shows the *net realizable value* of proven oil and gas reserves. The *income statement* has three sorts of items: (1) current income resulting from production or "lifting profit," which is the *revenue* from sales of oil and gas less the expense based on the current valuation amount at which these items had been carried on the balance sheet, (2) profit or loss from exploration efforts where the current value of new discoveries is revenue and all the exploration cost is expense, and (3) gain or loss on changes in current value during the year, which is in other contexts called a *holding gain or loss.*

residual income. In an external reporting context, this term refers to net income to common stock (= net income less *preferred stock dividends*). In *managerial accounting*, this term refers to the excess of income for a division or *segment* of a company over the product of the *cost of capital* for the company multiplied by the average amount of capital invested in the division during the period over which the income was earned.

residual security. A *potentially dilutive security. Options, warrants, convertible bonds,* and *convertible preferred stock.*

residual value. At any time, the estimated or actual, *net realizable value* (that is, proceeds less removal costs) of an *asset,* usually a depreciable *plant asset.* In the context of depreciation accounting, this term is equivalent to *salvage value* and is preferable to *scrap value,* because the asset need not be scrapped. Sometimes used to mean net *book value.* In the context of a *noncancelable* lease, the estimated value of the leased asset at the end of the lease period. See *lease.*

responsibility accounting. Accounting for a business by considering various units as separate entities, or *profit centers,* giving management of each unit responsibility for the unit's *revenues* and *expenses.* Sometimes called "activity accounting." See *transfer price.*

restricted assets. Governmental resources restricted by legal or contractual requirements for specific purpose.

restricted retained earnings. That part of *retained earnings* not legally available for *dividends.* See *retained earnings, appropriated.* Bond indentures and other loan contracts can curtail the legal ability of the corporation to declare dividends without formally requiring a retained earnings appropriation, but disclosure is required.

retail inventory method. Ascertaining cost amounts of *ending inventory* as follows (assuming FIFO): cost of ending inventory = (selling price of *goods available for sale − sales*) × *cost percentage.* Cost of goods sold is then computed from the inventory equation; costs of beginning inventory, purchases and ending inventory are all known. (When *LIFO* is used, the method is similar to the *dollar-value LIFO method*). See *markup.*

retail terminology. See *markup.*

retained earnings. Net *income* over the life of a corporation less all dividends (including capitalization through stock dividends); *owners' equity* less *contributed capital.*

retained earnings, appropriated. An *account* set up by crediting it and debiting *retained earnings.* Used to indicate that a portion of retained earnings is not available for dividends. The practice of appropriating retained earnings is misleading unless all capital is earmarked with its use, which is not practicable. Use of formal retained earnings appropriations is declining.

retained earnings statement. *Generally accepted accounting principles* require that whenever *comparative balance sheets* and an *income statement* are presented, there must also be presented a *reconciliation* of the beginning and ending balances in the *retained earnings account.* This reconciliation can appear in a separate statement, in a combined statement of income and retained earnings or in the balance sheet.

retirement method of depreciation. No entry is recorded for *depreciation expense* until an *asset* is retired from service. Then, an entry is made *debiting* depreciation expense and *crediting* the asset account for the cost of the asset retired. If the retired asset has a *salvage value,* the amount of the debit to depreciation expense is reduced by the amount of salvage value with a corresponding debit to cash, receivables, or salvaged materials. The "replacement system of depreciation" is similar, except that the debit to depreciation expense equals the cost of the new asset less the salvage value, if any, of the old asset. These methods were used by some public utilities. For example, if ten telephone poles are acquired in year one for $60 each and are replaced in year ten for $100 each when the salvage value of the old poles is $5 each, then the accounting would be as follows:

Retirement Method

Plant Assets	600	
Cash		600
To acquire assets in year one.		
Depreciation Expense	550	
Salvage Receivable	50	
Plant Assets		600
To record retirement and depreciation in year ten.		
Plant Assets	1,000	
Cash		1,000
To record acquisition of new assets in year ten.		

Replacement Method

Plant Assets	600	
Cash		600
To acquire assets in year one.		
Depreciation Expense	950	
Salvage Receivable	50	
Cash		1,000
To record depreciation on old asset in amount quantified by net cost of replacement asset in year ten.		

The retirement method is like *FIFO,* in that the cost of the first assets is recorded as depreciation and the cost of the second assets is put on the balance sheet. The replacement method is like *LIFO* in that the cost of the second assets determines the depreciation expense and the cost of the first assets remains on the balance sheet.

retirement plan. *Pension plan.*

return. A schedule of information required by governmental bodies, such as the tax return required by the *Internal Revenue Service.* Also the physical return of merchandise. See also *return on investment.*

return on investment. return on capital. *Income* (before distributions to suppliers of capital) for a period. As a rate, this amount divided by average total assets. *Interest*, net of tax effects, should be added back to *net income* for the numerator. See *ratio*.

revenue. The monetary measure of a service rendered. *Sales* of products, merchandise, and services, and earnings from *interest, dividends*, rents, and the like. Do not confuse with *receipt of funds*, which may occur before, when, or after revenue is recognized. Contrast with *gain* and *income*. See also *holding gain*. Some writers use the term *gross income* synonymously with *revenue*; such usage is to be avoided.

revenue center. A *responsibility center* within a firm that has control only over revenues generated; contrast with *cost center*. See *profit center*.

revenue expenditure. A phrase sometimes used to mean an *expense* in contrast to a capital *expenditure* to acquire an *asset* or to discharge a *liability*. Avoid using this phrase; use *period expense* instead.

revenue received in advance. An inferior term for *advances from customers*.

reversal (reversing) entry. An *entry* in which all *debits* and *credits* are the credits and debits, respectively, of another entry, and in the same amounts. It is usually made on the first day of an *accounting period* to reverse a previous *adjusting entry*, usually an *accrual*. The purpose of such entries is to make the bookkeeper's tasks easier. Suppose that salaries are paid every other Friday, with paychecks compensating employees for the 2 weeks just ended. Total salaries accrue at the rate of $5,000 per 5-day work week. The bookkeeper is accustomed to making the following entry every other Friday:

(1) Salary Expense 10,000
    Cash   10,000
    To record salary expense and salary
    payments.

If paychecks are delivered to employees on Friday, June 25, 1982, then the *adjusting entry* made on June 30 (or, perhaps, later) to record accrued salaries for June 28, 29, and 30 would be

(2) Salary Expense 3,000
    Salaries Payable   3,000
    To charge second quarter operations
    with all salaries earned in second quarter.

The Salary Expense account would be closed as part of the June 30 *closing entries*. On the next pay-day, July 9, the salary entry would have to be

(3) Salary Expense 7,000
    Salaries Payable 3,000
    Cash   10,000
    To record salary payments split between expense for the third quarter (7 days) and liability carried over from the second quarter.

To make entry (3), the bookkeeper must look back into the records to see how much of the debit is to Salaries Payable accrued from the previous quarter so that total debits are properly split between third quarter expense and the liability carried over from the second quarter. Notice that this entry forces the bookkeeper both (a) to refer to balances in old accounts and (b) to make an entry different from the one customarily made, entry (1).

The reversing entry, made just after the books have been closed for the second quarter, makes the salary entry for July 9, 1982, the same as that made on all other Friday pay-days. The reversing entry merely *reverses* the adjusting entry (2):

(4) Salaries Payable 3,000
    Salary Expense   3,000
    To reverse the adjusting entry.

This entry results in a zero balance in the Salaries Payable account and a *credit* balance in the Salary Expense account. If entry (4) is made just after the books are closed for the second quarter, then the entry on July 9 will be the customary entry (1). Entries (4) and (1) together have exactly the same effect as entry (3).

The procedure for using reversal entries is as follows: The required adjustment to record an accrual (*payable* or *receivable*) is made at the end of an *accounting period*; the closing entry is made as usual; as of the first day of the following period, an entry is made reversing the adjusting entry; when a payment is made (or received), the entry is recorded as though no adjusting entry had been recorded. Whether or not reversal entries are used affects the record-keeping procedures, but not the financial statements.

Also used to describe the entry reversing an incorrect entry before recording the correct entry.

reverse stock split. A stock split in which the number of shares *outstanding* is decreased. See *stock split*.

revolving fund. A *fund* whose amounts are continually expended and then replenished; for example, a *petty cash fund*.

revolving loan. A *loan* that is expected to be renewed at *maturity*.

right. The privilege to subscribe to new *stock* issues or to purchase stock. Usually, rights are contained in securities called *warrants* and the warrants may be sold to others. See also *preemptive right*.

risk. A measure of the variability of the *return on investment*. For a given expected amount of return, most people prefer less risk to more risk. Therefore, in rational markets, investments with more risk usually promise, or are expected to yield, a higher rate of return than investments with lower risk Most people use "risk" and "uncertainty" as synonyms. In technical language, however, these terms have different meanings. "Risk" is used when the probabilities attached to the various outcomes are known, such as the probabilities of heads or tails in the flip of a fair coin. "Uncertainty" refers to an event where the probabilities of the outcomes, such as winning or losing a lawsuit, can only be estimated.

risk-adjusted discount rate. In a *capital budgeting* con-

750

An Open Account, Ruled and Balanced
(Steps indicated in parentheses correspond to steps described in "ruling an account.")

	Date 1982	Explanation	Ref.	Debit (1)		Date 1982	Explanation	Ref.	Credit (2)		
	Jan. 1	Balance	✔	100	00						
	Jan. 13		VR	121	37	Sept. 15		J		42	
	Mar. 20		VR	56	42	Nov. 12		J	413	15	
	June 5		J	1,138	09	Dec. 31	Balance	✔	1,050	59	(3)
	Aug. 18		J	1	21						
	Nov. 20		VR	38	43						
	Dec. 7		VR	8	64						
(4)	1983			1,464	16	1983			1,464	16	(4)
(5)	Jan. 1	Balance	✔	1,050	59						

text, a decision maker compares projects by comparing their *net present values* for a given *interest* rate, usually the *cost of capital*. If a given project's outcome is considered to be much more or much less risky than the normal undertakings of the company, then the interest rate will be increased (if the project is more risky) or decreased (if less risky) and the rate used is said to be risk-adjusted.

risk premium. Extra compensation paid to an employee or extra interest paid to a lender, over amounts usually considered normal, in return for their undertaking to engage in activities more risky than normal.

ROI. *Return on investment*, but usually used to refer to a single project and expressed as a ratio: *income* divided by average *cost* of *assets* devoted to the project.

royalty. Compensation for the use of property, usually a patent, copyrighted material, or natural resources. The amount is often expressed as a percentage of receipts from using the property or as an amount per unit produced.

RRA. See *Reserve recognition accounting*.

rule of 69. An amount of money invested at r percent per period will double in 69/r + .35 periods. This approximation is accurate to one-tenth of a period for interest rates between 1/4 and 100 percent per period. For example, at 10 percent per period, the rule says that a given sum will double in 69/10 + .35 = 7.25 periods. At 10 percent per period, a given sum actually doubles in 7.27+ periods.

rule of 72. An amount of money invested at r percent per period will double in 72/r periods. A reasonable approximation but not nearly as accurate as the *rule of 69*. For example, at 10 percent per period, the rule says that a given sum will double in 72/10 = 7.2 periods.

rule of 78. The rule followed by many finance companies for allocating earnings on *loans* among the months of a year on the sum-of-the-months'-digits basis when equal monthly payments from the borrower are to be received. The sum of the digits from 1 through 12 is 78, so 12/78 of the year's earnings are allocated to the first month, 11/78 to the second month, and so on. See *sum-of-the-years'-digits depreciation*.

ruling (and balancing) an account. The process of summarizing a series of entries in an *account* by computing a new *balance* and drawing double lines to indicate the information above the double lines has been summarized in the new balance. The process is illustrated below. The steps are as follow. (1) Compute the sum of all *debit* entries including opening debit balance, if any—$1,464.16. (2) Compute the sum of all credit entries including opening credit balance, if any—$413.57. (3) If the amount in (1) is larger than the amount in (2), then write the excess as a credit with a check mark—$1,464.16 − $413.57 = $1,050.59. (4) Add both debit and credit columns, which should both now sum to the same amount, and show that identical total at the foot of both columns. (5) Draw double lines under those numbers and write the excess of debits over credits as the new debit balance with a check mark. (6) If the amount in (2) is larger than the amount in (1), then write the excess as a debit with a check mark. (7) Do steps (4) and (5) except that the excess becomes the new credit balance. (8) If the amount in (1) is equal to the amount in (2), then the balance is zero and only the totals with the double lines beneath them need be shown. This process is illustrated in the accompanying figure.

S

SAB. Staff Accounting Bulletin of the *SEC*.

salary. Compensation earned by managers, administrators, professionals, not based on an hourly rate. Contrast with *wage*.

sale. A *revenue* transaction where *goods* or *services* are delivered to a customer in return for cash or a contractual obligation to pay.

sale and leaseback. Phrase used to describe a *financing* transaction where improved property is sold but is taken back for use on a long-term *lease*. Such transactions often have advantageous income tax effects, but usually have no effect on *financial statement income*.

sales allowance. A reduction in sales *invoice* price usually given because the goods received by the buyer are not exactly what was ordered. The amounts of such adjustments are often accumulated by the seller in a temporary *revenue contra account* having this, or a similar, title. See *sales discount*.

sales basis of revenue recognition. *Revenue* is recognized, not as goods are produced nor as orders are received, but only when the sale (delivery) has been consummated and cash or a legal receivable obtained. Most revenue is recognized on this basis. Compare with the *percentage of completion method* and the *installment method*. Identical with the *completed contract method* but this latter term is ordinarily used only for *long-term* construction projects.

sales contra, estimated uncollectibles. A title for the *contra-revenue account* to recognize estimated reductions in income caused by accounts receivable that will not be collected. See *allowance for uncollectibles* and *allowance method*.

sales discount. Reduction in sales *invoice* price usually offered for prompt payment. See *terms of sale* and *2/10, n/30*.

sales return. The physical return of merchandise; the amounts of such returns are often accumulated by the seller in a temporary *revenue contra account*.

sales value method. *Relative sales value method.*

salvage value. Actual or estimated selling price, net of removal or disposal costs, of a used *plant asset* to be sold or otherwise retired. See *residual value*.

SAS. *Statement on Auditing Standards* of the *AICPA*.

SAV. *Supplemental actuarial value.*

schedule. Supporting set of calculations that show how figures in a statement or tax return are derived.

scientific method. *Effective interest method* of *amortizing bond discount* or *premium*.

scrap value. *Salvage value* assuming item is to be junked. A *net realizable value*. *Residual value*.

SEC. Securities and Exchange Commission, an agency authorized by the U.S. Congress to regulate, among other things, the financial reporting practices of most public corporations. The SEC has indicated that it will usually allow the *FASB* to set accounting principles but it reserves the right to require more disclosure than required by the FASB. The SEC's accounting requirements are stated in its *Accounting Series Releases* (*ASR*) and *Regulation S-X*. See also *registration statement* and *10-K*.

secret reserve. *Hidden reserve.*

Securities and Exchange Commission. *SEC.*

security. Document that indicates ownership or indebtedness or potential ownership, such as an *option* or *warrant*.

segment (of a business). As defined by *APB Opinion No. 30*, "a component of an *entity* whose activities represent a separate major line of business or class of customer . . . [It may be] a *subsidiary*, a division, or a department, . . . provided that its *assets*, results of *operations*, and activities can be clearly distinguished, physically and operationally for financial reporting purposes, from the other assets, results of operations, and activities of the entity." In *SFAS No. 14* a segment is defined as "A component of an enterprise engaged in promoting a product or service or a group of related products and services primarily to unaffiliated customers . . . for a profit."

segment reporting. Reporting of *sales*, *income* and *assets* by *segments of a business*, usually classified by nature of products sold but sometimes by geographical area where goods are produced or sold or by type of customers. Sometimes called "line of business reporting." *Central corporate expenses* are not allocated to the segments.

self-balancing. A set of records with equal *debits* and *credits* such as the *ledger* (but not individual accounts), the *balance sheet*, and a *fund* in nonprofit accounting.

self-insurance. See *insurance.*

selling and administrative expenses. *Expenses* not specifically identifiable with, nor assigned to, production.

semifixed costs. *Costs* that increase with activity as a step function.

semivariable costs. *Costs* that increase strictly linearly with activity but that are positive at zero activity level. Royalty fees of 2 percent of sales are variable; royalty fees of $1,000 per year plus 2 percent of sales are semivariable.

senior securities. *Bonds* as opposed to *preferred stock;* *preferred stock* as opposed to *common stock*. The senior security has a claim against *earnings* or *assets* that must be met before the claim of less senior securities.

serial bonds. An *issue* of *bonds* that mature in part at one date, another part on another date, and so on; the various maturity dates usually are equally spaced; contrast them with *term bonds*.

service basis of depreciation. *Production method.*

service department. A department, such as the personnel or computer department, that provides services to other departments, rather than direct work on a salable product; contrast with *production department*. Costs of service departments whose services benefit manufacturing operations must be *allocated* to as *product costs* under *absorption costing*.

service life. Period of expected usefulness of an asset; may not coincide with *depreciable life* for income tax purposes.

service potential. The future benefits embodied in an item that cause the item to be classified as an *asset*. Without service potential, there are no future benefits and the item should not be classified as an asset. *SFAS No. 3* suggests that the primary characteristic of service potential is the ability to generate future net cash inflows.

services. Useful work done by a person, a machine, or an organization. See *goods and services*.

setup. The time or costs required to prepare production equipment for doing a job.

SFAC. Statement of Financial Accounting Concepts from the *FASB*.

SFAS. *Statement of Financial Accounting Standards* from the *FASB*.

share. A unit of *stock* representing ownership in a corporation.

shareholders' equity. *Proprietorship* or *owners' equity* of a corporation. Because *stock* means inventory in Australian, British, and Canadian usage, the term "shareholders' equity" is usually used by Australian, British, and Canadian writers.

short-term. Current; ordinarily, due within one year.

shrinkage. An excess of *inventory* shown on the *books* over actual physical quantities on hand. Can result from theft or shoplifting as well as from evaporation or general wear and tear.

sight draft. A demand for payment drawn by a person to whom money is owed. The *draft* is presented to the borrower's (the debtor's) bank in expectation that the borrower will authorize its bank to disburse the funds. Such drafts are often used when a seller sells goods to a new customer in a different city. The seller is not sure whether the buyer will pay the bill. The seller sends the *bill* of lading, or other evidence of ownership of the goods, along with a sight draft to the buyer's bank. Before the goods can be released to the buyer, the buyer must instruct its bank to honor the sight draft by withdrawing funds from the buyers' account. Once the sight draft is honored, the bill of lading or other document evidencing ownership is handed over to the buyer and the goods become the property of the buyer.

simple interest. *Interest* calculated on *principal* where interest earned during periods before maturity of the loan is neither added to the principal nor paid to the lender. *Interest = principal × interest rate × time.* Seldom used in economic calculations except for periods less than 1 year; contrast with *compound interest*.

single-entry accounting. Accounting that is neither *self-balancing* nor *articulated*; that is, it does not rely on equal *debits* and *credits*. *No journal entries* are made. *Plugging* is required to derive *owners' equity* for the *balance sheet*.

single proprietorship. *Sole proprietorship*.

single step. Said of an *income statement* where *ordinary revenue* and *gain* items are shown first and totaled. Then all ordinary *expenses* and *losses* are totaled. Their difference, plus the effect of *income from discontinued operations* and *extraordinary items*, is shown as *net income*; contrast with *multiple-step* and see *proprietorship theory*.

sinking fund. *Assets* and their earnings earmarked for the retirement of bonds or other long-term obligations. Earnings of sinking fund investments are taxable income of the company.

sinking fund method of depreciation. The periodic charge is an amount so that when the charges are considered to be an *annuity*, the value of the annuity at the end of depreciable life is equal to the *acquisition cost* of the asset. In theory, the charge for a period ought also to include interest on the accumulated depreciation at the start of the period as

well. A *fund* of cash is not necessarily, or even usually, accumulated. This method is rarely used.

skeleton account. *T-account*.

slide. The name of the error made by a bookkeeper in recording the digits of a number correctly with the decimal point misplaced; for example, recording $123.40 as $1,234.00 or as $12.34.

soak-up method. The *equity method*.

Social Security taxes. Taxes levied by the federal government on both employers and employees to provide *funds* to pay retired persons (or their survivors) who are entitled to receive such payments, either because they paid Social Security taxes themselves or because the Congress has declared them eligible. See *Old Age, Survivors, Disability*, and *(Hospital) Insurance*.

sole proprietorship. All *owners' equity* belongs to one person.

solvent. Able to meet debts when due.

SOP. *Statement of Position* (of *AcSEC* of the *AICPA*).

sound value. A phrase used mainly in appraisals of *fixed assets* to mean *fair market value* or *replacement cost* in present condition.

source of funds. Any *transaction* that increases *working capital*.

sources and uses statement. *Statement of changes in financial position*.

SOYD. *Sum-of-the-years'-digits depreciation*.

special assessment. A compulsory levy made by a governmental unit on property to pay the costs of a specific improvement, or service, presumed not to benefit the general public but only the owners of the property so assessed. Accounted for in a special assessment fund.

special journal. A *journal*, such as a sales journal or cash disbursements journal, to record *transactions* of a similar nature that occur frequently.

special revenue debt. Debt of a governmental unit backed only by revenues from specific sources such as tolls from a bridge.

specific identification method. Method for valuing *ending inventory* and *cost of goods sold* by identifying actual units sold and in inventory and summing the actual costs of those individual units. Usually used for items with large unit value, such as jewelry, automobiles, and fur coats.

specific price changes. Changes in the market prices of specific *goods and services*; contrast with *general price level changes*.

specific price index. A measure of the price of a specific good or service, or a small group of similar goods or services, at one time relative to the price during a base period; contrast with *general price index*. See *dollar-value LIFO method*.

spending variance. In *standard cost systems*, the *rate* or *price variance* for *overhead costs*.

753

split. *Stock split.* Sometimes called "splitup."

splitoff point. The point where all costs are no longer *joint costs* but can be identified with individual products or perhaps with a smaller number of *joint products.*

spoilage. See *abnormal spoilage* and *normal spoilage.*

spread sheet. A *work sheet* organized like a *matrix* that provides a two-way classification of accounting data. The rows and columns are both labeled with *account* titles. An entry in a row represents a *debit* whereas an entry in a column represents a *credit.* Thus, the number "100" in the "cash" row and the "accounts receivable" column records an entry debiting cash and crediting accounts receivable for $100. A given row total indicates all debit entries to the account represented by that row and a given column total indicates the sum of all credit entries to the account represented by the column.

squeeze. A term sometimes used for *plug.*

SSARS. See *Statement on Standards for Accounting and Review Services.*

stabilized accounting. *Constant dollar accounting.*

stable monetary unit assumption. In spite of *inflation* that appears to be a way of life, the assumption that underlies *historical-cost/nominal dollar accounting*—namely that current dollars and dollars of previous years can be meaningfully added together. No specific recognition is given to changing values of the dollar in the usual *financial statements.* See *constant dollar accounting.*

Staff Accounting Bulletin. An interpretation issued by the Staff of the Chief Accountant of the *SEC* "suggesting" how the various *Accounting Series Releases* should be applied in practice.

standard cost. Anticipated *cost* of producing a unit of output; a predetermined cost to be assigned to products produced. Standard cost implies a norm: what costs should be. Budgeted cost implies a forecast, something likely, but not necessarily a "should," as implied by a norm. Standard costs are used as the benchmark for gauging good and bad performance. While a budget may similarly be used, it need not. A budget may simply be a planning document, subject to changes whenever plans change, whereas standard costs are usually not changed until technology changes or costs of labor and materials change.

standard cost system. *Product costing* using *standard costs* rather than actual costs. May be based on either *absorption* or *direct costing* principles.

standard price (rate). Unit price established for materials or labor used in *standard cost systems.*

standard quantity allowed. The quantity of direct material or direct labor (inputs) that should have been used if the units of output had been produced in accordance with preset *standards.*

standby costs. A type of *capacity cost,* such as property taxes, incurred even if operations are shut down completely. Contrast with *enabling costs.*

stated capital. Amount of capital contributed by shareholders. Sometimes used to mean *legal capital.*

stated value. A term sometimes used for the *face amount of capital stock,* when no *par value* is indicated. Where there is stated value per share, it may be set by the directors (in which case, capital *contributed in excess of stated value* may come into being).

statement of affairs. A *balance sheet* showing immediate *liquidation* amounts, rather than *historical costs,* usually prepared when *insolvency* or *bankruptcy* is imminent. The *going concern assumption* is not used.

statement of changes in financial position. As defined by *APB Opinion* No. 19, a statement that explains the changes in *working capital* (or cash) balances during a period and shows the changes in the working capital (or cash) accounts themselves. Sometimes called the "funds statement." See *dual transactions assumption* and *all financial resources.*

Statement of Financial Accounting Standards. SFAS. See *FASB.*

Statement of Financial Accounting Concepts. SFAC. One of a series of *FASB* publications in its *conceptual framework* for *financial accounting* and reporting. Such statements set forth objectives and fundamentals to be the basis for specific financial accounting and reporting standards.

statement of financial position. *Balance sheet.*

Statement of Position. SOP. A recommendation on an emerging accounting problem issued by the *AcSEC* of the *AICPA*. The AICPA's Code of Professional Ethics specifically states that *CPAs* need not treat SOPs as they do rules from the FASB, but a CPA would be wary of departing from the recommendations of a SOP.

statement of retained earnings (income). A statement that reconciles the beginning-of-period and end-of-period balances in the *retained earnings* account. It shows the effects of *earnings, dividend declarations*, and *prior-period adjustments.*

Statement on Auditing Standards. SAS. No. 1 of this series (1973) codifies all statements on auditing standards previously promulgated by the AICPA. Later numbers deal with specific auditing standards and procedures.

Statement on Standards for Accounting and Review Services. SSARS. Pronouncements issued by the *AICPA* on *unaudited financial statements* and unaudited financial information of nonpublic entities.

static budget. *Fixed budget.*

statutory tax rate. The tax rate specified in the *income tax* law for each type of income (for example, *ordinary income, capital gain or loss*).

step cost. Semifixed cost.

step-down method. The method for *allocating service department* costs that starts by allocating one service department's costs to *production departments* and to all other service departments. Then a second service department's costs, including costs allocated from the first, are allocated to pro-

754

duction departments and to all other service departments except the first one. In this fashion, the costs of all service departments, including previous allocations, are allocated to production departments and to those service departments whose costs have not yet been allocated.

sterilized allocation. Optimal decisions result from considering *incremental costs*, only. *Allocations* of *joint* or *common costs* are never required for optimal decisions. An allocation of these costs that causes the optimal decision choice not to differ from the one that occurs when joint or common costs are unallocated is "sterilized" with respect to that decision. The term was first used in this context by Arthur L. Thomas. Because *absorption costing* requires that all manufacturing costs be allocated to product, and because some allocations can lead to bad decisions, Thomas (and we) advocate that the allocation scheme chosen lead to sterilized allocations that do not alter the otherwise optimal decision. There is, however, no single allocation scheme that is always sterilized with respect to all decisions. Thus, Thomas (and we) advocate that decisions be made on the basis of incremental costs before any allocations.

stock. *Inventory. Capital stock.* A measure of the amount of something on hand at a specific time; in this sense, contrast with *flow*.

stock appreciation rights. The employer promises to pay to the employee an amount of *cash* on a certain future date. The amount of cash is the difference between the *market value* of a certain number of *shares* of *stock* in the employer's company on a given future date and some base price set on the date the rights are granted. This is a form of compensation used because both changes in tax laws in recent years and stock market performance have made *stock options* relatively less attractive. *GAAP* computes compensation based on the difference between market value of the shares and the base price set at the time of the grant. *Expense* is recognized as the holder of the rights performs the services required for the rights to be exercised.

stock dividend. A so-called *dividend* where additional *shares* of *capital stock* are distributed, without cash payments, to existing shareholders. It results in a *debit* to *retained earnings* in the amount of the market value of the shares issued and a *credit to capital stock* accounts. It is ordinarily used to indicate that earnings retained have been permanently reinvested in the business; contrast with a *stock split*, which requires no entry in the capital stock accounts other than a notation that the *par* or *stated value* per share has been changed.

stock option. The right to purchase a specified number of shares of *stock* for a specified price at specified times, usually granted to employees; contrast with *warrant*

stock right. See *right*.

stock split. Increase in the number of common shares outstanding resulting from the issuance of additional shares to existing shareholders without additional capital contributions by them. Does not increase the total *par* (or *stated*) *value of common stock* outstanding because par (or stated) value per share is reduced in inverse proportion. A three-

for-one stock split reduces par (or stated) value per share to one-third of its former amount. Stock splits are usually limited to distributions that increase the number of shares outstanding by 20 percent or more; compare with *stock dividend*.

stock subscriptions. See *subscription* and *subscribed stock*.

stock warrant. See *warrant*.

stockholders' equity. See *shareholders' equity*.

stores. *Raw materials*, parts, and supplies.

straight-debt value. An estimate of what the *market value* of a *convertible bond* would be if the bond did not contain a conversion privilege.

straight-line depreciation. If the *depreciable life* is n periods, then the periodic *depreciation* charge is $1/n$ of the *depreciable cost*. Results in equal periodic charges and is sometimes called "straight-time depreciation."

Subchapter S Corporation. A firm legally organized as a *corporation* but taxed as if it were a *partnership*.

subject to. Qualifications in an *auditor's report* usually caused by a *material* uncertainty in the valuation of an item, such as future promised payments from a foreign government or outcome of pending litigation.

subordinated. Said of *debt* whose claim on income or assets is junior to, or comes after, claims of other debt.

subscribed stock. A *shareholders' equity* account showing the capital that will be contributed as soon as the subscription price is collected. A subscription is a legal contract so that an entry is made debiting an owners' equity contra account and crediting subscribed stock as soon as the stock is subscribed.

subscription. Agreement to buy a *security*, or to purchase periodicals such as magazines.

subsequent events. *Post-statement events*.

subsidiary. Said of a company more than 50 percent of whose voting stock is owned by another.

subsidiary (ledger) accounts. The *accounts* in a *subsidiary ledger*.

subsidiary ledger. The *ledger* that contains the detailed accounts whose total is shown in a *controlling account* of the *general ledger*.

successful-efforts accounting. In petroleum accounting, the *capitalization* of the drilling costs of only those wells that contain oil. See *reserve recognition accounting* for an example.

summary of significant accounting principles. *APB Opinion* No. 22 requires that every *annual report* summarize the significant *accounting principles* used in compiling the annual report. This summary may be a separate exhibit or the first *note* to the financial statements.

sum-of-the-years'-digits depreciation. SYD. SOYD. An *accelerated depreciation* method for an asset with *depreciable life* of n years where the charge in period $i(i = 1, \ldots, n)$ is the fraction $(n + 1 - i)/[n(n + 1)/2]$ of the *depreciable cost*. If an asset has a depreciable cost of $15,000 and a 5-year depreciable life, for example, the depreciation charges would be $5,000 $(= 5/15 \times \$15,000)$ in the first year, $4,000 in the second, $3,000 in the third, $2,000 in the fourth, and $1,000 in the fifth.

sunk cost. *Costs* incurred in the past that are not affected by, and hence irrelevant for, current decisions, aside from *income tax* effects; contrast with *incremental costs* and *imputed costs*. For example, the *acquisition cost* of machinery is irrelevant to a decision of whether or not to scrap the machinery. The current *exit value* of the machine is the imputed cost of continuing to own it and the cost of, say, electricity to run the machine is an incremental cost of its operation. Sunk costs become relevant for decision making when *income taxes* (gain or *loss* on disposal of asset) are taken into account because the cash payment for income taxes depends on the tax basis of the asset.

supplemental actuarial value. SAV. *Present value* at a given time of a *pension plan's* unrecognized benefits assigned to employees for their service before that given time. Called "prior service cost" in *APB Opinion* No. 8; includes *past service cost*. Such obligations are not recognized as liabilities in the accounting records but must be disclosed in the notes to the financial statements; contrast with *normal cost*. This term is used in *SFAS* No. 35, but seems likely to be replaced by *accrued actuarial liability*.

supplementary statements (schedules). Statements (schedules) in addition to the four basic *financial statements* (including the retained earnings reconciliation as a basic statement).

surplus. A word once used but now considered poor terminology; prefaced by "earned" to mean *retained earnings* and prefaced by "capital" to mean *capital contributed in excess of par* (or *stated*) *value*.

surplus reserves. Of all the words in accounting, *reserve* is the most objectionable and *surplus* is the second most objectionable. This phrase, then, has nothing to recommend it. It means, simply, *appropriated retained earnings*.

suspense account. A *temporary account* used to record part of a transaction prior to final analysis of that transaction. For example, if a business regularly classifies all sales into a dozen or more different categories but wants to deposit the proceeds of cash sales every day, it may credit a sales suspense account pending detailed classification of all sales into sales, type 1; sales, type 2; and so on.

sustainable income. The part of *distributable income* (computed from *current cost* data) that the firm can be expected to earn in the next accounting period if operations are continued at the same levels as during the current period. *Income from discontinued operations*, for example, may be distributable but not sustainable.

S-X. See *Regulation S-X*

SYD. *Sum-of-the-years'-digits depreciation. SOYD.*

T

T-account. Account form shaped like the letter T with the title above the horizontal line. *Debits* are shown to the left of the vertical line, *credits* to the right.

take-home pay. The amount of a paycheck; earned wages or *salary* reduced by deductions for *income taxes, Social Security taxes*, contributions to fringe benefit plans, union dues, and so on. Take-home pay might be as little as 60 percent of earned compensation.

take-or-pay contract. As defined by *SFAS* No. 47, an agreement between a purchaser and a seller that provides for the purchaser to pay specified amounts periodically in return for products or services. The purchaser must make specified minimum payments even if it does not take delivery of the contracted products or services.

taking a bath. To incur a large loss. See *big bath*.

tangible. Having physical form. Accounting has never satisfactorily defined the distinction between tangible and *intangible assets*. Typically, intangibles are defined by giving an exhaustive list and everything not on the list is defined as tangible.

target cost. *Standard cost.*

tax. A nonpenal, but compulsory, charge levied by a government on income, consumption, wealth, or other bases for the benefit of all those governed. The term does not include fines or specific charges for benefits accruing only to those paying the charges, such as licenses, permits, special assessments, admissions fees, and tolls.

tax allocation: interperiod. See *deferred income tax liability*.

tax allocation: intrastatement. The showing of income tax effects on *extraordinary items, income from discontinued operations*, and *prior-period adjustments* along with these items, separately from income taxes on other income. See *net-of-tax reporting*.

tax avoidance. See *tax shelter*.

tax credit. A subtraction from taxes otherwise payable, contrast with *tax deduction*.

tax deduction. A subtraction from *revenues* and *gains* to arrive at taxable income. Tax deductions are technically different from tax *exemptions*, but the effect of both is to reduce gross income in computing taxable income. Both are different from *tax credits*, which are subtracted from the computed tax itself in determining taxes payable. If the tax rate is the fraction t of pretax income, then a *tax credit* of $1 is worth $1/t of *tax deductions*.

tax evasion. The fraudulent understatement of taxable revenues or overstatement of deductions and expenses or both; contrast with *tax shelter*.

tax exempts. See *municipal bonds*.

tax shelter. The legal avoidance of, or reduction in, *income taxes* resulting from a careful reading of the complex income tax regulations and the subsequent rearrangement

756

of financial affairs to take advantage of the regulations. Often the term is used pejoratively, but the courts have long held that an individual or corporation has no obligation to pay taxes any larger than the legal minimum. If the public concludes that a given tax shelter is "unfair," then the laws and regulations can be changed. Sometimes used to refer to the investment that permits tax avoidance.

tax shield. The amount of an *expense* that reduces taxable income but does not require *working capital*, such as *depreciation*. Sometimes this term is expanded to include expenses that reduce taxable income and use working capital. A depreciation deduction (or *R&D expense* in the expanded sense) of $10,000 provides a tax shield of $4,600 when the marginal tax rate is 46 percent.

Technical Bulletin. The *FASB* has authorized its staff to issue bulletins to provide guidance on financial accounting and reporting problems. Although the FASB does not formally approve the contents of the bulletins, their contents are presumed to be part of *GAAP*.

technology. The sum of a firm's technical *trade secrets* and *know-how*, as distinct from its *patents*.

temporary account. *Account* that does not appear on the *balance sheet*. *Revenue* and *expense* accounts, their *adjuncts* and *contras, production cost accounts, dividend distribution accounts*, and purchases-related accounts (which are closed to the various inventories). Sometimes called a "nominal account."

temporary difference. See *timing difference*.

temporary investments. Investments in *marketable securities* that the owner intends to sell within a short time, usually 1 year, and hence classified as *current assets*.

10-5-3 rule. See *3-5-10 rule*.

10-K. The name of the annual report required by the *SEC* of nearly all publicly held corporations.

term bonds. A *bond issue* whose component bonds all mature at the same time; contrast with *serial bonds*.

term loan. A loan with a *maturity* date, as opposed to a demand loan which is due whenever the lender requests payment. In practice bankers and auditors use this phrase only for loans for a year or more.

terms of sale. The conditions governing payment for a sale. For example, the terms *2/10, n(et)/30* mean that if payment is made within 10 days of the invoice date, a *discount* of 2 percent from *invoice* price can be taken; the invoice amount must be paid, in any event, within 30 days or it becomes overdue.

3-5-10 rule. For income tax purposes (since the income tax legislation of 1981), almost all *depreciable assets* are grouped into one of three classes: those to be depreciated for tax purposes over 3 years (such as automobiles), those to be depreciated for tax purposes over 5 years (such as most machinery and equipment), and those to be depreciated over 10 years. Because most assets have service lives for tax purposes of 3, 5, or 10 years, the rule has come to be known as the 3-5-10 rule. Officially it is designated as the Acceler-

ated Cost Recovery System (ACRS). For financial reporting the depreciable life is chosen as the best estimate of its useful life. Income tax *timing differences* for depreciation are created when a shorter life is used for tax reporting than for financial reporting.

throughput contract. As defined by *SFAS* No. 47, an agreement between a shipper (processor) and the owner of a transportation facility (such as an oil or natural gas pipeline or a ship) or a manufacturing facility that provides for the shipper (processor) to pay specified amounts periodically in return for the transportation (processing) of a product. The shipper (processor) is obligated to make cash payments even if it does not ship (process) the contracted quantities.

ticker file. A collection of vouchers or other memoranda arranged chronologically to remind the person in charge of certain duties to make payments (or to do other tasks) as scheduled.

time-adjusted rate of return. *Internal rate of return*.

time cost. *Period cost*.

time deposit. Cash in bank earning interest; contrast with *demand deposit*.

time series analysis. See *cross section analysis* for definition and contrast.

times-interest earned. Ratio of pretax *income* plus *interest* charges to interest charges. See *ratio*.

timing difference. A difference between taxable income and pretax income reported to shareholders that will be reversed in a subsequent period and requires an entry in the *deferred income tax* account. For example, the use of *accelerated depreciation* for tax returns and *straight-line depreciation* for financial reporting.

total assets turnover. *Sales* divided by average total *assets*. Contrast with *permanent difference*.

trade acceptance. A *draft* drawn by a seller which is presented for signature (acceptance) to the buyer at the time goods are purchased and which then becomes the equivalent of a *note receivable* of the seller and the *note payable* of the buyer.

trade credit. One business allows another to buy from it in return for a promise to pay later. As contrasted with consumer credit, where a business extends the privilege of paying later to a retail customer.

trade discount. A *discount* from *list price* offered to all customers of a given type; contrast with a *discount* offered for prompt payment and *quantity discount*.

trade payables (receivables). *Qayables* (*receivables*) arising in the ordinary course of business transactions. Most accounts payable (receivable) are of this kind.

trade secret. Technical or business information such as formulas, recipes, computer programs, and marketing data not generally known by competitors and maintained by the firm as a secret. A famous example is the secret formula for *Coca Cola* (a registered *trademark* of the company). Compare with *know-how*. Theoretically capable of having an infinite life, this intangible asset is capitalized only if purchased and then amortized over a period not to exceed 40 years. If it is developed internally, then no asset will be shown.

trade-in. Acquiring a new *asset* in exchange for a used one and perhaps additional cash. See *boot* and *trade-in transaction*.

trade-in transaction. The accounting for a trade-in depends whether or not the asset received is "similar" to the asset traded in and whether the accounting is for *financial statements* or for *income tax* returns. Assume that an old asset cost $5,000, has $3,000 of *accumulated depreciation* (after recording depreciation to the date of the trade-in), and hence has a *book value* of $2,000. The old asset appears to have a market value of $1,500, according to price quotations in used-asset markets. The old asset is traded-in on a new asset with a list price of $10,000. The old asset and $5,500 cash (*boot*) are given for the new asset. The generic entry for the trade-in transaction is:

```
New Asset . . . . . . . . . . . . . . . .    A
Accumulated Depreciation (Old Asset).  3,000
Adjustment on Exchange of Asset . .    B  or   B
   Old Asset  . . . . . . . . . . . . . . .         5,000
   Cash . . . . . . . . . . . . . . . . .           5,500
```

(1) The *list price* method of accounting for trade-ins rests on the assumption that the list price of the new asset closely approximates its market value. The new asset is recorded at its list price (A = $10,000 in the example); B is a *plug* (= $2,500 credit in the example). If B requires a *debit* plug, the Adjustment on Exchange of Asset is a *loss*; if a *credit* plug is required (as in the example), the adjustment is a *gain*.

(2) Another theoretically sound method of accounting for trade-ins rests on the assumption that the price quotation from used-asset markets gives a more reliable measure of the market value of the old asset than is the list price a reliable measure of the market value of the new asset. This method uses the *fair market value* of the old asset, $1,500 in the example, to determine B (= $2,000 book value − $1,500 assumed proceeds on disposition = $500 debit or loss). The exchange results in a loss if the book value of the old asset exceeds its market value and in a gain if the market value exceeds the book value. The new asset is recorded on the books by plugging for A (= $7,000 in the example).

(3) For income tax reporting, no gain or loss may be recognized on the trade-in. Thus the new asset is recorded on the books by assuming B is zero and plugging for A (= $7,500 in the example). In practice, firms that wish to recognize the loss currently will sell the old asset directly, rather than trading it in, and acquire the new asset entirely for cash.

(4) *Generally accepted accounting principles* (*APB Opinion No. 29*) require a variant of these methods. The basic method is (1) or (2), depending upon whether the list price of the new asset (1) or the quotation of the old asset's market value (2) is the more reliable indication of market value. If, when applying the basic method, a debit entry, or loss, is required for the Adjustment on Exchange of Asset, then the trade-in is recorded as described in (1) or (2) and the full

amount of the loss is recognized currently. If, however, a credit entry, or gain, is required for the Adjustment on Exchange of Asset, then the amount of gain recognized currently depends upon whether or not the old asset and the new asset are "similar". If the assets are not similar, then the entire gain is recognized currently. If the assets are similar and cash is not received by the party trading in, then no gain is recognized and the treatment is like that in (3); that is B = 0, plug for A. If the assets are similar and cash is received by the party trading in—a rare case—then a portion of the gain recognized currently. The portion of the gain recognized currently is the fraction *cash received/fair market value of total consideration received*. (When the list price method, (1), is used, the market value of the old asset is assumed to be the list price of the new asset plus the amount of cash received by the party trading in.)

The results of applying *GAAP* to the example can be summarized as follows:

More Reliable Information As To Fair Market Value	Old Asset Compared with New Asset	
	Similar	Not Similar
New Asset List Price	A = $7,500	A = $10,000
	B = 0	B = 2,500 gain
Old Asset Market Price . . .	A = $7,000	A = $ 7,000
	B = 500 loss	B = 500 loss

trademark. A distinctive word or symbol affixed to a product, its package or dispenser, which uniquely identifies the firm's products and services. See *trademark right*.

trademark right. The right to exclude competitors in sales or advertising from using words or symbols that may be confusingly similar to the firm's *trademarks*. Trademark rights last as long as the firm continues to use the trademarks in question. In the United States, trademark rights arise from use and not from government registration. They therefore have a legal life independent of the life of a registration. Registrations last 20 years and are renewable as long as the trademark is being used. Thus, as an asset, purchased trademark rights might, like land, not be subject to amortization if management believes that the life of the trademark is indefinite. In practice, accountants amortize a trademark right over some estimate of its life, not to exceed 40 years. Under *SFAS No. 2*, internally developed trademark rights must be *expensed*.

trading on the equity. Said of a firm engaging in *debt financing*: frequently said of a firm doing so to a degree considered abnormal for a firm of its kind. *Leverage*.

transaction. A *transfer* between the accounting *entity* and another party, or parties.

transfer. *SFAC No. 3* distinguishes "reciprocal" and "nonreciprocal" transfers. In a reciprocal transfer, or "exchange," the entity both receives and sacrifices. In a nonreciprocal transfer the entity sacrifices but does not receive (examples include gifts, distributions to owners) or receives but does not sacrifice (investment by owner in entity). *SFAC No. 3* suggests that the term "internal transfer" is self-contradictory and that the term "internal event" be used instead.

transfer agent. Usually a bank or trust company designated by a corporation to make legal transfers of *stock* (*bonds*) and, perhaps, to pay *dividends* (*coupons*).

transfer price. A substitute for a *market*, or *arm's-length, price* used in *profit center*, or *responsibility, accounting* when one segment of the business "sells" to another segment. Incentives of profit center managers will not coincide with the best interests of the entire business unless transfer prices are properly set.

translation gain (or loss). *Foreign exchange gain* (*or loss*).

transportation-in. *Freight-in.*

transposition error. An error in record keeping resulting from reversing the order of digits in a number, such as recording "32" for "23." If an error of this sort has been made in a number added in a total, then the incorrect total will differ from the correct total by a number divisible by nine. Thus if *trial balance* sums differ by a number divisible by nine, one might search for a transposition error.

treasury bond. A bond issued by a corporation and then reacquired; such bonds are treated as retired when reacquired and an *extraordinary gain or loss* on reacquisition is recognized. Also, a *bond* issued by the U.S. Treasury Department.

treasury shares. *Capital stock* issued and then reacquired by the corporation. Such reacquisitions result in a reduction of *shareholders' equity*, and are usually shown on the balance sheet as *contra* to shareholders' equity. Neither *gain* nor loss is recognized on transactions involving treasury stock. Any difference between the amounts paid and received for treasury stock transactions is debited (if positive) or credited (if negative) to *additional paid-in capital*. See *cost method* and *par value method*.

treasury stock. *Treasury shares.*

trial balance. A listing of *account balances*; all accounts with *debit* balances are totaled separately from accounts with *credit* balances. The two totals should be equal. Trial balances are taken as a partial check of the arithmetic accuracy of the entries previously made. See *adjusted, preclosing, postclosing, unadjusted trial balance*.

troubled debt restructuring. As defined in *SFAS No. 15*, a concession (changing of the terms of a *debt*) granted by a *creditor* for economic or legal reasons related to the *debtor's* financial difficulty that the creditor would not otherwise consider.

turnover. The number of times that *assets*, such as *inventory* or *accounts receivable*, are replaced on average during the period. Accounts receivable turnover, for example, is total sales on account for a period divided by average accounts receivable balance for the period. See *ratio*.

turnover of plant and equipment. See *ratio*.

two-T-account method. A method for computing either (1) *foreign exchange gains and losses* or (2) *monetary gains or losses* for *constant dollar accounting statements*. The left-hand *T-account* shows actual net balances of *monetary items* and the right-hand T-account shows implied (*common*) *dollar* amounts.

2/10, n(et)/30. See *terms of sale*.

U

unadjusted trial balance. *Trial balance* before *adjusting* and *closing entries* are made at the end of the period.

unappropriated retained earnings. *Retained earnings* not appropriated and therefore against which *dividends* can be charged in the absence of retained earnings restrictions. See *restricted retained earnings*.

uncertainty. See *risk* for definition and contrast.

uncollectible account. An *account receivable* that will not be paid by the *debtor*. If the preferable *allowance method* is used, the entry on judging a specific account to be uncollectible is to *debit* the allowance for uncollectible accounts and to *credit* the specific account receivable. See *sales contra, estimated uncollectibles*.

unconsolidated subsidiary. A *subsidiary* not consolidated and, hence, accounted for on the *equity method*.

uncontrollable cost. The opposite of *controllable cost*.

underapplied (underabsorbed) overhead. An excess of actual *overhead costs* for a period over costs applied, or charged, to products produced during the period. A *debit balance* remaining in an overhead account after overhead is assigned to product.

underlying document. The record, memorandum, *voucher*, or other signal that is the authority for making an *entry* into a *journal*.

underwriter. One who agrees to purchase an entire *security issue* for a specified price, usually for resale to others.

unearned income (revenue). *Advances from customers*; strictly speaking, a contradiction in terms.

unemployment tax. See *FUTA*.

unencumbered appropriation. In governmental accounting, portion of an *appropriation* not yet spent or *encumbered*.

unexpired cost. An *asset*.

unfavorable variance. In *standard cost* accounting, an excess of actual cost over standard cost assigned to product.

unfunded. Not *funded*. An obligation or *liability*, usually for *pension costs*, exists but no *funds* have been set aside to discharge the obligation or liability.

Uniform Partnership Act. A model law, enacted by many states, to govern the relations between partners where the *partnership* agreement fails to specify the agreed-upon treatment.

unissued capital stock. *Stock* authorized but not yet issued.

units of production method. The *production method of depreciation*.

unlimited liability. The liability of *general partners* or the sole proprietor for all debts of the *partnership* or *sole proprietorship*.

759

unqualified opinion. See *auditor's report*.

unrealized appreciation. An *unrealized holding gain*; frequently used in the context of *marketable securities*.

unrealized gross margin (profit). A *contra* account to *installment accounts receivable* used with the *installment method* of revenue recognition. Shows the amount of profit that will eventually be realized when the receivable is collected. Some accountants show this account as a *liability*.

unrealized holding gain. See *inventory profit* for definition and an example.

unrealized loss on marketable securities. An *income statement account* title for the amount of *loss* during the current period on the portfolio of *marketable securities* below the beginning-of-period *book value* of that portfolio. *SFAS No. 12* requires that losses caused by declines in price below market be *recognized* in the income statement, even though they have not been *realized*.

unrecovered cost. *Book value* of an *asset*.

usage variance. *Quantity variance*.

use of funds. Any transaction that reduces funds (however funds is defined).

useful life. *Service life*.

V

valuation account. A *contra account* or *adjunct account*. When *marketable securities* are reported at *lower-of-cost-or-market*, any declines in market value below cost will be credited to a valuation account. In this way, the acquisition cost and the amount of price declines below cost can both be shown. *SFAS No. 3* says a valuation account is "a separate item that reduces and increases the carrying amount" of an asset (or liability). The accounts are part of the related assets (or liabilities) and are neither assets (nor liabilities) in their own right.

value. Monetary worth; the term is usually so subjective that it ought not to be used without a modifying adjective unless most people would agree on the amount; not to be confused with *cost*. See *fair market value, entry value, exit value*.

value added. *Cost* of a product or *work in process*, minus the cost of the material purchased for the product or work in process.

value variance. *Price variance*.

variable annuity. An *annuity* whose periodic payments depend upon some uncertain outcome, such as stock market prices.

variable budget. *Flexible budget*.

variable costing. *Direct costing*.

variable costs. *Costs* that change as activity levels change. Strictly speaking, variable costs are zero when the activity level is zero. See *semivariable costs*. In accounting this term most often means the sum of *direct costs* and variable *overhead*.

variance. Difference between actual and *standard costs* or between *budgeted* and actual *expenditures* or, sometimes, *expenses*. The word has completely different meanings in accounting and statistics, where it is a measure of dispersion of a distribution.

variance analysis. The investigation of the causes of *variances* in a *standard cost system*. This term has a different meaning in statistics.

variation analysis. Analysis of the causes of changes in items of interest in financial statements such as net *income* or *gross margin*.

vendor. A seller. Sometimes spelled, "vender."

verifiable. A qualitative *objective* of financial reporting specifying that items in *financial statements* can be checked by tracing back to *underlying documents*—supporting *invoices*, canceled *checks*, and other physical pieces of evidence.

verification. The auditor's act of reviewing or checking items in *financial statements* by tracing back to *underlying documents*—supporting *invoices*, canceled *checks*, and other business documents—or sending out *confirmations* to be returned. Compare with *physical verification*.

vertical analysis. Analysis of the financial statements of a single firm or across several firms for a particular time, as opposed to *horizontal* or *time series analysis* where items are compared over time for a single firm or across firms.

vested. Said of an employee's *pension plan* benefits that are not contingent on the employee continuing to work for the employer.

volume variance. *Capacity variance*.

voucher. A document that signals recognition of a *liability* and authorizes the disbursement of cash. Sometimes used to refer to the written evidence documenting an *accounting entry*, as in the term *journal voucher*.

voucher system. A method for controlling *cash* that requires each *check* to be authorized with an approved *voucher*. No cash *disbursements* are made except from *petty cash funds*.

W

wage. Compensation of employees based on time worked or output of product for manual labor. But see *take-home pay*.

warrant. A certificate entitling the owner to buy a specified number of shares at a specified time(s) for a specified price. Differs from a *stock option* only in that options are granted to employees and warrants are issued to the public. See *right*.

warranty. A promise by a seller to correct deficiencies in products sold. When warranties are given, proper accounting practice recognizes an estimate of warranty *expense* and an *estimated liability* at the time of sale. See *guarantee* for contrast in proper usage.

wash sale. The sale and purchase of the same or similar *asset* within a short time period. For *income tax* purposes, *losses* on a sale of stock may not be recognized if equivalent stock is purchased within 30 days before or 30 days after the date of sale.

waste. Residue of material from manufacturing operations with no sale value. Frequently, it has negative value because additional costs must be incurred for disposal.

wasting asset. A *natural resource* having a limited *useful life* and, hence, subject to *amortization*, called *depletion*. Examples are timberland, oil and gas wells, and ore deposits.

watered stock. *Shares* issued for *assets* with *fair market value* less than *par* or *stated value*. The assets are put onto the books at the overstated values. In the law, for share to be considered watered, the *board of directors* must have acted in bad faith or fraudulently in issuing the shares under these circumstances. The term originated from a former practice of cattlemen who fed cattle ("stock") large quantities of salt to make them thirsty. The cattle then drank a lot of water before being taken to market. This was done to make the cattle appear heavier and more valuable than otherwise.

weighted average. An average computed by counting each occurrence of each value, not merely a single occurrence of each value. For example, if one unit is purchased for \$1 and two units are purchased for \$2 each, then the simple average of the purchase prices is \$1.50 but the weighted average price per unit is \$5/3 = \$1.67. Contrast with *moving average*.

weighted-average inventory method. Valuing either *withdrawals* or *ending inventory* at the *weighted average* purchase price of all units on hand at the time of withdrawal or of computing ending inventory. The *inventory equation* is used to calculate the other quantity. If the *perpetual inventory* method is in use, often called the "moving-average method."

where-got, where-gone statement. A term used by W.M. Cole for a statement much like the *statement of changes in financial position*.

window dressing. The attempt to make financial statements show *operating* results, or *financial position*, more favorable than would be otherwise shown.

with recourse. See *note receivable discounted*.

withdrawals. *Assets* distributed to an owner. *Partner's drawings*. See *inventory equation* for another context.

withholding. Deductions from *salaries* or *wages*, usually for *income taxes*, to be remitted by the employer, in the employee's name, to the taxing authority.

without recourse. See *note receivable discounted*.

work in process. Partially completed product; an *asset* that is classified as *inventory*.

work sheet. A tabular schedule for convenient summary of *adjusting* and *closing entries*. The work sheet usually begins with an *unadjusted trial balance*. Adjusting entries are shown in the next two columns, one for *debits* and one for *credits*. The horizontal sum of each line is then carried to the right into either the *income statement* or *balance sheet* columns, as appropriate. The *plug* to equate the income state-

ment column totals is the income, if a debit plug is required, or loss, if a credit plug is required, for the period. That income will be closed to retained earnings on the balance sheet. The income statement credit columns are the revenues for the period and the debit columns are the expenses (and revenue *contras*) to be shown on the income statement.

Work sheet is also used to refer to *schedules* for determining other items appearing on the *financial statements* that require adjustment or compilation.

working capital. *Current assets* minus *current liabilities*. The *statement of changes in financial position* usually explains the changes in working capital for a period.

working capital equation. The *balance sheet* states that $Assets = Equities$. The information in comparative balance sheets from the start and end of a period can be restated as:

$$\text{Change in Assets} = \text{Change in Equities}$$

This equation can be further broken down to say that

$$\begin{array}{ccc} \text{Change in} & & \text{Change in} \\ \text{Current Assets} & & \text{Current Liabilities} \\ \text{Plus} & = & \text{Plus} \\ \text{Change in} & & \text{Change in} \\ \text{Noncurrent Assets} & & \text{Noncurrent Equities} \end{array}$$

which is equivalent to:

$$\begin{array}{ccc} \text{Change in} & & \text{Change in} \\ \text{Current Assets} & & \text{Noncurrent Equities} \\ \text{Less} & = & \text{Less} \\ \text{Change in} & & \text{Change in} \\ \text{Current Liabilities} & & \text{Noncurrent Assets} \end{array}$$

The left-hand side of this equation is the change in *working capital* for the period. The items on the right-hand side cause the change in working capital during the period. The *statement of changes in financial position* typically shows the causes of the changes (right-hand side of the equation) at the top of the statement and the way working capital has changed (left-hand side of the equation) at the bottom of the statement.

working capital provided by operations. See *funds provided by operations*.

working papers. The schedules and analyses prepared by the *auditor* in carrying out investigations prior to issuing an *opinion* on *financial statements*.

worth. *Value*. See *net worth*.

worth-debt ratio. Reciprocal of the *debt-equity ratio*. See *ratio*.

write-down. *Write off*, except that not all the assets' cost is charged to expense or *loss*. Generally used for nonrecurring items.

write off. *Charge* an *asset* to *expense* or *loss*; that is, *debit* expense (or loss) and *credit* asset.

write-off method. A method for treating *uncollectible accounts* that charges *bad debt expense* and credits accounts receivable of specific customers as uncollectible amounts are identified. May not be used when uncollectible amounts are significant and can be estimated. See *sales contra, estimated uncollectibles* and the *allowance method* for contrast.

761

write up. To increase the recorded *cost* of an *asset* with no corresponding *disbursement* of *funds*; that is, *debit* asset and *credit revenue*, or perhaps, *owners' equity*. Seldom done because currently accepted accounting principles are based on actual transactions. When a portfolio of *marketable equity securities* increases in market value subsequent to a previously-recognized decrease, the *book value* of the portfolio is written-up—the debit is to the *contra account*.

Y

yield. *Internal rate of return* of a stream of cash flows. Cash yield is cash flow divided by book value. See also *dividend yield*.

yield to maturity. At a given time, the *internal rate of return* of a series of cash flows, usually said of a *bond*. Sometimes called the "effective rate."

Z

zero base(d) budgeting. ZBB. In preparing an ordinary *budget* for the next period, a manager starts with the budget for the current period and makes adjustments as seem necessary, because of changed conditions for the next period. Because most managers like to increase the scope of the activities managed and since most prices increase most of the time, amounts in budgets prepared in the ordinary, incremental way seem to increase period after period. The authority approving the budget assumes operations will be carried out in the same way as in the past and that next period's expenditures will have to be at least as large as the current period's. Thus, this authority tends to study only the increments to the current period's budget. In ZBB, the authority questions the process for carrying out a program and the entire budget for next period. Every dollar in the budget is studied, not just the dollars incremental to the previous period's amounts. The advocates of ZBB claim that in this way: (1) programs or divisions of marginal benefit to the business or governmental unit will more likely be deleted from the program, rather than being continued with costs at least as large as the present ones, and (2) alternative, more cost-effective, ways of carrying out programs are more likely to be discovered and implemented. ZBB implies questioning the existence of programs, and the fundamental nature of the way they are carried out, not merely the amounts used to fund them. Experts appear to be evenly divided as to whether the middle word should be "base" or "based."

zero salvage value. If the *salvage value* of a *depreciable asset* is estimated to be less than 10 percent of its *cost*, then the tax regulations permit an assumption of zero salvage value in computing *depreciation* for federal *income tax* purposes. This convention is often used in financial reporting as well, but seldom in textbooks.

Index